D0538596

American Casebook Series
Hornbook Series and Basic Legal Texts
Nutshell Series

of

WEST PUBLISHING COMPANY
P.O. Box 64526
St. Paul, Minnesota 55164-0526

ACCOUNTING

Faris' Accounting and Law in a Nutshell, 377 pages, 1984 (Text)

Fiflis, Kripke and Foster's Teaching Materials on Accounting for Business Lawyers, 3rd Ed., 838 pages, 1984 (Casebook)

Siegel and Siegel's Accounting and Financial Disclosure: A Guide to Basic Concepts, 259 pages, 1983 (Text)

ADMINISTRATIVE LAW

Davis' Cases, Text and Problems on Administrative Law, 6th Ed., 683 pages, 1977 (Casebook)

Davis' Basic Text on Administrative Law, 3rd Ed., 617 pages, 1972 (Text)

Gellhorn and Boyer's Administrative Law and Process in a Nutshell, 2nd Ed., 445 pages, 1981 (Text)

Mashaw and Merrill's Cases and Materials on Administrative Law-The American Public Law System, 2nd Ed., 976 pages, 1985 (Casebook)

Robinson, Gellhorn and Bruff's The Administrative Process, 3rd Ed., 978 pages, 1986 (Casebook)

ADMIRALTY

Healy and Sharpe's Cases and Materials on Admiralty, 2nd Ed., 876 pages, 1986 (Casebook)

Maraist's Admiralty in a Nutshell, 390 pages, 1983 (Text)

Sohn and Gustafson's Law of the Sea in a Nutshell, 264 pages, 1984 (Text)

AGENCY—PARTNERSHIP

Fessler's Alternatives to Incorporation for Persons in Quest of Profit, 2nd Ed., 326 pages, 1986 (Casebook)

AGENCY—PARTNERSHIP—Cont'd

Henn's Cases and Materials on Agency, Partnership and Other Unincorporated Business Enterprises, 2nd Ed., 733 pages, 1985 (Casebook)

Reuschlein and Gregory's Hornbook on the Law of Agency and Partnership, 625 pages, 1979, with 1981 pocket part (Text)

Seavey, Reuschlein and Hall's Cases on Agency and Partnership, 599 pages, 1962 (Casebook)

Selected Corporation and Partnership Statutes and Forms, 555 pages, 1985

Steffen and Kerr's Cases and Materials on Agency-Partnership, 4th Ed., 859 pages, 1980 (Casebook)

Steffen's Agency-Partnership in a Nutshell, 364 pages, 1977 (Text)

AGRICULTURAL LAW

Meyer, Pedersen, Thorson and Davidson's Agricultural Law: Cases and Materials, 931 pages, 1985 (Casebook)

ALTERNATIVE DISPUTE RESOLUTION

Kanowitz' Cases and Materials on Alternative Dispute Resolution, 1024 pages, 1986 (Casebook)

Teple and Moberly's Arbitration and Conflict Resolution, (The Labor Law Group), 614 pages, 1979 (Casebook)

AMERICAN INDIAN LAW

Canby's American Indian Law in a Nutshell, 288 pages, 1981 (Text)

Getches and Wilkinson's Cases on Federal Indian Law, 2nd Ed., 880 pages, 1986 (Casebook)

LAW SCHOOL PUBLICATIONS—Continued

ANTITRUST LAW

Gellhorn's Antitrust Law and Economics in a Nutshell, 3rd Ed., about 470 pages, 1986 (Text)

Gifford and Raskind's Cases and Materials on Antitrust, 694 pages, 1983 with 1985 Supplement (Casebook)

Hovenkamp's Hornbook on Economics and Federal Antitrust Law, Student Ed., 414 pages, 1985 (Text)

Oppenheim, Weston and McCarthy's Cases and Comments on Federal Antitrust Laws, 4th Ed., 1168 pages, 1981 with 1985 Supplement (Casebook)

Posner and Easterbrook's Cases and Economic Notes on Antitrust, 2nd Ed., 1077 pages, 1981, with 1984–85 Supplement (Casebook)

Sullivan's Hornbook of the Law of Antitrust, 886 pages, 1977 (Text)

See also Regulated Industries, Trade Regulation

ART LAW

DuBoff's Art Law in a Nutshell, 335 pages, 1984 (Text)

BANKING LAW

Lovett's Banking and Financial Institutions in a Nutshell, 409 pages, 1984 (Text)

Symons and White's Teaching Materials on Banking Law, 2nd Ed., 993 pages, 1984 (Casebook)

BUSINESS PLANNING

Painter's Problems and Materials in Business Planning, 2nd Ed., 1008 pages, 1984 (Casebook)

Selected Securities and Business Planning Statutes, Rules and Forms, 470 pages, 1985

CIVIL PROCEDURE

Casad's Res Judicata in a Nutshell, 310 pages, 1976 (text)

Cound, Friedenthal, Miller and Sexton's Cases and Materials on Civil Procedure, 4th Ed., 1202 pages, 1985 with 1985 Supplement (Casebook)

Ehrenzweig, Louisell and Hazard's Jurisdiction in a Nutshell, 4th Ed., 232 pages, 1980 (Text)

Federal Rules of Civil-Appellate Procedure—West Law School Edition, 607 pages, 1986

Friedenthal, Kane and Miller's Hornbook on Civil Procedure, 876 pages, 1985 (Text)

Kane's Civil Procedure in a Nutshell, 2nd Ed., 306 pages, 1986 (Text)

Koffler and Reppy's Hornbook on Common Law Pleading, 663 pages, 1969 (Text)

Marcus and Sherman's Complex Litigation—Cases and Materials on Advanced Civil Procedure, 846 pages, 1985 (Casebook)

CIVIL PROCEDURE—Cont'd

Park's Computer-Aided Exercises on Civil Procedure, 2nd Ed., 167 pages, 1983 (Coursebook)

Siegel's Hornbook on New York Practice, 1011 pages, 1978 with 1985 Pocket Part (Text)

See also Federal Jurisdiction and Procedure

CIVIL RIGHTS

Abernathy's Cases and Materials on Civil Rights, 660 pages, 1980 (Casebook)

Cohen's Cases on the Law of Deprivation of Liberty: A Study in Social Control, 755 pages, 1980 (Casebook)

Lockhart, Kamisar, Choper and Shiffrin's Cases on Constitutional Rights and Liberties, 6th Ed., 1266 pages, 1986 with 1986 Supplement (Casebook)—reprint from Lockhart, et al. Cases on Constitutional Law, 6th Ed., 1986

Vieira's Civil Rights in a Nutshell, 279 pages, 1978 (Text)

COMMERCIAL LAW

Bailey's Secured Transactions in a Nutshell, 2nd Ed., 391 pages, 1981 (Text)

Epstein and Martin's Basic Uniform Commercial Code Teaching Materials, 2nd Ed., 667 pages, 1983 (Casebook)

Henson's Hornbook on Secured Transactions Under the U.C.C., 2nd Ed., 504 pages, 1979 with 1979 P.P. (Text)

Murray's Commercial Law, Problems and Materials, 366 pages, 1975 (Coursebook)

Nickles, Matheson and Dolan's Materials for Understanding Credit and Payment Systems, about 1,000 pages, 1987 (Casebook)

Nordstrom and Clovis' Problems and Materials on Commercial Paper, 458 pages, 1972 (Casebook)

Nordstrom, Murray and Clovis' Problems and Materials on Sales, 515 pages, 1982 (Casebook)

Nordstrom, Murray and Clovis' Problems and Materials on Secured Transactions, about 500 pages, 1987 (Casebook)

Selected Commercial Statutes, 1389 pages, 1985

Speidel, Summers and White's Teaching Materials on Commercial and Consumer Law, 3rd Ed., 1490 pages, 1981 (Casebook)

Stockton's Sales in a Nutshell, 2nd Ed., 370 pages, 1981 (Text)

Stone's Uniform Commercial Code in a Nutshell, 2nd Ed., 516 pages, 1984 (Text)

Uniform Commercial Code, Official Text with Comments, 994 pages, 1978

UCC Article 9, Reprint from 1962 Code, 128 pages, 1976

UCC Article 9, 1972 Amendments, 304 pages, 1978

LAW SCHOOL PUBLICATIONS—Continued

COMMERCIAL LAW—Cont'd

Weber and Speidel's Commercial Paper in a Nutshell, 3rd Ed., 404 pages, 1982 (Text)

White and Summers' Hornbook on the Uniform Commercial Code, 2nd Ed., 1250 pages, 1980 (Text)

COMMUNITY PROPERTY

Mennell's Community Property in a Nutshell, 447 pages, 1982 (Text)

Verrall and Bird's Cases and Materials on California Community Property, 4th Ed., 549 pages, 1983 (Casebook)

COMPARATIVE LAW

Barton, Gibbs, Li and Merryman's Law in Radically Different Cultures, 960 pages, 1983 (Casebook)

Glendon, Gordon and Osakive's Comparative Legal Traditions: Text, Materials and Cases on the Civil Law, Common Law, and Socialist Law Traditions, 1091 pages, 1985 (Casebook)

Glendon, Gordon, and Osakwe's Comparative Legal Traditions in a Nutshell, 402 pages, 1982 (Text)

Langbein's Comparative Criminal Procedure: Germany, 172 pages, 1977 (Casebook)

COMPUTERS AND LAW

Maggs and Sprowl's Computer Applications in the Law, about 300 pages, 1987 (Coursebook)

Mason's An Introduction to the Use of Computers in Law, 223 pages, 1984 (Text)

CONFLICT OF LAWS

Cramton, Currie and Kay's Cases-Comments-Questions on Conflict of Laws, 3rd Ed., 1026 pages, 1981 (Casebook)

Scoles and Hay's Hornbook on Conflict of Laws, Student Ed., 1085 pages, 1982 with 1986 P.P. (Text)

Scoles and Weintraub's Cases and Materials on Conflict of Laws, 2nd Ed., 966 pages, 1972, with 1978 Supplement (Casebook)

Siegel's Conflicts in a Nutshell, 469 pages, 1982 (Text)

CONSTITUTIONAL LAW

Barron and Dienes' Constitutional Law in a Nutshell, 389 pages, 1986 (Text)

Engdahl's Constitutional Power in a Nutshell: Federal and State, 411 pages, 1974 (Text)

Lockhart, Kamisar, Choper and Shiffrin's Cases-Comments-Questions on Constitutional Law, 6th Ed., 1601 pages, 1986 with 1986 Supplement (Casebook)

CONSTITUTIONAL LAW—Cont'd

Lockhart, Kamisar, Choper and Shiffrin's Cases-Comments-Questions on the American Constitution, 6th Ed., 1260 pages, 1986 with 1986 Supplement (Casebook)—abridgment of Lockhart, et al. Cases on Constitutional Law, 6th Ed., 1986

Manning's The Law of Church-State Relations in a Nutshell, 305 pages, 1981 (Text)

Miller's Presidential Power in a Nutshell, 328 pages, 1977 (Text)

Nowak, Rotunda and Young's Hornbook on Constitutional Law, 3rd Ed., Student Ed., 1191 pages, 1986 (Text)

Rotunda's Modern Constitutional Law: Cases and Notes, 2nd Ed., 1004 pages, 1985, with 1986 Supplement (Casebook)

Williams' Constitutional Analysis in a Nutshell, 388 pages, 1979 (Text)

See also Civil Rights

CONSUMER LAW

Epstein and Nickles' Consumer Law in a Nutshell, 2nd Ed., 418 pages, 1981 (Text)

McCall's Consumer Protection, Cases, Notes and Materials, 594 pages, 1977, with 1977 Statutory Supplement (Casebook)

Selected Commercial Statutes, 1389 pages, 1985

Spanogle and Rohner's Cases and Materials on Consumer Law, 693 pages, 1979, with 1982 Supplement (Casebook)

See also Commercial Law

CONTRACTS

Calamari & Perillo's Cases and Problems on Contracts, 1061 pages, 1978 (Casebook)

Calamari and Perillo's Hornbook on Contracts, 3rd Ed., about 900 pages, 1987 (Text)

Corbin's Text on Contracts, One Volume Student Edition, 1224 pages, 1952 (Text)

Fessler and Loiseaux's Cases and Materials on Contracts, 837 pages, 1982 (Casebook)

Friedman's Contract Remedies in a Nutshell, 323 pages, 1981 (Text)

Fuller and Eisenberg's Cases on Basic Contract Law, 4th Ed., 1203 pages, 1981 (Casebook)

Hamilton, Rau and Weintraub's Cases and Materials on Contracts, 830 pages, 1984 (Casebook)

Jackson and Bollinger's Cases on Contract Law in Modern Society, 2nd Ed., 1329 pages, 1980 (Casebook)

Keyes' Government Contracts in a Nutshell, 423 pages, 1979 (Text)

Schaber and Rohwer's Contracts in a Nutshell, 2nd Ed., 425 pages, 1984 (Text)

LAW SCHOOL PUBLICATIONS—Continued

CONTRACTS—Cont'd

Summers and Hillman's Contract and Related Obligation: Theory, Doctrine and Practice, about 1060 pages, 1987 (Casebook)

COPYRIGHT

See Patent and Copyright Law

CORPORATIONS

Hamilton's Cases on Corporations—Including Partnerships and Limited Partnerships, 3rd Ed., 1213 pages, 1986 with 1986 Statutory Supplement (Casebook)

Hamilton's Law of Corporations in a Nutshell, 2nd Ed., about 465 pages, 1987 (Text)

Henn's Teaching Materials on Corporations, 2nd Ed., 1204 pages, 1986 (Casebook)

Henn and Alexander's Hornbook on Corporations, 3rd Ed., Student Ed., 1371 pages, 1983 with 1986 P.P. (Text)

Jennings and Buxbaum's Cases and Materials on Corporations, 5th Ed., 1180 pages, 1979 (Casebook)

Selected Corporation and Partnership Statutes, Regulations and Forms, 555 pages, 1985

Solomon, Stevenson and Schwartz' Materials and Problems on Corporations: Law and Policy, 1172 pages, 1982 with 1986 Supplement (Casebook)

CORPORATE FINANCE

Hamilton's Cases and Materials on Corporate Finance, 895 pages, 1984 with 1986 Supplement (Casebook)

CORRECTIONS

Krantz's Cases and Materials on the Law of Corrections and Prisoners' Rights, 3rd Ed., 855 pages, 1986 (Casebook)

Krantz's Law of Corrections and Prisoners' Rights in a Nutshell, 2nd Ed., 386 pages, 1983 (Text)

Popper's Post-Conviction Remedies in a Nutshell, 360 pages, 1978 (Text)

Robbins' Cases and Materials on Post Conviction Remedies, 506 pages, 1982 (Casebook)

CREDITOR'S RIGHTS

Bankruptcy Code, Rules and Forms, Law School and C.L.E. Ed., 838 pages, 1986

Epstein's Debtor-Creditor Law in a Nutshell, 3rd Ed., 383 pages, 1986 (Text)

Epstein and Landers' Debtors and Creditors: Cases and Materials, 2nd Ed., 689 pages, 1982 (Casebook)

LoPucki's Player's Manual for the Debtor-Creditor Game, 123 pages, 1985 (Coursebook)

CREDITOR'S RIGHTS—Cont'd

Riesenfeld's Cases and Materials on Creditors' Remedies and Debtors' Protection, 4th Ed., about 870 pages, 1987 (Casebook)

White's Bankruptcy and Creditor's Rights: Cases and Materials, 812 pages, 1985 (Casebook)

CRIMINAL LAW AND CRIMINAL PROCEDURE

Abrams', Federal Criminal Law and its Enforcement, 882 pages, 1986 (Casebook)

Carlson's Adjudication of Criminal Justice, Problems and References, 130 pages, 1986 (Casebook)

Dix and Sharlot's Cases and Materials on Criminal Law, 2nd Ed., 771 pages, 1979 (Casebook)

Federal Rules of Criminal Procedure—West Law School Edition, 463 pages, 1986

Grano's Problems in Criminal Procedure, 2nd Ed., 176 pages, 1981 (Problem book)

Israel and LaFave's Criminal Procedure in a Nutshell, 3rd Ed., 438 pages, 1980 (Text)

Johnson's Cases, Materials and Text on Criminal Law, 3rd Ed., 783 pages, 1985 (Casebook)

Kamisar, LaFave and Israel's Cases, Comments and Questions on Modern Criminal Procedure, 6th Ed., 1558 pages, 1986 with 1986 Supplement (Casebook)

Kamisar, LaFave and Israel's Cases, Comments and Questions on Basic Criminal Procedure, 6th Ed., 860 pages, 1986 with 1986 Supplement (Casebook)—reprint from Kamisar, et al. Modern Criminal Procedure, 6th ed., 1986

LaFave's Modern Criminal Law: Cases, Comments and Questions, 789 pages, 1978 (Casebook)

LaFave and Israel's Hornbook on Criminal Procedure, Student Ed., 1142 pages, 1985 with 1986 P.P. (Text)

LaFave and Scott's Hornbook on Criminal Law, 2nd Ed., Student Ed., 918 pages, 1986 (Text)

Langbein's Comparative Criminal Procedure: Germany, 172 pages, 1977 (Casebook)

Loewy's Criminal Law in a Nutshell, 302 pages, 1975 (Text)

Saltzburg's American Criminal Procedure, Cases and Commentary, 2nd Ed., 1193 pages, 1985 with 1986 Supplement (Casebook)

Uviller's The Processes of Criminal Justice: Investigation and Adjudication, 2nd Ed., 1384 pages, 1979 with 1979 Statutory Supplement and 1986 Update (Casebook)

LAW SCHOOL PUBLICATIONS—Continued

CRIMINAL LAW AND CRIMINAL PRO- CEDURE—Cont'd

Uviller's The Processes of Criminal Justice: Adjudication, 2nd Ed., 730 pages, 1979. Soft-cover reprint from Uviller's The Processes of Criminal Justice: Investigation and Adjudication, 2nd Ed. (Casebook)

Uviller's The Processes of Criminal Justice: Investigation, 2nd Ed., 655 pages, 1979. Soft-cover reprint from Uviller's The Processes of Criminal Justice: Investigation and Adjudication, 2nd Ed. (Casebook)

Vorenberg's Cases on Criminal Law and Procedure, 2nd Ed., 1088 pages, 1981 with 1985 Supplement (Casebook)

See also Corrections, Juvenile Justice

DECEDENTS ESTATES

See Trusts and Estates

DOMESTIC RELATIONS

Clark's Cases and Problems on Domestic Relations, 3rd Ed., 1153 pages, 1980 (Casebook)

Clark's Hornbook on Domestic Relations, 754 pages, 1968 (Text)

Krause's Cases and Materials on Family Law, 2nd Ed., 1221 pages, 1983 with 1986 Supplement (Casebook)

Krause's Family Law in a Nutshell, 2nd Ed., 444 pages, 1986 (Text)

Krauskopf's Cases on Property Division at Marriage Dissolution, 250 pages, 1984 (Casebook)

ECONOMICS, LAW AND

Goetz' Cases and Materials on Law and Economics, 547 pages, 1984 (Casebook)

See also Antitrust, Regulated Industries

EDUCATION LAW

Alexander and Alexander's The Law of Schools, Students and Teachers in a Nutshell, 409 pages, 1984 (Text)

Morris' The Constitution and American Education, 2nd Ed., 992 pages, 1980 (Casebook)

EMPLOYMENT DISCRIMINATION

Jones, Murphy and Belton's Cases on Discrimination in Employment, about 1120 pages, 1987 (Casebook)

Player's Cases and Materials on Employment Discrimination Law, 2nd Ed., 782 pages, 1984 (Casebook)

Player's Federal Law of Employment Discrimination in a Nutshell, 2nd Ed., 402 pages, 1981 (Text)

See also Women and the Law

ENERGY AND NATURAL RESOURCES LAW

Laitos' Cases and Materials on Natural Resources Law, 938 pages, 1985 (Casebook)

Rodgers' Cases and Materials on Energy and Natural Resources Law, 2nd Ed., 877 pages, 1983 (Casebook)

Selected Environmental Law Statutes, 965 pages, 1986

Tomain's Energy Law in a Nutshell, 338 pages, 1981 (Text)

See also Environmental Law, Oil and Gas, Water Law

ENVIRONMENTAL LAW

Bonine and McGarity's Cases and Materials on the Law of Environment and Pollution, 1076 pages, 1984 (Casebook)

Findley and Farber's Cases and Materials on Environmental Law, 2nd Ed., 813 pages, 1985 (Casebook)

Findley and Farber's Environmental Law in a Nutshell, 343 pages, 1983 (Text)

Rodgers' Hornbook on Environmental Law, 956 pages, 1977 with 1984 pocket part (Text)

Selected Environmental Law Statutes, 965 pages, 1986

See also Energy Law, Natural Resources Law, Water Law

EQUITY

See Remedies

ESTATES

See Trusts and Estates

ESTATE PLANNING

Kurtz' Cases, Materials and Problems on Family Estate Planning, 853 pages, 1983 (Casebook)

Lynn's Introduction to Estate Planning, in a Nutshell, 3rd Ed., 370 pages, 1983 (Text)

See also Taxation

EVIDENCE

Broun and Meisenholder's Problems in Evidence, 2nd Ed., 304 pages, 1981 (Problem book)

Cleary and Strong's Cases, Materials and Problems on Evidence, 3rd Ed., 1143 pages, 1981 (Casebook)

Federal Rules of Evidence for United States Courts and Magistrates, 337 pages, 1984

Graham's Federal Rules of Evidence in a Nutshell, 2nd Ed., about 450 pages, 1987 (Text)

Kimball's Programmed Materials on Problems in Evidence, 380 pages, 1978 (Problem book)

LAW SCHOOL PUBLICATIONS—Continued

EVIDENCE—Cont'd

Lempert and Saltzburg's A Modern Approach to Evidence: Text, Problems, Transcripts and Cases, 2nd Ed., 1232 pages, 1983 (Casebook)

Lilly's Introduction to the Law of Evidence, 490 pages, 1978 (Text)

McCormick, Sutton and Wellborn's Cases and Materials on Evidence, 6th Ed., about 1060 pages, 1987 (Casebook)

McCormick's Hornbook on Evidence, 3rd Ed., Student Ed., 1156 pages, 1984 (Text)

Rothstein's Evidence, State and Federal Rules in a Nutshell, 2nd Ed., 514 pages, 1981 (Text)

Saltzburg's Evidence Supplement: Rules, Statutes, Commentary, 245 pages, 1980 (Casebook Supplement)

FEDERAL JURISDICTION AND PROCEDURE

Currie's Cases and Materials on Federal Courts, 3rd Ed., 1042 pages, 1982 with 1985 Supplement (Casebook)

Currie's Federal Jurisdiction in a Nutshell, 2nd Ed., 258 pages, 1981 (Text)

Federal Rules of Civil-Appellate Procedure—West Law School Edition, 607 pages, 1986

Forrester and Moye's Cases and Materials on Federal Jurisdiction and Procedure, 3rd Ed., 917 pages, 1977 with 1985 Supplement (Casebook)

Redish's Cases, Comments and Questions on Federal Courts, 878 pages, 1983 with 1986 Supplement (Casebook)

Vetri and Merrill's Federal Courts, Problems and Materials, 2nd Ed., 232 pages, 1984 (Problem Book)

Wright's Hornbook on Federal Courts, 4th Ed., Student Ed., 870 pages, 1983 (Text)

FUTURE INTERESTS

See Trusts and Estates

IMMIGRATION LAW

Aleinikoff and Martin's Immigration Process and Policy, 1042 pages, 1985 (Casebook)

Weissbrodt's Immigration Law and Procedure in a Nutshell, 345 pages, 1984 (Text)

INDIAN LAW

See American Indian Law

INSURANCE

Dobbyn's Insurance Law in a Nutshell, 281 pages, 1981 (Text)

Keeton's Cases on Basic Insurance Law, 2nd Ed., 1086 pages, 1977

Keeton's Basic Text on Insurance Law, 712 pages, 1971 (Text)

INSURANCE—Cont'd

Keeton's Case Supplement to Keeton's Basic Text on Insurance Law, 334 pages, 1978 (Casebook)

York and Whelan's Cases, Materials and Problems on Insurance Law, 715 pages, 1982, with 1985 Supplement (Casebook)

INTERNATIONAL LAW

Buergenthal and Maier's Public International Law in a Nutshell, 262 pages, 1985 (Text)

Folsom, Gordon and Spanogle's International Business Transactions – a Problem-Oriented Coursebook, 1160 pages, 1986 (Casebook)

Henkin, Pugh, Schachter and Smit's Cases and Materials on International Law, 2nd Ed., about 1500 pages, 1987 with Documents Supplement (Casebook)

Jackson and Davey's Legal Problems of International Economic Relations, 2nd Ed., 1269 pages, 1986, with Documents Supplement (Casebook)

Kirgis' International Organizations in Their Legal Setting, 1016 pages, 1977, with 1981 Supplement (Casebook)

Weston, Falk and D'Amato's International Law and World Order—A Problem Oriented Coursebook, 1195 pages, 1980, with Documents Supplement (Casebook)

Wilson's International Business Transactions in a Nutshell, 2nd Ed., 476 pages, 1984 (Text)

INTERVIEWING AND COUNSELING

Binder and Price's Interviewing and Counseling, 232 pages, 1977 (Text)

Shaffer's Interviewing and Counseling in a Nutshell, 353 pages, 1976 (Text)

INTRODUCTION TO LAW STUDY

Dobbyn's So You Want to go to Law School, Revised First Edition, 206 pages, 1976 (Text)

Hegland's Introduction to the Study and Practice of Law in a Nutshell, 418 pages, 1983 (Text)

Kinyon's Introduction to Law Study and Law Examinations in a Nutshell, 389 pages, 1971 (Text)

See also Legal Method and Legal System

JUDICIAL ADMINISTRATION

Nelson's Cases and Materials on Judicial Administration and the Administration of Justice, 1032 pages, 1974 (Casebook)

JURISPRUDENCE

Christie's Text and Readings on Jurisprudence—The Philosophy of Law, 1056 pages, 1973 (Casebook)

LAW SCHOOL PUBLICATIONS—Continued

JUVENILE JUSTICE

Fox's Cases and Materials on Modern Juvenile Justice, 2nd Ed., 960 pages, 1981 (Casebook)

Fox's Juvenile Courts in a Nutshell, 3rd Ed., 291 pages, 1984 (Text)

LABOR LAW

Atleson, Rabin, Schatzki, Sherman and Silverstein's Collective Bargaining in Private Employment, 2nd Ed., (The Labor Law Group), 856 pages, 1984 (Casebook)

Gorman's Basic Text on Labor Law—Unionization and Collective Bargaining, 914 pages, 1976 (Text)

Grodin, Wollett and Alleyne's Collective Bargaining in Public Employment, 3rd Ed., (the Labor Law Group), 430 pages, 1979 (Casebook)

Leslie's Labor Law in a Nutshell, 2nd Ed., 397 pages, 1986 (Text)

Nolan's Labor Arbitration Law and Practice in a Nutshell, 358 pages, 1979 (Text)

Oberer, Hanslowe, Andersen and Heinsz' Cases and Materials on Labor Law—Collective Bargaining in a Free Society, 3rd Ed., 1163 pages, 1986 with Statutory Supplement (Casebook)

See also Employment Discrimination, Social Legislation

LAND FINANCE

See Real Estate Transactions

LAND USE

Callies and Freilich's Cases and Materials on Land Use, 1233 pages, 1986 (Casebook)

Hagman's Cases on Public Planning and Control of Urban and Land Development, 2nd Ed., 1301 pages, 1980 (Casebook)

Hagman and Juergensmeyer's Hornbook on Urban Planning and Land Development Control Law, 2nd Ed., Student Edition, 680 pages, 1986 (Text)

Wright and Gitelman's Cases and Materials on Land Use, 3rd Ed., 1300 pages, 1982, with 1987 Supplement (Casebook)

Wright and Wright's Land Use in a Nutshell, 2nd Ed., 356 pages, 1985 (Text)

LEGAL HISTORY

Presser and Zainaldin's Cases on Law and American History, 855 pages, 1980 (Casebook)

See also Legal Method and Legal System

LEGAL METHOD AND LEGAL SYSTEM

Aldisert's Readings, Materials and Cases in the Judicial Process, 948 pages, 1976 (Casebook)

Berch and Berch's Introduction to Legal Method and Process, 550 pages, 1985 (Casebook)

LEGAL METHOD AND LEGAL SYSTEM—Cont'd

Bodenheimer, Oakley and Love's Readings and Cases on an Introduction to the Anglo-American Legal System, 161 pages, 1980 (Casebook)

Davies and Lawry's Institutions and Methods of the Law—Introductory Teaching Materials, 547 pages, 1982 (Casebook)

Dvorkin, Himmelstein and Lesnick's Becoming a Lawyer: A Humanistic Perspective on Legal Education and Professionalism, 211 pages, 1981 (Text)

Greenberg's Judicial Process and Social Change, 666 pages, 1977 (Casebook)

Kelso and Kelso's Studying Law: An Introduction, 587 pages, 1984 (Coursebook)

Kempin's Historical Introduction to Anglo-American Law in a Nutshell, 2nd Ed., 280 pages, 1973 (Text)

Kimball's Historical Introduction to the Legal System, 610 pages, 1966 (Casebook)

Murphy's Cases and Materials on Introduction to Law—Legal Process and Procedure, 772 pages, 1977 (Casebook)

Reynolds' Judicial Process in a Nutshell, 292 pages, 1980 (Text)

See also Legal Research and Writing

LEGAL PROFESSION

Aronson, Devine and Fisch's Problems, Cases and Materials on Professional Responsibility, 745 pages, 1985 (Casebook)

Aronson and Weckstein's Professional Responsibility in a Nutshell, 399 pages, 1980 (Text)

Mellinkoff's The Conscience of a Lawyer, 304 pages, 1973 (Text)

Mellinkoff's Lawyers and the System of Justice, 983 pages, 1976 (Casebook)

Pirsig and Kirwin's Cases and Materials on Professional Responsibility, 4th Ed., 603 pages, 1984 (Casebook)

Schwartz and Wydick's Problems in Legal Ethics, 285 pages, 1983 (Casebook)

Selected Statutes, Rules and Standards on the Legal Profession, 276 pages, Revised 1984

Smith's Preventing Legal Malpractice, 142 pages, 1981 (Text)

Wolfram's Hornbook on Modern Legal Ethics, Student Edition, 1120 pages, 1986 (Text)

LEGAL RESEARCH AND WRITING

Cohen's Legal Research in a Nutshell, 4th Ed., 450 pages, 1985 (Text)

Cohen and Berring's How to Find the Law, 8th Ed., 790 pages, 1983. Problem book by Foster, Johnson and Kelly available (Casebook)

Cohen and Berring's Finding the Law, 8th Ed., Abridged Ed., 556 pages, 1984 (Casebook)

LAW SCHOOL PUBLICATIONS—Continued

LEGAL RESEARCH AND WRITING— Cont'd

Dickerson's Materials on Legal Drafting, 425 pages, 1981 (Casebook)

Felsenfeld and Siegel's Writing Contracts in Plain English, 290 pages, 1981 (Text)

Gopen's Writing From a Legal Perspective, 225 pages, 1981 (Text)

Mellinkoff's Legal Writing—Sense and Nonsense, 242 pages, 1982 (Text)

Ray and Ramsfield's Legal Writing: Getting It Right and Getting It Written, about 400 pages, 1987 (Text)

Rombauer's Legal Problem Solving—Analysis, Research and Writing, 4th Ed., 424 pages, 1983 (Coursebook)

Squires and Rombauer's Legal Writing in a Nutshell, 294 pages, 1982 (Text)

Statsky's Legal Research and Writing, 3rd Ed., 257 pages, 1986 (Coursebook)

Statsky and Wernet's Case Analysis and Fundamentals of Legal Writing, 2nd Ed., 441 pages, 1984 (Text)

Teply's Programmed Materials on Legal Research and Citation, 2nd Ed., 358 pages, 1986. Student Library Exercises available (Coursebook)

Weihofen's Legal Writing Style, 2nd Ed., 332 pages, 1980 (Text)

LEGISLATION

Davies' Legislative Law and Process in a Nutshell, 2nd Ed., 346 pages, 1986 (Text)

Nutting and Dickerson's Cases and Materials on Legislation, 5th Ed., 744 pages, 1978 (Casebook)

Statsky's Legislative Analysis and Drafting, 2nd Ed., 217 pages, 1984 (Text)

LOCAL GOVERNMENT

McCarthy's Local Government Law in a Nutshell, 2nd Ed., 404 pages, 1983 (Text)

Reynolds' Hornbook on Local Government Law, 860 pages, 1982 (Text)

Valente's Cases and Materials on Local Government Law, 3rd Ed., about 980 pages, 1987 (Casebook)

MASS COMMUNICATION LAW

Gillmor and Barron's Cases and Comment on Mass Communication Law, 4th Ed., 1076 pages, 1984 (Casebook)

Ginsburg's Regulation of Broadcasting: Law and Policy Towards Radio, Television and Cable Communications, 741 pages, 1979, with 1983 Supplement (Casebook)

Zuckman and Gayne's Mass Communications Law in a Nutshell, 2nd Ed., 473 pages, 1983 (Text)

MEDICINE, LAW AND

King's The Law of Medical Malpractice in a Nutshell, 2nd Ed., 342 pages, 1986 (Text)

MEDICINE, LAW AND—Cont'd

Shapiro and Spece's Problems, Cases and Materials on Bioethics and Law, 892 pages, 1981 (Casebook)

Sharpe, Fiscina and Head's Cases on Law and Medicine, 882 pages, 1978 (Casebook)

MILITARY LAW

Shanor and Terrell's Military Law in a Nutshell, 378 pages, 1980 (Text)

MORTGAGES

See Real Estate Transactions

NATURAL RESOURCES LAW

See Energy and Natural Resources Law

NEGOTIATION

Edwards and White's Problems, Readings and Materials on the Lawyer as a Negotiator, 484 pages, 1977 (Casebook)

Peck's Cases and Materials on Negotiation, 2nd Ed., (The Labor Law Group), 280 pages, 1980 (Casebook)

Williams' Legal Negotiation and Settlement, 207 pages, 1983 (Coursebook)

OFFICE PRACTICE

Hegland's Trial and Practice Skills in a Nutshell, 346 pages, 1978 (Text)

Strong and Clark's Law Office Management, 424 pages, 1974 (Casebook)

See also Computers and Law, Interviewing and Counseling, Negotiation

OIL AND GAS

Hemingway's Hornbook on Oil and Gas, 2nd Ed., Student Ed., 543 pages, 1983 with 1986 P.P. (Text)

Kuntz, Lowe, Anderson and Smith's Cases and Materials on Oil and Gas Law, 857 pages, 1986, with Forms Manual (Casebook)

Lowe's Oil and Gas Law in a Nutshell, 443 pages, 1983 (Text)

See also Energy and Natural Resources Law

PARTNERSHIP

See Agency—Partnership

PATENT AND COPYRIGHT LAW

Choate and Francis' Cases and Materials on Patent Law, 2nd Ed., 1110 pages, 1981 (Casebook)

Miller and Davis' Intellectual Property—Patents, Trademarks and Copyright in a Nutshell, 428 pages, 1983 (Text)

Nimmer's Cases on Copyright and Other Aspects of Entertainment Litigation, 3rd Ed., 1025 pages, 1985 (Casebook)

PRODUCTS LIABILITY

Noel and Phillips' Cases on Products Liability, 2nd Ed., 821 pages, 1982 (Casebook)

LAW SCHOOL PUBLICATIONS—Continued

PRODUCTS LIABILITY—Cont'd

Noel and Phillips' Products Liability in a Nutshell, 2nd Ed., 341 pages, 1981 (Text)

PROPERTY

Bernhardt's Real Property in a Nutshell, 2nd Ed., 448 pages, 1981 (Text)

Boyer's Survey of the Law of Property, 766 pages, 1981 (Text)

Browder, Cunningham and Smith's Cases on Basic Property Law, 4th Ed., 1431 pages, 1984 (Casebook)

Bruce, Ely and Bostick's Cases and Materials on Modern Property Law, 1004 pages, 1984 (Casebook)

Burke's Personal Property in a Nutshell, 322 pages, 1983 (Text)

Cunningham, Stoebuck and Whitman's Hornbook on the Law of Property, Student Ed., 916 pages, 1984, with 1987 P.P. (Text)

Donahue, Kauper and Martin's Cases on Property, 2nd Ed., 1362 pages, 1983 (Casebook)

Hill's Landlord and Tenant Law in a Nutshell, 2nd Ed., 311 pages, 1986 (Text)

Kurtz and Hovenkamp's Cases and Materials on American Property Law, about 1300 pages, 1987 (Casebook)

Moynihan's Introduction to Real Property, 254 pages, 1962 (Text)

Uniform Land Transactions Act, Uniform Simplification of Land Transfers Act, Uniform Condominium Act, 1977 Official Text with Comments, 462 pages, 1978

See also Real Estate Transactions, Land Use

PSYCHIATRY, LAW AND

Reisner's Law and the Mental Health System, Civil and Criminal Aspects, 696 pages, 1985 (Casebooks)

REAL ESTATE TRANSACTIONS

Bruce's Real Estate Finance in a Nutshell, 2nd Ed., 262 pages, 1985 (Text)

Maxwell, Riesenfeld, Hetland and Warren's Cases on California Security Transactions in Land, 3rd Ed., 728 pages, 1984 (Casebook)

Nelson and Whitman's Cases on Real Estate Transfer, Finance and Development, 2nd Ed., 1114 pages, 1981, with 1986 Supplement (Casebook)

Nelson and Whitman's Hornbook on Real Estate Finance Law, 2nd Ed., Student Ed., 941 pages, 1985 (Text)

Osborne's Cases and Materials on Secured Transactions, 559 pages, 1967 (Casebook)

REGULATED INDUSTRIES

Gellhorn and Pierce's Regulated Industries in a Nutshell, 2nd Ed., about 400 pages, 1987 (Text)

REGULATED INDUSTRIES—Cont'd

Morgan, Harrison and Verkuil's Cases and Materials on Economic Regulation of Business, 2nd Ed., 666 pages, 1985 (Casebook)

See also Mass Communication Law, Banking Law

REMEDIES

Dobbs' Hornbook on Remedies, 1067 pages, 1973 (Text)

Dobbs' Problems in Remedies, 137 pages, 1974 (Problem book)

Dobbyn's Injunctions in a Nutshell, 264 pages, 1974 (Text)

Friedman's Contract Remedies in a Nutshell, 323 pages, 1981 (Text)

Leavell, Love and Nelson's Cases and Materials on Equitable Remedies and Restitution, 4th Ed., 1111 pages, 1986 (Casebook)

McCormick's Hornbook on Damages, 811 pages, 1935 (Text)

O'Connell's Remedies in a Nutshell, 2nd Ed., 320 pages, 1985 (Text)

York, Bauman and Rendleman's Cases and Materials on Remedies, 4th Ed., 1029 pages, 1985 (Casebook)

REVIEW MATERIALS

Ballantine's Problems

Black Letter Series

Smith's Review Series

West's Review Covering Multistate Subjects

SECURITIES REGULATION

Hazen's Hornbook on The Law of Securities Regulation, Student Ed., 739 pages, 1985, with 1987 P.P. (Text)

Ratner's Securities Regulation: Materials for a Basic Course, 3rd Ed., 1000 pages, 1986 (Casebook)

Ratner's Securities Regulation in a Nutshell, 2nd Ed., 322 pages, 1982 (Text)

Selected Securities and Business Planning Statutes, Rules and Forms, 470 pages, 1985

SOCIAL LEGISLATION

Hood and Hardy's Workers' Compensation and Employee Protection Laws in a Nutshell, 274 pages, 1984 (Text)

LaFrance's Welfare Law: Structure and Entitlement in a Nutshell, 455 pages, 1979 (Text)

Malone, Plant and Little's Cases on Workers' Compensation and Employment Rights, 2nd Ed., 951 pages, 1980 (Casebook)

SPORTS LAW

Schubert, Smith and Trentadue's Sports Law, 395 pages, 1986 (Text)

LAW SCHOOL PUBLICATIONS—Continued

TAXATION

Dodge's Cases and Materials on Federal Income Taxation, 820 pages, 1985 (Casebook)

Dodge's Federal Taxation of Estates, Trusts and Gifts: Principles and Planning, 771 pages, 1981 with 1982 Supplement (Casebook)

Garbis and Struntz' Cases and Materials on Tax Procedure and Tax Fraud, 829 pages, 1982 with 1984 Supplement (Casebook)

Gelfand and Salsich's State and Local Taxation and Finance in a Nutshell, 309 pages, 1986 (Text)

Gunn's Cases and Materials on Federal Income Taxation of Individuals, 785 pages, 1981 with 1985 Supplement (Casebook)

Hellerstein and Hellerstein's Cases on State and Local Taxation, 4th Ed., 1041 pages, 1978 with 1982 Supplement (Casebook)

Kahn and Gann's Corporate Taxation and Taxation of Partnerships and Partners, 2nd Ed., 1204 pages, 1985 (Casebook)

Kragen and McNulty's Cases and Materials on Federal Income Taxation: Individuals, Corporations, Partnerships, 4th Ed., 1287 pages, 1985 (Casebook)

McNulty's Federal Estate and Gift Taxation in a Nutshell, 3rd Ed., 509 pages, 1983 (Text)

McNulty's Federal Income Taxation of Individuals in a Nutshell, 3rd Ed., 487 pages, 1983 (Text)

Posin's Hornbook on Federal Income Taxation of Individuals, Student Ed., 491 pages, 1983 with 1985 pocket part (Text)

Selected Federal Taxation Statutes and Regulations, 1429 pages, 1986

Solomon and Hesch's Cases on Federal Income Taxation of Individuals, about 800 pages, 1987 (Casebook)

Soboloff and Weidenbruch's Federal Income Taxation of Corporations and Stockholders in a Nutshell, 362 pages, 1981 (Text)

TORTS

Christie's Cases and Materials on the Law of Torts, 1264 pages, 1983 (Casebook)

Dobbs' Torts and Compensation—Personal Accountability and Social Responsibility for Injury, 955 pages, 1985 (Casebook)

Green, Pedrick, Rahl, Thode, Hawkins, Smith, and Treece's Advanced Torts: Injuries to Business, Political and Family Interests, 2nd Ed., 544 pages, 1977 (Casebook)

Keeton, Keeton, Sargentich and Steiner's Cases and Materials on Torts, and Accident Law, 1360 pages, 1983 (Casebook)

Kionka's Torts in a Nutshell: Injuries to Persons and Property, 434 pages, 1977 (Text)

TORTS—Cont'd

Malone's Torts in a Nutshell: Injuries to Family, Social and Trade Relations, 358 pages, 1979 (Text)

Prosser and Keeton's Hornbook on Torts, 5th Ed., Student Ed., 1286 pages, 1984 (Text)

See also Products Liability

TRADE REGULATION

McManis' Unfair Trade Practices in a Nutshell, 444 pages, 1982 (Text)

Oppenheim, Weston, Maggs and Schechter's Cases and Materials on Unfair Trade Practices and Consumer Protection, 4th Ed., 1038 pages, 1983 with 1986 Supplement (Casebook)

See also Antitrust, Regulated Industries

TRIAL AND APPELLATE ADVOCACY

Appellate Advocacy, Handbook of, 2nd Ed., 182 pages, 1986 (Text)

Bergman's Trial Advocacy in a Nutshell, 402 pages, 1979 (Text)

Binder and Bergman's Fact Investigation: From Hypothesis to Proof, 354 pages, 1984 (Coursebook)

Goldberg's The First Trial (Where Do I Sit?, What Do I Say?) in a Nutshell, 396 pages, 1982 (Text)

Haydock, Herr and Stempel's, Fundamentals of Pre-Trial Litigation, 768 pages, 1985 (Casebook)

Hegland's Trial and Practice Skills in a Nutshell, 346 pages, 1978 (Text)

Hornstein's Appellate Advocacy in a Nutshell, 325 pages, 1984 (Text)

Jeans' Handbook on Trial Advocacy, Student Ed., 473 pages, 1975 (Text)

Martineau's Cases and Materials on Appellate Practice and Procedure, about 550 pages, 1987 (Casebook)

McElhaney's Effective Litigation, 457 pages, 1974 (Casebook)

Nolan's Cases and Materials on Trial Practice, 518 pages, 1981 (Casebook)

Parnell and Shellhaas' Cases, Exercises and Problems for Trial Advocacy, 171 pages, 1982 (Coursebook)

Sonsteng, Haydock and Boyd's The Trialbook: A Total System for Preparation and Presentation of a Case, Student Ed., 404 pages, 1984 (Coursebook)

TRUSTS AND ESTATES

Atkinson's Hornbook on Wills, 2nd Ed., 975 pages, 1953 (Text)

Averill's Uniform Probate Code in a Nutshell, 425 pages, 1978 (Text)

Bogert's Hornbook on Trusts, 6th Ed., Student Ed., about 800 pages, 1987 (Text)

Clark, Lusky and Murphy's Cases and Materials on Gratuitous Transfers, 3rd Ed., 970 pages, 1985 (Casebook)

LAW SCHOOL PUBLICATIONS—Continued

TRUSTS AND ESTATES—Cont'd

Gulliver's Cases and Materials on Future Interests, 624 pages, 1959 (Casebook)

Gulliver's Introduction to the Law of Future Interests, 87 pages, 1959 (Casebook)—reprint from Gulliver's Cases and Materials on Future Interests, 1959

McGovern's Cases and Materials on Wills, Trusts and Future Interests: An Introduction to Estate Planning, 750 pages, 1983 (Casebook)

Mennell's Wills and Trusts in a Nutshell, 392 pages, 1979 (Text)

Simes' Hornbook on Future Interests, 2nd Ed., 355 pages, 1966 (Text)

Turano and Radigan's Hornbook on New York Estate Administration, 676 pages, 1986 (Text)

Uniform Probate Code, 5th Ed., Official Text With Comments, 384 pages, 1977

Waggoner's Future Interests in a Nutshell, 361 pages, 1981 (Text)

Waterbury's Materials on Trusts and Estates, 1039 pages, 1986 (Casebook)

WATER LAW

Getches' Water Law in a Nutshell, 439 pages, 1984 (Text)

WATER LAW—Cont'd

Sax and Abram's Cases and Materials on Legal Control of Water Resources in the United States, 941 pages, 1986 (Casebook)

Trelease and Gould's Cases and Materials on Water Law, 4th Ed., 816 pages, 1986 (Casebook)

See also Energy and Natural Resources Law, Environmental Law

WILLS

See Trusts and Estates

WOMEN AND THE LAW

Kay's Text, Cases and Materials on Sex-Based Discrimination, 2nd Ed., 1045 pages, 1981, with 1986 Supplement (Casebook)

Thomas' Sex Discrimination in a Nutshell, 399 pages, 1982 (Text)

See also Employment Discrimination

WORKERS' COMPENSATION

See Social Legislation

LOCAL GOVERNMENT LAW
CASES AND MATERIALS
Third Edition

By

William D. Valente
*Professor of Law, Villanova University
School of Law*

AMERICAN CASEBOOK SERIES

WEST PUBLISHING CO.
ST. PAUL, MINN., 1987

Library of Congress Cataloging in Publication Data

Valente, William D.
  Cases and materials on local government law.

  (American casebook series)
  Rev. ed. of: Local government law. 2nd ed. 1980.
  Includes index.
  1. Local government—Law and legislation—United
States—Cases. I. Valente, William D. Local government
law. II. Title. III. Series.

KF5300.A7V34 1987   342.73'09   86–28954
                        347.3029

ISBN 0–314–32761–4

Valente, Local Gov't Law, 3rd Ed. ACB

To
Elizabeth J. Valente

Preface To The Third Edition

In the six years since publication of the second edition, dramatic shifts in economic conditions and national policies produced equally dramatic changes in local government law. Decentralization of business regulation and diminished federal funding of state and local activities, increased local initiatives and control. Conversely, expanding federal oversight of many incidents of public employment and of civil rights violations heightened federal intrusion. The costs of compliance with federal mandates continue to be a factor in local planning. State imitation of federal oversight practices, especially in "cooperative" programs, further burden local programs. Finally, continuing developments in constitutional law place new limits upon the exercise of local police powers, especially in licensing controls. These cross currents provide the principal impetus for a substantially revised edition.

While this edition supplements and reorganizes the content of its predecessor, it pursues the same basic goal, i.e. to enable readers to cultivate a root understanding of local government structures, functions and jurisdiction; to explore various intergovernmental arrangements and relationships; and to do so from a perspective that views the many forms of local governments essentially as delivery systems of public services that operate at the "street level" of government action. In my view, these goals are best served by policy-oriented analyses of local government processes and of the legal devices that are available to public officials in the pursuit of particular programs. More intensive studies of selected topics are best deferred to later courses; after students have mastered the groundwork principles of local administration.

The list and sequence of covered topics do not differ materially from prior editions, but the original seven chapters have been redistributed into 11 chapters, in order to highlight certain subjects which, on reflection, appear to merit separate treatment. The material and space dedicated to each subject has also changed to accommodate more recent authorities, and to focus upon issues of emerging importance. The three introductory chapters were compressed to make room for more extensive treatment of interlocal arrangements, federal-state-local conflicts, anti-discrimination laws, and local licensing of businesses disfavored by the general community.

The changes in Chapter I primarily involve new data, on classification and distribution of local government units, from the 1982 census of governments. Chapter II adds some cases on the role of courts in fashioning substantive doctrines and litigation controls that peculiarly affect local units. Chapter III, again with some updating authorities, surveys state legislative control of local units. The materials in Chapter IV were revised to track current trends regarding state-local conflicts. Those in Chapter V survey interlocal cooperation and conflict, and legal barriers that continue to hamper attempts to reorganize the territory or authority of municipalities and special districts. The recent Washington decision on massive bond defaults (under failed nuclear power projects) add fresh urgency and vitality to seemingly technical doctrines on state, regional and local jurisdiction.

Chapter VI was completely overhauled to cover the increasingly specialized law on federal-state-local relations. Some 28 Supreme Court decisions, post 1980, have been added. They represent significant advances that affect many local government functions, viz. local elections, taxation, affirmative action programs, municipal franchises, and regulations that implicate First Amendment freedoms (cable television, business signs, adult book stores).

The chapter VII materials on licensing and land use include a new section on group occupancy of residential property, and new material on low cost housing and on restrictions against businesses that contribute to blight. Chapter VIII updates the local government revenue data by source and amount, and cases on tax caps and debt limitations. The supplemental cases in chapter IX primarily cover issues of collective bargaining, dispute settlement and union security under state public employee labor statutes.

In chapter X a new section has been added on "special duties" of municipalities in exceptional situations. The materials there also trace ongoing adoptions of modified modern versions of state law tort defenses of immunity, comparative negligence, time bars to suit, dollar limits on recovery, and indemnification of officers and employees by their employer governments.

The final chapter reviews the burgeoning law of federal tort liability for deprivation of federal rights under 42 U.S.C. Sec. 1983 primarily through sixteen decisions of the Supreme Court, that were rendered since 1980. Those cases comprise the bulk of this chapter and explain the procedural, substantive and remedial features of federal civil rights torts.

Throughout the text, the notes and annotations to principal cases were selected with a view to indicating spreads of authorities on certain points, and where evident, regional patterns of law that may arise from different socio-economic conditions rather than doctrinal disagreements. The case annotations are intended to facilitate independent research that cannot be pursued within the constraints of a particular course. This casebook is not measured for any set number of hours or to serve any fixed topical coverage or outline. Choices of study or omission must remain with the users, considering, inter alia, what materials are better studied in allied courses. As with prior editions, the footnotes to the principal cases have been omitted with few exceptions, and in the latter instance, case footnotes bear the same number as appears in the original court opinion.

WILLIAM D. VALENTE

Villanova, Pa.
1987

*

Acknowledgments

The time and resources required for this edition were generously provided by the Administration and particularly by the Law Library staff of Villanova University. Special thanks are also due to my students, especially to Nancy Mancheski, Lisa Basemore, and Sharon Sugerman, whose research assistance and editorial suggestions saved me months of effort and substantially improved the final product. As with past editions, faculty secretary, Joan Delong, supplied the patience and skill that was indispensible to completion of the manuscript.

Acknowledgments for copyrighted text materials appear in the pages that contain such material.

*

Summary of Contents

Appendices

Table of Contents

Appendices

*

Table of Cases

The principal cases are in bold type. Cases cited or discussed in the text are roman type. References are to pages. Cases cited in principal cases and within other quoted materials are not included.

Table of Authorities

Following are the authorities cited in the textual interstices of this casebook. Statutory authorities are not included in this Table.

*

LOCAL
GOVERNMENT LAW
CASES AND MATERIALS
Third Edition

*

Chapter I

INTRODUCTION

A. PERSPECTIVES ON THE STUDY OF LOCAL GOVERNMENT LAW

Local Government law is an amalgam of public and private law that is specially adapted to community governance. Viewed from the perspective of government structure and administration, it projects familiar patterns of constitutional and administrative law. Viewed from the perspective of individuals who are subject to government regulations or services, it projects an assortment of private law doctrines, e.g. those relating to contracts, torts, and property. A bifocal view of local government relations, however, would oversimplify and distort the reality. The interaction of public and private law in local government operations must be analyzed in terms of the peculiarities of local government jurisdiction and process. That analysis, whether in planning or executing local government decisions, requires lawyers, to be more than technicians or advocates. Whether acting as counsellors, administrators, judges, or legislators, they must also double, however informally, as architects of social policy.

This book attempts to develop a comprehensive view and understanding of local government practices, at some cost in intensity of coverage of specific subjects of that practice. Specialized studies, *viz.* public employee labor relations or taxation, are best undertaken after one understands the total field of municipal operations. In order to illumine that understanding, occasional references will be made in the following chapters to secondary authorities, *viz.* statistical summaries and legal commentary. However, these references, from a vast pool of literature, are very selective and limited, with a view to encouraging their use in a way that is practical for students.

The materials in the following chapters move from broad topical areas, such as local unit structure and organization, to specific activities of local units in providing services and regulatory oversight. The historical background and data in the initial chapters on local government developments, though familiar to many students, are intended to set the necessary frame of references for problems that are taken up in the succeeding chapters.

One basic theme of lawyering which should be evident from local government study has been summarized as follows: "McLuhan would say: the process defines the product. Yeats puts it better: 'O Body swayed to music, O brightening glance, How can we know the dancer from the dance?' Some would argue: law must be distinguished from the political system. * * * Yet drawing such a distinction is not a neutral act. * * * It disengages the dancer from the dance, the product from the process. There can be no neutral jurisprudence for one who wishes to define law in a democratic society." Cahn & Cahn, *The New Sovereign Immunity,* 81 Harv.L.Rev. 929, 970 (1968).

B. FORMS AND FUNCTIONS OF LOCAL GOVERNMENT UNITS

1. HISTORICAL DEVELOPMENT

Without its historical underpinnings, local government law would seem to be a "ragbag of details". The historical genesis and evolution of various local government units cannot be traced in any detail here, but a useful survey of that history will be found in O.M. Reynolds, Jr., Local Government Law. §§ 5–13 (1982). A number of lessons drawn from that history are still pertinent, to wit:

(1) Local government units, unlike state and federal governments, are not products of constitutional design, but of historical developments, originating in English law. The number and types of local government units continued to grow through successive stages of urbanization to perform ever increasing services and regulation. The modern patchwork of boroughs, towns, cities, counties, and special districts must be understood in the light of their particular uses in each of the states. The different needs that inspired the growth of such units explains the concurrence of different, sometimes overlapping, layers of local governments that operate in a common territory.

(2) Though similarly named, the legal incidents and powers of particular classes of local government vary, depending on their enabling charter laws, whether or not they are "incorporated", and rights gained by custom or prescription. Legal historians thus described local government law in England as "complex and chaotic." In the American environment, the English models underwent still further regional adaptations and variations.

(3) Local governments are not true sovereign governments, but political creatures and subdivisions of sovereign state governments. As such they possess no independent sovereign powers or authority, save those delegated to them by state constitutions and laws. In brief, they remain subject to the sovereign authority of the national and the state

governments. Increased centralization of government functions tends to decrease and displace local jurisdiction. Just as the ancient city-states lost their status in the Roman Empire, and the English boroughs ceased to be "states within states" with the rise of King and Parliament, so did municipalities suffer diminished powers in the welfare state. See e.g. Norton v. Shelby, p. 27 infra; J.C. Bollens and H.J. Schmandt, The Metropolis, p. 431 (1970).

Recent efforts to decentralize government, by ceding back to localities powers previously assumed by the national government and the states, still leave the local units subject in law to the superior jurisdiction of the federal and state legislatures, yet some degree of power-sharing is inevitable:

"It is impossible to govern a whole country exclusively from a single center. Nowhere, even in small states, is it attempted. To do so would mean * * * 'apoplexy at the center and paralysis at the extremities.' All modern states are divided and subdivided into local units." T. Reed, *Municipal Government In The United States*, p. 31 (1934).

(4) The supremacy of federal and state law (within constitutional constraints) over local government law poses perennial issues of pre-emption, i.e. when are local ordinances or regulations consistent with, and when are they in conflict with, or preempted by, higher law. Lawyers must constantly check the hierarchy of pertinent federal, state, and local law governing a particular activity to determine whether a given position is supported by the highest level of applicable law.

(5) Anglo-American local governments have a dual nature. For some purposes and activities they are treated like a private corporation with flexible powers authorized by written charters. For other purposes they remain political subdivisions and government units limited to the will of the sovereign state. The choice of relating to corporate or constitutional law is critical in many cases; but that choice is not always so clear as to eliminate discretionary lawmaking by courts. Conflicts of authority as to whether a particular municipal activity is "proprietary" or "governmental" provide clear examples of the confusing dual nature of local government units.

(6) The development of public policy that is to operate at the local level; and the choice of local, state, or federal agencies to implement such policies, is not a matter of preordained, uniform law, but often a product of political pressure by special interest groups to invest legal jurisdiction at one or another level of government. The shifting alliances between these groups, from one issue to another, also accounts for some variations in local government functional authority from one region to another.

The foregoing generalizations do not tell a very full story, but they do place in appropriate perspective the foundation principles by which the law rationalizes local government jurisdiction and operations.

2. LEGAL CLASSIFICATIONS OF LOCAL GOVERNMENT UNITS

a. Comment on Classification Terms and Criteria

The class labels employed to describe local government units, e.g., cities, towns, boroughs, special districts, provide helpful guidance but not precise indications of local government authority. Aside from a state's power to enlarge or delimit the structure and functions of any particular local government unit, such class labels do not account for distinct types of jurisdiction, i.e. "territorial" jurisdiction and jurisdiction over particular functions. The size and structure of such units have no fixed legal relation to their authorized functions. Further, the distinction between "general function" unit (police power) municipalities and "special function" special districts does not exclude the possibility of both municipalities and special districts exercising overlapping functions in the same area. Undue reliance upon class labels could, therefore, blur and confuse the analysis of competing jurisdictional claims of different local units that serve a common territory.

Reclassifications, subclassifications and different modes of classifications find their way into the law. The older authorities classified units into municipal corporations, sometimes called voluntary (cities, boroughs, towns and villages) and quasi-public corporations; sometimes called involuntary (counties, townships, special districts). 1 Dillon, *Municipal Corporations,* pp. 24, 65 (5th ed. 1911); O.M. Reynolds, Jr., Local Government Law § 6 (1982). Local governments are now classified in terms of their formal structure, their range of functions, population size and density, their dependence or independence with relation to other government agencies, and many other criteria. See e.g. U.S. Bureau of the Census, 1977 *Census of Governments,* V.–1, p. VI et seq. No single classification system adequately explains the variations found in different states among similarly named units. Also cities or towns with similar powers may adopt different plans of organization *viz.* commission, council, and mayor-council type governments; with or without a city or town manager.

Class terms, like city, town or district, absorb additional meanings in different places. The "New England" town is quite different in structure and function than townships in other parts of the country. The newest urban counties and metro-governments defy uniform fitting to historical classifications. These qualifications must be kept in mind in considering the following outline of local government structure.

b. Classification According to Structure

The following excerpt from the 1982 Census of Governments, p. VI, et seq. (U.S. Bureau of the Census) presents the data and distribution on classified units of local governments:

"There were 82,341 governmental units in the United States at the beginning of 1982. In addition to the Federal Government and the 50

State governments, there were 82,290 units of local government. Of these, 38,851 are general-purpose local governments—3,041 county governments, 19,076 municipal governments, and 16,734 township governments. The remainder (over one-half of the total) are limited-purpose local governments, including 14,851 school district governments and 28,588 special district governments.

"The average number of governmental units per State is 1,647 but Illinois has 6,467 while Hawaii has only 18. The following 10 States had more than 3,000 governments each: Illinois, Pennsylvania, Texas, California, Kansas, Minnesota, Ohio, Nebraska, New York, and Missouri. Together these 10 States account for nearly one-half (49 percent) of all governmental units in the Nation. * * *

"The total number of governmental units in 1982 was 2,428 more than that reported for the 1977 census, an overall increase of 3 percent. Virtually all of the increase is in special district governments, which increased 10 percent over the 5–year period.

"As shown by table A, there has been little change in the number of general-purpose governments compared with the previous four censuses. The number of county governments has remained relatively constant; the number of municipal governments continues to increase slightly, while the number of township governments continues to record small declines. However, there have been shifts in the distribution of these governments among the various population-size groupings, * * *. Limited-purpose governments, on the other hand, have had dramatic changes: School districts have decreased significantly, although the rate of decline has slowed in recent years; in contrast, there has been a substantial rise in the number of special district governments, which now comprise 35 percent of all governments, compared to 20 percent in 1962."

Table A. Governmental Units: 1972 to 1982

Type of government	1982	1977	1972
Total	82,341	79,913	78,269
U.S. Government	1	1	1
State governments	50	50	50
Local governments	82,290	79,862	78,218
County	3,041	3,042	3,044
Municipal	19,076	18,862	18,517
Township	16,734	16,822	16,991
School district	14,851	15,174	15,781
Special district	28,588	25,962	23,885

(1) Municipalities

The term "municipality" normally refers to the primary organization of general local government. It embraces a broad class of municipal corporations, including cities, boroughs, villages, and towns, other than New England towns. Municipalities exercise proprietary, as well as governmental functions, and have considerable leeway in choosing the range and level of urban services they provide.

(2) Counties

Descended from the old English shire, the county unit (called "borough" in Alaska, and "parish" in Louisiana) is, with limited exceptions, found in all territories of all the states except Connecticut, Rhode Island, and the District of Columbia. Typically, the county embraces the geographic territory of the other forms of local government as well as unincorporated territory. They vary greatly in their size, powers, and administrative organization.

Counties traditionally administer certain state functions, e.g. justice, property assessment, public roads and record keeping, and are distinguished from general purpose municipalities, under the heading of quasi-municipal or quasi-corporate units. Nevertheless, many local government functions are delegated to county governments, especially with respect to unincorporated areas where the county serves as the primary unit of local government. The area-wide jurisdiction and intermediate position of counties between the state and local governments has in recent decades increasingly rendered the county unit useful to provide area-wide services and to coordinate intergovernmental programs involving federal-local, state-local, and inter-local activity. See e.g. Johnson v. County of Fairfax, p. 190, infra; City of West Allis v. County of Milwaukee, p. 140, infra; Town of Lockport v. Citizens For Community Action, p. 350, infra. The potential for area-wide county functions has been generally blunted in some states, by obsolescent laws which freeze the growth of county governments. For a good summary of the status, potential, and regional differences in county government in the United States, see J.C. Bollens, *American County Government* (1969); Fairlie and Kneier, *County Government Administration* (1930).

(3) Townships

The terms "town" and "township" have no fixed uniform meaning, and have varied significance in different places. The role of townships varies among the states. In compact New England, the "New England Town" is a distinctly strong type of local government, with power being exercised largely through the popular democracy of the town meeting. The Bureau of the Census reports that township organization is, except for the state of Washington, largely confined to twenty-one north and north central states, with only Indiana having townships located throughout the state territory. In Massachusetts, Maine, New York, New Jersey, Pennsylvania, Rhode Island, and Wisconsin, townships, like counties, may provide municipal services to territory that is not incorporated into a municipality. In many states, townships are "unorganized" and therefore qualify only as geographic expressions, rather than as governing units. While their scope of government varies, most townships, except as above noted, provide very limited services to predominantly rural areas. See U.S. Bureau of the Census, *1982 Census of Governments*, V. 1. Stated in fiscal terms: "Only those of Michigan, New Jersey, New York, Pennsylvania and Wisconsin perform many significant functions. The townships in these five states spent almost $600 million in 1962, * * *. The remaining townships * * * primarily in rural areas * * * never had many functions, spending only $158 million in 1962." Committee for Economic Development (hereinafter cited as "CED"), Modernizing Local Government, 30 (N.Y.1966).

(4) Special Districts

Of the 82,290 local governments identified by the United States Census of Governments (1982), 28,588 were classified as special districts. Special districts are the most numerous, diverse and rapidly growing class of local governments, but, except for school districts, they are not usually created in all parts of the state. As indicated by the following section, the one feature that distinguishes the great variety of special districts is their lack of general government authority, and their limited functions to a single or small number of special purposes. Once considered "outside the normal structure of government," the increasing significance and explosive growth of special districts to serve particular areas or provide special facilities has invited refined classification of different types of special district. See, e.g., J.C. Bollens, *Special District Government in the United States* (1964); R. Smith, *Public Authorities, Special Districts, and Local Government* (1964); U.S. Advisory Commission on Intergovernmental Relations, *Special District Government in the United States* (1954). Special districts may be subclassified as "local" or "metropolitan"; and as "independent" or "dependent," i.e., requiring authorization or consent of their overlying municipalities.

Since the powers and purposes of special districts may be expanded by legislation or by contract arrangements, e.g., consolidation of different districts, or cumulative transfer of additional powers to a special district, it remains possible for entities that are originally special districts to evolve de facto as well as de jure into governments that approach, if not assume, the normal powers of a municipality. See, e.g., the cases on the New Jersey-New York Port Authority at p. 236, et seq. infra.

The Bureau of the Census has summarized district distribution as follows:

> "Special district governments are independent, limited-purpose governmental units (other than school district governments), which exist as separate entities with substantial administrative and fiscal independence from general-purpose local governments. As defined for census purposes, the term 'special district governments' excludes school district governments.

"Units counted by the Bureau of the Census as special district governments are found in every State and in the District of Columbia. * * *

"The 28,588 special district governments counted in 1982 reflect an increase of 2,626 or 10 percent since 1977. This continues the upward trend of the past few decades to create new governmental units to meet additional needs for government services and resources.

"The following States, each having at least 800 special district governments account for nearly 64 percent of all such local governments:

California	2,506
Colorado	1,030
Illinois	2,602
Indiana	897
Kansas	1,370
Missouri	1,195
Nebraska	1,157
New York	923
Oklahoma	916
Oregon	825
Pennsylvania	2,050
Texas	1,681
Washington	1,130

An additional 16 States have at least 300 special district governments.

* * *

"On a regional basis, the South gained 1,172 special districts—an increase of 20 percent. Special districts in the West region had the second highest gain—687 or 10 percent. The North Central region, containing the highest number of special districts, recorded a gain of 603 special districts for an increase of 7 percent. The Northeast, adding 164 special districts, had the smallest gain—4 percent.

"Approximately 43 percent of all special district governments reported property-taxing power.

"Special district governments inside SMSA's increased since 1977 by over 2,100 or 22 percent to 11,725 (chart G/8); 37. Special district governments outside SMSA's, recorded a much smaller intercensal gain.

* * *

"Of the 28,588 special district governments reported in 1982, over 91 percent performed a single function. Close to one-fourth of all special district governments are in the natural resources category, performing such functions as drainage and flood control, irrigation, and soil and water conservation. The next most frequent function performed by such units is fire protection, followed by housing and community development, and water supply. * * * "

Table G.   Special District Governments by
Function: 1982

Function	Number	Percent
Total	28,588	100.0
Single-function districts:		
Natural resources	6,232	21.8
Fire protection	4,560	16.0
Housing and community development	3,296	11.5
Water supply	2,637	9.2
Sewerage	1,631	5.7
Cemeteries	1,577	5.5
Education	960	3.4
Parks and recreation	924	3.2
Hospitals	775	2.7
Libraries	638	2.2
Highways	598	2.1
Health	451	1.6
Airports	357	1.2
Other	1,355	4.7
Multiple-function districts	2,597	9.1

c. Classification According to Function

As above noted, local units may be subdivided into general function units (e.g., municipalities) and special function units (e.g., special districts), with the general function unit class being associated with general governmental power, and the special function unit class being associated with a narrow authority to carry out a particular and specific function. Thus, there is less variation in the service and police power functions of general function units than there is in the special purposes served by special function units. The purposes for which special districts (other than school districts) are created vary greatly with the needs of different geographic, urban, suburban, and rural regions. See Table G, supra; ACIR, Special Districts, chapter 3 (1964).

C.   LOCAL GOVERNMENTS IN METROPOLITAN AREAS

"[in the past] There was little question where the city ended and the country began. Outside of city boundaries there were no large population concentrations, and government outside these boundaries was designed for a basically rural condition. * * * *The metropolitan area is in effect a new community.* * * * It ignores the political lines of districts, villages, town, cities, counties and states." CED, *Guiding Metropolitan Growth,* p. 13 (1960)

Few metropolitan areas in the United States are currently governed by a single local government. In addition to socio-economic interdependence, the Census Bureau has, for its classification of Standard Metropolitan Statistical Areas added the requirement of "a recognized large population nucleus.":

"Statistics are summarized for local governments and public school systems in standard metropolitan statistical areas (SMSA's) and New England county metropolitan areas (NECMA's), * * *

"Each SMSA and NECMA consists of a single county area or a group of contiguous counties that includes at least one 'central city' of 50,000 inhabitants or in some instances contiguous twin cities that together meet this population minimum. There are 146 SMSA's and NECMA's that are composed of a single county area. The other 159 SMSA's and NECMA's each consist of two or more county areas. There are 34 SMSA's and one NECMA that cross State boundaries.

"Slightly over 75 percent of the population of the United States reside within standard metropolitan statistical areas and New England county metropolitan areas—170.5 million persons of the nationwide total of 226.5 million counted in 1980. In 1982, these 305 areas encompassed 29,861 local governments, over 36 percent of all local governments in the Nation. In nine State areas, more than 50 percent of all local governments are within SMSA's. * * *

"A considerable portion—41 percent—of all special district governments is found in SMSA's and NECMA's, up from 37 percent in 1977.

"Public school systems within the 305 SMSA's and NECMA's totaled 6,541, or 40 percent of all systems. * * * All 189 school systems with enrollments of more than 25,000 are within metropolitan areas, as are two-thirds of the 3,693 systems with enrollments between 2,500 and 25,000. About 31 percent of the remaining 12,507 school systems with enrollments of less than 25,000 are situated within SMSA's and NECMA's and comprise nearly 60 percent of all public school systems in these areas.

*   *   *

"More than 36 percent of the municipal governments in the Nation were located in standard metropolitan statistical areas and New England county metropolitan areas in 1982, including all 419 municipal governments of 50,000 inhabitants or more, about half (49 percent). * * * " 1982 Census of Governments, Vol. VI, pp. XVIII–XIX (U.S. Bureau of the Census).

The basic factors that must be addressed for effective legal arrangements in the expanded metropolitan community are: population, physical resources, economic resources, and political forces.

1. POPULATION GROWTH AND MIGRATION

Population configurations largely determine public policies pertaining to levels of government service, taxes and the use of open space and natural resources.

The United States population doubled, between 1870 and 1900, then redoubled by 1950. It is now concentrated in 281 metropolitan areas (SMSAs) as defined by the U.S. Census Bureau. The larger SMSAs (over 100,000 inhabitants) contain more than 90% of the urban population. The vigor of metropolitan expansion and the influence of regional population shifts upon local government activity is evident from the following news release of the Census Bureau in December 1985:

"The population of the United States rose to 238,740,000 as of July 1, a growth rate of 5.4 percent over the last five years, the Census Bureau reported today. Southern and Western states accounted for more than 90 percent of the population increase of 12.2 million people, the bureau said. * * *

"California maintained its position as the most populous state, with 26,365,000 residents as of July 1. It was followed by New York, with 17,783,000; Texas, with 16,370,000; Pennsylvania, with 11,853,000, and Illinois with 11,535,000. Florida has moved into the No. 6 slot since 1980, with 11,366,000 residents, displacing Ohio, with a population of 10,744,000.

"Alaska continued to be the fastest-growing state, with a growth rate of 29.7 percent over the five-year period, but it is still the least populated state.

* * *

"Michigan, Ohio, Iowa, Pennsylvania, West Virginia and the District of Columbia have lost population since the census of April 1, 1980. * * * " (N.Y. Times, p. A15 (12–30–85).

Over half the SMSA population lives in the suburbs, and by the end of this century, the majority of all Americans will reside in the suburbs. Typically the more affluent, mobile whites move to the suburbs while the aged, low income and non-white groups move to and remain in the city. See ACIR, *Urban America and the Federal System* 1, 43–50 (1969). Thus although the black population group grew much faster than the white population in metropolitan areas between 1960–1970, the percentage of blacks residing in suburbia has little changed in recent years. The implications of such acute population disparities pose critical challenges to local governments.

2. PHYSICAL RESOURCES

Urban sprawl follows neither the profiles of nature nor artificial political boundaries. Control of the metropolitan environment requires a fiscal and physical capacity that far exceeds that of existing local jurisdictions. CED, *Guiding Metropolitan Growth* (1960). The sharing of natural resources, e.g. land, water and drainage; and the construction of artificial resources, e.g. highways and sewerage increasingly require intergovernmental cooperation, for which available legal means are ill adapted. Land use regulation, largely a matter of local zoning, is divorced from land development financing which is largely a matter of state and federal grant standards.

"Planning * * * has been preoccupied with land use. The result, too often, has been an attempt to achieve impossible goals through irrelevant means * * * Attempts have been made to control the location and flow of population through land policy. The apparent assumption behind such planning is that if everyone could be properly placed in the landscape, the economic and social pieces would necessarily fall into place." Kolestar, *The States and Urban Planning,* in *The States and the Urban Crisis,* Alan K. Campbell, Ed. (American Assembly) p. 134 (1970). See also ACIR—*Urban America and the Federal System* 47–52, 118–122 (1969).

3. ECONOMIC RESOURCES

America's wealth is centered in its SMSAs. Economic resources once concentrated in the core city and its immediate suburbs have been redistributed and deconcentrated throughout the metropolitan region. As new technologies widened the economic base, housing, retail and service industries followed the suburban market. The consequent relocation of jobs and related housing in turn modified the tax base and service levels of many government units. The regional patterns of business planning find little counterpart in local government, whose tax resources, schools, municipal services and land regulation directly interact with the metropolitan economy. See CED, *Guiding Metropolitan Growth* (1960). The "spillover" effects of these developments are familiar.

Area-wide government is easily justified by economic considerations, but political considerations present still other obstacles to local government restructuring.

4. POLITICAL BARRIERS

In 1982, over 80% of the municipalities of America had a population of less than 5000 persons per unit. U.S. Bureau of the Census, *1977 Census of Governments,* Vol. I, p. 2. Consolidation of local government units, however, has largely failed. Metropolitan reorganization affects many "potentially alienable groups" (*viz.* racial and economic classes, political parties, and local officials.) Lawmakers shy away from antagonizing such interest groups. Unchecked by an apathetic public,* these obstacles encourage a fallback to the piecemeal, "incremental," approach of taking small steps toward consolidation, with each step tailored to mollify opposition, by concessions to sectional politics and opinion.

The metropolitan community presents problems of federalism. Federated arrangements are not new to American law but the challenge to adapt techniques of federalism to the metropolis is fairly fresh. See e.g. ACIR, *Regional Decision Making: New Strategies For Substate Districts* (2 vols. 1973); ACIR, *Factors Affecting Voters Reaction to*

---

* "Proposals for government reorganization in metropolitan areas have faced a largely apathetic public. ＊ ＊ ＊ Within the 18 areas studied, only one in four (voters) bothered to cast a vote on the reorganizational proposal." ACIR, *Factors Affecting Voters Reactions to Government* *Reorganization in Metropolitan Areas,* p. 8 (1962). The poor rate of success of proposed metropolitan reforms is summarized in Lineberry, *Reforming Metropolitan Governance; Requiem or Reality,* 58 Georgetown L.Rev. 675 at 715 (1970).

Government Reorganization in Metropolitan Areas (1962); ACIR, *Urban America and the Federal System* (1969); *The States and the Urban Crisis,* pp. 5–7, 169 et seq. (1970).

Summary Note

"Substance v. Resources, Organization, and Politics.

* * *

"These interrelationships between substance, resources, the organizational system and political attitudes make it difficult to fully comprehend the nature of the urban crisis. * * * So much emphasis has been placed by scholars * * * on the fragmented, overlapping character of local government that this character had become, in the minds of many, the urban crisis. * * *

"Despite the dangers inherent in taking apart for analytical purposes the varied aspects of the urban crisis, it is essential that this be done if the analysis is to be manageable." Campbell and Shalala, *Problems Unsolved, Solutions Untried* in *The States and the Urban Crisis,* Alan K. Campbell, Ed. (American Assembly 1970), pp. 5, 6.*

Among the problems aggravated by fractionated local government are:

1. Multiple, uncoordinated legal jurisdiction over given functions;

2. Inability of general government units to plan and coordinate effective urban management;

3. Citizen inability to know, participate in, and control the particular agencies responsible for particular actions;

4. Non-accountability of appointive experts on district boards who need not stand for election.

The simplest solution would be either to eliminate special function units and transfer their functions to general function units, or where this is not feasible, to consolidate them into larger multifunctional districts with elected boards. See ACIR, *Government Structure, Organization and Planning in Metropolitan Areas,* pp. 26–30 (1961).

Chapter II

JUDICIAL OVERSIGHT AND CONTROL OF LOCAL GOVERNMENT UNITS

A. JUDICIAL REVIEW

The influence of the courts on every phase of law making is particularly strong in the field of local government law. It is the courts which determine which branches of public and private law apply to given situations. Whether dealing with the interpretation of constitutions, statutes, or case law, they constantly exercise considerable discretion. Without a clear understanding of discretionary techniques to adapt, reconcile or nullify existing laws, the rules appearing in later chapters would seem to lack consistency of purpose or rationality. As will be seen shortly, however, the purposes underlying various modes of judicial review do provide some rationalizing framework for rules that, standing alone, would be artificial and argumentative.

1. LEGISLATION—CONSTRUCTION AND APPLICATION

Since local governments draw their powers almost exclusively from written laws (i.e. state constitutions, statutes, ordinances and regulations) judicial construction of legislation plays a uniquely important part in local government disputes. The power of courts to determine the meaning and intent of positive legislation is generally exercised under and explained by canons of interpretation. In American law, however, there is no universally adopted doctrine or test of construction, but only an assortment of aids or canons that point in different directions. The following brief review of interpretive methods provides a background for the later discussion of cases that turn on issues of legislative interpretations.

It is obvious that "legislation has a name; it seeks to obviate some mischief, to supply an inadequacy, to effect a change of policy, to formulate a form of government" (Frankfurter, *Some Reflections on the*

Reading of Statutes, 47 Col.L.Rev. 527, 538 (1947)), but the elaboration of legislative purposes to diverse or changed conditions is often far from obvious. When lawmakers fail to anticipate a particular problem, or intentionally consign its solution to nonlegislative bodies under broad guidelines, discretionary gap-filling or implementation becomes unavoidable. In such situations, courts mediate competing public policies and interests, and their policy judgments on the proper thrust of the law are often more crucial than their techniques (canons of statutory construction) to explain the result.

For example, there is no automatic key to a choice between labelling a statute as mandatory or directory; as preemptive, subordinate or concurrent with other statutes; as penal (strict reading) or remedial (liberal reading); or as one of general grant or narrow limitation. Justice Frankfurter's observation that reading of legislation is less a science than a craft, and less a craft than an art, merely acknowledges that courts have a role to play in making law and policy.

While this subject of statutory construction merits extensive study elsewhere, (see e.g. *A Symposium On Statutory Construction,* 3 Vanderbilt L.Rev. 365 (1950)), the following excerpts serve present purposes.

"Under our traditions the Judge's role, while final, is still subordinate. To some extent at least, he must apply laws made by the people's representatives regardless of his own opinions; the pinch comes when the legislators had no discernible or particularized intention. In such a case the Judge may choose between looking to his own heart * * * and seeking to divine out of the confused, often conflicting and half conscious aspirations which lie behind the statutes some resultant of those forces in keeping with what was consciously contemplated. The former choice is not unthinkable. The adjudication of such cases might have been committed to the courts with no mandate save that they should not disregard whatever meaning is reasonably apparent. * * * Thus far, however, our law has made the second choice, casting the Judge as interpreter of the will of Congress." Cox, *Judge Learned Hand and the Interpretation of Statutes,* 60 Harv.L.Rev. 370, 372 (1947).* But as Mr. Justice Frankfurter pointed out the proportion of common law litigation to litigation involving statutory application in the first half of the twentieth century has drastically changed: given the explosive growth of statutory and administrative law at the state and local level, the significance of judicial interpretation of statutes can hardly be overemphasized.

"* * * [T]he shift in the thrust of the judicial function, * * * from concern with the common law to concern with statutory law, has inevitably brought into increasing prominence the principles and techniques of statutory interpretation. * * *" Nutting, Elliott, and Dickerson, *Legislation,* p. 407 (1969).

* Reprinted by permission of The Harvard Law Review Association, copyright © 1947.

While American courts are not bound by any single, dominant process of statutory construction, they are responsible to make consistent and rational use of interpretive principles. The task of the competent lawyer is to apprehend the kinds of occasions, the manner, and the extent to which these principles and techniques will be favored by the authorities.

a. Rules of Construction

Three general rules are often cited by commentators: the literal rule, the golden rule and the mischief rule. E.g., Nutting, Elliott, and Dickerson, supra, pp. 408, 409; Hart and Sachs, *The Legal Process* (Tent.Ed.1958), pp. 1144, 1145. The literal, or plain meaning rule is simple, but of limited use. "Where the language is plain and admits of no more than one meaning, the duty of interpretation does not arise," since "the sole function of the Courts is to enforce it (statute) according to its terms." Caminetti v. United States, 242 U.S. 468, 485–486, 37 S.Ct. 192, 61 L.Ed. 442 (1917). The rule is not helpful in the many cases where legislative language admits of more than one meaning. Few courts would apply a rule literally in order to achieve absurd results. Further, shifting conditions can cause shifting language implications in light of general statutory purpose. While one may always find an individual court or judge who is enthralled by particular language, the literal rule harkens toward the one-word, one-meaning fallacy. Words have many meanings; and draw their meaning from context. "[P]urpose and meaning commonly react upon each other." Landis, *A Note on Statutory Interpretation,* 43 Harv.L.Rev. 886, 887 (1930). "Every language thus presupposes a conceptual 'grid' or 'map' through which all experience is received. To adjust the one is inevitably to affect the other." Dickerson, *The Fundamentals of Legal Drafting,* p. 10 (1965).*

Greater flexibility and consistency between word meaning and legislative purpose is provided by the "golden rule" as expressed in the following excerpts from Riverwear Commissioners v. Adamson, 2 App. Cas. 742, 746 (H.L., 1877): " * * * the office of the Judges is not to legislate, but to declare the expressed intention of the legislature, even if that intention appears to the court injudicious; and I believe that is not disputed * * * that we are to take the whole statute together * * * giving the words their ordinary signification, unless when so applied they produce an inconsistency or an absurdity or inconvenience so great as to convince the court that the intention could not have been to use them in their ordinary signification, and to justify the court in putting on them some other signification, which, though less proper, is one which the court thinks the words will bear." Obviously, there is a good deal of room for differences of opinion as to (a) what results are sufficiently inconvenient or absurd and (b) what the words will bear.

See e.g. Holy Trinity Church v. United States, 143 U.S. 457, 12 S.Ct. 511, 36 L.Ed. 226 (1892).

Still more purposive and open-ended is the "mischief rule" stated in Heydon's Case, 76 Eng.Rep. 637 (Exchequer, 1584):

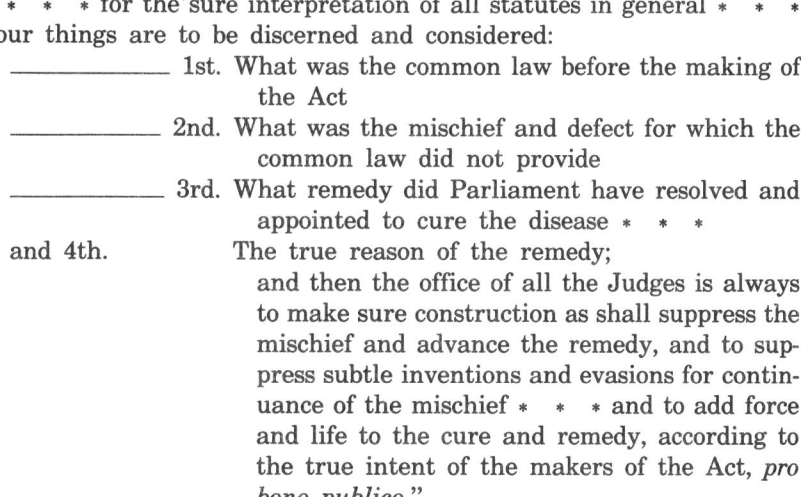

"* * * for the sure interpretation of all statutes in general * * * four things are to be discerned and considered:

        _____ 1st. What was the common law before the making of the Act

        _____ 2nd. What was the mischief and defect for which the common law did not provide

        _____ 3rd. What remedy did Parliament have resolved and appointed to cure the disease * * *

and 4th.   The true reason of the remedy;

and then the office of all the Judges is always to make sure construction as shall suppress the mischief and advance the remedy, and to suppress subtle inventions and evasions for continuance of the mischief * * * and to add force and life to the cure and remedy, according to the true intent of the makers of the Act, *pro bono publico.*"

It should be apparent to any student of constitutional and statutory law, that few judges are wed to any one of the cited rules, be they "liberal" or "conservative," and that the degree of activism and purposive interpretation of any individual may well vary and depend upon his or her policy bias in a particular kind of case. See, e.g., the uneven career of Dillon's Rule, discussed at p. 66, infra, which originally espoused restrictive statutory interpretation to limit implication of local government powers.

b. *Mandatory and Directory Statutes*

The judicial power to create substantive law and to advance public policy, in the guise of construing governing statutes, is well illustrated by the classification of statutes as "mandatory" or "directory." Whether a court will hold official action "void" for failure to follow a statute deemed mandatory, or merely voidable or valid, on a finding that the statute is only directory, often rests upon considerations other than specific legislative language and history.

YOUNKER BROS. v. ZIRBEL

Supreme Court of Iowa, 1943.
234 Iowa 269, 12 N.W.2d 219.

BLISS, JUSTICE.

[The taxpayer challenged increased tax assessments as void and beyond the statutory authority of the assessing Board of Revision. The governing statute provided that "The assessment shall be completed not later than April thirtieth" and that assessed taxpayers may protest increases between May 1 and May 30 of the year of assessment. The assessment was actually made and noticed to the plaintiff taxpayer after June 14.]

It may be noted, and, it is significant, that in the provisions specifying the various times or periods, at or in which, the duties of the Board are to be performed, there are no commands that they shall not be performed at any other times. Section 16 provides that the Board shall be in session * * * during the month of May. But Chapter 202 nowhere prohibits the performance of these duties at any other reasonable time not prejudicial to the rights of an owner or taxpayer. Any action of the Board in performing such a duty is nowhere in the statute declared to be void and of no effect. One of the duties within the power of the Board is to equalize assessments by raising or lowering individual assessments of real property. Section 22 does not expressly state when the power shall be exercised, but neither does it, or any other section, by expression or implication, rigidly limit the exercise of the power to the month of May. The provisions of the statute are directions, only, and are not prohibitory mandates to the Board, or inflexible limitations upon the exercise of its powers or the performance of its duties. The provisions of sections 16 and 21 are directory and not mandatory. This court has uniformly so held, in like or similar situations, whenever the issue has been presented to it. * * *

The general rule is well expressed by a quotation from 23 Am. & Eng.Ency. of Law, 458, in Hubbell v. Polk County, *supra*, 106 Iowa 618, 622, 76 N.W. 854, 856, to wit: "Statutory prescriptions in regard to the time, form, and mode of proceeding by public functionaries are generally directory, as they are not of the essence of the thing to be done, but are given simply with a view to secure system, uniformity, and dispatch in the conduct of public business." The thought is repeated in Hawkeye Lbr. Co. v. Board of Review, *supra*, 161 Iowa 504, 507, 143 N.W. 563, 565, as follows: "Ordinarily statutes which are for the guidance of officers in the conduct of business devolving upon them, designed to secure order, system, and dispatch in the proceedings, and in the disregard of which the rights of persons interested cannot be injuriously affected, are held to be directory." See supporting quotations therein from Cooley, Constitutional Limitations, 5th Ed., page 92, and 2 Sutherland on Statutory Construction, section 611. * * *

Chapter 202 of the 49th G.A. and Chapter 343 of the 1939 Code are public revenue statutes designed to provide funds for governmental use. They should be construed to effect that end, and the acts of the enforcing officers upheld unless clearly contrary to the statutory provisions, and substantially prejudicial to the rights of the owner or taxpayer. * * *

The language of Chapter 202 of the 49th G.A. should be construed as have other similar taxation statutes. The times and periods noted in sections 16 and 21 are general guides * * *. Time is not of the essence of the provisions ∗ ∗ ∗ The delay in increasing the assessments until June 14 has not prejudiced the appellant. While the aggrieved owner or taxpayer is required under Section 23 to file his protest between the inclusive dates of May first and May twentieth, if the original assessment is not raised, he is, of course, entitled to file a protest to the action of the Board if it increases his assessment subsequent to May thirty-first, as was done in this case. He is also entitled to appeal to the district court, as provided by statute, from a denial of his protest. The appellant has taken advantage of the rights of protest and of appeal accorded it under the statute. It may prosecute his appeal and test the correctness of the assessments by a trial on the merits. Neither the statute nor the conduct of the taxing officials has deprived it of any of its rights under the equal protection or due process clauses of the State or Federal Constitutions.

∗ ∗ ∗

The order of the trial court in annulling the writ is affirmed.

Notes

Accord. Parker v. Krick, 433 Pa. 514, 252 A.2d 648 (1969). In *Parker,* the court stated: "We are aware that this Court stated in dictum in *Taylor Borough Appeal,* supra, that the provisions of the act before us are mandatory. However, the Court there was discussing the time of appeal provisions of the Act to which contesting taxpayers are subject. There is no inconsistency in viewing those provisions, which are similar in nature to statutes of limitations, as being mandatory, while holding the provisions to which the board is subject as being directory within the rationale of *Pennsylvania Railroad.*" 252 A.2d at 649.

GANN v. HARRISBURG COMMUNITY UNIT SCHOOL DISTRICT

Appellate Court of Illinois, 1966.
73 Ill.App. 103, 218 N.E.2d 833.

GEORGE J. MORAN, JUSTICE.

[Appeal from dismissal of suit to void a special election that authorized the creation of a school district, on the grounds that one of the polling places was located outside the territory of the proposed school district, in violation of the governing election statute.]

∗ ∗ ∗

The statute ∗ ∗ ∗ expressly provides that the polling place for a particular precinct must lie within the boundaries of the precinct.
∗ ∗ ∗

Generally, an election should be held at the time and in the place provided by law in order that it have validity. Snowball v. People ex rel. Grupe, 147 Ill. 260, 35 N.E. 538. However, a distinction has been drawn between directory and mandatory provisions. Siedschlag v. May, 363 Ill. 538, 2 N.E.2d 836; People ex rel. v. Crossley, 261 Ill. 78, 103 N.E. 537. The failure to follow a mandatory provision will invalidate an otherwise valid election, while the failure to follow a directory provision will not. People ex rel. v. Graham, *supra.* This is not to say, however, that a directory provision may or should be disregarded, but only that an entire election will not be invalidated for the failure to follow such a provision. Hester v. Kamykowski, 13 Ill.2d 481, 150 N.E.2d 196. This analysis has been used not only for general elections, but also for special school elections. People ex rel. v. Kinsey, 294 Ill. 530, 128 N.E. 561; [citations omitted].

The determination whether a statutory provision is mandatory or directory has depended upon the following criteria: (1) Whether the statutory scheme expressly or impliedly provides that the failure to follow the provision shall render an election void; (2) whether the failure interfered in any way with the result of the election; (3) whether any person legally entitled to vote was not permitted to do so; (4) whether any person voted who was not a resident of the territory sought to be organized; (5) whether the polling place was chosen for any improper motive; and (6) whether any fraud occurred in or as a result of the selection of the polling place. People ex rel. v. Green, 265 Ill. 39, 106 N.E. 504; [citations omitted]. Generally, "statutory provisions regulating the conduct of an election are deemed directory after an election in which no improper voting has occurred." People ex rel. Elder v. Quilici, *supra,* 309 Ill.App. at 472, 33 N.E.2d at 495.

In this case, the statutory scheme does not expressly or impliedly provide that a failure to follow the provision shall render an election void. In addition, none of the adverse effects mentioned above were alleged to have occurred as a result of the failure. Nor was there any fraud alleged. Hence, the provision is directory, not mandatory, and the election need not be voided.

For the foregoing reasons, the judgment of the lower court is affirmed.

Judgment affirmed.

Notes

See also Veterans Finance Committee v. Betts, 55 Cal.2d 397, 11 Cal. Rptr. 103, 359 P.2d 471 (1961) (defective election notice held not to nullify election). In prior cases the same court held that proper notice of election to fill vacancies in elective office was necessary to validate special elections. People ex rel. Leverson v. Thompson, 67 Cal. 627, 9 P. 833 (1937); Kenfield v. Irwin, 52 Cal. 164 (1877). Do the contrasting classifications of the same statutory notice provisions hinge upon fact distinctions, upon hindsight balancing of public injuries to be endured under the available alternatives of finding a statute mandatory or directory? Are courts more likely to enjoin proposed official action than to overturn completed official action? See Hurd v. Nyquist, 72 Misc.2d 213, 338 N.Y.S.2d 702 (1972).

MULLEN v. BOARD OF SCHOOL DIRECTORS OF DuBOIS AREA S. DIST.

Supreme Court of Pennsylvania, 1969.
436 Pa. 211, 259 A.2d 877.

ROBERTS, JUSTICE. * * * Mullen was abruptly dismissed by appellant Board of School Directors [Board] from his position as a temporary professional employee of the DuBois Area School District. * * * Mullen brought an action in mandamus seeking reinstatement to his position * * * and related economic damages. * * * Mullen alleged that his dismissal was arbitrary and capricious and that he had no other adequate remedy because his dismissal had made it impossible for him to obtain employment as a teacher in any other school district.

The Board answered that Mullen's dismissal was the result of his unsatisfactory service as a teacher, that he had no valid and enforceable contract with the Board, and that he had other adequate remedies.

The trial court resolved all of the issues in favor of Mullen and ordered both reinstatement and payment of damages. We affirm.

* * *

The second issue in the case involves the validity of the contract between Mullen and the Board. The Public School Code requires that the hiring of a professional employee be effected by an affirmative vote of a majority of the members of the hiring board duly recorded in its minutes. The Board takes the position that there is no valid and enforceable contract covering Mullen's employment because there is no recorded vote of the Board with regard to that contract.

The facts concerning Mullen's hiring bear narration at this point. On January 22, 1966, while still a student, Mullen was interviewed by the superintendent of the DuBois Area School District. At the close of this interview Mullen signed a document which proclaimed itself to be a contract of employment. The instrument was subsequently signed by the President and Secretary of the Board. The exact nature of the authority given by the Board to the superintendent in hiring teachers is unclear, and their records are less than complete. However, we agree with the trial court's finding that "[i]t is quite clear that the Board did approve the appointment and accepted it. Further, its prior approval was followed by further acceptance of the contract." The Board clearly acquiesced in Mullen's appointment for over a year; at one point he was personally feted at a Board meeting for having received a favorable commendation from the Pennsylvania Department of Public Instruction on the handling of one of his courses.

We agree with the trial court that it would be "not only unconscionable but untenable at law, to maintain that the requirements for a valid and enforceable contract were not met in this case."

We are aware that there is a line of cases giving this statute a very strict construction. To the extent that they interpret the requirement that there be a formal vote recorded in the minutes as being mandatory we overrule them. In a way we are only returning to the interpretation given the predecessor of this statute in the first case which dealt with it. * * *

Neither are we inclined to eviscerate the force of the statute. However, it is clear beyond doubt that the expression of the board members' approval required by the statute can be evidenced in ways other than by a formal vote recorded in the minutes. To allow this does no violence to the purpose of the statute. * * * To hold that the lack of a formal vote recorded in the minutes, the presence or absence of which is entirely within the control of the Board, renders this contract null and void, would be to exalt form over substance. What possible value can there be in establishing rigid civil service requirements to protect public employees, if such legislation can be defeated by school board mistakes in the appointive process? We hold the requirement of a formal recorded vote to be directory only, although with the caveat that the proof from which Board approval can be inferred must be solid.

Any result other than the one we reach today would arm every school board in the Commonwealth with a tool by which they could regularly avoid otherwise valid contracts. All they would need do is fail to specifically record in their minutes the required vote; then at their whim, as in this case, a contract could be voided by acknowledgement of the failure. Such a situation is clearly violative of the avowed legislative policy of creating in this state an atmosphere hospitable to school teachers. * * *

The third and final question is this appeal is whether mandamus is proper. "Mandamus is an extraordinary writ which lies to compel the performance of a ministerial act or mandatory duty where there is a *clear* legal right in the plaintiff, a corresponding duty in the defendant, and a want of any other appropriate and adequate remedy." Travis v. Teter, 370 Pa. 326, 330, 87 A.2d 177, 179 (1952). This is such a case. The existence of a right in Mullen and a corresponding duty in the Board has been established. The only other condition is the absence of an adequate alternative remedy. None exists. Mullen has not been able to secure other satisfactory employment since his dismissal. We have concluded, as did the trial court, that he is entitled to restoration to his position, damages for lost salary * * * and a certification which would result in his becoming a "permanent professional employee." * * *

Judgment affirmed.

POMEROY, J., files a dissenting opinion in which Jones, J., joins.

POMEROY, JUSTICE (dissenting). I cannot agree with the conclusion of the majority that mandamus will lie in the present case, * * *. This is a basic issue which lies at the threshold of this case. As the majority recognizes, mandamus will lie only to compel performance of a ministerial act or a mandatory duty where there is a clear right-duty relationship between plaintiff and defendant. In this case, such a relationship between Mullen and the Board could have been created only by a valid and enforceable contract entitling Mullen to continued employment. Thus, the existence of such a contract is the crucial issue.

The standards for making a valid employment contract between a teacher and a school district are not the usual common law standards; they have been set forth in meticulous fashion by the legislature. The relevant statute is clear and unequivocal: "The affirmative vote of a majority of all the members of the board of school directors in every school district, duly recorded, showing how each member voted, *shall be required* in order to take action on the following subjects:—* * * Appointing or dismissing * * * teachers, * * * *Failure to comply with the provisions of this section shall render such acts of the board of school directors void and unenforceable.*" Act of September 28, 1951, P.L. 1546, § 1, 24 P.S. § 5–508. * * * Accordingly, the employment contract in question is void and unenforceable unless the quoted provision is, as the majority concludes, directory in nature.

Whether a particular statutory provision is mandatory or directory is determined by the intent of the legislature as ascertained by a consideration of the statute as a whole. See *e.g.* Prichard v. Willistown Twp. School District, 394 Pa. 489, 147 A.2d 380 (1959). The essential difference between mandatory and directory provisions is the effect given to acts performed in violation of the standard set forth: "A mandatory provision is one the omission to follow which renders the proceeding to which it relates illegal and void, while a directory provision is one the observance of which is not necessary to the validity of the proceeding." Deibert v. Rhodes, 291 Pa. 550, 554–555, 140 A. 515, 517 (1928): Pleasant Hills Borough v. Carroll, 182 Pa.Super. 102, 125 A.2d 466 (1956); and Kowell Motor Vehicle Registration Case, 209 Pa.Super. 386, 228 A.2d 50 (1969). In the present case, the legislature has prescribed that failure of a board to adhere to the statutory procedures for the appointment of teachers shall render such acts void and unenforceable. I can imagine no way in which the legislature could have better or more categorically expressed its intent that these procedures were to be considered mandatory * * *.

Secondly, it should be noted that the statutory requirement * * * has been on the books of the Commonwealth for over one hundred years. * * * Finally, it was retained in The Public School Code of 1949, Act of March 10, 1949, P.L. 30, Art. V, § 508, as amended, 24 P.S. § 5–508. As the majority recognizes, this requirement of the statute has been consistently construed by this and other courts as a mandatory provision. See Taggart v. Board of Directors of Canon-McMillan Joint School System, 409 Pa. 33, 185 A.2d 332 (1962); Commonwealth ex rel. Ake v. Blough, 330 Pa. 590, 200 A. 10 (1938); Commonwealth ex rel. Ricapito v. Bethlehem School District, 148 Pa.Super. 426, 25 A.2d 786 (1942); McCandless v. Summit Township School District, 55 Pa. Super. 277 (1913). The legislature chose to re-enact this provision in the face of this long-standing judicial interpretation. It is a settled canon of statutory construction that legislative reenactment of a statutory provision is presumptively a legislative adoption of the judicial interpretation previously given to the language in question. See Statutory Construction Act, Act of May 28, 1937, P.L. 1019, Art. IV, § 51, 46 P.S. § 551; Commonwealth v. Wetzel, 435 Pa. 468, 257 A.2d 538 (1969); and Commonwealth v. Sitkin's Junk Co., 412 Pa. 132, 194 A.2d 199 (1963). Particularly in view of this standard, I am unable to accept the view that the provision at hand is, in its intent, merely directory. This Court can overrule its own decisions, as the majority here frankly does; in so doing, however, it effectively negates a valid statutory provision, and that it cannot do.

Finally, it should be noted that the statutory requirement of a recorded affirmative vote applies not only to the appointment of teachers but also to a wide variety of other school board actions * * *. Cases holding the present provision to be mandatory as to these other actions by school boards are numerous. See Yoder v. School District of Luzerne Twp., 399 Pa. 425, 160 A.2d 419 (1960); In re Chester School District's Audit, 301 Pa. 203, 151 A. 801 (1930); Jackson v. Conneautville Borough School District, *supra,* and Matevish v. Ramey Borough School District, 167 Pa.Super. 313, 74 A.2d 797 (1950). I see no ground upon which we could logically find the affirmative recorded vote requirement mandatory as to some board actions and directory only as to other actions. While this case is decided on its own facts, it seems inevitable that the decision may have unwanted consequences in other areas.

Nothing I have here said is intended to condone in any way the negligent, or even improper, conduct of the School Board in the situation before us. Moreover, I recognize that certain problems of policy are inherent in a statute which subjects the substantive rights of one party to a second party's faithful observance of procedural requirements. But the choice of such a procedure is within the province of the legislature, and the legislature * * * spoke with unmistakable clarity. For this Court to hold that the words "void and unenforcible" mean "valid and enforceable" is, in my view, judicial legislation unwarranted by even the hard facts of this case.

Notes

1. How critical were the following factors: (a) whether it was practical to insist upon correction of the statutory deficiency; (b) the degree of departure from statutory requirements; (c) the materiality and consequence of the particular statutory violation, i.e. whether the statutory violation was relatively harmless or substantially subversive of primary legislative policy goals?

2. In Stana v. School District of City of Pittsburgh, 775 F.2d 122 (3d Cir.1985), the court refused to give a literal meaning to mandatory statutory language: "Stana argues that 24 Pa.Stat.Ann. § 21–2110, gives her a

substantive right to the position itself. She construes the statutory provision as depriving the school district officials of any discretion. * * * We do not think that the Supreme Court of Pennsylvania would construe § 21–2110 as compelling that result. We recognize that the statute is couched in mandatory language but several considerations impel us to conclude that, nonetheless, the School District retains some discretion to bypass one or more names from the [eligibility] list in an appropriate situation." Id. at 131.

2. JUDICIALLY DETERMINED DOCTRINES

a. *De Facto Government Action*

Occasionally, the purported authority and actions of local governments or their officers are challenged as void because of non-compliance with the preconditions of the statutes which authorize their creation and activities. When defects of legal qualification are discovered *after* substantial transactions were undertaken in reliance on the appearance of government authority, courts must choose between two divergent public policies, namely, enforcing all requirements of enabling statutes; or avoiding disruption and instability of public affairs or harsh forfeiture of just private claims. This dilemma is sometimes solved by curative legislation which, retroactively, confirms or validates the challenged transactions. Where validating statutes are not available or cannot be enacted timely to solve the immediate problem, courts have fashioned "de facto" doctrines which, in appropriate circumstances, preserve the legality of technically deficient action. The application of these doctrines turns upon the proper adjustment of the competing policies. The factors bearing upon that adjustment are noted in the following materials.

(1) De Facto Entities

By analogy to the law of private corporations, courts generally subscribe to the following statement, with respect to defectively organized governmental units:

"A public or municipal corporation de facto exists when there is:

"(1) Some law under which a corporation with powers assumed might lawfully have been created;

"(2) A colorable and bona fide attempt to perfect an organization under such a law;

"(3) User of the rights claimed to have been conferred by the law.

"This rule has been adopted in substance as applicable to private corporations. The same rule applies whether the corporation is a public or private one.

"The reason for this rule, as accepted in this state, emphasizes the importance of stability and certainty in matters involving public corpo-

rate franchises and the serious consequences which might follow if the existence of a municipal corporation should be called into question and, perhaps, determined void in actions between the corporation and private parties."
See Bowman v. Moorehead, 228 Minn. 35, 36 N.W.2d 7 (1949).

Courts will not apply the de facto doctrine in the face of explicit statutory prohibitions. Thus, de facto theory requires an outstanding law that authorizes de jure creation of the agency in question. "In the absence of a law authorizing the creation of a municipality de jure there can be none de facto." See Ocean Beach Heights, Inc., v. Brown-Crummer Investment Co., 302 U.S. 614, 58 S.Ct. 385, 82 L.Ed. 478, (1938). Courts are divided on the question whether an enabling statute which was presumed valid at the time of purported municipal action, but which was later declared unconstitutional, satisfies the "color of law" ground for de facto existence. Compare the *Ocean Beach* decision, supra, with Evans v. Anderson, 132 Minn. 59, 155 N.W. 1040 (1916). Cf. Norton v. Shelby County, 118 U.S. 425, 6 S.Ct. 1121, 30 L.Ed. 178 (1886).

De facto recognition was given to a town unit that operated for many years without challenge, until the discovery of oil under a public way raised a claim by an abutting landowner. Despite the absence of an endorsement on its petition for incorporation and the absence of a judge's initial on the docket entry of incorporation as required by governing statutes, the town's claim was sustained. Town of Maysville v. Magnolia Petroleum Co., 272 F.2d 806 (10th Cir.1959). In the *Bowman* case, supra, the court found the city of Moorehead to be "a valid de facto government under a revised charter," notwithstanding the failure of authorities to publish general notice of the proposed new charter in the manner prescribed by the state constitution. In *Ocean Beach*, supra, however, the court held that a de jure town could not claim de facto existence within disconnected territory in view of legal prohibitions against incorporation of disconnected tracts of land.

Procedural Barriers to Challenge Municipal Existence. Most states follow the rule that the issue of defective incorporation can only be raised by or with the consent of state officials. In the absence of specific enabling legislation, private plaintiffs lack standing to make a collateral attack upon the validity of municipal action, unless and until their rights and obligations are directly affected by the questioned government. See *Town of Maysville*, supra. The barrier to collateral attack is removed, however, where state law permits state citizens to bring such suits. Trimble v. People, 75 Ill. 561 (1874).

Statutory Validation. The power of state legislatures to validate and confer de jure status on de facto legal governments has been sustained (see *Town of Maysville*, supra; Perkins v. State, 367 S.W.2d 140 (Tex.1963)). That power, of course, extends only to actions that are otherwise constitutional.

(2) De Facto Officers

The de facto doctrine relating to the status and authority of de facto officers parallels, but is not identical to, that which applies to de facto government entities.

NORTON v. SHELBY COUNTY

Supreme Court of the United States, 1886.
118 U.S. 425, 6 S.Ct. 1121, 30 L.Ed. 178.

MR. JUSTICE FIELD delivered the opinion of the court.

[Following the decision of the highest court of the State of Tennessee the court held that the Board of Commissioners of Shelby County, organized under the Act of March 9, 1867, had no lawful existence; that it was an unauthorized and illegal body; that its members were usurpers of the functions and powers of the justices of peace of the county; that their action in holding a county court was void; and that their acts in subscribing to the stock of the Mississippi River Railroad Company and issuing bonds in payment therefor were void.]

This suit was brought to enforce payment of twenty-nine bonds for $1000 each, issued by the Board of Commissioners of Shelby County, * * *

* * *

But it is contended that if the act creating the board was void, and the commissioners were not officers *de jure*, they were nevertheless officers *de facto*, * * * This contention is met by the fact that there can be no officer, either *de jure* or *de facto*, if there be no office to fill. As the act attempting to create the office of commissioner never became a law, the office never came into existence. Some persons pretended that they held the office, but the law never recognized their pretensions, nor did the Supreme Court of the State. * * *

The doctrine which gives validity to acts of officers *de facto*, whatever defects there may be in the legality of their appointment or election, is founded upon considerations of policy and necessity, for the protection of the public and individuals whose interests may be affected thereby. Offices are created for the benefit of the public, and private parties are not permitted to inquire into the title of persons clothed with the evidence of such offices and in apparent possession of their powers and functions. For the good order and peace of society their authority is to be respected and obeyed until in some regular mode prescribed by law their title is investigated and determined. It is manifest that endless confusion would result if in every proceeding before such officers their title could be called in question. But the idea of an officer implies the existence of an office which he holds. It would be a misapplication of terms to call one an officer who holds no office, and a public office can exist only by force of law. This seems to us so obvious that we should hardly feel called upon to consider any adverse opinion on the subject but for the earnest contention of plaintiff's counsel that such existence is not essential, and that it is sufficient if the office be provided for by any legislative enactment, however invalid. Their position is, that a legislative act, though unconstitutional, may in terms create an office, and nothing further than its apparent existence is necessary to give validity to the acts of its assumed incumbent. That position, although not stated in this broad form, amounts to nothing else. It is difficult to meet it by any argument beyond this statement. An unconstitutional act is not a law; it confers no rights; it imposes no duties; it affords no protection; it creates no office; it is, in legal contemplation, as inoperative as though it had never been passed.

*   *   *

Numerous cases are cited in which expressions are used which, read apart from the facts of the cases, seemingly give support to the position of counsel. But, when read in connection with the facts, they will be seen to apply only to the invalidity, irregularity, or unconstitutionality of the mode by which the party was appointed or elected to a legally existing office. *   *   *

The case of The State v. Carroll, 38 Conn. 449, decided by the Supreme Court of Connecticut, upon which special reliance is placed by counsel, and which is mentioned with strong commendation as a landmark of the law, in no way militates against the doctrine we have declared, but is in harmony with it. *   *   * The court held that whether the law was constitutional or not, he was an officer *de facto*, and, as such, his acts were valid. The opinion of Chief Justice Butler is an elaborate and admirable statement of the law *   *   *; and it thus defines an officer *de facto:*

"An officer *de facto* is one whose acts, though not those of a lawful officer, the law, upon principles of policy and justice, will hold valid, so far as they involve the interests of the public and third persons, where the duties of the office are exercised:

"First. Without a known appointment or election, but under such circumstances of reputation or acquiescence as were calculated to induce people, without inquiry, to submit to or invoke his action, supposing him to be the officer he assumed to be.

"Second. Under color of a known and valid appointment or election, but where the officer had failed to conform to some precedent, requirement, or condition, as to take an oath, give a bond, or the like.

"Third. Under color of a known election or appointment, void because the officer was not eligible, or because there was a want of power in the electing or appointing body, or by reason of some defect or irregularity in its exercise, such ineligibility, want of power, or defect being unknown to the public.

"Fourth. Under color of an election or an appointment by or pursuant to a public, unconstitutional law, before the same is adjudged to be such."

Of the great number of cases cited by the Chief Justice none recognizes such a thing as a *de facto* office, or speaks of a person as a *de facto* officer, except when he is the incumbent of a *de jure* office. The fourth head refers not to the unconstitutionality of the act creating the office, but to the unconstitutionality of the act by which the officer is appointed to an office legally existing. That such was the meaning of the Chief Justice is apparent from the cases cited by him in support of the last position, * * *

It is evident, from a consideration of these cases, that the learned Chief Justice, in State v. Carroll, had reference, in his fourth subdivision, as we have said, to the unconstitutionality of acts appointing the officer, and not of acts creating the office. * * *

* * * Where no office legally exists, the pretended officer is merely a usurper, to whose acts no validity can be attached; and such, in our judgment, was the position of the commissioners of Shelby County who undertook to act as the county court, which could be constitutionally held only by justices of the peace. * * *

It remains to consider whether the action of the commissioners in subscribing for stock of the Mississippi River Railroad Company and issuing the bonds, * * * being originally invalid, was afterwards ratified by the county. The County Court, consisting of the justices of the peace, elected in their respective districts, alone had power to make a subscription and issue bonds. * * *

* * *

The question recurs whether any ratification can be inferred from the action of the County Court on the 11th and 16th of April, 1870, which was had before that Constitution took effect. At the meeting of the court on those days * * * less than a majority of the justices of the county were present; and the County Court under those circumstances could not even directly have authorized the subscription. * * *

* * * The original invalidity of the acts of the commissioners has never been subsequently cured. It may be, as alleged, that the stock of the railroad company, for which they subscribed, is still held by the county. If so, the county may, by proper proceedings, be required to surrender it to the company, or to pay its value; for, independently of all restrictions upon municipal corporations, there is a rule of justice that must control them as it controls individuals. * * * But questions of that nature do not arise in this case. Here it is simply a question as to the validity of the bonds in suit, and as that cannot be sustained, the judgment below must be Affirmed.

Notes

1. While the *Norton* rule prevails among the states (see e.g. In re Templeton, 399 Pa. 10, 159 A.2d 725 (1960)), there is a weak minority *contra.* Jersey City v. Department of Civil Service, 57 N.J.Super. 13, 153 A.2d 757 (1959); Lang v. Mayor of the City of Bayonne, 74 N.J.L. 455, 68 A.

90 (1907); see also Platte v. Dortch, 255 Ind. 157, 263 N.E.2d 266 (1970). It is interesting to note that the minority reads the lead case of State v. Carroll differently than the Norton court to uphold recognition of *de facto* officers in the absence of a legally existing office, on the ground that such recognition equally serves the policy of protecting the public in good faith dealings with apparent public officials.

A person elected to borough office on an election date prior to the date set by the governing election statutes was held to qualify as a *de facto* officer for the purpose of suing an adjoining township to protect the borough's interest. Borough of Pleasant Hills v. Jefferson, 359 Pa. 509, 59 A.2d 697 (1948). Is this case distinguishable from Norton and Templeton, supra?

2. **Appointments by De Facto Officers.** Third parties may not collaterally attack the action of a *de facto* officer which affects public employees. Detroit Police Officers Ass'n v. Detroit, 17 Mich.App. 700, 170 N.W.2d 260 (1969); Commonwealth ex rel. Palermo v. Pittsburgh, 339 Pa. 173, 13 A.2d 24 (1940).

3. **Conflicting Policies Affecting De Facto Official Action.** The Palermo opinion noted that the *de facto* doctrine would not apply to sustain action that personally benefits the *de facto* officer. Should courts, even in the absence of conflicts of interest or nepotism, abandon *de facto* analysis where contravening public policies outweigh the value of preserving the *de facto* action?

b. Classification of Municipal Activities: Governmental-Proprietary Distinctions

The legal effect of particular actions often hinges upon the characterization of those actions as "governmental" or "proprietary." When acting in governmental capacities, municipalities exercise delegated sovereign powers, which tend to be construed narrowly, and which are subject to "public" law doctrines. When acting in a proprietary capacity, they are exposed to private law doctrines, by analogy to the law governing private corporations. See generally, O. Reynolds, *Local Government Law*, p. 12 (1982); Antieau, *Municipal Corporations* § 5.06. The governmental-proprietary distinction has significant impact, not only in disputes between individuals and local governments, but also between different government units. The state's plenary power to appropriate property of its local government subdivisions is not defeated by the nature of local use, but if the property be held in a proprietary and not governmental capacity, the state may be held to compensate the local unit under federal constitutional law. See ch. III, § A, infra.

The governmental-proprietary distinction also affects conflicting claims by local governments over the same subject. The authority of one local entity to condemn the property of another may depend on the purpose (governmental or proprietary) for which the property is sought, and if governmental, whether it represents a "higher" use than that for which it is held by the putative condemnee. Further, assuming authority to condemn, the obligation of the taking unit to pay the surrendering unit compensation will also depend upon the governmental or proprietary use of the condemned land, unless express legislation by the state supersedes these judge-made standards. See ch. VII, § D.2, infra.

The distinction is also critical in cases involving local government tort immunity (see ch. X and state taxation of local government activity. See p. 32, et seq.

The efforts of courts to rationalize decisions based upon the above distinctions have become increasingly difficult and elusive as modern local governments increasingly assume service functions that were previously provided almost exclusively by private businesses and charities. As the public-private distinction becomes more blurred, the case authorities become more confusing. Nevertheless, the distinction endures.

PEOPLE EX REL. CHICAGO TITLE & TRUST CO. v. MISSION BROOK SANITARY DISTRICT

Appellate Court of Illinois, 1966.
76 Ill.App.2d 423, 222 N.E.2d 8.

Sullivan, Presiding Justice.

[Developer sued Sanitary District in mandamus to compel the District to approve his plans to connect sanitary sewers to the District's facilities. The District refused approval because Developer refused to take its water supply from the District, and opted to connect to the water lines of the local Village, whose water rates were better than 40% cheaper than the District's. The court affirmed judgment for the Developer.]

* * *

Furthermore, the operation of a sewage system differs from that of a waterworks system. * * * The court in Ruth v. Aurora Sanitary District, 17 Ill.2d 11, at page 20, * * * said:

"The governmental function granted to sanitary districts is the treatment and purification of sewage for the preservation of public health, * * *"

On the other hand, the operation of a waterworks system is a proprietary function of any municipality. * * *

Since the supplying of water is a proprietary function, the Sanitary District and the Village can operate water distribution systems with coequal jurisdiction.

* * *

Because of a lack of exclusivity of right to supply water to the property involved in this case, and a positive duty to supply sewage service to that same property, the Sanitary District was without right to deny its approval of plaintiffs' engineering plans * * *.

HOLDING

*   *   *

Judgment affirmed.

DEPARTMENT OF TREASURY v. EVANSVILLE

Supreme Court of Indiana, 1945.
223 Ind. 435, 60 N.E.2d 952.

YOUNG, JUDGE.

This case involves the liability of the city for the payment of gross income tax upon income derived from certain activities and the decision depends upon whether or not the activities are private or proprietary within the meaning of the 1937 amendment to the gross income tax act. * * * The 1937 amendment changed the definition of "person" to read as follows:

> "When used in this act, the term 'person' * * *, means and includes any * * * municipal corporation or any other political subdivision of the state engaged in private or proprietary activities or business, * * *." Burns' Ind.Stat.1933, § 64–2601.

The City of Evansville is engaged in the following activities from which it derives gross revenue:

It owns and operates two city markets in which it leases stalls and stands to farmers and others engaged in the operation of retail food establishments.

It * * * owns real estate * * * which it has improved and operates as a public wharf. * * *

It owns certain levee, street and park property which it leases to persons for farming and other uses. This includes street paving and repair equipment which it leases to contractors when not in use by the city.

It also owns and operates a municipal golf course as a part of its park system, in connection with which it collects fees * * *.

It also, in connection with its park system, leases concession stands and shelter houses from which sales are made of soft drinks and confections.

During the period here involved, it also sold and leased park and airport land.

During the period here involved, it made sales of miscellaneous, obsolete or wornout equipment * * *; also property acquired in a normal way by the park department, but no longer useful; also scrap and junk accumulated at the municipal airport.

It granted permits to persons desiring to cut into the city streets for utility connections and other purposes, and at the time of granting such permits charged the permittee a sum sufficient to pay the cost of replacing the cut pavement, which said sums were placed in the Street Department fund of the city.

The city operates a municipal airport at which gas and oil are sold and rental is received for the storage of planes. Income is also derived from soft drink concessions at the airport.

It owns and operates two cemeteries from which it derives revenue from the sale of lots and graves, containers for flowers and the installation of miscellaneous materials, foundations for stones and monuments, and service and sodding lots and graves. * * *

It owns and operates a rendering plant used for the reduction of dead animals * * *. By-products are sold in the open market.

* * * Some of these activities have resulted in net loss which has been paid from funds derived from taxes. We have not referred to these matters in stating the several items involved, because the tax involved is not a profits tax and the taxability of every item of income depends solely upon the nature and character of the activity involved and not upon whether a profit is realized, or from what source a deficit is met, or how the property used was acquired.

For the years 1937 to 1941, the City of Evansville paid gross income tax upon its gross receipts derived from all the foregoing activities. Thereafter it filed its statement and petition for refund, which was denied and this action was brought to recover the gross income tax so paid. The case was submitted upon a stipulation of facts and the court found that the city's receipts from its markets, wharf, golf course privileges, street repairs, sale of gas and oil at the airport, and sale of lots and graves and service and sodding in its cemeteries, were not taxable under the terms of the gross income tax law, as amended in 1937, and found that receipts from locker fees, park and airport concessions, sale of park and airport land, miscellaneous sales of park street and aviation scrap and junk and obsolete equipment, and sale of by-products of the rendering plant, are taxable under the gross income tax law as amended in 1937, and rendered judgment accordingly.

* * * There is no challenge of the lower court's actions upon the items held taxable. Therefore only the items held not taxable are before us, and the sole question is whether or not the income of the city derived from the items held not taxable constitute income from private or proprietary activities or business within the meaning of the 1937 amendment to the gross income tax law.

The rule is universally recognized that municipal corporations exist and act in a dual capacity—one public or governmental and the other private or proprietary. In its public or governmental capacity, it acts as the agent of the state for the benefit and welfare of the state as a whole, but when acting for the peculiar and special advantage of its inhabitants, rather than for the good of the state at large, the city is spoken of as acting in a private or proprietary capacity. [Citations omitted]

In the case of City of Kokomo v. Loy, *supra*, the appellee was injured working as an employee in a city park. * * * The suit was prosecuted upon the theory that the city was acting in its private and proprietary capacity in maintaining and conducting the park. The city contended that it was acting in a governmental capacity and was not liable. There was a verdict for the plaintiff which was affirmed, and Judge Lairy recognized the dual capacity in which cities may act, and pointed out the distinctions between the two capacities, and stated the accepted rule in the following language, 185 Ind. at pages 21 and 22, 112 N.E. at page 995:

> "Municipal corporations exist in a dual capacity, and their functions are twofold. In one they exercise the right springing from sovereignty, and while in the performance of the duties pertaining thereto, their acts are political and governmental. Their officers and agents in such capacity, though elected or appointed by them, are nevertheless public functionaries performing a public service, and as such they are officers, agents, and servants of the state. In the other capacity the municipalities exercise a private, proprietary or corporate right, arising from their existence as legal persons and not as public agencies. Their officers and agents in the performance of such functions act in behalf of the municipalities in their corporate or individual capacity, and not for the state or sovereign power."

* * *

The rule is stated in McQuillin on Municipal Corporations 2d Ed., Vol. I, Sec. 126, p. 381, as follows:

> "A municipal corporation proper has a twofold capacity or character—one governmental, the other private. It has a public character as regards the state at large in so far as it is its agent in government, and private (so-called) in so far as it is to promote local necessities and conveniences for its own community."

In the case of Chadwick v. City of Crawfordsville, 1940, 216 Ind. 399, at page 412, 24 N.E.2d 937, at page 943, 129 A.L.R. 469 involving taxation of utility property owned and operated by a municipality, this court used the following language:

> "When a municipality has been clothed with powers for the peculiar and special advantages of its inhabitants, rather than for the good of the state at large, the corporation has a private character, and its liability for torts *and otherwise* (our italics) is based upon the same principles as that of a private corporation, * * *."

* * *

While it is well established that governmental units act in a dual capacity * * * and while general rules and tests have been evolved and stated in the cases and text books to distinguish the two, none of these rules is conclusive, and a great deal of confusion has resulted in application, and uniformity in application has not been attained. Each case is a subject for individual determination in the light of its own facts. While this is true, the general rules to which we have called attention should always be considered, and consistency, so far as possible, should be the aim, else we will have no landmarks and cases will be decided according to the arbitrary fiat of the man who happens to be judge.

We have carefully considered the activities of the City of Evansville, which the trial court held to be not taxable and we have reached the conclusion that in operating and conducting its markets, its wharf, its golf course, its airport and its cemeteries, it is engaged in private and proprietary activities and its income from these sources is subject to gross income tax under the 1937 amendment to the gross income tax law. In all of these activities it is acting primarily for its own compact community rather than for the state at large. Each of these activities is of a general business nature frequently engaged in by private persons or corporations. In each instance the city is exercising a permissive privilege given by statute and is not performing a duty imposed by the legislature. In all of these activities consideration in the form of money flows to the city from those who are the immediate and direct participants and beneficiaries of the activities.

Ct. Held that items held not taxable by T. Ct. were taxable.

Four factors Ct. Considered in Arriving At This Concl.

This conclusion is not only consistent with the rules and tests herein discussed but is supported by authority. The operation of markets by a city has been held to be a proprietary activity. Reed v. Mayor, etc., of Baltimore, 1936, 171 Md. 115, 118 and cases cited 188 A. 15; [citations omitted]. The operation of a wharf likewise has been held to constitute a private or proprietary activity. Jeffersonville v. Gray, 1905, 165 Ind. 26, 29, and cases cited, 74 N.E. 611; McQuillin on Municipal Corporations, Second Edition, Vol. 6, Sec. 2849, p. 1183. The golf course * * * is a part of the park system * * *, and in Indiana it has been held that in operating their park systems municipalities exercise a private, proprietary and corporate right. City of Kokomo v. Loy, 1916, 185 Ind. 18, 112 N.E. 994; [citations omitted]. The operation of cemeteries by a city constitutes a proprietary activity. Mt. Hope Cemetery v. Boston, 1892, 158 Mass. 509, 519, 33 N.E. 695, 35 Am.St. Rep. 515; Hollman v. Platteville, 1898, 101 Wis. 94, 99, 76 N.W. 1119, 70 Am.St.Rep. 899; Toledo v. Cone, 1894, 41 Ohio St. 149, 161, 162. The operation of an airport by a city has been held to constitute a proprietary activity. Mobile v. Lartigue, 1930, 23 Ala.App. 479, 483, 127 So. 257; Coleman v. Oakland, 1931, 110 Cal.App. 715, 720, 295 P. 59; Peavey v. Miami, 1941, 146 Fla. 629, 636 and cases cited 1 So.2d 614; Christopher v. El Paso, 1936, Tex.Civ.App., 98 S.W.2d 394, 398; Pignet v. Santa Monica, 1938, 29 Cal.App.2d 286, 287, 84 P.2d 166; Blue v. City of Union, 1938, 159 Or. 5, 11, 75 P.2d 977.

This leaves for determination the taxability of the city's revenue from persons obtaining permits to cut street pavements for the convenience of such permittees.

In Indiana cities consistently have been held liable for torts committed in connection with the maintenance of their streets. Ordinarily this would mean a private or proprietary activity. But the basis for such liability as to street maintenance is at present in some confusion in Indiana. See Touhey v. City of Decatur, 1911, 175 Ind. 98, 100, 93

N.E. 40, 32 L.R.A., N.S., 350 for one theory and Aaron v. City of Tipton, 1941, 218 Ind. 227, 235, 32 N.E.2d 88, for another theory.

But the character of the activity from which the revenue here involved was received does not depend upon the capacity in which the city maintains its streets. This revenue all came from individual citizens desiring for their own personal, private interests to cut street pavements, and the city's activity in this connection was for the purpose of gratifying this private, personal desire of certain individuals, and took its color from this purpose and was, we think, a private and proprietary activity rather than the exercise of a public or governmental function. In this view such income is taxable under the 1937 amendment.

* * *

Having found that the activities discussed are taxable under the 1937 amendment of the gross income tax law, it follows that the court erred in ordering refunds.

The judgment is therefore reversed with instructions to sustain appellant's motion for a new trial and for further proceedings consistent with this opinion.

c. Equity Law

The uses of equity principles and remedies against government agencies are more circumscribed than in purely private disputes. Equitable relief is peculiarly discretionary and courts are slow to provide the same, notwithstanding strong individual appeals to justice, where countervailing public interests would be harmed by such relief. The reserve of equitable discretion enhances the role of courts in actions that are not directly controlled by statute or common law, e.g. those seeking restitution, injunctions, or the raising of estoppel barriers to normal relief. As will be seen later, courts are generally less inclined to grant particular forms of relief, e.g. estoppels against government action, than other forms, e.g. restitution, but they retain the power to tailor applications of equity law to the peculiar circumstances of each case. See e.g. Annots., Estoppel of State and Local Government in Tax Matters, 21 A.L.R. 4th 573 (1983); Applicability of Estoppel Against Government, 1 A.L.R.2d 338 (1948); Comment, *Never Trust A Bureaucrat: Estoppel Against The Government*, 42 So.Calif.L.Rev. 391 (1969); Heeton, *Zoning Estoppel*, 1971 Urban Annual Rev. 63; and case notes, at p. 40 (building encroachments); p. 716, n. 1 (defective municipal contracts); p. 19 (defective elections); p. 679 (defective bond issues).

NEW–MARK BUILDERS, INC. v. AURORA

Appellate Court of Illinois, 1967.
90 Ill.App.2d 98, 233 N.E.2d 44.

DAVIS, PRESIDING JUSTICE.

[Suit to compel the defendant City to approve plaintiff's request for the annexation of certain contiguous land. The trial court dismissed the plaintiff's petition and plaintiff appealed.]

* * *

The petition for mandamus alleged that the plaintiff was the owner of Unit No. 2 of Heritage Subdivision—the land which it seeks to have annexed * * *; that it was the owner of a larger parcel of land which it divided into three subdivisions: Heritage Green, Unit No. 1 of Heritage Subdivision and Unit No. 2 thereof; and that the three subdivisions were laid out, subdivided and were to be developed as one over-all project. The petition further stated that the preliminary plans for the three subdivisions were submitted to and disapproved by the Aurora Planning Commission in December of 1963; that the reason stated for the disapproval was that these plans did not provide open space for Indian Trail Road, which was to pass through the land comprising the proposed subdivisions; that thereafter the plaintiff revised its plans to provide open space for the proposed highway through the said subdivisions; and that the final plans for Heritage Green and Units Nos. 1 and 2 of Heritage Subdivisions were approved by the Aurora Planning Commission and then by the Aurora City Council.

The plaintiff's petition further asserted that Heritage Green and Unit No. 1 of Heritage Subdivision were thereafter annexed to the City of Aurora, but with no requirement that the plaintiff dedicate or construct the portion of Indian Trail Road passing through these subdivisions; that subsequently, the plaintiff filed its petition to annex Unit No. 2 of Heritage Subdivision which contained the same reservation in its plat of open space for the use of the proposed Indian Trail Road * * *; and that the City denied this petition, apparently on the grounds that the plaintiff must first dedicate and construct that portion of Indian Trail Road passing through this subdivision.

The plaintiff further alleged that Heritage Green and Unit No. 1 of Heritage Subdivision were developed and annexed to the City after all three of the subdivisions were approved by both the Planning Commission and the City Council; that the City at no time indicated prior to its annexation of Heritage Green and Unit No. 1 that it would impose as a condition precedent to the annexation of Unit No. 2 that there be a dedication and construction of Indian Trail Road passing through it; and that the City should be estopped to impose such a condition now.

The sole issue before us is whether the petition stated a cause of action * * *. The City contends that plaintiff's petition for annexation, filed under Ill.Rev.Stat.1965, ch. 24, Sec. 7–1–8, invoked its legislative power and authority; and that it had the absolute right to either accept or refuse the annexation. The City's position in this regard is well taken. The determination of whether a municipality should expand its boundaries is purely a legislative function which rests within the discretion of the legislative branch of the government. North v. Board of Education, 313 Ill. 422, 425, 145 N.E. 158 (1924); The City of Galesburg v. Hawkinson et al., 75 Ill. 152, 156–158 incl. (1874); La Salle Nat. Bank v. Village of Burr Ridge, 81 Ill.App.2d 209, 219, 225 N.E.2d 33 (1967).

The plaintiff contends that inasmuch as it had complied with all of the statutory and ordinance requirements for annexation, the City's determination as to whether it should annex pursuant to plaintiff's petition was purely a ministerial act and not a legislative act involving its discretion. In this respect the plaintiff cites People ex rel. American National Bank v. City of Park Ridge, 25 Ill.App.2d 424, 166 N.E.2d 635 (1960). That case, however, deals with the question of the approval of the resubdivision of certain property. The court there held that the approval by the City Council was a ministerial act when the appropriate statutes and ordinances have been complied with. Such is not the case with reference to the question of annexation, and the municipal authorities retain the discretionary right to either accept or reject the petition filed with it. Ill.Rev.Stat.1965, ch. 24, Sec. 7–1–8.

The plaintiff argues, however, that the City is estopped by its prior conduct to deny the annexation of Unit No. 2 of Heritage Subdivision. Under recognized law, the doctrine of estoppel, may in a proper case, be applied against a municipal corporation, even when it is acting in a governmental capacity. [Citations omitted.] Whether the doctrine of estoppel may be applied against a municipal corporation depends upon a consideration of all the circumstances of the case. Before the doctrine can be invoked, there must be some positive acts by the municipal officers which induced the action of the adverse party. Mere nonaction is not enough. Also, the doctrine may be invoked only to prevent injustice and fraud. If under all of the circumstances, the affirmative acts of the public body have caused another to take certain actions which have created a situation where it would be inequitable and unjust to permit the public body to, in effect, retract what it previously had done, the doctrine of estoppel may be applied against it. [Citations omitted.]

It appears from the petition before us that the plaintiff developed the three subdivisions under one comprehensive plan. When the first three plans were disapproved because of the failure to provide space for the proposed Indian Trail Road, they were revised to eliminate this defect; and thereupon the revised plans were approved * * *. Heritage Green and Unit No. 1 were then developed by plaintiff and annexed to the City of Aurora. Nothing was required with reference to Heritage Green and Unit No. 1 of Heritage Subdivision other than that open space be reserved for Indian Trail Road. The plaintiff then proceeded to develop Unit No. 2 in the same manner as the earlier units. The plaintiff contends that, in developing Unit No. 2, it relied upon the acceptance of Heritage Green and Unit No. 1 by the City on the basis of a reservation of open space for Indian Trail Road; and that upon the annexation of the prior units nothing further was required. It asserts that to refuse annexation at this time would be totally unjust in that it has expended large sums of money in the development of the total subdivision in reliance upon defendant's acts; and that to redesign the plat and redevelop the construction plans to meet the approval of the County in contrast to the City would cost substantial additional expenditures.

* * *

We believe that under the allegations of the petition, the plaintiff stated a cause of action, based upon the possibility of the application of the doctrine of estoppel against the City. It is apparent that the three subdivisions were designed and promoted as one over-all development, the nature of which was materially affected by the actions of the City in providing what was, and what was not, required for the acceptance of the respective plats. The prior annexations of these accepted plats of Heritage Green and Unit No. 1 of Heritage Subdivision might well induce the plaintiff to assume that Unit No. 2 would be accepted for annexation under the same terms and conditions as the prior subdivisions. Municipal corporations, as well as private corporations and individuals, are bound by the principles of fair dealing. [Citations omitted.]

* * * We believe that the petition for mandamus sets forth sufficient allegations to raise the possibility of the application of this doctrine. We are not suggesting that the doctrine either should, or should not, be applied against the defendant City in this case. That can only be determined from such facts as may be shown by the evidence to exist in the case. We do believe, however, that the petition states a cause of action. Therefore, the case should be reversed and remanded for further proceedings upon the petition, or such amendments as may be made thereto, and upon such answer and reply as may be filed in said proceeding.

Reversed and remanded.

Notes

1. **Estoppel.** In determining whether to apply the estoppel doctrine against public entities, courts balance the public interest against the citizen's equitable claim, and develop significant variations in the application of the equities. See e.g., pp. 40–42 infra.

"Sometimes the resulting disability has been characterized as an estoppel, sometimes as a waiver. The label counts for little. Enough for the present purposes that the disability has its roots in a principle more nearly ultimate than either waiver or estoppel, the principle that no one shall be permitted to found any claim upon his own inequity or take advantage of his own wrong." Justice Cardozo in R.H. Stearns Co. v. United States, 291 U.S. 54, 61–62, 54 S.Ct. 325, 328, 78 L.Ed. 647 (1934).

CITY OF RAPID CITY v. HOOGTERP

Supreme Court of South Dakota, 1970.
85 S.D. 176, 179 N.W.2d 15.

RENTTO, JUDGE.

The defendants Henry H. Hoogterp and Ruth C. Hoogterp, his wife, are the owners of a building located at 24 E. Main Street in Rapid City. Portions of the building are leased to the defendant Leonard Walla for business purposes. A land survey of the area made in 1967, in preparation for a program of improving and enlarging East Main Street, disclosed that defendants' building protruded into the street right-of-way. Plaintiff city thereupon instituted this suit to enjoin the obstructing portion of the structure as a nuisance.

In resisting the city's claim the position of the defendants is that their building does not encroach upon the street right-of-way. They base this on a survey of the ground which they had made and urge that the survey relied on by the city was erroneous. Additionally they urge that the city, because of its conduct, is estopped from claiming that their building encroaches upon the right-of-way. The court found that a portion of the building was in the right-of-way, but concluded that the city was estopped from having the nuisance abated.

* * *

Both parties appeal from the judgment. * * * Our statutes provide that abatement is one of the remedies against any nuisance. SDCL 21–10–5. They further provide that "No lapse of time can legalize a public nuisance, amounting to an actual obstruction of public right." SDCL 21–10–4. The estoppel which the court determined to be present in this case has the effect of making this latter statutory declaration inoperative.

The doctrine of equitable estoppel or estoppel in pais is bottomed on principles of morality and fair dealing and is intended to subserve the ends of justice. Security State Bank v. Gannon, 39 S.D. 232, 163 N.W. 1040. In considering the application of the doctrine of estoppel each case, in the nature of things, must stand on its own facts. Kraft v. Corson County, 72 S.D. 396, 34 N.W.2d 838. It seeks to accomplish that which is fair between man and man. First Church of Christ, Scientist v. Revell, 68 S.D. 377, 2 N.W.2d 674. It is one of those troublesome areas of the law where the difficulty is not in determining the governing principles, but in applying them to the facts.

This court has on several occasions indicated or recognized that the doctrine of estoppel is available against a municipal corporation. [Citations omitted.] However, estoppels against the public are little favored and should be used sparingly. They are applied against municipal corporations with caution and only when exceptional circumstances demand their application to prevent manifest injustice. 31 C.J.S. Estoppel § 141; 28 Am.Jur.2d, Estoppel & Waiver, § 129. The burden of establishing that such exceptional circumstances are present is on the party seeking the protection of the doctrine.

Because the disposition made of cases of this kind is dictated by the facts and circumstances of the particular case, the text statements concerning this field of law are largely generalizations. See 64 C.J.S. Municipal Corporations § 1753(c); 38 Am.Jur., Municipal Corporations, § 668. * * * More than municipal acquiescence in an obstruction should be required to give rise to an estoppel when the matter involved is a street easement in which the public has vested interest. Kuehl v. Bettendorf, 179 Iowa 1, 161 N.W. 28; Village of Newport v. Taylor, 225 Minn. 299, 30 N.W.2d 588. This view is in harmony with the mandate of SDCL 21–10–4.

The court's conclusion that the city was estopped to abate the encroachment complained of is based on these findings:

"A. The building situated on said lot, in its present dimensions, was constructed in the year 1919 and has existed in the same dimensions since that time;

"B. That, the Plaintiff City, through its officers, governing body and employees, at all times since the construction of said building knew of its existence from the time of its construction in 1919 to the present time;

"C. That, at least since 1947 and possibly since the year following its construction, said structure, as it now appears, has been taxed and taxes paid thereon by the Defendant owners and their predecessors in interest;

"D. That, in January, 1956, the Plaintiff City issued a permit to the Defendant owners for the repair of said building and interior thereof and from time to time, as shown by the Exhibits herein, issued miscellaneous permits for signs attached thereto, including what has been referred to as the porch, the second story of which has at all times been an enclosed portion of said main structure situated on said property in question herein; and

"E. That, at no time since the construction of said building, in its present form, in 1919, has the City, by or through any of its officers or governing body, made any objection of any kind to said encroachment on East Main Street in Rapid City, South Dakota, or claimed that such encroachment constituted a public nuisance, or has taken any action of any kind for the abatement thereof."

While the city was charged with knowledge of the existence of the building there is nothing to indicate it should have known that it occupied a part of the right-of-way of East Main Street. Nor is it claimed that the city knew of the survey which the defendant owners had made before they bought the property, showing that the building was all within the lines of the lot they were buying. In our view the circumstances here present do not justify the application of the rule of estoppel against the city.

The only South Dakota cases cited by the defendants in support of an estoppel are Missouri River Telephone Company v. City of Mitchell, *supra,* and Tubbs v. City of Custer, *supra.* We do not regard them as supporting an estoppel in the described circumstances. In each of these cases affirmative action by the cities involved was the basis for applying the rule of estoppel. As to decisions from other jurisdictions, they rely principally on the case of Bridges v. Incorporated Town of Grand View, 158 Iowa 402, 139 N.W. 917. Our study of that case persuades us that its holding resulted from factual circumstances not here present. The other foreign cases cited are similarly distinguishable. The annotation in 171 A.L.R. 94, referred to by them, specifically states that it does not generally extend to questions of estoppel in respect of encroachments of the kind here involved.

*   *   *

Accordingly, we reverse that portion of the judgment questioned by the appeal of the city and affirm the part challenged by the cross appeal of the defendants.

All the Judges concur.

Notes

1. For a contrary view, see Sioux City v. Johnson, 165 N.W.2d 762 (Iowa 1969). See Annot., 44 A.L.R.3d 257 (1972) for jurisdictional variations in treatment of the foregoing problem.

2. Should a court, at the suit of a resident, enjoin a town in the performance of its public duty (refuse burning) in order to abate an alleged nuisance? See Webb v. Rye, 108 N.H. 147, 230 A.2d 223 (1967).

HUDSON CITY CONTRACTING CO. v. JERSEY CITY INCINERATOR AUTHORITY

Supreme Court of New Jersey, 1955.
17 N.J. 297, 111 A.2d 385.

Burling, J.

[In a prior taxpayer suit the Authority was enjoined from paying plaintiff for refuse collection services under a contract that was let without competitive bidding and, therefore, held void. In the present suit, plaintiff sues in quasi-contract for the value of services rendered on the restitutionary theory of unjust enrichment.]

*   *   *

I.   Quasi-Contractual Liability of Municipal Corporations

The substantial question involved in this case is whether there may be any recovery on the *quantum meruit* for services performed under the *ultra vires* contract with the public corporation, the authority.

The basic rule, applied in the Scatuorchio case, *supra,* is that there can be no recovery under an express municipal contract entered into without observing the mandatory legal requirements specifically regulating the mode by which a municipal power is to be exercised. *Cf.* 10 McQuillin, Municipal Corporations (3d ed. 1950), sec. 29.26, p. 257.

* * *

The American law on this subject has incurred academic criticism for its apparent confusion. In 1911 it was said "The cases upon this subject are truly bewildering." Jerome C. Knowlton, The Quasi-Contractual Obligation of Municipal Corporations, 9 Mich.L.Rev. 671 (1911). It was suggested by Knowlton that favoritism and extravagance on the part of municipal officials call for limiting, rather than extending, the remedy of recovery by a contractor on the *quantum meruit. Id.,* p. 676. See also *Id.,* p. 683. Twenty-three years later it was observed, "The liability of municipal corporations in quasi-contracts, that is upon contracts implied in law, has never been satisfactorily worked out by our courts * * *" C.W. Tooke, Quasi-Contractual Liability of Municipal Corporations, 47 Harv.L.Rev. 11–3 (1934). The latter essay discusses the varying juridical philosophies on the subject and reaches the conclusion that " * * * there would seem to be no reason why a municipal corporation should not be held to respond upon principles of *quasi* -contract for services rendered or materials furnished under invalid contracts *intra vires* the corporation." *Id.,* p. 1171. A similar current analysis of the authorities on the subject demonstrates that no clear-cut solution has been attained. Chester James Antieau, The Contractual and Quasi-Contractual Responsibilities of Municipal Corporations, 2 St. Louis Univ. L.J. 230 (1953).

While these articles, as well as McQuillin's work, cited *ante,* and other authorities on the subject, point to seeming divergent judicial expression, the general principles, namely the contrapositive principles of public policy and unjust enrichment, appear to have general recognition. It is the application of these principles under varying constitutional and statutory provisions and factual circumstances that sets the scale of justice for or against the contractor. * * *

* * *

In New Jersey, recovery on the *quantum meruit* where a contract was invalid was approved in Armitage v. Essex Construction Co., 88 N.J.L.·640, 641, 96 A. 889 (E. & A.1916). In State v. Kuehnle, 85 N.J.L. 220, 227–228, 88 A. 1085, 1089 (E. & A.1913), the former Court of Errors and Appeals held "that, if the express contract was not binding, there was still an implied contract," and approved the rule that "a recovery against a municipal corporation (exists) upon an implied contract, where the express contract is set aside by the court." * * *

* * *

In summary, we find that the New Jersey law pertinent to this type of case is that where the contract was not within the corporate power no recovery may be had by the contractor either on express or implied contract; where the Legislature expressly prohibits the incurring of liability on contract or otherwise no recovery may be had either on express or implied contract; but where the power to contract lies within the competence of the municipal corporation and there has been an irregular exercise of that power *in good faith,* recovery on the *quantum meruit* may be had although the express contract is void. *Cf.* Potter v. Borough of Metuchen, 108 N.J.L. 447, 450–451, 155 A. 369 (Sup.Ct.1931).

The final facet of this subject is the extent to which recovery may be allowed. The ordinary rule for the measure of damages where the suit is based on the *quantum meruit* is the reasonable value of the services rendered. In the Burlington-Bristol Bridge Co. case, *supra,* (8 N.J., at page 475, 86 A.2d at page 221) the county was allowed to keep the bridge, *i.e.,* to retain the benefits of the contract, while the selling syndicate were required to "disgorge the profits which they received from this illegal transaction." (8 N.J. at pages 499–500, 86 A.2d at page 233). In the present case the benefits were received by the defendant authority (and incidentally by the City of Jersey City and the taxpayers therein). The services rendered cannot be restored to Hudson.

If the contracts were entered into and the services were performed by Hudson in good faith, the measure of damages in the present case is the reasonable expense of the performance of services actually rendered, but not in excess of its actual expenses, and deleting profits.

* * *

CONCLUSION.

In summary, we find that our decision in Scatuorchio v. Jersey City Incinerator Authority, *supra,* is not *res adjudicata,* and that the circumstances of this case would permit recovery on the *quantum meruit* provided the factor of good faith is developed and proven. In the absence of adequate presentation of the pertinent facts in the record palpably showing no dispute as to the fact of good faith or absence of good faith, summary judgment was premature.

For the reasons expressed in this opinion the judgment of the Superior Court, Law Division, is reversed. The cause is remanded to the Superior Court, Law Division, for further proceedings not inconsistent with this opinion.

3. JUDICIAL CONTROL OF THE LITIGATION PROCESS

Access to court review of local government action is conditioned in many cases by special pre-litigation requisites, some of which are statutory, and others of which are judge-made. The prerequisites operate selectively, i.e., only with respect to certain parties, particular municipal functions, or particular forms of actions. See generally, L. Jaffe, *Judicial Control of Administrative Actions,* chs. 5, 6, 11, 12 (1965). The more common grounds for limiting judicial review involve: standing to sue; exhaustion of administrative remedies; the doctrine against "collateral attack" of government actions; and the uses of special suits that grew out of ancient "prerogative writs." Other litigation prerequisites that relate to tort claims against local government entities are taken up in chapter X.

a. Standing to Sue

A party who has a special interest in, or suffers special injury by, government action, that is not common to other citizens, is generally accorded standing to sue for judicial relief. Where, however, suit is brought to redress an injury that is generally shared by the public, and to vindicate rights that are not purely private, the citizen or taxpayer standing to institute such a "public action" is subject to statutes and case law which vary from state to state. See generally, Yokley, *Municipal Corporations,* §§ 602–606 (1957); Note, *Taxpayer Suits, A Survey and Summary,* 60 Yale L.J. 895 (1960). The following excerpts from L. Jaffe, *Judicial Control of Administrative Action* (1965) * describe the law of public actions:

[handwritten margin notes: "Suit for Individ. Injury" and "Suit for Injury to Public"]

"The most significant prototype of the public action are the prerogative writ of mandamus and the bill in equity for an injunction, with the recently developed declaratory action as an appropriate alternative. Of some, but of considerably lesser significance is certiorari, and least important are prohibition and quo warranto." p. 462.

" * * * The taxpayer's suit was first directed to local action; its extension to state action came later, and now is not complete * * * The American states had become more and more committed to the public action. * * * It seems that a need for some external controls, at least of local authorities, is generally felt. * * * It is one interpretation of this development * * * but not the only one as we shall see, that it compensates for our inability to insure adequately controlled administration." pp. 474–5.

"There are then, approximately, 29 states which allow a citizen as such to test by Mandamus the legality of official conduct, and five more where that may be the case. In most all jurisdictions a taxpayer may enjoin a local action, and in at least 27 states, and it may be in 9 more, a taxpayer may enjoin state action, with many jurisdictions permitting such an attack, though the effect on expenditure and a fortiori on the taxpayer is nominal. * * * The Supreme Court has adjudicated appeals from state judgments in local taxpayer suits." p. 473.

b. Special Actions

Limitations on the uses of special actions rest upon certain common policies. The following summary of special actions, for example, echoes a recurrent theme that the relief sought in each form of action may usually be denied in the court's discretion where: (a) prior admin-

* Reprinted by permission of Little, Brown & Co., copyright © 1965.

istrative remedies have not been exhausted; (b) where other adequate relief is available; (c) where the public interest outweighs the party's interest in the remedy; or (d) where the requested review risks inappropriate judicial interference with the expert factual judgments of official administrators.

(1) Mandamus

Common Law Mandamus, or its statutory equivalent, is employed solely to compel the performance of an official duty that is ministerial and non-discretionary, and only where administrative appeal is not available, or where limited review "on the record" (by certiorari) would be undesirable. Courts may deny a mandamus remedy if they deem other available remedies to be adequate, or if the specific relief would cause unwarranted injury to the public interest. See Mullen p. 21, supra, L. Jaffe, supra, pp. 177–180, 424; Yokely, supra § 593; Switz v. Middletown, 23 N.J. 580, 130 A.2d 15 (1957). The states have not adopted a uniform test for the propriety of the mandamus remedy, and differ on the scope of review to be undertaken in mandamus cases. Some cases will dismiss a mandamus action on the ground that it should lie in certiorari, while another declines certiorari on the ground that mandamus is the proper remedy. L. Jaffe, supra, pp. 177–8, 183–191. Counsel must, therefore, carefully canvass the law of the governing state.

(2) Prohibition

This form of action is employed to have a higher court enjoin a lower court or a "quasi-judicial" body from exercising jurisdiction in a particular matter. Here also the adequacy of another remedy is ground for denying prohibition relief. L. Jaffe, supra, pp. 192–3; Pirillo v. Takiff, 462 Pa. 511, 341 A.2d 896 (1975).

(3) Quo Warranto

Used to challenge the right to hold a public office, this action, like mandamus, was one of the prerogative writs at common law. It may also be refused on a finding that another adequate remedy is available. Here also one finds division of judicial opinion as to when mandamus, rather than quo warranto, is appropriate in an office-holding dispute. The "courts are vested with a considerable degree of discretion in permitting * * * a petition in quo warranto * * *." Explicit statutory considerations often control in particular jurisdictions. Yokely, supra §§ 596–599; L. Jaffe, supra, p. 193.

(4) Declaratory Judgment

This form of action is created by state statutes to provide the limited relief of judicial statement of legal rights. Here again, the authorities are divided on the propriety of declaratory relief, *vis-a-vis* other special remedies. L. Jaffe, supra, pp. 159–194.

c. *Doctrine Against Collateral Attack*

The doctrine against collateral attack of colorable government action contains some of the same elements of the rules governing standing to sue and special forms of action. Broadly speaking, that doctrine bars private parties from challenging government actions unless they are either authorized by statute to do so; or possess special status that permits them to speak on behalf of the public. In their application of collateral attack doctrine to particular facts courts often arrive at diverse results, but the doctrine itself is well recognized: "And, it has always been the law in Oklahoma and elsewhere that 'where a municipal corporation is acting under color of law and its existence is not questioned by the state, it cannot be collaterally drawn in question by private parties; * * * the only recognized exception to this rule of immunity is where the attempted incorporation [action] is void *ab initio* for want of organic authority, or where the attempted exercise of corporate power is utterly void for lack of jurisdiction, * * * Another exception to immunity from private attack has been recognized where, as here, the corporation sues in its corporate name, alleging its corporate existence. The legal fact of the corporation may be drawn in issue by a denial, which, of course, places upon the plaintiff the duty of proving the fact of its existence. In these circumstances, the defense challenges the fact, not the legality of corporate existence, and it is, therefore, not a collateral attack." See Town of Maysville v. Magnolia Petroleum Co., 272 F.2d 806 (10th Cir.1959). See generally, 56 Am.Jr.2d § 36—Municipal Corporations (1971).

Chapter III

LEGISLATIVE SOURCES OF CONTROL

A. STATE LEGISLATIVE SUPREMACY

The states have been called the "fountainhead" and "keystone" of American government. National sovereignty arises from "the sovereign union of sovereign states," but concurrent state sovereignty is preserved by constitutional law. Local governments, as creatures of the states, lack inherent power; hence their existence, form, powers and property are generally subject to ongoing state control. The only limitations on such control are found in the higher sovereign expressions of state constitutions and federal law. 2 McQuillin, *Municipal Corporations*, §§ 4.01–4, 4.05, 4.132 (3d rev. ed. 1979); I Yokley, *Municipal Corporations* §§ 11, 59, 60 (1956).

1. CREATION AND DESTRUCTION OF LOCAL GOVERNMENT ENTITIES

HUNTER v. PITTSBURGH

Supreme Court of the United States, 1907.
207 U.S. 161, 177–180, 28 S.Ct. 40, 46–47, 52 L.Ed. 151.

MOODY, J.

[Pennsylvania statute authorizing consolidation of the adjoining cities of Pittsburgh and Allegheny upheld against the complaints that the statute enabled the majority citizens of Pittsburgh to annex Allegheny without its consent and to increase tax and property burdens of Allegheny citizens. The court made the following observations.]

* * * This court has many times had occasion to consider and decide the nature of municipal corporations, their rights and duties, and the rights of their citizens and creditors. [Citations omitted] We think the following principles have been established by them and have become settled doctrines of this court, to be acted upon wherever they are applicable. Municipal corporations are political subdivisions of the State, created as convenient agencies for exercising such of the governmental powers of the State as may be entrusted to them. For the purpose of executing these powers properly and efficiently they usually are given the power to acquire, hold, and manage personal and real property. The number, nature and duration of the powers conferred upon these corporations and the territory over which they shall be exercised rests in the absolute discretion of the State. Neither their charters, nor any law conferring governmental powers, or vesting in them property to be used for governmental purposes, or authorizing them to hold or manage such property, or exempting them from taxation upon it, constitutes a contract with the State within the meaning of the Federal Constitution. The State, therefore, at its pleasure may modify or withdraw all such powers, may take without compensation such property, hold it itself, or vest it in other agencies, expand or contract the territorial area, unite the whole or a part of it with another municipality, repeal the charter and destroy the corporation. All this may be done, conditionally or unconditionally, with or without the consent of the citizens, or even against their protest. In all these respects the State is supreme, and its legislative body, conforming its action to the state constitution, may do as it will, unrestrained by any provision of the Constitution of the United States. Although the inhabitants and property owners may by such changes suffer inconvenience, and their property may be lessened in value by the burden of increased taxation, or for any other reason, they have no right by contract or otherwise in the unaltered or continued existence of the corporation or its powers, and there is nothing in the Federal Constitution which protects them from these injurious consequences. The power is in the State and those who legislate for the State are alone responsible for any unjust or oppressive exercise of it.

*   *   *

OPINION OF THE JUSTICES

Supreme Court of Alabama, 1965.
277 Ala. 630, 173 So.2d 793, 796.

We have held that the State, through its Legislature, at its pleasure, may modify or withdraw all the governmental powers of a municipality, may expand or contract the territorial area, unite the whole or a part of it with another municipality, repeal the charter and destroy the corporation. All this may be done, conditionally or unconditionally, with or without the consent of the citizens, or even against their protest. In all these respects the State is supreme, and its legislative body, conforming its action to the State Constitution, may do as it will, *   *   *. Although the inhabitants and property owners may, by such changes, suffer inconvenience, and their property may be lessened in value by the burden of increased taxation, or for any other reason, they have no right, by contract or otherwise, in the unaltered or continued existence of the corporation or its powers, and there is nothing in the Federal Constitution which protects them from these injurious consequences.   *   *   * [Citing, *inter alia,* Hunter v. Pittsburgh, reported at p. 48.]

Notes

1. The principles enunciated in Hunter were reaffirmed in Reynolds v. Sims, 377 U.S. 533, 574–575, 84 S.Ct. 1362, 1388, 12 L.Ed.2d 506 (1964); Opinion of the Justices, 277 Ala. 630, 173 So.2d 793 (1965). See also Supervisors of the County of Boone v. Rainbow Gardens, 14 Ill.2d 504, 153 N.E.2d 16 (1958) and Madison Metropolitan Sewerage Dist. v. Committee on Water Pollution, 260 Wis. 229, 50 N.W.2d 424 (1951) (destruction of local units); Rhodes v. Asheville, 230 N.C. 134, 52 S.E.2d 371 (1949) (alteration of municipal powers). For a recent example of statutory destruction of existing units (county boards of education) and substitution of new units (intermediate public school units) see 24 Pa.Stat. §§ 9–925, 9–951.

2. **The Rejected Theory of Inherent Local Power.** "Local units of government have no inherent police power, and may exercise such power only to the extent that (1) it is expressly conferred by the state legislature; (2) it may be fairly implied from powers expressly granted; or (3) it is essential to the fundamental declared objects of local government. Ordinances passed pursuant to such power, absent a showing to the contrary, enjoy a presumption of validity." See Redwood Gym v. Salt Lake Cty. Com'n, 624 P.2d 1138, 1143 (Utah 1981). See also, State ex rel. Petit v. Wagner, 170 Ohio St. 297, 164 N.E.2d 574 (1960); City of Trenton v. New Jersey, 262 U.S. 182, 43 S.Ct. 534, 67 L.Ed. 937 (1923); State v. Burr, 65 Wash. 524, 526, 118 P. 639, 644 (1911); Town of Holyoke v. Smith, 75 Colo. 286, 226 P. 158 (1924); Cobo v. O'Bryant, infra p. 55; City of Detroit v. Division 26 of Amalgamated Ass'n, 332 Mich. 237, 242, 51 N.W.2d 228, 235–236 (1952). Compare State ex rel. Gebhardt v. City Council of Helena, 102 Mont. 27, 55 P.2d 671 (1936).

3. **State Control vs. Third Party Rights.** State control over municipalities cannot be exercised in a way that would abridge constitutional rights of third parties. See Columbia County v. Board of Trustees, infra, p. 52.

2. CONTROL OF LOCAL GOVERNMENT POWERS

STYRING v. SANTA ANA
District Court of Appeals of California, 1944.
64 Cal.App. 12, 147 P.2d 689.

[Appeal from a judgment requiring defendants to grant plaintiffs and other members of the fire department of the City of Santa Ana leaves "of absence from active duty of four working shifts in every month of such service" as required by an act of the legislature. Stats. 1895, p. 76 as amended, Deering's Gen. Laws, 1937, Act No. 2598.]

MARKS, JUSTICE. The city of Santa Ana is a municipal corporation of the fifth class organized under the municipal corporation act Stats. 1883, p. 93, as variously amended. This act serves as the charter of those municipalities incorporated under it. [Citations omitted] Section one of this act provides that cities "shall have the powers conferred, or that may be hereafter conferred, by law, upon municipal corporations of the class to which the same may belong." Thus the legislature has much more power to regulate the affairs of unchartered cities than it has over those organized under a charter which have authority " * * * to make and enforce all laws and regulations in respect to municipal affairs, subject only to the restrictions and limitations provided in their several charters, * * *." Sec. 6, Art. XI, Const. It follows that cases dealing with the rights of officers and employees of chartered cities are unimportant here and need not be noticed.

The act in question here (Stats.1895, p. 76, as amended) provides in part as follows:

"In every city, fire district, county fire district and fire protection district of this State where there is a regularly organized paid fire department, the board of supervisors, common council, commissioners or other body having the management and control of the same shall once each year grant to each regular or permanent member thereof, a leave of absence from active duty of not less than fifteen days in each year and in addition thereto a leave of absence from active duty of four working shifts in every month of such service. Leave of absence so granted, as aforesaid, must be arranged by said board, council, commission, commissioners or other governing body so as not to interfere with or in any way impair the efficiency of said department."

In Santa Ana there is a regularly organized paid fire department whose members have been given fifteen days leave of absence from active duty each year but have been refused leaves of absence from four working shifts each month.

* * *

Defendants argue that the act of 1895 must be construed as directory and not mandatory. * * *

The act of 1895 does not require a municipal corporation to maintain a regularly organized paid fire department. It merely requires a city which has such a department organized to give the firemen the leaves of absence from active duty there indicated which sufficiently distinguishes the instant case from the Shealor case.

The leaves of four working shifts a month from active duty is made obligatory by the act of 1895. Thus it becomes the duty of those having control of regularly organized paid fire departments in unchartered cities to arrange such leaves of absence "so as not to interfere with or in any way impair the efficiency of said department(s)." A duty resting on a public official which the law requires him to perform may be enforced by a writ of mandate.

The judgment is affirmed.

COLUMBIA COUNTY v. BOARD OF TRUSTEES

Supreme Court of Wisconsin, 1962.
17 Wis.2d 310, 116 N.W.2d 142.

HALLOWS, JUSTICE.

[Suit by the county and taxpayers to challenge the constitutionality of a state statute requiring all counties to join the state pension system and provide thereunder retirement benefits to their county employees.]

Standing on the threshold of the constitutional issues is the question whether the plaintiffs have the legal capacity to sue and the right to contest the constitutionality of Ch. 459, Laws of 1961. No doubt, counties and a taxpayer have the capacity to bring a suit for declaratory relief under sec. 269.56, Stats. Subsec. 13 thereof expressly so provides, and sec. 59.07, Stats., authorizes a county to commence and maintain an action to protect its interests. However, neither section abrogates the traditional rule that a county does not have the legal right or status as against the state or another state agency to contest the constitutionally of a statute. Upon the reasoning a city was a municipal corporation and a metropolitan sewerage district was a quasi municipal corporation, both being political subdivisions of the state * * * and as such were creatures of the legislature and an arm of the state, we held in Madison Metropolitan Sewerage Dist. v. Committee on Water Pollution (1951), 260 Wis. 229, 50 N.W.2d 424, that the city of Madison and the Metropolitan Sewerage District did not have any standing to contest the constitutionality of the state law there in question. While there is a distinction between a county and a village or city and the former is generally classified as a quasi municipal corporation rather than a municipal corporation, State ex rel. Bare v. Schinz (1927), 194 Wis. 397, 216 N.W. 509, the distinction is not material in this case.

A county * * * has no right to question the constitutionality of the acts of its superior and creator or of another arm or governmental agency of the state. A county or a governmental agency is created almost exclusively in the view of the policy of the state at large for purposes of political organization and civil administration in matters of state concern. McQuillin, Municipal Corporations, Vol. 1, sec. 112; Young v. Juneau County (1927), 192 Wis. 646, 212 N.W. 295. In two recent cases we have made an exception to the general rule after stating it as follows:

> "State agencies or public officers cannot question the constitutionality of a statute unless it is their official duty to do so or they will be personally affected if they fail to do so and the statute is held invalid."

In Fulton, we allowed the department of taxation, in the tax case brought by a private taxpayer, to raise in defense the question of constitutionality on the ground of an exceptional situation involving issues of great public concern. Likewise, in Associated Hospital Service, Inc. v. Milwaukee (1961), 13 Wis.2d 447, 109 N.W.2d 271, under the same reasoning, we allowed the city of Milwaukee to raise the question of constitutionality in a tax case brought by a taxpayer. It will be noted in both these cases, neither the city nor the state agency was suing the state of Wisconsin or another state agency. We are not disposed to extend the exception to the general rule to cover suits between two agencies of the state government or between an arm of the government and the state itself. Nor does this case involve any official duty of the county to raise the question of constitutionality or any personal liability if it fails to do so and the statute is held invalid.

In Madison Metropolitan Sewerage Dist. v. Committee on Water Pollution, *supra*, we also stated the taxpayer had no standing to sue because he had no other or higher right than that which the district or municipality itself could claim and his action was derivative in nature. However, the Madison Metropolitan Case is not controlling of the taxpayer's rights in this case. In essence, Ch. 459, Laws of 1961, is concerned with the operation and administration of a county as a political subdivision of the state. The county, in such capacity, does not represent the taxpayers, as we said a city might act in the Associated Hospital Case.

The injury to the individual taxpayer in this suit is distinct from the injury complained of or alleged by the county. If the taxpayer was attempting to protect the same interests which the county was attempting to protect if it could sue, the taxpayer's suit would be derivative. But here, the taxpayer alleged in his complaint a direct pecuniary loss to him as a taxpayer of the state of Wisconsin and to other taxpayers similarly situated. This allegation was admitted by the demurrer and meets the requirements of the taxpayer's action for his own injury as declared in S.D. Realty Co. v. Sewerage Comm. of City of Milwaukee (1961), 15 Wis.2d 15, 112 N.W.2d 177.

Unless an individual taxpayer can ground an action for an injury to himself and raise the question of unconstitutionality of the laws so affecting him, the legislature could with impunity violate the constitutional limitations of its powers by enacting statutes affecting counties and the taxpayers thereof and be free from challenge in the state courts, leaving only a taxpayer to sue in the federal courts in those instances where such violation of the state constitution also violated the rights guaranteed by the federal constitution * * *. The state's legislative control of municipalities, like other state power, is not entirely beyond the scope of some limitations imposed by the U.S. Constitution. Gomillion v. Lightfoot (1960), 364 U.S. 339, 81 S.Ct. 125, 5 L.Ed.2d 110. The authority of the legislature over a municipal corporation, while supreme, is subject to such limitations as may be prescribed by the state constitution. [Citations omitted]

We hold that while the counties cannot raise the issue of unconstitutionality against another agency of the state, the individual taxpayer and resident of one of the counties affected in his individual capacity by Ch. 459, Laws of 1961, has the capacity to bring this suit and the right to raise the constitutional issue on behalf of himself and the other taxpayers.

* * *

IMPAIRMENT OF CONTRACTS

The plaintiff's argument that the mandatory feature of Ch. 459, Laws of 1961, impairs the obligation of the contract prohibition in the federal and Wisconsin constitution is based upon the premise contributions to the Fund are additional compensation for services which have been rendered and paid for in full or currently increases the amount of compensation of existing contracts for future services. It is also contended the withholding of contributions of the employees without their express consent constitutes a violation of constitutional provisions and existing contracts with employees which inured to the benefit of the taxpayer as a third party beneficiary. This argument is neither manifest nor ineluctable.

From the standpoint of the counties, they have no privilege or immunities under the federal constitution which may be invoked against state legislation. [Citations omitted] Nor can an agency of the state raise the unconstitutionality of a state law under the state constitution against the state or one of its agencies. Madison Metropolitan Sewerage Dist. v. Comm., *supra*. See also State ex rel. Martin v. Juneau, *supra*. From the standpoint of county officers and employees, they do not hold their offices or positions by virtue of a contract. For this point, see Dandoy v. Milwaukee County, *supra*. Contracts made by the county with third persons for government purposes can be questioned on constitutional grounds only by the third party. Frederick v. Douglas County (1897), 96 Wis. 411, 71 N.W. 798; Milwaukee v. Milw. & Suburban Transport Corp. (1959), 6 Wis.2d 299, 94 N.W.2d 584.

No county employee here is questioning the impairment of any of his rights, but the plaintiff taxpayer seeks to do so on the theory that taxpayers are third party beneficiaries of such contracts so far as it concerns the right to services of the employees to be rendered at the specified contract compensation. This is an ingenious argument and if carried to its logical conclusion would allow any taxpayer to contest the modification or change in any contract between a municipality and a third person. Such contracts, when they do exist, are not third party beneficiary contracts for taxpayers within the doctrine of Tweeddale v. Tweeddale (1903), 116 Wis. 517, 93 N.W. 440, 61 L.R.A. 509.

Chapter 459, Laws of 1961, is hereby declared constitutional.

Notes

1. State legislative control applies to unincorporated administrative units, such as counties, and to special districts and authorities, as well as to municipalities. See City of New Bedford v. New Bedford, Woods Hole, Martha's Vineyard, and Nantucket Steamship Authority, 336 Mass. 651, 148 N.E.2d 637 (1958).

2. Where control of local functions carries with it control of local property, the classification of local property as governmental or proprietary can be critical as shown in the next section. The maze of multi-statute construction through which courts must often labor is illustrated by the opinion in City of Mesa, reported at p. 201.

COBO v. O'BRYANT

Supreme Court of Florida, 1959.
116 So.2d 233.

THORNAL, JUSTICE.

[Appellants sought to overturn a series of state enactments which changed the governing board of a municipally owned electric utility by adding citizen members and by limiting the terms of municipal officials who served "ex officio."]

* * *

Numerous points are assigned for consideration, however, the determining aspects of the problem are whether a Florida municipality is endowed with powers of local self-government, and, the extent of legislative control over the operation and management of property owned by a municipality in a proprietary capacity.

* * *

To support the decree of the Chancellor in both cases the appellees take the position that Florida municipalities do not enjoy any residuum of local self government. They assert that under Section 8, Article VIII of the Florida Constitution, F.S.A., municipalities in this state are creatures of the Legislature and are absolutely subject to legislative control.

In the interest of brevity we resist the temptation to elaborate upon the history of municipal government in this country. * * *

* * * Unfortunately for appellants, this Court disposed of the matter adversely to their contentions many years ago.

Our own research reveals that there has been a division of authorities on the subject. They can be reconciled, however, by an analysis of the different constitutional provisions of the several states governing the creation and functioning of municipalities.

* * *

Legislative authority over Florida municipalities is provided in Section 8, Article VIII, Florida Constitution, which reads as follows:

"The Legislature shall have power to establish, and to abolish, municipalities to provide for their government, to prescribe their jurisdiction and powers, and to alter or amend the same at any time. When any municipality shall be abolished, provision shall be made for the protection of its creditors."

In applying the quoted provision of the Constitution this Court has consistently adopted the generally accepted proposition that municipal corporations have no inherent right of self-government beyond legislative control of the state in the absence of some specific constitutional provision granting it to them. 62 C.J.S. Municipal Corporations § 184, p. 343; 37 Am.Jur. Municipal Corporations § 77, p. 691; McQuillin, Municipal Corporations, Vol. 2 (3rd Ed.), § 4.82; Rhyne, Municipal Law (1957) §§ 3–4, 4–2.

The appellants here insist that a state constitution in this country is a limitation upon, rather than a grant of power. This basic premise is correct but the application of the principle contended for by appellants does not follow. It is their contention that the provision of the Florida Constitution quoted above limits the powers of the Legislature thereby defined, and there being no organic limitation against municipal self-government a residuum of self-governing authority rests inherent in the people of the local community. This contention of appellants fails to take cognizance of several principles covered in this opinion, and particularly the proposition that there could be no municipal corporation in the absence of legislative action. In other words, the Legislature creates a municipality. It has the authority to abolish it and certainly has the power to regulate and control its government by statutory enactment.

* * *

In State ex rel. McMullen v. Johnson, 102 Fla. 19, 135 So. 816, this Court considered a local act regulating municipal elections in the City of Tampa. The act created a board of elections and named the persons who should constitute the first board. The statute was sustained against the attack that it interfered with a claimed right of local self-government. * * * In State ex rel. McMullen v. Johnson, supra, we recognized the proposition that palpable abuse of power when committed in the enactment of laws or the improper exercise of delegated authority conferred by law will be remedied by the Courts when such action encroaches upon the personal or property rights of individuals. The power exercised by the Legislature under Section 8, Article VIII, Florida Constitution, is not unbridled, in that the Legislature will not be permitted to enact statutes that violate some other provision of the organic law. However, until it is clearly demonstrated that some provision of the Constitution has been violated, a statute is clothed with a presumption of correctness.

Appellants here urge that the authority conveyed to the utility board and to the assistant city clerk could be abused to the detriment of the people of the community even though the people themselves have had no direct part in establishing these agencies of the city government. The answer to this contention is simply that under our representative system the people control their government through legislative representation. * * *

Further, supporting the position of the appellees and sustaining the decree of the Chancellor is City of Orlando v. Evans, 132 Fla. 609, 182 So. 264, 265. The Orlando case involved a statute which, for all practical purposes, was identical with the statutes now before us regarding the Key West Utilities Board. The Orlando Act appointed by name the original Board and endowed the Board with complete control and management of Orlando's municipally owned utilities. * * *

Appellants in the instant case appear to take some comfort from various dissenting opinions of the late Justice Armstead Brown, who was an ardent judicial advocate of the principle of local self-government and home rule. Despite our abounding respect for the ability and written eloquence of our late brother, we are compelled to point out that in each instance when he so capably advocated his concept of the doctrine, he was very much in the minority. * * *

* * *

With reference to the Key West Utilities Board, the appellants in that case contend also that the electric utilities are owned by the City of Key West in a proprietary, as distinguished from its governmental capacity. They then assert that the municipality enjoys all of the same privileges of ownership and control of property as does the individual citizen. To this end they contend that the Legislature, even under the board [broad] provisions of our Constitution, has no power to regulate or control municipally owned property which is held in a proprietary capacity.

City of Orlando v. Evans, *supra,* supplemented by State ex rel. Gibbs v. Couch, 139 Fla. 353, 190 So. 723, dispose of this contention adversely to the position of the appellants. It should be borne in mind that, while it has been said that a municipality may own property and exercise proprietary functions, nevertheless, the property remains public. So long as a statutory enactment recognizes this continued public nature of the property and merely sets up an agency for its operation and control in the continued interest of the public there can be no objection to such legislative action. We are not here holding that the Legislature could completely appropriate or divert to some different use, property owned by a municipality in its proprietary capacity. However, we are not here confronted with this problem. The Legislature in its wisdom merely established a municipal agency to operate the publicly owned property for the benefit of the public. Whether or not this Court deems such legislation wise or salutary is of no consequence at all. Granting the existence of the power to act, the wisdom of exercising it and the necessity for its exercise are matters for legislative determination. The view which we have taken here and in prior cases is consistent with decisions in point from other jurisdictions. Monoghan v. Armatage, 1944, 218 Minn. 108, 15 N.W.2d 241, appeal dismissed 1945, 323 U.S. 681, 65 S.Ct. 436, 89 L.Ed. 552; Town of Bridgie v. County of Koochiching, 1948, 227 Minn. 320, 35 N.W.2d 537; Orleans Parish School Board v. City of New Orleans, La.App.1952, 56 So.2d 280.

* * *

Finding as we do that the statutes under assault were not violative of any provisions of the Constitution the decrees of the Chancellor upholding the acts must be affirmed.

It is so ordered.

3. CONTROL OF LOCAL GOVERNMENT PROPERTY

HUNTER v. PITTSBURGH

Supreme Court of the United States, 1907.
207 U.S. 161, 179–180, 28 S.Ct. 40, 46–47, 52 L.Ed. 151.

[Case reported at p. 48]

* * *

It will be observed that in describing the absolute power of the State over the property of municipal corporations we have not extended it beyond the property held and used for governmental purposes. Such corporations are sometimes authorized to hold and do hold property for the same purposes that property is held by private corporations or individuals. The distinction between property owned by municipal corporations in their public and governmental capacity and that owned by them in their private capacity, though difficult to define, has been approved by many of the state courts (1 Dillon, Municipal Corporations, 4th ed., sections 66 to 66a, inclusive, and cases cited in note to 48 L.R.A. 465), and it has been held that as to the latter class of property the legislature is not omnipotent. If the distinction is recognized it suggests the question whether property of a municipal corporation owned in its private and proprietary capacity may be taken from it against its will and without compensation. Mr. Dillon says truly that the question has never arisen directly for adjudication in this court. But it and the distinction upon which it is based has several times been noticed. [Citations omitted] Counsel for plaintiffs in error assert that the City of Allegheny was the owner of property held in its private and proprietary capacity, and insist that the effect of the proceedings under this act was to take its property without compensation and vest it in another corporation, and that thereby the city was deprived of its property without due process of law in violation of the Fourteenth Amendment. But no such question is presented by the record, and there is but a vague suggestion of facts upon which it might have been founded. * * *

PROPRIETORS OF MT. HOPE CEMETERY v. BOSTON

Supreme Court of Massachusetts, 1893.
158 Mass. 509, 33 N.E. 695.

[Corporation formed pursuant to state statute directing City of Boston to transfer to the corporation, cemetary property known as Mt. Hope Cemetary, brought suit to compel the transfer of the property to it, without compensation. After noting that the state legislature could enforce such a transfer as to property held in a governmental capacity, but that it could not require such a transfer without condemnation and compensation, as to property held by the city in a proprietary capacity, the court turned to the task of deciding how the cemetary property should be classified.]

ALLEN, J.

* * *

* * * In the case before us, we have to determine whether the city of Boston's title to the Mt. Hope Cemetery is subject to legislative control; and this involves an inquiry, to some extent, into the usages and laws in this commonwealth relating to burying grounds, * * *

* * *

* * * the city, by St.1849, c. 150, was "authorized to purchase and hold land for a public cemetery in any town in this commonwealth, and to make and establish all suitable rules, orders, and regulations for the interment of the dead therein, to the same extent that the said city of Boston is now authorized to make such rules, orders, and regulations for the interment of the dead within the limits of the said city." Before any purchase under this statute was made, a general statute was passed, which included Boston, (St.1855, c. 257) providing that "each city and town in the commonwealth shall provide one or more suitable places for a burial ground within their respective limits and forbidding the use, for the burial of the dead, of any land in any city or town other than that already used or appropriated for that purpose, without permission. * * * Being under these positive duties, and having authority, under St.1849, c. 150, to go outside of the city limits for a burial ground, the city of Boston purchased the largest portion of the land of the Mt. Hope Cemetery in West Roxbury in 1857, * * *, and has expended large sums in the care and management thereof, and about 40 acres still remain unsold. There is no suggestion in argument that in any of these particulars it has acted beyond its powers.

We are not aware that the sale of burial rights in this cemetery has ever been limited to inhabitants of Boston. * * * St.1889, c. 265, requires the city to transfer to the newly-formed corporation, called the Proprietors of Mt. Hope Cemetery, without compensation, this cemetery, with the personal property pertaining thereto, and with the right to any unpaid balances remaining due for lots already sold, and the annual income of certain funds held for the perpetual care of lots. [If such transfer is made, all that the city would retain would be the right to bury such persons as it is or may be by law obliged to bury, in a certain prescribed portion of the cemetery.] * * * But it is apparent, from the considerations heretofore expressed, that this is not property which is held exclusively for purposes strictly public. The city of Boston is possessed of much other property which * * * is held for the benefit of the public, but in other respects is held more like the property of a private corporation. Notably among these may be mentioned its system of waterworks, its system of parks, its market, its hospital, and its library. [In establishing all of these, the city has not acted strictly as an agent of the state government, * * *, but rather with special reference to the benefit of its own inhabitants.] If its cemetery is under legislative control, so that a transfer of it without compensation can be required, it is not easy to see why the other properties mentioned are not also, * * *. In view of all these considerations, the conclusion to which we have come is that the cemetery falls within the class of property which the city owns in its private or proprietary character, as a private corporation might own it, and that its ownership is protected under the constitution of Massachusetts and of the United States, so that the legislature has no power to require its transfer without compensation. Const.Mass. (Declaration of Rights) art. 1; Const.U.S. 14th Amend.

* * *

It is contended in behalf of the petitioner that it is a public corporation, wholly under the control of the legislature. But it is an error to suppose that a corporation becomes a public one merely by receiving a charter from the legislature, by owing certain duties to the public, and by being subject to rules and regulations established in the exercise of the police power. * * * Certainly, there appears to be nothing binding the corporation to give any preference to inhabitants of Boston * * *. There is, therefore, no ground on which the petitioner can be said, in any just sense, to be a public corporation; and its duties to the inhabitants of Boston are, at best, but vague and shadowy.

* * * Petition dismissed.

Notes

1. The disparity in state treatment of like forms of public property is considerable. See generally, Annot., Power of Eminent Domain as Between State and Subdivision or Agency Thereof, 35 A.L.R.3d 1293 (1971); 2 McQuillin, *Municipal Corporations* §§ 4.132–4.138 (3d rev. ed. 1971).

A court could treat the same property differently for different purposes, *viz.* a municipal utility may be considered "private" or "proprietary" for condemnation purposes, but "public" or "governmental" with regard to immunity from tort liability. Since public interests are implicated in either case, the conceptual distinction invites erratic applications. See Parr, *State Condemnation of Municipally Owned Property: The Governmental Proprietary Distinction*, 11 Syracuse L.Rev. 27 (1960); Dau, *Problems in Condemnation of Property Devoted to Public Use*, 44 Tex.L.Rev. 1517, 1527–1530 (1966).

2. **Donated Property.** State control over property donated for specified uses may be limited by trust law. See Town of Winchester v. Cox, p. 64 fn. 2 infra.

3. **Federal Condemnation.** With respect to the federal government all local government property is "private" and must be compensated upon condemnation by the federal government. United States v. 50 Acres of

Land, 469 U.S. 105 S.Ct. 451, 87 L.Ed.2d 376 (1984). See Annot., Eminent Domain—Cost of Substitute Facilities as Measure of Compensation Paid to State or Municipality for Condemnation of Public Property, 40 A.L.R.3d 143 (1971).

4. **Cooperative Federal-State Projects.** When states undertake highway projects that are predominantly funded by federal grants, should they be permitted to take local government property without compensation? See State v. Salt Lake City Bd. of Education, infra p. 64 n. 4.

CITY OF CAMBRIDGE v. COMMISSIONER OF PUBLIC WELFARE   *"Govt al"*
Supreme Court of Massachusetts, 1970.
357 Mass. 183, 257 N.E.2d 782.

QUIRICO, JUSTICE.

[City sued State Commissioner of Public Welfare for a decree to preserve city liens which were declared abolished by state statute.]

* * * The city, acting under G.L. c. 118A, § 4, * * * took liens on a number of parcels of real estate, or on interests therein, owned by recipients of old age assistance, and recorded them in the registry of deeds. * * * The commissioner has released a number of such liens, "upon request of interested persons and for the purpose of clearing record titles of such liens." He has not asked the city to transfer any such liens to the Commonwealth, and has not offered to pay the city any consideration for them.

* * *

While this case was before the Superior Court and when the parties filed their briefs in this court, a substantial issue in the case was whether the comprehensive changes made in our welfare system and statutes by St.1967, c. 658, effective July 1, 1968, impliedly discharged or terminated the old assistance liens, so called, which were then held by municipalities and on which no judicial enforcement proceedings had been started. A related question was who was authorized to discharge or release such a lien, assuming that it was still in effect. These two questions have been effectively eliminated from this case by St.1969, c. 885, § 28, approved August 29, 1969, which provides that "[a]ll liens given by recipients to the cities and towns under any assistance program administered by the department of public welfare prior to the enactment of chapter six hundred and fifty-eight of the acts of nineteen hundred and sixty-seven are hereby abolished. A release of such liens shall be given by the treasurer of such city or town."

* * *

Thus the sole issue remaining is whether the Massachusetts Constitution permits the Legislature to abolish these old age assistance liens without requiring the Commonwealth to compensate the municipalities for their loss of the liens. In deciding this issue it may be helpful to restate the basic nature of our municipalities, their relationship to the

Commonwealth, and the power and authority of the Legislature to deal with the property of the municipalities. * * *

* * *

Property which a municipality has acquired and owns as an agency of the State, and which it holds solely for public uses, is subject to legislative control. It may be transferred to some other agency of government charged with the same duties, or it may be taken from the municipality by the Commonwealth and devoted to other public uses and purposes, without payment of compensation therefor. City of Worcester v. Commonwealth, 345 Mass. 99, 100, 185 N.E.2d 633; Massachusetts Turnpike Authy. v. Commonwealth, 347 Mass. 524, 526–529, 199 N.E.2d 175. Yet, the legislative power to take or transfer this type of property from a municipality is not unlimited. It may be exercised only for the accomplishment of some public purpose encompassed by Part II, c. 1, § 1, art. 4, of the Constitution. [Citations omitted]

Property which a municipality holds in its private or proprietary capacity is not subject to the same legislative control as the type of property described in the preceding paragraph. * * * As to this type of property a municipality has the same right to be compensated as an individual has under art. 10 of the Declaration of Rights of the Constitution. Proprietors of Mount Hope Cemetery v. Boston, 158 Mass. 509, 511, 519, 33 N.E. 695.

We now consider the question whether the liens here involved were acquired and held by the city in its governmental capacity as an agency of the State, or in its private or proprietary capacity. This question has arisen most frequently in cases where the ultimate issue was whether a municipality was subject to liability in tort for negligence * * *.

Although we are not here concerned with the question of municipal tort liability, the decisions in cases in which that question was involved and which held that the municipal administration of the general welfare laws was a governmental function furnish some guidance. The liens in question were acquired by the city in its administration of the old age assistance law before July 1, 1968. That law was then only a part of a large body of statutes establishing a comprehensive municipally administered welfare program for furnishing aid and assistance to various segments of the inhabitants of the Commonwealth. * * * The old age assistance part of the program was geared to the nation-wide Social Security laws under which the Federal government contributed to its expense as did the municipalities and the Commonwealth. See City of Worcester v. Quinn, 304 Mass. 276, 280, 23 N.E.2d 463, and 42 U.S.C.A. §§ 301–306 inclusive. [Citations omitted]

We hold that the old age assistance program as administered by municipalities prior to July 1, 1968, was a <u>purely governmental function</u> and that all property acquired or held by them in the discharge of that function was held in their governmental, and not in their private or proprietary, capacity. As such, that property, including the liens in question, was subject to legislative control. That right of control included the right to abolish the liens without compensation to the municipalities if it was done for the accomplishment of a public purpose.

*   *   *

A final decree is to be entered declaring: (a) that the liens acquired by the city of Cambridge under G.L. c. 118A, § 4, which were in effect before July 1, 1968, and on which it had not started judicial enforcement proceedings prior to that date, have been abolished; (b) that the city is not entitled to payment from the Commonwealth for the liens which have been abolished; and (c) that the treasurer of the city is required to give releases of the liens which have been abolished.

So ordered.

Notes

1. **Local vs. Regional Benefit Factors.** Should transfers of local property to regional or state units that perform the same function, without significant reduction of local benefits, be treated differently than property taken for uses that primarily serve non-local interests, *viz.* throughways? See e.g. Silver City Consolidated School District v. Board of Regents of N.M. Western College, 75 N.M. 106, 401 P.2d 95 (1965) (legislative transfer of high school property from state college to school district); Baier v. St. Albans, 128 W.Va. 630, 39 S.E.2d 145 (1946) (state takeover of county toll bridge); Chester County Inst. Dist. v. Commonwealth, 341 Pa. 49, 17 A.2d 212 (1941) (state takeover and operation of District mental hospitals); Hickey v. Burke, 78 Ohio App. 351, 69 N.E.2d 33 (1946).

In City of Worcester v. Commonwealth, 345 Mass. 99, 185 N.E.2d 633 (1962) the city sought compensation for school and park land that was taken for state highway purposes. Compensation was denied on a finding that the property was "governmental" and not "proprietary." Accord: City of New Rochelle v. State, 14 N.Y.2d 559, 198 N.E.2d 41 (1964). But the dissent in City of New Rochelle adopted a broader approach:

"Burke, Judge (dissenting).

"Although the Appellate Division was correct in characterizing sewage and drainage as governmental functions, that is not the end of the matter. The fact that this is an appropriation for the Thruway Authority puts it in a different light.   *   *   *

"The reasoning, such as it is, behind the governmental-proprietary distinction in the ordinary case is that a municipality holds some property as an agent of the entity that created it, the State, and for purposes proper to the State. Accordingly, it is said, there is no constitutional need for the State to pay its own creature when it retakes such governmentally held property for some other public purpose—it would be paying itself in effect, so the reasoning runs. Here, however, the whole scheme of the Thruway Act is to establish a quasi-public corporation as distinct as possible from the State—especially economically. [Citations omitted]

"I find it decisive that our statutes provide that the State Treasury shall not bear the cost of Thruway construction and maintenance. Subdivision 2 of section 357 of the Public Authorities Law, Consol. Laws, c. 43–A, requires the Thruway Authority to reimburse the State for Thruway expenses incurred by it. The report on public authorities submitted by the Temporary State Commission on the Co-ordination of State Activities (N.Y.Legis.Doc., 1956, No. 46) clearly states the controlling policy: 'The desire to find revenue sources other than additional taxes for the financing of capital improvements has been a recurrent reason given for the creation of public authorities in New York State. Local governments are limited by the State Constitution in their power to tax real property, and local government revenues have generally been considered inadequate to meet the increasing costs of services. The State government has such heavy demands upon its own revenue sources that the public authority device is attractive for projects which can be financed through user charges rather than from State appropriations. * * *'

"If, therefore, all Thruway expenses are to be borne exclusively by the users thereof through the payment of tolls, and not by the State Treasury, it is not very sensible to require this municipality, the State's creature, to bear such cost by the forced donation of property. The rational justification for the governmental-proprietary distinction as a measure of compensability for the taking of municipal property is elusive enough in the ordinary case and it is now removed from our law by legislation (General Municipal Law, Consol.Laws c. 24, § 3). To take it in its last days of life and press it into service against this claimant in the teeth of a statutory scheme so patently out of harmony with its presuppositions is a decision to which I cannot assent."

2. **Trust Property.** Where appropriated property had been privately granted, or dedicated for special local benefit purposes, courts have avoided the state ownership theory by impressing such property with trust obligations which require state compensation or the provision of equivalent benefits to preserve the interests of trust beneficiaries. See Town of Winchester v. Cox, 129 Conn. 106, 26 A.2d 592 (1942); Cummings v. St. Louis, 90 Mo. 259, 2 S.W. 130 (1886) infra.

3. **Legislative Cure of Hardships.** State legislatures may, in any event, require compensation for property taken by the state independently of the source and nature of the taking. State v. Human Relations Research Foundation, 64 Wash. 262, 391 P.2d 513 (1964).

4. **Judicial Cure by Strained Statutory Construction.** See State Road Comm. v. Salt Lake City Public Bd. of Educ., 13 Utah 2d 56, 368 P.2d 468 (1962):

"McDonough, Justice.

"The State Road Commission, in connection with the construction of a new freeway through Salt Lake City (Interstate Highway 15) found it necessary to condemn the Franklin School, belonging to the Salt Lake City Board of Education. * * *

* * *

"Plaintiff cites authorities for the proposition that one agency of the state, acting pursuant to statutory duty, is not required to pay compensation for taking public property held by another state agency. It relies on the case of the School District of Borough of Speers v. Commonwealth of Pennsylvania, wherein the court said:

" '(It) has always been held that the Commonwealth may take property of a political subdivision or agency without payment therefor, (citing authorities), the right to compensation in such cases being only a matter of grace or allowance by the Legislature.'

"Our consideration of that case and other authorities relied on indicates that the resolution of such a problem depends on the intent shown in the particular statute involved. Therefore the critical inquiry here is whether our legislature intended that a school board's property should be taken for highway purposes without being paid for it.

"The basis for the exercise of the power of eminent domain is set forth in Chapter 34, Title 78, U.C.A.1953. It is important to note that the act shows that the legislature had in mind that necessity may require that property devoted to one public use may be taken from its public owner if it was required for a different and more necessary public use. * * * It is true that the statute does not state specifically whether compensation is to be paid to the public agency from which it is taken. But without making any distinction between the method of taking public or private property, the statute requires any condemnor, whoever or whatever it may be, without any exception, to take all of the essential steps to condemnation. It is required that 'all owners' of the property taken should be named as defendants in the complaint; that the 'value of the property sought to be condemned' shall be 'separately assessed' and that the taker pay the sum of money so assessed 'within thirty days.'

"If there be any uncertainty as to the meaning and the proper application of the statute, * * * it is proper to look both to the purpose for which it was created, and to the practical aspects of its operation in order to assist in determining the legislative intent.

"The gravamen of the plaintiff's argument is that it should not be supposed that the legislature would require that one public agency, under the necessity of taking the property of another, should compensate it because that would be the same as taking public money out of one pocket and putting [it] into another. This argument may appear on the surface to have some merit, and it would in fact have some validity if the resources of the state could be regarded as one unified fund. But the argument is not sound, because that is not the fact. The fallacy is apparent when consideration is given to the means the legislature has created for the raising of the funds for the operation of the individual school districts in the state. It has provided a comprehensive and finely balanced plan for raising the funds for the various school districts and delegated responsibilities in connection with the raising and management of such funds to the various school boards. * * * If an individual state agency such as the Road Commission could reach over and take a property such as this Franklin School, worth several hundred thousand dollars, from a single school board, that would disrupt the balanced plan for the financing of schools. As a practical matter it would create insuperable obstacles for school boards in managing their schools. We see nothing either in the express words of the statute or in its nature or purpose which suggests that the legislature intended any such result.

"The incongruity is even more apparent when it is realized that this project is not just a state highway but is part of a federal interstate system which is being constructed not only for Utah but for the whole United States. This principle is recognized by the federal government, which is participating * * * to the extent of about 90% of the total cost. * * *

"From the language of the eminent domain statute, as well as upon the basis of its purpose and practical application, it is our conclusion that the legislature intended that public property of the character of this Franklin School should be taken and compensated for the same as if it had been taken from a private owner.

"Affirmed. No costs awarded."

Similar use of statutory construction to require compensation is found in State ex rel. State Highway Comm. v. Board of County Commissioners, 72 N.M. 86, 380 P.2d 830 (1963); State of N.J. by State Highway Comm. v. Cooper, 24 N.J. 261, 131 A.2d 756 (1957); School Dist. of the Borough of Speers v. Commonwealth, 383 Pa. 205, 117 A.2d 702 (1955).

4. DILLON'S RULE

Judicial preoccupation with preserving the "order of things," led commentators, notably Judge Dillon of Iowa, to promulgate, as an apparent corollary to the creature concept, a principle of strict construction known as *Dillon's Rule*. It reads:

"It is a general and undisputed proposition of law that *a municipal corporation possesses and can exercise the following powers, and no others:* First, those granted in *express words;* second, those *necessarily* or *fairly implied* in or *incident* to the powers expressly granted; third, those *essential* to the accomplishment of the declared objects and purposes of the corporation,—not simply convenient, but indispensable. Any fair, reasonable, substantial doubt concerning the existence of power is resolved by the courts against the corporation, and the power is denied. * * * *These principles are of transcendent importance, and lie at the foundation of the law of municipal corporations. * * *"* Dillon, *Municipal Corporations,* § 237(89) (5th ed. 1911)

That the foregoing is only an aid or canon of construction, and not an inflexible rule of law is clear from later statements of Judge Dillon:

"*The extent of the powers of municipalities * * * is one of* construction. * * * The rule of strict construction does not apply to the *mode adopted* by the municipality to *carry into effect powers*

* * * where the mode is not limited or prescribed by the legislature, and is left to the discretion of the municipal authorities. In such a case the usual test * * * is, Whether it is reasonable? and there is no presumption against the municipal action in such cases.

"The general principles of law, stated * * * are indisputably settled, but difficulty is often experienced in their application, on account of the complex character of municipal duties, * * * " Dillon, supra, § 239(91).

As so tempered, Dillon's Rule is not as restrictive as it may seem. As urbanization brought increasing need for greater local powers, Dillon's Rule has come under increased attack and has suffered increasing erosion. Consider the following techniques to avoid Dillon's Rule.

(1) The recognition of local autonomy by constitutional provision, "home rule," or "local option" charter supports liberal rather than strict construction of delegated powers. Greenberg v. Bradford, 432 Pa. 611, 248 A.2d 51 (1968) (power to prescribe compensation for policemen and firemen not conforming with statewide acts); Corpus Christi v. Continental Bus Systems, Inc., 445 S.W.2d 12 (Tex.1969) (power to conduct bus service beyond city limits); Bazell v. Cincinnati, 13 Ohio St. 2d 63, 233 N.E.2d 864 (1968) (power to build and lease a stadium); City of Grass Valley v. Walkinshaw, 34 Cal. 595, 212 P.2d 894 (1949) (power to tax for payment of bonded indebtedness); Beardsley v. Darlington, 14 Wis.2d 369, 111 N.W.2d 184 (1961) (power to erect television translator tower). For a discussion of the effect of home rule on Dillon's Rule, see Note, 59 Wash.L.Rev. 653 (1984).

(2) Where the municipal charter or legislative grant contains a general welfare or police power clause, the rule of liberal rather than strict construction applies. Krolick v. Lowery, 32 A.D.2d 317, 302 N.Y.S.2d 109 (1969) (upholding fire department regulation); Kligman v. Lautman, 98 N.J.Super. 344, 237 A.2d 483 (1967) (upholding street regulation ordinance). Even Iowa, Judge Dillon's home state, has espoused the liberal implication of powers under a general grant of police powers. Wilson v. Council Bluffs, 253 Iowa 162, 110 N.W.2d 569 (1961) (upholding ordinance for fluoridation of water). "[A]nd we have said the Dillon rule of strict construction no longer has application to statutes pertaining to local and internal affairs." Webster Realty Co. v. Fort Dodge, 174 N.W.2d 413, 421 (Iowa 1970) (upholding urban renewal project).

(3) Where delegated power involves a proprietary rather than governmental function, liberal construction is often favored. Bazell v. Cincinnati, *supra;* Nelson-Johnston & Doudna v. Metropolitan Utilities District, 137 Neb. 871, 291 N.W. 558 (1940).

(4) The state legislature may displace judicial rules of construction, *viz.* Statutory Construction Acts.

For other examples see generally 2 McQuillin, *Municipal Corporations,* §§ 10.18a–10.25 (3d rev. ed. 1979).

STATE OF UTAH v. HUTCHINSON

Supreme Court of Utah, 1980.
624 P.2d 1116.

STEWART, JUSTICE:

Defendant, a candidate for the office of Salt Lake County Commissioner, was charged with having violated § 1–10–4, Revised Ordinances of Salt Lake County, which requires the filing of campaign statements and the disclosure of campaign contributions.

*   *   *

A complaint charged defendant in two counts: (1) failure to report the name and address of a $6,000 contributor to his election campaign, and (2) failure to file supplemental campaign disclosures of the discharge of campaign debts and obligations.

Defendant filed a motion in a city court to dismiss the complaint on the ground that the ordinance was in violation of the Utah Constitution. The court granted the motion and held that Salt Lake County was without constitutional or statutory authority to enact the ordinance under which defendant was charged and dismissed the complaint.

An appeal was taken to a district court which affirmed the dismissal.

*   *   *

Defendant contends that because the Legislature has not specifically authorized counties to enact ordinances requiring disclosure of campaign contributions in county elections, Salt Lake County had no power to enact the ordinance in question. Alternatively, defendant contends that the ordinance is invalid because state statutes have preempted the field of regulation.

Concededly, the district court was correct in holding that the Legislature has not expressly authorized enactment of an ordinance requiring disclosure of campaign contributions in county elections. However, the Legislature has conferred upon cities and counties the authority to enact all necessary measures to promote the general health, safety, morals, and welfare of their citizens. Section 17–5–77, U.C.A. (1953).

*   *   *

The specific issue in this case is whether § 17–5–77 by itself provides Salt Lake County legal authority to enact the ordinance for disclosure of campaign contributions, or whether there must be a specific grant of authority for counties to enact measures dealing with disclosures of campaign financing to sustain the ordinance in question. Defendant claims that the powers of municipalities must be strictly construed and that because Salt Lake County did not have specific, delegated authority to enact the ordinance in issue, the ordinance is invalid.

The rule requiring strict construction of the powers delegated by the Legislature to counties and municipalities is a rule which is archaic, unrealistic, and unresponsive to the current needs of both state and local governments and effectively nullifies the legislative grant of general police power to the counties. Furthermore, although the rule of strict construction is supported by some cases in this State, it is inconsistent with other cases decided by this Court—a situation that permits a choosing from among conflicting precedents to support a particular result.

Dillon's Rule, which requires strict construction of delegated powers to local governments, was first enunciated in 1868. The rule was widely adopted during a period of great mistrust of municipal governments and has been viewed as "the only possible alternative by which extensive governmental powers may be conferred upon our municipalities, with a measurable limit upon their abuse."

The courts, in applying the Dillon Rule to general welfare clauses, have not viewed the latter as an independent source of power, but rather as limited by specific, enumerated grants of authority. See, i.e., American Fork City v. Robinson, 77 Utah 168, 292 P. 249 (1930); Salt Lake City v. Sutter, 61 Utah 533, 216 P. 234 (1923). More recently, however, reasoned opinion regarding the validity of the rule has changed.

* * *

Any vestige of inherent powers or liberality in construing delegated powers was soon swept away by the Dillon Rule. This rule was formulated in an era when farm-dominated legislatures were jealous of their power and when city scandals were notorious. It has been the authority, without critical analysis of it, for literally hundreds of subsequent cases.

As it arose, the strict construction doctrine applied to municipal corporations but it has been extended to local government generally and it must be faced in any approach to liberalizing local powers. This rule sends local government to State legislatures seeking grants of additional powers; it causes local officials to doubt their power, and it stops local governmental programs from developing fully. The strict construction rule stimulated home rule efforts and is largely responsible for the erosion of home rule. Because of its importance the rule should be examined critically from time to time.

* * *

If there were once valid policy reasons supporting the rule, we think they have largely lost their force and that effective local self-government, as an important constituent part of our system of government, must have sufficient power to deal effectively with the problems with which it must deal.

* * *

In a time of almost universal education and of substantial, and sometimes intense, citizen interest in the proper functioning of local government, we do not share the belief that local officials are generally unworthy of the trust of those governed. Indeed, if democratic processes at the grassroots level do not function well, then it is not likely that our state government will operate much better.

* * *

There are ample safeguards against any abuse of power at the local level. Local governments, as subdivisions of the State, exercise those powers granted to them by the State Legislature, Ritholz v. City of Salt Lake, 3 Utah 2d 385, 284 P.2d 702 (1955), and the exercise of a delegated power is subject to the limitations imposed by state statutes and state and federal constitutions. A state cannot empower local governments to do that which the state itself does not have authority to do. In addition, local governments are without authority to pass any ordinance prohibited by, or in conflict with, state statutory law. Salt Lake City v. Allred, 20 Utah 2d 298, 437 P.2d 434 (1968). Also, an ordinance is invalid if it intrudes into an area which the Legislature has preempted by comprehensive legislation intended to blanket a particular field.

In view of all these restraints and corrective measures, it is not appropriate for this Court to enfeeble local governments on the unjustified assumption that strict construction of delegated powers is necessary to prevent abuse.

* * *

* * * On the contrary, the history of our political institutions is founded in large measure on the concept—at least in theory if not in practice—that the more local the unit of government is that can deal with a political problem, the more effective and efficient the exercise of power is likely to be.

The wide diversity of problems encountered by county and municipal governments are not all, and cannot realistically be, effectively dealt with by a state legislature which sits for sixty days every two years to deal with matters of general importance. Thus the manner in which the Legislature operates militates in favor of a rule of judicial construction which permits localities to deal with their problems by local legislative action.

The general welfare provision, § 17–5–77, grants county commissioners of each county two distinct types of authority. In the first instance, power is given *to implement specific grants of authority.* Second, the counties are granted *an independent source of power to act for the general welfare of its citizens.* Thus § 17–5–77 provides authority to "pass all ordinances and rules and make all regulations, not repugnant to law, necessary for carrying into effect or discharging the powers and duties conferred by this title * * *." The second part of that section empowers counties to pass ordinances that are "necessary and proper to provide for the safety, and preserve the health, promote the prosperity, improve the morals, peace and good order, comfort and convenience of the county and the inhabitants thereof, and for the protection of property therein."

Nothing in § 17–5–77 or in Title 17 suggests that the general welfare clause should be narrowly or strictly construed.

* * *

The courts of other states have also held that a general welfare clause confers power in addition to and beyond that granted by specific statutory grants. Birkenfeld v. City of Berkeley, 17 Cal.3d 129, 130 Cal. Rptr. 465, 550 P.2d 1001 (1976); Leavenworth Club Owners Assoc. v. Atchison, 208 Kan. 318, 492 P.2d 183 (1971); City of Duluth v. Cerveny, 218 Minn. 511, 16 N.W.2d 779 (1944); Lehrhaupt v. Flynn, 140 N.J. Super. 250, 356 A.2d 35 (1976); City of Hobbs v. Biswell, 81 N.M. 778, 473 P.2d 917 (1970); Krolick v. Lowery, 32 A.D.2d 317, 302 N.Y.S.2d 109 (1969); Adams v. City of New Kensington, 357 Pa. 557, 55 A.2d 392 (1947); City of Pasco v. Dixson, 81 Wash.2d 510, 503 P.2d 76 (1972).

* * *

"The exercise of power conferred by a general welfare or general grant of power clause must be exercised by a municipal corporation, as a general rule, through an ordinance or other form of legislative enactment."

* * *

This power is not to be construed by specifically delegated powers. In City of Hobbs v. Biswell, supra, the Court of Appeals of New Mexico upheld a city ordinance regulating pawnbrokers under a general welfare provision similar to Utah's. Compare N.M.Stat.Ann. § 14–16–1 (1953) with Utah Code Ann. § 10–8–84 (1953). In referring to the authority of a municipality under the general welfare provision, the court stated: "The ordinance adopting authority of subsection B, often referred to as a general welfare clause, is independent of and in addition to ordinance adopting authority conferred by specific statutes." [473 P.2d at 919.]

The Supreme Court of Pennsylvania adopted a similar position in Adams v. City of New Kensington, 357 Pa. 557, 55 A.2d 392 (1947).

* * *

Closely in point with the facts of the instant case is Lehrhaupt v. Flynn, 140 N.J.Super. 250, 356 A.2d 35 (1976), which dealt with the validity of a financial disclosure ordinance adopted by a township without express authority for such action. The court stated: "[A]lthough there is no specific statutory authorization for municipal enactment of official financial disclosure ordinances, general power to adopt such local legislation is inherent in the broad delegation of police power * * *."

These cases state the rule which we adopt in this case. When the State has granted general welfare power to local governments, those governments have independent authority apart from, and in addition to, specific grants of authority to pass ordinances which are reasonably and appropriately related to the objectives of that power, i.e., providing for the public safety, health, morals, and welfare. Salt Lake City v. Allred, 20 Utah 2d 298, 437 P.2d 434 (1968). * * *

Broad construction of the powers of counties and cities is consistent with the current needs of local governments. The Dillon Rule of strict construction is antithetical to effective and efficient local and state government.

* * *

We therefore hold that a county has the power to preserve the purity of its electoral process. The county was entitled to conclude that financial disclosure by candidates would directly serve the legitimate purpose of achieving the goal that special interests should not be able to exercise undue influence in local elections without their influence being brought to light.

It is further argued as support for the unconstitutionality of the statute that the State of Utah has preempted the entire matter of regulating elections. We do not agree. The argument is not based on any direct conflict between the ordinance and a statute for there is none. Rather, the argument rests upon the existence of state legislation requiring campaign disclosures by candidates running for certain state offices. But that legislation does not evidence an intention on the part of the Legislature to preempt local ordinances dealing with local candidates.

* * *

The state restrictions pertain only to contribution disclosure requirements for state candidates for the offices of governor, secretary of state, and attorney general, § 20–14–7. The State Corrupt Practices in Elections Act leaves county governments to determine for themselves whether the circumstances necessitate the imposition of campaign contribution disclosure requirements for city or county offices.

The subject of campaign disclosure requirements is not one that reflects a need for uniformity. * * * The ordinances in this case do not conflict, directly or impliedly, with any state statute and are not for that reason unconstitutional.

In sum, the Dillon Rule of strict construction is not to be used to restrict the power of a county under a grant by the Legislature of general welfare power or prevent counties from using reasonable means to implement specific grants of authority. County ordinances are valid unless they conflict with superior law; do not rationally promote the public health, safety, morals and welfare; or are preempted by state policy or otherwise attempt to regulate an area which by the nature of the subject matter itself requires uniform state regulation. * * *

Finally, contrary to defendant's contentions, a grant of general welfare authority to counties does not violate Article I, § 24, or Article XI, § 4 of the Utah Constitution. Article I, § 24 requires the uniform operation of general laws. The general welfare clause, § 17–5–77, applies uniformly to all counties. The fact that each county may exercise that power differently is of no constitutional moment. * * *

* * * We rule only that the ordinance under which this action is brought is constitutional.

The judgment of the lower court is reversed, and the case is remanded for a trial on the merits.

CROCKETT, C.J., and HALL, J., concur.

MAUGHAN, JUSTICE (dissenting):

* * *

The District Court stated it had considered Salt Lake City v. Kusse and Salt Lake City v. Allred cases relied on by the County, and it acknowledged there was certain language in these cases, which suggested a county had a fairly broad power to enact ordinances under the general welfare clause of Section 17–5–77. The District Court explained after considering those cases, it discerned a substantial difference in the authority of a city or county to regulate driving under the influence and prostitution under the wording of the general welfare clause of Section 17–5–77, and in being able to regulate campaign financing in county elections. The District Court concluded:

"* * * Given its broadest meaning, the Court fails to see how this type of conduct can be regulated under language enabling ordinances 'such as are necessary and proper to provide for the safety, and preserve the health, promote the prosperity, improve the morals, peace and good order, comfort and convenience of the county and the inhabitants thereof, * * *' "

The ruling of the District Court was correct. The ordinances were ultra vires, and therefore void. There are no constitutional provisions conferring the police power concerning local matters on counties or non-chartered cities. These corporate political bodies have no inherent powers and none of the elements of sovereignty; they cannot go beyond the powers granted them and must exercise such powers in a reasonable manner. The exercise of the police power is an attribute of state sovereignty, a portion of which it may delegate, but not to relinquish, to municipalities, which have none of the elements of sovereignty.

Notes

1. **Dillon's Rule Under Home Rule Charters.** The adoption of home rule for municipalities has hastened the demise of Dillon's rule in many states. See e.g. Marshall Field & Co. v. South Barrington, 92 Ill.App. 3d 964, 47 Ill.Dec. 964, 415 N.E.2d 1277 (1981).

B. STATE CONSTITUTIONAL LIMITS ON LEGISLATIVE SUPREMACY

State legislative supremacy is tempered to a limited degree by state constitutions. The models adopted by each state to curb legislative interference vary, and cannot easily be generalized, especially since state constitutional provisions remain subject to continuing judicial interpretation, and to ongoing piecemeal amendment. For example, proposals to revise state constitutions appeared on the ballots of 37 states in 1972. See A.C.I.R., 14th Annual Report, p. 24 (1973); Sturm, *Thirty Years of State Constitution Making*, p. 107 (1970); Columbia U., *Constitutions of the United States—National and State* (1974); Columbia U., *Digest of State Constitutions* (1959); Winters, *State Constitutional Limitations* (1961). The constitutional prohibitions hereafter discussed must be considered against later constitutional development in each state. Constitutional prohibitions to curb legislative abuses can over time produce undesirable effects.

Comment: State Constitutions—Obstacles to Reform

"In all fifty states, the relationship of the cities and other local jurisdictions to the government of the state is defined by law, and the most permanent and most difficult-to-change rules of that relationship are found in the 50 state constitutions. * * *

"It is generally agreed that state constitutional provisions have inhibited the solution of urban problems in most states. The need for housing, social welfare and health services and job training, the vast need for better and more schools, the need for transportation facilities, the growing need for environmental controls in metropolitan regions have been caused by unprecedented immigration from rural areas into the cities since World War II, aggravated by a movement from the cities to the suburbs by the middle class. * * *

" * * * The continued presence of constitutional restrictions on the states' powers to act may itself be a clue to their readiness to do so.

* * *

"Constitutional restrictions placed on the state governments * * * disable the local governments as well, because the localities cannot look for help to the state when the state has effectively deprived itself of the capacity to render it. There are, however, many more direct constitutional limitations on the local governments' ability to act; these include constitutional restrictions on permissible structure of local government, on the range of powers, and on the scope of their fiscal powers. * * *" Grad, *The State's Capacity to Respond to Urban Problems: The State Constitution,* in, *The States And The Urban Crisis,* Alan K. Campbell, Ed., 27, 28, 41 (American Assembly 1970).*

1. SPECIAL LEGISLATION **

State constitutions commonly prohibit the enactment of "special legislation," but do so in widely differing terms. Among the policies served by these prohibitions are: avoidance of discrimination against

---

* Reprinted by permission of Prentice-Hall, Inc., Englewood Cliffs, N.J. Copyright © 1970 by The American Assembly, Columbia University.

** Distinctions, not here pursued, can be drawn between "special" and "local" legislation which in turn have a narrower significance than "special acts" and "private acts." See e.g. 2 McQuillin, *Municipal Corporations,* §§ 4.35, 4.47, 4.48 (3d rev. ed. 1979).

particular localities; avoidance of legislative interference in local affairs; and reduction of legislative burdens by minimizing multifarious statutes of selective application.

The range of state constitutional variations is illustrated by the following samples.

(1) *Illinois* (Article IV, § 13):

"SPECIAL LEGISLATION—The General Assembly shall pass no special or local law when a general law is or can be made applicable. Whether a general law is or can be made applicable shall be a matter for judicial determination."

(2) *Wisconsin* (Article IV, §§ 31, 32):

"Sec. 31. SPECIAL AND PRIVATE LAWS PROHIBITED. The legislature is prohibited from enacting any special or private laws in the following cases:

"1st. For changing the name of persons or constituting one person the heir at law of another.

"2nd. For laying, opening or altering highways, except in cases of state roads extending into more than one county, and military roads to aid in the construction of which lands may be granted by congress.

"3rd. For authorizing persons to keep ferries across streams at points wholly within this state.

"4th. For authorizing the sale or mortgage of real or personal property of minors or others under disability.

"5th. For locating or changing any county seat.

"6th. For assessment or collection of taxes or for extending the time for the collection thereof.

"7th. For granting corporate powers or privileges, except to cities.

"8th. For authorizing the apportionment of any part of the school fund.

"9th. For incorporating any city, town or village, or to amend the charter thereof.

"Sec. 32. GENERAL LAWS ON ENUMERATED SUBJECTS. The legislature shall provide general laws for the transaction of any business that may be prohibited by section thirty-one of this article, and all such laws shall be uniform in their operation throughout the state."

(3) *Pennsylvania* (Article III, § 32, Article IX, § 13(b)):

"Section 32. The General Assembly shall pass no local or special law in any case which has been or can be provided for by general law and specifically the General Assembly shall not pass any local or special law:

"1. Regulating the affairs of counties, cities, townships, wards, boroughs or school districts:

"2. Vacating roads, town plats, streets or alleys:

"3. Locating or changing county seats, erecting new counties or changing county lines:

"4. Erecting new townships or boroughs, changing township lines, borough limits or school districts:

"5. Remitting fines, penalties and forfeitures, or refunding moneys legally paid into the treasury:

"6. Exempting property from taxation:

"7. Regulating labor, trade, mining or manufacturing:

"8. Creating corporations, or amending, renewing or extending the charters thereof:

"Nor shall the General Assembly indirectly enact any special or local law by the partial repeal of a general law; but laws repealing local or special acts may be passed.*

* * *

"Local and special laws, regulating the affairs of the City of Philadelphia * * * shall be valid notwithstanding the provisions of section thirty-two of article three of this Constitution."

(4) *Summary:*

"All states, except for the northeastern states of Connecticut, Delaware, Massachusetts, and New Hampshire now have some constitutional provisions either restricting the use of special legislation or expressing a need for general legislation. * * *

"Of the provisions requiring that a general act be used, slightly over half of them require that a general law be used when applicable, possible, proper or practicable. One-third of the constitutions provide specifically that a general law must be used to organize or regulate cities; but of these, four include a provision permitting classification and one allows an exception where the city requests it. * * *"
Winters, *State Constitutional Limitations,* p. 85 (1961); ** see also Winters, *Classification of Municipalities,* 57 Nw.U.L.Rev. 279 (1962).

FEDERAL PAVING CORPORATION v. PRUDISCH

Supreme Court of Wisconsin, 1940.
235 Wis. 527, 293 N.W. 156.

WICKHEM, JUSTICE. The controversy involved in this case has been before the court in the cases of Bechthold v. Wauwatosa, 228 Wis. 544, 277 N.W. 657, 280 N.W. 320, and Federal Paving Corporation v. Wauwatosa, 231 Wis. 655, 286 N.W. 546. In the first case this court held a street paving contract under which plaintiff sought payment for the contract price void for failure to follow statutory prescriptions * * *. In the second, this court held that plaintiff could not maintain an action against the city for restitution of the reasonable value of

---

* Similar provisions with longer enumerations are found in many states. See e.g. Constitutions of California (Art. IV § 25) and Texas (Art. III § 56).

** Reprinted by permission of Michigan Legal Publications. Copyright © 1961 by The University of Michigan Law School, Ann Arbor.

the paving. Following the last of the two decisions, the legislature enacted sec. 62.215, Stats., which provides as follows:

"Authority to pay for public work done in good faith. (1) Whenever any city shall have received prior to January 1, 1939, and shall be enjoying any benefits or improvements furnished under any contract which shall have been or shall hereafter be declared as imposing no legal obligation upon such city, and which contract was entered into in good faith and was fully performed and the work accepted by the proper city officers, so as to impose a moral obligation upon such city to pay therefor, such city may, by resolution of its common council and in consideration of such moral obligation, pay to the person furnishing such benefits or improvements the fair and reasonable value of such benefits and improvements.

"(2) The fair and reasonable value of such benefits and improvements and the funds out of which such payment shall be made shall be determined by the common council of such city. Such payments may be made out of any available funds, and said common council shall have authority, if necessary, to levy and collect taxes in sufficient amount to meet such payment.

"(3) Where special assessments shall have been levied for the benefits or improvements mentioned in subsections (1) and (2) of this section, the common council of such city may validate such special assessments and apply the proceeds thereof towards payment for such benefits and improvements."

Acting under the authority of this section, the common council of the city of Wauwatosa adopted a resolution authorizing and directing the payment to plaintiff by the proper city officers the sum of $24,596.78. * * * The contention of the city treasurer and the intervening defendants was that sec. 62.215, Stats., is invalid as special legislation under sections 31 and 32 of Article IV, Constitution. The trial court sustained this position and held that while there may be classifications of cities, all classifications must satisfy all of the following requisites: (1) *They must be based upon substantial distinctions which make one class really different from another;* (2) *they must be germane to the purpose of the law;* (3) *they must not be based upon existing circumstances;* (4) *the law must apply equally to every member of the class;* (5) *the characteristics of each class should be so far different from those of other classes as to reasonably suggest the propriety of the substantially different legislation.* * Johnson v. Milwaukee, 88 Wis. 383, 60 N.W. 270. Upon the basis of rule (3), the trial court concluded that sec. 62.215, Stats., classified cities into those which prior to January 1, 1939, had entered into such contracts as are described in the section and those which after that date had entered such contracts; that the section was based upon existing circumstances and created a closed class; that no sufficient reason existed for the classification; and that the section was to be treated as a special law, void under the provisions of Article IV, sec. 31, sub. 9, which prohibits the legislature

---

* Emphasis supplied, not the court's.

from enacting any special or private law "for incorporating any city, town or village, or to amend the charter thereof." Although the matter is not free from difficulty, we conclude that the conclusions of the trial court were sound.

By its terms, sec. 62.215, Stats., applies to all cities, * * * The difficulty with appellant's contention is that although the terms of the section are in no way restricted, sec. 62.03 excludes from its provisions cities of the first class operating under special charters, and hence sec. 62.215 applies only to cities of the second, third and fourth classes. Thus, we are presented with the question whether a statute applicable only to cities of the second, third and fourth classes, * * * is a special act creating a closed class into which no other municipality may grow. That it does so seems to have been established in Johnson v. Milwaukee, 88 Wis. 383, 60 N.W. 270; Boyd v. Milwaukee, 92 Wis. 456, 66 N.W. 603; Burnham v. Milwaukee, 98 Wis. 128, 73 N.W. 1018; Cawker v. Central B.P. Co., 140 Wis. 25, 121 N.W. 888; and Neacy v. Drew, 176 Wis. 348, 187 N.W. 218. These cases have one circumstance in common. The curative acts considered in each case applied only to cities of the first class, and the city of Milwaukee is the only city of that class in the state. * * *

It was held that this curative act was unconstitutional * * * because the act applied only to Milwaukee, could never apply to any other city, and therefore was a special law. * * *

At this point it will be convenient to consider another group of cases which at first sight seem inconsistent with those referred to and give considerable color to plaintiff's contentions. These are Adams v. Beloit, 105 Wis. 363, 81 N.W. 869, 47 L.R.A. 441; State ex rel. Risch v. Board of Trustees, 121 Wis. 44, 98 N.W. 954; Wisconsin Cent. R. Co. v. Superior, 152 Wis. 464, 140 N.W. 79; State ex rel. Bloomer v. Canavan, 155 Wis. 398, 145 N.W. 44; Milwaukee v. Reiff, 157 Wis. 226, 146 N.W. 1130; State ex rel. Binner v. Buer, 174 Wis. 120, 182 N.W. 855. In each of these cases it was held that classification of cities is proper on the basis of population; that the fact that laws pertain only to cities of the first class and that there is only at present one such city do not affect their validity; and that in general the fact that a law applies only to a single class and excludes other classes of cities does not make it a special law repugnant to the constitutional provisions. * * *

In each of the cases cited, however, the law involved applied not merely to all cities presently in the class but to all cities which might grow into the class. In none of the cases was there any limitation of the law to past facts, * * * Once the propriety of classification on the basis of population was settled, no further problem was considered to remain.

* * *

In addition to the foregoing cases * * * should be considered * * * the case of Schintgen v. La Crosse, 117 Wis. 158, 94 N.W. 84, 87. That case involved the validity of Sec. 1210d, Stats. (1898), which provided for the reassessment of invalid special assessments for street improvements. * * * It was objected that so far as it pertains to past assessments the law was void because it constituted improper class legislation and hence was a special or private law and within the inhibition of sec. 31, Article IV, Constitution. * * *

While the court in the Schintgen case refers to the section as applicable to cities operating under a special charter, the law in fact applies to all void assessments by any municipality. * * * If a statute in terms applies to all cities, the circumstance that there may be no factual situation in some of the cities upon which it may operate does not disclose an attempted classification, good or bad.

* * * The White Construction Company case represents the considered judgment of this court upon facts so nearly parallel to this as to leave no escape from the conclusion that a curative act, which validates past transactions or permits recognition of liability on the basis of pre-existing facts, must be made applicable to all municipalities if it is to escape condemnation as a special act. * * *

* * *

Judgment affirmed, and cause remanded for further proceedings according to law.

NELSON, J., dissents.

Notes

1. **Classification Criteria.** Students should read the brief, informative article by Professor Winters entitled *"Municipal Classification,"* 57 Nw.U.L.Rev. 279 (1962). See also Comment, *A History of the Constitutionality of Local Laws in Texas,* 13 Baylor L.Rev. 37 (1961).

The five criteria stated in Federal Paving leave much play for *ad hoc* judgments regarding: (1) what constitutes a "substantial" distinction among different classes of local governments; (2) when a classification is sufficiently "germane" to the law's purposes; (3) when a classification is "closed"; (4) what constitutes "equal" application to all members of a covered class; (5) what local characteristics justify special legislative treatment. These elements are obviously interdependent and overlapping. The class of units, type of function, population, and numerous other special characteristics in each case bear upon the impact of each criterion. The comprehensive standard of reasonableness serves to organize these criteria in the formation of specific judgments.

2. **Curative Statutes.** Unless unwarranted discrimination is found, as in Federal Paving, curative statutes are not deemed "closed" although they apply only to existing and not future situations. They may be deemed general laws which apply uniformly to unique situations, or deemed laws covered by the exception—"where general laws cannot be made applicable." E.g. City of Mason v. West Texas Utility Co., 150 Tex. 18, 237 S.W.2d 273 (1951) (statute authorizing power company use of city streets for ten years after a city's incorporation); People ex rel. Black v. Armstrong, 286 Ill. 246, 121 N.E. 556 (1919) (statute providing that the oldest continuing

school district is validated where districts overlap); State v. Squires, 26 Iowa 340 (1868) (statute validating the organization of a particular school district).

3. **Local Option Statutes.** Statutes which allow local units the option to be governed or not governed by all or part of the statute are deemed general and not special legislation. See 2 McQuillin, *Municipal Corporations* § 4.49 (3d rev. ed. 1979).

4. **Open and Closed Classes.** Closed classes are generally taken as an earmark of special legislation. City of Scottsbluff v. Tiemann, 185 Neb. 256, 175 N.W.2d 74 (1970); Stout v. Democratic County Central Committee, etc., 40 Cal.2d 91, 251 P.2d 321 (1952); City of Fort Worth v. Bobbitt, 121 Tex. 14, 41 S.W.2d 228 (1931); Batistich v. Brennan, 45 N.J. 533, 213 A.2d 761 (1965).

A class is not closed, however, by the bare fact that the statute may, at any point in time, affect but one municipality:

> "Legislation is intended * * * to provide for the future. * * * At no distant day Pittsburg will probably become a city of the first class; * * * In the meantime, is the classification as to cities of the first class bad because Philadelphia is the only one of the class? We think not. Classification does 'not depend on numbers. * * *" Wheeler v. Philadelphia, 77 Pa. 338, 349, 350 (1875).

See also Lovell v. Democratic Central Committee, 230 Ark. 811, 327 S.W.2d 387 (1959); Omaha Parking Auth. v. Omaha, 163 Neb. 97, 77 N.W.2d 862 (1956); DuBois v. Gibbons, 2 Ill.2d 392, 118 N.E.2d 295 (1954); Devon v. San Antonio, 443 S.W.2d 598 (Tex.Civ.App.1969). *But see* Constitutions of Connecticut (Art. X, § 2) and Massachusetts (Art. VI, § 8), which require that statutory classes be applicable to two or more municipalities.

5. **Standards of Municipal Population or Organization.** Courts generally uphold as general and not special in nature, legislation which classifies municipalities according to their population, or their form of government organization. In a few states, the constitutions expressly state that classification by population does not constitute special legislation. Pa. Const. Art. III § 20; Vernon's Ann.Texas Const. Art. IX §§ 4, 5. These standards, however, do not invariably avoid condemnation as special legislation. Petition for Removal of Struck, 41 Ill.2d 574, 244 N.E.2d 176 (1969) (statute providing for recall of elective officials, and applicable to commission form, but not to managerial or aldermanic forms, of government— nullified as special legislation).

Problems —How would you characterize the following laws? A statute which authorizes county commissioners to dissolve any underlying town with an assessed property valuation below $40,000? See Town of Bridgie v. Koochiching, 227 Minn. 320, 35 N.W.2d 537 (1948). A statute which authorizes condemnation procedures for counties, but not for cities? See Bleamaster v. Los Angeles, 189 Cal.App.2d 274, 11 Cal.Rptr. 214 (1961). A statute which requires larger cities, but not smaller towns and villages, to contribute part of their traffic fines to the state driver education fund, for the use of all state residents? See Oklahoma City v. Griffin, 403 P.2d 463 (Okl.1965); but see Veail v. Louisville and Jefferson County Met. Sewer

Dist., 303 Ky. 248, 197 S.W.2d 413 (1946). A statute which enables cities of less than 4000 persons which are bounded by suburbs with a population seven times as large, to borrow funds for certain improvements? See City of Walnut Creek v. Silveira, 47 Cal. 804, 306 P.2d 453 (1957).

6. **Classification by Special Characteristics.** Legislation that is directed to problems that arise from special characteristics of a single or small number of local units may be upheld as reasonable, and thus a general law. In People ex rel. County of Du Page v. Smith, 21 Ill.2d 572, 173 N.E.2d 485 (1961) the court sustained a statutory classification that limited its operation to the characteristics of a single 5 county region of the state, because the unique population and territorial characteristics of that region justified the narrow classification.

In County of Cameron v. Wilson, 160 Tex. 25, 326 S.W.2d 162 (1959) the court sustained a statute which located a public park on an island that was generally usable only by residents of one county. The dissenter argued that all legislation based only upon geographic factors is necessarily local and special.

7. **Constitutional Exceptions to Special Legislation Barriers.** Many state constitutions authorize special legislation where a general law could not be made applicable to the subject at hand, or where the special legislation is provided at the initiative or by referendum of affected local units. See *e.g.* Constitutions of West's Florida Stat.Ann. (Art. III, § 10), Massachusetts Gen.Laws Ann. (Art. II, § 8), New Jersey Stat.Ann. (Art. IV, § 7 par. 10), Pennsylvania (Art. III, §§ 7, 32), Texas (Art. III, § 57). A few state constitutions also except prohibition statutes dealing with cities. Opinion of the Justices, 341 Mass. 760, 168 N.E.2d 858 (1960); Begley v. Board of Appeals, 349 Mass. 458, 208 N.E.2d 799 (1965).

The reasons for such exceptions also underlie grants of local home rule. "The task of obtaining authorizing legislation may be most difficult for the municipality when the legislature is restricted by an effective prohibition of local legislation. Although the authorization may eventually be forthcoming, the necessity of drawing legislation generally applicable throughout the state means that enactment may have to await crystallization of opinion on a statewide basis. * * * [T]here may be considerable delay between the time when one municipality needs power and the time when general legislation is politically feasible. Often, too, the strength of the opposition * * * may be increased by the required application of the legislation to areas where the problem is less acute or, perhaps, nonexistent.

"The need for flexibility in handling municipal problems has led, in most jurisdictions, to a substantial watering down of constitutional provisions prohibiting special legislation. * * * the problems created by constitutional efforts to force all municipalities into a single mold, or at best a limited number of molds, * * * raises other problems. * * *" Sandalow, *The Limits of Municipal Power Under Home Rule: A Role for the Courts,* 48 Minn.L.Rev. 643, 654 (1964).*

That generally applicable legislation cannot be honestly made to serve a need provided by special legislation in certain circumstances, is seen in the following excerpt from Albuquerque Metropolitan Arroyo Flood Control Authority v. Swinburne, 74 N.M. 487, 490, 394 P.2d 998, 1001–2 (1964):

> "It is apparent that in the Albuquerque area the flood conditions result largely from the density of the population. * * * No other area of the state has such a heavy concentration of improvements which cause the water to run off in such volume. No other area is so situated that there are no channels or other available devices to carry off the water which accumulates. * * * No other area in the state was required to raise such a large amount of money to meet federal demands for local participation with the federal government to handle such flood conditions. It was these special, unique and atypical conditions in the area described in this Act which gave rise to the * * * Arroyo Flood Control Act * * *. It is apparent that a general law could not have been made applicable."

Query—Where the statutory methods for remedying local problems are so burdensome as to deter local authorities and electors from implementing the statute, does a new statute which provides more acceptable alternatives, and which is admittedly "special" legislation, fall within the exception that "no general law * * * can be made applicable" to the subjects of the special law? See Solvang Municipal Imp. Dist. v. Jensen, 111 Cal.App. 2d 237, 244 P.2d 492 (1952).

ELIAS v. TULSA

Supreme Court of Oklahoma, 1965.
408 P.2d 517.

DAVISON, JUSTICE. * * * The zoning ordinance was enacted by the City pursuant to powers granted by an Act of the 1955 Legislature, 19 O.S.Supp.1955, Secs. 863.1–863.43.

Section 863.2 of the 1955 Act, supra, provided in pertinent part that any county having an assessed valuation of not less than $200,000,000 and having within its boundaries, a city of not less than 180,000 and not more than 240,000, according to the last or any future Federal Decennial Census, was authorized to form a cooperative planning commission with such city, and that:

> " * * * Such city is hereby empowered to adopt, amend, extend, add to or carry out a city plan for such city and such surrounding territory as lies within five (5) miles of the boundaries of such city, excluding, however, any other incorporated area as hereinafter provided, or any portion of an adjoining county having a population of not less than 43,143, and not more than 43,243 according to the last Federal Decennial Census or any future Federal Decennial Census * * * ".

* * *

Elias contends that the 1955 Act, supra, is in violation of Sec. 46, Art. 5, of the Oklahoma Constitution, prohibiting local or special laws regulating the affairs of counties and cities; and of Sec. 59, Art. 5, providing that laws of a general nature shall have uniform operation throughout the State, and where a general law can be made applicable, no special law shall be enacted; and was invalid as a special or local law because of failure to comply with Sec. 32, Art. 5, requiring publication notice prior to legislative consideration of such a law.

* * *

The City does not deny that the descriptive language in Sec. 863.2 * * * is applicable only to Tulsa County, and excludes the one county in the State having a city with a greater population (Oklahoma County) and excludes all other counties. In fact, the City admits that "the act when adopted in 1955 was a suit that fit only one party, and that was the Tulsa metropolitan area."

The determinative question presented to this court is whether the 1955 Act was a general law. In deciding whether an act is a general law as distinguished from a local or special law the answer to the problem depends fundamentally on whether there is a proper and legitimate classification, and each case must be decided on its own merits. Sheldon v. Grand River Dam Authority, 182 Okl. 24, 76 P.2d 355.

Classification by reference to population must be a legitimate one, and bear some reasonable relation to the subject matter, and must not be an arbitrary or capricious classification and used as a subterfuge for the purpose of passing a special law under the form of a general law. Key v. Donnell, 107 Okl. 157, 231 P. 546.

In Roberts v. Ledgerwood, 134 Okl. 152, 272 P. 448, we stated the factors to be considered in determining whether a legislative act was in fact general in its nature, as follows:

> "In order for a law to be general in its nature and to have a uniform operation, it is not necessary that it shall operate upon every person and every locality in the state. A law may be general and have a local application or apply to a designated class if it operates equally upon all the subjects within the class for which it was adopted. * * * But, where a statute operates upon a class, the classification must not be capricious or arbitrary and must be reasonable and pertain to some peculiarity in the subject-matter calling for the legislation. As between the persons and places included within the operation of the law and those omitted, there must be some distinctive characteristic upon which a different treatment may be reasonably founded and that furnishes a practical and real basis for discrimination."

* * *

As stated above the 1955 Act was "tailored" to apply to Tulsa County, even to the extent of excluding from the 5 mile perimeter strip that portion of an adjoining county having a population between 43,143 and 43,243, which could only refer to adjoining Creek County. Disregarding this exclusionary provision that was applicable only where there existed the combination of Tulsa and Creek Counties, the only other county in the State that in any way came close to falling within the statutory classification was Oklahoma County, which had Oklahoma City with a 1950 population of 243,504.

*   *   *

The 1955 Act does not reveal why the classification set forth therein made this zoning power available to the City of Tulsa, as the second largest city in the State with a population of 182,740, and failed to extend the same to the largest city with a population of only 3,504 inhabitants in excess of the statutory classification. The *   *   * "purposes" [of the Act] set forth certain general and specific conditions that are considered or deemed to be in need of improvement in cities falling within the classification, and specifically the City of Tulsa. These conditions relate generally to the welfare of the public and specifically to conditions that are a problem and in need of improvement in all large metropolitan cities. In fact it is recognized that problems of this nature tend to increase, rather than decrease, as a city becomes larger and the population becomes more concentrated. These conditions exist in Oklahoma City and in this respect it is not dissimilar to the City of Tulsa.

In Wilkinson v. Hale, *supra*, it is stated:

"Local or special laws are all those that rest on a false or deficient classification. Their vice is that they do not embrace all the class that they should naturally embrace. They create preference and establish inequality. They apply to persons, things, and places possessed of certain qualities or situations and exclude from their effect other persons, things, or places which are not dissimilar in this respect."

For the reasons stated it is our conclusion that the population classification in the Act was arbitrary and a subterfuge, and did not embrace all of the class that it should have naturally embraced.

The City urges that in considering the constitutionality of the 1955 Act this court should presume that the Legislature did not intend to violate the Constitution. We concede that this is the general rule of law. However, we have shown that the classification in the Act was arbitrary, capricious, and a subterfuge, designed to give the Act the appearance of a general law. In such a situation the presumption is overcome.

The City makes two additional contentions in support of the judgment of the lower court. It argues the Act is a general law because the population and assessed valuation classification is an "open" classification and that as cities in Oklahoma grow in the above respects, they will reach a position where they fall within the classification. It also argues that there was justification in making the Act apply only to Tulsa County and the Tulsa metropolitan area and excluding the larger [*sic*] City of Oklahoma City for the reason that there were fewer incorporated areas adjacent to the City of Tulsa than there was [*sic*] in the area surrounding Oklahoma City, and other differences, such as, difference in per capita earnings and the shape of the two counties.

It appears to us that there is an inconsistency in these two arguments that only serves to strengthen our conclusion that the classification in the 1955 Act was an arbitrary and unjustifiable classification. In the first place the classification was restrictive to the extent that it did not include Oklahoma County with a city of slightly larger population and similar enumerated statutory conditions. In the second place the classification based on alleged local conditions described as peculiar only to the City of Tulsa, negatives legislative intent to enact a general law having a uniform operation throughout the State, as required by Sec. 59, Art. 5, of the State Constitution. Under the present circumstances a holding that the classification in the 1955 Act was sufficient to render it a general law would make it permissible to adopt any arbitrary formula of population and valuation as a valid ground for a general law.

For the foregoing reasons we are of the opinion and hold, that Chapter 19Aa, S.L.1955, 19 O.S.Supp.1955, Secs. 863.1–863.43, is unconstitutional.

*   *   *

The judgment of the lower court is reversed with instructions to render judgment in accordance with the views herein expressed.

*   *   *

Notes

1. **Rational v. Arbitrary Classification.** "Perhaps the most important question in judging the validity of a classification is whether the particular classification is relevant [substantially] to the purpose of the statute." Winters, *Classification of Municipalities,* supra p. 84.

Equal protection principles have parallel application to the classification of equal and special legislation: "It is the essence of a classification that upon the class are cast * * * burdens different from those resting upon the general public. * * * Indeed, the very idea of classification is that of inequality, * * *" Atchison, Top. & S. Fe R.R. v. Matthews, 174 U.S. 96, 106, 19 S.Ct. 609, 613, 43 L.Ed. 909 (1899). "Here then is a paradox: The equal protection of the laws is a 'pledge of the protection of equal laws.' But laws may classify. * * * In tackling this paradox the Court has neither abandoned the demand for equality nor denied the legislative right to classify. It has taken a middle course. It has resolved the contradictory demands of legislative specialization and constitutional generality by a doctrine of reasonable classification." Tussman and ten-Broek, *The Equal Protection of the Laws,* 37 Calif.L.Rev. 341, 344 (1949).*

See Anderson v. Wagner, 79 Ill.2d 295, 37 Ill. Dec. 558, 402 N.E.2d 560, (1979), appeal dismissed 449 U.S. 807, 101 S.Ct. 54, 66 L.Ed.2d 11 (1980); semble: State ex rel. City of Charleston v. Bosely, 165 W.Va. 332, 268 S.E.2d 590 (1980).

At what point should courts refuse deference to legislative judgments on the propriety of population-range classes? Compare DuBois v. Gibbons,

* Reprinted by permission of California Law Review, Inc. Copyright © 1949.

2 Ill.2d 392, 118 N.E.2d 295 (1954) with People ex rel. Adamowski v. Wilson, 20 Ill.2d 568, 170 N.E.2d 605 (1960). On the issue of reasonableness are courts necessarily reviewing legislative discretion?

2. **Narrow Population Brackets.** Where a narrow, exclusionary population class serves no public purpose, the inference of special discrimination is readily drawn. See Annot., Statutory Classifications Based on Population, 98 A.L.R.3d 679 (1980). Haas v. Holloman, 327 P.2d 655 (Okl.1958) (statute providing judicial salary increase in counties with population between 17,000 and 18,000, and a net valuation of less than $16 million, effectively excluded all but one county in the state—held to be special legislation); State ex rel. Cotterill v. Bessenger, 133 So.2d 409 (Fla.1961) (nullified, as special legislation, a statute authorizing nudism regulation in counties with population between 36,700 and 38,000); see also Opinion of the Justices, 277 Ala. 630, 173 So.2d 793 (1965). But where population range classifications are relevant to statutory policies, the exclusionary effect does not per se render the act "special." See Town of Bridgie v. Koochiching *supra* p. 80; Great Lakes Properties, Inc. v. Rolling Hill Estates, 225 Cal.App.2d 525, 37 Cal.Rptr. 448 (1964) (upholding special procedures for annexation limited to state's most populous county). Courts uphold urban blight statutes that are limited to heavily populated cities. State on the Relation of Fatzer v. Urban Renewal Agency, 179 Kan. 435, 296 P.2d 656 (1956); Foeller v. Housing Authority, 198 Or. 205, 256 P.2d 752 (1953); Krause v. Peoria Housing Authority, 370 Ill. 356, 19 N.E.2d 193 (1939).

3. **Split Population Brackets.** Especially suspect and difficult to rationalize are statutes which create a series of population class brackets, and which treat intermediate population classes differently than the next higher and next lower bracket. A few examples follow. State v. Bargus, 53 Ohio St. 94, 41 N.E. 245 (1895) nullified as special legislation a statute which excepted from its coverage counties with populations between 31,940 and 31,960 and between 35,400 and 35,500. To like effect, see Anderson v. Wood, 137 Tex. 201, 152 S.W.2d 1084 (1941); Smith v. Lancaster, 269 Ala. 579, 114 So.2d 568 (1959). But courts may go to great lengths in upholding split or narrow population classes. Bailey v. Evansville-Vanderburgh Airport Authority, 240 Ind. 401, 166 N.E.2d 520 (1960).

4. **Multiple Population Classifications.** Arbitrary legislative manipulation of population classes is most evident in statutes which present dual classifications (e.g. cities of specified population within counties of specified population) as effective devices to close the class to future entrants. City of Scottsbluff v. Tiemann, 185 Neb. 256, 175 N.W.2d 74 (1970).

2. GENERAL LIMITS ON LEGISLATIVE DELEGATION

Even in the absence of express constitutional text, our traditions of "separation of powers" and the "rule of law" would prohibit delegation or redelegation of legislative power to coordinate or subordinate administrative bodies. Though notched with important exceptions, the delegation principle is an accepted part of constitutional law.

For a survey of developments on delegation principles, see Westbrook, *Nondelegation in Public Sector Law,* 30 St. Louis L.J. 331, 358–68 (1986).

The principle obviously does not forbid all delegation of powers to local governments. People ex rel. Adamowski v. Public Bldg. Commission of Chicago, 11 Ill.2d 125, 147, 142 N.E.2d 67, 79 (1957); Fish Creek Park Co. v. Bayside, 274 Wis. 533, 537, 80 N.W.2d 437, 439–440 (1957). Indeed some state constitutions empower state legislatures to delegate to local units lawmaking powers over subjects upon which the state legislatures themselves are forbidden to legislate directly. Exceptions are also made for local option statutes. Locke's Appeal, 72 Pa. 491 (1873); Bucino v. Malone, 12 N.J. 330, 96 A.2d 669 (1953).

In confining the lawmaking function to elected legislatures, courts must determine whether a statute delegates "lawmaking" or only "administrative" power; that is, whether statutory guidelines are adequate to insure reasonable administrative implementation under discernible legislated standards. In application, the question is one of degree. As a rule of thumb, it may be said that the willingness of courts to indulge broad statutory guidelines and broad delegations of discretion to administrators tends to increase as the statutory subject becomes more complex; and as the need for administrative expertise and flexibility increases. For the refinements on this generalization, students must refer to the cases, and to special texts on administrative law.

BELOVSKY v. REDEVELOPMENT AUTHORITY

Supreme Court of Pennsylvania, 1947.
357 Pa. 329, 54 A.2d 277.

[Facts and other portions of the opinion reported at p. 96 infra.]

* * * One of the [plaintiff's] assaults is directed against an alleged delegation of legislative powers contrary to the provision of Article II, section 1 of the Constitution,* P.S., it being claimed that insufficient standards are set up in the statute to guide the Authority in exercising the powers with which it is vested. The fact is, however, that the act contains as definite a description of what constitutes a blighted area as it is reasonably possible to express; in regard to such factors as the selection and the size of the areas to be redeveloped, the costs involved, and the exact form which the redevelopment in any particular case is to take, it was obviously impossible for the legislature to make detailed provisions or blueprints in advance for each operation. * * * The planning necessary to accomplish the purposes of the act must necessarily vary from place to place within the same city or county and from city to city and county to county. All that the legislature could do, therefore, was to prescribe general rules and reasonably definite standards, leaving to the local authorities the preparation of the plans and specifications best adapted to accomplish in each instance the desired result, a function which obviously can be performed only by administrative bodies. While the legislature cannot

* "The legislative power * * * shall be vested in a General Assembly * * *."

delegate the power to make a law, it may, where necessary, confer authority and discretion in connection with the execution of the law, it may establish primary standards and impose upon others the duty to carry out the declared legislative policy in accordance with the general provisions of the act. So far as Article II, section 1 of the Constitution is concerned the validity of the Urban Redevelopment Law finds support in many authorities: [citations omitted].

*   *   *

ROEHL v. PUBLIC UTILITY DIST. NO. 1 OF CHELAN COUNTY

Supreme Court of Washington, 1953.
43 Wash.2d 214, 261 P.2d 92.

HAMLEY, JUSTICE.

[Taxpayer suit to nullify and enjoin joint acquisition of electrical utility properties by five public utility districts pursuant to enabling statute which appellants attacked as unconstitutional on eight separate grounds. The following portion of the opinion deals with the delegation issue.]

*   *   *

The sixth question which is presented for our consideration is whether the joint purchase agreement and joint operating agreement contemplate an unlawful delegation of the powers of the district commissioners to a consulting engineer and an executive board.

Article III of the purchase agreement provides for the employment of an independent consulting engineer for the purpose of providing immediate and continuous "engineering counsel" in the operation of the joint system. Article III further provides that the consulting engineer shall prescribe the form of annual budgets to be adopted for the joint system, and an effective procedure for the control of expenditures under such budget. It is further provided that the consulting engineer shall make inventories of the properties and prepare valuations, establish the basis for the plant account records, and prepare and file periodic reports or surveys with respect to management, operation, maintenance, rates, sufficiency of power supply, and necessity for capital improvements.

Article II, § 2.2, of the purchase agreement provides that the consulting engineer shall certify the additional amounts to be added to the agreed purchase price by reason of net capital additions after June 30, 1952. The five districts agree to pay such additional amounts on a prorated basis specified in the section. Section 2.3 of article II provides that, on the acquisition date, the consulting engineer shall certify to each of the districts the initial estimated cost of the current assets, the allocation thereof to each individual district, and each district's share in the cost of the current assets which pertain to the joint system. Each district agrees to pay the amount so certified. *   *   *

Article V of the joint operating agreement confers additional duties upon the consulting engineer. Among other things, he is to determine the amount of production properties debt service according to a specified formula; redetermine such amount in connection with additional bond issues, and such redetermination "shall not be subject to the approval of the Executive Board;" and make similar redeterminations in the event changes occur which, in the opinion of the consulting engineer, make it necessary or desirable to redetermine such amounts. These latter redeterminations are subject to the approval of the executive board.

Article II of the joint operating agreement provides for the creation of an executive board, comprised of one commissioner from each of the five districts. The executive board is to serve as the agency of the districts in the performance of such duties as are assigned to it in the agreement, or may hereafter be assigned by the districts, in connection with the joint operation, management, improvement and extension of the joint system. Other district commissioners are entitled to attend the meetings of the executive board, but are not permitted to vote. Any district, however, may, by majority vote of its commissioners, bind its representative on the executive board as to how he shall cast his vote upon any item of business before the board.

Appellant contends that the provisions summarized above evidence an unlawful delegation of discretionary powers by the district commissioners to the consulting engineer and executive board. He cites no authority in support of this proposition.

Where the enabling legislation under which a municipal or quasi-municipal corporation derives its power confides legislative or discretionary functions in particular officials or boards, such functions may not be delegated to others. 2 McQuillin on Municipal Corporations, 3d Ed., 672, § 10.39; cases cited in 37 Am.Jur. 732, Municipal Corporations, § 118, note 14. Unless the enabling legislation provides otherwise, however, those in whom such functions repose may delegate to others the performance of duties of a purely ministerial or administrative nature. Storey v. Seattle, 124 Wash. 598, 215 P. 514.

The legislative and discretionary functions essential to the operation of an individual public utility district are confided in a commission, consisting of three elected members. Laws of 1931, chapter 1, §§ 4, 6(n). Chapter 227, Laws of 1949, contains no express provision relative to the exercise of legislative and discretionary functions in connection with the joint operation of integrated electric systems by two or more districts. However, § 2 thereof provides that any two or more public utility districts

"* * * shall have the power, by mutual agreement, to exercise jointly all powers granted to each individual district * * *."

Having in mind the above principle and statutory provisions, we do not believe that there has been an unlawful delegation of legislative and discretionary functions to the consulting engineer. He is given no power to make policy decisions of a legislative character. Nor is he given freedom to carry out or ignore, as his own discretion dictates, the basic policies formulated by the commissioners.

He will render consultative service and make recommendations on matters requiring engineering competence. He will perform a variety of tasks in connection with such matters as budgets, inventories, valuation, and surveys. In the making of certain certificates, he will, in a sense, be acting as an impartial fact finder as between the individual districts. In the making of certain determinations, he will be acting as a fact finder as between the districts, considered jointly, and the bondholders. In the latter capacity his determination will, with one minor exception, be subject to approval by the executive board.

In none of these respects will the consulting engineer, in our opinion, be exercising legislative or discretionary functions which have been vested in the individual district commissions, or in all the commissions, acting jointly. His duties are important, and they will require the exercise of judgment, but since they are administrative in character, there is no violation of the principle which appellant invokes.

We reach the same conclusion with regard to the executive board. This board will exercise management functions within the field assigned to it by the agreement or by the individual districts. In the exercise of such functions, each district retains full control over its own representative on the board. Municipal corporations frequently delegate management duties to an individual officer, committee, or board. Where, as here, the operation is to be the joint responsibility of several quasi-municipal corporations, the designation of a management board seems especially necessary. It is, therefore, an arrangement clearly within the contemplation of the enabling legislation—chapter 227, Laws of 1949.

[Dissenting opinion omitted.]

Notes

1. **The Control Factor in Subdelegation.** Without standards to assure control, as found in Roehl, the Washington Supreme Court voided an alleged joint agreement to acquire power facilities in Chemical Bank v. Washington Pub. Power Supply System, reported at p. 267, infra.

2. **Judicial Attitudes Toward Broad Delegations.** "The frequent attempts to vitiate legislation aimed at solving metropolitan area problems, by claiming an unconstitutional delegation has taken place, have met with notable lack of success." Winters, *State Constitutional Limitations,* 124–127 (1961).* The extent to which a court may go to find an adequate legislative standard was indicated by Mr. Chief Justice Hughes: "Appellants insist that the delegation of authority to the Commission is invalid because the stated criterion is uncertain. That criterion is the 'public

* Reprinted by permission of Michigan   The University of Michigan Law School, Legal Publications. Copyright 1961 by   Ann Arbor.

interest'. It is a mistaken assumption that this is a mere general reference to public welfare without any standard to guide determinations. The purpose of the Act, the requirement it imposes, and the context of the provision in question show the contrary." New York Central Securities Corp. v. United States, 287 U.S. 12, 24, 53 S.Ct. 45, 48, 77 L.Ed. 138 (1932).

Does a statute which empowers a public corporation to approve and regulate airports within twenty-five miles of two contiguous cities of the first class delegate lawmaking or administrative power? See State ex rel. Interstate Air-Ports, Inc. v. Minneapolis-St. Paul Metro Airports Commission, 223 Minn. 175, 25 N.W.2d 718 (1947).

3. EXPRESS LIMITS ON LEGISLATIVE DELEGATION

"The General Assembly shall not delegate to any special commission, private corporation or association, any power to make, supervise or interfere with any municipal improvement, money, property or effects, whether held in trust or otherwise, or to levy taxes or perform any municipal function whatever." Constitutions of West's Ann. California (Art. XI, § 13), Colorado (Art. V), So. Dakota (Art. III, § 26), Pennsylvania (Art. III, § 31), Wyoming (Art. III, § 37).

TOWN OF HOLYOKE v. SMITH

Supreme Court of Colorado, 1924.
75 Colo. 286, 226 P. 158.

TELLER, C.J. The plaintiff in error is a municipal corporation owning and operating an electric light and power plant, and the defendants in error, doing business in the town, were among its customers.

The town council established a schedule of rates for electric current, and the State Board of Public Utilities established a higher rate. The town brought suit to recover the higher rate, which the defendants had refused to pay.

* * *

The question then is: Does the act under consideration (chapter 127, Laws of 1913), if it gives the commission the power claimed for it, contravene the provision of the Constitution * * *. The provision reads as follows:

> "The General Assembly shall not delegate to any special commission, private corporation or association, any power to make, supervise or interfere with any municipal improvement, money, property or effects, whether held in trust or otherwise, or to levy taxes or perform any municipal function whatever."

In considering the question thus raised we are to take a broad view of the subject, and ascertain, if possible, the purpose for which this limitation on the power of the Legislature was imposed.

In Denver v. Telegraph Co., 67 Colo. 225, 184 P. 604, this court quoted from Cooley's Constitutional Limitations as follows:

" 'Narrow and technical reasoning is misplaced when it is brought to bear upon an instrument framed by the people themselves, for themselves, and designed as a chart upon which every man, learned and unlearned, may be able to trace the leading principles of government. The Constitution is to be construed as a frame of government or fundamental law,' and not as a mere statute."

To ascertain the meaning of this provision we may consider its historical background, the conditions existing when it was adopted, and what were the mischiefs against which it was intended to guard. [Citations omitted]

*   *   *

It is common knowledge that for years prior to the adoption of the state Constitution of Colorado the Legislatures of several states had repeatedly, by statutes, regulated the internal affairs of cities in those states, and that there had been great opposition to such legislation.

*   *   *

The right of the Legislature thus to interfere in municipal affairs, even though there was no constitutional provision against it, had been several times before the courts of several of the states. People v. Hurlbut, 24 Mich. 55, 9 Am.Rep. 103; People ex rel. Board of Park Com'rs v. Common Council of Detroit, 28 Mich. 228, 15 Am.Rep. 202; People ex rel. Atty. Gen. v. Common Council of Detroit, 29 Mich. 108; People ex rel. Wood v. Draper, 15 N.Y. 532; People ex rel. Bolton v. Albertson, 55 N.Y. 50; People v. Lynch, 51 Cal. 15, 21 Am.Rep. 677; and Philadelphia v. Fox, 64 Pa. 169.

Unquestionably these facts were had in mind when this provision was framed, and the people in adopting it intended to guard against the evils to which attention had been called by these cases.

It remains only to determine whether or not the people, by the language used, effected their purpose so far as the instant case is concerned. If they have done so, it is our duty so to declare. *   *   *

The operation of the electric light plant by the town of Holyoke is the performance of a municipal function, specifically authorized by statute. Section 8987, C.L.1921.

The evils to be avoided being such as have been above mentioned, we should, in applying this provision, give it a broad and reasonable, rather than a technical meaning, so as to accomplish its evident purpose. That the purpose was to prevent—generally speaking—any organization being authorized by law to control or interfere with municipal matters, whether it be the making of local improvements, the management of property, or the levying taxes, is clear. Nor can such organization be authorized to "perform any municipal function whatever."

The prohibition is not limited by the fact that the term "special commission" is used, for, if there is reason to prohibit a special commission, private corporation, or association from exercising the powers named, it exists as well as to a general commission. Indeed, it is difficult to see why a special commission would not be more desirable for the performance of municipal functions than a general commission, since it could be made local in its membership, and be assigned to duty in only one or a few municipalities. Such a commission would be far more likely to perform the assigned duties in a satisfactory manner than would be one having a large field to operate in or supervise.

This section in nowise deprives the Legislature of power to create special commissions for any purpose deemed necessary, and to delegate to them powers other than those mentioned in this section. The prohibition is not upon the creation of a special commission, private corporation, or association, but upon the delegation thereto of certain enumerated powers.

The subjects to which this protection extends by the terms of the section are such as properly fall within the domain of local self-government. If they are entitled to protection from an agency of the state exercising delegated powers of the kind enumerated, the right thus proposed to be protected would be violated as much by a general commission's doing the mentioned acts as by a special commission's doing the same things.

If the contention of counsel be correct, that the provision is to apply only to a commission specifically limited in time, or extent of operation, the manifest purpose of the provision would not be effected. It would be entirely possible for the Legislature to avoid the prohibition by creating a body to act permanently, and thus not be a special commission in the sense for which counsel contend, or to act through-out the state, if temporary in character. * * * It cannot be supposed that an instrument framed carefully, as are Constitutions, would so poorly protect the right of local self-government, if it were thought worthy of protection at all. * * *

We have heretofore placed a construction on this section which is conclusive upon the point under consideration. In Milheim et al. v. Moffat Tunnel Improvement Dist., 72 Colo. 268, 211 P. 649, we have this section under consideration and quoted with approval from In re Senate Bill, 12 Colo. 188, 21 P. 481, where it was held that the term "special commission" in this section referred—

> "to some body or association of individuals separate and distinct from the city government; that is, created for different purposes, or else created for some individual or limited object not connected with the general administration of municipal affairs."

This court has, therefore, twice held that a body distinct from the city government, created for a different purpose, or one not connected with the general administration of municipal affairs, is a special commission. It cannot be denied that the Public Utilities Commission is a body separate and distinct from the "city government," and that it is created for an object "not connected with the general administration of municipal affairs." The framers of the Constitution had in mind the possibility that the Legislature might attempt to create some special body to interfere with the management of municipal affairs, and wisely made provision to prevent such action.

When the Public Utilities Commission fixes rates to be charged by a lighting plant owned and operated by a municipality, it performs a municipal function. In Denver v. Telegraph Co., supra, we held that the regulation of rates by the Utilities Commission is the performance of a municipal function.

Counsel for plaintiff in error rely upon the case of Public Service Commission v. City of Helena, 52 Mont. 527, 159 P. 24, which sustained the Public Service Commission in its claim of the right to supervise a water system, owned by the city. In so doing the court held that the Commission was not a special commission under the terms of a constitutional provision like ours. The right of self-government, in the respect named, is denied on the ground that the principle of local self-government "does not exclude the state from the exercise of police power within a city of this state." It is to be observed that the question was not as to the state's power to act directly but as to its right to delegate the power. The opinion suggests a misapprehension of the scope of the right of self-government, as announced in the cases which sustain the right. * * *

* * *

On principle it would seem entirely unnecessary to give a commission authority to regulate the rates of a municipally owned utility. The only parties to be affected by the rates are the municipality and its citizens, and, since the municipal government is chosen by the people, they need no protection by an outside body. If the rates for electric light or power are not satisfactory to a majority of the citizens, they can easily effect a change, either at a regular election, or by the exercise of the right of recall.

These views are sustained by the case of McFadden v. Board of Supervisors, 74 Cal. 571, 16 P. 397, wherein it is held that a board of supervisors, which is authorized by law to fix the rates to be charged by corporations which sell or rent water to the general public, has no power to fix rates of a corporation which distributes water to its stockholders only. The ground of the rule is obvious.

* * * It should not be overlooked that a lighting system is owned and operated by a municipality, in a proprietary, and not in a governmental, capacity. As such it is not subject to legislative control.

* * *

In Town of Milwaukee v. City of Milwaukee, 12 Wis. 93, the court said of a town:

> "In its political or governmental capacity, it is liable at any time to be changed, modified or destroyed by the Legislature; but in its capacity of owner of property, designed for its own, or the exclusive use and benefit of its inhabitants, its vested rights of property are no more the subject of legislative interference or control, without the consent of the corporators, than those of a merely private corporation or person."

In City of Henderson v. Young, 119 Ky. 224, 83 S.W. 583, it is said:

"In the management and operation of its electric plant a city is not exercising its governmental or legislative powers, but its business powers, and may conduct it in the manner which promises the greatest benefit to the city and its inhabitants in the judgment of the city council."

In this case we are not called upon to decide as to the constitutionality of the act, but merely to determine its scope, in view of a constitutional provision. It is clear that if the act be construed as giving to the Public Utilities Commission the right to fix the rates in this case, it would to that extent be invalid, because in violation of the section of the Constitution above discussed.

Moreover, it being manifest that the fixing of rates to be charged by the town of Holyoke for electric current is not an exercise of the police power, it would seem that the Public Utilities Commission would have no authority in the premises, even were there no specific constitutional provision involved.

The judgment of the trial court is right, and is accordingly affirmed.

CAMPBELL and DENISON, JJ., dissent.

Notes

1. The term "municipal function" embraces both governmental and proprietary activity. By referring to the constitutional purpose of enhancing "self-government" the Holyoke opinion implied that a governmental function was involved; yet it later suggests that a utility operation is proprietary in nature. The instability, if not logical flaws, of the governmental-proprietary distinction is clear. Were municipal utilities purely proprietary, how could they escape state police power regulation which govern private utility corporations? Should the court have merely declared that the purpose of constitutional limits on delegation was met by local control over local utility rates; and that different kinds of utility regulation would call for discrete functional analysis? See p. 133, infra, 2 McQuillin, *Municipal Corporations,* §§ 4.156–4.158 (3d rev. ed. 1979). See State Water Pollution Control Board v. Salt Lake City, at p. 98, infra; Stewart v. Cheyenne, 60 Wyo. 497, 154 P.2d 355 (1944).

2. **Judicially Exempted Delegations to State Commissions.** Courts avoid extreme literal applications of constitutional text, and uphold commissions' powers that do no great violence to the historical purposes of nondelegation clauses, *viz.* statutory commissions to regulate local government reorganizations; statutory boards for special districts; commissions to assist local government. 2 McQuillin, supra, §§ 4.09–4.11.

Query—Where the state constitution authorizes municipal operation of public utilities, has all state legislative power over such utilities been withdrawn? Compare Pfau v. City of Cincinnati, 142 Ohio St. 101, 50 N.E.2d 172 (1943); City of West Allis v. County of Milwaukee, reported at p. 140, infra.

BELOVSKY v. REDEVELOPMENT AUTHORITY

Supreme Court of Pennsylvania, 1947.
357 Pa. 329, 54 A.2d 277.

HORACE STERN, JUSTICE.

[Taxpayer suit to nullify Urban Redevelopment Law which authorized creation of public corporations by cities and counties, with powers to acquire, finance and manage redevelopment sites and projects through private developers, subject to approval by the creating city or county.]

Legislation similar to these Pennsylvania statutes has been adopted in 23 other States.

* * *

The present attack upon the constitutionality of the Urban Redevelopment Law centers largely upon the grant therein made to the Redevelopment Authorities of the power to exercise the right of eminent domain. It is contended that the taking of property under the act is not for a public purpose and therefore cannot constitutionally be effected by resort to the power of eminent domain.

Dornan v. Philadelphia Housing Authority, 331 Pa. 209, 200 A. 834, may be regarded as the prototype of the present case since all the arguments now presented on this subject were there fully considered. The Urban Redevelopment Law closely parallels the provisions of the "Housing Authorities Law" of May 28, 1937, P.L. 955, 35 P.S. § 1541 *et seq.*, with which the Doran case was concerned. * * *

As is not unusual when the constitutionality of an important statute is assailed, attacks are here made upon alleged violations of a considerable number of constitutional provisions, possibly in the hope that a stray shot may find its way to some vital target. * * *

The act does not violate Article III, section 3 of the Constitution because of any deficiency in its title. The title is virtually a complete index of the provisions of the statute. Although, as plaintiff points out, there is no mention of the fact that the properties acquired by the Authority may be resold to private individuals after the redevelopment has been accomplished, the title does state that the Authorities have the power of the leasing and selling of property, and also that they may contract with private redevelopers.

The act does not offend the provision of Article III, section 20 of the Constitution that the legislature shall not delegate to any special commission or private corporation any power to make, supervise or interfere with any municipal improvement or perform any municipal function. The Redevelopment Authorities are purely administrative bodies enjoying no important power which is not subject to the approval of the city council or the county commissioners; the Authorities cannot independently exercise any municipal functions. Moreover they are public bodies and not special commissions or private corporations within the meaning of the constitutional prohibition: Tranter v. Allegheny County Authority, 316 Pa. 65, 77–79, 173 A. 289, 294, 295; Dornan v. Philadelphia Housing Authority, 331 Pa. 209, 230, 200 A. 834, 844; Williams v. Samuel, 332 Pa. 265, 274, 2 A.2d 834, 838, 839.

There is no violation of Article IX, sections 1 and 3 of the Constitution which provide that all taxes shall be uniform and that only certain prescribed property may be exempted from taxation. * * * The only tax exemption is that provided by the Urban Redevelopment Law in the case of the bonds issued by an Authority, and it has been held that bonds issued by such a governmental instrumentality are not the kind of property contemplated by the constitutional prohibition against exemption of any property from taxation other than that specified in the Constitution: Kelley v. Earle, 325 Pa. 337, 356, 190 A. 140, 149; Williams v. Samuel, 332 Pa. 265, 274, 275, 2 A.2d 834, 839.

The provisions of Article IX, section 8 and Article XV, section 2 of the Constitution concerning the debts of counties, cities and other municipalities and incorporated districts, and the incurring of liability by any municipal commission, are not violated by the Urban Redevelopment Law. A Redevelopment Authority is not a municipal commission. It is specifically provided by the act that neither the bonds nor any other obligations of an Authority shall be debts or liabilities of any municipality or of the Commonwealth. "In view of that declaration," as was said in Dornan v. Philadelphia Housing Authority, 331 Pa. 209, 231, 200 A. 834, 845, "it is difficult to understand how the act in any way impinges upon these constitutional provisions."

In the provision of the Redevelopment Cooperation Law authorizing loans or donations of money to Redevelopment Authorities there is no violation of Article IX, section 7 of the Constitution forbidding the legislature to authorize any county, city, borough, township or incorporated district to appropriate money for, or to loan its credit to, any corporation, institution or individual. This section of the Constitution has no application to a public corporation such as an Urban Redevelopment Authority, but is restricted to the appropriation of public funds to a purely private enterprise: [Citations omitted]

* * *

Decree dismissing the bill affirmed; * * *.

Notes

1. **Taxing Power and Delegation Issues.** The transfer of taxing power may be a significant factor, since nondelegation provisions are directed in part against control of municipal tax functions by non-elected state boards. Evans v. West Norriton Twp. Mun. Authority, 370 Pa. 150, 87 A.2d 474 (1952); Backman v. Salt Lake County, 13 Utah 2d 412, 375 P.2d 756 (1962); compare Board of County Commissioners of Albany Co. v. White, 79 Wyo. 420, 335 P.2d 433 (1959). Does this reflect the popular ideal—"no taxation without representation"?

2. **State v. Local Affairs.** A crucial issue is whether the state board is exercising control over "local affairs" or over statewide interests that apply to every locality. Had the state law in Belovsky authorized regional rather than municipal authorities, the court could have found no control over "local affairs" without making the questionable argument that the Authority was a "purely administrative" body subject to municipal control. See Fellom v. Redevelopment Agency of City and County of San Francisco, 157 Cal.App.2d 243, 320 P.2d 884 (1958); Santa Barbara County Water Agency v. All Persons and Parties, 47 Cal.2d 699, 306 P.2d 875 (1957), reversed Ivanhoe Irr. Dist. v. McCracken, 357 U.S. 275, 78 S.Ct. 1174, 2 L.Ed.2d 1313. The state's power to redefine a local affair as a statewide affair is seen in the transfer of functions from municipalities to county units and regional agencies.

3. **Public Authorities.** The increasing use of public authorities to operate or finance capital improvements has generally withstood challenges as unconstitutional special commissions. See the discussion on this point in Part IV of the Basehore opinion, reported at p. 704 infra.

STATE WATER POLLUTION CONTROL BOARD v. SALT LAKE CITY

Supreme Court of Utah, 1957.
6 Utah 2d 247, 311 P.2d 370.

CROCKETT, JUSTICE.

[State created Water Pollution Board by Legislature held to be a "special commission" under constitutional provision prohibiting Legislature from delegating to any "special commission" power to supervise or interfere with any municipal improvement.]

This case involves a controversy between The State Water Pollution Control Board and Salt Lake City concerning the City's failure to conform to certain of the Board's regulations pertaining to sewerage systems. The fundamental contention of the City is that it is not subject to these regulations.

The Water Pollution Board was created by the 1953 Legislature. Its declared purpose was to "Control, Prevent and Abate the Pollution of Surface and Underground Waters of the State." Pursuant to the Act, the Board adopted a set of regulations for sewerage systems to which some of the practices Salt Lake City has followed for many years do not conform.

The three regulations which provide the basis for the dispute here are these: (1) prohibiting any cross-connection between a drinking water system and a sewage system; (2) prohibiting the use of any public sewer pipe less than eight inches in diameter; and (3) requiring mechanical ventilation in all underground pump stations.

* * *

Regarding the latitude of the Board's sphere of authority: there seems to be no doubt that the Act was meant to give it jurisdiction over cities for certain purposes. * * *

The contention of the City is that if the Water Pollution Act is so construed as to give the Board authority to make and enforce such regulations over it as those in question here, the Act is contrary to Article VI, Section 29 of our Utah Constitution:

> "The legislature shall not delegate to any special commission, * * * any power to make, supervise or interfere with any municipal improvement, * * *."

It is evident that if the Board's position is correct, it would be supervising and in a sense "interfering" with the City's sewer and its operation. It is contended by the Board however, that because the constitutional restriction upon interference with activities of the City above referred to, speaks of "municipal improvements" and "municipal functions" it was meant only to apply to those activities of the municipality which it pursues in a private or proprietary capacity. It reasons that matters concerning health and sanitation to which water pollution relates are of a purely governmental nature and are thus subject to control by the Board, even if it be deemed a special commission.

As both parties argue in terms of the distinction between governmental and proprietary functions in order to include or exclude the sewage disposal regulations under the constitutional provision, it is appropriate to inquire into the meaning of the word "municipal" as there used. * * *

Where this distinction has been made the basis for interpreting constitutional provisions similar to our own, the cases lack uniformity in its application. Some have held that the constitutional provision safeguards the City's action insofar as the function is proprietary, but in others it is persuasively argued that if such distinction is to be made at all it should have just the opposite effect: That is, that it would be more logical that the framers intended the cities to have freedom in their governmental activities. The lack of any consistency of results reached in applying the tort liability cases to the instant problem makes plain that the tests there employed have no particular relevancy on the question here involved as to whether a special commission can supervise "municipal" activities of the City. * * *

If the constitutional provision was intended to assure the City freedom from outside supervision and control, it most certainly seems that it must be with respect to their primary and essential functions. Considering this purpose, it does not seem open to question that in the context of the constitutional provision here under consideration the term "municipal" as used in connection with municipal improvement and municipal function, was used in its broad sense and would include any activity properly engaged in by the city or municipality, whether governmental or proprietary. Sewage disposal is a function which is almost invariably left to cities to perform, and our statutes specifically grant them the power to "construct, reconstruct, maintain and operate, sewer systems, * * *."

* * *

It is to be noted that we are here dealing specifically with respect to the problem of sewerage disposal within Salt Lake City, and as affecting the inhabitants thereof. It is obvious that a community might so handle its sewage as to constitute a menace to the health of other communities or inhabitants of the state, *e.g.* by letting it escape into streams, or lakes or springs which form their head waters so that it would affect lower users. This is undoubtedly the reason for the general language in the statute granting the Water Pollution Board its powers to guard against pollution of "all * * * bodies * * * of water, * * * contained within * * * this state * * *." If the statute is so construed, the Board is endowed with authority to supervise and regulate such matters where they are conducted in a manner which threatens pollution of waters beyond the confines of the city. Such interpretation does not run afoul the constitutional provision hereinabove discussed relating to the City's independence of internal operation * * *.

It is finally pointed out by the Board that the constitutional provision only prohibits the legislature from delegating the powers involved to a "special commission, private corporation or association." It is contended that the Water Pollution Board is not a "special Commission" within the meaning of the Constitution. With this we do not agree. The same question was raised in the case of Logan City v. Public Utilities Commission, wherein it was held that the defendant was a "special commission" and in specifically rejecting a Montana case holding to the contrary stated:

> "But we think such a construction * * * is too narrow, and one which in effect impairs the very essence and purpose of it, deprives cities and towns of local self-government, * * *."

It appears that the only cases in which this court has found the Constitution inapplicable to the interfering agency are those similar to the case of Lehi City v. Meiling, wherein it was held that a Metropolitan Water District was not a "special commission." However, that and similar cases, are clearly distinguishable in that the Metropolitan Water District was initiated by the cities desiring the district and there was no direct delegation by the legislature to a board or agency which would allow it to interfere with any municipal improvement, property, or function.

The decision of the trial court is affirmed.   *   *   *

Note

On the problem of classifying metropolitan special districts as "special commissions" with relation to underlying municipalities, see the concurring opinion in Four County Metropolitan Cap. Imp. District v. Board of County Comm'rs., p. 136, infra.

4. OTHER STATE CONSTITUTIONAL LIMITATIONS

The policy against special legislative treatment of different localities is also served by the following constitutional limitation:

(1) Provisions that general laws shall be uniform in operation.

(2) Provisions requiring uniformity of taxation.

(3) Provisions barring state imposition of local taxes for local purposes.

(4) Provisions barring certain kinds of state assistance to local governments, *viz.* state assumption of municipal debts; state release of local inhabitants from taxes levied for local purposes; state involvement in internal local improvements.

Of the many questions left to interpretation by the foregoing provisions, the most fundamental is whether a legislative subject constitutes a "state" or "local" affair. Many facilities which are located within municipal bounds, (roads, bridges, airports) and many regulations which affect the local government operation, (employee wage and health standards) involve both local and state interests. See Winters, *State Constitutional Limitations,* p. 22. Compare e.g. the following cases which arose under the old Illinois Constitution. People ex rel. Gallenbach v. Franklin, 338 Ill. 560, 58 N.E.2d 555 (1944) invalidated a state statute which created a state annuity fund to be financed by assessment of covered cities.

People ex rel. Moshier v. City of Springfield, 370 Ill. 541, 19 N.E.2d 598 (1939), upheld a state statute which set minimum wages for city firemen. But see other minimum wage cases at p. 151, *infra.*

The financing of highway construction by state user taxes (motor vehicles and gasoline taxes) has been held not to constitute state aid to local improvements. State Highway Commissioner v. Detroit City Controller, 331 Mich. 337, 49 N.W.2d 318 (1951) but cf. State ex rel. City of Charleston v. Sims, 132 W.Va. 836, 54 S.E.2d 729 (1949).

Professor Winters notes the functional weighing of various factors under a broad "public purpose" test. The source and form of financing, the nature of the public facility, and its availability to persons other than the inhabitants of a given local unit are more significant than the incidental location and local use of a facility. See Winters, *State Constitutional Limitations,* pp. 24–31. See generally, *Comment, Wisconsin's Internal Improvement Prohibition: Obsolete in Modern Times,* 1961 Wis.L.Rev. 294.

Chapter IV

LOCAL GOVERNMENT ORGANIZATION

CITY OF CLEVELAND EX REL. NEELON v. LOCHER

Supreme Court of Ohio, 1971.
25 Ohio St.2d 49, 266 N.E.2d 831.

C. WILLIAM O'NEILL, CHIEF JUSTICE. * * * The municipal charter is basically the constitution of the municipality. Here, we have a charter provision which specifically directs that council shall enact appropriate legislation to effectuate the purpose of the charter provision. It is a clear legal mandate which places an affirmative duty on the council to act.

Although * * * mandamus does not lie to compel a legislative body to enact legislation on the basis that this would infringe on the doctrine of separation of powers, there are instances in which such a rule cannot apply. * * *

If the members of a legislative body can ignore, with impunity, the mandates of a constitution or a city charter, then it is certain that the faith of the people in constitutional government will be undermined and eventually eroded completely.

In the instant case, the city charter provision imposes a clear and mandatory duty on city council to enact legislation to provide for the enforcement of the charter provision creating a 48–hour work week for city employees.

The charter provision is clear on its face. If, because of the peculiar circumstances surrounding the operation of a fire department, such a work week is not feasible, the remedy lies in an amendment of the charter, not in a refusal to comply with the present clear dictates of the charter provision.

102

There being a mandatory duty on city council to enact such legislation, the judgment of the Court of Appeals denying a writ of mandamus is reversed and the writ is allowed.

Judgment reversed and writ allowed.

A. HOME RULE

The Home Rule Movement. The powers of local government are defined by state charter laws. Early charter laws were fairly inflexible, and narrowly defined delegated powers. By increasing local autonomy, home rule also affects the horizontal (interlocal) and vertical (local-state-federal) intergovernmental activities. See generally, Vanlandingham, *Municipal Home Rule in the United States,* 10 Wm. & Mary L.Rev. 269 (1968); F.P. Grad, *The State's Capacity to Respond to Urban Problems,* in *The States and The Urban Crisis,* 27 (Am.Assembly, 1970). As these authors point out, the merits and implementation of home rule remain subjects of continuing argument. See ACIR, *14th Annual Report,* p. 50 (1973).

The theory of absolute local home rule—what Mr. Justice Brewer termed "imperium in imperio" (City of St. Louis v. Western Union Tel. Co., 149 U.S. 465, 468, 13 S.Ct. 990, 991, 37 L.Ed. 810 (1833))—envisioned a dual state and local sovereignty, along the national model of federal and state governments. But neither the principle of independent, concurrent sovereignty, nor the attempts to develop bright-line divisions of state and local authority have prevailed.

"Save for a few states, such as Colorado and Utah which enumerate specific home rule powers along with a broad general grant of home rule authority, the laws of most states define home rule grant in vague language, such as 'frame and adopt a charter for its own government' (Mo.), 'all powers of local self-government' (Ohio), 'municipal affairs' (Cal.), 'all local municipal matters' (Colo.), 'property, affairs or government' (N.Y.), and 'local affairs and government' (Wis.). *Under such provisions, determination of which matters are state and which matters are local constitutes the crux of the home rule problem.* This determination, however, is in most instances exceedingly difficult. The Nebraska Supreme Court confessed: 'It is not easy in all cases to distinguish between municipal powers and state powers, and when they come within the classification of police powers, they are as impossible of accurate definition as the police power itself.' Determination of home rule powers is sometimes further complicated by the fact that the character of governmental functions changes. As noted by the California Court of Appeals: 'The term "municipal affairs" is not a fixed quantity, but fluctuates with every change in the conditions upon which it is to operate.' Local functions for this reason are sometimes judicially reclassified as state; and when reclassification occurs, the possible quantity of home rule is thereby decreased." Vanlandingham, supra, pp. 291–292.*

One commentator concluded that the idea of constitutional or legislative home rule really reflects a standard of "judicial home rule." Another suggested that home rule ultimately depends upon a "state of mind," i.e. the willingness of legislatures, courts, and local officials to press for what they consider the proper scope of local power. This would partly explain why some local governments make little use of their home rule powers, while others employ them extensively; why some state legislatures are liberal in granting home rule powers (e.g., Michigan, Texas) while others have taken little action. Home rule patterns change, but there is little correlation between the form of home rule authorization and the zeal with which it is pursued. See Vanlandingham, supra, pp. 282–83, 294–96; Fordham and Asher, *Home Rule Powers In Theory And Practice,* 9 Oh.St.L.J. 18, 20 (1968).

1. FORMS OF HOME RULE

Home rule has not been extended to like local governments by all states, nor defined in uniform terms by state laws. Judicial construction of home rule powers has been neither uniform, consistent, nor generally favorable to home rule *vis-a-vis* state jurisdiction. Compare e.g., the California provision (p. 122, infra) with the Wisconsin provision (p. 140, infra) and those of Massachusetts and Pennsylvania quoted below.

> "A distinction is often made between 'constitutional' home rule and legislative home rule, depending on the source of the home rule powers. As a result, a good deal of definitional confusion has arisen, because many state constitutions do not grant home rule powers to local governments directly, but rather authorize, or instruct, the legislature to go ahead and grant home rule powers.* Since there is no way to compel the legislature to legislate, there have been instances where a constitutional mandate to provide for local self-government powers has been wholly ignored. Thus, unless the constitution itself provides a method for the adoption * * * of a home rule charter, as well as an express grant of home rule powers, the legislature may be the true source of the municipality's powers * * *." F.P. Grad, *The State's Capacity To Respond To Urban Problems, in The States and The Urban Crisis,* Alan K. Campbell, Ed., 42–43 (American Assembly 1970).**

The National Municipal League has developed a model home rule provision that avoids the extremes of absolute or illusory home rule theories. It provides:

"A county or city may exercise any legislative power or perform any function which is not denied to it by its charter, is not denied to counties or cities generally, or to counties or cities of its class, and is within such limitations as the legislature may establish by general law."

Under the foregoing provision, the control of the definition of home rule powers is removed from the courts to state legislatures, and although this provision empowers states to restrict home rule activity, it has been defended as follows:

"* * * Proponents have had to concede, of course, that this so-called home rule approach does not give the municipalities any exclusive areas of protection, * * *. * * * It does not really provide home rule; it provides something far more important * * *. It provides a means to resolve and adjust the conflicting claims of the states and the municipalities in the solution of urban problems, and it deprives each group of the alibi that only the other has power to act. * * * [I]t does not preserve artificial boundaries * * * but recognizes the power of the state to make order out of chaos—if it really wants to do so—by putting together viable combinations for metropolitan government, overriding if necessary the parochial claims of some local jurisdictions." Grad, supra, p. 49.

By granting home rule for action which the legislature could have authorized and did not expressly reserve; and by preserving the residual powers of state legislatures to limit home rule, the model provision reverses the role of courts and the restrictive interpretations on the scope of local control. See e.g., American Municipal Association (National League of Cities), Model Constitutional Provision for Home Rule § 6 (1953); ACIR, State Legislative Program 185–6 (1963). The above model provision has been adopted in a number of states. See Vanlandingham, supra, 305–308; Hymen, Home Rule in New York, 15 Buff.L. Rev. 335, 360–364 (1965); Westbroch, Municipal Home Rule: An Evaluation of the Missouri Experience, 33 Mo.L.Rev. 45, 70 (1968).

MASSACHUSETTS

Amend. Art. II: "§ 6. Any city or town may, by the adoption, amendment, or repeal of local ordinances or by-laws, exercise any power or function which the general court has power to confer upon it, which is not inconsistent with the constitution or laws enacted by the general court in conformity with powers reserved to the general court by section eight, and which is not denied, either expressly or by clear implication, to the city or town by its charter. This section shall apply to every city and town, whether or not it has adopted a charter.

* * *

"§ 7. Nothing in this article shall be deemed to grant to any city or town the power to (1) regulate elections [other than purely local elections]; (2) to levy, assess and collect taxes; (3) to borrow money or pledge the credit of the city or town; (4) to dispose of park land; (5) to enact private or civil law governing civil relationships except as an incident to an exercise of an independent municipal power; or (6) to define and provide for the punishment of a felony or to impose imprisonment as a punishment for any violation of law; provided, however, that the foregoing enumerated powers may be granted by the general court in conformity with the constitution and with the powers reserved to the general court by section eight; nor shall the provisions of this article be deemed to diminish the powers of the judicial department of the commonwealth."

PENNSYLVANIA
Article IX, §§ 2, 3, 14

Sec. 2. Home rule

Municipalities shall have the right and power to frame and adopt home rule charters. Adoption, amendment or repeal of a home rule charter shall be by referendum. The General Assembly shall provide the procedure by which a home rule charter may be framed and its adoption, amendment or repeal presented to the electors. If the General Assembly does not so provide, a home rule charter or a procedure for framing and presenting a home rule charter may be presented to the electors by initiative or by the governing body of the municipality. A municipality which has a home rule charter may exercise any power or perform any function not denied by this Constitution, by its home rule charter or by the General Assembly at any time.

Sec. 3. Optional plans

Municipalities shall have the right and power to adopt optional forms of government as provided by law. The General Assembly shall provide optional forms of government for all municipalities. An optional form of government shall be presented to the electors by initiative, by the governing body of the municipality, or by the General Assembly. Adoption or repeal of an optional form of government shall be by referendum.

Sec. 14. Definitions

As used in this article, the following words shall have the following meanings:

"Municipality" means a county, city, borough, incorporated town, township or any similar general purpose unit of government which shall hereafter be created by the General Assembly.

Comment: Classification of State and Municipal Affairs

The construction of constitutional and statutory terms affecting state and local authority (e.g., special legislation, scope of delegations, fiscal authorizations; issues of conflict or preemption) hinges on the same issue that is raised in home rule disputes, namely: whether a particular matter constitutes a state or a local affair.

Since most home rule laws are not unconditional, mandatory, or self-executing, courts must interpret their scope and object. The conceptual labels used to explain their decisions do not free courts from the necessity of making the political judgment as to what is a local or statewide affair. "[I]n a complex society, state and local governments frequently have a concurrent interest in them, and they cannot be assigned to exclusive spheres save on the basis of arbitrary reasoning." Vanlandingham, *Municipal Home Rule in the United States,* 10 Wm. & Mary L.Rev. 269, 293 (1968).* These judgments shift over time. Home rule opinions reveal the process of adaptation whereby old rules are confined, extended, or reconstituted to serve new purposes; a process which has been aptly described as "pouring new wine into old bottles." See E. Levi, *An Introduction to Legal Reasoning* (1948).

Three separate issues require analysis, namely (1) whether a particular activity falls within the sphere of home rule; (2) whether an overlap of state and local law is legally consistent or conflicting; and (3) whether, in the event of inconsistency or conflict, the state or local law supersedes the other. Conflict and preemption doctrines are also studied in a later section.

BAZELL v. CITY of CINCINNATI, Supreme Court of Ohio, 1963. 13 Ohio St. 63, 68, 233 N.E.2d 864, 868–9. "The determination of what constitutes a public municipal purpose is primarily a function of the legislative body of the municipality * * * and such determination * * * will not be overruled by the courts except in instances where that determination is manifestly arbitrary or unreasonable."

* * *

STATE ex rel. BRELSFORD v. RETIREMENT BOARD of POLICE-MEN'S ANNUITY & BENEFIT FUND, 41 Wis.2d 77, 163 N.W.2d 153 (1968): "This [Wisconsin] constitutional provision does not leave it to the municipality concerned or the legislature to define what is a local affair or what is a matter of statewide concern. In the landmark Van Gilder decision, this court decided that 'In the event of a controversy * * * the court is required to make the ultimate determination.' * * * In an attempt to answer this question, it is proper for this court to look to relevant declarations of the legislature * * *. * * * It is this broad [legislative] declaration of public policy which is entitled to great weight by this court. * * *"

* Reprinted by permission of the William
and Mary Law Review. Copyright ©1968.

MARSHALL FIELD & CO. v. VILLAGE OF SOUTH BARRINGTON

Appellate Court of Illinois, First District, Second Div., 1981.
92 Ill.App.3d 360, 47 Ill.Dec. 964, 415 N.E.2d 1277.

DOWNING, JUSTICE:

Plaintiff Marshall Field & Co. (Field) filed an action for declaratory judgment (Ill.Rev.Stat.1979, ch. 110, par. 57.1) seeking a judicial determination of the validity of two resolutions of the defendant Village of South Barrington's government to issue revenue bonds in order to finance the construction of Field retail facilities located in West Dundee and Bloomingdale, Illinois. Following submission of the initial pleadings, Field moved for summary judgment. Both parties filed briefs, and the trial court granted Field's motion, declaring the proposed bond issues to be consonant with the Illinois Constitution and state law.

South Barrington appeals that finding, asserting two bases upon which the trial court allegedly should have invalidated the bond issues: (1) that South Barrington exceeded its constitutionally granted home rule authority in undertaking these particular bond proposals; * * *

South Barrington is a home rule unit in accordance with provisions of the Illinois Constitution. (Ill. Const.1970, art. VII, § 6.) On January 17, 1980, South Barrington adopted two resolutions which stated the village's intent to market two revenue bond issues not exceeding $9 million each for the purpose of financing the construction of Field retail facilities in the villages of West Dundee and Bloomingdale. Included in the resolutions were the following findings: (1) that the bond financing was necessary to insure the completion of the facilities, and (2) that the financing arrangements would "promote and further public purposes." Incorporated into the resolutions were memoranda of agreement between the village and Field. Among the representations therein were a restatement that the arrangements served the public purposes, a notation that Field wished to begin construction of the facilities only after "satisfactory assurances" that the proposed financing would be available, and an agreement that South Barrington would " * * * cooperate with the Company [Field] to endeavor to find a purchaser or purchasers for the bonds, and * * * will adopt such proceedings and authorize the execution of such documents as may be necessary or desirable for the authorization, issuance and sale * * * all as shall be authorized by law and mutually satisfactory to the Issuer and the Company." Also agreed to were that Field would be responsible for payment of the principal, interest, and premium on the bonds, and that the two projects together would result in 625 new jobs. * * *

* * *

On June 20, 1980, South Barrington's corporate counsel notified Field that the village would not proceed with the bond issues because of questions as to their legality. * * *

I.

South Barrington contends that the proposed bond issues exceeded the permissible scope of its home rule authority as granted by the constitution. It is argued that the funding by a home rule unit of a commercial facility located within the corporate boundaries of another municipality which is not a home rule unit does not "pertain to the government and affairs" of South Barrington, the home rule unit, as required by the constitution.

*   *   *

The constitution itself does not explicitly indicate whether the home rule authority granted therein may be exercised by a municipality outside of its corporate limits. *   *   * As originally submitted, the proposed article on home rule power stated that any eligible unit could "*   *   * *within its corporate limits,* exercise any power and perform any function pertaining to its government and affairs *   *   *." (Emphasis added.) (See 7 Proceedings 1577–78.) After some debate the proposal was adopted and referred to the Committee on Style, Drafting and Submission. This committee deleted the emphasized terminology without explanation. (See 7 Proceedings 1987, 1990.) No discussion of this change was undertaken by the convention delegates upon the second reading. The provision was finally adopted in this altered form.
*   *   *

From this "legislative history" of the provision, we conclude that the framers did not intend to limit home rule power solely to activities to be undertaken within the unit's boundaries. *   *   *

We have not been referred to nor have we discovered any legislative enactment pursuant to the just cited constitutional provisions which seeks to place such a territorial limitation on a home rule unit's power to raise financing through the issuance of revenue bonds.

The supreme court has determined that home rule units possess this capacity as well, not under the explicit terms of the Act, but under the constitution's grant of home rule power in Article VII. (*People ex rel. City of Salem v. McMackin* (1972), 53 Ill.2d 347, 365, 291 N.E.2d 807.) *   *   * Since the *McMackin* holding must stand for the proposition that such activity as is possible thereunder pertains to the acting body's government and affairs *   *   * we must conclude that, under *McMackin,* South Barrington would be capable of issuing revenue bonds to finance at least those types of projects specified in the Act, if the projects were located within 10 miles of its boundaries.

*   *   *

There remains the question of whether such activity is legal when the facility's location is within the 10 mile limit but also within the territorial boundary of another, non-home rule unit. *   *   *

South Barrington cites numerous cases in an effort to argue that this type of financing arrangement does not pertain to the government and affairs of the bond issuer. (See *e.g., People ex rel. Lignoul v. City of*

Chicago (1977), 67 Ill.2d 480, 10 Ill.Dec. 614, 368 N.E.2d 100; *City of Des Plaines v. Chicago & Northwestern Ry.Co.* (1976), 65 Ill.2d 1, 2 Ill.Dec. 266, 357 N.E.2d 433.) We find those cases distinguishable. There, the problems sought to be acted upon * * * were found to concern the region or state more than the specific local interests of the home rule body. Here, in contradistinction, the supreme court in *McMackin* has, by approving revenue bond financing as envisioned by the Act for home rule units, effectively ruled that such concerns do pertain to local interests. Additionally, the facts before us do not indicate the alleged contravention of the constitutional distinction between home rule and non-home rule *units* * * * West Dundee and Bloomingdale are essentially passive entities under the South Barrington plan. They are to take no part in administering the bond issues, have no direct financial concern, and, as we perceive the record, have done nothing more than acquiesce in the proposed financing scheme. No municipal power of any consequence is being either utilized by or usurped from these situs communities. Therefore, in view of the constitution's mandate that its grant of home rule authority is to be liberally construed (Ill. Const. 1970, art. VII, § 6(m)), we are of the considered opinion that the proposed bond issues of South Barrington are based upon a valid exercise of that municipality's home rule power.

a. Personnel

SONOMA COUNTY ORGANIZATION OF PUBLIC EMPLOYEES v. COUNTY OF SONOMA, ET AL.

Supreme Court of California, 1979.
23 Cal.3d 296, 152 Cal.Rptr. 903, 591 P.2d 1.

[Following state constitutional amendment (Proposition 13) which limited taxing powers and revenues of state and local governments, the state legislature enacted a statute to provide state grants to local governments, to make up for lost revenues, but conditioned them by a provision which declared void any cost of living increases to public employees in excess of such cost of living increases allowed to state government employees. The latter provision was challenged by unions representing public employees on two grounds, namely that the statute impaired obligations of bargained union contracts in violation of the federal and state constitution; and that the statute violated the home rule powers of the local government employers which negotiated and executed those bargained contracts. The California Supreme Court voided the statute on all of the plaintiffs' challenge grounds. The following portion of its opinion addresses the home rule claims.]

* * *

II

The next question for our determination is whether section 16280 violates article XI of the California Constitution because it interferes with the rights of chartered cities and counties to determine the compensation of their employees. Under section 5, subdivision (b), of article XI, chartered cities are granted "plenary authority * * * subject only to the restrictions" of that article to provide for the compensation of their officers and employees. Section 4, subdivisions (c) and (f), state that charter counties shall provide for the compensation of their officers and employees, and subdivision (g) states that a county charter making such provisions shall supersede inconsistent state laws.

There can be no doubt that there is a conflict between the provision of section 16280 invalidating wage increases agreed to by cities and counties and the ordinances or resolutions of the local agencies which ratified the agreements.

It has long been settled that, insofar as a charter city legislates with regard to municipal affairs, its charter prevails over general state law. (E.g., Ex parte Braun (1903) 141 Cal. 204, 209, 74 P. 780; Professional Fire Fighters, Inc. v. City of Los Angeles (1963) 60 Cal.2d 276, 291, 32 Cal.Rptr. 830, 384 P.2d 158.) However, as to matters of statewide concern, charter cities remain subject to state law. (Bishop v. City of San Jose (1969) 1 Cal.3d 56, 61–62, 81 Cal.Rptr. 465, 460 P.2d 137.) Similar rules apply to charter counties. (E.g., Pearson v. County of Los Angeles (1957) 49 Cal.2d 523, 535, 319 P.2d 624.)

What constitutes a strictly municipal affair is often a difficult question; ultimately it is an issue for the courts to determine. In Bishop v. City of San Jose, supra, 1 Cal.3d 56, 63, 81 Cal.Rptr. 465, 460 P.2d 137, we made it clear that while a court will accord great weight to the purpose of the Legislature in enacting general laws which disclose an attempt to preempt the field to the exclusion of local regulation, the fact that the Legislature has chosen to deal with a problem on a statewide basis is not determinative of whether the statute relates to a statewide concern.

Section 16281 contains not only a statement of legislative intent, but a declaration that the section relates to matters of statewide concern and supersedes inconsistent provisions in the charters of local entities. In view of the rule that the Legislature is not the final arbiter as to what constitutes a matter of statewide concern, this declaration cannot be deemed controlling.

As we note above, subdivision (b) of section 5 of article XI expressly grants "plenary authority" to cities to provide in their charters for the compensation of their employees. We recently held in Ector v. City of Torrance (1973) 10 Cal.3d 129, 132, 109 Cal.Rptr. 849, 850–851, 514 P.2d 433, 434–435, with regard to another matter * * * (i.e., the qualifications of employees) that "this is not the usual case in which the courts are without constitutional guidance in resolving the question whether a subject of local regulation is a 'municipal affair' and hence within the general home rule power vested in charter cities * * * Constitution [citation]. Here we have the benefit of a specific directive * * * We held that a state statute which prohibited charter cities from prescribing municipal residence requirements in their charters contravened this provision.

But even before section 5 of article XI was amended in 1970 to expressly provide "plenary authority" to charter cities over compensation paid their employees, it was held that the salaries of local employees of a charter city constitute municipal affairs and are not subject to general laws. * * * It seems clear to us, therefore, that both the language of the Constitution and prior authority support the proposition advanced by petitioners that the determination of the wages paid to employees of charter cities as well as charter counties is a matter of local rather than state-wide concern.

Respondents assert that the principles relied upon by petitioners apply only * * * in the absence of a conflict with state law, but that whenever such a conflict exists the question whether the state statute regulates a matter of state-wide concern "must be determined from the legislative purpose in each individual instance." (Citing Professional Fire Fighters, Inc. v. City of Los Angeles, supra, 60 Cal.2d 276, 294, 32 Cal.Rptr. 841, 384 P.2d 169.) This argument is without merit. * * *

But respondents' main reliance in support of their assertion that the substance of section 16280 constitutes a matter of statewide concern is the purported fiscal emergency discussed above. * * * [T]he gravamen of their argument appears to be that even if the determination of compensation to be paid to employees of charter cities and counties is ordinarily a matter of local concern, the consequences of allowing local governments to exercise these powers in the present circumstances would result in serious statewide problems * * *. Thus, they contend the question of whether local employees should be granted increases in wages is a matter of statewide concern, and the provisions of section 16280 prevail over local laws.

While this reasoning is debatable, we need not decide the issue, as respondents have failed to establish the fundamental premise of their argument. As is true with respect to the issue of impairment of contracts, respondents ground their claim upon the existence of a statewide emergency. We have demonstrated that they have not established that such a calamitous emergency exists and we therefore reject the argument that section 16280 prevails over the salary ordinances and resolutions enacted by charter cities and counties.

* * *

Let a peremptory writ of mandate issue directing respondent local entities to pay to their officers and employees the salary increases provided in the 1978–1979 agreements without regard to the invalid restrictions contained in sections 16280 and 16280.5.

* * *

CITY OF LaGRANDE v. PUBLIC EMPLOYEES
RETIREMENT BOARD ET AL.
CITY OF ASTORIA v. PUBLIC EMPLOYEES
RETIREMENT BOARD ET AL.

Supreme Court of Oregon, 1978.
281 Or. 137, 576 P.2d 1204, aff'd on reh. 284 Or. 173, 586 P.2d 765.

[Suit by cities to nullify provisions of state statute that required: *(handwritten: NATURE OF THE CASE)* (a) city police and fire personnel to be brought within the state's Public Employees Retirement System unless the city employers provided them with equal or better retirement benefits than the state system; and (b) said cities and other covered local governments to fund the costs of covering their respective employees under the state system. A closely divided court sustained the state law under a new test for distinguishing which matters are subject to paramount local home rule control or to paramount state legislative control.]

LINDE, JUSTICE.

* * *

The validity * * * of the statute was attacked in declaratory judgment proceedings brought by the Cities * * *. The cities claim *(handwritten: Cities' ARGUMENT)* that * * * the legislature has invaded a domain reserved to local discretion by the Oregon Constitution. * * * In granting review, we specifically asked the parties to discuss these questions:

> 1. In State ex rel. Heinig v. Milwaukie et al, 231 Or. 473, 373 P.2d 680 (1962), this court announced a test to be used in determining when the state can legislate on a matter of local concern. Should the *Heinig* test be refined or reconsidered and, if so, in what way?

> If the *Heinig* test is refined or reconsidered, what criteria might apply to define areas of state or local concern in the context of employe relations and employe benefits?

* * * For the reasons that follow, we conclude that * * * the legislature did not exceed constitutional bounds and accordingly reverse the decisions below.

* * *

I

The issues in these cases arise from two provisions of the Oregon Constitution that together provide "home rule" for cities and towns. * * * The pertinent part of article XI, section 2, provides:

> "The Legislative Assembly shall not enact, amend or repeal any charter or act of incorporation for any municipality, city or town. The legal voters of every city and town are hereby granted power to enact and amend their municipal charter, subject to the Constitution and criminal laws of the State of Oregon, * * *"

In article IV, section 1a (now 1(5)), the statewide initiative and referendum powers "reserved" to the people * * * were "further reserved to the qualified voters * * * as to all local, special and municipal legislation of every character in or for their municipality or district."

The relationship between the authority of the legislature and that of local governments under these provisions * * * has occupied this court in more than 75 cases. As might be expected, the court has employed a variety of formulations in explaining these decisions. This is only proper, since that relationship presents a number of distinct issues rather than a single issue. In any given case, it is necessary to distinguish whether it involves (1) the validity of a local act in the absence of a contrary state law; (2) the validity of a state law in the absence of a contrary local act; (3) the validity of a local act said to conflict with a state law; or (4) the validity of a state law said to conflict with a local act. To reduce the effect of the amendments on local authority * * * to a single formula would only obscure the fact that these are two different questions.

It is useful to recall the role of the amendments in the state's constitutional arrangements. With respect to local authority, their central object is to allow the people of the locality to decide upon the organization of their government and the scope of its powers under its charter without having to obtain statutory authorization from the legislature, as was the case before the amendments. * * * With respect to a state law, on the other hand, it is elementary that the legislature has plenary authority except for such limits as may be found in the constitution or in federal law. Thus the validity of a state law vis-a-vis local entities does not depend upon a source of authority for the law, nor on whether a locality may have authority to act on the same subject; it depends on the limitations imposed by article XI, section 2, supra.

Moreover, these constitutional provisions are concerned with the structural and organizational arrangements for the exercise of local self-government, with the power of local voters to enact and amend their own municipal charters * * * They address the manner in which governmental power is granted and exercised, not the concrete uses to which it is put. * * * [T]he amendments do not purport to divide areas of substantive policy between the levels of government. Accordingly, the accommodation of state and local authority most directly involves the amendments when a party invokes a state law as governing some process of local government, such as elections, the qualification and selection of local government personnel, taxation and finance or judicial procedures.

The important issue in the early disputes over the effects of the amendments was whether the prohibition of article XI, section 2, extended beyond laws changing a single municipal charter to laws amending such charters generally. * * *

Thus the court in 1917, * * * reached the conclusion that the legislature retained the power to enact general laws even if they affected the charters of all or many municipalities. * * *

* * * [T]he same issue was reexamined most recently in State ex rel. Heinig v. City of Milwaukie, 231 Or. 473, 479, 373 P.2d 680 (1962). There a state law requiring a city to establish a civil service system, * * * was defended on the ground that it applied to all cities. The court rejected the argument that this fact of itself took the law outside article XI, section 2. Instead, Justice O'Connell wrote,

> "we now expressly hold that the legislative assembly does not have the authority to enact a law relating to city government even though it is of general applicability to all cities in the state unless the subject matter of the enactment is of general concern to the state as a whole, that is to say that it is a matter of more than local concern to each of the municipalities purported to be regulated by the enactment. * * *"

HEINIG TEST

But even with respect to a law prescribing municipal modes of government, the court concluded, a general law might be valid if it served a predominant social interest extending beyond the local municipality. * * *

The quoted holding of *Heinig* states the rule for testing general laws for the processes of city government. The opinion in *Heinig* went further, explaining this holding by a view of the state and its cities as competing sovereignties that seemed to extend to all conflicts of state and local policy. But we do not think that article XI, section 2, extends that far, nor that the *Heinig* formula should be extended beyond the context of laws for city government * * * This is so for two reasons. First, constitutional provisions like those for home rule in the first instance are designed to formulate how government is to govern, not how judges are to exercise judicial review. * * * Judicial interpretations of such a provision must strive to articulate these directives and avoid formulations that * * * leave every policy dispute to judicial decision. Of course this does not mean that challenges * * * under the home rule provisions are beyond judicial review. * * * Rather, it bears on the proper interpretation of the provisions.

Reasons why

Secondly, * * * when such a challenge does reach a court, the court's decision must be derived from a constitutional standard, not from the court's own view of competing public policies. The accommodation of state and local authority over the processes of city government at least involves comparable interests * * *. These processes of government are the chief object of the municipal charters mentioned in article XI, section 2 * * *. When a comparison of competing policies is pressed beyond this to all conflicts between state and local acts, however, it must often involve a choice among values that have no common denominator either in or outside the constitution.

Outside the context of laws prescribing the modes of local government, both municipalities and the state legislature in many cases have enacted laws in pursuit of substantive objectives, each well within its respective authority, that were arguably inconsistent with one another. In such cases, the first inquiry must be whether the local rule in truth is incompatible with the legislative policy, either because both cannot operate concurrently or because the legislature meant its law to be exclusive. * * * However, when a local enactment is found incompatible with a state law in an area of substantive policy, the state law will displace the local rule. See, e.g., Winters v. Bisaillon, 152 Or. 578, 54 P.2d 1169 (1936), holding that the State Motor Vehicle Act displaced local speed limits and overruling a prior holding that city authority is paramount; Southern Pac. Co. v. Consolidated Freightways, Inc., 203 Or. 657, 281 P.2d 693 (1955) (same as to trains); Lovejoy v. City of Portland, 95 Or. 459, 188 P. 207 (1920) (licensing insurance agents); City of Woodburn v. Public Service Comm'n, 82 Or. 114, 161 P. 391 (1916) (utility rates); City of Klamath Falls v. Oregon Liquor Control Comm'n, 146 Or. 83, 29 P.2d 564 (1934) (liquor regulation); Fischer v. Miller, 228 Or. 54, 363 P.2d 1109 (1961) (hunting regulations). No state law in an area of substantive policy has ever been held subordinate to a contrary local rule since Kalich v. Knapp, * * * was overruled.

It is therefore pertinent to * * * determine whether the challenged law is addressed primarily to a concern of the state with the modes of local government or to substantive social, economic, or other regulatory objectives.

II

Petitioners contend, * * * that there is no issue of conflicting state and local laws in these cases because the pertinent policies of the Cities * * * are not found in the charter or the ordinances of either city. It is true that article XI, section 2, literally only forbids the legislative assembly to "enact, amend or repeal" such charters, * * * But cities sometimes place into charters specific actions on substantive matters that are unrelated to the city's governmental processes and, on the other hand, place rules for the conduct of government into ordinances, or perhaps resolutions, by-laws, or other forms of enactment allowed by the city's charter. It is not the label that matters but the role of the provision in local self-government.

The 1906 amendments were not designed to exalt form over substance * * *. They were designed, * * * to secure local control over the structure and organization of local government, and the capacity to act on a community's own initiative in any form, so long as the action * * * is not otherwise contrary to law. In the present cases, the City of La Grande had undertaken a pension and retirement program * * * through a private contractor, and Astoria had provided retirement benefits * * * through collective bargaining. Since it is not claimed that either scheme was unauthorized by the respective charters, they will be treated the same as their underlying charters for the purpose of examining whether an inconsistent state law unconstitutionally alters the cities' mode of government.

The provisions of ORS chapters 237 and 243 * * * do not fail the test stated above. The statutes plainly embody a legislative concern with securing the postemployment living standards of persons in these occupations * * * not with the cities' governmental organization. It is not essential to the legitimacy of this goal whether the legislature singled out police officers and firemen * * * nor whether its assumptions were well founded. In any event, the statutes are addressed to a statewide substantive, social objective rather than any asserted concern with the modes of local government.

The present legislation avoids the prescription of precise municipal organization involved in the two adverse decisions most nearly in point, Branch v. Albee, 71 Or. 188, 142 P. 598 (1914), and State ex rel. Heinig v. City of Milwaukie, supra. In *Branch* the challenged statute undertook to establish a police disability and pension fund "in cities of the state, having more than 50,000 inhabitants," to create in the act itself a city "board of police pension and relief," and to designate the precise license fees and fines to be used for the fund. Not surprisingly the court, * * * found this to be "an attempt to amend, *by indirection* the charter of the City of Portland" * * *. Similarly, while the statute involved in *Heinig* did not single out one city, it also undertook by the act itself to create municipal civil service commissions, to be composed of three members selected in the manner prescribed by the act * * *. Even apart from this direct prescription of an element in the city's administrative structure, the civil service law would have displaced the authority of the politically accountable local officials over the selection, assignment, discipline, and replacement of the employees, * * * and done so not as a matter of the community's policy or negotiated agreement but by direction from the state. This is a substantially different interference with local self-government from an obligation to provide a measure of economic security to public employees. Thus the act was held to be an intervention into the powers * * * specified in the Milwaukie city charter, unjustified by any independent statewide concern, and therefore in violation of article XI, section 2.

In contrast, the present statutes do not create any agencies of local government, nor do they direct local communities to do so. They oblige local governments to bring their police officers and firemen under the benefits provided respectively by the state's retirement system and a statewide insurance policy, but even that obligation is made contingent upon an option to provide equal or better benefits by other means of the local government's choice. ORS 237.620, ORS 243.055. The administrative machinery of these statutes is state administration, not compelled local administration.

III

Though the legislature in these laws has not mandated city administration in the manner that proved fatal in *Branch* and *Heinig*, its pursuit of its statewide social objective undeniably displaces the arrangements (or absence of arrangements) preferred by the local government. This is not uncommon, * * * Nor is it generally useful to define a "subject" of legislation and assign it to one or the other level of government. To treat "local personnel" as such a subject, for instance, would * * * raise doubt whether local employees also must be excluded from all state occupational qualifications or state protective laws, e.g., workers' compensation, wage and hour standards, safety standards, nondiscrimination, or child labor laws. * * * But if these doubts can be made to disappear by defining the "subject" of the same laws to be safety, or nondiscrimination, or job security, the definition merely marks the desired conclusion of an argument rather than its premise. A search for a predominant state or local interest in the "subject matter" of legislation can only substitute for the political process to which we have referred the court's own political judgment whether the state or the local policy should prevail. Moreover, * * * it misconceives the nature of a "state interest" to focus narrowly on the functions performed * * * to the exclusion of a concern with the employees as citizens. The "state" as such has no interest apart from that of its inhabitants, present and future * * *.

* * * Arguments presented in these cases, as in *Heinig,* point out that city police officers and firemen are sometimes assigned duties beyond their cities, but this is hardly needed to demonstrate a state concern. * * * The modern addition of home rule for counties would create additional complexities in employing a geographic criterion for allocating mutually exclusive constitutional authority.

* * *

Thus neither the form in which the local policy is cast, nor the "subject" of the state law, nor the existence of local boundaries can by itself determine the validity of a statewide law. Instead, we conclude that the following principles for resolving a conflict between such a law and an inconsistent local provision for the conduct of city government are consistent with our past interpretations of the "home rule" amendments:

When a statute is addressed to a concern of the state with the structure and procedures of local agencies, the statute impinges on the powers reserved by the amendments to the citizens of local communities. Such a state concern must be justified by a need to safeguard the interests of persons or entities affected by the procedures of local government.

Conversely, a general law addressed primarily to substantive social, economic, or other regulatory objectives of the state prevails over contrary policies preferred by some local governments if it is clearly intended to do so, unless the law is shown to be irreconcilable with the local community's freedom to choose its own political form. In that case, such a state law must yield in those particulars necessary to preserve that freedom of local organization.

As we have said the statutes challenged * * * in these cases are of the second, substantive kind. The provisions for financial security and * * * in the event of retirement, disability, or death address a social concern with * * * these classes of workers, not with local governments as such. Various categories of employees are not placed beyond the reach of the state's social legislation merely because their occupational functions—* * *—happen to be found in the public sector of local government. While the statewide retirement and insurance plans do displace other plans that local agencies have made, or might make, for these objectives, they are not irreconcilable with the freedom to charter their own governmental structures that are reserved to the citizens of Astoria and La Grande by article XI, section 2. Accordingly, the statutes are constitutional.

Reversed.

TONGUE, HOWELL and BRYSON, JJ., separate dissenting opinions.

TONGUE, JUSTICE, dissenting.

I agree that, as a general rule, dissenting opinions should be restrained and respectful. It is difficult to do so, however, when, because of a purely fortuitous change in the membership of this court, there is now a majority which, by a margin of one vote, has prevailed by an opinion which:

(1) Drastically upsets the long-existing balance of power between Oregon cities and the state legislature in the critical area of "home rule" by abandonment of the long-established concept that the "home rule" amendments * * * granted to Oregon cities exclusive power to legislate as to all matters of "local interest," * * * free from intervention by the state legislature, and with the courts as the arbiters of disputes * * * as to what are matters of "local interest."

* * *

(2) Substitutes * * * a new rule of "legislative supremacy," to the effect that the state legislature may legislate as to all matters which *it* deems to involve some state-wide interest, with the single exception of some matters involving the "structure and procedures of local agencies." * * *

(3) Overrules a line of unanimous decisions extending for a period of more than 40 years * * *. As a substitute, the majority has adopted a new * * * rule for which it cites no direct authority * * *.

(4) Permits the legislature to transfer to the cities the cost of expensive social programs of predominately local interest, * * * thus compelling Oregon cities to make expenditures, incur debts, or levy taxes to raise funds for such programs. * * *

(5) Uses this case as a vehicle for a "judicial *tour de force*" by the adoption of that new and unprecedented rule despite the fact that the majority could have sustained the validity of state laws requiring cities to provide pensions for police officers and firemen by application of the rule previously recognized by this court for application in such cases. * * *

(6) Decides this case upon the basis of a new and drastic rule not urged by any of the parties or amicus curiae in this case * * *.

* * *

NOTE

Does the *LaGrande* test—that looks to the factors of government structure, organization and processes—successfully avoid judicial balancing of state and local interests which is required by the test that looks to the subject matter of the legislation? Does it adequately protect local autonomy? See the analysis of Professor Andersen in 18 Urban Law Annual 129 (1980) entitled: *Resolving State/Local Governmental Conflict—A Tale of Three Cities.*

Did *LaGrande* put a gloss on the same court's decision in Haley v. City of Troutdale, reported infra at page 154?

b. *Fiscal Control*

WEEKES v. OAKLAND

Supreme Court of California, 1978.
21 Cal.3d 386, 146 Cal.Rptr. 558, 579 P.2d 449.

BY THE COURT.

May a chartered city, in the exercise of powers conferred by the home rule provision of the California Constitution (art. XI, § 5, subd. (a)), levy upon all persons employed within the city a tax measured by the compensation received from employers, notwithstanding an express statutory prohibition against municipal taxes "upon income"? (Rev. & Tax.Code, § 17041.5 * * *. This is the issue presented to us following the City of Oakland's adoption * * * of Municipal Code section 5–1.65, which provides for an "employee license fee" upon the "privilege of engaging in or following any business, trade, occupation or profession as an employee." The fee is measured by the employee's "gross receipts" for services performed in Oakland and consists generally of 1 percent of Oakland-derived earnings. (Oakland Mun.Code, § 5–1.65.) Thus, we examine the interplay of a state constitutional authorization, a statutory prohibition, and a municipal ordinance enacted by a chartered city.

Plaintiffs and interveners, all subject to the ordinance and potential taxpayers, assert that the levy, although denominated a "license fee," is essentially a municipal income tax, * * * in contravention of the * * * prohibition of section 17041.5: "Notwithstanding any statute, ordinance, regulation, rule or decision to the contrary, no city, county, city and county, governmental subdivision, district, public and quasi-public corporation, municipal corporation, whether incorporated or not or whether chartered or not, shall levy or collect or cause to be levied or collected any tax upon the income, or any part thereof, of any person, resident or nonresident. [¶] This section shall not be construed so as to prohibit * * * any otherwise authorized license tax upon a business measured by or according to gross receipts."

The city offers * * * first, that the license fee is not a tax upon income but a business or occupation tax measured by gross receipts; and second, that even if it is an income tax the levy is a legitimate exercise of a chartered city's revenue-raising power which the Legislature is without authority to prohibit.

We conclude that the fee is what it purports to be, namely, an occupation tax substantially resembling the type of municipal license fee long approved by us and expressly authorized by the final paragraph of section 17041.5. In view of our conclusion in this regard, we need not, and do not, reach the further question whether the Legislature is prevented by the home rule provision of the California Constitution from imposing an absolute ban upon revenue-raising measures of this nature enacted by chartered cities.

* * *

We also conclude that the City of Oakland is not barred from imposing its license tax upon state employees who work within the city (cf. Graves v. N.Y. ex rel. O'Keefe (1939) 306 U.S. 466, 486–487, 59 S.Ct. 595, 83 L.Ed. 927); nor does the tax discriminate unreasonably against Oakland residents who are employed in the city, merely because residents employed elsewhere are exempt. * * * The privilege of engaging in a trade, employment, or calling within a municipality is a nexus with the city sufficiently distinct from residence therein to justify separate tax treatment in this instance.

The judgment is reversed.

RICHARDSON, JUSTICE, concurring.

I concur. Although the case properly may be disposed of on the basis that the Oakland license tax is not an income tax, I would uphold the tax upon the additional ground that, in any event, the Legislature lacks power to proscribe municipal income taxes. I would reach and resolve the constitutional issue which the parties have raised in view of the unquestionable importance of this matter to numerous California cities. Additionally, a speedy resolution of the constitutional question is suggested by the need for judicial economy and the likelihood of future litigation over novel municipal levies that are business taxes by designation but arguably are disguised income taxes statutorily prohibited by Revenue and Taxation Code section 17041.5 (all statutory references are to that code unless otherwise indicated).

Stated concisely, that issue is whether the enactment of a revenue-raising tax based upon the income of persons within a city's jurisdictional reach is a municipal affair, insulated from legislative interference by article XI, section 5, subdivision (a), of the California Constitution.

Since 1879, California cities of designated population have had the power to adopt charters for local government (Cal. Const., art. XI, §§ 6, 8 (1879)), but it was not until 1896 that they acquired supremacy over local matters by virtue of a constitutional amendment which provided that "*respect to municipal affairs* [city charters] shall be subject to and controlled by general laws." (Cal. Const., art. XI, § 6 (1896), italics added.) * * *

The home rule provision, * * * is best construed as accomplishing two purposes: (1) it *grants* to chartered cities the authority to manage local affairs; and (2) it imposes a corresponding *restriction* upon the power of the state Legislature to interfere with or override decisions on municipal matters made at the local level. * * *

"On the other hand," we observed in Professional Fire Fighters, Inc. v. City of Los Angeles (1963) 60 Cal.2d 276, 291, 32 Cal.Rptr. 830, 839, 384 P.2d 158, 167, "the clear language of the constitutional provisions * * * deny to the state Legislature the right to interfere with a chartered city only with respect to matters which are exclusively municipal affairs." More recently we noted that "as to matters which are of statewide concern * * * home rule charter cities remain subject to and controlled by applicable general state laws regardless of the provisions of their charters, if it is the intent and purpose of such general laws to occupy the field to the exclusion of municipal regulation * * *." (Bishop v. City of San Jose (1969) 1 Cal.3d 56, 61–62, 81 Cal.Rptr. 465, 468, 460 P.2d 137, 140.) Thus, "When it appears that a municipal regulation [of a chartered city] and a general state law are in conflict, the controlling law will depend on whether the subject matter is a municipal affair or whether it is of statewide concern. If the matter is a municipal affair, local ordinances and regulations will be upheld despite conflict with the general state laws * * *." (City of Santa Clara v. Von Raesfeld (1970) 3 Cal.3d 239, 245, 90 Cal.Rptr. 8, 11, 474 P.2d 976, 979.)

It is conceded that taxation for local purposes is one of the powers conferred by direct constitutional grant under article XI, section 5 * * * and that such power, generally speaking, is very broad. * * * Municipal taxing power, however, like all powers granted by the home rule provision, is not unlimited but may be circumscribed or abrogated * * * (2) by other constitutional provisions reserving various powers over taxation to the state; and (3) by the limitations inherent in the concept of "municipal affairs."

Section 17041.5 purports to forbid any California city, chartered or not, to impose an income tax. Assuming for purposes of discussion that the Oakland employee license fee must be considered an income tax in direct conflict with that provision, plaintiffs contend that the state statute must prevail for two reasons. The power to levy an income tax, they assert, is expressly reserved to the Legislature by article XIII, sections 26, subdivision (a), and 33, * * * Alternatively, it is argued that enactment by California cities of a series of individual, uncoordinated local income taxes would have such a severe impact at the state level upon the mobility of California citizens, the location of commercial enterprises, and the operation of the state income tax system that municipal income taxation must, for practical purposes, be deemed a "matter of statewide concern," * * * I examine each of these contentions.

1. RESERVATION OF POWER UNDER ARTICLE XIII

Article XIII, section 26, subdivision (a), of the Constitution provides as follows: "Taxes on or measured by income may be imposed on persons, corporations, or other entities *as prescribed by law*." (Italics added.) Section 33 states, "The Legislature shall pass all laws necessary to carry out the provisions of this article."

Although article XIII deals expressly with income taxation and the broad grant of the home rule amendment does so only by implication, the traditional rule that specific constitutional provisions govern more general provisions is applicable only if section 26 is indeed specific on the precise point at issue: the identity of the governmental entities entitled to levy taxes upon income. * * * [P]laintiffs maintain that the two provisions, in combination, indicate a constitutional purpose that the power to impose income taxes shall rest exclusively with the state. I do not agree.

We have previously held that "Where the power of taxation has been lodged [by constitutional provision] in the state to the exclusion of municipalities and other entities of that character, it has customarily been done by specific language expressive of such a purpose" (Ainsworth v. Bryant (1949) 34 Cal.2d 465, 472, 211 P.2d 564, 568), and that even constitutional provisions which clearly are reservations of taxing power should be strictly construed, * * *.

* * *

With the adoption of the home rule amendment, * * * chartered cities choosing to take advantage of the grant acquired, with respect to local matters, "a power of taxation * * * concurrent with, not dependent upon, the state Legislature." (Comment, *The Municipal Income Tax and State Preemption in California*, supra, 11 Santa Clara Law. at p. 352; see Ex parte Braun, supra, 141 Cal. 204, 211–212, 74 P. 780.) * * *

Consequently, I would conclude that the power to enact an income tax is not reserved exclusively to the state Legislature by article XIII, sections 33 and 26, subdivision (a).

The inquiry should not, however, terminate at this point. Even if the power to tax income is not constitutionally reserved, the Legislature may appropriate that power to itself by statute unless a city income tax is a "municipal affair" within the meaning of article XI, section 5, subdivision (a), the home rule provision of the Constitution. On matters of statewide concern, statutes adopted by the Legislature are supreme, superseding all conflicting municipal ordinances. Is imposition of a local income tax properly a municipal affair?

2. "MUNICIPAL AFFAIRS"

The California Legislature first adopted a comprehensive state income tax system in 1935. * * * With the 1963 enactment of section 17041.5 proscribing local taxes "upon the income * * * of any person," it clearly expressed its intent to preempt the field of income taxation. The city, however, contends that the Legislature has no authority to prevent chartered cities from enacting a local tax measure designed to raise revenue for municipal purposes. I agree.

Since the adoption of the home rule amendment in 1896, the courts of this state have grappled with the definition of "municipal affair" * * * The exact scope of the term is of great significance, because we have said that a "city which [has] adopted * * * 'home rule' * * * thereby [has] gained exemption, *with respect to its municipal affairs,* from the 'conflict with general laws' restrictions of [section 5] * * * of article XI. [¶] As to matters which are of statewide concern, however, home rule charter cities remain subject to and controlled by applicable general state laws regardless of the provisions of their charters, if it is the intent and purpose of such general laws to occupy the field to the exclusion of municipal regulation * * *." (Bishop v. City of San Jose, supra, 1 Cal.3d 56, 61–62, 81 Cal.Rptr. 465, 468, 460 P.2d 137, 140, italics added.)

Expressing the precise contours of the foregoing concept is essentially a matter of allocating power among competing governmental entities, and it is a duty confided to the courts alone. * * * With "no alternative but to accept the invitation," and "without the benefit of guidance from history, constitutional tradition, or sharply delineated principle," (Sandalow, *The Limits of Municipal Power Under Home Rule: A Role for the Courts,* supra, 48 Minn.L.Rev. at p. 661), we soon concluded that "[n]o exact definition of the term 'municipal affairs' can be formulated," and have perforce been content to "give it meaning in each controverted case." (Butterworth v. Boyd, supra, 12 Cal.2d 140, 147, 82 P.2d 434, 438.)

Over the past 80 years, numerous subjects and activities have been found *not* to be "municipal affairs," and certain examples may be revealing. (E.g., Baron v. City of Los Angeles (1970) * * *, 469 P.2d 353 [city lobbyists regulation, insofar as it impinges upon state regulation of the practice of law]; City of Santa Clara v. Von Raesfeld, supra, 3 Cal.3d 239, * * * 474 P.2d 976 [intercity water pollution control project and its funding procedure]; Professional Fire Fighters, Inc. v. City of Los Angeles, supra, * * * 384 P.2d 158 [organizational rights of city employees]; Pipoly v. Benson (1942) * * * 25 P.2d 482 [regulation of highway traffic passing through city streets]; Bay Cities Transit Co. v. Los Angeles (1940) * * * 108 P.2d 435 [regulation of interurban transportation system]; Young v. Superior Court (1932) * * * 15 P.2d 163 [public improvement project extending beyond city limit]; CEEED v. California Coastal Zone Conservation Com. (1974) * * * 118 Cal. Rptr. 315 [regional land use planning]; Wilson v. City of San Bernardino (1960) * * * 9 Cal.Rptr. 431 [highway development]; County of San Mateo v. City Council (1959) * * *, 335 P.2d 1013 [annexation procedures]; cf., Century Plaza Hotel Co. v. City of Los Angeles (1970) * * * 87 Cal.Rptr. 166 [taxation/regulation of alcohol].)

With the possible exception of *Century Plaza,* supra, all of these decisions involved activities which were essentially *regulatory* in nature. On the specific issue of taxation for revenue only, numerous cases declare without equivocation or qualification that "the power of municipal corporations * * * to impose taxes for revenue purposes is strictly a municipal activity authorized by the state Constitution and subject only to those limitations appearing in the Constitution or the charter itself." (A.B.C. Distributing Co. v. City and County of San Francisco (1975) * * *. Indeed, the only case I have found which hints at any erosion of this principle is *Century Plaza,* supra, a decision which "relied upon the interrelationship of certain constitutional and statutory provisions" peculiar to that case, and seems to have turned upon the inherently regulatory effect of any tax on the sale or purchase of alcoholic beverages. * * *

Past adherence to the principle of local autonomy in tax matters, however is neither conclusive nor dispositive as to the issue before us. Matters once entirely local in nature may, in a society rapidly increasing in both complexity and interdependence, lose their "strictly local" character and become "matters of statewide concern." (Bishop v. City of San Jose, supra, 1 Cal.3d 56, 63, 81 Cal.Rptr. 465, 460 P.2d 137; * * * Pacific Tel. & Tel. Co. v. City & County of S.F. (1959) * * * 336 P.2d 514; CEEED v. California Coastal Zone Conservation Com., supra, * * * 118 Cal.Rptr. 315.) Plaintiffs argue that the unprecedented mobility of contemporary society, * * * and the growing disposition of businesses to treat local tax burdens as a key factor in location decisions will all combine to * * * magnify the effect of a local income tax, necessarily producing considerable impact at the state level. * * *

We have on occasion suggested that to be a "municipal affair," a particular matter must be "solely" or "exclusively" of local interest. (See Professional Fire Fighters, Inc. v. City of Los Angeles, supra, 60 Cal.2d 276, 291, 32 Cal.Rptr. 830, 384 P.2d 158.) Literal application of that standard would compel termination of the present inquiry * * * for it certainly cannot be said that the state interests urged herein are wholly fictitious. Judicial characterization of a particular matter as either a "municipal affair" or "of statewide concern," however, has always and necessarily been less a practical description of raw fact than a legal conclusion. * * * virtually anything touching upon the welfare and management of a municipality will also be of some concern to the state. * * * But article XI, section 5, by committing one class of affairs to local government and the other to the Legislature, compels a dichotomy when state and local enactments conflict. Classification, then, is unavoidable; how is it to be accomplished?

In *Bishop*, we stated quite plainly that the Legislature may not arrogate to itself a particular area of activity merely by asserting an interest. * * * If the home rule provision is not to be excised from the Constitution virtually at the will of the Legislature as we have said it is not, then the only reasonable and practicable means of distinguishing matters * * * is to weigh, in each case, the city's interest against the state's need to require uniformity, or to prohibit, control or coordinate the extraterritorial impact of the challenged municipal activity * * *

Applying this principle to the case before us, we must acknowledge that the Legislature's attempt to appropriate the field of income taxation is certainly an indication of the seriousness with which it views the potential statewide impact of local income taxes. * * * However, the Legislature's evaluation is not conclusive * * * and in the present instance I am not persuaded that the problems potentially generated by municipal income taxes are so sweeping that they can be resolved by nothing less than an absolute proscription of this type of tax.

* * * When a local tax measure threatens serious extraterritorial effects, * * * the Legislature may properly assert its supremacy to prevent or minimize them. But the sweep of the state's protective measures may be no broader than its interest.

Here, it is the "spillover" effect, not the local revenue ordinance itself, that is the proper concern of the Legislature. If a number of sister cities follow Oakland's lead, it is perhaps conceivable that the resulting network of uncoordinated local income taxes might cause such a heavy impact upon the ubiquitous California commuter as to impede intermunicipal business activities. None of the recitation of facts * * * presented to us, however, suggests that such external difficulties, * * * cannot be adequately controlled by means less stringent and intrusive than total prohibition. For example, there is available a mandatory credit and allocation system comparable to provisions of the Bradley-Burns Uniform Local Sales and Use Tax Law. (§§ 7200–7209; see also *Legislative Developments, The Limits of Municipal Income Taxation: The Response in Ohio* (1970) 7 Harv.J.Leg. 271 * * *.

Similarly, it is urged that businesses may be heavily influenced by the existence or nonexistence of a local income tax * * *. I am not persuaded that this danger so expands the state interest as to justify a flat prohibition of the city tax. Nor can I discern any potential impact upon the state income tax system, except insofar as the addition of local income tax liability increases the citizens' overall burden. * * *

Although I hasten to acknowledge that neither the economic wisdom nor the social propriety of a municipal tax measured by "income" lies within our purview, I cannot say that the mere existence of a tax such as the Oakland employee license fee threatens to disrupt a state legislative scheme or produce serious *and uncontrollable* adverse consequences outside the bounds of the taxing jurisdiction. Accordingly, an absolute prohibition of a particular type of revenue-raising tax is neither warranted nor tolerable under the home rule doctrine.

* * *

MOSK, JUSTICE, dissenting.

I dissent.

Although titled an "Employee License Fee Ordinance" the tax involved here is measured by a percentage of the gross income of all employees in Oakland. Thus this measure will have the dubious distinction of being the first municipal tax on the gross income of employees in the State of California, despite the clearly expressed intent of the Legislature that the state, and the state alone may impose a tax based on income. (Rev. & Tax.Code, § 17041.5.) Of one thing we can be certain: it will not be the last. * * *

* * * [T]he majority reach the remarkable conclusion that a tax on income is not an income tax. My views on the subject are less imaginative: since the burden of the tax is on the income of employees and not upon the receipts of a business, the ordinance does not create a license fee but an income tax.

* * * It is rare for the Legislature to prohibit municipal action; yet it has done so in this instance with unusual emphasis. "Notwithstanding any statute, ordinance, regulation, rule or decision to the contrary," declared the Legislature in 1963 and 1965, "no city * * * whether chartered or not, shall levy or collect * * * any tax upon the income, or any part thereof, of any person, resident or non-resident." (Rev. & Tax.Code, § 17041.5.) Legislative intent has seldom been expressed more clearly.

* * *

I am unimpressed by the constitutional argument raised by the city. Authority for the Legislature to retain the exclusive right to impose income taxes is contained in the state Constitution. Article XIII, section 26, permits imposition of income taxes and article XIII, section 33, authorizes the Legislature to "pass all laws necessary to carry out the provisions of this article." It is elementary that if home rule rights of chartered cities conflict with constitutionally bestowed authority of the State of California and its Legislature, the latter will prevail.

I would affirm the judgment of the trial court.

CITY OF ROCKFORD v. GILL

Supreme Court of Illinois, 1979.
75 Ill.2d 334, 26 Ill.Dec. 669, 388 N.E.2d 384.

UNDERWOOD, JUSTICE:

Plaintiff, the City of Rockford, filed suit * * * seeking a declaration that an ordinance levying taxes for library purposes in excess of the statutory limit was valid under the city's home rule powers. Defendant Paul P. Gill, the county clerk, had refused to extend the levy

* * * on the ground that it exceeded the maximum tax rate for library purposes permitted by section 3–1 of the Illinois Local Library Act (Ill.Rev.Stat.1975, ch. 81, par. 3–1). * * * The trial court granted the city's motion for summary judgment, the county clerk appealed, and the appellate court reversed and remanded, holding that despite its home rule power to tax, the city could not exceed the library tax rate fixed by the statute (60 Ill.App.3d 94, 17 Ill.Dec. 421, 376 N.E.2d 420). We allowed the city leave to appeal and we now reverse.

* * *

The Rockford Public Library is governed by the Act, which was first adopted in 1965. Despite the statutory limitation of .15%, the library board requested and the city adopted a tax-levy ordinance for library purposes in 1976 in an amount requiring a tax rate of .1604%. The ordinance recited that it was adopted pursuant to the procedures set forth in section 3–1 of the Act, but that the tax-rate limitation was inapplicable because the ordinance was enacted pursuant to the city's taxing power as a home rule municipality under article VII, section 6(a), of our 1970 Constitution. That section provides:

> "Except as limited by this Section, a home rule unit may exercise any power and perform any function pertaining to its government and affairs including, but not limited to, the power to regulate for the protection of the public health, safety, morals and welfare; to license; to tax; and to incur debt."

* * *

We agree with the appellate court that the issue here may be stated simply as whether a home rule municipality may levy a tax for library purposes in excess of the .15% limit imposed by the statute governing local libraries. In our judgment, however, an affirmative answer is clearly required by the earlier decisions of this court.

In *Kanellos v. County of Cook* (1972), 53 Ill.2d 161, 290 N.E.2d 240, this court held that pursuant to its power to incur debt (Ill. Const.1970, art. VII, sec. 6(a)) a home rule county could issue general obligation bonds without prior referendum approval by county voters, although a pre-1970 statute required such approval. * * * Noting that the concept of home rule was "totally foreign in the contemplation of legislation adopted prior to the 1970 Constitution" (53 Ill.2d 161, 166–67, 290 N.E.2d 240, 244), the court held that the prior statute was inapplicable to a home rule county. This court subsequently followed the rationale of *Kanellos* in a series of decisions approving ordinances adopted by home rule units pursuant to section 6(a) of article VII despite the fact that those ordinances conflicted with existing statutes enacted prior to the adoption of the 1970 Constitution. * * *

The appellate court in this case found that the General Assembly intended the library to be "a separate and independent taxing body whose finances and administration will remain apart from the exigencies of municipal politics." (60 Ill.App.3d 94, 100, 17 Ill.Dec. 421, 425, 376 N.E.2d 420, 424.) * * *

In focusing on this question, however, the appellate court misconceived the proper nature of the present inquiry. It is manifestly impossible to find a legislative intention to limit the city's home rule powers of taxation in a statute that pre-dates the 1970 Constitution because, as this court said in *Kanellos,* the concept of home rule was "totally foreign" to pre-1970 legislative contemplation. (53 Ill.2d 161, 166–67, 290 N.E.2d 240.) Nor does the 1978 amendment, * * *, support a different conclusion, for we have repeatedly held that a statute enacted after the adoption of the 1970 Constitution can restrict home rule taxing powers only if it is approved by a three-fifths majority of both houses (Ill. Const.1970, art. VII, sec. 6(g)) and specifically expresses a restrictive purpose. (*Stryker v. Village of Oak Park* (1976), 62 Ill.2d 523, 528, 343 N.E.2d 919; *Mulligan v. Dunne* (1975), 61 Ill.2d 544, 550, 338 N.E.2d 6; *Rozner v. Korshak* (1973), 55 Ill.2d 430, 435, 303 N.E.2d 389.) There is no contention that the amendment in question here meets these tests. Additionally, of course, section 6(h) of article VII authorizes the legislature to "provide specifically by law for the exclusive exercise by the State" of most home rule powers. (Ill. Const. 1970, art. VII, sec. 6(h).) * * *

RUGGERI v. ST. LOUIS

Supreme Court of Missouri, 1969.
441 S.W.2d 361.

JAMES A. MOORE, SPECIAL JUDGE.

[Suit to nullify ordinance establishing city tourism bureau and levying gross receipts tax on hotels, motels and restaurants. On plaintiffs' motion for summary judgment, trial court held ordinance valid. Appeal. Affirmed.]

* * *

Plaintiffs-appellants assert the trial court erred in holding the ordinance to be valid, specifically assigning error for the following:

* * *

Because the city has no power to levy and collect, as a license fee, a tax on restaurants to promote conventions and tourism.

Because the city has no authority whatever to levy and collect taxes for such purposes.

* * *

IV. POWER TO LEVY AND COLLECT, AS A LICENSE FEE, A TAX TO
PROMOTE TOURISM

Plaintiffs contend that a license fee or tax must be for regulation and not for revenue. In this they overlook two things. First, a license tax may be imposed for revenue purposes. Edmonds v. City of St. Louis, 348 Mo. 1063, 156 S.W.2d 619. Second, in the ordinance here, the revenue tax is an additional tax to the regulatory tax, separate and distinct. Ross v. City of Kansas City, Missouri, Mo., 328 S.W.2d 610 is not apposite as to this phase of the case.

We do not agree that the promotion of tourism is unrelated to the business of restaurants and, for that matter, of hotels and motels. Restaurants doing a volume of business above the exempt amount could readily be major beneficiaries of tourism.

V. POWER TO TAX AT ALL TO PROMOTE TOURISM

The final substantive attack upon the ordinance is that St. Louis has no authority, constitutional, statutory, or charter, to lay and collect a tax to promote conventions and tourism. True, the Constitution of Missouri grants no such power; nor does it forbid it. The General Assembly has adopted an analogous program for the state, supported by tax money. The Charter of St. Louis does not mention conventions, tourism, nor even Kiel Auditorium, but it does mention more than general welfare. It does so, not in a preamble, but in an enumeration of specific powers. Disregard the heading and read, "To do all things whatsoever expedient for promoting or maintaining the * * * trade, commerce or manufactures of the city or its inhabitants." Article I, Section 1(33).

Constitutional charter cities have been described as *imperium in imperio*. Whether this be a too grandiose description of the relation of such municipalities to state government need not be explored. It does suggest what is the fact—that such a municipality may legislate in a field occupied but not preempted by the state, provided the local legislation is not inconsistent with that of the state. Passler v. Johnson, Mo., 304 S.W.2d 903, 907[1]. See also Grant v. Kansas City, Mo., 431 S.W.2d 89.

The City of St. Louis has done so here. We now hold what was forecast in our previous decision in Ruggeri v. City of St. Louis, Missouri, Mo., 429 S.W.2d 765, 770. "[T]he City of St. Louis, through its official government, may provide a tax-supported scheme for advertising and promoting the city as a convention site and tourist attraction which shall be under the control and direction of the city government."

* * *

Notes

1. **Formalities and Substance of Home Rule Power.** Home rule jurisdiction does not necessarily preclude state control over the *manner* of its exercise. Thus, a home rule city conducting a referendum on local fiscal questions may be required by state law to put the ballot questions in dollars and cents to insure fair notice to electors. Distinctions between substance and form can be elusive. *Query*—Where a home rule charter sets a higher dollar minimum than state law, for municipal contracts that may be let without councilmanic approval, which governs? See State ex rel. Cronin v. Wald, 26 Ohio St.2d 22, 268 N.E.2d 581 (1971).

2. **Tax Authority Under Home Rule.** Many home rule statutes expressly limit the taxing powers of home rule units and preserve state control over local taxation. Absent express limitations, the extent to which courts are willing to imply particular fiscal powers as an incident of home

rule varies from state to state. The conservative position, is by no means outmoded. See Weber v. New York, 18 Misc.2d 543, 195 N.Y.S.2d 269, 274 (1959).

Liberal readings of fiscal home rule are found in California, Colorado, Missouri, and other states. See e.g. Berman v. Denver, 156 Colo. 538, 400 P.2d 434 (1965); City of Glendale v. Trondsen, 48 Cal.2d 93, 308 P.2d 1 (1957); City of Clute v. Linscomb, 446 S.W.2d 377, 379 (Tex.Civ.App.1969).

The deprivation of local fiscal initiative and autonomy may undercut the home rule unit's ability to deal with local problems. See Cohn, *Municipal Revenue Powers in the Context of Constitutional Home Rule,* 51 Nw.L.Rev. 27 (1957). But, unfettered local taxing power places local governments in competition with the state for available tax dollars.

c. *Utility Services*

PACIFIC TELEPHONE & TELEGRAPH CO. v. SAN FRANCISCO

Supreme Court of California, 1959.
161 Cal.2d 766, 336 P.2d 514.

McCOMB, JUSTICE.

[Telephone company suit for declaration of its right to maintain telephone lines in city streets pursuant to state franchise, contested by city's claim of authority to exclude such lines from its streets. Trial court ruling that location of such lines was a "municipal affair" and that city could exclude the transmission lines, reversed on appeal.]

* * *

We are of the opinion that the construction and maintenance of telephone lines in the streets and other public places within the city is today a matter of state concern and not a municipal affair.

* * *

In 1914 sections 6 and 8 of article XI of the Constitution were amended to give greater autonomy with respect to municipal affairs to cities whose charters were adopted or amended after 1914. After 1914 the city, by appropriate amendment to its charter, acquired autonomy with respect to all municipal affairs except to the extent that its charter limited or restricted such autonomy. [Citations omitted]

As to matters which are of state concern, however, freeholders' charter cities remained subject to and controlled by general state laws regardless of the provisions of their charters. * * *

* * *

It is likewise settled that the constitutional concept of municipal affairs is not a fixed or static quantity. It changes with the changing conditions upon which it is to operate. What may at one time have been a matter of local concern may at a later time become a matter of state concern controlled by the general laws of the state. [Citations omitted] * * *

*　*　* In 1957 the telephone company handled 250 million long distance messages in California. Of these, over 18 million were to telephones located in the San Francisco exchange and over 11 million were from telephones in that exchange.

*　*　* The geographical area of an exchange is based upon a community of business and social interests of people residing in that area, and thus its boundaries do not necessarily conform to the boundaries of cities. *　*　*

*　*　* Thus, the San Francisco-East Bay extended area includes 30 exchanges serving the residents of 53 cities as well as unincorporated areas located within the counties of Santa Clara, San Mateo, Alameda, Contra Costa and Marin.

*　*　*

*　*　* In order to provide these communication services, the telephone company must maintain telephone lines in the streets located within the city. A communication circuit cannot be established for a subscriber in the city without lines either along or across the streets. *　*　*

*　*　*

Pursuant to its Public Works Code, the city controls the particular location of and manner in which all public utility facilities, including telephone lines, are constructed in the streets and other places under the city's jurisdiction. *　*　*

Also, the telephone company concedes that its state franchise can be taxed by the city. The record shows that it paid the city for the fiscal year 1957–1958 nearly $4,000,000 in ad valorem taxes, which payment included taxes on such franchise.

Applying the above stated rules of law to the facts of the present case, it is apparent that *　*　* the right and obligation to construct and maintain telephone lines has become a matter of state concern. For this reason the city cannot today exclude telephone lines from the streets upon the theory that "it is a municipal affair."

*　*　*

Sunset Telephone & Telegraph Co. v. City of Pasadena, 161 Cal. 265, 118 P. 796, relied on by the city in support of its contention that placing telephone lines in the streets of a city is a municipal affair, was decided in 1911. *　*　*

*　*　*

In 1909 there was a vast difference in long distance telephone service. No long distance calls from San Francisco could be made to any place south of Los Angeles, north of Portland, or east of Reno. *　*　*

*　*　*

Clearly, there has been a vast change in conditions since the decision in Sunset Telephone & Telegraph Co. v. City of Pasadena, *supra*, in 1911, and it is evident that telephone service is not at the present time a municipal affair but is a matter of statewide concern.

City of San Diego v. Southern Cal. Tel. Co., 92 Cal.App.2d 793, 208 P.2d 27, also relied on by the city, wherein the court held that the construction and maintenance of telephone lines in streets is not a matter of state concern but is a municipal affair, is contrary to the views hereinabove expressed and is therefore disapproved.

The judgment is reversed.

PEOPLE EX REL. PUBLIC UTILITIES CO. v. MOUNTAIN STATES TEL. & TEL. CO.

Supreme Court of Colorado, 1952.
125 Colo. 167, 243 P.2d 397.

MOORE, JUSTICE. * * *

In the year 1919 this court handed down its decision in the case of the City and County of Denver v. Mountain States Telephone & Telegraph Co., 67 Colo. 225, 184 P. 604, in which by a four to three decision it was held that the telephone service being rendered by the company in the City and County of Denver, and the rates to be charged therefor, were matters "local and municipal" to the City, and that said service rates were proper subjects for exercise of the regulatory powers of the City granted in section 6, Article XX of the Colorado Constitution, which authorizes a home rule city to adopt a charter, "which shall be its organic law and extend to all its local and municipal matters."

* * *

The ultimate question for determination in this case is whether the Public Utilities Commission of the State of Colorado is the agency authorized to regulate the charges of the Telephone Company for the telephone exchange service furnished within the limits of the City. Counsel for the City and Sarpy contend, upon the authority of Denver v. Telegraph Co., *supra,* that the power to regulate the rates of the Telephone Company lies in the municipality, and under our holding in the recent case of Berman v. Denver, 120 Colo. 218, 209 P.2d 754, the exclusive method provided by law for the exercise of said regulatory power is by the initiation of an ordinance by the people of the City and County of Denver. If the early case of Denver v. Telegraph Co., *supra,* is to be followed under the rule of stare decisis, and if the rule announced in Berman v. Denver, *supra,* be then applied, these conclusions would seem to be well justified. * * * Unquestionably the issues there determined were decided by a very narrow preponderance of opinion. It is equally certain that the majority opinion was clearly out of harmony with the very great weight of authority as evidenced by the numerous cases decided by appellate courts throughout the country prior to that time. The case of Berman v. Denver, *supra,* likewise was decided by a divided court with two judges not participating.

* * * Although we now hold that the intracity business conducted by the Telephone Company is not a matter of local and municipal concern to the City and County of Denver, or any other home rule city,

it does not necessarily follow that the services of all public utilities, functioning in whole or in substantial part within a municipality, must thus be classified. Whether a particular business activity is a matter of municipal concern to a city depends upon the inherent nature of that activity and the impact and effect which it may or may not have upon the areas outside the municipality. It cannot properly be said that all services supplied by any public utility company within a municipality are matters of local or municipal concern * * * without reference to the kind of service offered, the nature and extent of the physical properties involved, or the demand for, and use of, the service in areas outside the city.

* * *

First and foremost we expressly overrule our decision in Denver v. Telegraph Co., *supra,* [67 Colo. 225, 184 P. 612], because at the time it was decided the rule announced was without adequate support in the law. * * *

* * *

No good purpose would be served by including in this opinion the numerous authorities from the various states which hold that telephone service has come to be generally recognized as not being local or municipal to any particular city or town; and that the only effective and logical regulation to which major telephone companies should be subjected is regulation upon a statewide basis. The weight of authority to this effect is overwhelming.

* * *

While the authority of the state to regulate the Telephone Company is unquestioned, such regulation must be reasonable and it seems to us grossly unreasonable to subject a telephone company to separate regulation by as many agencies as there are home rule cities operating in the state, and in addition thereto to provide regulation outside home rule cities by the Public Utilities Commission. * * *

* * *

Accordingly we now hold that the Public Utilities Commission of the State of Colorado is the sole agency authorized to regulate the business and rates of the Mountain States Telephone and Telegraph Company within the State of Colorado; that the regulation of the business of said company and the rates to be charged for service is not a "local or municipal" matter; and that municipalities operating as Home Rule Cities have no power, authority or jurisdiction to attempt such regulation.

The judgments are reversed and the causes remanded for entry of judgments consistent with the views herein expressed.

HOLLAND, JUSTICE (dissenting).

Is the majority opinion herein a defiance of the expressed will of the people, the sovereign power of the state, and does it, by not adhering to the stabilizing rule of stare decisis, strike down many

former decisions of the court and the interests affected thereby?
* * *

* * * Briefly stated, and without extended discussion, that decision in 1919 determined that the power of the regulation of telephone rates in the City and County of Denver was a local and municipal matter, which was capable of being delegated, and was delegated to Denver in express terms by the people in the Twentieth Article to the State Constitution.

* * *

* * * It must always be borne in mind that the people of the state have the exclusive right to place power and its exercise wherever they choose. They made a choice in the adoption of Article XX, and that was to take the original power vested in the legislature to make a charter for Denver, and give that power exclusively to the people of Denver. I doubt that the overwhelming weight of authority, as stated in the majority opinion, deals with this exact question. In most of the other states there is a reserve power in the constitution or it is extended to the legislative branch in the making of home-rule charters subject to such provisions. Summed up, the people of the state of Colorado said to the people of Denver, "You have all of the power that the legislature ever had to make your charter, you have made it, and we now approve it." This was the final and binding expression of the people.

* * *

Article XX of the Constitution, the home-rule amendment thereto, and the charter of the City and County of Denver are offspring of a common parentage, that of our original Constitution. What was then and there provided cannot be interfered with or nullified by the courts or the legislature or any of its creatures.

* * *

Notes

1. On the question whether a particular activity is of "predominant" state or local interest, compare Omaha Parking Authority in subparagraph (b) of this note with State Water Pollution Control Board v. Salt Lake City, p. 98, supra, where a state-created regional pollution control district was held not to supersede home rule regulation of sewerage. The ability to segregate local and "through" service lines, the allocability of local and extramunicipal service costs, and the administrative feasibility of dual regulation must be considered.

(a) *Utility Power Lines.* Power lines affecting areas outside a city are subject to paramount state jurisdiction, and a municipality may not, by zoning, force such lines underground without state commission approval. In re Public Service Electric & Gas Co., 35 N.J. 358, 173 A.2d 233 (1961). Home rule control over local service lines, while acknowledged, may also be subordinated to state jurisdiction where there is a conflicting state statute. State ex rel. Klapp v. Dayton Power & Light Co., 11 Ohio App.2d 64, 228 N.E.2d 673 (1962).

(b) *Public Carriers.*   Freight and passenger carriage, by rail or motor transport, present overlapping regulatory interests, but many of them involve no serious state-local conflict.   See e.g. City of Bedford Heights v. Tallarico, 25 Ohio St. 211, 267 N.E.2d 802 (1971).   When local regulation amounts to prohibition or exclusion from municipal areas, the jurisdictional conflict is squarely presented.   The size and location of the municipality may be significant factors.   Thus, municipal exclusion of public transit lines from its streets was held unlawful in In re Curtailment of Bus Service, 125 Neb. 825, 252 N.W. 407 (1934), while a local ban on bus passenger pickup and discharge in village streets was upheld in Village of Perrysburg v. Ridgeway, 108 Ohio St. 245, 140 N.E. 595 (1923).   The growing problems of mass traffic and transit in metropolitan areas are manifested in Omaha Parking Authority v. Omaha, 163 Neb. 97, 77 N.W.2d 862 (1956) where the court held the state parking authority statute superseded home rule authority to control city street franchises for public transit on city streets.

(c) *Municipally Owned Utilities.*   The law regarding municipal utility services is extremely varied.   12 McQuillin, *Municipal Corporations,* ch. 35 (3d rev. ed. 1970).   Differences in state legislation and classification of particular utilities as being governmental or proprietary in nature produce diverse case results.   Distinctions between residential and extraterritorial municipal services are taken upon later (p. 294 et seq.).

FOUR–COUNTY METROPOLITAN CAPITAL IMPROVEMENT DISTRICT v. BOARD OF COUNTY COM'RS

Supreme Court of Colorado, 1963.
149 Colo. 284, 369 P.2d 67.

MOORE, J.

[Statute establishing Four-County Metropolitan Capital Improvement District held unconstitutional.]

* * *

We readily agree that problems in urban areas exist * * * that "financing and construction of capital improvements" and the acquisition of "capital equipment in order to enable local government units to cope with the problems of urbanization" raise problems for which solutions are desirable.   We have no hesitancy, however, in asserting that any act of the legislature which is adopted as a means to bring about a solution of these local problems must not involve the exercise of legislative power which the people, by constitutional provision, have very clearly stated the General Assembly shall not have.

* * *

The statute in question purports to authorize the formation of Metropolitan Capital Improvement Districts.   It is quite evident that the only area in which such a district would be formed is the Denver urban area, and that the City and County of Denver and all three surrounding counties must be incorporated within the district. The statute provides that an election shall be held throughout the proposed district * * *. We take notice of the fact that * * * an election was held * * * and that each of the counties surrounding Denver rejected the proposed district. A sufficient number of voters in Denver to overcome the adverse vote in the adjoining counties approved the district and thus the Four-County Metropolitan Capital Improvement District was created and a Board of Directors selected as provided by the statute. Perhaps the most significant power of the district to be exercised by its directors, as provided by the statute, was as follows:

> "Section 14.—Power to levy tax—exemptions. (1) * * * the board of directors, for and on behalf of the district, shall have power to levy and provide for the collection of a sales and use tax at the rate of two per cent upon every transaction or other incident with respect to which a sales and use tax is now levied by the state pursuant to the provisions of article 6 of chapter 138, Colorado Revised Statutes 1953, as amended; provided, however, that no such tax shall be levied and collected upon: * * *"

* * *

Among other powers conferred upon the district, * * *, we find the following:

> "Section 13–(5) To acquire and dispose of real and personal property * * *.

> "(6) To have management, supervision and control of the construction of capital improvements and acquisition and installation of capital equipment requested by local units and undertaking in accordance with the terms of this act.

> "(7) To employ and retain such employees, agents, engineers and attorneys as may be necessary to carry out the functions of the district * * *.

> "(8) To have and exercise the power of eminent domain, both within and without the boundaries of the district."

* * *

It is indisputably clear that the district is a conduit through which to channel taxes earmarked for local "capital improvement" or "capital equipment" in the county or city areas where collected. It is also clear that this "conduit" district after exercising the powers of "management, supervision and control of the construction of capital improvements and acquisition and installation of capital equipment requested by local units" must forthwith thereafter convey the completed "capital improvement" or the "capital equipment" to the county or the city which made the request for its construction or purchase, and which supplied the money to pay for it. Indisputably the district becomes a conduit, created by statute, through which activity is channelled to accomplish objectives which for generations have been achieved by local officers directly responsible to the people, and upon whom the duty of discharging such local responsibilities has heretofore been placed by constitutional provision or municipal home rule charter provision, or both.

* * *

To remove all doubt concerning the nature of the powers granted to the City and County of Denver, the people amended the original Article XX and provided that home rule cities "are hereby vested with, and they shall always have, power to make, amend, add to or replace the charter of said city or town, which shall be its organic law and extend to *all its local and municipal matters."* (Emphasis supplied). Section 6 continues as follows:

"Such charter and the ordinances made pursuant thereto in such matters shall supersede within the territorial limits and other jurisdiction of said city or town any law of the state in conflict therewith. * * *"

After the adoption of Article XX all the home rule cities within the "Four-County District" (and there are several) had *all the power* that could be acquired by anyone to govern with relation to their local and municipal affairs. Only by constitutional amendment could this allocation of power be changed. * * * By the Home Rule Amendment the General Assembly had been deprived of *all* the power it might otherwise have had to legislate concerning matters of local and municipal concern. Particularly is this true where a home rule city has adopted a charter or ordinances governing such matters. * * *

* * *

Article XX above quoted, and the said charter provisions adopted pursuant thereto, precludes any state law purporting to superimpose the functioning of a "Four-County District" Board of Directors on the activities of the City and County of Denver in supplying their "local and municipal" needs for "capital improvements" and "capital equipment." There can be no doubt that the activities contemplated by the district board of directors involve "local and municipal matters."

* * * Thus it is apparent that the statute purports to empower the "Four-County District" to discharge the official functions of home rule cities with relation to local and municipal affairs. * * *

* * *

For the reasons above set forth we hold the statute in question to be unconstitutional, and direct that collection of the tax levied thereunder, and all other acts of the said Four-County District, terminate forthwith.

* * *

McWILLIAMS, JUSTICE (dissenting). The majority of this Court hold that Chapter 179 of the Session Laws of 1961 is unconstitutional solely on the ground that it is repugnant to Article XX of the Constitution of Colorado. I must respectfully dissent from this conclusion and shall briefly state my reasons therefor.

* * *

The question to be resolved is: May the General Assembly create or permit the creation of an independent governmental entity of a quasi-municipal character which is organized for a limited purpose to operate within the geographical confines of a municipality or home rule city, and to include said municipality or home rule city within its geographical boundaries? This question must be answered in the affirmative. In support of my conclusion, see Milheim v. Moffat Tunnel Dist., 72 Colo. 268, 211 P. 649; [citations omitted]

In my opinion the Milheim case has particular applicability to the present controversy. There the General Assembly created an independent governmental entity of a quasi-municipal nature for the purpose of building a capital improvement, and said independent governmental entity proceeded to include the City and County of Denver within its geographical boundaries. This independent governmental entity then levied a tax on all property owners within its district including the property owners in Denver, and built a capital improvement. In the instant case we also have an independent governmental agency of a quasi-municipal character which proposes to levy a sales tax and to construct capital improvements within its geographical boundaries. True, in the Milheim case the district was organized to construct only one capital improvement, but such is certainly not a controlling fact. Surely it would appear to be highly illogical to hold that an independent governmental agency which constructs one capital improvement is constitutional, but if it proposes to build more than one capital improvement, it is thereby rendered unconstitutional.

The concept of a metropolitan area is of recent origin, at least in Colorado. But that metropolitan areas do exist is a fact, and not a figment of imagination. Metropolitan areas because they are metropolitan areas create metropolitan problems which suggest, at least, metropolitan action looking toward their solution. * * *

In short, Article XX in my opinion does not clearly and beyond all reasonable doubt preclude the People through their General Assembly from trying to solve a specific metropolitan problem on a metropolitan basis, and such being the case we should not by judicial fiat thwart their efforts in this direction.

Nor do I agree with MR. JUSTICE SUTTON, * * *. Any contention that M.C.I.D. is a "special commission" within the meaning of the constitutional provision is specifically negated by Aurora v. Aurora Sanitation District; Milheim v. Moffat Tunnel District; People v. Lee, People ex rel. v. Letford, *supra.*

* * *

Notes

1. For a contrary result, based upon constitutional authorization to create a metropolitan services district by local referenda, see State on Information of Dalton v. Metropolitan St. Louis Sewer District, 365 Mo. 1, 275 S.W.2d 225 (1955).

2. Are the rationales of the two preceding principal cases, both written by the same judge, consistent? If so, on what basis?

2. COUNTY HOME RULE

CITY OF WEST ALLIS v. MILWAUKEE COUNTY
Supreme Court of Wisconsin, 1968.
39 Wis.2d 356, 159 N.W.2d 36 (1968), cert. denied 393 U.S. 1064, 89 S.Ct. 717,
21 L.Ed.2d 707 (1969).

HEFFERNAN, JUSTICE.

[Action by the city of West Allis and other municipalities challenging, as unconstitutional, a grant of power to Milwaukee county to construct an incinerator and waste-disposal system and to levy taxes to pay for the construction. The county's demurrer to the actions was sustained by order of the circuit court, and on appeal, affirmed.]

* * *

Plaintiffs contend that this grant to the counties violates art. XI, sec. 3, of the Constitution, which provides:

"Cities and villages organized pursuant to state law are hereby empowered, to determine their local affairs and government, subject only to this constitution and to such enactments of the legislature of state-wide concern as shall with uniformity affect every city or every village. The method of such determination shall be prescribed by the legislature. * * * "

In Van Gilder v. City of Madison, supra, we concluded that, when the legislature deals with matters that are primarily of state-wide concern, it may deal with them free of any restriction contained in the home-rule amendment. The legislature can thus make effective a law touching on a matter of state-wide concern in one city and not in another, provided that the classification is proper. The home-rule amendment does not limit the right of the legislature to deal with matters of state-wide concern, even if, in so dealing, some cities and not others are affected. * * *

* * * It should be pointed out, however, that in construing home-rule amendments, it has generally been concluded that the disposition of garbage is a matter of state-wide concern. 2 McQuillin, Municipal Corporations (1966 Rev.Vol.), sec. 4.98, p. 175. The trial judge, however, did not base his decision on the determination of whether or not a municipality was protected from the exercise of state power by its constitutional prerogatives of home-rule. He concluded, correctly, that the home-rule amendment was irrelevant to the issue in this case.

* * * The home-rule amendment, although empowering cities and villages to determine their "local affairs and government," further states that, "The method of such determination * * * shall be prescribed by the legislature." The legislature in sec. 66.01, Stats., prescribed the method by which those powers shall be exercised. We do not herein determine that no home-rule powers exist unless exercised by charter ordinance, but sec. 66.01 does make it clear that a city or village is to manifest its election not to be governed by a state law by the passage of a charter ordinance. The legislature intended the constitutional right * * * to be exercised by the passage of a charter ordinance electing not to be governed by a legislative enactment that would otherwise limit municipal activity.

The record fails to show that the municipalities herein attempted to exercise their home-rule powers by charter ordinance, the only way prescribed by statute. It is reasonable that they should not have done so, for there is no law applicable to them which they might seek to avoid. The law they object to delegated powers to Milwaukee county, an administrative branch of the state government itself. We see no evidence that the home-rule amendment was in any way intended to limit the power of the state to deal with its own agencies. Even assuming, without deciding, that the construction of incinerators and refuse-disposal facilities is a matter of local concern in a constitutional sense, it is apparent that the state is not thereby limited from conferring the same powers upon a county. * * *

It is undoubtedly true that our many-layered structure of local government sometimes results in an expensive duplication of function. This is the price that Wisconsin citizens have been willing to pay for substantial local autonomy. However, it has never been claimed that efficiency is the principal virtue of democracy. * * *

Nor do we see any objection properly cognizable by the courts in the fact that county facilities may be in part a duplication of municipal facilities. * * * The legislature, by its delegation of power to Milwaukee county, has determined that it is in the interests of the public generally to have what it hopes will be an adequate county-wide system of refuse disposal. No provision of the home-rule amendment precludes the legislature from exercising its judgment in that respect. * * *

Notes

1. **Harmonizing County and Municipal Home Rule.** The potential for interlocal conflicts and wasteful duplication problem was anticipated and avoided by a Pennsylvania statute which provides:

"No county which has adopted a home rule charter shall at any time thereafter exercise within any municipality in the county, a power or function being exercised by that municipality, except under all of the following conditions:

"(1) The exercise of such power or function by the county shall be authorized by ordinance of the governing body of the county, which ordinance * * * shall, within thirty days of its enactment, be filed with the clerk or secretary of each local municipality within the county.

"(2) The transfer of a power or function to the county from any local municipality within the county, as authorized by such ordinance, shall not become effective for at least fifteen months from the date of adoption of such ordinance.

"(3) Within one hundred twenty days from the adoption of such ordinance, the governing body of any local municipality, exercising on the date of the adoption of such ordinance any power or function authorized by ordinance of the county to be exercised by the county, may elect by ordinance to be excluded from the county exercise of such power or function. Within sixty days after the date of adoption by the governing body of a local municipality of an ordinance excluding such municipality from the exercise by the county of a power or function, or in the absence of any action of the governing body, the qualified voters of such municipality may initiate a petition requiring that the question of inclusion or exclusion from the exercise of such power or function by the county be submitted to a referendum of the electorate at the election held on the date of the next ensuing primary, municipal or general election.

* * *

"(4) The governing body of any local municipality may by ordinance, subsequent to the time limit for action as set forth in clause (3) of this section, request the county to be included in a municipal power or function being exercised by the county: Provided, however, That the county may specify the terms and conditions for acceptance or denial of the power or function requested by the local municipality to be exercised by the county, which shall be subject to court review if the local municipality determines that the terms and conditions as set forth by the county are unreasonable.

"(5) No assessment, tax, fee or levy in the nature thereof made by the governing body of a county in support of the exercise of a power or function as authorized by ordinance of the county, shall be applicable in any municipality within the county which is providing the same municipal power or function.

* * *

"(7) A local municipality may, by action of the governing body, or by initiative and referendum, withdraw from a power or function which it was exercising at the date of the adoption of the county home rule charter which it transferred to a county, provided it again assumes and exercises the power or function but may not vote on the question of withdrawing sooner than four years from the time the county assumed the power or function of the local municipality." Pa.Stat.Ann.Tit. 53, § 1–303.

MULTNOMAH KENNEL CLUB v. DEPARTMENT OF REVENUE

Supreme Court of Oregon, 1983.
295 Or. 279, 666 P.2d 1327.

JONES, JUSTICE.

Plaintiff Multnomah Kennel Club questions the right of Multnomah County to impose a business income tax on pari-mutual racing establishments. * * * Plaintiff questions the county's right to impose the business income tax under the Oregon Constitution and under ORS chapter 462 which plaintiff claims results in a state preemption of the field of income taxation of pari-mutuel betting establishments. * * *

* * * Multnomah County taxes all business within the county, including the plaintiff at the rate of six percent of net income. The Multnomah County Business Income Tax does not discriminate between income earned on concessions and income earned on pari-mutuel wagering; the tax is imposed upon all income of plaintiff regardless of its source.

Multnomah County is a constitutional home rule county and therefore has the power to exercise "authority over matters of county concern" Or.Const., Art. VI, § 10. Multnomah County's business income tax, Mult.County Ord. 121, § 12, codified at § 5.70.090, replaces its business license tax, Mult.County Code ch. 5.80. The purpose of this business income tax is expressly "to raise funds," * * *

The authority of a county to impose a business income tax is a matter of first impression for this court.

The first question for decision is whether Oregon's constitutional grant of county home rule authority gives counties the power to levy income taxes. * * *

* * *

Of the various forms of conflict possible between a state and local law, we deal here with "(3) the validity of a local act said to conflict with a state law."

For the years in question, the power of statutory home rule counties to levy taxes was expressly granted by ORS 203.120(5) (repealed as unnecessary by Or.Laws 1981, ch. 140, § 5). * * *

* * *

Although section 5 of 1981 Oregon Laws, chapter 140, repealed ORS 203.120(5), the power to tax was not repealed since it is a "matter of county concern" generally granted. * * *

Since the legislature has granted the power to statutory home rule counties to levy taxes, it follows logically that constitutional home rule counties such as Multnomah County have a like power to levy taxes. So, even in the absence of an express statutory grant, we hold it is an implicit power of a constitutional home rule county to levy taxes. The

Multnomah County Home Rule Charter implements a general grant of power "over matters of county concern to the fullest extent granted or allowed." * * *

Plaintiff contends the kind of tax selected is not a matter of county concern. Plaintiff's premise is that certain taxes (*e.g.*, on property, privileges, and occupations), are traditional local concerns while other taxes (*e.g.*, on sales and income), are traditional state concerns. That position is not an accurate generalization of municipal law, * * * Although Oregon municipalities have typically imposed certain taxes while the state has imposed different ones, this customary distinction between the "subjects" of state and local taxation does not create mutually exclusive constitutional authorities. *LaGrande*, 281 Or. at 153–55, 576 P.2d 1204.

* * *

As to plaintiff's first contention, we conclude that the constitutional grant of power to a home rule county includes the power to levy an income tax.

The second question raised by the plaintiff is whether the State of Oregon has pre-empted the field of income taxation of pari-mutuel betting establishments by enactment of ORS chapter 462.

ORS chapter 462 governs state licensing of race meets. * * *

* * *

The tax described in ORS chapter 462 ("The license fee *and tax * * * for the privilege of conducting the race meet*" (emphasis supplied)), is payable to the state racing commission. It is collected in aid of a regulatory program, different from a tax imposed *solely* for revenue purposes.

The state purpose of the Multnomah County Business Income Tax is the raising of revenue. It is not a "license" or "privilege" tax. * * *

* * *

We conclude Multnomah County has the authority and power under its home rule charter to impose a business income tax and that the tax does not conflict with the prohibition in ORS 462.100 against other privilege taxes for holding a race meet.

The Tax Court is affirmed.

SCHMIDT v. MASTERS

Court of Appeals of Oregon, 1971.
7 Or.App. 421, 490 P.2d 1029.

LANGTRY, J.

[Action challenging power of county to enact county-wide ordinance regarding waste collection and disposal.]

* * *

The County Home Rule Amendment to the Oregon Constitution (Art. VI, § 10, adopted in 1958), states that

> " * * * A county charter may provide for the exercise by the county of authority over matters of county concern."

Washington County accepted this general offer of authority in its charter in broad terms:

> " * * * to the full extent granted or allowed by the Constitution and laws * * * of * * * Oregon."

It takes no documentation to observe that urbanization of areas outside of incorporated cities and resultant need for more sophisticated services * * * has resulted in a confusing and inefficient proliferation of special service districts; that a major reason for offering to counties broadening of authority under home rule was the need for a more sophisticated form of government than existed for such areas, carrying with it authority to do in localities what needs to be done there. * * * We conclude that with reference to matters of local concern, the authority of a county under a home rule charter may be as broad as that of a city.

In Spencer et al. v. City of Medford et al., 129 Or. 333, 276 P. 1114 (1929), it was held that a city has the authority, under the general police power conferred on it by charter, to regulate and provide for the disposal of garbage, and that an ordinance doing that was valid, * * *.

In Dunn v. Gray, 238 Or. 71, 392 P.2d 1018 (1964), an exclusive sanitary service franchise had been granted by the City of Salem and such action was under challenge. Citing Spencer et al. v. City of Medford et al., *supra,* the court said:

> "A city has the unquestioned power to grant an exclusive license or franchise for the purpose of collecting and disposing of garbage."

We have no doubt that these holdings are as applicable to all solid waste collection and disposal as to garbage.

In Davidson Baking Co. v. Jenkins et al., 216 Or. 51, 337 P.2d 352 (1959), the Oregon Supreme Court settled any preexisting inconsistency in its opinions about whether a city may, under a general grant of power, have authority to do that which is not preempted by state law and is otherwise within the general ambit of authority of the particular city. This decision is equally applicable to home rule counties. We hold that unless the state has preempted the field of waste collection and disposal, the general grant of authority in the Washington County charter was a basis for Ordinance No. 59. * * * Nothing in the act indicates an intent by the state to license, franchise, limit or certificate individual waste collection businesses through any state agency except local units of government. It is idle to contend that this act preempts and eliminates local authority over local waste collectors.

* * *

Notes

1. Limited Adoptions of County Home Rule. After 22 years from the adoption of county home rule only 7 of Oregon's 36 counties adopted home rule charters. See Etter, *County Home Rule in Oregon,* 61 Ore.L.Rev. 3 (1982). Some states, e.g., New York and Pennsylvania, have recently experienced increased adoption of county home rule. For studies of problems encountered in different states adopting various forms of county home rule, see Freilich, Robards and Wilson, *Home Rule for the Urban County: Observations on the New Jackson County Constitutional Charter,* 39 U.M. K.C.L.Rev. 297 (1971); Glauberman, Note, *County Home Rule: An Urban Necessity,* 1 Urban Lawyer 170 (1969); Note *County Home Rule: An Approach to Metropolitan Problems in Michigan,* 6 U.Mich.L.J. 232 (1972). These problems essentially parallel those in municipal home rule concerning classification of local, county-wide and state-wide functions.

2. The Flexible Pennsylvania Model. Pursuant to constitutional redefinition of counties as "municipalities" (p. 106 supra), Pa.Act. 62 of 1972, 53 Pa.Stat. §§ 1–101 et seq. extended broad home rule powers to counties.

3. OPTIONAL CHARTER LAWS

In order to provide additional incentives to modernize local governments, many states have enacted optional charter laws which permit the local unit to adopt one of several statutory charters. See National Mun. League, *New Jersey's Optional Municipal Charter Law* (1964); Bucino v. Malone, 12 N.J. 330, 96 A.2d 669 (1953); McQuillin, *Municipal Corporations,* § 9.07 (3d rev. 1979).

> "One aspect of the Pennsylvania proposal which deserves comment is the fact that ＊ ＊ ＊ all existing county government arrangements are required to be included in any optional county government law ＊ ＊ ＊ so that the political establishment was able to propose a forward moving model ＊ ＊ ＊ while retaining reasonable assurances that counties that wanted to would be able to hold on to the patterns of the past." Grad, *The State's Capacity to Respond to Urban Problems, in The States and The Urban Crisis,* Alan K. Campbell, Ed., 57 (Am. Assembly 1970).＊

Summary Note

The ideal of local control has been tempered by state intervention where metropolitan interdependence becomes compelling:

> "Recent developments ＊ ＊ ＊ have divested the concept of home rule of much of the sanctity it possessed ＊ ＊ ＊ in the past. The values of maximum citizen participation and local control ＊ ＊ ＊ are in tension with the limited ability of small units of government to meet modern service standards, with the spread of public policy concerns to

＊ Reprinted by permission of Prentice-Hall, Inc., Englewood Cliffs, N.J. Copyright ⓒ 1970 by The American Assembly, Columbia University.

the metropolitan scale, and with the poor public performance that often results from divided authority. Effective local control—the goal of home rule advocates—often requires a larger jurisdiction than the typical local unit in a metropolitan area.

* * *

"The case for local home rule rests upon such considerations as controllability, accessibility to the public, and citizen participation—all of which are held to be promoted most successfully by small units of government. These are important values, but they must be balanced against other considerations. First, it is not clear whether they are in fact best served by small home rule units. Larger, more diverse communities also serve important political values in minimizing the likelihood that any one group will dominate the government and increasing the opportunity for all groups to have their interests respected. Other considerations center around economies of scale in performing urban functions and the need for adequate space to cope with many responsibilities. Still other limitations of local home rule arise from the close functional interrelationships that exist in metropolitan areas. Many problems have grown beyond city limits, but the city's power to cope with a situation ends abruptly at its boundary lines. In addition * * * individual communities may damage their neighbors' interests by their own policies—by excluding moderate-cost housing or polluting rivers, for example.

"The complexity of metropolitan problems and the inability of many smaller units to cope with them defeats the theory of local home rule and popular control * * *. Where everybody is concerned but no one unit has the power to act, what purpose is served by local popular control? The Commission shares the view expressed by Luther Gulick that municipal home rule in the mid-20th century is not the right to be left alone behind a legally defined bulwark, but rather the right to participate as an equal partner in arriving at decisions which affect community life. * * * Home rule, in the view of the Commission, is by no means an absolute principle of local government today, but must be modified within a metropolitan context." ACIR, *Metropolitan America—Challenge to Federalism*, 123, 124 (1966).

The metropolitan social structure tends to elevate the state interests in problems that have become regionalized. We seem then to have come full circle; where local home rule rather than state interference may become the obstacle to efficient local government. The notion now grows that home rule power may be asserted to oppose desirable reallocation of local powers to regional units. See e.g., F. Grad, *The State's Capacity to Respond to Urban Problems, in the States and the Urban Crisis*, pp. 45–48 (Am. Assembly 1970).

B. OVERLAPPING STATE AND LOCAL LAW— ISSUES OF CONCURRENCE, CONFLICT AND PREEMPTION

When are overlapping state and local laws to be given concurrent operation, as being mutually consistent, or require displacement of one by the other, as being mutually inconsistent, conflicting, or preemptive? See, e.g., Blease, *Civil Liberties and the California Law of Preemption,* 17 Hastings L.J. 517 (1966); Note, *Conflict Between State Statutes and Municipal Ordinances,* 72 Harv.L.Rev. 737 (1959); Ruud, *Legislative Jurisdiction of Texas Home Rule Cities,* 37 Tex.L.Rev. 682 (1959). No general answer or rationale can be offered to the foregoing questions. They involve a series of independent issues, each of which is materially affected by the facts and legal setting in each case.

Some cases swing upon legislated intent, that a law operate exclusively or "occupy the field," without regard to the possibility that coexistent laws could be consistent in their operation. In the absence of expressed legislative intent, a court may still imply such an intent from the design and history of the law.

Preemptive intent aside, courts must still determine if overlapping laws conflict each other, and even if not in direct conflict, if they are mutually "inconsistent," either totally, or with respect to limited situations. Such inconsistencies may be substantive or administrative (e.g., enforcement process), and may be material or immaterial in degree.

The construction and application of overlapping state and local laws thus requires successive analysis of issues regarding "intent," (as measured by legislative purposes) and by the consistent or inconsistent effects of their concurrent operation of the law. Unfortunately, these distinctions between express and implied legislative intent; between gradations of inconsistency ranging from absolute conflict to selective inconsistency of varying degrees, are often ignored and blurred by loose use of words like "preemption" to blanket any issue of displacement or concurrence of operation between state and local law.

1. CONFLICT

ORANGE COUNTY AIR POLLUTION CONTROL DISTRICT v. PUBLIC UTILITIES COMMISSION, RESPONDENT, SOUTHERN CALIFORNIA EDISON COMPANY, REAL PARTY IN INTEREST

Supreme Court of California, 1971.
4 Cal.3d 945, 95 Cal.Rptr. 17, 484 P.2d 1361.

[Reported at p. 288]

WHOLESALE LAUNDRY BD. OF TRADE
v. NEW YORK

Supreme Court, Appellate Div., New York, 1962.
17 A.D.2d 327, 234 N.Y.S.2d 862.

STEUER, JUSTICE. * * * The actions seek declaratory judgments to the effect that the New York City Minimum Wage Law (Local Law No. 59, 1962) is invalid. * * *

The local law in question provides that after its effective date every employer in the City of New York shall pay to his employees a wage of not less than $1.25 an hour and that on and after one year subsequent to the effective date the minimum wage shall be not less than $1.50 an hour.

Plaintiffs challenge this enactment on two grounds: * * * second, that the local law is invalid because it is inconsistent with statewide legislation on the same subject.

* * * The constitutional grant is limited to legislation not inconsistent with the laws of the state. It is implemented by the City Home Rule Law (L.1939, ch. 867, amending L.1924, ch. 363). The statute contains the following provision:

> "Sec. 11. (4). Nothing contained in this section shall be deemed by implication or otherwise to authorize an amendment or repeal of any provision of the labor law * * *."

* * *

Consequently, any purported enactment which offends in this connection lacks authorization and is invalid regardless of whether it might be embraced within the general powers granted to the municipalities by the constitution.

We conclude that the proposed legislation is inconsistent with Labor Law, Article 19 (L.1960, ch. 619, §§ 650–665), also called the Minimum Wage Act. This Act (§ 652, as amd. by L.1962, ch. 439) provides a minimum wage of one dollar per hour for the period October 1, 1960, to October 15, 1962; thereafter, and until October 15, 1964, a minimum wage of $1.15 an hour; and thereafter a wage of $1.25 an hour. As to each period, there is a provision that the wage is to prevail unless another wage is established in accord with the provisions of the article. Succeeding sections (653 et seq.) provide for an investigation by the Industrial Commissioner whether the wages paid in any occupation in accordance with the provisions of the law are adequate. If the commissioner has reason to believe that the minimum wage in any occupation is inadequate, he is directed to appoint a wage board to inquire into the question and make recommendations. These recommendations may vary as to locality within the same occupation (§ 656). After receipt of the wage board's findings and after provisions for hearing and review, a new and higher wage in the particular occupation and locality may be fixed by the commissioner.

That is the statewide legislation in the field and the question is whether the local law supersedes the state statute. It is the city's contention that a statute which extends but does not run counter to the state statute is not interdicted. Generally speaking, local laws which do not prohibit what the state law permits nor allow what the state law forbids are not inconsistent (People v. Lewis, 295 N.Y. 42, 64 N.E.2d 702). Thus, penal statutes in which the local law provides a greater penalty are not void for this reason (People v. Lewis, *supra*). However, where the extension of the principle of the state law by means of the local law results in a situation where what would be permissible under the state law becomes a violation of the local law, the latter law is unauthorized (Jewish Consumptives Relief Soc. v. Town of Woodbury, 230 App.Div. 228, 243 N.Y.S. 686, affd. 256 N.Y. 619, 117 N.E. 165). Here, that is plainly the case. The local law forbids a hiring at a wage which the state law permits and so prohibits what the state law allows. Semantic exercises in this connection cannot change the concept.

Furthermore, it is entirely clear that the state law indicates a purpose to occupy the entire field. And where that is found, local laws are prohibited (People v. Lewis, *supra,* 295 N.Y. at p. 51, 64 N.E.2d at p. 704). This is not only to be deduced from the restriction on any law that supersedes any provision of the labor law (City Home Rule Law, § 21), which indicates a general state policy to make the provisions of that law free from interference by local authorities. It is also, and more specifically, found in the State Minimum Wage Law itself. The provisions for amendment of the wage fixed formulate an elaborate machinery for the determination of an adequate wage in any occupation and in any locality, including the City of New York. It can hardly be argued that the state statute does not occupy the field. Nor can it reasonably be claimed that, after the fixation of a minimum wage according to the terms of the state law, the local law, if given recognition, would not, in terms supersede the state statute. As the ban in such an instance is absolute, the local law is found to be invalid.

The orders denying temporary injunctions should be reversed on the law and the motions granted without costs.

Orders, entered on November 9, 1962, denying temporary injunctions unanimously reversed, on the law, and the motions granted without costs. Settle order on notice.

All concur.

[Aff'd by Court of Appeals on above opinion, 12 N.Y.2d 998, 189 N.E.2d 623 (1963) with following dissents.]

DYE, JUDGE (dissenting). * * * The local law here challenged does not permit what the State law prohibits and is not inconsistent therewith but, rather, supplemental thereto and in aid of its stated policy. In dealing as it does with conditions peculiar to the City of New York involving the preservation and promotion of the health, safety and general welfare of its inhabitants resulting from inadequate wage rates, it constitutes a proper exercise of the City's police power (N.Y.

Const., art. IX, § 12; City Home Rule Law, Consol.Laws, c. 76, § 11, subd. 2; New York City Charter, § 27; People v. Lewis, 295 N.Y. 42, 64 N.E.2d 702). When the City Council acts to protect local needs it will be upheld, especially when such action is in aid and furtherance of the State law (People v. Sampsell, 248 N.Y. 157, 161 N.E. 454). It may not be said that the State has preempted the field simply because the State law is State-wide in its application, particularly when it does not forbid enactment of a local law such as this.

The judgments appealed from should be reversed, with costs, and judgment should be rendered in favor of the city declaring the City Minimum Wage Law to be valid and constitutional.

FULD, JUDGE (dissenting). I find nothing in the State Minimum Wage Law (Labor Law, Consol.Laws, c. 31, § 650) which gives evidence of any legislative design to exclude consistent local legislation and, since the New York City Minimum Wage Law * * * neither prohibits what the State statute affirmatively permits nor permits what it prohibits, I perceive no such conflict as to require the local law to be stricken as unconstitutional. There is no inconsistency between a city law and a State statute dealing with the same subject simply because the local law provides higher minima or standards than those prescribed by the State law. In the present case, both enactments are prohibitory, the only difference between them being that the local law goes further than, not counter to, the prohibition contained in the State statute.

* * *

Notes

1. **Accord:** Phoenix v. Kidd, 54 Ariz. 75, 92 P.2d 513 (1939). Compare *Wholesale Laundry* with Bishop v. San Jose, 1 Cal.3d 56, 81 Cal.Rptr. 465, 460 P.2d 137 (1969), which upheld home rule city minimum wage level that was lower than the state minimum; and with City of Baltimore v. Sitnick, 254 Md. 303, 255 A.2d 376 (1969), which upheld city minimum wage level that was higher than the state minimum. The *Sitnick* opinion states: "However, with regard to specific conflicts which appellees contend exist between various provisions * * * we find that the purported conflicts properly lend themselves to the characterization of supplementation of state law, rather than irreconcilable differences." Id. at 323–24, 255 A.2d at 385. Accord: Greenberg v. Bradford, 432 Pa. 611, 248 A.2d 51 (1968). *Query:* How does one determine whether a variation in state and local law is supplementation or an inconsistency? By their purposes, by their subject coverage, by their sanctions; by their administrative design and procedure? There is no uniform answer to these questions.

The oft-cited generalization-that "local laws which do not prohibit what the state law permits nor allow what the state law forbids are not inconsistent" raises more interpretive questions than it answers. Could it be argued that the ordinance in *Wholesale Laundry* would have been inconsistent with state law even if its terms were identical to the state labor law? Cf. Cleveland v. Betts, 107 Ohio App. 511, 148 N.E.2d 708 (1958).

The issues raised in *Wholesale Laundry* permit a conscious, judicial selection of a *quantitative standard* of conflict or preemption (i.e., the actual terms and coverage of the related statute and ordinance) or a *qualitative standard* (i.e., the impact of each law upon the other's operation and purposes). On the premise that state minimum wage laws are primarily intended to protect employees, which test is more appropriate? On the further premise that the cost of living and income levels are higher in urban centers than elsewhere in the state, should the courts uphold local law reflecting that difference, as consistent with the lower state minimum?

2. **Rent Control.** The perplexing shifts in economic conditions and state legislative responses affecting rent control law is further complicated by conditions attached to federal involvement in low rent housing. See Gramercy Spire Tenants' Association v. Harris, et al., 446 F.Supp. 814 (S.D. N.Y.1977) for a detailed review of state and federal issues and case lines in this area. *Gramercy,* in brief, held that to protect the federal interest against default of a federally insured mortgage on low cost housing facilities, the Department of Housing and Urban Development could (upon finding that compliance with city or state rent control ceilings jeopardized payment of the insured mortgage) selectively authorize higher rentals for the threatened facility, and to that extent, selectively preempt state and local rent control laws; further, however, that rent control laws created entitlements in the protected tenants which required that they be given a notice and hearing on proposed federal tolling of their controlled rents, before such preemption could take effect.

The following excerpt from the *Gramercy* opinion outlines the choppy history of state and local rent control in New York:

"In the present case, Associates ∗ ∗ ∗ became a party to a regulatory agreement with the Federal Housing Commissioner in August of 1962. At that time, since it was of post-1947 construction, Gramercy Spire Apartments was subject to neither New York State nor New York City rent control laws. ∗ ∗ ∗ The building came under the umbrella of local rent regulation only upon the passage by New York City of the Rent Stabilization Law ('RSL') of 1969, N.Y.C. Admin.Code §§ YY51–1.0 to YY51–7.0, which undertook to provide rent regulation for housing accommodations completed between February 1, 1947 and March 10, 1969. N.Y.C.Admin.Code § YY51–3.0(a) ∗ ∗ ∗ The administration of the 1969 law was confided largely in a Real Estate Industry Stabilization Association ('Stabilization Association'), N.Y.C.Admin.Code § YY51–6.0, of which Associates became a member. ∗ ∗ ∗

"The category of dwelling units afforded protection under the RSL, however, was significantly restricted by the passage of State legislation in 1971. Under the Vacancy Decontrol Law, 1971 Laws of N.Y., Ch. 371, all rent-controlled or rent-stabilized apartments which became vacant on or after July 1, 1971, were to be rented on a free-market basis. In 1974, however, pursuant to the Emergency Tenant Protection Act ('ETPA') and related legislation, 1974 Laws of New York, Ch.

576, New York State ended vacancy decontrol and considerably broadened the scope of potential local rent regulation. The ETPA was a form of local option legislation, which authorized the City of New York (and other specified localities) to declare the existence of a public emergency requiring the regulation of residential rents. The Act provided that upon the declaration of an emergency, all apartments which had theretofore been destabilized or exempt from rent stabilization—including apartments which had become vacant on or after July 1, 1971—were to be subject to the RSL. 1974 Laws of New York, Ch. 576 §§ 2, 4. Effective July 1, 1974, the New York City Council implemented the legislation, determining the existence of a public emergency for all classes of housing accommodations in New York City subject to control by the ETPA. N.Y.C. Council Resolution 276. The consequence, for purposes of the present case, is that Gramercy Spire apartments became fully subject to the provisions of the RSL. As Associates acknowledges, until the local rent control laws were preempted by HUD in respect to Gramercy Spire Apartments on April 6, 1976, Associates assumed that it was legally bound to comply with—and did comply with—both the RSL and ETPA * * *." 446 F.Supp. at 818–819.

3. **Broad vs. Narrow Frames for Decision.** Is "wage regulation" an adequate concept to distinguish state from local interests; or must the question be refined and limited to particular employees, activities, and relations that are in issue? Consider the specifics of local requirements on residency and non-alienage (City of Pasadena v. Charleville, 215 Cal.2d 384, 10 P.2d 745 (1932)); on state laws on workmen's compensation; on civil service; on the limits of officers' compensation; and on pension systems. As will appear in other parts of this book, functionally minded courts look more to the purpose and effect of local and state laws, than to abstract broad descriptions of state and local interests.

Some courts favor the view that the state legislation should control subjects of economic welfare, no matter how localized they be. See Wagner v. Mayor and Municipal Council of City of Newark, 24 N.J. 467, 132 A.2d 794 (1957) (holding that local rent control cannot be legislated consistently with a state rent control statute); City of New York v. State, 67 Misc.2d 513, 323 N.Y.S.2d 460 (1971) (holding that state rent decontrol laws displace the rent control ordinance of a home rule city.)

4. **Residency Requirements for Municipal Employment.** State and local laws pertaining to municipal employment raise many potential conflict and preemption issues. See McQuillin, *Municipal Corporations* § 12.59. (3d rev. ed. 1982); compare: Hesslegrave v. King, 45 Misc.2d 256, 256 N.Y.S.2d 753 (1965) (invalidating city requirement of local residency by all policemen), with In re Gagliardi's Appeal, 401 Pa. 141, 163 A.2d 418 (1960) (upholding borough ordinance which required policemen to reside in borough or be discharged, as consistent with state civil service statute which prohibited discharge from civil service except for specified causes, none of which related to residency).

State courts differ on the validity of residency requirements under their respective state constitutions. Compare: City of Memphis v. International Bhd. of Elect. Workers Union Local 1288, 545 S.W.2d 98 (Tenn.1976) (upheld), with Angwin v. Manchester, 118 N.H. 336, 386 A.2d 1272 (1978). On the federal constitutional question, see p. 356 infra.

STATE BY AND THROUGH HALEY v. TROUTDALE, ET AL.

Supreme Court of Oregon, 1977.
281 Or. 203, 576 P.2d 1238.

LINDE, JUSTICE.

The City of Troutdale asks us to reverse a decree enjoining it from enforcing a provision of a city building code ordinance which is more stringent than a corresponding provision of regulations promulgated by the state Director of Commerce.

The legislative assembly in 1973 authorized the Director to promulgate a state building code. Or.Laws 1973, ch. 834, *codified* in ORS 456.750—456.890. Pursuant to this enactment, the Director in 1974 adopted standards published by the International Conference of Building Officials * * *. One section of the Structural Specialty Code so incorporated by reference, * * * sets a standard permitting "single wall" as well as "double wall" construction. Thereafter, the city enacted an ordinance requiring homes constructed in Troutdale to use sheathing under siding, i.e. double wall construction.

The Director initiated this suit in the name of the state to enjoin the city from enforcing this requirement. The city defended on the grounds that its ordinance did not conflict with the state regulation and that, if it did conflict, the state law cannot constitutionally displace the ordinance. * * * We allowed review to consider the relationship between the state and local enactments.

* * *

II

The Court of Appeals found the statute and the ordinance to be irreconcilable and concluded that it had to determine whether the state or the city had the predominant interest in the disputed construction standard under the test of State ex rel. Heinig v. City of Milwaukee, 231 Or. 473, 373 P.2d 680 (1962). But that test expressly related to the validity of a state law concerning local modes of government, not to the validity of state and local regulations addressed to private persons. * * *

The construction standards at issue here regulate builders, not city governments. The statute contemplates but does not require that municipal officials will administer the state codes; if the municipality chooses not to do so, the state will do so through agencies of its own. ORS 456.800(4). Under the circumstances the statute can hardly be said to "enact, amend or repeal any charter or act of incorporation for any municipality, city or town," nor to prevent the voters of Troutdale from enacting or amending their own charter, as provided in article XI, section 2.

As stated in City of La Grande v. Public Employes' Retirement Board, Or., 576 P.2d 1204 (1978), decided today, this section and its companion "home rule" amendment, article IV, section 1(5), do not purport to allocate areas of substantive policy, such as building codes, between the levels of government. * * * When the validity of a local ordinance is at issue, as in this case, the first question is whether the ordinance is properly enacted within the powers of the city under its charter or a statute. The state does not challenge the Troutdale ordinance in this respect. Rather, the state claims that the city's "double wall" requirement is "in conflict with" or "contrary to" the state's building code. The claim is not that buildings complying with the ordinance would violate the state's regulations, but that the legislature has excluded regulations other than the state's.

On this issue the statutory provisions, taken as a whole, leave room for different conclusions. For instance, ORS 456.755(4) states that the statute or any "specialty code" adopted under it do not limit local safety standards for housing "except where the power of municipalities to enact any such regulations is expressly withheld by statute." ORS 456.775(1) provides:

> The state building code shall be applicable and uniform throughout this state and in all municipalities therein and no municipality shall enact or enforce any ordinance, rule or regulation in conflict therewith.

Again, it is undisputed that this section requires construction throughout the state to comply with the state code. But the state interprets the words "in conflict therewith" to include "in addition thereto", while the city argues that they mean only "incompatible with" and do not exclude additional requirements. A point favoring the state's view is that the statute provides a procedure for amending a state code to meet local conditions. ORS 456.785(4). On the other hand, ORS 456.755(1) describes the state code as designed only to establish "basic" uniform standards for "reasonable" safeguards for health, safety, welfare, and comfort. Consistent with this view of the state code as merely "basic," the Director himself described the state regulations he promulgated as being "minimum safety standards." OAR § 814–26–005, supra note 1.

As stated in *City of La Grande,* supra:

> "It is reasonable to interpret local enactments, if possible to be intended to function consistently with state laws, and equally reasonable to assume that the legislature does not mean to displace local civil or administrative regulation of local conditions by a statewide law unless that intention is apparent." [Citing cases.] 576 P.2d at 1211.

That approach is proper here. We are reluctant to assume that the legislature meant to confine the protection of Oregon residents exclusively to construction standards which it described as "basic" and which the administering agency describes as "minimum," and to place these beyond the power of local communities to provide additional safeguards for themselves. Certainly that intention is not unambiguously expressed. Until it is, we conclude that local requirements compatible with compliance with the state's standards are not preempted by ORS 456.750 et seq. The injunction against Troutdale's enforcement of its ordinance should have been denied.

Reversed.

TONGUE, J., specially concurring, joined by HOWELL and BRYSON, JJ.

TONGUE, JUSTICE, specially concurring.

I agree with the result reached by the majority opinion, but strongly disagree with its reasoning in reaching that result. More specifically, I agree with the holding by the majority that there is no "conflict" between the state building code and the city building code, but I disagree with the implicit, if not express, holding by the majority that this result can only be reached because the state did not "unambiguously express" an intention that the construction standards provided by the state building code be "exclusive" construction standards (rather than "minimum" standards), and that if such an intent had been "unambiguously expressed" it would have been "beyond the power of local communities to provide additional safeguards for themselves."

VICK v. PEOPLE

Supreme Court of Colorado, 1968.
166 Colo. 565, 445 P.2d 220.

KELLEY, JUSTICE. * * * plaintiffs in error (defendants), were charged and convicted * * * of "wagering upon games," * * * in violation of C.R.S.1963, 40–10–9. The defendants admit gambling, but claim their acts were lawful, because the gambling activity occurred in a casino licensed by the city pursuant to a valid city ordinance.

The defendants concede that there is a conflict between the ordinance and C.R.S.1963, 40–10–9, but claim that the ordinance supersedes the statute. The defendants rely upon City of Canon City v. Merris, 137 Colo. 169, 323 P.2d 614, and Woolverton v. City and County of Denver, 146 Colo. 247, 361 P.2d 982, in support of their argument.

The *Merris* decision involved a conflict between a state statute and an ordinance of Canon City relating to driving a motor vehicle while under the influence of intoxicating liquor. The court was concerned with the question of whether such an offense should be prosecuted under the ordinance or under state law. We held that it was a matter of state-wide concern; consequently, the statute controlled.

Woolverton involved the validity of an ordinance of the City and County of Denver which declared gambling to be a crime. The issue was whether the city ordinance and C.R.S.1963, 40–10–9, could coexist in view of the *Merris* decision. This court held that the statute and the ordinance were not mutually exclusive and permitted them to coexist.

Canon City and Denver are both home rule cities. Central City is not. Ordinances of home rule cities, created under Article XX of the Colorado Constitution, in matters of strictly local concern supersede state statutes relating to those matters, but, in matters of both local and state interest, the municipality does not have a superseding authority. In the latter situation, *Woolverton* holds that a home rule city had a supplemental authority which permitted its ordinance to coexist with the state statute, *so long as they are not in conflict.*

In Ray v. City and County of Denver, 109 Colo. 74, 121 P.2d 886, 138 A.L.R. 1485, this court observed that it "is a fundamental principle, that an ordinance which is in conflict with a state law of general character and state-wide application is invalid." Also, see Glendinning v. City and County of Denver, 50 Colo. 240, 114 P. 652. So, where the ordinance authorizes the doing of acts which the statute prohibits, the ordinance is invalid.

It is most difficult to understand the aid and comfort which the defendants derive from *Merris* and *Woolverton.* The philosophy and the rules of law enunciated in *Merris* and *Woolverton* would even invalidate an ordinance of a home rule city licensing gambling establishments if, as here, the ordinance conflicted with a state statute on the same subject. Central City, as a non-home rule city, has less legislative power and authority than a home rule city.

* * * Suffice it to say that Central City, by virtue of its ancient charter, has retained no authority which overrides or supersedes the state statutes on gambling.

* * *

The judgment is affirmed.

Notes

1. **Protective Safety and Morals Regulations.** The issue whether local laws are consistent and concurrently operative with state law, extends to ordinances that attempt to suppress certain activity as "nuisances" (see City of Piggot v. Eblen, and notes thereto, page 377, et seq., infra), and to regulation of noxious materials. See Town of Wendell v. Attorney General, 394 Mass. 518, 476 N.E.2d 585 (1985) (town regulation of pesticides held inconsistent with and precluded by state pesticide control law).

2. **Accord:** Blackman v. County Court in and for City and County of Denver, 169 Colo. 345, 455 P.2d 885 (1969) (home rule weights and measures ordinance upheld as consistent with state law on same subject); Vela v. People, 174 Colo. 465, 484 P.2d 1204 (1971) (home rule disturbance ordinance that contained broader prohibitions than state statute, upheld as not in conflict therewith). In *Vela,* the court observed that, had the ordinance pertained to a "purely local matter," the state statute would have been without effect within the home rule city. Id. at 1205. Preemption by a home rule municipality, where its ordinance expressly declared the intent to supersede a conflicting state law, was allowed where state law

was construed to permit the same. Bartle v. Zoning Bd., 391 Pa. 207, 137 A.2d 239 (1958) (zoning ordinance preempting state law).

2. PREEMPTION DOCTRINES

UNITED TAVERN OWNERS OF PHILADELPHIA v. SCHOOL DISTRICT OF PHILADELPHIA

Supreme Court of Pennsylvania, 1971.
411 Pa. 274, 272 A.2d 868.

O'BRIEN, JUSTICE. * * * The case presents only one question: May the City of Philadelphia validly enact an ordinance taxing the retail sales of liquor, malt, and brewed beverages?

The court below and the parties to this action have sought to discuss the doctrine of preemption as it applies to this case as two separate questions. First, has the state preempted the field through the enactment of the Liquor Code, * * *? Second, has the state preempted the field through the enactment of the Commonwealth sales tax, * * * which imposed a six-percent sales tax on liquor, and the enactment of the emergency act of June 9, 1936, P.L. 13, § 2, as amended, 47 P.S. § 795, which imposed an eighteen-percent tax on liquor sold by the liquor control board?

The chancellor concluded against the validity of the tax on both issues, finding that the Commonwealth had totally preempted the field of legislation pertaining to liquor by its enactment of the comprehensive state Liquor Code, 47 P.S. § 1–101 *et seq.*, and had also specifically preempted the area of taxation on the sales of liquor by the specific wording of the Sterling Act.

The court en banc agreed with the chancellor insofar as the preemptive effects of the Liquor Code were concerned, but the court en banc did not believe that the Sterling Act had preempted the field of taxation on the sales of liquor.

Although we agree with both the chancellor and the court en banc in their final conclusion * * * we disagree with their analysis of the issues involved. In our view, * * * the state Liquor Code alone is not a sufficient indication of the Commonwealth's intention to preempt the entire field of legislation affecting liquor. Only when consideration is given to the two taxes which exist on liquor and the specific preemption doctrine enacted as part of the Sterling Act, as well as to the Liquor Code, can the conclusion be reached that the City of Philadelphia is barred from authorizing the imposition of a tax on the retail sales of liquor in hotels, restaurants, taverns or clubs.

At this point, it would be well to restate the general principles involved * * *.

In Pennsylvania, cities have no power to act unless that power has been granted to them * * *. Moreover, even when cities have been given powers to act, if the state has preempted the field in a specific area, then in that area cities have no power despite the wording of the enabling act on which they rely.

Our most recent statement on this general subject of preemption appears in Harris-Walsh, Inc. v. Dickson City Boro., 420 Pa. 259, 268–269, 216 A.2d 329, 333–334 (1966). There, we quoted at length from our opinion in the landmark case of Western Pennsylvania Restaurant Ass'n v. Pittsburgh, 366 Pa. 374, 380–381, 77 A.2d 616 (1951):

> " '(1) There are statutes which expressly provide that nothing contained therein should be construed as prohibiting municipalities from adopting appropriate ordinances, not inconsistent with the provisions of the act or the rules and regulations adopted thereunder, as might be deemed necessary to promote the purpose of the legislation. On the other hand there are statutes which expressly provide that municipal legislation in regard to the subject covered by the state act is forbidden. Then there is a third class [of statutes] which, regulating some industry or occupation, are silent as to whether municipalities are or are not permitted to enact supplementary legislation or to impinge in any manner upon the field entered upon by the state; in such cases the question whether municipal action is permissible must be determined by an analysis of the provisions of the act itself in order to ascertain the probable intention of the legislature in that regard. It is of course self-evident that a municipal ordinance cannot be sustained to the extent that it is contradictory to, or inconsistent with, a state statute. [citing an authority] * * * municipalities in the exercise of the police power may regulate certain occupations by imposing restrictions which are in addition to, and not in conflict with, statutory regulations. [citing authorities]. But if the general tenor of the statute indicates an intention * * * that it should not be supplemented by municipal bodies, that intention must be given effect and the attempted local legislation held invalid. [citing authorities].' "

* * * The statute itself is silent as to whether municipalities are or are not permitted to enact taxation legislation relating specifically to the sales of liquor. The appellees disagree with this * * *. They further remind us of our opinion in the *Tahiti Bar, Inc. Liquor License Case,* 395 Pa. 355, 360, 150 A.2d 112, 115 (1959), where we said:

> "There is perhaps no other area of permissible state action within which the exercise of the police power of a state is more plenary than in the regulation and control of the use and sale of alcoholic beverages."

However, to concede plenary and exclusive control under the police power is not to concede the same under the taxation power.

In determining whether * * * the Commonwealth completely barred a municipality's enactment of an ordinance relating to the same field, we will refrain from striking down the local ordinance unless the Commonwealth has explicitly claimed the authority itself, or unless there is such actual, material conflict between the state and local powers that only by striking down the local power can the power of the wider constituency be protected.

As we said in Retail Master Bakers Ass'n v. Allegheny County, 400 Pa. 1, 3, 161 A.2d 36, 38 (1960):

" * * * [In such cases] the ordinance will not be stricken down unless it be clearly shown that the Legislature intended to pre-empt the field or unless the ordinance conflicts with the statute. * * * "

The appellees argue that there is irreconcilable conflict between the state Liquor Code and the ordinance. Arguing that "the power to tax involves the power to destroy," McCulloch v. Maryland, 4 Wheat. 316, 4 L.Ed. 579 (1819), * * *. Although that maxim is true, it is not applicable to our present situation. We are not dealing with an attempt on the part of Philadelphia to tax liquor so excessively that total prohibition is achieved. We are instead dealing with a specific ordinance seeking to raise revenue * * *.

For this reason, the *Sawdey Liquor License Case*, 369 Pa. 19, 85 A.2d 28 (1951), and *Hilovsky Liquor License Case*, 379 Pa. 118, 108 A.2d 705 (1954), which were emphasized by the appellees, the chancellor, and the court en banc, are not applicable to the present case. Both *Sawdey* and *Hilovsky* concerned zoning ordinances which attempted to bar operations by liquor licensees in commercially zoned areas merely because of their liquor sales. In this way the ordinances were attempts to "establish prohibition within the borders of the municipality without a vote of the electors on the question of local option as provided in Section 472 of the liquor code." *Hilovsky, supra,* at page 121, 108 A.2d at page 706. Consequently, the ordinances were in direct conflict with the Liquor Code and were invalid.

There is no showing that prohibition would result or that the holders of liquor licenses would be prevented from operating in Philadelphia. In fact, such a result was clearly not intended because * * * the Philadelphia School System would not obtain the revenues that this ordinance intended.

Consequently, if we were to examine the proposed taxation ordinance only in the light of the Liquor Code, we could not conclude that the legislature had clearly indicated that its statewide regulation of liquor was intended to preempt the field as to local taxation as well as regulation.

However, the enactment of the Liquor Code is not the only indication of the legislature's intent on this question. * * * One act specifically imposes an eighteen-percent tax on all liquors * * *.

The other act is the general statewide six-percent sales and use tax which is applicable to many items in addition to liquor. * * * As to liquor, every sale, whether or not for resale, is taxed when made by the Pennsylvania liquor store and is not taxed when resold by a dispenser. * * *

The real question * * * is whether, by the enactment of these two statutes, the legislature has intended to preempt the field of taxation specially imposed on the sale of liquor.

In the specific area of taxation, the legislature has given us further guidance to the solution of the difficult problem of reconciling the governmental relationship between state and local authorities by enacting a specific preemption provision in the enabling statute on which the authority must rely for the validity of this tax.

The Sterling Act, on which Philadelphia must rely for authority validating this enactment, provides as follows:

"* * * *except that such council shall not have authority to levy, assess and collect, or provide for the levying, assessment and collection of, any tax on a privilege transaction, subject or occupation or on personal property which is now or may hereafter become subject to a State tax or license fee.*" (Emphasis supplied.) Act of August 5, 1932, P.L. 45, § 1, 53 P.S. § 15971.

We hold today that because the sales of liquor are already subject to two state taxes, the state has preempted the specific field of liquor sales for taxation purposes and Philadelphia is barred from enacting the ordinance in question.

The court en banc and the appellants both contend that the opposite conclusion is required by our recent decision in Philadelphia Tax Review Bd. v. Smith, Kline & French Laboratories, 437 Pa. 197, 262 A.2d 135 (1970).

We do not agree. In *Smith, Kline* we interpreted "state license fee" to mean only those fees imposed for purposes of raising revenue. By so doing, we ascribed to the General Assembly the same philosophy of preemption, as contained in the various tax-enabling acts, which we have followed in developing our own preemption doctrine * * *. In the area of taxation, that philosophy means that if the local tax is not imposed directly on specific transactions on which the state is dependant for revenues, then the local ordinance poses no real threat to the state's revenue plans. * * *

In *Smith, Kline* we held that the registration fee required by the Drug, Device and Cosmetic Act was a regulatory measure not designed to produce revenue. Consequently, because the state had not preempted the field for purposes of raising revenue, the city was not barred from enacting a tax. In the case of sales of liquor, however there can be no doubt that the two taxes, one for eighteen percent, the other for six percent, are clearly designed to produce revenue for the state.

Appellants also contend that the ordinance in question does not violate the preemption provision of the Sterling Act because it is imposed on a different transaction than that on which the two state taxes are imposed. According to this argument the local tax would be imposed on the transaction between the holder of the retail liquor license, *i.e.,* the owner of the hotel or bar, and the consumer, whereas the state taxes are imposed on the transaction between the holder of the liquor license and his distributor, the state liquor store.

We do not accept this view. In our view, the state taxes on liquor are classic sales taxes. The only reason that the definition of sales in the case of liquor is different from the definition with regard to other items covered by the sales tax is because the existence of a statewide system of state-operated distribution centers for liquor made it possible to assure effective collection of the tax by imposing the tax on the sale at the state store.

The case of Cahill v. Philadelphia, 381 Pa. 611, 114 A.2d 99 (1955), cited by the appellants, is inapposite. In that case the Philadelphia Mercantile License Tax (Ordinance of December 9, 1950) was challenged as violative of the preemption provisions of the Sterling Act when imposed on the gross receipts of holders of state liquor licenses because of the license fees which such licensees are required to pay. However, that case dealt with a gross-receipts tax aimed at business generally, rather than specifically at liquor sales. Moreover, in *Cahill* we explained that even though the license fees which licensees are required to pay did generate revenue, that revenue was turned over to the municipality rather than being appropriated by the state. In this way, *Cahill* was similar to the case of McClelland v. Pittsburgh, 358 Pa. 448, 57 A.2d 846 (1948), because the state statute which was said to have preempted the taxation field was not a "state tax" within the statutory preemption provision since the tax was expressly imposed for county purposes.

Here, the state taxes were clearly imposed for statewide purposes, the state has preempted the field and the city tax is invalid under the Sterling Act.

* * *

BELL, C.J., and ROBERTS, J., concur in the result.

POMEROY, J., filed a dissenting opinion, in which EAGEN, J., joined.

* * *

POMEROY, JUSTICE (dissenting).

Under the so-called "Little Sterling Act" * * * the City Council of Philadelphia was given the power to authorize the Philadelphia School District Board of Education to impose any tax, for school purposes, which the city could impose for general revenue purposes. * * * Our inquiry, then, is directed to the extent of and limitations upon the city's power to tax.

* * *

1. As to the preemption issue, I agree with the majority that by enacting the Liquor Code, *supra,* the legislature did not indicate explicitly any intention that its statewide regulation of liquor (or brewed beverages) should preempt the field not only as to local regulation but also as to local taxation; neither do I see any indication that it meant to do so by implication. Moreover, we are not here concerned with a tax which is in reality regulation because so excessive as to be confiscatory. The appellee has not cited, nor does our research reveal, any cases where the doctrine of preemption as it exists in Pennsylvania has

been applied so that state regulation of an industry or other area of state interest has the effect of preventing local taxation of the regulated field.

I cannot, however, accede to the majority's proposition that preemption is a concept that, in Pennsylvania at least, is applicable to the field of taxation as well as that of regulation; specifically, that when the state enacts a specific tax for revenue purposes it thereby intends to occupy the field exclusively for itself. To my knowledge there had not heretofore existed in Pennsylvania a doctrine of preemption in the field of taxation, nor do I see any basis or need for creating one. Municipal subdivisions in Pennsylvania are creations of the sovereign state; they have no inherent power to tax, but only such as the state gives them. The Pennsylvania legislature has from time to time made specific grants of such power. With respect to the City of Philadelphia, that power has been delegated by the Sterling Act, *supra,* * * * The approach that has traditionally been followed, and which to me seems still to be proper and adequate, is simply to ascertain whether a tax levied by Philadelphia is or is not within its Sterling Act power. In practical effect, the inquiry becomes one of ascertaining whether the city is *without* such power because the "privilege, transaction, subject or occupation, or * * * personal property" sought to be taxed is already subject to a state tax or license fee.

The inquiry is thus not whether the state has imposed a tax in a particular area of taxation; it is whether a particular state tax and city tax are coincident with respect to a privilege, transaction, subject or occupation, or to personal property. * * *

* * * The Commonwealth chooses to tax only the liquor sales which are made by its State Stores, which must be by the unopened bottle (47 P.S. § 3–305(d)), and to tax only the brewed beverage sales which are made by the distributors thereof, which must in general be by packages containing not less than 24 containers (47 P.S. § 1–102). Neither the liquor sold at State Stores nor the malt or other brewed beverage sold by distributors may be consumed on the premises. In contrast, the proposed city tax is on the sale by licensees which sale must, in the case of liquor, be by "the glass, open bottle or other container, in any mixture" (47 P.S. § 4–406(a)) for consumption on the premises and, in the case of malt or other brewed beverages, by individual containers for consumption on the premises, or, if to "take out", in quantities not in excess of 144 ounces (two "six packs") in a single sale to one person (47 P.S. § 1–102).

The majority opinion, in rejecting the view that the transactions being taxed by the Commonwealth and the city, respectively, are not the same, gives as its reason that the Commonwealth taxes sales at the State Store level because of ease of collection through its own stores. Conceding that this may be the motivation for the arrangement, it appears to me quite irrelevant to the determination of whether the same transaction as the state taxes at State Stores is sought to be taxed by the city at places other than State Stores.

In sum, since the city has been granted by the Commonwealth the same power to tax as the Commonwealth itself possesses, since it is uncontradicted that the Commonwealth itself could enact a statute having the same content as the contested ordinance, and since the Commonwealth has not already taxed the over-the-counter sale of liquor and malt or brewed beverages, there is no basis for invalidating the ordinance as enacted by Philadelphia City Council. I would, therefore, reverse the decree of the court below and I accordingly dissent.

* * *

Notes

1. In view of the close division in United Tavern (two judges joined in the result but not in the opinion), the decision is of limited authority on the presumption of preemption by implication that is drawn from several statutes.

2. How would you evaluate the opinions in United Tavern on the following points?

(a) The tax enabling act by expressly preempting one subject, excluded any implication of intent to preempt any other subject. Per contra, is it more likely that in enacting the Sterling Act, the Pennsylvania legislature never contemplated the problem raised in United Tavern?

(b) Does the majority or dissent test (of consistent taxation) better minimize speculation on legislative intent?

(c) In construing "legislative intent" to effect a preemption, should courts "hug the shores" of statutory language, or venture what the legislature reasonably would have intended, had the question occurred to it? When the majority opinion "ascribed to the General Assembly the same philosophy of preemption as contained in the various tax-enabling acts which we have followed in developing our own preemption doctrine" was it employing a policy-oriented "construction"? Compare Rivera v. Fresno, 6 Cal.3d 132, 98 Cal.Rptr. 281, 490 P.2d 793 (1971) which upheld city utility users' tax as not falling within preemption provisions of the state use tax law.

3. **Uniformity of Regulation.** Local regulatory laws are subject to preemption where uniformity is required to avoid excessive burdens. State ex rel. McElroy v. Akron, 173 Ohio St. 189, 181 N.E.2d 26 (1962), appeal dismissed 371 U.S. 35, 83 S.Ct. 145, 9 L.Ed.2d 113 (1962).

4. **Preemption and Home Rule.** Liberally construed, home rule provisions may preclude even express preemption of local taxing authority by the state. In Security Life and Accident Co. v. Temple, 177 Colo. 14, 492 P.2d 63 (1972) a state law provided that gross premiums tax on insurance companies shall constitute all taxes collectible against them. It was held to be superseded by the ordinance of Denver which imposed local sales and use taxes on such companies. Generally, however, state power to preempt

subjects of local taxation is preserved by law even as to home rule municipalities. Glander and Dewey, *Municipal Taxation—A Study of the Preemption Doctrine,* 9 Ohio St.L.J. 72 (1948).

CITY OF BELLINGHAM v. SCHAMPERA

Supreme Court of Washington, 1960.
57 Wash.2d 106, 356 P.2d 292.

HILL, JUDGE.

 * * * John David Schampera was charged * * * with a violation of § 143 of ordinance No. 5777, as amended by ordinance No. 6952, prohibiting the driving of a motor vehicle while under the influence of intoxicating liquor. * * * He was * * * convicted and sentenced to ninety days in the county jail (fifty days of which were suspended), fined one hundred dollars, and his motor vehicle operator's license suspended for a period of six months.

He appeals to this court and challenges the validity of the Bellingham ordinance under which he was charged and tried. Basically, his contentions are three:

1. The state of Washington by RCW 46.56.010 (a part of the Washington motor vehicle act) * * * has precluded Bellingham, or any other city in Washington, from passing ordinances directed against the same offense.

2. If Bellingham can enact such legislation, it cannot, as a penalty for its violation, suspend the license of a motor vehicle operator inasmuch as the state has preempted the field of the issuance, regulation, and suspension of motor vehicle operators' licenses; * * *.

3. If Bellingham can enact such legislation, the particular ordinance now before the court is invalid because the maximum fine and prison term, which it prescribes for the violation of the ordinance, exceed the maximum fine and prison term allowed to be imposed by first class cities under RCW 35.22.470.

We disagree with the contention that Washington cities can not, by ordinance, prohibit driving within their limits by persons under the influence of, or affected by the use of, intoxicating liquor.

We agree that no Washington city can prescribe, as a penalty for a violation of its ordinances, the suspension of a motor vehicle operator's license.

We agree that the city of Bellingham can not impose penalties in excess of those provided by RCW 35.22.470, but we do not agree that this necessarily invalidates the ordinance; and hold that since the penalties of fine and imprisonment, which were imposed, were within the limits which the city could impose they will be affirmed.

* * *

We have recognized, in numerous cases involving various types of offenses, the right of a city to enact ordinances prohibiting and punishing the same acts which constitute an offense under state laws so long as the city ordinance does not conflict with the general laws of the state, or the state enactment does not show upon its face that it was intended to be exclusive. Seattle v. Hewetson, 1917, 95 Wash. 612, 164 P. 234 (prohibiting the sale of intoxicating liquor); Allen v. City of Bellingham, 1917, 95 Wash. 12, 163 P. 18 (regulating jitney busses); Seattle v. MacDonald, 1907, 47 Wash. 298, 91 P. 952, 17 L.R.A.,N.S., 49 (prohibiting gambling); Bellingham v. Cissna, 1906, 44 Wash. 397, 87 P. 481 (regulating speed of automobiles); City of Seattle v. Chin Let, 1898, 19 Wash. 38, 52 P. 324 (prohibiting lotteries).

* * *

Another section of our motor vehicle statute should also be in our thinking as we discuss this phase of the case. RCW 46.08.020 is as follows:

"Precedence over local vehicle and traffic regulations. The provisions of this title relating to vehicles shall be applicable and uniform throughout this state and in all cities and towns and all political subdivisions therein and no local authority shall enact or enforce any law, ordinance, rule, or regulation in conflict with the provisions hereof unless expressly authorized by law to do so and any laws, ordinances, rules, or regulations in conflict with the provisions of this title are hereby declared to be invalid and of no effect. Local authorities may, however, adopt additional vehicle and traffic regulations which are not in conflict with the provisions hereof. (1937 c. 189 § 2; RRS § 6360–2.)"

* * *

No case in this state has considered whether an ordinance, prohibiting driving while under the influence of intoxicating liquor is in "conflict" with our state law on the same subject, * * *.

The following cases from other states have held that ordinances prohibiting driving while under the influence of intoxicating liquor are invalid—either on the theory that such driving was not a matter of local concern, or that the ordinance was in conflict with state law, or that, if it was concurrent in its effect, the state had preempted the field. City of Canon City v. Merris, 1958, 137 Colo. 169, 323 P.2d 614; City of Billings v. Herold, 1956, 130 Mont. 138, 296 P.2d 263; City of Fargo v. Glaser, 1932, 62 N.D. 673, 244 N.W. 905; Clayton v. State, 1931, 38 Ariz. 135, 297 P. 1037 (rehearing) 38 Ariz. 466, 300 P. 1010; Helmer v. Superior Court of Sacramento County, 1920, 48 Cal.App. 140, 191 P. 1001.

The following cases have upheld such ordinances, as dealing with matters of local concern and not in conflict with the state law though operating concurrently: State ex rel. Coffin v. McCall, 1954, 58 N.M. 534, 273 P.2d 642; State v. Poynter, 1950, 70 Idaho 438, 220 P.2d 386; Mares v. Kool, 1946, 51 N.M. 36, 177 P.2d 532; Salt Lake City v. Kusse, 1939, 97 Utah 113, 93 P.2d 671; Shaw v. City of Norfolk, 1937, 167 Va. 346, 189 S.E. 335; Kistler v. City of Warren, 1937, 58 Ohio App. 531, 16

N.E.2d 948; State v. Hughes, 1930, 182 Minn. 144, 233 N.W. 874; Village of Struthers v. Sokol, 1923, 108 Ohio St. 263, 140 N.E. 519.

We find the reasoning of the latter group of cases more convincing, and particularly the New Mexico and Utah cases which construed acts quite similar to our own, *i.e.*, the Uniform Motor Vehicle Act; * * *. The court, in the Utah case, says (97 Utah at page 119, 93 P.2d at page 673):

> "We see nothing inconsistent between that part of the ordinance which prohibits driving while under the influence of liquor and the provisions of Title 57",

and follows that statement with the following quotations from Ohio and Wisconsin cases:

> " ' "In determining whether an ordinance is in 'conflict' with general laws, the test is whether the ordinance permits or licenses that which the statute forbids and prohibits, and vice versa." Village of Struthers v. Sokol, 108 Ohio St. 263, 140 N.E. 519. Judged by such a test, an ordinance is in conflict if it forbids that which the statute permits'. State [ex rel. Cozart] v. Carran, 133 Ohio St. 50, 11 N.E.2d 245, 246.

> " 'The statute, as well as the ordinance, in the case at bar, is prohibitory, and the difference between them is only that the ordinance goes farther in its prohibition—but not counter to the prohibition under the statute. The city does not attempt to authorize by this ordinance what the Legislature has forbidden; nor does it forbid what the Legislature has expressly licensed, authorized, or required. * * * Unless legislative provisions are contradictory in the sense that they cannot coexist, they are not to be deemed inconsistent because of mere lack of uniformity in detail. Bodkin v. State (1932 Neb. 535) 272 N.W. 547; City of Mobile v. Collins, 24 Ala.App. 41, 130 So. 369'. Fox v. City of Racine, 225 Wis. 542, 275 N.W. 513, 515."

We conclude that the ordinance of the city of Bellingham, here in question, was not in conflict with our state statute, and there is no indication that the legislature intended to pre-empt the field of legislation with which we are concerned in this phase of the appeal. The appellant's first contention is without merit. * * *

* * *

* * * It is urged by the appellant that the state has, by RCW 46.08.010, in specific terms pre-empted the field of the issuance, suspension, and revocation of motor vehicle licenses, * * *

State preempts licensing field. The provisions of this title relating to certificates of ownership, certificates of license registration, vehicle licenses, vehicle license plates and vehicle operator's licenses shall be exclusive and no political subdivision of the state shall require or issue any licenses or certificates for the same or a similar purpose, * * *.

Amicus curiae, representing the city of Auburn, argues that though the quoted statute pre-empts for the state the issuance of motor vehicle operators' licenses, it does not preclude a city from exercising suspensory power, if it has the implied power so to do.

Passing, for the moment, the pre-emption claim, we find not only no implied power to suspend licenses, but a specific limitation. Attention is again directed to RCW 35.22.470 * * *.

It is plain that the "punishment of all persons charged with violating any of the ordinances of said city", is not to exceed a fine of three hundred dollars or ninety days, or both. Whether the problem is approached from the standpoint of pre-emption by the state or lack of power on the part of the city, the result is the same—the city cannot, in the absence of express authority from the state, revoke a motor vehicle operator's license.

* * *

We turn now to a consideration of the cases relied upon by the respondent.

In Kistler v. City of Warren, 1937, 58 Ohio App. 531, 16 N.E.2d 948, 953, we have an express holding that the court could not suspend a motor vehicle operator's license for the violation of an ordinance, but that it could impose the penalty which the ordinance in that case evidently provided, *i.e.*, to suspend the convicted person "from the right to operate a motor vehicle within * * * the city of Warren for not more than one year."

We are not here concerned with an attempt to suspend the right of the appellant to operate a motor vehicle within the limits of the city of Bellingham, but with an ordinance that provides for the suspension of an operator's license for not less than thirty days and a judgment and sentence that suspends it for six months. This would prevent the appellant from driving anywhere in the state of Washington for that period of time.

Cases are cited, on behalf of the city, from states where statutes make the conviction of certain offenses in a municipal court the basis for a mandatory revocation of a driver's license, as in Smith v. City of Gainesville, Fla.1957, 93 So.2d 105, where it was held that in revoking the driver's license (of a person convicted of driving a motor vehicle while under the influence of intoxicating liquor) a municipal judge merely followed the mandate of a statute as an administrative representative of the state department of public safety at the municipal level; and a statute imposing the duty of such revocation on a municipal judge imposes a purely ministerial or administrative responsibility, and, therefore, does not constitute an improper delegation of judicial authority in determining a punishment to be imposed.

Comparable, perhaps, would be our own RCW 46.20.250 which provides that:

> "Mandatory revocation of license by court. Every court in fixing the penalty shall forthwith revoke the vehicle operator's license of a

person upon his conviction of any of the following crimes, when such conviction has become final:

"1. * * *

"2. * * *

"3. * * *

"4. * * *

"5. * * *

"6. Conviction or forfeiture of bail upon three charges of operating a vehicle while under the influence of or affected by the use of intoxicating liquor or of any narcotic drug, all within the preceding five years;

"7. * * *."

This is a mandate to "every court" to revoke a license under certain conditions regardless of what penalty the statute or ordinance violated may have provided.

* * *

The appellant is, therefore, correct in his contention that the portion of the judgment and sentence appealed from, which purports to suspend his driver's license for the violation of a city ordinance, is beyond the authority of the superior court to enter in this case and must be deleted.

* * *

As we have indicated, Bellingham ordinance No. 6952 carried the penalties for a first conviction * * * of a fine of not less than fifty, or more than five hundred dollars; and not less than five days or more than one year in jail. As we have also pointed out, the maximum penalties which the city could impose were

" * * * a fine not to exceed three hundred dollars or imprisonment not to exceed ninety days, or both such fine and imprisonment." RCW 35.22.470.

The question for consideration is whether there can be a valid sentence pronounced under an ordinance which authorizes a penalty in excess of that permitted by state statute. We have already pointed out, but here reiterate, that the fine and jail sentence imposed in this case, *i.e.*, one hundred dollars and ninety days, are within the permissible limits fixed by state statute, *i.e.*, RCW 35.22.470.

There is a division of authority on this question, but we adopt the majority and, we believe, the preferable rule: that an ordinance which authorizes a penalty in excess of that permitted by statute is not void, and a sentence pronounced under such an ordinance may be enforced to the extent that it is within the statutory limitations, if the city's legislative body would have enacted the ordinance knowing that only the lesser penalties could be imposed. See Kist v. Butts, 1942, 71 N.D. 436, 1 N.W.2d 612, 138 A.L.R. 1206.

* * *

We, therefore, hold that the sentence of a fine of one hundred dollars and a jail sentence of ninety days (with fifty days suspended) should be affirmed. * * *

Note

Following complaints by owners regarding weekend frolics of motorcyclists and dune buggies on their lands, the County of San Bernadino adopted an ordinance prohibiting off-road motor vehicle operation on private property without prior written permission of the owners, and penalizing such operation as a misdemeanor. In upholding the ordinance, the court found neither a conflict with state law, nor any implied preemption of the field by the state penal code. Sports Committee District 37 v. San Bernadino, 113 Cal.App.3d 155, 169 Cal.Rptr. 652 (1980). Compare, City of Portland v. Dollarhide, 71 Or. 289, 692 P.2d 162 (1984), wherein the Oregon Supreme Court held that a city ordinance would not impose a harsher minimum penalty for prostitution than set for the same crime by state law.

GALVAN v. SUPERIOR COURT

Supreme Court of California, 1969.
70 Cal.2d 851, 76 Cal.Rptr. 642, 452 P.2d 930.

PETERS, JUSTICE.

[Taxpayer and firearms owner in San Francisco attacked the constitutionality of San Francisco gun registration law.]

* * *

PREEMPTION—CONFLICT WITH STATE LAW

Galvan argues that the San Francisco gun law is void because the law directly conflicts with Penal Code section 12026, which states that "no permit or license" shall be required of any adult citizen (with certain limitations not at issue) to keep a concealable firearm at his residence or place of business.

The validity of the San Francisco law is governed by the California Constitution, article XI, section 11, which restricts local lawmaking to "all such local, police, sanitary and other regulations as are not in conflict with general laws." Any local law that directly conflicts with state legislation is void. [Citations omitted.]

Section 12026, however, prohibits licenses or permits. The section does not prohibit registration requirements. The meaning of "register" is "[t]o record formally and exactly; to enroll; to enter precisely in a list or the like." * * * The meaning of "license," however, is permission or authority to do a particular thing or exercise a particular privilege. [Citations omitted.]

Any requirement that an item be registered before it can be lawfully used involves, of course, "permission to do a particular thing," and to that extent "registration" is the same as "licensing." But the basic, and commonly held, distinction between licensing and registration is that licensing regulates activity * * * while registration catalogs all persons with respect to an activity, or all things that fall with certain classifications. * * *

Concededly, the distinction between licensing and registration has not always been reflected in all types of legislation. * * *

* * *

The authority vested by the ordinance in the chief of police to revoke "for cause" does not transform San Francisco's gun registration ordinance into a licensing law. * * * We are satisfied that the term "for cause" refers to the requirements for registration * * *.

We conclude that the San Francisco registration requirement does not conflict with the permit and licensing provision of section 12026 of the Penal Code.

PREEMPTION BY IMPLICATION

Galvan contends that even if the San Francisco gun law does not directly conflict with any state statute, the gun law is void because the state has preempted the entire broad field of weapons control. * * * Whenever the Legislature has adopted a general scheme for the regulation of a particular subject, no local legislation on that subject is permissible. (In re Lane, *supra,* 58 Cal.2d at p. 102, 22 Cal.Rptr. 857, 372 P.2d 897, and cases cited therein; Abbott v. City of Los Angeles, 53 Cal.2d 674, 682, 3 Cal.Rptr. 158, 349 P.2d 974, 82 A.L.R.2d 385.)

To determine whether the Legislature intended to occupy a particular field to the exclusion of all local regulation, we may look to the " 'whole purpose and scope of the legislative scheme.' " (In re Lane, *supra,* 58 Cal.2d at pp. 102–103, 22 Cal.Rptr. at p. 859, 372 P.2d at p. 899.)

In re Hubbard, *supra,* 62 Cal.2d 119, 128, 41 Cal.Rptr. 393, 399, 396 P.2d 809, 815, established three tests to determine whether a subject has been preempted by the Legislature. "(1) the subject matter has been so fully and completely covered by general law as to clearly indicate that it has become exclusively a matter of state concern; (2) the subject matter has been partially covered by general law couched in such terms as to indicate clearly that a paramount state concern will not tolerate further or additional local action; or (3) the subject matter has been partially covered by general law, and the subject is of such a nature that the adverse effect of a local ordinance on the transient citizens of the state outweighs the possible benefit to the municipality."

* * *

These statutes cannot reasonably be said to show a general scheme for the regulation of the subject of gun registration, and there is no basis for a conclusion that these statutes show a legislative intent to make the subject of gun registration immune from local regulation.

Galvan does not contend to the contrary; his position is that the registration statutes when coupled with the large number of statutes dealing with guns and other weapons show that the Legislature has preempted the entire broad field of gun control or weapons control and that gun registration as a subject included within the broad field of gun or weapons control must be deemed preempted.

Although Galvan cites a great number of statutes relating to weapons, these statutes do not show that the entire area of gun or weapons control has been so fully and completely covered by general law, in the words of *Hubbard*, "as to clearly indicate that [the subject] has become exclusively a matter of state concern." (62 Cal.2d at p. 128, 41 Cal.Rptr. at p. 399, 396 P.2d at p. 815.) There are various subjects that the legislation deals with only partly or not at all. We have already seen the limited statutory provisions for gun registration. Another example is, with regard to the related subject of licensing, the Legislature has not authorized or prohibited the licensing of rifles or shotguns.

* * *

The fact that there are numerous statutes dealing with guns or other weapons does not by itself show that the subject of gun or weapons control has been completely covered so as to make the matter one of exclusive state concern.

To approach the issue of preemption as a quantitative problem provides no guidance * * * and further confounds a meaningful solution to preemption problems by offering a superficially attractive rule of preemption that requires only a statutory nose-count. Thus, in the instant case, by grouping weapons licensing, registration and prohibitions, and offenses involving the use of firearms, the very volume of statutes might suggest that the Legislature has covered, and preempted the field. Language in In re Lane, *supra,* 58 Cal.2d 99, 110, 22 Cal.Rptr. 857, 863, 372 P.2d 897, 903 (concurring opinion), that "the general intent may be found in a multiplicity of statutes taken together" of course presupposed closely related statutes.

The task is, as shown in *Hubbard,* to determine whether the state has occupied a relevant field—an area of legislation which includes the subject of the local legislation, and is sufficiently logically related so that a court or a local legislative body, can detect a patterned approach to the subject. Thus, that the state has legislated concerning the possession of loaded firearms on government premises (*e.g.,* Pen.Code, §§ 171c–171e) indicates no patterned approach to the subject of prohibited users, such as prisoners or ex-felons or minors. A field cannot properly consist of statutes unified by a single common noun. (See Markus v. Justice's Court, 117 Cal.App.2d 391, 396–397, 255 P.2d 883 [local licensing of dogs not preempted by state].)

In In re Hubbard, *supra,* 62 Cal.2d 119, 125–126, 41 Cal.Rptr. 393, 396 P.2d 809, we recognized that the Legislature had preempted some areas of gambling such as horse-wagering (In re Loretizo, *supra,* 59 Cal. 2d 445, 447, 30 Cal.Rptr. 16, 380 P.2d 656), lotteries (People v. Cole, 226 Cal.App.2d 125, 127, 37 Cal.Rptr. 798), gambling houses (People v. Franks, 226 Cal.App.2d 123, 37 Cal.Rptr. 800), and certain games of chance, but we held that the Legislature had preempted neither all gambling, or more specifically, regulation of all games of chance. Similarly, here the numerous statutes cited by Galvan indicate that some areas of weapons control have been preempted, but because of the substantial areas left unregulated and the very limited regulation of gun registration, the statutes cannot be said to show that the entire field of gun or weapons control has been so completely covered as to indicate an intent on the part of the Legislature to make gun registration exclusively a subject of state concern.

The second standard set forth in *Hubbard* contemplates that the Legislature may preempt a field even though the statutes are not so comprehensive as to indicate an intent to occupy the field if there has been partial coverage of the field by general law couched in such terms as to indicate that there is a paramount state concern which will not tolerate further or additional local requirements. (62 Cal.2d at p. 128, 41 Cal.Rptr. 393, 396 P.2d 809.) No statute has been called to our attention which expressly states that gun registration or gun or weapons control is exclusively a matter of state concern. Although language in statutes might reasonably imply a legislative intention that a paramount state concern will not permit regulation by other agencies [citations omitted] we do not find such an implied legislative intent here.

* * *

The issue of "paramount state concern" also involves the question "whether substantial, geographic, economic, ecological or other distinctions are persuasive of the need for local control, and whether local needs have been adequately recognized and comprehensively dealt with at the state level." (Robbins v. County of Los Angeles, 248 Cal.App.2d 1, 9, 56 Cal.Rptr. 853, 859.)

That problems with firearms are likely to require different treatment in San Francisco County than in Mono County should require no elaborate citation of authority. * * *

We are persuaded by language in In re Hoffman, 155 Cal. 114, 118, 99 P. 517, 519: "The state in its laws deals with all of its territory and all of its people. * * * but it may often, and does often, happen that the requirements which the state sees fit to impose may not be adequate to meet the demands of densely populated municipalities, so that it becomes proper, and even necessary, for municipalities to add to state regulations provisions adapted to their special requirements."

The third standard presented in *Hubbard* is whether the subject matter has been partially covered by general law, and "the adverse effect of a local ordinance on the transient citizens of the state outweighs the possible benefit to the municipality." (62 Cal.2d at p. 128, 41 Cal.Rptr. at p. 399, 396 P.2d at p. 815; see also, In re Lane, *supra*, 58 Cal.2d at p. 111, 22 Cal.Rptr. 857, 372 P.2d 897 (concurring opinion).)

We find that the San Francisco gun law places no undue burden on transient citizens. Indeed, the ordinance was drafted to prevent such a burden. The law, applicable to firearms possessed by persons in San Francisco, provides for a seven-day exemption, and thus excludes those transients who might otherwise be burdened.

* * *

Finally, Galvan's reliance on In re Lane, *supra,* 58 Cal.2d 99, 22 Cal.Rptr. 857, 372 P.2d 897 is misplaced. *Lane,* defining the relevant field as "criminal aspects of sexual activity" (58 Cal.2d at p. 102, 22 Cal. Rptr. 857, 372 P.2d 897), invalidated a Los Angeles ordinance which attempted to make sexual intercourse between persons not married to each other a criminal act (*id.,* at p. 105, 22 Cal.Rptr. 857, 372 P.2d 897).

The conclusion in *Lane* that the Legislature had preempted the entire field of proscribed sexual activity and the inference that the Legislature intended that simple fornication not be a crime, was compelled by an analysis of the relevant Penal Code sections. * * *

The considerations involved in *Lane* do not apply to the instant case. The statutory pattern governing sexual behavior differs from that governing guns and other weapons, and there is no extensive coverage of gun registration as there is of criminal sex offenses; * * *

In summary, we find that the Legislature has not adopted a uniform statutory scheme governing gun registration, that the absence of provisions governing registration does not reflect a legislative intent to prohibit local registration, that the San Francisco gun law imposes no undue burden on transients, and that the differing community needs for gun registration within the state justifies local regulation of the subject. The San Francisco gun law is not void on grounds of state preemption.

Note

1. **Local Gun Control.** Municipal gun regulation has been upheld and not deemed preempted by state gun control laws, in several other states: Township of Chester v. Panicucci, 62 N.J. 94, 299 A.2d 385 (1973); City of Detroit v. Recorders Court Judge, 71 Mich.App. 414, 248 N.W.2d 566 (1977); Mosher v. Dayton, 48 Ohio St.2d 243, 358 N.E.2d 540 (1976); Junction City v. Lee, 216 Kan. 495, 532 P.2d 1292 (1975). But see contra: Schneck v. Philadelphia, 34 Pa.Cmwlth. 96, 383 A.2d 227 (1978). The argument that state or local laws on gun control infringe the constitutional right to bear arms has been consistently rejected by the courts. See, e.g., the cases last cited (other than Schneck); Quilici v. Morton Grove, 695 F.2d 261 (7th Cir.1982); Rinzler v. Carson, 262 So.2d 661 (Fla.1972).

Chapter V

INTERLOCAL GOVERNMENT
RELATIONS

A. TERRITORIAL AND BOUNDARY
CHANGES

One can not advance any single model for government organization. Reform strategies must be tailored to the situations encountered in each state. Most local governments, though too weak to provide current needs, are politically too strong to be eliminated by dissolution. Further, the forces favoring localism and centralism in metropolitan governance are differently balanced on specific issues. Poor public acceptance of comprehensive metropolitan reorganization is recorded in Lineberry, *Reforming Metropolitan Governance*, 58 Geo.L.J. 675 at 715 (1958). Among the techniques selectively employed to modernize local government, three predominate: 1—*Restructuring Government Units*— by annexation of territory or consolidation of smaller units; or by local federation with larger regional units. 2—*Reorganization of Functions*—by consolidation of selected metro-scale urban functions by means of metropolitan special districts; by special extraterritorial powers; by intergovernmental transfers of functions; or by interlocal cooperative arrangements. 3—*State Assistance and Control of Intergovernmental Activities*. These techniques are reviewed in the following articles. Reading any one or more of them will well repay a student's effort: *A Symposium: Restructuring Metropolitan Area Government*, 58 Georgetown L.Rev. 663 (1970); ACIR, *Regional Decisionmaking: New Strategies for Substate Districts* (2 Vols. 1973); ACIR, *Government Structures, Organization and Planning in Metropolitan Areas* (1961); ACIR, *Alternative Approaches to Governmental Reorganization in Metropolitan Areas* (1962); Note, *Stumbling Giants—A Path to Progress Through Metropolitan Annexation*, 39 N.Dame L.Rev. 56 (1963–64); Note, *The Urban County, A Study of New Approaches to Local Government in Metropolitan Areas*, 73 Harv.L.Rev. 526 (1960); D.C. Grant, *Urban Needs and State Response* in *The States and the Urban Crisis*

(Am.Assembly 1971); J.C. Bollens and H.J. Schmandt, *The Metropolis,* chapters 11–13 (1970); CED, *Reshaping Government in Metropolitan Areas* (1970).

1. ANNEXATION—CONSOLIDATION

Political unification of local governments into fewer structures of sufficient size and power to govern expanding urban centers may occur through territorial annexation; merger of adjoining municipalities; or absorption of underlying units into a single county unit. These methods of expansion have been authorized in most states by an assortment of separate, uncoordinated statutes. Hence, any analysis of the diverse processes of boundary change will require reference to all pertinent legislation in a given state.

Annexation was the favored and principal method of municipal growth in the pre-metropolitan age. Many of the original annexation laws are still in force, but have become barriers, rather than aids, to orderly growth. "During the 1950–1960 decade, only 22 of these 130 [largest] cities annexed as much as 30 square miles to their respective areas, * * *. Furthermore, 44 of the 130 largest cities experienced no change in area during the entire decade, while 36 others added only from 1 to 10 square miles of territory. * * * In only 12 of these [38] states, however, were there major cities with a territorial increase of 30 square miles or more. At the other extreme are states in which no major city added as much as 10 square miles of territory—New York State * * * New Jersey * * * Massachusetts, Michigan and Pennsylvania * * * Connecticut * * * and Minnesota * * * as well as 10 other states * * *. ACIR, *Government Structures,* supra, p. 22.

"Annexation legislation is in a chaotic condition in the United States. Diverse systems have been adopted in various states without logical justification for diversity. Annexation programs are poorly thought out. Few standards regarding the qualifications of territory to be annexable have been drafted, and those that are drafted are often inadequate or harmful to metropolitan interests. The practical mechanics of annexing territory are unnecessarily complex and seldom effectively implement any particular statutory method of annexation. * * * The principal difficulty * * * stems from the fact that few states have formulated any kind of consistent policy toward the metropolitan area * * *. Until a state has done this, it is useless to advocate any particular method of annexation as best * * *." F. Sengstock, *Annexation: A Solution to the Metropolitan Area Problem* 118 (1960); * see also Woodruff, *Systems and Standards of Municipal Annexation Review: A Comparative Analysis,* 58 Geo.L.Rev. 743 (1970).

Annexation is not entirely useless. It is still employed successfully by smaller municipalities, and interest in its potential for larger population centers has revived. A number of states have recently modern-

* Reprinted by permission of Michigan   The University of Michigan Law School, Legal Publications. Copyright © 1960 by   Ann Arbor.

ized their boundary laws. See Note—*Stumbling Giant, supra,* 62–63; ACIR, *Government Structures, supra,* 23–24; National League of Cities, *Adjusting Municipal Boundaries—Law and Practice* (1966).

Of the many questions which influence annexation policy, the following are prominent:

(a) Should annexation be controlled directly by statutory provisions, or by administrative regulations? Should the power of decision be vested in local residents, in local governments, or in independent tribunals?

(b) What procedures are best suited to administer annexation proposals?

(c) What annexation standards best assure intelligent growth and fair treatment of conflicting local interests?

(d) How broadly or strictly should courts review annexation determinations by local agencies?

Methods of Annexation. Studies indicate five principal means: by direct legislative act: by municipal action (ordinance or resolution); by popular approval (petition or referendum); by impartial tribunals (courts or administrative commissions); or by some combination of the foregoing. Most states use more than one of the foregoing means of annexation. State variations on these patterns are outlined in National League of Cities, *Adjusting Municipal Boundaries* (1966).

Direct Statutory Annexation. This method is largely unused due to constitutional prohibitions against special acts and special legislation. But some state constitutions (Alaska, Florida, Maryland, Montana and New York) specifically exempt municipal boundary changes from general prohibitions against special legislation. See F. Sengstock, *Annexation: A Solution To The Metropolitan Area Problem,* p. 11, n. 7; City of Long Beach v. Collins, 261 So.2d 498 (Fla.1972); Lee v. Jesup, 222 Ga. 530, 150 S.E.2d 836 (1966).

Delegation Problems. The adequacy of legislative guidelines to confine delegated discretion also arises in annexation disputes. Authorizations for annexations on findings that they are "in the public interest," "just and equitable," "reasonable," "necessary and convenient" or "desirable" receive a different reception in different jurisdictions. Compare: Town of Beloit v. Beloit, 37 Wis.2d 637, 155 N.W.2d 633 (1968) (nullifying annexation standard "in the public interest" as delegation of lawmaking discretion); City of Auburndale v. Adams Packing Ass'n, 171 So.2d 161 (Fla.1965); with, Common Council of Albany v. Town Board of Town of Bethlehem, 23 A.D.2d 381, 261 N.Y.S.2d 144 (1965) (upholding "public interest" standard as adequate); Smith v. Incorporated Town of Culver, 140 Ind.App. 508, 224 N.E.2d 59 (1967); State ex rel. Klise v. Riverdale, 244 Iowa 423, 436, 57 N.W.2d 63, 71 (1953).

Some courts apply stricter tests to statutes that authorize judicial annexation. Thus, the Wisconsin court nullified the "public interest" standard for judicial tribunals in Town of Beloit, supra, but upheld the same standard for an administrative commission:

"* * * it must be recognized that in the * * * Beloit case the court was dealing with the legislative delegation of legislative power to the judiciary. * * *

We are dealing here * * * with a delegation of that power to an administrative agency * * * The legislative agency or director is, in fact, an arm or agent of the legislature itself. * * * An administrative agency does not stand on the same footing as a court when considering the doctrine of separation of powers. * * * " Schmidt v. Department of Resources Development, 39 Wis.2d 46, 55–57, 158 N.W.2d 306, 311, 312 (1968).

Compare: Ruland v. Augusts, 120 Kan. 42, 242 P. 456 (1926) with City of Salina v. Thompson, 169 Kan. 579, 220 P.2d 147 (1950). The same distinction does not hold in Virginia. See the Johnston case, p. 190.

Party Standing to Challenge Boundary Changes. State laws also differ on the standing of different classes of citizens and government units to sue on such issues. See e.g., Fort Collins-Loveland Water District v. Fort Collins, 174 Colo. 79, 482 P.2d 986 (1971); Elkins v. Denver, 157 Colo. 252, 402 P.2d 617 (1965).

Retroactive Validation of Boundary Changes. As indicated at p. 26, municipal expansion may be validated by retroactive judicial process (*de facto* doctrine), or by retroactive legislation (validating statutes).

a. *Popular Determination*

CITY OF DOUGLAS v. JUNEAU
Supreme Court of Alaska, 1971.
484 P.2d 1040.

RABINOWITZ, JUSTICE. * * *

Appellant City of Douglas instituted a declaratory judgment action * * * seeking a declaration that AS 29.85.160(c), a portion of our statutes relating to unification of local government units, was violative of article X, section 9 of the Alaska Constitution, which establishes procedures for the adoption, amendment, or repeal of home rule charters. Appellees moved to dismiss the action. The motion was granted and this appeal followed.

CONSTITUTIONAL AND STATUTORY FRAMEWORK.

The purpose of the local government article of the Alaska Constitution is "to provide for maximum local self-government with a minimum of local government units, and to prevent duplication of tax-levying jurisdictions." All local government powers are constitutionally vested in boroughs and cities, and only they may tax. It is required that the entire state be divided into boroughs, but the details of the manner of their establishment, organization, and consolidation are left to the legislature. It is further provided that cities are parts of the boroughs in which they are located, and the manner of consolidation and dissolution of the cities is left to the legislature.

Turning to the statutory framework, the legislature has provided that an organized borough and all cities within it may unify into a single unit of home rule local government by following a prescribed procedure. Unification must be proposed by a petition for a referendum. The borough assembly then submits to the voters the questions of whether the borough and its cities should be unified, * * *. Unification requires a majority of votes in the first class and home rule cities of the borough taken together, as well as a majority of the votes in the remainder of the borough. In the event unification is approved, the charter commission elected at the same time prepares and proposes a home rule charter for the unified entity. An election is then held on the proposed charter; ratification requires concurrent majorities in the first class and home rule cities taken together, and in the remainder of the borough. If the charter is rejected, the charter commission proposes another, and if the second proposed charter is rejected, the unification process terminates. If the charter is ratified, it dissolves all pre-existing local governments in the unified area.

The City of Douglas was duly organized as a first class city under a home rule charter within the Greater Juneau Borough. At an election in February 1970, the voters in the borough ratified a charter pursuant to AS 29.85.160(c), purportedly unifying the City and Borough of Juneau and dissolving the City of Douglas as of July 1, 1970. A majority of the votes cast in the City of Douglas opposed ratification. Nevertheless, the charter was ratified under AS 29.85.160(c), because the favorable vote in the City of Juneau outweighed the negative vote in Douglas, their votes being counted together in the category of "remaining area of the Borough, composed of all first class and home rule cities."

CONSTITUTIONALITY OF AS 29.85.160(C).

The main thrust of appellants' contentions in this appeal is that AS 29.85.160(c) violates article X, section 9 of the Alaska Constitution. * * *

Appellants' theory is that this provision applies whenever the charter of a home rule city is repealed, * * *. Appellees say that article X, section 7 empowers the legislature to devise means for dissolution of home rule cities other than submission of charter repeal referenda to their voters. Article X, section 7 provides that:

> "Cities shall be incorporated in a manner prescribed by law, and shall be a part of the borough in which they are located. Cities shall have the powers and functions conferred by law or charter. They may be merged, consolidated, classified, reclassified, or dissolved in the manner provided by law."

Alaska's Constitution further provides that the terms "by law" and "by the legislature" are used interchangeably when related to law-making powers.

We think appellees' position is correct. Article X, section 7 leaves the legislature free to determine the manner of dissolution of cities. On the other hand, article X, section 9 grants to the qualified voters of a city the right to adopt, amend, or repeal a home rule charter. The distinction between dissolution of cities and adoption, amendment, or repeal of home rule charters is, in our view, of controlling significance. Article X, section 9 empowers first class cities to determine the local question of whether to have home rule without interference by others, but by virtue of article X, section 7, the legislature is authorized to decide the broader and quite different question of whether a home rule city should be dissolved, as well as the method or manner of dissolution. A similar policy distinction underlies the constitutional provision for establishment of a local boundary commission. In regard to the Local Boundary Commission, the minutes of the constitutional convention were examined in Fairview Public Utility District No. One v. City of Anchorage, 368 P.2d 540 (Alaska 1962). There it was said that the framers of the Alaska Constitution thought that "local political decisions do not usually create proper boundaries and that boundaries should be established at the state level." *Fairview* held that residents of a community have no constitutionally protected interest in its existence as a separate governmental unit, so the legislature may provide for its annexation without their consent. *Fairview* was followed by Oesau v. City of Dillingham, 439 P.2d 180 (Alaska 1968), upholding the Local Boundary Commission's dissolution of a fourth class city without a vote of its residents.

Though the Local Boundary Commission is not involved in unification of government units provided for under AS 29.85.010–210, the enabling constitutional provisions, as well as the *Fairview* and *Oesau* decisions, offer a cogent analogue for the constitutional distinction between article X, section 9, granting the qualified voters of a first class city the right to adopt, amend, or repeal a home rule charter, and article X, section 7, providing that cities may be merged, consolidated or dissolved in the manner provided by the legislature. It appears that this cleavage is reflective of a policy which has as its objective the placement of decisional responsibility for local problems within local control and decisional responsibility for broader problems in control of a broader community. Therefore, in light of the authorization provided by article X, section 7 for legislative enactment of a statutory system for the merger and consolidation, as well as the dissolution of cities, we hold that AS 29.85.160(c) is constitutional and does not violate the provisions of article X, section 9.   *   *   *

*   *   *

Appellants next argue that the legislature has unconstitutionally delegated its powers of dissolution. Conceding that article X, section 7 of the Alaska Constitution empowers the legislature to dissolve cities, it is argued that by placing this power in the legislature, the constitution impliedly prohibits the legislature from delegating the power to others. In the case at bar, we are not presented with an instance of impermissible delegation. As was indicated previously, article X, section 7 provides that cities may be "dissolved in the manner provided by law," a phrase interchangeable with "in the manner provided by the legislature." Since the provision says dissolved "in the manner" provided by the legislature, it empowers the legislature to construct any otherwise constitutional scheme for dissolution, rather than requiring the legislature to perform the dissolution.

* * *

Affirmed.

Notes

1. **Popular Self-Determination.** Annexation by popular approval is authorized in most states. The statutes vary as to: the kinds of annexation that require popular approval; the qualifications of electors; the effect of popular approval *viz.* as a prerequisite to action by annexation tribunals or as a final and binding determination. See, e.g., F. Sengstock, supra, 13–19. Municipal annexation requiring concurrent approval by electors of each affected (annexor and annexee) unit has been held constitutional. See, e.g., Town of Lockport v. Citizens for Community Action, 430 U.S. 259, 97 S.Ct. 1047, 51 L.Ed.2d 313 (1977). Accord: Holmes v. Little Rock, 285 Ark. 296, 686 S.W.2d 425 (1985). North Carolina provided a hybrid alternative to popular determination, with respect to unincorporated territory.

> "The 1959 legislation does an about face, removes annexation from the category of political questions to be decided by a vote of the people, and adopts a policy strongly favoring periodic annexation * * *. Briefly C. 1009 authorizes any municipality to annex contiguous and unincorporated land which meets any one of five specific standards [criteria of 'urban development'] * * *." Note—*North Carolina 1959 Sessions Laws,* 39 No.Car.L.Rev. at 210–212 (1960).

The North Carolina amendments protect annexee interests from improvident unilateral absorption by smaller municipalities (less than 5,000), by imposing conditions regarding planning and capacity to provide public services; and by providing judicial review to assure compliance with such prerequisites. Gen.Stats. North Carolina §§ 160.453.1–6; Lithium Corp. v. Bessemer, 261 N.C. 532, 135 S.E.2d 574, 578 (1964). See also City of Bettendorf v. Abeln, 261 Iowa 404, 154 N.W.2d 836 (1967); City of Bourbon v. Miller, 420 S.W.2d 296 (Mo.1967).

The revised local government article of the Pennsylvania Constitution (Art. IX, § 8) provided that, within two years of adoption, the General Assembly enact uniform legislation establishing *procedures* for municipal boundary changes; that electors could effect municipal boundary changes by concurrent majority vote of the electors in each affected municipality, without the approval of any governing body; but that the foregoing provisions should not prevent the General Assembly from authorizing additional methods of municipal boundary changes. When, however, the legislature defaulted on the constitutional mandate of enacting uniform boundary change procedures, the court held that the constitution voided all prior procedures, and left available for municipal boundary changes only the initiative and referendum procedure stated in the constitution. Middle Paxton Township v. Borough of Dauphin, 10 Pa.Cmwth. 431, 308 A.2d 208 (1973).

2. **Alternatives to Popular Determination.** The alternative methods outlined in City of Douglas, e.g., by legislative action or state agency boundary commissions, have variant counterparts in other states, as illustrated in the following pages.

3. **Extraterritorial Jurisdiction and Annexation Statutes.** Whether extraterritorial jurisdiction affects or is affected by annexation laws depends upon specific statutory and constitutional interpretation. See Sitton v. Lindale, 455 S.W.2d 939 (Tex.1970) holding that the annexation requirement of popular approval is unaffected by prior grant of extraterritorial jurisdiction; City of Ceres v. Modesto, 274 Cal.App.2d 545, 79 Cal. Rptr. 168 (1969) holding that such jurisdiction is not impliedly affected by annexation proceedings.

CITY OF ROME ET AL. v. UNITED STATES ET AL.

Supreme Court of the United States, 1980.
446 U.S. 156, 100 S.Ct. 1548, 64 L.Ed.2d 119.

Mr. Justice Marshall delivered the opinion of the Court.

At issue in this case is the constitutionality of the Voting Rights Act of 1965 and its applicability to electoral changes and annexations made by the city of Rome, Ga.

I

* * *

Section 5 of the Voting Rights Act of 1965 requires preclearance by the Attorney General or the United States District Court for the District of Columbia of any change in a "standard, practice, or procedure with respect to voting," 42 U.S.C. § 1973c (1976), * * * by jurisdictions that fall within the coverage formula set forth in § 4(b) of the Act, 42 U.S.C. § 1973b(b) (1976). In 1965, the Attorney General designated Georgia a covered jurisdiction under the Act, 30 Fed.Reg. 9897, and the municipalities of that State must therefore comply with the preclearance procedure, * * *.

It is not disputed that the 1966 changes in Rome's electoral system were within the purview of the Act. * * * Nonetheless, the city failed to seek preclearance for them. In addition, the city did not seek preclearance for 60 annexations made between November 1, 1964, and February 10, 1975, even though required to do so because an annexation constitutes a change in a "standard, practice or procedure with respect to voting" under the Act, Perkins v. Matthews, 400 U.S. 379, 91 S.Ct. 431, 27 L.Ed.2d 476 (1971).

In June 1974, the city did submit one annexation to the Attorney General for preclearance. The Attorney General discovered that other annexations had occurred, and, in response to his inquiries, the city submitted all the annexations and the 1966 electoral changes for preclearance. The Attorney General declined to preclear the provisions for majority vote, numbered posts, and staggered terms for city commission and board of education elections, as well as the residency requirement for board elections. * * * The Attorney General also refused to preclear 13 of the 60 annexations in question. He found that the disapproved annexations either contained predominately white populations of significant size or were near predominately white areas and were zoned for residential subdivision development. * * * [H]e determined that the city had not carried its burden of proving that the annexations would not dilute the Negro vote.

* * * At the same time, he refused to clear the annexations for city commission elections because, in his view, the residency requirement for city commission contained in the preexisting electoral procedures could have a discriminatory effect.

The city and two of its officials then filed this action, seeking relief from the Act based on a variety of claims. A three-judge court, * * * granted summary judgment for the defendants. 472 F.Supp. 221 (D.C.1979). We noted probable jurisdiction, * * * and now affirm.

A

The appellants contend that the city may exempt itself from the coverage of the Act. * * *

* * *

Section 4(a) also provides, however, a procedure for exemption from the Act. This so-called "bail out" provision allows a covered jurisdiction to escape the preclearance requirement of § 5 by bringing a declaratory judgment action * * * and proving that no "test or device" has been used in the jurisdiction "during the seventeen years preceding the filing of the action for the purpose or with the effect of denying or abridging the right to vote on account of race or color." The District Court refused to allow the city to "bail out" of the Act's coverage, holding that the political units of a covered jurisdiction cannot independently bring a § 4(a) bailout action. We agree.

* * * Rather, the city comes within the Act because it is part of a covered State. Under the plain language of the statute, then, it appears that any bailout action to exempt the city must be filed by, and seek to exempt all of, the state of Georgia.

The appellants seek to avoid this conclusion by relying on our decision in United States v. Board of Commissioners of Sheffield, Alabama, supra. That decision, however, did not even discuss the bailout process. In Sheffield, the Court held that when the Attorney General determines that a State falls within the coverage formula of § 4(b), any political unit of the State must preclear new voting procedures under § 5 * * *. In so holding, the Court necessarily determined that the scope of §§ 4(a) and 5 is "geographic" or "territorial," id., at 120, 126, and thus that, when an entire State is covered, it is irrelevant whether political units of it might otherwise come under § 5 as "political subdivisions." Id., at 126–129.

* * * Thus, our decision in that case is in no way inconsistent with our conclusion that * * *, the city is not a "political subdivision" for purposes of § 4(a) "bail out."

Nor did *Sheffield* suggest that a municipality in a covered State is itself a "State" for purposes of the § 4(a) exemption procedure. * * * Bound by this unambiguous congressional intent, we hold that the city of Rome may not use the bailout procedure of § 4(a).

* * *

Section 5 of the Act provides that the Attorney General must interpose objections to original submissions within 60 days of their filing. If the Attorney General fails to make a timely objection, the voting practices submitted become fully enforceable. * * *

The timing provisions of both the Act and the regulations are silent on the effect of supplements to requests for reconsideration. We agree with the Attorney General that the purposes of the Act and its implementing regulations would be furthered if the 60–day period provided by 28 CFR § 51.3(d) were interpreted to commence anew when additional information is supplied by the submitting jurisdiction on its own accord.

* * *

The appellants raise five issues of law in support of their contention that the Act may not properly be applied to the electoral changes and annexations disapproved by the Attorney General.

The District Court found that the disapproved electoral changes and annexations had not been made for any discriminatory purpose, but did have a discriminatory effect. The appellants argue that § 5 of the Act may not be read as prohibiting voting practices that have only a discriminatory effect. * * * By describing the elements of discriminatory purpose and effect in the conjunctive, Congress plainly intended that a voting practice not be precleared unless *both* discriminatory purpose and effect are absent. * * *

The appellants urge that we abandon this settled interpretation because in their view § 5, to the extent that it prohibits voting changes that have only a discriminatory effect, is unconstitutional. * * *

Congress passed the Act under the authority accorded it by the Fifteenth Amendment. The appellants contend that the Act is unconstitutional because it exceeds Congress' power to enforce that Amendment. They claim that § 1 of the Amendment prohibits only purposeful racial discrimination in voting, and that in enforcing that provision pursuant to § 2, Congress may not prohibit voting practices lacking discriminatory intent even if they are discriminatory in effect.

We hold that, even if § 1 of the Amendment prohibits only purposeful discrimination, the prior decisions of this Court foreclose any argument that Congress may not, pursuant to § 2, outlaw voting practices that are discriminatory in effect.

The appellants are asking us to do nothing less than overrule our decision in South Carolina v. Katzenbach, 383 U.S. 301, 86 S.Ct. 803, 15 L.Ed.2d 769 (1966), in which we upheld the constitutionality of the Act.

* * *

* * *

The Court's treatment in South Carolina v. Katzenbach of the Act's ban on literacy tests demonstrates that, * * * Congress may prohibit voting practices that have only a discriminatory effect. * * * This holding makes clear that Congress may, under the authority of § 2 of the Fifteenth Amendment prohibit state action that, though in itself not violative of § 1, perpetuates the effects of past discrimination.

Other decisions of this Court also recognize Congress' broad power to enforce the Civil War Amendments. In Katzenbach v. Morgan, 384 U.S. 641, 86 S.Ct. 1717, 16 L.Ed.2d 828 (1966), the Court held that legislation enacted under authority of § 5 of the Fourteenth Amendment would be upheld so long as the Court could find that the enactment " 'is plainly adapted to [the] end' " of enforcing the Equal Protection Clause and "is not prohibited by but is consistent with 'the letter and spirit of the constitution,' " regardless of whether the practices outlawed by Congress in themselves violated the Equal Protection Clause. Id., at 651. * * *

* * * In the present case, we hold that the Act's ban on electoral changes that are discriminatory in effect is an appropriate method of promoting the purposes of the Fifteenth Amendment, even if it is assumed that § 1 of the Amendment prohibits only intentional discrimination in voting. * * *

C

The appellants next assert that, even if the Fifteenth Amendment authorized Congress to enact the Voting Rights Act, that legislation violates principles of federalism articulated in National League of Cities v. Usery, 426 U.S. 833, 96 S.Ct. 2465, 49 L.Ed.2d 245 (1976). * * * To the contrary, we find no inconsistency between these decisions.

* * *

The decision in *National League of Cities* was based solely on an assessment of congressional power under the Commerce Clause, and we explicitly reserved the question "whether different results might obtain if Congress seeks to affect integral operations of State governments by exercising authority granted it under other sections of the Constitution such as * * * § 5 of the Fourteenth Amendment." Id., at 852, n. 17. The answer to this question came four days later in Fitzpatrick v. Bitzer, 427 U.S. 445, 96 S.Ct. 2666, 49 L.Ed.2d 614 (1976). That case presented the issue whether, in spite of the Eleventh Amendment, Congress had the authority to bring the States as employers within the coverage of Title VII of the Civil Rights Act of 1964, 42 U.S.C. § 2000e et seq., and to provide that successful plaintiffs could recover retroactive monetary relief. The Court held that this extension of Title VII was an appropriate method of enforcing the Fourteenth Amendment * * *.

We agree with the court below that *Fitzpatrick* stands for the proposition that principles of federalism that might otherwise be an obstacle to congressional authority are necessarily overridden by the power to enforce the Civil War Amendments "by appropriate legislation." * * * *National League of Cities*, then, provides no reason to depart from our decision in South Carolina v. Katzenbach. * * *

D

The appellants contend in the alternative that, even if the Act and its preclearance requirement were appropriate means of enforcing the Fifteenth Amendment in 1965, they had outlived their usefulness by 1975, when Congress extended the Act for another seven years. We decline this invitation to overrule Congress' judgment that the 1975 extension was warranted.

* * *

E

As their final constitutional challenge to the Act, the individual appellants argue that, because no elections have been held in Rome since 1974, their First, Fifth, Ninth, and Tenth Amendment rights as private citizens of the city have been abridged. In blaming the Act for this result, these appellants identify the wrong culprit. The Act does not restrict private political expression or prevent a covered jurisdiction from holding elections; rather, it simply provides that elections may be held either under electoral rules in effect on November 1, 1964, or under rules adopted since that time that have been properly precleared. * * * In these circumstances, the city's failure to hold elections can only be attributed to its own officials, and not to the operation of the Act.

IV

* * * we must address the appellants' contentions that the 1966 electoral changes and the annexations disapproved by the Attorney General do not, in fact, have a discriminatory effect. We are mindful that the District Court's findings of fact must be upheld unless they are clearly erroneous.

A

We conclude that the District Court did not clearly err in finding that the city had failed to prove that the 1966 electoral changes would not dilute the effectiveness of the Negro vote in Rome. * * * The 1966 change to the majority vote/runoff election scheme significantly decreased the opportunity for such a Negro candidate since, "even if he gained a plurality of votes in the general election, [he] would still have to face the runner-up white candidate in a head-to-head runoff election in which, given bloc voting by race and a white majority, [he] would be at a severe disadvantage." City of Rome v. United States, 472 F.Supp. 221, 224 (D.C.1979) (footnotes omitted).

* * *

The District Court also found that the city had failed to meet its burden of proving that the 13 disapproved annexations did not dilute the Negro vote in Rome. The city's argument that this finding is clearly erroneous is severely undermined by the fact that it failed to present any evidence shedding meaningful light on how the annexations affected the vote of Rome's Negro community.

* * *

Certain facts are clear, however. In February, 1978, the most recent date for which any population data were compiled, 2,582 whites and only 52 Negroes resided in the disapproved annexed areas. Of these persons, 1,797 whites and only 24 Negroes were of voting age, and 823 whites and only 9 Negroes were registered voters. We must assume that these persons moved to the annexed areas from outside the city, rather than from within the preannexation boundaries of the city, since the city, which bore the burden of proof, presented no evidence to the contrary. * * *

* * * By substantially enlarging the city's number of white eligible voters without creating a corresponding increase in the number of Negroes, the annexations reduced the importance of the votes of Negro citizens who resided within the preannexation boundaries of the city. In these circumstances, the city bore the burden of proving that its electoral system "fairly reflects the strength of the Negro community as it exists after the annexation[s]." City of Richmond v. United States, 422 U.S. 358, 371, 95 S.Ct. 2296, 2304, 45 L.Ed.2d 245 (1975). * * * Particularly in light of the inadequate evidence introduced by the city, this determination cannot be considered to be clearly erroneous.

The judgment of the District Court is affirmed.

It is so ordered.

Note

1. **Impact of Federal Laws Upon Reorganizations.** The Voting Rights Act of 1965 applies to local elections that reorganize electoral districts. Lockhart v. United States, 460 U.S. 125, 103 S.Ct. 998, 74 L.Ed.2d 863 (1983); NAACP v. Hampton Co. Election Comm., 470 U.S. 166, 105 S.Ct. 1128, 84 L.Ed.2d 124 (1985). The Supreme Court held that an annexation reducing the total political strength of a minority race in a city enlarged by annexation did not violate the Act so long as the post-annexation system fairly recognized the minority's political potential in the enlarged community by the use of ward rather than at-large elections.

City of Richmond v. United States, 422 U.S. 358, 95 S.Ct. 2296, 45 L.Ed.2d 245 (1975).

Changes in voting and representation pursuant to government reorganizations must comply with federal constitutional and statutory protections of voter rights, but strict constitutional standards have, however, been relaxed in dealing with local voting districts and boundary changes. See Abate v. Mundt, 403 U.S. 182, 91 S.Ct. 1904, 29 L.Ed.2d 399 (1971); Whitcomb v. Chavis, 403 U.S. 124, 91 S.Ct. 1858, 29 L.Ed.2d 363 (1971); Dixon, *Rebuilding The Urban Political System*, 58 Geo.L.Rev. 955, 974–984 (1970). See also the *Holt* case, p. 259 n. 1, infra, the similar rulings on the exercise of extraterritorial powers, and chapter VI, B.1, dealing with Interstate Districts. In City of Long Beach Resort v. Collins, 261 So.2d 498 (Fla.1972) the court rejected an equal protection attack against a statute that effected a merger of several cities without referendum, but which empowered electors of unincorporated areas to determine whether to join the same merger. The court held that the statutory merger did not deny residents of the consolidated cities equal protection of the laws.

b. *Municipal Approval*

HAMMONDS v. CORPUS CHRISTI, TEXAS

United States District Court, S.D.Texas, 1964.
226 F.Supp. 456.

GARZA, DISTRICT JUDGE. In this cause the Plaintiffs are suing the City of Corpus Christi, Texas, as Defendant, asking that two annexation ordinances of the Defendant be held void * * *.

The City of Corpus Christi is a home rule city and operates under a city charter under Article 11, Section 5, of the Constitution of the State of Texas, Vernon's Ann.St.

A city of over 5,000 inhabitants, such as Corpus Christi, Texas, has the power to adopt or amend its charter subject to such limitations as may be prescribed by the Legislature. Among the enumerated powers granted to such home rule cities by the Legislature is "the power to fix the boundary limits of said city, to provide for the extension of said boundary limits and the annexation of additional territory lying adjacent to said city, * * * according to such rules as may be provided by said charter." Vernon's Annotated Civil Statutes, Art. 1175, subd. 2.

Texas courts have held that the only limitation fixed by the Legislature on the power of a home rule city to annex additional territory is that the territory shall be adjacent to the city and not included within the boundaries of any other municipality. City of Houston v. State ex rel. City of West University Place, 142 Tex. 190, 176 S.W.2d 928; State ex rel. Pan American Production Co. v. Texas City, 157 Tex. 450, 303 S.W.2d 780 (1957), Reh. den.

The City of Corpus Christi has provided the different modes of annexing territory to the city, in Article 1, Sec. 2, of its city charter.

Acting under said city charter provisions, the City of Corpus Christi passed two annexation ordinances which are the ones under attack here. These two ordinances have already been under attack in the State courts, and the validity of said annexation ordinances has been upheld.

The cases in which the validity of said ordinances was attacked by the same attorney representing the Plaintiffs here were the cases of Pennington et al. v. City of Corpus Christi, Tex.Civ.App., 363 S.W.2d 502, and W.L.D. Winship et al. v. City of Corpus Christi [Case No. 15 of the Court of Civil Appeals for the Thirteenth Judicial District of Texas), 373 S.W.2d 844, * * *.

* * *

The annexation of lands to a city or town has been held without exception to be purely a political matter, entirely within the power of the Legislature of the State to regulate.

* * *

In a very fine article on the annexation of new territory by Texas cities, Truman O'Quinn, in 39 Texas Law Review 172, points out that under our present Texas Constitution and statutes, home rule cities in Texas are unbridled in their method of annexation and their actions thereunder.

Although we may disagree with the mode of annexation or annexations themselves, the remedy of those aggrieved is not in the courts, but in the State Legislature.

* * *

It is, therefore, ordered, adjudged and decreed by the Court that this action be and the same is hereby dismissed.

Notes

1. **Municipal Self-Determination.** As shown by the *Hammonds* and *City of Douglas* cases, annexation is generally considered a matter of state-wide, and not purely local, interest, even as to home rule cities. See also Rogers v. Denver, 161 Colo. 72, 419 P.2d 648, 649 (1966); State ex rel. Bowen v. Kreugel, 67 Wash.2d 673, 409 P.2d 458 (1965). For a rare exception, see State ex inf. Hannah v. St. Charles, 676 S.W.2d 508 (Mo. 1984).

Excessive unilateral annexation permits land-grabbing by competing cities and can undermine planned growth. Areas vulnerable to such practices are induced to incorporate defensively into small units, thereby hemming in the core cities. Examples of such counterproductive developments, and of statutory correctives are discussed in Chapman, *The Texas Municipal Annexation Act,* 29 Tex.Bar Journal 165 (1966); Claunch, *Land-Grabbing—Texas Style,* 42 National Mun.Rev. 494 (1953). See also note 4 below.

2. **Anti-Incorporation Laws—Buffer Zones.** "Part of the problem lies in the ease with which new municipalities may be incorporated on the urban fringe, strangling the growth of central cities and compounding the

task of constructing local governments that are metropolitan both in function and jurisdiction." Mandelker, *Municipal Incorporation on the Urban Fringe,* XVIII La.L.Rev. 628 (1958); * see also, ACIR, supra, p. 39. A number of states, notably, Arizona, Georgia, Idaho, Nebraska, New Mexico, North Carolina, Ohio, and Wyoming have enacted legislation to prohibit preemption of fringe territory by suburban annexations, or by new suburban incorporation. See e.g. Fort Lauderdale v. Hacienda Village, Inc., 172 So.2d 451 (Fla.1965) (prevention of suburban annexation in metro area); Kelley v. Willowbrook, 38 Ill.App.2d 112, 186 N.E.2d 369 (1962) (limiting incorporation in border areas). Other statutory and decisional authorities are collected in Note—*Stumbling Giant,* supra, 87–89.

3. **Border Area Controls.** Different annexation powers are commonly extended to different types of municipalities. Thus legislatures may grant *unilateral* annexation powers only to home rule or large cities, or with respect to unincorporated land that is urban in character, i.e., ready for urban development. See e.g. People ex rel. Redford v. Burley, 86 Idaho 519, 388 P.2d 996 (1964) (contiguous platted land); City of Millard v. Omaha, 185 Neb. 617, 177 N.W.2d 576 (1970); State ex rel. Kreamer v. Overland Park, 192 Kan. 654, 391 P.2d 128 (1964).

4. **Inter-County Annexations.** Some states prohibit annexation across county lines. Ark.Stat. § 19–307; Official Code Ga.Ann. § 36–36–23; cf. Kans.Stat.Ann. 12–502. Others expressly authorize municipal annexation in a foreign county. See West's Ann.Cal.Gov.Code, § 35305; Minn.Stat.Ann. § 413.15; Neb.Rev.Stat. § 17–406; Or.Rev.Stat. § 222.111. Courts in other states hold that the factor of cross-county territory should be considered though the governing statute is silent on that subject. See In re Conewago Township, 209 Pa.Super. 426, 431, 228 A.2d 212, 214 (1967); Town of Mt. Carmel v. Kingsport, 217 Tenn. 298, 397 S.W.2d 379 (1965). Should power to annex land in another county be implied? Compare: Barton v. Omaha, 180 Neb. 752, 145 N.W.2d 444 (1966) (metropolitan city denied such power) with, Board of County Commissioners of Jefferson County v. Denver, 150 Colo. 198, 372 P.2d 152 (1969) (constitutional home rule city held to have such power).

c. *Impartial Tribunals*

JOHNSTON v. FAIRFAX

Supreme Court of Appeals of Virginia, 1970.
211 Va. 378, 177 S.E.2d 606.

I'ANSON, JUSTICE. This proceeding was instituted * * * by petitioners Edward C. Johnston and one hundred and eight-one other persons, constituting more than fifty-one per centum of the qualified voters residing in an area of Fairfax County adjacent to the City of Falls Church, seeking its annexation to the City of Falls Church. * * * The city favored annexation of the area, and the county opposed it. Subsequently, Elizabeth A. Blystone and twenty-three

* Reprinted by permission of Louisiana Law Review. Copyright © 1958.

other persons, residents of the city, intervened in favor of the annexation, and J.W. Marriott, Jr., Richard E. Marriott, and Eugene Hooper, owners of a tract of land containing approximately 33 acres zoned for high-rise apartments and commercial use in the area sought to be annexed, intervened in opposition.

* * * The court held, Judge Haas dissenting, that the petitioners had not carried the burden of proving the necessity for and expediency of the annexation, and dismissed the petition. * * *

* * *

The area sought to be annexed is a 200–acre tract, * * *. Most of the area is zoned for single-family residences. Two Falls Church city schools are located in the area. The two schools and a recreation area connected with one of them occupy 22 percent of the land. The vacant land consists of three parcels of approximately 44 acres.

The streets in the annexation area are extensions of the city's system. For the most part they lack curbs, gutters and sidewalks. There are no street lights in the area except those erected by the city near its schools. Trash and garbage are collected by the county and private collectors. The area is sewered partly by the county and partly by the city, and sewage is treated in the county's sewage treatment plant. The city purchases water from an agency of the federal government and sells it to the residents. Fire protection is provided by the city's volunteer fire department, which is integrated with the county's fire department and is financed by the city and Fairfax and Arlington Counties. The county provides police protection.

Falls Church became a city of the second class on August 16, 1948. * * * Approximately 11,500 persons live within its two-square-mile area. There were 114 acres of unimproved land in the city when this proceeding was instituted. The city has an efficient and well-managed school system, * * *. It has a library, recreation areas, and equipment for removal of snow from its streets. Approximately one-third of its streets do not have curbs and gutters. The city does not have a sewage disposal plant, a sanitary land-fill, or an incinerator, and is dependent upon the county through contracts to render the services provided by such facilities. It has no hospital, and its residents use the hospital facilities of Fairfax and Arlington Counties and the District of Columbia. It has a part-time health officer, and its welfare cases are handled through the Department of Public Welfare of the county. The business area of the city is composed mostly of retail stores. A major portion of its residents shop in large shopping centers and department stores in the adjacent counties of Arlington and Fairfax. * * *

The County of Fairfax is a large county with an area of approximately 400 square miles and a population of over 416,000. It operates under the urban county executive form of government, and provides to its residents all the services and facilities that are usually furnished by a municipality, except in its undeveloped rural areas. It has an excellent school system * * * It has a large and efficient police department, a large library with many branches throughout the county, and a park authority to administer its many parks. In 1967 it embarked on a county-wide program of street lighting. Under this program all the residential areas and major highway systems will be completely lighted. Schools and other public facilities are in close proximity to the proposed annexation area. One of its schools is located in the City of Falls Church. * * *

There is some community of interest between the annexation area and the city. Approximately 19 percent of the people in the annexation area work in Falls Church. Some of the residents attend church in the city, are members of its civic clubs, use the city's library, bank there, are served by its doctors and dentist, and patronize its stores. * * *

* * *

Appellants contend that the court erroneously required them to prove that the annexation was in the best interests of the county. * * *

Subsection (b) of Code § 15.1–1041 sets forth the general guide for determining whether the corporate limits of a particular municipality should be expanded. It reads as follows:

"The court shall determine the necessity for and expediency of annexation, considering the best interests of the county and the city or town, the best interests, services to be rendered and needs of the area proposed to be annexed, and the best interests of the remaining portion of the county." * * *

In City of Roanoke v. County of Roanoke, 204 Va. 157, 161–162, 129 S.E.2d 711, 714 (1963), we said that the onus is upon the city to show the necessity for and expediency of annexation, taking into consideration the best interests of the county, the city, and the area sought to be annexed.*

What was obviously meant by the language used in the three cases above referred to and in the present case was that the proponents of annexation must prove the necessity for and expediency of annexation, and in making this determination the court is to take into consideration the best interests of the county, the city, and the territory to be annexed, and to "balance the equities" of all interests affected by the proceeding.

It appears from the opinion of the majority of the annexation court that after it considered the best interests of all the entities affected and balanced the equities, it found that the appellants had not proved the necessity for and expediency of the annexation in that it was not in the best interests of the city and the territory to be annexed. Hence we find no justification for a reversal of this case on the point raised.

---

* A similar standard is provided by Wash.Rev.Code §§ 55.13, 173 (1965).

The appellants next argue that the court's majority opinion erroneously construed Code § 15.1–1041(b), by requiring the city to prove that the municipal services of the city were equal to or better than services offered by the county.

Appellant's argument is based on a statement, taken out of context, in the written opinion of the majority of the court, that "with certain minor exceptions, the services furnished by Fairfax County are equal to or superior to the services rendered by the City of Falls Church."
* * *

Code § 15.1–1041(b) requires the court to consider the "services to be rendered and needs of the area proposed to be annexed." This the court did, and its comment * * * does not indicate that the majority of the court required appellants to prove that the services to be rendered by the city would be equal to or superior to the services rendered by the county. * * *

Lastly, the appellants contend that the court erred in holding that they had not borne the burden of proving the necessity for and expediency of annexation.

Appellants say that since this proceeding was instituted by "79 percent" of the qualified voters of the area sought to be annexed, their wishes "should be given the weight of a jury verdict on the question of need and services to be rendered." We do not agree.

While the wishes of the qualified voters of an area proposed to be annexed should be given consideration in determining the best interests of the parties affected, such do not control the decision of the court. Fairfax County v. Town of Fairfax, 201 Va. 362, 369, 111 S.E.2d 428, 433 (1959).

Before an annexation court may extend a city's boundaries the court must be satisfied, and the evidence must support the findings, that the proposed annexation is both necessary and expedient. County of Norfolk v. City of Portsmouth, 186 Va. 1032, 1045, 45 S.E.2d 136, 142 (1947). This principle is applicable in all annexation proceedings, whether they are brought, as in the present case, by fifty-one per centum of the qualified voters of the area sought to be annexed under Code § 15.1–1034, or by a city under the provisions of Code § 15.1–1033. Mowry v. City of Virginia Beach, 198 Va. 205, 209, 93 S.E.2d 323, 326 (1956).

* * *

No single factor controls in determining the necessity for and expediency of annexation. Fairfax County v. Town of Fairfax, *supra*, 201 Va. at 368, 111 S.E.2d at 433.

On appeal, a presumption of correctness attends the decision of the annexation court on all questions of fact. The decision will not be disturbed by us unless it is plainly wrong or is without credible evidence to support it. City of Roanoke v. County of Roanoke, *supra*,

204 Va. at 161, 129 S.E.2d at 714; Rockingham County v. Timberville, *supra,* 201 Va. at 307, 110 S.E.2d at 393–394.

In addition to hearing the evidence *ore tenus* the annexation court judges visited and studied the areas affected. They saw the physical properties under the control of the city and had an opportunity to observe and study the services rendered by the municipality. They observed and studied the services that were being rendered by the county and the needs of the area sought to be annexed.

* * *

We find that there is credible evidence to sustain the holding of the majority of the annexation court, and the judgment is

Affirmed.

Notes

1. **Annexation Standards.** In the absence of explicit statutory standards should courts assess the public interest by considering the interests of the entire region that is affected by annexation, and not merely those of the annexor and annexee territory? Wisconsin employs a "rule of reason" which precludes mechanical application of narrow standards where such could defeat the goal of orderly growth. City of Beloit v. Beloit, Turtle, and Rock, 47 Wis.2d 377, 177 N.W.2d 361 (1970).

The most commonly employed annexation standards are discussed in Note, *Stumbling Giant,* supra, 81–89; F. Sengstock, *Annexation: A Solution to the Metropolitan Area Problem,* 42–50; Woodruff, *Systems and Standards of Municipal Annexation Review: A Comparative Analysis,* 58 Geo.L.Rev. 743, 744 et seq. (1970). See also Annot., *What Land is Contiguous or Adjacent to Municipality so as to be Subject to Annexation,* 49 A.L.R. 3d 589 (1973).

2. **Judicial Determinations.** Virginia courts admittedly exercise legislative discretion in annexation proceedings (City of Falls Church v. Board of Supervisors, 193 Va. 112, 114, 68 S.E.2d 96, 98 (1951), but the leading case of Henrico County v. Richmond, 106 Va. 282, 55 S.E.2d 683 (1903), upheld statutory delegation of annexation decisions to special courts. Since Virginia courts are empowered to modify and redraw annexation proposals, are they not resolving political questions akin to those reviewed by the United States Supreme Court in the electoral districting cases? Cf. Campbell v. Lincoln, 182 Neb. 459, 155 N.W.2d 444 (1968); City of Ceres v. Modesto, 274 Cal.App.2d 545, 79 Cal.Rptr. 168 (1969). For a favorable appraisal of the Virginia system, see C. Bain, *Annexation in Virginia* 210 et seq. (1966).

Several states have adopted the Virginia approach. Ark.Stat. § 19–302; West's Ann.Ind.Code § 48–701(a); Kentucky Rev.Stat. 81.110; Neb. Rev.Stat. § 16–108. Idaho, Mississippi, South Dakota, Tennessee, Utah and Wyoming also have statutes employing judicial panels in specified circumstances. See Woodruff, supra, 765 n. 94.

VILLAGE OF FARMINGTON v. MINNESOTA MUNICIPAL COMMISSION

Supreme Court of Minnesota, 1969.
284 Minn. 125, 170 N.W.2d 197.

[Finding that consolidation of Lakeville Township with Lakeville Village was in best interest of public, held not to constitute a determination that such consolidation would better serve entire area than annexation of part of Lakeville Township by Village of Farmington; and, thus, insufficient to support Commission's consolidation order.]

ROGOSHESKE, JUSTICE. This appeal requires us to review orders of the District Court of Dakota County (1) affirming * * * an order of the Minnesota Municipal Commission granting a petition to consolidate Lakeville township with the village of Lakeville; and (2) affirming the commission's statutory denial of a petition to annex 195 acres of the township to the adjoining village of Farmington.

On April 13, 1965, a majority of landowners by number and area filed a petition pursuant to Minn.St. c. 414, which created the Minnesota Municipal Commission, to have 195 acres of unplatted and unincorporated land in Lakeville township annexed to the village of Farmington. Both the village of Farmington and the township of Lakeville are located in Dakota County, * * * Farmington, which then had a population of about 2,500, is located in Empire township, * * *. The 195-acre tract sought to be annexed is irregular in shape. * * * This tract contains 13 parcels of land and has a population of 45. * * *

After the village council of Farmington set a date for public hearing on the petition to annex, objections were filed by Lakeville township and the village of Lakeville, thereby automatically transferring jurisdiction over the petition to the Minnesota Municipal Commission. * * *

On July 2, 1965, a resolution and petition for consolidation of the village of Lakeville and the entire Lakeville township into a single new municipality, which included the 195 acres involved in the Farmington annexation petition, were filed with the commission pursuant to § 414.02, subd. 5(1). The 48-square-mile of Lakeville township, which includes the village of Lakeville, contains 30,720 acres, 144 of which comprise the village. At the time the consolidation petition was filed, the estimated populations of the township and the village were 3,208 and 982, respectively.

* * *

* * * Counsel for Farmington, Lakeville township, and the village of Lakeville stipulated that the testimony and exhibits introduced in the hearings conducted on each of the petitions would become part of the record in both proceedings. No further hearings were held on either petition.

* * *

On October 20, 1966, the commission issued findings of fact, conclusions of law, and an order consolidating Lakeville township and the village of Lakeville into a single new municipality. Separate appeals from this order were filed in the District Court of Dakota County * * *. The district court affirmed the consolidation order * * * and affirmed the statutory denial of the annexation petition as reasonable in the face of the evidence supporting consolidation.

All appellants below appealed * * *.

* * *

1. Appellants argue that the Minnesota Municipal Commission did not have jurisdiction either to consider or to act upon the consolidation petition until it had disposed of the annexation petition, since the latter was filed first. In support of that position, they cite State ex rel. Harrier v. Village of Spring Lake Park, 245 Minn. 302, 71 N.W.2d 812. In that case, incorporation proceedings were begun relative to unincorporated land * * *. This situation resulted from the existence of independent statutory procedures for incorporation and annexation which could be utilized simultaneously, * * *. In order to prevent such perverse results, we adopted a "first-in-time-first-in-right" rule, holding that the incorporation proceeding, which was commenced first, had priority over the annexation proceeding, which was commenced later even though completed first.

The entire complexion of the problem * * * has, however, been changed by the enactment of c. 414 creating the Minnesota Municipal Commission as an independent administrative agency vested with broad powers to facilitate the orderly growth of Minnesota municipalities. The commission has jurisdiction over both consolidation and annexation proceedings * * * Thus, unlike the situation which prevailed at the time of the Spring Lake Park case, the ultimate decision on both petitions can now be made by a single administrative agency. Since the * * * basis necessary for the application of the "first-in-time-first-in-right" rule does not exist, it cannot be accepted as controlling in this case.

Moreover, c. 414 authorizes the chairman of the commission to consolidate "separate hearings in the interest of economy and expedience" and vests in the commission broad powers to increase or decrease the area proposed for annexation. * * * It is clear therefore that the legislature necessarily intended to authorize simultaneous consideration of such petitions. * * *

While no formal order consolidating the hearings on the petitions was made, * * * it was stipulated that the evidence and exhibits submitted regarding each were to be considered by the commission as evidence pertaining to both. * * * we hold that the commission had jurisdiction to consider and act upon the petitions in any sequence it deemed appropriate to carry out its administrative function and the underlying purpose of c. 414.

2. In considering appellants' claims that the commission's failure to grant annexation and its order of consolidation are unjustified by the evidence and therefore arbitrary and capricious, an understanding of the statutory provisions governing the proceedings under review is necessary.

The 1959 act creating the commission was intended to recodify and revise traditional procedural and substantive laws governing incorporation of new municipalities and changes in the boundaries of existing municipalities in Minnesota. It was designed to eliminate many of the difficulties which had arisen under prior statutes * * * by delegating to the commission, as a statewide administrative agency, broad powers to facilitate the orderly growth of Minnesota municipalities * * *.

While the commission is given discretionary power to approve or reject annexation petitions, § 414.03, subd. 4, provides that after a hearing, when required under c. 414, "the commission *shall* approve if it finds that the property to be annexed is now, or is about to become, urban or suburban in character." (Italics supplied.) This same section sets forth as a "guide" * * * 10 "factors" concerning which it requires the commission to make findings. The commission also has almost unlimited discretionary authority to alter the boundaries of the area to be annexed and to approve annexation of the area so altered. * * *

Section 414.02, subd. 5, grants the commission similar, although more limited and less clearly expressed, powers with respect to proceedings for the consolidation of an existing municipality and all or part of an adjoining township. * * * More important to this case is the statutory mandate requiring a denial of consolidation "if it appears that annexation * * * would better serve the interests of the area" sought to be incorporated by consolidation. § 414.02, subd. 3. As we interpret this provision, it manifests a strong legislative preference for annexation of unincorporated areas. Applied to this case, where all of the unincorporated area of Lakeville township was found by the commission to be or about to become urban or suburban in character, annexation of the area adjoining Farmington as proposed or as modified by the commission is to be preferred over consolidation with Lakeville.

The question thus arises as to the basis for the commission's approval of consolidation rather than annexation of the area adjoining Farmington. * * *

Had the chairman of the commission ordered consolidated hearings of these petitions pursuant to § 414.01, subd. 5, the problem confronting us might not have arisen, for the commission could then have justifiably delayed its decision of the consolidation petition pending the outcome of the appeal. * * *

As noted, § 414.02, subd. 5, requires the commission, in passing upon a consolidation petition, to make findings * * *. That section requires that "the commission *shall* approve the petition for incorporation if it finds that the property to be incorporated is now, or is about to become, urban or suburban in character." (Italics supplied.) The commission did specifically find that "[t]he entire area to be incorporated is or is about to become urban or suburban in character," and this finding, although challenged, is adequately supported by the record. Having made this determination, the commission * * * compelled to approve consolidation unless "it appears that annexation to an adjoining municipality would better serve the interests of the area." § 414.02, subd. 3. This legislative policy preferring annexation of unincorporated lands expressly requires the commission to consider and make a specific finding upon the question of whether annexation to an adjoining municipality would better serve the interests of all or any part of the area involved in the consolidation petition than consolidation would. Indeed, such a finding is required even though a conflicting petition seeking annexation * * * has not been filed. * * * The commission, in our opinion, made no specific finding on this issue. * * *

* * *

As reluctant as we usually are to interfere with the actions of an administrative agency in a case such as this, we are compelled to remand the entire matter to the district court with directions to vacate the commission's consolidation order and remand it to the commission. * * * we also direct the district court to vacate its order * * * and remand it to permit the commission to consolidate the proceedings, reconsider the entire matter, and make such findings as are required by §§ 414.02, subd. 3, and 414.03, subd. 4, based upon the record herein and upon such other evidence as the parties might now submit.

* * *

Notes

1. **Annexation vs. Consolidation.** Legislative preference for annexation over consolidation may rest upon the following considerations. Consolidation historically required concurrent majorities in each unit to be merged. Consolidation poses a threat kindred to defensive incorporations. Boundary commissions may be better positioned to assure provident annexations than to prevent improvident consolidations. The integration of all obligations and assets held by consolidated units may prove more troublesome than the transfer of physical territory. See Bouldin v. Homewood, 277 Ala. 665, 174 So.2d 306 (1965).

2. **State-wide vs. Local Boundary Commissions.** The impartial tribunals established in various states to administer boundary laws fall into three general categories: (1) preexisting local agencies carrying out other primary duties, e.g. county commissions or county courts; (2) mixed panels of municipal, county, and outside officials, See e.g., the Virginia annexation courts, the California and Washington local boundary commissions (West's Ann.California Government Code §§ 54780–54782; West's Rev.Code Wash. Ann. 58.(1); Mid-County Future Alternatives Committee v. Portland Metropolitan Area Local Govt. Boundary Comm'n, 300 Or. 14, 706 P.2d 924

(1985); and (3) a central commission of state-wide jurisdiction. See e.g., Alaska Stat. 07.10.010–40, 44.19.250, 44.19.260. For a review of the use of these devices, see Note—*The Minnesota Municipal Commission—Statewide Administrative Review of Municipal Annexations and Incorporations*, 50 Minn.L.Rev. 911 at 916–918 (1966); Johnson, *The Wisconsin Experience With State Level Review of Municipal Incorporations, Consolidations and Annexations*, 1965 Wis.L.Rev. 462. Liberal states have authorized commissions to initiate or modify boundary proposals on their own motion. See *Notes on 1969 Amendments on Minnesota's Incorporation, Consolidation, Annexation and Detachment Statutes*, 54 Minn.L.Rev. 1052 (1970); and the Oesau case following these notes.

Many commentators favor a specialized statewide commission which can develop comprehensive expertise and consistent statewide policies. See F. Sengstock, *Annexation: A Solution To The Metropolitan Area Problem*, 118–119; Note, supra, 50 Minn.L.Rev. at 916–918 (1966).

3. **Procedural Gambits to Forestall Boundary Changes.** Uncoordinated boundary change statutes that permit a prior petition to place a moratorium on later related proposals invite artificial races to the courthouse. While the Farmington view prevails in some jurisdictions (see e.g. State ex rel. Hannan v. DeCourcey, 18 Ohio St.2d 73, 247 N.E.2d 465 (1969)), the majority appears to follow the older rule of exclusionary jurisdiction. Fuller v. San Bernardino Valley Mun. Water Dist., 242 Cal. App.2d 52, 51 Cal.Rptr. 120 (1966); Landis v. Roseburg, 243 Or. 44, 411 P.2d 282 (1966); City of Joplin v. Shoal Creek Drive, 434 S.W.2d 25 (Mo.1968).

OESAU v. DILLINGHAM

Supreme Court of Alaska, 1968.
439 P.2d 180.

DIMOND, JUSTICE. * * * Article X, Section 7 of the Alaska Constitution provides that cities may be dissolved "in a manner prescribed by law." The legislature has provided for the dissolution of cities * * *. These statutes generally provide for dissolution upon an election when the population of a city drops below a certain number, or upon a court order after a finding that a city has ceased to function as a city government. Since none of these methods was followed * * * appellants maintain that Wood River was not dissolved "in the manner provided by law", and therefore still exists as a municipal corporation in its own right.

The local boundary commission has the constitutional authority to "consider any proposed local government boundary change." It may present any such proposed change to the legislature, and the change becomes effective "forty-five days after presentation or at the end of the session, whichever is earlier, unless disapproved by a resolution concurred in by a majority of the members of each house."

In Fairview Public Utility District No. 1 v. City of Anchorage we held that the authority vested in the local boundary commission by the Constitution was sufficient to effect, by means of a local government boundary change proposed by the commission, the annexation to the City of Anchorage of the Fairview Public Utility District No. 1, an area entirely surrounded by the city. The situation here is not dissimilar. The fourth class city of Wood River was encompassed within the boundaries of the second class City of Dillingham. Although the boundary commission's proposal was to confirm the boundaries of the City of Dillingham and to dissolve the city of Wood River, rather than to annex Wood River to Dillingham, the effect is the same. When the legislature failed to disapprove of the commission's proposal, the commission's local boundary change, which consisted of the abolition of the boundary of Wood River and the confirmation of the boundary of the City of Dillingham, had the effect of making Wood River a part of the City of Dillingham.

When the boundary commission's proposal for boundary change became effective, the city of Wood River was dissolved, even though the statutory procedures for dissolution of cities were not followed. The basic purpose for creating the boundary commission * * * was to obviate the type of situation that existed here where there was a controversy over municipal boundaries which apparently could not be settled at the local level. * * * When the boundary change became effective, the city of Wood River was extinguished as a municipal corporation and its property, powers and duties were then vested in the City of Dillingham.

The judgment is affirmed.

Notes

1. New Mexico has a statewide boundary commission, but its discretion is more limited by statute. N.M.Stat.Ann. § 14-7-12. The Local Agency Formation Commission of California is required to pass upon the formation and dissolution of municipalities and special districts, as well as upon annexations. West's Ann.Cal.Gov.Code § 54773 et seq.; San Mateo County Harbor District v. Board of Supervisors of San Mateo County, 273 Cal.App.2d 195, 77 Cal.Rptr. 871 (1969).

2. **Effects of Annexation—Adjustment Problems.** Once completed, annexation gives rise to a host of special problems concerning the disposition of assets and obligations of the affected units; the applicability of tax, regulatory and other laws in the annexed territory; and the rights of private parties having claims to franchises, public employment, or other interests in the annexed area. The subject is too specialized to treat in this book, but the following case illustrates the dislocating effects of annexation.

CITY OF MESA v. SALT RIVER PROJECT AGRICULTURAL IMPROVEMENT AND POWER DISTRICT

Supreme Court of Arizona, 1962.
92 Ariz. 91, 373 P.2d 722.

WILLIAM W. NABOURS, SUPERIOR COURT JUDGE.

[Action by the City of Mesa against the Salt River Project Agricultural Improvement and Power District to determine their respective rights to supply electrical energy in areas within and adjacent to the corporate limits of the City. The District by counterclaim sought to restrain the City from competing with the District or interfering with its operations. From a judgment in favor of the District the City appeals.]

* * *

* * * In October 1917, the City acquired the electrical distribution system of the Southside Gas and Electric Company serving the town, together with water and gas distribution systems and since has furnished all three utilities to its residents. * * *

The District is an agricultural improvement district organized * * * for the purpose of reclaiming lands susceptible of irrigation. The predecessor in interest to the District was the Salt River Valley Water Users Association, incorporated in 1903, under the General Corporation Laws of the Territory of Arizona. At the time of its organization the townsites of Phoenix, Tempe and Mesa were excluded from its boundaries. * * *

In 1929 the Central Arizona Light & Power Company, the City of Mesa and the District served electrical energy in Maricopa County. In general the service areas of the Central Arizona Light & Power Company were the incorporated areas of Maricopa County excluding the City of Mesa. The service of the City was confined to its incorporated limits with certain exceptions not of importance here. Prior to 1929 the Salt River Valley Water Users Association provided some retail electric service in rural areas, and supplied power at wholesale to Central Arizona Light & Power Company, and after 1922 and until 1949 to the City. In 1928 the Salt River Valley Water Users Association embarked upon a plan to provide electric service to rural areas in the Salt River Valley not then being served. Hydro-generating plants were constructed on the Salt River and a transmission system covering the entire area was shortly thereafter completed. Funds for this program were provided by the issuance of bonds.

* * *

The great growth and development of the Salt River Valley and Maricopa County consistent with suburban living has resulted in the District greatly expanding its facilities and service. In the years following the adoption of the District's rural electrification program tens of thousands of people established homes within the District's boundaries and the District has increased and continues to increase its generative and distributive facilities. Its bonded indebtedness at the time of trial was $55,000,000. As a result of the District's expanding its lines and increasing its services and facilities together with the annexations made by the City whereby it extended its incorporated limits, the District is now serving customers within the City whom the City wishes to supply by its electrical services and facilities. The District refuses either to remove, abandon or sell its facilities now valued at over $900,000 in the areas in dispute or to desist from serving new customers where it has been doing business, claiming the right to continue to serve without competition and to expand its service therein without limit.

The City claims as a minimum that it has the exclusive right to serve all areas within its corporate limits, even though the same were acquired or extended by annexation and were being served by the District prior to annexation. It urges that a municipal corporation has the exclusive control of its streets and alleyways and only the City can authorize the use of such streets and alleys for public utility purposes, and that no municipality or political subdivision may acquire a franchise to serve or a right to use the City's streets and alleyways within its territorial limits without its consent.

The District's exact status escapes a simple definition. It is not a "public service corporation" as set forth in the Constitution, Art. 15, § 2, A.R.S. and is not subject to regulation by the corporation commission as to its services and rates. State ex rel. Jones v. MacDonald, 76 Ariz. 401, 265 P.2d 454. It is denominated a political subdivison of the state and entitled to all the immunities and benefits granted to municipalities by the Constitution or statutes, Constitution, Art. 13, § 7 [Amendment of 1940]. Yet as a political subdivision its powers are obviously limited to the purposes justifying its political existence. * * * But whatever may be the District's exact status, plainly, the effect of selling electricity to the ultimate consumer at retail is to place the District in the position of engaging in business as a public utility for this is a business traditionally affected with public interest.

Essentially, three principal questions are raised by the overlapping of interest. First, can the District be required to terminate its electric service within the disputed areas by reason of the City's annexation. * * *

The District asserts an unrestricted right to use the streets and alleyways of the City * * *. As to the Constitution, the District claims by reason of Art. 13, § 7 thereof that its powers are as broad and its immunities equal to those of a municipal corporation. Still the District may not claim by this provision more than a municipality could claim under like circumstances. Elsewhere in either the organic law, the statutes or the common law must be found support for the claimed right.

The District in part rests its claim to a continued use of the City's streets and alleyways on A.R.S. § 45–936, subd. A wherein the sale of electric power by the District is authorized in order to reduce the cost of irrigation. The District here is really claiming two rights: first, the right to sell electric power and second, to that end, the right to utilize the streets and alleyways within the incorporated limits of the City without its consent. The first, if construed to include the latter, would conflict with the express language of A.R.S. § 9–240, subd. B, providing that the common councils of cities shall have the right to exercise *exclusive* control over their streets, alleys, avenues and sidewalks. Such a right can not be inferred as it clashes with accepted statutory construction.

The accepted principle is that courts will not render an interpretation of statutes which makes them contradictory to each other but must, if sound reason and good conscience allow, construe statutes in harmony. S.H. Kress & Co. v. Superior Court of Maricopa County, 66 Ariz. 67, 182 P.2d 931. If there is inferred from the right to sell power the right to use the City's streets and alleys for that purpose, the two statutes would be contradictory and not in harmony. A construction denying the inference sought to be given harmonizes the express right to sell electricity with the exclusive control of streets and alleyways lodged in the City.

The District further claims the right to use the City's streets and alleyways on the language of A.R.S. § 45–938, subd. C, providing:

> "C. The district shall have the use of and a right of way is expressly granted to it to locate, construct and maintain *the works* over, through and upon any of the lands which are the property of the state or any subdivision or institution thereof." (Italics supplied.)

It is to be noticed that subsection C refers to "the works". This is a reference to the preceding subsection A which authorizes the District to construct, " * * * *any of the works* necessary to carry out any provision of this chapter, across any stream of water, watercourse, street, avenue, highway, railway, canal, ditch or flume which * * * the district may intersect * * *."

Statutes must be construed as a whole * * *. Together subsections A and C do not import a special grant of power to enter into the distribution of electricity as a business in competition within the City without its consent. The whole of A.R.S. § 45–938 simply grants a right of way to pass over, through and upon any lands * * * where the works of the District intersect or cross. Such a statute does not confer a right to construct works longitudinally in a street. Town of New Castle v. Lake Erie & W.R. Co., 155 Ind. 18, 57 N.E. 516.

While the claim of the District to the use of the streets and alleys of the City does not find support in either Art. 13, § 7 of the Constitution of Arizona or the legislative enactments referred to, it is nonetheless certain that the District may not be required by the City to terminate its operations in the annexed areas without just compensation. * * * The District thus has been projected in a major fashion into the business of supplying electric power at retail to the ultimate consumer.

While we reject the claim of the District to the use of the streets and alleys within the incorporated limits of the City based upon the Constitution, Art. 13, § 7 and the statutes, A.R.S. §§ 45–936 and 45–938, this does not mean that the City may compel the District to terminate its services in the disputed areas simply because of their incorporation within the municipal limits. * * * The District by its investment has committed itself to a public utility undertaking plainly accepting the grant of the state to engage in that business. By such conduct a property right has been created which is protected by the Constitution, Art. 2, § 25 forbidding the enactment of any law impairing the obligation of contract. Russell v. Sebastian, 233 U.S. 195, 34 S.Ct. 517, 58 L.Ed. 912; and see Blount v. MacDonald, 18 Ariz. 1, 155 P. 736.

* * *

If the District has been using private rights of way or a claimed easement, the use is permissive and property within the meaning of Art. 2, § 17, Constitution of Arizona forbidding the taking or damaging thereof without just compensation. The City can not under the guise of a legislative grant to enlarge its corporate limits impair rights so protected.

We therefore hold that the District may not without just compensation be ousted from doing business in the disputed areas nor from the streets and alleys taken over by the City at the time of annexation or thereafter. What we have said is not, however, to be understood as exempting the District from the effect of reasonable regulatory ordinances controlling the uses of its highways and alleys.

Second, it is the City's position that if it may not oust the District from doing business, it has the right to compete with it in the disputed areas. While ordinarily two municipal corporations may not occupy the same territory and exercise the same authority and control over it and the population at the same time, South Park Com'rs v. Chicago City Ry. Co., 286 Ill. 504, 122 N.E. 89, and see 2 McQuillin, Municipal Corporations § 7.08 (3rd ed. 1949), this is true only as to governmental functions and not those of a proprietary nature. Public Utility District No. 1 v. Town of Newport, 38 Wash.2d 221, 228 P.2d 766. Here both parties are engaged in what is normally considered to be a proprietary or business function. Taylor v. Roosevelt Irr. Dist., 71 Ariz. 254, 226 P.2d 154, and could freely compete unless sound reasons required a contrary conclusion.

The right to compete with the District in the disputed localities has been expressly denied by the legislature in its enactment of A.R.S. § 9–516, subd. A. This statute clearly expresses the public policy of the estate forbidding the competition of the City with the District in this language:

"A. It is declared as the public policy of the state that when adequate public utility service under authority of law is being rendered in an area, within or without the boundaries of a city or town, a competing service and installation shall not be authorized, instituted, made or carried on by a city or town unless or until that portion of the plant, system and business of the utility used and useful in rendering such service in the area in which the city or town seeks to serve, has been acquired."

* * *

The City predicates its right to compete with the District upon a claim of exclusive power to franchise utility undertakings within the confines of its incorporated limits. This claim is opposed to the general rule enunciated in 12 McQuillin, Municipal Corporations § 34.10 (3rd ed. 1950):

"The power to grant franchises resides in the state; and a city, in granting a franchise, acts as agent for the state * * *."

This must necessarily be true since all powers of government are lodged in the people, Constitution, Art. 2, § 2, exercised by the state subject to constitutional limitations. State ex rel. Davis v. Osborne, 14 Ariz. 185, 125 P. 884. The City derives its powers from the Constitution and the legislature and has only such powers as are expressly granted or can be reasonably implied therefrom. Town of Holbrook v. Nutting, 57 Ariz. 360, 114 P.2d 226.

* * *

It is urged that A.R.S. § 9–516, if construed to prevent the City from competing with the District within the limits of the City, is unconstitutional. This is predicated upon the language of Art. 13, § 5 of the Constitution which it is asserted gives to the City the unrestricted right to engage in the electric utility service within and without its corporate limits. Art. 13, § 5 reads:

"Every municipal corporation within this State shall have the right to engage in any business or enterprise which may be engaged in by a person, firm, or corporation by virtue of a franchise from said municipal corporation."

The consequences of the City's argument might follow if we were to hold the City was without the means to acquire the District's property in the incorporated area by eminent domain but we do not so hold.

This brings us to the third major question presented in this appeal. It is the City's position that if by annexation the District is not ousted from doing business and using the streets and alleys of the City and if it may not compete with the District, then it may acquire the District's facilities by eminent domain. In this we think the City is correct and that the trial court erred.

* * *

We have heretofore noted that the District's power to sell electricity is a power incidental to its primary purpose of providing water for irrigation. Property may be taken which is already appropriated to some public use if it appears that the public use to which it is to be applied is a more necessary public use. A.R.S. § 12–1112, subsection 3. * * *

The authority of the City to acquire by condemnation the interests of the District is clear from an examination of A.R.S. §§ 9–521 and 9–522. * * *

The District argues that by subsection B of A.R.S. § 9–516 the City's right is restricted to acquiring the facilities of a "public service corporation" by eminent domain. We do not think this necessarily follows. A.R.S. § 9–522 was originally enacted in 1943 and A.R.S. § 9–516 was enacted in 1954—Chapter 105, Laws of 1954. Chapter 105, section 2 of the Laws of 1954 was specifically named as an amendment to Art. 6, Ch. 16 of the Code of 1939 "by adding" the subsection under consideration. Since no repeal was declared in the Act, presumably the legislature did not consider the contents as in conflict with other portions of the same chapter. [Chapter 16 of the 1939 Code as supplemented].

The District's interpretation would effect a repeal by implication of that portion of A.R.S. § 9–522, initially Chapter 31, Laws of 1943, which authorizes the acquisition of electric light or power plants or systems as utility undertakings. While a statute may be repealed by implication as well as by direct language, such repeals are not favored and will not be indulged if there is any other reasonable construction. Southern Pac. Co. v. Gila County, 56 Ariz. 499, 109 P.2d 610. It is only when by no reasonable construction can two statutes be operative that the latter act repeals the former by implication. Burnside v. Douglas School Dist. No. 27, 33 Ariz. 1, 261 P. 629.

* * *

The foregoing settles the principal issues arising between the parties to this litigation. * * *

In 1949 the City applied to the Arizona Power Authority for a Purchase Certificate and was granted a certificate for the following described areas: * * * The City maintains that such Power Purchase Certificate is authority for the City to serve in the disputed localities and prohibits the District from serving such areas. The District maintains that the certificate is void as it exceeds the statutory authority granted under the Power Authority Act.

A.R.S. § 30–154 provides that certificates shall be granted as a matter of right in certain instances, * * *

The Act within itself does not give the Commission authority to confer the right to engage in the distribution of electric energy. Its only function is to distribute available power to operating units. Any certificate granted by it to a city or town must be limited to the provisions contained in the statute. The District having been established in those areas which now the City seeks to serve, the Commission has no authority to grant electric power to the City for that purpose.

To the extent that such certificate purports to embrace those areas herein disputed it is ineffectual to confer any rights.

* * *

The judgment of the court below is affirmed in part and in part reversed, with directions to enter a further judgment consistent with this decision.

* * *

Notes

1. **Municipal Annexation of District Service Territory.** But see contra: Missouri Pub. Serv. v. Platte-Clay Elec. Co-op, 700 S.W.2d 838 (1985). "Considering the variety and complexity of statutory arrangements, the need for legislation that comprehensively * * * works out the consequences of municipal annexation of special district territory becomes evident. The present statutes are characteristically scattered throughout statute books under titles governing municipal annexation or the formation, functioning and alteration of districts. * * * Moreover, states * * * often have no statutes at all particularly dealing with annexation of district territory. Others have statutes applicable to a few, but not all, of the several kinds of districts which exist in the state. Many * * * are quite new, a fact which indicates that the need for legislative solution * * * is becoming more urgent * * *." Note, *Problems Created by Municipal Annexation of Special District Territory,* 1967 Wash.U.L.Q. 560, 583–4.*

The case and statute laws of the states reveal a number of different solutions including the following:

(a) Automatic dissolution of the district whose entire territory is annexed by a competing municipality. In re Sanitary Board of East Fruitvale Sanitary District, 158 Cal. 453, 111 P. 368 (1910); but see City of Downey v. Downey City Water District, 202 Cal.App.2d 786, 21 Cal.Rptr.2d 370 (1962). This common law merger-by-annexation doctrine has been modified by statutes. For a reversal of the common-law rule, and preservation of concurrent municipal and district existence, see City of Aurora v. Aurora Sanitation District, 112 Colo. 406, 149 P.2d 662 (1944). For a statutory scheme permitting discretionary determination by a county board, on continued district operations in expanded municipal limits, based upon prevailing circumstances, see West's Ann.Cal.Gov. Code § 56400. Even in states which have legislated the common law rule, special statutory provisions are made to adjust municipal rights and obligations. See Note, supra, 1967 Wash.U.L.Q. 565–567. See Note 5 infra.

(b) Automatic ouster of special districts from the annexed territory. State on Inf. Flaxel v. Chandler, 180 Or. 28, 175 P.2d 448 (1946); Weather-Wax et al. v. Grays Harbor County, 116 Wash. 212, 199 P. 303 (1921).

(c) Optional power by the annexing municipality to oust the district from the annexed territory upon payment to the district of compensation

* Reprinted by permission of Washington University Law Quarterly copyright ©1967.

for district facilities, as in City of Mesa, supra. Morgan County Rural Electric Membership Corp. v. Public Service Co. of Ind., 253 Ind. 541, 255 N.E.2d 822 (1970); Franklin Power & Light Co. v. Middle Tenn. Elec. Membership Corp., 222 Tenn. 182, 434 S.W.2d 829 (1968). But see: Cass County Elect. Cooperative, Inc. v. Wold Properties, Inc., 249 N.W.2d 514 (N.D.1976).

2. **Annexation by Special Districts.** Generally speaking, the impediments to district expansion by annexation are similar to those which limit municipal annexation. See M. Pock, *Independent Special Districts: A Solution To The Metropolitan Area Problems* ch. IX (1962). "Annexation procedures for metropolitan districts appear to suffer from the same basic deficiencies as those of conventional units of local government. * * * The situation is further aggravated by the fact that some districts are entirely lacking in powers of territorial expansion. * * * It is, * * * impossible to make an accurate evaluation of annexation in any but the individual case, since such evaluation depends on too many variables, not the least of which being that the need for expansion is in all cases a function of * * * the particular specialized purposes subserved by the district. One fact, however, seems to be unassailable * * *: so far, not a single metropolitan district has been able, since its formation, to extend its boundaries through annexation to include the entire metropolitan area in which it might well function." Id. 183–184.* The enlargement of such districts has been achieved in a limited number of instances by special legislative enactment. Id. 163.

3. **District Consolidations.** Consolidation of special district units is, with the exception of school districts, rare, due to a void of legislation on the subject.

4. **Automatic District Expansion.** Where District territory is defined by statute to coincide with municipal or county limits, municipal or county expansion by annexation may automatically enlarge the District's territory. Some statutes so provide, e.g. West's Rev.Code Wash.Ann. § 35.61.020; M. Pock, supra, 171. Should the reasons for municipal annexation presumably justify similar expansion of district territory? Should the district board be empowered to reject such concurrent annexations? Compare West's Ann.California Public Utility Code § 13911 with Vernon's Ann.Texas Civil Stat. Art. 7880–75a.

5. **Municipal Incorporation of District Territory.** The authorities are not in agreement on whether districts serving unincorporated territory are automatically dissolved upon incorporation of such territory as a new municipality. See Airport Authority of City of Millard v. Omaha, 185 Neb. 623, 177 N.W.2d 603 (1970).

2. CITY–COUNTY CONSOLIDATION

"The County is at once the most underresearched and most controversial unit in the American federal system. * * * [it] has been variously described as 'the dark continent of American politics,' 'the

* Reprinted by permission of Michigan   The University of Michigan Law School,
Legal Publications copyright © 1962 by   Ann Arbor.

headless wonder,' and 'the local government of the future.' It is not without irony, therefore, that while some have urged that the county be the basis of a 'new constitutional form for metropolis,' Connecticut has abolished county government for a similar reason—local government modernization." Lineberry, *Reforming Metropolitan Governance: Requiem or Reality,* 58 Geo.L.J. 675, 683 (1970).* Perhaps both verdicts are correct, depending *inter alia* on the size of a state, and whether the projected metropolitan area crosses county lines.

The county unit can, under appropriate laws, serve as an areawide government, either as an enlarged municipality (city-county consolidation); or as the upper tier of urban federation (p. 213 et seq.); or as a transferee of selected municipal functions from underlying units (p. 261 et seq.).

Consolidation requires extension of city boundaries to the county limits, and a complete or partial merger of the two governments. A core city which is not coterminal with the county may affect consolidation even though smaller municipalities in the county elect to be excluded from the consolidated government.

The bias against consolidation and in favor of interlocal arrangements is largely a matter of local politics, but interest in city-county consolidations persists.

LENNOX v. CLARK
Supreme Court of Pennsylvania, 1953.
372 Pa. 355, 93 A.2d 334.

HORACE STERN, CHIEF JUSTICE. Broadly speaking we are here called upon to decide the effect wrought upon the officers and employees of the former Philadelphia county offices by the City-County Consolidation Amendment of the Constitution, P.S., (adding section 8 to Article XIV thereof), the First Class City Home Rule Act of April 21, 1949, P.L. 665, 53 P.S. § 3421.1 *et seq.*, and the Philadelphia Home Rule Charter adopted by the electors April 17, 1951, effective January 7, 1952. * * * The appeals here presented concern the offices of the Sheriff, Register of Wills, County Commissioners, Recorder of Deeds, Clerk of the Court * * *, Prothonotary * * * Board of Revision of Taxes and Registration Commission. * * *

* * *

Notwithstanding the consolidation of the city effected by the Act of February 2, 1854, P.L. 21, 53 P.S. § 6361, the structure of the government of Philadelphia continually grew more and more complex and ultimately completely outmoded. Instead of a unified system there existed dual governments. Entirely different rules and regulations prevailed in the city and the county offices; * * * These anomalies flourished in spite of the fact that all the offices and departments, city

* Reprinted by permission of Georgetown Law Journal. Copyright © 1970.

and county, participated in the government of the same compact area and its inhabitants. * * * It is no wonder, therefore, that over a great number of years there has been considerable popular agitation for the correction of this patch-work system and its uneconomic division of functions, and it was presumably in response to that agitation that the City-County Consolidation Amendment, the First Class City Home Rule Act and the Home Rule charter came into being, bringing in their train the problems that have given rise to the present appeals.

The specific issues with which we are here confronted are these: (1) whether the civil service provisions of the Charter now apply to the employees of the former county offices; (2) whether the Charter prohibitions against political activities * * * now extend to officers and employees of the former county offices; (3) whether the former county officers now are subject to the Charter prohibition against the appointment of private solicitors * * *; (4) whether the former county officers are now bound by * * * the Charter to give the information prescribed therein to the Director of Finance, the City Controller and the Personnel Director. Or whether, as to all these matters, further legislation by the General Assembly or the City Council is necessary to effect those results. * * *

* * *

* * * It is believed that all such confusion would be immediately dissipated if two important distinctions were kept clearly in mind,—the one between the effect of the consolidation on the *personnel* of the county offices and its effect on the *duties* or *functions* performed by such offices, and the other between the consolidation of the city and county governments and the proposed "streamlining" of the city government following that consolidation. These distinctions, it is hoped, will become entirely clear in the course of this discussion.

We start with the City-County Consolidation Amendment itself. It provides in clause (1) that "In Philadelphia all county offices are hereby abolished, and the city shall henceforth perform all functions of county government within its area through officers selected in such manner as may be provided by law." The crucial words there to be noted are "*hereby*" and "*henceforth.*" The county offices are abolished, not at some indefinite time in the future * * * but "*hereby*," * * *. It will be further noted that all the functions of county government * * * are *thenceforth* to be performed by the city; the city is to take over *then and there,* as part of its own government, the performance of the functions of the county government. * * * Here again the amendment is manifestly self-executing, for the change from county to city officers is to take place *upon adoption of the amendment*—which, incidentally, occurred on November 6, 1951—and therefore without the necessity of any further action, legislative or otherwise. Thus the county offices were effectually brought into the structure of the municipal government. And of course, when the county officers became city officers their employees automatically became thereby city employees. * * *

What then was the effect on such personnel? * * *

* * * [I]t would be wholly incredible to suppose that the only accomplishment intended by the City-County Consolidation Amendment was the merely puerile one of a change of titles, * * * Its real and designed result was that * * * they automatically became subject thereby to the laws then in effect governing and regulating city officers and employees, and also, of course, to any such laws as might thereafter become effective.

What, then, were the laws * * * that were in force on November 6, 1951 * * *? They were the laws contained in the First Class City Act of June 25, 1919, P.L. 581, 53 P.S. § 2901 *et seq.* * * *

These provisions of the 1919 Act * * * were quickly superseded by the provisions on these same subjects contained in the Home Rule Charter, which * * * became effective on January 7, 1952. Section 7–301 of the Charter provided that all officers and employees of the city, all departments, all independent boards and commissions and all departmental boards and commissions should, with certain exceptions, be under civil service. * * * Section 8–103 provided that it was the duty of each officer or department and each independent board and commission of the city * * * to comply with all requests made by the Director of Finance for information dealing with the budget. Section 8–104 provided that each department board and commission of the city * * * should transmit to the City Controller, the Director of Finance, and the Personnel Director, certain information in regard to their officers and employees. Section 10–107, clauses (3), (4) and (5) forbade the appointed officers, and the employees of the city * * * from engaging in any of the political activities therein specified, and *all* city officers from engaging in certain of those activities. Section 4–400(a) provided that the Law Department of the city should have the power and duty of furnishing legal advice to all officers, departments, boards and commissions * * * and section 8–410 provided that whenever any officer * * * should require legal advice concerning his or its official business it should be the duty of such officer, * * * to refer the same to the Law Department, and to follow the advice so received; * * *

On January 7, 1952, therefore, *all* city officers and employees became immediately subject to these provisions of the Charter * * *

Some point has been made of the fact that the former county officers in a few instances performed certain duties on behalf of the Commonwealth and to that extent were acting in the capacity of an officer, agent or employee of the State. [Citations omitted.] However, just as the rendition of that service did not militate against their general status as *county* officers, so now its continued rendition does not conflict with their general status as *city* officers.

The court below held that the civil service provisions of the Charter were applicable to the former county officers and their employees, that the Charter prohibitions against their political activities were also applicable, and that the officers were bound to supply the information required by sections 8–103 and 8–104. In all these respects we are in accord with its decision. ✱ ✱ ✱

✱ ✱ ✱ The one phase is completed in that the county offices are now a part of the municipal government and that all their officers and employees are now city officers and employees and as such bound by the provisions of the Charter concerning such officers and employees. But their *activities* or *functions* are not changed; ✱ ✱ ✱ Since clause (7) of the City-County Consolidation Amendment provides that the county officers are to continue, now as city officers to perform their duties "until the General Assembly shall otherwise provide," it would seem that any proposed reorganizations, regroupings, abolitions, or mergers, of the former county offices, designed the more advantageously to incorporate their functions into the existing municipal structure, must wait upon action by the General Assembly. Whether, however, the legislature has already abrogated its power in that regard and vested it exclusively in the city by the provisions of Article II, section 17, of the Home Rule Act or otherwise, is a question not involved in the present appeals, and as to which, therefore, we express no opinion.

This brings us to a consideration of the appeals involving ✱ ✱ ✱ the Prothonotary of the Courts of Common Pleas and the Register of Wills, which require individual treatment because ✱ ✱ ✱ they are each the subject of a special provision of the Constitution, and also because they are so closely integrated in the judicial branch of the government. As to the Prothonotary, it is provided in Article V, section 7 of the Constitution that "For Philadelphia there shall be ✱ ✱ ✱ one prothonotary for all said courts, to be appointed by the judges of said courts, ✱ ✱ ✱; the said prothonotary shall appoint such assistants as may be necessary and authorized by said courts; ✱ ✱ ✱." While it is true that by Article XIV, section 1, of the Constitution, the prothonotary is designated as a county officer, and that clause (7) of the City-County Consolidation Amendment provides that ✱ ✱ ✱ all county officers should become officers of the City of Philadelphia, the question arises whether, in view of Article V, section 7, the Prothonotary should be considered a county officer *within the intendment* of the City-County Consolidation Amendment. It is an established principle of constitutional construction that, where a conflict exists between a specific constitutional provision which is applicable to a particular case and certain general provisions which, were it not for such conflict, might apply, the specific provision will prevail. [Citations omitted] Here, such a conflict does exist because, if ✱ ✱ ✱ the City-County Consolidation Amendment were to be deemed applicable to the Prothonotary, clause (7) thereof would enable the General Assembly or the City Council, ✱ ✱ ✱ so to emasculate his functions as practically to abolish his office altogether, and, ✱ ✱ ✱ its mere existence would constitute an encroachment upon the independence and the functioning of the judiciary. * * * It is because of the constitutional status specially given the Prothonotary * * * that we are led to conclude that the office of the Prothonotary does not fall within the scope of the City-County Consolidation Amendment, and that therefore, not being transformed into a city office, it has not become subject to the provisions of the Charter.

The same consideration * * * apply with equal, if not greater, force to that of the Register of Wills, since it has been held that he is a judge and that his probate of wills constitutes a judicial act. [Citations omitted] He too is the subject of a specific provision in the Constitution. * * * Accordingly it is our opinion that the office of the Register of Wills was not converted by the City-County Consolidation Amendment into a city office and therefore has not become subject to the provisions of the Charter.

We pass to the questions * * * concerning the offices of the Board of Revision of Taxes and the Registration Commission.

The Board of Revision of Taxes is not referred to in the Constitution at all. * * * Is it a county office? Its members now contend that it is a State Agency, and therefore is not affected by the City-County Consolidation Amendment. * * *

When we come to view the subject on the basis of history, reason and logic, it is abundantly clear that the Board of Revision of Taxes of Philadelphia is a county office. * * *

* * * The State long since became unconcerned with county assessments of property as the basis of any State Tax. Performing, therefore, a purely local function * * *, there is no ground whatever for viewing the Board other than as a county office, and, as such, transformed by the City-County Consolidation Amendment into a city office. Certainly the mere fact that it was specifically established by an act of the legislature does not make it a State agency; all nonconstitutional offices are necessarily so created.

All considerations thus applying to the Board of Revision of Taxes apply even more forcefully to the Registration Commission. * * * The Registration Commission is no more a State agency than is the Board of Revision of Taxes. * * * We conclude, therefore, that the members of the Registration Commission are city officers, that their employees are city employees, and that members and employees alike are bound by the provisions of the Charter. * * *

FRAZER v. CARR

Supreme Court of Tennessee, 1962.
210 Tenn. 565, 360 S.W.2d 449.

TOMLINSON, SPECIAL JUSTICE.

[Against challenges to the consolidation of Nashville City and Davidson County, on the grounds that the consolidation violated state constitutional provisions on special legislation, delegation of legislative power and uniformity of taxation, the Court sustained the consolidation. * * *]

This is a suit filed under the declaratory judgment law. Its purpose is to have declared void the recently established Metropolitan Government by a consolidation of all, or substantially all, of the governmental and corporate functions of Davidson County, * * * and of Nashville, its principal city. Section 6–3702 T.C.A.

Thus was created, * * * a governmental entity, based upon a Metropolitan Charter, § 6–3711 T.C.A. Its governing body is a metropolitan council vested with "all the authority and functions of the governing bodies of the county and cities being consolidated, with such exceptions and with such additional authority as may be specified elsewhere in this chapter", § 6–3711(k) T.C.A.

*   *   *

* * * The classification is reasonable because we all know that it is in these large counties that the problem of the large cities as to the ever increasing population just beyond the corporate limits becomes more acute, complex, and confusing.

*   *   *

In this connection, it is quite untenable to say that the efficacy and acceptance of a law can not be decided by a vote of the people in an election held for that purpose when authorized by the constitution. Whatever may have been the law on this question prior to the 1953 constitutional amendment, it was no longer the law after the adoption of that 8th amendment.

*   *   *

Next, it is insisted that this charter "violates Article II, Sections 28 and 29 of the Tennessee Constitution. Section 28 provides that all property shall be so taxed as to be equal and uniform throughout the state. * * *

*   *   *

The metropolitan government created two service districts; to-wit, (1) the general service district, embracing the total area of the county, and (2) the urban service district, consisting "of the total area of the principal city."

Provision is made for the levying by the governing body of the metropolitan government of taxes (1) to meet the needs of the general services district, and (2) of the urban services district. Since the metropolitan government is a consolidation of the urban government and of the county government, it is in exact keeping with that which has always been true in this state, that one tax is levied for the municipal government according to its needs, and another for the county in accordance with its needs.

*   *   *

The improvement sought by the 8th Amendment was a consolidation of the municipal and county governments into a metropolitan government, with the authority of both the previous governmental entities.

For these delegates to have intended, * * *, that the Metropolitan Government levy the same tax in the county area as that to be levied in the urban area, would not have resulted "in the opening of another gate to the future development and progress * * *." That "gate" would have been closed with a resounding bang by the voters in the county had they been saddled with taxes for services which they knew could not be rendered them, and the members of the convention necessarily knew this; and thus knew the amendment would "die aborning", if such an unjust and unequal tax should have been intended.

Notes

1. **Other Modern Models.** The 1968 consolidation of City of Jacksonville and DuVal County, Florida, is similar to Nashville-Davidson, and withstood similar constitutional challenges. See Jackson v. Consolidated Government of City of Jacksonville, 225 So.2d 497 (Fla.1969). Together with the partial 1947 consolidation of Baton Rouge and Baton Rouge Parish (La.—LSA–Constitution Art. XIV, § 3(a)) these developments prompted the following observation:

> "Each included a single county and a single city. Each occurred in the South in * * * not heavily populated area that had few local governments. Each excluded small municipalities [at their option]. All three have service and tax differential zones. All have an independent chief executive with considerable authority. All render a number of major services on an area-wide basis.

> * * *

> "Each [has] * * * a governing board comprised of at-large and district members, the latter being the decided majority."

J.C. Bollens and H.J. Schmandt, *The Metropolis* 303, 304 (1970).*

The consolidation of Indianapolis and Marion County in 1970 (effected by legislative fiat (West's Ann.Ind.Code 48–9109 to 48–9507)) closely proximated the Nashville and Jacksonville experience in providing dual tax and service zones, a single executive and legislature, and provision to permit smaller municipalities to opt out of the consolidation. Constitutional challenges were equally unsuccessful in Indianapolis. See Dortch v. Lugar, 255 Ind. 545, 266 N.E.2d 25 (1971); Note—*Decentralization of Metropolitan Government: Reform in Indianapolis,* 4 J.Law Reform, 310 (1970).

City-county consolidation is authorized by the Oregon constitution (Or. Const. Art. XI, § 2a(2)) and implemented by legislation (ORS 199.705 to 199.775). A charter study commission proposal to consolidate Portland-Multnomah County was rejected by the electorate.

Though the Washington State Constitution authorizes city-county consolidation through adoption of home rule charters by interested counties

* Reprinted by permission of Harper & Row, Publishers, Inc. Copyright © 1970.

(Wash. Const.Amend. 58, 1 Wash.Legis.Serv. 6 (1973)), the union of Seattle and King County has yet to be achieved. See 61 Nat'l.Civic Rev. 417, 419 (1972).

For city-county consolidations proposals in several other states, see 61 Nat'l.Civic Rev. 417, 419 (1972); Book of The States 1970–71, pp. 276, 277.

2. **City-County Separation.** Although employed to promote urban government, city-county separation is the converse of consolidation. It involves detachment, rather than merger, of territory; and proliferation, rather than reduction, of existing units. By state-wide law, Virginia makes all first class cities separate units independent of the counties from which they are carved. "A fundamental characteristic of the independent [city-county] separation is that it performs within its jurisdiction all of the functions normally provided by the county." C.W. Bain, *A Body Incorporating City-County Separation In Virginia* 26 (1967). Professor Bain also points out that, by a gradual absorption of county functions over a long period of time, the city of Boston achieved the same result as city-county separation. Id. p. 34. Among the criticisms leveled at the Virginia model, the following are prominent. The system permits cities to compete with counties for territory by annexation of developed suburbs, resulting in diminished county area, population, and revenues. Finally, the Virginia system fosters creation of additional municipalities when states are being urged to reduce the number of local governments.

B. INTEGRATING PARTICULAR FUNCTIONS

1. FEDERATION OF LOCAL UNITS

MIAMI SHORES VILLAGE v. COWART

Supreme Court of Florida, 1958.
108 So.2d 468.

[Suit by Miami Shores Village against Board of Commissioners of Dade County seeking to nullify County Board ordinance that established Metropolitan Traffic Code to replace and supersede traffic ordinances of underlying municipalities, and that required violations of said Code to be tried exclusively in a Metropolitan Court. The Village appealed from an adverse decision below.]

ROBERTS, JUSTICE. This is another in a series of cases arising in Dade County since May 21, 1957, questioning the validity of various actions taken by the Board of County Commissioners of Dade County * * * under the purported authority of the Home Rule Charter adopted on that date by the voters of Dade County. See Dade County v. Kelly, Fla.1958, 99 So.2d 856; Chase v. Cowart, Fla.1958, 102 So.2d 147; Dade County v. Young Democratic Club of Dade County, Fla.1958, 104 So.2d 636. Under these decisions it is settled that the Charter and the ordinances adopted thereunder "must be consistent with and must do no violence to the provisions of Article VIII, Section 11, Florida Constitution, pursuant to which the charter is adopted." Dade County v. Dade County League of Municipalities, Fla.1958, 104 So.2d 512, 516.

The issues made and decided in the instant suit were not, however, limited to the validity vel non of the Metropolitan Traffic Code. In addition to upholding the validity of the Code the Chancellor found and declared that the Dade County Home Rule Charter and county ordinances adopted thereunder "shall in cases of conflict supersede all municipal charters and city ordinances, except in those instances where the charter of Dade County specifically provides otherwise." The Chancellor also found and declared that § 1.01A(18) of the Home Rule Charter, providing the methods by which a municipality may transfer to the Board a municipal service or function, "imposes no limitation or restriction upon the [Board] in the exercise of any of the powers enumerated in Section 1.01 of the Charter." It is this decree that we review on this appeal.

Pertinent here are the following provisions of the so-called Home Rule Amendment to the Florida Constitution, * * *

"Section 11(1). The electors of Dade County, Florida, are granted power to adopt, revise, and amend from time to time a home rule charter of government for Dade County, Florida, under which the Board of County Commissioners of Dade County shall be the governing body. This charter:

* * *

"(b) May grant full power and authority to the Board of County Commissioners of Dade County to pass ordinances relating to the affairs, property and government of Dade County and provide suitable penalties for the violation thereof; to levy and collect such taxes as may be authorized by general law and no other taxes, *and to do everything necessary to carry on a central metropolitan government in Dade County.*

* * *

"(d) *May* provide a method by which any and all of the functions or powers of any municipal corporation or other governmental unit in Dade County *may* be transferred to the Board of County Commissioners of Dade County.

* * *

"(g) *Shall* provide a method by which each municipal corporation in Dade County shall have the power to make, amend or repeal its own charter. *Upon adoption of this home rule charter by the electors this method shall be exclusive and the Legislature shall have no power to amend or repeal the charter of any municipal corporation in Dade County.*" (All emphasis above is supplied, and paragraph designations are as in Florida Statutes 1957, F.S.A.)

In Gray v. Golden, Fla.1956, 89 So.2d 785, 791, this court declined to sustain a decree of the lower court holding, inter alia, that the provisions of the Resolution proposing the Home Rule Amendment were so inconsistent, conflicting and contradictory as to invalidate the entire proposed amendment. In so doing this court said: "Properly construed we think the proposed amendment defines a comprehensive plan for home rule in Dade County; we think its apparent conflicts may be reconciled within the confines of the proposed amendment." .

On this appeal it is contended on behalf that the Home Rule Charter, as interpreted by the Board and by the Chancellor in the decree upholding such interpretation, instead of "reconciling" such inconsistencies, has perpetuated them. * * *

The appellees contend that the Home Rule Amendment, and the Charter adopted pursuant thereto by the electors of Dade County, were designed to and did establish a system of metropolitan government described by the Chancellor in his decree as follows:

> "The system of local government in Dade County has been termed by experts in political science as the 'federated plan' of metropolitan government. This concept of local government recognizes the fact that virtually all activities of local government are inter-related, and contemplates a division of governmental functions between a central metropolitan government and the existing municipalities within the territorial area, and is designed to provide a method for accomplishment of community problems by means of concerted cooperation between the two levels of local government. The type of metropolitan government adopted for Dade County allocated to the municipalities specific rights of self determination and home rule in municipal affairs, and reserved to the county government the power to pass ordinances or county-wide laws relating to the affairs, property and government throughout the county, and all other powers necessary to carry on a central metropolitan government in the territorial area of Dade County. It recognizes the most vital single problem facing Dade County; that is, the urgent need for the establishment of an area-wide framework for effective local government."

When interpreted in the light of the purpose sought to be accomplished, we find no conflicts or inconsistencies among the several provisions of the Home Rule Amendment quoted above, nor in the Home Rule Charter adopted by the electors of Dade County. The Home Rule Amendment, § 11(1)(b), supra, authorized the Charter to "grant full power and authority to the Board of County Commissioners of Dade County to pass ordinances relating to the affairs, property and government of Dade County * * * and to do everything necessary to carry on a central metropolitan government in Dade County." This means that the Charter could authorize the Board to regulate on a county-wide basis according to a uniform plan those municipal services or functions that are susceptible to, and could be most effectively carried on under, a regulatory plan applicable to the entire metropolitan area—or it means nothing insofar as the authority to "carry on a central metropolitan government in Dade County" is concerned; and we must assume that every sentence of a constitution is designed to have some effect. See In re Advisory Opinion to the Governor, Fla.1957, 96 So.2d 904, 905.

When § 11(1)(b) is so interpreted, there is no inconsistency among the three constitutional provisions quoted above. Thus, the provision of

§ 11(1)(d), *supra,* authorizing the Charter to provide for the transfer to the Board by a municipality of "any and all" of its municipal functions or powers, must have been included in the Home Rule Amendment for the purpose of authorizing the municipalities to transfer to the Board, and the Board to perform, (1) purely local municipal functions or powers not susceptible to regulation on a county-wide basis under a uniform plan, or (2) other municipal services that are susceptible to and may have been regulated on a county-wide basis, but which could be provided as well at the local level by the local administrative body as by the Board on a county-wide basis, *e.g.,* garbage collection.

Completing the "comprehensive plan for home rule in Dade County," * * * guarantees to the municipalities complete autonomy— freedom from interference by either the Legislature or the Board— insofar as their purely local municipal functions or powers are concerned. The question of what is or is not a purely local function or power of a municipality is a mixed question of law and fact to be determined judicially if, as and when the authority of the Board is controverted.

In summary, then, we construe the above-quoted provisions of the Home Rule Amendment as requiring the Charter to provide for municipal autonomy as to the purely local functions or powers of the municipalities in Dade County; and as authorizing regulation and control by the Board on a county-wide basis of those municipal functions and services that are susceptible to, and could be most effectively carried on under, a uniform plan of regulation applicable to the county as a whole.

* * * The particular regulation here brought into question—an ordinance establishing uniformity of traffic control and enforcement throughout the metropolitan area—is specifically authorized by § 1.01A(1) of the Home Rule Charter and is in accord with the intent and purpose of the constitutional authority granted by the Home Rule Amendment.

* * *

The decree of the Chancellor here reviewed, holding that the Home Rule Charter and county ordinances adopted thereunder "shall in cases of conflict supersede all municipal charters and city ordinances, except in those instances where the charter of Dade County specifically provides otherwise," and that § 1.01A(18) of the Charter "imposes no limitation or restriction upon the [Board] in the exercise of any of the powers enumerated in Section 1.01 of the Charter", is correct if it be assumed that the Charter power sought to be exercised by the Board is consistent with and does no violence to the provisions of the Home Rule Amendment as discussed and defined herein. As so limited, the decree of the Chancellor should be and it is hereby

Affirmed.

STURGIS, WALLACE E., ASSOCIATE JUDGE (specially concurring).

* * *

* * * It is difficult to imagine a field in which a central metropolitan government could more effectively function than in that of removing the confusion, inequalities, and inequities resulting from a multiplicity of independent municipal ordinances governing the control of traffic and parking in highly congested and contiguous metropolitan areas.

The concept of home rule should be cherished and nurtured. However, the conclusion is inescapable that over-purification of this concept would establish a rule of laissez faire rather than of reason, would promote the anarchy of untrammeled individuality.

THOMAS, JUSTICE (concurring in part and dissenting in part).

I agree with most of the opinion but I do not agree with the application to the present problem of the principles announced, and that traffic control should be wholly taken from the municipalities.

From the preamble of the Metropolitan Charter it appears that both metropolitan government and control by municipalities over their local affairs were intended to be preserved. * * *

I think control of traffic is a problem for the municipalities except possibly traffic on arterial roads under Section 1.01A(1) which provides that the Board of County Commissioners shall have power to regulate traffic on "arterial roads."

Notes

1. **A Comparison of Reform Models.** (a) *Miami and Nashville.* What Nashville and Indianapolis accomplished by single governments, with separate local and metro service and tax zones, Miami achieved through separate tiers of local and metro governments. Neither model avoids the problem of classifying local and metro affairs. Cf. People ex rel. Younger, p. 227.

(b) *Miami and Kansas City.* These federations present an interesting comparison on the subjects assigned to local (municipal) and area-wide (county) jurisdiction. The Florida Constitution invests Dade County with power to regulate county government as a whole, within and without incorporated areas (West's Florida Stat. Ann. Constitution, Art. VIII, § 11(b)). The Dade County Charter (§§ 5.01, 5.02) suggests, and the judicial interpretation of the Florida Constitution imposed, a limitation on county powers to those functions which are "susceptible to * * * and most effectively carried on under a regulatory plan applicable to the entire metropolitan area." The dividing line between municipal and metropolitan functions is, therefore, subject to ultimate judicial determination. See, e.g., City of Miami Beach, p. 222.

In Kansas, city and county jurisdiction is formally defined by the Jackson County Charter which confers "all powers permissible for a county to have under the Constitution and laws of Missouri." (Jackson County Charter, Art. I, § 3). The 1970 Missouri Constitutional Amendment authorizes the county charter to "provide for the vesting and exercise of legislative power pertaining to any and all services and functions of any municipality or political subdivision, except school districts, throughout the county, within and as well as outside incorporated areas; *and any such charter shall set forth the limits within which the municipalities may exercise the same powers collaterally or coextensively.*" (Vernon's Ann. Missouri Stat. Constitution Art. VI, § 18(c)) [Emphasis supplied]. On a literal reading, this constitutional grant would enable the county to assume and displace all municipal functions. The constitution may, however, be read to *require* that the charter specify those powers which municipalities "may" (meaning can or should) retain over local affairs. Under the first reading, if the county charter provided for no municipal jurisdiction, the courts could enforce county preemption power. Under the second reading, the court (as in Florida) would have to determine whether the county charter properly assigned local functions and jurisdiction to underlying municipalities. The Jackson County Charter will therefore, require judicial clarification. See Freilich, Robards, Wilson, *Home Rule for the Urban County: Observations on the New Jackson County Constitutional Charter*, 39 U.M.K.C.L.Rev. 297 (1971).

(c) *Miami and Toronto.* The Municipality of Toronto, serving two million persons in a 241 square mile area, was created by legislative action in 1954, without popular referendum. In federating 13 municipalities consisting of Toronto City, five townships, four towns, and three villages. The metro worked so well that, by subsequent amendments, its 13 constituent local units were consolidated into five boroughs and one city. The metropolitan governing council was streamlined to provide proportional district representation and at-large representation. The range of functions provided by the Toronto metro is far more comprehensive than any provided in the United States. Considered "the first urban federation in America," the Toronto government provides major services that include area-wide planning, licensing standards and regulations, a metro police force, parking system, school board, and pooled financial services. While the Miami and Toronto federations share common objectives the difference in their *scale* of metropolitan services and control is such that commentators normally conclude that true federation, as illustrated by Toronto, has never been achieved in the United States. See Grant, *Urban Needs and State Response:* in, *The States and the Urban Crisis, Alan K. Campbell, Ed. (American Assembly 1970)* 71–73; J.C. Bollens, H.J. Schmandt, The Metropolis, 339–346.

"The best known examples of metropolitan federation are the governments of Greater London and Metropolitan Toronto. * * * The closest thing to metropolitan federation * * * in the United States is the Metro government of Dade County in Miami. * * * The heart of this plan is the retention of the existing municipalities—Miami plus 27 suburban cities—to perform purely local functions * * *. The political opposition and financial limitations have made it impossible for Dade County to assume anything like the package of area-wide functions hoped for by the original advocates. In practice, Dade County's metro is more nearly a 'municipalized county' than it is a federation of municipalities, since the cities as such are not represented on the Board of Commissioners." Grant, supra 72.*

CITY OF MIAMI BEACH v. MUTUAL BENEFIT LIFE INS. CO.

District Court of Appeals of Florida, 1970.
239 So.2d 272.

PER CURIAM. The City of Miami Beach appeals from a final judgment of the circuit court holding that the city had no authority to change a provision of the South Florida Building Code, the building code for both the incorporated and unincorporated areas of Dade County, Florida. See § 8–1, Code of Metropolitan Dade County.

The trial court correctly held that under Article 1, § 1.01A(13) of the Metropolitan Dade County Home Rule Charter, the Board of County Commissioners has the exclusive authority to adopt, enforce, amend, or modify building and related technical codes governing construction in both the incorporated and unincorporated areas of Dade County, Florida. See: Miami Shores Village v. Cowart, Fla.1959, 108 So.2d 468; City of Miami Beach v. Cowart, Fla.1960, 116 So.2d 432; City of Coral Gables v. Burgin, Fla.1962, 143 So.2d 859; City of Coral Gables v. Dade County, Fla.App.1966, 189 So.2d 530.

* * *

2. METROPOLITAN SPECIAL DISTRICTS

The term metropolitan special district is not a strictly legal classification, but is employed to isolate from the mass of special districts, those which are truly metropolitan in scope. Relatively few special districts are even multi-county, much less metropolitan, in area, and more than 90% of all districts were still single-purpose entities in 1962. M. Pock, *Independent Special Districts: A Solution to the Metropolitan Area Problem*, 16, 17, 79 (1962). The primitive development of metropolitan districts as a class is partly explained by the fact that they have not been accorded legal recognition save in a few states; that they receive no consistent classification under sporadic special statutes *; and that they are often created to meet specific needs at different stages of population expansion across municipal, county, and state lines. See e.g. Tobin, *The Legal and Governmental Status of the Metropolitan Special District*, XIII U.Miami L.Rev. 129 (1958); Note, *Special Districts and Deficient Local Government in Salt Lake Metropolitan Area*, 7 Utah L.Rev. 229 (1960). In recent years, greater attention has been given to improved organization of metropolitan special districts. See Tobin, *The Metropolitan Special District: Inter-County Metropolitan Government of Tomorrow*, XIV U.Miami L.Rev. 333–335 (1960). In proposing reform legislation to the states for expanded use of metropolitan special districts, the U.S. Advisory Commission recommended, inter alia: that states employ general, rather than special

* California has some 200 laws authorizing formation of special districts, most of which qualify as special legislation, that are not reprinted in the California Code. See Hagman, *Regionalized Decentralism*, 58 Georgetown L.Rev. 901, 914–915 (1970).

legislation to insure a consistent policy for such districts; that they enact standards for the formation of metropolitan districts; that they identify the urban functions that are appropriate for metro district jurisdiction; that they favor multi-functional districts serving related purposes (such as water, irrigation, drainage, power and sewers); that they require district-municipal coordination in the planning and operation of related facilities; and that they be made accountable to the public by election of district officials, and by referenda on major district fiscal proposals. See, ACIR, *Government Structure, Organization and Planning in Metropolitan Area* 26–30 (1961); M. Pock, supra 191–193.

The foregoing recommendations have yet to find their way into the law of many states. State legislatures apparently find it easier to forego the search for a state-wide policy, and to adopt the expedient of authorizing local creation of municipal authorities (Sause, *Municipal Authorities, The Pennsylvania Experience* (1962); R. Smith, *Special Districts and Local Governments* (1964). A few states, however, have enacted measures to foster multiple function metropolitan districts. See e.g., Michigan Comp. Laws Ann. Constitution Art. 7, § 28, quoted at p. 262; Tobin, *The Metropolitan Special District:* supra, pp. 333, 350, 353.

STATE v. METROPOLITAN ST. LOUIS SEWER DISTRICT

Supreme Court of Missouri, 1955.
365 Mo. 1, 275 S.W.2d 225.

HYDE, JUDGE. * * * There is no dispute about the facts. The issue to be decided is whether the plan under which the District is organized and operating attempts to confer powers in excess of the constitutional authority under which the District was formed.

Sec. 30(a), Art. VI * * * authorizes the people of St. Louis City and St. Louis County "to establish a metropolitan district or districts for the functional administration of services common to the area included therein"; and provides that this power "shall be exercised by the vote of the people of the city and county upon a plan prepared by a board of freeholders". The freeholders were properly selected to prepare a plan * * * and the plan prepared by them has been adopted by the voters. Relator contends the entire plan should be held unconstitutional and void * * *.

Sec. 30(b) provides that, upon adoption by the voters the plan "shall become the organic law of the territory therein defined, and shall take the place of and supersede all laws, charter provisions and ordinances inconsistent therewith relating to said territory." The authority to prepare such a district plan is a broad grant of legislative power to the freeholders (with confirmation by the voters) similar to the grants in Sections 18, 19 and 20, Article VI, giving certain counties and cities the right to frame, adopt and amend their own charters. It is even greater because their plan supersedes conflicting laws. It is a recognition of the fact that the St. Louis Metropolitan area has many problems which require "services common to the area"; * * *.

The District Plan adopted in this case provides for its incorporation and government (Art. 1), its boundaries and extensions (Art. 2), its powers (Art. 3), enforcement of its ordinances (Art. 4), its board of trustees (Art. 5), its executive director (Art. 6), its finances (Art. 7), its personnel (Art. 8), its improvements (Art. 9), its elections (Art. 10) and amendments (Art. 11). * * *

Relator says the Constitution only authorizes the establishment of a metropolitan district, "for the functional administration of services common to the area included therein", and contends the above enumerated powers attempted to be granted in the plan are far in excess of requirements for that purpose. Relator argues for a narrow definition of the term "functional administration" and says that a valid plan could only confer powers which were directly related to the operation of sewer facilities in the area included in the plan. Powers which relator specifically claims are beyond the authority to operate sewer facilities are those stated in Sec. 3.030 to establish building lines or floodway reservation lines along or adjacent to any watercourse or stream and to prevent building without permission within such lines, which relator says confers zoning powers; and those stated in Sec. 3.040 to police and clean out channels of streams to prohibit dumping therein and to require removal of material deposited within the lines fixed by the District. Relator further claims the District includes areas which do not have common sewer problems because they drain through different watersheds. Relator also says "the following may not properly be considered within the scope of the constitutional limitation of 'functional administration': (1) The condemnation of property authorized by Section 3.020(6) of the plan; (2) Unlimited borrowing authorized by Section 3.020(13); (3) The bonding of the District, authorized by Section 3.020(15); (4) The issuance of tax anticipation warrants, authorized by Section 3.020(14); and (5) The taking over by the District, without compensation, of all sewers in the area covered, under Section 3.010."

However, the constitutional authority is not merely to prepare and adopt a plan for operation of sewer facilities. It does not say services common to sewers. Instead it authorized a plan for operation of "services common to the area". This is a very broad term and is not limited to any particular kind of services. Moreover, the authority is for a plan which "shall become the organic law of the territory" on the subjects and purposes of the plan. Our view is that all services, common to the area for the protection of the public health and welfare in connection with drainage and sewage disposal, may be properly established for such a district as this. * * * It is easy to understand what floods caused by inadequate drainage can do to sewage disposal. We hold the powers authorized by the plan * * * are within the constitutional authority and valid.

Relator's claim that the plan attempts to include in the District areas, which have no common problems of sewage disposal is based on the inclusion of three county areas that do not drain through the City. These are the Lemay Sewer District, which has a sewer system draining directly into the Mississippi River * * *; the Gravois Creek watershed which drains into the River Des Peres * * *, and the Coldwater Creek watershed which drains a part of the County north of the City and flows into the Missouri River * * *. However, the area to be included in such a district is a matter of legislative discretion (in this case of the freeholders with the approval of the voters) subject, of course, to the limitation that it must not be arbitrary and unreasonable. [Citations omitted.] As stated in relator's exhibit "disease communicating insects and microbes recognize no political boundaries of county, city, or village." Thus, health hazards of raw sewage, septic tank effluent or inadequately treated sewage affect areas other than those of the watershed through which they drain. It is suggested that one large disposal plant for sewage from areas draining into the Mississippi south of the City would be the most effective and economical way to protect the people of the City and those of adjacent areas of the County. As to the area north of the City, draining into the Missouri River, not only are these same factors present but also this sewage must flow down the Mississippi past the City and the waterworks which supply the City. We therefore, hold that it does not appear unreasonable to include these areas in the District and that the plan is not invalidated by their inclusion.

The other powers objected to, namely, condemnation, 3.020(6), incurring debts, 3.020(13), issuance of tax anticipation warrants, 3.020(14), and issuance of bonds, 3.020(15), are essential powers of such a district. Our Legislature has always given drainage and sewer districts the power of condemnation and they could not function without it. * * * We hold these contested powers, with the limitations placed on them are proper and valid powers * * *.

The provision of Sec. 3.010 for taking over all existing sewers, constructed by public agencies, is likewise a necessary, proper and valid provision. These sewers are not private property; they have been built for public purposes under the police power of the state. They are public property and their transfer to this District is a mere transfer of custodianship. Veail v. Louisville and Jefferson County Metropolitan Sewer District, 303 Ky. 248, 197 S.W.2d 413. We have stated similar principles as to property of school districts. See School District of Oakland v. School District of Joplin, 340 Mo. 779, 102 S.W.2d 909. The transfer is only from one public trustee to another. * * *

Notes

1. The Vernon's Ann. Missouri Stat. Constitution Art. VI, § 30(b), making that district charter "the organic law of the territory * * * which shall supersede all laws, charter provisions and ordinances inconsistent

therewith * * *" goes much farther than most states in conferring governmental powers on metropolitan districts.

2. **Consolidation of Districts.** The principal case *indirectly* achieved a consolidation of the Lemay Sewer District, and the absorption of other preexisting public sewers in the metropolitan district. For an example of *direct* merger of separate unifunctional special districts into one multifunctional district, see Solvang Municipal Improvement District v. Jensen, 111 Cal.App.2d 237, 244 P.2d 492 (1952) which upheld consolidation of a sanitary, fire and lighting district. Geographic consolidation may also be accomplished by creating very large regional districts, such as the Metropolitan Water District of Southern California, or by merger of like single-function districts into one entity. See Smith-Hurd, Ill.Ann.Stat. c. 105, § 333 *et seq.* which consolidated several smaller park districts into the Chicago Park District.

3. (a) *Constitutional Status.* The constitutional provision in the principal case was specially directed to St. Louis, and is not typical. Neither is the following authorization of the Michigan Constitution (Art. VII, § 27); "Notwithstanding any other provision of this Constitution the legislature may establish in metropolitan areas additional forms of government or authorities with powers, duties and jurisdictions as the legislature shall provide. Wherever possible, such additional forms of government or authorities shall be designed to perform multi-purpose functions rather than a single function."

While several state constitutions refer to new forms of local government (Pennsylvania Constitution Art. 9, § 5; South Carolina Constitution Art. II, § 5; West's Rev. Code Washington Constitution Art. VIII, § 7), the lack of such references has not been considered a limitation on the plenary power of the state to create metropolitan districts. See e.g. authorities noted in M. Pock, supra, p. 20, n. 37.

(b) *Statutory Status.* Metropolitan district legislation follows no consistent pattern. A statute may classify such districts as "municipal corporations" (see also People v. Chicago Transit Authority, 392 Ill. 77, 64 N.E.2d 4 (1945); 5 Or.Rev.Stat. 777.010); as state agencies (West's Ann.California Health and Safety Code § 24350.1); or as public corporations, whether for municipal, public utility, or public service purposes (36 Pa.Stat. § 3503; West's Ann.California Harbor and Navigation Code § 6290; Erickson v. Metropolitan Utilities District, 171 Neb. 654, 107 N.W.2d 324 (1961)). Each of the varied functions of metropolitan districts may be treated by separate statutes. Thus one textwriter breaks down the law of special districts solely by type of service rendered. See 3A Antieau, *Local Government Law* chs. (D) to (P).

(c) *Judicial Treatment.* Tracking the variations in constitutional and statutory law, courts also differ on the status of metropolitan districts. They have been held to be municipal, quasi-municipal, or corporate in nature, depending upon the issues presented, and the purposes they serve. Compare e.g. Milheim v. Moffett Tunnell Imp. District, 72 Colo. 268, 211 P. 649 (1922) (holding the district to be a municipal corporation); Madison Metropolitan Sewerage District v. Committee on Water Pollution, 260 Wis. 229, 50 N.W.2d 424 (1951) (treating the district as a quasi-municipal corporation); People of the State of New York v. New Jersey, 256 U.S. 296, 41 S.Ct. 492, 65 L.Ed. 937 (1921) (viewing the district as a state agency). "The political character is primarily determined by the tasks assigned to them. * * * This aura of uncertainty surrounding the governmental status of special districts will persist so long as the legislature is either unaware of their significance or views them as temporary solutions that are not worthy of integration into the local government code." M. Pock, supra 23, 24.*

Thus, courts continue to resolve a host of issues, *viz.* whether and when such districts are entitled to governmental tort immunity; whether and when they are subject to the county or municipal home rule powers; whether and when they are covered by state laws governing the qualifications, salaries, pensions and other incidents of public office and employment or by general laws governing the powers, duties and limitations of various classes of state subdivisions. On the division of authority relating to tort liability immunity for different types of districts, see Antieau, *supra;* Annot., 160 A.L.R. 1165 (1946). On the diverse application of municipal debt limitations to district borrowing power, compare City of Lehi v. Meiling, 87 Utah 237, 48 P.2d 530 (1935), and Minn.Stat.Ann. § 445.17(10), with State v. Metropolitan St. Louis Sewer District, supra, 275 S.W.2d at 231 (omitted from above reported opinion). Compare also Anderson Appeal, 408 Pa. 179, 182 A.2d 514 (1962) (holding the Delaware River Port Authority, created by interstate compact, to be a state agency, and as such immune from liability for consequential damages from the construction of its facilities) *with* Philadelphia v. Southeastern Pennsylvania Transportation Authority, 441 Pa. 518, 272 A.2d 921 (1971) (holding that Authority, (created by statute as a separate body politic) was engaged in proprietary functions, so that the Commonwealth was not a real party in interest.) Cf. Pullman Inc. v. Volpe, 337 F.Supp. 432 (E.D.Pa.1971). For a convenient survey of the welter of authorities on the legal status of special metropolitan districts, see Tobin, *The Legal and Governmental Status of the Metropolitan District XIII,* U. Miami L.Rev. 129, 130–151 (1958).

4. **Inter-County Federation Through Use of a Metropolitan Special District.** In multi-county metropolitan areas, inter-local transfers of functions from constituent municipalities to overlying counties cannot produce effective metropolitan solutions. The inter-county and interstate metropolitan special districts may, however, effect a metropolitan federation, where authorized by statute, to receive transfers of municipal functions. A legislative model to create a large metropolitan district as an upper-tier unit is provided by the statute which established the Metropolitan Municipality of Seattle. West's Rev. Code Wash. Ann. Ch. 35.58. The statute empowered the district, upon approval of affected voters, to expand its functions to provide water supply, public transportation, garbage disposal, park services, and planning. The failure of the voters to implement this authorization, and their rejection of the addition of the transportation function to the district, is another example of the popular determination dilemma. On the one hand, elections are necessary to assure district board

accountability to the public; but, on the other they often serve to defeat district development. Popular determination is favored by most legislatures as a political expedient, and not by reason of constitutional requirements. See M. Pock, supra, 41, n. 128.

For other general statutes authorizing intrastate, multifunctional metropolitan districts, see, West's Ann.Cal.Pub.Util.Code §§ 11501–14509; Colo.Rev.Stat. Ch. 89, Art. 3; Conn.Gen.Stat.Ann. §§ 7–333 to 7–339; Mich. Comp.Laws Ann. ch. 119.

3. REGIONAL COUNCILS

Numerous regional agencies that are not truly governmental participate in the implementation of federal and state assistance grants. Though bearing names like "district" or "council of government—," they are neither constitutional nor political in origin, and are not local governments or political subdivisions of the state. Their structure, service area and project activities are determined largely by regulations geared to the needs of a particular program rather than a particular local unit. Often cutting across local jurisdictional lines, such agencies cannot act independently, but depend upon the cooperation of participating local governments. They do, however, influence local government policy in that interlocal cooperation is often a prerequisite to receipt of federal and state grants. See generally, Sundquist, *The Multicounty Agency in Nonmetropolitan America,* 58 Geo.L.Rev. 839 (1970); ACIR, *Urban America* and *The Federal System* 28, 29, 41 (1969).

The federal government is the prime, though not exclusive, stimulus for the creation of regional agencies. These vary in their territory, forms and functions according to particular statutes e.g. Appalachian Regional Development Act of 1965, 40 U.S.C.A.App. § 101 et seq.; Food and Agriculture Act of 1962, 74 Stat. 1187, codified in scattered sections of Titles 7 and 16 U.S.C.A. (Resource, Conservation and Planning); Public Works and Economic Development Act of 1965, 42 U.S.C.A. § 3121 *et seq.* (Economic Development); Economic Opportunity Act of 1964, 42 U.S.C.A. § 2701 (Health services and community action programs).

In its survey of 40 separate federal urban aid programs, involving 13 federal departments and agencies, the Advisory Commission concluded: "Among the major findings * * * are that almost all * * * aids are available to special purpose units of government at the state or local level as well * * * and almost half are available to nongovernmental persons or groups. * * * Through one means or another * * * a little more than one-quarter of the surveyed programs provide that aided projects should not be inconsistent with comprehensive plans for urban development * * *. About one-quarter operate under interagency agreements for sharing review responsibilities for plans and projects, and another quarter have legislatively established working relationships." ACIR, *Impact of Federal Urban Development Programs on Local Government Organization and Planning* iii–iv (1964).

Metropolitan Councils of Government (COGs). Federal policy often requires grant projects to be planned, reviewed and approved by COGs. See e.g. Demonstration Cities and Metropolitan Development Act, 42 U.S.C.A. § 3334. With limited exceptions, these councils are voluntary associations of local governments that lack fiscal or regulatory authority. Their proposals require the approval of each constituent government. COGs have been damned as powerless "fronts" to serve sectional interests and praised as hopeful beginnings to evolve new metro government forms. See generally, Comus, *Council of Government Approach,* 22 Vanderbilt L.Rev. 811 (1969); Zimmerman, *Metropolitan Ecumenism,* 44 J.Urban Law 433 (1967); *Metropolitan Government: Minnesota's Experience With a Metropolitan Council,* 53 Minn.L.Rev. 122 (1968).

> "While regional government does not appear to be a real political possibility, formation of voluntary regional councils of local governments * * * is a growing phenomenon. In the year * * * to June 30, 1969, eighty new regional councils were formed in both metropolitan and nonmetropolitan areas. * * * The National Service to Regional Councils reported that thirty-three states have active programs to develop regional planning districts and cooperative programs. In at least eleven states, these agencies are receiving financial assistance from the state to encourage their efforts." G. Blair, *State-Local Relations in 1968–69, The Book of the States* (1970–71) pp. 274, 275; * see especially, ACIR, *Regional Decisionmaking: New Strategies for Substate Districts* (2 Vols.—1973).

C. INTERSTATE COMPACTS— INTERSTATE DISTRICTS

Many interstate districts are created by compact to regulate activities formerly left to local governments. Their increasing use for developing shared natural resources, for controlling pollution, and for improving metropolitan services, is seen in the fact that most outstanding compacts came into effect after 1960. See Council of State Governments, *Interstate Compacts 1783–1970, A Compilation* (1971); Note, *Congressional Supervision of Interstate Compacts,* 75 Yale L.J. 1416 (1966); M. Ridgeway, *Interstate Compacts* (1971).

The interpretation and validity of interstate compacts present federal questions that are subject to ultimate determination by courts. State of West Virginia ex rel. Dyer v. Sims, 341 U.S. 22, 71 S.Ct. 557 (1951). A detailed review of the history and law regarding the Compact Clause is beyond the scope of this text, but the opinions and authorities cited in the Multistate Tax Commission case, infra, reviews the many uses and legal issues generated by the Compact Clause.

The possible uses of interstate compacts may be put are far from exhausted. It would seem a small step for states, which by compact now create interstate special function districts,* to create an interstate city. A compact might even be employed to carve out and create, as a new state, a present interstate metropolitan region. Neither the language of the Compact Clause, nor its early use to carve out the states of Kentucky and West Virginia, preclude such radical restructuring. See Tobin, *The Interstate Metropolitan District and Cooperative Federalism* 36 Tulane L.Rev. 67, 74 (1961); Engdahl, Interstate Urban Areas and Interstate Agreements, 58 Geo. L.J. 799 (1970).

Where different states submit an agreement to Congress for approval, does congressional approval nevertheless give the agreement the status of a federal statute? The issue has not fully resolved by judicial decision. Where cities in different states execute agreements pursuant to joint state laws, with congressional consent, there is uncertain authority on the question whether such compacts become the (supreme) "law of the union" as to supersede state jurisdiction over municipal actions that are governed by such agreements. The Supreme Court has alternately indicated approval and rejection of "the law of the union" doctrine relative to compacts. See Petty v. Tennessee-Missouri Bridge Commission, 359 U.S. 275, 79 S.Ct. 785, 3 L.Ed.2d 804 (1959); Engdahl, supra, at 815, n. 76 *.

Other problems arise on the necessity and effect of congressional consent. If Congress conditions its consent on terms which are breached, the legal consequences of such breaches are not fully delineated by any line of decisions. Congress may expressly reserve power to alter or revoke its consent, but whether reserved power is absolute, or subject to judicial limitation, e.g., by an estoppel, is not settled. It seems clear, however, that Congress may by independent general legislation supersede any inconsistent compact provisions. Courts are not likely to raise an estoppel against Article I legislative powers of Congress from an isolated consent to a compact. The Tobin opinion, p. 247, infra, illustrates the need for further clarification on the foregoing questions.

PEOPLE EX REL. YOUNGER v. EL DORADO

Supreme Court of California, 1971.
5 Cal.3d 480, 96 Cal.Rptr. 553, 487 P.2d 1193.

SULLIVAN, JUSTICE.

[Mandamus to compel county payments to bi-state agency formed by interstate compact.]

* * *

* Even interstate school districts created by compact have been upheld. See Dresden School District v. Norwich Town School District, 124 Vt. 227, 203 A.2d 598 (1964).

* It is clear, however, that the interpretation of local ordinances passed pursuant to an Interstate Compact may present a federal question subject to federal court review and jurisdiction. See League To Save Lake Tahoe v. BJK Corp., 547 F.2d 1072 (9th Cir.1976).

The controversy * * * focuses upon the Lake Tahoe Basin—an area of unique and unsurpassed beauty situated high in the Sierras along the California-Nevada border. * * *

* * * Only recently has the public become aware of the delicate balance of the ecology, and of the complex interrelated natural processes which keep the lake's waters clear and fresh, preserve the mountains from unsightly erosion, and maintain all forms of wildlife at appropriate levels. Today, and for the foreseeable future, the ecology of Lake Tahoe stands in grave danger before a mounting wave of population and development.

In an imaginative and commendable effort to avert this imminent threat, California and Nevada, with the approval of Congress (Pub.Law 91–148, 83 Stat. 360), entered into the Tahoe Regional Planning Compact (Compact) the provisions of which are found in Government Code section 66801. The basic concept of the Compact is a simple one—to provide for the region as a whole the planning, conservation and resource development essential to accommodate a growing population within the region's relatively small area without destroying the environment.

To achieve this purpose, the Compact establishes the Tahoe Regional Planning agency with jurisdiction over the entire region. (§ 66801, art. III, subd. (a).) The Agency has been given broad powers to make and enforce a regional plan of an unusually comprehensive scope. * * *

The Agency is given the power to "adopt all necessary ordinances, rules, regulations and policies to effectuate the adopted regional * * *." plan. (§ 66801, art. VI, subd. (a).) While ordinances so enacted establish minimum standards applicable throughout the region, local political subdivisions may enact and enforce equal or higher standards. "The regulations shall contain general, regional standards including but not limited to the following: water purity and clarity; subdivision; zoning; tree removal; solid waste disposal; sewage disposal; land fills, excavations, cuts and grading; piers, harbors, breakwaters; or channels and other shoreline developments; waste disposal in shoreline areas; waste disposal from boats; mobile home parks; house relocation; outdoor advertising; flood plain protection; soil and sedimentation control; air pollution; and watershed protection. Whenever possible without diminishing the effectiveness of the * * * general plan, the ordinances, rules, regulations and policies shall be confined to matters which are general and regional in application, leaving to the jurisdiction of the respective states, counties and cities the enactment of specific and local ordinances, rules, regulations and policies which conform to the * * * general plan." (Id.) The Compact also provides that "[v]iolation of any ordinance of the [A]gency is a misdemeanor." (§ 66801, art. VI, subd. (f).) Finally, it states that "all public works projects shall be reviewed prior to construction and [except for certain state public works projects] approved by the [A]gency as to the project's compliance with the adopted regional general plan." (§ 66801, art. VI, subd. (c).)

The governing body of the Agency is composed of ten members, five from California and five from Nevada. The Boards of Supervisors of El Dorado and Placer Counties and the City Council of the City of South Lake Tahoe each appoint one member; * * * The Boards of County Commissioners of the Counties of Douglas, Ormsby and Washoe in the State of Nevada each select one member; * * *. The Administrator of the California Resources Agency, or his designee, and the Director of the Nevada Department of Conservation and Natural Resources, or his designee, are *ex officio* members of the board. Finally, the Governors of California and Nevada each appoint one member, who "shall not be a resident of the region and shall represent the public at large." (§ 66801, art. III, subd. (a).)

The Compact permits the Agency to receive fees for its services, gifts, grants and other financial aids. It also provides for Agency financing as follows: " * * * the agency shall establish the amount of money necessary to support its activities * * *. The agency shall apportion not more than $150,000 of this amount among the counties within the region on the same ratio to the total sum required as the full cash valuation of taxable property within the region in each county bears to the total full cash valuation of taxable property within the region." * * *

* * *

II

We turn to the merits. The counties first contend that the Compact violates former sections * * * of the California Constitution. * * *. Generally speaking, these sections confer upon specified local governmental bodies broad powers over purely local affairs. But, as we shall point out, the Compact is unaffected by any of the above provisions since its subject matter is a regional, rather than local, concern.

* * *

* * * Only an agency transcending local boundaries can devise, adopt and put into operation solutions for the problems besetting the region as a whole. * * *

A

* * * The counties argue that the Compact gives the Agency power to adopt local, police and sanitary ordinances, rules and regulations, violations of which are declared misdemeanors by section 66801, article VI, subdivision (f). According to their argument, "[t]hese powers have been granted to respondent counties by the California Constitution and there is, therefore, a violation of Article XI, section 11, of the California Constitution in any attempt to grant these same powers to the Agency." In support of this contention, the counties cite In re Werner (1900) 129 Cal. 567, 574, 62 P. 97; and Gilgert v. Stockton Port District (1936) 7 Cal.2d 384, 60 P.2d 847.

* * *

Certain broad language in *Werner* and *Gilgert* appears to support the proposition that no power to make regulations having a local effect may be conferred upon public corporate bodies not enumerated in section 11. (See Brooks, The Metropolis, Home Rule, and the Special District, Part II (1960) 11 Hastings L.J. 246, 256–259.) * * *

The instant case is clearly distinguishable from *Werner* and *Gilgert* since the Legislature has not delegated to the Agency the power of enacting penal legislation. It is the Legislature itself which has properly declared that: "Violation of any ordinance of the agency is a misdemeanor." (§ 66801, art. VI, subd. (f).)

Nor has the Legislature, as it is claimed, granted to the Agency the same powers which have been granted to respondent counties by section 11. * * * It is sufficient to point out that the powers exercised by respondents are for local purposes, within the limits of the county. But, as we have explained, the broad powers conferred upon the Agency are not for *local* purposes, but solely to achieve the *regional* goal of preserving the Lake Tahoe Basin—a goal which local bodies have been unable to attain. * * *

The counties argue that the powers of zoning and planning conferred on the Agency deal with matters which traditionally have been of exclusively local concern. (See Gov.Code, § 65800 *et seq.*) But such argument ignores the very language of the Compact. Section 66801, article VI, subdivision (a), which sets forth the Agency's powers, provides that the governing body shall adopt all necessary ordinances, rules and regulations "to effectuate the adopted *regional* and interim plans"; that all such ordinances, rules and regulations shall establish minimum standards "applicable *throughout the basin*"; that the regulation shall contain "*general, regional* standards" including "zoning"; and that the ordinances, rules and regulations shall be confined to matters "which are general and regional in application * * *" (All italics added.) * * *

* * *

The counties next contend that the Compact legislation unconstitutionally imposes a tax on them in violation of former section 12 of article XI (now § 37 of art. XIII). * * *

Contrary to the above claim, we have held that "[t]he limitations of section 12 do not prevent the Legislature from authorizing a district to impose taxes for a state purpose, Joint Highway Dist. No. 13 of California v. Hinman, 220 Cal. 578, 588, * * *, nor for a purpose that transcends the boundaries of the various municipalities that may be included within the limits of a larger district. (Citations omitted)

* * *

C

Finally, we consider the claim that the Compact violates former section 13 of article XI. * * * The counties assert that the Agency is a "special commission" within the purview of the section and that the Legislature has unconstitutionally delegated to it the power to "interfere with" county improvements and to "perform" municipal functions. We find no merit in the contention.

* * *

Although section 13 was intended primarily to prevent legislative interference with the financial affairs of municipalities, its prohibition extends to other forms of interference. (Comment, *supra*, 55 Cal.L.Rev. 728, 761; Peppin, Municipal Home Rule in California: IV (1946) 34 Cal. L.Rev. 644, 682–684.) However, our cases have recognized "that the section was intended to prohibit only legislation interfering with purely local matters. Special commissions have been upheld if they either fulfill a more than local purpose, under the 'larger municipality' doctrine, or promote a 'statewide purpose.'" * * *

In upholding the establishment of sanitary districts we said: "[W]hile generally the question of sanitation is a municipal affair, in many instances it is one of broader scope, which cannot be adequately handled by the municipal authorities of a single town. Therefore it cannot be said to be a 'local' or 'municipal' affair within the inhibition of sections 12 and 13 of the constitution * * *." * * *

* * * The Compact does not give the Agency power to build or maintain local parks or other improvements; it merely grants the Agency authority to assure that public works which are planned, built and maintained by appropriate local bodies do not interfere with the fulfillment of the regional plan. Any restriction upon local improvements is merely incidental to the execution of the Agency's regional duties. Consequently, the Compact does not violate former section 13 of article XI of the California Constitution.

* * *

LADUE LOCAL LINES, INC. v. BI–STATE DEV. AGENCY OF MO.–ILL. MET. D.

United States Court of Appeals, Eighth Cir., 1970.
433 F.2d 131.

LAY, CIRCUIT JUDGE. This action was brought under the anti-trust laws * * *. Plaintiff Ladue Local Lines, Inc., is a Missouri corporation engaged in private bus transportation in the metropolitan St. Louis area, which includes parts of eastern Missouri and western Illinois. Suit was brought against the Bi-State Development Agency of the Missouri-Illinois Metropolitan District (hereinafter Bi-State), organized and operating under the laws of Missouri and Illinois. Plaintiff claims that defendant's monopolistic control of the public transportation market has destroyed Ladue's business by excluding it from bidding and servicing schools and school systems. Bi-State moved to dismiss on the ground that it was a body politic created by and under the laws of the States of Illinois and Missouri and the United States, exercising the powers of those sovereigns and therefore not subject to suit under the antitrust laws of the United States.

The district court * * * granted the motion to dismiss. * * * We affirm the dismissal. * * *

* * * As established by the compact, the governing body of the Bi-State Development Agency consists of ten commissioners, five voters of each state, all of whom reside within the bi-state district. Each state reserves the right to provide by law for the veto power of its governor over the action of any commissioner. In 1949, when the compact was initiated, the defendant was given powers, *inter alia*, to plan, own and maintain bridges, tunnels, airports and terminal facilities; to help coordinate streets, highways, parkways, parking areas, water supply and sewerage and disposal works, recreational and conservation facilities and land use patterns. The agency was empowered to charge and collect fees for the use of the facilities and was given the general power to perform all other necessary and incidental functions. Provision was also made for the exercise of such additional powers as conferred upon it by the legislatures of the states or by act of Congress.[2]

In 1959 the compact was amended by identical Missouri and Illinois statutes. The Missouri statute, Mo.Rev.Stat. § 70.373 (1959), V.A.M.S., reads in part:

"In further effectuation of that certain compact of * * * the Bi-State Development Agency * * * is authorized to exercise the following powers in addition to those heretofore expressly authorized * * *

* * *

"(1) To acquire and to plan, construct, operate and maintain, or lease * * * *passenger transportation facilities,* and air, water, rail, motor vehicle and other terminal facilities."[3] (Emphasis ours.)

* * *

" * * * it must follow that no monopoly or combination in a legal sense can arise from the fact that the duly authorized agents of the State are alone allowed to perform the duties devolving upon them by law." Olsen v. Smith, 195 U.S. 332, 344–345, 25 S.Ct. 52, 55, 49 L.Ed. 224 (1904).

In Parker v. Brown, 317 U.S. 341, 351, 63 S.Ct. 307, 313, 87 L.Ed. 315 (1943), the Supreme Court expanded this reasoning: * * * Thus, it appears that the proposition is settled that the antitrust laws do not apply to state government or activities undertaken pursuant to legislative mandate.

The plaintiff urges, however, that bussing of school children is not a recognized governmental function, that it is proprietary in nature and

---

2. The consent of Congress to this compact was required by Article I, Section 10, clause 3 of the Constitution of the United States, which provides in part: "No state shall, without the consent of Congress * * * enter into any agreement or compact with another state * * *."

3. Congress approved the exercise of these additional powers in Pub.L. No. 86–303, § 2, 73 Stat. 582 * * *.

therefore Bi-State should not enjoy sovereign immunity. * * * We think this approach misconceives the true issue before us. * * *

* * *

When a state determines that it is in the public interest to operate a public transportation system as a monopoly, or when two states enter into a congressionally approved compact to do so, the antitrust laws do not apply, whether the operation is labeled proprietary or governmental. * * *

* * *

Judgment affirmed.

Note

1. Cf. Hecht v. Pro-Football, Inc., 444 F.2d 931 (D.C.Cir.1971), where the court held the anti-trust laws applicable to a government agency on the theory that it was performing a proprietary, rather than governmental, function. There the federal agency owned a sports stadium and leased it to the Washington Redskins under a restrictive covenant that prevented any other professional football club from leasing the same facility. Since the lease did not serve a "governmental" function, the court held that the agency was not exempt from federal anti-trust laws.

SGAGLIONE v. PORT OF NEW YORK AUTHORITY

Supreme Court of New York, 1970.
61 Misc.2d 1058, 307 N.Y.S.2d 714.

CHARLES A. LORETO, JUSTICE. This is a proceeding * * * against The Port of New York Authority seeking the annulment of its decision relating to the method of promotion to the title of sergeant of a policeman of its police force.

The respondent is a bi-state agency created by interstate compact * * * and by legislation it is declared "a body, both corporate and politic". Its bi-state transportation operations are indeed impressive and vast, including six interstate vehicular crossings, the George Washington Bridge, the Lincoln and Holland Tunnels, the Bayonne Outerbridge Crossing and Goethals Bridge; two New York Marine terminals (Erie Basin and Brooklyn), the New Jersey Marine terminals (Newark, Elizabeth & Hoboken); two New Jersey airports (Newark and Teterboro); two New York airports (Kennedy and La Guardia); two inland freight terminals, one in New York and another in New Jersey. In addition, the interstate commuter railroad named the Port of Authority Trans-Hudson Corporation (PATH), which includes the Hudson River tunnels for their passage and the huge project now under construction in lower Manhattan, named the "World Trade Center".

As a separate and distinct body politic in the operation of these extensive * * * facilities, understandably a large number of employees are required, among whom necessarily is a police force which is of significant size, now numbering 850 police officers, 100 sergeants, 40 lieutenants, eight captains and one inspector.

Prior to 1969, promotion of its police officers to the rank of sergeant was by process of written competitive examination * * *.

On May 19, 1969, respondent issued an announcement stating that there would be a police officer's superior evaluation with the purpose of determining "the eligibility of police personnel for promotion to positions of police sergeant and police lieutenant * * *. The announcement further stated that the eligible list for sergeant would be permanent * * * and not ranked on the basis of marks or grades * * *. By reason of this change, petitioner is an aggrieved police officer.

* * *

In support of the contention that the Authority's action is a radical departure from the standard throughout the country, the petitioner has shown wherever the police force is of a significant size, advancement of the police officer to the next higher rank of sergeant has been and is pursuant to written competitive examination, with a list of limited duration. * * *

* * * But the Authority in its employment practices has not been expressly made subject to the Civil Service statutes of the states of New York and New Jersey. * * *

The source of the Authority's power is found in the 1921 compact between the States of New York and New Jersey, which provides in Article XIV, McK.Unconsol.Laws, § 6415:

"* * * the port authority * * * may appoint such officers and employees as it may require for the performance of its duties, and shall fix and determine their qualification and duties."

The Authority is truly sui generis. In view of its unique nature as a body politic, the creation of two sovereign states—with broad and explicit powers, this court doubts that it may be equated with the usual departmental body or agency, whose exercise of discretionary powers is often the subject of judicial review. [Citations omitted]

Nevertheless, one may query whether the Authority is endowed with the complete freedom of private business in its employment practices. * * *

This court does not doubt that the Authority may exercise its sound judgment in its employment and promotion policies, and it may even utilize what it denotes as management evaluation in supplementing any written examination for promotion of a police officer to the rank of sergeant. But in doing this by purportedly transferring the position of police sergeant from the class of "operating personnel" to that of "managerial and professional personnel", in this court's opinion, the Authority misbrands the duties of police sergeant. There is nothing in the listed duties of police sergeant which can correctly be termed as dealing with policy—duties ordinarily entrusted to a higher level of employee, whose salary tends in a measure to justify the responsibility of policy making.

* * *

Treating the Authority's resolution as one subject to judicial review, the statement in Matter of Wanetick v. State Liquor Authority, 8 A.D.2d 706, 707, 185 N.Y.S.2d 690, 691, cited by the petitioner, reads: "When reasons are enumerated, such reasons, when challenged, will be scrutinized, to ascertain if the conclusion reached is or may be rationally supported."

* * *

In paragraph VI of its answer the Authority "admits that, among other reasons, the Authority's action in proceeding by the said 'evaluation' in the selection of Sergeant in its police force is based on its determination that the said position is *both* supervisory and managerial and is ranked in the junior management classification as set forth by the Personnel Department of the Authority" (italics supplied).

* * *

Merely in attributing here the status "managerial" to a sergeant does not visit him with such powers. It is the actual work performed by the employee, not the title, which determines his position, * * *.

Thus it appears that of two reasons explicitly assigned for the promotional change, one is sustained and the second is found wanting.

* * *

In the court's opinion, even if Wanetick were applicable, it would not impose the requirement that all reasons given by the Authority for its action be sustained. The consideration of the reasons given does serve the purpose of inquiring into the good faith of the Agency.

* * *

The test where abuse of discretion is at issue is "whether there is any rational basis for the decision of the authority". (Matter of Austin v. Rohan, 8 A.D.2d 647, 185 N.Y.S.2d 11.) The court cannot agree that the record is bereft of showing any rational basis for the Authority's action.

* * *

It should be noted that the parties have in effect presented proof directed to the entire petition and answer, and in view of the foregoing opinion, the petition should be dismissed.

AGESEN v. CATHERWOOD

Court of Appeals of New York, 1970.
26 N.Y.2d 521, 311 N.Y.S.2d 886, 260 N.E.2d 525.

BREITEL, JUDGE. * * * employees of the Port of New York Authority engaged in the building and mechanical trades, * * * urge the applicability to their employment of New York's prevailing rate of wage legislation (Labor Law, Consol.Laws, c. 31, § 220).

* * *

The problem is presented because of the special character of the Port of New York Authority, a public authority created by compact between two States and approved by Congress as required by the

United States Constitution (L.1921, ch. 154, § 1, McK.Unconsol.Laws, § 6400 *et seq.;* N.J.S.A. § 32:1–1 *et seq.;* 42 U.S.Stat. 174; U.S. Const., art. I, § 10, subd. 3).

* * *

First, article XIV of the applicable compact between the States of New York and New Jersey reads: "The port authority * * * may appoint such officers and employees as it may require for the performance of its duties, and shall fix and determine their qualifications and duties" (L.1921, ch. 154, § 1). This language does not expressly empower the Authority to fix salaries. The fixing of salaries, however, * * * is undoubtedly one of its implied powers. Certainly, as to employees not covered by prevailing wage statutes, there would otherwise be no power anywhere to fix their salaries, a consequence hardly conceivable and not tolerable.

Secondly, a disparate wage scale dependent upon the geographic location of work sites, although occasionally burdensome, is not necessarily "unworkable." Presumably, similar problems were involved, and surmounted, in the Authority's Workmen's Compensation coverage, since both New York and New Jersey each have independent statutes and agencies (see N.J.S.A. §§ 34:1A–11 to 34:1A–13, 34:15–1 *et seq.;* Workmen's Compensation Law, Consol.Laws, c. 67, esp. § 140 *et seq.*).

Consequently, the inapplicability of section 220 of the Labor Law results not from any express exclusion or inherent unworkability, but rather from a general intent, amply reflected in the compact, that the internal operations of the Authority be independent of the direct control of either State acting without the concurrence of the other. Section 220, enacted long before the creation of the Authority, should not be construed to impose a unilateral regulation of the wages of only a fraction of the Authority's employees, namely, those building and mechanical workers who, it is alleged, work solely on projects within the State of New York.

The distinction between the internal operations and conduct affecting external relations of the Authority is crucial in charting the areas permitting unilateral and requiring bilateral State action. New York and New Jersey have each undoubted power to regulate the external conduct of the Authority, and it may hardly be gainsaid that the Authority, albeit bistate, is subject to New York's laws involving health and safety, insofar as its activities may externally affect the public (see 1949 Ops.Atty.Gen. 118–121).

Indeed, given sufficient social or economic justification, the lines of external and internal operation may shift, justifying increased regulation as the impact outside the Authority becomes more pronounced. Finally, even as to internal matters, the two States, by bi-lateral action, may always regulate Authority action, when unilateral action is ineffective or impractical.

Although the Authority's participation in New York's Workmen's Compensation and State Employees' Retirement systems constitute qualified exceptions to the scheme of internal autonomy, these exceptions are not controlling. * * *

* * *

Accordingly, the order of the Appellate Division should be affirmed without costs.

Notes

1. **Open-Ended Compacts.** Congress and state legislatures can provide advance blanket consent for compact parties to add functions to multistate authorities.

The Port Authority of New York and New Jersey has continually grown in this fashion. See, N.Y.—McKinney's Uncons.Laws Amended 1972, C. 531, § 1 et seq.; 65 N.Y.—McKinney's Consolidated Laws of New York, Part 2, § 6404.

2. **Mammoth Authorities as Super-Governments.** (a) *Size of Operations.* Many metropolitan districts far exceed the geographic size, employment rolls, fiscal budgets, and service operations of most municipalities, and even by most individual states. See, e.g., *Annual Report of Financial Transactions Concerning Special Districts of California—Fiscal Year 1966–67,* at 242, 257 (1967). The Delaware River Port Authority embraces 10 major counties, two in Pennsylvania and eight in New Jersey, and provides extraterritorial services in still others. 36 Pa.Stat. § 3503 at XII.

(b) *Limits on State Control.* Individual state legislatures lack unilateral control over interstate districts. All state parties must agree by joint legislation to changes of interstate authority powers.

UNITED STATES STEEL CORP. v. MULTISTATE TAX COMMISSION

Supreme Court of the United States, 1978.
434 U.S. 452, 54 L.Ed.2d 682.

[Class action by multistate corporate taxpayers seeking declaration that Multistate Tax Compact was invalid and a permanent injunction against its operation.]

MR. JUSTICE POWELL delivered the opinion of the Court.

The Compact Clause of Art. I, § 10, cl. 3, of the Constitution provides that "No State shall, without the Consent of Congress, * * * enter into any Agreement or Compact with another State, or with a foreign Power * * *." The Multistate Tax Compact, which established the Multistate Tax Commission, has not received congressional approval. This appeal requires us to decide whether the Compact is invalid for that reason. We also are required to decide whether it impermissibly encroaches on congressional power under the Commerce Clause and whether it operates in violation of the Fourteenth Amendment.

I

The Multistate Tax Compact was drafted in 1966 and became effective, according to its own terms, on August 4, 1967, after seven States had adopted it. * * * Its formation was a response to this Court's decision in Northwestern States Portland Cement Co. v. Minnesota, 358 U.S. 450, 79 S.Ct. 357, 3 L.Ed.2d 421 (1959) * * *.

In *Northwestern States,* this Court held that net income from the interstate operations of a foreign corporation may be subjected to state taxation, provided that the levy is nondiscriminatory and is fairly apportioned to local activities that form a sufficient nexus to support the exercise of the taxing power. This prompted Congress to enact a statute, Act of Sept. 14, 1959, Pub.L. 86–272, 73 Stat. 555, which sets forth certain minimum standards for the exercise of that power. * * *

While Congress was wrestling with the problem, the Multistate Tax Compact was drafted. It symbolized the recognition that, as applied to multistate businesses, traditional state tax administration was inefficient and costly to both State and taxpayer. * * *

To these ends, Art. VI creates the Multistate Tax Commission, composed of the tax administrators from all the member States. Section 3 of Art. VI authorizes the Commission (i) to study state and local tax systems; (ii) to develop and recommend proposals for an increase in uniformity and compatibility of state and local tax laws in order to encourage simplicity and improvement in state and local tax law and administration; (iii) to compile and publish information that may assist member States in implementing the Compact * * * and (iv) to do all things necessary and incidental to the administration of its functions pursuant to the Compact.

* * * These regulations are advisory only. * * * They have no force in any member State until adopted by that State in accordance with its own law.

Article VIII applies only in those States that specifically adopt it by statute. It authorizes any member State or its subdivision to request that the Commission perform an audit on its behalf. * * * Information obtained by the audit may be disclosed only in accordance with the laws of the requesting State. Moreover, individual member States retain complete control over all legislation and administrative action affecting the rate of tax, the composition of the tax base (including the determination of the components of taxable income), and the means and methods of determining tax liability and collecting any taxes determined to be due.

Article X permits any party to withdraw from the Compact by enacting a repealing statute. * * *

In 1972, appellants brought this action * * *. Their complaint challenged the constitutionality of the Compact on four grounds: (1) the Compact, never having received the consent of Congress, is invalid under the Compact Clause; (2) it unreasonably burdens interstate commerce; (3) it violates the rights of multistate taxpayers under the Fourteenth Amendment; and (4) its audit provisions violate the Fourth and Fourteenth Amendments. * * *

* * * Turning to the merits, the District Court first rejected the contention that the Compact Clause requires congressional consent to every agreement between two or more States. * * * The District Court found neither enhancement of state political power nor encroachment upon federal supremacy. Concluding that appellants' Commerce Clause, Fourth Amendment, and Fourteenth Amendment claims also lacked merit, the District Court granted summary judgment for appellees.

* * *

II

Read literally, the Compact Clause would require the States to obtain congressional approval before entering into any agreement among themselves, irrespective of form, subject, duration, or interest to the United States. The difficulties with such an interpretation were identified by Mr. Justice Field in his opinion for the Court in Virginia v. Tennessee, *supra*. His conclusion that the Clause could not be read literally was approved in subsequent dicta, but this Court did not have occasion expressly to apply it in a holding until our recent decision in New Hampshire v. Maine, *supra*.

Appellants urge us to abandon Virginia v. Tennessee and New Hampshire v. Maine, but provide no effective alternative other than a literal reading of the Compact Clause. At this late date, we are reluctant to accept this invitation to circumscribe modes of interstate cooperation that do not enhance state power to the detriment of federal supremacy. * * *

Article I, § 10, cl. 1, of the Constitution—the Treaty Clause—declares that "No State shall enter into Any Treaty, Alliance or Confederation * * *." Yet Art. I, § 10, cl. 3—the Compact Clause—permits the States to enter into "agreements" or "compacts," so long as congressional consent is obtained. The Framers clearly perceived compacts and agreements as differing from treaties. The records of the Constitutional Convention, however, are barren of any clue as to the precise contours of the agreements and compacts governed by the Compact Clause. * * *

Whatever distinct meanings the Framers attributed to the terms in Art. I, § 10, those meanings were soon lost. In 1833, Mr. Justice Story perceived no clear distinction among any of the terms. * * *

The Court's first opportunity to comment on the scope of the Compact Clause, Holmes v. Jennison, 14 Pet. 540, 10 L.Ed. 579 (1840), proved inconclusive. * * *

* * *

In [Virginia v. Tennessee] the Court held that Congress tacitly had assented to the running of a boundary between the two States. In an extended dictum, however, Justice Field took the Court's first opportunity to comment upon the Compact Clause since the neglected essay in Holmes v. Jennison. * * *

> "Looking at the clause in which terms 'compact' or 'agreement' appear, it is evident that the prohibition is directed to the formation of any combination tending to the increase of political power in the states, which may encroach upon or interfere with the just supremacy of the United States." Id., at 519, 13 S.Ct., at 734.

* * *

Although this Court did not have occasion to apply Justice Field's test for many years, it has been cited with approval on several occasions. * * * Moreover, several decisions of this Court have upheld a variety of interstate agreements effected through reciprocal legislation without congressional consent. * * * While none of these cases explicitly applied the Virginia v. Tennessee test, they reaffirmed its underlying assumption: not all agreements between States are subject to the strictures of the Compact Clause. * * *

* * *

This was the status * * * until two Terms ago, when we decided New Hampshire v. Maine, 426 U.S. 363, 96 S.Ct. 2113, 48 L.Ed.2d 701 (1976). In that case we specifically * * * held that an interstate agreement locating an ancient boundary did not require congressional consent. We reaffirmed Justice Field's view that the "application of the Compact Clause is limited to agreements that are 'directed to the formation of any combination tending to the increase of political power in the States, which may encroach upon or interfere with the just supremacy of the United States.'" 426 U.S. at 369, 96 S.Ct., at 2117, * * * This rule states the proper balance between federal and state power with respect to compacts and agreements among States.

* * * It is true that most multilateral compacts have been submitted for congressional approval. But this historical practice, which may simply reflect considerations of caution and convenience * * * is not controlling. It is also true that the precise interstate mechanism involved in this case has not been presented to this Court before.

Appellants further urge that the pertinent inquiry is one of potential, rather than actual, impact upon federal supremacy. We agree. But the multilateral nature of the agreement and its establishment of an ongoing administrative body do not, standing alone, present significant potential for conflict with the principles underlying the Compact Clause. The number of parties to an agreement is irrelevant if it does not impermissibly enhance state power at the expense of federal supremacy. As to the powers delegated to the administrative body, we think these also must be judged in terms of enhancement of state power in relation to the Federal Government. See Virginia v. Tennessee, 148

U.S., at 520, 13 S.Ct., at 734 (establishment of commission to run boundary not a "compact"). We turn, therefore, to the application of the Virginia v. Tennessee rule to the Compact before us.

III

On its face the Multistate Tax Compact contains no provisions that would enhance the political power of the member States in a way that encroaches upon the supremacy of the United States. * * * Group action in itself may be more influential than independent actions by the States. But the test is whether the Compact enhances state power *quo ad* the National Government. This pact does not purport to authorize the member States to exercise any powers they could not exercise in its absence. Nor is there any delegation of sovereign power to the Commission; each State retains complete freedom to adopt or reject the rules and regulations of the Commission. Moreover, as noted above, each State is free to withdraw at any time. * * *

A

Appellants contend initially that the Compact encroaches upon federal supremacy with respect to interstate commerce. * * *

* * *

* * * Appellees make no showing that increased effectiveness in the administration of state tax laws, * * * threatens federal supremacy. * * *

B

Appellants further argue that the Compact encroaches upon the power of the United States with respect to foreign relations. * * *

This contention was not presented to the court below and in any event lacks substance. * * * The Commission, as auditing agent, adopts the method only at the behest of a State requesting an audit. To the extent that its use contravenes any foreign policy of the United States, the facial validity of the Compact is not implicated.

C

Appellants' final Compact Clause argument charges that the Compact impairs the sovereign rights of nonmember States. * * *

We find no support for this conclusion. It has not been shown that any unfair taxation of multistate business * * * will redound to the benefit of any particular group of States or to the harm of others. * * * Risks of unfairness and double taxation, then, are independent of the Compact.

* * *

IV

Appellants further challenge, on relatively narrow grounds, the validity of the Multistate Tax Compact under the Commerce Clause and the Fourteenth Amendment. * * * Specifically, they claim that the Commission induced eight States to issue burdensome requests for production of documents and to deviate from the provisions of state law by issuing arbitrary assessments against taxpayers who refuse to comply with these harassing production orders.

These allegations do not establish that the Compact is in violation either of the Commerce Clause or the Fourteenth Amendment. We observe first that this contention was not presented to the court below.

* * *

Even if appellants' factual allegations were supported by the record, they would be irrelevant to the facial validity of the Compact. As we have noted above, it is only the individual State, not the Commission, that has the power to issue an assessment—whether arbitrary or not. If the assessment violates state law, we must assume that state remedies are available. * * *

V

We conclude that appellants' constitutional challenge to the Multistate Tax Compact fails. We affirm the judgment of the District Court.

Affirmed.

MR. JUSTICE WHITE, with whom MR. JUSTICE BLACKMUN joins, dissenting.

The majority opinion appears to concede, as I think it should, that the Compact Clause reaches interstate agreements presenting even *potential* encroachments on federal supremacy. In applying its Compact Clause theory to * * * the Multistate Tax Compact, however, the majority is not true to this view. For if the Compact Clause has any independent protective force at all, it must require the consent of Congress to an interstate scheme of such complexity and detail as this. The majority states it will watch for the mere *potential* of harm to federal interests, but then approves the Compact here for lack of *actual* proved harm.

* * *

II

Congressional consent to an interstate compact may be expressed in several ways. In the leading case of Virginia v. Tennessee, 148 U.S. 503, 13 S.Ct. 728, 37 L.Ed. 537 (1893), congressional consent to a compact setting a boundary was inferred from years of acquiescence to that line by the Congress in delimiting federal judicial and electoral districts. *Id.,* at 522, 13 S.Ct., at 735. Congressional consent may also be given in advance of the adoption of any specific compacts, by general consent resolutions, as was the case for the highway safety compacts, 72 Stat. 635 (1958), and the Crime Control Compact Act of 1934, 48 Stat. 909.

Congress does not pass upon a submitted compact in the manner of a court of law deciding a question of constitutionality. Rather, the requirement that Congress approve a compact is to obtain its political judgment: is the agreement likely to interfere with federal activity in the area, is it likely to disadvantage other States to an important extent, is it a matter that would better be left untouched by state and federal regulation? It comports with the purpose of seeking the political consent Congress affords that such consent may be expressed in ways as informal as tacit recognition or prior approval, that Congress be permitted to attach conditions upon its consent, and that congressional approval be a continuing requirement.

In the present case, it would not be possible to infer approval from the congressional reaction to the Multistate Tax Compact. Indeed, the history of the Congress and the Compact is a chronicle of jealous attempts of one to close out the efforts of the other.

On the congressional side of this long-lived battle, bills to approve the Compact have been introduced 12 separate times, but all have faltered before arriving at a vote. * * *

* * *

A hostile stalemate characterizes the present position of the parties: the Multistate Tax Compact States opposing the federal Congress and, since the proposed new tax treaty, the federal Executive as well. No one could view this history and conclude that the Congress has acquiesced in the Multistate Tax Compact.

But more is demonstrated by this long dispute underlying the present case: not only has Congress failed to acquiesce in the Multistate Tax Compact, both Congress and the Executive have clearly demonstrated that there is a federal interest in the rules for apportioning multistate and multinational income. * * *

* * *

IV

For appellant's many suggestions of extraordinary authority wielded by the Multistate Tax Commission, the majority has but one repeated answer: that each member State is free to adopt the procedures in question just as it could as if the Compact did not exist.

This cannot be an adequate answer even for the majority, which holds that "Agreements effected through reciprocal legislation may present opportunities for enhancement of state power at the expense of the federal supremacy similar to the threats inherent in a more formalized 'compact.'" * * * In recognizing Compact Clause concerns even in reciprocal legislation, the majority correctly lays the premise that the absence of an autonomous authority would not be controlling.

* * *

The Compact Clause is an important, intended safeguard within our constitutional structure. It is functionally a conciliatory rather than a prohibitive clause. All it requires is that Congress review interstate agreements that are capable of affecting federal or other States' rights. In the Court's decision today, a highly complex multistate compact, detailed in structure and pervasive in its effect on the important area of interstate and international business taxation, has been legitimized without the consent of Congress. If the Multistate Tax Compact is not a compact within the meaning of Art. I, § 10, then I fear there is very little life remaining in that section of our Constitution.

I respectfully dissent.

TOBIN v. UNITED STATES

United States Court of Appeals, District of Columbia Cir., 1962.
113 U.S.App.D.C. 110, 306 F.2d 270.

BASTIAN, CIRCUIT JUDGE. Austin J. Tobin, the Executive Director of the Port of New York Authority, was charged by information and convicted in the District Court of criminal contempt of Congress, under 2 U.S.C.A. § 192, for refusing to produce certain documents called for by a subpoena issued by Subcommittee No. 5 of the Committee on the Judiciary of the United States House of Representatives.

The Port of New York Authority is a bi-state agency established * * * by compacts between the States of New York and New Jersey to provide for the efficient administration of the New York harbor, which is divided geographically between the two states. Pursuant to the compact clause of the Constitution, Congress consented to the compacts but expressly retained, among other matters, "the right to alter, amend or repeal" its resolutions of approval. * * *

In February of 1960, the Judiciary Committee initiated an investigation of the Authority on an informal basis. The Authority cooperated with the Committee investigators except as to disclosing certain documents alleged to relate exclusively to the internal administration of the Authority. After this refusal events moved swiftly to a climax.

On June 1, 1960, the Chairman of the Committee obtained from the House subpoena power in connection with matters "involving the activities and operations of interstate compacts." * * *

Appellant conferred with the Board of Commissioners of the Authority, as well as with the Governors of both New York and New Jersey, and the consensus of their opinion was that the investigation being attempted was too broad to be valid. * * * Discounting these objections, the Subcommittee issued the subpoena in question. * * *

After being denied the opportunity to appear before the Subcommittee, the Governors wrote identical letters to their respective representatives on the Board of Commissioners of the Authority, instructing them to direct appellant not to comply with the subpoena. The Board of Commissioners so directed appellant on June 27, 1960. * * * It was against this background that appellant refused to comply with the demands of the subpoena * * *. Thereafter, the Subcommittee recommended to the full Committee that appellant be cited by the House for contempt. This recommendation was adopted by the Judiciary Committee, * * * and subsequently by the House itself. Charged by information, appellant waived his right to jury trial and was convicted of contempt of Congress by District Judge Youngdahl.

Appellant advances several arguments in support of the position that his conviction cannot stand. For present purposes, * * * we list but two of his arguments:

> "1. That Congress does not have the power, * * * to 'alter, amend or repeal' its consent to an interstate compact, which was the stated purpose of the Subcommittee's investigation.

> "2. That 'the subpoena issued by the Subcommittee, demanding documents relating to the internal administration of the Port Authority * * * was an unconstitutional invasion of powers reserved to the states * * *'."

Because of the view we take of this case, appellant's first contention demands some elaboration. In granting its consent Congress can attach certain binding conditions, * * *. However, the vital condition precedent to the validity of any such attached condition is that it be constitutional. If Congress does not have the power under the Constitution, then it cannot confer such power upon itself by way of a legislative fiat imposed as a condition to the granting of its consent.

In the present case, therefore, Congress's express reservation of the right "to alter, amend or repeal" its initial consent to the creation of the Authority is meaningless unless Congress has the power under the Constitution "to alter, amend or repeal" its consent to an interstate compact. The compact clause of the Constitution does not specifically confer such power upon Congress. No case has been cited to us, nor have we been able to find any case through our own research, holding that Congress has such constitutional power. Nor do we find any to the contrary. Since no such power appears expressly in the compact clause, any holding that it exists and that Congress possesses it must be predicated on the conclusion that it exists as an implied power.

We have addressed ourselves at some length to this issue in order to show the gravity of passing upon even only one of the constitutional questions posed by this case. Moreover, in view of appellant's argument, * * * we are even less inclined to reach the constitutional issues involved here. We have no way of knowing what ramifications would result from a holding that Congress has the implied constitutional power "to alter, amend or repeal" its consent to an interstate compact. * * *

Appellant argues that congressional consent becomes irrevocable once it is given under the compact clause since Congress thereby removes the constitutional ban against the formation of interstate compacts and thus, to that extent, restores the states to the inherent sovereignty they enjoyed prior to the adoption of the Constitution. This does not mean that once congressional consent is obtained the particular compact becomes a law unto itself, immune * * * from future congressional supervision. It simply means that the states are restored to that much of their original sovereignty as would permit them to enter into compacts with each other. To this extent, and to this extent alone, does congressional consent restore them to sovereignty—sovereign in the narrow sense of being free to conclude an interstate compact, not sovereign in the broad sense of being free of the Constitution.

Accordingly, if a particular compact happens to be operational in nature (as exemplified by the compact creating the Authority) as opposed to one static in nature (as exemplified by an agreement to settle a disputed boundary line, * * *) Congress is not without power to control the conduct of the former. Under our system of government the Constitution is paramount, and the Constitution gives to Congress certain plenary powers, as for example those in the field of interstate commerce and that of national defense. With the choice of acting pursuant to any or all of these plenary powers continuously available to it, Congress has at its disposal abundant authority to supervise and regulate the activities of operational compacts in such a way as to insure that no violence is done by these compacts to more compelling federal concerns.

* * *

A contempt of Congress prosecution is not the most practical method of inducing courts to answer broad questions broadly. Especially is this so when the answers sought necessarily demand far-reaching constitutional adjudications. To avoid such constitutional holdings is our duty, particularly in the area of the right of Congress to inform itself. United States v. Rumely, 345 U.S. 41, 73 S.Ct. 543, 97 L.Ed. 770 (1953). * * *

Accordingly, the first issue we must decide is whether Congress gave the Judiciary Committee of the House (and therefore its Subcommittee No. 5) authority sufficient to permit the Subcommittee to conduct the sweeping investigation undertaken in the instant case. * * *

* * *

The authority thus granted to the Committee is couched in general terms. In the present case, the Committee stretched these general terms in order to justify about as specific an investigation of the Port of New York Authority as can be envisaged. We are inclined to believe the House did not intend these general terms to be stretched quite so far. * * *

* * * Therefore, we think the Subcommittee's investigative authority, as thus construed, was exhausted by the information actually tendered by appellant in compliance with the subpoena, for such information adequately disclosed all that the Authority had done in the areas under inquiry. The information refused to the Subcommittee related only to the *why* of Authority activity and, consequently, was outside the scope of the Subcommittee's authority to investigate.

We feel inclined to add a few words in conclusion. If Congress should adopt a resolution which in express terms authorizes and empowers the Committee and its duly authorized Subcommittee to initiate an investigation of the Port of New York Authority as deep and as penetrating as the one attempted here, a challenge of the congressional power so to provide would of course present constitutional issues which we should have to meet and decide. Therefore, we emphasize that all we are saying here is that a due regard for the responsibility of administering justice prompts us to avoid serious constitutional adjudications until such time as Congress clearly manifests its intention of putting such a decisional burden upon us.

* * *

Reversed.

Notes

1. See Case Note, Tobin v. United States, 8 Vill.L.Rev. 237 (1962); Note, *Congress And The Port of New York Authority: Federal Supervision of Interstate Compacts,* 70 Yale L.J. 812 (1961).

2. **Choice of Law Problems.** (a) New York and New Jersey, by compact, created a Joint Commission with authority to conduct investigations and issue subpoenas. By subsequent joint enactment, they also empowered the Commission to compel testimony by granting witnesses immunity from criminal prosecution in either state. Thereafter, New Jersey modified its general laws to extend the privilege of refusing to testify for fear of self-incrimination under the laws of any other state or foreign government. In a Commission hearing a witness from New Jersey refused to testify on self-incrimination grounds notwithstanding the Commission's grant of immunity from prosecution in the compact states. Which law controls? See In re Application of Waterfront Commission of New York Harbor, 39 N.J. 436, 189 A.2d 36 (1963).

(b) By interstate compact, Pennsylvania and New Jersey created a Bridge Commission to construct bridge approaches. The states limited the Commission's power of eminent domain over local government property "unless consented to by the affected municipality." The Commission undertook to construct approaches in Easton, Pennsylvania and in Morrisville, New Jersey. Morrisville refused to consent, and the Easton City Council passed a resolution consenting to the construction of bridge approaches over the city ways. The Commission proceeded with its work on the claim that it did not require Morrisville's consent. Citizens of Easton sued to enjoin construction of overpasses over Easton's streets and alleged: (1) under its city charter Easton could consent to the Commission condemnation only by an ordinance approved by voter referendum. (2) that the Commission could not proceed without the consent of Morrisville; (3) that the Pennsylvania waiver statute violated the compact and was without effect, and (4) that a Pennsylvania statute waiving the city's consent condition was invalid as "local and special legislation." What result? See Henderson v. Delaware River Joint Toll Bridge Commission, 362 Pa. 475, 66 A.2d 843 (1949).

D. CONSOLIDATING PARTICULAR FUNCTIONS

An alternative remedy to structural changes is to consolidate particular functions of the existing government units. Functional consolidation may take the form of (a) state mandated transfers of selected urban functions to state or area-wide units; (b) state authorization of inter-local transfers of functions, at the option of local governments; (c) state authorization of informal or contract arrangements whereby area functions are performed jointly or by one of neighboring units on behalf of all. These options have different appeal in different urban contexts. Small states like Hawaii (*viz.*, state-wide education district), Connecticut (whose counties were abolished) and Massachusetts may find the first option more suitable than would larger states. Where political conditions prevent *interlocal transfers of functions*, area-wide functional consolidation *of limited scope and duration* may still be feasible under *interlocal service contracts*. The differences between transfers of function and interlocal contracts, often blurred by their similarities, are legally significant.

1. EXTRATERRITORIAL POWERS

One of the older methods of unifying functions across municipal boundaries is the piecemeal grant of specific extraterritorial power. The grant of extraterritorial jurisdiction to municipalities without voting approval or representation rights of the affected extraterritorial residents has been upheld against constitutional challenge under the one-man one-vote principle in the absence of any special law governing racial discrimination. Compare City of Rome, p. 182, supra, with Holt Civic Club v. Tuscaloosa, 439 U.S. 60, 99 S.Ct. 383, 58 L.Ed.2d 292 (1978).

As noted in the *Holt* case, p. 259 n. 1, infra, some "35 states authorize their municipal subdivisions to exercise governmental power beyond their corporate limits. Comment, The Constitutionality of The Exercise of Extraterritorial Powers by Municipalities. 45 Chi.L.Rev. 151 (1977)." Like other makeshift substitutes, this technique is freighted with legal problems.

How strictly or liberally should courts construe legislation regarding: (1) the scope of activities authorized beyond municipal boundaries; (2) the degree of authorized extraterritorial regulation and enforcement; (3) delegations of related powers to other municipalities and state agencies; (4) the extraterritorial power, if any, to be implied from expressed powers? These questions can only be answered with reference to particular activity (*viz.* providing services; imposing regulations; acquiring land).

Where extraterritorial power is granted *ad hoc* a narrow function or activity, the limits of each such grant is unrelated to other grants of extraterritorial jurisdiction. See e.g., Phay, *The Municipal Corporation and Conflicts Over Extraterritorial Acquisitions: The Need For Land Planning,* 17 Vanderbilt L.Rev. 347 (1964); Bouwsma, *The Validity of Extraterritorial Municipal Zoning,* 8 Vanderbilt L.Rev. 806 (1953); Kneier, *State Supervision Over Municipally Owned Utilities,* 49 Columbia L.Rev. 180 (1949); Sengstock, *Extraterritorial Powers in the Metropolitan Area* (1962). These authors note that there is no single theoretical foundation for the analysis of municipal extraterritorial powers. See Becker, *Municipal Boundaries and Zoning, Controlling Regional Land Development,* 1966 Wash.U.L.Q. 1, 23–58 (detailed analysis of state statutes and decisions on extramural land controls); Kneier, supra, 199–200 (tabulation and comparison of state statutes on extramural utility regulation); Sengstock, supra 32 et seq. (comparison of state statutes on extraterritorial municipal utility operations); and at pp. 52 et seq. (comparison of state statutes on extraterritorial police and sanitary regulations).

While patterns of judicial "balancing" of competing interests may be drawn from the decisional law (see Phay, *supra*), the reasoning of extraterritorial power cases is not easily harmonized. There is general agreement on the point, namely, that the grant of extraterritorial municipal power is an inadequate device for consolidating area-wide functions.

*   *   *

"A study of extraterritorial powers leads to these conclusions: the multiplicity of local governments within the metropolitan area *   *   * is an impediment to the solution of metropolitan area problems; extraterritorial powers *   *   * have failed and will fail to overcome that impediment. The problems of the metropolitan area will not be permanently solved by the employment of extraterritorial powers. Other solutions should be sought." Sengstock, supra, p. 72.

CITY OF PUEBLO v. FLANDERS

Supreme Court of Colorado, 1950.
122 Colo. 571, 225 P.2d 832.

STONE, JUSTICE. This action was brought to enjoin the officers of the city of Pueblo from furnishing fire protection to property located outside the city limits, and the trial court granted a writ of injunction declaring that, "The maintenance and operation of a fire department by a municipality is exercising a governmental function and therefore has no extraterritorial powers; *   *   * "

In reviewing this judgment and writ, we are confronted with a question novel in this jurisdiction and, so far as our study discloses, without precedent elsewhere. In such a case it is particularly unfortunate that the questions involved are not explored in the briefs.

*   *   * In the record before us there is evidence of occasional response by the fire department to calls outside the city limits over a term of years; there is evidence also of action by the city council at various times prohibiting such response, * * *. We think the showing here insufficient to justify the drastic remedy of injunctive relief, but are not content to rest our decision on that ground alone.

* * *

The injunction here issued by the trial court does not concern contract obligations to supply fire protection to outside areas * * *, but only the discretionary use of such equipment at such times as may be deemed advisable by the appropriate city officials.

It will be noted that the injunction here issued by the trial court contains no exception, * * *. It applies, regardless of the location, nature or threatened consequences of the fire, and regardless of whether its extinguishment might save the city itself from serious conflagration.

* * *

We do not challenge the rule that in exercising a governmental function a municipality generally has no extraterritorial powers, except as they may be delegated by the legislature, but the authority of permissive statute is essential, not because the city may otherwise not act outside its limits, but rather because it does not have the power to enforce its actions upon the people or property against which it acts in invitum, in the absence of statute. The question here before us does not concern the right to enforce a municipal power against properties or citizens outside the city limits, but rather the right of city officials to volunteer service outside. The distinction, we think is fundamental, and in cases involving actions of municipal authorities outside the city limits, it is important to distinguish which question may be involved: the power to enforce the authority of the municipality as against property or people outside its borders, or the right of municipal officers to act outside the city limits where no enforcement of authority is involved. The former right, if existing at all, is absolute; the latter is discretionary and dependent on purpose and result. The former, as raised in People v. Raims, 20 Colo. 489, 39 P. 341, is dependent on legislative delegation of authority; the latter is dependent on whether or not the use of the city's officers or facilities or funds is, or is not, for the benefit of the municipality. Admittedly the operation of a fire department within the city limits is a proper municipal activity. Its purpose is to benefit the city, and, where there is no conflict of rights, its relation to that purpose, rather than arbitrary city boundary lines, must determine the extent of its use.

As to the second ground, we cannot agree with the unsupported declaration of the trial court that the welfare and public interest of the municipality and the taxpayers therein are neither promoted nor protected by permitting the city's fire department to accept calls for the extinguishment of fire outside the municipality's corporate limits, even where public buildings are not involved. In many cases prompt action in extinguishing a small fire outside the city limits may prevent its increase and spread across the city line with disastrous results to the city and its taxpayers. The destruction by fire of a factory located outside the city limits may deprive resident taxpayers of means of livelihood and they and the city suffer loss thereby. Mutual assistance by neighboring cities may well work to the advantage of each. * * * On the other hand, there are doubtless many cases where large districts refuse to become annexed to the city, and the burden of furnishing fire protection to such areas becomes an imposition on the city and its taxpayers, and discretion might well require refusal of fire service except where there is danger of the fire spreading across the city lines.

A similar issue was raised in connection with the purchase by the City of New York of land outside the city for use as a public park. * * * and in Matter of Application of Mayor, etc., of N.Y., 99 N.Y. 569, 2 N.E. 642, 648, the court said, *inter alia*, "It appears to be conceded * * * that the acquisition and maintenance of public parks, securing pure air and healthful rest and recreation to the people, is a 'city purpose' when executed within the corporate limits; and the sole contention is that it ceases to be a 'city purpose' when, * * * it moves outside of those boundaries. * * * that test of a city purpose which asks if the property bought and the money spent go outside of the corporate boundaries must be abandoned. It will not serve for a rule. * * * While, as was said in one of the cases cited, it is impossible to formulate a perfect definition of what is meant by a city purpose, * * *." So we think the question here is not whether the actual service rendered by the fireman is within or without the city limits, but rather it is whether the predominant purpose is to benefit the city. In Hansen v. City of Havre, 112 Mont. 207, 114 P.2d 1053, 1058, 135 A.L.R. 1278, challenge was raised by a taxpayer as to the right of the city to assess property in a special improvement district within a city for improvements made without the city for control of flood waters, or for the purpose of paying for property without the city condemned for that purpose, and the court said: "The thing to be accomplished is improvement of conditions within the city and the improvement district. The fact that property must be acquired and the work performed outside the city is but incidental. The property to be benefited is not that outside the city but that within the city and within the improvement district."

Municipal police are usually employed * * * by the city, and the taxpayers might with equal justice, as in the case of firemen, demand that their activities be carried on exclusively within the city boundaries; * * * However, in addition to the powers granted to the police by the legislature, it is a matter of common knowledge that, when a vicious crime is committed * * *, it is part of the regular work of the police of other cities, using city equipment and on city time, to go to the place of the crime, although without any authority to act there, for the purpose of assisting the local police in solving the crime and apprehending the criminal. While this assists the local police, its main purpose is, and must be, the protection of the city by which the visiting police are employed. * * * It would seem difficult to sustain them if the activities of fire departments were entirely restricted within the municipal limits.

While we have found no case involving precisely the question here raised, there are numerous cases in which the legality of extraterritorial service by a municipal fire department is recognized or assumed. See, Anno., 122 A.L.R. 1158. * * *

In Hubert v. Granzow, 131 Minn. 361, 155 N.W. 204, 205, where a similar question was raised in an action for negligence against members of a fire department, the court said: "It is probably true that no legal duty is imposed upon a city fire department to assist in extinguishing fires outside the city; but it is a matter of common knowledge that such departments almost invariably respond when called upon in such cases. Actuated by motives of humanity rather than by the mandate of strict legal duty, they seldom refuse to give their services to their neighbors in case of need. While the law may not impose a legal duty upon them to assist in extinguishing fires outside the city, it certainly does not forbid them from doing so."

In McCarthy v. Mason, 132 Me. 347, 171 A. 256, 258, the court quoted the above expression of the Minnesota case and said: "We concur. * * *"

* * *

In Barclay-Westmoreland Trust Co. v. Borough of Latrobe, 131 Pa. Super. 513, 200 A. 271, an insurance carrier challenged the award of compensation to dependents of a fireman who was killed after responding to a fire alarm, and being sent to rescue some people marooned by flood waters outside the city. No objection was made on the ground of his having been employed outside the city limits, and it was held that the fact that he was engaged in other work than fighting a fire was not material; that it is well known when disastrous floods have occurred members of the fire department rendered valuable service in rescuing persons in jeopardy; that this was expected of firemen, and that it was generally regarded as work incidental to their duties.

Finally, in exploring this question, we are persuaded that law must be more than isolated logic. * * * The rule sought here and adopted by the trial court is niggardly and antisocial, contrary to long recognized custom, and, in the long view, detrimental, as we think, to the city and its taxpayers. * * *

HAYS, JUSTICE (dissenting).

* * *

The general rule, to which there are few, if any, exceptions, is stated in 62 C.J.S., Municipal Corporations, § 141, page 283, as follows: "As a general rule the powers of a municipal corporation cease at municipal boundaries and cannot, without plain manifestation of legislative intention, be exercised beyond its limits, at least as far as governmental functions are concerned, even though it may have acquired property outside of its geographical limits. Within and subject to its constitutional limitations, the legislature, however, may, and often does, authorize the exercise of powers beyond municipal limits, and in accordance with the terms of the authorization, a municipal corporation may operate beyond its boundaries."

This rule is followed in: City of Detroit v. Oakland Circuit Judge, 237 Mich. 446, 212 N.W. 207; Light v. City of Danville, 168 Va. 181, 190 S.E. 276, 285; Miller v. Fowle, 92 Cal.App.2d 409, 206 P.2d 1106, 1108.

In the opinion in the City of Detroit case, it was said:

"* * * The writer is in full accord with as extensive a grant as may be of the right of home rule, so called, to cities. But such grant must obtain expression by legislative enactment or in the Constitution. * * * and it is a far cry to urge that the permission, given them by the Constitution to acquire parks within and without their corporate limits, *ipso facto,* and without any prescribed procedure of any sort, gives them such permission by the exercise of the right of eminent domain." [237 Mich. 446, 212 N.W. 209.]

* * *

As a result of the illegal practice of going out of the city limits to extinguish fires at the expense of the taxpayers of Pueblo, the city council adopted a resolution, which provides: "That on and after June 1st, 1947, that the service of the fire department shall be confined to territory within the city limits, and, the commissioner of public safety in charge of the fire department, be and he is, hereby directed to act accordingly."

The above resolution is still in force and effect, but seems to have been ignored and disregarded, as is shown by the following excerpts from the trial court's findings:

* * *

Certainly the misuse by public officials of city property is just as illegal as the misuse of money which we condemned in McNichols v. City and County of Denver, 120 Colo. 380, 209 P.2d 910.

We are presented with a shocking situation. According to the Commissioner of Safety the "Pueblo fire equipment and number of firemen employed by the department are insufficient to care for the present needs of the city itself." As stated by the same commissioner, the department needed "an increased appropriation for 1949 amounting to approximately one-fourth more than the appropriation the department received for 1948."; the city council by reason of the shortage of equipment and manpower, by resolution in terms prohibited the use of such equipment and firemen outside the city boundaries in order that such equipment and firemen could at all times be ready for the extinguishment of fires within the city.

Regardless of the foregoing, and also of the fact that there is no statute regulating the use of fire equipment, or defining the power, duties and responsibilities of a city in performing its governmental activities beyond its corporate limits, this court now vests chiefs of fire departments with the absolute and uncontrolled discretion to say when and under what circumstances such equipment and such firemen shall be used to extinguish fires outside of the limits of a city.

Owners of property situate outside of the city may lawfully provide for fire protection for themselves and their property without relying upon the gratuitous services of a city, * * *. They may, for instance, create a fire protection district * * * or may avail themselves of the provisions of the annexation laws, and thus secure ample fire protection for themselves and their property.

HOLLAND, J., concurs in this dissenting opinion.

Notes

1. **Implied Extraterritorial Power.** A liberal construction was advanced in Miller v. St. Joseph, 485 S.W.2d 688 (Mo.App.1972) where the city and a stockyards association agreed that the city would extend fire protection to stockyards beyond the city's borders, with the association paying to the city $75,000 annually in advance. The court upheld the agreement, reasoning that it benefited the city and its residents by preventing fire that might spread to the city, and by preserving plants which were essential to the employment of city residents. Contra: Jefferson County Fiscal Ct. v. Jefferson County ex rel. Grauman, 278 Ky. 785, 129 S.W.2d 554 (1939).

2. **Physical Limits.** Where a statute authorizes extraterritorial acquisition of land but provides no distance limit for its exercise, may a northern city purchase property in Florida to be used as a home for its aged citizens? See Sabaugh v. Dearborn, 16 Mich.App. 182, 167 N.W.2d 826 (1969).

ROBERSON v. MONTGOMERY

Supreme Court of Alabama, 1970.
285 Ala. 421, 233 So.2d 69.

MADDOX, JUSTICE.

The City of Montgomery filed this action, in equity, asking the court to enjoin respondents from operating automobile junkyards in two separate locations on the ground that such operations constituted "public nuisances" and that such operations violated city zoning ordinances. It was stipulated that both operations were located on land outside the corporate limits of Montgomery but within its police jurisdiction.

· * * * The main question presented by this appeal, * * *, is: "Did the trial court err in finding that the City of Montgomery was entitled to enforce its zoning ordinances outside its corporate limits?" After careful study of our statutes dealing with municipal zoning, and planning, we must conclude that the trial court did err and that enabling legislation from which the city derives its power to enact zoning regulations did not authorize the city to enforce zoning beyond the municipal corporate limits.

* * *

* * * The question then is whether the Legislature has granted extraterritorial zoning authority to the city.

Act No. 480, Acts of Alabama, 1961, grants to the Planning Commission of the City of Montgomery all the powers, duties, and responsibilities of city planning and zoning commissions as provided in Chapter 16, Title 37, Code of Alabama (1940), as amended.

Title 37, § 772, provides:

"Each municipal corporation in the state of Alabama may divide the territory *within its* corporate limits into business, industrial, and residential zones or districts * * *." (Emphasis added)

Title 37, § 776, provides that for the purpose of promoting the public peace, order, safety or general welfare, "the local legislative body *may divide the municipality into districts*." (Emphasis added)

While Title 37, § 9, grants to the City of Montgomery the power to enforce police or sanitary regulations in adjoining territory within three miles of the corporate limits, this power does not extend to zoning regulations which are specifically provided for in other statutes. * * *.

Our own decision in City of Homewood v. Wofford Oil Co., 232 Ala. 634, 169 So. 288 (1936), seems to recognize that Title 37, § 9, is not all encompassing. We there said:

"It is not to be inferred that a city may exercise any and every police power over the zone outside its corporate limits, styled its 'police jurisdiction,' which it may exercise within its corporate limits."

* * *

We now come to the city's argument that since its planning commission has all the powers, duties and responsibilities of city and regional planning and zoning commissions as provided in Chapter 16, Title 37, Code of Alabama, 1940, as amended, it has the authority to regulate the use of these two parcels outside its corporate limits under the provisions of §§ 791, 794 and 797 of Title 37. These statutes do explicitly grant to the city the right to do "planning" and further grant to the city some degree of control extraterritorially, especially with regard to subdivisions located within five miles of the city limits and with regard to certain "public" structures and "public" developments located within "any areas outside of its boundaries which, in the commission's judgment, bear relation to the planning of such municipality."

While the Legislature has given to municipalities certain extraterritorial control in these "planning" statutes, the general powers of a municipality to "zone" are contained in Title 37, §§ 772–785, Code of Alabama, 1940, as amended.

* * *

As we read Title 37, §§ 786–814, Code of Alabama, 1940, as amended, the Legislature primarily intended to confer upon municipalities the power to perform "city and regional planning." Section 791, which sets out the general powers and duties of a planning commission, is specific in stating that city planning commissions have the authority to draft a master *plan* and *make recommendations* * * *. The commission's recommendations may include a zoning *plan.* * * * We hold that the city was without authority to enforce extraterritorially the zoning ordinance here involved.

We do not here decide the question of whether or not a city may enjoin the operation of a public nuisance located outside its corporate limits but within its police jurisdiction. Appellants candidly admit the city has such authority if a public nuisance exists. Neither do we decide the constitutional question of whether a municipality can enforce extraterritorial zoning if granted such authority by the Legislature. See Extraterritorial Zoning: Reflections on Its Validity, 32 Notre Dame Lawyer 367 (1957).

* * * we must reverse the judgment of the trial court and remand the case to that court for proceedings not inconsistent with this opinion.

Reversed and remanded.

On Rehearing

Maddox, Justice. On application for rehearing, the City of Montgomery asks that we withdraw our original opinion * * *. The Alabama League of Municipalities and the Central Alabama Regional Planning Commission have also filed briefs as amicus curiae, each contending that our original opinion * * * is erroneous. We have carefully reviewed our statutes on city and regional planning, and we are still convinced that the City of Montgomery was without legislative authority to enforce its zoning ordinances outside its corporate limits.

* * *

Notes

1. The constitutionality of grants of extraterritorial authority was resolved favorably to the City in Holt Civic Club v. Tuscaloosa, 439 U.S. 60, 99 S.Ct. 383, 58 L.Ed.2d 292 (1978).

2. Compare the reasoning of the principal case with the following: In City of West Frankfort v. Fullop, 6 Ill.2d 609, 129 N.E.2d 682 (1955) the city brought suit to enjoin oil drilling operations around a lake eight miles beyond its borders. The city owned and operated the lake for a municipal water system and had passed an ordinance prohibiting oil drilling near the lake to protect the water supply from pollution. The defendant oil operators obtained dismissal of the action, but the appeal court reversed. It found the city's authority to enact the ordinance in statutes which authorized extraterritorial condemnation of water supply property and which authorized the city to prevent pollution of its water supply within ten miles of its corporate limits. "That these jurisdictional grants by the legislature appear in eminent domain waterworks statutes does not limit the exercise of jurisdiction to cases in which the city is condemning; for there would be no need for such power as to property condemned and owned by the city.

Regulatory jurisdiction is required only over property of others, and this is implicit in these statutory grants." Id. at 612, 129 N.E.2d at 685. To the objection that the ordinance unconstitutionally deprived defendants of their property, the court ruled that protection of the public water supply was within the police power. It was careful, however, to leave open for review the sufficiency of evidence as to the need for a total prohibition on drilling. See also City of Shreveport v. Conrad, 212 La. 737, 33 So.2d 503 (1947) (upholding conviction under city ordinance that prohibited air flight over a city water source that was located beyond city limits).

2. INTERLOCAL TRANSFERS OF FUNCTIONS

BOROUGH OF WEST CALDWELL v. CALDWELL

Supreme Court of New Jersey, 1958.
26 N.J. 9, 138 A.2d 402.

HEHER, J.

[Under extraterritorial powers granted by statute, Caldwell Borough executed a contract with West Caldwell to construct and operate a sewage disposal system within West Caldwell for the use of both boroughs. More than 50 years later West Caldwell desired to withdraw from the contract and Caldwell disputed its right to do so. The contract was silent as to its duration. The court held West Caldwell was bound to the contract for a "reasonable time" (in terms of Caldwell's amortizing its investment in the facility) and made the following observations.]

* * * The safeguarding of the public health is thus an essential governmental function within the police power of the State [citations omitted] and it is axiomatic that the State's delegation to the municipalities and other agencies for local governmental administration of the power and responsibility of providing sewerage and sanitation facilities to this end cannot be abdicated or renounced or surrendered to another such agency without legislative permission. The Legislature is the exclusive source of the municipality's authority, both in its governmental and corporate or proprietary character; and the power is to be exercised as given. * * *

The corollary theorem is that a municipality cannot bind itself by a perpetual contract, or a contract of unreasonable duration, unless by legislative sanction. *Compare* Westminster Water Co. v. Westminster, 98 Md. 551, 56 A. 990, 64 L.R.A. 630 (Ct.App.1904). And this is *a fortiori* true where, as here, the subject matter of the contract bears on the legislative or governmental function of the local subdivisions of government, involving as it does the exercise of the police power in the vital area of health and sanitation in fulfillment of the public need attendant on growth in population and new and different land uses and the expansion of old uses. R.S. 40:63–68(b) and (c), N.J.S.A., have no such quality or scope; these provisions plainly do not contemplate the surrender or abridgement of the local police power by such measures in perpetuity or for an unreasonable period of time. It is to be presumed that the Legislature intended not to subvert, but to maintain the local police power in all its vigor to serve public necessity, comfort and convenience as it arises, and meantime to invoke such measures as would be ample under the then existing conditions. We have here two contiguous local subdivisions of the State Government acting in the common interest under a grant of power by the Legislature for the general public good and welfare; and the contractual undertaking is to be assessed accordingly. We are concerned here with a basically continuing governmental power that is not exhausted by its exercise at a given time.

Governmental power to regulate and control the use of highways in the public interest cannot be surrendered or impaired by contract. (Citations omitted) So also, in the field of public health and sanitation.

And the construction and other costs incurred by Caldwell in reliance upon the 1955 agreement, if such was indeed the case, may well be an element to be considered with all the facts and circumstances in resolving the factual issue of reasonable time for the continuance of the agreement as so modified.

Reversed and remanded for judgment accordingly.

Notes

1. *Semble.* City of Grandview Heights v. Columbus, 174 Ohio St. 473, 190 N.E.2d 453 (1953) (as to interlocal service contract). The problems raised in Caldwell are readily solved by constitutional or statutory provisions authorizing local governments to redelegate their powers to other government units. See e.g., *Transfer of Functions Between Municipalities and Counties,* ACIR State Legislative Program § 2.205 (1975 cum.) In designing such legislation, difficult policy choices must be made. For instance, should, local governments be permitted to surrender, by transfer, a portion of their jurisdiction unqualifiedly and irrevocably; or only within prescribed limits? Should transfer decisions be made exclusively at the local level? Where transfers of functions must be made under a contract procedure which requires state approval of the contract, what legislative guidelines should direct administrative review? Should transfers of functions be governed generally by one law; or selectively by statutes dealing specifically with particular functions. See e.g. West's Ann.California Government Code §§ 51330–51335, 5150, 5156. How do the following laws meet the foregoing questions?

West's Florida Stat.Ann. Constitution Art. 8, § 4: *Transfer of Powers*—By law or by resolution of the governing bodies of each of the governments affected, any function or power of a county, municipality or special district may be transferred to or contracted to be performed by another county, municipality or special district, after approval by vote of the electors of the transferor and approval by vote of the electors of the transferee, or as otherwise provided by law.

Pennsylvania Constitution Art. 9, § 5: Intergovernmental cooperation—A municipality by act of its governing body may, or upon being required by initiative and referendum in the area affected shall * * * delegate or transfer any function, power or responsibility to, one or more other governmental units including other municipalities or districts, the Federal government, any other state or its governmental units, or any newly created governmental unit.

Michigan Comp.Laws Ann. Constitution Art. 7, § 28: Governmental functions and powers; joint administration, costs and credits, transfers—The legislature by general law shall authorize two or more counties, townships, cities, villages or districts, or any combination thereof among other things to: * * * transfer functions or responsibilities to one another or any combination thereof upon the consent of each unit involved; * * *.

Mich.Comp.Laws Ann. §§ 124.531–124.536: An Act to provide for intergovernmental transfers of functions and responsibilities.

Sec. 1. As used in this act:

* * *

(b) "Political subdivision" means a city, village, other incorporated political subdivision, county, school district, community college, intermediate school district, township, charter township, special district or authority.

* * *

Sec. 2. Two or more political subdivisions are authorized to enter into a contract with each other providing for the transfer of functions or responsibilities to one another or any combination thereof upon the consent of each political subdivision involved.

* * *

Sec. 4. A contract shall include:

(a) A description of the functions or responsibilities to be transferred.

(b) The effective date of the contract.

(c) The term of operation under the contract.

(d) The manner in which the affected employees, if any, of the participating political subdivisions shall be transferred, reassigned or otherwise treated subject to the following:

* * *

Sec. 5. A joint board or commission may be established by the political subdivisions involved to supervise the execution of a contract.

Sec. 6. A contract may be amended by agreement of the parties thereto in the same manner as the original contract was made. A contract may be terminated by joint action of all parties, or by an individual party not less than 1 year after its notice thereof in writing to all other parties.*

---

* Michigan also employs a piecemeal statutory approach in authorizing joint intergovernmental contracting for particular purposes. See Gaut v. Southfield, 388 Mich. 189, 200 N.W.2d 76 (1972).

CITY OF PASADENA v. LOS ANGELES

Court of Appeals of California, 1965.
235 Cal.App.2d 153, 45 Cal.Rptr. 94.

KINGSLEY, JUSTICE.

[Action to sustain the validity of a contract between plaintiff City and defendant County relating to the enforcement of state health laws within plaintiff city. From a judgment in favor of the city, the county and the other defendants appealed.]

I

Under the provisions of the Health and Safety Code of this state, the state, the counties, and incorporated cities each play a part in the enactment and enforcement of rules and laws governing public health. The Legislature directly enacts laws of general statewide application; The State Board of Public Health may "adopt * * * rules and regulations consistent with law for the protection of the public health." (Health & Saf.Code, § 102); the board of supervisors of each county "shall take such measures as may be necessary to preserve and protect the public health in the unincorporated territory of the county, * * *." (Health & Saf.Code, § 450); and the governing body of a city "shall take such measures as may be necessary to preserve and protect the public health, * * * (Health & Saf.Code, § 500.)

Enforcement of these sundry statutes, rules, regulations, orders and ordinances is similarly diverse. Enforcement of the state statutes and rules, and of county orders and ordinances, in unincorporated portions of a county, is vested in a county health officer (Health & Saf. Code, § 452). Within the boundaries of an incorporated city, the enforcement of all state statutes, rules and regulations, and of municipal ordinances, is vested in a city health officer. (Health & Saf.Code, § 504.) The salary and expenses of each local health officer—county, town or city—is paid by the local agency which appoints him. (Health & Saf.Code, §§ 450 and 504.)

Recognizing the desirability of combining at least some of these functions, the Legislature has enacted certain enabling provisions. An incorporated city may transfer to the county health officer the power and duty of enforcing, within the city, all of the state-created laws and rules (Health & Saf.Code, § 476), in which case the costs of local enforcement of these laws becomes a county expense. In addition, a board of supervisors and an incorporated city may contract for the enforcement within the city of the municipal ordinances by the county health officer (Health & Saf.Code, § 480), the expenses of the enforcement of these municipal ordinances remaining with the city (Health & Saf.Code, § 482). Thirdly, a county may contract with a city for the enforcement, by the city's health officer, of state and county rules and laws in "any unincorporated territory adjacent to the city, * * *."

(Health & Saf.Code, § 483), the expenses of such enforcement being still borne by the county (Health & Saf.Code, § 484).

In the instant case, the City of Pasadena, having duly cast upon the County of Los Angeles the obligation to enforce state laws in the city at the county's expense, pursuant to * * * section 476, then entered into a contract with the county under which the powers and duties previously transferred to the county health officer would again be performed by the health officer of the city, but now under the supervision and control of the county health officer and at the county's expense. The fiscal officer of the county having refused to pay the first installment of the moneys called for under this contract, the city instituted the present action to determine the validity of the contract.

* * *

In the light of Avan v. Municipal Court (1965) 62 Cal.2d 630, 43 Cal.Rptr. 835, 401 P.2d 227, we have no doubt of the basic power of the city and the county to enter into the contract in question. In Avan, the city public defender had been called on by the court to represent an indigent defendant in a misdemeanor prosecution pending in the municipal court—a duty which the law cast on the county, but which the county officer could not perform, since the law limited him to appearing in felony cases. The court held that payment to the city officer, by the county, under these circumstances was not only proper, but a duty compellable by mandate. We recognize that there are two differences between Avan and the case at bench. (1) In Avan, payment was made to the officer. * * * (2) In Avan, the county officer involved was unable to perform the county's duty because a statute restricted him from acting. * * * Since the county was obligated to see that the state health laws were enforced, it had the power to arrange for the necessary personnel. * * *

It is not contended that the contract increases the cost of enforcement of the state health laws within the boundaries of Pasadena * * *, nor that it enriches the City of Pasadena beyond the sum necessary to reimburse that city for the moneys it must pay * * * for carrying out the county's obligations.

We can see no difference between the reimbursement by a county of a city for the services of a city public defender who performs a county duty, and the reimbursement by a county of a city for the services of a city health officer who performs a county duty.

III

The county argues that, once the city had cast the duty of enforcing state health laws on the county, the subject of such enforcement became one of unconcern to the city and that the contract was, therefore, ultra vires. The outline of the statutes in this field, above set forth, shows the fallacy in this position. The city still retains its concern for the enforcement within its boundaries of all of the health laws, whomsoever enacts them; the city may reinvest itself with the power and duty to enforce state law by a resolution terminating its action under section 476 (Health & Saf.Code, § 477). * * *

We hold that the contract before us was one within the legitimate contractual powers of the city and that, unless otherwise made unlawful, it was valid and binding on both parties.

IV

It is argued, however, that the Legislature has indicated an intent that a contract such as the one herein involved should not be made. * * * The Legislature has recognized the difficulties inherent in the enforcement of health laws by small geographical areas. As the county itself points out, disease and contamination do not start and stop at the boundaries of local governmental units. A solution appropriate for one city in one part of the state may not be appropriate for another city in another part of the state. We regard the legislative purpose as being to allow to the cities and counties concerned the broadest power to make such local arrangements for enforcement as the discretion of the several city and county governments might dictate. * * *

* * *

Notes

1. **The Lakewood Plan.** "One of the most formal, and by far the most common of all types of intergovernmental contracts, is the 'Lakewood Plan' under which a county government, for a service charge, performs selected * * * municipal functions for cities (and other areas) within its jurisdiction. Although similar * * * cooperation between counties and cities have a long history, the particular name of the plan is derived from what was probably the first comprehensive county-city scheme of contracting—the agreement in 1954 by the County of Los Angeles, California to perform, for such charges, a wide variety of services for the city of Lakewood. * * * Services rendered under a Lakewood Plan contract are performed by only one of the contracting bodies, usually a more comprehensive governmental entity such as a county * * *. This arrangement results in a 'vertical' system of contracting—contracts among governmental bodies of varying political levels. * * * The Lakewood Plan contract contemplates a two-party agreement * * *. Service and payment arrangements, however, can be effectuated by creation of other entities, with or without taxing powers. Included among such entities are joint powers authorities, non-profit corporations, special purpose districts, and county service areas. * * * Since saving money and providing effective services are the primary justifications * * * to enter into a Lakewood Plan arrangement, 'cost determination' is an essential element of both levels of government. Unless costs are accurately and readily explainable, the county will be subject to accusations of overstaffing and giving away services and the cities will be liable to criticism for overpaying." Kuyper, *Intergovernmental Cooperation: An Analysis of the Lakewood Plan,* 58 Geo. L.J. 777 at 780–81, 793, 796–97 (1970).*

By its wholesale, package-service offerings, the Lakewood Plan enhances the role of the county as an area-wide government unit with *de facto* transferred municipal powers, even though any attempt to restructure such a servicing county formally into a metropolitan municipality would raise fierce political opposition. The success of vertical interlocal cooperation will vary, depending upon cost effectiveness factors, *viz.* the size of the county to effect substantial economies of scale and the willingness of underlying municipalities to join the county's service group. See Note, *The Urban County: A Study of New Approaches to Local Government in Metropolitan Areas,* 73 Harv.L.Rev. 526, 545, 558 (1960).

3. INTERLOCAL CONTRACTS

"Intergovernmental contracts and agreements are the most widely used formal method of accommodating governmental problems to geographic boundaries. They provide a formal yet flexible and adaptable method for public jurisdictions of all types and at all levels to cooperate and share responsibility for providing public services and facilities. They constitute a method of adaptation which bypasses basic structural and organization problems, and the issue of allocating the responsibility among levels of government. Finally, they stress consolidation of services, rather than consolidation of governments." ACIR, *A Handbook for Interlocal Agreements and Contracts,* p. 18 (1967) (hereinafter cited as Handbook).

Interlocal contracts have developed rapidly. The two major types are service purchase contracts under which one local government provides services to another; and joint enterprise contracts whereby two or more local units jointly undertake a particular operation or project for their common needs. These two forms call for different powers, duties, and obligations, hence their design and wording must be tailored to the specific intention and legal powers of each party government. Thus, in Port of Peninsula v. E.H. Bendiksen Co., 71 Wash.2d 530, 429 P.2d 859 (1967) a purported joint powers agreement was found to be an interlocal service contract, and as such, void for the servicing unit's lack of authority to provide extraterritorial service.

Under the impetus of model legislation proposed by the U.S. Advisory Commission on Intergovernmental Relations and by the Council of State Governments, an increasing number of states (45 as of 1970) have enacted Interlocal Cooperation Acts, (see Table of State Statutes, *Handbook,* supra, p. 23). In several states constitutional amendments authorize such contracts. *Id.* 29; 1975 (cum.) ACIR, *State Legislative Program* § 2.204, ACIR, *14th Annual Report,* p. 51 (1973). "Not all * * * state statutes are equally broad, either as to powers which may be exercised * * * or units of government which may participate. * * * A detailed analysis and comparison is contained in Leigh Grosenick, *'A Comparative Analysis of Joint Exercise of Powers Legislation in the United States'* (Unpublished Masters Thesis, University of Minnesota, 1965)." *Handbook,* supra, p. 23.

CHEMICAL BANK v. WASHINGTON PUB. POWER SUP. SYSTEM

Supreme Court of Washington, 1983.
99 Wash.2d 772, 666 P.2d 329.

BRACHTENBACH, JUSTICE.

The Washington Public Power Supply System (WPPSS) issued revenue bonds to obtain funds to construct two nuclear generating plants known as WNP–4 and WNP–5. Bonds in the face amount of approximately $2.25 billion have been issued; repayment with interest will cost approximately $7.2 billion. Chemical Bank is the trustee for the bondholders.

Construction of the two plants was undertaken. On January 22, 1982 WPPSS terminated construction of both plants. At that time WNP–4 was approximately 24 percent completed and WNP–5 approximately 16 percent completed. Costs to date had almost reached the original estimated total cost for complete construction of both plants. WPPSS alleges that termination was necessary due to its inability to obtain adequate financing to complete the projects.

Chemical Bank brought a declaratory judgment action against WPPSS and the participants (defined hereafter) seeking a determination that the participants owe to WPPSS sufficient funds to pay the bonds, with interest. In general WPPSS has responded to the suit by substantially agreeing with Chemical Bank as to the rights and obligations of the various parties. Most of the participants, however, have interposed numerous defenses to any payment obligation.

* * * We granted discretionary review on limited issues on which the trial court granted summary judgment in favor of the bond trustee and stayed further trial on other issues until this appeal was decided. On some of those issues we reverse.

To understand the complex issues, a recital of facts is necessary. WPPSS is a "joint operating agency" established in 1957 under RCW 43.52. It is a municipal corporation. RCW 43.52.250. Its members are 19 public utility districts and four cities, Ellensburg, Richland, Seattle and Tacoma. It has authority to acquire, build, operate and own power plants and systems for the generation and transmission of electricity. RCW 43.52.300. WPPSS also has authority to issue revenue bonds payable from the revenues of the utility properties operated by it. RCW 43.52.3411. It may not levy taxes or issue general obligation bonds. RCW 43.52.391.

In the early 1970's WPPSS started construction of three nuclear generating projects, WNP–1, WNP–2 and WNP–3. Those projects were developed in conjunction with a number of participating public utilities from several northwestern states, including Washington. In 1974 WPPSS decided to construct two additional plants, WNP–4 and WNP–5, financing of which is the subject of this litigation. WNP–4 is owned entirely by WPPSS; WNP-5 is owned 90 percent by WPPSS and 10 percent by Pacific Power & Light Company, a privately owned utility.

Besides WPPSS and Pacific Power & Light Company, there are 88 "Participants" in these two projects: 9 Washington cities, 19 Washington public utility districts, 1 Washington irrigation district, 7 Oregon cities, 4 Oregon peoples utility districts, 5 Idaho cities, and 43 rural electric cooperatives, of which 13 are in Washington. The remainder of the REC's are in Idaho, Montana, Nevada, Oregon and Wyoming. Each of the participants in WNP-4 and WNP-5 signed an identical 63-page "Participants' Agreement", dated July 14, 1976.

A 117-page "Bond Resolution" was adopted by WPPSS on February 23, 1977 providing a plan for the construction of both plants and providing for the issuance of revenue bonds.

Each Participants' Agreement provided that "[s]upply System hereby sells, and the Participant hereby purchases, its Participant's Share of Project Capability."

"Project Capability" is defined in section 1(v) of the agreement as:

"the amounts of electric power and energy, if any, which the Projects are capable of generating at any particular time * * *"

The Participants' Agreement requires each participant to pay monthly its proportionate share of a "Billing Statement" issued annually by WPPSS and based upon an "Annual Budget." The "Annual Budget" is to be adopted by WPPSS commencing with the "Date of Continuous Operation" * * * *OR* the date 1 year after the termination of a project. The Bond Resolution in turn similarly requires WPPSS to collect and set aside funds sufficient to make payments on the bonds. Termination thus established a trigger date for various payments, and gave rise to this lawsuit.

The Participants' Agreement purports to require payment to WPPSS whether or not the projects are ever completed, operable or operating. * * *

The Bond Resolution requires WPPSS to collect charges for electricity and capability, which are adequate to provide for payment of the revenue bonds "whether or not the generation or transmission of power * * * is suspended, interrupted or reduced for any reason whatever * * *"

Thus, if the agreements are valid, and subject to interpreting the contract, the participants collectively could pay approximately $7 billion for nuclear plants which will never generate any electricity. Ultimately the ratepaying consumers of the participants would pay for the nonexistent electricity.

The method of financing WNP-1, 2 and 3 differs from that involved in WNP-4 and 5. The Bonneville Power Administration, a federal agency, facilitated financing of the first three plants through complex "net-billing" agreements that allocated the risk of noncompletion to the federal agency. *Springfield v. Washington Pub. Power Supply Sys.*, 564 F.Supp. 90 at 95 (D.Or.1983). * * *

The rates charged by WPPSS or public utility districts are not subject to the rate-making supervision of the State Utilities and Transportation Commission. RCW 43.52.450; RCW 54.16.040.

As noted above, various participants interposed numerous defenses to the Chemical Bank action and cross claims against WPPSS. Among those defenses were (1) allegations that at least some participants did not have authority to enter into the agreement; and (2) that proper interpretation of the agreement did not require payment as sought by WPPSS and the bond trustee. * * *

After hearing extensive oral argument and considering voluminous briefs and affidavits (the record is nearly 7,000 pages) the trial court entered an order on summary judgment motions on November 16, 1982 which provided *inter alia:* * * *

2. * * * the language of the Participants' Agreement provides that the participants are obligated to pay WPPSS their respective shares of decommissioning costs incurred by WPPSS, whether or not any of the projects has been or ever will be completed or placed into operation. * * *

3. * * * WPPSS had statutory authority to enter into the Participants' Agreement and Bond Resolution and to issue the bonds pursuant thereto.

4. * * * the Washington participants (other than Vera) had statutory authority to enter into the Participants' Agreement. * * * The court reserves decision as to whether Vera and the other participants had authority to enter into the Participants' Agreement * * *.

5. * * * any obligations of the Washington participants under the Participants' Agreement do not violate Washington constitutional or statutory limitations on the incurring of debt. Such obligations do not constitute debt within the meaning of such limitations, and even if such limitations were otherwise applicable they would be rendered inapplicable by reason of the special fund doctrine under Washington law.

6. * * * any obligations of the Washington participants under the Participants' Agreement do not violate Washington constitutional or statutory limitations on the lending of credit.

7. * * * the Participants' Agreement does not constitute or provide for any unlawful delegations of power or authority by Washington participants.

8. The Interstate Compact Clause of the United States Constitution is not applicable to the Participants' Agreement.

* * *

We are asked to decide whether the Participants' Agreement and the Bond Resolution, hereinafter referred to as the agreement, were contracts within the statutory authority of the Washington participants.[2] * * *

Initially, some principles of statutory construction are relevant to the court's analysis. * * * The resolution of the authority issue requires an examination of the entire statutory scheme governing each category of participant to determine whether they had the express power to enter into this agreement. Absent express statutory authorization, we must also consider whether participation in the agreement may be based upon necessary or implied powers. * * * [W]e ultimately must decide whether the present agreement conforms to the statutes. Our conclusion in this case is therefore based upon an examination of all Washington statutes authorizing the purchase of electricity, the acquisition or construction of generating facilities, joint operating agencies, and joint development of energy generating projects.

I. PURCHASE OF ELECTRICITY

The Washington participants have explicit statutory authority to buy electricity on behalf of citizens. For example, each of the 19 Washington Public Utility Districts (PUD's) involved in this litigation is authorized to: "purchase, within or without its limits, electric current for sale and distribution within or without its limits * * *" RCW 54.16.040.

Similarly, the nine Washington municipal participants could purchase electricity, * * * The first class cities of Tacoma and Richland were authorized to: "provide for lighting the streets and all public places, and for furnishing the inhabitants thereof with gas or other lights * * *" RCW 35.22.280(15). Centralia, the only participant exercising second class city powers, had the authority to: "provide for lighting the streets and all public places of the city and for furnishing the inhabitants of the city with gas, electric, or other light * * *" RCW 35.23.440(44). As third class cities, Blaine and Ellensburg had the power to: "establish, lay out, alter, keep open, open, widen, vacate, improve and repair streets, sidewalks, alleys, squares and other public highways and places within the city, and to drain * * * light the same * * *" RCW 35.24.290(3). In practically identical language, towns such as McCleary and Steilacoom were authorized to secure electricity. RCW 35.27.370(4). The final category of municipal participants, code cities, includes Port Angeles and Sumas. A code city may: "provide utility service within and without its limits and exercise all

2. * * * The authority of the Idaho, Oregon, Wyoming and Nevada participants is currently being litigated in their respective states.

An Oregon trial court has held that Oregon cities and PUD's lacked authority and the agreement was contrary to public policy. Defazio v. Springfield Utility Board, cause 16–81–11344 (Lane County Cir.Ct. Nov. 5, 1982). That case is on appeal. The Idaho Supreme Court has entered an order prohibiting collection of funds until the matter is decided on the merits. Asson v. City of Burley, cause 82–174 (Sup.Ct. Nov. 3, 1982). The Wyoming Rate Commission has ruled that rates may not be increased to pay the WPPSS debt.

powers to the extent authorized by general law for any class of city or town." RCW 35A.80.010.

In addition to these categorical grants of enumerated powers, the PUD's and cities were authorized, under the statutory provisions that created WPPSS, to: "enter into contracts or compacts with any operating agency or a publicly or privately owned public utility for the purchase and sale of electric energy or falling waters." RCW 43.52.410. Thus, the various statutes clearly provide for Washington PUD's, cities and towns to purchase and sell electricity.

Initially, we must decide whether this agreement is authorized as a purchase of electricity by the participants. * * * The agreement expressly provides for the possibility that no electricity will be generated and that participant payments will be due even if the project is not completed. The unconditional obligation to pay for no electricity is hardly the purchase of electricity. We hold that an agreement to purchase project capability does not qualify as a purchase of electricity.

II. ACQUISITION OF ELECTRIC GENERATING FACILITIES

Another type of express authority granted to cities and towns is the power to construct, acquire and operate electric generating facilities. RCW 35.92.050. * * * Under this provision the municipalities clearly had the authority to build or buy their own plants. *Jones v. Centralia*, 157 Wash. 194, 289 P. 3 (1980). In almost identical language, the PUD's are granted the express authority to construct, acquire and operate electric generating facilities. RCW 54.16.040. The respective powers of the PUD's and cities are similar and therefore subject to a similar construction. *State ex rel. PUD 1 v. Wylie*, 28 Wash.2d 113, 127–30, 182 P.2d 706 (1947). Under the provisions, the participants clearly could construct, acquire and operate generating facilities.

In construing these provisions, however, this court has never found authority for a project in which the participants did not have an ownership interest. *E.g., Roehl v. PUD 1*, 43 Wash.2d 214, 261 P.2d 92 (1953); *State ex rel. PUD 1 v. Schwab*, 40 Wash.2d 814, 246 P.2d 1081 (1952). Under this agreement, section 1.1(*o*) of the Bond Resolution expressly provides that only WPPSS and Pacific Power & Light Company retain any ownership interest in the projects. In comparison, the participants do not retain an ownership share in this project but only contracted to buy from WPPSS a share of project capability. * * * The "electric power and energy, if any" language indicates that the parties anticipated a possible share of no power. * * * In effect, the participants unconditionally guaranteed WPPSS bonds with no guaranty of electricity in return.

Some states have provided statutory authority for such unconditional guaranties and courts have recognized the validity of projects developed under those provisions. *Johnson v. Piedmont Mun. Power Agency*, 277 S.C. 345, 287 S.E.2d 476 (1982). That recognition, however, is based upon very explicit statutory authority. South Carolina's "Joint Municipal Electric Power and Energy Act" provides an example:

> "Any municipality which is a member of the joint agency may contract to buy from the joint agency power and energy required for its present or future requirements, including the capacity and output of one or more specified projects. * * * *any such contract may provide that the municipality so contracting shall be obligated to make the payments required by the contract whether or not a project is completed, operable or operating notwithstanding the suspension, interruption, interference, reduction or curtailment of the output of a project or the power and energy contracted for,* and that such payments under the contract shall not be subject to any reduction, whether by offset or otherwise. * * * "

(Italics ours.) S.C.Code Ann. § 6–23–110 (Law.Co-op.Supp.1982). Several other states have similar statutes. Mass.Ann.Laws, ch. 164A, § 3(b) (Law.Co-op.1979); Me.Rev.Stat.Ann. tit. 35, § 4103(1)(B) (Supp.1982); N.C.Gen.Stat. § 159B–12 (1982); Va.Code § 15.1–1611 (1981); Vt.Stat. Ann., tit. 30, § 604 (Supp.1982). This state has no such statute.

Nonetheless, rather than ruling that an ownership interest is an absolute requirement when acquiring or constructing generating facilities, we will examine the present agreement to determine whether the participants retained sufficient control over the project to constitute the equivalent of an ownership interest. In the present case, several provisions of the agreement limit the participants' role in management to an extent inconsistent with control of any facilities acquired or constructed. * * * The inclusion of such items suggests a degree of control and involvement in management, yet section 15 also sets out a procedure for committee consideration of WPPSS proposals that precludes meaningful deliberation on the part of the committee. With limited exceptions, that procedure requires that 20 percent of the participants register their *disapproval* of any WPPSS proposal within 15 days or that proposal "shall be deemed approved." Considering the complexity of the various budgetary items, construction decisions and financing arrangements involved in a project of this scope, it seems unlikely that a part-time committee of representative participants could provide significant input to the management of the projects with such rigid procedural requirements. It appears to this court that such limited involvement in project management does not satisfy the type of ownership control envisioned in the statutes.

It should be noted that we recognize the necessity and propriety of establishing representative committees to manage and oversee joint development projects. *E.g., Roehl v. PUD 1,* 43 Wash.2d 214, 261 P.2d 92 (1953); *PUD 1 v. Taxpayers of Snohomish Cy.,* 78 Wash.2d 724, 479 P.2d 61 (1971). Our concern is not with the use of such committees in general; it is with the structuring of such committee procedures in a way that does not allow sufficient participant involvement in project management to control their risk. Thus, although this court recognizes the need for delegating duties in the context of joint development agreements, *e.g., Roehl,* 43 Wash.2d at 238–40, 261 P.2d 92; *Snohomish Cy.,* 78 Wash.2d at 731, 479 P.2d 61, we are not prepared to sanction a virtual abdication of all management functions and policy decisions to an operating agency such as WPPSS. Here, the participant's committee apparently served as a rubber stamp for WPPSS' decisions, resulting in two terminated projects, less than 25 percent complete, at a cost of $2.25 billion, or almost $7 billion over the 30–year repayment period. As a matter of public policy, the enormous risk to ratepayers must be balanced by either the benefit of ownership or substantial management control.

Also, there is language common to each set of statutes indicating the Legislature intended that cities and PUD's should retain significant control over the use of any facilities acquired. * * * While the public entities had the statutory authority to construct or acquire electric generating facilities, that authority is conditioned upon either an ownership interest or their active participation in the management of these facilities. Here, the municipal and PUD participants were not acquiring or constructing generating facilities as set out in the statutes because under the agreement they ceded virtually all of their ownership interests and most of the management responsibilities to WPPSS.

The need for a municipality or PUD to retain ownership and control over public construction projects is also evident from earlier decisions * * *.

* * *

* * * This court, however, held that the new joint acquisition statute allowed two or more districts to acquire integrated electric facilities beyond district lines. *Roehl,* at 237, 261 P.2d 92.

* * * The court also addressed the issue of PUD control over the project, concluding that the executive board, consisting of one member from each utility, was responsible for overall project management and policy decisions, while the consulting engineer only performed administrative tasks relating to project operation. *Roehl,* at 240–41, 261 P.2d 92. That same degree of participant control is not present in this case because most of the policy decisions and management control are delegated to WPPSS, the operating agency, rather than any executive committee.

Applying the language of the acquisition or construction statutes and the principles derived from the cases construing that language, we do not believe the participants retained sufficient ownership interests or management responsibilities under this agreement to constitute acquisition or construction of an electric generating facility.

III. IMPLIED POWERS

On separate grounds, respondents urge, * * * that the express authority to acquire or construct generating facilities and provide electricity carries with it an implied power to pay for that service.

Municipality of Metro Seattle v. Seattle, 57 Wash.2d 446, 459–60, 357 P.2d 863 (1960). In *Metro* this court upheld the City of Seattle's power to pledge city revenues to a countywide agency in order to pay for sewage disposal service. Since the statutes authorized the cities to provide sewage services and systems, we held: "[i]t must follow that with the power to provide a sewer system there is implied the power to pay for it, unless otherwise prohibited by the charter or statute." *Metro,* at 460, 357 P.2d 863. In the present case, the trial court extended this reasoning and concluded that the implied power to pay also included the power to make financing arrangements such as the present agreement. We disagree.

The services the city contracted for in *Metro* were to be paid as the services were provided, *Metro,* at 458–59, 357 P.2d 863, which is significantly different from the type of unconditional pledge of revenues contained in this agreement. Also, the countywide agency agreed to process and dispose of the sewage in part through the use of the city's existing sewage treatment plants. *Metro,* at 449, 357 P.2d 863. Since the city continued to own the sewage treatment facilities, the revenues pledged were actually paid back to the city for the use of its facilities and these funds helped pay for those plants. That arrangement is distinguishable from the present agreement because here the pledges of revenues are not conditioned upon the receipt of services and in *Metro* the city owned the facility used to provide the services.

This court subsequently adopted a more stringent test for a municipality seeking to incur indebtedness based upon general grants of authority to provide services. In *Edwards v. Renton,* 67 Wash.2d 598, 602, 409 P.2d 153 (1965), we held that the power to borrow money: "should not and will not be inferred or implied from a general statutory authority permitting municipalities to enter into contracts or to incur indebtedness." Moreover, a municipal corporation's powers are limited to those conferred in express terms or those necessarily implied. *In re Seattle,* 96 Wash.2d 616, 629, 638 P.2d 549 (1981). If there is any doubt about a claimed grant of power it must be denied. *Port of Seattle v. State Utils. & Transp. Comm'n,* 92 Wash.2d 789, 794–95, 597 P.2d 383 (1979). The test for necessary or implied municipal powers is legal necessity rather than practical necessity. *Hillis Homes, Inc. v. Snohomish Cy.,* 97 Wash.2d 804, 808, 650 P.2d 193 (1982). * * *

The parties argue that first class cities have greater powers than other municipalities, which precludes a narrow statutory construction. Generally, first class cities may exercise powers that do not violate a constitutional provision, legislative enactment, or the city's own charter. *Winkenwerder v. Yakima,* 52 Wash.2d 617, 622–23, 328 P.2d 873 (1958). These broad powers are derived from first class cities' status as "home rule" municipalities, *i.e.,* cities that frame their own charters and consequently retain broad control over local matters. Const. art. 11, § 10. In some states, the home rule powers of municipalities result in considerable autonomy from state control. *E.g., Board of Cy.*

Comm'rs v. Thornton, Colo., 629 P.2d 605, 609–10 (1981). In Washington, the courts have interpreted the home rule powers of first class cities more narrowly. Professor Trautman perceptively characterized these limitations:

> "The conclusion to be drawn is that in Washington a home rule city is subordinate to the legislature as to any matter upon which the legislature has acted, whether it be regarded as of state, local, or joint concern. In the event of an inconsistency, the statute prevails.
> * * *"

Trautman, *Legislative Control of Municipal Corporations in Washington,* 38 Wash.L.Rev. 743, 772 (1963). * * *

The development of generating facilities through the joint efforts of municipalities and other public bodies is a subject of at least joint state and local interest. As reflected in both legislative enactments, *e.g.,* RCW 54.44, and decisions of this court, *e.g., Shorts v. Seattle,* 95 Wash. 538, 164 P. 241 (1917), the State is vitally interested in the diverse municipal powers that might be employed in this type of project. Because of the obvious state interest, either an express or implied delegation of power is necessary to find sufficient authority.

The holding in *Hillis* vitiates the arguments that this type of bond guaranty was a necessity to sell the bonds in the investment market. That may well be true, but necessity does not provide authority. Accordingly, we do not believe that this agreement is authorized as an implied power to pay for an admittedly proper municipal service.

IV. JOINT OPERATING AGREEMENTS

Another possible independent source of express power is the joint operating statutes under which WPPSS was created. RCW 43.52. As quoted previously, these provisions clearly authorize the participants to purchase "electric energy." RCW 43.52–410. By comparison, a joint operating agency is authorized to contract with any municipal corporation or public utility "for any term relating to the purchase, sale, interchange or wheeling of power". RCW 43.52.391. * * * If WPPSS were simply selling the electric energy, the participants obviously would be authorized to buy it. However, since the terms of the agreement encompass only a potential share of any electricity that might be generated, it is not accurate to analyze the participants' authority in terms of purchasing electric energy. Since the statutes do not provide for the purchase of electric energy that may not be generated, we can discern no basis for the participants' authority in RCW 43.52.

V. JOINT DEVELOPMENT AGREEMENTS

A final category of express authority that could be involved in this type project, but was not employed in the present case, is contained in the: "Nuclear, Thermal, Electric Generating Power Facilities—Joint Development", RCW 54.44. Under this statute, public entities explicitly are authorized to enter into agreements for the joint development of nuclear, thermal, or electric generating facilities. *See, e.g., PUD 1 v. Taxpayers of Snohomish Cy.,* 78 Wash.2d 724, 479 P.2d 61 (1971). Although there is no indication in the record as to why this chapter was not used, there are statutory requirements under RCW 54.44 notably absent from this agreement. * * *

A second statutory requirement under RCW 54.44 is that each participant is responsible only for its own debts and obligation in the facility. RCW 54.44.030. In contrast, section 17(c) of the Participants' Agreement explicitly requires that participants assume the obligations of defaulting participants. * * * Such an assumption of liability is expressly forbidden under the joint development provisions of RCW 54.44.030. * * *

Although other state courts have upheld such step-up provisions despite the lack of express statutory authority, *e.g., Frank v. Cody,* 572 P.2d 1106, 1111–12 (Wyo.1977), we are not persuaded that a similar conclusion is appropriate here. In *Cody* the court found the participants retained an ownership interest in the joint project and a significant role in managing the project. *Cody,* at 1111. Moreover, default may have been less likely since payments were only due after the utility services were delivered. *Cody,* at 1113–14. *Accord, Goreham v. Des Moines Metro Area Solid Waste Agency,* 179 N.W.2d 449, 457 (Iowa 1970). Here, the lack of an ownership interest coupled with the "dry hole" risk preclude a similar result.

* * *

VI. CONCLUSION

We recently reaffirmed the application of the ultra vires doctrine in the area of government contracts. *Noel v. Cole,* 98 Wash.2d 375, 655 P.2d 245 (1982). As a general rule, the unauthorized contracts of governmental entities are rendered void and unenforceable under the ultra vires doctrine. *Noel,* at 378, 655 P.2d 245. The doctrine applies to government action to "protect the citizens and taxpayers * * * from unjust, ill-considered, or extortionate contracts, or those showing favoritism * * * " 10 E. McQuillin, *Municipal Corporations* § 29.02, at 200 (3d ed. 1981). * * * In *Noel* this court held a logging contract between the State Department of Natural Resources and a private company ultra vires because of the parties' failure to conform to mandatory statutory procedures.

* * *

Although we have discussed our conclusions throughout the opinion, it is helpful to summarize. It should be apparent that this agreement does not satisfy the statutory scheme governing the public participants. (1) The agreement is not a standard contract for the purchase of power because the payments are due irrespective of whether any electric current is delivered. (2) It is not the type of acquisition or construction * * * authorized by the statutes or previously recognized by this court, because the participants retained no ownership interest, * * * and a very limited role in management of the project.

(3) It is not an exercise of an implied power to pay for municipal services because there was no guaranty the services would be provided * * *. (4) Finally, it is not a joint operating agreement within the provisions of RCW 43.52 because those provisions limit the participants' ability to buy anything more than "electric energy."

* * * An attempt to structure an agreement under the joint operating agency statutes or to base it upon implied powers does not alter that basic authority and the participants simply are not authorized to guarantee another party's ownership of a generating facility in exchange for a possible share of any electricity generated. Therefore, we hold that the Washington PUD's and Washington municipal participants lacked authority to enter into this agreement.

The trial court ruling * * * is reversed.

WILLIAM H. WILLIAMS, C.J., ROSELLINI, DIMMICK and PEARSON, JJ., and MORGAN, J. PRO TEM., concur.

DORE, JUSTICE (concurring). * * *

* * *

UTTER, JUSTICE (dissenting).

* * *

Notes

1. **State Law Variations.** As the principal case indicates, a state's legislature could (as in South Carolina) authorize delegation of managerial control to an outside entity. Whether that has been done raises an issue of statutory construction.

2. **Managerial Versus Administrative Controls.** The distinction between unauthorized surrender of managerial control, vis-a-vis valid delegation of administrative details, discussed in the principal case, turns essentially on matters of degree. The specific project agreements, rather than the language of enabling statutes, may be decisive, as illustrated in the following case.

CITY OF OAKLAND v. WILLIAMS

Supreme Court of California, 1940.
15 Cal.2d 542, 103 P.2d 168.

SHENK, JUSTICE.

[Suit to compel Auditor of City of Oakland to execute contract with six other contiguous cities for special study of sewerage disposal problems.]

* * *

* * * These cities are contiguous and presently discharge their sewage by many outlets into San Francisco Bay, * * *. By reason of the proximity of these outlets, dispersion has proved highly unsatisfactory, and admittedly a grave condition exists threatening both health and property. Specifically, it is alleged that the prevailing method of sewage disposal of said municipalities has caused the illness of persons

required to work in the general vicinity, has resulted in damage to nearby property and ships, and has caused a pollution of shellfish. The State Board of Public Health has by resolution declared the sewage-laden mud flats of the East Bay to be a public nuisance and has urged the several named municipalities to take action looking to the early abatement thereof.

* * * each of the named municipalities in 1937 appointed an official to a body known as the East Bay Executives' Association, whose province it was to investigate and find the facts. * * * These investigations and studies disclosed that the problem could not be satisfactorily solved by independent action of each of the municipalities, but, instead, required a joint survey and investigation of conditions in all the area and of the suitability of different methods of disposal to the peculiar circumstances there existing. It was also reported that such a survey would require approximately seven months and would involve an expenditure of $60,000. Thereupon the seven named municipalities, by appropriate action of their governing bodies, approved such recommendation and respectively authorized the execution of a proposed agreement among them looking to such joint survey and study and directed the appropriate officers to execute the same on their behalf, each agreeing to pay its share of the expenses incident thereto. * * * Admittedly, ample funds remain in the Oakland treasury for the performance and discharge of its obligation under the contract here involved, but Williams, as auditor, nevertheless has refused to counter-sign the contract on the ground generally that the City of Oakland is without authority under its charter to enter into such a contract with its neighboring cities for a joint survey of the sewage disposal problem. * * *

Preliminarily, it is well to state that * * * any independent action of one or more of said cities * * * would, because of the action of the tides and currents of San Francisco Bay, still leave unabated the obnoxious nuisance and health menace resulting from sewage deposited on the common shores by the neighboring cities continuing to discharge their sewage into the bay. This and the further fact that there is a present interlocking or common use of certain sewers and outfalls * * * makes it readily apparent that the proposed joint solution of the problem is the only feasible and practical one. Therefore, the Executive Association above mentioned proposed a form of contract * * * by which said cities would contract with one of their number to do the work * * * subject to the approval and supervision of an executive committee whose membership would consist of one representative from each of the contracting cities. * * * By its terms the City of Berkeley will become the sponsor of the proposed survey and the depository of the funds * * * to be paid toward the cost and completion of such survey. All contentions of Williams to the contrary notwithstanding, it may generally be stated that by the terms of the agreement the City of Berkeley is to be the employer of all persons engaged upon the survey. * * * But, in order to give each of the cities * * * the right to approve the expenditures * * * the City of Berkeley agrees that none of the money will be disbursed except upon approval of the executive committee * * *. However, the executive committee itself is without authority to incur any expense, execute any contract or employ any person. The committee's approval is merely a condition precedent to the exercise of the powers conferred by the agreement on the City of Berkeley. * * *

The statute under which the above contract was drafted was enacted in 1921 (Stats.1921, p. 542) and is entitled "An act providing for the joint exercise of powers by counties, by municipalities or by municipalities and counties." Section 1 thereof, among other things, provides that two or more municipalities "by agreement entered into respectively by them and authorized by their legislative bodies, may jointly exercise any power or powers common to the several contracting parties." * * *

* * *

In substance, Williams, as auditor of the City of Oakland, urges that the statute above referred to authorizing the joint exercise by municipalities of powers "common" to them does not contemplate or permit the joint exercise of powers that may be separately or independently exercised by them, * * *. Such a construction of the statute is strained and would render it meaningless. * * * The statute means nothing if it does not mean that cities may contract in effect to delegate to one of their number the exercise of a power or the performance of an act in behalf of all of them, and which each independently could have exercised or performed. A statute thus authorizing the joint exercise of powers separately possessed by municipalities cannot be said to enlarge upon the charter provisions of said municipalities. It grants no new powers but merely sets up a new procedure for the exercise of existing powers. * * * The 1921 statute merely provides a procedure whereby this power may be exercised by cooperative action. This type of statute is not unusual in this state. In other instances, the Legislature has authorized two or more governmental agencies to contract, whereby one is empowered to perform a governmental function for another. See, among others, Stats.1895, p. 219, Deering's Gen.Laws, Act 8464; Stats.1915, p. 329, Deering's Gen.Laws, Act 5616. * * *

It is next urged that the Oakland charter contemplates joint action in two particulars not here pertinent and that such specific mention necessarily excludes the assumption that other and unmentioned powers may be jointly exercised. However, we are satisfied that the admitted exception to the cited rule here governs, *i.e.,* where the charter is silent a city may exercise powers conferred upon it by general law, provided such general powers are not inconsistent with those granted by the charter. We find no such inconsistency in this case. * * *

Much of what we have just above stated is equally applicable to the contention that the City of Berkeley is without power to authorize the proposed agreement * * *.

The point is made that said contract provides for an unlawful delegation by Oakland of the handling and disposition of a substantial amount of the public tax funds and in the determination of the particular purpose for which they may be expended. In this connection it is urged that an unbridled discretion is vested in the City of Berkeley or the executive committee, or both, as to the type of survey to be carried on, and that it may develop that Oakland tax funds are being expended in studying the tideland flats of the other contracting cities. Obviously, if a joint survey is to be successfully effected some administrative discretion must be conferred * * *. The City of Oakland, through its council, has itself exercised the function and discretion of determining whether to enter into the contract for a joint survey * * *. It cannot be said that the delegation of the administrative function of checking the expenditure of money in accomplishment of the desired purpose infringes upon any constitutional or charter provision.

* * *

An assault is made upon the contract based on the declaration that it would permit the expenditure of Oakland tax funds for non-municipal purposes in that a portion of said funds may assertedly be expended outside the territorial limits of Oakland and for the purpose of surveying the tidelands of one or more of the other contracting cities. It is hinted that such result would likewise run counter to the constitutional inhibition against the gift of public funds. We cannot approve the contention. * * * It is urged that cities daily expend their funds in a legal manner in the enforcement of various state laws which in the strict sense of the word do not involve municipal purposes but, on the contrary, involve public purposes or state affairs. Be that as it may, we are satisfied that if in the solution of their respective municipal sewage problems it becomes necessary, as here, for several contiguous cities to contribute to the conduct of a joint survey of the entire affected area, the expenditure of the funds of each such city in this manner is a proper municipal expenditure.

We are likewise constrained to reject the argument that the joint survey agreement does violence to the civil service provisions of the charter of the City of Oakland. This contention is in effect premised upon the theory that the City of Berkeley is not, under the agreement, to carry out the survey and that the persons to be engaged in the project must therefore necessarily be employees of the City of Oakland and subject to its civil service requirements. Earlier in this opinion we rejected this theory, pointing out that the City of Berkeley under the agreement was to be the sponsor of the survey and was to enter into all necessary contracts and obligations, pay all appropriate expenses out of the sewage disposal fund and employ all persons essential to the project, subject only to the approval of the executive committee. This being so, the civil service provisions of the City of Oakland are without relevancy * * *.

In principle, the disposition made of the last point is equally applicable to the contention * * * that the joint survey agreement runs counter to section 38 of the Oakland charter prohibiting the city from employing any person "holding any office or position of profit under the government of this state, or any other state of the United States, or of any nation, government or country". As stated just above * * * persons engaged in the survey will be employees of the sponsor city Berkeley. * * *

The contention is made that the joint survey agreement does violence to section 125 and other sections of the Oakland charter calling for competitive bids on public work contracts. We cannot accede to the application of said charter provisions under an agreement such as we have here, in which one of the several contracting cities undertakes to carry on the survey. If the conceivably conflicting charter provisions of all the contracting cities were held to be applicable and relevant, the effect would be to vitiate the statute authorizing joint and cooperative action. In other words, there could only be joint action under such a theory when the charter provisions of all contracting cities are identical. To state the matter is to reveal its absurdity.

* * *

What we have said adequately disposes of the points urged by Auditor Williams * * *.

Let a peremptory writ of mandate issue directing Harry G. Williams, as auditor of the City of Oakland, to countersign the agreement and to endorse thereon his certificate, as required by sections 125 and 131 of the city charter.

Notes

1. There is a conflict of authority on the question whether each contracting unit, or only one of them, must possess the power to perform the contract. See e.g. Comment, *Interlocal Cooperation, The Missouri Approach* supra, pp. 450–451; Kaufman v. Swift County, 225 Minn. 169, 30 N.W.2d 34 (1947) (holding that all parties to a contract for joint hospital operation must individually possess the power to operate such a hospital; Council of State Governments, *Suggested State Legislation Program for 1957,* p. 94 (1956) (indicating intent of cooperation statute to authorize interlocal agreement where only one of the units has such power).

2. **Intergovernmental Cooperation—State Law Variations.** The case law is sparse, hence the statutes of each state must be carefully checked. See *Handbook,* supra, p. 6 et seq.; Merrill, *Our Unrealized Resource—Intermunicipal Cooperation,* 23 Okl.L.Rev. 349 (1970); Comment, *Interlocal Cooperation: The Missouri Approach,* 33 Mo.L.Rev. 442 (1968).

Where an interlocal contract is covered by both general enabling legislation and by a statute regulating the particular subject of the contract, any inconsistency between them must be resolved by the courts. See e.g., Mercy v. Seattle, 71 Wash.2d 556, 429 P.2d 917 (1971).

Are home rule powers exclusively limited to the home rule territory, or may the home rule unit exercise those powers beyond its boundaries pursuant to interlocal contract? Schmoll v. Housing Authority of St. Louis, 321 S.W.2d 494 (Mo.1959) held that it may.

Does interlocal cooperation legislation authorize a municipality to render services free of charge, or to grant tax exemption to another governmental unit? Housing Authority of Seattle v. Seattle, 56 Wash.2d 10, 351 P.2d 117 (1960) held yes (by legislative intent). City of Danville Municipal Housing Comm. v. Danville, 319 S.W.2d 460 (Ky.1959) held—no (by construction of the agreement).

Statutory authority to enter into long-term interlocal contracts empowers a city council to bind the discretion of successor councils with regard to the subject matter of the contract. See Terminal Enterprises, Inc. v. Jersey City, 54 N.J. 568, 258 A.2d 361 (1969).

In MacCalman v. Bucks, 411 Pa. 316, 191 A.2d 265 (1963) several municipalities faced with a crisis on sewerage outlets but lacking the legal or fiscal power to construct new sewer facilities, contracted with a Sewer Authority for the latter to construct and operate the needed disposal plant. To make the deal viable, the overlying county agreed to pay the Authority specified annual subsidies until such time as increased usage and revenues of the new lines rendered county subsidy unnecessary to liquidate authority loans. The court upheld the agreement against the charge that the county acted ultra vires in subsidizing other local governments, and reasoned that the county expenditures were for a proper public purpose. *Semble:* Johnson v. Louisville, 261 S.W.2d 429 (Ky.1953); *cf.* Town of Williamsport v. Washington County Sanitary District, 247 Md. 326, 231 A.2d 40 (1967) (service contract by the Town for sewerage services by the District upheld as expenditure for proper public purpose, nonconstat obligation of the District to provide such services under general law). See also City of Grandview Heights v. Columbus, p. 261 n. 1 supra.

3. **Debt Limit Factors.** Municipalities disabled by constitutional debt limitations from directly financing essential service facilities may, by interlocal service contracts lease service facilities under annual "Rental" payments which are treated as current expenses rather than long-term capital debt. See, e.g. Bair v. Layton City Corp., 6 Utah 2d 138, 307 P.2d 895 (1957); Hillard v. Mobile, 253 Ala. 676, 47 So.2d 162 (1950).

4. **Service Contracts, Joint Enterprise Contracts and Transfers of Function Compared.** Under a service contract, the serviced municipality runs a risk that the servicing unit will favor its own needs in the event of a shortage of resources. A municipality which lacks the resources to undertake joint obligations may have no choice but to take that risk. But even with adequate resources, a municipal administration may find it easier to execute a service contract than to obtain required consents and agreements on joint ventures or on transfers of function.

Governments may by appropriate contract terms reserve policy control on given activities, while policy control may be lost by transfers of function, unless the enabling law authorizes the transferring unit to revoke and terminate the transfer on short notice. See e.g. the Michigan statute at p. 262; 53 Pa.Stat. §§ 484–89.

ROLLOW v. WEST

Supreme Court of Oklahoma, 1971.
479 P.2d 962.

MCINERNEY, JUSTICE.   The Southern Oklahoma Development Association (SODA) is a voluntary association of seven counties, and some cities and towns within the counties, organized pursuant to the Interlocal Cooperation Act, 74 O.S.Supp.1970, §§ 1001–1008 (S.L.1965).   It seeks to exercise the power of eminent domain to condemn three buildings in downtown Ada for a parking lot on behalf of the Southern Oklahoma Development Trust, a public trust created pursuant to 60 O.S.1961, § 176 *et seq.*   The landowners lodge this action to prohibit the condemnation for the asserted reason that SODA has no power of eminent domain.

Our inquiry need extend no further than to determine whether SODA is granted the power of eminent domain under the Interlocal Cooperation Act.   We hold that a separate legal or administrative entity, created by agreement of the signatory local governmental units or public agencies, is not vested with the power of eminent domain by the Interlocal Cooperation Act.

The Act by its terms contemplates cooperation or joint exercise between the various governmental entities of activities permitted of the individual entities.   The Act does not create *new* powers to be exercised *independently* by the legal or administrative agency.   74 O.S.Supp.1970, § 1004.   We find no clear legislative authority in the Interlocal Cooperation Act to justify the taking of property in derogation of the rights of citizens.

It follows that the power of eminent domain is not granted to SODA by the Act.   The mere statutory authorization for voluntary associations of public agencies created by written agreement is not a *specific* enactment by the Legislature designating the occasions, the modes, and the agencies by and through which the fundamental power to exercise the right of eminent domain may be placed in operation. Harn v. State, 184 Okl. 306, 87 P.2d 127 (1939).

Our conclusion is limited solely to the condemnation question presented and does not affect the validity of the bond issue approved in Application of Southern Oklahoma Development Trust, Okl., 470 P.2d 572 (1970).

The writ is granted.

All the Justices concur.

(1) *State Assistance and Control of Interlocal Cooperation.*—Prior to 1965, only five states had state offices for local government affairs. Since then, more than twenty-seven states established local government offices, often at the cabinet level, usually entitled Department of Community Affairs.   The operations of these agencies range from advisory and technical services to direct action programs, grants in aid,

planning projects, and administrative review of specified local functions. To the extent that they allocate incentive grants and exercise supervisory powers, their leverage on interlocal cooperation is significant. See generally *1970–71 Book of the States,* p. 272; Grant, *Urban Needs and State Response,* and J. Kolestar, *The States and Urban Planning,* both in, *The States and the Urban Crisis* at pp. 77–88, 115–120 (American Assembly 1970). State departments of community affairs are not upper-tier governments, but their rapid growth marks the increasing role of states in promoting interlocal cooperation.

E. INTERLOCAL CONFLICTS

Territorial and functional overlaps of local government units occasion interlocal conflicts on a variety of subjects. These conflicts typically involve exercise of police powers, public facilities, service areas, and land use control. They may arise between municipalities, between upper and lower tier governments, or general and special function units at the local and regional levels. They include disputes between two subdivisions that assert jurisdiction over a third subdivision. As previously noted, this conflict potential inheres in, but is not limited to, the use of special extraterritorial powers.

In reading the following materials consider whether decisional rules on interlocal conflicts adequately accommodate the competing needs of conflicting local governments.

1. POLICE POWER REGULATIONS

CITY OF GALVESTON v. GALVESTON COUNTY

Court of Civil Appeals of Texas, 1942.
159 S.W.2d 976.

CODY, JUSTICE. This appeal involves a conflict of jurisdiction between the City of Galveston and the County of Galveston over the Seawall Boulevard, and the sidewalks adjacent thereto—insofar as the same is situated within the corporate limits of the City. It is, as we view it, a case of the first impression, and comes before us in the form of an appeal from an order granting to the County a temporary injunction restraining the City, and its co-defendant, Dual Parking Meter Company, "from installing, placing or erecting parking meters on the land and premises known as the seawall and Seawall Boulevard and sidewalks, and from drilling and boring holes in or tearing up portion or part of the surface of said seawall and Seawall Boulevard and sidewalks thereof." * * *

The seawall, the Seawall Boulevard, its flanking sidewalks, and the containing wall, form component parts of the defensive barrier erected against the storm waters of the Gulf. They were erected by the County Commissioners' Court of Galveston County under authority of R.S. Articles 6830 and 6831, * * *. Article 6830, so far as here relevant,

reads: "The county commissioners' court of all counties * * * bordering on the coast of the Gulf of Mexico, shall have the power and are
authorized from time to time to establish, locate, erect, construct,
extend, protect, strengthen, maintain, and keep in repair and otherwise
improve any sea wall or breakwater, levees, dikes, floodways and
drainways, and to improve, maintain and beautify any boulevard erected in connection with such seawall * * *." And Article 6831, so far
as here relevant, reads: "Said county commissioners' court * * *
shall have the power to impose such additional uses and burdens upon
all streets, alleys, public highways and other public grounds as they
may deem necessary for the location, erection, construction and maintenance of seawalls, * * * and to license, regulate or grant such
additional uses of said seawalls, breakwaters, levees, dikes, floodways or
drainways as will not impair their efficiency." The greater part of the
seawall, the Boulevard, and its flanking sidewalks, was, under a proper
exercise of the jurisdiction thus conferred upon the Commissioners'
Court, constructed within the corporate limits of the City. [citations
omitted] County v. Gresham, Tex.Civ.App., 220 S.W. 560.

    * * * The greater part of the seawall proper, of course, fronts on
the Gulf, and the containing-wall parallels the seawall, and the space
between the seawall and the containing wall is filled in with sand.
Over the top of this sand-fill is constructed the pavement of the Seawall
Boulevard, with its flanking sidewalks. The pavement of the
Boulevard, and the sidewalks, protect the sand-fill from the action of
the storm-waters which are cast up over the seawall. Anything that
happened to the pavement of the Boulevard or sidewalks, such as
breaking holes in them, which would have the effect of subjecting the
sand-fill to the action of the storm waters, and its consequent washing
away, and undermining of the pavement, would not only result in great
expense to repair and restore the Boulevard, but it would interfere with
the efficiency of the barricade as planned and constructed. The jurisdiction to protect and maintain the seawall, * * * is thus expressly
committed to the commissioners' court; * * *

    On the other hand, the Boulevard * * * is unquestionably (so far
as here involved) a street within the City of Galveston, and a heavily
travelled one. The County makes no contention that the City hasn't
jurisdiction to police the vehicular traffic upon the Boulevard, or the
pedestrian use of the adjacent sidewalks.

    In the exercise of its police jurisdiction over the traffic upon a part
of the Boulevard, the City proposed to install parking meters, whereupon the County brought suit to restrain it from so doing. Upon the trial,
the City introduced evidence from which it could have been reasonably
inferred that the parking meters as installed would not endanger the
efficiency of the seawall * * *. The City contended that the meters
thus installed would not constitute hazards to the strength of the
seawall, or the sand-fill, etc., first because they were readily removable
in the event of an approaching hurricane; and when removed would

leave only four small holes of about three-quarters of an inch in diameter, and about two and a half inches in depth, with the metal shields in them to prevent the entry of water to the sand-fill, and second, that if a standard could not be readily detached it could be knocked down by pulling the lag screws from the holes without tearing up the pavement, and the holes would be too small to allow water to the sand-fill, and thus undermine the pavement. It was shown that it is always known pretty far in advance if a storm is approaching in the direction of Galveston; * * *. The evidence of the County was to the effect that logs and trees and other debris would be washed over the seawall by the storm waters which might be caught and held by the meters against the pavement, holes might be made in the pavement and allow the water to get to the sand-fill or the meters would be torn up by the debris being forced there against, and make holes in the pavement or walks and thus enable the storm waters to undermine the pavement and sidewalks.

The learned trial judge found that it was difficult to predict what objects would stand or be destroyed, or the manner in which destruction would be accomplished, by the pounding of wind and waves during a hurricane. He found that the County Commissioners and the County Engineer were sincere in their opinion that the meters, if installed, would endanger and constitute a hazard to the safety of the Boulevard during a major storm, and that they had, in good faith in the exercise of their discretion, come to this conclusion. But he found further that it was difficult and unsatisfactory to make a finding on such a theoretical point, on which experts differ, and in effect declined to find as a fact whether the installation of the meters would endanger the safety of the Boulevard; he found that the evidence produced by the County was insufficient to convince him of the anticipated destruction, * * * but expressed the opinion that the parking meters would be torn from their base before they could cumulate appreciable debris, without breaking up or cracking the concrete through to the sand-fill. He concluded as a matter of law, in effect, that the determination of the County Commissioners in the exercise of the discretion vested in them to protect, etc., the Boulevard, that the erection of the parking meters would endanger the seawall under the facts of this case, was binding on the Court.

The City predicates its appeal on these two points:

"1. The City was improperly enjoined from the erection * * * solely upon the grounds that the determination of the Commissioners' Court of Galveston County * * * was conclusive of the question as to the authority of the City to install them.

"2. The erection and maintenance of the seawall with its adjacent Boulevard and sidewalks by Galveston County * * * are insufficient grounds upon which to enjoin the City from using the parking meters in the performance of its duties in the regulation of vehicular traffic upon the Boulevard as one of the public streets * * * in the absence of a finding by the Court that the installation and use of such meters will in fact seriously affect the efficacy of the Boulevard and its sidewalks as protections to the seawall, the limitation of the City's jurisdiction over traffic control being dependent upon the existence of such fact and not merely upon the judgment of the Commissioners' Court relative thereto."

* * *

* * * The Seawall Boulevard, at the points thereof involved here, is subject both to the authority of the City Council acting within the sphere of its jurisdiction and to the authority of the Commissioners' Court acting within the sphere of its jurisdiction. * * * Thus we have a conflict of jurisdiction.

However, in the very nature of things, the jurisdiction of the County Commissioners' Court and that of the City Council over the Boulevard are reconcilable. * * * Now the primary purpose for which the Boulevard was constructed was that it should serve to protect, support and brace the seawall. Indeed, the seawall and the containing-wall, together with the Boulevard, inclusive of the sand-fill and the covering pavement and cement walks, form component parts of a complex whole; and such whole is primarily dedicated to being used as a barrier to storm waters from the Gulf, and to this use it must be primarily devoted. The right therefore of the public to the use of the Boulevard as a street or highway within the City of Galveston is subordinate and inferior to the right of its use as an integral part of the barrier erected against storm waters from the Gulf. So, when the Commissioners' Court decided that the proposed installation of the parking meters would constitute a lessening of the efficiency of the Boulevard as a barrier against storm waters in the event of a major storm, it was unquestionably acting within the sphere of its jurisdiction. That is not to say that the City Council was not acting within the sphere of its jurisdiction when it decided to install the parking meter; but that the jurisdiction of the City, which in this instance serves but a subordinate right of the public, must yield to the jurisdiction of the Commissioners' Court which in this instance serves a superior right of the public.

It follows that, when the jurisdiction of the City has yielded to the jurisdiction of the County relative to the determination of whether or not the parking meters should be installed on the Boulevard, and such fact is made to appear to the Court, the Court must treat the determination made by the City as beyond the sphere of its jurisdiction or at least as having been superseded, and the determination made by the County as being within the County's jurisdiction. Consequently, the court is not in the position of being required to weigh the reasonableness of the determination by the City * * * against the reasonableness of the determination by the County * * *. The mere occurrence of the conflict of jurisdiction with reference to this particular determination by the County apprises the Court that the jurisdiction of the City has yielded to that of the County. However the determination by the County, acting within the sphere of its jurisdiction, is not necessarily conclusive upon the courts, and we do not understand that the trial court so held. Such determination can be challenged as being so unreasonable, fanciful and arbitrary, as to be void. But, as against such challenge, if it be made to appear that such determination is supported by substantial evidence, as contradistinguished from a preponderance of the evidence on the one hand, or the mere scintilla of evidence on the other, such determination will not be held void. The Court in effect found, as appears above, that the City failed to prove there was no substantial evidence to support the County's determination.

* * *

No reversible error of law being made to appear, and no abuse of discretion by the trial court having been shown in the granting of the temporary injunction, the judgment of the court below will be affirmed.

Affirmed.

Note

1. Cf. City of West Allis v. Milwaukee, p. 140, supra.

ORANGE COUNTY AIR POLLUTION CONTROL DISTRICT v. PUBLIC UTILITIES COMMISSION

Supreme Court of California, 1971.
4 Cal.3d 945, 95 Cal.Rptr. 17, 484 P.2d 1361.

PETERS, JUSTICE. We are presented in this case with an issue of some importance to urban California: Whether the authority conferred upon the Public Utilities Commission to grant permission to construct and operate privately owned electric generating units supersedes, in cases of conflict, the authority conferred upon an air pollution control district to condition construction of such units upon compliance with district emission controls.

We conclude that neither the commission nor the district has exclusive or paramount authority. Subject to judicial review provided by law, a utility must comply with the rules and regulations of both the commission and the district.

* * *

The commission has historically been the agency charged by the Legislature with regulation of privately owned public utilities. * * *

The Legislature has used its authority to confer broad powers upon the commission. The commission "may supervise and regulate every public utility in the State" (Pub.Util.Code, § 701), may order construction or modification of facilities or equipment (Pub.Util.Code, §§ 761, 762, 768), and may fix standards of service to be furnished (Pub.Util. Code, § 770). No privately owned utility may construct an electric generating unit or plant without first obtaining a certificate of public convenience and necessity from the commission. (Pub.Util.Code, § 1001.) Finally, public utilities are directed to obey and comply with all commission orders as to any matter affecting its business as a public utility. (Pub.Util.Code, § 702).

Air pollution control districts were created by the Legislature in 1947 to protect the state's "primary interest in atmospheric purity" (Health & Saf.Code, § 24198). The air pollution control district is *the* agency charged with enforcing both statewide and district emission controls. (§ 24224.) The districts may also require that a permit be obtained before any building is constructed or equipment is erected or operated, and may condition the permit upon a showing that the proposed facility will comply with applicable emission controls. (§§ 24263, 24264.)

The district's enforcement powers are broad. The district air pollution control officer may enter any building or premises to ascertain compliance with emission controls. (§ 24246.) He may require an applicant for or holder of any permit to provide information disclosing the nature, extent, quantity, or degree of air contaminants which are or may be discharged. (§ 24269.) A permit may be denied or suspended for refusal to furnish information or failure to comply with applicable emission standards. (§§ 24264, 24270, 24276.) Failure to obtain a permit, operate a facility in accord with the terms of a permit, or otherwise obey *any* order, rule or regulation of an air pollution control district constitutes a misdemeanor. (§§ 24253, 24279, 24280, 24281.) Any violation of statewide or district regulations by any state or local governmental agency or public district may also be enjoined in a civil action. (§ 24254.)

Southern California Edison Company, real party in interest herein, sought permission to construct and operate two new steam electric generating units (utilizing fossil fuels) at its Huntington Beach generating station. On August 1, 1969, Edison applied to the commission for a certificate of public convenience and necessity covering its proposed construction. On September 30, 1969, Edison similarly applied to the Orange County Air Pollution Control District for a permit covering the proposed new units.

The district took action on Edison's application first. ＊ ＊ ＊ On November 18, 1969, the control officer denied the application, stating that the information submitted was not adequate to show that the units would not violate Health and Safety Code, section 24243.

＊ ＊ ＊

On December 23, 1969, the district's governing board adopted rule 67, which sets forth specific emission control requirements applicable to all nonmobile fuel burning equipment. ＊ ＊ ＊ On December 29, 1969, the control officer denied Edison's original application on the independent ground that the proposed facility would not comply with rule 67.

＊ ＊ ＊

The commission held hearings on Edison's application on 19 days between December 17, 1969, and March 9, 1970. The district participated in these hearings, presenting evidence and argument in opposition to the application. The commission was aware that Edison's application had been denied by the district based on rules 20 and 67. Nevertheless, on June 23, 1970, a week after the hearing board's final decision, the commission granted Edison's application and further directed Edison to begin construction immediately. (Decision No. 77400, June 23, 1970, rehearing denied, Decision No. 77552, July 28, 1970.)

In its decision the commission did not contradict the district's finding that Edison would not comply with rule 67. * * * Without discussion or citation, however, the commission characterized this statutory authority as that of a "local agency."

Having made this assumption, the commission then asserted that its jurisdiction was paramount: "The cases are clear that in matters involving more than strictly local interest the broader regulatory authority, in this case the State through its Public Utilities Commission, should prevail. (California Water and Telephone Co. v. Los Angeles County, 253 Cal.App.2d 16 [16 Cal.Rptr. 618]; Los Angeles Railway Corp. v. Los Angeles, 16 Cal.2d 779, [108 P.2d 430].) [¶] As to concurrent jurisdiction, it may well exist as to some matters but * * * if * * * there is a direct confrontation with the jurisdiction exercised by this Commission * * * the jurisdiction of this Commission in the matter is either exclusive or paramount. That was essentially the determination made in the *California Water and Telephone Company* and the *Los Angeles Railway Corp.* cases."

The commission correctly stated that local ordinances are controlled by and subject to general state laws and the regulations of statewide agencies regarding matters of statewide concern. * * *

Where its jurisdiction conflicts with *other* than a local agency, commission directives have not been given such controlling effect. * * *

Perhaps an even more relevant issue is jurisdiction to regulate the health and sanitation of common carrier employees. While the commission has been said to have such jurisdiction (37 Ops.Cal.Atty.Gen. (1961) 31, 33), the Industrial Welfare Commission and the Division of Industrial Safety have been held to have *concurrent* jurisdiction over such matters. The Attorney General's opinion makes it clear that a common carrier must not only obtain an operating permit from the commission (Pub.Util.Code, § 1001) and comply with commission orders (*id.,* § 702), but must *also* comply with pertinent orders of the Industrial Welfare Commission or the Division of Industrial Safety. "[O]wners of common carriers must comply with the orders of *each* of the agencies so empowered." (37 Ops.Cal.Atty.Gen. at p. 36; italics added.)

When the Legislature considered the problem of air pollution control in 1947, it was no doubt aware of the jurisdictional limitations of local city and county governments. It is obvious that air is not a matter of purely local concern, and that the effective control of air pollution therefore should be undertaken on a nonlocal basis.

* * * The Legislature declares that air quality is a matter of statewide importance (§ 24198), and that *"it is not practical or feasible to prevent or reduce such air contaminants by local county and city ordinances."* (§ 24199, subd. (b), italics added.) The Legislature therefore creates a *new* agency to deal with this non-local matter, the air pollution control district. (§ 24200.) The district, through its officer, is to enforce all statewide standards concerning air pollution (§ 24224, subd. (a)) * * * The Legislature expressly declares that all such rules are to be enforceable against *"any state or local governmental agency* or public district, or any officer or employee thereof," and any violation of an air pollution control district rule by such public agency or public district "may be enjoined in a civil action brought in the name of the people of the State of California." (§ 24254, italics added.)

Edison contends that districts have only local powers because they function only with the consent of the county board of supervisors (§§ 24202, 24205), have boundaries coextensive with that of the county (§ 24201), and have as officers the entire board of supervisors sitting ex officio (§ 24220). What is most significant, however, is the care with which the Legislature separated the legal status of the air pollution control district from that of the county. One prime reason that the board of supervisors must give in its resolution declaring that a district is needed is that *"it is not practical to rely upon the enactment or enforcement of local county and city ordinances to prevent or control * * * such pollution."* (§ 24205, subd. (b), italics added.) The board must appropriate separate funds for the operation of the district (§ 24209), deposit such funds in a separate treasury (*id.*), and record the appropriation as a legal charge against the county (§ 24210). The district is a separate corporate and political body from the county (§ 24211), * * *.

The Legislature did not, it is true, intend to occupy the field completely in delegating powers over pollution to air pollution control districts. Aware that some local ordinances of cities and counties might be valid but for the Legislature's intervention, and not wishing to abrogate any power that local governments might have, the Legislature declared that it did not mean to prohibit the "enactment or enforcement by any county or city of any local ordinance stricter than the provisions of this article and stricter than the rules and regulations adopted [by a district]. * * * " (§ 24247; see also §§ 24248, 24249.) The possible validity of local pollution controls, however, obviously has no effect on the validity of district regulation of nonlocal matters.

It might be contended that the Legislature did not consider the possibility that air pollution control districts might regulate the emissions of public utilities. The possibility of such legislative inadvertence is unlikely. * * * It is extremely doubtful that the Legislature, in considering the need for districts with broad powers over private and public "persons," did not contemplate district regulation of power plants. There is also no evidence that the Legislature contemplated a patchwork structure in which districts might regulate the emissions of municipally owned utilities but not those of privately owned utilities, and in the absence of such evidence we are unwilling to reach such a result.

We conclude that the Legislature has established one statutory scheme for the general regulation of public utilities, another for the general regulation of air pollution. As in the field of industrial health and sanitation (37 Ops.Cal.Atty.Gen. 31), the commission must share its jurisdiction over utilities regulation where that jurisdiction is made concurrent by another (especially a later) legislative enactment. Here the Legislature has itself enacted specific emission control standards and has erected a comprehensive statutory structure for the adoption of further controls. These controls without doubt apply to public utilities. * * * Where the district has found that a proposed or existing facility does not comply with applicable regulations, the commission may not order a utility to violate district rulings.

Rather, the Legislature has clearly provided a means by which the utility may challenge a district ruling. "Any person deeming himself aggrieved * * * may maintain a special proceeding in the superior court, to determine the reasonableness and legality of any action of the hearing board." (§ 24322.) * * * If a court for any reason finds that a discharge in excess of that permitted by district rules and regulations is necessary, it may so order. (§ 24291.) There is thus little likelihood that the horrific nightmare envisioned by the commission—inadequate electrical service—will become a reality.

The commission has acted in excess of its jurisdiction in purporting to overrule the Orange County Air Pollution Control District's denial of Edison's application. The order of the commission is annulled, without prejudice to Edison's right to seek judicial review of the district's order pursuant to section 24322.

Notes

1. **Interstatutory Construction.** Cf. City Transportation Co., Inc. v. Pharr, 186 Tenn. 217, 209 S.W.2d 15 (1948) where a city-chartered bus carrier successfully sued to exclude a state licensed bus line from the city, on a finding that the statute authorizing the city to charter public carriers operated to divest the state licensing jurisdiction within the city.

In City of Opa-Locka v. Metropolitan Dade County, 247 So.2d 755 (Fla. App.1971) the city tax on leasehold interests at the Dade County Airport Authority, which operated partly within the city, was void on findings that the leasehold interests, like property held directly by the Airport Authority, were tax exempt, and that the city lacked taxing jurisdiction over this aspect of the Authority's airport operation.

2. **Judicial Construction of Implied Powers and Immunities.** In order to reconcile overlapping regulatory powers of municipalities and

special districts, courts are often without express legislative guidelines. See e.g. State on Inf. Dalton v. Metropolitan St. Louis Sewer District, 365 Mo. 1, 275 S.W.2d 225 (1955) reported at p. 223; cf. State Water Pollution Control Board v. Salt Lake City, reported at p. 98.

2. MUNICIPAL UTILITIES

CITY OF MESA v. SALT RIVER PROJECT AGRICULTURAL IMPROVEMENT AND POWER DISTRICT

Supreme Court of Arizona, 1962.
92 Ariz. 91, 373 P.2d 722.

[Reported at p. 201, *supra*]

Notes

1. **Countervailing Doctrine and Public Policies.** (a) There is no neat rule to govern interlocal utility conflicts. On one hand, raiding of established service area by a competing utility invites wasteful duplication and undermines the primary local utility. On the other, competitive utility services may be necessary to assure essential services where the primary local utility is unable or unwilling to construct required facilities. Neither state legislatures, nor the courts, have produced a consistent body of law to reconcile these considerations.

(b) Statutes may prohibit extramural municipal utility services. Cf. Louisiana Gas Service Co. v. St. Tammany Gas Utility Dist. No. 1, 189 So. 2d 304 (La.App.1965), but as shown by City of Mesa and the cases noted therein, this solution evaporates where the service area of an outside district is annexed to a municipality which operates its own utility services.

(c) Statutes are often vague on the question of "exclusive" service rights, hence courts fit the law to immediate need. In City of Cold Springs v. Campbell County Water District, 334 S.W.2d 269 (Ky.1960) the City of Covington executed an interlocal contract to supply the City of Cold Springs with water service by way of a pipeline running through the territory of the Campbell County Water District. Persons in an area where the district had no facility to provide water service desired to tap into the city water line. When the city undertook to provide such service, the district commenced building its own service facility for that area, and sued to enjoin the city from providing water service within the district. The court ruled that the district did not have "exclusive" rights, and that if "raiding" were involved, the State Public Utility Commission was empowered to prevent the same. The dissenting opinion objected that the court was destroying the territorial integrity of the water district. Compare Alderwood Water District v. Pope & Talbott, Inc., 62 Wash.2d 319, 382 P.2d 639 (1963) where the court enjoined a water district from supplying service to the plaintiff district's territory, on the ground that the statute impliedly prohibited duplication of service and "inter-district raiding." But in City of Covington v. Board of Commissioners, Canton County Water District, 371

S.W.2d 20 (Ky.1963) a State Public Utility Commission ruling that water districts should not be licensed to provide service that duplicated the service of the City of Covington, was reversed on appeal. The court found that the proposed service facilities would not be duplicative since the facilities of either body were not adequate substitutes for those of the other. The court added that, should the City of Covington decide not to supply water, the State Public Utility Commission would be powerless to prevent the discontinuance.

Where two local governments are authorized to provide the same services in the same area, a court may settle the service controversy by allowing consumers to elect the unit from which they wished to receive service by construing the service as "proprietary" and not confined by jurisdictional statutes. People v. Mission Brook Sanitary Dist., reported at p. 31. See also Jackson County Public Water Supply District No. 1. v. Ong Aircraft Corp., 409 S.W.2d 226 (Mo.App.1966).

2. **Service Discrimination.** The common law or its statutory rule that public utilities must provide nondiscriminatory services at reasonable rates, and this requisite is normally overseen by a state public utility commission. But with respect to municipally owned utilities, there is a wide variation in statutory and case law on the existence or extent of state agency jurisdiction. Kneier, *State Supervision Over Municipally Owned Utilities*, 49 Col.L.Rev. 180 (1940); 12 McQuillin, *Municipal Corporations*, ch. 35 (3d rev. ed. 1970). Greater local autonomy is allowed with respect to residential service on the view that municipal residents exercise sufficient political control to assure adequate utility operation. In re Complaint of Morris Twp., 49 N.J. 194, 229 A.2d 516 (1967); Georgia Public Service Commission v. Albany, 180 Ga. 355, 179 S.W. 369 (1935). As to service beyond city limits, the case for public utility commissions' jurisdiction is much stronger.

The Pennsylvania court recently articulated a balanced approach:

"So long as a municipality provides utility services *inside* its boundaries, the Legislature specifically excluded such operations from the jurisdiction of the Commission. See 66 P.S. § 1102(9), (15) and (17). However, once the municipality provides utility services *outside* its boundaries, the jurisdiction of the Commission attaches, and the municipality is in the same position and subject to the same control as a privately owned public utility. Public Utility Law, Act of May 28, 1937, P.L. 1053. See 66 P.S. §§ 1141 and 1171.

"The Legislature also provided a procedure for the municipality to obtain a certificate of public convenience so that it can delineate the scope and extent of its extraterritorial service area.

"Municipalities have ample legislative protection against the possibility of unwanted extensions. As we held in our opinion in the case of Borough of Akron v. Pa. P.U.C., filed simultaneously with this opinion, the Commission may not unilaterally order an extension beyond a certificated area after it issues a certificate of public convenience. Therefore if the Borough of Phoenixville does not desire its water and sewer utility service lines to extend beyond the service area it now physically services, it has available to it the certification route provided by the Legislature. So long as Phoenixville continues to render uncertificated extraterritorial service, it will be within the discretionary power of the Commission, on the basis of reasonableness, to determine questions of extensions of service." Borough of Phoenixville v. Pennsylvania Public Utility Commission, 3 Pa.Cmwth. 56, 59–62, 280 A.2d 471, 473–4 (1971).

In Mayor and Council of Rockville v. Goldberg, 275 Md. 563, 264 A.2d 113 (1970) the court held that the city may be compelled to extend service beyond its boundaries only where it has previously held itself out as a public utility within such area.

Absent explicit statutory controls, some states make little distinction between local and extraterritorial operation. Compare City of Corpus Christi v. Continental Bus System, Inc., 445 S.W.2d 12 (Tex.Civ.App.1969) (private bus line denied injunction against city bus line competing on routes outside city limits) with City of Colorado Springs v. Public Utilities Commission, 126 Colo. 265, 248 P.2d 311 (1952) (extraterritorial municipal water service held not a utility activity that is subject to state commission jurisdiction); People v. Mission Brook Sanitary Dist., p. 31, supra; Annot. 60 A.L.R.3d 714–718 (1974).

3. Assuming that a municipality is willing to provide service beyond its borders, may it condition such service upon the customer's purchase of other lines of its utility service? See Edris v. Sebring Utility Comm., 237 So.2d 585 (Fla.App.1970) (held such a tie-in condition to be unjustified and discriminatory).

Where a municipality charges higher service rates to non-residents, the courts generally require economic justification for the differential. City of Texarkana v. Wiggins, 151 Tex. 100, 246 S.W.2d 622 (1952) (higher charges held to be discriminatory). Contra: Barr v. First Taxing Dist. of City of Norwalk, 151 Conn. 53, 192 A.2d 872 (1963) and Faxe v. Grandview, 48 Wash.2d 342, 294 P.2d 402 (1956) (differential upheld as based on financial justification, with burden of proving discrimination upon plaintiff consumers). Reasonable discrimination between resident and non-residents in the replacement of service facilities has also been upheld. City of Bremerten v. Kitsap County Sewer District, 71 Wash.2d 689, 430 P.2d 956 (1967).

3. LAND USE CONFLICTS

VILLAGE OF BLUE ASH v. CINCINNATI

Supreme Court of Ohio, 1962.
173 Ohio St. 345, 182 N.E.2d 557.

[The city, pursuant to general constitutional grant of power to condemn extraterritorial land for airport purposes, undertook to condemn lands forming part of the village streets. The village sued to enjoin the city.]

DOYLE, JUDGE. We here review the judgment of the Court of Appeals which, in effect, holds that the city of Cincinnati has a legal right to appropriate a public street in an adjacent municipal corporation, over the objection of such municipal corporation, for the construction of an airport.

* * *

Section 4, Article XVIII of the Constitution of Ohio, provides:

"Any municipality may acquire, construct, own, lease and operate within or without its corporate limits, any public utility the product or service of which is or is to be supplied to the municipality or its inhabitants, * * *. The acquisition of any such public utility may be by condemnation or otherwise * * *."

It is obvious that this provision in the Constitution is self-executing (Link v. Public Utilities Commission, 102 Ohio St. 336, 131 N.E. 796) and gives general powers to the city of Cincinnati to acquire property by eminent domain within or without its corporate limits for the construction of a public utility. We entertain no doubt that the proposed airport in the instant case must be classed as a public utility which may be operated by the city in its proprietary capacity. City of Toledo v. Jenkins et al., Board of Tax Appeals, 143 Ohio St. 141, 54 N.E.2d 656.

It is observed, however, that when this provision in the Constitution was adopted in 1912, the creators thereof were thinking in terms of electric power, water, and railroads, * * * Airports with two- and three-mile runways necessary to accommodate jet planes, if thought of at all by the framers of the Constitution, were but figments of the imagination. The use of aircraft in commerce came years later.

As a result of the development of aircraft as instruments of commerce after the adoption of the provision in the Constitution, legislation was enacted to specifically meet the problems of the new era. In the chapter, "Specific Powers" (given to municipal corporations), Section 717.01, Revised Code, provides:

"Each municipal corporation may:

* * *

"(V) Acquire by purchase, gift, devise, bequest, lease, condemnation proceedings, or otherwise, real or personal property, and thereon and thereof to establish, construct * * * equip, maintain, and operate airports * * *; no municipal corporation may take or disturb property or facilities belonging to any public utility or to a common carrier engaged in interstate commerce, which property or facilities are required for the proper and convenient operation of such utility or carrier, unless provision is made for the restoration, relocation or duplication of such property or facilities elsewhere at the sole cost of the municipal corporation * * *."

In the chapter of the Code treating on "Appropriation of Property" by municipal corporations, the Legislature enacted Section 719.01, Revised Code, which reads in part:

"Any municipal corporation may appropriate, enter upon, and hold real estate * * *:

* * *

"(O) For establishing airports * * *, either within or without the limits of a municipal corporation * * *.

* * *

Again, in Section 719.02, Revised Code, the Legislature has provided for the appropriation of property outside the municipal corporation limits for airport purposes.

Both under the Constitution and the statutes, the city of Cincinnati is empowered to build and operate an airport; and, although the powers of the city are derived directly from the Constitution, the statutes do not in any way restrict the constitutional grant of power but implement it, as it was the Legislature's right to do.

In considering the city of Cincinnati's claimed constitutional right to appropriate the village street involved in this case, we must appraise it against a background of constitutional purposes. * * * It appears certain that the framers of the Constitution were not thinking in terms of the appropriation of a city hall or of an established public cemetery or of the creation of an airport with two-to-three-mile runways. A constitution cannot be made to mean different things at different times. Although the policy of one age may ill suit the policy of another, the Constitution must not be subject to such fluctuations. If it becomes undesirable in a present age, it should be amended.

Contrary to the claim of the city of Cincinnati, the village of Blue Ash asserts a right to keep its street as it now exists free from appropriation by a neighbor municipal corporation, on the basis of a right which falls squarely within the frame of the Ohio Constitution.

Section 3, Article XVIII, Constitution of Ohio, reads as follows:

"Municipalities shall have authority to exercise all powers of local self-government and to adopt and enforce within their limits such local police, sanitary and other similar regulations, as are not in conflict with general laws."

* * *

The streets and highways as to which the Constitution and statutes have given municipalities the power to "regulate" and "control" are not "public utilities," as that term is used under Ohio laws; they are "public and governmental institutions maintained for the free use of all citizens of the state," the maintenance of which engages the municipality in the performance of a governmental function as distinguished from a proprietary function. City of Wooster v. Arbenz, 116 Ohio St. 281, 156 N.E. 210, 52 A.L.R. 518; Standard Fire Ins. Co. v. City of Fremont, 164 Ohio St. 344, 131 N.E.2d 221. It appears from the foregoing that the question, reduced to its simplest terms, may be stated: Can a grant of authority to one municipal corporation, acting as a proprietor, to condemn property within or without its corporate limits, for the purpose of establishing a public utility, be exercised by appropriating property of another municipal corporation which is used by the latter municipality in the performance of a governmental function?

It is a general rule, and one of long standing, that when a condemnor, * * * seeks to exercise its power with respect to property already devoted to public use, its action may be enjoined if the proposed use will either destroy the existing use or interfere with it to such an extent as is tantamount to destruction, unless the law has authorized the acquisition either expressly or by necessary implication. The manner in which the property was originally acquired has no bearing upon the operation of the general rule. [Citations omitted].

It cannot be seriously contended that the Constitution has expressly authorized the taking of a street of one municipal corporation by another municipal corporation for public utility purposes of the latter. * * *

It requires no argument to prove that the use of the property for airport runway purposes is inconsistent with the use of the property for street purposes. * * * This is not a case of a public utility crossing a highway under circumstances where the same land may possibly be used for the purposes of the public utility as well as for highway purposes.

Determining as we do that the Constitution does not expressly confer a right to appropriate a dedicated street for airport purposes, can it be said that it does so by necessary implication?

* * *

This case must be controlled by legal principles and not by considering the practical effect of an airport for the city of Cincinnati at the expense of a public street in the village of Blue Ash. Each are municipal corporations, and if property of one, * * * can be taken by the other for an airport, while acting in its proprietary capacity, it would make possible the destruction of a municipal corporation, or at least a part thereof, by another municipal corporation for its convenience and economy. Such power cannot be found by implication in the Constitution. * * *

The exact question under consideration has not heretofore been considered by this court. However, questions involving the proposed taking of property devoted to public use have frequently arisen under various factual situations. In Board of Education of City of Akron v. Proprietors of Akron Rural Cemetery, 110 Ohio St. 430, 144 N.E. 113, paragraph two of the syllabus reads:

"Property already appropriated in the proper exercise of the power of eminent domain, cannot be taken for another use which will wholly defeat or supersede the former use unless power to make such second appropriation be expressly granted. Railroad [Co.] v. [Village of] Belle Centre, 48 Ohio St. 273, 27 N.E. 464, approved and followed."

Other decisions of this court have followed the general rule extant in this country, that property already devoted to public use cannot be taken for another public use, at least if such use is an inconsistent one, without authority expressly given or necessarily implied.

It has been urged by the city of Cincinnati that under the circumstances of this case "the paramount public need for the property * * * must be determined by the court and the property can, as a matter of law, be acquired by Cincinnati if the paramount public need for the property * * * is for airport purposes rather than street purposes."

* * * The limits to which the court's power may extend are not governed by principles of equity, thereby giving power to a court to base its judgment upon a paramount public need in a contest between two sovereign governments, each possessing the power of eminent domain. The limit of the court's power is to enjoin an unlawful or improper exercise of the power of eminent domain * * *. Injunction, in this class of cases, is a matter of strict right, not of equitable discretion.

The judgment of the Court of Appeals is reversed, and the judgment of the Court of Common Pleas granting the injunction is affirmed.

Judgment reversed.

ZIMMERMAN, TAFT, MATTHIAS and O'NEILL, JJ., concur.

WEYGANDT, C.J., and BELL, J., dissent.

* * *

BELL, JUDGE (dissenting). The authority granted by the people to a municipality by Sections 4, 5, 6 and 12, Article XVIII of the Constitution, is a plenary one, and the Legislature is without power to impose restrictions or limitations thereon. [Citations omitted]

Similarly, the authority granted by Section 3, Article XVIII, is a plenary one subject only to the limitations provided therein. [Citations omitted]

Concededly, there is no constitutional provision that expressly warrants the application of one constitutional grant of authority to the exclusion of the other.

Private property can be appropriated only on the theory that a paramount need for a public purpose requires the annihilation of private rights in that property. Such must, of necessity, be the criterion for determining whether public property acquired and used under a constitutional grant of authority can be appropriated for another public use under another equally effective grant of constitutional authority. Such a criterion, in my opinion, is eminently more desirable than further perpetuating the already over-extended differentiation between governmental and proprietary functions of a municipality.

Whether there is such an overwhelming public need that will permit Cincinnati to acquire this property already devoted to a public use by Blue Ash is not before us. Similarly, the question of whether the street system of Blue Ash will be "destroyed" or interfered with "to such an extent as is tantamount to destruction" is not before us. (The allegations of the answer of Cincinnati, admitted for the purpose of demurrer, are to the effect that such will not be the case.) The need of Cincinnati and the effect on Blue Ash are questions to be determined in a hearing on the merits ＊　＊　＊. If Cincinnati can prove the allegations of its second amended answer that the street involved is essential to the construction of the airport, and that the public need therefor is greater than the public need for the street as it is now used, in my opinion the Constitution clearly grants Cincinnati the right to make the appropriation.

The issues were raised below in a court of equity. Cincinnati may or may not be able to prove the allegations of its second amended answer. It should be given the opportunity to try. If it can, the court has it within its power to see that the rights of Blue Ash are protected so far as the flow of traffic on Plainfield Road or another street or streets constructed in its place is concerned.

＊　＊　＊ Certainly the Constitution should not mean one thing at one time and something else at another time. Nor should it be used as a vehicle for impeding progress by interpreting it in the light only of conditions which existed at the time of its adoption. ＊　＊　＊

Notes

1. **Accord:** King County v. Seattle, 68 Wash.2d 688, 414 P.2d 1016 (1966); contra: Howard v. Atlanta, 190 Ga. 730, 10 S.E.2d 190 (1940) (applying a rule of "reasonable necessity" in upholding a street condemnation).

Two years prior to its decision in Blue Ash, the Ohio court exhibited some resilience in avoiding its own general rule. In Village of Richmond Heights v. Board of County Commissioners, 112 Ohio App. 272, 166 N.E.2d 143 (1960) (which is discussed at length in the Board of Supervisors Opinion, infra at p. 305), the Village sued to enjoin the county from condemning for airport expansion, village lands which had been acquired for municipal buildings and a park. It appeared that the village selected the site with a view to blocking airport expansion in the direction of the village. While enjoining the condemnation of the parcel needed for municipal buildings, the court refused to enjoin condemnation of the remainder, on findings that the village failed to show a clear right to injunctive relief, and that the injury to the county from an injunction would far exceed injury to the village resulting from its refusal.

2. **Circular Condemnations.** Where each neighboring government is vested with co-equal powers to condemn the other's land, what is to prevent retaliatory or circular condemnations? In Cemetery Co. v. Warren School Township, 236 Ill. 171, 139 N.E.2d 539 (1951) a school district undertook to condemn the land of a cemetery district. Noting that both districts held equal power to condemn each other's property, the court refused to balance their respective public interests; ruled that such balancing was a matter for the legislature, and remanded the case on procedural grounds.

CITY OF DANIA v. CENTRAL AND SOUTHERN FLORIDA FLOOD CONTROL DISTRICT

District Court of Appeal of Florida, 1961.
134 So.2d 848.

SHANNON, JUDGE.

[Proceeding by Flood Control District to condemn city land. The Circuit Court denied the city's motion to dismiss, and the city petitioned for certiorari.]

* * *

We have set out the acts of the legislature which, in part, deal with the subject of eminent domain.

Flood control districts are clearly creatures of the legislature, having no power or authority other than that conferred upon them by statute. Thus, it is only from the statutes that these districts have the power of eminent domain. The power to condemn real property which is being put to a public use by a municipal corporation is not contained in any such statute, nor can we construe the above quoted statutes as giving this authority. [Citations omitted]

* * *

In McQuillin on Municipal Corporations, 3d Ed., Vol. 11, § 32.67, the following is found:

"The rule then being that property already devoted to a public use cannot be taken for another public use, at least if such use is an inconsistent one, without legislative authority expressly given or 'necessarily implied,' it becomes important to determine, if possible, when authority can be considered to be necessarily implied. * * * "

Inasmuch as no Florida cases have been cited us and we have found none bearing directly on the question, we have, of necessity, studied the decisions of other jurisdictions. From these cases it is clear that the rule is as set out above in the quoted textual material. In some cases the "doctrine of prior use" is explicitly relied upon by the courts. There are some exceptions but these exceptions, in our opinion, do not apply to the instant case.

In New York the rule is well expressed in Central Hudson Gas & Electric Corp. v. Morgenthau, 1932, 234 App.Div. 530, 256 N.Y.S. 97, 100, * * *.

In Illinois the rule is expressed in City of Moline v. Greene, 1911, 252 Ill. 475, 96 N.E. 911, 912, 37 L.R.A., N.S., 104, * * *.

In the New Jersey case of Township of Weehawken v. Erie Railroad Company, 1956, 20 N.J. 572, 120 A.2d 593, 596, in a well-reasoned opinion, in which Chief Justice Vanderbilt concurred, it was stated:

"The doctrine of prior use is well recognized. * * * Simply stated, the rule denies exercise of the power of condemnation where the proposed use will destroy an existing public use or prevent a proposed public use unless the authority to do so has been expressly given by the Legislature or must necessarily be implied * * *.

"* * * The rule stems from the recognition that municipal and many private corporations possess general powers of condemnation delegated by the Legislature. If one such body may acquire land used or held for a public purpose by another corporation under a general power of condemnation, the latter would logically be free to re-acquire the same property * * *."

On this general subject see New Jersey Turnpike Authority v. Parsons, 1949, 3 N.J. 235, 69 A.2d 875, an opinion written by Chief Justice Vanderbilt.

In connection with the question under consideration and in support of our decision, see Texas Turnpike Authority v. Shepperd, 1955, 154 Tex. 357, 279 S.W.2d 302; and Illinois Cities Water Company v. City of Mt. Vernon, 1957, 11 Ill.2d 547, 144 N.E.2d 729, 68 A.L.R.2d 384.

It is the holding of this court that the Central and Southern Florida Flood Control District has no authority to condemn the property described in the petition for condemnation.

The petition for certiorari is granted and the order rendered by the court below, dated August 29, 1960, be and the same is hereby quashed.

Certiorari granted.

* * *

SANDLER, HARRY N., ASSOCIATE JUDGE (dissenting).

* * *

* * * While it is true that such is the general rule, there are several well established exceptions. One of the exceptions to which the general rule is subject is stated in 12 Florida Jurisprudence, Eminent Domain, Section 53, as follows:

"Under the general authority to condemn for public use, property devoted to one public use may be condemned for another which is of superior rank in respect of public necessity, or which may be exercised consistently with the use first attaching."

Another exception to the general rule is that the condemning authority has the power to take a portion of the tract in question because the use to which it will be put is compatible with the current use of the property. The rule stated in 29 C.J.S. Eminent Domain § 74, page 865, is as follows:

"*New use consistent with prior use.* The rule that power to take property devoted to a public use must be conferred expressly or by necessary implication applies only where the second use will destroy or injure the use to which the land was originally appropriated. So, in the absence of some statutory provision expressly or by implication forbidding it, property devoted to one public use may under general statutory authority be taken for another public use, where the taking will not materially impair or interfere with or is not inconsistent with the use already existing, and is not detrimental to the public. It is not material that some inconvenience may result to the prior occupant, if the conditions are such that the two uses can stand together."

* * *

It appears from the transcript that the district takes in seventeen counties in whole or in part, and comprises about 15,500 square miles. The purpose of condemning the tract in question is to widen an already existing canal necessary for drainage purposes. In order to determine the effect of the taking of the tract in question upon the entire tract used by the city, the taking of testimony is necessary. This testimony may develop that the entire tract may be destroyed for use by the city or, on the contrary, that the need of the tract sought to be condemned is superior to the use made of it by the city, or that the taking of such tract may not materially interfere with the operation of the existing use. I would return the case to the trial court with directions to take testimony to determine these questions. For these reasons I respectfully dissent from the majority opinion.

ON REHEARING.

ALLEN, JUDGE.

* * *

Since we now hold, on rehearing, that the order sought to be quashed was proper and that certiorari should necessarily be denied, we would further suggest the lower court, on the remand of this case, take testimony to determine whether the taking of the City of Dania's property for widening the canal will materially impair or interfere with the public use to which it is now subjected by the city.

Certiorari denied.

SHANNON, C.J., concurs.

SANDLER, HARRY N., ASSOCIATE JUDGE (concurring specially).

I concur in the opinion prepared by JUDGE ALLEN on rehearing except that in the suggestion to the trial court to take testimony, I would include the question of the need of the tract sought to be condemned being superior to the use made of it by the city, this question in my opinion being inherent in this case.

Notes

1. **Ranking Public Uses.** San Bernardino County Flood Control District v. Superior Court, 269 Cal.App.2d 514, 75 Cal.Rptr. 24 (1969) involved a dispute wherein a Water Control District opposed a Flood Control District Project to pave certain water courses. The Water District argued that paving the water courses would interfere with its functions by preventing water seepage into the soil. In ruling for the Flood Control District, the court found that the Water District's use of the water course was not a "more necessary" use than that of the Flood Control District.

Where statutes authorize taking of lands in public use for "higher" or "more necessary" uses, courts are obliged to engage in explicit balancing of conflicting governmental interests. See e.g., Arizona Rev.Stat. § 12–

1112(3); West's Ann.Cal.Code Civ.Proc. § 1241(3); Idaho Code § 7–703; Mont.Code Ann. § 93–9904(3); Nev.Rev.Stat. § 37.030(3); Utah Code Ann. 1953, 78–34–3(3).

Courts may avoid absolute use preferences. In Buffalo Sewer Authority v. Cheektowoga, 20 N.Y.2d 47, 228 N.E.2d 386 (1967) the court, in a suit by the Authority to enjoin the Town from discharging sewerage into the Authority's system, noted that the Town would have no means of disposing of its sewerage under an absolute injunction. It accordingly qualified its injunction by a condition that the Authority and the Town arrive at a mutually agreeable solution to their common sewerage problems. For a general review of the subject, see Matteoni, *Taking Property Already Dedicated to Public Use: Priorities of Public Use*, 20 Hastings L.J. 551 (1969); Dau, *Problems in Condemnation of Property Devoted to Public Use*, 44 Tex.L.Rev. 1517 (1966); Annot., 35 A.L.R.3d 1293 (1971).

2. **Land Regulation Conflicts.** The municipality in which extraterritorial condemnation is attempted often raises the objection that the intended use violates local zoning and land use regulations. While the response to such objection is not uniform, it has not been effective in warding off condemnations. See e.g., Scottsdale v. Municipal Court of Tempe, 90 Ariz. 393, 368 P.2d 637 (1962) (upholding condemnation by Scottsdale City of land in Tempe City, for construction of a sewage plant, in violation of Tempe's zoning laws); *semble:* City of Plano v. Allen, 395 S.W. 2d 927 (Tex.1965); City of Des Plaines v. Metropolitan Sanitary District of Greater Chicago, 48 Ill.2d 11, 268 N.E.2d 428 (1971) and O'Connor v. Rockford, 3 Ill.App.3d 548, 279 N.E.2d 356 (1971) (immunizing extraterritorial municipal condemnor from domestic zoning laws).

Where the purpose of the condemnation is deemed "proprietary" should a court construe the condemnation statute as not intended to authorize takings in conflict with domestic zoning? Cf. City of Treasure Island v. Decker, 174 So.2d 756 (Fla.App.1965).

Where the proposed facility is deemed to be "governmental" in nature, may the domestic city enjoin its operation, as a nuisance? See Township of Scotch Plains v. Westfield, 83 N.J.Super. 323, 199 A.2d 673 (1964). See the later discussion of "Zoning Conflicts" in Chapter VII, p. 551.

On the nature of a "public use" that qualifies for interlocal immunity, see Board of Education of Union Free School District v. Pace College, 27 A.D.2d 87, 276 N.Y.S.2d 162 (1966); Tuomey Hospital v. Sumter, 243 S.C. 544, 134 S.E.2d 744 (1964).

3. **County Condemnations.** County eminent domain powers vary according to their purposes. In carrying out a state function, county powers may be equivalent to that of the state itself; while condemnations for local purposes will depend in part upon the charter status of the county, i.e. home rule county, consolidated county, or a federated municipalized county. Counties may also enjoy some advantage in relation to intergovernmental immunity from local condemnation and zoning authority. Compare: Appelbaum v. St. Louis County, 451 S.W.2d 107 (Mo.1970) (condemnor county with home rule power held immune from local zoning restrictions) with, St. Louis County v. Manchester, 360 S.W.2d 638 (Mo.

1962) (home rule city barred by home rule county zoning restrictions from erecting a sewage plant outside the city).

RUTGERS, THE STATE UNIVERSITY v. PILUSO

Supreme Court of New Jersey, 1972.
60 N.J. 142, 286 A.2d 697.

[Opinion reported at p. 553]

Notes

Disputes involving school districts can be distinguished from conflicts with state universities. The Rutgers opinion covers many points relied upon in other cases to grant or deny school districts immunity from municipal regulation.

Hall v. Taft, 47 Cal.2d 177, 302 P.2d 574 (1956) held a local school district immune from municipal building regulations on several grounds, one of which was that the school district was a statewide agency. Per contra, school district immunity was denied in Port Arthur Independent School District v. Groves, 376 S.W.2d 330 (Tex.1964). There the court found no inconsistency between local regulation of school buildings, and the execution of a state educational function. The same result was reached in School District of Philadelphia v. Zoning Board of Adjustment, 417 Pa. 277, 207 A.2d 864 (1965).

In Southwest Delaware County Municipal Authority v. Aston, 413 Pa. 526, 198 A.2d 867 (1964), the court held that the school district land was immune from special assessment for a new sewer line operated by the local sewer Authority, but that the school district was not immune from the regulation regarding use and payment for the Authority's sewer line.

Could a school district compel another local government unit to supply sewer service? Cf. Travaini v. Maricopa County, 9 Ariz.App. 228, 450 P.2d 1021 (1966) (city compelled to provide sewer service to the county hospital within its territory).

BOARD OF SUPERVISORS OF PRINCE WILLIAM COUNTY v. BOARD OF COUNTY SUPERVISORS OF FAIRFAX COUNTY

Supreme Court of Appeals of Virginia, 1966.
206 Va. 730, 146 S.E.2d 234.

GORDON, JUSTICE. This condemnation proceeding was instituted by Fairfax county. Subsequently, Prince William county filed a petition to intervene in the proceeding as a party condemning. This appeal is from an order denying that petition.

* * *

On January 3, 1962, Fairfax county filed a petition * * * seeking to acquire * * * all properties owned by The Alexandria Water Company, located in Fairfax and Prince William counties, * * *.

The right of Fairfax county to condemn these properties was vigorously contested by the Water Company and by Prince William county, * * *

The Water Company defended the petition for condemnation on the ground (among others) that Fairfax county had not obtained a certificate of public convenience and necessity from the State Corporation Commission * * *. The Water Company took the position that Code § 25–233 (Va.Code Ann. § 25–233 (Repl. vol. 1964)) required the issuance of such a certificate, since Fairfax county sought to acquire the water system for the benefit of the Fairfax County Water Authority.

Before the court ruled on this defense, the State Corporation Commission at the instance of the Water Company issued a declaratory judgment to the effect that the provisions of Code § 25–233 were applicable to the condemnation proceeding.

We reversed the order of the Commission. Board of Supervisors of Fairfax County v. Alexandria Water Company, 204 Va. 434, 132 S.E.2d 440 (1963). We found that Fairfax county, and not the Fairfax County Water Authority, was the real party plaintiff in the condemnation proceeding, and held that the proceeding could be maintained by Fairfax county without a certificate from the Commission.

* * * We rejected, moreover, the argument of the Water Company that, since Fairfax county proposed to transfer the properties to the Fairfax County Water Authority, the requested condemnation was not for a proper public purpose.

On July 3, 1964, Prince William county filed its petition * * * praying that it be permitted to condemn the portion of the water works system located in Prince William county. It adhered to its previous position that condemnation of the system was not in the public interest. * * *

* * *

The lower court applied the general rule that, where two persons would otherwise have equal right to condemn the same property, the right of the person who first institutes condemnation proceedings is superior—that is, the institution of condemnation proceedings by one such person precludes the right of the other person to condemn the same property. Connolly v. Des Moines & Cent. Iowa Ry. Co., 246 Iowa 874, 68 N.W.2d 320 (1955); City of Chehalis v. City of Centralia, 77 Wash. 673, 138 P. 293 (1914).

In its brief, Prince William county recognizes this general rule, but seeks to avoid the rule on the ground that it "has heretofore been utilized, for all practical purposes, exclusively in contests * * * between * * * utility companies". But the rule has been applied in cases of contests between political subdivisions. City of Chehalis v. City of Centralia, *supra*. We see no reasonable basis, moreover, for distinguishing contests between public utilities from contests between political subdivisions.

In its brief, Prince William county cites only one case, Village of Richmond Hts. v. Board of County Com'rs, 112 Ohio App. 272, 166 N.E. 2d 143 (1960), that supports the application of equitable principles to determine the relative rights of two political subdivisions to acquire and retain the same property. The village brought suit in equity to enjoin the county from condemning land previously purchased by the village for alleged public purposes—municipal buildings and a park. The court, having found that the village and the county had "equal rights to appropriate property for public purposes", refused to give priority to the village merely because it had acquired the property first.

The court noted that equity should "balance the relative conveniences of the parties" in granting or denying an injunction. It found that the complainant-village had failed to show a clear right to an injunction with respect to the portion of the land intended for use as a park; nor had the village shown that, if the county were permitted to condemn the land intended for use as a park, the injury to the village would exceed the injury that would be inflicted upon the county * * *. An injunction was issued prohibiting the county from proceeding with the condemnation of the portion of the land dedicated by the village for municipal buildings, leaving the county free to condemn the other portion.

One of the three judges who sat in the case filed a concurring opinion, in which he agreed with the result but disagreed with the reasoning of the majority. He was of opinion that a court of equity should not " 'compare and weigh the greater or more paramount necessity of the conflicting appropriations,' nor * * * [should] it 'make an equitable adjustment of the rights of the contending parties.' " (112 Ohio App. 272, 292, 166 N.E.2d 143, 157). * * * He agreed with the holding of the majority because the village had not shown that the land, except for the portion to be used for municipal buildings, was held by the village with a bona fide intention of use for recreational purposes within a reasonable time.

Village of Richmond Hts., unlike the present case, involved the right of one political subdivision to condemn property owned by another political subdivision. Insofar as that case may be relevant here, we find the reasoning of the concurring judge—that the relative necessity of the conflicting appropriations should not be weighed, nor an equitable adjustment of the rights of the parties made—consonant with Virginia practice and procedure.

We hold that the lower court was correct in applying the rule of first in time, first in right in this case, and in refusing to determine the issue by the application of equitable principles. * * *

Equity is not the proper forum for condemnation proceedings. Such proceedings should be maintained on the common law side of the court. See Brown v. May, 202 Va. 300, 117 S.E.2d 101 (1960); Dove v. May, 201 Va. 761, 113 S.E.2d 840 (1960).

* * *

Prince William county asks us to read into the statutes an authorization for the condemnation court to determine the relative rights of two competing condemnors by the application of equitable principles. In effect, it is asking us to interpret the condemnation statutes as authorizing the court to determine whether the greater public convenience and necessity would be promoted by the condemnation of part of the water works system by Fairfax county or by Prince William county.

* * * There is no statute that would have authorized the court to deny the prayer of the petition upon a finding that the greater public interest would be served by the continued ownership and operation of the water system by the Water Company. Nor is there any statute that would have authorized the court to determine, by applying equitable principles or determining the greater public convenience and necessity, whether a portion of the water system should be owned and operated by Fairfax county or Prince William county.

Two cases decided by the Supreme Court of Washington illustrate the necessity of statutory authority to enable a court to determine, upon the basis of the greater public benefit, the relative rights of competing condemnors. In City of Chehalis v. City of Centralia, *supra*, 77 Wash. 673, 138 P. 293 (1914), the court applied the rule of first in time, first in right; but in State ex rel. Kennewick Irr. Dist. v. Superior Court for Walla Walla County, 118 Wash. 517, 204 P. 1 (1922), the court decided in favor of the condemnor who had proved that its condemnation of the property would result in the greater public benefit. The statutes governing the condemnation proceeding in *Chehalis* contained no provision authorizing the court to weigh the public benefit; but when *Kennewick* was decided, the governing statutes had been amended so as to provide: "In condemnation proceedings the court shall determine what use will be for the greatest public benefit, and that use shall be deemed a superior one." It should be noticed that the court in *Kennewick* did not determine the issue by applying principles gratuitously borrowed from equity, but followed the statutory mandate that the greater public benefit be determined.

Not only do the Virginia statutes fail to give authority for a condemnation court to determine the substantive question of greater public benefit, they do not even provide for intervention as a party condemning. * * *

For the reasons assigned, the order is

Affirmed.

Notes

1. The first-in-time, first-in-right rule on competing condemnations of non-governmental property has been applied elsewhere. See Town of Somerset v. Dighton Water District, 347 Mass. 738, 200 N.E.2d 237 (1964); Public Utility District No. 1, of Pend Oreille County v. Newport, 38 Wash. 2d 221, 228 P.2d 766 (1951) (concurring opinion).

Chapter VI

FEDERAL–STATE–LOCAL RELATIONS

A. Introductory Note

The pervasive impact of federal law upon local government activity rests upon the three-fold sources: the federal constitution; federal statutes that directly regulate specified subjects or that impose conditions on optional acceptance of federal subsidies; and federal preemption and displacement of otherwise valid local laws. Since all federal law, constitutional, statutory, or administrative, supersedes inconsistent state or local laws by virtue of the Supremacy Clause of the federal constitution, federal-local relations largely hinge on case rulings whether overlapping laws are "consistent" in the myriad situations that implicate federal-local interests.

Constitutional limitations regarding due process, equal protection and substantive individual liberties directly limit the means by which local government policies may be pursued. Federal civil rights statutes (ch. XI, infra) further extend those restrictions with regard to identified subgroups of the population.

Beyond protection of civil rights, the federal power to regulate interstate commerce and to spend for the national welfare extends to most subjects of local government. The fact that federal power is not always wielded with a mandatory stick, but often exerted with the carrot of conditional federal grants, does not materially lessen its force. While recent moves toward federal deregulation slowed the expansion of federal influence, they have not materially lessened it.

The following materials provide some illustrations of the paths by which federal law conditions local government power and practices.

B. FEDERAL SOURCES OF LOCAL GOVERNMENT JURISDICTION

CITY OF TACOMA v. TAXPAYERS

Supreme Court of the United States, 1958.
357 U.S. 320, 78 S.Ct. 1209, 2 L.Ed.2d 1345.

MR. JUSTICE WHITTAKER delivered the opinion of the Court.

This is the latest episode in litigation beginning in 1948 which has been waged in five tribunals and has produced more than 125 printed pages of administrative and judicial opinions. It concerns the plan of the City of Tacoma, a municipal corporation in the State of Washington, to construct a power project on the Cowlitz River, a navigable water of the United States, in accordance with a license issued by the Federal Power Commission under the Federal Power Act. The question presented for decision here is whether under the facts of this case the City of Tacoma has acquired federal eminent domain power and capacity to take, upon the payment of just compensation, a fish hatchery owned and operated by the State of Washington, by virtue of the license issued to the City under the Federal Power Act and more particularly § 21 thereof. The project cannot be built without taking the hatchery because it necessarily must be inundated by a reservoir that will be created by one of the project's dams.

* * *

We come now to the core of the controversy between the parties, namely, whether the license issued by the Commission under the Federal Power Act to the City of Tacoma gave it capacity to act under that federal license in constructing the project and delegated to it federal eminent domain power to take, upon the payment of just compensation, the State's fish hatchery * * * in the absence of state legislation specifically conferring such authority.

* * *

It is no longer open to question that the Federal Government under the Commerce Clause of the Constitution (Art. 1, § 8, cl. 3) has dominion, to the exclusion of the States, over navigable waters of the United States. [Citations omitted] Congress has elected to exercise this power under the detailed and comprehensive plan for development of the Nation's water resources, which it prescribed in the Federal Power Act, to be administered by the Federal Power Commission. [Citations omitted]

* * *

* * * It can hardly be doubted that Congress, acting within its constitutional powers, may prescribe the procedures and conditions under which, and the courts in which, judicial review of administrative orders may be had. *Cf.* Labor Board v. Cheney California Lumber Co., 327 U.S. 385, 388, 66 S.Ct. 553, 554, 90 L.Ed. 739. So acting, Congress in § 313(b) prescribed the specific, complete and exclusive mode for judicial review of the Commission's orders. Safe Harbor Water Power Corp. v. Federal Power Comm'n, 124 F.2d 800, 804, cert. denied, 316 U.S. 663, 62 S.Ct. 943, 86 L.Ed. 1740. * * * Hence, upon judicial review of the Commission's order, all objections to the order, to the license it directs to be issued, and to the legal competence of the licensee to execute its terms, must be made in the Court of Appeals or not at all. For Congress, acting within its powers, has declared that the Court of Appeals shall have "exclusive jurisdiction" to review such orders, and that its judgment "shall be final," subject to review by this Court upon certiorari or certification. Such statutory finality need not be labeled *res judicata*, estoppel, collateral estoppel, waiver or the like either by Congress or the courts.

The State participated in the hearing before the Commission. It there vigorously objected to the issuance of the license upon the grounds, among others, "[t]hat the reservoirs which would be created by the proposed dams would inundate a valuable and irreplaceable fish hatchery owned by the State" and, hence, necessarily require the taking of it by the City under the license sought; that the City had not complied with the applicable laws of the State respecting construction of the project and performance of the acts necessarily incident thereto (note 11); and that the City was not authorized by the laws of the State to engage in such business. The Commission rejected these contentions of the State and made all the findings required by the Act to support its order granting the license (note 9). * * * The State then petitioned the Commission for a rehearing, reviving the foregoing contentions and raising others. The petition was denied.

Thereafter, the State, following the procedures prescribed by § 313(b), petitioned the proper Court of Appeals for review of the Commission's findings and order. After full hearing, that court rejected all contentions there raised by the State, did not disturb any of the Commission's findings, and affirmed its order without modification. Washington Department of Game v. Federal Power Comm'n, 207 F.2d 391. It made particular mention of, and approved, the Commission's finding, as rephrased by the court, that the City had submitted "such evidence of compliance with state law as, in the Commission's judgment, would be 'appropriate to effect the purposes of a Federal license on the navigable waters of the United States.'" *Id.,* at 396.

Moreover, in its briefs in the Court of Appeals, the State urged reversal of the Commission's order on the grounds that the City "has not shown, nor could it show, that [it] has availed itself of * * * *any right to take or destroy the property of the State* of Washington [and that] Tacoma, as a creature of the State of Washington, *cannot act* [under the license] in opposition to the policy of the State or in derogation of its laws." (Emphasis added.) In rejecting these contentions—that the City does not have "any right to take or destroy property of the State" and "cannot act" in accordance with the terms of its federal license—the Court of Appeals said:

> "Again, we turn to the First Iowa case, *supra*. There, too, the applicant for a federal license was a creature of the state and the chief opposition came from the state itself. Yet, the Supreme Court permitted the applicant to act inconsistently with the declared policy of its creator, and to prevail in obtaining a license.

> "Consistent with the First Iowa case, *supra*, we conclude that the state laws cannot prevent the Federal Power Commission from issuing a license *or bar the licensee from acting under the license* to build a dam on a navigable stream since the stream is under the dominion of the United States." *Id.*, at 396. (Emphasis added.)

* * * After the Court of Appeals' judgment was rendered, the State petitioned this Court for a writ of certiorari which was denied. 347 U.S. 936, 74 S.Ct. 626, 98 L.Ed. 1087.

These were precisely the proceedings prescribed by Congress in § 313(b) of the Act for judicial review of the Commission's findings and order. They resulted in affirmance. That result, Congress has declared, "shall be final."

But respondents say that the Court of Appeals did not decide the question of legal capacity of the City to act under the license and, therefore, its decision is not final on that question, but left it open to further litigation. They rely upon the following language of the opinion:

> "However, we do not touch the question as to the legal capacity of the City of Tacoma to initiate and act under the license once it is granted. There may be limitations in the City Charter, for instance, as to indebtedness limitations. Questions of this nature may be inquired into by the Commission as relevant to the practicability of the plan, but the Commission has no power to adjudicate them." *Id.*, at 396–397.

We believe that respondents' construction of this language is in error. The questioned language expressly refers to possible "indebtedness limitations" in the City's Charter and "questions of this nature," not to the right of the City to receive and perform, as licensee of the Federal Government under the Federal Power Act, the federal rights determined by the Commission and delegated to the City as specified in the license. * * *

* * *

We conclude that the judgment of the Court of Appeals, upon this Court's denial of the State's petition for certiorari, became final under § 313(b) of the Act, and is binding upon the State of Washington, its Directors of Fisheries and of Game, and its citizens, including the taxpayers of Tacoma; and that the objections and claims to the contrary asserted in the cross-complaints * * * in this bond validation suit, were impermissible collateral attacks upon, and *de novo* litigation between the same parties of issues determined by the final judgment of the Court of Appeals. Therefore, the judgment of the Supreme Court of Washington is reversed and the cause is remanded for further proceedings not inconsistent with this opinion.

Reversed and remanded.

Notes

1. See also City of Davenport v. Three-fifths of An Acre of Land, 147 F.Supp. 794 (S.D.Ill.1957) which upheld delegation of federal eminent domain power to a municipality in connection with its authority to construct a bridge over a federal navigable waterway.

2. Following the *Tacoma* decision, an attempt to block the city's project by adopting a state initiative which purported to divest the city of jurisdiction to build the controversial dam, failed. City of Tacoma v. Taxpayers of Tacoma, 60 Wash.2d 66, 371 P.2d 938 (1962).

The City of Seattle and Public Utility District No. 1, a special district serving the Seattle area, filed competing applications with the Federal Power Commission (FPC) to develop power generating facilities in and for the same territory. While the license proceedings were taking place, a taxpayer sued the City in the state court to enjoin it from condemning any property of the District. When the FPC granted the license to the City, but before the District exhausted its appeal from the FPC decision, the state trial court dismissed the taxpayer action. The state supreme court reversed and remanded. Following remand, federal court upheld the FPC (Public Utility District No. 1 of Pend Oreille v. Federal Power Commission, 113 U.S.App.D.C. 363, 308 F.2d 318 (1962) and the state trial court again dismissed the action. On appeal, the state supreme court again reversed, (Beezer v. Seattle, 60 Wash.2d 239, 373 P.2d 796 (1962)), and was again reversed in turn 376 U.S. 224, 84 S.Ct. 709, 11 L.Ed.2d 656 (1964). Cf. Eden Memorial Park Ass'n v. Department of Public Works, 59 Cal.2d 412, 29 Cal. Rptr. 790, 380 P.2d 390 (1963) (upholding federal highway condemnation by state agency, contra state statute prohibiting the taking); United States v. Certain Parcels of Land in Peoria County, Ill., 209 F.Supp. 483 (S.D.Ill. 1962), affirmed 314 F.2d 825 (7th Cir.1963) (upholding federal power to condemn municipally owned land at request of State Department which lacked authority to make such condemnation directly, but which sought to carry out state participation under federal grant program approved by the state legislature).

3. **Ecology v. Power Factors.** Ecological implications of power development produced a shift in the Supreme Court standards of review for federal agency licensing under (7–b) of the Federal Power Act. In Udall v. Federal Power Commission, 387 U.S. 428, 87 S.Ct. 1712, 18 L.Ed.2d 869 (1967) the court abandoned the limited review of Tacoma, and reversed the Federal Power Commission on findings that the Commission failed properly to weigh all competing local and extra-local public interests before licensing the dam in question. Noting that the dam would destroy fisheries and disrupt the river ecology, the court ruled: "The question whether the proponents of a project 'will be able to use' the power supplied is relevant to the issue of the public interest. So too is the regional need for the

additional power. But the inquiry should not stop there. A license * * * empowers the licensee * * * in effect, to appropriate water resources from the public domain. The grant of authority to the Commission to alienate federal water resources does not, of course, turn simply on whether the project will be beneficial to the licensee. * * * The test is whether the project will be in the public interest. And that determination can be made only after an exploration of all issues relevant to the 'public interest', including future power demand and supply, alternate sources of power, the public interest in preserving reaches of wild rivers and wilderness areas, the preservation of anadromous fish * * *, and the protection of wild life." 387 U.S. at 450, 87 S.Ct. at 1724. Accord: Scenic Hudson Preservation Conference v. Federal Power Commission, 354 F.2d 608 (2d Cir.1965), (FPC licensing order reversed for failure to consider all factors and available alternatives affecting the public interest).

4. May a city, by contract, delegate its municipal authority to the federal government? City of Middlesboro v. Kentucky Utilities Co., 284 Ky. 833, 146 S.W.2d 48 (1940). Held-No. There the city's contract with the TVA for power supply vested de facto control over the city's operation in the TVA.

1. INTERSTATE DISTRICTS

[See discussion of Interstate Compacts, ch. V, Sec. C, supra.]

In People ex rel. Younger v. El Dorado, reported at p. 230, supra, the Court observed:

"The Counties of El Dorado and Placer also contend that the Compact is void because it denies their residents equal protection of the laws * * *.

"The counties' first argument is essentially this: Since the Legislature has provided for initiative, referendum and recall for *counties* but has made no such provision for the [interstate] Agency, there is an unreasonable and arbitrary classification * * *. The point seems to be that although the citizens of El Dorado and Placer Counties *do* have such rights in respect to their counties, they are constitutionally entitled to an additional bundle of similar rights in respect to the Agency. We can discern no merit in this line of argument.

* * *

"Nor can we discern any constitutional infirmity in the appointment, rather than the election of the governing body of the Agency. (See § 66801, art. III, subd. (a).) Certainly such a scheme of organization is not without precedent. * * * Indeed, in the instant case, the selection of the governing body by appointment would appear to be a necessary consequence of the interstate nature of the Agency.

"The counties' 'one person, one vote' argument is also lacking in merit. They urge that the Agency exercises 'general governmental powers' and that, therefore, under Avery v. Midland County (1968) 390 U.S. 474, 88 S.Ct. 1114, 20 L.Ed.2d 45 and its progeny, the governing board of the Agency must be apportioned in a manner which conforms with the 'one person, one vote' requirement of the Fourteenth Amendment.

"Clearly, the members of the governing board of the Agency do not represent equal numbers of residents of the region. * * * Furthermore the 11,998 residents of the City of South Lake Tahoe are, in a sense, represented twice, since both that city and El Dorado County within which it is located have a member on the Agency. Finally, the *ex officio* members and the members appointed by the governors do not represent residents at all, but rather 'the public at large.' If the Agency's governing board must be selected on a 'one person, one vote' basis, it obviously fails the test. [Citations omitted]

"However, the members of the Agency's governing board are appointed, not elected. In Sailors v. Board of Education (1967) 387 U.S. 105, 87 S.Ct. 1549, 18 L.Ed.2d 650, the United States Supreme Court upheld a similar system of appointing members of a county school board over the objection that it violated the 'one person, one vote' principle. * * *

* * *

"Although *Sailors* was decided prior to *Avery,* it was cited with approval in the latter case and in Hadley v. Junior College District (1970) 397 U.S. 50, 90 S.Ct. 791, 25 L.Ed.2d 45. *Sailors* represents the continuing view of the United States Supreme Court that 'one person, one vote' applies to elected, but not to appointed, officials. Since the governing board of the Agency is filled by appointment, we think that 'the principle of "one man, one vote" has no relevancy' to this case.

"The counties, however, contend that *Sailors* is distinguishable because there the Supreme Court found that the school board 'performs essentially administrative functions; and while they are important they are not legislative in the classical sense.' (Fn. omitted.) (387 U.S. at p. 110, 87 S.Ct. at p. 1553). Here as shown above, the Agency exercises a broad spectrum of powers of which some—for example, the enactment of ordinances to implement the regional plan—have normally been seen as legislative.

"*Sailors* held that where *nonlegislative* offices are filled by appointment rather than by election, the 'one person, one vote' principle is inapplicable, but expressly reserved the question as to whether apportionment would be required where *legislative* or *quasi-legislative* offices are filled by appointment. (387 U.S. at pp. 109–110, 87 S.Ct. 1549.) To the best of our knowledge, no reported decision has resolved that question, but some guidance can be gained from Hadley v. Junior College District, supra, 397 U.S. 50, 90 S.Ct. 791.

"*Hadley* dealt with *elective* offices and held that 'one person, one vote' applies to the election of school board officials. Rejecting the argument that 'one person, one vote' was inapplicable because the school board exercised only administrative functions, the court stated: 'Such a suggestion would leave courts with an equally unmanageable principle since governmental activities "cannot easily be classified in the neat categories favored by civics texts" * * *.' (397 U.S. at pp. 55–56, 90 S.Ct. at p. 795.) Thus, with regard to *elective* offices the court has refused to distinguish on the basis of the type of function performed by the officer.

"We think that any administrative-legislative distinction in *appointive* offices should also be rejected. Surely, it is just as difficult to fit the governmental activities performed by appointed officers into neat categories, as it is to classify the functions of elected officials. * * *

"The members of the Agency's governing board are appointed; consequently, the fact that they do not 'represent' equal numbers of people does not deny those who are 'underrepresented' equal protection of the laws.

"Furthermore, we perceive significant state interests which justify the Compact's provisions for appointment of the Agency's governing board. In the first place, the Agency presents unique problems because of its interstate nature. If the board were apportioned on the basis of population within the region, Nevada would be accorded more votes than California, * * *. California * * * would be less interested in the Agency if its votes were less than equal to Nevada's. Secondly, persons not residing within the Tahoe Basin have a very real and direct interest in the actions of the Agency. Aside from the general interest of the people of this state, including its vacationers, in the preservation of Lake Tahoe, it is common knowledge that many nonresidents own vacation homes and other property within the region. They will, of course, be directly affected by any planning or zoning by the Agency. Finally, the Compact represents an innovative attempt to deal with a problem directly affecting nonresidents of the Tahoe Basin, as well as residents. * * * ·

"As the United States Supreme Court has said: "The *Sailors* and *Dusch* [Dusch v. Davis (1967) 387 U.S. 112, 87 S.Ct. 1554, 18 L.Ed.2d 656] cases demonstrate that the Constitution and this Court are not roadblocks in the path of innovation, experiment, and development among units of local government. We will not bar what Professor Wood has called "the emergence of a new ideology and structure of public bodies, equipped with new capacities and motivations * * *."' (Avery v. Midland County, supra, 390 U.S. 474, 485, 88 S.Ct. 1114, 1120.) The Compact, imbued with the new ideology of environmental protection, has fashioned for the Agency a structure and machinery designed to deal with the special problems threatening the area. We find nothing in the concept of equal protection of the laws which forbids such a commendable effort."

Note

1. **Local Expenditure of Federal Funds.** State law directing local governments to expend federal payments to such governments, was held invalid as preempted by federal law which provided that the funds be used "for any governmental purpose." Lawrence County v. Lead-Deadwood School District, 469 U.S. 256, 105 S.Ct. 695, 83 L.Ed.2d 635 (1985).

C. FEDERAL LIMITS ON LOCAL JURISDICTION

1. LOCAL REGULATION AND TAXATION TOUCHING FEDERAL AND STATE FUNCTIONS

Ever since the landmark decision in *McCulloch v. Maryland,* 17 U.S. (4 Wheat.) 316, 4 L.Ed. 579 (1819) (which voided a state tax upon the Bank of the United States) the principle that a state or its subdivisions may not directly tax or regulate federal government functions remains undisputed. In application, however, that principle has not yielded any single, bright-line rule. The scope of federal government immunity from state or local laws, varies with diverse situations: "But the limits of the immunity doctrine are, for present purposes, as significant as the rule itself." See United States v. New Mexico, 455 U.S. 720, 734, 102 S.Ct. 1373, 1382, 71 L.Ed.2d 580, 591 (1982).

Scope of Federal Immunity from Regulation. State and local regulations of federal activities may be expressly authorized by Congress. Cf. Hancock v. Train, 426 U.S. 167, 96 S.Ct. 2006, 48 L.Ed.2d 555 (1976) (Federal Clean Air Act requirement that federal installations comply with state air pollution requirements). Absent such consent, the constitutional issue is squarely raised, namely, whether state or local regulation conflicts with the federal function. The question is necessarily one of degree: "Neither the Supremacy Clause nor the Plenary Powers Clause bars all state regulations which may touch the activities of the federal government. See Penn Dairies v. Pennsylvania Milk Control Commission, 318 U.S. 261, 63 S.Ct. 617, 87 L.Ed. 748 (1943); Alabama v. King and Boozer, 314 U.S. 1, 9, 62 S.Ct. 43, 45, 86 L.Ed. 3, 6 (1941), and cases cited." See Hancock v. Train, supra, 426 U.S. at p. 179, 180.

Licensing requirements for federal contractors have been voided as unconstitutional interferences (Hancock v. Train, supra; Leslie Miller, Inc. v. Arkansas, 352 U.S. 187, 77 S.Ct. 257, 1 L.Ed. 231 (1956)), as have state minimum milk price regulations as applied to federal milk purchases for consumption at military bases. Paul v. United States, 371 U.S. 245, 83 S.Ct. 426, 9 L.Ed.2d 292 (1963).

Even in the absence of direct interference, the Supreme Court has voided state regulations under a motivation test, namely, where the regulation is found to be "hostile to federal interests." North Dakota v. United States, 460 U.S. 300, 103 S.Ct. 1095, 75 L.Ed.2d 77 (1983). As will appear shortly, similar tests have been applied to state and local taxation touching federal activities.

Scope of Federal Immunity from Taxation. Courts have upheld state and local taxation of federal employees and contractors (Graves v. New York ex rel. O'Keefe, 306 U.S. 466, 59 S.Ct. 595, 83 L.Ed. 927 (1939); James v. Dravo Contracting Co., 302 U.S. 134, 58 S.Ct. 208, 82 L.Ed. 155 (1937)), and sales taxes on materials purchased by a contractor acting under a federal contract. (United States v. Mexico, 455 U.S. 720, 102 S.Ct. 1373, 71 L.Ed.2d 580 (1982); United States v. Boyd, 378 U.S. 39, 84 S.Ct. 1518, 12 L.Ed.2d 713 (1964); Alabama v. King and Boozer, 314 U.S. 1, 62 S.Ct. 43, 86 L.Ed. 3 (1941), cf. McKee General Contractor, Inc. v. Bureau of Revenue, 80 N.M. 453, 457 P.2d 701 (1968) (federal consent statute). But a state taxes on sales to those contractors who are designated as agents for the federal government were found to be unconstitutional direct taxes on instrumentalities of the United States. United States v. Tax Comm. of Mississippi, 421 U.S. 599, 95 S.Ct. 1872, 44 L.Ed.2d 404 (1975); Kern-Limerick, Inc. v. Scurlock, 347 U.S. 110, 74 S.Ct. 403, 98 L.Ed. 546 (1954).

In United States v. Fresno, 429 U.S. 452, 97 S.Ct. 699, 50 L.Ed.2d 683 (1977) a county tax on improvements made on tax-exempt federal land by an employee living thereon was upheld, even though the U.S. Forest Service allowed the tenancy as part of the employee's compensation. In United States v. Detroit, 355 U.S. 466, 78 S.Ct. 474, 2 L.Ed.2d 424 (1958), a state tax on a lessee of federal property was upheld as not being a tax on federal property.

Nondiscriminatory local taxes on federal employees have also been upheld. See e.g. Patrick v. Frankfort, p. 405, infra.

As with discriminatory regulations, discriminatory taxes touching federal activity will also be voided as unconstitutional. Memphis Bank & Trust Co. v. Garner, 459 U.S. 392, 103 S.Ct. 692, 74 L.Ed.2d 562 (1983) (state bank tax that discriminated against holders of federal securities and investments, vis-a-vis holders of state securities).

Federal Enclaves. Where Congress has not acted to make federal law exclusive in federal territory, and where state law does not impede federal sovereignty, state law may still operate within federal territory. James Stewart & Co. v. Sadrakula, 309 U.S. 94, 60 S.Ct. 431, 84 L.Ed. 596 (1940) (wrongful death recovery under state law by a construction worker on a federal post office project within the city). Accord: Vasina v. Grumman Corp., 644 F.2d 112 (2d Cir.1981); Stokes v. Adair, 265 F.2d 662 (4th Cir.1959), cert. denied 361 U.S. 816, 80 S.Ct. 56, 4 L.Ed.2d 62 (1959). These rulings apply a fortiori to local government ordinances and regulations. For a good analysis of the enclave problem see Note, 101 U.Pa.L.Rev. 124 (1952). The following excerpt summarizes the situation.

"CONTROL OVER ACTIVITY ON UNITED STATES LANDS: THE PROBLEM OF THE FEDERAL ENCLAVE"—The United States government owns almost one-fourth of the land within the continental boundaries. * * * In addition, the United States has acquired substantial areas of land which it uses for such purposes as post-offices, armories, parks, power and navigation projects, military camps, and atomic energy installations.

These federal islands within the states present complex and significant governmental problems. * * *

The beginning (but by no means the end) of a solution to these problems turns on whether the United States acquired the land in question under circumstances which authorize the United States to exercise "exclusive" jurisdiction. Under Article I, § 8 of the Constitution, "The Congress shall have Power. * * * To exercise exclusive Legislation" over the District of Columbia and "to exercise like Authority over all places purchased by the Consent of the Legislature of the State in which the same shall be, for the Erection of Forts, Magazines, Arsenals, Dockyards, and other needful Buildings. * * *" This requirement that the state legislatures consent to the acquisition of places which will fall within the exclusive jurisdiction of the United States does not limit the power of the United States to purchase land which is needed to carry on its activities, or even to acquire such land by eminent domain. Kohl v. United States, 91 U.S. 367 (1875). But if the state legislature has not consented, the acquisition does not withdraw the federal lands from the jurisdiction of state law and law enforcement. For example, a person committing a crime on such federal property may be prosecuted in the state courts under state law, and contracts made and torts committed on such federal property may be governed by state law.

More troublesome problems arise with respect to lands acquired in a manner which gives "exclusive" federal control. The federal government has no complete body of law to govern the myriad of legal problems which may arise on such lands * * *. Consequently, a legal vacuum may result which has been partially filled by an assortment of legal devices.

> "* * * It has been suggested that Congress either develop a complete body of law governing the federal enclaves, or re-cede jurisdiction to the states. Can the problem be solved by the federal courts without legislation?" Barrett and Bruton, Constitutional Law, Cases and Materials 515–517 (4th ed. 1973); see also ACIR, *State Legislative Program* (1970 cum.) 88–22–00 (pp. 1–3) regarding concurrent, partial and exclusive federal jurisdiction and proprietary status of some federal lands, and which proposes legislation to resolve such issues.

Other Federal Interests. Local regulations that impact upon subjects of superior federal jurisdiction, viz. interstate commerce, must also be adjudicated in light of their specific impact. As noted elsewhere, not every local regulation will be inconsistent with or preempted by federal law. Compare, e.g., Huron Portland Cement Co. v. Detroit, 362 U.S. 440, 80 S.Ct. 813, 4 L.Ed.2d 852 (1960) (Detroit's Smoke Abatement Code, as applied to federally licensed ships in interstate commerce, did not unconstitutionally burden interstate commerce) with Ray v. Atlantic Richfield Co., 435 U.S. 151, 98 S.Ct. 988, 55 L.Ed.2d 179 (1978), (state regulation of design of oil tankers held unenforceable under the federal Ports and Waterways Safety Act of 1972 which requires the Secretary of Transportation to regulate design and construction); Northern States Power Co. v. Minnesota, 447 F.2d 1143 (8th Cir.1971) (state regulations of radiation from nuclear plants nullified nonconstat absence of express federal preemption); but nondiscriminatory state taxation of imported goods was upheld by the Supreme Court not to violate the Export-Import Clause of the Constitution. Michelin Tire Corp. v. Wages, 423 U.S. 276, 96 S.Ct. 535, 46 L.Ed.2d 495 (1976). See the Burbank case, p. 340, infra, and accompanying notes.

2. FEDERAL REGULATIONS TOUCHING STATE AND LOCAL GOVERNMENT ACTIVITIES

The principles governing federal government immunity from local laws are not the same as those governing local government immunity from federal laws. The more comprehensive federal power is evident in modern Supreme Court decisions that uphold federal imposition upon local governments and their employees of: (a) federal wage and hour standards (Garcia, infra); (b) federal antitrust laws (City of Los Angeles v. Preferred Communications, Inc., p. 337, infra); (c) Federal taxes upon local government operations (Massachusetts v. United States, 435 U.S. 444, 98 S.Ct. 1153, 55 L.Ed.2d 403 (1978) (federal aircraft registration taxes); semble: Usery v. Allegheny County Institution District, 544 F.2d 148 (3d Cir.1976); United States v. Washington Toll Bridge Authority, 307 F.2d 330 (9th Cir.1962), cert. denied 372 U.S. 911, 83 S.Ct. 724, 9 L.Ed.2d 71 (1963) (federal taxation of local government bridge operation); New York v. United States, 326 U.S. 572, 582–84, 66 S.Ct. 310, 314, 315, 90 L.Ed. 326 (1946) (federal excise tax on mineral water sales by state and its subdivisions); (d) total prohibition against setting a mandatory retirement age, except for certain specified security personnel, 1983 Amendment to Age Discrimination in Employment Act; (e) federal constitutional restraints upon public employee bargaining laws. See, e.g., Chicago Teachers Union, chapter IX, p. 858, infra.

Where federal and local laws overlap in governing the same subject, the issue whether both apply concurrently or whether federal law preempts local law depends upon their respective construction and operation, i.e. whether the federal law was intended to preempt local law or whether there is conflict or inconsistency between federal and local law in the circumstances. The preemption principles discussed at p. 148 et seq. (with regard to state-local overlaps) have parallel application here. Only by interpreting the intent and impact of specific legislation can these issues be resolved. See City of Burbank, p. 340 infra.

GARCIA v. SAN ANTONIO METROPOLITAN TRANSIT AUTHORITY

Supreme Court of the United States, 1985.
469 U.S. 528, 105 S.Ct. 1005, 83 L.Ed.2d 1016.

[In 1976, the Supreme Court decided, 5–4, that Congress could not constitutionally impose federal wage and hour employment standards upon state and local government employers in activities that were deemed to involve traditional state functions. *National League of Cities v. Usery*, 426 U.S. 833, 96 S.Ct. 2465, 49 L.Ed.2d 245 (1976). In *Garcia*, the Court, again by 5–4 vote, overruled *National League* under the following opinion which redefines the meaning and import of the Tenth Amendment.]

JUSTICE BLACKMUN delivered the opinion of the Court.

* * *

In the present cases, a Federal District Court concluded that municipal ownership and operation of a mass-transit system is a traditional governmental function and thus, under *National League of Cities,* is exempt from the obligations imposed by the FLSA. Faced with the identical question, three Federal Courts of Appeals and one state appellate court have reached the opposite conclusion.

Our examination of this "function" standard * * * now persuades us that the attempt to draw the boundaries of state regulatory immunity in terms of "traditional governmental function" is not only unworkable but is inconsistent with established principles of federalism and, indeed, with those very federalism principles on which *National League of Cities* purported to rest. That case, accordingly, is overruled.

I

The history of public transportation in San Antonio, Tex., is characteristic of the history of local mass transit in the United States generally. Passenger transportation for hire within San Antonio originally was provided on a private basis by a local transportation company. * * * The city continued to rely on such publicly regulated private mass transit until 1959, when it purchased the privately owned San Antonio Transit Company and replaced it with a public authority known as the San Antonio Transit System (SATS). SATS operated until 1978, when the city transferred its facilities and equipment to appellee San Antonio Metropolitan Transit Authority (SAMTA), a public mass-transit authority organized on a countywide basis. * * * SAMTA currently is the major provider of transportation in the San Antonio metropolitan area; * * *.

As did other localities, San Antonio reached the point where it came to look to the Federal Government for financial assistance in maintaining its public mass transit. * * *

The principal federal program to which SATS and other mass-transit systems looked for relief was the Urban Mass Transportation Act of 1964 (UMTA), Pub.L. 88–365, 78 Stat. 302, as amended, 49 U.S.C. App. §§ 1601 *et seq.,* which provides substantial federal assistance to urban mass-transit programs. * * *

The present controversy concerns the extent to which SAMTA may be subjected to the minimum-wage and overtime requirements of the FLSA. When the FLSA was enacted in 1938, its wage and overtime provisions did not apply * * * to employees of state and local governments. * * * In 1961, Congress extended minimum-wage coverage * * *. Five years later, Congress extended FLSA coverage to state and local-government employees for the first time by withdrawing the minimum-wage and overtime exemptions from * * *, mass-transit carriers whose rates and services were subject to state regulation. * * *

* * * Congress simultaneously brought the States and their subdivisions further within the ambit of the FLSA by extending FLSA coverage to virtually all state and local-government employees. * * * SATS complied with the FLSA's overtime requirements until 1976, when this Court, in *National League of Cities,* [held] that the FLSA could not be applied constitutionally to the "traditional governmental functions" of state and local governments. * * *

Matters rested there until September 17, 1979, when the Wage and Hour Administration of the Department of Labor issued an opinion that SAMTA's operations "are not constitutionally immune from the application of the Fair Labor Standards Act" under *National League of Cities.* * * * On November 21 of that year, SAMTA filed this action against the Secretary of Labor in the United States District Court for the Western District of Texas. It sought a declaratory judgment that, contrary to the Wage and Hour Administration's determination, *National League of Cities* precluded the application of the FLSA's overtime requirements to SAMTA's operations. * * * [On] the same day that SAMTA filed its action, appellant Garcia and several other SAMTA employees brought suit against SAMTA in the same District Court for overtime pay under the FLSA.

* * *

Appellees have not argued that SAMTA is immune from regulation under the FLSA on the ground that it is a local transit system engaged in intrastate commercial activity. In a practical sense, SAMTA's operations might well be characterized as "local." Nonetheless, it long has been settled that Congress' authority under the Commerce Clause extends to intrastate economic activities that affect interstate commerce. [*Hodel v. Virginia Surface Mining; Heart of Atlanta Motel, Wickard v. Filburn; Darby.*] * * * Any constitutional exemption from the requirements of the FLSA therefore must rest on SAMTA's status as a governmental entity rather than on the "local" nature of its operations.

The prerequisites for governmental immunity under *National League of Cities* were summarized by this Court in *Hodel, supra.* Under that summary, four conditions must be satisfied * * *. First, it is said that the federal statute at issue must regulate "the 'States as States.'" Second, the statute must "address matters that are indisputably 'attribute[s] of state sovereignty.'" Third, state compliance with the federal obligation must "directly impair [the States'] ability 'to structure integral operations in areas of traditional governmental functions.'" Finally, the relation of state and federal interests must not be such that "the nature of the federal interest * * * justifies state submission." * * *

The controversy in the present cases has focused on the third *Hodel* requirement—that the challenged federal statute trench on "traditional governmental functions." * * *

Thus far, this Court itself has made little headway in defining the scope of the governmental functions deemed protected under *National League of Cities*. In that case the Court set forth examples of protected and unprotected functions, see 426 U.S., at 851, 854, n. 18, 96 S.Ct., at 2474, 2475 n. 18, but provided no explanation of how those examples were identified. The only other case in which the Court has had occasion to address the problem is *Long Island*. We there observed: "The determination of whether a federal law impairs a state's authority with respect to 'areas of traditional [state] functions' may at times be a difficult one." * * * The accuracy of that statement is demonstrated by this Court's own difficulties in *Long Island* in developing a workable standard for "traditional governmental functions." * * *

* * * In *South Carolina*, it expressed its concern that unlimited state immunity from federal taxation would allow the States to undermine the Federal Government's tax base by expanding into previously private sectors of the economy. * * * Although the need to reconcile state and federal interests obviously demanded that state immunity have some limiting principle, the Court did not try to justify the particular result it reached; it simply concluded that a "line [must] be drawn," * * * and proceeded to draw that line. * * * [This] inability to give principled content to the distinction between "governmental" and "proprietary," no less significantly than its unworkability, led the Court to abandon the distinction. * * *

[The] distinction the Court discarded as unworkable in the field of tax immunity has proved no more fruitful in the field of regulatory immunity under the Commerce Clause. * * *

We believe, however, that there is a more fundamental problem at work here, a problem that explains * * * why an attempt to draw similar distinctions with respect to federal regulatory authority under *National League of Cities* is unlikely to succeed regardless of how the distinctions are phrased. The problem is that neither the governmental/proprietary distinction nor any other that purports to separate out important governmental functions can be faithful to the role of federalism in a democratic society. The essence of our federal system is that within the realm of authority left open to them under the Constitution, the States must be equally free to engage in any activity that their citizens choose for the common weal, no matter how unorthodox or unnecessary anyone else—including the judiciary—deems state involvement to be. Any rule of state immunity that looks to the "traditional," "integral," or "necessary" nature of governmental functions inevitably invites an unelected federal judiciary to make decisions about which state policies it favors and which ones it dislikes. * * * [States] cannot serve as laboratories for social and economic experiment, see *New State Ice Co. v. Liebmann*, 285 U.S. 262, 311, 52 S.Ct. 371, 386, 76 L.Ed. 747 (1932) (Brandeis, J., dissenting), if they must pay an added price when they meet the changing needs of their citizenry by taking up functions that an earlier day and a different society left in private hands. * * *

We therefore now reject, as unsound in principle and unworkable in practice, a rule of state immunity from federal regulation that turns on a judicial appraisal of whether a particular governmental function is "integral" or "traditional." * * * If there are to be limits on the Federal Government's power to interfere with state functions—as undoubtedly there are—we must look elsewhere to find them. * * *

III

The central theme of *National League of Cities* was that the States occupy a special position in our constitutional system and that the scope of Congress' authority under the Commerce Clause must reflect that position. Of course, the Commerce Clause by its specific language does not provide any special limitation on Congress' actions with respect to the States. * * * It is equally true, however, that the text of the Constitution provides the beginning rather than the final answer to every inquiry into questions of federalism, for "[b]ehind the words of the constitutional provisions are postulates which limit and control." *Monaco v. Mississippi,* 292 U.S. 313, 322, 54 S.Ct. 745, 748, 78 L.Ed. 1282 (1934). *National League of Cities* reflected the general conviction that the Constitution precludes "the National Government [from] devour[ing] the essentials of state sovereignty." * * * In order to be faithful to the underlying federal premises of the Constitution, courts must look for the "postulates which limit and control."

What has proved problematic is not the perception that the Constitution's federal structure imposes limitations on the Commerce Clause, but rather the nature and content of those limitations. One approach to defining the limits on Congress' authority to regulate the States under the Commerce Clause is to identify certain underlying elements of political sovereignty that are deemed essential to the States' "separate and independent existence." *Lane County v. Oregon,* 7 Wall. 71, 76, 19 L.Ed. 101 (1869). This approach obviously underlay the Court's use of the "traditional governmental function" concept in *National League of Cities,* * * *.

We doubt that courts ultimately can identify principled constitutional limitations on the scope of Congress' Commerce Clause powers over the States merely by relying on *a priori* definitions of state sovereignty. In part, this is because of the elusiveness of objective criteria for "fundamental" elements of state sovereignty, a problem we have witnessed in the search for "traditional governmental functions." There is, however, a more fundamental reason: the sovereignty of the States is limited by the Constitution itself. A variety of sovereign powers, for example, are withdrawn from the States by Article I, § 10. Section 8 of the same Article works an equally sharp contraction of state sovereignty by authorizing Congress to exercise a wide range of legislative powers and (in conjunction with the Supremacy Clause of Article VI) to displace contrary state legislation. * * * Finally, the developed application, through the Fourteenth Amendment, of the greater part of the Bill of Rights to the States limits the sovereign authority that States otherwise would possess to legislate with respect to their citizens and to conduct their own affairs.

The States unquestionably do "retai[n] a significant measure of sovereign authority." * * * They do so, however, only to the extent that the Constitution has not divested them of their original powers and transferred those powers to the Federal Government. * * *

* * *

When we look for the States' "residuary and inviolable sovereignty," The Federalist No. 39, * * * (J. Madison), in the shape of the constitutional scheme rather than in predetermined notions of sovereign power, a different measure of state sovereignty emerges. Apart from the limitation on federal authority inherent in the delegated nature of Congress' Article I powers, the principal means chosen by the Framers to ensure the role of the States in the federal system lies in the structure of the Federal Government itself. It is no novelty to observe that the composition of the Federal Government was designed in large part to protect the States from overreaching by Congress. The Framers thus gave the States a role in the selection both of the Executive and the Legislative Branches of the Federal Government. The States were vested with indirect influence over the House of Representatives and the Presidency by their control of electoral qualifications and their role in presidential elections. * * * They were given more direct influence in the Senate, where each State received equal representation and each Senator was to be selected by the legislature of his State. * * * The significance attached to the States' equal representation in the Senate is underscored by the prohibition of any constitutional amendment divesting a State of equal representation without the State's consent. * * *

* * * In short, the Framers chose to rely on a federal system in which special restraints on federal power over the States inhered principally in the workings of the National Government itself, rather than in discrete limitations on the objects of federal authority. State sovereign interests, then, are more properly protected by procedural safeguards inherent in the structure of the federal system than by judicially created limitations on federal power.

* * *

We realize that changes in the structure of the Federal Government have taken place since 1789, not the least of which has been the substitution of popular election of Senators by the adoption of the Seventeenth Amendment in 1913, and that these changes may work to alter the influence of the States in the federal political process. Nonetheless, against this background, we are convinced that the fundamental limitation that the constitutional scheme imposes on the Commerce Clause to protect the "States as States" is one of process rather than one of result. Any substantive restraint on the exercise of Commerce

Clause powers must find its justification in the procedural nature of this basic limitation, and it must be tailored to compensate for possible failings in the national political process rather than to dictate a "sacred province of state autonomy." [*EEOC v. Wyoming*]. * * *

* * *

IV

* * * The political process ensures that laws that unduly burden the States will not be promulgated. In the factual setting of these cases the internal safeguards of the political process have performed as intended.

* * *

* * * In sum, in *National League of Cities* the Court tried to repair what did not need repair.

We do not lightly overrule recent precedent. We have not hesitated, however, when it has become apparent that a prior decision has departed from a proper understanding of congressional power under the Commerce Clause. [*Darby*] Due respect for the reach of congressional power within the federal system mandates that we do so now. *National League of Cities v. Usery*, 426 U.S. 833, 96 S.Ct. 2465, 49 L.Ed.2d 245 (1976), is overruled. * * *

JUSTICE POWELL, with whom THE CHIEF JUSTICE, JUSTICE REHNQUIST and JUSTICE O'CONNOR join, dissenting.

The Court today, in its 5–4 decision, overrules [*National League of Cities*] * * * [Because] I believe this decision substantially alters the federal system embodied in the Constitution, I dissent.

I

There are, of course, numerous examples over the history of this Court in which prior decisions have been reconsidered and overruled. There have been few cases, however, in which the principle of *stare decisis* and the rationale of recent decisions were ignored as abruptly as we now witness. The reasoning of the Court in *National League of Cities,* and the principle applied there, have been reiterated consistently over the past eight years. Since its decision in 1976, *National League of Cities* has been cited and quoted in opinions joined by every member of the present Court. * * *

* * *

Whatever effect the Court's decision may have in weakening the application of *stare decisis,* it is likely to be less important than what the Court has done to the Constitution itself. A unique feature of the United States is the *federal* system of government guaranteed by the Constitution and implicit in the very name of our country. Despite some genuflecting in Court's opinion to the concept of federalism, today's decision effectively reduces the Tenth Amendment to meaningless rhetoric when Congress acts pursuant to the Commerce Clause. * * *

[To] leave no doubt about its intention, the Court renounces its decision in *National League of Cities* because it "inevitably invites an unelected federal judiciary to make decisions about which state policies it favors and which ones it dislikes." * * * In other words, the extent to which the States may exercise their authority, when Congress purports to act under the Commerce Clause, henceforth is to be determined from time to time by political decisions made by members of the federal government, decisions the Court says will not be subject to judicial review. * * *

II

* * *

A

[Much] of the Court's opinion is devoted to arguing that it is difficult to define *a priori* "traditional governmental functions." *National League of Cities* neither engaged in, nor required, such a task. * * *

* * *

In reading *National League of Cities* to embrace a balancing approach, Justice BLACKMUN quite correctly cited the part of the opinion that * * * [weighed] the seriousness of the problem addressed by the federal legislation at issue * * * [against] the effects of compliance on State sovereignty. * * *

* * *

Today's opinion does not explain how the States' role in the electoral process guarantees that particular exercises of the Commerce Clause power will not infringe on residual State sovereignty. * * *

The Court apparently thinks that the State's success at obtaining federal funds for various projects and exemptions from the obligations of some federal statutes is indicative of the "effectiveness of the federal political process in preserving the States' interests. * * *" But such political success is not relevant to the question whether the political *processes* are the proper means of enforcing constitutional limitations. * * * The States' role in our system of government is a matter of constitutional law, not of legislative grace. "The powers not delegated to the United States by the Constitution, nor prohibited by it to the States, are reserved to the States, respectively, or to the people." U.S. Const., Amend. 10.

* * *

More troubling * * * is the result of its holding, *i.e.*, that federal political officials, invoking the Commerce Clause, are the sole judges of the limits of their own power. This result is inconsistent with the fundamental principles of our constitutional system. See, *e.g.*, The Federalist No. 78 (Hamilton). At least since *Marbury v. Madison* it has been the settled province of the federal judiciary "to say what the law is" with respect to the constitutionality of acts of Congress. * * *

III

A

In our federal system, the States have a major role that cannot be preempted by the national government. * * * Indeed, the Tenth Amendment was adopted specifically to ensure that the important role promised the States by the proponents of the Constitution was realized.

* * *

* * * [So] strong was the concern that the proposed Constitution was seriously defective without a specific bill of rights, including a provision reserving powers to the States, that in order to secure the votes for ratification, the Federalists eventually conceded that such provisions were necessary. * * *

C

The emasculation of the powers of the States that can result from the Court's decision is predicated on the Commerce Clause as a power "delegated to the United States" by the Constitution. * * * It is clear from the debates leading up to the adoption of the Constitution that the commerce to be regulated was that which the states themselves lacked the practical capability to regulate. * * * Indeed, the language of the clause itself focuses on activities that only a national government could regulate: commerce with foreign nations and Indian tribes and "*among*" the several states.

* * *

D

In contrast, the Court today propounds a view of federalism that pays only lip service to the role of the States. * * * Indeed, the Court barely acknowledges that the Tenth Amendment exists. * * * that "[t]he powers not delegated to the United States * * * are reserved to the States." U.S. Const., Amend. 10. The Court recasts this language to say that the States retain their sovereign powers "only to the extent that the Constitution has not divested them of their original powers and transferred those powers to the Federal Government." * * * This rephrasing is not a distinction without a difference; rather, it reflects the Court's unprecedented view that Congress is free under the Commerce Clause to assume a State's traditional sovereign power, and to do so without judicial review of its action. Indeed, the Court's view of federalism appears to relegate the States to precisely the trivial role that opponents of the Constitution feared they would occupy.

* * *

The Court maintains that the standard approved in *National League of Cities* "disserves principles of democratic self-government." * * * In reaching this conclusion, the Court looks myopically only to persons elected to positions in the federal government. It disregards entirely the far more effective role of democratic self-government at the state and local levels. * * * Federal legislation is drafted primarily by the staffs of the congressional committees. * * * Federal departments and agencies customarily are authorized to write regulations. * * *

* * * My point is simply that members of the immense federal bureaucracy are not elected, know less about the services traditionally rendered by States and localities, and are inevitably less responsive to recipients of such services, than are state legislatures, city councils, boards of supervisors, and state and local commissions, boards, and agencies. It is at these state and local levels—not in Washington as the Court so mistakenly thinks—that "democratic self-government" is best exemplified.

* * *

JUSTICE REHNQUIST, dissenting.

I join both Justice Powell's and Justice O'Connor's thoughtful dissents. * * * But under any one of these approaches the judgment in this case should be affirmed, and I do not think it incumbent on those of us in dissent to spell out further the fine points of a principle that will, I am confident, in time again command the support of a majority of this Court.

JUSTICE O'CONNOR, with whom JUSTICE POWELL and JUSTICE REHNQUIST join, dissenting.

The Court today surveys the battle scene of federalism and sounds a retreat. Like Justice Powell, I would prefer to hold the field and, at the very least, render a little aid to the wounded. * * *

* * *

In my view, federalism cannot be reduced to the weak "essence" distilled by the majority today. * * * [The] true "essence" of federalism is that the States as *States* have legitimate interests which the National Government is bound to respect even though its laws are supreme. * * * If federalism so conceived * * * [is] to remain meaningful, this Court cannot abdicate its constitutional responsibility to oversee the Federal Government's compliance with its duty to respect the legitimate interests of the States.

* * *

* * * Because virtually every *state* activity, like virtually every activity of a private individual, arguably "affects" interstate commerce, Congress can now supplant the States from the significant sphere of activities envisioned for them by the Framers. It is in this context that recent changes in the workings of Congress, such as the direct election of Senators and the expanded influence of national interest groups, * * * become relevant. These changes may well have lessened the weight Congress gives to the legitimate interests of States as States. As a result, there is now a real risk that Congress will gradually erase the diffusion of power between state and nation on which the Framers based their faith in the efficiency and vitality of our Republic.

* * *

[It] is worth recalling * * * [*McCulloch*]. * * * "Let the end be legitimate, let it be within the scope of the constitution," Chief Justice Marshall said, "and all means which are appropriate, which are plainly adapted to that end, which are not prohibited, but consist with the letter *and spirit* of the constitution, are constitutional." (emphasis added). The *spirit* of the Tenth Amendment, of course, is that the States will retain their integrity in a system in which the laws of the United States are nevertheless supreme. * * *

It is not enough that the "end be legitimate"; the means to that end chosen by Congress must not contravene the spirit of the Constitution. * * *

* * * [The] Court today * * * [washes] its hands of all efforts to protect the States. In the process, the Court opines that unwarranted federal encroachments on state authority are and will remain " 'horrible possibilities that never happen in the real world.' " * * * There is ample reason to believe to the contrary.

The last two decades have seen an unprecedented growth of federal regulatory activity, as the majority itself acknowledges. * * * For example, recently the Federal Government has, with this Court's blessing, undertaken to tell the States the age at which they can retire their law enforcement officers, and the regulatory standards, procedures, and even the agenda which their utilities commissions must consider and follow. * * * [*EEOC* * * *; FERC* * * *] The political process has not protected against these encroachments on state activities, even though they directly impinge on a State's ability to make and enforce its laws. With the abandonment of *National League of Cities,* all that stands between the remaining essentials of state sovereignty and Congress is the latter's underdeveloped capacity for self-restraint.

* * *

It has been difficult for this Court to craft bright lines defining the scope of the state autonomy protected by *National League of Cities.* Such difficulty is to be expected * * * I would not shirk the duty acknowledged by *National League of Cities* and its progeny, and I share Justice Rehnquist's belief that this Court will in time again assume its constitutional responsibility. * * *

Notes

1. **Congressional Response.** The Fair Labor Standards Amendments of 1985, Pub.L. No. 99–150, 1985 U.S.Code Cong. & Ad.News (99 Stat.) 787 (to be codified at 29 U.S.C.A. § 201 et seq.) was enacted to buffer the effect of Garcia. The Act provides that a state or local government may provide an employee with additional vacation time in lieu of overtime compensation at the rate of one and a half hours for each excess hour worked up to a limit of 240 hours for all employees other than workers in areas of public safety or emergency response and for seasonal employees who may accrue up to 480 hours of compensable time off. Overtime hours

in excess of those limits must still be paid for at the rate required by the F.L.S.A.

2. **Participation vs. Regulation.** When acting as regulators local governments are subject to Commerce Clause restraints against burdening interstate commerce, but when acting as "market participants" they are not subject to such restraints. White v. Massachusetts Council of Construction Employers, Inc., 460 U.S. 204, 103 S.Ct. 1042, 75 L.Ed.2d 1 (1983) (upholding city requirement that city-federal projects employ at least 50% bona-fide residents of Boston).

COMMUNITY COMMUNICATIONS CO. v. BOULDER

Supreme Court of the United States, 1982.
455 U.S. 40, 102 S.Ct. 835, 70 L.Ed.2d 810.

[Suit by cable television broadcaster to enjoin enforcement of City ordinance that temporarily forbade extension of plaintiff's service area into previously unserved parts of the City of Boulder. The trial court granted the plaintiff's injunction request, and was reversed by the Court of Appeals. The Supreme Court in turn reversed the Court of Appeals decision.]

Justice Brennan delivered the opinion of the Court.

The question presented in this case, * * * is whether a "home rule" municipality, * * * enjoys the "state action" exemption from Sherman Act liability announced in *Parker v. Brown*, 317 U.S. 341, 63 S.Ct. 307, 87 L.Ed.2d 315 (1943).

I

Respondent city of Boulder is organized as a "home rule" municipality under the Constitution of the State of Colorado. The city is thus entitled to exercise "the full right of self-government in both local and municipal matters," and with respect to such matters the City Charter and ordinances supersede the laws of the State. * * * In 1964 the City Council enacted an ordinance granting to Colorado Televents, Inc., a 20-year, revocable, nonexclusive permit to conduct a cable television business within the city limits. This permit was assigned to petitioner in 1966, and since that time petitioner has provided cable television service to the University Hill area of Boulder, an area where some 20% of the city's population lives, and where, for geographical reasons, broadcast television signals cannot be received.

From 1966 until February 1980, * * *, petitioner's service consisted essentially of retransmissions of programming broadcast from Denver and Cheyenne, Wyo. Petitioner's market was therefore confined to the University Hill area. However, markedly improved technology became available in the late 1970's, enabling petitioner to offer many more channels of entertainment than could be provided by local broadcast television. Thus presented with an opportunity to expand its business into other areas of the city, petitioner in May 1979 informed the City Council that it planned such an expansion. But the new technology offered opportunities to potential competitors, as well, and in July 1979 one of them, the newly formed Boulder Communications Co. (BCC), also wrote to the City Council, expressing its interest in obtaining a permit to provide competing cable television service throughout the city.

The City Council's response, after reviewing its cable television policy, was the enactment of an "emergency" ordinance prohibiting petitioner from expanding its business into other areas of the city for a period of three months. The City Council announced that during this moratorium it planned to draft a model cable television ordinance and to invite new businesses to enter the Boulder market under its terms, but that the moratorium was necessary because petitioner's continued expansion during the drafting of the model ordinance would discourage potential competitors from entering the market.

Petitioner filed this suit in the United States District Court for the District of Colorado, and sought, *inter alia,* a preliminary injunction to prevent the city from restricting petitioner's proposed business expansion, alleging that such a restriction would violate § 1 of the Sherman Act. The city responded that its moratorium ordinance could not be violative of the antitrust laws, either because that ordinance constituted an exercise of the city's police powers, or because Boulder enjoyed antitrust immunity under the *Parker* doctrine. The District Court considered the city's status as a home rule municipality, but determined that that status gave autonomy to the city only in matters of local concern, and that the operations of cable television embrace "wider concerns, including interstate commerce * * * [and] the First Amendment rights of communicators." 485 F.Supp. 1035, 1038–1039 (1980). Then, assuming, *arguendo,* that the ordinance was within the city's authority as a home rule municipality, the District Court considered *City of Lafayette v. Louisiana Power & Light Co.,* 435 U.S. 389, 98 S.Ct. 1123, 55 L.Ed.2d 364 (1978), and concluded that the *Parker* exemption was "wholly inapplicable," and that the city was therefore subject to antitrust liability. 485 F.Supp., at 1039. Petitioner's motion for a preliminary injunction was accordingly granted.

On appeal, a divided panel of the United States Court of Appeals for the Tenth Circuit reversed. 630 F.2d 704 (1980). * * * It distinguished the present case from *City of Lafayette* on the ground that, in contrast to the municipally operated revenue-producing utility companies at issue there, "no proprietary interest of the City is here involved." 630 F.2d, at 708. * * * We reverse.

II

A

Parker v. Brown, 317 U.S. 341, 63 S.Ct. 307, 87 L.Ed. 315 (1943), addressed the question whether the federal antitrust laws prohibited a State, in the exercise of its sovereign powers, from imposing certain anticompetitive restraints. These took the form of a "marketing program" adopted by the State of California for the 1940 raisin crop; that program prevented appellee from freely marketing his crop in interstate commerce. *Parker* noted that California's program "derived its authority * * * from the legislative command of the state," *id.*, at 350, 63 S.Ct., at 313, and went on to hold that the program was therefore exempt, by virtue of the Sherman Act's own limitations, from antitrust attack:

* * *

The availability of this exemption to a State's municipalities was the question presented in *City of Lafayette, supra.* In that case, petitioners were Louisiana cities empowered to own and operate electric utility systems both within and beyond their municipal limits. Respondent brought suit against petitioners under the Sherman Act, alleging that they had committed various antitrust offenses in the conduct of their utility systems, to the injury of respondent. Petitioners invoked the *Parker* doctrine as entitling them to dismissal of the suit. The District Court accepted this argument and dismissed. But the Court of Appeals for the Fifth Circuit reversed, holding that a "subordinate state governmental body is not *ipso facto* exempt from the operation of the antitrust laws," *City of Lafayette v. Louisiana Power & Light Co.*, 532 F.2d 431, 434 (1976) (footnote omitted), and directing the District Court on remand to examine "whether the state legislature contemplated a certain type of anticompetitive restraint," *ibid.*

This Court affirmed. In doing so, a majority rejected at the outset petitioners' claim that, * * * "Congress never intended to subject local governments to the antitrust laws." * * * A plurality opinion for four Justices then addressed petitioners' argument that *Parker*, properly construed, extended to "all governmental entities, whether state agencies or subdivisions of a State, * * * simply by reason of their status as such." 435 U.S., at 408, 98 S.Ct., at 1134. The plurality opinion rejected this argument. * * * The plurality opinion said:

> "Cities are not themselves sovereign; they do not receive all the federal deference of the States that create them. *Parker*'s limitation of the exemption to 'official action directed by a state,' is consistent with the fact that the States' subdivisions generally have not been treated as equivalents of the States themselves. * * *"

The opinion emphasized, however, that the State as sovereign might sanction anticompetitive municipal activities and thereby immunize municipalities from antitrust liability. Under the plurality's standard, the *Parker* doctrine would shield from antitrust liability municipal conduct engaged in "pursuant to state policy to displace competition with regulation or monopoly public service." 435 U.S., at 413, 98 S.Ct., at 1137. This was simply a recognition that a State may frequently choose to effect its policies through the instrumentality of its cities and towns. It was stressed, however, that the "state policy" relied upon would have to be "clearly articulated and affirmatively expressed." *Id.*, at 410, 98 S.Ct., at 1135. This standard has since been adopted by a majority of the Court. *New Motor Vehicle Board of California v. Orrin W. Fox Co.,* 439 U.S. 96, 109, 99 S.Ct. 403, 411–12, 58 L.Ed.2d 361 (1978); *California Retail Liquor Dealers Assn. v. Midcal Aluminum, Inc.,* 445 U.S. 97, 105, 100 S.Ct. 937, 943, 63 L.Ed.2d 233 (1980).

B

Our precedents thus reveal that Boulder's moratorium ordinance cannot be exempt from antitrust scrutiny unless it constitutes the action of the State of Colorado itself in its sovereign capacity, see *Parker,* or unless it constitutes municipal action in furtherance or implementation of clearly articulated and affirmatively expressed state policy, see *City of Lafayette, Orrin W. Fox Co.,* and *Midcal.* Boulder argues that these criteria are met by the direct delegation of powers to municipalities through the Home Rule Amendment to the Colorado Constitution. It contends that this delegation satisfies both the *Parker* and the *City of Lafayette* standards. We take up these arguments in turn.

(1)

Respondent city's *Parker* argument emphasizes that through the Home Rule Amendment the people of the State of Colorado have vested in the city of Boulder " '*every power* theretofore possessed by the legislature ＊ ＊ ＊ in local and municipal affairs.' " ＊ ＊ ＊ Thus, it is suggested, the city's cable television moratorium ordinance is an "act of government" performed by the city *acting as the State* in local matters, which meets the "state action" criterion of *Parker.*

We reject this argument: ＊ ＊ ＊ The *Parker* state-action exemption reflects Congress' intention to embody in the Sherman Act the federalism principle that the States possess a significant measure of sovereignty under our Constitution. But this principle contains its own limitation: ＊ ＊ ＊

＊ ＊ ＊

The dissent in the Court of Appeals correctly discerned this limitation upon the federalism principle: "We are a nation not of 'city-states' but of States." 630 F.2d, at 717. *Parker* itself took this view. ＊ ＊ ＊ We turn then to Boulder's contention that its actions were undertaken pursuant to a clearly articulated and affirmatively expressed state policy.

(2)

Boulder first argues that the requirement of "clear articulation and affirmative expression" is fulfilled by the Colorado Home Rule Amendment's "guarantee of local autonomy." It contends, quoting from *City of Lafayette,* 435 U.S., at 394, 415, 98 S.Ct., at 1127, 1138, that by this means Colorado has "comprehended within the powers granted" to Boulder the power to enact the challenged ordinance, and that Colorado has thereby "contemplated" Boulder's enactment of an anticompetitive regulatory program. ＊ ＊ ＊

But plainly the requirement of "clear articulation and affirmative expression" is not satisfied when the State's position is one of mere *neutrality* * * * A State that allows its municipalities to do as they please can hardly be said to have "contemplated" the specific anticompetitive actions for which municipal liability is sought. Nor can those actions be truly described as "comprehended within the powers *granted*," * * * The relationship of the State of Colorado to Boulder's moratorium ordinance is one of precise neutrality. * * * Thus, in Boulder's view, it can pursue its course of regulating cable television competition, while another home rule city can choose to prescribe monopoly service, while still another can elect free-market competition: and all of these policies are equally "contemplated," and "comprehended within the powers granted." Acceptance of such a proposition—that the general grant of power to enact ordinances necessarily implies state authorization to enact specific anticompetitive ordinances—would wholly eviscerate the concepts of "clear articulation and affirmative expression" that our precedents require.

III

Respondents argue that denial of the *Parker* exemption in the present case will have serious adverse consequences for cities, and will unduly burden the federal courts. But this argument is simply an attack upon the wisdom of the longstanding congressional commitment to the policy of free markets and open competition embodied in the antitrust laws. * * * Moreover, judicial enforcement of Congress' will regarding the state-action exemption renders a State "no less able to allocate governmental power between itself and its political subdivisions. It means only that when the State itself has not directed or authorized an anticompetitive practice, the State's subdivisions in exercising their delegated power must obey the antitrust laws." *City of Lafayette,* 435 U.S., at 416, 98 S.Ct., at 1138. * * *

* * *

The judgment of the Court of Appeals is reversed, and the action is remanded for further proceedings consistent with this opinion.

It is so ordered.

Notes

1. **Legislative and Judicial Responses to Limit the Impact of Boulder.**

(a) *By Congress.* In response to the threat raised by *Boulder,* of ruinous treble damage antitrust suits against municipalities, Congress enacted the Local Government Antitrust Act of 1984, Pub.L. No. 98–544 (U.S.Code Cong. & Ad.News, 98 Stat. 2750), which prohibits recovery of monetary damages from local governments as an antitrust remedy; and immunizes from such damage claims any person or official action that was directed by a local government and taken while acting in one's "official capacity."

In 1984, Congress enacted the Cable Communications Policy Act, Pub. L. No. 98–549, 98 Stat. 2779, which authorized state and municipal regulation of cable television. Congress, however, "weasel worded" on the question whether its authorization was intended to delimit the antitrust law with respect to cable television: "The Committee is aware of Community Communications Co. v. Boulder * * *. While this Committee does not through this statute, to revise the federal antitrust law, the Committee intends that Title VI be construed to establish a scheme of regulation for cable franchising." See 5 U.S. Code Cong. & Ad. News, 90th Cong., 2d Sess. 1984, at p. 4696. As a masterpiece of doubletalk, and legislative fobbing off of a problem to the courts, the foregoing quotation has few rivals. The new law does, however, provide some further support for the "state action" exemption which was rejected in *Boulder.*

(b) *By State Legislatures.* Where the state legislature affirmatively addresses the subject of cable television with a statute authorizing local franchise of cable television, and with some specific legislative finding and direction (even though some discretion is left to the local authorities) the antitrust exemption is preserved. In Preferred Communications, Inc. v. Los Angeles, 754 F.2d 1396 (9th Cir.1985), the Circuit Court noted that in Town of Hallie v. Eau Claire, 471 U.S. ___, 105 S.Ct. 1713, 85 L.Ed.2d 24 (1985), the Supreme Court held that, once state anticompetition policy is shown, active state supervision of local regulation is not necessary to maintain the exemption; and that the state legislature need not explicitly declare its intention to displace competition with regulation. Per Hallie, the fact that state authorization of local regulation is not mandatory, but discretionary, is not controlling. Accord: Southern Motors Carriers Rate Conference, Inc. v. United States, 471 U.S. ___, 105 S.Ct. 1721, 85 L.Ed.2d 36 (1985).

(c) *By Judicial Distinctions.* Following *Boulder,* the Supreme Court affirmed the view that local regulation that does not involve private parties or concerted action by government with private parties, is not covered by the federal antitrust Act. See, e.g., Fisher v. Berkeley, 475 U.S. ___, 106 S.Ct. 1045, 89 L.Ed.2d 206 (1986) (fixing local rent ceilings); Hybud Equipment Corp. v. City of Akron, 654 F.2d 1187 (6th Cir.1981) (city monopoly on recycleable garbage—upheld).

2. **First Amendment Aspects of Cable TV Regulation.** Municipalities that are exempt from the federal antitrust law in regulating and limiting the amount of cable television franchises within their territory, still face the question whether and to what extent the First Amendment confines their licensing power. That important question was addressed, but left largely unanswered in City of Los Angeles v. Preferred Communications, Inc., ___ U.S. ___, 106 S.Ct. 2034, 90 L.Ed.2d 480 (1986). While recognizing that city limitation of access to public utility poles by putative cable television competitors raised First Amendment issues, the court remanded the case for trial on the issue whether the city was justified in granting such access only to one station on an "auction" competition basis.

CITY OF LOS ANGELES, DEPARTMENT OF WATER AND POWER v. PREFERRED COMMUNICATIONS, INC.

___ U.S. ___, 106 S.Ct. 2034, 90 L.Ed.2d 480 (1986).

JUSTICE REHNQUIST delivered the opinion of the Court.

* * * Preferred Communications, Inc., sued * * * City of Los Angeles (City) and the Department of Water and Power (DWP) in the United States District Court for the Central District of California. The complaint alleged a violation of respondent's rights under the First and Fourteenth Amendments, and under §§ 1 and 2 of the Sherman Act, by reason of the City's refusal to grant respondent a cable television franchise and of DWP's refusal to grant access to DWP's poles or underground conduits used for power lines. The District Court dismissed the complaint * * *. The Court of Appeals for the Ninth Circuit affirmed with respect to the Sherman Act, but reversed as to the First Amendment claim. 754 F.2d 1396 (1985). We granted certiorari with respect to the latter issue, * * *.

Respondent's complaint against the City and DWP alleged, *inter alia*, the following facts: Respondent asked Pacific Telephone and Telegraph (PT & T) and DWP for permission to lease space on their utility poles in order to provide cable television service in the South Central area of Los Angeles. * * * These utilities responded that they would not lease the space unless respondent first obtained a cable television franchise from the City. * * * Respondent asked the City for a franchise, but the City refused to grant it one, stating that respondent had failed to participate in an auction that was to award a single franchise in the area. * * *

The complaint further alleged that cable operators are First Amendment speakers, * * * that there is sufficient excess physical capacity and economic demand in the south central area of Los Angeles to accommodate more than one cable company, * * * and that the City's auction process allowed it to discriminate among franchise applicants based on which one it deemed to be the "best." * * * Based on these and other factual allegations, the complaint alleged that the City and DWP had violated the Free Speech Clause of the First and Fourteenth Amendments, §§ 1 and 2 of the Sherman Act, the California Constitution, and certain provisions of state law. * * *

The City did not deny that there was excess physical capacity to accommodate more than one cable television system. But it argued that the physical scarcity of available space on public utility structures, the limits of economic demand for the cable medium, and the practical and esthetic disruptive effect that installing and maintaining a cable system has on the public right-of-way justified its decision to restrict access to its facilities to a single cable television company. * * *

The Court of Appeals for the Ninth Circuit affirmed in part and reversed in part. * * * It upheld the conclusion that petitioners were immune from liability under the federal antitrust laws. * * * But it reversed the District Court's dismissal of the First Amendment claim, * * * It held that, taking the allegations in the complaint as true, * * * the City violated the First Amendment by refusing to issue a franchise to more than one cable television company when there was sufficient excess physical and economic capacity to accommodate more than one. * * *

We agree with the Court of Appeals that respondent's complaint should not have been dismissed, * * * but we do so on a narrower ground than the one taken by it, * * * The City, while admitting the existence of excess physical capacity on the utility poles, the rights-of-way, and the like, justifies the limit on franchises in terms of minimizing the demand that cable systems make for the use of public property. The City characterizes these uses as the stringing of "nearly 700 miles of hanging and buried wire and other appliances necessary for the operation of its system." * * * The City also characterizes them as "a permanent visual blight," * * * and adds that the process of installation and repair of such a system in effect subjects City facilities designed for other purposes to a servitude which will cause traffic delays and hazards and esthetic unsightliness. Respondent in its turn replies that the City does not "provide anything more than speculations and assumptions," * * *

We of course take the well-pleaded allegations of the complaint as true for the purpose of a motion to dismiss, * * * Ordinarily such a motion frames a legal issue * * *. But this case is different from a case between private litigants for two reasons: first, it is an action of a municipal corporation taken pursuant to a city ordinance that is challenged here, and, second, the ordinance is challenged on colorable First Amendment grounds. The City has adduced essentially factual arguments to justify the restrictions on cable franchising imposed by its ordinance, but the factual assertions of the City are disputed at least in part by the respondent. We are unwilling to decide the legal questions posed by the parties without a more thoroughly developed record of proceedings in which the parties have an opportunity to prove those disputed factual assertions * * *.

We do think that the activities in which respondent allegedly seeks to engage plainly implicate First Amendment interests. * * * Thus, through original programming or by exercising editorial discretion over which stations or programs to include in its repertoire, respondent seeks to communicate messages on a wide variety of topics and in a wide variety of formats. * * * Cable television partakes of some of the aspects of speech and the communication of ideas as do the traditional enterprises of newspaper and book publishers, public speakers and pamphleteers. * * *

Of course, the conclusion that respondent's factual allegations implicate protected speech does not end the inquiry. "Even protected speech is not equally permissible in all places and at all times." * * * Moreover, where speech and conduct are joined in a single course of action, the First Amendment values must be balanced against competing societal interests. See, *e.g., Members of the City Council v. Taxpayers for Vincent, supra,* 466 U.S., at 805–807, 104 S.Ct. 2129–2130, *United States v. O'Brien,* 391 U.S. 367, 376–377 (1968). We do not think, however, that it is desirable to express any more detailed views on the proper resolution of the First Amendment question raised by the respondent's complaint and the City's responses to it without a fuller development of the disputed issues in the case. We think that we may know more than we know now about how the constitutional issues should be resolved when we know more about the present uses of the public utility poles and rights-of-way and how respondent proposes to install and maintain its facilities on them.

The City claims that no such trial of the issues is required, because the City need not "generate a legislative record" in enacting ordinances which would grant one franchise for each area of the City. * * * "Whether a limitation on the number of franchises * * * is 'reasonable,'" the City continues, "thus cannot turn on a review of historical facts." * * * The City supports its contention in this regard by citation to cases such as *United States Railroad Retirement Board v. Fritz,* 449 U.S. 166, 179, 101 S.Ct. 453, 461, 66 L.Ed.2d 368 (1980), and *Schweiker v. Wilson,* 450 U.S. 221, 236–237, 101 S.Ct. 1074, 1083–1084, 67 L.Ed.2d 186 (1981).

The flaw in the City's argument is that both *Fritz* and *Wilson* involved Fifth Amendment equal protection challenges to legislation, rather than challenges under the First Amendment. Where a law is subjected to a colorable First Amendment challenge, the rule of rationality which will sustain legislation against other constitutional challenges typically does not have the same controlling force. * * * This Court "may not simply assume that the ordinance will always advance the asserted state interests sufficiently to justify its abridgement of expressive activity." *Taxpayers for Vincent,* 466 U.S., at 803, n. 22, *Landmark Communications, Inc. v. Virginia,* 435 U.S. 829, 843–844 (1978).

We affirm the judgment of the Court of Appeals * * *, and remand the case to the District Court so that petitioners may file an answer and the material factual disputes between the parties may be resolved.

It is so ordered.

JUSTICE BLACKMUN, with whom JUSTICE MARSHALL and JUSTICE O'CONNOR join, concurring.

I join the Court's opinion on the understanding that it leaves open the question of the proper standard for judging First Amendment challenges to a municipality's restriction of access to cable facilities.

Different communications media are treated differently for First Amendment purposes. Compare, *e.g., Miami Herald Publishing Co. v. Tornillo,* 418 U.S. 241, 94 S.Ct. 2831, 41 L.Ed.2d 730 (1974), with *FCC v. League of Women Voters,* 468 U.S. 364, ___, 104 S.Ct. 3106, 3118, 82 L.Ed.2d 278 (1984) (slip op. 15). In assessing First Amendment claims concerning cable access, the Court must determine whether the characteristics of cable television make it sufficiently analogous to another medium to warrant application of an already existing standard or whether those characteristics require a new analysis. As this case arises out of a motion to dismiss, we lack factual information about the nature of cable television. Recognizing these considerations, * * * the Court does not attempt to choose or justify any particular standard. It simply concludes that, in challenging Los Angeles' policy of exclusivity in cable franchising, respondent alleges a cognizable First Amendment claim.

CITY OF BURBANK v. LOCKHEED AIR TERMINAL INC.

Supreme Court of the United States, 1973.
411 U.S. 624, 93 S.Ct. 1845, 36 L.Ed.2d 547.

[The Supreme Court held that city ordinance prohibiting jet aircraft from taking off between the hours of 11 p.m. and 7 a.m. was invalid because Congress, by its enactment of Federal Aviation Act and the Noise Control Act, preempted state and local control over aircraft noise.]

MR. JUSTICE DOUGLAS delivered the opinion of the Court.

* * *

The Court in Cooley v. Board of Wardens, 12 How. 299, 13 L.Ed. 996, first stated the rule of pre-emption which is the critical issue in the present case. Speaking through Justice Curtis, it said:

"Now the power to regulate commerce, embraces a vast field, containing not only many, but exceedingly various subjects, quite unlike in their nature; some imperatively demanding a single uniform rule, operating equally on the commerce of the United States in every port; and some, like the subject now in question, as imperatively demanding that diversity, which alone can meet the local necessities of navigation. * * * Whatever subjects of this power are in their nature national, or admit only of one uniform system, or plan of regulation, may justly be said to be of such a nature as to require exclusive legislation by Congress." *Id.,* at 319.

* * * The only regularly scheduled flight affected by the ordinance was an intrastate flight of Pacific Southwest Airlines originating in Oakland, California, and departing from Hollywood-Burbank Airport for San Diego every Sunday night at 11:30 p.m.

* * *

The Federal Aviation Act of 1958, 72 Stat. 737, 49 U.S.C.A. § 1301 *et seq.,* as amended by the Noise Control Act of 1972, 86 Stat. 1234, and the regulations under it, 14 CFR Pts. 71–77, 91–97, are central to the question of pre-emption.

Section 1508 provides in part, "The United States of America is declared to possess and exercise complete and exclusive national sovereignty in the airspace of the United States * * *." By § 1348 the Administrator of the Federal Aeronautics Act (FAA) has been given broad authority to regulate the use of the navigable airspace, "in order to insure the safety of aircraft and the efficient utilization of such airspace * * *" and "for the protection of persons and property on the ground. * * *"

The Solicitor General, though arguing against pre-emption, concedes that as respects "airspace management" there is pre-emption. That, however, is a fatal concession, for as the District Court found: "The imposition of curfew ordinances on a nationwide basis would result in a bunching of flights in those hours immediately preceding the curfew. This bunching of flights during these hours would have the twofold effect of increasing an already serious congestion problem and actually increasing, rather than relieving, the noise problem by increasing flights in the period of greatest annoyance to surrounding communities. Such a result is totally inconsistent with the objectives of the federal statutory and regulatory scheme." * * *

* * * FAA has occasionally operated curfews. See Virginians for Dulles v. Volpe, D.C., 344 F.Supp. 573. But the record shows that FAA has consistently opposed curfews, unless managed by it, in the interests of its management of the "navigable airspace."

* * *

The Notice Control Act of 1972, 86 Stat. 1234, which was approved October 27, 1972, provides that the Administrator "after consultation with appropriate Federal, State, and local agencies and interested persons" shall conduct a study of various facets of the aircraft "noise" problems and report to the Congress within nine months, *i.e.*, by July 1973. The 1972 Act by amending § 611 of the Federal Aviation Act, also involves the Environmental Protection Agency (EPA) in the comprehensive scheme of federal control of the aircraft noise problem. Under the amended § 611(b)(1) the FAA, after consulting with EPA, shall provide "for the control and abatement of aircraft noise and sonic boom, * * *.

* * *

There is to be sure no express provision of pre-emption in the 1972 Act. That, however, is not decisive. As we stated in Rice v. Santa Fe Elevator Corp., 331 U.S. 218, 230, 67 S.Ct. 1146, 1152, 91 L.Ed. 1447:

"Congress legislated here in a field which the States have traditionally occupied. * * * So we start with the assumption that the historic police powers of the States were not to be superseded by the Federal Act unless that was the clear and manifest purpose of Congress. * * * Such a purpose may be evidenced in several ways. The scheme of federal regulation may be so pervasive as to make reasonable the inference that Congress left no room for the states to supplement it. * * * Or the Act of Congress may touch a field in which the federal interest is so dominant that the federal system will be assumed to preclude enforcement of state laws on the same subject. * * * Likewise, the object sought to be obtained by the federal law and the character of obligations imposed by it may reveal the same purpose. * * * Or the state policy may produce a result inconsistent with the objective of the federal statute."

It is the pervasive nature of the scheme of federal regulation of aircraft noise that leads us to conclude that there is pre-emption. * * *

* * *

Our prior cases on pre-emption are not precise guidelines in the present controversy, for each case turns on the peculiarities and special features of the federal regulatory scheme in question. *Cf.* Hines v. Davidowitz, 312 U.S. 52, 61 S.Ct. 399, 85 L.Ed. 581; Huron Portland Cement Co. v. Detroit, 362 U.S. 440, 80 S.Ct. 813, 4 L.Ed.2d 852. Control of noise is of course deep-seated in the police power of the States. Yet the pervasive control vested in EPA and in FAA under the 1972 Act seems to us to leave no room for local curfews or other local controls. * * *

* * *

Affirmed.

MR. JUSTICE REHNQUIST, with whom MR. JUSTICE STEWART, MR. JUSTICE WHITE, and MR. JUSTICE MARSHALL join, dissenting.

The Court concludes that congressional legislation dealing with aircraft noise has so "pervaded" that field that Congress has *impliedly* pre-empted it, and therefore the ordinance of the city of Burbank here challenged is invalid under the Supremacy Clause of the Constitution. * * *

* * *

Appellees do not contend that the noise produced by jet engines could not reasonably be deemed to affect adversely the health and welfare of persons constantly exposed to it; control of noise, sufficiently loud to be classified as a public nuisance at common law, would be a type of regulation well within the traditional scope of the police power possessed by States and local governing bodies. Because noise regulation has traditionally been an area of local, not national, concern, in determining whether congressional legislation has, by implication, foreclosed remedial local enactments "we start with the assumption that the historic police powers of the States were not to be superseded by the Federal Act unless that was the clear and manifest purpose of Congress." Rice v. Santa Fe Elevator Corp., 331 U.S. 218, 230, 67 S.Ct. 1146, 1152, 91 L.Ed. 1447 (1947). * * * Unless the requisite pre-emptive intent is abundantly clear, we should hesitate to invalidate state and local legislation for the added reason that "the state is powerless to remove the ill effects of our decision, while the national government, which has the ultimate power, remains free to remove the burden." Penn Dairies, Inc. v. Milk Control Commission, 318 U.S. 261, 275, 63 S.Ct. 617, 624, 87 L.Ed. 748 (1943).

* * *

The Court of Appeals found critical to its decision the distinction between the local government as airport proprietor and the local government as a regulatory agency, which was reflected in the views of the Secretary of Transportation outlined in the Senate Report on the 1968 Amendment. Under its reasoning, a local government unit that owned and operated an airport would not be pre-empted by § 611 from totally, or, as here, partially, excluding noisy aircraft from using its facilities, but a municipality having territorial jurisdiction over the airport would be pre-empted from enacting an ordinance having a similar effect. If the statute actually enacted drew this distinction, I would of course respect it. But since we are dealing with "legislative history," rather than the words actually written by Congress into law, I do not believe it is of the controlling significance attributed to it by the court below.

The pre-emption question to which the Secretary's letter was addressed related to "the field of noise regulation insofar as it involves controlling the *flight* of aircraft" (emphasis added), and thus included types of regulation quite different from that enacted by the city of Burbank that would be clearly precluded. See American Airlines, Inc. v. Town of Hempstead, *supra.* But more important is the highly practical consideration that the Hollywood-Burbank Airport is probably the only airport in the country used by federally certified air carriers that is not owned and operated by a state or local government. * * * It simply strains credulity to believe that the Secretary, the Senate Committee, or Congress intended that all airports except the Hollywood-Burbank Airport could enact curfews.

Considering the language Congress enacted into law, the available legislative history, and the light shed by these on the congressional purpose, Congress did not intend either by the 1958 Act or the 1968 Amendment to oust local governments from the enactment of regulations such as that of the city of Burbank. The 1972 Act quite clearly intended to maintain the status quo between federal and local authorities. * * *

* * *

The history of congressional action in this field demonstrates, I believe, an affirmative congressional intent to allow local regulation. But even if it did not go that far, that history surely does not reflect "the clear and manifest purpose of Congress" to prohibit the exercise of "the historic police powers of the States" which our decisions required before a conclusion of implied preemption is reached. * * *

Notes

1. **Alternative Relief.** Federal preemption of airport operation regulation does *not* preempt private alternative relief against the City operator

in a nuisance cause of action. Greater Westchester Homeowners Association v. Los Angeles, 160 Cal.Rptr. 733, 603 P.2d 1329 (1979).

2. **Environmental Laws.** Not all aircraft operation regulations are preempted by federal law. In People of State of California v. Department of Navy, 431 F.Supp. 1271 (N.D.Cal.1971), the court granted the state an injunction prohibiting Navy planes from emitting pollution on the grounds that: (1) the federal anti-pollution statutes did not expressly preempt the subject to the extent of banning state pollution regulation, and permitted concurrent operation of the state pollution laws consistent with E.P.A. standards; and (2) there was no implied preemption since the state was not regulating airways as such, but pollution emission. Local authorities may not, however, discriminate against airlines by selective imposition of noise standards. British Airways Bd. v. Port of Authority of New York and New Jersey, 564 F.2d 1002 (2d Cir.1977) (Concord II).

The power of states and their subdivisions to regulate air transit, consistent with federal legislation, has been expressly recognized by some federal aviation acts. Such recognition does not, however, eliminate the constitutional ban against unreasonable burdens on interstate commerce. Compare e.g. City of Shreveport v. Conrad, 212 La. 737, 33 So.2d 503 (1947) (upheld ordinance that prohibited airplane flights over a lake which the city employed for water supply), with Allegheny Airlines Inc. v. Cedarhurst, 238 F.2d 812 (2d Cir.1956) (nullified ordinance which prohibited airplane flights over the village at less than 1,000 feet, as contra preemptive federal statute on air traffic regulation). Compare also State v. MaNaney, 1950 U.S.Av. 144 (Baltimore City Crim.Cts.1950) (ordinance prohibiting airplane flights for commercial advertising purposes, over occupied sports stadium upheld as reasonable measure to protect lives and property) with People v. Coffrin, 126 N.Y.S.2d 329 (Mag.Ct.1953) (ordinance prohibited aircraft towing advertising banners held unconstitutional as conflicting with state and federal law); and with American Airlines, Inc. v. Audubon Park, 407 F.2d 1306 (6th Cir.1969) (ordinance prohibiting city overflight below 750 feet, held unconstitutional burden on interstate commerce and as conflicting with federal regulation on landing approaches). But cf. People v. Altman, 61 Misc.2d 4, 304 N.Y.S.2d 534 (1969).

Expanding federal antipollution legislation requires increasingly complex analysis, since federal law may displace state and local law, for some purposes, but not for others. See, e.g. City of Milwaukee v. Illinois and Michigan, 451 U.S. 304, 101 S.Ct. 1784, 68 L.Ed.2d 114 (1981); United States v. Dixie Carriers, Inc., 627 F.2d 736 (5th Cir.1980).

In Metropolitan Sanitary District of Greater Chicago v. United States Steel Corp., 41 Ill.2d 440, 243 N.E.2d 249 (1968) the court upheld the district's control of pollution in Lake Michigan and found that Congress did not intend to preempt the field by the Federal Water Pollution Control Act (33 U.S.C.A. § 466 et seq. (as amended 33 U.S.C.A. § 1251 et seq.)), but intended to encourage water pollution control by local governments. See Annot., Validity of Anti-Water Pollution Ordinances, 32 A.L.R.3d 215 (1970 and Supp.1985).

The ad hoc classification of laws that do or do not involve preemption is seen in two cases wherein state legislatures sought to regulate oil tankers. In Chevron U.S.A. v. Hammond, 726 F.2d 483 (9th Cir.1984), the court upheld, as not preempted an Alaska statute which prohibited oil tankers from discharging ballast from their cargo tanks into state territorial waters, since federal law permits discharge of ballast within 50 miles of shore, so long as it does not produce visible oil traces on the water surface or adjoining shoreline. The court distinguished Ray v. Atlantic Richfield Co., 435 U.S. 151, 98 S.Ct. 988, 55 L.Ed.2d 179 (1978), wherein the Supreme Court invalidated a state safety regulation on oil tankers, as preempted by the federal Ports and Waterways Safety Act of 1972. The Ninth Circuit found that Congress did not intend to preempt the field of pollutant discharges in state territorial waters, and noted that the Clean Water Act and other federal maritime protection statutes envisioned extensive state participation in regulatory efforts.

3. **Partial (Selective) Preemption.** See discussion of Chevron U.S.A. v. Hammond, supra. In Pacific Gas and Elec. Co. v. State Energy Resources Conservation & Development Comm'n, 461 U.S. 190, 103 S.Ct. 1713, 75 L.Ed.2d 752 (1983), the Supreme Court rejected a challenge to a California statute that imposed a moratorium on construction of federally licensed nuclear power plants until adequate capacity to dispose of its nuclear waste was provided. The Court held that the Atomic Energy Act of 1954 (42 U.S.C.A. § 2011 et seq.) preempted only safety and "nuclear" aspects of energy generation; that Congress intended to preserve dual regulation by states of nuclear power plants; and that the regulation in question did not interfere with federal law. See generally, Annot., State Regulation of Nuclear Power Plants, 82 A.L.R.3d 751 (1978 and Supp.1985).

4. **Conflict.** A state advertising ban that conflicted with specific FCC regulations was voided as preempted by federal law. Capital Cities Cable, Inc. v. Crisp, 467 U.S. 691, 104 S.Ct. 2694, 81 L.Ed.2d 580 (1984).

CITY OF BOSTON v. HARRIS

United States Court of Appeals, First Circuit, 1980.
619 F.2d 87.

PER CURIAM.

This case presents for the first time the question of whether new Department of Housing and Urban Development (HUD) regulations governing housing subsidized under the National Housing Act, 48 Stat. 1246, June 27, 1934 (now codified at 12 U.S.C. §§ 1701–1750g (1976) validly preempt local rent control regulation. Unlike those considered in a long line of past cases, the newly promulgated HUD regulations which we must consider, 24 C.F.R. §§ 403.1, 403.8, et seq. (1979), specifically preempt all local rent control laws as applied to federally subsidized insured projects. We hold that the HUD regulations were validly promulgated and thus operate through the Supremacy Clause, U.S.Const. Art. VI, cl. 2, to preempt local rent control regulations in these instances. We also conclude that HUD procedures and regulations satisfied the tenants' due process rights.

BACKGROUND

The rental housing which both parties seek to regulate in this case is federally insured subsidized units developed under the National Housing Act (NHA), 12 U.S.C. §§ 1701 et seq. (1976). * * * The NHA programs administered by HUD are intended to stimulate the development of low and moderate income housing by providing subsidies or insured mortgages designed to lower the cost of building a project and thus lower the rent which owners must charge to make a fair return on their investments. The rental housing which the City of Boston purports to regulate involves four HUD programs combining insured mortgages and subsidized rents.

The first of these four programs, section 202 of the Housing Act of 1959, 12 U.S.C. § 1701q (1976), allows HUD to make 3% loans for 50 year terms to eligible developers to provide housing facilities for elderly or handicapped families with inadequate income to pay private market housing rentals. * * * In order to insure that section 202 objectives are met, HUD requires an applicant to enter into a regulatory agreement providing that the Secretary of HUD shall establish rental levels and tenant eligibility.

The second of these four programs, * * * establishes a subsidized mortgage program. Section 221(d)(3) assists "private industry in providing housing for low and moderate income families and displaced families." * * *

Again, Congress provided the Secretary with broad discretion to manage and control the rental housing. * * * HUD is authorized to control rents and operation through a regulatory agreement, although the Secretary may defer to other federal or local law. 12 U.S.C. § 1715(d)(3) (Supp.1978). While a project owner may apply for rent increases, the Secretary controls the determination and strict limitations are placed on the permissible return on investment. Once more, defaults on mortgages directly cause the mortgagee to draw upon the insurance fund. 12 U.S.C. § 1715(g).

A third program * * * is designed to encourage private enterprise to develop rental and cooperative housing for lower income families and provide periodic subsidy payments to the mortgagee which effectively reduced the interest payments on the mortgage to 1% on qualified rental housing. 12 U.S.C. § 1715z–1(c) (1976). The Secretary is expressly directed by Congress to establish rental charges. The Secretary may also enter into regulatory agreements and establish necessary rules and procedures. Id. at section 1715z–1(h) (1976).

The final program here involved is a Rent Supplement Program (RSP), * * * which empowers the Secretary to make annual payments on behalf of eligible low income families or individuals unable to afford section 221(d)(3) rents. The maximum payment which the Secretary can make for an eligible tenant is that amount by which the rent

approved by the Secretary exceeds 25 percent of the tenant's income.
* * *

In examining these four programs it becomes apparent that their success "requires a flexible exercise of administrative discretion." *Hahn v. Gottlieb,* 430 F.2d 1243, 1246 (1st Cir.1970). Moreover, Congress has granted the Secretary broad general rule making authority for the NHA and again in each specific section. * * * Although the Secretary originally permitted local governments to operate their rent control programs freely, the Secretary nonetheless engaged extensively in the regulation of rent in HUD insured and subsidized projects through leases and regulatory agreements. * * * Rental increases are only permissible for justifiable increased costs and, in general, HUD allows a landlord to receive a six percent return on equity. *Kargman v. Sullivan,* 552 F.2d 2, 4 (1st Cir.1977).

While Congress was coping with rental housing problems through the NHA, local government concerned with spiraling rents began imposing direct limits on the amount of rent which a landlord could charge. One of the earliest programs of local rent control was that instituted by the City of Boston in 1970, * * * Under the local legislation, the City of Boston's rent control legislation sets maximum rents for covered projects. * * * The governing principle is to maintain maximum rents at levels which will yield landlords a fair net return on operating income from the rental unit. * * *

While Boston's procedure for setting maximum rents has similarities to HUD's rent setting formula, we have previously noted that differences exist. *Kargman v. Sullivan,* 552 F.2d 2, 5 (1st Cir.1977). Nevertheless, this circuit decided that no such actual, impermissible conflict existed between local regulation and the NHA provisions as effected preemption. *Id.* at 6, 13–14. *Kargman,* however, specifically left open the question we face here: whether a HUD regulation could preempt local rent control. *Id.* at 6.

As noted, HUD originally left the field open for local rent control of its subsidized insured projects. In 1975, however, HUD promulgated an interim rule, 40 Fed.Reg. 8189 (1975), to deal with the problems it found local rent control was causing. * * *

The interim rules were adopted later in 1975 and *bar all local rent control applying to subsidized insured projects.* 24 C.F.R. §§ 403.1, 403.8–403.10 (1979); 40 Fed.Reg. 8189, 8190 (1975). As to unsubsidized housing which HUD insures, local regulation is permitted except where HUD determines that such local control jeopardizes its economic interest in the project. 24 C.F.R. §§ 403.1–403.7; *see also Gramercy Spire Tenants' Association v. Harris,* 446 F.Supp. 814, 821 (S.D.N.Y.1977).

After promulgation of 24 C.F.R. §§ 403.1–403.10 (1979), the City of Boston filed suit against the Secretary of HUD challenging the constitutionality of HUD's preemptive regulation. Certain tenants * * * also intervened as plaintiffs. * * * Since the lower court had earlier determined that HUD's regulations were valid and had the full effect of federal law, * * * it granted the defendant's motion for summary judgment. 461 F.Supp. at 1203.

Plaintiffs-tenants appealed arguing (1) that the Secretary acted in excess of delegated authority * * * because Congress never intended to authorize the Secretary to preempt local rent control and (2) that the preemption regulation deprived tenants in federally subsidized insured housing of their entitlement to the protection of rent control without due process. * * *

I.

In analyzing whether HUD's regulations validly preempt Boston's local rent control ordinance, we start with the obvious fact, conceded by plaintiffs, that HUD's regulations and Boston's local rent control ordinances directly conflict. Indeed, the very object of the challenged regulations is to provide for the displacement of local rent controls. * * * Thus, the only question remaining is whether the Secretary had the authority to promulgate the regulation.

Plaintiffs place much reliance on *Kargman v. Sullivan*, 552 F.2d 2 (1st Cir.1977), *reh. denied*, 558 F.2d 612 (1st Cir.1977). That case, unlike this one, presented no actual conflict between the operation of HUD's subsidized insured housing programs and Boston's rent control for the regulations now challenged * * * were not then in effect. In large part that case turned upon the burden of proof and evidence presented at a time when the Secretary's own policies were unclear and, indeed, had vacilated. * * * Because it was not established that Boston's rent regulation caused mortgage defaults in HUD insured projects, the court concluded that the laws could co-exist. The Court specifically noted, however, that

> "[T]his is not a case where a national administrator, surveying all of his problems of dealing with local rent control, had concluded that the federal program nationally is jeopardy because of varying approaches to setting rent ceilings, or administrative entanglements, or the risk that local regulation would discourage participation in the program."

Id. at 5.

The very situation stated not to exist in the above quotation now exists. The Secretary has surveyed the situation nationally and has concluded that preemption of local rent control is necessary to protect HUD insured subsidized projects from default. * * *

The Secretary promulgated the regulations under the authority of 42 U.S.C. § 3535(d) (1976). That section gives the Secretary broad powers under the NHA to "make such rules and regulations as may be necessary to carry out [her] functions, powers, and duties." *Id.* * * * Federal regulation of rents accord the government a voice in securing the economic viability of federally subsidized insured housing. Thus, the Secretary's preemptive regulation, in light of Congress' delegation, is consistent with and advances the purposes of the Act * * * and is therefore valid. * * *

II.

We turn next to plaintiffs' due process argument. In promulgating 24 C.F.R. §§ 403.1–403.10 (1979), HUD examined the housing situation nationally and drafted a rule to deal with a series of problems. In other words, HUD engaged in legislative rule-making rather than in an adjudicatory function. Thus, HUD complied with the necessary due process requirements for this action when it proceeded in conformity with 5 U.S.C. § 553 (1976) which requires public notice and hearing prior to the regulation's promulgation.

The question of what procedural requirements HUD must meet when landlords seek to have their rent increased has been answered before. 24 C.F.R. § 401 (1979) * * * provides for written notice to the tenants, an opportunity to comment and a written response from HUD explaining its actions. This provides sufficient protection of plaintiff's interests. This court previously determined that tenants in subsidized housing were not entitled to an administrative hearing or judicial review of agency decisions on rent increases. *Hahn v. Gottlieb*, 430 F.2d 1243, 1249 (1970). Similarly, several other circuits found that tenants had no due process rights in the adjustment of rents in NHA housing. * * * Moreover, in those cases which did find that tenants must be accorded some rights, the courts imposed only nominal notice and hearing requirements now satisfied by HUD's regulations. *Marshall v. Lynn, supra; Geneva Towers Tenants' Organization v. Federated Mortgage Investors*, 504 F.2d 483 (9th Cir.1974). Consequently, tenants here are assured of due process when their landlord petitions for rental increases. *Accord Gramercy Spire Tenants' Association v. Harris*, 446 F.Supp. 814 (S.D.N.Y.1977); *Argo v. Hills*, 425 F.Supp. 151 (E.D.N.Y. 1977), *aff'd*, 578 F.2d 1366 (2d Cir.1978); *515 Associates v. City of Newark*, 424 F.Supp. 984 (D.N.H.1977).

Accordingly, the decision of the district court is affirmed.

* * *

Note

1. **A Different Kind of Preemption.** The Sherman Anti-Trust Act does not preempt municipal laws setting rent ceilings, since such laws do not involve private or concerted activity within the meaning of the federal law. Fisher v. Berkeley, __ U.S. __, 106 S.Ct. 1045, 89 L.Ed.2d 206 (1986). Even if such flaws were construed to fall within the anti-trust statute, they might still qualify for exemption under the state action exemption.

a. *Local Elections*

TOWN OF LOCKPORT, NEW YORK, ET AL. v. CITIZENS FOR COMMUNITY ACTION AT THE LOCAL LEVEL, INC., ET AL.

Supreme Court of the United States, 1977.
430 U.S. 259, 97 S.Ct. 1047, 51 L.Ed.2d 313.

MR. JUSTICE STEWART delivered the opinion of the Court.

New York law provides that a new county charter will go into effect only if it is approved in a referendum election by separate majorities of the voters who live in the cities within the county, and of those who live outside the cities. A three-judge Federal District Court held that these requirements violate the Equal Protection Clause of the Fourteenth Amendment.　＊　＊　＊

I

County government in New York has traditionally taken the form of a single-branch legislature, exercising general governmental powers. General governmental powers are also exercised by the county's constituent cities, villages, and towns. The allocation of powers among these subdivisions can be changed, and a new form of county government adopted, pursuant to referendum procedures specified in Art. IX of the New York Constitution and implemented by § 33 of the Municipal Home Rule Law. Under those procedures a county board of supervisors may submit a proposed charter to the voters for approval. If a majority of the voting city dwellers and a majority of the voting noncity dwellers both approve, the charter is adopted.

In November 1972, a proposed charter for the county of Niagara was put to referendum. The charter created the new offices of County Executive and County Comptroller, and continued the county's existing power to establish tax rates, equalize assessments, issue bonds, maintain roads, and administer health and public welfare services. No explicit provision for redistribution of governmental powers from the cities or towns to the county government was made. The city voters approved the charter by a vote of 18,220 to 14,914. The non-city voters disapproved the charter by a vote of 11,594 to 10,665. A majority of those voting in the entire county thus favored the charter.

The appellees, ＊ ＊ ＊ filed suit pursuant to 42 U.S.C. § 1983 ＊ ＊ ＊ seeking a declaration that the New York constitutional and statutory provisions governing adoption of the charter form of county government are unconstitutional. ＊ ＊ ＊

II

The impact of the Equal Protection Clause on the exercise of the electoral franchise under state law is hardly a novel concern of the federal judiciary. It was made clear more than 15 years ago in Baker v. Carr, 369 U.S. 186, 82 S.Ct. 691, 7 L.Ed.2d 663, that the subject is a justiciable one, and ever since the seminal case of Reynolds v. Sims, 377

U.S. 533, 84 S.Ct. 1362, 12 L.Ed.2d 506, it has been established that the Equal Protection Clause cannot tolerate the disparity in individual voting strength that results when elected officials represent districts of unequal population, since "the fundamental principle of representative government in this country is one of equal representation for equal numbers of people, without regard to race, sex, economic status, or place of residence within a State." Id., at 560–561, 84 S.Ct., at 1381.

* * * "Reasoning by analogy," the court held, in short, that the dual-majority requirement of New York law "is unconstitutional because it violates the one man, one vote principle." 386 F.Supp., at 7. * * *

* * * The Court concluded that in voting for their legislators, all citizens have an equal interest in representative democracy, and that the concept of equal protection therefore requires that their votes be given equal weight. * * *

The equal protection principles applicable in gauging the fairness of an election involving the choice of legislative representatives are of limited relevance, however, in analyzing the propriety of recognizing distinctive voter interests in a "single-shot" referendum. * * * The policy impact of a referendum is also different in kind from the impact of choosing representatives—instead of sending legislators off to the state capitol to vote on a multitude of issues, the referendum puts one discrete issue to the voters. That issue is capable, at least, of being analyzed to determine whether its adoption or rejection will have a disproportionate impact on an identifiable group of voters. * * * This question has been confronted by the Court in two types of cases: those dealing with elections involving "special-interest" governmental bodies of limited jurisdiction, and those dealing with bond referenda.

The Court has held that the electorate of a special-purpose unit of government, such as a water storage district, may be apportioned to give greater influence to the constituent groups found to be most affected by the governmental unit's functions. Salyer Land Co. v. Tulare Water Dist., 410 U.S. 719, 93 S.Ct. 1224, 35 L.Ed.2d 659. But the classification of voters into "interested" and "noninterested" groups must still be reasonably precise, as Kramer v. Union School Dist., 395 U.S. 621, 89 S.Ct. 1886, 23 L.Ed.2d 583, demonstrates. * * *

* * *

These decisions do not resolve the issues in the present case. Taken together, however they can be said to focus attention on two inquiries: whether there is a genuine difference in the relevant interests of the groups that the state electoral classification has created; and, if so, whether any resulting enhancement of minority voting strength nonetheless amounts to invidious discrimination in violation of the Equal Protection Clause.

III

The argument that the provisions of New York law in question here are unconstitutional rests primarily on the premise that all voters in a New York county have identical interests in the adoption or rejection of a new charter, and that any distinction, therefore, between voters drawn on the basis of residence and working to the detriment of an identifiable class is an invidious discrimination. If the major premise were demonstrably correct—if it were clear that all voters in Niagara County have substantially identical interests in the adoption of a new county charter, regardless of where they reside within the county—the District Court's judgment would have to be affirmed under our prior cases. Cipriano v. City of Houma, supra. That major premise, however, simply cannot be accepted. To the contrary, it appears that the challenged provisions of New York law rest on the State's identification of the distinctive interests of the residents of the cities and towns within a county rather than their interests as residents of the county as a homogeneous unit. This identification is based in the realities of the distribution of governmental powers in New York, and is consistent with our cases that recognize both the wide discretion the States have in forming and allocating governmental tasks to local subdivisions and the discrete interests that such local governmental units may have *qua* units. Reynolds v. Sims, 377 U.S., at 580, 84 S.Ct., at 1391; Abate v. Mundt, 403 U.S. 182, 91 S.Ct. 1904, 29 L.Ed.2d 399; Mahan v. Howell, 410 U.S. 315, 93 S.Ct. 979, 35 L.Ed.2d 320.

General-purpose local government in New York is entrusted to four different units: counties, cities, towns, and villages. * * *

The New York Legislature has conferred home rule and general governmental powers on all of these subdivisions, and their governmental activities may on occasion substantially overlap. The cities often perform functions within their jurisdiction that the county may perform for noncity residents; similarly villages perform some functions for their residents that the town provides for the rest of the town's inhabitants. Historically towns provided their areas with major social services that more recently have been transferred to counties; towns exercise more regulatory power than counties; and both towns and counties can create special taxing and improvement districts to administer services. * * *

Acting within a fairly loose state apportionment of political power, the relative energy and organization of these various subdivisions will often determine which one of them in a given area carries out the major tasks of local government. Since the cities have the greatest autonomy within this scheme, changes serving to strengthen the county structure may have the most immediate impact on the functions of the towns as deliverers of government services. * * *

The provisions of New York law here in question clearly contemplate that a new or amended county charter will frequently operate to transfer "functions or duties" from the towns or cities to the county, or even to "abolish one or more offices, departments, agencies or units of government." * * * The creation of the offices of County Executive and Commissioner of Finance clearly reflects this purpose. Such anticipated organizational changes, no less than explicit transfers of functions, could effectively shift any pre-existing balance of power between town and county governments toward county predominance. In terms of efficient delivery of government services, such a shift might be all to the good, but it may still be viewed as carrying a cost quite different for town voters and their existing town governments from that incurred by city voters and their existing city governments.

The ultimate question then is whether, given the differing interests of city and noncity voters in the adoption of a new county charter in New York, those differences are sufficient under the Equal Protection Clause to justify the classifications made by New York law. Phoenix v. Kolodziejski, 399 U.S. 204, 90 S.Ct. 1990, 26 L.Ed.2d 523; Salyer Land Co. v. Tulare Water Dist., 410 U.S. 719, 93 S.Ct. 1224, 35 L.Ed.2d 659; Hill v. Stone, 421 U.S. 289, 95 S.Ct. 1637, 44 L.Ed.2d 172. If that question were posed in the context of annexation proceedings, the fact that the residents of the annexing city and the residents of the area to be annexed formed sufficiently different constituencies with sufficiently different interests could be readily perceived. The fact of impending union alone would not so merge them into one community of interest as constitutionally to require that their votes be aggregated in any referendum to approve annexation. Cf. Hunter v. Pittsburgh, 207 U.S. 161, 28 S.Ct. 40, 52 L.Ed. 151. Similarly a proposal that several school districts join to form a consolidated unit could surely be subject to voter approval in each constituent school district.

Yet in terms of recognizing constituencies with separate and potentially opposing interests, the structural decision to annex or consolidate is similar in impact to the decision to restructure county government in New York. In each case, separate voter approval requirements are based on the perception that the real and long-term impact of a restructuring of local government is felt quite differently by the different county constituent units that in a sense compete to provide similar governmental services. Voters in these constituent units are directly and differentially affected by the restructuring of county government, which may make the provider of public services more remote and less subject to the voters' individual influence.

The provisions of New York law here in question no more than recognize the realities of these substantially differing electoral interests. Granting to these provisions the presumption of constitutionality to which every duly enacted state and federal law is entitled, we are unable to conclude that they violate the Equal Protection Clause of the Fourteenth Amendment.

For the reasons stated in this opinion the judgment is reversed.

Notes

1. **Revising Electoral Units.** As noted in Lockport, a state or local government may not give unequal weight to its citizens' votes by creating electoral districts with substantial population disparities, unless there is a public interest justification to toll the one-man, one-vote principle. See

also Abate v. Mundt, 403 U.S. 182, 91 S.Ct. 1904, 29 L.Ed.2d 399 (1974); City of Eastlake v. Forest City Enterprises, Inc., p. 560, infra; Annot., State Legislative Apportionment, 77 L.Ed.2d 1496 (1985).

2. **Interstate Districts.** The one-man, one-vote principle does not apply to the creation of governing boards of interstate districts by interstate compacts. See chapter V, § C.

3. **Differential Representation in Multimember Districts and at Large Elections.** As the following case shows, the above noted constitutional principles apply as well to mixed district electoral systems.

4. **Federal Voting Rights Act.** As reported in City of Rome, p. 182, supra, any rule that involves a "standard practice * * * with respect to voting" cannot be adopted by a local government unit until approved or "precleared" by a federal agency specified by the Voting Rights Act. Hence a County Board of Education rule which required employees seeking elective office to take a leave of absence was enjoined for lack of the requisite prior federal approval. Dougherty County, Ga. Bd. of Education v. White, 439 U.S. 32, 99 S.Ct. 368, 58 L.Ed.2d 269 (1978).

ROGERS v. LODGE

Supreme Court of the United States, 1982.
458 U.S. 613, 102 S.Ct. 3272, 73 L.Ed.2d 1012.

* * *

II

At-large voting schemes and multimember districts tend to minimize the voting strength of minority groups by permitting the political majority to elect *all* representatives of the district. A distinct minority, whether it be a racial, ethnic, economic, or political group, may be unable to elect any representatives in an at-large election, yet may be able to elect several representatives if the political unit is divided into single-member districts. The minority's voting power in a multimember district is particularly diluted when bloc voting occurs and ballots are cast along strict majority-minority lines. While multimember districts have been challenged for "their winner-take-all aspects, their tendency to submerge minorities and to overrepresent the winning party," *Whitcomb v. Chavis,* 403 U.S. 124, 158–159, 91 S.Ct. 1858, 1877, 29 L.Ed.2d 363 (1971), this Court has repeatedly held that they are not unconstitutional *per se. Mobile v. Bolden, supra,* 446 U.S., at 66, 100 S.Ct., at 1499; * * *. The Court has recognized, however, that multimember districts violate the Fourteenth Amendment if "conceived or operated as purposeful devices to further racial discrimination" by minimizing, cancelling out or diluting the voting strength of racial elements in the voting population. *Whitcomb v. Chavis, supra,* 403 U.S., at 149, 91 S.Ct., at 1872. See also *White v. Regester, supra,* 412 U.S., at 765, 93 S.Ct., at 2339. Cases charging that multimember districts unconstitutionally dilute the voting strength of racial minorities are thus subject to the standard of proof generally applicable to Equal Protection Clause cases. *Washington v. Davis,* 426 U.S. 229, 96

S.Ct. 2040, 48 L.Ed.2d 597 (1976), and *Arlington Heights v. Metropolitan Housing Dev. Corp.*, 429 U.S. 252, 97 S.Ct. 555, 50 L.Ed.2d 450 (1977), made it clear that in order for the Equal Protection Clause to be violated, "the invidious quality of a law claimed to be racially discriminatory must ultimately be traced to a racially discriminatory purpose." *Washington v. Davis, supra,* 426 U.S., at 240, 96 S.Ct., at 2048. Neither case involved voting dilution, but in both cases the Court observed that the requirement that racially discriminatory purpose or intent be proved applies to voting cases by relying upon, among others, *Wright v. Rockefeller,* 376 U.S. 52, 84 S.Ct. 603, 11 L.Ed.2d 512 (1964), a districting case, to illustrate that a showing of discriminatory intent has long been required in *all* types of equal protection cases charging racial discrimination.   *   *   *

Notes

1. **Desegregation and Redistricting.** The Equal Protection command that limits local reorganization elections also confines local government redistricting of areas that are under court desegregation orders. Federal courts have enjoined school district reorganizations that would frustrate desegregation decrees. Wright v. Council, Emporia, 407 U.S. 451, 92 S.Ct. 2196, 33 L.Ed.2d 51 (1972); United States v. Scotland Neck City Bd. of Educ., 407 U.S. 484, 92 S.Ct. 2214, 33 L.Ed.2d 75 (1972). Indeed, courts may order consolidation of particular school districts for the purpose of curing unconstitutional racial segregation. See e.g., Evans v. Buchanan, 555 F.2d 373 (3d Cir.1977), cert. denied sub nom. Delaware State Bd. of Educ. v. Evans, 434 U.S. 880, 98 S.Ct. 235, 54 L.Ed.2d 160 (1977).

2. **Voter Qualifications.** Under the Equal Protection Clause, eligibility to vote may not be restricted to special citizen classes unless there is a special constitutional justification, for limiting the franchise.

Residency. The Supreme Court nullified state laws which required residence of more than 90 days in the local voting district, as a condition of eligibility to vote. Dunn v. Blumstein, 405 U.S. 330, 92 S.Ct. 995, 31 L.Ed. 2d 274 (1972); Danforth v. Christian, 351 F.Supp. 287 (W.D.Mo.1972). See also MacLeod and Wilberding, *State Voting Residence Requirements and Civil Rights,* 38 Geo.Wash.L.Rev. 93, 96–97 (1969); Note, *A Constitutional Analysis of Student Residency Laws,* 18 Vill.L.Rev. 461 (1973).

Property Ownership. Limitation of voting rights to property owners and taxpayers is *prima facie* suspect under the equal protection clause, but may be validated by a justifying state interest. Compare, e.g., Phoenix v. Kolodziejski, 399 U.S. 204, 90 S.Ct. 1990, 26 L.Ed.2d 523 (1970), with Salyer Land Co. v. Tulare Lake Basin Water Storage District, 410 U.S. 719, 93 S.Ct. 1224, 35 L.Ed.2d 659 (1973) (exclusion of citizens other than property owners from a special district election, where the district served only such owners and was financed exclusively by assessments upon their property, held constitutional); accord: Ball v. James, 451 U.S. 355, 101 S.Ct. 1811, 68 L.Ed.2d 150 (1981).

b. *Local Government Office and Employment*

Eligibility and preference criteria for appointment to office or employment, viz. citizenship, residence, military service; and affirmative action standards of public employment often implicate federal law.

Citizenship. Citizenship requirements to hold offices that partake of important government functions has been upheld as not violating the constitutional rights of aliens, who are lawfully admitted for residence in the United States, e.g., Cabell v. Chavez-Salido, 454 U.S. 432, 102 S.Ct. 735, 70 L.Ed.2d 677 (1982) (deputy probation officer); Foley v. Connellie, 435 U.S. 291, 98 S.Ct. 1067, 55 L.Ed.2d 287 (1978) (state troopers); Amback v. Norwick, 441 U.S. 68, 99 S.Ct. 1589, 60 L.Ed.2d 49 (1979) (public school teachers). But exclusion of aliens from other employments not deemed to require citizenship allegiance is unconstitutional. Sugarman v. Dougall, 413 U.S. 634, 93 S.Ct. 2842, 37 L.Ed.2d 853 (1973) (general civil service); Bernal v. Fainter, 467 U.S. 216, 104 S.Ct. 2312, 81 L.Ed.2d 175 (1984) (notary public). Thus the validity of citizenship requirements for local government employment will depend upon the particular position or public function that is in question.

Residency. State law variations on residency requirements for local government officers and employees; and the constitutional limits on such residency restrictions, are reviewed in later coverage of public offices and public employees (p. 783, et seq.). As there noted, some limits are imposed by the federal Constitution upon the adoption of residency requirements by state and local governments.

Veterans. The grant of veteran preferences or preferential ratings in civil service positions has been sustained (Personnel Administrator of Massachusetts v. Feeney, 442 U.S. 256, 99 S.Ct. 2282, 60 L.Ed.2d 870 (1979)), but discrimination among different veterans groups, based upon their residence at the time of entry into military service, was voided as unconstitutional discrimination. Hooper v. Bernalillo County Assessor, ___ U.S. ___, 105 S.Ct. 2862, 86 L.Ed.2d 487 (1985).

Minority Groups. The settled constitutional principle that public authorities may not invidiously discriminate against certain groups in affording access to public office or employment, has not resulted in any universal standard of discrimination. For example, the constitutional scrutiny applied to racial discrimination is somewhat higher than that applied to gender discrimination. Those differences have, however, been somewhat minimized by federal civil rights statutes which prohibit employment discrimination in federally aided activities on the basis of race, gender, age, handicap, religion or national origin. See, e.g., Titles VI, VII, and IX, of the Act of 1964, 42 U.S.C.A. § 2000 et seq.; the Rehabilitation Act of 1973, 29 U.S.C.A. § 794; the Age Discrimination in Employment Act, 29 U.S.C.A. § 621. Such prohibitions extend to allowance of fringe benefits, such as pregnancy related benefits and pension plans. See, e.g., Arizona Governing Committee v. Norris, 463 U.S. 1073, 103 S.Ct. 3492, 77 L.Ed.2d 1236 (1983). With respect to age, public employers may no longer force retirement *by reason of age alone,* and must with limited exceptions, permit *qualified* employees to continue to work. The impact of federal employment discrimination law (over and above state and local fair employment laws) has become so pervasive as to constitute a separate specialty in public administration.

Affirmative Action Preferences in Public Employment and Contracts. The extent to which local governments may or must give preferential access to public positions, to designated citizen groups remains unsettled in many areas of government employment. The impact of constitutional and statutory law upon "affirmative action," varies with the context of each program. For example, court ordered and legislated affirmative action programs that favor a particular group in order to undo past unconstitutional discrimination have been upheld, both as constitutional, and as not violative of statutes barring class discrimination in employment (e.g., Title VII of the Civil Rights Act of 1964). See, Fullilove v. Klutznick, 448 U.S. 448, 100 S.Ct. 2758, 65 L.Ed.2d 902 (1980). However, in the absence of any finding of past constitutional injury to the preferred minority, the Justices of the Supreme Court continue to be closely divided on the extent to which local officials may grant preferential employment or contract opportunities to undo the effects of past public or private discriminations. Compare e.g. Local 28 of Sheet Metal Workers v. EEOC, ___ U.S. ___, 106 S.Ct. 3019, 92 L.Ed.2d 344 (1986); Local No. 93, Int'l Ass'n of Firefighters v. Cleveland, ___ U.S. ___, 106 S.Ct. 3063, 92 L.Ed.2d 405 (1986) with Wygant v. Jackson Bd. of Education, ___ U.S. ___, 106 S.Ct. 1842, 90 L.Ed.2d 260 (1986); Firefighters Local Union v. Stotts, 467 U.S. 561, 104 S.Ct. 2576, 81 L.Ed.2d 483 (1984); Hicklin v. Orbeck, 437 U.S. 518, 98 S.Ct. 2482, 57 L.Ed.2d 377 (1978). Cf. Regents of U. of California v. Bakke, 438 U.S. 265, 98 S.Ct. 2733, 57 L.Ed.2d 750 (1978). See also the notes on public contract preferences and bid laws in ch. VIII, pp. 730–764, infra. Controversy continues over the reach of these decisions so that their impact in other contexts will require continuing clarification.

The validity of affirmative action programs is affected by such factors as: (1) a finding of past injury, for which affirmative action is the remedy; (b) an exercise of legislative power to promote equality, even in the absence of official discrimination; (c) judicial decision to characterize affirmative action preferences as lawful policy "goals," or as unlawful discriminatory "quotas"; (d) the limited scope (in time or scale) and impact (upon third parties) of affirmative action policies, e.g., whether they may be treated as nondiscriminatory or *"de minimis,"* and (e) the source of affirmative action, e.g., a collective bargaining agreement, or consent decree. It is evident that no single test exists for the legality of minority preferences in all contexts. Compare, e.g., the *Stotts* case supra, where the Supreme Court invalidated a consent decree modification to maintain affirmative action employment goals by preventing layoff of minority workers with less seniority than white workers firemen; *with* Local 93 v. Cleveland, supra, where the Court upheld a consent decree that established temporary fixed ratios of minority to majority employees to be promoted in the city's fire department, as an affirmative action remedy for past discrimination.

The foregoing problems are further complicated by varying degrees of scrutiny, and different standards of proof, which the courts apply (1) to different forms of discrimination (e.g., racial or gender), and (2) under different sources of law (e.g., the Fourteenth Amendment or Title VII of the Act of 1964. See, e.g., Washington v. Davis, 426 U.S. 229, 96 S.Ct. 2040, 48 L.Ed.2d 597 (1976); Furnco Constr. Corp. v. Waters, 438 U.S. 567, 98 S.Ct. 2943, 57 L.Ed.2d 957 (1978). The validity of voluntary affirmative action may also vary with different classifications and job security incidents (e.g. tenure) attached to different positions by state and local laws. See generally Annot., Minority Employment Preferences, 26 A.L.R.Fed. 633 (1976 and Supp.1985); Annot., Gender Based Classifications, 60 L.Ed.2d 1188 (1980); Annot., What Constitutes Reverse or Majority Discrimination on Basis of Sex or Race, 26 A.L.R.Fed. 13 (1976).

Political Affiliation. In 1980, the United States Supreme Court adopted a new constitutional rule for the validity of political patronage dismissals of public employees, namely, that employee dismissal based solely upon political party affiliation unconstitutionally abridges rights of association, unless "the hiring authority can demonstrate that party affiliation is an appropriate requirement for the effective performance of the public office [employment] involved." Branti v. Finkel, 445 U.S. 507, 100 S.Ct. 1287, 63 L.Ed.2d 574 (1980). The Court there recognized that "it is not always easy to determine whether a position is one in which political affiliation is a legitimate factor to be considered" and that "party affiliation is not necessarily relevant to every policy-making or confidential position." Manifestly, this test leaves much room for interpretation by public officials and by courts. See, e.g., Ness v. Marshall, 660 F.2d 517 (3d Cir.1981) which upheld the firing of (republican) city solicitors by a newly elected (democratic) mayor.

Other Qualifications Implicating Federal Law. Constitutional limits on the uses of other eligibility prerequisites to public employment or officeholding, (e.g. loyalty oaths, property ownership, minimum age) are discussed in the later chapters on public employees and public officers.

Public Employee Freedom to Criticize Public Officials. As noted at page 816 infra, public employees enjoy constitutional rights of freedom of speech. The Supreme Court, however, has also noted that First Amendment protection of employee criticism of official superiors or official practices is limited to criticisms that: (a) involve matters of "public concern," and (b) is not subordinated by counterbalancing "interests of the State, as an employer, in promoting the efficiency of public services. * * *" See Pickering v. Board of Education, 391 U.S. 563, 568, 88 S.Ct. 1731, 1734, 20 L.Ed.2d 811 (1968). The balancing formula is elusive, because public employee criticism of official actions often implicate both matters of public concern and of personal employee interest, especially when expressed among fellow workers in the work place. In the *Pickering* case, supra, employee criticism in the public press of the employer's financial policies was held to be citizen speech on a matter of public concern, and, therefore, constitutionally protected. More recently, however, the court held an employee who polled fellow employees regarding office morale, confidence in superiors, and attitudes toward transfer policies was not civic speech on a matter of public concern, but a personal employee grievance that did not qualify for constitutional protection. Connick v. Myers, 461 U.S. 138, 103 S.Ct. 1684, 75 L.Ed.2d 708 (1983). Since the employee failed on the threshold issue of proving that speech was protected, the Court found it unnecessary to inquire into the employer's motives for discharging him. Even had the speech been found to involve "public concern," the employee would still have to overcome further defenses that (1) the speech was sufficiently disruptive to justify suppression; and (2) the discharge resulted from a constitutional purpose of preserving the state's interest, rather than an unconstitutional motive of punishing protected speech. See, e.g., Mt. Healthy City School Dist. Bd. v. Doyle, 429 U.S. 274, 97 S.Ct. 568, 50 L.Ed.2d 471 (1977).

In the words of the Supreme Court, the key to resolving the foregoing balancing factors lies in consideration of "the content, form and context of a given statement." Applying the above standards to varied circumstances, lower courts have differed in their judgments as to the nature and circumstances of critical speech that qualify for constitutional protection. See the authorities reported in Bernheim, *Free Speech for Public Employees: The Supreme Court Strikes a New Balance*, 31 *West Ed.Law Rptr.* 7 (1986). Such differences are understandable since the question whether either party is acting more from personal grievance than from a proper civic interest of the general community necessarily raises issues of subjective motivation of the actors, on which individual judges can reasonably disagree. Courts may, however, be more sympathetic to group expression of grievances on employment policies or practices, when uttered by collective bargaining representatives, since that expression also implicates rights of association and statutory policies on collective negotiations. See, e.g., Gavrilles v. O'Connor, 579 F.Supp. 301 (D.Mass.1984).

c. *Public Services and Benefits*

Federal constitutional and statutory standards of fairness (due process) and of nondiscrimination (equal protection) govern local administration of public benefits. Official compliance, however, is complicated by the fact that not every public service is one to which an individual or group can claim a legal "right" of access. See e.g. San Antonio Ind. Sch. District v. Rodriguez, 411 U.S. 1, 93 S.Ct. 1278, 36 L.Ed.2d 160 (1973) (unequal public education per pupil expenditures between school districts). Nor does every disparity of public services or benefits between individuals or groups amount to unconstitutional discrimination. Cf. Dandridge v. Williams, 397 U.S. 471, 90 S.Ct. 1153,

25 L.Ed.2d 491 (1970) (flat cap on welfare payments regardless of family size). The required level of public benefits is resolved, to a limited extent by statutes that mandate equal or comparable benefits to all covered individuals. Absent such legislation, however, courts must decide whether or when the refusal, suspension, or termination of a publicly provided service or benefit must be preceded by notice and hearing, as a matter of due process, and when such action violates equal protection. These issues take somewhat different form in cases of individual claims, unrelated to group identification, and claims alleging discrimination against identifiable minority groups.

Due Process. Due process requires prior notice and hearing to consumers of governmentally provided services where the individual has some legal "entitlement" or constitutionally protected property interest; or alleges the broad due process right not to be denied a publicly offered service without any rational government basis. Thus, a municipal utility could not cut off services for nonpayment of utility bills where state law forbade such action without prior notice and hearing. Memphis Light, Gas & Water Division v. Craft, 436 U.S. 1, 98 S.Ct. 1554, 55 L.Ed.2d 30 (1978). See also Escalera v. New York City Housing Authority, 425 F.2d 853 (2d Cir.1970) (public housing authority must provide hearing to tenant who objects to eviction). Nor can city water service be denied to an applicant without a rational government basis for such denial, or terminate for nonpayment of utility bills without notice to and hearing for that user. Davis v. Weir, 497 F.2d 139 (5th Cir.1974). A violation of both due process and equal protection was found where local authorities refused to reinstate a tenant's water service because the landlord failed to pay the water bill. Sterling v. Maywood, 579 F.2d 1350 (7th Cir.1978), cert. denied 440 U.S. 913, 99 S.Ct. 1227, 59 L.Ed.2d 462 (1979).

With regard to constitutional due process, the Supreme Court has repeatedly noted that the required elements of procedural due process will vary with the weight given by the Court to asserted interests, and with the context in which those interests are affected;

> "More precisely, our prior decisions indicate that identification of the specific dictates of due process generally require consideration of three distinct factors: first, the private interest that will be affected by the official action; second, the risk of an erroneous deprivation of such interest * * *, and the probable value, if any, of additional or substitute procedural safeguards; and finally, the Government's inter-est, including the function involved and the fiscal or administrative burdens that the additional or substitute procedural requirement would entail." See Mathews v. Eldridge, 424 U.S. 319, 334–35, 96 S.Ct. 893, 903, 47 L.Ed.2d 18, 33 (1976).

Equal Protection Services. Public authorities must provide similar treatment to similarly situated persons. If a local government violates that duty by denying comparable service without a rational basis, or by discriminating between identified classes of citizens, a court may remedy the constitutional deprivation by ordering the extension of such services to the injured individual or class. See generally O. Reynolds, *Local Government Law,* pp. 347, 348 (1982); Annot., *Discrimination in the Provision of Municipal Services,* 51 ALR3d 950 (Supp.1985); Annot., *Power of Municipalities to Charge Nonresidents Higher Fees Than Residents,* 57 ALR3d 998 (Supp.1985). The determination whether or not refusals of public services rests upon a rational basis; or involve group discrimination, turns on fact analysis, unless the law, on its face, creates invidious classifications. With respect to individual claims of discrimination, compare, e.g., Seifert v. Brooklyn, 101 N.Y. 136, 4 N.E. 321 (1886) (refusal to extend utility lines—held rational) with Home Owners' Loan Corp. v. Logan City, 97 Utah 235, 92 P.2d 346 (1939) (refusal to permit connection to existing line—overturned).

With respect to denials of service access to identified citizen classes at a specific site, courts usually exercise heightened judicial scrutiny, especially where the class is a racial minority. Compare, e.g., Abbott v. Highlands, 52 N.C.App. 69, 277 S.E.2d 820 (1981) (failure of town to provide equal sewer services to residents of newly annexed area, held not to violate equal protection, absent any discrimination against a suspect class; and where alternative services were provided to new residents by other legislation) with Johnson v. Arcadia, 450 F.Supp. 1363 (M.D.Fla.1978) (failure to provide comparable municipal services to black community held to constitute systematic racial discrimination and violation of equal protection); *semble:* Dowdell v. Apopka, 511 F.Supp. 1375 (M.D.Fla.1981); United Farmworkers of Florida Housing Project, Inc. v. Delray Beach, 493 F.2d 799 (5th Cir.1974) (refusal to extend water and sewer service to proposed low income housing project for farm workers).

Greater difficulty is encountered where service is not denied to a specific site, but to entire general neighborhoods. The complaint that people on the wrong side of the tracks get the worst public services whether of streets and utility facilities, sanitation services, police or fire protection, or other public benefits finds no easy solution in the law. In Hawkins v. Shaw, 437 F.2d 1286 (5th Cir.1971), the court ordered the town to improve roads and services to the poor black section of the city. Later courts have not followed *Hawkins* as a model or landmark approach; and have not undertaken to equalize services by neighborhood, in the absence of clear proofs of intentional official discrimination. The reason was recently noted by Professor Dworkin:

> "But cities have compound responsibilities and overall rather than inherently compartmentalized budgets: spending more on parks and fire service, in order to provide equality of result there, means spending less on other services, such as medical care or welfare programs, and so damaging equality in other ways. In these circumstances it is hardly plain that the fundamental duty to treat all residents with equal concern means providing exactly the same benefits for each neighborhood, service by service no matter what the cost to the city's

overall ability to serve its residents in other ways." See R. Dworkin, "A New Route To Equality," *The Atlantic,* March, 1986, p. 108.

In sum, neither the federal Constitution, nor federal civil rights statutes require *absolute* equality in the provision of local government services; and the dividing line between permissible disparities and impermissible denials or degrees of disparity is not always clear or obvious.

With regard to public welfare benefits, local governments cannot require that applicants reside within the jurisdiction for any period of time that is either "unreasonable" or so deters the right of travel as to be considered a "penalty" for its exercise. Cf. Hooper v. Bernalillo County Assessor, 472 U.S. ___, 105 S.Ct. 2862, 86 L.Ed.2d 487 (1985) (voiding veterans' tax exemption that excluded new residents); Hicklin v. Orbeck, 437 U.S. 518, 98 S.Ct. 2482, 57 L.Ed.2d 397 (1978) (voiding employment preference of residents over nonresidents). The problem with benefit preferences arises from fact characterization on issues of reasonableness, "penalties," and "compelling state interests" in determining which particular welfare conditions are justified.

d. Regulation of Business and the Environment

(1) Land Use Regulations

The traditional powers of local government to regulate development and uses of real estate have been increasingly challenged under the 14th Amendment. The materials in Chapter VI illustrate how pervasively federal law qualifies property regulations by local governments. With regard to regulatory *methods,* federal law limitations are indicated in the following sections.

(2) Local Licensing and Inspection

The *Garcia, Boulder* and *Burbank* cases, pp. 320–345, *supra,* cover local regulations of matters that are subject to federal jurisdiction. Page 356, *supra,* covers government employment practices that are limited by federal law. Many federal laws also apply to local regulations of private business. When these are resisted as interfering with freedom of expression; freedom from unreasonable search and seizure; freedom from invidious discrimination; or denial of procedural due process, for example, courts balance private interests against those of local governments.

Speech-Related Subjects. Business regulations that affect speech activities present no problem where the locus of that activity is not in a "public forum," i.e., in areas reserved exclusively for designated public functions (e.g., West Gallery Corp. v. Salt Lake City Bd. of Commissioners, p. 410, infra; Adderley v. Florida, 385 U.S. 39, 87 S.Ct. 242, 17 L.Ed.2d 149 (1966) (upholding trespass conviction for demonstration on county jail property); Lehman v. Shaker Heights, 418 U.S. 298, 94 S.Ct.

2714, 41 L.Ed.2d 770 (1974)); or areas where such expressive activity is incompatible with higher public interests. See Members of City Council v. Taxpayers for Vincent, p. 384, n. 3, infra.

Entertainment & Literature. Local regulation of movies, adult bookstores, and periodicals often aim either to suppress or restrict the exhibition and distribution of material that is deemed harmful. To the extent that material fits the constitutional definition of "obscene" its public use is not deemed to qualify for First Amendment protection. Miller v. California, 413 U.S. 15, 93 S.Ct. 2607, 37 L.Ed.2d 419 (1973) (mass mailer); Paris Adult Theatre I v. Slaton, 413 U.S. 49, 93 S.Ct. 2628, 37 L.Ed.2d 446 (1973) (films). The difficulty lies in determining what materials are obscene under Supreme Court tests, which differ for adults and for minors. New York v. Ferber, 458 U.S. 747, 102 S.Ct. 3348, 73 L.Ed.2d 1113 (1982) (child pornography). Thus, while for adults, "Nudity alone does not place otherwise protected material outside the mantle of the First Amendment." See Schad v. Mount Ephraim, 452 U.S. 61, 66, 101 S.Ct. 2176, 2181, 68 L.Ed.2d 671, 678 (1981) (ordinance barring public display of sexually explicit materials "harmful to minors" unless kept in sealed wrappers, upheld); Upper Midwest Booksellers Ass'n v. Minneapolis, 780 F.2d 1389 (8th Cir.1985).

Local laws that restrict public exhibitions of nudity to particular zones or places, without effectively prohibiting them, may qualify as reasonable time, place and manner regulations, as hereafter discussed, if they serve a legitimate government purpose by means narrowly tailored to achieve that purpose. Compare e.g. the Schad case, supra, which outlawed total prohibition, with City of Renton v. Playtime Theatres, ___ U.S. ___, 106 S.Ct. 925, 89 L.Ed.2d 29 (1986) wherein the Supreme Court sustained an ordinance that barred adult movie theatres from locating within 1000 feet of certain residences, churches, schools and parks.

Censorial Regulations. Regulations that discriminate between different speech content cannot qualify as time, place or manner regulations. "[A]bove all else, the First Amendment means that government has no power to restrict expression because of its message, its ideas, its subject matter, or its content." See Police Dept. v. Mosley, 408 U.S. 92, 95, 92 S.Ct. 2286, 2290, 33 L.Ed.2d 212, 216 (1972) (voiding ordinance that barred picketing near school building, but exempting picketing arising out of labor dispute). Still, there are exceptions to this broad language, viz. the Court's treatment of obscenity as not a species of constitutional "speech"; and zoning restrictions that limit the locations of "adult" book stores and "adult" theatres. See, e.g., Young v. American Mini Theatres, 427 U.S. 50, 96 S.Ct. 2440, 49 L.Ed.2d 310 (1976) (upholding city zoning location restrictions on businesses dealing in sexually explicit, though not obscene materials).

Time, Place and Manner Regulations. Where expression occurs in a "public forum" or "limited public forum" the regulation must be justified on one of two general bases. Local regulations that are designed solely to serve "housekeeping" purposes, i.e., preserve the rights of others, by limiting the time, place and manner of expression (without prohibiting it altogether), need only be "reasonable" in order to pass constitutional muster. See, e.g., the above discussion of "entertainment" businesses; Heffron v. International Society for Kirshna Consciousness, 452 U.S. 640, 101 S.Ct. 2559, 69 L.Ed.2d 298 (1981) (upholding restriction of distribution of literature and fund solicitations to particular time and place, at state fair). "The crucial question is whether the manner of expression is basically incompatible with the normal activity of a particular place at a particular time." See Grayned v. Rockford, 408 U.S. 104, 116, 92 S.Ct. 2294, 2303, 33 L.Ed.2d 222, 232 (1972) (upholding ordinance that barred demonstrations adjacent to public school buildings while classes were in session). The lower courts are not agreed on the outer limits of ordinances barring door-to-door canvassing. *Compare*, e.g., Wisconsin Action Coalition v. Kenosha, 767 F.2d 1248 (7th Cir. 1985) *with* Pa. Alliance for Jobs and Energy v. Council of the Borough of Munhall, 743 F.2d 182 (3rd Cir. 1984).

Subordinating Government Interests. Where speech-burdening laws cannot be justified as reasonable "time, place or manner" regulations, local officials must prove that they are *necessary* to achieve a *compelling* government interest to prevent serious disorder or injury, *and* that the means adopted by the regulation to achieve that purpose are no broader in their impact upon individual or business rights of expression than is required by the government's purpose. Otherwise, the regulation is presumptively unconstitutional and void. To meet that heavy burden, it is not enough to show that speech is "offensive" or that officials fear that it may provoke disorder. They must rather show a present likelihood of substantial disorder. See, e.g., Collin v. Smith, 578 F.2d 1197 (7th Cir.1978), affirmed sub nom. Smith v. Collin, 439 U.S. 916, 99 S.Ct. 291, 58 L.Ed.2d 264 (1978) (voiding city ordinances that prohibited street marches by the American Nazis through Jewish neighborhood); Cohen v. California, 403 U.S. 15, 91 S.Ct. 1780, 29 L.Ed.2d 284 (1971) (reversing conviction for wearing jacket bearing vulgar, offensive words in county courthouse).

Commercial Speech. Business communications are also constitutionally protected, though to a lesser degree than other forms of speech. See, e.g., the following Metromedia case and the notes thereto.

Vague and Overbroad Regulations. The First Amendment restricts the *manner* in which local regulations and ordinances may be drafted, published and applied. If their terms are unduly "vague" or "overbroad" they may be stricken for that reason alone. See, e.g., Coates v. Cincinnati, 402 U.S. 611, 91 S.Ct. 1686, 29 L.Ed.2d 214 (1971) (ordinance punishing conduct "annoying to persons thereby," struck down as unconstitutionally vague); cf. Central States Theater Corp. v. Sar, 245 Iowa 1254, 66 N.W.2d 450 (1954) (striking down licensing law for lack of adequate guidelines); Schaumburg v. Citizens for a Better Environment, 444 U.S. 620, 100 S.Ct. 826, 6 L.Ed.2d 73 (1980) (holding unconstitutional, an ordinance that barred solicitations by organizations that used less than 75% of receipts for "charitable purposes"—as overbroad). See note 2, following Delight Wholesale, p. 385, infra; Annot., Vagueness as Invalidating Ordinances Dealing with Disorderly Persons, 12 A.L.R.3d 1448 (1967 & Supp.1985).

Prelicensing Procedures. Licensing procedures may not unduly burden First Amendment rights, either in terms of time, costs, or access to courts for review of licensing decisions. See e.g. Freedman v. Maryland, 380 U.S. 51, 85 S.Ct. 734, 13 L.Ed.2d 649 (1965); Southeastern Promotions, Ltd v. Conrad, 420 U.S. 546, 95 S.Ct. 1239, 43 L.Ed.2d 448 (1975) (voiding city refusal to exhibit "Hair" musical, as invalid prior restraint without procedural safeguards required by Freedman v. Maryland, supra).

The difficulties encountered in applying constitutional tests—what courts refer to as "line-drawing" between permissible and impermissible government regulations, are manifest from the fact that the Supreme Court Justices themselves often disagree as to whether a particular situation satisfied any of the above tests. Illustrations of these difficulties are provided in sections B and C of the following chapter VII, with respect to local regulations of physical signs, fund solicitations, adult entertainments, and curfew laws.

The need for legal counsel by local government officials, to assure compliance with First Amendment principles in the formulation and enforcement of official regulations has been sharpened by the exposure of local governments and their officials to heavy monetary liability for deprivation of constitutional rights under the newly emergent federal tort doctrines that are discussed in chapter XI, infra.

METROMEDIA, INC. v. SAN DIEGO

Supreme Court of the United States, 1980.
449 U.S. 897, 101 S.Ct. 2882, 69 L.Ed.2d 800.

SYLLABUS *

Appellee city of San Diego enacted an ordinance which imposes substantial prohibitions on the erection of outdoor advertising displays within the city. The stated purpose of the ordinance is "to eliminate hazards to pedestrians and motorists brought about by distracting sign displays" and "to preserve and improve the appearance of the City." The ordinance permits onsite commercial advertising (a sign advertising goods or services available on the property where the sign is located), but forbids other commercial advertising and noncommercial advertising using fixed-structure signs, unless permitted by 1 of the ordinance's 12 specified exceptions, such as temporary political cam-

* The syllabus constitutes no part of the opinion of the Court but has been prepared by the Reporter of Decisions for the conve- nience of the reader. See United States v. Detroit Lumber Co., 200 U.S. 321, 337, 26 S.Ct. 282, 287, 50 L.Ed. 499.

paign signs. Appellants, companies that were engaged in the outdoor advertising business in the city when the ordinance was passed, brought suit in state court to enjoin enforcement of the ordinance. The trial court held that the ordinance was an unconstitutional exercise of the city's police power and an abridgment of appellants' First Amendment rights. The California Court of Appeal affirmed, but the California Supreme Court reversed, holding, *inter alia,* that the ordinance was not facially invalid under the First Amendment.

Held: The judgment is reversed, and the case is remanded. (opinion of White, J.); (opinion of Brennan, J.).

26 Cal.3d 848, 164 Cal.Rptr. 510, 610 P.2d 407, reversed and remanded.

Justice White, joined by Justice Stewart, Justice Marshall, and Justice Powell, concluded that the ordinance is unconstitutional on its face.

(a) As with other media of communication, the government has legitimate interests in controlling the noncommunicative aspects of billboards, but the First and Fourteenth Amendments foreclose similar interests in controlling the communicative aspects of billboards. Because regulation of the noncommunicative aspects of a medium often impinges to some degree on the communicative aspects, the courts must reconcile the government's regulatory interests with the individual's right to expression.

(b) Insofar as it regulates commercial speech, the ordinance meets the constitutional requirements of Central Hudson Gas & Electric Corp. v. Public Service Comm'n, 447 U.S. 557, 100 S.Ct. 2343, 65 L.Ed.2d 341. Improving traffic safety and the appearance of the city are substantial governmental goals. The ordinance directly serves these goals and is no broader than necessary to accomplish such ends.

(c) However, the city's general ban on signs carrying noncommercial advertising is invalid under the First and Fourteenth Amendments. The fact that the city may value commercial messages relating to on-site goods and services more than it values commercial communications relating to off-site goods and services does not justify prohibiting an occupant from displaying his own ideas or those of others. Furthermore, because * * * some noncommercial messages may be conveyed on billboards throughout the commercial and industrial zones, the city must allow billboards conveying other non-commercial messages throughout those zones. * * *

(d) Government restrictions on protected speech are not permissible merely because the government does not favor one side over another on a subject of public controversy. Nor can a prohibition of all messages carried by a particular mode of communication be upheld merely because the prohibition is rationally related to a nonspeech interest. * * *

Justice Brennan, joined by Justice Blackmun, concluded that in practical effect the city's ordinance constitutes a total ban on the use of billboards to communicate to the public messages of general applicability, whether commercial or noncommercial, and that under the appropriate First Amendment analysis a city may totally ban billboards only if it can show that a sufficiently substantial governmental interest is directly furthered thereby and that any more narrowly drawn restriction would promote less well the achievement of that goal. Under this test, San Diego's ordinance is invalid. * * *

Notes

1. See *Carlin Springs,* and notes thereto, page 380 infra; City of Lakewood v. Colfax Unlimited Ass'n, 634 P.2d 52 (Colo.1981) (ban on bus bench political ads invalidated).

2. **Total Ban on Billboards.** Compare Maurice Callahan & Sons, Inc. v. Outdoor Advertising Board, 12 Mass.App.Ct. 536, 427 N.E.2d 25 (1981) where court upheld a municipality-wide ban on off-premises commercial billboards. The court noted that the plurality opinion in *Metromedia* indicated a total (nondiscriminatory) ban would be constitutional; and that the town bylaw was no broader than necessary to meet its substantial interests in traffic safety and aesthetics.

3. **Headshops.** Regulation of store displays that advertise drug paraphernalia for sale was held not to infringe First Amendment freedom of speech. Village of Hoffman Est. v. Flipside, 455 U.S. 489, 102 S.Ct. 1186, 71 L.Ed.2d 362 (1982).

HOMETOWN CO–OPERATIVE APARTMENTS v. HOMETOWN

United States District Court, District of Illinois, 1981.
515 F.Supp. 502.

ASPEN, DISTRICT JUDGE:

Plaintiff Hometown Co-operative Apartments, an Illinois not-for-profit corporation brought this action pursuant to the Civil Rights Act of 1871, as amended, 42 U.S.C. § 1983, challenging the constitutionality of an amendment to the municipal building code of defendant, the City of Hometown, Illinois, making it unlawful for a new owner or lessee of residential property to occupy the premises unless a certificate of housing inspection without any deficiencies has been issued for the property within the prior three months. The ordinance provides that the building department is to issue a certificate of inspection within fourteen days after gaining access to the property whether by consent or by warrant. Each day of occupancy without a valid certificate of inspection constitutes a separate offense punishable by a fine of not less than ten nor more than five hundred dollars.

Plaintiff seeks injunctive relief against the enforcement of the ordinance and a declaratory judgment that the ordinance authorizes unreasonable searches in violation of the fourth amendment as applied to the states through the fourteenth amendment due process clause. This matter is presently before the Court on the parties' cross-motions for summary judgment pursuant to Fed.R.Civ.P. 56. The parties agree, and we so find, that there are no material facts in dispute and that the question before the Court is of a purely legal nature.

This is not the first time these parties have been before the Court with respect to the constitutionality of a Hometown ordinance that authorizes point of sale inspections of residential property. Last year, this Court held that the predecessor of Hometown's present ordinance was "unconstitutional under the fourth amendment insofar as it fail[ed] to provide for a warrant as a prerequisite for the point of sale inspection." Hometown Cooperative Apartments v. City of Hometown, 495 F.Supp. 55, 60 (N.D.Ill.1980). Following our ruling, the City of Hometown amended its ordinance by specifically providing that:

> "(e) [w]here no consent has been given to enter or inspect any property, no entry or inspection shall be made without the procurement of a warrant from the Circuit Court of Cook County."

* * * The City also made other changes in the ordinance not relevant here. We must now decide whether the inclusion of a warrant procedure in the ordinance covering situations in which a property owner or tenant refuses to consent to an inspection remedies the earlier constitutional defect.

In Camara v. Municipal Court, 387 U.S. 523, 87 S.Ct. 1727, 18 L.Ed. 2d 930 (1967), the Supreme Court held "that administrative searches of the kind at issue here are significant intrusions upon the interests protected by the Fourth Amendment, that such searches when authorized and conducted without a warrant procedure lack the traditional safeguards which the Fourth Amendment guarantees to the individual." 387 U.S. at 534, 87 S.Ct. at 1733. * * * Courts in other jurisdictions have similarly upheld the constitutionality of code enforcement inspections and ordinances similar to the one involved in the case at bar as long as a warrant is required when the owner or occupant of the property refuses to voluntarily consent to the inspection. Currier v. City of Pasadena, 48 Cal.App.3d 810, 121 Cal.Rptr. 913, cert. denied, 423 U.S. 1000, 96 S.Ct. 432, 46 L.Ed.2d 375 (1978); Wilson v. City of Cincinnati, 46 Ohio 2d 138, 346 N.E.2d 666 (1976).

By providing for a warrant procedure in cases in which a new owner or lessee of property refuses to consent to an inspection by the building department, the City of Hometown has remedied the fatal flaw in its earlier point of sale inspection ordinance. The property owner is no longer forced to choose between consenting to a warrantless search or subjecting himself or herself to substantial fines for failure to procure a certificate of inspection. If the property owner or tenant refuses to consent to the inspection, the city must procure a warrant in order to gain access to the property. To this extent, the Hometown ordinance is now in accord with the fourth amendment proscription of unreasonable searches and seizures.

The plaintiff maintains, however, that the ordinance—even as amended—is unconstitutional * * *. Since the ordinance flatly prohibits occupancy of a residence as a new owner or tenant without a valid certificate of inspection, plaintiff contends that, in a situation where the city does not or cannot procure a warrant, the property owner must either consent to a warrantless search or risk substantial fines just as before the ordinance was amended.

Plaintiff's argument assumes that there will be situations in which the City of Hometown either will refuse to seek a warrant, presumably in bad faith and contrary to the letter and spirit of the ordinance, or will be unable to procure one, and that in such circumstances, the city will force a property owner or tenant to consent to a warrantless search on the threat of substantial penalty. This speculation and conjecture as to possible future events is inappropriate at this time, however, in light of the facial validity of the Hometown ordinance as discussed above.

*   *   *

Speculation about the possibility of future unconstitutional acts of officials under a statute is insufficient to create a ripe case or controversy. * * *

In the same vein, the possibility that circumstances will arise in the future, as postulated by the plaintiff herein, in which residents of the City of Hometown will be forced to consent to inspections against their will because the city either refuses to seek a warrant or is unable to procure one under the relatively liberal standards set down in the ordinance consistent with *Camara*, does not state a case or controversy ripe for judicial determination.

Accordingly, for the reasons set forth in this opinion, defendant's motion for summary judgment is granted and plaintiff's motion for summary judgment is denied. It is so ordered.

Notes

1. **Home Visits by Welfare Workers.** A welfare recipient cannot claim a Fourth Amendment violation for loss of benefits arising from her refusal to permit a visit to her home by a social worker, where there is no forced visitation or criminal investigation or consequence to such refusal. Such visit conditions on the receipt of welfare were held by the Supreme Court to be (a) not a "search" and (b) not unreasonable, even assuming arguendo some aspects of a search. Wyman v. James, 400 U.S. 309, 91 S.Ct. 381, 27 L.Ed.2d 408 (1971).

2. **Other Licensing Issues.**

(a) **Government Searches & Seizures.** Constitutional limits on official inspections, searches and seizures, whether of the person or property of private parties are delineated by cases that make refined and complex distinctions between different scenarios for search or seizure by public authorities. See generally, W. LaFave, *Search and Seizure* (1978). In extraordinary cases, viz. true emergencies that cannot await the procurement of a search warrant, the Constitution permits warrantless inspections and searches. For nonemergency inspections to enforce fire, safety, health and other local and state codes, the Supreme Court has lowered the constitutional requirements, but still insists upon at least formal reliance upon a search warrant.

(b) **Discriminatory Licensing.** Licensing laws that unreasonably classify and discriminate between applicant classes on the basis of personal traits, such as race, gender, religion or alienage have been voided under the Equal Protection Clause, and under federal civil rights statutes. On unconstitutional discrimination against transient merchants, see State v. Schmidt, p. 394, infra. On gender discrimination, see Sail'er Inn, Inc. v. Kirby, 5 Cal.3d 1, 95 Cal.Rptr. 329, 485 P.2d 529 (1971); Paterson Tavern and Grill Owners Association, Inc. v. Hawthorne, 57 N.J. 180, 270 A.2d 628 (1970); Commonwealth v. Burke, 481 S.W.2d 52 (Ky.1972). On unconstitutional ethnic discrimination in administrating licensing laws, see Yick Wo v. Hopkins, 118 U.S. 356, 6 S.Ct. 1064, 30 L.Ed. 220 (1886). On unconstitutional discrimination in setting licensing fees, see United States Fidelity & Guaranty Co. v. Newberry, 257 S.C. 433, 186 S.E.2d 239 (1972). See also, Weber Basin case, p. 402, infra, on discriminatory taxes.

Discrimination in regulations on signs and on fund solicitation groups is treated in the Carlin case, p. 380, Delight Wholesale, p. 385, infra, and in the notes thereto.

(c) **Employment Discrimination.** See cases and discussion on employment discrimination p. 356, supra.

(d) **Due Process Standards.** Where local officials undertake to deny, suspend or revoke local licenses, their procedures are constrained by the requirements of due process. See Midwest Teen Centers, Inc., p. 408, infra.

(e) **Curfew Laws.** See discussion in ch. VII, pp. 388–392, infra.

Chapter VII

LOCAL POLICE POWERS

"But what are the police powers of a State? They are nothing more or less than the powers of government inherent in every sovereignty to the extent of its dominions." Taney, C.J., in License Cases, 46 U.S. (5 How.) 504, 582, 12 L.Ed. 256 (1847).

A. INTRODUCTORY NOTE

The power to govern—all men and subjects—under changing times and circumstances, is subject only to the limits constitutionally imposed upon states by the people. It is dynamic and has never been, nor could be, defined with specificity, for any such attempt would imply limits on the sovereign police power to govern for the common good.

> "An attempt to define its reach or trace its outer limits is fruitless, for each case must turn on its own facts. * * * Public safety, public health, morality, peace and quiet, law and order—these are some of the more conspicuous examples of the traditional application of the police power to municipal affairs. Yet they merely illustrate the scope of the power and do not delimit it." Berman v. Parker, 348 U.S. 26, 32, 75 S.Ct. 98, 102, 99 L.Ed. 27 (1954). "It is always easier to determine whether a particular case comes within the general scope of the [police] power, than to give an abstract definition of the power itself which will be in all respects accurate." See Stone v. Mississippi, 101 U.S. 814, 818, 25 L.Ed. 1079 (1879).

Except where the police power is expressed directly by the sovereign people in accordance with their constitutions, it is vested in the legislature. See generally 6 McQuillin, *Municipal Corporations,* §§ 24:02, 24:03 (1969 rev. ed.). Since local governments have no independent sovereignty, they possess only those police powers that are delegated to them by the state. Where not expressed specifically, municipal police power may be based upon the "general welfare" clauses in municipal charters, or implied from the very act of creating a local government. Adams v. New Kensington, 357 Pa. 557, 55 A.2d 392 (1947). As noted in State of Utah v. Hutchinson, p. 68, supra:

"These cases state the rule which we adopt in this case. When the State has granted general welfare power to local governments, those governments have independent authority apart from, and in addition to, specific grants of authority to pass ordinances which are reasonably and appropriately related to the objectives of that power, i.e., providing for the public safety, health, morals, and welfare. Salt Lake City v. Allred, 20 Utah 2d 298, 437 P.2d 434 (1968). * * * "

Municipalities do not have coextensive police powers. Police power delegation to a constitutional home rule city may well be broader than those granted to a legislatively chartered town. See People v. Osborne, 17 Cal.App.2d Supp. 771, 59 P.2d 1083 (1936); State v. Musser, 67 Idaho 214, 176 P.2d 199 (1946); Ex parte Gammel, 89 Okl.Cr.Crim. 400, 208 P.2d 961 (1949). Judicial construction or implication of police powers under particular laws may also be affected by the size and needs of different classes of local government. Municipal police power is not the equivalent of state police power. City of Baltimore v. Silver, 263 Md. 439, 283 A.2d 788 (1971). Absent a restriction under its constitution, the state may revoke and transfer police powers from local government units. Robin v. Incorporated Village of Hempstead, 38 A.D.2d 758, 329 N.Y.S.2d 678 (1972); Terminal Enterprises, Inc. v. Jersey City, 54 N.J. 568, 258 A.2d 361 (1969).

B. DIRECT LEGISLATIVE COMMANDS

GOLDBLATT v. HEMPSTEAD

Supreme Court of the United States, 1962.
369 U.S. 590, 82 S.Ct. 987, 8 L.Ed.2d 130.

MR. JUSTICE CLARK delivered the opinion of the Court.

The Town of Hempstead has enacted an ordinance regulating dredging and pit excavating on property within its limits. Appellants, who engaged in such operations * * * claim that it in effect prevents them from continuing their business and therefore takes their property without due process of law in violation of the Fourteenth Amendment. The trial court held that the ordinance was a valid exercise of the town's police power. * * * We noted probable jurisdiction, 366 U.S. 942, and having heard argument we now affirm the judgment.

Appellant Goldblatt owns a 38–acre tract within the Town of Hempstead. At the time of the present litigation appellant Builders Sand and Gravel Corporation was mining sand and gravel on this lot, a use to which the lot had been put continuously since 1927. Before the end of the first year the excavation had reached the water table leaving a water-filled crater which has been widened and deepened to the point that it is now a 20-acre lake with an average depth of 25 feet. The town has expanded around this excavation, and today within a radius of 3,500 feet there are more than 2,200 homes and four public schools with a combined enrollment of 4,500 pupils.

The present action is but one of a series of steps undertaken by the town * * * to regulate mining excavations within its limits. A 1945 ordinance, No. 16, provided that such pits must be enclosed by a wire fence and comply with certain berm and slope requirements. Although appellants complied with this ordinance, the town sought an injunction against further excavation as being violative of a zoning ordinance. This failed because appellants were found to be "conducting a prior non-conforming use on the premises. * * *." 135 N.Y.L.J., issue 52, p. 12 (1956). * * *

In 1958 the town amended Ordinance No. 16 to prohibit any excavating below the water table and to impose an affirmative duty to refill any excavation presently below that level. The new amendment also made the berm, slope, and fence requirements more onerous.

In 1959 the town brought the present action to enjoin further mining by the appellants on the grounds that they had not complied with the ordinance, as amended, * * *. Appellants contended, *inter alia*, that the ordinance was unconstitutional because (1) it was not regulatory of their business but completely prohibitory and confiscated their property without compensation, (2) it deprived them of the benefit of the favorable judgment arising from the previous zoning litigation, and (3) it constituted *ex post facto* legislation. * * *

Concededly the ordinance completely prohibits a beneficial use to which the property has previously been devoted. However, such a characterization does not tell us whether or not the ordinance is unconstitutional. It is an oft-repeated truism that every regulation necessarily speaks as a prohibition. If this ordinance is otherwise a valid exercise of the town's police powers, the fact that it deprives the property of its most beneficial use does not render it unconstitutional. Walls v. Midland Carbon Co., 254 U.S. 300, 41 S.Ct. 118, 65 L.Ed. 276 (1920); Hadacheck v. Sebastian, 239 U.S. 394, 36 S.Ct. 143, 60 L.Ed. 348 (1915); Reinman v. Little Rock, 237 U.S. 171, 35 S.Ct. 511, 59 L.Ed. 900 (1915); Mugler v. Kansas, 123 U.S. 623, 88 S.Ct. 273, 31 L.Ed. 205 (1887); see Laurel Hill Cemetery v. San Francisco, 216 U.S. 358, 30 S.Ct. 301, 54 L.Ed. 515 (1910). * * *

Nor is it of controlling significance that the "use" prohibited here is of the soil itself as opposed to a "use" upon the soil, cf. United States v. Central Eureka Mining Co., 357 U.S. 155, 78 S.Ct. 1097, 2 L.Ed.2d 1228 (1958), or that the use prohibited is arguably not a common-law nuisance, *e.g.,* Reinman v. Little Rock, *supra.*

This is not to say, however, that governmental action in the form of regulation cannot be so onerous as to constitute a taking which constitutionally requires compensation. Pennsylvania Coal Co. v. Mahon, 260 U.S. 393, 43 S.Ct. 158, 67 L.Ed. 322 (1922); * * *. There is no set formula to determine where regulation ends and taking begins. Although a comparison of values before and after is relevant, see Pennsylvania Coal Co. v. Mahon, *supra,* it is by no means conclusive, see

Hadacheck v. Sebastian, *supra,* where a diminution in value from $800,000 to $60,000 was upheld. How far regulation may go before it becomes a taking we need not now decide, for there is no evidence in the present record which even remotely suggests that prohibition of further mining will reduce the value of the lot in question. Indulging in the usual presumption of constitutionality * * * we find no indication that the prohibitory effect of Ordinance No. 16 is sufficient to render it an unconstitutional taking if it is otherwise a valid police regulation.

The question, therefore, narrows to whether the prohibition * * * is a valid exercise of the town's police power. The term "police power" connotes the time-tested conceptional limit of public encroachment upon private interests. Except for the substitution of the familiar standard of "reasonableness," this Court has generally refrained from announcing any specific criteria. The classic statement of the rule in Lawton v. Steele, 152 U.S. 133, 137, 14 S.Ct. 499, 501, 38 L.Ed. 385 (1894), is still valid today:

> "To justify the State in * * * interposing its authority in behalf of the public, it must appear, first, that the interests of the public * * * require such interference; and, second, that the means are reasonably necessary for the accomplishment of the purpose, and not unduly oppressive upon individuals."

Even this rule is not applied with strict precision, for this Court has often said that "debatable questions as to reasonableness are not for the courts but for the legislature * * *." *E.g.,* Sproles v. Binford, 286 U.S. 374, 388, 52 S.Ct. 581, 585, 76 L.Ed. 1167 (1932).

The ordinance in question was passed as a safety measure * * *. To evaluate its reasonableness we therefore need to know such things as the nature of the menace against which it will protect, the availability and effectiveness of other less drastic protective steps, and the loss which appellants will suffer from the imposition of the ordinance.

A careful examination of the record reveals a dearth of relevant evidence on these points. One fair inference * * * is that since a few holes had been burrowed under the fence surrounding the lake it might be attractive and dangerous to children. But there was no indication whether the lake as it stood was an actual danger to the public or whether deepening the lake would increase the danger. In terms of dollars or some other objective standard, there was no showing how much, if anything, the imposition of the ordinance would cost the appellants. In short, the evidence produced is clearly indecisive on the reasonableness of prohibiting further excavation below the water table.

Although one could imagine that preventing further deepening of a pond already 25 feet deep would have a *de minimis* effect on public safety, we cannot say that such a conclusion is compelled by facts of which we can take notice. Even if we could draw such a conclusion, we would be unable to say the ordinance is unreasonable; for all we know, the ordinance may have a *de minimis* effect on appellants. Our past cases leave no doubt that appellants had the burden on "reasonableness." *E.g.,* Bibb v. Navajo Freight Lines, 359 U.S. 520, 529, 79 S.Ct. 962, 967, 3 L.Ed.2d 1003 (1959) (exercise of police power is presumed to be constitutionally valid); Salsburg v. Maryland, 346 U.S. 545, 553, 74 S.Ct. 280, 284, 98 L.Ed. 281 (1954) (the presumption of reasonableness is with the State); United States v. Carolene Products Co., 304 U.S. 144, 154, 58 S.Ct. 778, 784, 82 L.Ed. 1234 (1938) (exercise of police power will be upheld if any state of facts either known or which could be reasonably assumed affords support for it). This burden not having been met, the prohibition of excavation on the 20-acre-lake tract must stand as a valid police regulation.

* * *

Appellants' other contentions warrant only a passing word. The claim that rights acquired in previous litigation are being undermined is completely unfounded. A successful defense to the imposition of one regulation does not erect a constitutional barrier to all other regulation. * * *

Appellants also contend that the ordinance is unconstitutional because it imposes under penalty of fine and imprisonment such affirmative duties as refilling the existing excavation and the construction of a new fence. This claim is founded principally on the constitutional prohibitions against bills of attainder and *ex post facto* legislation. These provisions are severable, both in nature and by express declaration, from the prohibition against further excavation. Since enforcement of these provisions was not sought in the present litigation, this Court under well-established principles will not at this time undertake to decide their constitutionality. * * * That determination must await another day. We pass only on the provisions of the ordinance here invoked, not on probabilities not now before us, and to the extent the judgment is affirmed.

Notes

1. Cf. Lyon Sand & Gravel Co. v. Oakland, 33 Mich.App. 614, 190 N.W.2d 354 (1971) which nullified a prohibition against gravel mining in a rural area.

2. **Presumptions and Burdens.** In view of the high private losses threatened by the town's ordinance, and the lack of evidence on crucial fact questions, should the court in Goldblatt have remanded the case for taking of testimony? Compare the approach taken in United States Fidelity & G. Co. v. Newberry, 257 S.C. 433, 186 S.E.2d 239 (1972).

3. **Regulation v. Condemnation.** The taking vs. regulation issue is discussed in the Penn-Central case, p. 434 infra.

KAUKAS v. CHICAGO

Supreme Court of Illinois, 1963.
27 Ill.2d 197, 188 N.E.2d 700.

SOLFISBURG, CHIEF JUSTICE.

[Owners of apartment building challenged an ordinance which prohibited use of glass panel doors as a secondary means of exit. The Supreme Court held the ordinance was not unreasonable and did not deprive owners of their property without due process of law, even though their building complied with ordinances in effect at time of its original construction, and even though compliance with the new ordinance would cost between $5,000 and $10,000.]

* * *

The legislature has provided that municipalities may prescribe the strength and manner of constructing buildings, and may cause all buildings which are in a dangerous fire condition to be put in a safe fire condition. (Ill.Rev.Stat.1959, chap. 24, pars. 23–70, 23–72.) There was considerable evidence in the present case dealing with the question of whether glass panel doors as a secondary means of exit are safe.

* * *

* * * It is clear that a city may lawfully make building requirements applicable to buildings in existence at the time the ordinance was enacted, even though these buildings complied with the ordinance in effect at the time the new ordinance was enacted. [Citations omitted] The question in these cases is whether the public welfare demands retroactive application and whether the property owners affected suffer unreasonable exactions as compared with the resulting public benefits. * * * We think it is clear that * * * a reasonable basis exists for the determination by the city council that the public safety required application of this ordinance to existing buildings. The only remaining question, therefore, is whether the burden upon the property owners is so great compared to the public benefit that the ordinance must be held invalid. No hard and fast rules can be laid down in such cases. * * * In Queenside Hills Realty Co. v. Saxl, 328 U.S. 80, 66 S.Ct. 850, 90 L.Ed. 1096, the United States Supreme Court upheld a New York statute providing that existing buildings must install certain new fire prevention equipment. The complaint filed in the trial court alleged that the building in question had a market value of about $25,000 and the cost of complying with the law would be about $7,500. * * * In the United States Supreme Court the property owner argued that its building was largely fireproof and that any fire hazard * * * was adequately safeguarded by fire alarms, constant watchman service and other safety arrangements. The Supreme Court stated that the legislature might choose not to take the chance * * * and might adopt the most conservative course which science and engineering offer and held that it was for the legislature to decide what regulations are needed * * *. The court pointed out that many types

of social legislation diminish the value of the property which is regulated and stated that in no case does the owner of a property acquire immunity against exercise of the police power because the property had been constructed in full compliance with the existing laws. * * *

In the present case it appears that * * * the plaintiffs had a total in excess of $59,000 invested in the building. The evidence is not clear * * * but according to the evidence it can be said that the cost of compliance would be somewhere between $5,000 and $10,000. When this cost is measured against the total cost of the building and considered in connection with the fact that the installation * * * would protect the tenants from the danger of fire, we think it is clear that the ordinance is not unreasonable * * * and does not deprive the owners of their property without due process of law.

The plaintiffs also contend that the ordinance deprives them of their property without just compensation. A short answer to this contention is found in Goldblatt v. Town of Hempstead, 369 U.S. 590, 82 S.Ct. 987, 8 L.Ed.2d 130, 133, * * *.

Judgment reversed.

CITY OF PIGGOTT v. EBLEN

Supreme Court of Arkansas, 1963.
236 Ark. 390, 366 S.W.2d 192.

HOLT, JUSTICE. The appellant, the City of Piggott, Arkansas, enacted Ordinance 209 declaring that: "* * * Pinball machines or other gaming devices are a public nuisance * * *". The ordinance further provides that it is unlawful for any business establishment or individual to possess pinball machines in any manner within the city. A violation of this ordinance is punishable by a fine of not less than $5.00 nor more than $25.00 per day.

* * * These appellees, the machine owner and location owners, brought suit in chancery court seeking injunctive relief and a declaratory judgment invalidating the ordinance.

* * *

* * * Act 167 of 1931 [Ark.Stat. § 84-2601] provides that the business of owning, operating, or leasing such machines is a privilege for which licenses can be required and taxes imposed. Its validity was approved in Thompson v. Wiseman, 189 Ark. 852, 75 S.W.2d 393. Act 137 of 1933 [Ark.Stat. § 84-2602] defines such machines as: "* * * any machine, * * * which is operated by placing in same through a slot, or any kind of opening or container, and coin, * * * before such machine operates or functions."

Act 201 of 1939, as amended, [Ark.Stat. § 84-2611] specifically provides that amusement games played on pinball machines are lawful even though free games be given upon certain scores being made. * * * This Act [Ark.Stat. § 84-2614] further provides that where the state tax has not been paid the machine is declared to be a public nuisance subject to seizure and sale by the state upon an order by the Pulaski Chancery Court if the owner does not redeem the machine within ten (10) days by paying the tax due and the costs. No such power is granted to municipalities if a municipal tax is not paid. Act 60 of 1949 [Ark.Stats. §§ 41–1122, 41–1123] makes it unlawful to permit any person under eighteen (18) years of age to play or operate a pinball machine and provides for a fine of not less than $25.00 and not more than $500.00 for violation thereof. Act 120 of 1959 [Ark.Stat. § 84–2622] provides that the business of owning, operating, or leasing coin operated amusement devices is a privilege subject to a state tax, and Ark.Stat. § 84–2625 imposes an annual license fee of $250.00 and expressly prohibits any municipality from levying such a privilege tax on the basis of this Act.

Thus, it is readily apparent that a conflict exists between the questioned ordinance and the statutes. * * *

* * * The statutes of our state, being paramount and supreme, have preempted the appellant in this field of legislation and, therefore, render the ordinance a nullity.

The appellant contends that the use of the pinball machines by minors [school children under eighteen (18)] constitutes a public nuisance and, therefore, pursuant to Act 24 of 1897 [Ark.Stat. § 19–2305] empowering municipal corporations to prevent and abate nuisances the city can validly abate the alleged nuisance by this ordinance. In this case three adult witnesses testified that they had observed children under the age of eighteen (18) playing these machines between school hours. Two of these minors testified that they had played the machines on many occasions. There is no evidence of gambling on these machines. Appellant is not empowered, of course, to declare something to be a public nuisance which the state has clothed with legality because the state law is paramount and supreme. Therefore, this contention is not valid.

Further, we have held in many cases that the mere declaration in a city ordinance that a certain act constitutes a nuisance does not make it such in fact. [Citations omitted.] * * *

We have held that although pool halls might be regulated by a city council to prevent them from becoming public nuisances, such authority would not permit a city to suppress completely the existence of a lawful business by imposing an annual license fee of $600,000 and requiring a bond of $1,000.00 conditioned upon the observance of certain regulations. Bryan v. City of Malvern, 122 Ark. 379, 183 S.W. 957.

* * * The fact that this ordinance cannot stand does not leave appellant helpless and disarmed in suppressing the alleged illegal acts. It is not denied in this case that no request or effort was ever made to invoke any of our penal laws that might be applicable to the facts in this case. The statutes which presently legalize the existence of pinball machines also make it a violation of the law to permit any person

under eighteen (18) years of age to play them. [Ark.Stats. §§ 41–1122, 41–1123, *supra*] The owners of those establishments which permit children under eighteen (18) years of age to play these machines are subject to these provisions.

The trial court was correct in declaring the questioned ordinance invalid as being contrary to the Constitution and Statutes of this state. The decree is affirmed.

Notes

1. **"Nuisance" Prohibitions.** At common law, the courts developed nuisance doctrines as part of real property and tort law to enjoin continuing trespasses. Under their police powers, state and local legislatures declare as "nuisances" many activities which do not fall within the judicially developed definitions of nuisance. See Delight Wholesale Co. v. Overland Park, infra; City of Nokomis v. Sullivan, reported at p. 479, infra, which set forth the general rule that legislation which defines nuisances need only be shown to have a reasonable relationship to the public welfare. Thus, while certain elements of common law and statutory nuisance may coalesce in particular cases, legislated nuisances are not to be analyzed in common law terms.

2. **Nuisance and Preemption.** See generally, Ch. IV–B. See also City of Tacoma v. Naubert, 5 Wash.App. 856, 491 P.2d 652 (1971) which nullified a city ordinance prohibiting the sale of erotic materials to minors, on the ground that a state statute against such sales (which provided different defenses) had expressly preempted that field of local police power. Double police power regulations, where not inconsistent or conflicting, may be imposed on the same subject, e.g. municipal regulation of pawnbrokers under a city ordinance notwithstanding a later statute regulating pawnbrokers. City of Hobbs v. Biswell, 81 N.M. 778, 473 P.2d 917 (1970) "An enactment may duplicate or complement statutory regulations * * * [t]here is no withdrawal of municipal authority by implication unless the later state statute * * * is irreconcilable with the prior legislative grant authorizing municipal regulation." Id. at 780, 473 P.2d at 920. See also St. Louis v. Goldman, 467 S.W.2d 99 (Mo.App.1971) (upholding conviction and fine under city disorderly conduct ordinance, notwithstanding state criminal law covering the same offense,); Tamiami, p. 399, Mogolefsky, p. 396.

3. **Land Use v. Activity Regulation.** The view that different police power limitations apply to land use, vis a vis activity regulations was expressly rejected in Bruner v. Danville, 394 S.W.2d 939 (Ky.1955). There, the court held that the city could refuse to license, and thus prohibit, public dances: "But, says the city, these [cited] were 'land use' cases, and they are different. Why? The freedom to engage in a lawful business is no less important * * * than the liberty to utilize property as he sees fit. * * * No authority is cited for the suggested distinction in degree of protection between the two, and we are confident that there is none." Id. at 942.

4. **Regulation v. Prohibition.** State courts tend to disfavor total prohibitions in the absence of a clear need to go that far. See e.g., *Delight Wholesale Co.*, reported at p. 385 and cases noted thereunder.

5. **Implied Police Powers.** An omitted portion of the opinion in Piggott upholds the implication of police powers. For implied police powers found in the general welfare clauses of municipal charters, see City of Hobbs v. Biswell, 81 N.M. 778–79, 473 P.2d 917, 918–19 (1970) where the court stated:

> "These subdivisions of § 14–17–1, supra, confer a 'police power' upon municipalities to protect their inhabitants and preserve peace and order within the municipal limits. * * *

> " 'General welfare' power and 'police' power are concepts which, if independent of one another, tend to merge. * * * "

6. **Promoting the Public Welfare.** The police power to "preserve" the public interest includes the power to "promote" public welfare by affirmative as well as protective measures, e.g. the use of public industrial development bonds as a police power measure to promote general welfare by stimulating the local economy, p. 704 et seq., infra.

RUGGERI v. ST. LOUIS

Supreme Court of Missouri, 1969.
441 S.W.2d 361.

[Reported at p. 129]

CARLIN v. PALM SPRINGS

Court of Appeals, Fourth District, California, 1971.
14 Cal.App.3d 706, 92 Cal.Rptr. 535.

KERRIGAN, ASSOCIATE JUSTICE. Plaintiffs have owned and operated a small hotel in Palm Springs for many years. They have done business under the fictitious name of "6⁵⁰ Hotel" since 1956. In 1967 the City Council of Palm Springs adopted a comprehensive sign ordinance. One of the provisions of the ordinance prohibits, in effect, the use of an outside business sign that makes reference to prices or rates. Under the ordinance "rate signs" are deemed to be public nuisances *per se.*

Several years prior to the enactment of the ordinance, the plaintiffs attached to the main entrance of their hotel, * * * a permanent sign displaying the official name of the business as "6⁵⁰ Hotel." Subsequent to the adoption of the sign ordinance, the city officials * * * determined that plaintiffs' sign was a "rate sign" and ordered its removal.

* * * The purpose of the action was to secure a judicial declaration that the sign ordinance was unconstitutional * * *.

* * * appraisers, architects, businessmen and planning officials testified on behalf of the city. The substance of their testimony was that aesthetics are of essential importance to a community; that rate

signs are detrimental to aesthetics; that aesthetic values cannot be separated from economic factors; that rate signs tend to proliferate, if permitted, and proliferation would adversely affect the quality of the civic environment and the city's attraction to tourists; ＊ ＊ ＊.

Plaintiffs called a formidable number of witnesses, including the former Planning Director of Riverside County. The essence of their testimony was that there was no connection between "rate signs" and the general welfare of the community ＊ ＊ ＊.

Following a lengthy trial, the court found, in substance, that the city of Palm Springs is a desert resort; that being tourist-oriented, the use of advertising signs has a direct bearing on the economic and aesthetic well-being of the community and, consequently, the general welfare of the community; that rate signs give rise to false advertising and hard-core commercialization which have a detrimental impact on the general welfare of the city; that a separate classification of rate signs is reasonable; that plaintiffs' business sign is a rate sign and is therefore violative of the ordinance. The court concluded the Palm Springs sign ordinance to be constitutional and enforceable against the plaintiffs, and entered judgment accordingly.

While plaintiffs' assault on the judgment is stated in varying ways, the crucial issue on appeal is whether the ordinance is unconstitutional as being violative of equal protection and free speech concepts or whether it represents a valid exercise of the police power.

This is a case of first impression in this state. It presents a clear conflict between an individual's right to conduct a business and to advertise his business as opposed to a municipality's right to exercise its police powers. ＊ ＊ ＊

＊ ＊ ＊

The ordinance does not absolutely proscribe the posting or advertising of hotel and motel rates. While it prohibits outside rate signs, it permits a limited posting of rates of accommodations in the interior of hotels; such rates may be indicated by a single sign or attraction board not to exceed 18 inches by 24 inches located no closer than one foot to the inside of a window when facing public view, in letters and numbers not to exceed ¾ inches in height. (Section 8152.09.)

The constitution expressly confers on cities and towns the power to make and enforce within their limits all such "local, police, sanitary and other regulations as are not in conflict with general laws." (Calif. Const., art. XI, § 11.) The power thus delegated to municipalities is as broad as that of the Legislature itself, providing the power is exercised within the confines of the city and is not in conflict with the state's general laws. (People v. Taylor, 33 Cal.App.2d Supp. 760, 761, 85 P.2d 978.)

In the exercise of its police power, the city has broad discretion in determining what is reasonable in endeavoring to protect the public health, safety, morals, and general welfare. (McKay Jewelers, Inc. v.

Bowron, 19 Cal.2d 595, 600, 122 P.2d 543.) The test as to whether a law enacted pursuant to the police power is arbitrary and discriminatory in its conception and application is whether it has any reasonable tendency to promote the public health, morals, safety or general welfare of the community. * * *

The reasonable regulation of signs and billboards constitutes a valid exercise of the police power. [Citations omitted] The size, location, and other physical attributes of signs may be regulated in the interest of public safety. [Citation omitted] The number of signs which may be posted, affixed or installed by a landowner or occupier may be limited. [Citation omitted] Signs that overhang or encroach upon a public highway or public property may be restricted or prohibited. [Citation omitted] Signs used to advertise prices, which may tend to deceive, are subject to the police power. [Citation omitted] Advertising on public streets through the use of the exterior of delivery vehicles for advertising of a business other than that of the vehicle owner may be regulated. (Railway Express Agency v. People of State of New York, 336 U.S. 106, 69 S.Ct. 463, 93 L.Ed. 533.)

* * * it is likewise true that the classification of advertising signs must not be arbitrarily made * * * but must be based upon some distinction, natural, intrinsic or constitutional, which suggests a reason for, and justifies, the particular legislation. [Citation omitted] However, there is a presumption in favor of the validity of the classification created by statute or ordinance. [Citation omitted] Where the validity of the legislative classification is fairly debatable, the legislative judgment must be allowed to control. [Citation omitted] The burden of proof rests upon the person attacking the statute to establish that there is no public nexus between such legislation and what it attempts to correct * * *

Counterbalancing the government's right to regulate signs is the right of a property owner to make a reasonable use of his land or the right of a businessman to conduct a business. The right to advertise is a property right. * * * The right to advertise also represents the exercise of the right of free speech.

While no California appellate tribunal has ever been confronted with the validity of a rate sign statute, in Viale v. Foley, 76 Nev. 149, 350 P.2d 721, a Nevada regulation prohibiting rate signs for hotels and motels was held constitutional. Conversely, in Eskind v. City of Vero Beach (Fla.), 159 So.2d 209, the reviewing court * * * ruled it to be unconstitutional; Vero Beach, like Palm Springs, is a tourist town; * * *.

Applying the foregoing constitutional, statutory and case law to the ordinance under review, it is obvious that a rate sign cannot be classified separately from a non-rate sign on the basis of public health, safety, or morals. If there is any justification for the ordinance, it may be upheld only in that it promotes the general welfare. * * *

The city contends that the power to regulate rate signs may be founded on aesthetics alone. While there is California authority that the city's police power does not include the power to legislate solely on aesthetic grounds [citations omitted], it is unnecessary to decide whether the judgment can be upheld solely for reasons of good taste inasmuch as the record reflects that there is not necessarily any difference whatsoever between a business sign classified as a "rate sign" and a business sign characterized as a "non-rate sign." From an aesthetic standpoint, there is no difference between a sign which reads, "Sam's Hotel," and "Hotel 6^{50}," or between a sign reading, "Swim suits" and "Swim suits $5.88."

Aesthetics should be considered as a factor, together with other factors, in support of an ordinance. [Citations omitted] The trial court herein found that the economic and commercial well-being of the city is directly connected with the good appearance of the community. * * * The city contends that its prohibition against rate signs is supportable in that rate signs create an atmosphere of "bargain basement commercialism" inimical to the general welfare of a resort community, and that economics and aesthetics are mutually supporting factors.

The argument is not persuasive. * * * While the two concepts are virtually inseparable, we cannot perceive, as previously indicated, any aesthetic difference between a sign reading, "Sam's Hotel" and "Hotel 6^{50}." * * * There is no natural, intrinsic, or constitutional distinction permitting the classification of rate and nonrate signs. * * * A rate sign is ugly only in the eye of a competitor. The ordinance in question creates an invalid classification under the guise of aesthetics.

The city argues that under its ordinance the posting of rates by a hotel owner is not prohibited but is merely regulated as the ordinance permits a hotel owner to post his rates inside the building. The same argument has been made and rejected before. In People v. Osborne, 17 Cal.App.2d Supp. 771, 59 P.2d 1083, a municipal ordinance prohibited barbers from displaying a rate sign visible from outside the shop; in striking down the ordinance as unconstitutional, the court indicated that "the only apparent purpose of such provision is to make it necessary for a prospective customer to advance so far within the portals * * *, before learning the prices * * *, as to discourage him from a departure should those prices seem to him more than he should pay." (p. 776, 59 P.2d p. 1086.)

Nor can the ordinance under review be justified on the basis that such signs are necessarily deceptive or fraudulent in nature. The uncontradicted evidence before the trial court reflects that misrepresentation of prices or false advertising of rates were not issues in the case. * * * While there was some evidence indicating that some merchants had engaged in deceptive practices, the state has provided that criminal penalties may be imposed on anyone posting any untrue, misleading, deceptive or fraudulent business advertisement. (See Bus. & Prof.Code, §§ 17562–17568.)

In a final attempt to justify the ordinance, the city urges that there is testimony indicating that the rate sign ordinance can be upheld on economic grounds in that tourists, having made reservations at a luxury hotel at a $20 a day rate, are disgruntled at having to pay a higher rate or cancel their reservations upon discovering the existence of accommodations at a much lower rate. The argument is specious. It is common knowledge that luxury hotels charge higher prices for accommodations because of the conveniences, services and appointments accorded therein * * *. The foregoing argument indicates that the city is partial to the owners of the luxury hotels. In the event the ordinance tends to favor one class of businessmen over another, it is discriminatory. (See Eskind v. City of Vero Beach, *supra* (Fla.), 159 So. 2d 209, 211–212.)

The judgment is reversed.

Notes

1. **Judicial v. Legislative Judgments.** While *Carlin* paid lip service to legislative deference and presumptions of validity, the result manifests a willingness to second-guess legislative judgment. How can the principal opinion be reconciled with the restrained approach taken by the court in Goldblatt (p. 372)?

2. **Free Speech v. Sign Regulation.** In Linmark Associates, Inc. v. Willingboro, 431 U.S. 85, 97 S.Ct. 1614, 52 L.Ed.2d 155 (1977), the Supreme Court invalidated an ordinance that prohibited residential "sale" signs, as excessive suppression of constitutionally protected speech. In Schoen v. Hillside, 155 N.J.Super. 286, 382 A.2d 704 (1977), the court held that provisions limiting the content and color of residential "For Sale" signs were invalid under Linmark; but that the following provisions of the same ordinance were valid: requirement that sale signs be removed within 30 days after execution of sale; prohibition of "Sold" signs; and limitations on the size, color and placement of "Garage Sale" signs. Re abatement of nonconforming billboards and signs under zoning amortization laws, see Notes following the *LaChappelle* case, p. 540 infra.

3. **Off-Premises Sign Regulations.** The regulation of off-premises advertising displays calls for balancing of different public and private interests. In contrast to the cases in the prior note, compare City of Escondido v. Desert Outdoor Advtg. Co., 8 Cal.3d 785, 106 Cal.Rptr. 172, 505 P.2d 1012 (1973) where the court upheld a general ordinance prohibiting signs along a freeway, and rejected the argument that the city could only regulate such signs by a zoning ordinance; Members of City Council v. Taxpayers for Vincent, 466 U.S. 789, 104 S.Ct. 2118, 80 L.Ed.2d 772 (1984), which upheld ordinance that prohibited posting of political campaign posters on street utility poles. See Annotations: 73 A.L.R.3d 1162 (1977); 80 A.L.R.3d 687 (1978).

4. **Discriminatory Fees and Taxes.** Discriminatory fees may be invalidated as unconstitutional. U.S. Fidelity & Guaranty Co. v. Newberry,

257 S.C. 433, 186 S.E.2d 239 (1972). The discrimination principle applies to taxation as well as regulatory fees. See Weber Basin, reported at p. 378. Some courts uphold heavy regulation fees against businesses that are deemed "harmful" even though such fees may deter or oppress the "harmful" business. See e.g. Bunzel v. Golden, 150 Colo. 276, 372 P.2d 161 (1962) (pin-ball machine licensing).

DELIGHT WHOLESALE CO. v. OVERLAND PARK

Supreme Court of Kansas, 1969.
203 Kan. 99, 453 P.2d 82.

HATCHER, COMMISSIONER. This is an appeal from a judgment denying relief in an action to enjoin the enforcement of an ordinance prohibiting huckstering and peddling on the public streets of Overland Park, Kansas.

* * *

Some years prior to the enactment of the ordinance the plaintiff, Delight Wholesale Company, had granted franchises of territory within the city of Overland Park to dealers who sold frozen novelties purchased from it, from jeeps furnished by it, on the streets of Overland Park. The jeeps were leased by the dealers. During 1965, the plaintiff, Robert Fuller, Jr., was such a dealer.

* * *

From the record it is disclosed that the city's witnesses conceded that the drivers of the vehicles from which frozen goodies were sold were not careless or reckless. They were considered to be good drivers. Neither is a sanitation or health problem presented.

Mr. Bennett, president of the city council, testified that there were two conditions creating the problem they were trying to correct—the safety of the younger citizens in the area and the nuisance value. We quote from his testimony:

* * *

"A. I think the primary reason the ordinance was passed was for the safety reason. *If it was for nuisance value alone, I would not have voted for the ordinance.*

* * *

We are inclined to agree with the president of the City Council that the nuisance feature alone would not justify the ordinance.

We would not attempt to give a precise definition of the word "nuisance". It is generally considered to be something that interferes with the rights of others. (Hofstetter v. George M. Myers, Inc., 170 Kan. 564, 228 P.2d 522, 24 A.L.R.2d 188.) A public nuisance is one which annoys an entire community. (State ex rel. Thompson v. Coler, 75 Kan. 424, 89 P. 693.) In Wilburn v. Boeing Airplane Co., 188 Kan. 722, 366 P.2d 246, we held:

"Although perhaps incapable of precise definition, the word 'nuisance' is generally held to mean something which interferes with the rights of persons, whether in person, property, or enjoyment of property or comfort, and to mean an annoyance, that which annoys or causes trouble or vexation, that which is offensive or noxious, or something that works harm, inconvenience or damage. What may or may not constitute a nuisance in a particular case depends upon many things, and each case must of necessity depend upon its own particular facts and circumstances." (Syl. 6.)

A dyspeptic or a recluse might find some things offensive which would not be at all obnoxious to the general public. It is difficult for us to consider the operation of an ice cream vehicle as genuinely offensive or obnoxious.

The question of public safety presents a more difficult problem. The trial court also found that the safety of the children was endangered * * *.

The appellant argues on appeal that the city lacked the power and authority to enact the ordinance; the ordinance as enacted is not a proper and valid exercise of police power and is unreasonable and arbitrary; the ordinance violates the 14th Amendment to the Constitution of the United States and Section 1 of the Bill of Rights of the Constitution of the State of Kansas, and the adoption of a regulatory ordinance would satisfy the legitimate object.

All of the above contentions may be disposed of by the answer to a single question—is the prohibition of the legitimate business reasonably necessary for the welfare and safety of the children of Overland Park? If the answer is yes the ordinance is valid. If the answer is no the ordinance is void for each and all of the reasons listed by appellants.

* * *

However, while the police power is wide in its scope and gives a governmental body broad power to enact laws to promote the health, morals, security and welfare of the people, and further, a large discretion is vested in it to determine for itself what is deleterious to health, morals or is inimical to public welfare, it cannot under the guise of the police power enact unreasonable and oppressive legislation or that which is in violation of the fundamental law. [Citations omitted]

Huckstering and peddling of vegetables, fruits and ice cream products have long been recognized as legitimate businesses. However, the right to so sell is not absolute and may be regulated or withheld, if necessary, for public safety and welfare.

* * *

If children in the streets of residential districts are to be protected, the regulation must be applied to all those using vehicles on the street.

The city has ample power to regulate hucksters and peddlers without prohibition. Although not intended to be exhaustive, they may be prohibited from selling on the freeways, thoroughfares and busy streets; they may be kept away from schools and hospitals, and they may be reasonably regulated as to the hours during which they sell.

The appellant calls our attention to certain cases from foreign jurisdictions, particularly Trio Distributor Corp. v. City of Albany, 2

N.Y.2d 690, 163 N.Y.S.2d 585, 587, 143 N.E.2d 329, 330, where the court was dealing with an ordinance requiring vendors in the streets to be accompanied by attendants having the sole duty of protecting children from hazards of vehicle traffic. In the opinion the court stated:

> "Although reasonable regulation of itinerant peddling in the streets of municipalities is permitted, 'When regulation becomes destruction, it ceases to be regulation.' * * * A peddler's ordinance cannot be used by indirection to prevent the conduct of lawful business. * * * An ordinance will be invalidated purporting to regulate a lawful activity, where its purpose is 'to prohibit by onerous and exasperating restrictions, under the guise of regulation'. * * *"
> [Citations omitted.]

However, our separate research has disclosed a decision from the Supreme Court of Illinois (Good Humor Corp. v. Village of Mundelein, 33 Ill.2d 252, 211 N.E.2d 269, 14 A.L.R.3d 887.) where the court in a well reasoned opinion held an ordinance similar to the one before us valid.

We must apply the general rules to the facts and circumstances as they exist in this state and as they exist in the streets of our residential areas. The facts as they exist in a more heavily populated state might well justify a different conclusion than would be reached here.

* * *

We are forced to conclude that the business of huckstering and peddling may be controlled by reasonable regulations, and the absolute prohibition of such legitimate enterprises is arbitrary and unreasonable. The ordinance is therefore void.

The judgment is reversed and remanded to the trial court with instructions to enjoin the enforcement of the ordinance.

* * *

Notes

1. **Accord:** State v. Byrd, 259 N.C. 141, 130 S.E.2d 55 (1963) (nullifying prohibition of street sales of ice cream from mobile trucks); Frecker v. Dayton, 153 Ohio St. 14, 90 N.E.2d 851 (1950); but cf. Borough of Harrington Park v. Hogenbirk, 52 N.J.Super. 223, 145 A.2d 161 (1958) (upholding ban on use of streets for vending stands.) Authorities on the regulation of different forms of sale activity along public streets are collected in Annot: 14 A.L.R.3d 896 (Supp.1985).

2. **Solicitation Ordinances.** Municipal regulation of door-to-door solicitations has been narrowed by Supreme Court decisions to limited justified public purposes, by means that are the least intrusive upon First Amendment liberties. Village of Schaumberg v. Citizens for a Better Environment, 444 U.S. 620, 100 S.Ct. 826, 63 L.Ed.2d 73 (1980) (voided ordinance that barred door-to-door charitable solicitations). Accord: Connecticut Citizens Action Group v. Southington, 508 F.Supp. 43 (D.Conn. 1980) (ordinance limiting solicitation hours, from 8:00 a.m. to 6:00 p.m. held unconstitutionally overbroad). See also, Carey v. Brown, 447 U.S. 455, 100

S.Ct. 2286, 65 L.Ed.2d 263 (1980). Antisolicitation laws can be tailored to meet First Amendment limitations. See, e.g. Heffron v. International Society for Krishna Consciousness, 452 U.S. 640, 101 S.Ct. 2559, 69 L.Ed.2d 298 (1981) which upheld confinement of religious solicitations to a designated physical area of state fair grounds. These rulings require reevaluation of prior state court decisions.

Further problems arise where an ordinance exempts religious solicitations from bans on commercial solicitations. The Tenth Circuit has voided such an ordinance because it required the court to determine what is religious, and what is secular. Espinosa v. Rusk, 634 F.2d 477 (10th Cir. 1980). The vagaries of such a distinction are apparent from two other cases. In one the court found that solicitation of funds, accompanied by lollipops for companion children, constituted a "sale" within the ordinance ban; while another court reached the opposite conclusion where the solicitation was accompanied by an offer of flowers. Compare: People v. Wood, 93 Misc.2d 25, 402 N.Y.S.2d 726 (1978), with, Evans v. Fullard, 444 F.Supp. 1334 (W.D.Pa.1978).

Drafting problems are posed by suits that challenge antisolicitation ordinances as unconstitutionally vague, whether in their terms, or in their standards to guide licensing officials. An ordinance that barred door-to-door solicitation without a license which was to be granted whenever a municipal official found the solicitation to be "in the best interests" of the village was held void for vagueness. New York Public Interest Research Group v. Roslyn Estates, 498 F.Supp. 922 (E.D.N.Y.1979). Compare Village of Hoffman Est. v. Flipside, Hoffman Est., 455 U.S. 489, 102 S.Ct. 1186, 71 L.Ed.2d 362 (1982) (headshop licensing ordinance—held not vague).

3. **Area Zone Prohibitions.** The validity of specific area prohibitions turns on the reasonable relationship to public welfare. Compare Carter v. Palm Beach, 237 So.2d 130 (Fla.1970) (nullifying ban on surfboards from 13 mile stretch of town beaches) with McDonald v. Newsome, 437 F.Supp. 796 (E.D.N.C.1977) (upholding ordinance ban on surfboarding in coastal waters within 500 feet of fishing piers, and from waters designated by owners of riparian rights in such waters); Hass v. Kirkland, 78 Wash. 2d 929, 481 P.2d 9 (1971) (upholding ban against building locations on piers). See discussion of "adult" entertainment, ch. VI, §§ 363–365.

4. **Massage Parlors and the Constitution.** See Redwood Gym, p. 413, infra.

AMERICAN CIVIL LIBERTIES UNION OF WEST TENNESSEE, INC. v. CHANDLER

United States District Court, W.D. Tennessee, 1978.
458 F.Supp. 456.

ORDER ON APPLICATION FOR PRELIMINARY RELIEF

WELLFORD, DISTRICT JUDGE.

This is an action under 42 U.S.C.A. § 1983 for damages and injunctive relief arising out of a nighttime curfew imposed in the City of Memphis during August of 1978. Plaintiffs claim that the curfew and the City Ordinance upon which it is based, both on its face and as applied, deny their rights under the First Amendment, including travel, speech and assembly.

*   *   *

*   *   * Freedoms of travel and speech may be subject to reasonable limitations as to time and place, and under appropriate circumstances a nighttime curfew may be a lawful and effective means of controlling or preventing imminent civil disorder.

*   *   *

After carefully considering the pleadings, the proof adduced at the hearing of this matter, and the arguments of the parties, we have concluded that the extraordinary relief sought must be denied.

BACKGROUND

At approximately 11:00 p.m. on August 10, 1978, members of the Memphis Police Association, a union representing Memphis police officers, began a strike. *   *   *

On the morning of August 11, in response to the police strike, the threat of a firemen's strike, and the threat of serious public disorder, Mayor Wyeth Chandler proclaimed a state of civil emergency and imposed a general curfew between the hours of 8:00 p.m. and 6:00 a.m. The declared state of emergency and the curfew remain in effect, although the curfew has been modified to run from 10:00 p.m. until 6:00 a.m.

The instant action was brought by Mary Wilder and the American Civil Liberties Union of West Tennessee, Inc. on August 15. *   *   * It is their contention that the ordinance under which Chandler acted in imposing the curfew is unconstitutional on its face, and as applied, and that Chandler failed to act in accordance with the terms of the ordinance in proclaiming the emergency and ordering the curfew.

*   *   *

In considering an application for preliminary injunctive relief, the court must consider the degree of likelihood that the applicant will prevail at the plenary hearing on the merits. *   *   *

CONSTITUTIONALITY OF THE ORDINANCE ON ITS FACE

In declaring the civil emergency and imposing the curfew, the Mayor acted under Memphis City Code § 22–91 et seq. *   *   *

The exercise of the mayor's power to order curfews and other restrictions is limited to those instances in which he has proclaimed a civil emergency. In turn, the power to proclaim such emergencies is narrowly limited to situations involving riots or unlawful assemblies characterized by violence or an imminent threat of violence; extraordinary disasters; and instances where deliberate acts of destruction or personal injury pose a threat to the public at large.

While first amendment rights, *   *   * are accorded special protection, they are not absolute. The ordinance at issue here permits a limitation on the exercise of such rights only in very unusual circumstances where extreme action is necessary to protect the public from immediate and grave danger. Additionally, the ordinance is not designed to regulate in any way, nor would it appear to have the effect of regulating, the content of speech or other form of expression. Rather, it is a regulation of conduct, not designed to limit or control the expression of ideas, which unfortunately has an incidental impact on the exercise of first amendment rights.

The court considers it highly unlikely that the ordinance will ultimately be found unconstitutional on its face.

COMPLIANCE WITH THE ORDINANCE

Plaintiffs have contended that Chandler acted beyond his authority under the ordinance, in declaring a state of civil emergency and a curfew. We believe it likely that Chandler acted within his authority as mayor, under this ordinance.

Under § 22–91(a)(3), the mayor may declare a civil emergency when, in his judgment, the deliberate acts of one or more persons have caused property damage, death, or injury, and such acts constitute a threat to the peace of the public.

The police had begun their strike the night before Chandler issued his proclamation. On that night, the strikers had picketed several police stations. As patrolmen returned to the stations following the completion of their shifts, they joined the strikers. Access to the stations was blocked by police cars which were parked across driveways. These vehicles and others were disabled by the striking officers, who slashed tires, locked the keys to the vehicles in their trunks, and left lights and other electrical equipment on to run down batteries. The strikers also carried weapons, and threatened persons who attempted to cross their picket lines with bodily harm.

At the end of the night, roughly 950 policemen and sergeants were on strike. This left approximately 200 supervisory personnel and a handful of non-striking policemen to protect police stations and property, and to provide regular police protection for the City.

Additionally, on the morning of August 11, Chandler was aware of the threat of a renewed strike by Memphis firemen. During the first day of the firemen's earlier strike in July, 1978, over 200 fires occurred throughout Memphis. This number greatly exceeded the normal number of fires to be expected. These fires caused severe and widespread property damage.

We believe that the Mayor could have determined on August 11 that the acts of the striking policemen * * * would leave Memphis with entirely inadequate police protection, and that this situation could be expected to lead to virtually unrestrained criminal activities throughout the City. Additionally, we believe that * * * he could also have considered a variety of other factors, such as the possibility of a firemen's strike with consequences as severe as those of the July strike, in deciding whether to exercise his emergency and curfew powers.

Under the facts recited above, we also consider it quite likely that Chandler could have acted within the terms of § 22–91(a)(1).   *   *   *

CONSTITUTIONALITY OF THE ORDINANCE AS APPLIED

There can be no question that, in ordinary circumstances, the imposition of a general curfew would unconstitutionally abridge rights guaranteed by the first amendment. The circumstances presented in this care are clearly not ordinary circumstances.   *   *   *

As noted above, the situation which the City faced on August 1 was a grave one.   *   *   *

*   *   *

Certainly on the present record, we may conclude that there was a factual basis for Chandler's decision.   *   *   * It would appear to be without dispute that the Mayor acted in good faith in ordering the curfew. There is no indication that the curfew was imposed for any reason other than to maintain order.

*   *   *

The only remaining consideration is whether the curfew has been imposed in the least restrictive manner necessary to preserve order. We note that the curfew has been imposed only during nighttime hours, when the most serious threat of crime and violence is present. As conditions have allowed, the City has modified the curfew hours so as to make them less restrictive.   *   *   *

While the curfew which has been imposed is a drastic measure, the court cannot say at this time that a less restrictive measure would be sufficient to counter the grave dangers presented.

For all the foregoing reasons, we believe it likely that the curfew will not be found an unconstitutional application of the ordinance.

*   *   *

CONCLUSION

Having considered all the foregoing, it is the opinion of the court that the issuance of the preliminary injunctive relief sought by the plaintiffs would constitute an abuse of our equitable powers. The motions for a temporary restraining order or a preliminary injunction are accordingly denied.

Notes

1. **Curfew Laws.** Judicial treatment of emergency curfew proclamations has varied. A curfew imposed by the Commissioner for the District of Columbia was upheld as not violating constitutional rights of speech, assembly and travel, notwithstanding lack of Congressional authorization, when imposed to prevent imminent disorder. Glover v. District of Columbia, 250 A.2d 556 (D.C.App.1969). Cf. Ervin v. State, 41 Wis.2d 194, 163 N.W.2d 207 (1968). (Mayoral curfew proclamation, as authorized by state

statute—upheld). But see Walsh v. River Rouge, 385 Mich. 623, 189 N.W. 2d 318 (1971) which nullified an emergency curfew by the mayor on finding that the state law vested such power exclusively in the state Governor. The authorities on curfew statutes, ordinances and proclamations are collected in Annot., 59 A.L.R.3d 321 (1974).

    2. **Juvenile Curfews.** Curfew restrictions that are not based upon a present or imminent emergency have not been extensively litigated, but also raise constitutional issues; "Although juvenile curfew ordinances are fairly common, only three federal cases to our knowledge have confronted the constitutionality of such ordinances. See Naprstek v. City of Norwich, 545 F.2d 815 (2d Cir.1976); McCollester v. City of Keene, 514 F.Supp. 1046 (D.N.H.1981); Bykofsky v. Borough of Middletown, 401 F.Supp. 1242 (M.D. Pa.1975), aff'd mem., 535 F.2d 1245 (3d Cir.), cert. denied 429 U.S. 964, 97 S.Ct. 394, 50 L.Ed.2d 333 (1976)." Johnson v. Opelousas, 658 F.2d 1065 at 1071 (5th Cir.1981). *Johnson* voided the ordinance as unnecessarily overbroad in its coverage, though it recognized that a narrowly drawn curfew for juveniles might pass muster. But see, People v. Chambers, 66 Ill.2d 36, 4 Ill.Dec. 308, 360 N.E.2d 55 (1976) which sustained a juvenile curfew ordinance against an overbreadth challenge.

C. ADMINISTRATIVE REGULATIONS— LICENSES AND PERMITS

    "The requirement that a license be obtained before conducting business or activity has long been recognized as a valid exercise of the police power." Sunset Amusement Co. v. Board of Police Com'rs, of L.A., 7 Cal.3d 64, 101 Cal.Rptr. 768, 496 P.2d 840, 845 (1972). Licensing laws and regulations may be designed to achieve a number of related police power objectives. By controlling performance of designated activity, they prohibit unlawful and unsafe practices. By prescribing examination and eligibility requirements for occupations, they insure competent products and services. By registering pertinent information on licensees, they facilitate enforcement. By providing inspections and legal sanctions, they induce compliance. By providing fair procedures of notice and hearing, they assure minimal constitutional due process. By levying license fees, they generate funds for the costs of regulation, or for general public revenue, or for both.

BELLEVILLE CHAMBER OF COMMERCE v. BELLEVILLE

Supreme Court of New Jersey, 1968.
51 N.J. 153, 238 A.2d 181.

    PER CURIAM. In 1964 the Town of Belleville adopted an ordinance which required that most local retail trades and services be licensed annually to do business in the community. The ordinance contemplated that an application for license could be denied (1) where the applicant failed to satisfy the Town's zoning ordinance, sanitary code, building code or fire prevention code or (2) where the applicant's

Provisions of the Ordinance

character, background or demeanor were such as to lead the Town to the finding that he was not qualified to conduct the particular trade or service. The ordinance was attacked in the Law Division by the Chamber of Commerce and some merchants. * * *

Ordinance attacked

An appeal to the Appellate Division was taken by the Town. * * * In the first place, it disagreed with the Law Division's view that the licensing ordinance could not set forth standards or conditions based on compliance with the Town's zoning ordinance and building, sanitary and fire codes. It saw no reason why the licensing ordinance could not lawfully provide for inspections designed to insure that other local ordinances and codes were being fully complied with or why the costs of such inspections should not be provided for by the imposition of reasonable charges or fees under the licensing ordinance. 93 N.J. Super. 392 at p. 398, 226 A.2d 23. We consider the Appellate Division's position in this regard as eminently sound * * *.

Appellate Division first holding

Secondly, the Appellate Division found that the record did not establish that the fees set forth in the ordinance were unreasonable or discriminatory as to any individual plaintiff. 93 N.J.Super. at p. 402, 226 A.2d 23. We subscribe to that finding although we do so without prejudice to any later proceeding by an applicant or licensee who seeks to establish, upon a more complete and individualized showing, that a particular fee is unreasonable or discriminatory as applied to his own situation. The record indicates that * * * all of the license fees collected amounted to merely $18,818 and that this amount probably did not cover the full costs of the various inspections made under the ordinance. As the Appellate Division correctly found, the total income from the licenses was at least "reasonably related to the expense of administration and regulation of the licensed businesses as a whole" (93 N.J.Super. at p. 401, 226 A.2d at p. 28) and was well within the bounds of the judicial precedents. [Citations omitted] * * *

Appellate Division Second holding

Actions not barred by this holding

Thirdly, the Appellate Division properly rejected the Law Division's holding that the ordinance could not apply to automobile dealers, automobile service stations and coal dealers because they were licensed by the State. 93 N.J.Super. at p. 404, 226 A.2d 23. We find nothing incompatible in the particular State and municipal licensing requirements nor do we find anything in any of the pertinent State licensing enactments which suggests a legislative intent to preempt the field entirely. [Citations omitted]

Appellate Division Third Holding

We granted the plaintiffs' application for certification (49 N.J. 363, 230 A.2d 396 (1967)), not because we had any doubts as to the soundness of the Appellate Division's judgment, but because we were disturbed by the sweep and obscurities of the ordinance provisions relating to the applicant's background, character and demeanor. * * * Many cases may be found upholding municipal requirements for character and background approvals as conditions precedent to municipal licenses for the conduct of local businesses; but each of those cases dealt with an individual type of business whose nature made it evident that the

Why Ct took the appeal

approval was appropriate for the protection or advancement of the public health, safety, morals or general welfare. * * *

* * * Other cases in our State and elsewhere have similarly recognized the validity of character and background requirements in selective ordinances regulating junkyards, taxicabs, auctions, bowling alleys, taverns, and other highly regulable fields of activity. [Citations omitted] But none of the cited holdings goes so far as to suggest that such requirements may be imposed universally on all local trades; and to the contrary there have been many instances in which courts have stricken legislative attempts to impose such requirements on businesses deemed to be innocuous and substantially unrelated to the public welfare. [Citations omitted]

* * * However we consider it inappropriate that the matter be pursued here since the record does not deal individually with or shed individual light on any of the named businesses, and the briefs deal not at all or only superficially with the controlling legal issue. * * *

Affirmed but without prejudice

On the limited record and issues submitted to us by the parties, the judgment of the Appellate Division must of course be affirmed but without prejudice to any later proceeding and supportive showing by an applicant or licensee who considers himself individually aggrieved by the terms of the ordinance. In the meantime the Town might be well advised to reconsider its ordinance in the light of this opinion and the authorities it cites. In any redraft, particular care should be taken to describe those individual trades and services which are deliberately found to warrant character and background requirements and to set forth, along with adequate provision for hearing, suitable standards in detailed and informative terminology. (Citations omitted)

Affirmed.

STATE v. SCHMIDT

Supreme Court of Minnesota, 1968.
280 Minn. 281, 159 N.W.2d 113.

OTIS, JUSTICE. This is an appeal from a conviction for violating an ordinance of the city of Brainerd requiring transient merchants to obtain a permit to do business in that city and requiring nonresidents to post a bond. The issue is whether such an ordinance is valid. We hold it is not.

The facts are not in dispute. Defendant, Robert Theodore Schmidt, is a resident of St. Cloud, * * *. He is employed by Wearever Aluminum Inc. of New Kensington, Pennsylvania, to solicit orders for the sale of cooking utensils in the city of Brainerd and in ten other Minnesota communities. Defendant was charged by the city of Brainerd with having made sales * * * in violation of Ordinance No. 469, * * *. The municipal court of Brainerd found defendant guilty and imposed a sentence of $50 or 15 days. * * *

The trial court held that the discrimination between residents and nonresidents of Crow Wing County with respect to the bond requirement was proper because it protected citizens who deal with solicitors not otherwise amenable to suit in the same manner as resident salesmen. The court felt that a $250 bond was nominal and within the police power of the city to exact from nonresident solicitors. Minn.St. 437.02.

1. Because it denies defendant equal protection of the laws and imposes a burden on interstate commerce, we hold the ordinance unconstitutional. The city of Brainerd argues that the bond required of nonresidents by Section 7 of the ordinance is valid because it provides some financial security for Brainerd citizens in the event a dispute arises over sales consummated by a nonresident solicitor. Local solicitors, it is argued, are amenable to suit for breach of contract or fraud. * * * The fallacy of the city's argument lies in the assumption that salesmen living in Crow Wing County are necessarily solvent and financially responsible, whereas their counterparts in Benton County and elsewhere are more likely to be without assets from which to satisfy a judgment. The record does not support this assumption.

We have held in a number of cases that ordinances governing itinerant merchants and transient vendors cannot be sustained if they do not apply equally to residents and nonresidents of the municipality. * * *

In so far as the ordinance directs that a bond shall be exacted from all but residents of Crow Wing County, we have no difficulty in applying the rule consistently followed and hold that the classification is arbitrary and unreasonable.

2. With respect to the effect of the ordinance on interstate commerce, the law is equally well settled. Beginning with Town of Green River v. Fuller Brush Co. (10 Cir.) 65 F.2d 112, 88 A.L.R. 177, state and Federal courts have been called on to review the validity of a great many "Green River" ordinances which prohibit or license house-to-house peddling. Prior to Green River, the United States Supreme Court in Real Silk Hosiery Mills v. City of Portland, 268 U.S. 325, 45 S.Ct. 525, 69 L.Ed. 982, held unconstitutional an ordinance requiring a peddler's bond where the ordinance did not discriminate against non-residents, but provided for both a license and a bond from all house-to-house solicitors. This, the United States Supreme Court held, imposed an unconstitutional burden on interstate commerce. * * *

* * * The defendant here does business in at least 11 Minnesota communities. To require him to apply for a permit, undergo an investigation by the chief of police, and post a bond in each community would be an intolerable and unreasonable imposition on the operation of a legitimate business. Defendant does not object to registering and furnishing each community with complete information regarding his business, his background, and his method of operation. We agree that such an ordinance would be valid. So too would a statute requiring a

statewide bond and license. But, for the reasons we have stated, the present ordinance of the city of Brainerd cannot be sustained.

Nor does Section 12, authorizing applications for relief from the effect of the ordinance, preserve its validity. In our opinion the process of applying to the city council, undergoing an investigation, and taking the necessary steps to persuade the city to relieve the applicant of the necessity for otherwise complying with the ordinance, are burdens which are as vexatious as the procedures which the applicant would thereby seek to avoid.

Reversed.

Note

Accord: City of Racine v. Weyhe, 241 Wis. 133, 5 N.W.2d 747 (1942) (license fee of $10 per day upon itinerant photographers nullified).

The legality of placing a quota on licenses for particular activities is not subject to a flat rule. In Kipperman v. Markham, 47 Ill.2d 285, 265 N.E.2d 166 (1970), the denial of a realtor's license, because the number of licenses authorized by the ordinance had been issued, was held improper. The court distinguished cases which permitted such a limitation Strub v. Deerfield, 19 Ill.2d 401, 167 N.E.2d 178 (1960), held that the municipality could limit the number of persons licensed to conduct scavenger operations, and Yellow Cab Co. v. Chicago, 396 Ill. 388, 71 N.E.2d 652 (1947) held that the city could limit the number of taxicab licenses issued. The scavenger case involved matters directly and intimately related, and like the taxicab case, it involved the use of public streets for private gain. See City of Chicago v. Vokes, 28 Ill.2d 475, 479, 193 N.E.2d 40 (1963).

1. DUAL REGULATION

MOGOLEFSKY v. SCHOEM

Supreme Court of New Jersey, 1967.
50 N.J. 588, 236 A.2d 874.

HALL, J. The plaintiffs are real estate salesmen duly licensed by the New Jersey Real Estate Commission. * * * One of its methods of securing residential property to sell is to have its salesman go from house to house in a community, without prior invitation or appointment, soliciting sales listings. While so doing * * * plaintiffs were arrested for violating the city's ordinance regulating canvassers and solicitors, * * *. Admittedly the plaintiffs had not obtained or even applied for such permits.

During the pendency of the charges * * * plaintiffs instituted the first-captioned action * * * to have the ordinance declared null and void * * *. The theory was that the state had preempted all regulation of real estate brokers and salesmen by the enactment of the statute providing for the licensing of such persons at the state level. N.J.S.A.

45:15–1, *et seq.* They do not contend that the city's ordinance is invalid *per se* * * *.

The defendants, taking the view that the real estate license law did not in any way supersede the municipal power to regulate generally soliciting and canvassing, moved for summary judgment. * * *

Thereafter, the plaintiff Berman applied for a permit, offering to comply with all the requirements of the ordinance therefor. His application was rejected because of the violation complaint against him, * * *. Thereupon he commenced the second-captioned action * * * asking that the city be enjoined from the enforcement of the ordinance against him because the municipality arbitrarily refused to issue him a permit even if he fully complied with the ordinance. * * *

* * *

It is conceded that this kind of regulation, applying to all who seek to solicit the sale of goods and the furnishing of services from householders, without invitation or advance appointment * * *, is a valid exercise of the municipal police power. * * * In essence, the extent of the municipality's interest on behalf of its residents is that it, or some other governmental agency, has been satisfied of the moral character and business responsibility of those who ring doorbells for purposes of solicitation without advance invitation or appointment.

The New Jersey real estate license statute * * * represents a very salutary effort to upgrade on a state-wide basis the qualifications and quality of those who * * * act as agents in dealing with other people's property and frequently their funds. * * * There are both general and special educational requirements which must be met in advance, N.J.S.A. 45:15–9 and 10.1, and licensure is granted only upon successful passage of an examination administered by the Real Estate Commission * * *. All applicants must furnish satisfactory evidence of good moral character, N.J.S.A. 45:15–9, and are subject to license revocation, suspension or fine for many kinds of misconduct, N.J.S.A. 45:15–17, as well as to statutory penalties for violations of the act which the commission may sue for, N.J.S.A. 45:15–23. The statute, N.J.S.A. 45:15–12.1, makes it mandatory for the commission to refuse a license "to any person known by it to have been, within five years theretofore, convicted of forgery, embezzlement, obtaining money under false pretenses, extortion, criminal conspiracy to defraud, or other like offense or offenses", requires a revocation of a license already issued upon conviction in or outside of this state for any such offense during the license term, N.J.S.A. 45:15–19.1, and authorizes the suspension of a license upon indictment therefor pending the trial of the charge, N.J. S.A. 45:15–19.2. Each license must be renewed annually and we are advised the licensee is directed to disclose in his renewal application any pertinent events which have occurred during the license year.

* * *

It should also be mentioned that the commission does not issue any identification cards to licensees, so that a soliciting salesman or broker would have nothing authoritative to show householders or police evidencing that he held a state real estate license, if no municipal permit is to be allowed. * * *

We thoroughly agree with the Appellate Division that the state real estate license law does not preempt all exercise of municipal police power over licensees. While a municipality may not require a person to obtain a local license to carry on a business or profession when he has already been licensed under state law, Coculo v. City of Trenton, 85 N.J.Super. 523, 205 A.2d 340 (App.Div.1964), it may exercise appropriate police power over amenable aspects of the conduct of that business for the protection of purely local interests by general or specific local legislation. Chaiet v. City of East Orange, 136 N.J.L. 375, 56 A.2d 599 (Sup.Ct.1948). * * *

* * *

The Appellate Division concluded that the Clifton ordinance does infringe on the real estate license law in permitting the local chief of police to override the Real Estate Commission's implicit finding, in issuing a license, that the licensee is of satisfactory moral character and business responsibility. * * * We agree that the statute evidences a preemption by the state as to evaluation and conclusion with respect to that element.

* * *

In order to make a practical accommodation of the interests involved, we arrive at the following conclusion * * *.

A licensed real estate salesman or broker making uninvited personal solicitations for listings from residents is subject to Clifton's solicitor's ordinance applying to all engaging in that method of doing business * * *. He must apply for and obtain a permit and pay the $3.00 fee. The municipality may use its usual form of permit and a form of application therefor which does not go beyond the inquiries specified in the ordinance and may require the taking of fingerprints and a photograph. When such a person makes application, he should present proof that he is a licensed real estate salesman or broker. The municipality may investigate, promptly, to the extent of checking on the applicant's criminal record and may withhold issuance of the permit meanwhile. If that check is negative, the permit shall then issue forthwith. If the check discloses a criminal record, the municipal authorities shall be limited to reporting the same to the commission, along with any other related information known to them. The commission's obligation will then be to review such a report and decide whether it calls for any reconsideration of its prior finding of good moral character. If the report does not so dictate, the commission shall promptly so advise the municipality and the permit shall then issue at once. If the report does indicate the need for commission action, presumably by a proceeding to revoke, suspend or refuse to renew the license, the municipality shall be so advised and the permit may be withheld pending the outcome thereof.

We see no reason why the Clifton ordinance should not be so construed and applied * * *.

As far as the other aspects of the present litigation are concerned, we see no justification to deny permits for subsequent years to these plaintiffs because of any prior violation of the ordinance since we have considerably limited its requirements as to them. The second suit is now clearly moot. And it should go without saying that no convictions of them for violation of the ordinance (now pending on appeal in the Passaic County Court) can stand.

The judgment of the Appellate Division is accordingly modified and the cases are remanded to the Chancery Division for entry of judgments declaratory of the views herein expressed. * * *

* * *

Note

State Licensed Activity. While states may expressly prohibit a municipality from regulating anyone holding a state license or certificate (Boulevard Apts., Inc. v. Hasbrouch Hts., 111 N.J.Super. 408, 268 A.2d 359 (1970)), preemption or conflict with state law will not be implied from the bare fact of dual licensing. In the *Boulevard Apts.* decision the court carefully distinguished *Mogolefsky* by narrowly interpreting the exclusion of the preemption statute: "Of course, where the purpose and effect of the State and local licensing requirements are dissimilar, there is no parallel licensing within the ambit of N.J.S.A. 40:52–1." Id. at 416, 268 A.2d at 363.

TAMIAMI TRAIL TOURS, INC. v. ORLANDO

Supreme Court of Florida, 1960.
120 So.2d 170.

ROBERTS, JUSTICE. We are here concerned with the validity of an ordinance, * * * purporting to regulate the loading and unloading of freight within the city, in its application to the petitioners, * * * who are interstate common carriers operating in this state under certificates of public convenience and necessity issued to them by the Florida Railroad and Public Utilities Commission ("the Commission" hereafter). The ordinance in question requires the owner or operator of a truck or trucks using the freight loading and unloading zones established by the city on its streets to apply for a "tag permit" for each such truck. Application for the permit is made to the City Tax Collector, who issues the permit "upon the payment of Ten Dollars ($10.00) for the first permit issued to an applicant and One Dollar ($1.00) for each succeeding permit issued to the same applicant." The permit is good for one year, and application therefor must be made and a new permit issued each year for each such truck.

The basis of petitioners' complaint ✱ ✱ ✱ is that ✱ ✱ ✱ they are required to and do pay the mileage tax prescribed by § 323.15; and that under the express provisions of § 323.15, such mileage tax "shall be in lieu of all other taxes and *fees of every kind, character and description,* state, county or municipal, including excise and license taxes levied or imposed against such auto transporation companies, or the operation of such business and facilities thereof, or their property ✱ ✱ ✱." (Emphasis supplied.) ✱ ✱ ✱

✱ ✱ ✱

By petition for certiorari the petitioners contend that the decision of the appellate court is in direct conflict with the decision of this court in Mercury Cab Owners Association v. Miami Beach Air Transport, Inc., Fla.1955, 77 So.2d 837. In that case this court held that a carrier operating under a certificate of public convenience and necessity issued by the Commission could not be compelled to secure such a certificate from the City of Miami Beach as a condition to carrying on its operations within the city. ✱ ✱ ✱ It appears to be conceded that if the permit fee was, in fact, in the nature of a tax, it is violative of Ch. 323, *supra,* and rightly so. See Anderson v. Wentworth, 1918, 75 Fla. 300, 78 So. 265; Langston v. Lundsford, 1936, 122 Fla. 813, 165 So. 898.

Before discussing this question it should be noted that the petitioners are not objecting to the city's regulation of traffic under its police power by the establishment of freight zones, but merely to the imposition upon them of a fee for the use of such freight zones. They point out that ✱ ✱ ✱ the Legislature has provided for the payment by the State Comptroller from the mileage taxes collected from petitioners the sum of $25 annually to each city and town in which any such company maintains a depot, warehouse, station or agent; that each of them maintains a station in the City of Orlando; that the city has received annually this sum based upon each of their certificates; that, presumably, the Legislature considered this sum ample for the cost of any police or traffic regulation inuring to the benefit of the petitioners; and that, if this sum is in fact insufficient, the proper way to correct the insufficiency is by amendment of § 323.16(1), *supra.*

The conclusion is also irresistible that, if the City of Orlando can exact this type of fee from the petitioners, then all cities on the route of a carrier can repeat the procedure, thereby building up an overhead for the carrier that obviously was not contemplated in the rate fixed or approved for such carrier by the Commission.

Assuming, arguendo, however, that in the exercise of its police power to regulate and control traffic the city could enact a *licensing* ordinance regulating the operations of the petitioners for this purpose, the fact remains that the ordinance shows on its face that the requirement for the permit and fee has nothing whatsoever to do with regulating the loading and unloading of freight and/or traffic.

It is, of course, well settled that the power to regulate includes the power to license *as a means of regulating,* and that a reasonable license fee may be charged in an amount sufficient to bear "the expense of issuing the license and the cost of necessary inspection or police surveillance connected with the business or calling licensed, and all the incidental expenses that are likely to be imposed upon the public in consequence of the business licensed." State ex rel. Harkow v. McCarthy, 1936, 126 Fla. 433, 171 So. 314, 317. But it is only in those cases where regulation is the primary purpose of a licensing ordinance or statute that the exaction of a fee therefor can be especially referred to the police power. 2 Cooley on Taxation (3d ed.) p. 1127. And where a license is required and a fee exacted solely for revenue purposes and the payment of such fee gives the right to carry on the business without any further conditions, it is a tax. See Bateman v. City of Winter Park, 1948, 160 Fla. 906, 37 So.2d 362; 33 Am.Jur., Licenses, § 19, p. __.

Here, * * * the ordinance does not require that such zones be used for the loading and unloading of freight; it merely prohibits the use thereof without a "tag permit". No standards are prescribed by the guidance of the City Tax Collector in granting or denying a permit to use the freight zones—such standards being a *sine qua non* to the validity of a true regulatory licensing ordinance or statute. See State ex rel. Ware v. City of Miami, Fla.App.1958, 107 So.2d 387, and cases cited. Nor does it provide for any regulation of the licensee or "permittee", once the permit is issued, which is the usual concomitant of a license proper and one of the distinctions between a regulatory fee exacted under the police power and a tax. See Bateman v. City of Winter Park, *supra,* 37 So.2d 362. The permits are issued and the fee collected by the *City Tax Collector*—further confirmation, if confirmation were needed, that the fee is exacted solely for revenue purposes.
* * *

The conclusion is therefore inescapable that, insofar as its provisions relating to "tag permits" are concerned, the ordinance in question is naught but an attempt to impose an excise tax upon petitioners and others similarly situated, either for the privilege of using the city's freight zones or upon the operation of their business within the city. This it obviously cannot do, under the express provisions of Ch. 323, quoted above, and the decisions of this court first above cited. For decisions of other courts reaching the same conclusion in similar cases see Eastern Ohio Transport Corp. v. City of Wheeling, 1943, 115 W.Va. 293, 175 S.E. 219; City of Pineville v. Meeks, 1934, 254 Ky. 167, 71 S.W.2d 33; City of Phoenix v. Sun Valley Bus Lines, 1946, 64 Ariz. 319, 170 P.2d 289; Payne v. Massey, 1946, 145 Tex. 237, 196 S.W.2d 493.

The parking-meter decisions * * * are readily distinguishable. Ordinances providing for the establishment and maintenance of a parking-meter system of traffic control appear to be *sui generis,* since parking meters operate *per se* to "regulate traffic and keep such traffic as liquid as is reasonably possible." See State ex rel. Harkow v. McCarthy, 1936, 126 Fla. 433, 171 So. 314, 316. The deposit of the fee in the parking meter automatically licenses or permits the driver to use the metered parking space for the authorized number of minutes, and the parking meter acts as a mechanical policeman to monitor the use of the space. Thus, the parking meter fee is not merely an incident of and attributable to the "license" to use the parking space—the payment thereof operates as an integral and working part of the parking-meter system of traffic control. It is, literally, a "regulatory" fee, * * *. On the contrary, the requirement for the tag permit and fee made by the ordinance in question is not "regulatory" in any sense of the word, as shown above; and the only resemblance between a parking-meter fee and the "tag permit" fee here involved is that "those who enjoy the privilege" of parking in a metered space or a freight zone, pay for such privilege. Absent the primary purpose of regulation as in the case of the parking-meter fee, the exaction of the fee for use of the freight zone can be none other than a tax on such privilege. * * *

It might be noted that the petitioners do not contend that they may use the metered parking spaces available to the public as a whole without paying the parking-meter fee, and rightly so. * * * Similarly, petitioners could not avoid the payment of a toll for the use of a toll bridge or toll road exacted by the State from the public as a whole * * * In its commonly accepted sense a toll is "a proprietor's charge for the passage over a highway or bridge, exacted when and as the privilege of passage is exercised," Carley & Hamilton v. Snook, 1930, 281 U.S. 66, 50 S.Ct. 204, 207, 74 L.Ed. 704; and since such a toll would be exacted by the State on behalf of the true proprietors—the unpaid bondholders—we do not conceive it to be a "license, fee or tax" in lieu of which the auto mileage tax is imposed upon petitioners. *Cf.* Cahoon v. Smith, 1930, 99 Fla. 1174, 128 So. 632.

For the reasons stated above, the decision of the District Court of Appeal here reviewed is quashed with directions to reverse the decree of the trial court and remand the cause to the trial court for the entry of a decree in accordance with this opinion.

Note

Partial and Selective Preemption. *Tamiami* and *Mogolefsky* illustrate how the overlap of state and local regulations may be partially consistent and partially inconsistent. Since legislatures cannot predict or prescribe the precise bounds of inconsistent overlap, courts etch out the area of partial or selective preemption by individual decisions.

2. REVENUE AND REGULATORY CHARGES

WEBER BASIN HOME BUILDERS ASSOCIATION v. ROY CITY

Supreme Court of Utah, 1971.
26 Utah 2d 215, 487 P.2d 866.

CROCKETT, JUSTICE. Weber Basin Home Builders, land developers, sought a declaratory judgment that an ordinance adopted by Roy City in 1968 increasing its building permit fee by $100 was ultra vires, discriminatory and unconstitutional. There was no dispute as to the facts. * * * the court sustained the plaintiff's contentions. Defendant appeals.

* * * Prior to the enactment of this ordinance the building permit charge for a single family dwelling was a flat fee of $12 plus two cents for each square foot of dwelling and garage or carport. The ordinance added $100 to the flat fee, so that it is now $112.

The City has made no claim * * * that a major purpose of the increase was to bring the permit fee in line with the costs of regulating building construction. On the contrary, it is conceded that the purpose was to obtain additional money for the City's general fund; * * *. The City does contend that the collection of this additional money is necessary to improve its water and sewer systems because of the construction of new homes.

As a prefatory foundation to considering the problem presented in this case it is appropriate to have in mind that there is a distinction between the authority of a city to charge a fee for the granting of a license or a permit to carry on business therein, and the authority to impose a tax. How such exactions should be classified depends upon their purpose. If the money collected is for a license to engage in a business and the proceeds therefrom are purposed mainly to service, regulate and police such business or activity, it is regarded as a license fee. On the other hand, if the factors just stated are minimal, and the money collected is mainly for raising revenue for general municipal purpose, it is properly regarded as the imposition of a tax, and this is so regardless of the terms used to describe it. In some states where the power granted cities does not expressly authorize the collection of a license fee for the purpose of raising revenue generally, the courts have held that the charge for such licensing must bear some reasonable relationship to the cost of regulating the business so licensed. It is reasoned that even though license fees sufficient to cover such costs are a necessary concomitant of the police power, fees in excess thereof are in reality a form of taxation, which may not be imposed by the city without express authorization of the legislature.[4]

It is to be recognized that there are situations where the ordinance is neither completely fish nor fowl, as coming within either of the above mentioned classifications, but is a hybrid in that it partakes of both. That appears to be the situation found in the ordinance here in question. It is justified under our Utah law, due to the particular wording of our statute, and previous decisions based thereon.

Sec. 10–8–80, U.C.A.1953, provides:

> "*License fees and taxes. They* [cities] *may raise revenue* by levying and collecting a license fee or tax on any business within the limits of the city, and regulate the same by ordinance; * * *. All such license fees and taxes shall be uniform in respect to the class upon which they are imposed."

4. See, *e.g.*, Merrelli v. City of St. Clair Shores, 355 Mich. 575, 96 N.W.2d 144; Daniels v. Borough of Point Pleasant, 23 N.J. 357, 129 A.2d 265; generally, 51 Am. Jur.2d, Licenses and Permits, Sec. 113.

Some years ago in the case of Ogden City v. Crossman [5] in construing a predecessor statute whose relevant parts are the same as Sec. 10–8–80, this court upheld a $5 annual license tax on each telephone within the city against the challenge that it was an illegal attempt to raise revenue under the guise of the police power. The court said:

"* * * Under the circumstances, where, by the constitution and statute, express authority is given to raise revenue by levying and collecting a license fee or tax upon any private corporation or business within the limits of the city, and regulate the same by ordinance, *it is held that the municipality is not limited to the mere expense of the regulation, but that it may impose a reasonable license tax for the purpose of obtaining revenue necessary to meet the general expenses of such municipality.* But the state [city] could not, under such circumstances, impose a license tax beyond the necessities of the city, nor one so excessive as to prohibit or destroy the occupation or business upon which it is imposed. * * *"

Consistent with the rationale of the Crossman case is Davis v. Ogden City [6] wherein we held that Sec. 10–8–80 empowered a city to impose and collect a license fee on the business of practicing law, even though the city is without power to regulate such practice.

* * * it is not now open to question that in our state a city may impose and collect a license fee on business operated therein, both for the purpose of regulation and of raising revenue for general municipal purposes. However, whether it be regarded as a license fee, or as a tax, or as a mixture of the two, it cannot be imposed in any such manner as to violate constitutional principles, which include equal and nondiscriminatory treatment and protection under the law.[8]

The critical question here is whether the ordinance in its practical operation results in an unjust discrimination by imposing a greater burden of the cost of city government on one class of persons as compared to another, without any proper basis for such differentiation and classification. It is not to be doubted that each new residence has its effect in increasing the cost of city government; nor that due to the steadily increasing costs of everything, * * *, the city would have authority to raise the fees charged for such services from time to time. Nevertheless, in that connection, the new residents are entitled to be treated equally and on the same basis as the old residents.

Similar in principle is the case of Daniels v. Borough of Point Pleasant, wherein the New Jersey court in striking down the same kind of ordinance, speaking through Chief Justice Vanderbilt, stated:

What the Borough * * * is attempting to do here is to defray the general cost of government under the guise of reimbursement for the special services * * *. The philosophy of this ordinance is that the tax rate of the Borough should remain the same *and the new people*

---

5. 17 Utah 66, 53 P. 985.

6. 117 Utah 315, 215 P.2d 616, 223 P.2d 412, 16 A.L.R.2d 1208.

8. See Secs. 2 and 7, Art. I, Utah Const.; Amdt. XIV, U.S.Const.

coming into the municipality should bear the burden of the increased costs of their presence. This is so totally contrary to tax philosophy as to require it to be stricken down.

Under the undisputed facts as presented to the trial court: * * * it was his opinion that the increase placed a disproportionate and unfair burden on new households in Roy City, as compared to the old ones, * * *; and that consequently it was discriminatory and constitutionally impermissible. We are not disposed to disagree with that conclusion. (All emphasis added.)

Affirmed. * * *

Notes

1. In Boulevard Apartments, Inc. v. Hasbrouck Hts., 111 N.J.Super. 408, 268 A.2d 359 (1970) (also decided on preemption grounds) the court held an annual licensing fee of $10 per unit in multiple dwellings presumptively valid, and that the licensee had the burden of proving that it was unreasonable or prohibitive. Quoting from Country Farms, Bellington v. East Windsor, 17 N.J. 558, 566, 112 A.2d 268, 273 (1955), the court stated: "A tax complementing the license fee proper is legally sufficient if it be reasonably related to the value of the public services and facilities offered the users of the regulated areas and the benefits of the regulations themselves and the consequent government supervision and control, and thus a correlated exercise of both the police and the taxing powers conformably to the statutory grant." Id. at 413, 268 A.2d at 361. "Any excess over the cost of regulation would have to be reasonably related to the value of various public services and facilities afforded plaintiffs." Id. at 414, 268 A.2d at 362. Is the stated burden of proof impractical if not impossible for small licensees; or even for large licensed operations?

2. **Classification of Levies.** Where a municipality is not given coextensive powers to levy both regulatory and general revenue charges upon the same subject, the classification of the levy can be crucial. In City of Richmond Heights v. LoConti, 19 Ohio App.2d 100, 250 N.E.2d 84 (1969), the court nullified a flat annual license charge of $100 on juke box distributors as being out of proportion to any regulatory burden created by the licensed activity. See also Eugene Theatre Co. v. Eugene, 194 Or. 603, 243 P.2d 1060 (1962).

PATRICK v. FRANKFORT

Supreme Court of Kentucky, 1976.
539 S.W.2d 275.

STERNBERG, JUSTICE.

This is an action by employees of the United States of America challenging the validity of the Frankfort, Kentucky, occupational tax ordinance (Frankfort Ordinance No. 23, 1971 Series, Sec. 2(a)). The questioned ordinance provides as follows:

"5.04.020 Occupational License Fee.

"(a) Every person, * * * in any occupation, business, trade, profession or other activity in the city shall pay unto the city treasury * * * an *annual occupational* and business *license fee* for the privilege of engaging in said activities, which license fee shall be *measured by* one per cent *of the net annual salaries or wages* earned by any licensee so compensated for work done * * * or rendered within the city and the net profits, per annum, of all licensees who are engaged in business from that portion of such business conducted in the city." (Emphasis added).

There are two issues presented by appellants, which are (1) does the ordinance levy an income tax in contravention of Section 181 of the Kentucky Constitution, and (2) does the ordinance impose a fee on the privilege of being employed by the United States of America?

The sources from whence cometh the authority of the City of Frankfort to levy an occupational tax are Section 181 of the Kentucky Constitution and KRS 92.281.

Appellants allege that the subject tax is in truth and fact an income tax, that an income tax is an excise tax, and that Section 181 of the Kentucky Constitution forbids the levy of such an excise tax by the city. They thus conclude that the tax is in violation of Section 181 of the Kentucky Constitution and therefore void. On the other hand, the city contends that the tax is a license tax levy against the privilege to engage in occupations, trades, professions, and businesses within the city limits of Frankfort and that a license tax is a permissible form of excise tax levy, the amount of tax being determined by applying the rate against the net salary or wages.

The issues are not new or novel, but do require a review and analysis of what has heretofore been written. * * * In City of Louisville v. Sebree, 308 Ky. 420, 214 S.W.2d 248, the Court of Appeals had before it an ordinance which imposed an annual tax or license fee for the privilege of engaging in any business, occupation, calling, profession, or labor within the city. In the course of the opinion, it is stated:

* * *

"Since a municipality's power to tax is only that which the legislature has granted it, and the legislature in granting the power must conform to constitutional limitations, we must first look to the authority of the Board of Aldermen for the particular action taken here.

Section 181 of the Constitution provides that the General Assembly may 'delegate the power to * * * cities * * * to impose and collect license fees on * * * franchises, trades, occupations and professions.' "

KRS 92.281 authorized cities of all classes to levy and collect any and all taxes provided for in Section 181 of the Kentucky Constitution. In City of Louisville v. Sebree, supra, the court went on to say:

"The principal storm center of the controversy, as we have said, is whether or not this ordinance imposes an income tax, the taxpayers' argument being that the city has no authority to levy such a tax. We need not pass upon the question of the existence or absence of that power.

Confusion in the case may arise from placing so much emphasis on the measure of the tax as to subordinate or lose sight of its true character. * * *."

* * *

In analyzing the type of tax presented in the Louisville ordinance, the court said:

"* * * The definition or classification may be a matter of approach or point of view. * * * The psychological impact loses force when emphasis is placed on what is made subject to taxation rather than on the measure of the tax and the basis of computation. Or if the word 'receipts', which, in truth, is the more appropriate term, be used instead of 'income.' If graduated stated sums had been provided instead of a per centum of receipts or net profits, the source of such sums would in all probability have been the same. And that way of fixing the tax could scarcely be regarded as illegal. * * *"

After its analysis, the court concluded:

"We, therefore, hold the tax is not an income tax and that its imposition is within the powers of the city of Louisville."

* * *

In Sims v. Board of Education of Jefferson County, Ky., 290 S.W.2d 491, the Court of Appeals had before it House Bill 404 of the regular session of the 1956 General Assembly, which authorized a Board of Education containing a city of the first class to impose occupational license fees not exceeding one-half of one percent on wages, salaries, and other earnings of individuals and on net profits of businesses. Objection was made that the Act violated Section 181 of our Kentucky Constitution in that it authorized cities to levy income taxes. In the course of the opinion the court said:

"* * * While it is true that the amount of the license fee each individual and each company must pay is measured by the income earned by those taxpayers and, therefore, the tax has some of the attributes of an income tax, the question is no longer an open one. * * *"

It will be noted that the ordinance under attack in the instant case is substantially the same as those that have heretofore come before the Court of Appeals and which were discussed in City of Louisville v. Sebree, supra: [citation] and Sims v. Board of Education of Jefferson County, Ky., supra. The genius of the times will not permit this court to do other than to affirm the holdings in those cases.

Next, we turn our attention to the second issue raised by appellants, and that is that the ordinance attempts to impose a fee for the privilege of being employed by the United States of America.

In Howard v. Commissioners of the Sinking Fund, 344 U.S. 624, 73 S.Ct. 465, 97 L.Ed. 617, the Supreme Court of the United States had before it the identical question now presented. * * *

* * *

"* * * In the instant case, the Kentucky Court of Appeals correctly stated that the question was whether the tax was an income tax within the meaning of the federal law. We hold that the tax authorized by this ordinance was an income tax within the meaning of the Buck Act. The City, it is conceded, can levy such a tax within its boundaries outside the federal area. By virtue of the Buck Act, the tax can be levied and collected within the federal area, just as if it were not a federal area."

Howard v. Commissioners of the Sinking Fund, supra, is dispositive of the other issue raised on this appeal.

We hold that the challenged Frankfort, Kentucky, ordinance is a levy of such a license fee that is not prohibited by the Kentucky Constitution. Further, we hold that the appellants are subject to the tax the same as if they were not federal employees.

The judgment is affirmed.

* * *

Notes

1. **Contra:** In Board of Trustees, Minturn v. Foster Lumber Co., Inc., 190 Colo. 479, 548 P.2d 1276 (1976), the Supreme Court of Colorado, contrary to the principal case, held that a two percent tax on all construction businesses and occupations was an unauthorized "income tax" although denominated an occupation tax in the town ordinance. Compare the *Weeks* case, p. 120, *supra,* which dealt with business receipts taxes.

2. On the possible distinctions between occupation taxes and regulatory fees, see City of Richmond v. Fary, 210 Va. 338, 171 S.E.2d 257 (1969); City & County of Denver v. Duffy Storage & Moving Co., 168 Colo. 91, 450 P.2d 339 (1969).

3. REFUSAL, SUSPENSION, AND REVOCATION

MIDWEST TEEN CENTERS, INC. v. ROSEVILLE
Court of Appeals of Michigan, 1971.
36 Mich.App. 627, 193 N.W.2d 906.

LESINSKI, CHIEF JUDGE. Plaintiff, Midwest Teen Centers, Inc., brought this action for money damages against defendant City of Roseville, a municipal corporation, alleging wrongful revocation of a dance hall permit. The trial court, * * * granted defendant's motion for summary judgment * * *. Plaintiff appeals as of right.

* * *

On October 9, 1968, the Roseville City Council revoked this permit. Plaintiff contends that the defendant failed to follow the procedure outlined in condition 19 for the revocation of this permit, and in so doing denied plaintiff due process of law.

Plaintiff claims that this permit was a contract between itself and defendant, and when defendant violated condition 19 it entitled plaintiff to money damages resulting from the wrongful revocation.

Our examination of the law in this case has failed to reveal any authority whatsoever that would establish that this permit is a contract. * * *

The granting of this dance hall permit was clearly an exercise of the City of Roseville's police power. There is no evidence of any consideration running from plaintiff to defendant which is a basic ingredient of any contract. Payment of a simple license or permit fee is not such consideration as will support the existence of a contractual relationship. There is no indication that this permit was anything more than a written promise to enjoy the privilege of operating a teen club, in Roseville, on the terms named for the period specified, subject to the City's absolute right to revoke this privilege, pursuant to the procedure in condition 19. * * *

The fact that this Court has determined that this permit is in actuality a license in no way detracts from plaintiff's right to have procedural due process observed in its revocation. * * *

In Eastwood Park Amusement Co. v. Mayor of East Detroit, *supra,* 325 Mich. at 72, 38 N.W.2d 77, the Michigan Supreme Court again reiterated a licensee's right to procedural due process in the revocation of his license. * * *

On appeal from the grant of defendant's motion for summary judgment, we must accept as true all of plaintiff's material allegations of fact. [Citations omitted] On this basis the record would indicate that the plaintiff was afforded none of the procedural safeguards outlined by the Michigan Supreme Court in the Prawdzik and Eastwood Park Amusement Co. cases.

* * *

Notes

1. **Due Process and Damages.** An omitted portion of the above case, denying damages for denial of due process, has been rendered obsolete by later developments in federal remedies under federal civil rights statutes. See, e.g., the *Carey* case, ch. 11, p. 982, infra.

2. **Revocation.** Generally speaking, the power to revoke a license may be exercised, inter alia, for the same reasons and on the same grounds

that support an initial denial of a license. See O'Bar v. Rainbow County, 269 Ala. 247, 112 So.2d 790 (1959) (revocation of night club license).

3. **Suspension.** Licensing boards have discretion as to the length of suspensions for infractions of license regulations, and will be upheld so long as they do not act arbitrarily. Bearden Co. v. Tulsa, 471 P.2d 449 (Okl. 1970).

WEST GALLERY CORP. v. SALT LAKE CITY BD. OF COMMISSIONERS

Supreme Court of Utah, 1978.
586 P.2d 429.

HALL, JUSTICE:

This appeal concerns a single issue of constitutional law: Does a Salt Lake City licensing ordinance which permits the City to suspend an adult theatre license if the licensee violates the City's obscenity ordinance during the license term infringe upon rights of free speech guaranteed by the constitutions of the United States and the State of Utah? It is noteworthy that we are not called upon to discuss any issue of procedural due process or improper breadth of administrative discretion. Plaintiff-Appellant asserts that since the ordinance provides for license revocation as a consequence of obscenity ordinance violation it is an unconstitutional interference with freedom of speech.

* * *

Examination of the pronouncements of the federal judiciary, and particularly the Supreme Court, does not lead to the conclusion that prior restraint, as a means of controlling *obscenity,* is constitutionally unacceptable. The initial case on the point is Near v. Minnesota [4] which dealt with a State's attempt to enjoin the continued publication of a periodical which had, from its inception, been loaded with scandalous and libelous statements about public officials and others. * * * In Times Film Corp. v. Chicago,[5] the court interpreted the quoted language of *Near,* as we do now, to permit the imposition of previous restraint in the control of obscenity under certain circumstances.

Gallery argues that the use of the licensing authority to punish individuals for past crimes is somehow abhorrent to constitutional principles. We do not see that the license suspension under review is primarily a punishment for past crimes. It is rather a means of assuring that the people who make the initial decision about the display of erotic films are not people who have already demonstrated an insensitivity to the statutory criteria for acceptability. A license is a privilege, not a right, and the licensing authority can and has been used to deter misconduct, even where freedom of speech is involved. A prominent example thereof is the longstanding practice of revoking various professional licenses for misconduct.

---

4. 283 U.S. 697, 51 S.Ct. 625, 75 L.Ed. 1357 (1931).

5. 365 U.S. 43, 81 S.Ct. 391, 5 L.Ed.2d 403 (1961).

The States have traditionally used licensing authority to control protest demonstrations and parades, activity which clearly falls within First Amendment shelter.

* * *

On the question of whether the interests of the public require interference with the business of exhibiting motion pictures, the U.S. Supreme Court has recently declared that the threat of public exposure to obscene movies can be found to "endanger the public safety." In Paris Adult Theatre v. Slaton,[8] the court said:

"The States have the power to make a morally neutral judgment that public exhibition of obscene material, or commerce in such material, has a tendency to injure the community as a whole, to endanger the public safety, or to jeopardize, in Chief Justice Warren's words, the States' 'right * * * to maintain a decent society.'"

The City can constitutionally make and has made a judgment that the exhibition of obscene motion pictures endangers the public safety; and the police power is invoked, in the classic phrase, to protect "the public health, safety and welfare."

On the question of whether the means (suspension of license for violation of obscenity ordinance) is reasonably necessary for accomplishment of the purpose, there are two federal cases which are relevant. In Times Film Corp. v. Chicago, supra, the court, in upholding an ordinance which required an applicant for a movie license to submit a copy of each film to the police commissioner for preview, said "it is not for the court to limit the State in its selection of the remedy it deems most effective to cope with such a problem."

In 106 Forsyth Corp. v. Bishop,[9] a license suspension was upheld as an appropriate remedy under circumstances substantially the same as those before the court now. The Supreme Court denied certiorari. No other federal appellate decisions appear to be on point.

We do not perceive that every citizen has the unrestricted right to operate an adult theatre, or, indeed, to speak his mind without restriction reasonably related to protection of coordinate public rights. We hold that the license suspension under scrutiny does not violate federal or state constitutional guarantees.

Affirmed, Costs to Defendants-Respondents.

MAUGHAN, JUSTICE (dissenting):

The ordinance under which appellant's license was revoked no doubt infringes upon rights of free speech under the Federal and State Constitutions. The question we are faced with is whether the infringement is so significant it is constitutionally intolerable.

* * *

The majority opinion attempts to rely on language in Near v. Minnesota creating "exceptions" to the prior restraint doctrine. The

8.   413 U.S. 49, 93 S.Ct. 2628, 37 L.Ed.2d   9.   482 F.2d 280 (5th Cir.1973).
446 (1973).

language referred to is of course, pure dicta, and in no way supports the result in this case. As noted, ante, the United States Supreme Court has allowed limited censorship systems to exist in the area of obscenity, as long as adequate safeguards exist assuring "prompt judicial review" of alleged obscene material. But the Court has *never* condoned the outright closure of an operation such as allowed in this case today.

* * *

Paris Adult Theatre v. Slaton also fail to support the majority opinion. * * * No issue of prior restraint was presented in the case, since no restraint on the exhibition of the film was imposed until after a full judicial determination by the Georgia Supreme Court.

Contrary to the impression given in the majority opinion, there is no authority emanating from the United States Supreme Court approving the result in this case. In addition, as the cited cases in Mr. Justice Wilkins' dissenting opinion show, our sister states have overwhelmingly rejected such action as unconstitutional. * * *

I find no meaningful distinction between defendant's license revocation in this matter and the use of a "nuisance" injunction to close a business based on prior obscenity conviction, which I addressed in my dissenting opinion in Ogden City v. Eagle Books, Utah, 586 P.2d 436 (1978), decided this date, and which I concluded was an unconstitutional incursion into free speech. In both instances the result is the same—an absolute prohibition on the distribution of presumptively protected material—and in both instances this result is constitutionally infirm.

Defendant bases its argument overwhelmingly on the case of 106 Forsyth Corporation v. Bishop, 362 F.Supp. 1389 (M.D.Ga.1972), aff'd 482 F.2d 280 (CA5 1973), cert. denied 422 U.S. 1044, 95 S.Ct. 2660, 45 L.Ed.2d 696 (1974). Plaintiff admits that *Forsyth* supports defendant's contention but argues that *Forsyth* is an "aberration"; a characterization I believe to be correct.

Forsyth is contrary to all the cases decided before it [2] and has been specifically rejected by every court that has subsequently considered it.[3]

2. People ex rel. Busch v. Projection Room Theater, 17 Cal.3d 42, 130 Cal.Rptr. 328, 550 P.2d 600 (1976), cert. denied, 429 U.S. 922, 97 S.Ct. 320, 50 L.Ed.2d 289 (1976); State ex rel. Ewing v. Without A Stitch, 37 Ohio St.2d 95, 307 N.E.2d 911 (1974); Kingsley Books, Inc. v. Brown, 354 U.S. 436, 77 S.Ct. 1325, 1 L.Ed.2d 1469 (1957); State ex rel. Cahalan v. Diversified Theatrical Corp., 396 Mich. 244, 240 N.W. 2d 460 (1976); General Corp. v. State ex rel. Sweeton, 294 Ala. 657, 320 So.2d 668 (1975); cert. denied, 425 U.S. 904, 96 S.Ct. 1494, 47 L.Ed.2d 753 (1976); Mitchem v. State ex rel. Schaub, 250 So.2d 883 (Fla., 1971); Sanders v. State, 231 Ga. 608, 203 S.E.2d 153 (1974); State v. A Motion Picture Entitled "The Bet," 219 Kan. 64, 547 P.2d 760 (1976); Gulf States Theatres of Louisiana, Inc. v. Richardson, 287 So.2d 480 (La., 1974); State ex rel. Field v. Hess, 540 P.2d 1165 (Okla., 1975); New Rivieria Arts Theatre v. State ex rel. Davis, 219 Tenn. 652, 412 S.W.2d 890 (1967); Grosjean v. American Press Co., 297 U.S. 233, 56 S.Ct. 444, 80 L.Ed. 660 (1936); Cantwell v. State of Connecticut, 310 U.S. 296, 60 S.Ct. 900, 84 L.Ed. 1213 (1940).

3. Alexander v. City of St. Paul, 303 Minn. 201, 227 N.W.2d 370 (1975); Hamar Theatres, Inc. v. City of Newark, 150 N.J. Super. 14, 374 A.2d 502 (1977); City of Delevan v. Thomas, 31 Ill.App.3d 630, 334 N.E.2d 190 (1975).

A subsequent Fifth Circuit case, Universal Amusement Co. v. Vance, 559 F.2d 1286 (CA5 1977) dealing with a nuisance injunction to close a theater after pornography conviction, reached a result contrary to *Forsyth*. The court in *Vance* clearly recognized the "prior restraint" problem and the *Vance* decision raises doubts as to the future vitality of *Forsyth* even within the Fifth Circuit (though granting by the Court en banc of rehearing in *Vance* leaves resolution of this matter within that circuit unsettled).

Note

Porn Shops and The First Amendment. As the majority and dissenting opinions illustrate, there is considerable variation in judicial balancing of interests in the area of commercial obscenity regulations. Compare e.g. Arcara v. Cloud Books Inc., 478 U.S. ___, 106 S.Ct. 3172, 92 L.Ed.2d 568 (1986) (upholding a padlock ordinance against a bookstore that was a place of prostitution) with City of Paducah v. Investment Enterprises, 791 F.2d 463 (6th Cir.1986) (voiding ordinance that provided for license revocation of dealers in pornography).

See the Notes post the following Redwood Gym.

REDWOOD GYM v. SALT LAKE CTY. COM'N
Supreme Court of Utah, 1981.
624 P.2d 1138.

HALL, JUSTICE:

Plaintiffs appeal the declaratory judgment of the trial court which upheld the constitutionality of the Salt Lake County "massage parlor" ordinance.

* * * The relevant sections of that enactment read as follows:

"*Sec. 15–18–1. Definitions.* For the purpose of this chapter the following terms shall have the meanings prescribed:

"(2) 'Masseur' shall mean any person who gives massage for hire; provided that any person who is duly licensed by the Department of Registration to practice the healing arts shall not be included in this definition.

"(4) 'Employee' means the operator, owner, or manager of a massage establishment and any person performing massages at or on the premises of a massage establishment and also any agent or independent contractor who gives massages at a massage establishment.

"*Sec. 15–18–3. Requirements for the Issuance of a License.* Each individual desiring a massage establishment license or a masseur license shall: (1) Be an individual at least 21 years of age. * * *

"*Sec. 15–18–4. Sanitary Premises.* All applications for a massage establishment license shall be referred to the Salt Lake City-County Board of Health for investigation and a license shall be granted only after a finding by the Salt Lake City-County Board of Health that the proposed premises are sanitary enough to conduct business therein without jeopardizing the public health.

"*Sec. 15–18–5. Prohibited Acts.* The following acts are prohibited:

"(1) It shall be unlawful for a masseur to administer, for hire, to any person of the opposite sex, a massage, a fomentation, or a bath. It shall be unlawful for any massage establishment to cause or permit in or about his place of business, an employee to administer a massage upon any person of the opposite sex. This section shall not apply to any treatment administered by any person licensed to practice a healing art or profession under the provisions of Utah Code Annotated, 1953, or any other law of this state.

"(2) It shall be unlawful to serve, to store, or allow to be consumed, any alcoholic beverages on the licensed premises of a massage establishment.

"(3) It shall be unlawful for a masseur to touch or offer to touch or massage the genitalia of customers.

"*Sec. 15–18–7. Civil Sanctions.* Any unlawful conduct, whether the omission to perform an act required by this ordinance, or the performance of an act prohibited by this ordinance, shall be cause for revocation or suspension of a massage establishment's license or masseur's license. The holder of a massage establishment license may have his or her license revoked or suspended for any and all violations of the provisions of this ordinance committed by his or her employees.

"*Sec. 15–18–8. Penal Sanctions.* The person convicted of violations of this chapter of the Revised Ordinances of Salt Lake County may be fined not to exceed $299.00, imprisoned in the Salt Lake County Jail not to exceed six months, or both."

It is conceded that the purpose of the enactment was to prevent the sale of sexual favors and prostitution in establishments holding themselves out to the public as massage parlors. * * *

Plaintiffs, an aggregate of unincorporated business entities operating as massage establishments in Salt Lake County, filed a complaint with the trial court on December 5, 1978, * * *. A stipulation was submitted to the court on March 7, 1979, indicating that the plaintiffs were duly licensed businesses in Salt Lake County, that licensed masseurs in the County numbered approximately 140 (of whom approximately 130 are women), and that the vast majority of massage parlor patrons are men. The stipulation further stated that if the ordinance were enforced, it would cause financial hardship on the owners and employees of massage parlors within the County.

Following hearing * * *, the trial court denied plaintiffs' motion for summary judgment and granted defendants' motion dismissing plaintiffs' complaint. * * *

Plaintiffs first assert that the Salt Lake County Commission acted in excess of legislatively-delegated powers in enacting the subject ordinance. * * * The Utah code provides that counties * * * may license for purpose of regulation and revenue all and every kind of business not prohibited by law * * *; * * *

Plaintiffs first point out that the foregoing statutory provision, while enabling a county commission to license every legal form of business for purposes of regulation and revenue, does not permit the suppression and prohibition of business establishments save those enumerated within the body of the statute itself. * * *

Plaintiffs' assertion * * * is not dissimilar to arguments which have been raised in other cases asserting that diverse business regulations were so severe as to amount to deprivation of property without due process. The general rule * * * is that the power to regulate for the general welfare, inherent in the police power of the State (and delegated by legislative enactment to cities and counties), does not constitute an abridgment of the due process rights of proprietors of business establishments provided it is applied in a necessary and proper fashion. * * * Such regulations as are necessary and proper to the protection of the welfare, morals, health, and well-being of the public shall not constitute suppression or prohibition for purposes of the above provision.

* * *

Plaintiffs first assert that the provision of the enactment forbidding the administration of massages to members of the opposite sex is an unnecessary regulation of Salt Lake County's massage parlor business establishments. The purpose of the provision being the curtailment of prostitution, argue plaintiffs, it is rendered superfluous by an extensive body of state law prohibiting the practice of prostitution, and providing penalty therefor.

It is not the function of this Court to evaluate the wisdom or practical necessity of legislative enactments. The form of the challenged provision, when read in conjunction with the minutes of the public meeting held prior to its enactment, clearly evidenced a concern on the part of the Commission that the state statutory framework, unsupplemented by local ordinances, presented insurmountable enforcement problems in the case of massage parlors. We will not presume to second-guess the soundness of that decision.

* * *

In the instant case, the County has been given express power to make rules and regulations, not repugnant to law, necessary and proper to improve the morals, preserve the health, peace and good order among its citizenry. The practice of prostitution within the County has presented a clear threat to the attainment of those goals, and its prevention in the seclusion of a seemingly legitimate massage parlor has proven sufficiently difficult that an ordinance of the sort here in question must be regarded as having been enacted pursuant to power fairly implied from the express provision of state law.

* * *

Plaintiffs argue, however, that any attempt by a county to regulate in the interest of combatting prostitution is improper, in that state law has preempted the field. It is argued that, by prohibiting the massage of a member of the opposite sex, and imposing civil and criminal penalties on the violation of such prohibition, the defendant Commission has created a new crime, non-existent under the comprehensive prostitution laws of Utah, and should therefore be declared invalid. In this regard, we are urged to accept the rationale of *Lancaster v. Municipal Court for Beverly Hills.*

This Court has previously ruled that local governments may legislate by ordinance in areas previously dealt with by state legislation, provided the ordinance in no way conflicts with existing state law * * *. In the case of *Salt Lake City v. Allred,* this Court stated that a local governmental body is at liberty to legislate for the prevention of prostitution and other sexual offenses, notwithstanding state legislation in the same area, so long as both statutory and ordinance law have a common purpose, and are not in conflict. Moreover, such conflict is not created by the fact that an ordinance denounces as unlawful an act upon which state law is silent, or pronounces a penalty therefor.

* * *

On the basis of the foregoing, we hold that the opposite-sex massage provision is not invalid by reason of preemption by state law.

In addition to their contention that the opposite-sex massage provision of the subject ordinance was enacted in excess of the powers delegated by enabling legislation, plaintiffs assert that its enforcement would necessarily place them at odds with other provisions of state law. Specifically mentioned are Utah's Anti-discrimination Act and civil rights legislation. The anti-discrimination provision referred to states that:

> "It shall be a discriminatory or unfair employment practice * * * [f]or an employer to refuse to hire, to discharge, to promote, demote, or terminate, or to discriminate in matters of compensation against any person otherwise qualified, because of race, color, sex, age, if the individual is 40 years of age or older, religion, ancestry, national origin, or handicap."

For purposes of this provision, the term "employer" is specially defined:

> " 'Employer' means the state or any political subdivision or board, commission, department, institution or school district thereof, and every other person employing 25 or more employees within the state;
> * * * "

This Court does not engage in the rendering of advisory opinions. Absent some overriding consideration of public policy, a party must demonstrate standing to raise an issue in order to secure a ruling thereon.

In the instant case, plaintiffs have not shown, by stipulation, affidavit, or otherwise, that any one of the massage parlors seeking declaratory relief below employed 25 or more individuals. Therefore, plaintiffs have failed to demonstrate standing to challenge the application of the Anti-discrimination Act, as it does not appear that any of their number is an "employer" for purposes of the statute.

As mentioned above, plaintiffs also rely on that portion of Utah's civil rights legislation which states that:

> "All persons within the jurisdiction of this state are free and equal and are entitled to full and equal accommodations, advantages, facilities, privileges, goods and services in all business establishments and in all places of public accommodation, and by all enterprises regulated by the state of every kind whatsoever, without discrimination on the basis of race, color, sex, religion, ancestry or national origin."

Plaintiffs reason that application of the opposite-sex massage provision, in light of the present makeup of the massage trade in Salt Lake County, will constrain massage parlors to turn away male customers, in violation of the foregoing statutory provision.

The assertion is without merit. Nothing in the challenged ordinance provisions requires a massage parlor to refuse service to a customer based on his or her gender. All individuals, male or female, are entitled to the services of a licensed masseur, provided the masseur is not a member of the opposite sex. If there exists in the county at present a dearth of licensed male masseurs, and an overabundance of male massage parlor patrons, such cannot be characterized a defect in the ordinance in question. The statute invoked by plaintiffs cannot be so read as to entitle a member of the public to a massage by a member of the opposite sex.

Plaintiffs next challenge the opposite-sex massage provision on the basis of guarantees of equal protection of the law afforded under the Constitutions of the United States and of the State of Utah. They argue that the prohibition of massaging a member of the opposite sex creates an arbitrary and unreasonble classification in violation of such constitutional guarantees.

It has been established to a certainty, as plaintiffs concede, that an ordinance such as the one in question here does no violence to federal guarantees of equal protection. We regard the rulings of the U.S. Supreme Court in this area dispositive of the present question, * * *.

Plaintiffs urge us, however, to apply a more rigid standard with regard to Utah's equal protection provision. This we likewise decline to do, and hold that the challenged provision complies with requirements of equal protection.

Where a legislative enactment creates no inherently suspect classification and touches upon no fundamental interest as recognized by the Constitution, it satisfies the exigencies of equal protection if the classification made thereby has a rational basis in a legitimate legislative objective. The opposite-sex massage provision clearly meets such a standard. * * *

Plaintiffs urge us, however, to regard the opposite-sex massage provision as touching both upon a fundamental interest and a suspect classification. We feel such contentions to be without merit.

Plaintiffs suggest that the ordinance provision creates a classification based on sex, which is or should be inherently suspect under Utah law. Without ruling upon the latter portion of this contention, we observe that no sex classification is created. Not all legal provisions which take gender into consideration create such sex-based classifications. The terms of the opposite-sex massage provision do not place either sex at an inherent legal disadvantage vis-a-vis the other. Men and women are afforded an equal right to practice as licensed masseurs, or to patronize massage parlors. Only the massage of a member of one sex by a member of the other sex is forbidden. * * *

We likewise reject plaintiffs' assertion that the conduct of a massage parlor business, or any other trade or occupation, constitutes such a fundamental interest that state legislation may not create classifications touching thereon absent a compelling state interest. Were we to accept such an assertion, all laws relating to commerce, trade, occupational requirements, etc., would be subject to reevaluation and a probable invalidation. The right to pursue a trade or occupation is indeed basic in our society, but does not constitute such a fundamental interest that it is immune from reasonable legal restrictions and classifications. Plaintiffs issue a further constitutional challenge to the opposite-sex massage provision in the form of a charge that it constitutes a bill of attainder in violation of guarantees afforded by the Constitution of the State of Utah. * * *

A bill of attainder is one which imposes guilt, and inflicts punishment, upon an identifiable individual or group without judicial process. The enactment here under consideration bears none of these characteristics. It is directed at all individuals within Salt Lake County who operate, or are employees at, a massage parlor. Unlike the ordinance considered in the *Hart* decision, the instant provision does not impose an automatic legislative penalty, but merely prohibits a certain act, and provides civil and criminal remedies for a violation thereof. No identifiable individual or group is, by operation of the ordinance alone, the subject of legislative punishment without due process.

Plaintiffs' remaining contentions deal with other sections of the enacted ordinance. Prior to their examination, we are compelled to make certain preliminary observations regarding the propriety of their presentation to this Court at the present time. It has been previously observed that this Court does not render advisory opinions. One application of this principle is the doctrine of ripeness for adjudication. * * * Where there exists no more than a difference of opinion regarding the hypothetical application of a piece of legislation to a situation in which the parties might, at some future time, find themselves, the question is unripe for adjudication.

* * * In short, the "controversy" which the parties lay before this Court, with the exception of that surrounding the opposite-sex massage provision, is nothing more than an academic debate regarding possible infringements on the legal rights of an unidentified business entity in the event that, at some future time, the provisions of the ordinance were applied under a set of hypothetical circumstances. This being the case, we deem it unwise to render an opinion in the matter at present.

* * *

The decision of the trial court is hereby affirmed.

Note

Divisions of Authority. Courts recognize that ordinances and regulations on the operation of massage parlors fall within local police powers, but they are divided on the limits of regulation under the Fourteenth Amendment, or under Title VII of the 1964 Civil Rights Act regarding discrimination in employment.

A majority of courts in accord with the principal case reject the argument that massage parlor businesses implicate rights or classifications so fundamental or suspect as to require strict scrutiny. Pollard v. Cockrell, 578 F.2d 1002 (5th Cir.1978); Harper v. Lindsay, 454 F.Supp. 597 (S.D.Tex. 1978). Accordingly, parties attacking such controls must show that the questioned law or regulation is arbitrary in its purpose or in the means adopted to achieve that purpose. Courts have upheld ordinances limiting hours of operation; allowing warrantless inspections of massage parlor premises; requiring a written register and record of massage parlor patrons by name, age and address (see Pollard, supra); and provisions regulating the dress of massage parlor employees. See Harper, *supra*. The court in *Harper* noted that the decisions consistently sustained such regulations even though they might restrict business opportunities or even contribute to termination of massage parlor business. 454 F.Supp. at 601.

A minority of courts concluded that important constitutional rights were threatened by such regulations. Myrick v. Board of Pierce County Commissioners, 101 Wash.2d 140, 677 P.2d 146 (1984); Corey v. Dallas, 352 F.Supp. 977, 983 (N.D.Tex.1972), reversed on other grounds 492 F.2d 496 (5th Cir.1974); Cianciolo v. Members of City Council, 376 F.Supp. 719 (E.D. Tenn.1974); Fehlhaber v. Thompson, Civil 1031 (E.D.N.C. Sept. 9, 1974) (unpublished opinion).

The minority view, however, seems to be weakened by the cases like the principal case, which upheld bans on cross-sex massages. Colorado Springs Amusements, Ltd. v. Rizzo, 524 F.2d 571 (3d Cir.1975); City of Independence v. Wright, 267 Ind. 471, 371 N.E.2d 1298 (1978). In cases that sustained the constitutionality of ordinances banning customer massages by a member of the opposite sex, the Supreme Court dismissed appeals taken from those decisions "for want of a substantial federal question." Smith v. Keator, 285 N.C. 530, 206 S.E.2d 203 (1974), appeal dismissed 419 U.S. 1043, 95 S.Ct. 613, 42 L.Ed.2d 636 (1974); Rubenstein v. Cherry Hill, 417 U.S. 963, 94 S.Ct. 3165, 41 L.Ed.2d 1136 (1974); Kisley v.

Falls Church, 212 Va. 693, 187 S.E.2d 168 (1972), appeal dismissed 409 U.S.
907, 93 S.Ct. 237, 34 L.Ed.2d 169 (1972). See Annots., Sex-Oriented Busi-
nesses-Licensing, 8 A.L.R.4th 130 (Supp.1985); Massage Salon-Treatment
by Opposite Sex, 51 A.L.R.3d 936 (Supp.1985).

Local laws against cross-sex massages also raised the issue of gender
employment discrimination under Title VII of the 1964 Civil Rights Act,
since the standard of discrimination under Title VII is not coterminus with
that of Equal Protection, and since the delineation of Title VII sex discrimination remains undeveloped, the lower courts have divided in their reasoning and results. Some found that the cross-sex employee assignment ban to
be gender-neutral, and not contrary to Title VII. Aldred v. Duling, 538
F.2d 637 (4th Cir.1976); Blackman v. Goodman, 457 F.Supp. 391 (W.D.N.C.
1978). Others, however, noted that most massage parlor customers are
males who prefer female masseuses; and found sexually disparate impacts
in employment opportunities of male and female employees sufficient to
have a discrimination effect. See e.g. Cianciolo v. Members of City Council,
supra; Stratton v. Drumm, 445 F.Supp. 1305 (D.Conn.1978). See, also,
Joseph v. House, 353 F.Supp. 367, 374–5 (E.D.Va.1973), affirmed sub nom.
Joseph v. Blair, 482 F.2d 575 (4th Cir.1973), cert. denied 416 U.S. 955, 94
S.Ct. 1968, 40 L.Ed.2d 305 (1974). Applicable rulings in this area develop
slowly and remain unsettled, especially since Title VII does not cover
businesses with less than 15 employees. See Colorado Springs Amusements v. Rizzo, 524 F.2d 571 (3d Cir.1975).

CITY OF DETROIT v. MASHLAKJIAN

Court of Appeals of Michigan, 1969.
15 Mich.App. 236, 166 N.W.2d 493.

LEVIN, JUDGE. The defendant George Mashlakjian appeals his
conviction of operating a public lodging house without a license.
* * * Its owner Harry Kemsuzian testified he operated it from 1939
to 1961 and annually obtained a license authorizing him to do so from
the city of Detroit. In 1961 Kemsuzian leased the hotel to the defendant George Mashlakjian.

Mashlakjian testified that he obtained a license for the years 1961–
1962 and 1962–1963 without difficulty. The license obtained for the
year 1962–1963 expired June 30, 1963. A Detroit police officer testified
that he took an application for a renewal of that license from Mashlakjian on May 15, 1963, 1½ months before * * * it was due to expire.

Two years later, on May 20, 1965, Mashlakjian was ticketed for
operating without a license. At the time the ticket was issued, no
action had been taken by the city on his renewal application for 1963–
1964. Mashlakjian did not apply for a renewal for the license year in
which the ticket was issued (1964–1965) until the day after the ticket
was issued, i.e., May 21, 1965. The police officer testified that Mashlakjian's May 21, 1965, application for a 1964–1965 license and the $55
filing fee paid therewith were "accepted." * * *

* * *

Mashlakjian's application for 1963-1964 could well be viewed as a continuing application for a one year license, so that when the city failed to act thereon before the expiration of the period for which it was applied, it became an application for a license for the next annual license period, *i.e.*, for the year 1964-1965, the license year in which the ticket was issued and specific renewal application made the following day. * * * Accordingly, we proceed on the assumption that Mashlakjian's application for renewal was pending throughout.

It is now well established that a licensing authority issuing occupational licenses may not refuse, revoke or suspend a license without informing the applicant or licensee of the reasons for the proposed negative action and giving him an opportunity to be heard thereon. Thus, whether called a renewal or a new application, Mashlakjian was entitled to notice and to an opportunity to be heard before denial of his application. This was his right both as a matter of constitutional principle [1] and under provisions of city of Detroit ordinances.

In Gilchrist v. Bierring (1944), 234 Iowa 899, 14 N.W.2d 724, the licensing authority asserted that there was no need to grant a hearing to one seeking renewal of a license * * * because, the license having expired, the licensee's rights thereupon were extinguished. In rejecting that contention the Iowa Supreme Court made the following observations which we now adopt (pp. 914-916, 14 N.W.2d p. 732):

"The right to earn a living is among the greatest of human rights * * *. Due process of law is satisfied only by such safeguards as will adequately protect these fundamental, constitutional rights of the citizen. Where the state confers a license to engage in a profession, trade or occupation, not inherently inimical to the public welfare, such license becomes a valuable personal right which cannot be denied or abridged in any manner except after due notice and a fair and impartial hearing before an unbiased tribunal. * * * "

* * *

See, also, Bankers Life & Casualty Co. v. Cravey (1952), 208 Ga. 682, 69 S.E.2d 87, where the Georgia Supreme Court refused to draw a distinction in regard to notice and hearing requirements between revocation of and refusal to renew a license.

1. Applications for license:

Willner v. Committee on Character and Fitness (1963), 373 U.S. 96, 105, 83 S.Ct. 1175, 10 L.Ed.2d 224 (hearing does not satisfy requirements of procedural due process if applicant is not informed of reasons for his proposed rejection and given an opportunity to rebut those reasons); Bennett v. Arizona State Board of Public Welfare (1963), 95 Ariz. 170, 388 P.2d 166 (child care license application); Milligan v. Board of Registration in Pharmacy (1965), 348 Mass. 491, 204 N.E.2d 504 (application for pharmacy license); Brown v. Murphy (1962), 34 Misc. 2d 151, 224 N.Y.S.2d 423 (application for tow truck driver's license).

Revocation of license:

Prouty v. Heron (1953), 127 Colo. 168, 255 P.2d 755 (engineer's license); Bechler v. Parsekian (1961), 36 N.J. 242, 176 A.2d 470, 478 (driver's license).

Generally:

1 Davis, Administrative Law Treatise, §§ 7.18, 7.19, p. 493, *et seq.*; 9 McQuillin on Municipal Corporations (3d ed. rev.), § 26.89, p. 208.

Mashlakjian's filing of the application for renewal had the effect of preserving the *status quo* until the city acted thereon in the manner required by law. In Parker v. Board of Barber Examiners (La.App. 1955), 84 So.2d 80, Louisiana's Court of Appeals speaking through Judge Albert Tate, Jr. ruled that, with the possible exception of a public emergency requiring immediate action, the procedural due process to which an occupational licensee is entitled requires not only notice and an opportunity to be heard but preservation of the *status quo* until completion of the review process.

If the city does not choose timely to act on a renewal application it should not be heard to say that the licensee's rights are at an end and that it can, thus, put the renewal applicant out of business without notice or hearing. It is not too much to expect that the city which seeks to enforce the law itself obey the law.

Occupational licenses are required by innumerable governmental authorities for countless endeavors. The periods for which they are issued are generally 1 and not more than 2 or 3 years. We know from our own experience as practitioners that an application for renewal is commonly filed toward the end of the license period and that frequently no action is taken by the licensing authority until after the date on which, by its terms, the license is due to expire. Licensing authorities ordinarily do not expect that their licensees whose applications have not been acted upon before the expiration of the license period will suspend operations until the licensing authority is able and willing to get around to considering the renewal application and act thereon. The city of Detroit is not atypical in that respect.

Commerce cannot and should not cease because of a logjam in a licensing department, * * *.

The city's reliance on Poulos v. New Hampshire (1952), 345 U.S. 395, 73 S.Ct. 760, 97 L.Ed. 1105, 30 A.L.R.2d 987, is misplaced. In *Poulos* a permit was improperly denied a preacher who sought permission to conduct religious services in a city park. Nevertheless, the Supreme Court held the preacher could not use the park without a permit.

This case of Mashlakjian differs from *Poulos* in 2 respects. Poulos sought an original grant of a license, while Mashlakjian applied for renewal of a license to run a long-established business. Poulos obtained a decision from the administrative body and acted in defiance thereof. Mashlakjian never heard from the city of Detroit and had a right to suppose that his application was still pending * * * in our judgment, to continue to operate his long-established business until the city * * * took steps to revoke his license if that be its purpose.

To affirm this conviction would be to say that the city's silence constituted an effective denial of a renewal without regard to the fact that the city failed to make any attempt to comply with constitutional and ordinance-imposed notice and hearing requirements. * * *

The conviction and sentence are vacated and the defendant discharged.

Notes

1. **Summary Revocations.** In limited instances a license may be made revocable at the will of the licensing authority. 9 McQuillin, *Municipal Corporations,* § 26.88 (3d rev. ed. 1978). In activities classified as harmful or dangerous, the weight of authority supports an exception to the general requirement that notice and hearing be given in connection with the revocation of a license. Walker v. Clinton, 244 Iowa 1099, 59 N.W.2d 785 (1953); Smith v. Iowa Liquor Control Commission, 169 N.W.2d 803 (Iowa 1969); Annot., 35 A.L.R.2d 1067 (1954). The much cited *Walker* case upheld revocation by city council, without notice or hearing, of a beer license, in the absence of any statutory requirement for a hearing. In approving *Walker,* the later *Smith* opinion noted, however, that the revocation must be reasonable, even though no hearing be required. As to what constitutes a dangerous activity, the courts are not in agreement. See e.g. House of Tobacco, Inc. v. Calvert, 394 S.W.2d 654, 656 (Tex.1965).

The bias against certain businesses, particularly liquor, also weights judicial review. In Sabes v. Minneapolis, 265 Minn. 166, 120 N.W.2d 871 (1963), the court upheld revocation of a restaurant-bar license on informal evidence of prostitution activity at the place of business. The court turned away the admitted fact that inadequate notice had been given of the revocation hearing, with the finding that the licensee was not prejudiced by the defective notice. But see Fascination Inc. v. Hoover, 39 Cal.2d 260, 246 P.2d 656 (1952) which disapproved denial of an amusement license for an activity that was thought to involve gambling devices, since the applicant was not given a hearing.

2. **Summary Civil and Criminal Sanctions.** Police powers delegated to local governments include the power to sanction local violations by summary fines and imprisonment. See Redwood Gym, p. 413, supra; City of Bellingham, p. 165, supra; Dunn v. Mayor and County of the City of Wilmington, 219 A.2d 153 (Del.1966). Summary fines are usually considered civil penalties in aid of enforcing civil regulations, rather than criminal penalties. Imprisonment for periods of less than six months are also deemed "petty" offenses that do not require jury trials. See Baldwin v. New York, 399 U.S. 66, 90 S.Ct. 1886, 26 L.Ed.2d 437 (1970).

4. STANDARDS FOR ADMINISTRATIVE DISCRETION

SUNSET AMUSEMENT CO. v. BOARD OF POLICE COMMISSIONERS OF LOS ANGELES

Supreme Court of California, 1972.
7 Cal.3d 64, 101 Cal.Rptr. 768, 496 P.2d 840.
Appeal dismissed 409 U.S. 1121, 93 S.Ct. 940, 35 L.Ed.2d 254 (1973).

Burke, J.

[Court upheld the denial of renewal license for a skating rink, as supported by substantial evidence that licensee failed to provide adequate parking, and control of patrons, leading to public disturbances. The court rejected licensee's claim that the proceeding involved Fourteenth Amendment rights that would require greater precision in regulatory standards.]

* * *

Nevertheless, where First Amendment activities are involved, this court has subjected licensing ordinances to strict scrutiny. (Citations omitted) In *Burton*, we were faced with the validity of the same subdivision of section 103.29 (then subd. (b)) involved herein, as applied to an exhibitor of motion picture films to the public. In our analysis * * * we noted that "The crucial factor here is our zealous solicitude for rights falling within the protection of the First Amendment," since in that category of cases, " 'precision of regulation must be the touchstone' [citations] and the standards set forth [in the ordinance] must be 'susceptible of objective measurement' [citations]" (Pp. 690–691, 68 Cal. Rptr. p. 725, 441 P.2d p. 285.) We concluded that the subdivision in question here contained "overly broad standards [which] are fraught with the hazard that an applicant will be denied his rights to free speech and press through exercise of the power of the board, in its discretion, to refuse a permit because of the content of the films which the applicant exhibits in his theater." (P. 692, 68 Cal.Rptr. p. 726, 441 P.2d p. 286.)

It is apparent that the rule announced in *Burton* applies only to those situations in which the operation of a licensing ordinance impinges upon the exercise of First Amendment activities, rather than ordinary commercial enterprises. [Citations omitted] Thus, in Daniel v. Board of Police Commissioners, 190 Cal.App.2d 566, 573, 12 Cal.Rptr. 226, the court upheld section 103.29 against a claim of vagueness and lack of standards in the context of the denial of a license for premises upon which food and beverages were sold and live entertainment provided. * * * Nevertheless, presumably because the *Daniel* case did involve the licensing of "live entertainment" possibly protected by the First Amendment [Citations omitted] we disapproved *Daniel*, but only "insofar as its language may be deemed inconsistent with the results * * * announced" in *Burton*. (68 Cal.2d at p. 693, 68 Cal. Rptr. at p. 727, 441 P.2d at p. 287.)

Therefore, we conclude that insofar as *Daniel* involved activities not falling within the ambit of the First Amendment, that case correctly held that the language of section 103.29 furnishes adequate standards to guide the Board in licensing matters and is not unconstitutionally vague. [Citations omitted] It should be kept in mind that there are an infinite variety of activities or conduct which could result in potential or actual danger to the "peace, health, safety, convenience, good morals, and general welfare" of the public. A municipality cannot reasonably be expected to isolate and specify those precise activities or conduct which are intended to be proscribed. As stated in *Daniel*, quoting from an earlier case, "To make a statute sufficiently certain to comply with constitutional requirements [of due process of law] it is not necessary that it furnishes detailed plans and specifications of the acts or conduct prohibited." [Citations omitted] The fact that an ordinance seems to vest unlimited discretion in the licensing agency does not necessarily invalidate the ordinance, for "the same might be said of almost any licensing board established under the laws of this state; discretion is not uncontrolled and unguided if it calls for the exercise of judgment of a high order. [Citations.]" * * *

It is significant that petitioners do not contest the foregoing conclusion. Instead, they contend that the operations of a roller skating rink are entitled to First Amendment protection. They claim that such activities include the "entertainment" or "amusement" of their patrons, whose rights of free speech and assembly assertedly would be affected by the licensing ordinance. However, no case has ever held or suggested that simple physical activity falls within the ambit of the First Amendment, * * *

Note

See Central States Theatre Corp. v. Sar, 245 Iowa 1254, 66 N.W.2d 450 (1954) which struck down a statute that authorized discretionary denial by local officials of theatre licenses, without adequate guidelines; Soof v. Highland Park, 30 Mich.App. 400, 186 N.W.2d 361 (1971) (ordinance limiting issuance of license for coin-operated motion picture machines to persons found by city council to be "suitable" and to have "good moral character," and to be "law abiding citizens", was unconstitutional on its face for lack of adequate guidelines to confine discretion of licensing authorities.

D. LAND USE PLANNING AND CONTROL

As a fixed resource, land has always been subject to the sovereign power, but the increasing complexity of land management in metropolitan areas requires a broad assortment of legal devices. These devices provide the means to allocate land management costs between individual owners and the public. The maintenance of a just balance of these burdens is a government responsibility. Should particular use of land that is disfavored by the community be prohibited by law (*viz.* as a nuisance), with resulting loss borne by the owner, or should the government, in order to terminate that use, be required to compensate the owner? When should heavier taxes be imposed upon uses which inconvenience or adversely affect the public? Should licensing fees and regulations be imposed upon certain users, or their business customers, to meet the cost of government services and when should those services be provided at public expense? These questions cannot be answered in the abstract. Issues of fairness on spreading social costs, depend on particular facts.

A corresponding challenge to insuring fairness is posed by the power of owners to direct land use development through private arrangements, *viz.* deed restrictions and covenants running with the land. Private governance of land at some point runs counter to public welfare. Here also, "fairness" supplies no hard rules, but only a guideline for ongoing adjustment between private and public controls. As urban lands becomes more scarce, and pressure increases to socialize land enjoyment, the balance point between private right and public good may be expected to shift.

1. PLANNING: PURPOSES AND MEANS

"Municipal planning, in a word, is the accommodation through unity in construction, of the variant interests seeking expression in the local physical life to the interest of the community as a social unit. Planning is a science and an art concerned with land economics and land policies in terms of social and economic betterment. The control essential to planning is exercised through government ownership or regulation of the use of the locus." Grosso v. Board of Adjustment, 137 N.J.L. 630, 631–632, 61 A.2d 167, 168 (1948).

" 'Comprehensive planning includes * * * (A) preparation, as a guide for long-range development of general physical plans with respect to the pattern and intensity of land use and the provision of public facilities, * * *; (B) programming of capital improvements * * *; (C) long-range fiscal plans for implementing such plans * * *; and (D) proposed regulatory and administrative measures which aid in achieving coordination of all related plans of the departments or subdivisions of the governments concerned and intergovernmental coordination of related planned activities * * *." Demonstration Cities And Metropolitan Development Act of 1966, 42 U.S.C.A. § 3338(5) (1970).

" * * * the fragmentation of governmental entities exercising land use planning powers, and the increased * * * impact of private actions have created a situation in which land-use management, decisions * * * are being made on the basis of expediency, tradition, short term economic considerations, and other factors which are often unrelated to the real concerns of a sound national land-use policy. * * *" *A National Land Use Policy,* S. 3345, 91st Cong.2d Sess. § 401 (1970).

Area wide planning takes many forms, both in theory and legal implementation. Different plans lay different stress on land economics, human renewal, economic development and "advocacy" planning. Planning experts do not agree on what should be included in or excluded from master plans (see e.g. Bassett, *The Master Plan,* 5–64 (1938)). The "comprehensive plan" under zoning law differs from master plans conceived for other purposes. It is necessary, therefore, to determine the kind of planning that is under discussion at any time.

Government planning has been accurately described as a "mixed profession" because its implementation requires the concert of planning theory and practice with legal theory and practice. But even while implementing planning goals, the legal process often limits them. This section covers the legal bases for land use control by local government, but the proper study of planning law must be left to specialized texts and courses. See generally C. Haar, *Land-Use Planning* (1976 3d ed.); D. Hagman, *Urban Planning and Land Development Control Law* ch. 1 (1975). Land development must also satisfy numerous environmental statutes, some of which are noted at p. 344, supra.

Patterns of local administration of land use controls requires careful attention. They vary with different forms of local governments and with diverse planning statutes. Administrative practice must be mastered for efficient law practice, because there are layers of state and local planning laws.

BURNS' INDIANA STATUTES ANNOTATED (1964)

§ 53–744.—After adoption of the master plan and ordinance, the city council, the board of county commissioners or other governing body within the territorial jurisdiction of the commission shall be guided by and give consideration to the general policy and pattern of development set out in the master plan in the:

1. Authorization, construction, alteration or abandonment of public ways, public places, public structures or public utilities;

2. Authorization, acceptance or construction of water mains, sewers, connections, facilities or utilities.

§ 53–753.—Within the corporate limits of a city, a structure shall not be located and an improvement location permit for a structure on platted or unplatted lands shall not be issued unless the structure and its location conform to the master plan and ordinance. A structure shall not be located and an improvement location permit shall not be issued for a structure on unincorporated lands within the jurisdiction of the commission unless the structure and its location conform to the master plan and ordinance, except that, if the lands lie within a county which has adopted a master plan and ordinance, then the city master plan and ordinance shall not apply and the structure must conform to the county master plan and ordinance. See also Me.Rev.Stat., tit. 30, § 4952(2)D; Mich.Com.Laws Ann. § 125.30; N.J.Stat.Ann. 40:55–1.13; Pa.Stat. tit. 53, § 10105.

2. PUBLIC OWNERSHIP AND USE

a. *Acquisition by Purchase or Gift*

The authority of local governments to acquire property for public purposes is well settled. When authorized, the purchase or lease of land presents few major problems. Where land is donated to the local government, for a public use, the determination of the public estate and obligations requires construction of the grantor's "intent," and application of special doctrines. Doctrines governing inter vivos grants do not control grants by will. Nor do laws on dedications for essential public uses, e.g. streets, govern gifts for less vital uses, e.g. public parks. The classification of donative transfers, as dedications or trusts, predetermine their effect, as do interpretation of use conditions, e.g. as covenants, conditions subsequent, or reservations of private interests. The following materials illustrate some interpretive problems arising from gift transfers.

WATSON v. ALBUQUERQUE

Supreme Court of New Mexico, 1966.
76 N.M. 566, 417 P.2d 54.

CARMODY, CHIEF JUSTICE. Plaintiffs appeal from the trial court's dismissal of a declaratory judgment suit, which sought to have a right-of-way called Caminito del Lado, N.W., declared to be a public street, twenty-eight feet in width.

* * * it is only necessary for us to consider whether or not there was a common-law dedication of the street.

The findings of the trial court are substantially as follows: The land is a right-of-way in the City of Albuquerque, which deadends at one extreme but has an outlet at the other. The street is shown on two plats, one filed in 1891 showing a 16–foot right-of-way, and the other filed in 1911 showing a right-of-way of twenty-eight feet. The 1911 plat contained no dedication and is deficient in other respects. Some of the deeds to lots were issued with reference to the 1911 plat, but the property owners of certain of these lots did not rely upon the plat and at least some of them built in accordance with the 1891 plat * * *. The name of the street was suggested by the plaintiffs and accepted by the city as a matter of accommodation. The right-of-way of approximately sixteen feet has been maintained on an irregular basis by the City of Albuquerque; it has also been used by the city for the purpose of collecting garbage, by certain public utility companies for the erection of power poles, and has never been assessed for taxes. The city commission rejected any attempted dedication of the right-of-way as a public street.

The trial court concluded that there had been no common-law dedication and no common-law acceptance of the right-of-way of the public street. A similar conclusion was made with reference to a statutory dedication, but * * * it is admitted by plaintiffs that there was not a proper statutory dedication.

At common law, there must be both an offer of dedication by the owner and an acceptance by the city to constitute a complete dedication, [citations omitted]. It is well settled that an owner of property cannot, simply by making a plat, impose the burden of dedication upon a municipality. The offer of dedication cannot bind the city until it has been accepted, [citations omitted]. The city's liability by acceptance arises only when it has done some act which unequivocally shows an intent to assume jurisdiction over the property dedicated, De Castello v. City of Cedar Rapids, 1915, 171 Iowa 18, 153 N.W. 353. Appellant refers us to several cases in which, under the facts there stated, it was determined that the city had exercised dominion and control in such a way as to signify an acceptance. However, the cases cited are quite distinguishable or state a rule which is not applicable under findings in this case * * *.

The fact that a city has, on an irregular basis, plowed or repaired a street, does not, by itself, establish an acceptance by the city, La France v. Town of Altmont, 1950, 277 App.Div. 917, 98 N.Y.S.2d 518. Nor does the use of the right-of-way by the city for collection of garbage, Sarty v. Millburn Township, 1953, 28 N.J.Super. 199, 100 A.2d 309, or installation of a street sign, People v. Underhill, 1895, 144 N.Y. 316, 39 N.E. 333, or the giving of permission to a utility company to erect poles in the right-of-way under a general franchise. In re Wallace, Barnes and Matthews Aves. in City of New York, 1917, 222 N.Y. 139, 118 N.E. 506, or the omission by the city to assess the right-of-way for taxes, West Hialeah Mfg. Co. v. City of Hialeah (Fla.App.1961), 134 So.2d 505; Johnson v. City of Niagara Falls, 1920, 230 N.Y. 77, 129 N.E. 213, by themselves establish an acceptance by the city.

The burden was here on the plaintiff to prove acceptance by the city, 11 McQuillen, Municipal Corporations, 3d ed., § 33.59, and such proof must be "clear, satisfactory and unequivocal," Robinson v. Town of Riveria, 1946, 157 Fla. 194, 25 So.2d 277; Board of County Com'rs of Highlands County v. F.A. Sebring Realty Co. (Fla.1953), 63 So.2d 256; City of Beckley v. Crouch, 1929, 107 W.Va. 342, 148 S.E. 198; 11 McQuillen, Municipal Corporations, 3d ed., § 33.54.

The trial court not only heard the witnesses but viewed the premises, and, on the basis of the facts found, we do not believe that it committed any error in concluding that the acts of the defendant did not show an exercise of dominion and control over the right-of-way in such a manner as to constitute an acceptance of a public street as a matter of law, as claimed by the plaintiffs. Of course, the issue of whether there had been acts which would constitute an acceptance is a question of fact, City of Carlsbad v. Neal, supra, although what constitutes acceptance under any given state of facts is a question of law, 11 McQuillen, Municipal Corporations, 3d ed., § 33.59.

The judgment will be affirmed. It is so ordered.

Notes

1. **Private Platting of Public Streets.** Developers map and plat public areas in subdivided tracts for several reasons. The recording of streets on a plat provides general information to prospective lot buyers; serves as a convenient record reference for legal descriptions in deeds to subdivided lots; may indicate private easements for dominant estates in abutting lots; or may dedicate to the general public the areas shown as public streets. The effect of recording subdivisions varies among different states. Compare e.g. the principal case with Volpe v. Marina Parks, Inc., 101 R.I. 80, 220 A.2d 525 (1966) where the platting of streets was held to

constitute "an incipient dedication of such streets"; and *with* Velasco v. Goldman Builder, Inc., 93 N.J.Super. 123, 225 A.2d 148 (1966) where still stronger significance was attached to plat recordation: "It has been held that when a real estate developer plats a tract of land into building lots and prepares a map disclosing streets abutting such lots, if he conveys by reference to the map, and the purchaser relies thereon, an intent to dedicate may be assumed. [Citations omitted]. But the prevailing rule in New Jersey is not uniformly followed in foreign jurisdictions." Id. at 135, 225 A.2d at 154. See generally Note, *Public Ownership of Land Through Dedication,* 75 Harv.L.Rev. 1406 (1962).

2. **Acceptance of Dedication.** It is not always clear (a) whether an implied dedication is based upon a finding of its "acceptance", or detrimental reliance upon the offer of dedication; and (b) whether such acceptance or reliance refers to actions of a municipality or to the conduct of the general public. In *Velasco,* supra, the plaintiffs sued to establish rights of way on the theory that their developer-grantor had dedicated the way as a public street. It was conceded that the developer made no express dedication or filed a plat showing the street, and that no formal act of acceptance was taken by the municipality. The Appellate Court nevertheless ruled that plaintiffs were entitled to prove other actions in support of their claim. "If the conduct ＊ ＊ ＊ manifested an offer to dedicate the McGuire Street extension ＊ ＊ ＊ and ＊ ＊ ＊ they [developers] acquiesced in its continued public use, the doctrine of equitable estoppel may preclude them from denying the dedication. When a land owner so acts as to raise in others a well-founded belief that he intends to donate to the public the easement, and such persons change their situation in consequence of such belief, he is estopped from denying, as against them, the intended dedication." 93 N.J. Super. at 136, 225 A.2d at 155.

While public use alone suffices in some states to effect acceptance of a dedication, isolated individual use will not create public easements—even where a recorded subdivision plat creates servitudes of passage in favor of abutting lot owners. In Parish of Jefferson v. Doody, 167 So.2d 489 (La. App.1964) the municipality failed to prove sufficient public use for acceptance of an alleged dedication. Had the dedication in Parish been a statutory dedication, no such problem would arise. Village of Folson v. Alford, 204 So.2d 100 (La.App.1967) (dedication by compliance with applicable statutes cannot be lost by non-user).

3. **Common Law and Statutory Dedications.** A common law dedication confers only a surface easement, while statutory dedications usually confer the entire fee, including underlying mineral wealth (see Smith v. Melbourne, 211 So.2d 66 (Fla.App.1968)). See also Belgum v. Kimball, 163 Neb. 774, 81 N.W.2d 205 (1957) (oil pool underlying highway dedicated by statute belonged to the city, and not the abutting owners).

An abortive attempt at statutory dedication may still give rise to a common law dedication—but with different results. In Pilgrim v. Chamberlain, 91 Ill.App.2d 233, 234 N.E.2d 75 (1968) defective compliance with statutory procedure resulted in a common law dedication of only that portion of the disputed strip that was actually used as a roadway. Consequently, the municipality could not eject the abutting owners from that part of the way which was never put to public use. But in Smith v. Melbourne, *supra,* the court held that the defective statutory dedication effected a common law dedication of the same width as the attempted statutory dedication, notwithstanding the city's use of only part of the disputed strip.

4. **Diverting Property from Dedicated Purposes.** The legal consequences of altering the use for which property is granted turn on a number of factors.

(a) Courts are less rigid in construing restrictions on publicly dedicated land than on privately dedicated land. See e.g. Hames v. Polson, 123 Mont. 469, 215 P.2d 950 (1950). In Paepcke v. Public Building Commission of Chicago, 46 Ill.2d 330, 263 N.E.2d 11 (1970) a dedication by the state of land to the city for park purposes was construed as authorizing the city to divert its use to school purposes.

(b) Street dedications create private as well as public rights. Once a street dedication is accepted, the city may not, by abandonment of the street, extinguish the independently created rights of abutting owners to ingress and egress over that street, unless it condemns and pays for those rights. Flake v. Thompson, Inc., 249 Ark. 713, 460 S.W.2d 789 (1970). However, where a *reservation* of private rights of user in land (as a public street) is inconsistent with the public grant, it may be held void. Hooker v. Grosse Point, 328 Mich. 621, 44 N.W.2d 134 (1950).

(c) Individual rights in parks and squares turn on still other principles. Under trust principles, a local government may not divert parks and squares to private uses; and absent special circumstances such attempts may be enjoined. Hames v. Polson, supra (attempt to lease park land to a country club); Hoffman v. Pittsburgh, 365 Pa. 386, 75 A.2d 649 (1950) (attempt by city to sell privately dedicated public square to a private party). But a court may permit, as consistent with the gift of park land, a lease of the subsurface, which requires permanent connecting entrances and exits on the surface of the park grounds. City and County of San Francisco v. Linares, 16 Cal.2d 441, 106 P.2d 369 (1940). The degree of deviation that a court will consider consistent with the primary grant, depends largely upon its construction of the trust. Compare: the *Linares,* case with City of Hermosa Beach v. Superior Court, 231 Cal.App.2d 295, 41 Cal.Rptr. 796 (1964) where the city was enjoined from installing a roadway along a beach devised to the city for public recreational use under a will which forbade automobiles on the beach, with Ward v. Mayor and City Council of Baltimore, 267 Md. 576, 298 A.2d 382 (1973) (permitting construction of throughway across park funded by a private trust). The authorities are collected in Annot., 60 A.L.R.3d 581 (1974).

(d) Where the grantor's heirs seek to forfeit and terminate a trust for a breach of condition, other factors come into play. Courts disfavor termination and forfeiture of public trust property to heirs of a long deceased grantor, but much depends upon the nature and wording of the restriction; the gravity of the breach; and whether the breach was rendered unavoidable by changing circumstances. Trust termination issues primarily involve judicial construction of the grantor's "intent". If a restriction be deemed a "covenant" and not a "condition," forfeiture may be avoided. Clark v. Grand Rapids, 334 Mich. 646, 55 N.W.2d 137 (1952).

The absence of express reverter or defeasance clauses in grant documents could be "construed" to negative any intention to terminate the public right for breach of a condition. City of Steubenville ex rel. Blackburn v. Targoss, 3 Ohio App.2d 21, 209 N.E.2d 486 (1965); Wilbur v. University of Vermont, 129 Vt. 33, 270 A.2d 889 (1970); Hagaman v. Board of Education of Woodbridge Twp., Middlesex County, 112 N.J.Super. 221, 270 A.2d 736 (1970).

Courts often declare that changed conditions may necessitate some departures from original trust terms in order to maintain the grantor's "primary" intent. Thus, in Wilbur v. University of Vermont, supra, the trust condition of limited enrollment was admittedly breached, but the court refused to terminate the gift on findings that admission of excess students was consistent with the settlor's primary intent to aid students; that limited enrollment was no longer practical; and that, in any event, the remedy for the alleged breach would be suit for compliance and not for forfeiture. In Trustees of Dartmouth College v. Quincy, 357 Mass. 521, 258 N.E.2d 745 (1970), the city trustee of a school established by charitable trust only for girls born in the city, was permitted to admit girls born elsewhere, upon payment of tuition, on the reasoning that such action would make it possible for the financially troubled school to survive and to carry out the trustees primary objective. Said the court: "In some cases, indeed, subordinate provisions, originally may have been imposed, not to facilitate the achievement of a general charitable purpose, but for the personal gratification of the donor in respects wholly irrelevant to any effective execution of a public purpose. There is strong ground for disregarding such subordinate details if changed circumstances render them obstructive of, or inappropriate to, the accomplishment of the principal charitable purpose. See DiClerico, Cy Pres: A Proposal for Change, 47 B.U.L.Rev. 153, 192–195, where it is suggested that (a) noncompliance with detailed provisions of a charitable trust should not give rise to a transfer to an alternative trust, if such provisions are not of controlling importance in relation to the general framework of the testator's scheme, and (b) a "gift over * * * [should] be resorted to only when it appears to the court that more benefit to the community would be derived from the alternative disposition and that nobody would be substantially damaged by terminating the original trust" (p. 194).

"A donor who brings into existence a charitable institution must recognize that most institutions are likely to change with time, that they will become sterile if they remain static, and that they must be adaptable to new public considerations and unpredictable economic circumstances. For this reason, the intention to make mandatory even detailed restrictions on the conduct of such institutions is not lightly to be inferred. If it appears that the unduly restrictive effect was in fact intended, provisions no longer appropriate must be tested against the requirements of current public policy concerning the donor's fundamental charitable objectives." Id. at 533–34, 258 N.E.2d at 753.

Judicial discretion has its limits. In Evans v. Abney, 396 U.S. 435, 90 S.Ct. 628, 24 L.Ed.2d 634 (1970), the Supreme Court affirmed the state court ruling that, under the law of Georgia, a public park entrusted by will to the city for use only by whites, reverted to the grantor's heirs, notwithstanding the absence of any reverter clause in the will, since the trust could not be constitutionally executed. Another warning against excessive reliance upon the policy against forfeiture is provided by People ex rel. King v. Lorenz, 34 Ill.2d 445, 216 N.E.2d 123 (1966). There the city defended a suit to revoke a dedication of land. The city argued that a dedication condition that the city construct an access road, was insubstantial since later changes in the design of a proposed highway would achieve substantially the same result, and that the plaintiffs should be limited to recovery of damages. The city lost.

b. *Eminent Domain*

"The power of eminent domain is an attribute of sovereignty. It is an inherent power of the state; not derived from, but limited by, the fundamental principles of the constitution." Miller v. Tacoma, 61 Wash.2d 374, 378 P.2d 464, 469 (1963). Eminent domain powers are not easily defined. Neither constitutions nor statutes answer the base questions: (1) what burdens on property rights—corporeal and otherwise—may, on the one hand, be imposed by police power regulations, without compensation; and what, on the other hand, constitutes a compensable "taking" of "property"? (2) what purposes or uses qualify as a "public use" within the condemnation power? (3) how much land may be lawfully taken for a particular public use? (4) how is "just compensation" to be measured? Helpful analyses of these issues, and of the underlying problem of "fairness" in determining when to individualize (by regulation) and when to socialize (by condemnation) the cost of public land arrangements, are found in Bosselman, Callies, Banta, *The Taking Issue—An Analysis of the Constitutional Limits of Land Use Control* (U.S. Council on Environmental Quality 1973); Michaelman, *Property, Utility and Fairness: Comment on Ethical Foundations of "Just Compensation" Law,* 80 Harv.L.Rev. 1165 (1967); Sax, *Takings, and the Police Power,* 74 Yale L.J. 36 (1964); Sax, *Takings, Private Property and Public Rights,* 81 Yale L.J. 149 (1971).

Local governments, lacking sovereign powers, can only exercise those eminent domain powers as are delegated to them by the federal or state government. It is, therefore, necessary to determine the purposes and limits of local condemnation powers under enabling legislation.

(1) "Property" and "Taking"

PENN CENTRAL TRANSPORTATION CO. v. NEW YORK CITY

Supreme Court of the United States, 1978.
438 U.S. 104, 98 S.Ct. 2646, 57 L.Ed.2d 631.

MR. JUSTICE BRENNAN delivered the opinion of the Court.

The question presented is whether a city may, as part of a comprehensive program to preserve historic landmarks and historic districts, place restrictions on the development of individual historic landmarks—in addition to those imposed by applicable zoning ordinances—without effecting a "taking" requiring the payment of "just compensation." Specifically, we must decide whether the application of New York City's Landmarks Preservation Law to the parcel of land occupied by Grand Central Terminal has "taken" its owners' property in violation of the Fifth and Fourteenth Amendments.

I

A

Over the past 50 years, all 50 States and over 500 municipalities have enacted laws to encourage or require the preservation of buildings and areas with historic or aesthetic importance. * * *

New York City, responding to similar concerns and acting pursuant to a New York State enabling act, adopted its Landmarks Preservation Law in 1965. * * * The city acted from the conviction that "the standing of [New York City] as a world-wide tourist center and world capital of business, culture, and government" would be threatened if legislation were not enacted to protect historic landmarks and neighborhoods from precipitate decisions to destroy or fundamentally alter their character. * * *

The New York City law is typical of many urban landmark laws in that its primary method of achieving its goals is not by acquisitions of historic properties, but rather by involving public entities in land use decisions affecting these properties and providing services, standards, controls, and incentives that will encourage preservation by private owners and users. While the law does place special restrictions on landmark properties as a necessary feature to the attainment of its larger objectives, the major theme of the Act is to ensure the owners of any such properties both a "reasonable return" on their investments and maximum latitude to use their parcels for purposes not inconsistent with the preservation goals.

The operation of the law can be briefly summarized. The primary responsibility for administering the Act is vested in the Landmarks Preservation Commission (Commission), * * * The Commission first performs the function, * * * of identifying properties and areas that have "a special character or special historical or aesthetic interest or value as part of the development, heritage, or cultural characteristics of the city, state or nation." * * * If the Commission determines, after giving all interested parties an opportunity to be heard, that a building or area satisfies the ordinance's criteria, it will designate a building to be a "landmark," * * * situated on a particular "landmark site," * * * or will designate an area to be a "historic district," * * *. After the Commission makes a designation, New York City's Board of Estimate * * * may modify or disapprove the designation, and the owner may seek judicial review of the final designation decision. * * *

Final designation as a landmark results in restrictions upon the property owner's options concerning use of the landmark site. First, the Act imposes a duty upon the owner to keep the exterior features of the building "in good repair." * * * Second, the Commission must approve in advance any proposal to alter the exterior architectural features of the landmark or to construct any exterior improvement on the landmark site, * * *.

* * *

Although the designation of a landmark and landmark site restricts the owner's control over the parcel, designation also enhances the economic position of the landmark owner in one significant respect. Under New York City's zoning laws, owners of real property who have not developed their property to the full extent permitted by the applicable zoning laws are allowed to transfer development rights to contiguous parcels on the same city block. See New York City, Zoning Resolution Art. I., ch. 2, § 12–10 (1978) (definition of "zoning lot"). A 1968 ordinance gave the owners of landmark sites additional opportunities to transfer development rights to other parcels. * * *

B

This case involves the application of New York City's Landmark Preservation Law to Grand Central Terminal (Terminal). The Terminal * * * is one of New York City's most famous buildings. * * *

The Terminal is located in midtown Manhattan. * * * The Terminal itself is an eight-story structure which Penn Central uses as a railroad station and in which it rents space not needed for railroad purposes to a variety of commercial interests. The Terminal is one of a number of properties owned by appellant Penn Central in this area of midtown Manhattan. The others include the Barclay, Biltmore, Commodore, Roosevelt, and Waldorf-Astoria Hotels, the Pan-American Building and other office buildings along Park Avenue, and the Yale Club. At least eight of these are eligible to be recipients of development rights afforded the Terminal by virtue of landmark designation.

On August 2, 1967, following a public hearing, the Commission designated the Terminal a "landmark" and designated the "city tax block" it occupies a "landmark site." * * *

On January 22, 1968, appellant Penn Central, to increase its income, entered into a renewable 50-year lease and sublease agreement with appellant UGP Properties, Inc. (UGP), * * *. Under the terms of the agreement, UGP was to construct a multistory office building above the Terminal. * * *

Appellants UGP and Penn Central then applied to the Commission for permission to construct an office building atop the Terminal. Two separate plans, * * * both apparently satisfying the terms of the applicable zoning ordinance, were submitted to the Commission for approval. * * * After four days of hearings at which over 80 witnesses testified, the Commission denied this application as to both proposals.

The Commission's reasons for rejecting certificates respecting Breuer II Revised are summarized in the following statement: "To protect a landmark, one does not tear it down. To perpetuate its architectural features, one does not strip them off." Record 2255. Breuer I, * * * In conclusion, the Commission stated that it

> "has no fixed rule against making additions to designated buildings—it all depends on how they are done * * *. But to balance a 55-story office tower above a flamboyant Beaux-Arts facade seems nothing more than an aesthetic joke. Quite simply, the tower would overwhelm the Terminal by its sheer mass. * * *" *Id.,* at 2251.

* * * Because the Terminal site enjoyed a tax exemption, remained suitable for its present and future uses and was not the subject of a contract of sale, there were no further administrative remedies available to appellants. * * * Further, appellants did not avail themselves of the opportunity to develop and submit other plans * * * Instead, appellants filed suit * * * claiming, *inter alia,* that the application of the Landmarks Preservation Law had "taken" their property without just compensation in violation of the Fifth and Fourteenth Amendments and arbitrarily deprived them of their property without Due Process of law in violation of the Fourteenth Amendment. * * * The trial court granted the injunctive and declaratory relief, but severed the question of damages for a "temporary taking."

Appellee, the city, appealed, and the New York Supreme Court, Appellate Division, reversed. 50 A.D.2d 265 (1975). * * *

The New York Court of Appeals affirmed. 42 N.Y.2d 324, 397 N.Y.S.2d 914, 366 N.E.2d 1271 (1977). * * *

* * *

II

The issues presented by appellants are (1) whether the restrictions imposed by New York City's law upon appellants' exploitation of the Terminal site effect a "taking" of appellants' property for a public use within the meaning of the Fifth Amendment, which of course is made applicable to the States through the Fourteenth Amendment, see Chicago B. & Q.R. Co. v. Chicago, 166 U.S. 226, 239, 17 S.Ct. 581, 585, 41 L.Ed. 979 (1897) and, (2) if so, whether the transferable development rights afforded appellants constitute "just compensation" within the meaning of the Fifth Amendment. We need only address the question whether a "taking" has occurred.

A

* * * The question of what constitutes a "taking" for purposes of the Fifth Amendment has proved to be a problem of considerable difficulty. While this Court has recognized that the "Fifth Amendment's guarantee [is] designed to bar Government from forcing some people alone to bear public burdens which, in all fairness and justice, should be borne by the public as a whole," Armstrong v. United States, 364 U.S. 40, 49, 80 S.Ct. 1563, 1569, 4 L.Ed.2d 1554 (1960), this Court, quite simply, has been unable to develop any "set formula" for determining when "justice and fairness" require that economic injuries caused by public action be compensated by the Government, rather than remain disproportionately concentrated on a few persons. See Goldblatt v. Hempstead, 369 U.S. 590, 594, 82 S.Ct. 987, 990, 8 L.Ed.2d 130 (1962). Indeed, we have frequently observed that whether a particular restriction will be rendered invalid by the Government's failure to pay for any losses proximately caused by it depends largely "upon the particular circumstances [in that] case." United States v. Central Eureka Mining Co., 357 U.S. 155, 168, 78 S.Ct. 1097, 1104, 2 L.Ed.2d 1228 (1958); see United States v. Caltex, Inc., 344 U.S. 149, 156, 73 S.Ct. 200, 203, 97 L.Ed. 157 (1952).

In engaging in these essentially ad hoc, factual inquiries, the Court's decisions have identified several factors that have particular significance. The economic impact of the regulation on the claimant and, particularly, the extent to which the regulation has interfered with distinct investment backed expectations are of course relevant considerations. See Goldblatt v. Hempstead, supra, 369 U.S. at 594, 82 S.Ct. at 990. So too is the character of the governmental action. A "taking" may more readily be found when the interference with property can be characterized as a physical invasion by Government, see *e.g.,* Causby v. United States, 328 U.S. 256 (1946), than when interference arises from some public program adjusting the benefits and burdens of economic life to promote the common good.

* * *

More importantly for the present case, in instances in which a state tribunal reasonably concluded that "the health, safety, morals or general welfare" would be promoted by prohibiting particular contemplated uses of land, this Court has upheld land use regulations that destroyed or adversely affected recognized real property interests. See Nectow v. City of Cambridge, 277 U.S. 183, 188, 48 S.Ct. 447, 448, 72 L.Ed. 842 (1928). Zoning laws are of course the classic example * * *.

* * *

Again, Hadacheck v. Sebastian, 239 U.S. 394, 36 S.Ct. 143, 60 L.Ed. 348 (1915), upheld a law prohibiting the claimant from continuing his otherwise lawful business of operating a brickyard in a particular physical community on the ground that the legislature had reasonably concluded that the presence of the brickyard was inconsistent with neighboring uses.   *   *   *

Goldblatt v. Hempstead, *supra,* is a recent example. There, a 1958 city safety ordinance banned any excavations below the water table and effectively prohibited the claimant from continuing a sand and gravel mining business that had been operated on the particular parcel since 1927. The Court upheld the ordinance against a "taking" challenge, although the ordinance prohibited the present and presumably most beneficial use of the property and had, like the regulations in *Miller* and *Hadacheck,* impacted severely on a particular owner.   *   *   *

Pennsylvania Coal Co. v. Mahon, 260 U.S. 393 (1922), is the leading case for the proposition that a state statute that substantially furthers important public policies may so frustrate distinct investment-backed expectations as to amount to a "taking." There the claimant had sold the surface rights to particular parcels of property, but expressly reserved the right to remove the coal thereunder. A Pennsylvania statute, enacted after the transactions, forbade any mining of coal that caused the subsidence of any house, unless the house was the property of the owner of the underlying coal and was more than 150 feet from the improved property of another. Because the statute made it commercially impracticable to mine the coal, *id.,* at 414, and thus had nearly the same effect as the complete destruction of rights claimant had purchased from the owners of the surface land, see *id.,* at 414–415, the Court held that the statute was invalid as effecting a "taking" without just compensation.   *   *   *

Finally, Government actions that may be characterized as acquisitions of resources to permit or facilitate uniquely public functions have often been held to constitute "takings." Causby v. United States, *supra,* is illustrative. In holding that direct overflights above the claimant's land, that destroyed the present use of the land as a chicken farm, constituted a "taking," *Causby* emphasized that Government had not "merely destroyed property [but was] using a part of it for the flight of its planes." Id., 328 U.S., at 262–263, n. 7, 66 S.Ct. at 1066. See also Griggs v. Allegheny County, 369 U.S. 84, 82 S.Ct. 531, 7 L.Ed.2d 585 (1962) (overflights held a taking); Portsmouth Co. v. United States, 260 U.S. 327, 43 S.Ct. 135, 67 L.Ed. 287 (1922) (United States' military installations repeated firing of guns over claimant's land is a taking); United States v. Cress, 243 U.S. 316, 37 S.Ct. 380, 61 L.Ed. 746 (1917) (repeated floodings of land caused by water project is taking); but see YMCA v. United States, 395 U.S. 85, 89 S.Ct. 1511, 23 L.Ed.2d 117 (1969) (damage caused to building when federal officers who were seeking to protect building were attacked by rioters held not a taking). See generally Michelman, 80 Harv.L.Rev. 1165, 1226–1229 (1967); Sax, 74 Yale L.J. 36 (1963).

B

In contending that the New York City law has "taken" * * * appellants make a series of arguments, * * *. Before considering these, we emphasize what is not in dispute. * * * appellants do not contest that New York City's objective of preserving structures and areas with special historic, architectural, or cultural significance is an entirely permissible governmental goal. They also do not dispute that the restrictions imposed on its parcel are appropriate means of securing the purposes of the New York City law. * * * They accept * * * both that the parcel of land occupied by Grand Central Terminal must, in its present state, be regarded as capable of earning a reasonable return, and that the transferable development rights afforded appellants by virtue of the Terminal's designation as a landmark are valuable, even if not as valuable as the rights to construct above the Terminal. In appellants' view none of these factors derogate from their claim that New York City's law has effected a "taking."

They first observe that the air space above the Terminal is a valuable property interest, * * *. They urge that the Landmark Law has deprived them of any gainful use of their "air rights" above the Terminal and that * * * the city has "taken" their right to this superadjacent air space, thus entitling them to "just compensation" measured by the fair market value of these air rights.

Apart from our own disagreement with appellants' characterization * * * the submission that appellants may establish a "taking" simply by showing that they have been denied the ability to exploit a property interest that they heretofore had believed was available for development is quite simply untenable. * * * "Taking" jurisprudence does not divide a single parcel into discrete segments and attempt to determine whether rights in a particular segment have been entirely abrogated. * * *

Secondly, appellants, focusing on the character and impact of the New York City law, argue that it effects a "taking" because its operation has significantly diminished the value of the Terminal site. * * *

Stated baldly, appellants' position appears to be that the only means of ensuring that selected owners are not singled out to endure financial hardship for no reason is to hold that any restriction imposed on individual landmarks pursuant to the New York scheme is a "taking" requiring the payment of "just compensation." Agreement with this argument would of course invalidate not just New York City's law, but all comparable landmark legislation in the Nation. We find no merit in it.

It is true * * * that both historic district legislation and zoning laws regulate all properties within given physical communities whereas landmark laws apply only to selected parcels. But, contrary to appellants' suggestions, landmark laws are not like discriminatory, or "reverse spot," zoning: that is, a land use decision which arbitrarily singles out a particular parcel for different, less favorable treatment than the neighboring ones. * * * In contrast to discriminatory zoning, * * * the New York City law embodies a comprehensive plan to preserve structures of historic or aesthetic interest wherever they might be found in the city, * * *.

Equally without merit is the related argument that the decision to designate a structure as a landmark "is inevitably arbitrary or at least subjective because it basically is a matter of taste," * * *.

* * * It is of course true that the Landmark Law has a more severe impact on some landowners than on others, but that in itself does not mean that the law effects a "taking." Legislation designed to promote the general welfare commonly burdens some more than others.

* * *

Appellants' final broad-based attack would have us treat the law as an instance, like that in United States v. Causby, *supra,* * * *. Apart from the fact that *Causby* was a case of invasion of airspace that destroyed the use of the farm beneath and this New York City law has in no wise impaired the present use of the Terminal, the Landmark Law neither exploits appellants' parcel for city purposes nor * * * arises from any entrepreneurial operations of the city. * * * The Landmarks Law's effect is simply to prohibit appellants or anyone else from occupying portions of the airspace above the Terminal, * * *. This is no more an appropriation of property by Government for its own uses than is a zoning law prohibiting, for "aesthetic" reasons, two or more adult theatres within a specified area, * * *.

C

Rejection of appellants' broad arguments is not however the end of our inquiry, * * * We now must consider whether the interference with appellants' property is of such a magnitude that "there must be an exercise of eminent domain and compensation to sustain [it]." Pennsylvania Coal Co. v. Mahon, 260 U.S., at 413, 43 S.Ct., at 159. That inquiry may be narrowed to the question of the severity of the impact of the law * * * and its resolution in turn requires a careful assessment of the impact of the regulation on the Terminal site.

Unlike the governmental acts in *Goldblatt, Miller, Causby, Griggs,* and *Hadacheck,* the New York City law does not interfere in any way with the present uses of the Terminal. * * * More importantly, on this record, we must regard the New York City law as permitting Penn Central not only to profit from the Terminal but to obtain a "reasonable return" on its investment.

Appellants, moreover, exaggerate the effect of the Act on its ability to make use of the air rights above the Terminal in two respects. First, it simply cannot be maintained, on this record, that appellants have been prohibited from occupying *any* portion of the airspace above the Terminal. While the Commission's actions in denying applications to construct an office building in excess of 50 stories above the Terminal may indicate that it will refuse to issue a certificate of appropriateness for any comparably sized structure, nothing that the Commission has said or done suggests an intention to prohibit *any* construction above the Terminal. * * * Since appellants have not sought approval for the construction of a smaller structure, we do not know that appellants will be denied any use of any portion of the airspace above the Terminal.

Second, to the extent appellants have been denied the right to build above the Terminal, it is not literally accurate to say that they have been denied *all* use of even those pre-existing air rights. Their ability to use these rights has not been abrogated; they are made transferable to at least eight parcels in the vicinity of the Terminal, one or two of which have been found suitable for the construction of new office buildings. Although appellants and others have argued that New York City's transferable development rights program is far from ideal, the New York courts here supportably found that, at least in the case of the Terminal, the rights afforded are valuable. While these rights may well not have constituted "just compensation" if a "taking" had occurred, the rights nevertheless undoubtedly mitigate whatever financial burdens the law has imposed on appellants and, for that reason, are to be taken into account in considering the impact of regulation. * * *

On this record we conclude that the application of New York City's Landmark Preservation Law has not effected a "taking" of appellants' property. The restrictions imposed are substantially related to the promotion of the general welfare and not only permit reasonable beneficial use of the landmark site but afford appellants opportunities further to enhance not only the Terminal site proper but also other properties.

Affirmed.

Notes

1. **Historic Preservations.** Restrictions to preserve historic areas have been consistently upheld on economic (tourism) and aesthetic grounds. See generally Annot., Validity * * * of Statute or Ordinance Protecting Historical Landmarks, 18 A.L.R. 4th 990 (1982); McNeely v. Board of Appeals, 358 Mass. 94, 261 N.E.2d 336 (1970); City of Santa Fe v. Gamble-Skogmo Inc., 73 N.M. 410, 389 P.2d 13 (1964); M & N Enterprises, Inc. v. Springfield, 111 Ill.App.2d 444, 250 N.E.2d 289 (1969). But these considerations are subject to nullification if pressed to unreasonable extremes. City of West Palm Beach v. State ex rel. Duffey, 158 Fla. 863, 30 So.2d 491 (1947); City of Milford v. Schmidt, 175 Neb. 12, 120 N.W.2d 262 (1963). Compare Hankins v. Rockleigh, 55 N.J.Super. 132, 150 A.2d 63 (1959) with State ex rel. Stoyanoff v. Berkeley, 458 S.W.2d 305 (Mo.1970).

The right to restrict building alteration was extended to non-historic districts in Faulkner v. Chestertown, 290 Md. 214, 428 A.2d 879 (1981).

2. **Government Property.** A city's attempt to designate state-owned structures as historic landmarks was held unconstitutional, ultra vires, and in conflict with state law. State v. Seattle, 94 Wash.2d 162, 615 P.2d 461 (1980). A similar attempt to subject federal instrumentalities to local historic preservation law failed in Don't Tear it Down, Inc. v. Pennsylvania Avenue Development Corp., 642 F.2d 527 (D.C.Cir.1980). The court held that the congressional statute empowering the District of Columbia to designate historic preservation sites was not intended to supersede an earlier federal act that authorized demolition of certain Capital areas by a nonmunicipal agency.

3. **Freezes on Private Use and Enjoyment.** While public plans and plotting of a private tract as a planned street can limit its exploitation by the owner, the general rule is that such action alone does not constitute a "taking" of the property. See Annot., 37 A.L.R.3d 127 (1971). Where, however, the governing authority undertakes by official notification, or denial of building permits, to prevent the sale or improvement of land proposed to be reserved for public use, such action, depending upon varying statutory controls may constitute a "taking". In re Land for L.R. 1062 & 1068, 422 Pa. 72, 221 A.2d 289 (1966); Grosso v. Board of Adjustment of Millburn Tp. in Essex County, 137 N.J.L. 630, 61 A.2d 167 (1948). General tests of invasion or deprivation of beneficial use of private property do not supply universal answers as to the permissible degree of delay that is required for a taking. See the opinion in Charles v. Diamond, p. 528, supra.

In addition to statutory variations, much will depend upon counterbalancing public benefits and necessity. See Note, *Problems of Advance Land Acquisition,* 52 Minn.L.Rev. 1175, at 1185–88 (1968).

4. **Condemnation of Land Subject to Servitudes.** Dominant estates in land created by private restrictions, covenants, easements or other servitudes may be compensable depending upon (a) state property law; and (b) the extent of statutory modification of such interests. See e.g. Annot., 4 A.L.R.3d 1137 (1965). The following excerpt outlines the jurisdictional variations:

United States v. Certain Land in the City of Augusta, County of Kennebec, State of Maine, 220 F.Supp. 696 (D.Me.1963) [Federal proceedings to condemn land that was subject to a restrictive covenant limiting its use to residential purposes. Owners of neighboring lots claimed compensation for the destruction of their interests in the land sought to be taken.]

" * * * The authorities are divided on the question of whether the extinguishment of an equitable servitude is a taking of private property for which federal and state constitutional provisions require that compensation be paid when the land to which it is attached is taken for public use. The state decisions are in hopeless and irreconcilable conflict, although the majority view favors compensation. The federal rule has not yet been authoritatively settled. * * * And the only recent federal cases which have dealt with the question have treated the rights created by such restrictions as compensable property interests in the context of federal eminent domain proceedings. Adaman Mut. Water Co. v. United States, 278 F.2d 842 (9th Cir.1960); United States v. 11.06 Acres of Land, 89

F.Supp. 852 (E.D.Mo.1950). This is the view adopted by the commentators and by the American Law Institute. 2 American Law of Property, op. cit. supra §§ 9.24 and 9.40; Restatement, Property §§ 539, comment (a) and 566 (1944); Comment, Real Property—Compensation for Abrogation of a Restrictive Covenant by Public Authority, 53 Mich.L.Rev. 451 (1955)." Id. at p. 700. See also Arkansas State Highway Commission v. McNeill, 238 Ark. 244, 381 S.W.2d 425 (1964) where the court noted that, if compensation should be allowed, there would be nothing to prevent the landowners from entering into a restrictive agreement as soon as a government project became known, and then from claiming compensation.

JUST v. MARINETTE COUNTY

Supreme Court of Wisconsin, 1972.
56 Wis.2d 7, 201 N.W.2d 761.

HALLOWS, CHIEF JUSTICE. Marinette County's Shoreland Zoning Ordinance Number 24 * * * became effective October 9, 1967, and follows a model ordinance published by the Wisconsin Department of Resource Development * * *. See Kusler, Water Quality Protection For Inland Lakes in Wisconsin: A Comprehensive Approach to Water Pollution, 1970 Wis.L.Rev. 35, 62–63. The ordinance was designed to meet standards and criteria for shoreland regulation which the legislature required to be promulgated * * *. The legislation, secs. 59.971 and 144.26, Stats., authorizing the ordinance was enacted as a part of the Water Quality Act of 1965 by ch. 614, Laws of 1965.

* * * The state shoreland program is unique. All county shoreland zoning ordinances must be approved by the department of natural resources prior to their becoming effective. 6 Wis.Adm.Code, sec. NR 115.04, May, 1971, Register No. 185. If a county does not enact a shoreland zoning ordinance which complies with the state's standards, the department of natural resources may enact such an ordinance for the county. Sec. 59.971(6), Stats.

There can be no disagreement over the public purpose sought to be obtained by the ordinance. * * * The Marinette county shoreland zoning ordinance * * * states the uncontrolled use of shorelands and pollution of navigable waters of Marinette county adversely affect public health, safety, convenience, and general welfare and impair the tax base.

The shoreland zoning ordinance divides the shorelands of Marinette county into general purpose districts, general recreation districts, and conservancy districts. A "conservancy" district is required by the statutory minimum standards and is defined in sec. 3.4 of the ordinance to include "all shorelands designated as swamps or marshes on the United States Geological Survey maps which have been designated as the Shoreland Zoning Map of Marinette County, * * *". The ordinance provides for permitted uses and conditional uses. One of the conditional uses requiring a permit * * * is the filling, drainage or dredging of wetlands * * *.

In April of 1961, several years prior to the passage of this ordinance, the Justs purchased 36.4 acres of land in the town of Lake along the south shore of Lake Noquebay, * * *.

The land owned by the Justs is designated as swamps or marshes on the United States Geological Survey Map and is located within 1,000 feet of the normal high-water elevation of the lake. Thus, the property is included in a conservancy district and, by sec. 2.29 of the ordinance, classified as "wetlands." Consequently, in order to place more than 500 square feet of fill on this property, the Justs were required to obtain a conditional-use permit from the zoning administrator of the county and pay a fee of $20 or incur a forfeiture of $10 to $200 for each day of violation.

In February and March of 1968, six months after the ordinance became effective, Ronald Just, without securing a conditional-use permit, hauled 1,040 square yards of sand onto this property and filled an area approximately 20-feet wide * * *. It is not seriously contended that the Justs did not violate the ordinance and the trial court correctly found a violation.

The real issue is whether the conservancy district provisions and * * * restrictions are unconstitutional because they amount to a constructive taking of the Justs' land without compensation. * * *

To state the issue in more meaningful terms, it is a conflict between the public interest in stopping the despoilation of natural resources, * * * and an owner's asserted right to use his property as he wishes. * * * The distinction between the exercise of the police power and condemnation has been said to be a matter of degree of damage to the property owner. In the valid exercise of the police power * * *, the damage suffered by the owner is said to be incidental. However, where the restriction is so great the landowner ought not to bear such a burden for the public good, the restriction has been held to be a constructive taking even though the actual use or forbidden use has not been transferred to the government so as to be a taking in the traditional sense. [Citations omitted] * * *

* * *

This case causes us to reexamine the concepts of public benefit in contrast to public harm and the scope of an owner's right to use of his property. In the instant case we have a restriction on the use of a citizens' property, not to secure a benefit for the public, but to prevent a harm from the change in the natural character of the citizens' property. * * * The state of Wisconsin under the trust doctrine has a duty to eradicate the present pollution and to prevent further pollution in its navigable waters. This is not, in a legal sense, a gain or a securing of a benefit by the maintaining of the natural *status quo* of the environment. What makes this case different from most condemnation or police power zoning cases is the interrelationship of the wetlands, the swamps and the natural environment of shorelands to the purity of the water and to such natural resources as navigation, fishing, and scenic beauty. ＊ ＊ ＊

The exercise of the police power in zoning must be reasonable and we think it is not an unreasonable exercise of that power to prevent harm to public rights by limiting the use of private property to its natural uses.

This is not a case where an owner is prevented from using his land for natural and indigenous uses. The uses consistent with the nature of the land are allowed and ＊ ＊ ＊ and still others permitted by special permit. ＊ ＊ ＊ The changing of wetlands and swamps to the damage of the general public by upsetting the natural environment and the natural relationship is not a reasonable use of that land which is protected from police power regulation. ＊ ＊ ＊ We realize no case in Wisconsin has yet dealt with shoreland regulations and there are several cases in other states which seem to hold such regulations unconstitutional; but nothing this court has said or held ＊ ＊ ＊ indicate that destroying the natural character of a swamp or a wetland ＊ ＊ ＊ for human habitation is a reasonable use ＊ ＊ ＊ when the new use, although of a more economical value to the owner, causes a harm to the general public.

＊ ＊ ＊

Cases wherein a confiscation was found cannot be relied upon by the Justs. In State v. Herwig (1962), 17 Wis.2d 442, 117 N.W.2d 335, a "taking" was found where a regulation which prohibited hunting on farmland had the effect of establishing a game refuge and resulted in an unnatural, concentrated foraging of the owner's land by waterfowl. In State v. Becker, *supra,* the court held void a law which established a wildlife refuge (and prohibited hunting) on private property. In Benka v. Consolidated Water Power Co. (1929), 198 Wis. 472, 224 N.W. 718, the court held if damages to plaintiff's property were in fact caused by flooding from a dam constructed by a public utility, those damages constituted a "taking" within the meaning of the condemnation statutes. In Bino v. Hurley (1955), 273 Wis. 10, 76 N.W.2d 571, the court held unconstitutional as a "taking" without compensation an ordinance which, in attempting to prevent pollution, prohibited the owners of land surrounding a lake from bathing, boating, or swimming in the lake. In Piper v. Ekern (1923), 180 Wis. 586, 593, 194 N.W. 159, 162, the court held a statute which limited the height of buildings surrounding the state capitol to be unnecessary for the public health, safety, or welfare and, thus, to constitute an unreasonable exercise of the police power. In all these cases the unreasonableness of the exercise of the police power lay in excessive restriction of the natural use of the land or rights in relation thereto.

Cases holding the exercise of police power to be reasonable likewise provide no assistance to Marinette county in their argument. In More-Way North Corp. v. State Highway Comm. (1969), 44 Wis.2d 165, 175 N.W.2d 749, the court held that no "taking" occurred as a result of the state's lowering the grade of a highway, which necessitated plaintiff's reconstruction of its parking lot and loss of 42 parking spaces. In Wisconsin Power & Light Co. v. Columbia County (1958), 3 Wis.2d 1, 87 N.W.2d 279, no "taking" was found where the county, in relocating a highway, deposited gravel close to plaintiff's tower, causing it to tilt. In Nick v. State Highway Comm., supra, the court held where property itself is not physically taken by the state, a restriction of access to a highway, while it may decrease the value of the land, does not entitle the owner to compensation. In *Buhler* the court held the mere depreciation of value was not sufficient ground to enjoin the county from enforcing the ordinance. In Hasslinger v. Hartland (1940), 234 Wis. 201, 290 N.W. 647, the court noted that "(a)ssuming an actionable nuisance by the creation of odors which make occupation of plaintiffs' farm inconvenient * * * and impair its value, it cannot be said that defendant has dispossessed plaintiffs or taken their property."

The Justs rely on several cases from other jurisdictions which have held zoning regulations involving flood plain districts, * * * to amount to a taking because the owners of the land were prevented from improving such property for residential or commercial purposes. * * * In Dooley v. Town Plan & Zon. Com. of Town of Fairfield (1964), 151 Conn. 304, 197 A.2d 770, the court held the restriction on land located in a flood plain district prevented its being used for residential or business purposes and thus the restriction destroyed the economic value to the owner. The court recognized the land was needed for a public purpose as it was part of the area in which the tidal stream overflowed when abnormally high tides existed, but the property was half a mile from the ocean and therefore could not be used for marina or boathouse purposes. In Morris County Land I. Co. v. Parsippany-Troy Hills Tp. (1963), 40 N.J. 539, 193 A.2d 232, a flood basin zoning ordinance was involved which required the controversial land to be retained in its natural state. The plaintiff owned 66 acres of a 1,500–acre swamp * * *. There was an extraneous issue that the freezing regulations were intended as a stop-gap until such time as the government would buy the property under a flood-control project. However, the court took the view the zoning had an effect of preserving the land as an open space as a water-detention basin and only the government or the public would be benefited, to the complete damage of the owner.

In State v. Johnson (1970), Me., 265 A.2d 711, the Wetlands Act restricted the alteration and use of certain wetlands without permission. The act was a conservation measure enacted under the police power to protect the ecology of areas bordering the coastal waters. The plaintiff owned a small tract of a salt-water marsh which was flooded at high tide. By filling, the land would be adapted for building purposes. The court held the restrictions against filling constituted a deprivation of a reasonable use of the owner's property and, thus, an unreasonable exercise of the police power. In MacGibbon v. Board of Appeals of Duxbury (1970), 356 Mass. 635, 255 N.E.2d 347, the plaintiff owned seven acres of land which were under water about twice a month in a shoreland area. He was denied a permit to excavate and fill part of his property. The purpose of the ordinance was to preserve from despoilage natural features and resources such as salt marshes, wetlands, and ponds. The court took the view the preservation of privately owned land in its natural, unspoiled state for the enjoyment and benefit of the public by preventing the owner from using it for any practical purpose was not within the limit and scope of the police power and the ordinance was not saved by the use of special permits.

It seems to us that filling a swamp not otherwise commercially usable is not in and of itself an existing use, which is prevented, but rather is the preparation for some future use which is not indigenous to a swamp. * * *

A recent case sustaining the validity of a zoning ordinance establishing a flood plain district is Turnpike Realty Company v. Town of Dedham (June, 1972), 72 Mass. 1303, 284 N.E.2d 891. The court held the validity of the ordinance was supported by valid considerations of public welfare, * * *. The ordinance provided that lands which were subject to seasonal or periodic flooding could not be used for residences or other purposes and prohibited the erection of structures or buildings which required land to be filled. This case is analogous to the instant facts. * * *

The Justs argue their property has been severely depreciated in value. * * * While loss of value is to be considered in determining whether a restriction is a constructive taking, value based upon changing the character of the land at the expense of harm to public rights is not an essential factor or controlling.

We are not unmindful of the warning in Pennsylvania Coal Co. v. Mahon (1922), 260 U.S. 393, 416, 43 S.Ct. 158, 160, 67 L.Ed. 322:

"* * * We are in danger of forgetting that a strong public desire to improve the public condition is not enough to warrant achieving the desire by a shorter cut than the constitutional way of paying for the change."

This observation refers to the improvement of the public condition, the securing of a benefit not presently enjoyed and to which the public is not entitled. The shoreland zoning ordinance preserves nature, the environment, and natural resources as they were created and to which the people have a present right. * * *

* * *

Notes

1. **Accord:** Candlestick Properties, Inc. v. San Francisco Bay Conservation and Development Commission, 11 Cal.App.3d 557, 89 Cal.Rptr. 897 (1970).

The Supreme Court recently approved the rule that zoning restrictions which do not deny an owner "economic viable use of his land", though perhaps not the most profitable, is not a compensable taking, in the form in inverse condemnation. Agins v. Tiburon, 447 U.S. 255, 100 S.Ct. 2138, 65 L.Ed.2d 106 (1980).

For an excellent study of the constitutional limits on land regulation without compensation, see Bosselman, Callies, and Banta, *The Taking Issue* (Council on Environmental Quality 1973). Those authors concluded: " * * * state courts have decided literally hundreds of cases, each of which determines whether the value of a particular land use regulation does or does not outweigh the loss of property value to a particular land owner. * * * In general this [review] * * * shows a general tendency of the courts to uphold well thought out regulations, though there are very few subjects on which one cannot find cases going both ways on very similar facts. * * * Nevertheless, the commentators have found a few tendencies * * * The one most often described is the tendency of the courts to prefer regulations that control those uses of land that were treated as 'nuisances' under the traditional common law. * * * A dramatic upsurge of concern over the environment took place in the late sixties * * *. We discovered an interesting trend * * * there is a strong tendency on the part of the courts to approve land use regulations if the purpose of the regulation is statewide or regional in nature rather than merely local. Id. at 322–323.

2. **Time Development Regulations.** How long may a municipality delay land development until it can supply street, sewerage and other utility facilities? See, Golden v. Planning Board of Town of Ramapo, reported at p. 529 and the notes thereto.

MARTIN v. PORT OF SEATTLE

Supreme Court of Washington, 1964.
64 Wash.2d 309, 391 P.2d 540.

FINLEY, JUDGE. This is an "inverse condemnation" action brought by 196 property owners against the Port of Seattle, a municipal corporation, as owner of the Seattle-Tacoma International Airport. The respondent property owners seek damages for an alleged taking or damaging of their property for public use caused by nearby low altitude flights of jet aircraft landing and taking off from the airport. * * *

* * *

* * * the gravamen of the complaint is the noise and vibration created by the aircraft rather than physical invasion * * *.

* * * The plaintiffs claim that, when jet aircraft pass over or in close proximity, conversation is halted, radio and television reception is disrupted, and the sound obliterated. The jets cause vibrations in the houses and of their contents, rendering it necessary to hammer the nails back into the siding of some of the homes * * * and to tighten light fixtures periodically. Sleep is disrupted, outdoor entertainment almost impossible, and the noise painful to many. The noise also causes fear * * *. It is asserted that the respondents cannot sell their homes, and that the property values are substantially reduced.

The trial court held that the plaintiffs had stated a claim for relief. The theory which forms the basis of this holding may be set out as follows. The property owners were conceptually divided into two groups, one group comprising those having land which was subjected to direct overflights * * * the second, those as to which no overflights were shown. Respecting the first group, the trial court held that the overflights amounted to a *taking* of an air easement without just compensation in violation of Art. I, § 16, Amendment 9, of the Washington Constitution and Amendment XIV of the United States Constitution. As to the second group, the trial court held that the regular low flights near by amounted to a *damaging* of the properties without payment of just compensation in violation of Art. I, § 16, Amendment 9, of the Washington Constitution. * * *

We are substantially in agreement with the trial court. However, this court will not in this case stress any of the proposed distinctions between the "taking" and the "damaging" of a property right * * *. As the Washington Constitution affords or provides a basis for compensation in either instance, subtle efforts at legal refinement * * * can be expected to be more difficult and treacherous than convincing or utilitarian.

There seems little doubt that the noise of jet aircraft * * * can amount to a taking or damaging of property for which Amendment 9 of the Washington Constitution requires that compensation be made. The term "property," as used in that provision, was defined in Ackerman v. Port of Seattle (1960), 55 Wash.2d 400, 348 P.2d 664, 77 A.L.R.2d 1344, to include the unrestricted right to use, enjoy, and dispose of the land. It was there held that the frequent flights over the land of the plaintiffs amounted to a taking * * *. The defendant in Ackerman was the same entity here involved.

An identical result follows in the instant case * * *. It should be noted that the Federal Government has developed the practice of affirmatively moving to condemn so-called "air easements" in connection with the operation of their air bases. See United States v. 15,909 Acres, 176 F.Supp. 447 (S.D.Cal.1958). It also appears that the right of a property owner to proceed against the federal government on a theory that the noise of jet aircrafts have "taken" his right to use and enjoyment of land is well established, recognized, and accepted. [citations] Some state courts recognize that the noise of jet aircraft, and its interference with the use of land * * * are additional elements of compensable damage includable in the payments required for the land or airspace actually physically taken in the action. [citations]

The appellants resist the conclusions * * * with a series of arguments which may be roughly grouped within three broad contentions: (1) That the Congress of the United States has placed all navigable airspace within the public domain, with the result that no use of such airspace by the public can result in liability; (2) that there can be no "taking or damaging" in the constitutional sense in the absence of a direct overflight of the plaintiff's land; and (3) that recovery based upon an alleged interference with the exercise or enjoyment of property rights must be limited to those instances where a *substantial* interference is shown, as opposed to a mere "incidental" damaging. These contentions will be considered in the above sequence.

* * * In the Federal Aviation Act of 1958, the "navigable airspace" of the United States was expressly extended to include any and all airspace "needed to insure safety in take-off and landing of aircraft." It is the position of the appellant that such legislation creates such an unrestricted right of use as to prevent any action for trespass or for nuisance, * * *. This approach, however, overlooks the fact that recovery * * * is supported upon reasoning akin to eminent domain, * * * and not upon any consideration of whether that taking should be classed as "wrongful" or tortious under any common-law theory. * * *

* * *

The appellants next contend that the terms "taking and damaging" of the Washington Constitution provide recovery in only those instances where a property right is taken by the passage of the aircraft directly over the land of the plaintiff. This requirement, * * * is presently stressed by some federal courts * * *. Batten v. United States (10th Cir.1962), 306 F.2d 580. We are unable to accept the premise * * *. The plaintiffs are not seeking recovery for a technical trespass * * *.

Both United States v. Causby (1946), 328 U.S. 256, 66 S.Ct. 1062, 90 L.Ed. 1206, and Griggs v. Allegheny County (1962) 369 U.S. 84, 82 S.Ct. 531, 7 L.Ed.2d 585, allowed recovery for repeated low-level flights over private land. While a direct overflight or invasion in airspace is in fact involved in each case, it is not clear that the reasoning and approach of those cases is so limited. Realistically, it must be conceded that a major part of the damage in either case was engendered by noise and vibration, whether or not accompanied by a physical displacement of air above the property. * * * Again in Griggs, the loss of sleep due to noise and vibration was stressed as an important factor in allowing recovery, * * *. The reliance placed upon the high noise level by the Supreme Court in both decisions, without detectable preoccupation with its angle of incidence, strongly indicates that the holdings are not limited to those instances where the aircraft passes directly over the land.

* * * We must agree that the problem of balancing the interests involved, public and private, seems much the same whether a physical trespass is or is not involved.

* * *

We hold that no overflight or direct physical invasion of the airspace over the land is necessary in order to maintain an action under the "taking or damaging" provisions of the state constitution.

* * * It is argued that the interference * * * must be shown to be a "substantial" interference before it can amount to a "taking" * * *. The terms "substantial injury" and "substantial interference" appear commonly in the decided cases, sometimes as if it were the *sine qua non* of recovery. The terms are not pertinent, however, in the "inverse condemnation" context, * * *. It differs from eminent domain only in that the landowner institutes the action, rather than the entity possessing the condemnation power. * * *

When this action is analyzed in this manner, the term "substantial" is of dubious relevancy or utility. It connotes a balancing of the interests of the public in general against those of the individual. * * * In eminent domain, and in inverse condemnation, such a balancing does not have to be accomplished as a distinct process, simply because the individual seeks no recovery for his individual suffering * * *. But in inverse condemnation the measure of recovery is injury to market value, and that alone.

Therefore, the balance of interest inherently struck in this type of action comes about in the following manner. If the individual is unusually sensitive, and sustains a greater injury than might be suffered by the general public from such interference, the public interest in maintaining the flights leaves him to one remedy—to sell his property and move. This is no different than it would be had his land been condemned for forced sale to the state. But whichever way the state exacts such a "sale," it must pay the individual the amount he suffers in the diminishment of the value of his land, as reflected by the decrease in the amount he can receive in a sale to a willing buyer. Such lowering of market value reflects not the personal injury to the individual, but the lesser desirability of the land to the general public; *i.e.,* to a ready, able, and willing buyer. When the land of an individual is diminished in value for the public benefit, then justice, and the constitution, require that the public pay.

* * *

Upon the reasoning hereinbefore set out, we therefore hold that the plaintiffs * * * have stated a claim upon which relief can be granted. The judgment should be affirmed in conformity with the conclusions reached herein. It is so ordered.

Notes

1. **Contra:** Ferguson v. Keene, 108 N.H. 409, 238 A.2d 1 (1968); Louisville and Jefferson County Air Board v. Porter, 397 S.W.2d 146 (Ky. 1965). Legislatures may, as a matter of sovereign grace, authorize compensation for cases that are doubtful under decisional law, but clear on the equities.

2. **Tort Alternative to Condemnation.** In Ferguson v. Keene, supra, the court denied a condemnation claim, but upheld the claim for nuisance damages. Accord: Greater Westchester Homeowners Association v. Los Angeles, 26 Cal.3d 86, 160 Cal.Rptr. 733, 603 P.2d 1329 (1979), cert.

denied 449 U.S. 820, 101 S.Ct. 77, 66 L.Ed.2d 22 (1980) (nuisance action for damage from excessive aircraft noise from city airport held not federally preempted). Damages in tort law might well exceed compensation for condemnation. What reasons could dictate a preference for a condemnation claim?

3. **Noise Pollution and Condemnation.** Industrial technology, particularly in transport and industry, has increased the volume and constancy of noise and vibrations, and interference with land enjoyment. The airport cases provide analogies for inverse condemnation claims for highway noise and vibrations where new highways accommodate heavy trucks and mass auto traffic. But airport cases may be distinguished by their special effects on a smaller segment of the populace. See Northcut v. State Road Dept., 209 So.2d 710 (Fla.App.1968). Nevertheless, some recent cases developed a rationale for inverse condemnation in highway cases. See Annot., 51 A.L.R.3d 860 (1973); Note, *Eminent Domain and the Environment*, 56 Cornell L.Q. 651 (1971).

4. **Destruction of Access to Public Ways.** Whether impairment of existing access to streets or highways constitutes a form of inverse condemnation largely depends on the impact of such loss under particular circumstances. A total cutoff would constitute a "taking" State ex rel. State Highway Dept. v. 14.69 Acres of Land, 226 A.2d 828 (Del.1967). But if *suitable* substitute access is provided, the claim for injury or damage may be defeated. If other access remains, the burden of circuitous travel must be "substantial" to support recovery. Cf. Priestly v. State, 23 N.Y.2d 152, 242 N.E.2d 827 (1968); Breidert v. Southern Pacific Co., 61 Cal.2d 659, 39 Cal.Rptr. 903, 394 P.2d 719 (1964); Stoebuck, *The Property Right of Access Versus The Power of Eminent Domain*, 47 Tex.L.Rev. 733 (1969); Clarke, *Easement and Partial Taking Valuation Problems*.

5. **Impairment of Use or Investment.** When no acreage is taken, but the grade or elevation between the public way and abutting land is altered as to substantially affect the land value, is this inverse condemnation? As to neighboring, but not immediately abutting owners should the foregoing question be resolved any differently? Case authorities are collected and analyzed in Annot., 2 A.L.R.3d 995 (1965); 43 A.L.R.2d 1072 (1955).

6. **Denial of Damages on Indirect Taking Claims.** For a new thesis that the only relief to burdensome regulations that do not directly interfere with property (but only with its usefulness) is injunction and not damages, see People v. Minjares, 153 Cal.Rptr. 224, 591 P.2d 514 (1979). A similar view was adopted in New York as to unconstitutional building freezes. See Charles v. Diamond, noted at p. 528, infra.

7. **Zoning Restrictions as a "Taking".** The authorities are also divided on the question whether zoning restrictions, viz. height of buildings and other objects near airports constitute a comparable "taking." Annot, Zoning Regulations Limiting Use of Property Near Airport, 18 A.L.R.4th 542 (1982).

(2) Public Use

BERMAN v. PARKER

Supreme Court of the United States, 1954.
348 U.S. 26, 75 S.Ct. 98, 99 L.Ed. 27.

[Owner sued to enjoin condemnation of his department store as part of an area redevelopment project. The Enabling Act declared that conditions in the District of Columbia were injurious to public health, safety, morals and welfare; that a comprehensive plan of redevelopment should be effected; that project area redevelopment plans are a public use; that the District redevelopment agency could acquire, by eminent domain or otherwise, real property to eliminate and prevent recurrence of blighted areas; and that the agency could redevelop the area for public use, and sell or lease improved areas (including low rent housing) and any remaining unimproved areas to private parties, with the restriction that such property be used in conformity with the redevelopment plan. The Act further provided that preference be given to private enterprise in carrying out the plan. The Act was attacked as unconstitutional on the ground that plaintiff's property was not blighted; that no public use was served by taking this unblighted business property, and that the taking thereof for possible resale to other individuals exceeded the condemnation power.]

Mr. JUSTICE DOUGLAS delivered the opinion of the Court.

* * *

The power of Congress over the District of Columbia includes all the legislative powers which a state may exercise over its affairs. * * * We deal, in other words, with what traditionally has been known as the police power. An attempt to define its reach or trace its outer limits is fruitless, for each case must turn on its own facts. The definition is essentially the product of legislative determinations addressed to the purposes of government, purposes neither abstractly nor historically capable of complete definition. Subject to specific constitutional limitations, when the legislature has spoken, the public interest has been declared in terms well-nigh conclusive. In such cases the legislature, not the judiciary, is the main guardian of the public needs * * * whether it be Congress legislating concerning the District of Columbia * * * or the States legislating concerning local affairs. * * * This principle admits of no exception merely because the power of eminent domain is involved. The role of the judiciary in determining whether that power is being exercised for a public purpose is an extremely narrow one. See Old Dominion Co. v. United States, 269 U.S. 55, 66, 46 S.Ct. 39, 40, 70 L.Ed. 162; United States ex rel. T.V.A. v. Welch, 327 U.S. 546, 552, 66 S.Ct. 715, 718, 90 L.Ed. 843.

* * * Miserable and disreputable housing conditions may do more than spread disease and crime and immorality. They may also suffocate the spirit * * *. They may indeed make living an almost insufferable burden. They may also be an ugly sore, a blight on the community which robs it of charm, * * * The misery of housing may despoil a community as an open sewer may ruin a river.

We do not sit to determine whether a particular housing project is or is not desirable. The concept of the public welfare is broad and inclusive. See Day-Brite Lighting, Inc. v. Missouri, 342 U.S. 421, 424, 72 S.Ct. 405, 407, 96 L.Ed. 469. The values it represents are spiritual as well as physical, aesthetic as well as monetary. * * * If those who govern the District of Columbia decide that the Nation's Capital should be beautiful as well as sanitary, there is nothing in the Fifth Amendment that stands in the way.

* * * Here one of the means chosen is the use of private enterprise for redevelopment of the area. Appellants argue that this makes the project a taking from one businessman for the benefit of another businessman. But the means of executing the project are for Congress and Congress alone to determine, once the public purpose has been established. * * * What we have said also disposes of any contention concerning the fact that certain property owners in the area may be permitted to repurchase their properties for redevelopment in harmony with the over-all plan. That, too, is a legitimate means which Congress and its agencies may adopt, if they choose.

In the present case, Congress and its authorized agencies attack the problem of the blighted parts of the community on an area rather than on a structure-by-structure basis. That, too, is opposed by appellants. They maintain that since their building does not imperil health or safety nor contribute to the making of a slum or a blighted area, it cannot be swept into a redevelopment plan by the mere dictum of the Planning Commission or the Commissioners. * * * The experts concluded that * * * the area must be planned as a whole. * * * The entire area needed redesigning so that a balanced, integrated plan could be developed for the region, including not only new homes but also schools, churches, parks, streets, and shopping centers. In this way it was hoped that the cycle of decay of the area could be controlled and the birth of future slums prevented. Cf. Gohld Realty Co. v. Hartford, 141 Conn. 135, 141–144, 104 A.2d 365, 368–370; Hunter v. Redevelopment Authority, 195 Va. 326, 338–339, 78 S.E.2d 893, 900–901. * * *

* * * If owner after owner were permitted to resist these redevelopment programs on the ground that his particular property was not being used against the public interest, integrated plans for redevelopment would suffer greatly. * * *

* * * Once the question of the public purpose has been decided, the amount and character of land to be taken for the project and the need for a particular tract * * * rests in the discretion of the legislative branch. * * *

* * *

The rights of these property owners are satisfied when they receive that just compensation which the Fifth Amendment exacts as the price of the taking.

The judgment of the District Court, as modified by this opinion, is affirmed.

Notes

1. **Aesthetic Zoning.** Berman marked a radical extension of prior law, and provided strong impetus to the view that government may zone and regulate for aesthetic purposes. State courts have adopted the Berman rationale in redeveloping blighted areas, e.g. Simco Stores v. Redevelopment Authority, 455 Pa. 438, 317 A.2d 610 (1974).

2. **Redevelopment and Leasehold Interests.** A compensable "taking" of leasehold rights was found in Devines v. Maier, 665 F.2d 138 (7th Cir.1981).

MILLER v. TACOMA

Supreme Court of Washington, 1963.
61 Wash.2d 374, 378 P.2d 464.

[The majority opinion affirmed dismissal of plaintiff's complaint which challenged an urban renewal law that authorized area-wide condemnation for redevelopment projects, with power in the authorities to resell large portions of the condemned area to other private parties. The following dissenting opinion sharpened the issues presented.]

ROSELLINI, JUDGE (dissenting).

* * *

In no case has this court ever held that the power of eminent domain may be used to take private property for immediate private use, even where there may be an ultimate public benefit. * * *

* * *

In Berman v. Parker, 348 U.S. 26, 75 S.Ct. 98, 99 L.Ed. 27, it was decided upon a unique and novel theory that the exercise of the power of eminent domain is only incidental to the police power. "Public use" is confused with "public welfare." * * *

Many other cases are decided upon the theory that the power of eminent domain may be exercised for a public purpose, a public benefit, or the public welfare, disregarding the requirement of our constitution that it be for a public use. Typical of these is Gohld v. City of Hartford, 141 Conn. 135, 104 A.2d 365. * * *

* * *

Finally, we have consistently and uniformly construed the language of amendment 9, Art. 1, § 16 * * * as prohibiting the taking * * * unless the public has a fixed and definite use of the property, and not simply a use which may incidentally or indirectly promote the public interest or general prosperity. * * *

* * *

The act also discloses that one of the dominant aims of the legislature was to provide for the transferring of the greatest portion of the renewal area to private enterprise.

* * *

* * * Under our constitution, the government does not have this power. * * *

Two ways that could legitimately achieve the stated goal

If urban renewal is a necessary and needed instrument of government to correct blighted areas * * *, the problem may be solved in one of two ways: municipal corporations may exercise their police power to condemn as a nuisance anything that is injurious * * *; or the people may amend the constitution to define urban renewal as a public use. * * *

Dissent's Holding

* * * Unless the people are willing to change the constitution so as to permit it, one man's property should not be taken by the government and turned over to another to aid in the fulfillment of a utopian ideal of the state.

* * *

I would reverse the judgment of the trial court.

Notes

1. **Prevention vs. Cure.** How far in advance of threatened blight may land be condemned for redevelopment? See People ex rel. Gutnecht v. Chicago, 3 Ill.2d 539, 547–9, 121 N.E.2d 791, 796 (1954).

2. **"Public Use".** The concept of "public use" has had an uneven development. Two broad views developed on the general test. "Under one rule, an 'actual use' by the public is required. To the courts adopting the other rule, a 'beneficial use' to the public is sufficient. * * * However, in the cases relying on the 'beneficial use' theory, the courts have held that elimination of blight was the controlling purpose and, although there was a possibility of resale or lease of the land to private persons, this was still a part of the public use, * * * in cases relying upon the 'actual use' theory, primary emphasis is placed on the fact that the area in question was to be acquired by the public and used by it * * *. Sale of the land to private redevelopers after clearance was deemed proper * * * because the public should not retain title to land for which it no longer has any use. * * * In urban redevelopment cases, public use could only end if there were no regulation regarding subsequent use and development of the cleared land. Without regulation * * * the long term result could then only be conjectural, and this conjectural result could * * * be an argument for invalidating the original condemnation * * *." State ex rel. Allerton Parking Corp. v. Cleveland, 4 Ohio App.2d 57, 64–67, 211 N.E.2d 203, 208–210 (1965); affirmed 6 Ohio St. 165, 216 N.E.2d 876 (1966).

The foregoing summary does not reflect the division of authority as to the kinds of "urban redevelopment" that satisfy both views of public use. Many courts distinguish area-wide condemnation to restore housing needs, from area-wide condemnation strictly to redevelop commercial districts, and from area-wide condemnation of non-blighted sections to provide industrial districts. In the last two categories, divisions in treatment may result from differences in state constitutions (compare e.g. Virginia Constitution Art. I § 11, which empowers the legislature to define public use, with Vernon's Ann. Missouri Stat. Constitution Art. I § 28, which, like Washington, makes public use a judicial question); or from judicial disagreement on the proper ambit of "public use." Put another way, they disagree on the proper roles of government in land management.

(a) *Industrial and Commercial Promotion.* Hogue v. Port of Seattle, 54 Wash.2d 799, 341 P.2d 171 (1959) held that condemnation of developed agricultural and residential areas to provide industrial sites was not for a public use, and, therefore, unconstitutional. But cf. Schenck v. Pittsburgh, 364 Pa. 31, 70 A.2d 612 (1950) wherein condemnation of an existing commercial area to rebuild commercial structures for ultimate sale or lease to private business was upheld as a public use.

In contrast to Hogue, Courtesy Sandwich Shop v. Port of New York Authority, 12 N.Y.2d 379, 240 N.Y.S.2d 1, 190 N.E.2d 402 (1963), appeal dismissed 375 U.S. 78, 84 S.Ct. 194, 11 L.Ed.2d 141 (1963) adopted the Berman "public purpose" rationale and upheld, over vigorous dissent, a statute authorizing the Port Authority to condemn a valuable lower Manhattan area for development of a World Trade Center. The competitive advantage taken by the Authority in its real estate management, at the expense of private realtors, was deemed incidental to its primary purpose of port development. Hogue and Courtesy Shop highlight the difference between limiting public "use" to public "necessity," or expanding it to public "purpose."

The [police] power to redevelop business sites by voluntary public purchase is generally upheld. See Mitchell v. North Carolina Ind. Dev. Fin. Auth., 273 N.C. 137, 159 S.E.2d 745 (1970); Note, *The Public Purpose of Municipal Financing for Industrial Redevelopment,* 70 Yale L.J. 789 (1961).

(b) *Public Parking Facilities.* Is condemnation of private parking lots for use as public parking facilities a public use? Ogden City v. Stephens, 21 Utah 2d 336, 445 P.2d 703 (1968) answered in the affirmative. See also State ex rel. Hawks v. Topeka, 176 Kan. 240, 270 P.2d 270 (1954). Compare City and County of San Francisco v. Ross, 44 Cal.2d 52, 279 P.2d 529 (1955) with Larsen v. San Francisco, 152 Cal.App.2d 355, 313 P.2d 959 (1957); cf. Foltz v. Indianapolis, 234 Ind. 656, 130 N.E.2d 650 (1955).

Club Joliet, Inc. v. Manchester, 110 N.H. 172, 262 A.2d 844 (1970) applied the public purpose reasoning of Berman v. Parker to condemnation and financing of parking facilities as part of an area redevelopment plan.

(c) *Private Benefits in Public Uses.* The off-street public parking cases illustrate problems that arise where condemned property is put to combined public and private uses. Denihan Enterprises Inc. v. O'Dwyer, 277 A.D. 407, 100 N.Y.S.2d 512 (1950) considered a challenge to a proposed condemnation on the ground that the property taken was intended for private use under long term lease to a developer which would construct a garage facility on the tract, with the right to lease 30% of the floor space for commercial purposes. The court's response is fairly typical:

"We understand that the fact that a private interest may be benefitted by a condemnation project does not render it illegal where the public good is enhanced, Matter of Murray v. LaGuardia, 291 N.Y. 320, 52 N.E.2d 884, but that is a relative matter and one of proper proportions and purposes. It is possible that a trial of the action may dissipate any doubts as to the legality of the arrangement, but it is also possible that a trial may reveal that the project on the whole is not authorized by sound condemnation principles and is so imbued with a private purpose and private use of the land to be condemned as to render the proposed condemnation and contract arrangements invalid. * * *" Id. 515.

In Wilmington Parking Authority v. Ranken, 34 Del.Ch. 439, 105 A.2d 614 (1954) the court upheld a lease of a public parking facility under which 40% of the space would be devoted to commercial uses. Such terms were found necessary to raise the funds needed to construct the parking project. Compare e.g. Price v. Philadelphia Parking Authority, 422 Pa. 317, 221 A.2d 138 (1966) (Parking Authority lease which granted "air rights," without competitive bidding, was nullified) with Seligsohn v. Philadelphia Parking Authority, 412 Pa. 372, 194 A.2d 606 (1963) (upheld authority condemnation and leasing of site for public parking and department stores) and with Basehore v. Hampden Indus. Development Authority, 433 Pa. 40, 248 A.2d 212 (1968) (condemnation for leasing of industrial sites upheld).

(3) Excess and Advance Condemnation

There are many reasons, not all good, why condemning authorities take more land than is necessary for an improvement, or take it well in advance of the time when needed. For a critique of such practices, and the authority thereon, see generally Note, *Excess Condemnation—To Take or Not to Take—Functional Analysis,* 15 N.Y.Law Forum 119 (1969). Excess condemnations have been described, according to the condemnor's primary motivation, as "protective," "remnant," and "recoupment." These inexact classifications are discussed in the following cases.

STATE EX REL. STATE HWY. DEPT. v. 9.88 ACRES OF LAND

Supreme Court of Delaware, 1969.
253 A.2d 509.

WOLCOTT, CHIEF JUSTICE.

[Appeal from an order denying the right of the State Highway Department to condemn 14.76 acres of excess land.]

Due to the construction of Interstate Route 495, the Highway Department sought to condemn 9.88 acres of land owned by Christiana Marine, Inc. The taking of the 9.88 acres * * * will result in a complete denial of land access to 14.76 acres of land also belonging to Christiana Marine, Inc. * * *

The Highway Department amended its complaint to include the taking of the 14.76 acres on May 5, 1967, presumably after the decision of this court in State ex rel. State Highway Department v. 14.69 Acres of Land, Del., 226 A.2d 828, and in reliance on 17 Del.C. § 175, adopted June 22, 1956. Section 175, in pertinent part, provides as follows:

" * * * the Department may, in its discretion, acquire an entire lot, block, or tract of land, if, by so doing, the interest of the public will be best served, even though said entire lot, block, or tract is not immediately needed for the right-of-way proper."

The Highway Department concedes that it has no immediate need for the additional 14.76 acres, nor has it any plans for its future use. It seeks to condemn the * * * excess acreage on the ground that the compensation it will be required to pay by the condemnation of the 9.88 acres will approximate the cost of the entire tract since access from the land will be denied by the taking of the 9.88 acres. This reason is, of course, an economic one.

* * *

* * * We think, however, that § 175 does not aid the Highway Department in its contention. We point out that the quoted portion of the section limits the acquisition of an entire tract of land only when it is "in connection with the acquisition of property or property rights for any controlled-access facilit[ies], * * *."

The Highway Department advances the so-called recoupment theory * * *. This theory is one which seeks to diminish the over-all cost of a particular public improvement by the condemnation of other abutting or adjacent property not actually needed for the particular improvement, with the ability ultimately to sell such excess property.

* * *

We consider the attempt by the Highway Department to take this excess 14.76 acres as falling squarely within the so-called recoupment theory. The recoupment theory is rejected by at least the majority of the states which still adhere to the doctrine that private property may be taken for public purposes only when the taking authority has an immediate public use * * *, or has plans for a public use of the property in the foreseeable future. In our opinion, the Highway Department has no foreseeable future use for this excess land and, consequently, may not take it through the power of eminent domain. [Citations omitted]

The Highway Department relies on a somewhat comparable statute of New Jersey (N.J.S.A. 27:7A–4.1) * * *.

We think the New Jersey act is broader in scope than is 17 Del.C. § 175. Since § 175 is, of necessity, limited by the general doctrine of condemnation long established in this state * * *, the absence of such future plans of necessity precludes a condemnation.

The Highway Department's contention * * * may be an attempt to apply the so-called "remnant" theory, described in 6 A.L.R.3d 317 and 2 Nichols on Eminent Domain (3d Ed.) § 7.5122. Whether or not this theory is good law in this State in a proper case need not be decided at this time because the facts here do not fall within its scope. To come within that theory, the "remnant" must be practically worthless. We do not agree that the 14.76 acres is rendered practically useless or worthless by the taking of the 9.88 acres; although the tract remaining will be landlocked, it is still worth $100 to $200 per acre, according to the appraisers.

* * * It desires to acquire the land solely for the purpose of reselling it at some undisclosed future time in order to recoup part of the payment for just compensation. We think this cannot be done constitutionally. * * *

For the foregoing reasons, the judgment below is affirmed.

Notes

1. **Contra.** People ex rel. Dept. of Public Works v. Superior Court, 68 Cal.2d 206, 65 Cal.Rptr. 342, 436 P.2d 342 (1968) upheld excess condemnation of 54 acres of farmland that became landlocked by the direct taking of 65/100 of an acre for highway right of way, with the following observation:

"The department points out that if it is allowed to condemn the entire parcel the Rodonis will receive full value for their property, the risk of excessive severance damages will be eliminated, and ultimately it will be able to reduce the cost of the freeway by selling the part of the parcel not needed for freeway purposes.

"The Rodonis challenge the excess condemnation on the ground that taking property for such a purely economic purpose violates article I, section 14 of the California Constitution * * *. They contend that excess condemnation must be limited to parcels that may properly be deemed remnants * * *. In their view, 54 acres * * * cannot be deemed a remnant of .65 acres. They insist that the state pay severance damages for the landlocked parcel and allow them to retain it, * * *.

* * *

"We hold that section 104.1 validly authorizes the trial court to proceed with the action to condemn the 54 acres. We also hold, however, that it must refuse to condemn the property if it finds that the taking is not justified to avoid excessive severance or consequential damages. * * *

* * *

"Although a parcel of 54 landlocked acres is not a physical remnant, it is a financial remnant: its value as a landlocked parcel is such that severance damages might equal its value. Remnant takings have long been considered proper. 'The reasoning behind the "remnant theory," * * * is that * * * fragments of lots would remain of such shape and size as to render them separately valueless, with the result that the city would be required to pay for the whole, although it took only a part, and with the further result that because of the lack of such value, the city would thereafter be deprived of collecting taxes on these remnants.' (Annot., 6 A.L.R.3d 297, 317 (1966); see also, 2 Nichols, Eminent Domain (3d ed. 1963) § 75122[1] p. 718.) There is no reason to restrict this theory to the taking of parcels negligible in size and to refuse to apply it to parcels negligible in value.

* * *

"When, as in this case, the property is not needed * * *, the question of public use turns on a determination of whether the taking is justified to avoid excessive severance or consequential damages. Accordingly, if the court determines that the excess condemnation is not so justified, it must find that it is not for a public use."

* * *

2. In State ex rel. State Highway Dept. v. 14.69 Acres, 226 A.2d 828 (Del.1967) the condemnation for a cloverleaf interchange and its future expansion "as traffic warranted" was deemed valid if expansion was reasonably probable within a reasonable time; even though no specific plan existed to so use the land in the foreseeable future. See Mandelker & Waite, *A Study of Future Acquisition and Reservation of Highway Rights of Way* 63 (mm; U.S. Bureau of Public Roads, June 1963).

On advance condemnation for future parking areas and school sites, see City of Chicago v. Newberry Library, 7 Ill.2d 305, 131 N.E.2d 60 (1956); Board of Education of the City of Grand Rapids v. Baczewski, 340 Mich. 265, 65 N.W.2d 810 (1954); Note, *Problems of Advance Land Acquisition,* 52 Minn.L.Rev. 1175 (1968); Annot., 6 A.L.R.3d 293 (1966).

3. **Private Initiative and Consents in Land Use Law.** On laws that authorize private parties to initiate condemnation proceedings to achieve public purposes *compare* Linggi v. Garovotti, 45 Cal.2d 20, 286 P.2d 15 (1955) with H.A. Bosworth & Son Inc. v. Tamiola, 24 Conn.Sup. 328, 190 A.2d 506 (1963).

On legislation making official permits contingent upon consent of affected private parties, see Zisook v. Maryland-Drexel Neighborhood R. Corp., 3 Ill.2d 570, 121 N.E.2d 804 (1954); Cusack Co. v. Chicago, 242 U.S. 526, 37 S.Ct. 190, 61 L.Ed. 472 (1916); and Annot., 21 A.L.R.2d 551 (1952).

4. **Procedural Distinctions Between Public Use and Public Necessity.** The distinction between the legitimacy of the purpose (public use) and of the quantum of land required for that purpose (public necessity) gives rise to different judicial review in some jurisdictions. Legislative or administrative determination of the *amount* of land required is prima-facie valid in most states. See State Road Dept. v. Southland, Inc., 117 So.2d 512 (Fla.App.1960).

(4) Just Compensation

"Most—perhaps ninety-eight percent—of the land acquired by eminent domain is obtained without litigation, by private negotiation; * * *. Even in those few cases which come to court, public use and necessity are seldom in issue. Only the adequacy and the justness of the compensation is questioned * * *." G. Lefcoe, *Land Development Law Cases and Materials,* 108–109 (1966).* In determining just compensation, it is necessary to decide, *inter alia,* the time at which the real estate is to be valued; the standards of valuation (e.g. market value, current or highest potential use); and the standards for damage

* Reprinted by permission of The Bobbs-
Merrill Company, Inc. Copyright ©1966.

claims (i.e. direct, consequential, and severance damages). See Freilich, *Solving the "Taking" Equation: Making the Whole Equal the Sum of Its Parts,* 15 Urban Lawyer. 447 (No. 2, 1983).

MERCED IRRIGATION DISTRICT v. WOOLSTENHULME

Supreme Court of California, 1971.
4 Cal.3d 478, 93 Cal.Rptr. 833, 483 P.2d 1.

TOBRINER, JUSTICE.

* * * A recurring issue * * * is whether, and to what extent, such increases in land values attributable to the proposed project comprise a proper element of the "just compensation" to be paid to a land owner if his land is ultimately taken for a project. * * *. Evidence introduced at trial revealed that, during this pre-improvement stage, land in the area had not sold for higher than $125 an acre.

In the late 1950's the district began evolving plans for a new Lake McClure project * * * By 1962 the district had begun a quest for federal funds * * *, and early in 1963 several newspaper articles informed the public that the completed Lake McClure project would include recreational facilities, such as camping, boating and fishing. The trial court found that about January 1, 1963, the public, * * *," did know of the general recreation plans, and that, as a result, property values in the area began to increase * * *. The court also found that by January 1, 1965 the plans for the project had progressed to a point where it became "reasonably probable" that the present parcel of defendant's land would be taken for the project. During 1965 and 1966, a flurry of land sales occurred in the area at prices ranging from $250 to $600 an acre. * * *

* * *

*The trial court did not err in permitting the jury * * * to consider the "project enhanced" value which accrued to defendant's property prior to the time that it was reasonably probable that the property would be taken for the improvement.*

* * *

* * * it has long been established that in general "the compensation required is to be measured by the market value of the property * * *" at the time of the taking. [Citations omitted] * * *

The "market value" of a given piece of property, of course, reflects a great variety of factors independent of the size, nature, or condition of the property itself. * * *

Sometimes, however, property which has increased in value, out of an initial anticipation that the land would be *outside* of a public improvement, must *itself* be taken for the construction or creation of that public improvement. Since the instant case presents that situation, our first issue must be to determine whether * * * the owner * * * should be compensated for the loss of this increase in value—an increase that occurs prior to the time that it is known the particular piece of property will be included in the project.

We note at the outset that, although this court has not spoken directly to the issue in the past, the majority rule in other jurisdictions is that such "project enhanced" value does constitute a proper element of value for which the landowner is entitled to be compensated. (See 4 Nichols on Eminent Domain (3d ed. 1962) § 12.3151[2], pp. 209–210.) Most notably, the United States Supreme Court has consistently construed the "just compensation" clause of the Fifth Amendment of the Federal Constitution to countenance the landowner's recovery of this "project enhanced value" unless his property was itself "probably within the scope of the project from the time the Government was committed to it." [Citations omitted] The courts of our sister states have generally embraced a like position. (See, *e.g.*, Williams v. City and County of Denver (1961) 147 Colo. 195, 200, 363 P.2d 171, 174; Cole v. Boston Edison Co. (1959) 338 Mass. 661, 666, 157 N.E.2d 209, 212; Andrews v. State of New York (1961) 9 N.Y.2d 606, 217 N.Y.S.2d 9, 176 N.E.2d 42; Rowan v. Commonwealth (1918) 261 Pa. 88, 94–95, 104 A. 502, 504–505; Stafford v. City of Providence (1873) 10 R.I. 567, 571–572, 14 Am.Rep. 710, 714–715; State By and Through Road Commission v. Wood (1969) 22 Utah 2d 317, 318–320, 452 P.2d 872, 873–874.)

* * *

* * * The value of land can be said to increase "by reason of the proposed improvement" (County of Los Angeles v. Hoe (1955) 138 Cal. App.2d 74, 78, 291 P.2d 98, 100) for at least three distinct reasons: (1) the worth of *property known to be within the project* may rise when the land is valued *as part of* the proposed improvement rather than as a separate tract of land; (2) the value of *property expected to be condemned* may rise because of the anticipation that the condemnor will be required to pay an inflated price for the land at the time of condemnation; and (3) the value of *property expected to be outside of the proposed improvement* may rise because it is anticipated that the land will reap the benefits resulting from *proximity* to the coming project. Although past California decisions have not found it necessary to distinguish between these various "increases in value," the district's contention in the instant case brings the need for such analysis into sharp focus.
* * *

* * * The beneficial purpose to be derived by the condemnor's use of the property is not to be taken into consideration in determining market values, for it is wholly irrelevant." [Citations omitted] * * *

We turn to the second aspect of "project enhanced value" * * * An increase in the value of property which can reasonably be expected to be condemned can generally be explained only as a result of speculation by potential purchasers that the condemnor may be compelled to pay an artificially inflated price for the property. (See Palmer, Manual of Condemnation Law (1961) § 154.) Although this speculation does, in a sense, affect "actual market value," (see 1 Orgel on Valuation Under

Eminent Domain (2d ed. 1953) § 83, pp. 355 et seq.), this is not the "open market" value contemplated by our controlling decisions [citations omitted]. Almost all courts universally agree that such an increase in value, based on a purchaser's conjecture of what the condemnor may ultimately be required to pay, is not a proper element of "fair market value" for "just compensation" purposes. [Citations omitted] * * * In our view this type of "enhanced" value is clearly not a legitimate element of just compensation * * *.

The (1) "enhanced value" arising from the condemnor's potential use of the property itself for the project, as in *Neale,* and (2) the "enhanced value" resulting from speculation * * * are clearly distinguishable, however, from (3) the increase in land values of property which is expected to be adjacent to or near a proposed project. * * *

The difference between the project enhanced value of the adjacent property and that of the other two situations discussed above is that the rise in value of the adjacent property is a legitimate element of its "fair open market value." * * *

The courts have long held that benefits of government activities, reflected in market value, compose part of just compensation for land. * * *

* * * Just compensation, the condemnor asserts, is only intended to put the landowner in the same position he would have held if the project had not been built; * * *

* * * In positing such a purpose to our constitutional provision, however, the district has subtly assumed away the entire question at issue. * * * Nevertheless, the long-established recognition of "market value at the time of the taking" * * * reflects a deeply rooted judgment that * * * the state bears the responsibility of meeting the reasonable market evaluations of potential sellers or purchasers. * * * He should be assured that if his property is ultimately condemned, the condemnor will compensate him * * * at the price at which he could have sold the land on the open market just prior to the taking.

* * *

In light of this analysis and the weight of authority, we now hold that increases in value, attributable to a project but reflecting a reasonable expectation that property will not be taken for the improvement, should properly be considered in determining "just compensation."

* * *

The trial court properly instructed the jury to exclude all "project enhancement" accruing after it was probable that the land to be valued would be taken for the project.

* * *

Notes

1. **Time of "Taking" for Purpose of Determining Compensation.** The time point for measuring just compensation varies with each state's policy and procedures. Special statutes may apply to designated types of taking. Valuation may take place upon adoption of a public resolution of necessity to condemn; when condemnation is reasonably probable; upon issuance of the summons (West's Ann.Cal.Civ.Proc.Code § 1249) or declaration of taking (26 Pa.Stat. § 1–402; Lombard Park District v. Chicago Title & Trust Co., 103 Ill.App.2d 1, 242 N.E.2d 440 (1968)); when public possession of condemned land is taken; upon public deposit of proposed damages; or at time of trial, or final decree. See Comment, *Date of Valuation in Eminent Domain: Irreverence for Unconstitutional Practice,* 30 U.Chi.L. Rev. 319, 326 (1963). Where exceptional circumstances are present, such as a wrongful public entry, special rules come into play. See Annot., 2 A.L.R.3d 1038 (1965).

May a legislature bar enhancement value on transactions or improvements that occur after the resolution of necessity to take such land? See 26 Pa.Stat. § 1–604; State ex rel. Willey v. Griggs, 89 Ariz. 70, 358 P.2d 174 (1960); cf. Dong v. State ex rel. Willey, 90 Ariz. 148, 367 P.2d 202 (1961).

2. **Value Standards.** Property value may be established on the basis of market data, investment return potential (i.e., determining capital value from the net income it may produce), or replacement value. For a review of the authorities on these methods, see *Notes on Intergovernmental Condemnation,* p. 467 infra.

"Just compensation" required by the 5th Amendment does *not* require payment of replacement cost of the condemned property, but merely the fair market value. United States v. 50 Acres of Land, 105 S.Ct. 451 (1984).

(a) *Market Standards.* The majority of jurisdictions employ a market value standard which contemplates valuation of the highest and best use to which the property is adaptable. The restoration standard that measures loss according to the actual use is not generally followed. "[T]he most common example is found in farmland situated in the direction of growth of nearby municipalities. Long before * * * development becomes an actuality, the land may have a value substantially greater than the present value for agricultural purposes * * *." See Lombard Park District v. Chicago Title & Trust Co., 103 Ill.App.2d 1, 5–6, 242 N.E.2d 440, 443 (1968). As the following notes indicate, special situations may require the application of other standards.

(b) *Partial Takings—Offsetting Benefits Against Damages.* Contrary to *Merced,* some jurisdictions allow the condemnor to deduct or offset the value of "special benefits" which public improvement brings to the remaining uncondemned parcel.

"The condition of benefit law at the state's level can only be described as chaotic. A few states do not permit any deduction for benefits and in the others there are wide differences both as to the types of benefits and the amount of benefits that may be deducted. * * *

"The situation is further complicated by the confusion in state court decisions attempting to distinguish between 'special' and 'general' benefits." *Study of Compensation and Assistance for Persons Affected by Real Property Acquisition in Federal and Federally Assisted Programs,* The Staff of Subcomm., Number 31, House Committee on Public Works, 88 Cong., 2d Sess. pp. 71–72 (1965).

"There is probably more judicial discord as to what is or is not special benefit than in any other area of the law of eminent domain. Where there is an actual physical improvement * * * such as the draining of a swamp, it is easy to see a special benefit. It is equally easy to recognize, at the other end of the spectrum, a general benefit such as an improved system of highways, since everybody in the community benefits * * *. The difficulty lies in the amorphous gray area between these two extremes." Taylor v. State ex rel. Herman, 12 Ariz.App. 27, 30, 467 P.2d 251, 254 (1970). See also Peacock, *The Offset of Benefits Against Losses in Eminent Domain Cases in Texas: A Critical Appraisal,* 44 Tex.L.Rev. 1564 (1966); Haar and Hearing, *The Determination of Benefits in Land Acquisition,* 51 Calif.L.Rev. 833, 851 (1963).

(c) *The Effect of Land Use Controls.* "Zoning plays a very important part in ascertaining the market value of property in condemnation proceedings. The doctrine of reasonable probability of rezoning has been adopted in all jurisdictions where the issue has been presented and its effect is still growing. As the importance of land use controls increases, there will be an enlargement of the interaction between condemnation proceedings and land use controls in determining true value of property." Zipser, *Zoning Classification and Eminent Domain,* 1 The Urban Lawyer 89, 101 (No. 1, 1969).* How do real estate experts qualify to testify on the probability of rezoning residential districts? See Lombard Park District v. Chicago Title & Trust Co., 103 Ill.App.2d 1, 242 N.E.2d 440 (1968); Snyder v. Commonwealth, 412 Pa. 15, 192 A.2d 650 (1963); People ex rel. Dept. of Public Works v. Donovan, 57 Cal.2d 346, 351–355, 19 Cal.Rptr. 473, 476, 369 P.2d 1, 4 (1962); Annot., 9 A.L.R.3d 291 (1966).

(d) *Consequential Damages.* While legislatures may authorize compensation for economic losses that are not strictly proprietary, the constitutional mandate covers only injury to proprietary interests. The question—which economic losses are only "consequential" thus becomes crucial. See Risinger, *Direct Damages: The Lost Key to Constitutional Just Compensation,* 15 Seton Hall L.Rev. 483 (1985). Items such as lost rentals, revenue potential of improvements, fixtures and equipment, removal costs, loss of patronage or good will, must be checked against the law of each jurisdiction.

(e) *Abandonment of Condemnation Proceedings.* The effect of abandonment is also subject to detailed treatment in state eminent domain codes. See e.g. West's Ann.Cal.Civ.Proc.Code § 1255(a); 26 Pa.Stat. § 1–410; Almota Farmers Elevator and Warehouse Co. v. United States, 409 U.S. 470, 93 S.Ct. 791, 35 L.Ed.2d 1 (1973); Community Redevelopment

Agency of Los Angeles v. Abrams, 15 Cal.3d 813, 126 Cal.Rptr. 473, 543 P.2d 905 (1976).

(5) Intergovernmental Condemnations

Condemnation of publicly owned property by other government authorities raises complex jurisdictional issues. Legislative authority must be found for the particular exercise of eminent domain, but that authority may be implied from express powers. See e.g., United States v. Carmack, 329 U.S. 230, 67 S.Ct. 252, 91 L.Ed. 209 (1946).

The supremacy clause authorizes federal taking of state and local governmental property, but such property is deemed private and compensable under the Fifth Amendment. United States v. Wheeler, 66 F.2d 977 (8th Cir.1933). Where a federal taking relieves the condemnee government of a costly public responsibility (*viz.* property devoted to the same public use) and there is no need for the condemnee to replace the taken property, the state or its subdivisions may be held (on a "restoration" standard) to suffer no compensable damage. See e.g., United States v. Board of Education of Mineral County, 253 F.2d 760 (4th Cir.1958); United States v. New York, 168 F.2d 387 (2d Cir.1948); Woodville, Okl. v. United States, 152 F.2d 735 (10th Cir.1946), cert. denied 328 U.S. 842, 66 S.Ct. 1021, 90 L.Ed. 1617 (1946). The same rules seem to apply where Congress delegates federal power of eminent domain to municipal agencies. Thus, state subdivisions may, by delegation of federal power, effect intralocal condemnations which they might not do under state law. See State of Okl., ex rel. Phillips v. Guy F. Atkinson Co., 313 U.S. 508, 61 S.Ct. 1050, 85 L.Ed. 1487 (1949); United States v. Carmack, 329 U.S. 230, 67 S.Ct. 252, 91 L.Ed. 209 (1946).

As noted earlier, the state has plenary power to take any lands of its subdivisions and municipalities, unless restricted by its own constitution or statutes. In such cases, compensation is generally made only for local government property held in a proprietary capacity; but cases are in confusion as to when property is held in either capacity. Legislatures may, as a matter of grace, authorize compensation; and a number of courts avoid the governmental-proprietary difficulty by "finding" legislative intent to provide compensation, regardless of the function served by condemned land. See Annot., 35 A.L.R.3d 1293 (1971).

3. PUBLIC REGULATION

a. Nuisance

Long before the emergence of land use legislation, courts exerted a limited control over land use by nuisance doctrines. "The law of nuisance plies between two antithetical extremes: The principle that every person is entitled to use his property for any purpose that he sees fit, and the opposing principle that everyone is bound to use his property in such a manner as not to injure the property or rights of his neighbor. For generations, courts, * * * have ruled on these extremes according to the wisdom of the day, and many have recognized that the contemporary view of public policy shifts from generation to generation." Antonik v. Chamberlain, 81 Ohio App. 465, 78 N.E.2d 752, 759 (1947). In finding that a use is reasonable or a nuisance, courts assess the social value of land uses, and, to that extent, direct land use policy.

Nuisance concepts may be expanded by legislation: "It has been held * * * that there is *no limitation of legislation from enlarging the category of public nuisances,* or declaring places or property used to the detriment of, or to the injury of the health, morals or welfare of the community as public nuisances, *although not such at common law * * *.*" See City of Philadelphia to Use of State Paving & Constr. Co. v. Watt, 162 Pa.Super. 433, 57 A.2d 591 (1948).

SPUR INDUSTRIES, INC. v. DEL E. WEBB DEVELOPMENT CO.

Supreme Court of Arizona, 1972.
108 Ariz. 178, 494 P.2d 700.

[Suit to enjoin cattle feedlot operation in an area that was agricultural, prior to plaintiff's purchase and development of nearby land as a retirement community settlement.]

CAMERON, VICE CHIEF JUSTICE. * * * Although numerous issues are raised, we feel that it is necessary to answer only two questions. They are:

1. Where the operation of a business, such as a cattle feedlot is lawful in the first instance, but becomes a nuisance by reason of a nearby residential area, may the feedlot operation be enjoined in an action brought by the developer of the residential area?

2. Assuming that the nuisance may be enjoined, may the developer of a completely new town or urban area in a previously agricultural area be required to indemnify the operator of the feedlot who must move or cease operation because of the presence of the residential area created by the developer?

* * *

It is noted, however, that neither the citizens of Sun City nor Youngtown are represented in this lawsuit and the suit is solely between Del E. Webb Development Company and Spur Industries, Inc.

MAY SPUR BE ENJOINED?

The difference between a private nuisance and a public nuisance is generally one of degree. A private nuisance is one affecting a single individual or a definite small number of persons in the enjoyment of private rights not common to the public, while a public nuisance is one affecting the rights enjoyed by citizens as a part of the public. To constitute a public nuisance, the nuisance must affect a considerable number of people or an entire community or neighborhood. City of Phoenix v. Johnson, 51 Ariz. 115, 75 P.2d 30 (1938).

Where the injury is slight, the remedy for minor inconveniences lies in an action for damages rather than in one for an injunction. Kubby v. Hammond, 68 Ariz. 17, 198 P.2d 134 (1948). Moreover, some courts have held, in the "balancing of conveniences" cases, that damages may be the sole remedy. See Boomer v. Atlantic Cement Co., 26 N.Y.2d 219, 309 N.Y.S.2d 312, 257 N.E.2d 870, 40 A.L.R.3d 590 (1970), and annotation comments, 40 A.L.R.3d 601.

Thus, it would appear * * * that, at most, residents of Youngtown would be entitled to damages rather than injunctive relief.

We have no difficulty, however, in agreeing with the conclusion of the trial court that Spur's operation was an enjoinable public nuisance as far as the people in the southern portion of Del Webb's Sun City were concerned.

§ 36–601, subsec. A reads as follows:

"§ 36–601. Public nuisances dangerous to public health

"A. The following conditions are specifically declared public nuisances dangerous to the public health:

"1. Any condition or place in populous areas which constitutes a breeding place for flies, rodents, mosquitoes and other insects which are capable of carrying and transmitting disease-causing organisms to any person or persons."

By this statute, before an otherwise lawful (and necessary) business may be declared a public nuisance, there must be a "populous" area in which people are injured:

"* * * A business which is not per se a public nuisance may become such by being carried on at a place where the health, comfort, or convenience of a populous neighborhood is affected. * * * What might amount to a serious nuisance in one locality by reason of the density of the population, or character of the neighborhood affected, may in another place and under different surroundings be deemed proper and unobjectionable. * * *." MacDonald v. Perry, 32 Ariz. 39, 49–50, 255 P. 494, 497 (1927).

It is clear that as to the citizens of Sun City, the operation of Spur's feedlot was both a public and a private nuisance. They could have successfully maintained an action to abate the nuisance. Del Webb, having shown a special injury in the loss of sales, had a standing to bring suit to enjoin the nuisance. Engle v. Clark, 53 Ariz. 472, 90 P.2d 994 (1939); City of Phoenix v. Johnson, *supra.* The judgment of the trial court permanently enjoining the operation of the feedlot is affirmed.

MUST DEL WEBB INDEMNIFY SPUR?

A suit to enjoin a nuisance sounds in equity and the courts have long recognized a special responsibility to the public when acting as a court of equity: * * *

In addition to protecting the public interest, however, courts of equity are concerned with protecting the operator of a lawfully, albeit noxious, business from the result of a knowing and willful encroachment by others near his business.

In the so-called "coming to the nuisance" cases, the courts have held that the residential landowner may not have relief if he knowingly came into a neighborhood reserved for industrial or agricultural endeavors and has been damaged thereby: * * *

* * *

" * * * a party cannot justly call upon the law to make that place suitable for his residence which was not so when he selected it. * * *." Gilbert v. Showerman, 23 Mich. 448, 455, 2 Brown 158 (1871).

Were Webb the only party injured, we would feel justified in holding that the doctrine of "coming to the nuisance" would have been a bar to the relief asked by Webb, and, on the other hand, had Spur located the feedlot near the outskirts of a city and had the city grown toward the feedlot, Spur would have to suffer the cost of abating the nuisance as to those people locating within the growth pattern of the expanding city: * * *

We agree, however, with the Massachusetts court that:

"The law of nuisance affords no rigid rule to be applied in all instances. It is elastic. It undertakes to require only that which is fair and reasonable under all the circumstances. In a commonwealth like this, which depends for its material prosperity so largely on the continued growth and enlargement of manufacturing of diverse varieties, 'extreme rights' cannot be enforced. * * *." Stevens v. Rockport Granite Co., 216 Mass. 486, 488, 104 N.E. 371, 373 (1914).

There was no indication in the instant case at the time Spur and its predecessors located in western Maricopa County that a new city would spring up, full-blown, alongside the feeding operation and that the developer of that city would ask the court to order Spur to move because of the new city. * * *

Del Webb, on the other hand, is entitled to the relief prayed for (a permanent injunction), not because Webb is blameless, but because of the damage to the people who have been encouraged to purchase homes in Sun City. It does not equitably or legally follow, however, that Webb, being entitled to the injunction, is then free of any liability to Spur if Webb has in fact been the cause of the damage Spur has sustained. It does not seem harsh to require a developer * * * to indemnify those who are forced to leave as a result.

Having brought people to the nuisance to the foreseeable detriment of Spur, Webb must indemnify Spur for a reasonable amount of the cost of moving or shutting down. It should be noted that this relief to Spur is limited to a case wherein a developer has, with foreseeability, brought into a previously agricultural or industrial area the population which makes necessary the granting of an injunction against a lawful business and for which the business has no adequate relief.

It is therefore the decision of this court that the matter be remanded to the trial court for a hearing upon the damages sustained by the defendant Spur as a reasonable and direct result of the granting of the permanent injunction. Since the result of the appeal may appear novel and both sides have obtained a measure of relief, it is ordered that each side will bear its own costs.

Affirmed in part, reversed in part, and remanded for further proceedings consistent with this opinion.

Notes

1. **Standing to Sue on Public and Private Nuisances.** The court found the nuisance to be both public and private, but if the nuisance was only private, could Webb assert standing to complain of a public nuisance? Cf. the Boomer opinion, p. ___. "Generally, a public nuisance cannot be the subject of an action by an individual citizen unless he can show special injury apart from that suffered by the public." See Comment, *Zoning and the Law of Nuisance*, 29 Fordham L.Rev. 749, 750 (1961).*

2. **Balancing the Equities.** As the principal case shows, courts do not use a simple two-sided scale to balance the equities between plaintiffs and defendants. The balance of individual and social equities relates to the time of land occupation; to neighborhood changes; to comparative hardship to litigants and the general public; and to the ability to eliminate nuisance effects by less drastic means than injunction. See generally, Annot.; 40 A.L.R.3d 601 (1971).

Why did the Spur court not apply its reasoning to buyers who came equally late, with equal notice of the area's character and the feedlot? Had Spur produced proofs that his feedlot assured a needed meat supply to the Sun City residents, should the result have changed? Had it so desired, could the court deny relief without violating the statutory declaration of a public nuisance? Cf. Hall v. Muckleroy, 411 S.W.2d 390 (Tex.Civ.App. 1967); Schiller v. Raley, 405 S.W.2d 446 (Tex.Civ.App.1966). In nuisance suits to enjoin agricultural activities, may public concern to preserve agricultural lands as food sources neutralize the claims of "populous" settlements?

The Time Factor—In Schlotfelt v. Vinton Farmer's Supply Co., 252 Iowa 1102, 109 N.W.2d 695 (1961) the court enjoined operation of a feed and fertilizer plant with the observations: "It is uncontradicted that the plaintiff 'was there first' * * * it required a much clearer case to justify a

* Reprinted by permission of Fordham Law Review, Lincoln Center, 140 West   62nd St., New York, N.Y. 10023 copyright © 1960 by Fordham University Press.

court of equity in interfering with the business long present than with the new business. * * * Priority of occupation is a circumstance of considerable weight, and it militates strongly in favor of the plaintiff here. * * * Id. at 1104–1111, 109 N.W.2d at 698–699.

The Locality Factor—"A fair test as to whether the operation * * * industry constitutes a nuisance has been said to be the reasonableness of conducting it in the manner, at the place, and under the circumstances in question." See Riter v. Keokuk Electro-Metals Co., 248 Iowa 710, 722, 82 N.W.2d 151, 158 (1957) (refusal to enjoin metal plant near residences in industrial section). See also McCarty v. Macy & Co., 167 Cal.App.2d 164, 334 P.2d 156 (1959) (nearby residents denied relief from grain mill operation located near railroad right of way in business and commercial area); York v. Stallings, 217 Or. 13, 341 P.2d 529 (1959) (injunction denied to plaintiffs in semirural residential area which contained little used rail branch line that foreshadowed future commercial development).

Halfway Houses—Landowners objections that rehabilitation centers will reduce their property value have been held insufficient to establish a nuisance. Nicholson v. Connecticut Half-Way House, Inc., 153 Conn. 507, 218 A.2d 383 (1966) (Boarding house for state prison parolees).

BOOMER v. ATLANTIC CEMENT COMPANY, INC.
Court of Appeals of New York, 1970.
26 N.Y.2d 219, 309 N.Y.S.2d 312, 257 N.E.2d 870.

BERGAN, JUDGE. Defendant operates a large cement plant near Albany. These are actions for injunction and damages by neighboring land owners alleging injury to property from dirt, smoke and vibration emanating from the plant. A nuisance has been found after trial, temporary damages have been allowed; but an injunction has been denied.

The public concern with air pollution * * * is currently accorded ever wider recognition * * *.

But there is now before the court private litigation in which individual property owners have sought specific relief from a single plant operation. The threshold question * * * is whether the court should resolve the litigation between the parties now before it as equitably as seems possible; or whether, seeking promotion of the general public welfare, it should channel private litigation into broad public objectives.

* * *

It seems apparent that the amelioration of air pollution will depend on technical research in great depth; on a carefully balanced consideration of the economic impact of close regulation; and of the actual effect on public health. It is likely to require massive public expenditure and to demand more than any local community can accomplish and to depend on regional and interstate controls.

A court should not try to do this on its own as a by-product of private litigation and it seems manifest that the judicial establishment is neither equipped in the limited nature of any judgment it can pronounce nor prepared to lay down and implement an effective policy for the elimination of air pollution. This is an area beyond the circumference of one private lawsuit. It is a direct responsibility for government and should not thus be undertaken as an incident to solving a dispute between property owners and a single cement plant—one of many—in the Hudson River valley.

The cement making operations of defendant have been found by the court at Special Term to have damaged the nearby properties of plaintiffs * * *. That court * * * accordingly found defendant maintained a nuisance and this has been affirmed at the Appellate Division. * * *

The ground for the denial of injunction, notwithstanding the finding both that there is a nuisance and that plaintiffs have been damaged substantially, is the large disparity in economic consequences of the nuisance and of the injunction. * * *

The rule in New York has been that such a nuisance will be enjoined although marked disparity be shown in economic consequence between the effect of the injunction and the effect of the nuisance.

The problem of disparity in economic consequence was sharply in focus in Whalen v. Union Bag & Paper Co., 208 N.Y. 1, 101 N.E. 805. A pulp mill entailing an investment of more than a million dollars polluted a stream in which plaintiff, who owned a farm, was "a lower riparian owner". The economic loss to plaintiff from this pollution was small. This court, reversing the Appellate Division, reinstated the injunction granted by the Special Term against the argument of the mill owner that in view of "the slight advantage to plaintiff and the great loss that will be inflicted on defendant" an injunction should not be granted (p. 2, 101 N.E. p. 805). * * *

* * *

* * * Thus, if within Whalen v. Union Bag & Paper Co., *supra* which authoritatively states the rule in New York, the damage to plaintiffs in these present cases from defendant's cement plant is "not unsubstantial", an injunction should follow.

* * *

The court at Special Term also found the amount of permanent damage attributable to each plaintiff, for the guidance of the parties * * *. The total of permanent damages to all plaintiffs thus found was $185,000. * * *

This result * * * is a departure from a rule that has become settled; but to follow the rule literally in these cases would be to close down the plant at once. This court is fully agreed to avoid that immediately drastic remedy; the difference in view is how best to avoid it.*

---

* Respondent's investment in the plant is in excess of $45,000,000. There are over 300 people employed there.

One alternative is to grant the injunction but postpone its effect to a specified future date to give opportunity for technical advances to permit defendant to eliminate the nuisance; another is to grant the injunction conditioned on the payment of permanent damages to plaintiffs which would compensate them for the total economic loss to their property present and future caused by defendant's operations. For reasons which will be developed the court chooses the latter alternative.

* * *

The parties could settle this private litigation at any time if defendant paid enough money and the imminent threat of closing the plan would build up the pressure on defendant. If there were no improving techniques found, there would inevitably be applications * * * for extensions of time * * * on showing of good faith efforts to find such techniques.

Moreover, techniques to eliminate dust and other annoying by-products of cement making are unlikely to be developed * * * within any short period * * *.

For obvious reasons the rate of the research is beyond control of defendant. If at the end of 18 months the whole industry has not found a technical solution a court would be hard put to close down this one cement plant * * *.

On the other hand, to grant the injunction unless defendant pays plaintiffs such permanent damages as may be fixed by the court seems to do justice between the contending parties. * * *

The nuisance complained of * * * may have other public or private consequences, but these particular parties are the only ones who have sought remedies and the judgment proposed will fully redress them. The limitation of relief granted is a limitation only within the four corners of these actions and does not foreclose public health or other public agencies from seeking proper relief in a proper court.

It seems reasonable to think that the risk of being required to pay permanent damages to injured property owners * * * would itself be a reasonable effective spur to research for improved techniques to minimize nuisance.

The power of the court to condition * * * the continuance of an injunction on the payment of permanent damages seems undoubted. * * *

* * *

The present cases and the remedy here proposed are in a number of other respects rather similar to Northern Indiana Public Service Co. v. W.J. & M.S. Vesey, 210 Ind. 338, 200 N.E. 620 decided by the Supreme Court of Indiana. * * * An injunction and damages were sought, but an injunction was denied and the relief granted was limited to permanent damages "present, past, and future" (p. 371, 200 N.E. 620).

* * *

It was held that in this type of continuing and recurrent nuisance permanent damages were appropriate. See, also, City of Amarillo v. Ware, 120 Tex. 456, 40 S.W.2d 57 where recurring overflows from a system of storm sewers were treated as the kind of nuisance for which permanent depreciation of value of affected property would be recoverable.

* * *

Thus it seems fair to both sides to grant permanent damages to plaintiffs which will terminate this private litigation. The theory of damage is the "servitude on land" of plaintiffs imposed by defendant's nuisance. (See United States v. Causby, 328 U.S. 256, 261, 262, 267, 66 S.Ct. 1062, 90 L.Ed. 1206, where the term "servitude" addressed to the land was used by Justice Douglas relating to the effect of airplane noise on property near an airport.)

The judgment, by allowance of permanent damages * * * would preclude future recovery by plaintiffs or their grantees (see Northern Indiana Public Serv. Co. v. W.J. & M.S. Vesey, *supra,* p. 351, 200 N.E. 620).

This should be placed beyond debate by a provision of the judgment that the payment * * * of permanent damages found by the court shall be in compensation for a servitude on the land.

Although the Trial Term has found permanent damages * * * on remission the court should be entirely free to re-examine this subject. It may again find the permanent damage already found; or make new findings.

* * *

JASEN, JUDGE (dissenting). I agree with the majority that a reversal is required here, but I do not subscribe to the newly enunciated doctrine of assessment of permanent damages, in lieu of an injunction, where substantial property rights have been impaired by the creation of a nuisance. * * *

* * *. In permitting the injunction to become inoperative upon the payment of permanent damages, the majority is, in effect, licensing a continuing wrong. It is the same as saying to the cement company, you may continue to do harm to your neighbors so long as you pay a fee for it. * * *

It is true that some courts have sanctioned the remedy here proposed * * * but none of the authorities relied upon by the majority are analogous to the situation before us. In those cases, the courts, * * * grounded their decision on a showing that the use to which the property was intended to be put was primarily for the public benefit. Here, on the other hand, it is clearly established that the cement company is creating a continuing air pollution nuisance primarily for its own private interest with no public benefit.

This kind of inverse condemnation (Ferguson v. Village of Hamburg, 272 N.Y. 234, 5 N.E.2d 801) may not be invoked by a private person or corporation for private gain or advantage. Inverse condemnation should only be permitted when the public is primarily served in the taking or impairment of property. [Citations omitted] * * *.

Nor is it constitutionally permissible to impose servitude on land, without consent of the owner, by payment of permanent damages where the continuing impairment of the land is for a private use. [Citations omitted]

* * *

I would enjoin the defendant cement company * * * unless, within 18 months, the cement company abated this nuisance.

* * *

Notes

1. **Condemnations Through Nuisance Injunction.** A miscalculated executory abatement of an alleged nuisance may amount to a taking of property. (See the following principal cases.) Can Boomer be justified (a) under traditional nuisance law? (b) as a matter of constitutional law and due process? (c) by social necessity?

Assuming the court could not rationally enjoin an essential industry, or provide adequate interim damages for continuing injury, did it have any other alternatives?

2. **Public Welfare Factors.** Where the reasonableness of use is measured solely by economic gains and burdens, courts would be hard put to enjoin many nuisances. Since industrial technology has so far outrun pollution technology, the question remains—how activist should courts be in advancing nuisance theory to supplement legislated environmental controls?

(a) *Nuisances Per Se.* Courts have the power to prohibit certain uses as nuisances, per se, under all circumstances. The doctrine has been confined to few activities (e.g. gambling, disorderly houses, cemetery uses in residential areas). The authorities are in conflict on what uses constitute nuisances per se, and on the question whether activity that is authorized by legislation may be held a nuisance per se. Funeral homes permitted by the zoning code were held to be nuisances per se. Rigsby v. Burton, 293 Ala. 459, 305 So.2d 366 (1974). See Annot., Funeral Home as Private Nuisance, 8 A.L.R.4th 324 (1981); Connecticut Bank and Trust Co., p. 477.

(b) *Comparative Injury Doctrine.* In the following cases the courts refused to enjoin industrial activities as nuisances either because their economic importance made them "reasonable", or, more often, because the injury to the public interest from an injunction would outweigh the benefit to the plaintiffs. *National Defense Industries:* Riter v. Keokuk Electro-Metals, Co., 248 Iowa 710, 82 N.W.2d 151 (1957); Pritchett v. Wade, 261 Ala. 156, 72 So.2d 533 (1954); Heppenstall Co. v. Berkshire Chemical Co., 130 Conn. 485, 35 A.2d 845 (1944). *Primary Local Industries:* (providing employment or large tax revenues)—Riter v. Keokuk Electro-Metals Co., supra; Koseris v. J.R. Simplot Co., 82 Idaho 263, 352 P.2d 235 (1960); York v. Stallings, 217 Or. 13, 341 P.2d 529 (1959); *but see* Board of Com. v. Elm Grove Mining Co., 122 W.Va. 442, 9 S.E.2d 813 (1940) where the court enjoined mining activities stating: " * * * no measure of necessity, usefulness, or public benefit will protect" a nuisance endangering public health. Id. at 451, 9 S.E.2d at 817.

Government Facility Nuisances, see Smith v. Ann Arbor, 303 Mich. 476, 6 N.W.2d 752 (1942) (publicly operated dump); Barber v. School District No. 51, Clay County, 335 S.W.2d 527 (Mo.App.1960) (discharge of school sewage onto plaintiff's land), *semble:* Johnson v. Independent School District, No. 1, Buffalo, 239 Mo.App. 749, 199 S.W.2d 421 (1947); Antonik v. Chamberlain, 81 Ohio App. 465, 78 N.E.2d 752 (1947) (airport operation open to the public). But see Webb v. Rye, 108 N.H. 147, 230 A.2d 223 (1967) (public dump), and Brainard v. West Hartford, p. 479 n. 1, *infra.*

Hazardous Activities—How far from residences should gun clubs be, to avoid injunction as nuisances? See Smith v. Western Wayne County Conservation Ass'n, 380 Mich. 526, 158 N.W.2d 463 (1968); Annot., 26 A.L.R.3d 661 (1969).

3. **Intermediate Relief.** While courts must decide the issue of nuisance *vel non,* they are free to fashion their decrees to accommodate interests of each party. Just as zoning legislation may provide a grace period to eliminate a disfavored use, so nuisance injunctions may allow a grace period to end prohibited uses. See e.g. Pendoley v. Ferreira, 345 Mass. 309, 187 N.E.2d 142 (1963). The court may condition grant or denial of injunction upon corrective measures *viz.* limiting hours of business or operation (Altman v. Ryan, 435 Pa. 401, 257 A.2d 583 (1969); installation of special equipment or buffer arrangements (Patton v. Westwood Country Club Co., 18 Ohio App.2d 137, 247 N.E.2d 761 (1969)); noise reduction (Nair v. Thaw, 156 Conn. 445, 242 A.2d 757 (1968)); emission controls modification (Hansen v. Independent School District No. 1 in Nez Perce County, 61 Idaho 109, 98 P.2d 959 (1940).

CONNECTICUT BANK & TRUST CO. v. MULARCIK

Superior Court of Connecticut, 1961.
22 Conn.Sup. 415, 174 A.2d 128.

MacDONALD, JUDGE. Plaintiffs, * * * seeks to enjoin the defendants, as owners of a sand and gravel bank on adjoining property, from carrying out their announced plan of operating, * * * a rock crusher and stone screener. Although the locality is admitted by defendants to be "heavily residential," there are several commercial establishments in the immediate vicinity * * * which is located on heavily traveled United States route 6 * * *. There also are a quarry, where blasting is conducted, and a sand and gravel operation, involving a large stone crusher, about a mile away.

It is unfortunate for those who wish to preserve the residential quiet and beauty * * * that they did not obtain * * * the status preservative of an appropriate zoning ordinance, for the only basis upon which further industrial or commercial intrusions can be enjoined is upon that of nuisance, more specifically, in this instance, a "private nuisance," * * *. It is the position of plaintiffs in the instant case that the establishment of a rock crushing and stone screening * * * would constitute, per se, an absolute nuisance regardless of the manner in which it is operated * * *.

In support of this position, plaintiffs rely heavily on the case of Jack v. Torrant, 136 Conn. 414, 71 A.2d 705, 709 involving the granting of an injunction against the operation of a funeral home on North Street in Litchfield—widely known as one of the most beautiful residential streets in the United States * * *. However, one of the concluding paragraphs in the opinion * * * points out some very important distinctions between that case and the present situation: * * *. In the Torrant case, the court found that the funeral home already had operated for about eight months * * *.

* * * In other words, no claim is or could be made here that the proposed use of defendants' property sought to be enjoined is inappropriate as the first commercial intrusion into the immediate neighborhood, as in the Torrant case. Rather, the claim for relief boils down to the proposition that the use of a stone crusher and screener might make noise which might disturb the neighborhood and that this very possibility is affecting the value of real estate in the vicinity.

Since the machine in question has not yet been operated on defendants' property, there was not and, of course, could not have been, any evidence as to the noise it makes, but neither was any evidence offered by plaintiffs as to the noise made by similar machines similarly situated. The plaintiff Davis mentioned that he could hear a stone crusher located over a mile from his home, but the only evidence as to a comparison with the defendants' machine was the statement that the former was very much larger than the latter. The experts * * * introduced by defendants, testified that the advanced scientific construction of defendants' machine made it so silent that the operation could not be heard beyond the boundaries of defendants' land, and although their testimony obviously was biased * * *, it was not contradicted or rebutted by plaintiffs.

Whether or not noise in itself, constitutes a nuisance is a question of fact dependent on the nature and character of the noise, * * * Here, there has been absolutely no evidence as to what, if any, noise will be created * * *

* * *

It is true, as claimed by plaintiffs, that when a threat of substantial future injury is inherent in a present condition of adjoining land it may constitute a present nuisance which should be enjoined. See Danbury & Norwalk R. Co. v. Norwalk, 37 Conn. 109; Wetherell v. Town of Newington, 54 Conn. 67, 5 A. 858; Brainard v. Town of West Hartford, 18 Conn.Sup. 218, 223. But, on the other hand, " '[i]t is obviously not fit that the power of [the] court should be invoked, * * * for every * * * speculative violation of one's rights.' " Taylor v. Cooke, 113 Conn. 162, 166, 154 A. 349, 350. In Brainard v. Town of West Hartford, *supra,* city cited by plaintiffs * * *, the threatened use of the land adjoining that of plaintiff was a public dump, which obviously presents a threat of nuisance of which a court could, for all practical purposes, take judicial notice. Such elements are not present and have not been shown to be imminent or even likely in this case.

* * * The plaintiffs have failed to make out a case of actionable nuisance or even imminent threat of actionable nuisance, and their application for a temporary injunction, accordingly, is denied.

Note

1. In Brainard v. West Hartford, 140 Conn. 631, 103 A.2d 135 (1954), which the principal case noted without disapproval, the residents near the site of a proposed town dump obtained an injunction over the objections that their suit was premature; founded upon unproven fears; and that the plaintiff should seek relief before the zoning board.

CITY OF NOKOMIS v. SULLIVAN

Supreme Court of Illinois, 1958.
14 Ill.2d 417, 153 N.E.2d 48.

SCHAEFER, JUSTICE. An ordinance of the city of Nokomis * * * declares that "the use of any premises in the City of Nokomis in such a manner as to create sewerage thereon not discharged into the sewerage system is hereby declared to be a nuisance; every water closet or privy * * * used in any building not connected with the sewerage system of said City is hereby declared to be a nuisance, provided that this section shall be inapplicable to premises where connection with the sewerage system is not feasible. * * *" The ordinance requires that connection with the sewerage system be made within one year after connection became feasible, but not later than January 1, 1954.

* * * The relief requested was a permanent injunction restraining the defendants "from using any water closet or privy, * * * located on the prescribed premises * * * not connected with the sewerage system" of the city.

* * *

While the constitutional question as to the power of a municipality to require connections with its sewer system has not heretofore been decided in this State, it has frequently been decided elsewhere. In 1912 the Supreme Court of the United States said, "it is the commonest exercise of the police power of a state or city to provide for a system of sewers, and to compel property owners to connect therewith." Hutchinson v. City of Valdosta, 227 U.S. 303, 308, 33 S.Ct. 290, 292, 57 L.Ed. 520, 523. * * * Each of these decisions is grounded, * * * upon the proposition that the continued use of privies and cesspools is a nuisance when a less hazardous means of disposition is available.

* * * In the present case the defendants' motion to strike took the position that a municipality has no power to declare that to be a nuisance which is not a nuisance in fact. Apparently the thought was

that because there are conditions under which privies and cesspools may be useful facilities, their use can never be prohibited as a nuisance without a showing that the particular privy or cesspool involved is itself noisome, offensive and hazardous to public health. That position is unsound. It has often been pointed out that the benefit to the public health that is afforded by a public sewer system is lost unless all can be required to use it. Spear v. Ward, 199 Ala. 105, 74 So. 27; Nourse v. City of Russellville, 257 Ky. 525, 78 S.W.2d 761. * * *

* * * So here, the facility that at one time represented an advance over more primitive methods, can be prohibited when a safer method becomes available. * * * To protect the public health, as well as to promote public safety, a legislative body may adopt "the most conservative course which science and engineering offer." Queenside Hills Realty Co. v. Saxl, 328 U.S. 80, 83, 66 S.Ct. 850, 851, 90 L.Ed. 1096, 1098.

Frequent efforts to state the precise effect of a municipal declaration that a particular thing or activity is a nuisance have proved unsatisfactory. * * * The ultimate question has been reasonableness of the questioned use of the property in the light of all of the surrounding circumstances. [Citations omitted] In this case, when the relatively small cost of compliance is weighed against the serious risks involved in noncompliance, it is clear that the ordinance is not invalid.

The General Assembly has delegated to cities and villages the power "To define, prevent and abate nuisances." Ill.Rev.Stat.1957, chap. 24, par. 23–61. * * *

We hold, therefore, that the ordinance is within the powers granted to the city by the General Assembly, and that the defendants are not deprived of due process under the State or Federal constitution because they are required to connect with the city sewer system. S.H.A. Const. art. 2, § 2; U.S. Const.Amend. 14.

* * *

Notes

1. **Legislative Definition of Nuisance.** Since the nuisance was neither a nuisance per se, nor necessarily actionable in fact, the label "nuisance" as used in the above ordinance really denotes generalized health regulations rather than a concept of specific injury, as was the case at common law.

In City of Philadelphia to Use of State Paving & Constr. Co. v. Watt, 162 Pa.Super. 433, 57 A.2d 591 (1948) an owner of a private driveway connecting two streets, attacked, as unconstitutional, a statute which authorized local health boards to declare broken common driveways to be nuisances, and to require their repair. The Court upheld the statute: "This was a private driveway but the fact that it connected two city streets was an invitation to the public to make use of it. * * * Conditions which *tend* to prejudice public safety or health are as much subject to abatement as are nuisances which have actually resulted in public injury. [Citation omitted]" Id. at 437–439, 57 A.2d at 593–4.

(1) Nuisance Controls for Substandard Housing

Most cities are doubly plagued with a housing shortage on the one hand, and thousands of abandoned or sub-standard housing units on the other. The radical solution of areawide clearance and reconstruction has not been fully effected or effective. Neither has selective rehabilitation of individual properties at public expense. The alternative of forcing rehabilitation by property owners, on grounds of nuisance abatement, presents formidable legal problems. Philadelphia and Wilmington developed a variation on the public and private initiative in housing repair, under the appealing title "Homesteading." See note p. 486.

CITY OF CHICAGO v. BUSCH

Appellate Court of Illinois, 1971.
132 Ill.App.2d 486, 270 N.E.2d 249.

LEIGHTON, JUSTICE.

[Reversing decree for demolition of apartment building.]

* * *

From the sparse and somewhat confused record before us, it appears that by an order of February 21, 1968 the trial court found that the building at 3824 West Jackson Boulevard "[f]ails to conform in certain instances to the minimum standards of health and safety as set forth in the applicable ordinances of the City of Chicago." Because the building was "unfit for human habitation," defendants were ordered to vacate the entire building and board it up. * * * On March 21, 1968 when Busch appeared, he expressed consent to the order. * * * The cause was then continued from time to time until June 5, 1968.

* * * A building inspector was called who testified to the inspection he made of the building the day before. He found it was not boarded * * *. For the balance of the hearing there was a colloquy between the trial judge and Busch concerning the building, its sale to Fields and the desire of the new owner to proceed with rehabilitation. The cause was then continued one week.

When it was before the court again * * * [t]he same building inspector * * * reported that the building was boarded front and rear. The cause was then continued to July 10. On that date Busch reported to the court that "[w]e understand from the architect that the permit will be out either tomorrow or the next day." * * * The cause was then continued to July 24, 1968. On that day Busch and Fields were in court. * * * The trial judge asked who was going to do the work. Fields responded, saying he was going to do it himself. * * * The court then continued the case to September 18, 1968.

On September 11, however, * * * the case was called on "[t]he City's motion for a hearing instanter." * * * The trial judge reviewed the history of the case and then for the first time said that plaintiff was requesting a decree of demolition. When Busch asked to be told the basis for the decree, the trial judge said, "[t]he basis is that you have a building that is vacant and boarded, and that Statute states that a vacant and boarded building is no defense, * * *." The court then continued the case one week * * *.

On September 18, the "prove up" was heard. * * *

* * * The trial judge * * * reminded Busch of the failure to proceed with rehabilitation. * * * the court said, "Let the record show that from the testimony and evidence the decree of demolition is allowed with lien and or judgment to attach for cost of demolition and court cost." * * * A short time later the trial judge was informed that the building had been demolished; and on December 13, 1968, a judgment was entered against defendants Busch and Feigenholtz in the sum of $2,335.00 for the expenses of demolition plus court costs.

* * * defendants contend it was plaintiff's burden to prove that the demolished building was dangerous beyond repair. * * * Defendants point out that in City of Aurora v. Meyer, 38 Ill.2d 131 at 137, 230 N.E.2d 200 at 204 the Supreme Court speaking of the statutory basis for this suit, section 11–31–1 of the Illinois Municipal Code, said,

> "[T]he plain implication of the act involved here is that if the property can be repaired with comparatively little expense the city ought to adopt this course rather than complete demolition, that only in cases where the structure is substantially beyond repair is an order for demolition contemplated. * * * The cost of repairs may well be a small fraction of the building's value. The court should find from the evidence what the specific defects are which render the building dangerous and unsafe. * * *"

* * *

* * * Under authority of section 11–31–1 of the Illinois Municipal Code, property may be ordered destroyed under certain conditions but only if the danger cannot be abated in any other way. It is only in cases where an absolute necessity exists that courts adopt the drastic method of correction by ordering destruction of private property. Childs v. Anderson, 344 Mich. 90, 73 N.W.2d 280 (1955); Echave v. City of Grand Junction, 118 Colo. 165, 193 P.2d 277 (1948). In every instance the remedy * * * is limited to the necessities of the case. Where hazardous conditions can be remedied by repair without major reconstruction * * * the building may not be destroyed. *Compare* Albert v. City of Mountain Home, 81 Idaho, 74, 337 P.2d 377 (1959). * * *

* * * The record is silent concerning the value of the property, the costs of the repairs or the condition of the structure so it could be determined whether it was beyond repair.

The record before us reflects a primary concern * * * about defendants' failure to rehabilitate the building. * * * We see an anomaly in defendants, in apparent good faith, seeking a permit, plaintiff issuing one and at the same time insisting on demolition of defendants' property without proof that its complete destruction was necessary, only because the owners (as plaintiff argues in this court) "[w]ere obviously incapable of repairing the building." Our review of the record leads us to conclude that the necessity for the demolition decree was not proved. * * * Accordingly, we reverse the decree of demolition and the judgment against defendants and remand the cause with directions that the trial court take further proceedings consistent with the views herein expressed. * * *

Notes

1. **Demolition of Unsafe Houses.** Horton v. Gulledge, 277 N.C. 353, 177 S.E.2d 885 (1970) held that the city could not demolish an unfit dwelling without giving the owner a reasonable opportunity to bring it into compliance with law, even though the cost of doing so would equal or exceed 60% of the value of the unrepaired building. The use of standards of percentage of depreciation to determine when a nuisance should be abated is reviewed in the study by Professor Grad, cited below. Compare City of Pittsburgh v. Kronzek, 2 Pa.Cmwlth. 660, 280 A.2d 488 (1971) (upholding demolition ordinance and orders).

Busch raises a number of typical questions. The principal question is—who is playing games with legal technicality? Where the owner appears to be stalling, should the court (a) fine him for code violations; (b) enter interim orders for repairs with a time deadline, under threat of contempt for noncompliance? A post-complaint sale by owner to third party could be a ploy to relieve owner of such pressures. The ploy would be doubly effective if the new owner were not financially responsible, and might take forever to find the required money. A court is not likely to sanction a "poor" owner for failure to repair a losing investment, especially if the violations stem from tenant neglect or vandalism. An owner could convey out to a party who could not be found. Abandoned properties with such transferees make demolition slow and costly. If market values shift back to the profit point, elusive owners (whether real or straw) may then reappear and redeem their investment. Compare the approach in the following principal case. For an excellent discussion of problems raised by demolition programs, see Frank P. Grad, Legal Remedies For Housing Code Violations, pp. 56–61 (Research Rep. No. 14, Nat'l. Comm. On Urban Problems 1968).

2. Some of the problems encountered in the principal case might be avoided by more carefully drawn ordinances and procedures. See Annot., 43 A.L.R.3d 916 (1972); Whiting v. Pasadena, 255 Cal.App.2d 372, 63 Cal. Rptr. 174 (1967).

3. **Nuisance Abatement and Municipal Liability.** The demolition in Busch occurred before final determination that it was unlawful. Should this render the city liable in damages to the owner? In Albert v. Mountain

Home, 81 Idaho 74, 337 P.2d 377 (1959) the court awarded damage to an owner whose property was demolished after city council declared it a public nuisance, and after the city mailed a notice to the owner to abate the nuisance or suffer demolition. " * * * Where the city orders a building summarily destroyed which is not a nuisance per se, it does so at its peril, * * * Because the nuisance could be abated * * *, the city went beyond its authority in ordering the building destroyed. The defendant acted at its peril, and having done so it must respond in damages." Id. 79–80, 337 P.2d at 380–381. See also Annot., 14 A.L.R.2d 73 (1950). *Semble:* In Hepner v. Township Committee of Twp. of Lawrence, 115 N.J.Super. 155, 278 A.2d 513 (1961) (owner granted injunction and damages for a demolition rendered unlawful for lack of mandatory statutory notices, notwithstanding the fact that he had indirect actual notice of proceedings). "Strict compliance with the notice requirements is mandatory in any proceeding where, as here, an intrusion of a substantial property right may result." Id. at 161–2, 278 A.2d at 516. Accord: Michaud v. Bangor, 159 Me. 491, 196 A.2d 106 (1963). Where, however, legislative authorization of demolition is a cumulative, rather than an exclusive remedy for nuisance abatement, the city may still demolish a hazardous property as a public nuisance under common law, without compliance with statutory procedures. See Perepletchikoff v. Los Angeles, 174 Cal.App.2d 697, 345 P.2d 261 (1959).

IN RE DEPARTMENT OF BUILDINGS OF CITY OF NEW YORK

Court of Appeals of New York, 1964.
14 N.Y.2d 291, 251 N.Y.S.2d 441, 200 N.E.2d 432.

FULD, JUDGE. Acting under the authority of the so-called 1962 Receivership Law (Multiple Dwelling Law, § 309, as amd. by L.1962, ch. 492), the Department of Buildings * * * petitioned for and obtained an order from the Supreme Court designating the Commissioner of Real Estate as receiver of the rents, issues and profits of the premises located at 221 West 21st Street. The Appellate Division unanimously affirmed, and the appellants, the owner and mortgagee of the premises involved, appeal * * * urging, primarily, that the statute is unconstitutional.

* * *

The receiver, expressly vested with "all of the powers and duties of a receiver appointed in an action to foreclose a mortgage", is to proceed "with all reasonable speed" to remove the nuisance "constituting a serious fire hazard or a serious threat to life, health or safety" and apply the rents which he is to collect from the property to the cost of removing or remedying such nuisance, * * *. If the income from the property proves insufficient, the Department of Real Estate shall advance to the receiver—"from a fund to be known as the multiple dwelling section three hundred nine operating fund" (subd. 9)—any sums necessary to cover such cost and shall have a lien against the property for the sums so advanced (subd. 5, par. d, cl. 1). This lien, the statute goes on to recite (subd. 4, par. a), "shall have priority over all other liens and encumbrances except taxes, assessments and mortgages recorded previously to the existence of such lien," except as otherwise provided in subdivision 5. * * *

The statute further provides that a mortgagee or lienor who at his own expense removes the nuisance shall have a lien "equivalent" to the lien granted to the receiver * * * The receiver shall be discharged * * * when the nuisance has been removed * * *.

The premises in question, * * * consist of a five-story rent-controlled building containing 10 apartments. On July 10, 1963, the respondent, following the procedure prescribed by the statute, certified that a nuisance existed on the premises, directed its removal and in its order * * * recited that, if the dangerous conditions were not removed or remedied within 21 days, it would apply for the appointment of a receiver "with rights * * * superior to that of the owner, mortgagees and lienors". The certificate listed the violations and conditions which constituted the nuisance. When later reinspections showed no change in the situation, the respondent, on September 10, 1963, applied to the Supreme Court for the appointment of a receiver * * *.

On September 12, 1963, the return day of the order to show cause, the owner appeared by counsel and the mortgagee * * *. The court was advised that no one was then living in the building, that a number of the tenants who had been forced to vacate the premises intended to return as soon as the building was rendered safe and that the owner had started to do the necessary work. * * * Instead of adjourning the motion for 30 days, * * * the court granted the motion for the appointment of a receiver but "stayed" his appointment until October 15 (a period of 33 days) to give the owner an "opportunity" to eliminate the violations * * *. The essential repairs not having been completed by that date, the owner was given further time, until November 20, to complete the task. And, when it appeared on this date that considerable work still remained to be done * * * the court signed the order appointing the receiver.

It is the appellants' position (1) that the statute is unconstitutional in that it impairs the rights of appellant mortgagee under his prior mortgage contract (U.S.Const. art. I, § 10); (2) that they were denied a proper hearing; and (3) that, in any event, the facts failed to warrant the appointment of a receiver.

* * *

If the legislation before us "is addressed to a legitimate end and the measures taken are reasonable and appropriate to that end", it may not be stricken as unconstitutional, even though it may interfere with rights established by existing contracts. (Home Bldg. & Loan Assn. v. Blaisdell, 290 U.S. 398, 438, 54 S.Ct. 231, 240, 78 L.Ed. 413.) It is "fundamental", we wrote in the Durham Realty Corp. case (230 N.Y. at p. 442, 130 N.E. at p. 605), that "the state may establish regulations reasonably necessary to secure the general welfare of the community by the exercise of its police power, although the rights of private property are thereby curtailed and freedom of contract is abridged." (See, also, Guttag v. Shatzkin, 230 N.Y. 647, 130 N.E. 929.) * * *

* * * As the statute now reads, it provides that the receiver's lien shall have priority over an existing mortgage only if the mortgagee is given notice * * *. Instead of being relegated to the sidelines, to "sit idly by", the mortgagee has an opportunity to participate in the proceedings from beginning to end. * * *

It is evident, therefore, that the due process objection * * * has been completely obviated by the Legislature in enacting the 1962 law.

* * *

When weighed against the vital public purposes sought to be achieved, the interference with the mortgagee's rights * * * may not be said to be so unreasonable or oppressive as to preclude the State's exercise of its police power. * * *

Concluding, as we do, that the statute is constitutional, we turn briefly to the appellants' further plaints.

As we have already observed, section 309 authorizes the appointment of a receiver only if there exists in the multiple dwelling in question "a nuisance * * * which constitutes a serious fire hazard or is a serious threat to life, health or safety". Although the statute does not in so many words provide for a hearing on that issue, the recitals in subdivision 5 (par. c, cl. 3) * * * "import a hearing" at which the owner and mortgagee will have an opportunity to present evidence in opposition to the application. (*Cf.* Thompson v. Wallin, 301 N.Y. 476, 494, 95 N.E.2d 806, 814.)

* * *

Before drawing this opinion to a close, it may not be inappropriate to note * * * that the statute allows them to terminate the receivership, once the nuisance has been eliminated, by reimbursing the receiver (or the Department of Real Estate) for the cost of ridding the property of such nuisance and that, if the removal of the dangerous conditions constituting the nuisance is disputed, the appellants are free to apply to the Supreme Court for a determination of that issue.

* * *

Notes

1. **Abatement Repair Costs.** May the owner nevertheless contest the recovery sought by the city, on the ground that the particular repairs were not necessary to abate the nuisance, or that their costs were unreasonable? If so, which party should have the burden of proof on these questions? Cf. Town of Woodbury v. Perrone, 17 A.D.2d 662, 230 N.Y.S.2d 367 (1962).

2. Various legal schemes for rehabilitating urban housing are reviewed in Schreiberg, *Abandoned Buildings: Tenant Condominiums and Community Redevelopment,* 2 Urban Lawyer 186 (1970).

3. **Urban Homesteading.** "The 1960 United States Census disclosed that there were approximately four (4) million vacant and abandoned

buildings and dwellings within the boundaries of our cities, beyond the point of rehabilitation. This same census also disclosed the existence of another five (5) million vacant, but rehabilitatable structures. From all indications, the 1970 census confirms the prediction that this condition has worsened further.

"City governments, through the execution of liens, judgments, tax delinquency, gifts, abandonment etc., are the actual or constructive owners of many of these structures."

*　*　*

"In several large cities, attempts have been made to develop our New Frontiers into low-income housing. In almost every instance, the high cost has simply priced these dwellings out of the financial reach of low-income families. Other attempts have been made to develop these Frontiers into luxury apartments. The purpose here has been mainly to lure back into the city persons, who for one reason or another, have fled to the suburbs. This latter plan has also met with very limited success.

"It is now crystal clear that presently employed profit-making oriented programs for developing our Frontiers have failed; and new approaches to this problem are needed. Perhaps a lesson from the pages of our history can furnish a clue.

"In 1862 the Congress of the United States enacted the Federal Homestead Act. Under this Act, the Federal Government gave land, on our then Frontiers, free to Citizens who would settle on the land and cultivate it. Obviously, this was not, nor intended to be, a profit-making oriented venture. It was an effort to develop our Frontiers, *　*　*. The success of the Federal Homestead Act of 1862 is indisputable.

"Perhaps an adoption or modification of this government-people venture is a possible answer to developing our Nation's present Frontiers. URBAN HOMESTEADING could be that adoption.

"Under URBAN HOMESTEADING citizens would be given City owned lots, after vacant and unrehabilitatable structures would have been cleared away, in addition to being given rehabilitatable structures. In both instances, the complete vesting of title in the lots or rehabilitatable structures would be contingent upon the new owners building on the land or bringing the rehabilitatable structures up to living standards, within an agreed specified period of time.

*　*　*

"*　*　* In effect what URBAN HOMESTEADING does is to make a conditional 'gift of ownership' of City owned property to an individual, and then applies presently available Federally funded programs to the improvement and rehabilitation of these properties.

"Let us now apply URBAN HOMESTEADING to the Frontiers in Philadelphia."

In July 1973 the city of Philadelphia enacted a homesteading ordinance along the lines above suggested by Councilman Coleman.

b. *Subdivision Controls*

(1) Official Maps

"In the kit of land planning tools, the official map is the tool least well known. Zoning, master plans, subdivision controls, building codes, slum clearance and blight rehabilitation measures are all * * * more familiar. Yet the official map is one of the oldest tools, one of the simplest and one which is currently enjoying considerable popularity. * * * It is one way, * * * to fix building lines. The official map may plat future as well as existing streets. * * * Other familiar methods are: (1) Setback provisions in zoning ordinances; (2) Set-back ordinances as such * * *; (3) Set-backs established on plats as a condition of subdivision approval; (4) Set-back provisions in privately established deed restrictions * * *; (5) The now virtually obsolete method of purchasing set-back easements through eminent domain proceedings. * * * [t]he master plan is not binding upon landowners; the official map is * * *. Official map acts, like zoning acts, are in general constitutional though specific applications * * * may * * * be unconstitutional. * * * There was an overwhelming consensus on the part of municipal officials that only proposed major streets should be mapped; minor streets should be controlled through subdivision plat approval." Kucirek & Beuscher, *Wisconsin's Official Map Law*, 1957 Wis.L.Rev. 176–215.* For a general discussion of the history and developing uses of official maps, see State ex rel. Miller v. Manders, 2 Wis.2d 365, 86 N.W.2d 469 (1957).

"The adoption of an official map specifically identifies and maps future locations for * * * public uses and officially reserves the sites for future public acquisition * * * By prohibiting or restricting development within the areas needed for public uses, it assures that where negotiated settlements are not possible, condemnation proceedings can be used to avoid costly acquisition.

"Over 40 States have some type of official map legislation on their books, but in only 26 does it include power actually to reserve land for streets and in only 13 to reserve land for park and playground areas. In the other cases, an official map is merely a specific indication of where public uses are intended and serves no other legal purpose." 1970 (cum.) ACIR *State Legislative Program* 31–35–00, p. 1.

A state by state summary of official map statutes, and chart comparisons is compiled in Anderson & Roswig, *Planning, Zoning and Subdivision: A Summary of Statutory Law In The 50 States* (1966).

A recent Pennsylvania statute (53 Pa.Stat. §§ 10401–10408) indicates other principal features of official mapping statutes. The official map provides public notice of the location lines of proposed streets, water courses and public grounds, may be amended by official action, and includes indirect amendment by approval of new subdivision plats.

The official map does not obligate the municipality to condemn land or improve streets; but building permits will not issue for improvements within the lines of, or setback limits from, lands mapped for mentioned public uses, except in stated special circumstances. Land reservation by mapping, without condemnation, however, will lapse one year after an owner submits written notice of his intention to build, subdivide or otherwise develop such land, unless within that time, the governing body acquires the land by purchase, gift or condemnation.

The decisions of each state must be checked for variations in mapping authority and procedures. Compare Miller v. Beaver Falls, 368 Pa. 189, 82 A.2d 34 (1951) (denying authority to map or plot private property for public playgrounds) *with* Jenad, p. 495, n. 2; see also Rochester Business Institute, Inc. v. Rochester, 25 A.D.2d 97, 267 N.Y.S.2d 274 (1966) (refused to allow improvement of unimproved mapped street but suggested that if loss to the private owner was substantial, compensation would be required). * * *

Uncoordinated official mapping by individual local governments, some of which may not have exercised their mapping powers, limits the utility of this technique in planning regional facilities, such as freeways. See e.g. Mandelker, *Planning The Freeway: Interim Controls In Highway Programs,* 1964 Duke L.J. 439.

(2) Subdivision by Private Developers

Subdivision laws are related to mapping and zoning, and partake of elements of both. They determine the layout of unimproved land and impose conditions for its development, in the public interest. Municipal planning acts usually include all three devices of mapping, subdivision and zoning law:

"The Municipal Planning Act, N.J.S.A. 40:55–1.1 *et seq.,* and the Official Map and Building Permit Act are *in pari materia* and must be read together. [Citations omitted.] The planning board's duty is to protect the public and future owners of property in the subdivision by requiring, among other conditions, adequate road facilities. The Official Map and Building Permit Act similarly protects the public and future owners by conditioning the grant of a building permit on certification * * * that the building lot abuts a suitably improved street. N.J.S.A. 40:55–1.39. * * *

"We believe the planning board is authorized to condition approval on the ability of the subdivider to comply with the Official Map and Building Permit Act * * * N.J.S.A. 40:55–1.20. The Municipal Planning Act exists to 'facilitate sound and orderly future municipal growth along preconceived lines.' Lake Intervale Homes, Inc. v. Parsippany-Troy Hills, 28 N.J. 423, 435, 147 A.2d 28, 35 (1958); Levin v. Livingston Tp., 35 N.J. 500, 507, 173 A.2d 391 (1963). Where a proposed subdivision requires action by divers municipal agencies, it would be the antithesis of 'a systematic development contrived to promote the common interest,' * * * to hold that the planning board cannot act as a coordinating body." See Noble v. Chairman and

Members of Twp. Committee of Mendham Twp. 91 N.J.Super. 111, 119–20, 219 A.2d 335, 340 (1966); Petition for certification denied 48 N.J. 120, 223 A.2d 497 (1966).

State subdivision statutes are digested and compared in Anderson and Roswig, *Planning, Zoning and Subdivision: A Summary of Statutory Law In The 50 States (1966).*

In earlier times, subdivision ordinances enabled land developers to record plats (maps showing precise boundary lines of lots, streets, alleys, etc. proposed for a particular tract of land) in order to improve title records and facilitate legal descriptions of subdivided parcels. Over time, these ordinances added other conditions for recording and approving subdivision plans, *viz.* conformity of the plat to the official map and to zoning requirements; provision for dedication of lands for streets and other essential public facilities (water, sewerage, drainage); and, most recently, the dedication of lands within the subdivision for parks or schools, or, "in lieu thereof" the payment of certain fees and charges. Also implicit, if not explicit, is the requirement that subdivision plats comply with zoning and general welfare regulations. See generally, *Melli, Subdivision Control in Wisconsin,* 1953 Wis.L.Rev. 389. The issues to be anticipated by counsel to subdividers must be left to real property courses, but to note a few: the legislature cannot define or treat a "subdivision" in a way that is not rationally related to authorized public purposes (cf. Noble v. Chairman and Members of Twp. Committee of Mendhem Township, 91 N.J.Super. 111, 219 A.2d 335 (1966), petition for certification denied 98 N.J. 120, 223 A.2d 497 (1966). It may not arbitrarily require a plat recordation for "every" conveyance, irrespective of "size" of tract or number of lots involved. Kass v. Lewin, 104 So.2d 572 (Fla.1958). Certain types of subdivisions are exempted by statute from subdivision regulations, such as subdivision of land into parcels over 10 acres for agricultural purposes (53 Pa. Stat. § 10107(21); or of land which has existing access to public highways (West's Ann.Cal.Bus. and Prof.Code § 11535(c)); or tracts smaller than a specified land area. Exemptions are often worded so vaguely as to invite evasions by subdividers, viz. division of a large development tract, prior to platting, into tracts smaller in area than the minimum lot size covered by the ordinance; and developing each smaller tract as an exempt subdivision separately. Such attempts may be judicially nullified as unlawful evasions. See e.g. Pratt v. Adams, 229 Cal.App.2d 602, 40 Cal.Rptr. 505 (1964).

In the cases which follow, courts upheld the imposition of *reasonable* conditions to various types of subdivision approval and zoning classifications. Legal distinctions are maintained, however, between conditions and exactions applicable to subdivision approvals, on one hand, and zoning regulations, on the other. Compare e.g., the Associated Builders case which follows, with Scrutton (p. 513 infra).

ASSOCIATED HOME BUILDERS OF GREATER EAST BAY, INC. v. WALNUT CREEK

Supreme Court of California, 1971.
4 Cal.3d 633, 94 Cal.Rptr. 630, 484 P.2d 606.

MOSK, JUSTICE. * * * In this class action * * * Associated Home Builders of the Greater East Bay, Incorporated (hereinafter called Associated) challenges the constitutionality of section 11546 as well as legislation passed by the City of Walnut Creek to implement the section. * * *

Section 11546 of the Business and Professions Code provides:

"The governing body of a city or county may by ordinance require the dedication of land, the payment of fees in lieu thereof, or a combination of both, for park or recreational purposes as a condition to the approval of a final subdivision map, provided that:

* * *

"(b) The ordinance includes definite standards for determining the proportion of a subdivision to be dedicated and the amount of any fee to be paid in lieu thereof.

"(c) The land, fees, or combination thereof are to be used only for the purpose of providing park or recreational facilities to serve the subdivision.

"(d) The legislative body has adopted a general plan containing a recreational element, and the park and recreation facilities are in accordance with definite principles and standards contained therein.

"(e) The amount and location of land to be dedicated or the fees to be paid shall bear a reasonable relationship to the use of the park and recreational facilities by the future inhabitants of the subdivision.

"(f) The city or county must specify when development of the park or recreational facilities will begin.

"(g) Only the payment of fees may be required in subdivisions containing fifty (50) parcels or less.

"The provisions of this section do not apply to industrial subdivisions."

Section 10–1.516 of the Walnut Creek Municipal Code, * * * refers to a general park and recreational plan adopted by the city.

* * *

Section 11546 and the city's ordinance are designed to maintain and preserve open space for the recreational use of the residents of new subdivisions. The adoption of a general plan (subd. (d)) avoids the pitfall of compelling exactions from subdividers of land which may be inadequate in size or unsuitable in location or topography for the facilities necessary to serve the new residents. Under the legislative scheme, the park must be in sufficient proximity to the subdivision which contributes land to serve the future residents. Thus subdividers, providing land or its monetary equivalent, afford the means for the

community to acquire a parcel of sufficient size and appropriate character, located near each subdivision which makes a contribution, to serve
the general recreational needs of the new residents.

* * * One purpose of requiring payment of a fee in lieu of
dedication is to avoid penalizing the subdivider who owns land containing an area designated as park land on the master plan. It would, of
course, be patently unfair and perhaps discriminatory to require such a
property owner to dedicate land, while exacting no contribution from a
subdivider in precisely the same position except for the fortuitous
circumstance that his land does not contain an area which has been
designated as park land on the plan.

CONSTITUTIONALITY OF SECTION 11546

Associated's primary contention is that section 11546 violates the
equal protection and due process clauses of the federal and state
Constitutions in that it deprives a subdivider of his property without
just compensation. It is asserted * * * that such contributions are
used to pay for public facilities enjoyed by all citizens of the city and
only incidentally by subdivision residents, and that all taxpayers should
share in the cost of these public facilities. Thus, it is asserted, the
future residents of the subdivision, * * * will be required to pay for
recreational facilities the need for which stems not from the development of any one subdivision but from the needs of the community as a
whole.

In order to avoid these constitutional pitfalls, claims Associated, a
dedication requirement is justified only if it can be shown that the need
for additional park and recreational facilities is attributable to the
increase in population stimulated by the new subdivision alone and the
validity of the section may not be upheld upon the theory that all
subdivisions to be built in the future will create the need for such
facilities.

In Ayres v. City Council of City of Los Angeles (1949) 34 Cal.2d 31,
207 P.2d 1, we rejected similar arguments. * * *

We held that the city was not acting in eminent domain * * *.
We held, further, that the conditions were not improper because their
fulfillment would incidentally benefit the city as a whole or because
future as well as immediate needs were taken into consideration
* * *. We do not find in Ayres support for the principle urged by
Associated that a dedication requirement may be upheld only if the
particular subdivision creates the need for dedication.

Even if it were not for the authority of Ayres we would have no
doubt that section 11546 can be justified * * *. The elimination of
open space in California is a melancholy aspect of the unprecedented
population increase which has characterized our state in the last few
decades. Manifestly governmental entities have the responsibility to
provide park and recreation land to accommodate this human expan-

sion despite the inexorable decrease of open space available to fulfill such need.

* * *

We see no persuasive reason in the face of these urgent needs * * * to hold that a statute requiring the dedication of land by a subdivider may be justified only upon the ground that the particular subdivider upon whom an exaction has been imposed will, solely by the development of his subdivision, increase the need for recreational facilities to such an extent that additional land for such facilities will be required.

Associated next contends that even if it be conceded that no showing of a direct relationship between a particular subdivision and an increase in the community's recreational needs is required, nevertheless the subdivider cannot be compelled to dedicate land for such needs, or pay a fee, unless his contribution will necessarily and primarily benefit the particular subdivision. Whether or not such a direct connection is required by constitutional considerations, section 11546 provides the nexus which concerns Associated. The act requires that the land dedicated or the fees paid are to be used only for the purpose of providing park or recreational facilities to serve the subdivision (subd. (c)) and (subd. (e)) that the amount and location of land or fees shall bear a reasonable relationship to the use of the facilities by the future inhabitants of the subdivision.

Another assertion by Associated is that the only exactions * * * which may be valid are those directly related to the health and safety of the subdivision residents and necessary to the use and habitation of the subdivision, such as sewers, streets and drainage facilities. While it is true that such improvements are categories directly required by the health and safety of subdivision residents, it cannot be said that recreational facilities are not also related to these salutary purposes. * * * As shall appear hereinafter several other jurisdictions have upheld exactions similar to those imposed by section 11546 on the ground that the influx of new residents increases the need for park and recreational facilities.[7]

Associated next poses as an eventuality that, if the requirements of section 11546 are upheld * * * a city or county could also require contributions from a subdivider for such services as added costs of fire and police protection, the construction of a new city hall, or even a general contribution to defray the additional cost of all types of governmental services necessitated by the entry of the new residents.

7. The only case cited by Associated which declared a statute similar to section 11546 to be unconstitutional recognized the need for recreational facilities caused by the influx of new residents but held that the need for such facilities must be "specifically and uniquely attributable" to the subdivider's activities and that the record did not indicate that this requirement had been met. (Pioneer Trust & Sav. Bank v. Village of Mount Prospect (1961), 22 Ill.2d 375, 176 N.E.2d 799, 802.) We have rejected this rationale in our previous discussion.

This proposition overlooks the unique problem involved in utilization of raw land. * * * The development of a new subdivision in and of itself has the counterproductive effect of consuming a substantial supply of this precious commodity, while at the same time increasing the need for park and recreational land. In terms of economics, subdivisions diminish supply and increase demand. * * *

Associated claims that section 11546 constitutes a special burden upon the future inhabitants * * * It is asserted that a double tax will be imposed on the new residents because they must not only pay for the initial cost of the park but will also be required to assume property taxes which will be used for its development and maintenance. Double taxation occurs only when "two taxes of the same character are imposed on the same property, for the same purpose, by the same taxing authority within the same jurisdiction during the same taxing period." (Rhyne, Municipal Law, p. 673.) Obviously the dedication or fee required of the subdivider and the property taxes paid by the later residents of the subdivision do not meet this definition. * * *

Another contention by Associated is that section 11546 arbitrarily imposes its requirements only upon subdividers whereas those who do not subdivide are free from its exactions. The example is suggested of an apartment house built on land which is not subdivided. * * * This point has some arguable merit in the sense that the apartment builder, by increasing the population of an area, may add to the need for public recreational facilities * * *. However, the apartment is generally vertical, while the subdivision is horizontal. * * * This significant distinction justifies legislatively treating the builder of an apartment house who does not subdivide differently than the creator of a subdivision.

Finally, Associated attacks the constitutionality of subdivision (f) of section 11546, which specifies that a city or county must state when development of park or recreational facilities will begin. It is claimed that the city could in one case postpone development for 10 years and in another begin development within a year, and that this discretion amounts to an arbitrary delegation of power to the local governmental body and a denial of due process and equal protection of the laws. Obviously, the need for park and recreational facilities will vary from one community to another and from one neighborhood to another within the same community. The city's resolution 2225 provides that improvements to the parks shall be made as the subdivision area develops and park facilities become necessary. Constitutional considerations do not require a more precise standard; the courts are available to redress any unreasonable delay in development.

Many of the issues raised by Associated have been discussed in the cases and law reviews. The clear weight of authority upholds the constitutionality of statutes similar to section 11546. While Illinois has held an ordinance requiring a subdivider to dedicate land for park purposes to be unconstitutional (Pioneer Trust & Savings Bank v.

Village of Mount Prospect, *supra,* 22 Ill.2d 375, 176 N.E.2d 799, 801–802), Montana has reached a contrary conclusion (Billings Properties, Inc. v. Yellowstone County (1964), 144 Mont. 25, 394 P.2d 182). New York and Wisconsin have affirmed the validity of statutes requiring either dedication or a fee in lieu thereof (Jenad, Inc. v. Village of Scarsdale, *supra,* 18 N.Y.2d 78, 271 N.Y.S.2d 955, 218 N.E.2d 673; Jordan v. Village of Menomonee Falls (Wis.1965), *supra,* 28 Wis.2d 608, 137 N.W.2d 442). In Connecticut the dedication requirement has been upheld but the requirement that a fee be paid in lieu of dedication was struck down on the ground that its use was not confined for the benefit of the subdivision but to the contrary the fees could be utilized to purchase park land for the residents of the entire town (Aunt Hack Ridge Estates, Inc. v. Planning Commission of Danbury (1967), 27 Conn. Sup. 74, 230 A.2d 45, 47).

The rationale of the cases affirming constitutionality indicate the dedication statutes are valid under the state's police power. * * *

* * *

It may come to pass, as Associated states, that subdividers will transfer the cost of the land dedicated or the in-lieu fee to the consumers who ultimately purchase homes in the subdivision, thereby to some extent increasing the price of houses to newcomers. While we recognize the ominous possibility that the contributions required by a city can be deliberately set unreasonably high in order to prevent the influx of economically depressed persons into the community, a circumstance which would present serious social and legal problems, there is nothing to indicate that the enactments of Walnut Creek in the present case raise such a spectre. The desirability of encouraging subdividers to build low-cost housing cannot be denied and unreasonable exactions could defeat this object, but these considerations must be balanced against the phenomenon of the appallingly rapid disappearance of open areas in and around our cities. We believe section 11546 constitutes a valiant attempt to solve this urgent problem, and we cannot say that its provisions or the city's enactments pursuant to the section are constitutionally deficient.

The judgment is affirmed.

Notes

1. "Statutes requiring dedication of park and playground land as a condition precedent to the approval of plats are in force in one form or another in most all states." Billings Properties, Inc. v. Yellowstone County, 144 Mont. 25, 32, 394 P.2d 182, 187 (1964). See e.g. 53 Pa.Stat. § 10501 et seq. See Annot., Subdivision Exactions, 43 A.L.R.3d 862 (1972); discussion of "exactions" in Scrutten at p. 516, *infra.*

2. Courts are divided on the legality of fund exactions which are put into a general fund for recreational lands of the entire municipality. Compare: Jenad, Inc. v. Scarsdale, 18 N.Y.2d 78, 271 N.Y.S.2d 955, 218

N.E.2d 673 (1966), with Haugen v. Gleason, 226 Or. 99, 359 P.2d 108 (1961); Kelber v. Upland, 155 Cal.App.2d 631, 318 P.2d 561 (1957).

FRANK ANSUINI, INC. v. CRANSTON
Supreme Court of Rhode Island, 1970.
107 R.I. 63, 264 A.2d 910.

POWERS, JUSTICE.

[Civil complaint to strike down * * * a regulation * * * requiring, as a condition precedent to final plat approval, the voluntary donation for recreation purposes of at least seven per cent of the land to be divided. The Court struck down the flat percentage fee.]

* * *

* * * In *Pioneer, supra,* citing *Ayres, supra,* the rule is stated to be that a developer may be required to donate only such portion of the land to be divided as may be needed for such public uses as will result from the activities specifically and uniquely attributable to him.

On the other hand, it has been held that the legislature may require a stated percentage donation in which case the burden is on each would-be developer to show that the stated percentage is unreasonable as to him. Billings Properties, Inc. v. Yellowstone County, *supra;* Jordan v. Village of Menomonee Falls, *supra;* Jenad, Inc. v. Village of Scarsdale, *supra;* Aunt Hack Ridge Estates, Inc. v. Planning Commission of Town of Danbury, *supra.*

It is on these later cited cases that defendant seeks support for the validity of the challenged regulation. We are of the opinion, however, that the rule as enunciated in *Pioneer* is the more reasonable and should apply in this jurisdiction. It seems obvious to us that a fixed percentage requirement will inevitably create inequities, which will be less likely to arise under the specifically and uniquely attributable formula.

* * *

Notes

1. **Accord:** Krughoff v. Naperville, 68 Ill.2d 185, 10 Ill.Dec. 185, 369 N.E.2d 892 (1977). See also Brazer v. Mountainside, 55 N.J. 456, 262 A.2d 857 (1970) where the court voided an exaction requirement (fifty foot right of way for a road extension) which would take 20% of the total area of a small development, and which was not essential to service subdivision residents. East Neck Estates, Ltd. v. Luchsinger, 61 Misc.2d 619, 305 N.Y.S.2d 922 (1969) nullified, as confiscatory, a dedication requirement which would reduce the value of the subdivider's plat from $208,000 to $118,000.

2. How reasonable is a requirement that the subdivider pay an "outlet sewer charge" of $400. per acre, as a condition of recording his development plan, where city officials had discretion to require or waive that charge as to each subdivision submission? See Longridge Estates v. Los Angeles, 183 Cal.App.2d 533, 6 Cal.Rptr. 900 (1960). Compare Zastrow

v. Village of Brown Deer, 9 Wis.2d 100, 100 N.W.2d 359 (1960) which upheld the requirement.

WEST PARK AVE., INC. v. OCEAN
Supreme Court of New Jersey, 1966.
48 N.J. 122, 224 A.2d 1.

WEINTRAUB, C.J. * * *

I

Plaintiff acquired 60 lots * * * which lots were part of a subdivision plan. After completing a model home, plaintiff erected signs advertising its tract, whereupon plaintiff was told by municipal officials that it could not use a billboard or receive further building permits or certificates of occupancy unless it agreed to pay to the defendant Board of Education the sum of $300 per house. =$18,000⁰⁰

As we have said, the trial court found that plaintiff yielded unwillingly to this imposition. That finding, we think, was inescapably correct. Plaintiff feared it could not survive if its project stood still during a period of litigation. It also sensed a danger of hostile enforcement of ordinances bearing upon the construction of homes. This was especially understandable because of the boldness with which the dollar demand was made, for the municipality did not so much as adopt an ordinance to give color to the exaction. * * *

* * *

In point of time, those transactions followed close upon our decision in Daniels v. Borough of Point Pleasant, 23 N.J. 357, 129 A.2d 265 (1957), in which we struck down an ordinance which attempted to impose a tax for revenue purposes upon new construction. In form the ordinance increased the fees for building permits. We said (at p. 362, 129 A.2d p. 267):

" * * * The philosophy of this ordinance is that the tax rate of the borough should remain the same and the new people coming into the municipality should bear the burden of the increased costs of their presence. This is so totally contrary to tax philosophy as to require it to be stricken down; see Gilbert v. Town of Irvington, 20 N.J. 432, 120 A.2d 114 (1956). * * *

The Legislature has not been unaware of the overall problem. It dealt with it in its statute relating to subdivisions. N.J.S.A. 40:55–1.21 reads:

"Before final approval of plats the governing body may require * * * the installation, or the furnishing of a performance guarantee in lieu thereof, of any or all of the following improvements it may deem to be necessary or appropriate: street grading, pavement, gutters, curbs, sidewalks, street lighting, shade trees, surveyor's monuments, water mains, culverts, storm sewers, sanitary sewers or other means of sewage disposal, drainage structures, and such other subdivision improvements as the municipal governing body may find necessary in the public interest."

But with respect to the impact of housing developments upon the educational scene, the Legislature went no further than to provide that the governing body or planning board "shall be permitted to reserve the location and extent of *school sites,* public parks and playgrounds shown on the master plan or any part thereof for a period of one year after the approval of the final plat or within such further time as agreed to by the applying party," but "Unless during such one-year period or extension thereof the municipality shall have entered into a contract to purchase or instituted condemnation proceedings according to law, for said school site, park or playground, the subdivider shall not be bound by the proposals for such areas shown on the master plan." N.J.S.A. 40:55–1.20. (Italics supplied.)

* * *

It is not our purpose to prejudge the constitutional power of the Legislature to authorize municipalities to impose charges such as the one here involved. * * * Rather our point is that the Legislature has not committed that authority to local government.

There being no statutory authorization, it is clear the municipality could not have lawfully exacted the charges here involved. * * *

Defendants argue that even if the payments were illegally extorted, * * * nonetheless plaintiff ought not recover for reasons to which we now turn.

II

* * *

* * * Defendants' position boils down to the proposition that one who buys with notice of municipal lawlessness thereby becomes bound by it. Thus understood, defendants' position is frivolous. * * *

III

Next, defendants say plaintiff's payments, although in fact made unwillingly, were nonetheless "voluntary" in law because plaintiff failed to resist the illegal demand by suit. * * *

* * *

Some authorities dispute the validity of the requirement that the victim of duress show he had no feasible remedy available to him. See S.P. Dunham & Co. v. Kudra, 44 N.J.Super. 565, 570–571, 131 A.2d 306 (App.Div.1957). * * *

* * *

In the case before us an unlawful demand was made with a consciousness of its unlawfulness. If it were crucial, we would not hesitate to say that plaintiff had no feasible remedy, * * *. But we prefer to say the wrong of the municipality was so palpable that it would be against good morals to permit defendants to complain that plaintiff was not valiant enough. * * *

* * *

For these reasons, we are satisfied that plaintiff is entitled to judgment. We note that this result is supported by decisions elsewhere. See Rosen v. Village of Downers Grove, 19 Ill.2d 448, 167 N.E.2d 230, 235 (Sup.Ct.1960); Gordon v. Village of Wayne, 370 Mich. 329, 121 N.W.2d 823 (Sup.Ct.1963); Ridgemont Development Co. v. City of East Detroit, 358 Mich. 387, 100 N.W.2d 301 (Sup.Ct.1960); cf. Kelber v. City of Upland, 155 Cal.App.2d 631, 318 P.2d 561 (D.Ct.App.1958); Haugen v. Gleason, 226 Or. 99, 359 P.2d 108 (Sup.Ct.1961); Theatre Control Corp. v. City of Detroit, 370 Mich. 382, 121 N.W.2d 828 (Sup.Ct.1963).

The judgment is reversed and the matter remanded to the trial court with directions to enter judgment in favor of plaintiff for $17,700 together with interest.   *   *   *

c. Building Codes

Building codes regulate the design, materials, and methods of construction. Together with health, fire, and housing codes, they are intended to promote safe and sanitary structures. To the extent that building codes promote uniform and modern construction standards, they serve the public welfare, but experience has shown that such codes may also retard efficient and economical construction, especially when they are employed to favor parochial business or labor interests by imposing obsolete and wasteful work, materials and safety standards. Some codes prohibit the use of plastic plumbing, dry wall construction and other labor and cost-saving devices, and impede technological advances in the construction industry. The diversity of building code requirements, administration and enforcement among thousands of municipalities entrusted with such functions, also prevents exploitation of mass production techniques, *viz.* prefabrication, standard components, and modular construction.

As of 1966 only five states (California, Indiana, North Carolina, Ohio and Wisconsin) * had statutes authorizing mandatory building construction codes, and four states (Connecticut, Minnesota, New Jersey and New York) provided for model state codes which local governments could, at their option, adopt. See ACIR, *Building Codes: A Program for Intergovernmental Reform,* p. 24 et seq. (1966).

More recently several states enacted Industrialized Housing Laws to deal specifically with industrialized housing. These laws permit industrialized housing that meets state qualification standards to be marketed and used throughout the state, without the need to comply with local building codes. See e.g. Ohio Rev.Code ch. 3781; West's Ann. Cal.Health and Safety Code, §§ 19960–19997; Wash.Laws 1970, ch. 44; Virginia Acts 1970, c. 305; 35 Pa.Stat. §§ 1651.1–1651.12.

Where building codes are confiscatory and unreasonable (*e.g.* by requiring a lavatory in each room of a rented unit), they are subject to nullification. Safer v. Jacksonville, 237 So.2d 8 (Fla.1970); Gates Co.

* Connecticut became the first state to establish a mandatory state-wide building code for all types of structures. Conn.Gen. Stat.Anno. § 19–395 ff. (1969).

Housing Appeals Bd. v. Columbus, 10 Ohio St.2d 48, 225 N.E.2d 222 (1967). The court in each case decides whether challenged code provisions satisfy due process or bear a reasonable relationship to the public welfare. Kaukas v. Chicago, 27 Ill.2d 197, 188 N.E.2d 700 (1963). Will the following building code requirements pass constitutional muster: that wood houses be painted on the exterior; that each room have two electrical outlets; that all bathrooms have heating facilities? See City of Columbus v. Stubbs, 223 Ga. 765, 188 S.E.2d 392 (1967); cf. Boden v. Milwaukee, 8 Wis.2d 318, 99 N.W.2d 156 (1959).

Housing codes are intended to insure minimum living standards and are enforced by rent and occupancy controls, inspections, injunctions and demolition. See Community Renewal Foundation, Inc. v. Chicago Title & Trust Co., 44 Ill.2d 284, 255 N.E.2d 908 (1970); the demolition cases, p. 481 et seq.; Annot., Housing Standards, 20 A.L.R. 4th 1246 (1983).

d. Zoning

(1) General Standards

Zoning laws prescribe the kinds of land uses and construction that are permitted in designated "districts." They are more comprehensive and flexible than subdivision regulations. Aptly termed "the workhorse" of the planning movement, zoning is a modern regulatory technique which is far from fully or adequately developed. Widespread zoning was ushered in by the model state Standard Zoning Enabling Act (U.S. Department of Commerce Rev.Ed.1926). Its constitutionality was established in Village of Euclid v. Ambler Realty Co., 272 U.S. 365, 47 S.Ct. 114, 71 L.Ed. 303 (1926), as a legitimate exercise of state police power. See R.M. Anderson, B.B. Roswig, *Planning, Zoning and Subdivision: A Summary of Statutory Law In The 50 States* (1966).

The primary test of zoning legality is the vague, but universal, requirement of state enabling laws that the local government zone "in accordance with" a comprehensive plan. This legislative standard, validates the delegation of zoning authority, and serves to limit its exercise. But while the legislative standard is uniform, judicial definition and application thereof is not. See generally, O. Reynolds, Local Government Law, § 118 (1982).

(a) Euclidean Zoning—

CLEAVER v. BOARD OF ADJUSTMENT OF TREDYFFRIN TOWNSHIP

Supreme Court of Pennsylvania, 1964.
414 Pa. 367, 200 A.2d 408.

BELL, CHIEF JUSTICE. The question involved is the validity and constitutionality of the amended zoning ordinance of Tredyffrin Township, Chester County.

An equally divided Board of Adjustment affirmed *ex necessitate* the issuance of a building permit for the erection of a garden type of apartment * * *. Thereafter the Court of Common Pleas of Chester County * * * held the amendatory ordinance (a) invalid because of lack of conformity with Tredyffrin's comprehensive plan, and (b) unconstitutional because it was spot zoning.

* * *

The action here complained of is the down zoning of the tract in suit from R-3 *to R-4*. R-3 allows * * * no apartment use whatever. R-4 permits garden or group type apartments. C-1 (Commercial), * * * permits various business uses such as retail store, bank, restaurant, certain kind of shops, and any *use permitted in R-4.* * * *

To answer the questions involved we must consider (a) the Constitution, and (b) the law pertaining to zoning, including a comprehensive plan.

THE RIGHT OF PROPERTY OWNERS AND THE POWERS OF
GOVERNMENT

The law governing the Constitutionality of zoning legislation may be thus summarized:

The Constitution of the United States in the Fifth Amendment and in the Fourteenth Amendment, and the Constitution of Pennsylvania in Article I, § 1, P.S., ordain and guarantee the right of private property. * * *

* * *

In Lhormer v. Bowen, 410 Pa. 508, page 512, 188 A.2d 747, page 749, the Court aptly said:

"* * * As stated in Lened Homes, Inc., v. Dep't of Licenses, * * * 386 Pa. [50] at page 54, 123 A.2d [406] at page 407: ' "An owner of property is still entitled in Pennsylvania to certain unalienable constitutional rights of liberty and property. These include a right to use his own home [or property] in any way he desires, provided he does not (1) violate any provision of the Federal or State Constitutions; or (2) create a nuisance; or (3) violate any covenant, restriction or easement, or (4) violate any laws or zoning or police regulations which are constitutional." ' See also, Andress v. Zoning Board, 410 Pa. 77, 188 A.2d 709 (1963)."

Nevertheless, it is well settled that that Constitutionally ordained right of property is and must be subject and subordinated to the Supreme Power of Government—generally known as the Police Power—to regulate or prohibit an owner's use of his property provided such regulation or prohibition is clearly or reasonably necessary to preserve or protect the health or safety or morals and general welfare of the people: [citations omitted].

* * * The dividing line between a regulation (by zoning legislation) and a "taking" is in many cases shadowy and difficult to draw or delineate. * * *

It may be helpful to add that an Ordinance is presumed to be valid and Constitutional and the burden of proving otherwise is upon one who challenges it: [citations omitted]. However, zoning regulations must be strictly construed because in derogation of a property owner's Constitutional rights: [citations omitted].

GENERAL ZONING POWERS, STANDARDS AND RESTRICTIONS

1. Municipalities are not sovereigns; they have no original or fundamental power of legislation; a municipal or councilmanic body can enact only the ordinances and exercise only the zoning powers which are authorized by the Legislature, and the Legislature can delegate or grant only those legislative and zoning powers which are Constitutionally permitted: [citations omitted].

2. Certain and definite and valid standards for zoning must be prescribed in the Legislative Act and in the zoning ordinance: [citations omitted].

3. Zoning classifications are largely within the sound discretion and judgment of the pertinent legislative or zoning body, subject to the provisions and limitations of the Constitution. Health, and safety, and morals, and general welfare are the indispensable sine qua non for a zoning ordinance. Moreover, in connection with general welfare, the nature, the size, and the particular and the general character of the property in question and of the neighborhood and the district, are important factors which, among others, must be considered by the zoning authorities: [citations omitted].

4. * * * The final decision in zoning matters rests in the legislative body and not in a planning commission, and a township or borough or county or city may adopt or modify or reject any comprehensive or master plan which is prepared by a planning commission: DiSanto v. Zoning Board of Adjustment, 410 Pa. 331, 189 A.2d 135, *supra;* Gratton v. Conte, 364 Pa. 578, 73 A.2d 381, *supra.*

5. A comprehensive plan is ordinarily separate and distinct from an ordinance, but it is possible for an ordinance in and of itself to be a comprehensive plan, unless the Legislature or the legislative body clearly otherwise provides. [Citations omitted]

6. A comprehensive plan does not contemplate or require a "master-plan" which *rigidly* provides for or attempts to answer in minute detail every possible question regarding land utilization or restriction. Neither a zoning ordinance nor a comprehensive plan is absolutely rigid, static and unchangeable; either or both may be amended, supplemented, changed, modified or repealed—in the sound discretion of the legislative body and in accordance with statutory and other pertinent legal and Constitutional requirements—as conditions or changing circumstances may require: Furniss v. Lower Merion Township, 412 Pa. 404, 194 A.2d 926; Donahue v. Zoning Board of Adjustment, 412 Pa. 332, 194 A.2d 610, *supra.*

7. Public hearings and public approval are often wise, but are mandatory only when required by the Legislature or by the Legislative body: * * *

8. Spot zoning is unconstitutional: French v. Zoning Board of Adjustment, 408 Pa. 479, 184 A.2d 791; Putney v. Abington Twp., 176 Pa.Super. 463, 108 A.2d 134; Boyle's Appeal, 179 Pa.Super.Ct. 318, 116 A.2d 860.

COMPREHENSIVE PLAN

All parties concede that the Land Use Plan for Tredyffrin Township issued by the Planning Commission in 1961, fulfills the legal requirements of a Comprehensive Plan. * * * On the other hand, appellees argue that although apartments, under the literal provisions of the "P" Professional zoning classification could, consistently with the plan, be erected on the property, in suit, the *permitted* apartment-uses under this amended ordinance failed to conform to the plan. Appellees' principal objections are that apartment-uses in R–4(a) permit too great a population *density* per square foot, and (b) fail sufficiently to restrict set-back and spacing of buildings.

Appellees take too narrow a view of the Township's Land Use Plan in particular and of the function of a Comprehensive Plan in general. The plan takes into consideration, *inter alia,* present conditions and the foreseeable likely future development of the Township. * * *

It is clear that the Tredyffrin Land Use Plan (a) permits a defined range of choices in the zoning of appellant's property (as well as neighboring properties), and (b) *does not command* particular requirements of population density or set-back or spacing for apartments thereon, and (c) clearly envisages and permits a proper zoning of the property here in question for apartments.

We find that the lower Court was in error.

SPOT ZONING

The lower Court first * * * held that the ordinance was unconstitutional because it amounted to "spot" zoning. With this conclusion, we disagree. It is very difficult to define "spot" zoning. Zoning is a legislative division of a community into areas or districts in each of which only certain designated uses of land and/or buildings are permitted. Generally speaking, spot zoning is the arbitrary and unreasonable classification and zoning of *a small parcel of land.* This small parcel of land is usually set apart or carved out of a surrounding or a large neighboring tract, with no reasonable justification for the differential zoning.

* * *

Assuming, arguendo, that this 11 acre tract is small enough to fall under the ban of "spot" zoning, we find that the ordinance with respect thereto is valid and Constitutional. We first note that the proposed apartment is on land immediately adjacent to the main line tracks of the Pennsylvania Railroad with their very heavy traffic. Furthermore, a large part of the surrounding land has the same or virtually the same classification as the tract in suit. As above pointed out, the land immediately to the East and to the South, as well as two small pieces nearby to the West, are classified C–1. *All R–4 uses are permitted in C–1 districts.* Thus the *uses* permitted by the down zoning under attack are substantially similar to those permitted on numerous adjoining properties. Moreover, the lower Court found—and no one on appeal has argued to the contrary—that a high pressure pipeline under 3.8 acres of the tract (in the shape of an "L"), renders the building of dwellings upon it impractical. Thus a change from R–3 to R–4, and appellants' contemplated development, have at first blush, a reasonable basis.

* * *

We conclude that in invalidating Tredyffrin's amendatory zoning ordinance, the lower Court committed an error of law.

Judgment reversed.

Notes

1. **"Euclidean Zoning".** The division of municipal territory into geographic districts which serve as "zoning envelopes" for land use classifications is termed euclidean zoning.

"Cumulative" zoning refers to the system whereby uses permitted in a higher restricted area are permitted in less restricted districts, so that the least restricted district is open to the greatest number of classified uses. Noncumulative zoning establishes districts for fixed uses and permits districting for exclusive classes of land use, *viz.* exclusive industrial use districts. See Grubel v. MacLaughlin, 286 F.Supp. 24 (D.Virgin Islands 1968).

2. **Spot Zoning.** Spot zoning is vulnerable on constitutional grounds, as in Cleaver, or as an "ultra vires" act, not in conformity with a comprehensive plan. See *Kozesnik,* p. 505 which follows. Since reasonableness lies at the heart of both claims, what are the advantages of constitutional attack over nonconstitutional attack? See Comment, Doctrine of Special Legislation In Pa. Zoning Law, 22 Vill.L.Rev. 106 (1977) for theory of treating spot zoning as a species of "special legislation". On the legal import of the "size" of the spot zoned, see Carpionato v. Town Council of North Providence, 104 R.I. 490, 244 A.2d 861 (1968).

3. **Presumption of Validity.** There is some confusion in the authorities on the meaning and strength of the presumption of validity of zoning ordinances. On the "debatable question" rule, that an ordinance will not be nullified if there is a "debatable" question as to its reasonableness, judges debate whether a question is debatable. See Raabe v. Walker, 10 Mich.App. 383, 159 N.W.2d 759 (1968), reversed 383 Mich. 165, 174 N.W.2d 789 (1970).

Where courts balance private and public injury or benefit, the effect of the presumption is equally uncertain. The following cases involve the reasonableness of restricting uses for the purpose of maintaining buffer zones: Cole-Collister Fire Protection District v. Boise, 93 Idaho 558, 468 P.2d 290 (1970) (voiding refusal to down-zone residential property); accord: Davis v. Rockford, 60 Ill.App.2d 325, 208 N.E.2d 110 (1965); Summers v. Glen Cove, 17 N.Y.2d 307, 270 N.Y.S.2d 611, 217 N.E.2d 663 (1966). But see, State v. Gallop Building, 103 N.J.Super. 367, 247 A.2d 350 (1968) (indirectly upholding requirement of 20 foot buffer of tree screens at front of business property). Both case lines stress the importance of the character of the affected neighborhood. See Annot., 40 A.L.R.3d 272 at 397 et seq. (1971).

The authorities vary on the applicability of the presumption with respect to (a) rezoning; (b) spot zoning; (c) the grant of special exceptions. Annot., 40 A.L.R.3d 372 at 389–94 (1971).

"In Roseta v. County of Washington, Or., 458 P.2d 405, decided this day, we held that where the county amends a zoning ordinance to permit a use inconsistent with the * * * the original ordinance the presumption of regularity * * * is not applicable. The same principle was recognized in Smith v. County of Washington, 241 Or. 380, 406 P.2d 545 (1965). As we explained in the Smith case, ' * * * the antithetical character of spot zoning * * * tends to neutralize, if not to overcome, the presumption in the particular case.'" Archdiocese of Portland v. Washington, 254 Or. 77, 82, 458 P.2d 682, 685 (1969).

The Supreme Court of Oregon seems to have taken a further step in reversing the presumption of validity where the zoning change involves a single parcel. Fasano v. Board of County Comm'rs, 264 Or. 574, 507 P.2d 23 (1973).

KOZESNIK v. MONTGOMERY TOWNSHIP

Supreme Court of New Jersey, 1957.
24 N.J. 154, 131 A.2d 1.

WEINTRAUB, J.

[Minnesota Mining & Manufacturing Company (3M) desired to mine and process rock on a site lying partly in Hillsborough and partly in Montgomery Townships. Each town respectively rezoned its portion of the tract to permit quarrying in Hillsborough, and a rock processing plant in Montgomery. Suit was brought to nullify each of these down-zoning changes.]

* * *

Although for reasons hereinafter expressed we feel compelled to set aside the amendatory ordinances of both townships, we are satisfied that the basic plan may lawfully be achieved. Our purpose here is to consider those objections, valid and invalid, which will bear upon the course the municipalities may take if they should determine to further the program.

There of course is nothing invidious in the circumstance that the townships cooperated in a matter of common interest. * * *

The Hillsborough Ordinance

Hillsborough amended its ordinance to create a limited industrial zone wherein it authorized residential and agricultural uses * * * and additionally permitted "Quarries." * * *

* * *

* * * In short, the ordinance is so framed that for all practical purposes the industrial activity authorized is pinpointed to the extraction and processing of diabase rock for limited ultimate use.

* * *

I

Plaintiffs contend the amendment is not "in accordance with a comprehensive plan." There are a number of facets to this attack. The first is that there can be no comprehensive plan unless it is evidenced in writing *dehors* the zoning ordinance itself.

Hillsborough has not adopted a master plan under the Planning Act, * * *.

* * *

No doubt good housekeeping would be served if a zoning ordinance followed and implemented a master plan * * *, but the history of the subject dictated another course. Initially regulations concerning land use were merely prohibitory or restrictive with respect to specific noxious or dangerous activities. Thereafter a more comprehensive approach developed in the form of zoning, * * * R.S. 40:55–30, N.J. S.A. Finally came the Planning Act, which envisions the development of a plan looking to and guiding future development with provision for the location of public improvements, control over subdivisions, and the like. * * *

Thus the historical development did not square with the orderly treatment of the problem which present wisdom would recommend. And doubtless the need for immediate measures led the Legislature to conclude that zoning shall not await the development of a master plan. * * *

It is thus clear that the "comprehensive plan" of the zoning statute is not identical with the "master plan" of the Planning Act * * *. The Zoning Act nowhere provides that the comprehensive plan shall exist in some physical form outside the ordinance itself. * * *

* * * Without venturing an exact definition, it may be said for present purposes that "plan" connotes an integrated product of a rational process and "comprehensive" requires something beyond a piecemeal approach, both to be revealed by the ordinance considered in relation to the physical facts and the purposes authorized by R.S. 40:55–32, N.J.S.A. Such being the requirements of a comprehensive plan, no reason is perceived why we should infer the Legislature intended by necessary implication that the comprehensive plan be portrayed in some physical form outside the ordinance itself. A plan may readily be

revealed in an end-product—here the zoning ordinance—and no more is required by the statute.

The comprehensive plan embraced by an original zoning ordinance is of course mutable. * * * and if the ordinance as thus amended reveals a comprehensive plan, it is of no moment that the new plan so revealed differs from the original one.

* * *

* * * It seems to us that the amendment presented a fairly debatable issue, and hence we cannot interfere with the legislative judgment * * * that the authorization of the industrial use is appropriately a part of the comprehensive plan.

III

It is urged that if quarrying is permitted, it is arbitrary to exclude other industrial uses and so-called "higher" uses, such as commercial ones.

We are not unmindful that in the infancy of zoning it was the general practice to permit higher uses in the less restricted district. The statute, however, does not so command. * * * Hence, in seeking a well-balanced community, * * * a municipality may conclude its welfare is better served by avoiding motley activities within its districts. See Roney v. Board of Supervisors of Contra Costa County, 138 Cal.App.2d 740, 292 P.2d 529 (Ct.App.1956). In every case the question is one of reasonableness under the circumstances. * * *

The problem is the familiar one of classification. Thus where the facts were found to demonstrate that it was unreasonable to exclude commercial activity from a light industrial district, the restriction was held invalid, Katobimar Realty Co. v. Webster, 20 N.J. 114, 118 A.2d 824 (1955), whereas when a reasonable basis existed for differentiating between motels and boarding or rooming houses, the exclusion of the former was upheld. Pierro v. Baxendale, *supra* (20 N.J. 17, 118 A.2d 401). In both cases this court divided 4 to 3, but the division did not reflect disagreement as to basic principle but rather as to the application of the principle to the facts of the case.

* * *

Ordinarily a single industrial activity would not constitute a defensible class, but the proposition is general and not universal. It is true that where a municipality determines a district is suitable for general industrial uses, it may not reserve the power to decide upon individual applications which industrial uses will be admitted. Rockhill v. Township of Chesterfield, 23 N.J. 117, 128 A.2d 473 (1957). Such, however, is not the situation before us. * * *

* * *

* * * For reported instances in which authorization of a single use has been upheld, see Higbee v. Chicago, Burlington & Quincy R. Co., 235 Wis. 91, 292 N.W. 320, 128 A.L.R. 734 (Sup.Ct.1940), where an ordinance authorizing a passenger depot was upheld, and Holt v. City of

Salem, 192 Or. 200, 234 P.2d 564 (Sup.Ct.1951), in which an ordinance permitting the erection of a substation for the distribution of electric power was sustained.

The ordinance is attacked as "spot zoning."

The testimony discloses that the diabase rock extends far beyond the limits of the new district, and this being so, plaintiffs seek application of the general proposition that all property in like circumstances * * * We again have a general proposition which must yield to realities.

* * * The final test must be whether the municipality is seeking to advance the community interest rather than some private or sectional advantage. Raskin v. Town of Morristown, *supra* (21 N.J. 180, 121 A.2d 378).

* * *

* * * The evidence indicates that the portion here selected had unique advantages apart from the special quality of the rock, namely, a lesser quantity of overburden coupled with suitable facings for quarrying. Additionally, Hillsborough was entitled to decide how much of its area could be subjected to the impact of these operations consistent with its total interest. * * *

Plaintiffs emphasize the fact the ordinance conforms to 3M's proposal. That it does, is not in itself a vitiating circumstance. Nor does the ownership of property nor its size constitute the controlling test of so-called spot zoning. If the purpose is solely to serve the private interests of the owner, there is a perversion of power, but if the intention is to further the welfare of the entire municipality as part of a comprehensive plan * * *, it is of no moment that private interests are simultaneously benefited.

* * *

But plaintiffs say that if the zone itself is properly fixed, yet it is arbitrary to include therein lands which cannot meet the minimum requirements for a quarrying permit.

The district embraces 950 acres, of which 3M controls 684.32 acres. It will be recalled that a permit may not issue for quarrying unless the applicant holds 200 contiguous acres and that 400 contiguous acres are required for both quarrying and rock processing. * * * In short, only 3M can quarry and the remaining acreage could so be utilized only if sold to 3M.

If the design were to compel a sale to 3M, the invalidity of the ordinance would be indisputable. But although the mentioned facts invite circumspection, yet the reasonableness of the acreage requirements were not challenged by any proof and we cannot reject the affirmative evidence that they are intended to safeguard the public. If the ordinance committed all of the district to the industrial use alone and thus prevented any utilization of the acreage not owned by 3M, a far different question would be presented. But these lands remain zoned as heretofore for residential and agricultural uses. * * *

Hillsborough manifestly found that quarry operations hold a significant potential for deleterious influence upon the enjoyment of neighboring property. This * * * is the basis of the restrictions * * * fixing certain distances between phases of the operations and homes. The difficulty is that protection is afforded only for "any dwelling *existing at the introduction of this ordinance*." The owners of the remaining acreage are entitled to like protection. * * *

* * * Rather, we have a situation in which some property owners are required * * * to absorb part of the burden of an industrial use of acknowledged capacity to harm, and this upon the irrelevant circumstance whether their properties are or are not improved at the time of the introduction of the ordinance. The imposition is unreasonable and the classification arbitrary.

* * *

The Montgomery ordinance does not permit residential or agricultural use in the limited industrial district and hence, unlike the Hillsborough ordinance, authorizes but a single use, * * * Since quarrying is not permitted in Montgomery, the integration can only be with quarrying in Hillsborough. Thus the sole use permitted is conditioned upon affiliation with a quarrying operation elsewhere. 3M alone can meet the requirement. * * *

Kozesnik complains that his property cannot be put to the single authorized use * * * It was frankly conceded before us that there is nothing he can do with his property. That a restraint against all use is confiscatory and beyond the police power and statutory authorization is too apparent to require discussion. [Citations omitted]

* * *

Ordinarily the invalidity of an ordinance as to a small parcel will not vitiate the treatment of the entire district within which it is situated. [Citations omitted] This principle is applicable where it may reasonably be assumed that the local legislative body would have intended the district to remain as legislated notwithstanding such partial invalidity. Here, however, the physical circumstances are such that we cannot say with assurance that the township would have so intended. * * * Since Kozesnik's acreage is not within an agricultural or residential district, it is not afforded that protection, and we of course cannot amend the ordinance * * *. Hence, we must conclude that the ordinance is invalid * * *.

Notes

1. **The Comprehensive Plan.** " * * * zoning may easily degenerate into a talismanic word, like the 'police power', to excuse all sorts of arbitrary infringements * * *. To assure that this does not happen, our courts must require local zoning authorities to pay more than mock obeisance to the statutory mandate * * *. * * * Exactly what consti-

tutes a 'comprehensive plan' has never been made clear. * * * No New York case has defined the term * * *. Nor have our courts equated the term with any particular document. We have found the 'comprehensive plan' by examining all relevant evidence. * * * These policies may be garnered from any available source * * *. In the case at bar, the search * * * is relatively easy. It may be found both in the village's zoning ordinance and in its zoning map." See Udell v. Haas, 21 N.Y.2d 463, 470–472, 288 N.Y.S.2d 888, 894–896, 235 N.E.2d 897, 901–902 (1968).

If zoning is not coextensive with the police power, nor confined to any particular plan document, but is rather part of a rational process of planning that may be evidenced by many things, what objective gauge other than reasonableness is there in jurisdictions like Pennsylvania, New Jersey and New York, to determine when there is conformity to a comprehensive plan? For examples of judicial disagreement on the precise nature of a comprehensive plan, see Annot., 40 A.L.R.3d 372 at 379–81 (1971).

(b) Floating Zones vs. Spot Zoning

RODGERS v. TARRYTOWN
Court of Appeals of New York, 1951.
302 N.Y. 115, 96 N.E.2d 731.

FULD, JUDGE.

[Action to challenge zoning amendment which created a new residential use classification for garden apartments, but which did not specify the physical district locations for the new use classification. The placement of the new use districts could, upon application by landowners, be fixed by later amendment to the zoning map.]

The village's zoning aim being clear, the choice of methods to accomplish it lay with the board. * * * That it called for separate legislative authorization for each project presents no obstacle or drawback * * *.

* * *

* * * It will still be for the board to decide * * * that the *grant* of such a classification accords with the comprehensive zoning plan and benefits the village as a whole. * * *

The charge of illegal "spot zoning" * * * is without substance. * * * If, therefore, an ordinance is enacted in accordance with a comprehensive zoning plan, it is not "spot zoning," even though it (1) singles out and affects but one small plot [citations omitted] or (2) creates in the center of a large zone small areas or districts devoted to a different use. * * *

* * *

* * * In sum, the 1947 amendment was merely the first step * * * and specifically provided for further action on the part of the board. That action was taken by the passage of the 1948 ordinance

which fixed the boundaries of the newly created zone and amended the zoning map accordingly. *   *   *

*   *   *

Notes

1. **Floating Zones.** In Donahue v. Zoning Board of Adjustment, 412 Pa. 332, 194 A.2d 610 (1963) the court sustained a new classification (Apartment House District) to be located by later ordinance amendment to the zoning map, upon application of land owners. Three years earlier the same court nullified a flexible, selective zoning ordinance, which left the determination of the new district location to the local zoning board. Eves v. Zoning Board of Adjustment of Lower Gwynedd Tp., 401 Pa. 211, 164 A.2d 7 (1960). Had the ordinance in Eves contained legislative guidelines on locations for floating zones, would that have sufficed to show a comprehensive plan? See 412 Pa. at 336 n. 5, 194 A.2d at 612 n. 5, and the following Cheney opinion.

Floating zones have been analogized to "special exceptions" from general zoning pursuant to legislative standards. See p. 542 et seq.; Beall v. Montgomery County Council, 240 Md. 77, 212 A.2d 751 (1965); Reno, *Non-Euclidean Zoning: The Use of the Floating Zone*, 23 Md.L.Rev. 105 (1963).

(c) Density Zoning—Planned Unit Development

CHENEY v. VILLAGE 2 AT NEW HOPE, INC.

Supreme Court of Pennsylvania, 1968.
429 Pa. 626, 241 A.2d 81.

[In sustaining the validity of a planned unit development, the court offered the following explanation.]

ROBERTS, JUSTICE. Under traditional concepts of zoning the task of determining the type, density and placement of buildings which should exist within any given zoning district devolves upon the local legislative body. *   *   *

This general approach to zoning fares reasonably well so long as development takes place on a lot-by-lot basis, and so long as no one cares that the overall appearance of the municipality resembles the design achieved by using a cookie cutter on a sheet of dough. However, with the increasing popularity of large scale residential developments, particularly in suburban areas, it has become apparent *   *   * that land can be more efficiently used, and developments more aesthetically pleasing, if zoning regulations focus on density requirements rather than on specific rules for each individual lot. Under density zoning, the legislature determines what percentage of a particular district must be devoted to open space, for example, and what percentage used for dwelling units. The task of filling in the particular district with real houses and real open spaces then falls upon the planning commission usually working in conjunction with an individual large scale developer. See Chrinko v. South Brunswick Twp., Planning Bd., 77 N.J.Super. 594, 187 A.2d 221 (1963). The ultimate goal of this so-called density or cluster concept of zoning is achieved when an entire self-contained little community is permitted to be built within a zoning district, with the rules of density controlling * * *

* * *

Notes

1. Though long familiar to planners, the PUD has come into vogue only recently. Treating the planned unit as an independent zoning entity, unconstrained by preset controls, offers a number of advantages. Public officials and developers can plan varied and creative designs for each community cluster. Clustering of compatible, mixed uses enhances intensity of use by commonly shared open space and by greater density of occupancy units. Clustering could reduce public costs of municipal improvements (shorter roads, water and sewer lines); of unit building costs, and hopefully of sales prices. Thus PUDs could encourage private development by enhancing investment return. By combining planning, subdivision and zoning review process,—the time span for official consents, financial commitments and development completion may be shortened, with attendant reduction of investment risk. See generally R.W. Burchell, *Planned Unit Development* (1973); ACIR, *Urban and Rural America: Policies for Future Growth* 111, 115–117 (1968); Comment, *Planned Unit Development*, 35 Mo.L.Rev. 27 (1970); Symposium, *Planned Unit Development*, 114 U.Pa.L.Rev. 2 (1965).

2. **Legal Status of PUD Under Existing Laws.** Although PUD developments are found in some 23 states (see R.W. Burchell, op. cit., supra) their validity has been challenged. See Orinda Homeowners Committee v. Board of Supervisors, 11 Cal.App.3d 768, 90 Cal.Rptr. 88 (1970) (upheld); Annot., 43 A.L.R.3d 888 (1972). A number of states have enacted PUD legislation. Ark.Stats. § 19–2829(b); Conn.Gen.Stat.Ann. §§ 8–2, 8–25; Ky.Rev.Stat. 100.203(1)(e); N.J.Stat.Ann. 40.55–54; N.Y.—McKinney's Town Law §§ 270 et seq.; 53 Pa.Stat. § 10704 et seq. It may be argued that the older zoning legislation authorizes PUD process, on the ground that the broadened discretion exercised by planning officials is still controlled by adequate legislative guidelines. See Chrinko v. South Brunswick Twp. Planning Bd., 77 N.J.Super. 594, 187 A.2d 221 (1963); Note, *Planned Unit Development*, 37 Mo.L.Rev. 27 (1970). Krasnowiecki, *Planned Unit Development: A Challenge to Established Theory and Practice of Land Use Control*, 114 U.Pa.L.Rev. 47, 78–85 (1965). Nevertheless, the threat of invalidation has induced proposals for a model act for planned unit development. Babcock, *An Introduction to the Model Enabling Act for Planned Residential Development*, 114 U.Pa.L.Rev. 136 (1965).

3. **Density Control and Discrimination.** Density controls (e.g. minimum lot, floor and building areas; minimum public facilities) may be engineered to exclude or segregate low income groups from housing opportunities. PUD regulation and administration may also be abused to foster class discrimination, *viz.* as a variant of high cost apartment house zoning.

4. **Aesthetic Zoning.** "We accept beauty as a proper community objective, attainable through the use of the police power. We are mindful of the reasoning of most courts that have upheld the validity of ordinances regulating outdoor advertising and of the need felt by them to find some basis in economics, health, safety, or even morality. See Thomas Cusack Co. v. City of Chicago, 242 U.S. 526, 37 S.Ct. 190, 61 L.Ed. 472 (1917). We do not feel so constrained. Hawaii's constitution provides: 'The State shall have power to conserve and develop its natural beauty, objects and places of historic or cultural interest, sightliness and physical good order, and for that purpose private property shall be subject to reasonable regulation.' (Article VIII, Section 5)" State v. Diamond Motors Inc., 50 Hawaii 33, 34, 429 P.2d 825, 827 (1967).

The goal of aesthetics presents definitional and valuation problems. See e.g. Reid v. Architectural Board of Review of City of Cleveland Heights, 119 Ohio App. 67, 192 N.E.2d 74 (1963) (denial of permit based on board disapproval of design of residential structure); Annot., 21 A.L.R.3d 1222 (1968); Masotti and Selfon, *Aesthetic Zoning and The Police Power,* 46 J.Urban L. 773 (1969); Comment, *Zoning Aesthetics and the First Amendment,* 64 Colum.L.Rev. 81 (1964).

5. **Billboard and Sign Regulation.** The police power to limit and prohibit billboards and signs for aesthetic purposes has gained acceptance. Each case must be decided on its facts, particularly with reference to the size, type and location of the sign in question. Cf. Metromedia, p. 365, supra; Klicker v. State, 293 Minn. 149, 197 N.W.2d 434 (1972); City of Escondido v. Desert Outdoor Advtg., Inc., 8 Cal.3d 785, 106 Cal.Rptr. 172, 505 P.2d 1012 (1973) and the notes following Carlin v. Palm Springs, p. 380, supra.

(d) Conditional Zoning

SCRUTTON v. SACRAMENTO

Court of Appeal, Third District, 1969.
275 Cal.App.2d 412, 79 Cal.Rptr. 872.

FRIEDMAN, ACTING PRESIDING JUSTICE.

Mrs. Bessie Scrutton, the plaintiff, brought a declaratory relief action against the County of Sacramento and appeals from a summary judgment favoring the county.

Mrs. Scrutton owns a parcel of land in suburban Sacramento County. ∗ ∗ ∗ In May 1964 Mrs. Scrutton filed an application with the County Planning Commission seeking to have the property rezoned from agricultural to multiple family residential to permit its development for residential apartment units.

The planning commission recommended that the application be approved subject to conditions. Section 23(H) of the county's basic zoning ordinance provides: "The Board of Supervisors may impose conditions to the zoning reclassification of property where it finds that said conditions must be imposed so as not to create problems inimical to the public health, safety and general welfare of the County of Sacramento."

Among the requirements proposed by the planning commission were that Mrs. Scrutton dedicate a 10–foot right of way for widening Whitney Avenue and improve it with pavement, sidewalk, curbs and gutters; that on the east edge of her property she dedicate a 27–foot strip to form the west half of Foster Way; that she join an assessment district which would improve the west half of Foster Way with paving, sidewalk, curbs and gutters.

The board of supervisors then held a hearing to consider the application. The board expressed agreement with the conditions recommended by the planning commission, except that it imposed the additional requirement that Mrs. Scrutton pave Foster Way at her own expense instead of financing the work through a neighborhood assessment district. Before adopting the rezoning ordinance sought by Mrs. Scrutton, the board of supervisors tendered a deed and contract for her signature. According to the board's usual procedures, it would not formally adopt the rezoning ordinance until the applicant returned the executed deed and contract. Under the contract proffered Mrs. Scrutton, she would commit herself to comply with all the conditions imposed by the county, and any failure on her part would cause the property's reversion to agricultural zoning.

Mrs. Scrutton had no objection to the county's requirement for dedication and improvement of the Whitney Avenue frontage. Although she had originally been willing to go along with the demand for dedicating a 27–foot strip along Foster Way, she objected to the supervisors' demand that she pave the latter at her own expense (amounting to about $13,000). She refused to sign the proposed contract, then filed this declaratory relief action to test the validity of the supervisors' demands for dedicating the Foster Way frontage and paving it at her own expense.

* * *

Although somewhat indirectly, Mrs. Scrutton's complaint charges that the Foster Way improvement project is unreasonably aimed at accommodating public needs unconnected with her own apartment development. * * *

"Conditional zoning" is an appropriate phrase to describe a zoning change which permits use of a particular property subject to conditions not generally applicable to land similarly zoned. (1 Anderson, American Law of Zoning (1968) § 8.20, pp. 610–614.) Plaintiff contends that the conditional rezoning attempted here exceeds Sacramento County's authority under state law and violates that law's uniformity demand. * * * The state statutes' silence on conditional rezoning is not a denial of power to pursue that practice. The practice must find its own justification as an appropriate exercise of the local police power.

So-called "Euclidean" zoning divides the community into homogeneous land use zones. Individual parcels may often be allowed a justified escape from this rigid grouping without detriment to zoning objectives. Rezoning an individual parcel is simply one of a variety of techniques for achieving flexibility in land use. (See 1 Anderson, *op. cit.*, § 8.17, pp. 604–608.) * * * The power to impose such conditions has been upheld in connection with the approval of subdivisions (Ayres v. City Council of City of Los Angeles, 34 Cal.2d 31, 41–42, 207 P.2d 1, 11 A.L.R.2d 503; City of Buena Park v. Boyar, 186 Cal.App.2d 61, 66–67, 8 Cal.Rptr. 674); with the grant of building permits (Southern Pac. Co. v. City of Los Angeles, 242 Cal.App.2d 38, 45–48, 51 Cal.Rptr. 197; Sommers v. City of Los Angeles, 254 Cal.App.2d 605, 610, 62 Cal.Rptr. 523), and with the grant of zoning variances (Bringle v. Board of Supervisors, 54 Cal.2d 86, 88–89, 4 Cal.Rptr. 493, 351 P.2d 765; see comment, 20 Hastings L.J. 735). The power to impose conditions on rezoning furthers the well-being of landowners generally, promotes community development and serves the general welfare. * * * Reasonably conceived conditions harmonize the landowner's need with the public's interest. In New York, the authority to reclassify subject to reasonable conditions has been upheld as a manifestation of the general authority to reclassify without conditions. (Church v. Town of Islip (1960) 8 N.Y.2d 254, 203 N.Y.S.2d 866, 168 N.E.2d 680, 683.) The same police power which supports the imposition of reasonable conditions upon other kinds of change in land use sustains the power of California counties to engage in "conditional rezoning."

* * *

* * * We conclude that section 23(H) is a valid expression of Sacramento County's zoning power.

Quite aside from the validity of section 23(H), plaintiff attacks the county's action as "contract zoning" by which the county, in exchange for the landowner's covenants, would bargain away a portion of its future power over zoning. The police power to zone and rezone may not be restricted by contract. (Acker v. Baldwin, 18 Cal.2d 341 at p. 345, 115 P.2d 455; * * * The phrase "contract zoning" has no legal significance and simply refers to a reclassification of land use in which the landowner agrees to perform conditions not imposed on other land in the same classification. No reported California decision deals with it. It has been criticized and defended, nullified in some states, sustained in others. (See, *e.g.*, Baylis v. City of Baltimore (1959) 219 Md. 164, 148 A.2d 429; Sylvania Electrical Products, Inc. v. City of Newton (1962) 344 Mass. 428, 183 N.E.2d 118; Bucholz v. City of Omaha (Neb. 1963) 174 Neb. 862, 120 N.W.2d 270; Church v. Town of Islip, *supra;* see generally, 1 Anderson, op. cit., § 8.21, pp. 616–620; 67 Dick.L.Rev. 109; 3 Gonzaga L.Rev. 197; 23 Md.L.Rev. 121; 12 Syracuse L.Rev. 230; 41 Temple L.Q. 267; 12 U.C.L.A.L.Rev. 897.)

All contracts are made with reference to possible exercises of the police power and with the possibility of its exercise as an implied term. * * * Here the county itself does not become party to an express contract. Yet, when the zoning agency exacts a concomitant contract from the landowner, it holds out an implied or moral assurance that it will not quickly reverse or alter its decision. In a sense this assurance tends to freeze the property's status. * * * "[W]e deal here with actualities, not phrases." (Church v. Town of Islip, *supra*, 203 N.Y.S.2d at p. 869, 168 N.E.2d at p. 683.) * * * The contract zoning procedure pursued here entails neither a formal nor a practical surrender of the police power.

Plaintiff has a valid objection to the reversion feature of the proposed rezoning. In effect, the proposed contract declares that the landowner's breach of covenant will be met by automatic reversion from the multiple residential to the original agricultural classification or by reversion through action of the board of supervisors. The reversion would amount to a second rezoning. Automatic reversion would violate the procedural directions of state law, which demands that rezoning be accomplished through notice, hearings and planning commission inquiry. (Gov.Code, §§ 65853–65857; Richter v. Board of Supervisors, *supra*, 259 Cal.App.2d at p. 105, 66 Cal.Rptr. 52; Hein v. City of Daly City, 165 Cal.App.2d 401, 405–406, 332 P.2d 120.)

Even if procedural directions were followed, the reversion would violate substantive limitations upon the supervisors' legislative power. * * * Although the courts do not ordinarily inquire into legislative motivation, the proceedings on their face would characterize the reversion ordinance as a forfeiture rather than a legislative decision on land use. (*Cf.* Kissinger v. City of Los Angeles, 161 Cal.App.2d 454, 460–462, 327 P.2d 10.) An ordinance so conceived is not a valid exercise of zoning power.

The county, nevertheless, has alternative remedies. Other enforcement devices are possible and judicial remedies available, based upon such theories as breach of contract, breach of restrictive covenant and breach of equitable servitude. (See 12 U.C.L.A.L.Rev., *supra*, at pp. 907–912.)

Lastly the inquiry focuses on validity of the specific demands attacked by Mrs. Scrutton's suit—that she dedicate a 27 by 650–foot strip as the western half of Foster Way and install pavement, gutter, curb and sidewalk at her own expense.

As noted earlier, the police power permits the imposition of reasonable conditions * * * Not all conditions are valid. A grant of public privilege may not be conditioned upon the deprivation of constitutional protections. * * * An arbitrarily conceived exaction will be nullified as a disguised attempt to take private property for public use without resort to eminent domain or as a mask for discriminatory taxation. * * *

Although "reasonableness" has been postulated as the hallmark of validity, a more precise standard is available. An utterance in Ayres v. City Council, *supra*, 34 Cal.2d at page 42, 207 P.2d at page 8 supplies it * * * The Ayres' formulation may be generalized by the statement that conditions imposed on the grant of land use applications are valid if reasonably conceived to fulfill public needs emanating from the landowner's proposed use.

The California decisions illustrate two kinds of need: the community's protection against potentially deleterious effects of the landowner's proposal (*e.g.,* Ayres v. City Council, *supra,* 34 Cal.2d at pp. 38–39, 207 P.2d 1) and the community's need for facilities to meet public service demands created by the proposal (*e.g.,* Bringle v. Board of Supervisors, *supra,* 54 Cal.2d at p. 89, 4 Cal.Rptr. 493, 351 P.2d 765; * * * While decisions invalidating the exaction rely upon theories of constitutional invasion, their springboard is the lack of relationship between the exaction and the proposed use * * *

The relationship between the condition exacted by the public authority and the use proposed by the landowner presents a factual inquiry for the trial court. In order to show a lack of relationship, the landowner must present evidence. (Bringle v. Board of Supervisors, *supra,* 54 Cal.2d at p. 89, 4 Cal.Rptr. 493, 351 P.2d 765.) The court can seldom if ever resolve this inquiry without taking evidence. * * *

The county's supporting affidavits, on the other hand, fell short of the target. * * * They contained no showing that Mrs. Scrutton's apartment project would generate traffic or other conditions on Foster Way which would reasonably necessitate widening and improving the street at her sole expense.

It is true that some of the courts have justified the exaction not only for its fulfillment of public needs caused by the proposed development, but also because it would benefit the landowner financially. (See discussion 52 Cornell L.Q. 871, 890–903; 20 Hastings L.J., *supra,* at pp. 740–743.) Standing alone, the landowner's economic benefit supplies inadequate underpinning for the exaction. * * * The landowner should be free to reject the paternalism which forces him into an exaction conceived for his personal benefit. * * *

The fulfillment of public needs emanating from the proposed land use is the *sine qua non* of the exaction's reasonableness.

* * *

The judgment is reversed and the cause remanded to the trial court for proceedings compatible with the views expressed in this opinion.

Note

1. **Contract Zoning.** Perhaps, the most flexible rezoning device is that whereby owners, neighbors and public officials bargain the terms and conditions of rezoning, with an agreement by the developer to subject the rezoned site to restrictions that are not required by law. See e.g. Sylvania Electric Products, Inc. v. Newton, 344 Mass. 428, 183 N.E.2d 118 (1962); cf. Bucholz v. Omaha, 174 Neb. 862, 120 N.W.2d 270 (1963); Church v. Islip, 8 N.Y.2d 254, 203 N.Y.S.2d 866, 168 N.E.2d 680 (1960). The practice has been disapproved in some jurisdictions as inconsistent with legislative control of zoning standards and comprehensive planning. See Hartnett v. Austin, 93 So.2d 86 (Fla.1956), and authorities cited in Sylvania Electric,

supra. See generally, Trager, *Contract Zoning*, 23 Md.L.Rev. 121 (1963); Strine, *The Use of Conditions in Land Use Control*, 67 Dick.L.Rev. 109 (1963); Comment, *The Use and Abuse of Contract Zoning*, 12 U.C.L.A.L.Rev. 897 (1965).

COLWELL v. HOWARD COUNTY
Court of Special Appeals of Maryland, 1976.
31 Md.App. 8, 354 A.2d 210.

LOWE, JUDGE.

On April 28, 1970 an amendment was adopted adding Sections 22A.01–22A.05 as part of Howard County's "Euclidean" Zoning Regulations. It provided that whenever the zoning map of Howard County was amended, "such amendment shall be subject to the following conditions":

.01 A Site Development Plan must be submitted to the Howard County Office of Planning and Zoning within 2 years, or the property shall revert to its prior classification.

* * *

.03 Building permits must be applied for within one year of site plan approval for a building or buildings * * * or the zoning of the property shall be void and shall revert to the prior classification.

.04 Substantial construction under the building permits must be underway within 3 years or the property shall revert to its original classification.

.05 Although the Zoning Board may grant one one-year extension if recommended by the Planning Board, if a property should revert, no further substantially similar petition may be considered for 1 year.

In short, Howard County now warns its successful zoning applicants to "use it or lose it."

FACTS

Appellant, Harry C. Colwell, owns certain lands in Howard County for which he and/or his predecessor in interest sought and obtained a zoning classification change from R–20 (residential) to R–A–1 (apartments). * * *

Two years later, * * * appellant was notified * * * that unless a Site Development Plan was filed pursuant to the aforesaid regulations, his zoning classification would revert to its former status. In response to that notice, Colwell filed a Bill of Complaint for Declaratory Judgment in the Circuit Court for Howard County, questioning the validity of the reverter provisions of the above quoted sections * * *

His primary contention * * * that the provision under which his land reverted to its previous zoning classification is nothing more than an enactment of conditional zoning which he argues is repugnant to both law and reason. He cites as authority for this proposition Hausmann & Johnson, Inc. v. Berea Bd. of Bldg. Code App., 40 Ohio App.2d 432, 320 N.E.2d 685 and Scrutton v. County of Sacramento, 275 Cal. App.2d 412, 79 Cal.Rptr. 872. * * *

With the exception of the applicability of the term "conditional," we fail to see how any of the authorities cited relate to the issue before us. All of the cases appellant cites as authority involved *contractual* agreements made between individuals and the zoning authority. * * *

The primary objection to conditional zoning then, is that it permits a use of particular property in a zoning district subject to restrictions *other than those applicable to all land similarly classified.* Mayor and City Council of Baltimore v. Crane, Md., 352 A.2d 786 (No. 131, September Term, 1975, filed 3/3/76); Anderson, *American Law of Zoning,* § 8.20. The evils inherent in conditional zoning *agreements* are clearly not inherent in a regulation that applies equally to all rezoned properties. We are not persuaded by appellant's attempt to analogize these distinct types of conditions on rezoning. The "use it or lose it" concept is an effective tool for controlling premature land development. Additionally, it serves to inhibit manipulative zoning by avaricious land speculators who are often unconcerned about the effect of development on a community. In short, it has a rational relationship to the purposes of zoning regulations and is a reasonable exercise of police powers. See Md.Code, Art. 66B, § 4.03.

Uniformity vs. Retroactivity

* * * appellant further contends that the requirement that zoning be uniform is violated since properties zoned *after* the enactment of the regulation are subject to reversion to their former classification and properties zoned *before* the enactment of the regulation are not.

Appellant's argument highlights a traditional legislative dilemma. * * * If legislation applies both past and present, it is caught in the whirlpool of retroactivity. If it avoids that whirlpool by applying the law prospectively only, the monster demanding uniformity lies in wait.

We find no fault with the legislative decision * * * to apply the regulation prospectively only. * * *

The Use It or Lose It Rationale

Notwithstanding that appellant's immediate concern rests with the reversion * * * for failure to submit a site plan within two years of the zoning change, we will also consider the validity of the additional requirements that application be made for a building permit within one year of approval of a site plan, § 22A.03, and that substantial construction must be commenced within three years of the permit's issuance. Although there are few cases dealing with the "use it or lose it" concept of zoning, its validity has been acknowledged and approved in scattered cases, usually when reversion has taken place as a result of the lapse of a specified time period following the issuance of a permit.

In Sherwood Lanes, Inc. v. City of San Angelo, 511 S.W.2d 597, the Court of Civil Appeals of Texas held that it was within the scope of legislative power of a city commission to prescribe that special permits authorized by ordinance would be inoperative if not accepted and used within one year from the enactment of the ordinance.

In Upton v. Gray, 269 Cal.App.2d 352, 74 Cal.Rptr. 783, the California Court of Appeal was asked to interpret a zoning ordinance which provided that any building permit would expire within one year of issuance unless the use for which it was granted was established within that period of time. Although they never dealt directly with the validity of such a requirement, the court recognized the rationale behind it * * *.

The Supreme Court of New Jersey in Houdaille Constr. Mats., Inc. v. Bd. of Adjustment, 92 N.J.Super. 293, 223 A.2d 210, held inter alia that the condition that a special use permit be accepted within 60 days was invalid and arbitrary, "in the absence of a general provision in the ordinance requiring all building or use permittees to signify acceptance within that time period." However, the court also held that "[t]he municipality can by a reasonable ordinance provision limit the life of a building or use permit duly granted." See also Kurowski v. Board of Adjustment of City of Bayonne, 11 N.J.Super. 433, 78 A.2d 429.

When Zoning Vests as a Right

Although no Maryland case to our knowledge has treated the question raised here directly, it is clear * * * that appellant's contention that he was denied due process is without merit. For appellant to have been denied due process, he must have had a vested right to the zoning classification which he lost by operation of law and passage of time. The Court of Appeals has held that the obtention of a building permit * * * does not create a vested right constitutionally insulated against a change in the zoning ordinance forbidding that particular use. Ross v. Montgomery County, 252 Md. 497, 504, 250 A.2d 635.

Rockville Fuel v. Gaithersburg, 266 Md. 117, 291 A.2d 672, reiterates the generally accepted rule that there is no vested right in zoning until construction is substantially begun, or as colloquially phrased, "the shovel is in the ground." * * * Surely, if a landowner's right to a particular zoning classification is not yet vested, it does no violence to his constitutional rights to require through a generally applied, properly enacted law, that a zoning change be utilized within a reasonable time period.

The Moratorium

Appellant would have us believe that his sole reason for noncompliance with the two-year limitation is that:

"A sewer moratorium has been declared which prevents the development of the property as rezoned, * * *

* * * Appellant does not attack the sewer moratorium directly. Rather, he contends that by virtue of the moratorium, the County has rendered it impossible for him to comply with the site plan requirement. Upon analysis, this argument militates more favorably for the County than for appellant.

Assuming, as we must, that the sewer moratorium was imposed for the health, safety and welfare of the people of Howard County, it follows that the reverter clause in the zoning ordinance also serves that purpose since it operates as a mechanism by which the zoning authorities can reconsider the rezoning of land after the moratorium is lifted. For example, the sewerage difficulties which led to the imposition of the moratorium may very well compel restricting the density of development in the area in which appellant's land is located. * * *

Judgment affirmed. Costs to be paid by appellant.

(e) Exclusionary Zoning

"The arsenal of tools for the process of exclusion is steadily growing. Lower percentage land occupancy—larger minimum plots—minimum house sizes—complicated building codes—limiting number of building permits issued per year—non-look-alike clauses (including a recent New Jersey ordinance against interior look-alikes)—costlier road specifications (for the sake of cost)—high permit fees—excessive development specifications—rigid enforcement of regulations in hardship cases—excessive bonding or cash deposit requirements—requirements for completion of improvements prior to granting of building permits—refusal to accept bonds instead of cash—confiscation of park lands as condition for subdivision approval—special development exactions for parks, schools, etc., for new houses only—extensive off-site improvements as condition for approval—installation of facilities far beyond the requirements of a subdivision to solve existing or anticipated municipal problems—refusal to permit construction of sewage plants where health authorities prohibit septic tanks—terroristic upzoning, subsequent to the purchase of land by a developer—open threats of reprisals if relief is sought in the courts—ex post facto regulations—and a veritable host of others. Even if relief in the courts were sought, a two or three year court fight can be afforded by few developers and nothing in recent court history would encourage them to undertake the cost. A developer is not innocent until proven guilty but is guilty unless proven innocent 'beyond debate'." Lloyd, *Public Control of Private Land Use*, 12 Local Government Law Service Letter 2–3 (A.B.A. Dec.1962).

SURRICK v. ZONING HEARING BD. OF THE TOWNSHIP OF UPPER PROVIDENCE

Supreme Court of Pennsylvania, 1977.
476 Pa. 182, 382 A.2d 105.

Nix, Justice.

* * * The dispositive issue is whether the township ordinance unconstitutionally excludes multi-family dwellings. The Commonwealth Court, in affirming the lower court's order, held that it did not. For the reasons set forth below, we disagree.

The history and facts of this case are as follows. Appellant sought to build apartments and townhouses on a 16.25 acre tract of land * * *. The tract is located in an area designated A–1 Residential under the township ordinance, which permits only single family dwellings on one-acre lots. Appellant initially had applied to the Board of Supervisors of the Township to rezone the 12.25 acre tract to B–Business, the only ordinance classification permitting multi-family housing, * * *. The requested rezoning was denied * * *. Thereafter, appellant revised his plans to include the four acres of ground owned by him. He sought building permits, which were denied by the Building Inspector. An appeal was then taken to the Board requesting a variance and including a challenge to the constitutionality of the ordinance. The Board held hearings and subsequently denied the requested variance. It was this denial which ultimately resulted in the instant appeal.

Upper Providence Township is a western suburb of Philadelphia, located about 12 miles from the center of the city. * * * The 1970 census set the township's population at slightly over 9,200; the total acreage of the township is approximately 3,800 acres. Approximately one-quarter of the township land is undeveloped. * * *

The zoning ordinance in question has classified 43 acres, or 1.14% of the total township acreage, as a B district; in this B district apartments are permitted along with other essentially commercial uses, and the record shows that the B district is already substantially developed. * * *

Article I Section 1 of the Pennsylvania Constitution protects the citizen's right to the enjoyment of private property, and governmental interference with this right is circumscribed by the due process provisions of the Fifth and Fourteenth Amendments to the United States Constitution. * * * In reviewing zoning ordinances, this Court has stated that an ordinance must bear a substantial relationship to the health, safety, morals, or general welfare of the community. * * *

Thus, without expressly labelling it as such, this Court has employed a substantive due process analysis in reviewing zoning schemes and has concluded implicitly that exclusionary or unduly restrictive zoning techniques do not have the requisite substantial relationship to the public welfare. See Concord Twp. Appeal, 439 Pa. 466, 268 A.2d 765 (1970); *Girsh Appeal, supra.*

In Twp. of Willistown v. Chesterdale Farms, Inc., 462 Pa. 445, 341 A.2d 466 (1975), this Court reaffirmed its conviction that suburban communities which find themselves in the path of urban-suburban growth cannot establish residential enclaves by excluding population growth. *Willistown* in fact was no departure from precedent but merely a culmination of prior case law which had invalidated zoning techniques which seriously impeded or effectively "zoned out" population growth. See National Land and Investment Co. v. Easttown Twp. Bd. of Adjustment, *supra* (invalidating a four acre lot minimum); *Girsh Appeal, supra* (invalidating a zoning ordinance which totally excluded apartments); *Concord Twp. Appeal, supra* (invalidating two and three acre lot minima). In *Willistown,* this Court was confronted with a zoning ordinance amendment which permitted multi-family dwellings on 80 acres out of a total of 11,589 acres in the township. In striking down this land-use scheme as "tokenism" and thus exclusionary, we extended the prohibition in *Girsh* to include not only *total* exclusion of multi-family dwellings but also *partial* exclusion, or "selective admission." Twp. of Willistown v. Chesterdale Farms, Inc., 462 Pa. 445, 448–49, 341 A.2d 466, 468 (1975). * * *

This Court's ruling in *Willistown* rested upon the premise of *Girsh* that where a municipal subdivision "is a logical place for development to take place, it should not be heard to say that it will not bear its rightful part of the burden." *Appeal of Girsh, supra,* 437 Pa. at 245, 263 A.2d at 399. It also embraces the more basic proposition that a political subdivision cannot isolate itself and ignore the housing needs of the areas surrounding it. To implement these concepts, we adopted the "fair share" principle, which requires local political units to plan for and provide land-use regulations which meet the legitimate needs of all categories of people who may desire to live within its boundaries. * * *

Some commentators have expressed concern that judicial adoption of the "fair share" test will thrust courts into the role of super boards of adjustment, thereby usurping a function that is more properly legislative or administrative in nature. Such concern shows a misconception of what we contemplate our role will be. In establishing the "fair share" standard, this Court has merely stated the general precept which zoning hearing boards and governing bodies must satisfy by the full utilization of their respective administrative and legislative expertise. We intend our scope of review to be limited to determining whether the zoning formulas fashioned by these entities reflect a balanced and weighted consideration of the many factors which bear upon local and regional housing needs and development.

* * *

The initial inquiry must focus upon whether the community in question is a logical area for development and population growth.

Girsh Appeal, supra; National Land and Investment Co. v. Easttown Twp. Bd. of Adjustment, *supra.* The community's proximity to a large metropolis and the community's and region's projected population growth figures are factors which courts have considered in answering this inquiry. * * *

Having determined that a particular community is in the path of urban-suburban growth, the present level of development within the particular community must be examined. Population density data and the percentage of total undeveloped land and the percentage available for the development of multi-family dwellings are factors highly relevant to this inquiry. * * *

Assuming that a community is situated in the path of population expansion and is not already highly developed, this Court has, in the past, determined whether the challenged zoning scheme effected an exclusionary result or, alternatively, whether there was evidence of a "primary purpose" or exclusionary intent to zone out the natural growth of population. * * * Because the *Willistown* "fair share" test compels judicial examination of the *actual effect* of a zoning ordinance * * * evidence of exclusionary motive or intent, whether direct or circumstantial, is not of critical importance. Thus, *Willistown* marked an implicit departure away from judicial inquiry into the motives underlying a particular zoning ordinance. Our primary concern now is centered upon an ordinance's exclusionary impact.

In analyzing the effect of a zoning ordinance, the extent of the exclusion, if any, must be considered. Is there *total* exclusion of multi-family dwellings, * * *, or is the exclusion *partial*? If the zoning exclusion is partial, obviously the question of the ordinance's validity is more difficult to answer. * * * Where the amount of land zoned as being available for multi-family dwellings is disproportionately small in relation to these latter factors, the ordinance will be held to be exclusionary.

It now remains to apply this analytical matrix to the facts of the instant case * * *. There can be little doubt that Upper Providence Township is a logical area for development and population growth. * * * The record shows that the township is not a high density population area; roughly one-quarter of the township land is undeveloped. Thus the township's present level of development does not preclude further development of multi-family dwellings. * * *

The zoning ordinance in question results in a partial exclusion of multi-family dwellings, providing, as it does, 1.14% of the township land for development of multi-family dwellings. It is also significant that multi-family dwellings are only one of more than a dozen other uses permitted on this fraction of land. * * * The above analysis leads inescapably to the conclusion that the facts of the instant case are legally indistinguishable from those in *Willistown.* Thus we hold that Upper Providence Township has not provided a "fair share" of its land for development of multi-family dwellings. Twp. of Willistown v. Chesterdale Farms, Inc., *supra.*

We therefore direct that zoning approval for appellant's land be granted and that a building permit be issued conditional upon appellant's compliance with the administrative requirements of the zoning ordinance and other reasonable controls and regulations which are consistent with this opinion. *Id.*

ROBERTS, JUSTICE, concurring.

I concur in the result. The Township's allocation of land clearly is not reasonable. * * * I cannot agree, however, with the majority's use of the notion of "fair share."

* * * To the contrary, the "fair share" theory has never commanded a majority of this Court. Strong reasons exist for this Court to continue its refusal to endorse "fair share."

In Willistown, the plurality looked to Southern Burlington County NAACP v. Township of Mount Laurel, 67 N.J. 151, 336 A.2d 713 (1975), appeal dismissed and cert. denied, 423 U.S. 808, 96 S.Ct. 18, 46 L.Ed.2d 28 (1975), where the Supreme Court of New Jersey relied upon "fair share" in striking down an exclusionary zoning scheme. * * *

In Oakwood at Madison, Inc. v. Township of Madison, 72 N.J. 481, 371 A.2d 1192 (1977), the New Jersey Court was called upon to explicate its decision in *Mount Laurel.* So divisive, apparently, was the attempt to translate the broad propositions of "fair share" announced in *Mount Laurel* into concrete and manageable standards, that the Court could not reach a decision until after hearing argument four times over a period of nearly four years. * * *

Mount Laurel relied in part on our own cases, * * * in striking down exclusionary zoning, but in introducing "fair share" went far beyond anything this Court had ever decided or suggested. * * *

The crucial distinction between our cases and those of New Jersey is that "fair share" transforms courts, both trial and appellate, into what Mr. Justice Pomeroy in his dissent in *Willistown* called "super boards of adjustment" and "planning commissions of last resort." * * *

Our own case law has proved adequate to the task of preventing unconstitutional exclusionary zoning schemes without involving our judiciary in the endless complications engendered by *Mount Laurel* in New Jersey. We would do well to continue to steer clear of "fair share."

Notes

1. How fully developed must a community be, before it is exempt from the obligation to zone for moderate and low income housing?

2. **The Fair Share Quagmire.** The warnings of concurring Justice Roberts in the principal case were confirmed by the second Mount Laurel

case (Southern Burlington County NAACP v. Mount Laurel Tp., 92 N.J. 158, 456 A.2d 390 (1983). The New Jersey Supreme Court, lost patience with the failure of municipalities and the state legislature to alleviate housing restrictions (which it considered rejection of its "fair share" mandate) and ruled as follows: (a) "bona-fide efforts" will not suffice, but municipalities must *in fact* provide realistic opportunities for construction of a fair share of moderate income housing; (b) that the numerical fair share of a region's lower income housing needs must include bonuses, set-asides and cooperation to obtain federal housing subsidies; (c) that municipalities must remove excessive restrictions and exactions, and use affirmative measures to zone for mobile homes and least-cost housing; (d) that three judges be selected to preside over all Mount Laurel type litigation with directions to void ordinances to effect compliance with the instant mandate; (e) that trial courts are authorized to hire masters, and experts in order to conclude all issues at trial.

The court allowed that fully developed municipalities may phase in the mandated zoning changes (to provide a "fair share" of lower cost housing) over a period of years—whatever that means. The New Jersey legislators have introduced bills to counter the court's legislation.

How then shall the courts determine the "fair share" burden of a local government? How balance the divergent interests of population seeking entry, on the one hand, and internal facilities, fiscal capacity, protection and preservation of the physical environment, on the other? Some cases suggest that such balances can only be struck rationally at a regional or statewide level.

3. **Minimum Lot, Location and Building Area Requirements.** On the issue of exclusionary impact, there is no settled rule on the outside limit for lot size restrictions. Compare Schere v. Freehold, 119 N.J.Super. 433, 292 A.2d 35 (1972); Kavanewsky v. Zoning Board of Appeals of Town of Warren, 160 Conn. 397, 279 A.2d 567 (1971) (nullifying large lot requirements), with Steel Hill Development Co. v. Sanbornton, 469 F.2d 956 (1st Cir.1972); Salamar Builders Corp. v. Tuttle, 29 N.Y.2d 221, 325 N.Y.S.2d 933, 275 N.E.2d 585 (1971) (upholding large lot requirements). See Annot., 48 A.L.R.3d 1210, at 1228–1240 (1973); 96 A.L.R.2d at 1327, 1409 (1964). On exclusionary zoning in general, see Symposium. *Exclusionary Zoning,* 22 Syracuse L.Rev. 465 (1971).

4. **The Other Side.** In Agins v. Tiburon, 447 U.S. 255, 100 S.Ct. 2138, 65 L.Ed.2d 106 (1980), the Supreme Court upheld the City's ordinance that restricted development of 5 acre plot with a magnificent view of the San Francisco Bay, to 5 single family dwellings, to protect residents from unnecessary ill effects of urbanization.

5. **Standing to Sue.** (a) *Non-residents.* Where the developer does not initiate a zoning challenge, should non-residents who seek housing be accorded standing to sue? See Note, *Extending Standing to Non-residents—A Response to the Exclusionary Effects of Zoning Fragmentation,* 24 Vand.L.Rev. 341 (1971); Annot., 48 A.L.R.3d 1210, 1215–16 (1973). The Supreme Court, in Warth v. Seldin, 422 U.S. 490, 95 S.Ct. 2197, 45 L.Ed.2d 343 (1975), held that such standing should not be granted in federal challenges to exclusionary zoning ordinances; unless a plaintiff who chal-

lenges zoning practices alleges specific, concrete facts demonstrating that such practices harm him, and that he personally would benefit from the court's intervention. Under state law challenges, however, some state courts have been more open to non-resident standing. On other aspects of developer-initiated suits vis-a-vis non-resident suits, see J. Hyson, *The Problem of Relief in Exclusionary Zoning*, 12:1 Urban Law Annual 21 (1976).

(b) *Civic Associations.* The cases are mixed on the standing of property owners and civic associations to challenge zoning changes and decisions. See Annot., 8 A.L.R.4th 1087 (1981).

6. **Remedial Activism.** Courts are aware that a bare decree invalidating an ordinance would leave municipalities free to perpetuate exclusionary practices. Is this sufficient ground for courts to order the issuance of a building permit? See Hyson, supra. The Pa. Municipal Planning Code authorizes a landowner, in lieu of challenging the validity of a statute before a zoning board, to petition the municipal governing board for a curative amendment to remove the alleged legal defect in the law, with the right of appeal to the courts. This alternative approach would permit relief, while attempting to preserve the continuity of land use laws. See Ellick v. Board of Supervisors, 17 Pa.Cmwlth. 404, 333 A.2d 239 (1975). A broadside attack on all zoning ordinances in an entire county, as being unreasonably exclusionary, is one which courts are not inclined to entertain. E.g., Commonwealth v. Bucks, 8 Pa.Cmwlth. 295, 302 A.2d 897 (1973). Such radical law revision is better left to the state legislature.

7. **Fiscal Zoning.** In Molino v. Mayor and Council of Borough of Glassboro, 116 N.J.Super. 195, 281 A.2d 401 (1971) the court nullified an ordinance that was admittedly designed to exclude children from the community because they would require more schools and higher borough taxes. See also Rutgers University v. Piluso, reported at p. 553, infra.

8. **Density Controls.** Under Surrick, the exclusionary *effect* controls the zoning issue, but the intent to achieve rational interim growth proved decisive, notwithstanding admitted exclusionary effect, in the Ramapo case, which follows. Mere exclusionary effect of a zoning ordinance without proof of discriminatory intent is insufficient to establish a constitutional violation against racial minorities. Arlington Heights v. Metropolitan Housing Development Corp., 429 U.S. 252, 97 S.Ct. 555, 50 L.Ed.2d 450 (1977).

9. **Absolute Exclusions of Particular Uses.** Mobile Homes and Trailer Parks: the courts are in conflict. Pioneer Trust & Sav. Bank v. McHenry, 41 Ill.2d 77, 241 N.E.2d 454 (1968); Cohen v. Freehold, 119 N.J. Super. 433, 292 A.2d 35 (1972). The New Jersey Supreme Court has shown little sensitivity to local impositions on mobile home residents. See e.g., Monmouth Junction Mobile Home Park, Inc. v. South Brunswick Township, 107 N.J.Super. 18, 256 A.2d 721 (1969) sustaining cumulative taxes upon mobile home spaces; Annot., 42 A.L.R.3d 598 (1972); Bartke and Gage, *Mobile Homes: Zoning and Taxation*, 55 Cornell L.Rev. 491 (1970).

A zoning ordinance that restricted use of a zoned area for mobile home parks exclusively by elderly persons (over 52 years of age) was upheld in New Jersey as not violating the substantive due process or equal protection rights of younger persons. Taxpayers Ass'n v. Weymouth, 71 N.J. 249, 364 A.2d 1016 (1976).

Public Service and Charitable Facilities—Hospitals, homes for children, schools and churches affect basic human needs, but courts strike different balances as to each service facility, depending, *inter alia,* upon the urgency of need, local development and traffic conditions. See e.g., New York Institute of Tech., Inc. v. Ruckgaber, 65 Misc.2d 241, 317 N.Y.S.2d 89 (1970) (college facilities in residential area upheld against zoning); Note, *Zoning Against The Public Welfare,* 71 Yale L.J. 720 (1962); Note, *The Immunity of Schools From Zoning,* 14 Syracuse L.Rev. 644 (1963); Note, *Churches and Zoning,* 70 Haw.L.Rev. 1428 (1957); Annot., 138 A.L.R.2d 1287 (1942). Some courts void absolute exclusion of churches from zoned residential areas as an abridgement of freedom of religion under the federal constitution. E.g., Church of Christ v. Metropolitan Bd. of Zoning, 175 Ind.App. 346, 371 N.E.2d 1331 (1978).

CHARLES v. DIAMOND

Court of Appeals of New York, 1977.
41 N.Y.2d 318, 392 N.Y.S.2d 594, 360 N.E.2d 1295.

[Landowner suit claiming that village unreasonably delayed making sewer improvements without which he could not legally construct apartment building.]

At the threshold, we note that this case does not involve the potentially troublesome issue of whether mere failure to provide municipal services can result in an inverse condemnation for which the municipality must pay compensation. Much more is involved here than merely an asserted failure to provide a service due equally to all members of the community. It is, of course, old law that a municipality is under no obligation to furnish sewers to particular property owners. * * * Although municipal sewage disposal obligations have been discussed at great length in the tort realm, and little mentioned elsewhere, it is virtually beyond question that an individual property owner has no right to insist that the municipality provide him with a system, at least where the problem is unique to his land and can be remedied at his expense. (Cf. 45 N.Y.St.Dept.Rep. 666 [Inf.Opn. of Atty. Gen.].) Article 14 of the Village Law provides for the optional construction of sewers in a village, with the cost to be borne entirely by the village, entirely by the owners of the property benefited or by the village and the property owners jointly, at the option of the village. It is also old law that once a municipality has acted to provide a sewer and its improvement causes damage, the municipality is liable to compensate for the injuries sustained. (Seifert v. City of Brooklyn, 101 N.Y. 136, 4 N.E. 321, *supra.*)

In this case, it is undisputed that the village provided a sewage disposal system and that local law requires that if a sewer is provided, it must be used. Moreover, the local law requires sewer-connected toilet facilities if the property is intended for any human use. The vice of the situation is that the municipality requires the use of public sewers if the property is to be developed for human use and yet has not provided an adequate system for meeting the requirement imposed by the ordinance. Hence, the claim is more than an undifferentiated demand for municipal service due to all citizens equally. The contention, stripped to its essence, is that the sewer ordinance is being applied unconstitutionally to petitioner's property, thereby frustrating nearly all reasonable development.

* * *

GOLDEN v. PLANNING BD. OF TOWN OF RAMAPO

Court of Appeals of New York, 1972.
30 N.Y.2d 359, 334 N.Y.S.2d 138, 285 N.E.2d 291.

SCILEPPI, J.

[In the face of a projected population boom, the town adopted a master plan and capital budget for phased growth of its municipal improvements that were to be built in a series of steps over a 12 to 18 year period. It adopted a zoning ordinance to implement the plan, under which a new use, "Residential Development Use," was created for housing developers. The new use required a special permit which could not issue until minimum municipal facilities and services were available, or unless such facilities were provided at developer's expense. No change was made in existing use and territorial districts.]

* * *

The standards for the issuance of special permits are framed in terms of the availability to the proposed subdivision plat of five essential facilities or services: specifically (1) public sanitary sewers * * *; (2) drainage facilities; (3) improved public parks or recreation facilities, including public schools; (4) State, county or town roads * * *; and, (5) firehouses. No special permit shall issue unless the proposed residential development has accumulated 15 development points, to be computed on a sliding scale of values assigned to the specified improvements under the statute. Subdivision is thus a function of immediate availability to the proposed plat of certain municipal improvements; the avowed purpose of the amendments being to phase residential development to the Town's ability to provide the above facilities or services.

Certain savings and remedial provisions are designed to relieve potentially unreasonable restrictions. Thus, the board may issue special permits vesting a present right to proceed with residential development in such year as the development meets the required point minimum, but in no event later than the final year of the 18-year capital plan. The approved special use permit is fully assignable, * * *. A prospective developer may advance the date of subdivision approval by agreeing to provide those improvements which will bring the proposed plat within the number of development points required by the amendments. And applications are authorized * * * for a reduction of the assessed valuation. Finally, upon application to the Town Board, the development point requirements may be varied should the board determine that such a variance or modification is consistent with the on-going development plan.

The undisputed effect of these integrated efforts * * * is to provide an over-all program of orderly growth and adequate facilities through a sequential development policy * * *. The owners of the subject premises argue, and the Appellate Division has sustained the proposition, that the primary purpose of the amending ordinance is to control or regulate population growth within the Town. * * * We disagree.

* * * Our concern is, * * * with the effects of the statutory scheme taken as a whole * * *.

* * *

* * * the challenged amendments are proper zoning techniques, exercised for legitimate zoning purposes. * * *

Of course, zoning historically has assumed the development of individual plats and has proven characteristically ineffective in treating with the problems attending subdivision and development of larger parcels, * * *. To this end, subdivision control (Town Law, §§ 276, 277) purports to guide community development in the directions outlined here, while at the same time encouraging the provision of adequate facilities for the housing, distribution, comfort and convenience of local residents * * *

It is argued, nevertheless, that the timing controls * * * are not legislatively authorized * * *.

It is, indeed, true that the Planning Board is not in an absolute sense statutorily authorized to deny the right to subdivide. That is not, however, what is sought * * *. Denial of subdivision plat approval, invariably amounts to a prohibition against subdivision, albeit a conditional one [citations omitted]; and to say that the Planning Board lacks the authority to deny subdivision rights is to mistake the nature of our inquiry which is essentially whether development may be conditioned pending the provision by the municipality of specified services and facilities. * * *

* * *

Recognition of communal and regional interdependence, in turn, has resulted in proposals for schemes of regional and State-wide planning, in the hope that decisions would then correspond roughly to their level of impact [citations omitted]. Yet, as salutary as such proposals may be, the power to zone under current law is vested in local municipalities, and we are constrained to resolve the issues accordingly. What does become more apparent * * * however, is that though the issues are framed in terms of the developer's due process rights, those rights cannot, realistically speaking, be viewed separately and apart from the rights of others " 'in search of a [more] comfortable place to live.' " (Concord Twp. Appeal, 439 Pa. 466, 474, n. 6, 268 A.2d 765, 768, *supra;* National Land & Inv. Co. v. Easttown Twp. Bd. of Adj., 419 Pa. 504, 527–528, 215 A.2d 597, *supra;* see, generally, Sager, Tight Little Islands: Exclusionary Zoning, Equal Protection and the Indigent, 21 Stan.L.Rev. 767; Roberts, Demise of Property Law, 57 Cornell L.Rev. 1).

There is, then, something inherently suspect in a scheme which, apart from its professed purposes, effects a restriction upon the free mobility of a people until some time in the future when projected facilities are available to meet increased demands. * * *

Of course, these problems cannot be solved by Ramapo or any single municipality, * * *.

Hence, unless we are to ignore the plain meaning of the statutory delegation, this much is clear: phased growth is well within the ambit of existing enabling legislation. * * *

The subject ordinance is said to advance legitimate zoning purposes as it assures that each new home built in the township will have at least a minimum of public services * * *. The town argues that various public facilities are presently being constructed but that for want of time and money it has been unable to provide such services and facilities at a pace commensurate with increased public need. It is urged that * * * the subject regulations go further and seek to avoid the increased responsibilities and economic burdens which time and growth must ultimately bring [citations omitted].

* * * What segregates permissible from impermissible restrictions depends in the final analysis upon the purpose of the restrictions and their impact in terms of both the community and general public interest * * *

What we will not countenance, then, under any guise, is community efforts at immunization or exclusion. But, far from being exclusionary, the present amendments merely seek * * * to provide a balanced cohesive community dedicated to the efficient utilization of land. The restrictions * * * represent a bona fide effort to maximize population density consistent with orderly growth. True, other alternatives * * * may be available, but the choice as how best to proceed * * * cannot be faulted.

Perhaps even more importantly, timed growth, unlike the minimum lot requirements recently struck down by the Pennsylvania Supreme Court as exclusionary, does not impose permanent restrictions upon land use [citations omitted]. Its obvious purpose is to prevent premature subdivision absent essential municipal facilities * * *.

We only require that communities confront the challenge of population growth with open doors. Where in grappling with that problem, the community undertakes * * * to provide required municipal services in a rational manner, courts are rightfully reluctant to strike down such schemes. * * *

* * *

We are reminded, however, that these restrictions threaten to burden individual parcels for as long as a full generation and that such a restriction cannot, in any context, be viewed as a temporary expedient. * * *

Every restriction on the use of property entails hardships for some individual owners. * * * The fact that the ordinance limits the use of, and may depreciate the value of the property will not render it unconstitutional, however, unless it can be shown that the measure is either unreasonable in terms of necessity or the diminution in value is such as to be tantamount to a confiscation (see, *e.g.*, Vernon Park Realty v. City of Mount Vernon, 307 N.Y. 493, 499, 121 N.E.2d 517, 520). * * *

Without a doubt restrictions upon the property in the present case are substantial in nature and duration. They are not, however, absolute. The amendments contemplate a definite term, * * *. * * *, in the absence of proof to the contrary, we must assume the Town will put its best effort forward in implementing the physical and fiscal timetable outlined under the plan. Should subsequent events prove this assumption unwarranted, or should the Town * * * fail in its primary obligation to these landowners, there will be ample opportunity to undo the restrictions upon default. * * *

Thus, unlike the situation presented in Arverne Bay Constr. Co. v. Thatcher, 278 N.Y. 222, 15 N.E.2d 587, *supra*, the present amendments propose restrictions of a certain duration and founded upon estimate determined by fact. * * * The proposed restraints, * * * are within the limits of necessity.

In sum, where it is clear that the existing physical and financial resources of the community are inadequate to furnish the essential services and facilities which a substantial increase in population requires, there is a rational basis for "phased growth" and hence, the challenged ordinance is not violative of the Federal and State Constitutions. Accordingly, the order appealed from should be reversed and the actions remitted to Special Term for entry of a judgment declaring section 46–13.1 of the Town Ordinance constitutional.

BREITEL, JUDGE (dissenting). The limited powers of district zoning and subdivision regulation delegated to a municipality do not include the power to impose a moratorium on land development. * * *

But there is more involved in these cases than the arrogation of undelegated powers. Raised are vital constitutional issues, and, most important, policy issues trenching on grave domestic problems of our time, without the benefit of a legislative determination which would reflect the interests of the entire State. The policy issues relate to needed housing, * * * and the exclusion in effect or by motive of walled-in urban populations of the middle class and the poor. The issues are raised by a town ordinance, which, as one of the Appellate Division Justices noted below, reflect a parochial stance without regard to its impact on the region or the State, especially if it become a valid model for many other towns similarly situated.

* * *

Decisive of the present appeals, however, is the absence in the town of legislative authorization to postpone growth, let alone to establish unilaterally phased population levels, through the expedient of barring residential development for scheduled periods of up to 18 years. * * *

* * *

Finally, there is the technique sought to be exercised by Ramapo—a technique partaking somewhat of the motivation for and methods used in holding zones.

Holding zones, that is, areas reserved for future development, if legislatively authorized and carefully circumscribed, can validly and effectively implement land planning. Both the interests of localities areas can be reconciled. Indeed, it has been suggested by the National Commission on Urban Problems that enabling legislation grant communities such power. The devising and authorization of new powers, one of which is to create holding or delayed development zones, is a chief concern of the State Office of Planning Coordination. * * * Notably, in delayed development schemes limitations are invariably suggested, limitations absent in the Ramapo ordinance (e.g., 3– to 5–year limits, regional and State agency review, provision for compensation). Such limitations may be essential if the delegation is to be valid constitutionally. * * *

Either by legislation limited by decisional rule, or by decisional rule alone a limited amount of restraint in time has been held valid in controlling development, even without compensation. Thus, in the State of Washington it was suggested that the legislatively authorized right to impress "holding zones" on private property beyond the immediate reaches of present development, must be reasonably limited in its duration (State ex rel. Randall v. Snohomish County, 79 Wash.2d 619, 488 P.2d 511; see, also, Westwood Forest Estates v. Village of South Nyack, 23 N.Y.2d 424, 428–429, 297 N.Y.S.2d 129, 132–133, 244 N.E.2d 700, 702–703). Significantly, the time limitations should be brief, or reasonably fixed, and justified by emergency or statutory authorization.

* * * The crux of the matter in these cases is that before wrestling with the constitutional issues the Ramapo ordinance is destroyed at the threshold. It lacks statutory authorization, and this despite the fact that its reach is more ambitious than any before essayed even with enabling legislation.

* * *

The exclusionary effect of local efforts to preserve the country's Edens has been largely noted. * * * To leave vital decisions controlling the mix and timing of development to the unfettered discretion of the local community invites disaster.

* * *

Accordingly, I dissent and vote to affirm the orders in both cases.

Notes

1. The timed development technique is being adopted elsewhere. In California such a plan was upheld against constitutional challenges that it (a) infringed property rights, (b) unreasonably burdened interstate commerce, and (c) infringed the right to travel. See Construction Industry Ass'n v. Petaluma, 552 F.2d 897 (9th Cir.1975), cert. denied 424 U.S. 934, 96 S.Ct. 1148, 47 L.Ed.2d 342 (1976). See also Associated Home Builders v. Livermore, reported in Note, p. 563, n. 1 infra.

(f) Group Occupancy Restrictions

The extent to which municipalities can exclude particular individuals from common occupancy of dwellings as a family home, in areas zoned for residential use, remains the subject of continuing case conflict and development. At the level of federal constitutional law, the Supreme Court has sustained an ordinance in a small community that prohibited occupancy by more than two unrelated persons (Village of Belle Terre v. Boraas, 416 U.S. 1, 94 S.Ct. 1536, 39 L.Ed.2d 797 (1974)), but it also held that a city could not constitutionally limit the concept of "family" for zoning purposes to a nuclear family, as to forbid occupancy in a family residential zone by first cousins living with their grandmother. Moore v. East Cleveland, 431 U.S. 494, 97 S.Ct. 1932, 52 L.Ed.2d 531 (1977). More recently, the Supreme Court refused to extend the concept of "family" constitutionally to the mentally retarded, (by treating them as a suspect class.) Nevertheless, it found that even under the minimal test (rational basis) of equal protection, municipal exclusion of a group home for the mentally retarded was unconstitutional as applied because the municipality permitted group homes for the aged, and the Court found no rational distinction between the aged and the retarded. City of Cleburne v. Cleburne Living Center, ___ U.S. ___, 105 S.Ct. 3249, 87 L.Ed.2d 313 (1985).

Lower courts are in conflict on the application of the above constitutional standards to zoning laws. In many instances, case divisions are explained on independent state law grounds, i.e. state constitutions and laws that are not comparable to those of sister states. Variations also arise from the different nature of groups that seek to live in a family residential setting, viz., religious communities, the aged, physically or mentally handicapped groups, and rehabilitative residential centers for delinquents, parolees, addicts, alcoholics or others.

Several recent cases have affirmed the power of municipalities to exclude group homes from residential districts. Penobscot Area Housing Development Corp. v. Brewer, 434 A.2d 14 (Me.1981); Civitans Care, Inc. v. Board of Adjustment, 437 S.2d 540 (Ala.App.1983); In re McGinnis, 68 Pa.Cmwlth. 57, 448 A.2d 108 (1982). A strong contrary trend, however, has been developing to permit group occupancies by persons not related by blood, marriage or adoption, on the ground that: their exclusion would violate constitutional rights (e.g., Charter Township of Delta v. Dinolfo, 419 Mich. 253 (1984) (rights of religious community under state constitution); accord: Holy Name Hospital v. Montroy, 153 N.J.Super. 181, 379 A.2d 299 (1977)); or that the term, "family", as used in the zoning law included persons not related by blood or marriage, who share other characteristics of a permanent household, rather than an institutional arrangement. See, e.g., City of Santa Barbara v. Adamson, 164 Cal.Rptr. 539, 610 P.2d 436 (1980); *semble:* Costley v. Caromin House, Inc., 313 N.W.2d 21 (Minn.1981) (six retarded adults living with a house parent); accord: City of West Monroe v. Ouachita Association for Retarded Children, Inc., 402 So.2d 259 (La. App.1981) (group home for retarded adults supervised by married couple); Linn County v. Hiawatha, 311 N.W.2d 95 (Iowa 1981) (mentally disabled children). With respect to unrelated occupants, see Annot., Limit on Number of Persons in Residence, 12 A.L.R.4th 238 (1982).

Local zoning restrictions on group occupancy have also been voided where inconsistent, preemptive state laws authorize group residential placement for certain groups. See, e.g., Region 10 Client Management, Inc. v. Hampstead, 120 N.H. 885, 424 A.2d 207 (1980) (state law authorizing community placement of retarded citizens); Incorporated of Freeport v. Association for Help of Retarded Children, 94 Misc.2d 1048, 406 N.Y.S.2d 221 (1977); White Plains v. Ferraioli, 34 N.Y.2d 300, 357 N.Y.S.2d 449, 313 N.E.2d 756 (1974) (children in foster homes). See also Oliver v. Zoning Commission, 31 Conn.Sup. 197, 326 A.2d 841 (1974). With respect to the mentally ill, see Annot., Halfway Houses, 100 A.L.R.3d 876 (1981).

(2) Exceptional Standards

(a) Nonconforming Uses

JONES v. LOS ANGELES

Supreme Court of California, 1930.
211 Cal. 304, 295 P. 14.

LANGDON, J.

We have thus arrived at this conclusion: The ordinance in question, in so far as it prohibits the establishment of hospitals for the treatment of nervous diseases in certain districts in the city of Los Angeles, and permits their establishment in other specified districts, is valid. * * * This much is clear, we feel, with respect to the *establishment of new businesses* of this character in the prohibited districts. But does the same result necessarily follow with regard to existing businesses in these districts? * * *

We have already emphasized the fact that courts, in their consideration of zoning legislation, have not deemed themselves bound by their prior decisions on the legislative regulation or prohibition of nuisances.

General Rule on Zoning (margin note)

* * * They decide nothing more than this: The right to engage in a lawful and not dangerous business in a certain area may be taken away in pursuance of a reasonable zoning scheme. They do not decide that an established and not dangerous business, operating in a lawful manner in a certain territory, may be eradicated in pursuance of a reasonable zoning scheme. That problem, * * * has, * * * only been squarely presented to appellate courts in a few instances. The reason for the paucity of decisions is illuminating: Zoning laws have almost invariably been prospective in nature. Indeed, in some states, including Kansas, Ohio, Wisconsin, Illinois, Massachusetts, Maine, and New Hampshire, the enabling statutes * * * expressly provide that no retroactive ordinances shall be passed. See Baker, Legal Aspects of Zoning, p. 158, note 220.

As a matter of practice, also, those who have drafted ordinances * * * have permitted existing, nonconforming uses to remain. They are very generally agreed that the destruction of an existing nonconforming use would be a dangerous innovation of doubtful constitutionality, and that a retroactive provision might jeopardize the entire ordinance. * * *

* * *

* * * We are asked to uphold a municipal ordinance which destroys valuable businesses, built up over a period of years. If we do so on the ground that this is a proper exercise of the police power in the enactment of zoning legislation, then it follows that the same thing may be done to apartment houses, flats, or stores. The establishment of many lawful and not dangerous businesses in a city would then become an extremely hazardous undertaking. At any time, in pursuance of a reasonable plan for its future development, the city could prohibit the continuance of the businesses, and make property valueless which was previously constructed and devoted to a useful purpose. * * * Only a paramount and compelling public necessity could sanction so extraordinary an interference with useful business.

Policy Reason Against Allowing Ordinance Which Destroys Right To Operate Certain Business (margin note)

* * *

We repeat, therefore, that the ordinance involved herein is to be supported upon principles of zoning and not as a prohibition directed against actual nuisances. * * * And here the distinction between the power to prohibit nuisances and the power to zone is exceedingly important. The power over nuisances is more circumscribed in its objects; but once an undoubted menace to public health, safety, or morals is shown, the method of protection may be drastic. * * *

Scope of Power in Nuisance Cases (margin note)

* * * Granting that a zoning ordinance may operate retroactively where there is clearly an element of nuisance, it does not follow that a similar disposition may be made of every type of non-conforming use dealt with in zoning. 39 Yale L.J. 738. * * *

* * *

We do not mean to hold that those engaged in the zoning of cities must always be faced with the impossibility of eradicating the nonconforming uses. In some jurisdictions this problem has been dealt with by provisions against alteration or enlargement of existing structures, or rebuilding after their destruction. See State v. Hillman, 110 Conn. 92, 147 A. 294; Appeal of Ward, 289 Pa. 458, 137 A. 630; City of Earle v. Shackleford, 177 Ark. 291, 6 S.W.(2d) 294. But ordinarily the added benefit to the majority of the residents of the restricted district should not be received at the expense of others. If the city desires to abolish the nonconforming use, this may be a legitimate object of the police power, but the means of its exercise must not include the destruction of the property interest without compensation. * * *

* * *

It follows that the present ordinance is * * * invalid in its ⟩ *Holding* application to these plaintiffs.

The judgment is therefore reversed.

Notes

1. **Problems of Definition and Application.** Nonconforming exceptions protect uses and not expectations, but the authorities are not uniformly clear as to the nature and extent of protected uses. In Conway v. Greenville, 254 S.C. 96, 173 S.E.2d 648 (1970) a nonconforming use of *part* of a ten-acre tract for a construction business * * * was held to entitle the owner to use the entire tract for similar use in later years. "The question of whether a partial use of a tract for a business purpose preempts the entire tract for such purpose must necessarily be determined from the facts of each case. The fact that the non-conforming use did not embrace the entire tract is not conclusive of the issue. It is generally stated that 'the criterion is whether the nature of the incipient non-conforming use, in the light of the character and adaptability to such use of the entire parcel, manifestly implies an appropriation of the entirety to such use prior to the adoption of the restrictive ordinance.' Annot: 87 A.L.R.2d 22. Rathkoff, The Law of Zoning and Planning, Section 2, p. 60–3; * * *" But see Martin v. Cestone, 33 N.J.Super. 267, 110 A.2d 54 (1954) (owner of four adjoining lots could not extend his pre-zoning non-conforming use from one of the lots to the other three). Consider the following comment from Town of Bridgewater v. Chuckran, 351 Mass. 20, 217 N.E.2d 726, 727–8 (1966):

"Recent cases have emphasized three tests for determining whether current use of property fits within the exemption granted to nonconforming uses. (1) Whether the use reflects the 'nature and purpose' of the use prevailing when the zoning by-law took effect. [Citations omitted] (2) Whether there is a difference in the quality or character, as well as the degree, of use. [Citations omitted] (3) Whether the current use is 'different in kind in its effect on the neighborhood.' City of Medford v. Marinucci Bros. & Co., Inc., 344 Mass. 50, 60, 181 N.E.2d 584, 590, and cases cited. We think that Chuckran's current use of his land with respect to his concrete mixing business is barred when tested by these standards.

"The original nature and purpose of the use which was exempted * * * was * * * as a house builder's main yard in which the mixing of concrete was merely incidental to the general business. In so far as the land is now used as a ready mixed concrete manufactory and center for supply to others, the original nature and purpose of the enterprise has changed. See Town of Lexington v. Bean, 272 Mass. 547, 553, 172 N.E. 867.''

A more liberal scope of non-conforming use is permitted by Pennsylvania's explicit doctrine of "natural expansion."

Pennsylvania courts have adopted the following rationale:

" 'We have consistently held that a lawful nonconforming use * * * may validly be expanded by a reasonable accessory use which is not detrimental to the public health, welfare and safety. [Citing authorities]. Pennsylvania's ruling in this respect is premised upon the view that the owner of property to which a lawful nonconforming use has attached enjoys a vested property right thereto which may not be abrogated, unless it is a nuisance, or abandoned, or is extinguished by eminent domain [Citing authorities], and that a zoning ordinance cannot preclude a natural and reasonable expansion thereof.' " Silver v. Zoning Board of Adjustment, 435 Pa. 99, 255 A.2d 506 (1969).

2. **Right to Repair or Rebuild.** The degree and character of repairs that are permissible involves both *ad hoc* judgments, and a determination of legislative intent. Compare e.g. Selligman v. Von Allman Bros., Inc., 297 Ky. 121, 179 S.W.2d 207 (1944) (replacement of frame walls with brick walls held impermissible) with Granger v. Board of Adjustment, 241 Iowa 1356, 44 N.W.2d 399 (1950) (major repairs to nonconforming building held not to destroy nonconforming use, on finding that zoning legislation was not intended to force a gradual extinction of nonconforming uses through wear and tear). When a nonconforming structure is destroyed by casualty, the right to continue or reconstruct a nonconforming facility depends upon specific provisions of zoning laws and the degree of destruction. See generally Annot. 57 A.L.R.3d 419 (1974).

3. **Abandonment of Nonconforming Uses.** A temporary nonuser for nonconforming purposes does not automatically terminate the nonconforming use, unless the use is changed. There must be intent to abandon, either actual or constructive. City of Bowling Green v. Miller, 335 S.W.2d 893 (Ky.1960); State v. Accera, 36 N.J.Super. 420, 116 A.2d 203 (1955). Should zoning ordinances specify a period of nonuser that will constitute abandonment? See Franmor Realty Corp. v. LeBoeuf, 201 Misc. 220, 104 N.Y.S.2d 247 (1951). The various factors affecting discontinuance issues are reviewed in Annot., 57 A.L.R.3d 279 (1974).

4. **Retroactive Application of Zoning Changes to Building Permits or Pending Permit Applications.** To be distinguished from nonconforming exemptions on existing uses, are situations where builders claim exemption on the basis of building permits or applications that were issued or filed under prior permissive zoning law.

Where the zoning law addresses these questions by a "savings clause" to preserve the position of extant permits or applications at the time of the new enactment, these questions are resolved, or narrowed by legislative specification of the circumstances under which exemptions will be granted. Since there is wide variation in savings clause criteria in judicial application of estoppel and vested rights theory (in the absence of "savings clauses") counsel must carefully consult the specific statutory and case law in each locality.

The rule that a given use will not qualify for constitutional protection as a "nonconforming use", unless it precedes the zoning law which prohibits it, is subject to certain exceptions based upon vested rights theory or equitable estoppel doctrine. Under either ground, the majority of jurisdictions grant exception only where there was a "substantial" commitment or reliance upon the prior zoning law. What constitutes sufficiently substantial reliance or financial commitment under prior zoning law—is the subject of some conflict of authority. See the authorities collected in 1 Anderson, *American Law of Zoning* §§ 6.19 to 6.27; Annots., Zoning Ordinance, Retroactive Effect on Issued Building Permit, 49 A.L.R.3d 13 (1973, Supp.1985); Retroactive Effect of Zoning Regulations * * * on Pending Application for Building Permit, 50 A.L.R.3d 596 (1973, Supp. 1985); Zoning—Building Under Construction, 89 A.L.R.3d 1051 (1979, Supp.1985).

While some states take a different view, the following rules appear to predominate in a majority of jurisdictions. The mere filing of a building permit prior to the passage of a downzoning ordinance does not, alone, create a vested right or nonconforming use, so that the permit may be denied or revoked under the law following the permit application filing. Anderson, supra, § 6.23. Where, however, the permit is validly issued and outstanding, and the permit recipient, in good faith, takes substantial steps (by way of financial commitment or actual construction) in reliance thereon, courts have exempted the permit recipient from the new law. Anderson, supra, § 6.25. The mere purchase of land, or filing of a plat approval is not deemed by most states to be sufficiently substantial to give rise to exemption from new zoning laws (Anderson, supra, §§ 6.20, 6.21) unless the new zoning ordinance expressly preserves the rights of holders of validly issued and outstanding building permits regardless of the degree of commitments undertaken in reliance thereon. Anderson, supra, § 6.27. In applying the foregoing rules, whether under a theory of constitutionally protected vested rights or of reasonable detrimental reliance in equity; or as an exception intended by the new ordinance, outcomes may turn on particular circumstances regarding the permit holder's reason to know about pending zoning law changes (good faith issue) and on the degree of progress toward construction. Legal counsel must, therefore, consult each states' case treatment of those factors.

Permit rights aside, local entities may be liable in damages for negligent issuance of unauthorized, and later revoked, permits for obligations incurred in reliance on the permit. In a few seminal cases, the courts of Washington recognized such a cause of action, over the objections of local government immunity and of the claimant's lack of entitlement to the permit in the first instance. J & B Development Co. Inc. v. King County, 100 Wash.2d 299, 669 P.2d 468 (1983). Other jurisdictions may reject the view of the Washington court that the county officials owed a "special" duty to permit applicants, and that their duty was ministerial and not discretionary, hence not covered by local government tort immunity.

LACHAPELLE v. GOFFSTOWN

Supreme Court of New Hampshire, 1967.
107 N.H. 485, 225 A.2d 624.

KENISON, CHIEF JUSTICE.

[Appeal from decision upholding ordinance which provided that nonconforming use of residential property may not continue for more than one year, unless the property be completely screened from public view.]

*   *   *

There is a conflict in the decisions on the power of a municipality to terminate a nonconforming use after a definite period of time stated in the zoning ordinance. Annot. 42 A.L.R.2d 1146; see the divided opinion in Harbison v. City of Buffalo, 4 N.Y.2d 553, 176 N.Y.S.2d 598, 152 N.E.2d 42; Note, The Abatement of Pre-Existing Nonconforming Uses Under Zoning Laws: Amortization, 57 Nw.U.L.Rev. 323 (1962); Note, Termination of Nonconforming Uses—Harbison to the Present, 14 Syracuse L.Rev. 62 (1962). Nevertheless "the greater weight of authority, both early and late, sustains the right to bring the nonconforming use to its predestined terminal point, provided, of course, the termination provisions are reasonable as to time and directed toward some reasonable aspect of land use regulation under properly delegated police power." 2 Yokley, Zoning Law and Practice, s. 16–14, p. 282 (3d ed. 1965). Hillman, Local Government in 1964 Annual Survey of American Law 627, 636. The trend of decisions is clearly in favor of approving the amortization theory as a tool necessary for orderly community development. *   *   *

Decisions approving the termination of nonconforming uses after a definite period of time are substantial. Grant v. Mayor and City Council of Baltimore, 212 Md. 301, 129 A.2d 363; City of Los Angeles v. Gage, 127 Cal.App.2d 442, 274 P.2d 34; Standard Oil Co. v. City of Tallahassee, 183 F.2d 410 (5th Cir.1950); State ex rel. Dema Realty Co. v. McDonald, 168 La. 172, 121 So. 613; State ex rel. Dema Realty Co. v. Jacoby, 168 La. 752, 123 So. 314; Wolf v. City of Omaha, 177 Neb. 545, 129 N.W.2d 501. In City of Seattle v. Martin, 54 Wash.2d 541, 342 P.2d 602, a one-year period for the termination of a use of an open lot was approved. In Spurgeon v. Board of Comm'rs of Shawnee County, 181 Kan. 1008, 317 P.2d 798, a two-year period for the removal of auto-wrecking yards and junk yards was upheld. The recent case of Eutaw Enterprises, Inc. v. City of Baltimore, 241 Md. 686, 217 A.2d 348 (1966) involved an 18-month termination provision in a zoning ordinance applicable to a check-cashing agency in a residential district as a nonconforming use. The provision was held to be valid and reasonable as applied to the plaintiff in view of the additional factor that the plaintiff continued his check-cashing activities during the litigation period of some five years. See also, Rhyne, Municipal Law, pp. 922–923 (1957); 2 Metzenbaum, Zoning 1256 (1966 supp.); 1 Antieau, Municipal

Corporations, s. 724 (1966); 6 Powell, Real Property, s. 869, pp. 120–121 (1965); Bair and Bartley, A Model Zoning Ordinance 35 (3d ed. 1966).
* * *

The plaintiff relies on City of Akron v. Chapman, 160 Ohio St. 382, 116 N.E.2d 697, 42 A.L.R.2d 1140 and Hoffmann v. Kinealy, (Mo.) 389 S.W.2d 745, which held that the abatement of nonconforming uses by a time limitation was unconstitutional. Both of these cases have not escaped criticism. 67 Harv.L.Rev. 1283 (1954); 11 Villanova L.Rev. 189 (1965); 44 Tex.L.Rev. 368 (1965); 45 Neb.L.Rev. 636 (1966). * * *

* * *

In the present case the record supports the findings, rulings, and decree of the court below, holding that the exception sought by the plaintiff under the zoning ordinance was properly denied. The ordinance in effect adopted the provisions of RSA 267:1 and 267:2 as applied to nonconforming uses, and we conclude that as applied to the plaintiff and his use of the property, it is valid and constitutional.

Appeal dismissed.

Notes

1. **Amortizing Nonconforming Uses.** " 'Stated in its simplest terms, amortization contemplates the compulsory termination of a nonconformity at the expiration of a specified period of time, which period is equaled *(sic)* to the useful economic life of the nonconformity.' * * * 'The basic idea is to determine the remaining normal useful life of a pre-existing nonconforming use. * * *" Note, 44 Cornell L.Q. 450, 453 (1959).*

"Several cases in other jurisdictions have approved the termination of pre-existing nonconforming uses by the amortization technique. However, there are a number of decisions to the opposite effect, and it may be fairly said that there is a 'decided lack of accord' in this area." See Hoffmann v. Kinealy, 389 S.W.2d 745, 750–51 (Mo.1965). See also Fell, *Amortization of Nonconforming Uses,* 24 Md.L.Rev. 323 (1964); Comment, *The Abatement of Pre-existing Nonconforming Uses Under Zoning Laws: Amortization,* 57 N.W.U.L.Rev. 323 (1962); Annot., 22 A.L.R.3d 1134 (1968). Different standards of useful life will apply to different structures and activities. See e.g. Shifflett v. Baltimore County, 247 Md. 151, 230 A.2d 310 (1967).

Whether particular means of setting an amortization period are reasonable, depends on the nature of the involved property.

"Plaintiff's witness testified that because of exposure of the signs to the elements, plaintiff is constantly repairing them * * * 'because all we can do is maintain it.' However, these repairs actually add to the useful life of the signs, and plaintiff claims that the signs have a book value which * * * cannot in most instances be further depreciated.' * * *

* Reprinted by permission of Cornell Law Quarterly/Cornell Law Review copyright ©1959 by Cornell University.

"It is apparent that plaintiff has totally failed to show arbitrariness and unreasonableness with respect to the 31 signs which its evidence indicated had already been fully amortized. Although essential maintenance repairs may be said to prolong to a degree the useful life of any structure, and are permitted to those that are nonconforming (Ricciardi v. County of Los Angeles (1953) 115 Cal.App.2d 569, 576[5], 252 P.2d 773), the repairs cannot be relied upon to defeat zoning legislation which looks to the future and the eventual liquidation of nonconforming uses. (Livingston Rock etc. Co. v. County of Los Angeles, *supra*, 43 Cal.2d 121, 127[4], 272 P.2d 4.) It may also be noted that there is no showing that if * * * these signs have been repaired * * * they cannot be used elsewhere. * * *

"With respect to the other 11 signs, not yet fully amortized, removal should await expiration of a reasonable amortization period in order to permit plaintiff to recover their original cost." National Advertising Co. v. Monterey, 1 Cal.3d 875, 464 P.2d 33 (1970).

The New York Court of Appeals recently upheld an ordinance requiring removal of all nonconforming billboards three years after its adoption, with leave to owners to apply for an additional three-year extension. Suffolk Outdoor Advertising Co. v. Hulse, 43 N.Y.2d 483, 402 N.Y.S.2d 368, 373 N.E.2d 263 (1977).

2. **Abatement of Nonconforming Uses.** "Certainly the spirit of zoning ordinances always has been and still is to diminish and decrease nonconforming uses * * * and to that end municipalities have employed various approved regulatory methods such as prohibiting the resumption of a nonconforming use after its abandonment or discontinuance, prohibiting the rebuilding or alteration of nonconforming structures or structures occupied for nonconforming uses, and prohibiting or rigidly restricting a change from one nonconforming use to another * * *." Hoffmann v. Kinealy, 389 S.W.2d 745, 748, 750 (Mo.1965). See LaChappelle, p. 540, infra.

3. **Earth Resource Industries.** How should courts determine the scope of a nonconforming use, and the permissible period for its amortization, for mining properties that involve large, but indeterminate underground resources? How should courts relate the scope of nonconforming use to pollution effects, or to an energy crisis? In determining reasonable period for investment return, are these public interest factors relevant? Should restriction against new surface building prevent exploitation of natural resource since surface outlets are indispensable to resource recovery? Do these unique aspects of mining argue for a liberal construction of "natural expansion?" Compare New Hope Limestone Co. v. Solebury Township Board of Adjustment, 10 Bucks Co.L.Rep. 279 (Pa.1960) with Struyk v. S. Braen's Sons, 9 N.J. 294, 88 A.2d 201 (1952); Town of Billerica v. Quinn, 320 Mass. 687, 71 N.E.2d 235 (1947).

(b) Special Exceptions

Certain land uses cannot be reasonably controlled on the inflexible basis of legislated zoning districts. Zoning ordinances usually authorize special uses, (also referred to as "special exceptions," "conditional uses" or "accessory uses"), under special procedures.

"Where the governing body in the zoning ordinance, has stated special exceptions to be granted or denied by the board pursuant to express standards and criteria, the board shall hear and decide requests for such special exceptions in accordance with such standards and criteria. In granting a special exception, the board may attach such reasonable conditions and safeguards, in addition to those expressed in the ordinance, as it may deem necessary to implement the purposes of this act and the zoning ordinance." Pennsylvania Statutes Annotated, title 53, § 10913.

"We have sanctioned application of the 'special' or 'conditional' use zone technique for those 'infrequent uses which are beneficial, but potentially inconsistent with normal uses in the various zones * * *' * * * But our approval of this technique does not mean that a determination to permit or deny a special or conditional use is beyond judicial review. * * * We have adopted the specific standard that 'the denial of a special use permit must bear a real and substantial relation to the public health, safety, morals or general welfare.' * * * Because a special or conditional use zoning ordinance does not allocate any particular zones for the establishment of these unique uses as a matter of right, the local zoning authorities are vested with broad powers in determining the suitability of a given site for a proposed * * * use." Pioneer Trust and Savings Bank v. McHenry, 41 Ill.2d 77, 83, 241 N.E.2d 454, 459 (1968).

Problems in the administration and review of special exceptions were outlined by Professor Mandelker: "Confusion about the role of exceptions and variances is endemic to zoning, reflecting the confusion over underlying purposes, and shows little sign of being resolved. The variance is an administratively authorized departure from the terms of the zoning ordinance, granted in cases of unique and individual hardship, in which a strict application of the terms of the ordinance would be unconstitutional. * * * By way of contrast, an exception is a use permitted by the ordinance in a district in which it is not necessarily incompatible, but where it might cause harm if not watched. Exceptions are authorized under conditions which will insure their compatibility with surrounding uses. Typically a use which is the subject of a special exception demands a large amount of land, may be public or semi-public in character and might often be obnoxious or offensive. * * * Hospitals * * * are one example * * *. A filling station in a light commercial district is another * * *. What distinguishes the exception from the variance is the absence of a hardship requirement. * * * Sometimes the exception is treated as more and sometimes as less lenient in character than the variance. * * * Nevertheless, the fundamental purpose of the exception is to serve in an ancillary role as an allocator of land use. * * * Most of the cases have held the use exception constitutional." Mandelker, *Delegation of Power and Function in Zoning Administration,* 1963 Wash.U.L.Q. 60, 60–73.*

Indiscriminate or inconsistent grants of special exceptions and variances is attacked, as undermining comprehensive planning and creating evils akin to widespread nonconforming uses. See e.g. Dukeminier & Stapleton, *The Zoning Board of Adjustment: A Case Study in Misrule,* 50 Ky.L.J. 273 (1962). On the other hand, mechanical application of euclidean zoning standards has proven too inflexible. As Professor Mandelker points out, courts have not solved these problems, especially with regard to the standards to confine administrative discretion. See generally, Comment, *Judicial Control Over Zoning Boards of Appeal: Suggestions For Reform,* 12 U.C.L.A.L.Rev. 937 (1965); Gaylord, *Zoning: Variances, Exceptions And Conditional Use Permits In California,* 5 U.C.L.A.L.Rev. 179 (1958).

ARCHDIOCESE OF PORTLAND v. WASHINGTON

Supreme Court of Oregon, 1969.
254 Or. 77, 458 P.2d 682.

O'CONNELL, J.

[Held that county board of commissioners did not act arbitrarily in denying conditional use permit for construction of church, school and gymnasium in area zoned residential, on ground that the proposed use would create access and traffic problems.]

* * *

The tract upon which plaintiff sought a conditional use permit to build its proposed church and school structures contains approximately 12 acres * * *. The application was made under the Washington County zoning ordinance which * * * makes provision for the granting of conditional use permits as follows:

* * *

"1903–6   Churches and Accessory Uses Zones Allowed

[The zone classification of plaintiff's property is included in the list of zones allowed.]

" * * *

"1903–33   Schools, Nursery, Public, Parochial or Private Zone Allowed

[The zone classification of plaintiff's property is included in the list of zones allowed.]"

* * *

On appeal plaintiff contends that the trial court erred (1) in finding that there was substantial evidence to support defendants' denial of plaintiff's application, and (2) in its finding that there was no discrimination against plaintiff in denying its application when permits had been granted to all other applicants under the same or less favorable conditions.

* * *

* * * It is known that zone changes are commonly made simply because the change is requested and no one in the neighborhood has an objection to it. Knowing this it would not be realistic to presume in a particular case that the governing board acted regularly in the sense that it duly considered the effect which the change would have on the comprehensive plan.

The same considerations do not obtain however when, as in the case before us, the governing board passes upon an application for a conditional use. The original ordinance itself expressly provides for the specified "conditional uses" * * *. In this sense the granting of an application for a conditional use does not constitute a deviation from the ordinance but is in compliance with it. The Washington County ordinance expressly declares that "A conditional use shall not be construed to be a zone change * * *." * * *

Thus the Washington County ordinance provides for such compatible uses as auditoriums, boat moorages, cemeteries, churches, colleges, community buildings, golf courses, greenhouses, hospitals, libraries, etc. Because these uses are generally compatible with the design of the zone the possibility that a permitted use will not comport with the comprehensive plan is not as great as it is when a variance or amendment is sought. Nor is there the same likelihood that such uses will be sought for and obtained as a matter of special privilege by those seeking private gain as there is where a variance or amendment is requested.

But more important * * * is the fact that the ordinance itself reveals the legislative plan forecasting the likelihood that certain specified uses will be needed to maximize the use of land in the zone for residential purposes. The Board's discretion is thus narrowed to those cases in which an application falls within one of the specified uses. The fact that these permissible uses are pre-defined and have the legislative endorsement * * * as a tentative part of the comprehensive plan for the area limits the possibility that the Board's action in granting a permit will be inimical to the interests of the community.
* * *

Absent the dangers incident to "spot zoning" the presumption of legislative regularity can be given its full effect. Under such circumstances the only function of this court and the trial court * * * is to decide whether the Board acted arbitrarily or capriciously. It is not our function to weigh the evidence for the purpose of determining whether in our judgment the Board correctly decided that the use sought would result in a detriment to the community as a whole. It is possible, as plaintiff contends, that the Board erred in concluding that the proposed use would cause traffic congestion or a fire hazard or other harm to the citizens in that area of the county. But the members of the Board, as representatives of the people who elected them, have the privilege of erring * * * as long as they abide by the required procedures and their conclusion is not patently irrational. * * *

* * * There is enough in the record to assure us that the Board did not act arbitrarily or capriciously. * * *

Plaintiff contends that the equal protection provisions of the Fourteenth Amendment of the United States Constitution and Article I, § 20 of the Oregon Constitution were violated by the Board's action in that previously all other applicants had been granted permits under circumstances which were the same or less favorable than those involved in plaintiff's proposed use. * * *

Implicit in the plaintiff's contention is the assumption that the Board of County Commissioners of Washington County is bound by the action of previous Boards of County Commissioners in that county. This assumption is not sound. Each Board is entitled to make its own evaluation of the suitability of the use sought by an applicant. The existing Board is not required to perpetuate errors of its predecessors. Even if it were shown that the previous applications were granted by the present Board, there is nothing in the record to show that the conditions now existing also existed at the time the previous applications were granted.

* * *

The judgment of the trial court is affirmed.

Notes

1. **Burden of Proof.** Compare Jacobi v. Zoning Board of Adjustment, 413 Pa. 286, 196 A.2d 742 (1964) where the court affirmed a special exception for a church-school complex, stating: "Implicit in appellants' argument is the thought that an applicant * * * has the burden of establishing that the proposed use will not adversely affect * * * the community. On the contrary, once the requisite facts and conditions detailed in the ordinance are found to exist * * * the applicant is 'entitled to the special exception unless there was legally sufficient competent evidence to support a finding that the grant * * * was adverse to the public interest.'" Id. at 290, 196 A.2d at 745. But see Crane v. Board of County Commissioners, 175 Neb. 568, 122 N.W.2d 520 (1963).

2. **Delegation Standards and Administrative Discretion.** While courts tend to accept "general welfare" as an adequate guideline for special exceptions, the ordinance texts and cases vary on the guidelines to be followed. See High Meadows Park Inc. v. Aurora, 112 Ill.App.2d 220, 250 N.E.2d 517 (1969); Annot., 58 A.L.R.2d 1083 (1958); Mandelker, *Delegation of Power and Function in Zoning Administration,* 1963 Washington U.L.Q. 60 at 74–80.

3. **Discretionary Conditions Imposed By Zoning Boards.** While some courts use the terms "conditional" and "special" uses interchangeably with special exceptions, the former terms have a much broader usage. The authority to grant special exceptions must be legislatively authorized, while the discretion to allow special uses under that authority is often adminis-

trative. In Farina v. Zoning Bd., Town of Trumball, 157 Conn. 420, 254 A.2d 492 (1969), the Board's condition of the widening of a street for the grant of special exception was overturned on the ground that street regulation authority was vested in another city department. Two years later, the same court upheld a similar condition based upon the different manner in which the board made its findings. See Reps, *Legal and Administrative Aspects of Conditional Zoning Variances and Exceptions,* 2 Syracuse L.Rev. 54 (1950); Note, *Zoning Variances and Exceptions Subject to Conditions,* 12 Syracuse L.Rev. 230 (1960).

(c) Variances

OTTO v. STEINHILBER
Court of Appeals of New York, 1939.
282 N.Y. 71, 24 N.E.2d 851.

FINCH, JUDGE. The question presented on this appeal is whether, upon the record in this case, there are shown the requisite elements which would authorize the Board of Appeals to grant a variance in the application of the zoning laws upon the ground of unnecessary hardship.

The property in question fronts on the north side of Merrick road in the incorporated village of Lynbrook, Nassau county. * * * Property on Merrick road is zoned for commercial purposes to a depth of 150 feet on either side of the road. The adjoining area is zoned for residential purposes. Thus the major portion of the land in question is within a class "A" residential zone. * * * Intervener applied to the Board of Appeals for a variance * * * so that he might erect a large roller skating rink upon both the commercial and the residential portions of his land. A roller skating rink is a permissible commercial use. * * *

* * *

* * * Where the property owner is unable reasonably to use his land because of zoning restrictions, the fault may lie in the fact that the particular zoning restriction is unreasonable in its application to a certain locality, or the oppressive result may be caused by conditions peculiar to a particular piece of land. In the former situation, the relief is by way of direct attack upon the terms of the ordinance [citations omitted]. In order to prevent the oppressive operation of the zoning law in particular instances, when the zoning restrictions are otherwise generally reasonable, the zoning laws usually create a safety valve under the control of a Board of Appeals, which may relieve against "unnecessary hardship" in particular instances. [Citations omitted] This the statute accomplishes in the following language: "Where there are practical difficulties or unnecessary hardship in the way of carrying out the strict letter of such ordinance, the board of appeals shall have the power in passing upon appeals, to vary or modify the application of any of the regulations or provisions of such ordinance

relating to the use, construction or alteration of buildings or structures, or the use of land, so that the spirit of the ordinance shall be observed, public safety and welfare secured and substantial justice done." Village Law, § 179–b. *Cf.* New York City Zoning Resolution, § 21. As a result of these provisions, "there has been confided to the board a delicate jurisdiction and one easily abused." People ex rel. Fordham Manor Reformed Church v. Walsh, *supra,* 244 N.Y. at page 290, 155 N.E. at page 578.

Before the Board may exercise its discretion and grant a variance upon the ground of unnecessary hardship, the record must show that (1) the land in question cannot yield a reasonable return if used only for a purpose allowed in that zone; (2) that the plight of the owner is due to unique circumstances and not to the general conditions in the neighborhood which may reflect the unreasonableness of the zoning ordinance itself; and (3) that the use to be authorized by the variance will not alter the essential character of the locality. Bassett, op. cit. *supra,* pp. 168, 169.

In the case at bar the applicant has failed to introduce any evidence whatever tending to show that the portion of his land which is located in the residential zone may not be reasonably employed in conformity with the zoning regulations governing Class "A" districts. The most which can be said for the cause of the intervener is that, if the variance were granted he could make an immediate profitable use of the entire tract. Intervener contends that the lack of access to the street from the rear portion constitutes an element showing unnecessary hardship. Intervener further contends that after the erection of the rink insufficient land will remain on either side to permit a street of the width required by the Village Law, § 719–*l* for access to the residential portion of his property. * * * He fails to show in any manner how the provisions of the statute quoted would prevent the creation of a right of way to the rear portion. For all that is shown, another use of the commercial property, or even a rearrangement of the rink building confined to the commercial portion, would seem to leave ample space for a village street. For the lack of any facts whatever from which it may reasonably be inferred that the zoning restrictions, requiring residential use of the rear portion of the land, would amount to an unnecessary hardship, a grant of a variance by the Board of Appeals was improper.

Furthermore, there is no evidence to show that the situation in which intervener finds himself, * * * is unique and distinct from that of the other owners whose properties front on the Merrick road. * * * Because of the heavy traffic upon that highway it was but a reasonable regulation to permit commercial uses of the property fronting upon the highway. Obviously there have to be some limits to this commercial zone. The extent thereof is primarily a legislative question and has been resolved in the zoning law to be no more than 150 feet away from the Merrick road. * * * If this be a hardship, then the vice is in the legislation itself and is not to be remedied by piecemeal exemption * * *. Thus, the variance granted by the Board of Appeals does not comply with the remaining two of the three prerequisites mentioned above, that the hardship to be alleviated not only be one peculiar to the applicant, but also that the relief granted shall not alter the essential character of the neighborhood heretofore devoted to residential purposes. In that event the commercial zone would to all intents and purposes extend not 150 feet, but for several hundred feet beyond.

* * *

The order of the Appellate Division confirming the determination of the Board of Appeals, should be reversed, the determination of the Board of Appeals annulled, and the application of the intervener denied, with costs in all courts.

LEHMAN, J. (dissenting). Where the major part of a large parcel of land lies in a residence district but has access only to a street in a business district, the unnecessary hardship and practical difficulties of strict enforcement of the zoning ordinance seem to me obvious.

* * *

Notes

1. **Variance Theory.** (a) *Requisite Grounds.* Most states require *unnecessary hardship* for the grant of a variance, and adopt the test of the principal case—that the applicant prove that the zoning restriction prevents any reasonable return on a conforming use; or that it amounts to virtual confiscation of the property. 2 Rathkopf, *The Law of Zoning and Planning,* p. 45–14 (3d ed. 1972). A looser test was provided by the New Jersey statute which authorized use variances on findings of "special reasons" "in particular cases" where "relief can be granted without substantial detriment to the public good and will not substantially impair the intent and purpose of the zone plan and zoning ordinance." N.J.Stat.Ann. 40:55–39(d); DeSimone v. Greater Englewood Housing Corp. No. 1, 56 N.J. 428, 267 A.2d 31 (1970). "It is long settled law in this state that this unique provision does not require that the particular premises cannot feasibly be used for a permitted use * * *. 'Special reasons' is a flexible concept * * * which specifically include promotion of * * * the general welfare. * * * So variances have been approved * * * because they significantly further the general welfare. * * * We specifically hold * * * semi-public housing * * * to furnish housing for * * * underprivileged segments * * * is a special reason adequate to * * * ground a use variance." Id. at 440–42, 267 A.2d at 37–39; contra: Farah v. Sachs, 10 Mich.App. 198, 157 N.W.2d 9 (1968).

(b) *Unique Hardship.* The view that the hardship must be unique to the particular property, and not to the owner or the general public is generally established. Tavares v. Zoning Bd. of Bristol, 103 R.I. 186, 235 A.2d 883 (1967); Priest v. Griffin, 284 Ala. 97, 222 So.2d 353 (1969); Serio v. Mayor and City Council of Baltimore, 208 Md. 545, 119 A.2d 387 (1956); Peterson v. Vasak, 162 Neb. 498, 76 N.W.2d 420 (1956). In theory, financial hardship alone will not suffice. MacLean v. Zoning Bd. of Adjustment of Borough of Crafton, 409 Pa. 82, 185 A.2d 533 (1962). A corollary holding of MacLean, also followed in other states, is that self-imposed hardship cannot be unique. One who purchases real property is deemed to know of its restrictions and cannot thereafter alter it in a way that would create unique hardship.

Where the statute describes the kind of uses for which variance may issue, other uses may be held beyond the board's power to entertain. Clarke v. DiDio, 226 So.2d 23 (Fla.App.1969); State ex rel. Sheridan v. Hudson, 400 S.W.2d 425 (Mo.App.1966).

Courts have not been as strict in allowing variances on building restrictions. See 3 Anderson, *American Law of Zoning* § 1445 et seq. (1968). In such cases a showing of practical difficulty may pass muster. See O'Neill v. Zoning Bd. of Adjustment of Philadelphia County, 434 Pa. 331, 337–338, 254 A.2d 12, 16 (1969) (dictum); R–N–R Associates v. Zoning Board of Review of City of Providence, 100 R.I. 7, 210 A.2d 653 (1965); but see Rochester Housing Authority v. Anderson, 51 Misc.2d 511, 273 N.Y.S.2d 448 (1966); Cary v. Board of Appeals of Worcester, 340 Mass. 748, 166 N.E.2d 690 (1960). See generally, Note, *Building Size, Shape and Placement Regulations: Bulk Control Zoning Reexamined*, 60 Yale L.J. 506 (1961).

(c) *Variance Consistency With Comprehensive Plans.* The third requirement of the principal case—that the variance not alter the character of the locality—is sometimes expressed by the requirement that it do no violence to the comprehensive plan of the municipality. Cow Hollow Improvement Club v. DiBene, 245 Cal.App.2d 160, 53 Cal.Rptr. 610 (1966); Carlton v. Board of Zoning Appeals of City of Indianapolis, 252 Ind. 56, 245 N.E.2d 337 (1969); Parsons v. Board of Zoning Appeals of City of New Haven, 140 Conn. 290, 99 A.2d 149 (1953). *Query*—If denial of a variance would raise constitutional objections, can the comprehensive plan test prevail?

2. **Variance Allowances in Practice.** The gap between variance theory and practice, is substantially documented by numerous field studies. See e.g. Shapiro, *The Zoning Variance Power—Constructive in Theory, Destructive in Practice,* 29 Md. 1 (1969); Haar, *Land Use Planning* 295–96 (1971); Note, *Administrative Discretion in Zoning*, 82 Harv.L.Rev. 668, at 671–72 (1969). Liberal and inconsistent allowances of variances tend to undermine comprehensive planning (see Heady v. Zoning Bd. of Appeals, for Town of Milford, 139 Conn. 463, 467, 94 A.2d 789, 791 (1953)), while strict application tends to impose economic hardship and produce blight and unproductive land uses.

Reform proposals go in opposite directions, depending on one's view of the competence and integrity of zoning administrators. Few variance decisions are appealed to the courts (Shapiro, supra, n. 89), as courts discourage appeals by limiting review to the record of board findings.

(3) Conflicts of Law in Zoning

(a) Intergovernmental Conflicts

Governments occupy substantial amounts of land, and the application of local land regulations to property of other government units was briefly touched upon in a previous section. See n. 2 following Penn Central, p. 434 supra. Intergovernmental zoning conflicts depend upon special statutes and common law doctrines that have less relation to land use planning than to general allocations of government powers.

Federal activities—With regard to the federal government, see the note at p. 317. Among the questions to be considered are: whether local zoning would interfere with federal functions; and whether the federal government has elected to waive any right to immunity. Omaechevarria v. Idaho, 246 U.S. 343, 38 S.Ct. 323, 62 L.Ed. 763 (1918) (state regulation of grazing on federal land held valid as a protective measure, consistent with federal ownership); Tim v. Long Branch, 135 N.J.Law 549, 53 A.2d 164 (1947) (federal conversion of property contra local zoning held valid). Similar questions arise for federal licensees that claim immunity under the federal cover.

State Activities—The operation of local zoning laws upon state facilities, agencies and licensees is equally checkered. There is no simple rule on the question whether state agency and local zoning authority are co-equal as to require courts to effectuate both to the fullest extent possible, or whether one source supersedes the latter. See Hill v. Collingswood, 9 N.J. 369, 88 A.2d 506 (1952). Thus a state liquor control board was held not to have exclusive authority over liquor business locations as to divest the zoning authority on business sites of a city. City of Norfolk v. Tiny House, Inc., 222 Va. 414, 281 S.E.2d 836 (1981).

Statutory interpretations vary with different kinds of regulations, facilities and functions. See e.g. West's Ann.Cal.Gov.Code § 53091 (exempting school districts, but not other government agencies from local zoning); Comment, *The Inapplicability of Municipal Zoning to Governmental Land Uses*, 19 Syracuse L.Rev. 698 (1968). Zoning restrictions on the *location* of a state building may be deemed inconsistent with state law, while local regulation of its actual *construction* may not. The safest course is to consult precedents dealing with particular agencies and activities, than upon general principles.

Some generalizations have been attempted in recent studies. See Note, *Governmental Immunity From Local Zoning Ordinances*, 84 Harv. L.Rev. 869 (1971); Note, *Municipal Power to Regulate Building, Construction, and Land Use by Other State Agencies*, 49 Minn.L.Rev. 284 (1964). Both notes criticize the mechanical application by majority jurisdictions of state sovereign immunity to municipal zoning, (e.g.

County of Los Angeles v. Los Angeles, 212 Cal.App.2d 160, 28 Cal.Rptr. 32 (1963)) and they cite a substantial minority of states which favor a reasonableness test which balances competing state and local interests. Port Arthur Ind. School District v. City of Groves, 376 S.W.2d 330 (Tex. 1964); Town of Oronoco v. Rochester, 293 Minn. 468, 179 N.W.2d 426 (1972); City of Richmond v. Board of Supervisors of Henrico County, 199 Va. 679, 101 S.E.2d 641 (1958); St. Louis County v. Manchester, 360 S.W.2d 638 (Mo.1962). Here, as elsewhere, judicial adaptation strives to minimize intergovernmental conflict where legislatures fail to define state immunity policy. See e.g. Annot. 74 A.L.R.3d 136 (1976). Some recent statutes adopt balancing tests. See e.g. N.Car.Gen.Stat. § 160A–390; Or.Rev.Stat. 227.286; West's Ann.Cal.Gov.Code §§ 53090–53091 (subjecting local state agencies to municipal zoning); Burns Ind.Ann. Stat. § 53–939 (1964) (creating rebuttable presumption on that state building construction contra local zoning is not in the public interest); N.J.Stat.Ann. 40:55–50; State v. Jersey Central Power & Light Co., 55 N.J. 363, 262 A.2d 385 (1970).

" * * * Rather than rely on artificial abstractions * * * courts should examine the composite factual context * * * to determine whether the [zoning] violation should be tolerated. * * *

* * * courts should place the burden of proof on that party who is seeking to establish the reasonableness of the proposed zoning evasion * * * courts would in effect establish a rebuttable presumption of governmental nonimmunity from local zoning regulation. Such a presumption could be overcome by a showing that the function the political subdivision sought to perform was critical * * *, that alternative locations for the proposed * * * facility * * * was the least violative of the comprehensive plan and the least detrimental to contiguous property. * * * Further, where an independent state-wide planning commission vested with the responsibility of making comprehensive land-use decisions has sanctioned the violation, the decisional burden should be reversed." Note, supra, 84 Harv.L.Rev. at 883–884.*

Interlocal Activities—Where the state grants extramural powers to a local government, many courts uphold the authority of that local government to erect facilities in violation of another government's zoning laws. See Notes, 84 Harv.L.Rev. at 874 et seq.; 49 Minn.L.Rev. at 299 et seq.

Courts have not developed comprehensive solutions where the state confers extramural zoning and subdivision controls on a local unit. See Becker, *Municipal Boundaries and Zoning, Controlling Regional Land Development,* 1966 Wash.U.L.Q. 1: **

" * * * extraterritorial zoning as authorized has not been and cannot be used to promote the orderly and efficient development of a metropolitan area. * * * It neither necessitates nor encourages joint efforts to plan and regulate regional growth; if anything, extra-territorial zoning permits a local community to adopt self-serving answers to pressing problems which may have regional ramifications. The absence of any requirement * * * which carves out a standard of reasonableness * * * to guide communities and courts alike, neces-sarily translates extraterritorial zoning into largely self-protective reg-ulation of fringe areas. * * * The answer must lie elsewhere. Perhaps it lies in regional or metropolitan government with the power to zone as well as plan." Id. 55–57.

The problem of extramunicipal zoning may be resolved by statuto-ry authorization of intermunicipal zoning suits. Town of Bedford v. Mount Kisco, 34 A.D.2d 687, 312 N.Y.S.2d 617 (1970); but see Town of Huntington v. Town Board of Oyster Bay, 57 Misc.2d 821, 293 N.Y.S.2d 558 (1968). There is considerable divergence of authority. See general-ly Annot., 49 A.L.R.3d 1126 (1973); Note, *Zoning: Looking Beyond Municipal Boundaries,* 1965 Wash.U.L.Q. 107 (1965); Note, *The Ag-grieved Person Requirement in Zoning,* 8 Wm. & Mary L.Rev. 294 (1967).

Municipal Exemption From Its Own Zoning Law—A municipality is generally held exempt from its own zoning ordinances on uses of its land for governmental purposes. Kedroff v. Springfield, 127 Vt. 624, 256 A.2d 457 (1969); cf. Hunke v. Foote, 84 Idaho 391, 373 P.2d 322 (1962) (city bound by its zoning law on property dedicated to proprieta-ry activity). Re lessees of municipal property, see Annot. 84 A.L.R.3d 1187 (1978).

RUTGERS, STATE UNIVERSITY v. PILUSO

Supreme Court of New Jersey, 1972.
60 N.J. 142, 286 A.2d 697.

HALL, J. The question presented by this litigation is whether Rutgers, The State University, ("Rutgers") is subject to the zoning ordinance provisions of a municipality in which one of its campuses is located—here Piscataway Township, Middlesex County. Although the provision precisely involved is a limitation on the permissible number of housing facilities for student families, the broader issue necessarily present encompasses the matter of intergovernmental land use regula-tion in general as well as the particular status of Rutgers. The Law Division, granting Rutgers' motion for summary judgment, held that it is an instrumentality of the state and immune from local zoning enactments. 113 N.J.Super. 65, 272 A.2d 573 (1971). * * *

The township as a whole is a large, sprawling area—until fairly recently mostly unimproved land with few centers of population, but now, typical of so many such municipalities in the northeastern New Jersey suburban ring, in the throes of extensive development of all kinds. Many housing developments, a few garden apartments, and a very considerable number of industrial establishments adjacent to new Interstate Highway Route 287 have come in, and there is room for a lot more of each. This growth has necessitated great extensions of municipal services and facilities, including schools, which must be principally financed, under New Jersey's present tax system, out of local property taxes. The result has been financial and other growing pains.

The township's present zoning ordinance, enacted in 1964 * * * reflects the usual means employed by this type of municipality in attempting to meet local financial problems by land use regulation, *i.e.*, so-called "fiscal zoning." The legally dubious stratagems of zoning wide expanses of vacant land for industrial use only, requiring large lots for undeveloped residential land, and rigidly regulating multi-family dwellings are all utilized to restrict private growth to land uses which will produce few school children and show a "tax profit."

* * *

The ordinance provision here precisely involved is found among the permitted accessory uses in the E-R zone and reads as follows:

> Dormitories for matriculated students; dormitories and other housing facilities for use by matriculated students and their families, provided, however, that such facilities do not exceed 500 units.

In other words, the township purported to allow unlimited housing facilities for unmarried students, but to arbitrarily restrict the number of those which could be used by married students and their families.

In 1969 Rutgers had reached the maximum of 500 student family housing units in Piscataway. It sought to build 374 more garden apartments in the middle of the Kilmer section * * * Building permits were refused because of the ordinance restriction. The university then sought a variance, which the Board of Adjustment denied.

* * *

Rutgers' proofs demonstrated the public need for the proposed housing beyond question, although in the view we take of the case that matter is of little relevance. * * *

The local interest * * * is in one respect somewhat difficult to fathom and in another, quite obvious. The campus is physically well insulated and substantially self-sufficient from the municipal service point of view. * * * It has its own police force for routine purposes (see N.J.S.A. 18A:6–4.2 to 4.–11). * * * The presence of the campus in the township nonetheless does have a local impact. For one thing, municipal traffic policing is undoubtedly required * * * by reason of the thousands of students and staff using the campus * * *.

As to university residential growth, the reason for the 500 unit limitation on student family housing is made exceedingly plain by the township's evidence * * *. That reason is "fiscal zoning" in its most baneful aspect. The township fears that if the 500 units limitation does not stand * * * the township will be required to build a new elementary school to accommodate the increased number of children of married students who will live in them. And such construction will, of course, under the present fiscal scheme, have to be at the expense of Piscataway taxpayers. While this result may be burdensome to property owners, * * * residential limitations imposed for such a reason may well be beyond the bounds of legitimate land use regulation.

* * *

The question of what governmental units or instrumentalities are immune from municipal land use regulations, and to what extent, is not one properly susceptible of absolute or ritualistic answer. Courts have, however, frequently resolved such conflicts in perhaps too simplistic terms and by the use of labels rather than through reasoned adjudication of the critical question of which governmental interest should prevail in the particular relationship or factual situation.

* * *

Thus, speaking generally, black letter law frequently says: "Absent a waiver expressed by, or necessarily inferred from, the language of a state statute, a state is not amenable to the zoning regulations of its political subdivisions" and "[a] public corporation or authority created by the state to carry out a function of the state is not bound by local zoning regulations," 2 Anderson, American Law of Zoning § 9.06 at 115, 117 (1968), thereby turning the matter on the scope of the political authority of the governmental unit seeking exemption. Often the decision is reached on the basis of whether the function, use or activity as to which exemption is claimed is "governmental" or "proprietary." Whether the claimant has been granted the right of eminent domain has been found to be conclusive in some cases.

Our own prior cases in the field, * * * cannot be said to have adopted any absolute criteria as decisive. * * *

* * *

The rationale which runs through our cases and which we are convinced should furnish the true test of immunity in the first instance, albeit a somewhat nebulous one, is the legislative intent in this regard with respect to the particular agency or function involved. That intent, rarely specifically expressed, is to be divined from a consideration of many factors, with a value judgment reached on an overall evaluation. All possible factors cannot be abstractly catalogued. The most obvious and common ones include the nature and scope of the instrumentality seeking immunity, the kind of function or land use involved, the extent of the public interest to be served thereby, the effect local land use regulation would have upon the enterprise concerned and the impact upon legitimate local interests. * * * In some instances one factor will be more influential than another or may be so significant as to completely overshadow all others. No one, such as the granting or withholding of the power of eminent domain, is to be thought of as ritualistically required or controlling. And there will undoubtedly be cases, as there have been in the past, where the broader public interest is so important that immunity must be granted even though the local interests may be great. The point is that there is no precise formula or set of criteria which will determine every case mechanically and automatically.

With regard to a state university * * * there can be little doubt that, as an instrumentality of the state performing an essential governmental function for the benefit of all the people of the state, the Legislature would not intend that its growth and development should be subject to restriction or control by local land use regulation. Indeed, such will generally be true in the case of all state functions and agencies.

It is, however, most important to stress that such immunity in any situation is not completely unbridled. Even where it is found to exist, it must not, as this court said in Washington Township v. Village of Ridgewood, *supra* (26 N.J. at 584–586, 141 A.2d 308), be exercised in an unreasonable fashion so as to arbitrarily override all important legitimate local interests. This rule must apply to the state and its instrumentalities as well as to lesser governmental entities entitled to immunity. For example, it would be arbitrary, if the state proposed to erect an office building in the crowded business district of a city where provision for off-street parking was required, for the state not to make some reasonable provision in that respect. And, at the very least, even if the proposed action of the immune governmental instrumentality does not reach the unreasonable stage for any sufficient reason, the instrumentality ought to consult with the local authorities and sympathetically listen and give every consideration to local objections, problems and suggestions in order to minimize the conflict as much as possible. See Town of Bloomfield v. New Jersey Highway Authority, *supra* (18 N.J. at 248, 113 A.2d 658). As far as Rutgers' proposal here, * * * is concerned, we fail to see the slightest vestige of unreasonableness as far as Piscataway's local interests are concerned or in any other respect. * * * The possible additional local cost of educating children living in the housing is clearly not a legitimate local interest from any proper land use impact point of view.

This brings us to the final point in the case, upon which the township principally relies. It urges in effect that under the "Rutgers, the state university law," N.J.S.A. 18A:65–1 to –35, L.1956, c. 61, the entity thereby created is not such an instrumentality of the state as to qualify it for immunity from local land use regulation on that basis. The contention appears to be that only a contract relationship was thereby established between the state and the Board of Trustees of the prior institution and that the Legislature did not intend to confer immunity. The point confuses the *method of creation* of Rutgers, as the state university, which was by legislative contract, with the *nature of the entity that resulted,* from the standpoint of the problem before us.

* * *

The whole picture demonstrates to us beyond any doubt that the Legislature must be said to have intended that the growth and development of Rutgers, as a public university for the benefit of all the people of the state, was not to be thwarted or restricted by local land use regulations and that it is immune therefrom. * * * The township urges that the failure to grant the university the power of eminent domain and the omission from the statute of a provision that all other inconsistent laws should be deemed inapplicable compel a contrary conclusion. As previously indicated, the absence of the right of eminent domain is not decisive. * * *

* * *

The judgment of the Law Division is affirmed.

Note

Cf. Board of Educ. v. Gloucester, 127 N.J.Super. 97, 316 A.2d 480 (1976); City of Charleston v. Board of Educ., 158 W.Va. 141, 209 S.E.2d 55 (1974) where school district suits to prevent rezoning of areas by the township were dismissed.

(b) Incompatible Private Use Restrictions

The extent to which land use may be controlled by privately created restrictions depends, in large part, upon the property law and public policy of a given state. Classification of a privately created use limitation—as a covenant (purely personal, or running with the land); as condition or grant; as a legal or equitable interest; and as negative burdens or affirmative duties—affect enforceability and standing of particular individuals to invoke or challenge that restriction. The law does not favor private restrictions on land use, but that proposition is not absolute. "The law has developed in such a way as to permit courts wide latitude in determining which covenants are enforceable." See Lundberg, *Restrictive Covenants and Land Use Control: Private Zoning,* 34 Mont.L.Rev. 199 (1973). Some of the doctrines which favor or disfavor private land controls are indicated below, but the courts have not perfected principles to deal with all private property restrictions.

Board of Education of Central School Dist. No. 1 of Towns of Walton, Hamden, etc. v. Miles, 15 N.Y.2d 364, 259 N.Y.S.2d 129, 207 N.E.2d 181 (1965). Where the grant of land to an academy limits its use for an academy, with a reverter to the grantor upon cessation of such use, the court ruled that the reverter condition could not be constitutionally terminated by a later statute. Semble: Burger v. St. Paul, 241 Minn. 285, 291–292, 64 N.W.2d 73, 77 (1954). But in Hendlin v. Fairmount Const. Co., 8 N.J.Super. 310, 72 A.2d 541 (Ch.1950), the court avoided enforcement of a private restriction by interpreting the same as a purely personal covenant between the parties at its creation, and therefore not enforceable by successors to the property.

In Shulman v. Serrill, 432 Pa. 206, 246 A.2d 643 (1968), building restriction on limiting its use to single family buildings was held binding notwithstanding (1) the rule of constructing restrictions strictly against the grantor; (2) the commercialization of the surrounding area; (3) the township rezoning of the restricted tract to permit office and multiple dwelling use; and (4) interior conversion of some buildings on the restricted tract, for office use. The court held that the zoning ordinance could not constitutionally abrogate the restriction, and that any change in use could not affect the *building* restriction which was independent of concurrent use restrictions. Under the doctrine of changed conditions (whereby courts may refuse to enforce restrictions whose purpose and value has been substantially thwarted by area changes) the court found that the proved changes did not so alter the character of the neighborhood as to render the value of the restriction unsubstantial. Accord: Western Land Co. v. Truskolaski, 88 Nev. 200, 495 P.2d 624 (1972) (citing similar authorities from Arizona, Colorado, Illinois, Nebraska and New Mexico); but cf. Hirsch v. Hancock, 173 Cal. App.2d 745, 343 P.2d 959 (1959) (applying the doctrine of changed conditions to defeat a restriction).

Where the private restriction is more restrictive, than the zoning ordinance, courts generally adhere to the rule that a zoning law cannot abrogate the restriction. See e.g. Morgan v. Matheson, 362 Mich. 535, 107 N.W.2d 825 (1961); Frey v. Poynor, 369 P.2d 168 (Okl.1962); Berger, *Conflicts Between Zoning Ordinances and Restrictive Covenants: A Problem In Land Use Policy,* 43 Neb.L.Rev. 449 (1964); Comment, *The Effect of Private Restrictive Covenants On Exercise Of The Public Powers of Zoning And Eminent Domain,* 1963 Wis.L.Rev. 321.

In Aluminum Co. of America v. Kohutek, 455 S.W.2d 789 (Tex. 1970) Alcoa acquired a large subdivision for a development, and by recorded restriction, prohibited any subsequent purchaser from placing a house trailer on any lot in Lynnhaven. In a suit to enforce the restriction, Alcoa prevailed. Compare, Crane Neck Ass'n v. New York City, 61 N.Y.2d 154, 472 N.Y.S.2d 901, 460 N.E.2d 1336 (1984), where the court refused to enforce private deed restrictions against use for single families, by mentally disabled state wards, on the ground that the restriction violated public policy favoring such placement.

When should courts thereby give legal sanction to private zoning to protect the investment interests; and when should such practices be limited or barred by public policy? See Comment, *Democracy In The New Towns: The Limits of Private Government,* 36 U.Chi.L.Rev. 379 (1969).

(c) Regional Planning and Controls

Legislation to insure orderly use of open space and natural resources that are shared by neighboring municipalities (by regional planning) is spotty and limited. One of the more comprehensive approaches was taken by the New York State Urban Development Act, N.Y.—McKinney's Unconsol. Laws §§ 6251–6285, which created a government controlled corporation with broad statewide powers of planning and development, including the power to intermix public and private participation in its projects. This power to involve citizen, as well as developer and local government participation in planning, financing and managing projects was bolstered by the crucial power to supersede, where necessary, local zoning and building codes. The improvements achieved under that law are summarized in Brandon, *Integrating Recreation and Open Space Facilities Into Urban Development Projects,* 24 Syracuse L.Rev. 929 (1973).

The Act proved too successful for many local interests. A coalition of disgruntled local units succeeded in enacting a "ripper" amendment to the State Urban Development Act whereby the power of the Development Corporation to override local zoning and building codes was effectively eviscerated. See McKinney's Session Laws of N.Y.1973—cl. 446.

State creation of regional planning agencies is more evident in specialized laws of six or seven states, under the impetus of federal incentive grants, and the National Land Use Policy Act of 1971. See Bosselman and Callies, *The Quiet Revolution in Land Use Control* (U.S. Council on Environmental Quality, 1971). That study also notes additional studies on "The Emerging Role of the State in Land Use Management" under the sponsorship of the Council of State Governments, and on a Model Land Development Code by the American Law Institute. Id. 327.

(4) Zoning Procedure and Due Process

Zoning board powers are stated in broad terms, leaving to the Board the task of formulating more specific rules and regulations. Leaving aside exceptional procedures, *viz.* those governing PUDs or special exceptions, zoning procedure is fairly uniform. When a permit for a particular use or alteration of property is denied under a zoning or related codes, challenges to such denials are raised by appeals to the local zoning board.

Upon filing of appeal, an administrative hearing is set and prescribed hearing notices are published, *viz.* by newspaper publication or posters prominently displayed at the affected property site. The hearing must be open to the public, but is not controlled by legal rules of procedure or evidence, and in most states does not require full board presence. Zoning board members need not be lawyers or property specialists. They usually render their findings by summary "form" opinions which lack specification of the crucial grounds of the board's conclusions. The difficulty of identifying the true ground of decision from the record is compounded by the fact that board members may act on their personal knowledge and investigations, including private conversation with municipal officials. Applicants may never learn of, or have the opportunity to controvert, such sources. Since courts presume the validity and good faith of zoning board discretion, the opportunities for unfair process are substantial.

Nevertheless, courts are bound to review and remedy denials of due process. These arise in ways too numerous to consider here, but the importance of due process issues in zoning administration is clear. On the adequacy of notices (in terms of addressees, time given, medium of issuance, and content), see Annot., 38 A.L.R.3d 167 (1971). On the right of cross-examination in zoning proceedings, see Annot., 27 A.L.R.3d 1304 (1969). On the impartiality of board members (*viz.* who have conflicts of interest or who are privately "reached" by communications outside the hearings), see Jarrott v. Scrivener, 225 F.Supp. 827 (D.D.C.1964), noted 12 U.C.L.A.Rev. 969 (1965). On the right of a board to refuse to hear offered evidence, see Hot Shoppes, Inc. v. Clouser, 231 F.Supp. 825 (D.D.C.1964). See generally Note, *Board of Zoning Appeals Procedure: Informality Breeds Contempt,* 16 Syracuse L.Rev. 568 (1965); Dukeminier & Stapleton, *The Zoning Board of Adjustment: A Case Study In Misrule,* 50 Ky.L.J. 273 (1962); Comment, *Judicial Control Over Zoning Boards of Appeal: Suggestions For Reform,* 12 U.C.L.A.L. Rev. 937 (1965).

EASTLAKE v. FOREST CITY ENTERPRISES, INC.

Supreme Court of the United States, 1976.
426 U.S. 668, 96 S.Ct. 2358, 49 L.Ed.2d 132.

MR. CHIEF JUSTICE BURGER delivered the opinion of the Court.

The question in this case is whether a city charter provision requiring proposed land use changes to be ratified by 55% of the votes cast violates the due process rights of a landowner who applies for a zoning change.

The city of Eastlake, Ohio, a suburb of Cleveland, has a comprehensive zoning plan codified in a municipal ordinance. Respondent, a real estate developer, acquired an eight-acre parcel of real estate in Eastlake zoned for "light industrial" uses at the time of purchase.

In May 1971, respondent applied . . . for a zoning change to permit construction of a multifamily, high-rise apartment building. The Planning Commission recommended the proposed change to the City Council, which under Eastlake's procedures could either accept or reject the Planning Commission's recommendation. Meanwhile, by popular vote, the voters of Eastlake amended the city charter to require that any changes in land use agreed to by the Council be approved by a 55% vote in a referendum. The City Council approved the Planning Commission's recommendation for reclassification of respondent's property to permit the proposed project. Respondent then applied to the Planning Commission for "parking and yard" approval for the proposed building. The Commission rejected the application, on the ground that the City Council's rezoning action had not yet been submitted to the voters for ratification.

Respondent then filed an action in state court, seeking a judgment declaring the charter provision invalid as an unconstitutional delegation of legislative power to the people. While the case was pending, the City Council's action was submitted to a referendum, but the proposed zoning change was not approved by the requisite 55% margin. Following the election, the Court of Common Pleas and the Ohio Court of Appeals sustained the charter provision.

The Ohio Supreme Court reversed. 41 Ohio St.2d 187, 324 N.E.2d 740 (1975). Concluding that enactment of zoning and rezoning provisions is a legislative function, the court held that a popular referendum requirement, lacking standards to guide the decision of the voters, permitted the police power to be exercised in a standardless, hence arbitrary and capricious manner. Relying on this Court's decisions in Washington ex rel. Seattle Trust Co. v. Roberge, 278 U.S. 116, 49 S.Ct. 50, 73 L.Ed. 210 (1928), Thomas Cusack Co. v. Chicago, 242 U.S. 526, 37 S.Ct. 190, 61 L.Ed. 472 (1917), and Eubank v. Richmond, 226 U.S. 137, 33 S.Ct. 76, 57 L.Ed. 156 (1912), but distinguishing James v. Valtierra, 402 U.S. 137, 91 S.Ct. 1331, 28 L.Ed.2d 678 (1971), the court concluded that the referendum provision constituted an unlawful delegation of legislative power.

We reverse.

I

The conclusion that Eastlake's procedure violates federal constitutional guarantees rests upon the proposition that a zoning referendum involves a delegation of legislative power. A referendum cannot, however, be characterized as a delegation of power. Under our constitutional assumptions, all power derives from the people, who can delegate it to representative instruments which they create. See, *e.g.,* The Federalist No. 39 (J. Madison). In establishing legislative bodies, the people can reserve to themselves power to deal directly with matters which might otherwise be assigned to the legislature. Hunter v. Erickson, 393 U.S. 385, 392, 89 S.Ct. 557, 561, 21 L.Ed.2d 616 (1969).

The reservation of such power is the basis for the town meeting a tradition which continues to this day in some States as both a practical and symbolic part of our democratic processes. The referendum, similarly, is a means for direct political participation, allowing the people the final decision, amounting to a veto power, over enactments of representative bodies. The practice is designed to "give citizens a voice on questions of public policy." James v. Valtierra, *supra,* 402 U.S., at 141, 91 S.Ct., at 1333.

In framing a state constitution, the people of Ohio specifically reserved the power of referendum to the people of each municipality within the State.

* * *

To be subject to Ohio's referendum procedure, the question must be one within the scope of legislative power. The Ohio Supreme Court expressly found that the City Council's action in rezoning respondent's eight acres from light industrial to high-density residential use was legislative in nature. Distinguishing between administrative and legislative acts, the court separated the power to zone or rezone, by passage or amendment of a zoning ordinance, from the power to grant relief from unnecessary hardship. The former function was found to be legislative in nature. * * *

II

*   *   * Under Eastlake's procedure, the Ohio Supreme Court reasoned, no mechanism existed, nor indeed could exist, to assure that the voters would act rationally in passing upon a proposed zoning change. This meant that "appropriate legislative action [would] be made dependent upon the potentially arbitrary and unreasonable whims of the voting public." 41 Ohio St.2d, at 195, 324 N.E.2d, at 746. The potential for arbitrariness in the process, the court concluded, violated due process.

*   *   *

In basing its claim on federal due process requirements, respondent also invokes Euclid v. Ambler Realty Co., 272 U.S. 365, 47 S.Ct. 114, 71 L.Ed. 303 (1926), but it does not rely on the direct teaching of that case. Under *Euclid,* a property owner can challenge a zoning restriction if the measure is "clearly arbitrary and unreasonable, having no substantial relation to the public health, safety, morals, or general welfare." *Id.,* at 395. If the substantive result of the referendum is arbitrary and capricious, bearing no relation to the police power, then the fact that the voters of Eastlake wish it so would not save the restriction. As this Court held in invalidating a charter amendment enacted by referendum:

> "The sovereignty of the people is itself subject to those constitutional limitations which have been duly adopted and remain unrepealed." Hunter v. Erickson, 393 U.S., at 392, 89 S.Ct., at 561.

But no challenge of the sort contemplated in Euclid v. Ambler Realty is before us. The Ohio Supreme Court did not hold, and respondent does not argue, that the present zoning classification under Eastlake's comprehensive ordinance violates the principles established in Euclid v. Ambler Realty. If respondent considers the referendum result itself to be unreasonable, the zoning restriction is open to challenge in state court, where the scope of the state remedy available to respondent would be determined as a matter of state law, as well as under Fourteenth Amendment standards. That being so, nothing more is required by the Constitution.

*   *   *

Our decision in James v. Valtierra, upholding California's mandatory referendum requirement, confirms this view. Mr. Justice Black, speaking for the Court in that case, said:

> "This procedure ensures that *all the people* of a community will have a voice in a decision which may lead to large expenditures of local governmental funds for increased public services *   *   *." 402 U.S., at 143 (emphasis added).

*   *   * As a basic instrument of democratic government, the referendum process does not, in itself, violate the Due Process Clause of the Fourteenth Amendment when applied to a rezoning ordinance. Since the rezoning decision in this case was properly reserved to the people of Eastlake under the Ohio Constitution, the Ohio Supreme Court erred in holding invalid, on federal constitutional grounds, the charter amendment permitting the voters to decide whether the zoned use of respondent's property could be altered.

The judgment of the Ohio Supreme Court is reversed, and the case is remanded for further proceedings not inconsistent with this opinion.

Reversed and remanded.

MR. JUSTICE POWELL, dissenting.

There can be no doubt as to the propriety and legality of submitting generally applicable legislative questions, including zoning provisions, to a popular referendum. But here the only issue concerned the status of a single small parcel owned by a single "person." This procedure, affording no realistic opportunity for the affected person to be heard, even by the electorate, is fundamentally unfair. The "spot" referendum technique appears to open disquieting opportunities for local government bodies to bypass normal protective procedures for resolving issues affecting individual rights.

MR. JUSTICE STEVENS, with whom MR. JUSTICE BRENNAN joins, dissenting.

* * *

Notes

1. For a critique of the above case, see Rosenberg, *Referendum Zoning*, 53 U.Cinn.L.Rev. 381 (1984). California recently upheld an initiative ordinance prohibiting further residential building permits until local school and utility facilities complied with specified standards. Prior notice of hearing procedures required by statute for enactments of the city council were held inapplicable to action by electors under powers reserved to them by the state constitution. Associated Home Builders v. Livermore, 18 Cal. 3d 582, 135 Cal.Rptr. 41, 557 P.2d 473 (1976). The court there reaffirmed the view that community measures for orderly development need only be reasonable, and not justified by a compelling state interest, to withstand constitutional challenge.

Chapter VIII

FINANCING LOCAL GOVERNMENT

The shortfall of local government revenues lies at the heart of urban problems. The mismatch between fiscal need and fiscal powers is summarized by the canard that the federal government has all the money, the local governments—all the problems, and the state government—all the legal powers. Fiscal limitations are not uniform for all municipalities and special districts. Nor are they so absolute as to preclude legal innovations to enhance fiscal capacity. It is necessary, therefore, to determine what specific limitations apply to a particular government unit or function, before deciding what financing options are available to achieve its particular goals.

Preceding chapters covered some of the constitutional and statutory restrictions on local fiscal powers. In this chapter, attention is directed to the specific means by which local revenues are raised and expended. Fiscal controls guide official action, but also alert private parties to the limits within which they may safely do business with local governments. Since finance laws are designed to protect the public fisc and taxpayers, the allowance of private claims for government work rests less on the justness of the claim than on lawful authorization.

A. BUDGETING, APPROPRIATIONS, AUDITING, EARMARKING

The budget is the starting point and basic framework of fiscal planning and control. It is more than an estimate to equate probable income with authorized outgo. The principles that comprise budget law, set the basic conditions, and dollar limits, for lawful taxation and expenditure. Budget control promotes responsible planning, fiscal stability, official accountability, and taxpayer information on the costs and priorities of a particular administration. Budget law originally developed as a check on official irresponsibility but deficit spending has become more necessary as the levels and range of public spending and public services expand.

Budgets are classified in several ways: the "operating" budget governs normal current operations during a specified (usually annual) budget period; a "capital" budget covers long term planning and financing of capital projects, and "special fund" budgets are funded from special project grants and revenues. Budget appropriations are made with different degrees of specificity. "Lump sum" budgets allot dollar amounts to a broad class of activities, sometimes to an entire operating department. A "line item" budget allots amounts by specific items of expenditure. Lump sum appropriations contemplate greater discretion and flexibility in the executive branch in alloting dollars from lump appropriations to specific transactions; while line-by-line budget appropriations reserve greater control to the legislative body over item priorities in public spending. Budgets are also based on different accounting systems, i.e., cash basis, accrual basis, or modified cash-accrual basis.

There are three basic types of budget: Executive, Legislative, or Administrative. Depending upon governing legislation, budgets may be formulated and administered by the chief executive, by the local legislature, by a special board or commission, or by some combination of these. Many large cities and most states employ the executive type budget which, though subject to legislative adoption or approval, is prepared and administered by the executive branch. Commission and Councilmanic budget administrations are, however, found in many municipalities and in county government.

Procedure

While local variations abound in fiscal procedures, the following comments outline the general steps taken in the formulation and adoption of an executive type budget. An estimate is made of the amount of revenues that will be available for expenditure in the upcoming budget period, taking into account surpluses from prior years, and the amount of anticipated collections from taxes, special assessments, user charges, license charges, grants and other income. Each department prepares a detailed budget request, listing by item and amount its proposed expenditures, broken down into payments which are mandatory (*viz.* interest on outstanding obligations) and those which are not. These estimates are reviewed, modified, and incorporated by the chief executive into a proposed budget and submitted, together with a budget message, for review and approval by the legislature.

The budget message, an important part of the budget submission, translates the mass of figures into intelligible terms and explains the spending policies, priorities, and justifications advanced by the executive, for requested spending authorizations and for such taxes or borrowing that is required to fund the budget. This submission may also disclose inaccuracies and maladministration of preceding budgets. In effect, the budget submission requests, directly or by implication, that the legislature enact laws to produce needed funds and to make appropriations in the amounts and classes stated in the budget.

Upon receipt of the budget submission, the legislative body may hold public hearings, review, and, within legal limits, modify the budget prior to approving or adopting the same. The law and practice on budget approval, adoption, or certification varies from jurisdiction to jurisdiction. In some, the budget is adopted prior to the enactment of appropriations. In others, the budget adoption ordinance also serves as the enactment of appropriations required by the budget. See Flaherty v. Craig, 226 N.Y. 76, 123 N.E. 157 (1919). In others, the law may require *all* budget appropriations to be enacted at one time (see Krahmer opinion, p. 567). However achieved, legislative appropriations must be made before budgeted amounts may be expended.

Appropriations

An appropriation sets aside a specified sum for a named purpose. It acts as both an authorization to incur obligations, and as an allocation of available funds to pay the same. Most local governments are subject to the rule that funds may not be paid out until appropriated in accordance with law. However, some flexibility is provided (where permitted), by budget appropriations for "contingencies;" by amending, supplementing, or transferring prior appropriations; and by exceptional rules to cover "emergencies." The appropriations requirement deters fund diversion and unlawful debt creation.

Accounting and Auditing

Compliance with appropriations limits is assured by accounting controls, as administered by officers other than those charged with spending authority. In a small municipality these accounting functions may be vested in one office, but in larger cities, it is common to have accounting and auditing functions assigned to different offices, *e.g.* to a Director of Finance, a Treasurer, and a Comptroller.

By maintaining account balances showing encumbered and unencumbered amounts of a given appropriation, the accounting officer can, and is often required to, verify in advance of any departmental commitment, whether there are sufficient uncommitted appropriations to cover a proposed transaction. Preliminary checks may also be required by other officers, *viz.* the city solicitor, to assure that the transaction is lawful in other respects. If these preliminary, sometimes called preaudit, checks are satisfied, the accounting officer may then "encumber" and reserve that amount of the uncommitted appropriation to cover the proposed service or contract. The act of encumbering an appropriation assures availability of funds for payment of covered transactions.

After the work, for which appropriated sums were encumbered, is completed, a "post-audit" review is made, as a double check on compliance with fiscal controls, and also to verify that the unit received full performance and value for its payments. Post-audit also enhances legislative review of the fiscal performance of the executive branch. Post-audits are often performed by an elected Controller, as an independent guardian against waste or fraud.

Earmarking

Some municipal funds are legislatively or constitutionally earmarked as "special funds", and are restricted to specified uses. Money belonging to a special fund is separately accounted for and is normally payable only to discharge obligations for which the fund was created. See Wileden, *Earmarking: Good or Bad?*, 33 State Government 251 (1960); Nowak v. Wereszynski, 21 A.D.2d 427, 250 N.Y.S.2d 981 (1964); Bilby v. McKenzie, 112 Cal. 143, 44 P. 341 (1896).

See generally, ACIR, *City Financial Emergencies* (1973); 15 McQuillin, *Municipal Corporations* ch. 39 (3d rev.ed. 1970); J. Phillips, *Municipal Governments and Administration in America,* 436–461 (1960); Pennsylvania Economy League, *Philadelphia Government,* 302–316 (1963).

KRAHMER v. McCLAFFERTY
Superior Court of Delaware, 1972.
288 A.2d 678.

O'HARA, JUDGE. Plaintiff, a taxpayer of the City of Wilmington, has initiated this suit * * * to compel the defendants, members of The Council of the City of Wilmington ("Council"), to enact an annual operating budget ordinance in compliance with the Home Rule Charter of the City of Wilmington ("Charter"). Defendants have moved for judgment on the pleadings. * * *

The Charter, § 2–300, requires defendants to adopt, on or before May 31 of each year, an annual operating budget for the fiscal year beginning July 1 thereafter. § 2–300(2) specifically provides:

"* * * shall make appropriations to [specified branches of city government] * * * and for all other items which are to be met out of the revenue of the city. All appropriations shall be made in lump sum amounts and according to the following classes of expenditures for each office, department, board or commission: (a) personal services, (b) materials, supplies and equipment, (c) debt service, (d) such additional classes as the mayor shall recommend in his proposed annual budget ordinance."

In 1971 prior to the deadline Council passed an annual operating budget ordinance which, in addition to other items, provided for an appropriation of $310,564.00 for "materials, supplies and equipment". The complaint alleges that in actual fact defendants intended to spend only about $49,510.00 for materials, supplies and equipment and the balance was intended for other purposes.

The complaint further contends that the defendants, members of the majority party, proposed by this device to, in effect, hold back an appropriated fund which Council could from time to time during the fiscal year appropriate to other uses for the purposes of gaining partisan political advantage.

Prior to the passage of the budget ordinance, Council was advised by the City Solicitor that it was not empowered to create such a "contingency fund", it not having been recommended by the Mayor. Disregarding such advice, defendants proceeded to the enactment of the ordinance * * *. Subsequent thereto the Mayor vetoed the appropriation alloted for materials, supplies and equipment and returned the ordinance to Council with a message pointing out what the Mayor designated as the illegality of the action of Council. * * * Thereafter the defendants overrode the Mayor's veto and passed the ordinance, including the questioned item, by a two-thirds vote. * * *

The provisions of § 2–300(2) would seem to be a clear and unequivocal direction and authorization that Council had to make *all* its appropriations at once in the annual operating budget ordinance. This conclusion is reenforced by examination of § 2–301 which provides that "the Council may not make any operating appropriations in addition to those included in the annual operating budget ordinance (with specified exceptions not here applicable)".

The obligations imposed by § 2–300 are, generally speaking, mandatory and when violated may be enforced by mandamus. 15 McQuillin, Municipal Corporations (3rd Ed.1970); 55 C.J.S. Mandamus § 139. The defendants herein rely, however, upon the general rule that a court may not inquire into the legislative motives of a legislative body. * * * Defendants rely heavily upon the decision in Klaw v. Pau-Mar Construction Company, 11 Terry 487, 135 A.2d 123 (1957) and McQuail v. Shell Oil Company, 40 Del.Ch. 410, 183 A.2d 581 (1962). In both of these decisions, involving zoning questions, our Delaware Courts have indicated that they "will not inquire into the motives of members of a municipal legislative body in order to determine the validity of an ordinance enacted by them within the scope of their admitted powers".

Balanced against these decisions is that of Piekarski v. Smith, 38 Del.Ch. 402, 153 A.2d 587 (1959). In the *Piekarski* case the Wilmington City Council had passed a resolution which was attacked on grounds of fraud and bad faith and the Court had the following to say * * *:

> "The legal basis for the contention that the resolution was adopted 'in bad faith' is found in an exception to the general rule that courts will not inquire into the motives of or inducements to legislators that may influence them in the passage of acts or resolutions. * * * The exception is that the validity of municipal ordinances or resolutions may be attacked if fraud or bad faith is proved. This rule is recognized

in Delaware, although in none of the decided cases was any fraud or bad faith found."

The Court must here assume to be true plaintiff's contention that defendants were fully informed of the limitation of their Charter powers and deliberately set out to evade them and that in carrying out that evasion they deliberately enacted an ordinance that was not the truth. If either of these facts can be proved "fraud or bad faith" would be established.

Defendants, however, argue that "fraud or bad faith" means a conflict of interest, or that it can be shown only by an ordinance which is "void on its face" * * *.

* * * To thus limit the powers of the Court in dealing with human misconduct would be an artificial limitation on the general powers of the judiciary to cope with wrongful action on the part of public officials.

There are many instances wherein "bad faith" has been construed by the courts in terms other than "conflict of interest". * * *

* * *

The final argument of defendants is to the effect that plaintiff mistakenly relies upon the isolated language of § 2–300(2) requiring that Council must make all of its appropriations at once in the annual operating budget ordinance. Defendants argue that this narrow a restriction of Council's powers is not required by the language of subsection (2) and, in fact, is in conflict with the provisions of § 2–300(6) which reads as follows:

"The annual operating budget ordinance may be amended after its passage to authorize the transfer of items but the aggregate of the appropriations made by it may not be increased and transfer of budget items may not be made during the last four months of any fiscal year, except upon the recommendation of the mayor."

Defendants argue that subsection (6), by limiting Council's power to transfer budgetary items during the last four months of any fiscal year except upon the recommendation of the Mayor, is implicit recognition that Council has the power to make such transfers during the first eight months without such recommendation. The Court believes that defendants strain the language of subsection (6) to reach this conclusion. * * *

The Wilmington Charter is substantially copied from the Philadelphia Home Rule Charter, and the key provision of § 2–300 is identical in all material respects with the corresponding provision of the Philadelphia Charter. It is significant that in the annotations to the Philadelphia Home Rule Charter the following language is found with regard to the purpose of subsection (6):

"Subsection (6) is intended to serve as a check on the present practice of transferring items of the budget at the end of the fiscal year. Some agencies, finding at the end of the fiscal year that they have surplus funds left under certain items, have from time to time requested and received authorization from the Council for spending those surpluses for other purposes. This sub-section prohibits such transfers during the last four months of any fiscal year except upon the recommendation of the Mayor."

This Court believes that such definition of the purposes of subsection (6) is correct and that defendants' attempt to rely upon it to expand its otherwise restricted powers is incorrect.

* * *

For the reasons herein stated this Court concludes that the plaintiff has alleged a sufficient factual basis which, if established, would form the basis for the issuance of the Writ of Mandamus requested. Having reached this conclusion it follows that defendants' motion for a judgment on the pleadings must be denied.

It is so ordered.

Notes

1. **Amendment and Transfer of Budget Appropriations.** Statutory and charter authorization to effect budget amendments and appropriation transfers are commonplace. Such transfer may be made only from available current revenues. McVeigh v. Jackson, 335 Mich. 391, 56 N.W.2d 231 (1953). Should smaller units of local government be permitted to transfer appropriations with less formality and restriction than large cities? See Laux v. Harvey's Lake, 2 Pa.Cmwlth. 297, 276 A.2d 366 (1971). The tendency of courts to favor flexible redirection of funds by smaller government units is illustrated by Ashley v. Rye School District, 111 N.H. 54, 274 A.2d 795 (1971). After the budget was adopted, the school board passed a resolution to appropriate funds for a teacher's aide position, even though, by prior resolution, it had voted not to hire school aides. The court upheld the appropriation as falling within the original budget item entitled "for the support of schools."

2. **Inflated Appropriations and Taxation.** Recent taxpayer revolts have produced "cap" laws in some states which limit the total amount of each new annual budget to a small percentage increase over the last annual budget. Exceptions are made for emergencies and specially authorized expenditures. See e.g., N.J.Stat.Ann. 40A:4–45.3.

In the principal case, the plaintiffs faced a heavy burden of proving legislative fraud and bad faith. Were less onerous lines of attack open to them?

In People ex rel. Brenza v. Morrison Hotel Corp., 4 Ill.2d 542, 123 N.E.2d 488 (1955) a taxpayer attacked an appropriation, *inter alia,* as a device to levy excessive taxes and to accumulate unnecessary revenues. Regarding the excessiveness of appropriations, the court ruled: " * * * [L]evies which result in unnecessary accumulation of funds are invalid. The authority to levy a tax * * * is intended to provide for the needs of the ensuing year and not to provide a fund for possible future needs * * *. A tax levy in an amount largely in excess of the requirements * * * during the ensuing year is illegal and void. As to the case at bar, however, these general rules have been rendered inapplicable by * * * the Libraries Act * * * which expressly authorize the accumulation of funds for the purposes in question." Id. at 547–48, 123 N.E.2d at 492. See also People ex rel. Gill Co. v. Schiek, 368 Ill. 353, 14 N.E.2d 223 (1938).

3. **Tax Levies in Excess of Budget Estimates.** Under statute limiting tax levies and expenditures to amounts stated in the budget, the city council, *after* adoption of the budget, increased the estimate of needed taxes. The court held that it could not do so and that plaintiff could sue to restrain issuance of warrants for expenditures in excess of the original tax estimates. Clark v. Des Moines, 222 Iowa 317, 267 N.W. 97 (1936). Where actual expenses exceed budget estimates, may city council legislate additional "interim" taxes? Not if the tax enabling statute is strictly construed and the court finds no emergency. See Mastrangelo v. Buckley, 433 Pa. 352, 250 A.2d 447 (1969). Cf. Tate v. Antosh, p. 574, infra.

4. **Budget Impasses.** Where due to councilmanic indecision or stalemate, the local legislature fails to adopt a budget in accordance with law, special remedies must be provided to prevent a collapse of government. Where a water district failed to adopt a budget or appropriations resolution to cover its contract obligations, the court ruled that its certification for tax levies could not legalize contract payments. Fortunately, the state legislature covered that contingency by a special statute which provided that in the absence of proper budget appropriation, ninety percent of the amounts in the last appropriations ordinance for the purposes therein specified should be deemed appropriated for the uncovered year. Shannon Water and Sanitation District v. Norris & Sons Drilling Co., 29 Colo.App. 48, 477 P.2d 476 (1970).

"Where the Council fails or refuses to act on the proposed budget, * * *, the Mayor's budget becomes the operating budget, by operation of law. The City must have funds to operate and the failure or refusal of the Council to perform its charter obligation cannot be permitted to create a crisis." City and County of Denver v. Blue, 179 Colo. 351, 500 P.2d 970, 974 (1972).

Where the commissioners of a near insolvent borough could not agree on a budget, one county court ordered them to agree under threat of judicial removal from office. See Report, *"Pass Budget or Be Fired,"* The Philadelphia Sunday Bulletin, p. 1, 2/21/71.

DUFF v. SOUTHBRIDGE

Supreme Judicial Court of Massachusetts, 1950.
325 Mass. 224, 90 N.E.2d 12.

SPALDING, JUSTICE. This is an action of contract to recover for labor and materials furnished by the plaintiff to the defendant under a written contract. From a finding for the plaintiff the defendant appealed. * * *

* * *

Pertinent evidence agreed to by the parties includes the following: At the annual town meeting in 1940 of the town of Southbridge (hereinafter called the town) it was voted "That the town raise and appropriate the sum of five thousand ($5,000) dollars to rebuild that part of Elm Street known as Lebanon Road * * *, the same to be taken from the tax levy of 1940." On June 10, 1940, a contract was executed between the plaintiff and the defendant by the terms of which the plaintiff agreed to do certain work on the road in accordance with a schedule of prices set forth in the contract. The contract was validly executed, all conditions precedent to its execution having been complied with by both parties. * * * The plaintiff began work on the road in June, 1940, and at that time the town had not expended any of the appropriation. "As the work progressed, the plaintiff submitted bills which were approved by the engineer and the board of selectmen and for which the plaintiff received payment." These payments amounted to $3,871.88. When the plaintiff submitted bills in excess of the appropriation they were approved by the engineer, but the board of selectmen of the town did not approve them, "being in doubt as a matter of law, whether the plaintiff could recover more than $5,000." All of the work was performed under the direction of the engineer who at all times here material was an agent of the town. "It is agreed that the total bills submitted by the plaintiff were as follows: $6,758.89 for unit price items and $3,921.74 [sic] for extras, making a total of $9,680.83 [sic] of which the plaintiff has received $3,871.88." It is also agreed that the charges were proper and that "unless the plaintiff is precluded from recovering more than $5,000 as a matter of law, [he] is entitled to recover the whole amount set forth in his declaration," namely, $5,808.84 together with interest in the amount of $1,394.12 or a total of $7,202.96. The judge found for the plaintiff for the total amount of his claim.

General Laws (Ter.Ed.) c. 44 (the municipal finance act), § 31, provides that "No department of any city or town, except Boston, shall incur liability in excess of the appropriation made for the use of such department, except in cases of extreme emergency involving the health or safety of persons or property, and then only by a vote in a city of two thirds of the members of the city council, and in a town by a vote of two thirds of the selectmen." "One purpose of this statute was to set rigid barriers against expenditures in excess of appropriations." McCarthy v. Malden, 303 Mass. 563, 565, 22 N.E.2d 104, 107. As we said recently in construing a similar provision in the city charter of Boston, "Persons dealing with a municipality must take notice of limitations of this kind upon the contracting power of the municipality and are bound by them and cannot recover upon contracts attempted to be made in violation of them." [Citations omitted] In the case at bar the sum appropriated was $5,000. This set the outside limit of the town's liability to the plaintiff, and the judge erred in ordering judgment for an amount which exceeded that sum. * * * There was no extreme emergency here, and the plaintiff is not aided by the exception in § 31 which permits a municipality to incur liability in excess of the appropriation "in cases of extreme emergency involving the health or safety of persons or property." See, Safford v. Lowell, 255 Mass. 220, 225, 151

N.E. 111; Continental Construction Co. v. Lawrence, 297 Mass. 513, 514–515, 9 N.E.2d 550, 111 A.L.R. 699. But even if there were, the plaintiff's claim would still not come within that exception because it does not appear that the liability in excess of the appropriation was incurred by "a vote of two thirds of the selectmen" as required by § 31.

* * *

* * * The provisions of § 31 could not be circumvented by proof that the town had resources with which to pay the amount of the plaintiff's claim.

It is to be noted that the plaintiff has been paid only $3,871.88 whereas the amount of the appropriation was $5,000. On a retrial of the case the plaintiff would be entitled to recover the difference between these amounts less such sums as have been validly paid or incurred to persons having rights in the appropriation prior to those of the plaintiff. Consequently the evidence offered by the town showing what was paid or incurred to others would be admissible. But in determining the unexpended balance of the appropriation available to satisfy the town's liability to the plaintiff, the plaintiff is entitled to show the true state of the account and to have deducted only such sums as were paid or incurred in accordance with law. Anchor Steel Co. v. Granville, 318 Mass. 688, 691, 63 N.E.2d 564. Thus it would be open to the plaintiff to show that the payment of $560.72 to G.C. Winter Company for soil pipe used on the job was made under a contract which was entered into in violation of article VII of the town by-laws. * * * It is plain that the contract with the Winter Company was made in violation of the town by-law and was invalid. Burt v. Municipal Council of Taunton, 272 Mass. 130, 133–134, 172 N.E. 230. The payments made under it by the town, therefore, ought not to be included in the amounts chargeable against the appropriation. Anchor Steel Co. v. Granville, 318 Mass. 688, 691–692, 63 N.E.2d 564.

The case is remanded for further proceedings in conformity with this opinion.

Order denying motion to dismiss appeal affirmed.

Order for judgment reversed.

Notes

1. **Emergencies and Contingencies.** Apparently the Duff court was not willing to adopt a legislative declaration of "emergency." But see McCray v. Boulder, 165 Colo. 383, 439 P.2d 350 (1968) where the court, with great discomfort, upheld an exceptional appropriation as an emergency on the bare fact of a legislative declaration. Absent legislative guidelines, an emergency is what the court says it is. As the "emergency" concept may be abused, so may the use of "contingency" accounts. Should outside limits be placed by law on the use or amount of contingency appropriations?

2. **Unencumbered Surplus.** To the extent that general revenues exceed budget appropriations, should local government be empowered to make supplemental budget appropriations from the surplus? The law is

not uniform on this question. It is clear, however, that unencumbered surplus may not be expended unless covered by a lawful appropriation. Kingsley v. Denver, 126 Colo. 194, 247 P.2d 805 (1952).

Unencumbered surplus remaining at the end of a budget year is generally applied to the ensuing budget, and to the calculation of revenue estimates. See City of Tucson v. Tucson Sunshine Climate Club, 64 Ariz. 1, 164 P.2d 598 (1945).

TATE v. ANTOSH

Commonwealth Court of Pennsylvania, 1971.
3 Pa.Cmwlth. 144, 281 A.2d 192.

BOWMAN, PRESIDENT JUDGE. Although not so posed by the parties to these consolidated appeals, the fundamental issue is whether the judiciary—to enforce an admitted obligation of the City of Philadelphia to certain of its employees—may direct the legislative branch of the government of that city to appropriate funds to meet such obligations. Prior decisional law makes solution of the issue difficult. Compounding the difficulty is the impact, if any, of recent legislation on the subject of labor relations between public employees and their government employer.

The essential facts are not in dispute * * *. For the fiscal year July 1, 1970 to June 30, 1971, the City had appropriated $2,725,000 for disability payments to City employees who were or became eligible therefor as a result of service connected injury as prescribed by Civil Service Regulation 32.

In substance, this regulation provides that employees totally and permanently disabled shall receive full salary for three years; those permanently and partially disabled shall be placed in secondary positions and shall receive as supplemental pay the difference between the salary of the secondary position and that of their prior regular pay. * * *

On January 15, 1971, when it became apparent that budgeted funds for payment of Regulation 32 benefits would soon become exhausted, eligible city employees were so notified in writing by the city personnel director based upon advice given to him by the finance director. The letter concluded that no payments would be made after the fund was exhausted.

This advice precipitated the suits in question * * *.

After hearing, the lower court entered orders enjoining defendants from discontinuing payments to eligible employees and directing them to appropriate funds for the purpose of financing such payments. These appeals followed * * *.

Before the lower court and here, the City maintains a single position * * *.

Citing O'Donnell v. Philadelphia, 385 Pa. 189, 122 A.2d 690 (1956) and Baxter v. Philadelphia, 385 Pa. 424, 123 A.2d 634 (1956) as controlling, it argues that the exhaustion of the appropriated funds for these purposes bars judicial remedy.

O'Donnell involved a declaratory judgment proceeding by a labor union and several city employees as a class suit to recover wages for work performed in excess of 40 hours each week during the year 1952; their claim rested partly on an ordinance and partly on a labor agreement, both of which reduced the work week from 48 to 40 hours with provision for overtime payment. However, upon adoption of the Home Rule Charter effective January 7, 1952, the Civil Service Commission, acting under authority of the Charter, reinstated the hours of work as those in force during 1951. * * * After concluding that the particular plaintiffs were not parties to the labor agreement in question, the Court proceeded to state:

> "[T]here is another and conclusive reason why the order of the lower court must be affirmed, this reason being that Council never made any appropriation to provide for overtime pay on the basis of a 40-hour week in pursuance of either the agreement or the ordinance, except partially for the Union members employed in the Department of Public Works. That there can be no recovery against the city in the absence of such an appropriation is so fundamental and so well established as to preclude the necessity of discussion. * * * The Home Rule Charter contains numerous sections—for example, 6–104, 6–106, 6–400(a), and 8–200(3)—to like effect. As for the decisional law on the subject, case after case has laid down the same rule, which was called by Judge Thayer 'the palladium of Philadelphia taxpayers': * * *"

To overcome this formidable pronouncement supported by a host of precedent, appellees advance two independent arguments: (a) that the administration of justice and the public interest require a contrary result and (b) that the instant claims are based upon negotiated labor contracts under new statutory law which make the pronouncement of *O'Donnell* obsolete. They also emphasize that the claims in question are for *benefits* and not for *wages,* urging that this fact distinguishes the instant cases from *O'Donnell* and its predecessor decisions, all of which were concerned with wage claims or third party contract claims.

* * *

* * * Appellees say Commonwealth ex rel. Carroll v. Tate, 442 Pa. 45, 274 A.2d 193 (1971) supports judicial enforcement of appellees' rights under such circumstances.

In our opinion, *Carroll* cannot be so extended. It declared that the judiciary as a co-equal and independent branch of government possesses the power to compel the executive and legislative branches of government to provide the reasonably necessary funds for the functioning and administration of the judicial branch. * * * While police officials particularly are certainly involved in and essential to the enforcement of the law, they are not of the judicial system in the "administration of justice". * * *

Although we cannot accept appellees' first argument, we are persuaded by their second argument that the circumstances of these cases render the *O'Donnell* holding inapplicable.

In these appeals we are confronted with the question of whether the City of Philadelphia may avoid payment of Regulation 32 benefits which it agreed to pay to its employees by mere failure of its legislative branch, the City Council, to appropriate sufficient funds to cover its liabilities under the regulation for fiscal 1970–71. Clearly we are dealing with a "bargained for" benefit * * * and we must examine the origin and nature of the employer-employee agreements creating these benefits and the resulting legally enforceable duty of the City of Philadelphia to provide such benefits.

I

As the Pennsylvania Constitution of 1968 recognizes and makes special provisions germane to collective bargaining and settlement of labor disputes between policemen and firemen and their government employer not accorded to other public employees, all of the appellees in these consolidated appeals cannot be lumped together in resolving the issue * * *. Therefore, we shall first examine the position of the uniformed employees under relevant constitutional and statutory provisions and then proceed to the non-uniformed employees' claims.

The Act of June 24, 1968, P.L.—, Act No. 111, 43 P.S. § 217.1 et seq. extends to policemen and firemen throughout the Commonwealth the right to bargain collectively with their government employer. This act implements Article III, Section 31 of the Pennsylvania Constitution of 1968, P.S., which generally prohibits the delegation of legislative power. As amended in 1968, however, it further provides:

> "Notwithstanding the foregoing limitation or any other provision of the Constitution, the General Assembly may enact laws which provide that the findings of panels or commissions, selected and acting in accordance with law for the adjustment or settlement of grievances or disputes or for collective bargaining between policemen and firemen and their public employers shall be binding upon all parties and shall constitute a mandate to the head of the political subdivision which is the employer * * *." Section 7 of the Act of 1968, *supra*, 43 P.S. § 217.7 contains identical language.

Thus, all political subdivisions of the Commonwealth are constitutionally and statutorily mandated to put into effect, to the extent possible under their delegated authority, an award of an arbitration panel. As long as a political subdivision may legally perform a duty mandated by such award, it must perform such duty.

The powers of the City of Philadelphia are contained in its Home Rule Charter. This Charter was enacted pursuant to the enabling legislation * * * contained in the Act of April 21, 1949, P.L. 665, 53 P.S. § 13101 *et seq.* * * *

However, Section 18 of the same act provides:

"Notwithstanding the grant of powers contained in this act, no city shall exercise powers contrary to, or in limitation or enlargement of, powers granted by acts of the General Assembly which are—

* * *

"(b) Applicable in every part of the Commonwealth.

"(c) Applicable to all the cities of the Commonwealth." 53 P.S. § 13133.

The grievance procedures set forth in Article III, Section 31 of the Pennsylvania Constitution and the 1968 implementing legislation are within the ambit of Section 18 of the 1949 enabling act. Therefore, the City of Philadelphia may not act in derogation of any of the rights guaranteed to policemen and firemen by the Constitution and its implementing legislation applicable to all political subdivisions of the Commonwealth.

* * *

Simply because City Council refuses to appropriate sufficient funds to effectuate payment, the City as a public employer is not relieved of its duty to follow the mandate of the arbitration panel. The appropriation of funds does not involve the performance of any illegal act on the part of the City. * * *

In the Washington Arbitration Case, 436 Pa. 168, 177, 259 A.2d 437, 442 (1969), our Supreme Court has stated:

"The essence of our decision is that an arbitration award may only require a public employer to do that which it could do voluntarily. We emphasize that this does not mean that a public employer may hide behind self-imposed legal restrictions. An arbitration award which deals only with proper terms and conditions of employment serves as a mandate to the legislative branch of the public employer, and if the terms of the award require affirmative action on the part of the Legislature, they must take such action, if it is within their power to do so."

* * * In the instant case, the City of Philadelphia is specifically vested with the power to make emergency appropriations to perform a legal duty. The issue of what additional duties would be imposed upon the City government by a judicial order directing the appropriation of requisite funds is not before this Court. We note, however, that our Supreme Court has spoken by way of dicta that the powers of the courts are broad enough to require a local government to raise taxes to provide the funds necessary for complete performance under the directives of an arbitration award benefiting policemen and firemen.

"Furthermore, if we do hear a case in which the tax millage, as a matter of record, cannot permissibly be raised so as to provide sufficient funds to pay the required benefits to the employees, it will still be open to this Court to rule that the Act of June 24, 1968 impliedly authorizes a court-approved millage ceiling increase to pay the arbitration award where necessary, or to hold that the municipal budget must be adjusted in other places in order to provide resources for police-

men's or firemen's salaries."   Harney v. Russo, 435 Pa. 183, 193, 255
A.2d 560, 565 (1969).

II

The non-uniformed employees of the City of Philadelphia, * * *
are protected by no constitutional provision comparable to Article III,
Section 31. The rights and duties of these employees and their public
employer are contained in a collective bargaining agreement which
became effective on February 20, 1968. * * *

Two provisions of the negotiated agreement are essential to a full
examination of appellees' rights. A section entitled "Service Incurred
Disability" specifically includes the benefit provisions for permanent
and total disability and permanent and partial disability contained in
Regulation 32.

The second provision of the labor agreement which affects the
rights and duties here contested is the "Savings Clause".

> "In the event that any provisions are found to be inconsistent with,
> altered or conditioned by provisions of the Civil Service Regulations,
> the *Home Rule Charter* or other statutes, then the provisions of such
> Regulations, Charter or other statutes shall prevail." [Emphasis sup-
> plied.]

The non-uniformed employees have on the one hand acquired a
legally enforceable contract right against the City in terms of specific
disability benefits. On the other hand, the enforcement of such benefits may not necessitate illegal or unauthorized action on the part of the
City.

The Home Rule Charter is explicit in its prohibition of any payment of City funds due under an otherwise legal contract absent a
previous appropriation for the purpose. Section 8–200(3), Philadelphia
Home Rule Charter. * * *

The enforceability of contract rights for wages by public employees
has been proscribed by the *O'Donnell* and *Baxter* decisions cited above.
However, we are of the considered opinion that both the logic and the
underlying rationale of those decisions are clearly inappropriate to the
instant facts and circumstances.

We are not here concerned with the payment of wages to public
employees under a contract for which no appropriation has been made
as was the case in *O'Donnell.* "Bargained for" benefits are the subject
of this controversy which must represent a continuing obligation of the
City even though such obligation is not susceptible to exact calculation
and projection for any fiscal period. The emergency appropriation
provision of the Home Rule Charter contemplates and provides for a
method of funding unforeseen financial contingencies. No City employee can be expected to undertake the colossal task of examining a
proposed city budget cast only in general terms and lump-sum appropriations to assure himself that there will be sufficient funds to pay his
potential disability benefits. He is not an individual making a contract

with the City for his unique services but rather a part of a large and complex collective bargaining process which renders former case law on the subject of public employee labor contracts inapposite, at least as to benefits of the kind with which we are here concerned.

* * *

We thus conclude that the City of Philadelphia has a judicially enforceable duty to its uniformed and non-uniformed employees to pay to those employees the Regulation 32 disability benefits to which they became entitled during the fiscal year 1970–1971, * * * and that it must appropriate sufficient funds to perform this duty notwithstanding the exhaustion of the appropriation for such purpose in its 1970–1971 budget. However, until such an appropriation is made by the legislative branch of the government of the City of Philadelphia, there was and is no duty upon its executive officers, named as defendants in these suits, to continue payment of disability benefits upon exhaustion of the funds appropriated therefor. To compel them to do so would require them to perform an illegal act. We must, therefore, reverse the various orders of the lower court directing continuation of payment of such benefits by the named defendants absent funds appropriated for this purpose.

The orders of the lower court are otherwise affirmed.

Notes

1. **Mandatory and Nonmandatory Appropriations.** The Carroll case, cited in the principal opinion, mandated the city to appropriate additional funds for the operation of courts. Was it based on "emergency" or did the court violate separation of powers by overriding legislative discretion?

If, on remand of the principal case, city council refused to enact additional taxes to fund the mandated appropriations for disability benefits, should the court then mandamus the city to enact new taxes? Cf. the Mastrangelo case, note 3, p. — supra. The subject is covered in Annot., 59 A.L.R.3d 569 (1974).

2. **Appropriations and Salary Determinations.** Does an excessive budget appropriation (of $13,000) for annual salary of the city manager effect a raise in his past salary of $11,000 per year? See Councillors of Brockton v. Gildea, 343 Mass. 631, 180 N.E.2d 77 (1962). Under the laws governing some municipalities, the positions and salary rates in city employment, as fixed by adopted budget appropriations, may not be changed during the budget year, except by a formal supplement budget, and by appropriations amendment. Allen v. Cambridge, 316 Mass. 351, 55 N.E.2d 925 (1944); cf. Duff v. Southridge, reported at p. 571. Should an authorized initiative resolution by the electorate, to raise city employees' salaries retroactively supersede lower salary budget appropriations previously enacted by city council? See City of Las Vegas v. Ackerman, 85 Nev. 493, 457 P.2d 525 (1969).

3. **Appropriations Limitations.** See also Kingsley v. City and County of Denver, 126 Colo. 194, 247 P.2d 805 (1952).

May a city lawfully make a contract not covered by the existing appropriations, on the express agreement that it will be paid only if and when the expenditure is authorized by appropriations in the next budget period? Compare Butler v. Hatfield, 277 Minn. 314, 152 N.W.2d 484 (1967) (held—yes), with State ex rel. Point Towing Co. v. McDonough, 150 W.Va. 724, 149 S.E.2d 302 (1966) (held—no). See Comment, 52 Minn.L.Rev. 892 (1968).

FLORA CRANE SERVICE, INC. v. ROSS

Supreme Court of California, 1964.
61 Cal.2d 199, 37 Cal.Rptr. 425, 390 P.2d 193.

SCHAUER, JUSTICE. Plaintiff appeals from a judgment denying a peremptory writ of mandate * * * to compel various officers of the City and County of San Francisco (hereinafter called "the city") to take the steps set forth in the city charter to certify the availability of funds for payment under a contract for the performance of public improvements.

The dispositive issue is whether at the time mandate was sought the defendant city controller was under a clear ministerial duty to make such certification. For the reasons hereinafter delineated we have concluded that the controller was under such a duty; that he had no lawful excuse for refusing to perform it; and hence that the judgment should be reversed.

The matter was submitted * * * upon the pleadings alone, * * *. Our knowledge of the facts is therefore limited to such pleadings and exhibits.

On August 10, 1959, the defendant director of property of the city caused to be published a call for bids for the razing of five city-owned buildings * * *. The call for bids declared, inter alia, that "The award of contract will be made subject to certification by the City's Controller * * *."

Plaintiff * * * submitted its bid for $4,920, together with the required deposit check in the amount of $1,000. On September 21, 1959, a notice was published declaring that on September 14 the department of public works had approved an "award of contract" by the director of property to plaintiff, "said Company being the lowest regular and responsible bidder therefor in response to a published call for sealed bids * * *."

On October 19, 1959, a written form of contract embodying this agreement and prepared by the city was signed by plaintiff, and by the director of property on behalf of the city, and approved by the director of public works and the chief administrative officer and, as to form, by the city attorney. The contract provided, inter alia, that it "is made subject to the following terms and conditions:

"(1) Said work shall be commenced by the Company within ten calendar days after being notified by the Director of Property that the City's Controller has certified this contract, * * *."

No such certification by defendant controller was made, however, and no notification, either of certification or noncertification, was given to plaintiff by the director of property. Plaintiff nevertheless * * * began the work * * * and completed the same on May 16, 1960. There is no contention that the work was unsatisfactory.

A "Request for Allotment and Certification of [the subject] Contract" was first presented to the controller on July 6, 1960. * * * On July 13, 1960, the controller determined and so informed the director of property that he was "unable to certify [the subject contract] as to funds because of nonconformance with the provisions of Section 86 of the Charter of the City and County of San Francisco."

It is admitted in the pleadings that at the time of the award of contract there were sufficient unencumbered funds to the credit of a valid appropriation to pay the whole amount of $4,920; and that at the time of filing the application for mandate unencumbered funds in the amount of $2,988.51 remained to the credit of such appropriation and sufficient other monies were available for transfer from surplus or reserve funds to make up the total of $4,920.

* * *

* * * The dispositive issue, therefore, is whether at the time mandate was sought defendant controller was under a clear ministerial duty to certify the existence of available funds for the purpose of paying plaintiff under the subject contract. It is not denied that if the controller was under such a duty, then his co-defendants were under consequential—and equally compellable—duties to perform the remaining official acts prayed for in this proceeding.

The general powers and duties of the controller are set forth in sections 64 to 68 of the city charter, * * *. More specifically relevant here are the provisions of the second paragraph of charter section 86 (*ante*, fn. 2), declaring that no obligation involving the expenditure of money shall be incurred or authorized by any city officer or board "unless the controller first certify that there is a valid appropriation from which the expenditure may be made, and that sufficient unencumbered funds are available in the treasury to the credit of such appropriation to pay the amount of such expenditure when it becomes due and payable." * * * That duty, moreover, is a ministerial one, for the controller is required only to determine *as a matter of fact* whether "there is" such an appropriation and whether such funds "are available" in the treasury. A determination of this nature "is a matter of mere calculation requiring no exercise of discretion" (Balding v. Eich (1932) 120 Cal.App. 491, 496[2], 7 P.2d 1073). * * *

* * *

The same conclusion has consistently been reached in our sister jurisdictions, where it is held that a city auditor or controller may be compelled by mandate to certify that sufficient unencumbered funds have been appropriated to pay the claimant under a contract with the municipal body. (See, *e.g.,* State ex rel. Board of Education v. D'Aulisa (1947) 133 Conn. 414, 52 A.2d 636, 639[3]; People ex rel. P.J. Carlin Const. Co. v. Prendergast (1917) 99 Misc. 8, 163 N.Y.Supp. 583, 585[1]; F.W. Mark Const. Co. v. Hadley (1927) 290 Pa. 544, 139 A. 157, 158–159; *cf.* State ex rel. Benz v. District Court (1884) 32 Minn. 181, 19 N.W. 732, 734.)

* * * Here the reason given by defendant controller for refusing to make the requested certification was "non-conformance with the provisions of Section 86" of the charter. In support of that position it is stressed that section 86 requires the controller to "first certify" the existence of the necessary funds before an obligation of the city "shall be incurred or authorized"; that here the controller did not do so because the contract papers were not presented to him until after the work was done; and that his refusal to certify at the latter date was justified by the final paragraph of section 86, which declares that "All obligations incurred * * * contrary to the provisions of this section, shall be void, and any claim or demand against the city and county based thereon shall be invalid." Defendants rely on the many decisions holding that "the mode of contracting as prescribed by the municipal charter, is the measure of the power to contract; and a contract made in disregard of the prescribed mode is unenforceable" * * *

Defendants' argument, however, misses the point; and the decisions and principles relied on, though well settled in our law, are irrelevant to the case at bench. In each of those decisions a purported contract with a municipal body was entered into in disregard of one or more charter provisions relating to the mode of contracting (*e.g.,* requirement of competitive bidding), and the contractor thereafter sought to recover against the city *on that contract.* Here, to the contrary, plaintiff is not suing on contract, but rather is seeking by writ of mandate to compel the defendant controller to perform a ministerial duty which is a prerequisite to the validity of the contract itself. * * *

It is contended, however, that plaintiff has no remedy because at the time the request for certification was made (and *a fortiori* at the time the application for mandate was filed) it was too late for the controller to "first certify" the availability of the necessary funds to pay plaintiff on the subject contract. It is argued that the obligation in question had already been "incurred" and hence that by the very terms of section 86 the controller was no longer under a compellable duty to certify.

The city may not so easily profit by its own inaction. * * *

As plaintiff correctly contends, that duty arose without the need for a specific request therefor by plaintiff; *i.e.,* the controller had an affirmative duty to act in this regard, and cannot now excuse his nonperformance by saying that plaintiff did not make a timely request for certification. While such duty to act is not expressly set forth in the charter, it appears by analogy in the affirmative duty of the controller, imposed by section 85, to audit and process all claims against the city. It appears also by operation of the basic principle that "All things that in law or usage are considered as incidental to a contract, or *as necessary to carry it into effect,* are implied therefrom * * *." (Italics added.) (Civ.Code, § 1656.) Under that principle the "award of contract" to plaintiff may be deemed to have included an implied covenant by the city to take whatever steps were required to "carry it into effect," and in particular a covenant to submit the matter to the controller for his determination under section 86.

Moreover, the exhibits in the record before us (relevant portions of which are quoted hereinabove) clearly indicate that it is the city's practice to place this duty to act upon the controller rather than the individual contractor. * * * As quoted at the outset, the formal contract in the case at bench expressly recites that plaintiff was to begin work thereunder within ten days "after being notified by the Director of Property that the City's Controller has certified this contract * * *." The clear implication of this language is that in due course the city will submit the contract to the controller for action under charter section 86, and plaintiff will be "notified" of the latter's determination. Bearing out this interpretation is the fact that in the present case the controller's notice of refusal to certify is in the form of an interdepartmental memorandum addressed not to plaintiff but to the director of property. Indeed, it would be absurd to assume that a timely demand by plaintiff was a necessary prerequisite to submission of the matter to the controller for certification while all the other steps in the same contracting process * * * were performable without any request whatever on plaintiff's part.

To summarize, in the present case the charter requirements relating to competitive bidding were, as they must be, strictly followed; an award of contract was made to plaintiff as the lowest responsible bidder; at that time there was a valid appropriation from which such an expenditure could legally have been made and there were sufficient unencumbered funds standing to the credit of that appropriation to pay plaintiff on the subject contract. In such circumstances the controller was under a clear ministerial duty compellable by mandate to make his certification pursuant to section 86 of the charter, and the unexplained delay in submitting the contract to him for that purpose is chargeable to the city and does not justify the controller's refusal to perform such duty. To permit the city to prevail in the circumstances established here would reward it for its own neglect.

Nor does this conclusion open the door to fraudulent imposition of contractual liabilities on the city, by defeating or in any way impairing the operation of charter section 86. Insofar as here relevant, that provision is a measure of fiscal control designed principally to protect the city and its taxpayers from incurrence of liabilities in excess of specifically appropriated and encumbered funds in the treasury. Ordinarily, of course, the controller will fulfill his duty and the certification will be timely made. In the rare event, as in this case, that the contractor nevertheless performs the work before receiving formal notice of the certification, he does so at his peril, *i.e.,* at the risk that when certification is thereafter sought there may no longer be sufficient unencumbered funds available to the credit of a valid appropriation from which to pay such expenditure; in that case the city will be placed under no contractual liability for the work performed, since mandate does not lie to compel a public officer to authorize expenditures when the proper funds are lacking. [Citations omitted] Here, however, such funds were admittedly available, and the controller had no lawful reason to refuse to so certify.

For the reasons stated the judgment is reversed.

EDWARDS v. RENTON

Supreme Court of Washington, 1965.
67 Wash.2d 598, 409 P.2d 153.

HAMILTON, JUDGE.

[Held that where city had entered into an *ultra vires* agreement with shopping center owners, to reimburse owners for installation of traffic control signal, in violation of budget and bid statutes, and where the city accepted traffic signal as installed, the shopping center owners were entitled to recover the reasonable value of the signal in absence of any evidence of bad faith, fraud, or collusion.]

* * *

* * * Funds, however, had not been appropriated in the 1960 city budget for the installation of such a signal * * *. The cost of the signal and its installation was $18,200, * * *. The installation was accepted by the city and integrated into its over-all traffic control system.

No bids for the design, manufacture, and installation of the signal were called for.

The city council, in making up the city's 1961 budget, appropriated funds for the purpose of reimbursing plaintiffs. A question thereafter arose as to the propriety of the contemplated reimbursement. When plaintiffs demanded repayment, the city refused and this suit followed.

The trial court concluded that the failure to call for bids and the failure to budget funds for the installation of the signal during 1960, the year the obligation was incurred, contravened RCW 35.23.352 and RCW 35.33.120, respectively, and rendered any agreement by the city to reimburse plaintiffs invalid and unenforceable. The trial court futher concluded that, since the city had accepted the traffic signal and derived and retained the traffic control benefits thereof, plaintiffs were, upon equitable principles, entitled to recover the reasonable value of the benefits flowing to the city from the improvement. * * *

* * *

Stripped to the bare bones, the transaction between plaintiffs and the City of Renton amounted to a borrowing of funds by the city for the installation of an improvement for which moneys had not been regularly appropriated.

Municipal corporations do not possess inherent power to borrow money. Authority to do so must be found in appropriate legislative provisions. * * * Though the purpose for which the funds were to be expended can be characterized as infra vires, the manner in which the funds were obtained was ultra vires, and the purported repayment agreement was accordingly void.

Even if the foregoing were not true, it can hardly be gainsaid that the "financial arrangement" here undertaken contravenes the purpose, intent and spirit of the pertinent municipal budget and bid statutes.

The purposes, generally, of statutory municipal budgeting requirements are to inculcate sound business principles and practices into the municipal economy, with particular reference to avoidance of waste, extravagance, and ill-considered expenditures, and to give the members of the tax paying public a better understanding of the financial affairs of the municipality and the anticipated disposition of public moneys. 15 McQuillin, Municipal Corporations § 39.39, at 125 (3d ed. 1950); 2 Antieau, Municipal Corporation Law § 15.31, at 453 (1965).

And, the objects of statutory bidding requirements in connection with the letting of municipal contracts are to prevent fraud, collusion, favoritism, and improvidence in the administration of public business, as well as to insure that the municipality receives the best work or supplies at the most reasonable prices practicable. 10 McQuillin, Municipal Corporations § 29.29 (3d ed. 1950); 1 Antieau, Municipal Corporation Law § 10.11, at 688 (1965).

It should be axiomatic that plans, schemes, or devices which thwart or circumvent the wholesome objects and purposes of such statutory provisions are invalid.

We turn now to the second issue presented by this appeal, that is, the extent, if any, of plaintiffs' right to recover the moneys or benefits advanced. A solution to this issue is complicated by the fact that, though the city had power to otherwise lawfully contract for the installation of the traffic signal, the particular financial arrangement with plaintiffs was ultra vires * * *. Thus, any recovery allowed plaintiffs cannot rest on the void and unenforceable contract; it must rest, if at all, upon a theory of quasi-contract or unjust enrichment.

There is some division and conflict of authority on the question of whether and when a recovery may be had against a municipality for money, goods, or services furnished to and retained by a municipality under an ultra vires contract. The greater weight of authority would appear to deny recovery, particularly where the contract involved is clearly beyond the scope of the municipal powers, is prohibited by constitutional or statutory provisions, or is contrary to public policy [citations omitted]. There is, however, respectable authority * * * which permit a recovery where the public improvement furnished to and retained by the municipality is within the scope of its authority to provide, although the contract by which the benefit was supplied is ultra vires yet not *malum in se, malum prohibitum,* or manifestly violative of public policy.

A review of our own cases satisfies us that we fall into the latter category. In Abrams v. City of Seattle, 173 Wash. 495, 23 P.2d 869 (1933), an action brought to enjoin the City of Seattle from making certain payments in favor of private entrepreneurs who had advanced money, labor, and material for the construction of an electrical substation on city owned property under an ultra vires lease arrangement, we expressed our view as follows, at 500, 23 P.2d at 871:

> "Conceding that the lease was void, still the municipality may not escape payment of the reasonable value of what it actually received as a result of the enterprise of the lessee. It did have the power to erect a substation on the property. It could have let a contract for that purpose which would have been valid and binding. Had it done so, even though such contract had been void for want of regularity in any particular (such as failing to advertise for bids), still the city would have been required to pay the reasonable value of the building, although no recovery could have been had on the contract. Green v. Okanogan County, 60 Wash. 309, 111 P. 226, 114 P. 457; Mallory v. Olympia, 83 Wash. 499, 145 P. 627, 629. In the latter case the court says:
>
> " * * *
>
> "This court has endeavored to hold municipalities to the same standard of right and wrong that the law imposes upon individuals. [Citations omitted] In Green v. Okanogan County, 60 Wash. 309, 111 P. 226, 114 P. 457, it was sought to enjoin the execution of a contract on the ground that it had not been let in accordance with the requirements of the statute. The court found that the controlling statutes were, in fact, violated and that the contract was void. * * * Yet, notwithstanding, we said:
>
> " 'This court has adopted the more equitable doctrine of allowing the parties, where the contract, if entered into in conformity with the statutes, would not have been unlawful, to retain from the moneys received by them a sum equivalent to the reasonable value of the property the county acquires and retains in virtue of the execution of the void contract. * * * So in this case, since the county has accepted and made use of the bridge, it is liable to the builders for its reasonable value.' "

* * *

In the instant case, the City of Renton could have, by appropriate action, lawfully and regularly installed the traffic control device, albeit not as expeditiously as it was installed under the arrangement with plaintiffs. * * * On the other hand, plaintiffs can hardly be characterized as innocent victims * * *, for it is commonly recognized that one dealing with a municipality is chargeable with knowledge of the extent of the municipality's authority. Be this as it may, however, the traffic signal has in fact been installed; it has been accepted by the city and integrated into its traffic control system; the traffic safety factors inherent in the control of the complex intersection involved have redounded to the benefit of the motoring public; and the city council has, by including an appropriate item in the 1961 budget, indicated the city's willingness to reimburse plaintiffs to the extent lawfully authorized. Aside from the fact that plaintiffs were desirous of having the traffic signal installed in time for the opening of their shopping center, we find no evidence of bad faith, fraud, or collusion involved in the transaction, and the trial court found none.

Under the circumstances outlined, we are satisfied that the approach adopted in the Abrams case, *supra*, is apropos. By this approach, plaintiffs would be entitled to recover from the City of Renton the reasonable value of the traffic signal, as opposed to the trial court's determination that their recovery should be limited to the reasonable value of the traffic control benefits which the trial court conceived to have been derived by the city from the installation.

In so holding, we recognize, as heretofore indicated, that there is ample authority from other jurisdictions which would deny any recovery to plaintiffs under the circumstances here outlined, *e.g.,* Town of Worland v. Odell & Johnson, 79 Wyo. 1, 329 P.2d 797 (1958); and that still other jurisdictions would limit any recovery to the value of the actual benefit conferred, as distinguished from the reasonable value of the improvement supplied, *e.g.,* Luther v. Wheeler, 73 S.C. 83, 52 S.E. 874, 4 L.R.A.,N.S., 746 (1905). In applying the approach of the Abrams case, *supra*, to the instant case, we do so with the understanding that the transaction involved is devoid of any bad faith, fraud, or collusion and that "financial arrangements" such as here evidenced are not usually indulged in by political subdivisions of the state. Should the contrary ever appear, it could well be that the dictates of public policy would require a more stringent approach.

* * *

The judgment of the trial court limiting plaintiffs' recovery to the value of benefits is reversed. The cause is remanded to the trial court for the introduction of such further evidence * * * upon the issue of the reasonable value of the traffic signal and its installation as of March, 1960. * * *

* * *

Notes

1. **Equitable Relief.** According to Edwards, how many standards of quasi-contractual recovery are to be found among the states? The availability of equitable relief turns largely on judicial discretion, as influenced by the subject matter of the transaction (i.e. borrowing, construction,

services or supplies); by the stage of completion of work or the extent of its receipt and use at the time of suit; and by the degree of fault on the part of the contractor and the local government. See related notes at pp. 699 n. 3, 705 n. 1; Antieau, *Municipal Corporation Law* §§ 10:01–10:08 (1972); Annot., 33 A.L.R.3d 397, 1164 (1970).

B. REVENUE

The revenue raising position of local governments is dependent upon state and federal law. As of 1982 the federal government collected almost 84% of all personal and corporate income taxes, and almost 60% of all per capita tax revenue, while the state governments collected about 86% of all income and sales taxes levied at the state and local levels. See *1985 Statistical Abstract of the United States*, p. 264. The 82,300 local taxing jurisdictions rely upon state and federal assistance, as well as local sources of revenue. State and federal assistance now accounts for almost two-thirds of total local government revenues.

While the contributions of states to their local governments are substantial, the bulk of state funds are channelled to special functions, primarily education, welfare and highway uses.

Combined state and local expenditures almost doubled between 1975 and 1982. Although their revenues also increased, long-term borrowing and debt skyrocketed in that period from 220 billion to 399 billion dollars. *1985 Statistical Abstract*, p. 261.

The taxing base of local government, in relation to the tax sources of federal and state governments, is described in the following data.

FIGURE 5

Tax Revenue, by Source and Level of Government for 1976

[in millions of dollars]

All Government

Type of Tax	Total	Federal	State	Local
Individual Income	348,896	298,111	45,708	5,078
Corporation Income	64,240	49,207	14,006	1,027
Sales and gross receipts	148,228	54,592	78,800	14,836
Property	81,918	—	3,113	78,805

Source: *1985 Statistical Abstract of the United States* (U.S. Bureau of the Census) Table No. 439, p. 265.

The property tax remains the dominant source of local government tax revenue, (with the exception of special districts other than school districts) although local property taxes have declined, relative to total revenues, by about 10% between 1972 and 1982. 1982 Census of Governments, Vol. 4 Government Finances (U.S. Bureau of the Census).

While state governments have withdrawn from property taxation, local governments rely on it. Having yielded the bulk of property tax revenues to their subdivisions, state governments place increasing reliance upon income and sales taxes, but those nonproperty taxes are also being increasingly employed by local governments.

As of 1981, general sales taxes constituted the most remunerative nonproperty local tax, and accounted for about 48% of municipal tax revenues. See Table 5 of *1982 Census of Governments,* (Vol. 4, Government Finances). Local sales taxes have been adopted in a majority of states, and "More than half, 26, of the nation's 48 largest cities used the local sales tax in 1972." ACIR, Local Revenue Diversification pp. 31, 32, 34 (1974).

While local income taxes are not as prevalent as sales taxes, their growing use is impressive. See Table IV–1 of ACIR, Loc.Rev.Diversification, supra, p. 53.

1. PROPERTY TAXATION

Property taxes remain the largest, and most unpopular, local taxes in the nation. The property tax imposes a fixed charge upon property, irrespective of its use or value to its particular owner, and weighs heavily upon low income and elderly taxpayers.* Except in periods of unusual inflation, property taxes rise faster than property values, making it one of the most regressive forms of taxation. Finally, property tax laws are subject to abusive and discriminatory administration.

"A somewhat exclusive characteristic of property tax administration is that few officials feel under no obligation to enforce the tax law as written. In some States, in fact, compliance by the assessors with the constitution and statutes would be a cause for general consternation. The average assessor makes himself a sort of one-man legislature. He—not the State constitution and the State legislature—defines local taxing and borrowing power and determines the value of a veterans' or homestead tax exemption by the level at which he decides to assess property. He is likely, also, to administer his own version of the personal property tax. * * *

* * *

" * * * Underassessment exists when assessors assess property at levels below that legally required by constitution or statute, * * * As further complications, the degree of underassessment usually varies widely among the local assessment districts within a State and the basis used by the State agency for assessing centrally assessed property may be different from some or all of the local bases.

"Despite this anarchic condition, assessed valuation is used by the States as a base for numerous important regulatory purposes, including those limiting the taxing and borrowing powers of local governments and determining the amounts of tax exemption for veterans,

---

* Some 30 states have enacted or authorized "circuit breaker" legislation to provide property tax relief when it reaches a designated percentage of the taxpayer's income. See Significant Features of Fiscal Federalism—1985–86 (U.S. Advisory Comm'n on Intergovernmental Relations) p. 109.

homestead owners, etc. * * * Assessed valuation also has been used widely as a base for the distribution of State school aid and * * * to compensate for inter-community differences in fiscal ability. With this policy stultified by interarea variations in the extent of underassessment, the States have been turning to various methods of interarea equalization of assessment levels. * * *

* * *

"The States have long had a propensity, which is continuing, to fritter away the property tax base by concealed subsidies in the form of special tax exemptions to promote private causes of questionable public importance, provide welfare aid, advance undertakings for social and economic reform, and reward public service. Typically these special tax exemptions are mandatory upon local taxing jurisdictions; they have to be honored by them, regardless of their revenue cost or the preference of the particular community. * * *

* * *

"In many States the hierarchy of administrative and judicial review and appeal agencies for the protection of the property tax payers is elaborate; but actual protection * * * is illusory because, first, the tribunals to which the taxpayer must appeal are not well constituted and staffed for the purpose and second, the burden of proving his case is too onerous and costly. The small taxpayer, in particular, is helpless if he has no simple, inexpensive, and dependable recourse. * * * " ACIR, *The Role of the States in Strengthening the Property Tax,* Vol. 1, pp. 4, 9–11, 24 (1963).

County boards of tax equalization and revision do not, despite their titles, equalize tax assessments in all respects. In some instances local assessments are revised only for purposes of levying county taxes, or for purposes of determining allotment of state funds that are distributed on the basis of property valuation throughout the state, or for the purpose of determining local debt ceilings, or to establish the rates of other forms of taxation. See e.g., Welch: *A New Multiple-Purpose Equalization Program,* 1949 National Tax Association Procs. 260.

Property tax reform is most dramatically seen in laws which place a cap on allowable taxes, but new laws to require more equitable standards and procedures for property tax administration are equally significant. A summary of these state-by-state developments is compiled in ACIR, The Property Tax In The Changing Environment (1974).

AMADOR VALLEY JOINT UNION HIGH SCHOOL DIST. v. STATE BD. OF EQUALIZATION

Supreme Court of California, 1978.
22 Cal.3d 208, 149 Cal.Rptr. 239, 583 P.2d 1281.

RICHARDSON, JUSTICE.

In these consolidated cases, we consider multiple constitutional challenges to an initiative measure which was adopted by the voters of this state at the June 1978 primary election. This measure, designated on the ballot as Proposition 13 and commonly known as the Jarvis-Gann initiative, added article XIII A to the California Constitution. * * * As will be seen, the new article changes the previous system of real property taxation and tax procedure by imposing important limitations upon the assessment and taxing powers of state and local governments.

Petitioners, * * * are various governmental agencies and concerned citizens, each of whom has alleged actual or potential adverse effects resulting from the adoption and ultimate operation of the article. * * * The issues herein presented are of great public importance and should be resolved promptly. * * * We do not consider or weigh the economic or social wisdom or general propriety of the initiative. Rather, our sole function is to evaluate article XIII A legally * * * We further emphasize that we examine only those principal, fundamental challenges to the validity of article XIII A as a whole.

* * *

It is a fundamental precept of our law that, * * * "the people reserve to themselves the powers of initiative and referendum." (Cal. Const., art. IV, § 1.) It follows from this that, "[t]he power of initiative must be liberally construed * * * to promote the democratic process."

* * *

The new article contains four distinct elements. The first imposes a limitation on the *tax rate* applicable to real property: "The maximum amount of any ad valorem tax on real property shall not exceed one percent (1%) of the full cash value of such property. * * *" (§ 1, subd. (a).) (This limitation is made specifically inapplicable, * * * to property taxes or special assessments necessary to pay prior indebtedness approved by the voters.) The second is a restriction on the *assessed value* of real property. Section 2, subdivision (a), provides: "The full cash value means the County Assessors valuation of real property as shown on the 1975–76 tax bill under 'full cash value', or thereafter the appraised value of real property when purchased, newly constructed, or a change in ownership has occurred after the 1975 assessment. * * *" Subdivision (b) permits a maximum 2 percent annual increase in "the fair market value base" of real property to reflect the inflationary rate.

The third feature limits the method of changes in *state* taxes: "From and after the effective date of this article, any changes in State taxes enacted for the purpose of increasing revenues * * * whether by increased rates or changes in methods of computation must be imposed by an Act passed by not less than two-thirds of all members * * * of the Legislature, except that no new ad valorem taxes on real property, or sales or transaction taxes on the sales of real property may be imposed." (§ 3.) The fourth element is a restriction upon *local* taxes: "Cities, Counties and special districts, by a two-thirds vote of the qualified electors of such district, may impose special taxes on such district, except ad valorem taxes on real property or a transaction tax or sales tax on the sale of real property within such City, County or special district." (§ 4.)

* * *

We examine petitioners' specific contentions.

1. CONSTITUTIONAL REVISION OR AMENDMENT

The petitioners' primary argument is that article XIII A represents such a drastic and far-reaching change in the nature and operation of our governmental structure that it must be considered a "revision" of the state Constitution rather than a mere "amendment" thereof. * * * Because a revision may not be achieved through the initiative process, petitioners' first contention strikes at the very validity of article XIII A in its inception and in its entirety. Were we to conclude that the Proposition 13 initiative constituted a revision not an amendment, that would end our inquiry; the initiative would be invalid for its failure to meet the constitutional requirements of a revision.

* * *

We think it significant that prior to 1962 a constitutional revision could be accomplished *only* by the elaborate procedure of the convening of, and action by, a constitutional convention (art. XVIII, § 2). This fact suggests that the term "revision" * * * was intended to refer to a substantial alteration of the entire Constitution, rather than to a less extensive change in one or more of its provisions. * * *

While the Constitution itself does not specifically distinguish between revision and amendment, we are considerably aided in an evaluation of petitioners' primary argument by our earlier analysis of the issue in McFadden v. Jordan (1948) 32 Cal.2d 330, 196 P.2d 787 (cert. den. 336 U.S. 918, 69 S.Ct. 640, 93 L.Ed. 1080). In *McFadden,* we struck down an initiative measure which would have added 21,000 words to our then existing 55,000–word constitution. We held that the initiative was "revisory rather than amendatory in nature," because of the "far reaching and multifarious substance of the measure * * *" (p. 332, 196 P.2d p. 788) which dealt with such varied and diverse subjects as retirement pensions, gambling, taxes, oleomargarine, healing arts, civic centers, senate reapportionment, fish and game, and surface mining. We noted that the proposal would have repealed or substantially altered at least 15 of the 25 articles which then comprised the Constitution (P. 345, 196 P.2d 787.)

* * *

In addition, although the subject of taxation was only one of many covered by the *McFadden* initiative, nevertheless we observe that the proposed taxation amendment would have accomplished, *by itself,* a far more substantial change in the state's taxation scheme than that effected by Proposition 13. The far reaching nature of the *McFadden* measure is demonstrated by the fact that it not only would have destroyed the power of cities and counties to tax and regulate their own budgets and expenditures (p. 344, 196 P.2d 787), but also the 2 percent gross receipts tax proposed therein was to have been *the only tax* permitted to any agency on real or personal property, or on any business enterprises. (Pp. 336–337, 196 P.2d 787.)

*   *   *

Taken together our *   *   * decisions mandate that our analysis in determining whether a particular constitutional enactment is a revision or an amendment must be both quantitative and qualitative in nature. *   *   *

In both its quantitative and qualitative aspects, however, article XIII A appears demonstrably less sweeping than the initiative measure at issue in *McFadden*. As noted above, the *McFadden* measure consisted of 21,000 words and covered many different subjects, whereas XIII A comprises approximately 400 words and, *   *   * is limited to the single subject of taxation (with particular emphasis upon real property taxation). *   *   *

Our review of petitioners' description of numerous asserted changes indicates that the claims may be based upon possible errors in petitioners' interpretation of the new article. *   *   *

In addition, petitioners assume that article XIII A will annul or amend the various "home rule" provisions of the state Constitution (art. XI, §§ 3–7), an assumption we discuss and reject below. *   *   * we decline to hold that article XIII A accomplished a revision of the Constitution by reason of its *quantitative* effect upon the existing provisions of that document.

Petitioners insist, however, that the new article also will have far reaching *qualitative* effects *   *   * in two principal particulars, namely, (1) the loss of "home rule" and (2) the conversion of our governmental framework from "republican" to "democratic" form. A close analysis of XIII A convinces us that its probable effects are not as fundamentally disruptive as petitioners suggest.

a.) *Loss of home rule.* The principle of home rule involves, essentially, the ability of local government *   *   * to control and finance local affairs without undue interference by the Legislature. *   *   * It is undeniably true that a constitutional limitation upon prevailing local taxation rates and assessments will have a potentially limiting effect upon the management and resolution of local affairs. *   *   * To conclude, however, that the mere imposition of tax limitations, per se, accomplishes a constitutional revision would in effect bar the people from ever achieving *any* local tax relief through the initiative process. Petitioners have cited to us no authorities which support such a broad proposition, and our own research, disclosing only one case, indicates a contrary rule. (See School Dist. of City of Pontiac v. City of Pontiac (1933) 262 Mich. 338, 247 N.W. 474, 477 [initiative measure adopting a 1½ percent tax limitation on assessed value, and requiring two-thirds approval of electorate to increase taxes, was a constitutional amendment, not a revision].)

Petitioners insist, however, that article XIII A has an additional effect * * * the Legislature is thereby empowered, at its whim, and upon whatever conditions it may impose, to pick and choose among the local agencies, rewarding "deserving" agencies with substantial amounts while penalizing others by reduced awards. Certainly nothing on the face of the article, however, abrogates home rule to this extent, * * * For several reasons, petitioners' fears in this connection seem illusory and ill-founded.

First, it is clear that even prior to the adoption of article XIII A, the Constitution authorized the Legislature to "provide maximum property tax rates and bonding limits for local government" (art. XIII, § 20), to provide similar limits for school districts (*id.*, § 21), and to grant exemptions from real property taxation in favor of certain specified classes of property (*id.*, § 4). Thus, from the standpoint of legislative control, the new article appears potentially no more threatening to home rule than these preexisting constitutional limitations.

Second, wholly unlike the *McFadden* initiative, article XIII A neither destroys nor annuls the taxing power of local agencies. Although revenues derived from real property taxes may well be substantially reduced by reason of the new tax rate and assessment restrictions (§§ 1, 2), local agencies retain full authority to impose "special taxes" (other than certain real property taxes) if approved by a two-thirds vote of the "qualified electors." (§ 4.) Although the interpretation of the foregoing quoted provisions is not presently before us, it seems evident that section 4 assists in preserving home rule principles by leaving to *local* voters the decision whether or not to authorize "special" taxes to support *local* programs.

Third, article XIII A does not by its terms empower the Legislature to direct or control local budgetary decisions or program or service priorities, * * * The mere fact of reduction in local revenues does not lead us necessarily to the conclusion that local agencies have forfeited control over allocations and disbursements of their remaining funds.

* * *

b.) *Loss of republican form of government.* Continuing their thesis that XIII A is a constitutional revision * * * petitioners next maintain that the operation of the article, and particularly section 4 thereof, will result in a change from a "republican" form of government (*i.e.*, lawmaking by elected representatives) to a "democratic" governmental plan (*i.e.*, lawmaking directly by the people).

Contrary to petitioners' assertion, however, we are convinced that article XIII A is more modest both in concept and effect and does not change our basic governmental plan. * * * Other than in the limited area of taxation, the authority of local government * * * remains wholly unimpaired. * * *

* * * We conclude that article XIII A fairly may be deemed a constitutional amendment, not a revision.

* * *

3. EQUAL PROTECTION OF THE LAWS

Petitioners' equal protection argument against article XIII A is directed at two aspects of the article. They contend that (1) the "rollback" of assessed valuation (§ 2, subd. (a)) assertedly will result in invidious discrimination between owners of similarly situated property, and that (2) the two-third voting requirement for enacting "special taxes" by local agencies (§ 4) unduly discriminates in favor of those voters casting negative votes. As will appear, we hold that neither contention has merit.

a.) *1975–1976 Assessment Date.* As we have noted, section 2, subdivision (a), of article XIII A provides that "The full cash value [to which the 1 percent maximum tax applies] means the County Assessors valuation of real property as shown on the 1975–76 tax bill under 'full cash value', or thereafter, the appraised value of real property when purchased, newly constructed, or a change in ownership has occurred after the 1975 assessment. * * * Petitioners emphasize that, by reason of the "rollback" of assessed value to the 1975–1976 fiscal year, two substantially identical homes, located "side-by-side" and receiving identical government services, could be assessed and taxed at different levels depending upon their date of acquisition. Such a disparity in tax treatment, petitioners claim, constitutes an arbitrary discrimination in violation of the federal equal protection clause (amend. XIV, § 1).

* * *

The general principles applicable to the determination of an equal protection challenge to state tax legislation were recently summarized by the United States Supreme Court as follows: "We have long held that [w]here taxation is concerned and no specific federal right, apart from equal protection, is imperiled, the States have large leeway * * *. A state tax law is not arbitrary although it 'discriminate[s] in favor of a certain class * * * if the discrimination is founded upon a reasonable distinction, or difference in state policy,' not in conflict with the Federal Constitution. [Citation.] This principle has weathered nearly a century of Supreme Court adjudication * * *." (Kahn v. Shevin (1974) 416 U.S. 351, 355, 356, 94 S.Ct. 1734, 1737, 40 L.Ed.2d 189.)

Consistent with the foregoing expression * * *, the high court has recognized the wide flexibility permitted states * * *, holding that "The latitude of discretion is notably wide in the classification of property for purposes of taxation *and the granting of partial or total exemptions upon grounds of policy.*" (Royster Guano Co. v. Virginia (1920) 253 U.S. 412, 415, 40 S.Ct. 560, 562, 64 L.Ed. 989, italics added; see Haman v. County of Humboldt (1973) 8 Cal.3d 922, 925–927, 106 Cal.Rptr. 617, 506 P.2d 993.) There exists no "iron rule of equality, prohibiting the flexibility and variety that are appropriate" to reasonable schemes of taxation. [citations] So long as a system of taxation is supported by a rational basis, and is not palpably arbitrary, it will be upheld despite the absence of "a precise, scientific uniformity" of taxation. [citations]

Petitioners, in response, rely upon a line of cases which hold, as a general proposition, that the intentional, systematic *undervaluation* of property similarly situated with other property assessed at its full value constitutes an improper discrimination in violation of equal protection principles. * * *

The foregoing cases, however, involved constitutional or statutory provisions which *mandated* the taxation of property on a *current value* basis. These cases do not purport to confine the states to a current value system under equal protection principles * * *.

By reason of section 2, subdivision (a), of the article, except for property acquired prior to 1975, henceforth all real property will be assessed and taxed at its value *at date of acquisition* rather than at current value (subject, of course, to the 2 percent maximum annual inflationary increase provided for in subdivision (b)). This "acquisition value" approach to taxation finds reasonable support in a theory that the annual taxes which a property owner must pay should bear some rational relationship to the original cost of the property, rather than relate to an unforeseen, perhaps unduly inflated, current value. Not only does an acquisition value system enable each property owner to estimate with some assurance his future tax liability, but also the system may operate on a fairer basis than a current value approach. * * * Seen in this light, and contrary to petitioners' assumption, section 2 does not unduly discriminate against persons who acquired their property after 1975, for those persons are assessed and taxed in precisely the same manner as those who purchased in 1975, namely, on an acquisition value basis predicated on the owner's free and voluntary acts of purchase. This is an arguably reasonable basis for assessment. (We leave open for future resolution questions regarding the proper application of article XIII A to involuntary changes in ownership or new construction.)

In addition, the fact that two taxpayers may pay different taxes on substantially identical property is not wholly novel to our general taxation scheme. For example, the computation of a sales tax on two identical items of personalty may vary substantially, depending upon the exact sales price and the availability of a discount. * * * [t]he framers of article XIII A chose not to "roll back" assessments any earlier than the 1975–1976 fiscal year. For assessment purposes, persons who acquired property prior to 1975 are deemed to have purchased it during 1975. These persons, however, cannot complain of any unfair tax treatment in view of the substantial tax advantage they will reap from a return of their assessments from current to 1975–1976 valuation levels. * * * The selection of the 1975–1976 fiscal year as a base year, although seemingly arbitrary, may be considered as comparable to utilization of a "grandfather" clause wherein a particular year is chosen as the effective date of new legislation, in order to prevent inequitable results or to promote some other legitimate purpose. [citations] Similar provisions are routinely upheld by the courts. [citations]

Petitioners insist, however, that property of equal *current* value must be taxed equally, regardless of its original cost. This proposition is demonstrably without legal merit, for our state Constitution itself expressly contemplates the use of "a value standard other than fair market value * * *." (Art. XIII, § 1, subd. (a).) Moreover, the Legislature is empowered to grant total or partial exemptions from property taxation on behalf of various classes (e.g., veterans, blind or disabled persons, religious, hospital or charitable property; see art. XIII, § 4), despite the fact that similarly situated property may be taxed at its full value. In addition, homeowners receive a partial exemption * * * which is unavailable to other property owners. * * * We cannot say that the acquisition value approach incorporated in article XIII A, * * * is wholly arbitrary or irrational. Accordingly, the measure under scrutiny herein meets the demands of equal protection principles.

b.) *Two-thirds Voting Requirement.*

* * * We may quickly dispose of the contention. Petitioners rely upon our decision in Westbrook v. Mihaly, *supra,* 2 Cal.3d 765, 87 Cal. Rptr. 839, 471 P.2d 487, wherein we held that a two-thirds requirement for approval of county general obligation bonds violated federal equal protection principles. However, our *Westbrook* opinion was vacated by the United States Supreme Court (Mihaly v. Westbrook (1971) 403 U.S. 915, 91 S.Ct. 2224, 29 L.Ed.2d 692) and the cause was remanded for our reconsideration in the light of Gordon v. Lance (1971) 403 U.S. 1, 91 S.Ct. 1889, 29 L.Ed.2d 273, a case which upheld a 60 percent vote requirement primarily because no "discrete and insular minority" was singled out for special treatment by application of the voting requirement. Thus, *Westbrook* no longer represents the controlling law on the subject. (See Coffineau v. Eu (1977) 68 Cal.App.3d 138, 143, 137 Cal. Rptr. 90.) * * *

4. RIGHT TO TRAVEL

Petitioners insist that the constitutional right to travel [citation] is impaired by the provisions of article XIII A. They reason that since any "nonresidents or newly arrived residents" will have to pay greater property taxes than "established" residents article XIII A will deter property owners from moving to another location, thereby inhibiting travel.

As we have explained * * * no penalty is imposed on the owner. The change from a current value system to an acquisition value method is intended to benefit *all* property owners, past and future, resident and nonresident, by reducing inflationary increases in assessments, by limiting tax rates, and by permitting the taxpayer to make more careful and accurate predictions of future tax liability. * * * Certainly, travel is inhibited to no greater extent by the new system, * * *. Accordingly, we hold that the right to travel is not unconstitutionally impaired by article XIII A.

5. IMPAIRMENT OF CONTRACTS

Petitioners forcefully argue that the operation of article XIII A inevitably will result in the default of various contractual obligations which were incurred by local agencies and districts prior to the enactment of the new article. At the least, petitioners contend, the new restrictions upon the local tax power will "depreciate" the security on which the various obligees have relied for repayment of public obligations held by them. It is claimed, therefore, that article XIII A constitutes an unlawful impairment of contract under the federal Constitution (art. 1, § 10, subd. (1)).

Petitioners observe that section 1, subdivision (b), of article XIII A, in apparent anticipation of the argument, contains a specific exception in favor of those holding evidence of certain prior indebtedness: "The limitation provided for in subdivision (a) [the 1 percent maximum tax] shall not apply to ad valorem taxes or special assessments to pay the interest and redemption charges *on any indebtedness approved by the voters* prior to the time this section becomes effective." (Italics added.) Petitioners point, however, to certain municipal obligations which were not required to be approved by the voters, including pension and health plan benefits, labor and other municipal contracts, and redevelopment agency bonds. The latter category, particularly, involves a special risk of impairment, according to petitioners, for redevelopment agencies rely exclusively upon property tax revenues for the retirement of their bonds.

Redevelopment bonds are secured by a pledge of so-called "tax increment" revenues generated by increases in the assessed value of the redeveloped property. (Cal. Const., art. XVI, § 16; Health & Saf. Code, §§ 33670, 33671; see Redevelopment Agency v. County of San Bernardino (1978) 21 Cal.3d 255, 257, 259, 145 Cal.Rptr. 886, 578 P.2d 133.) As we explained in *San Bernardino,* "In essence this section [art. XVI, § 16] provides that if, after a redevelopment project has been approved, the assessed valuation of taxable property in the project increases, the taxes levied on such property in the project area are divided between the taxing agency and the redevelopment agency. The taxing agency receives the same amount of money it would have realized under the assessed valuation existing at the time the project was approved, while the additional money resulting from the rise in assessed valuation is placed in a special fund for repayment of indebtedness incurred in financing the project." (*Id.,* at p. 259, 145 Cal.Rptr., at p. 888, 578 P.2d, at p. 135, italics omitted.)

According to petitioners, article XIII A will have a dual adverse effect upon redevelopment agency revenues because both the 1 percent maximum tax and the "rollback" of assessments to the 1975–1976 valuation will combine to reduce substantially tax increment revenues.

It is further contended that the problem thereby posed is acute, and the implications widespread.   Tax increment bonds are being used to finance 250 redevelopment projects in 121 cities and 3 counties.   None of these bonds was specifically approved by the voters, and thus none of them is exempt from the 1 percent maximum tax restriction.

There are two troublesome aspects to petitioners' impairment argument, involving both timing and standing.   First, it is readily apparent that petitioners' impairment of contracts argument is prematurely raised.   Nothing on the face of article XIII A requires local agencies to default either in meeting their preexisting contracts or in liquidating their outstanding bonds.   As we have seen the ultimate operation of the article may result in a substantial reduction in the amount of available revenues, but as yet no direct impairment of any contract or bond has occurred by virtue thereof.   No party to any contract or bondholder has so contended.   As we have noted above, courts will avoid reaching constitutional objections when it is not absolutely necessary to the disposition of the case before them.   (Bayside Timber Co. v. Board of Supervisors, *supra* 20 Cal.App.3d 1, 6, 97 Cal.Rptr. 431.)

In the present cases, despite the reduction of revenues from property taxation, doubtless many local public entities will retain sufficient funds to meet preexisting contractual or bonded indebtedness rather than suffer default; allocation of surplus state funds (see Stats.1978, chs. 292, 332) may assist other entities in these efforts.

As for redevelopment agencies, and other local agencies and districts relying upon property tax revenue for the retirement of bonds and other prior indebtedness which have not been voter approved, we note that the Legislature has created the Local Agency Indebtedness Fund to promote a public policy of protecting "the credit of the state and local agencies *by assuring that no bond of a local agency goes into default.*"   (Gov.Code, § 16496, added by Stats.1978, ch. 292, § 18, italics added.)   The new fund is designed to provide loans with a maximum three-year term for the purpose of preventing defaults on bonds during the 1978–1979 fiscal year "while local agencies are reorganizing revenue sources which support payments on such bonds."   (*Id.*, § 16496.5.) This legislation applies to bonds "which have not been specifically approved and authorized by the voters of the local agency prior to June 6, 1978" (*id.*, § 16497, subd. (c)), including redevelopment bonds secured by tax increment revenues (*id.*, § 16499, subd. (b), as amended by Stats. 1978, ch. 332, § 22).   The legislation thus fills the gap not covered by the constitutional exemption.

Petitioners properly observe that the new legislation does not specify from what sources a state loan to a redevelopment agency might be repaid (as tax increment revenues presumably are reserved to the bondholders).   Yet, as we have previously noted, the loans are made to prevent bond defaults while new revenue sources are being explored. We cannot assume on the face of the present record that no new revenue sources will be found or legislatively created.   Thus, for all of the foregoing reasons, we are not able to conclude that default or prior contractual obligations is an *inevitable* consequence of article XIII A.

Petitioners extend their impairment argument, however, contending that the new restrictions upon the local taxing power necessarily have resulted in a present "depreciation" of the security relied upon by the various obligees for repayment of their obligations, and that accordingly the impairment issue is ripe for our consideration. According to petitioners, any substantial restriction placed upon the taxing power of local governments accomplishes an immediate unlawful impairment of preexisting obligations, at least insofar as the discharge of these obligations may depend upon the availability of adequate tax revenues.

The authorities on which petitioners rely for the foregoing proposition are not in point. There is a line of cases holding generally that "a State may not authorize a municipality to borrow money and then restrict its taxing power *so that the debt cannot be repaid.* [Citations.]" (United States Trust Co. v. New Jersey (1977) 431 U.S. 1, 24, fn. 22, 97 S.Ct. 1505, 1519, 52 L.Ed.2d 92, and cases cited, italics added.) These cases do not suggest, however, that an unlawful impairment occurs immediately upon imposition of the tax restriction, without regard to its ultimate effect upon the repayment of preexisting debts. The *United States Trust Co.* decision, on which petitioners primarily rely, involved a legislative repeal of *an express covenant* which had assured to bondholders that monies pledged as security for repayment would not be used to subsidize rail passenger transportation. The high court explained that "The parties [to a municipal contract] may rely on the continued existence of adequate statutory remedies for enforcing their agreement, *but they are unlikely to expect that state law will remain entirely static.* Thus, a reasonable modification of statutes governing contractual remedies is much less likely to upset expectations than a law *adjusting the express terms of an agreement.* In this respect, the repeal of the 1962 covenant is seen as a serious disruption of the bondholders' expectations." (*Id.,* at pp. 20–21, fn. 17, 97 S.Ct. at pp. 15, 17, italics added.)

Nor does the recent case of Allied Structural Steel Co. v. Spannaus (1978) 438 U.S. 234, 98 S.Ct. 2716, 57 L.Ed.2d 727, assist petitioners, for in that case the challenged statute expressly modified the employees' pension rights which previously had been fixed by contract. In the present case, article XIII A on its face neither directly repudiates any express covenant with municipal obligees nor immediately impairs any contract right. As described by the high court in *Allied,* the federal contract clause (art. I, § 10) applies only to a "substantial impairment of a contractual relationship." (*Id.,* at p. ___, 98 S.Ct. at p. 2723.) In the absence of a factual record disclosing any present, specific and substantial impairment of contract attributable to the adoption of article XIII A, we must reject petitioners' impairment of contract challenge because it is premature.

A second defect in the impairment argument relates to petitioners' standing to assert the claim. It is noteworthy that, unlike the situation presented in the *United States Trust Co.* and *Allied* cases, none of the petitioners herein are municipal obligees, bondholders or creditors alleging an actual or potential impairment of their rights. In this connection, it is doubtful that petitioners possess the requisite standing to assert the invalidity of article XIII A on impairment of contract grounds. (See, *e.g.,* Brock v. Superior Court (1939) 12 Cal.2d 605, 613–614, 86 P.2d 805; In re Davis (1966) 242 Cal.App.2d 645, 666, 51 Cal. Rptr. 702; 5 Witkin, Summary of Cal.Law (8th ed. 1974) Constitutional Law, § 44 *et seq.*) As expressed in an earlier case, " * * * no obligation of any contract with the appellant has been impaired, and in the absence of the showing of injury on its part, it may not be heard." (Irrigation District v. Wutchumna W. Co. (1931) 111 Cal.App. 688, 696, 296 P. 933, 937.)

We conclude that the challenge to article XIII A based upon the federal contract clause is premature and must await a case in which the contract rights of an obligee have been demonstrably impaired by the operation of the new article.

* * *

Having carefully considered them, we have concluded that article XIII A survives each of the substantial challenges raised by petitioners.
* * *

Notes

1. **Alternative Revenue.** Some of the California tax shortfall led to increased use of special fees for certain services, viz. trash collection, recreational facilities (see "California Discovers Tax-Cut Mania Has a Corollary: Fee Fever," Wall St. Jrnl. 6–1–79, p. 1), and of special assessments. Challenges to these forms of exaction, as contravening Proposition 13, were turned back by the California courts. See, e.g., Mills v. Trinity, 108 Cal.App.3d 656, 166 Cal.Rptr. 674 (1980).

2. For other means of placing a cap on government taxes, see note 2, following Krahmer case, supra.

IDAHO TELEPHONE CO. v. BAIRD

Supreme Court of Idaho, 1967.
91 Idaho 425, 423 P.2d 337.

SMITH, JUSTICE. * * *

In their complaint appellants alleged that specific provisions of Idaho Session Laws * * *, relating to revenue and taxation, are violative of Idaho's Constitution, as well as the due process and equal protection clauses of the United States Constitution. Appellants further alleged that respondents lack authority to assess appellants' property at a higher ratio of full cash value than applies to other taxable property within the State. Upon the filing of respondents' answer,

both appellants and respondents moved for judgment on the pleadings.
* * *

Chapter 312 of the 1965 Session Laws effected a general revision of the ad valorem property tax laws. The purpose * * * was to equalize assessed valuations among the counties, and not to raise additional revenue. I.C. § 63–100. To this end, chapter 312 added I.C. § 63–101A, which provides as follows:

"All property within the jurisdiction of this state for the purpose of assessment and taxation is hereby classified as follows:

Class 1. Real Property,

Class 2. Personal Property, and

Class 3. Operating Property."

Operating property is defined * * * to include:

" * * * all franchises, rights of way, roadbeds, tracks, pipe lines, terminals, rolling stock, equipment, power stations, power sites, lands, reservoirs, generating plants and substations, all immovable or movable property operated in connection with any public utility * * *."

I.C. § 63–101B * * * imposes different ratios of assessment against appellants' operating property than prevails in the assessment of Class 1, Real Property, or Class 2, Personal Property. I.C. § 63–101B reads:

"The term 'assessed value' as used in this title shall mean a percentage of 'full cash value' as the later term is hereinafter defined.

"Class 1, real property, * * * shall be assessed at twenty per cent (20%) of its full cash value.

"Class 2, personal property, * * * shall be assessed at twenty per cent (20%) of its full cash value.

"Class 3, operating property, * * * shall be assessed at forty per cent (40%) of its full cash value."

* * *

Idaho Constitution, Art. VII, § 2 reads as follows:

"Revenue to be provided by taxation.—The legislature shall provide such revenue as may be needful, by levying a tax by valuation, so that every person or corporation shall pay a tax in proportion to the value of his, her, or its property, except as in this article hereinafter otherwise provided. * * *"

Art. VII, § 3, provides:

"Property to be defined and classified.—The word 'property' as herein used shall be defined and classified by law."

Finally, Art. VII, § 5, reads:

"Taxes to be uniform—Exemptions.—All taxes shall be uniform upon the same class of subjects within the territorial limits, of the authority levying the tax, and shall be levied and collected under general laws, which shall prescribe such regulations as shall secure a just valuation for taxation of all property, real and personal: provided, that the legislature may allow such exemptions from taxation from time to time as shall seem necessary and just, * * *."

* * *

It must be kept in mind that the Constitution of the State of Idaho is not a delegation of power to the legislature but is a limitation on the power it may exercise, and that the legislature has plenary power in all matters for legislation except those prohibited by the constitution. [Citations omitted]

"A statute cannot declare a public policy contrary to the Constitution." Boise-Payette Lumber Co. v. Challis Independent School Dist. No. 1, 46 Idaho 403, 408, 268 P. 26, 27 (1928). * * *

The court must identify a specific prohibition in the constitution before it may justifiably declare a legislative enactment unconstitutional. * * *

* * *

Idaho Constitution, Art. VII, §§ 2, 3 and 5, * * * must be construed *in pari materia*.

Appellants' principal argument is that the Idaho Constitution, Art. VII, relating to finance and revenue, dictates a uniform rule for property taxation within jurisdictions levying the tax.

A constitutional rule of uniform ad valorem taxation forbids legislative classifications of property for the purpose of imposing a greater burden of ad valorem taxation on one class than on another; that is, all property not exempt from taxation must be assessed at a uniform percentage of actual cash value, and a single fixed rate of taxation must apply against all taxable property. See 1 Cooley, Taxation, §§ 298 and 299 (4th ed. 1924).

We interpret the language of Art. VII, § 2 * * *—as meaning that every property owner shall receive equal treatment under the ad valorem tax laws; * * *.

This court has previously held that the requirement of Art. VII, § 2, of uniform ad valorem taxation, is violated when one class of property is systematically assessed at a higher percentage of actual cash value, thereby subjecting the taxpayer to a higher rate of taxation, than applies to other property within the taxing jurisdiction. [Citations omitted]

The language of Art. VII, § 2 * * * appears in the constitutions of several other jurisdictions. The Constitution of New Hampshire, Article Fifth, Part Second, requires "proportional and reasonable assessments, rates, and taxes." The New Hampshire Supreme Court has held that such language compels uniform and equal property taxation. Opinion of the Justices, 99 N.H. 532, 114 A.2d 327 (1955); Bemis Bros. Co. v. City of Claremont, 98 N.H. 446, 102 A.2d 512 (1954). California's Constitution, Article XIII, Section 1, provides that "All property in this State * * * shall be taxed in proportion to its value * * *." California's Supreme Court regards that language as compelling an equal and uniform taxation of all property in the state. [Citations omitted]

The proportionality requirements in the 1875 Missouri Constitution, Art. X, § 4; the Illinois Constitution, Art. IX, § 1, S.H.A., and the Massachusetts Constitution, pt. 2, Chapter 1, Article 4, have similarly been construed as imposing a uniform rule of taxation upon the taxing authorities. [Citations omitted]

Our interpretation of the provisions of Idaho Constitution, Art. VII, § 2, is manifestly supported by reference to the debates at the 1889 Idaho Constitutional Convention. * * * It was unanimously assumed that properties not wholly exempt would be subject to taxation on an equal basis with all other taxable property. * * *

Respondents would concede *arguendo* that Art. VII, § 2 states the rule of uniformity as to ad valorem taxes, but contend that the clause "except as in this article hereinafter otherwise provided" permits an exception for discriminatory classifications under Sections 3 and 5. * * * Common sense refutes any fiction that the Convention intended to destroy ab initio its own constitutional mandate. * * *

Respondents present persuasive arguments that Art. VII, §§ 3 and 5, of the constitution permit classification such as exists under the statutes challenged by appellants. Art. VII, § 3, providing that "property" shall be classified by law, lends prima facie support to respondents' contention. Classification of property, however, may be effected for a variety of purposes; classification for one purpose may contravene the rule of uniform ad valorem taxation, while another classification scheme does not. For example, even in jurisdictions where the rule of uniformity is acknowledged to prevail, the legislatures or state tax commissions may promulgate reasonable classifications so as to provide different methods for determining the true value of disparate species of property. The overriding rule of uniformity does not preclude classification for such purposes, since the end of uniformity is promoted by applying sophisticated valuation methods to distinctive classes of property. To demand absolute uniformity in methods of valuation would defeat the prior, supreme requirement of equality and uniformity. The constitutional mandate is satisfied if the methods are not obviously designed to produce discriminatory burdens upon different classes of property. [Citations omitted]

Art. VII, § 3, therefore, affirms the power of the state legislature to make reasonable classifications of property for certain purposes. However, the exercise of that power is bounded by the constitutional requirement of uniformity embodied in Art. VII, § 2.

Respondents contend that Art. VII, § 5, implicitly authorizes the state legislature to classify property and to impose differing rates of assessments and levies against the various classes defined by law. Section 5 requires that all taxes be uniform upon the same class of subjects * * *. This court has repeatedly held that the uniformity clause of section 5 does not apply to excise or poll taxes. [Citations omitted] Since all taxes are categorized as either (1) capitation or poll taxes; (2) excise taxes, or (3) taxes on property, [citations omitted] those holdings necessarily limit the application of Art. VII, § 5 to property taxes exclusively. Respondents proceed to argue, * * * that section 5 only requires uniformity within each class, * * *. [Citations omitted]

However, respondents further contend if section 5 contemplates classes of property, and only requires that property taxes be uniform within each class, then it follows that the legislature may prescribe disparate rates of assessment or taxation between the several distinct classes of property. In those jurisdictions where the constitutional phraseology—"taxes shall be uniform upon the same class of subjects"—stands unqualified by any other constitutional restraint against unequal taxation, respondents' argument is demonstrably correct. The Pennsylvania Constitution, Art. IX, § 1, P.S., for example, embodies a uniformity clause identical to that of Idaho Constitution, Art. VII, § 5, except that the Pennsylvania clause is not secondary to any rule of uniformity. The Pennsylvania Supreme Court has accordingly upheld classification for purposes of discriminatory assessments of property. City of Williamsport v. Brown, 84 Pa. 438 (1877); Roup's Case, 81½ Pa. 211 (1876).

The Delaware Constitution, Art. VIII, § 1, Del.C.Ann., also requires that taxes be "uniform upon the same class of subjects," without further restriction upon assessment and taxation. The Delaware courts have consistently upheld discriminatory classifications of property. Philadelphia, B. & W.R. Co. v. Mayor & City Council, 30 Del. Ch. 213, 57 A.2d 759 (1948); State v. Pinder, 30 Del. 416, 108 A. 43 (1919). See also Mont. Const., Art. XII, § 11; Yellowstone Pipe Line Co. v. State Bd. of Equalization, 138 Mont. 603, 358 P.2d 55 (1960); Hilger v. Moore, *supra.*

Respondents observe that the uniformity clause of Art. VII, § 5 of the Idaho Constitution, is worded identically with Art. X, § 3, of Colorado's 1876 Constitution. Indeed, the Idaho Framers deliberately patterned portions of Article VII, relating to finance and revenue, upon corresponding provisions of the Colorado Constitution. II Idaho Constitutional Convention, 1656–57, 1722–23. For that reason, respondents contend that this court should adopt the construction placed upon the uniformity clause by the Colorado courts. See In re Schriber, 19 Idaho 531, 114 P. 29, 37 L.R.A.,N.S., 693 (1911); Stein v. Morrison, 9 Idaho 426, 75 P. 246 (1904). * * *

We cannot agree with that contention. First, the Colorado Constitution contains no clause, comparable to Article VII, § 2, of the Idaho Constitution, * * *. This substantial difference in itself sufficiently distinguishes the line of Colorado cases decided under the uniformity clause. Second, even if the Colorado decisions were pertinent * * * no Colorado case has squarely held that Colorado's legislature may classify property for the purpose of imposing unequal or discriminatory rates of assessment or taxation. * * * Finally, we note that the people of Colorado deemed it expedient in 1956, to amend. Art. X, § 3 of their 1876 Constitution, so as expressly to provide for property classifications, as follows: "All taxes shall be uniform upon each of the various classes of real and personal property located within the territorial limits of the authority levying the tax * * *." Idaho has not adopted a similar amendment.

Respondents' arguments place undue emphasis upon the permissive implications of Idaho's Constitution, Art. VII, § 5, without adequate reference to the additional restraints imposed by the rule of uniform ad valorem taxation in Article VII, § 2. * * *

Art. X, § 3, of the Missouri Constitution, for example, provides as follows:

> "Taxes may be levied and collected for public purposes only, and shall be uniform upon the same class of subjects within the territorial limits of the authority levying the tax. All taxes shall be levied and collected by general laws".

But the taxation of property in Missouri was further limited in Art. X, § 4, of the 1875 Missouri Constitution, which provides that "All property subject to taxation shall be taxed in proportion to its value." The Missouri Supreme Court has ruled that section 4 imposed a rule of uniformity in the taxation of all property. [Citations omitted]

The Georgia Constitution, prior to the amendments of 1937, stated that:

> "All taxation shall be uniform upon the same class of subjects, and *ad valorem* on all property subject to be taxes, within the territorial limits of the authority levying the tax, and shall be levied and collected under general laws." Article VII, Section 2, Paragraph 1.

The Georgia Supreme Court held in Mayor and Alderman etc. v. Weed, 84 Ga. 683, 11 S.E. 235, 8 L.R.A. 270 (1890), that the ad valorem clause distinguished Georgia's Constitution from Pennsylvania's, so that there could be no classification of property for purposes of imposing different rates of taxation. Accord, Featherstone v. Norman, 170 Ga. 370, 153 S.E. 58, 70 A.L.R. 449 (1930).

Respondents attempt to distinguish numerous cases decided under the Idaho Constitution and code holding that the constitutional requirements of uniformity proscribe systematic discrimination, either through undervaluation or overvaluation of one property or class of property as compared to other property. [Citations omitted] * * *

*   *   *

Inasmuch as the rule of uniform ad valorem taxation prevails under the constitutional mandate of Idaho Constitution, Art. VII, §§ 2 and 5, we are constrained to hold that Idaho Session Laws 1965, chap. 312, § 4, codified as I.C. § 63–101B, purporting to classify operating property for the purpose of imposing a higher ratio of assessment against such classification of property, than prevails against other classes of property, violates that constitutional requirement of uniformity. Under this view of the case, we deem it unnecessary to dispose of appellants' further assignments of error * * *.

Respondents lack authority to assess appellants' property at a higher ratio of full cash value than applies to other taxable property in this State; the assessment of appellants' property should be reduced accordingly. [Citations omitted]

* * *

Notes

1. See Newhouse, *Governmental Uniformity and Equality in State Taxation* (Mich.Leg.Studies 1959).

2. **Equal Protection and the Rule of Uniformity.** "It is safe to say the equal protection clause of the federal constitution, and state constitutional provisions pertaining to equality and uniformity of taxation are substantially similar and that, in general, what violates one will contravene the other and vice versa." Associated Ry. Equipment Owners v. Wilson, 167 Kan. 608, 619, 208 P.2d 604, 612 (1949); National Tea Co. v. State, 205 Minn. 443, 445, 286 N.W. 360, 362 (1939).

Equal protection does not require equality of burden on taxpayers. A city ordinance imposing a $100 charge on real property owners for each parcel of real estate as separately listed on the tax rolls was held not to violate equal protection, notwithstanding a disproportionate impact. Acorn v. New Orleans, 377 So.2d 1206 (La.1979), appeal dismissed 446 U.S. 961, 100 S.Ct. 2934, 64 L.Ed.2d 819 (1980).

Where discrimination by taxpayer class cannot be proved, a court can still nullify a local levy as "oppressive", where the impact is harshly destructive of a single business. Continental Bank and Trust Co. v. Farmington City, 599 P.2d 1242 (Utah 1979).

3. **Overlapping Tax Administration.** "Assessed values are determined by both State and local government officials. In most states the taxable value of * * * utility property is set by the State taxing agency. * * * Local assessors determine the assessed value of all other taxable real and personal property under their jurisdiction. Local assessment organization differs * * * varying from that in 28 States in which the county is the primary assessing unit to that in 12 States with hundreds of city, village, and township assessors. Hawaii is the only State that provides completely centralized administration of the property tax * * *.

"In the 28 States with primarily county assessment there is considerable overlapping of assessment functions. Ten permit cities to do their own assessing, * * * and in Texas even school districts may do their own assessing. * * * In 20 States property tax collection is exclusively a county function, and the county collector bills the taxes for all jurisdictions in the county—municipalities, school districts, and special districts, as well as the county. Another eight States * * * allow cities to do their own collecting. * * * In the New England States, as well as in Michigan, New Jersey, New York, Pennsylvania, and Wisconsin, the property taxes are collected by cities, towns, villages, and boroughs, and in the case of New

York, by school districts.   *   *   * " ACIR, *Tax Overlapping In The United States* 90–92 (1964).

4. **Federal Abstention on Unconstitutional Tax Claims.** In 1981, The Supreme Court ruled that local taxpayers alleging unconstitutional (unequal) property tax assessments cannot seek immediate relief in federal court, but must pursue their state *administrative* remedies. See Fair Assessment In Real Estate Association, Inc. v. McNary, p. 964, infra.

SKINNER v. NEW MEXICO STATE TAX COMMISSION

Supreme Court of New Mexico, 1959.
66 N.M. 221, 345 P.2d 750.

CARMODY, JUSTICE.   This is an appeal by plaintiffs, as taxpayers, *   *   *.

The sole question involved is whether a tax equalization program in a county, commenced but not completed in a single year, violates the New Mexico constitutional provision requiring equal and uniform taxes.

The facts are not complicated.   In January, 1957, the newly elected county assessor decided to equalize the real estate assessments of Bernalillo County on the basis of sixteen percent of actual market value.   Being limited as to funds and personnel, he was in 1957 only able to reappraise or revalue about twenty per cent of approximately 120,000 pieces of property in the county.   As a result, when the assessment roll was prepared for 1957, reappraisal values were used for more than 20,000 pieces of property, but with regard to the remaining eighty percent the 1956 valuations were utilized without change.
*   *   *

In connection with the reappraisal values *   *   * the record fails to indicate any intentional or systematic discrimination.   On the contrary, there was apparently an honest effort to equalize all properties that time, ability and circumstances would permit.   *   *   * Plaintiffs' assessments, however, were substantially increased, and they contend that as a result they will pay taxes on a wholly different basis than the other eighty per cent of the property owners in the county.   It is therefore urged that there is a violation of the New Mexico constitution, art. VIII, § 1, which reads:

"Taxes levied upon tangible property shall be in proportion to the value thereof, and taxes shall be equal and uniform upon subjects of taxation of the same class.   (As amended November 3, 1914.)"

The trial court concluded that the equalization program was a continuing process, that it was not contemplated that it could be completed within any given year, and that there was no contravention of the constitutional provision.

Appellants do not seriously protest their valuations nor claim that they are higher than the law allows, but, in effect, say that their assessments cannot be raised unless and until all other property in the county is similarly treated. As an adjunct to this argument, it is also urged that the so-called continuing process of reappraisement is without tangible or legal support and that the same may depend upon the whim of the assessor. This argument is based, at least in part, upon the fact * * * that the assessor who inaugurated the program was defeated for re-election and that there is no showing in the record that the program will be carried forward.

The problem involved is not new, although this court has not heretofore directly passed upon the question.

In New Mexico, it has long been the rule that a taxpayer who is not assessed more than the law provides has no cause for complaint in the courts in the absence of some well-defined and established scheme of discrimination or some fraudulent action, [Citations omitted]. The taxpayer's remedy is to have the assessing authority raise the value on the property claimed to be, valued too low to a level with his own, [citations omitted]. These two rules must be construed together, and if there is illegal discrimination * * * our courts will grant relief * * *.

Here, appellants have shown no discrimination or fraud, nor did they ask that all other property be immediately raised in assessed value. * * *

As stated heretofore, the valuations for the prior year varied greatly. * * * We cannot speculate as to this, and the burden is on the plaintiff to prove that an unreasonable number of typical or representative properties were assessed at a level considerably under the sixteen per cent figure. * * *

This is not a case where one or a few taxpayers are arbitrarily assessed at a higher level than others, as in Sioux City Bridge Co. v. Dakota County, Neb., 1923, 260 U.S. 441, 43 S.Ct. 190, 67 L.Ed. 340, 28 A.L.R. 979; nor where a single industry is discriminated against, as in Greene v. Louisville & Interurban R. Co., 1917, 244 U.S. 499, 37 S.Ct. 673, 61 L.Ed. 1280, Ann.Cas. 1917E, 88. It is more analogous to the situation in Sunday Lake Iron Co. Township of Wakefield, 1918, 247 U.S. 350, 38 S.Ct. 495, 62 L.Ed. 1154, where a reappraisal program was commenced but in one year re-assessment was completed on mining properties only. There, the Supreme Court of the United States refused to interfere and allowed the assessment to stand, even though there was an obvious but temporary inequality.

The decisions of the various state courts that have had this question before them for determination are not at all uniform, and it would unduly lengthen this opinion to discuss them all. * * * For other recent similar, although not identical, decisions, see May Department Stores Co. v. State Tax Commission, Mo.1958, 308 S.W.2d 748; and Rogan v. County Commissioners of Calvert County, 1950, 194 Md. 299, 71 A.2d 47.

There are a few cases from other jurisdictions which seem to rule to the contrary, but we do not feel that they are persuasive.

We hold under the facts in this case that there is no showing of a violation of the constitutional provision here involved. * * *

* * * In event there is a failure to so continue, appellants would be fully justified in taking such action as might be required to force a corresponding revaluation of all of the other property in the county. * * *

The judgment of the district court will be affirmed, and it is so ordered.

* * *

Notes

1. **Accord:** Appelman v. Beach, 94 N.M. 237, 608 P.2d 1119 (1986). See also Tax Assessment—Standing to Challenge, 9 A.L.R.4th 428 (1981).

2. The practice of applying discretionary percentages of value, provided the percentages are uniform, has been upheld in many states.

"Despite § 273.11, which provides that as a basis of taxation all property shall be assessed at its full and true value in money and not according to any lower standard of value, it is the practice in this state, as it is in most states, to assess property systematically and uniformly at a percentage of its full and true value. In accord with this well-established practice petitioners' property was assessed on a percentage basis. Section 272.03, subd. 8, defines 'full and true value' as:

" ' * * * the usual selling price at the place where the property to which the term is applied shall be at the time of assessment; being the price which could be obtained at private sale and not at forced or auction sale.'

"Under this definition the full and true value means the fair market value of such property—the price that could be obtained in a private sale between a willing seller and a willing buyer.

"The primary issue of invalidity because of inequality in assessment rests upon plaintiffs' contention that the assessor failed to apply to all commercial property in his taxing district a uniform percentage of market value. * * *

* * *

"Apparently the trial court assumed that if petitioners' property was taxed upon a percentage base which was substantially the same as the *average* percentage applied to other commercial properties, they were not adversely affected. This assumption is wholly illusory as a basis for a finding of uniformity * * *. Some taxpayers may be taxed as low as 10 percent of market value and others as high as 60 or 70 percent and yet the average could be 37.16. It is true that the county assessor testified that he had *tried to follow* the percentage established by state surveys * * *. This testimony is entitled to little weight in view of other positive testimony unmistakably showing that a variation from 28 to 40 percent of market value was used. * * *

* * *

"Although petitioners were unfairly and unequally assessed because of the assessor's applying to their property a percentage substantially higher than that applied to the market value of other commercial property, it is clear that the full and true taxable value so ascertained was, in any event, less than the property's actual market value. In the light of our holding in State v. Cudahy Packing Co., supra, the question arises whether petitioners, despite such inequality of assessment, have any standing to complain as long as their property was assessed at a full and true value less than its actual or real market value. In the Cudahy case, decided 50 years ago, this court refused to grant relief to a taxpayer whose property was assessed at its approximate market value even though other property of the same class was assessed at far less than market value. The Cudahy case is clearly wrong * * *." Hamm v. State, 255 Minn. 64, 68–69, 95 N.W.2d 649, 652–653 (1959). But see State ex rel. Beggrow v. Atkisson, 170 So.2d 455, (Fla. App.1964) which required the city property tax assessment to be made at "just value" i.e., 100% .

3. **Uniform Assessments.** Sparks v. McCluskey, 84 Ariz. 283, 327 P.2d 295 (1958) invalidated reassessment of plaintiff's property, on a different basis than the prior basis which was continued for other taxpayers of the district. Sparks did not involve a county-wide reassessment. Should this distinction be determinative? Cf. State ex rel. Barlow v. Kinnear, 70 Wash.2d 482, 423 P.2d 937 (1967) where the State Tax Commission was upheld in ordering county assessors to use a uniform percentage of true value, but was held to have acted improperly in failing to require the use of the percentage figure specified by the state constitution.

4. **Uniformity Requirements on Nonproperty Taxes.** A Pennsylvania Court recently struck down a multi-county occupation tax by a multi-county school district, as violating the Uniformity Clause of the state constitution. Carl v. Southern Columbia Area School District, 41 Pa. Cmwlth. 527, 400 A.2d 650 (1979). The court found that the multi-county school district residents were paying different amounts for the same service, due to county variations in their "assessed valuations".

5. **Standing as Aggrieved Taxpayer.** The fact that a person was not the owner at the time of tax assessment (but becomes such and liable thereon before the time for payment) does not deprive him of standing to sue on the ground of improper assessment. Langford v. Newton, 119 N.H. 470, 403 A.2d 414 (1979).

VILLAGE OF RIDGEFIELD PARK v. BERGEN COUNTY BOARD OF TAXATION

Supreme Court of New Jersey, 1960.
31 N.J. 420, 157 A.2d 829.

WEINTRAUB, C.J. The Village of Ridgefield Park and several of its taxpayers filed a complaint * * * against the Bergen County Board of Taxation and the assessors of each of the other municipalities in

Bergen County, seeking certain relief with respect to the assessment of real and personal property. * * *

Plaintiffs allege that in the Village of Ridgefield Park all real and personal properties were assessed at true value * * * but the county board and the defendant assessors have "willfully, deliberately and intentionally failed, neglected and refused to perform their duties and obligations" to achieve the same treatment of property in the remaining municipalities of the county. This allegation must of course be accepted as true on a motion addressed to the face of the pleadings. * * *

I.

It is urged that (1) the issuance of a *mandamus* would be contrary to the public interest and (2) plaintiffs should be remitted to an administrative remedy.

Both propositions were presented in Switz v. Middletown Township, 23 N.J. 580, 130 A.2d 15 (1957). * * * The Constitution does not require that all real property taxed locally or for local use shall be assessed at true value. Rather it requires all such real property to be assessed "according to the same standard of value," which may be a percentage of true value. But the statute, N.J.S.A. 54:4–1, provides that unless exempted it shall be subject to taxation "at its true value." The Constitution does not require that all personal property * * * shall be assessed at true value. But, again, the statute just cited provides that all taxable tangible personal property shall be assessed "at its true value." See also R.S. 54:3–13, N.J.S.A. and N.J.S.A. 54:3–22; N.J.S.A. 54:4–12, 23, 47.

In Switz we discussed the long history of widespread failure to comply with the legislative mandate. * * *

In Switz a majority of the court concluded the issuance of *mandamus* to achieve assessment at true value should there be delayed for a period of two years. The manifold problems * * * were weighed, and because of them the right of the plaintiff to relief was suspended for the stated period to the end that the Legislature would have an adequate opportunity to explore the subject. More than two years have elapsed and we assume the necessary facts are on hand for such action by the Legislature * * *. In the circumstances, we may not delay the right of plaintiffs to enforcement of the existing statutory policy * * *.

As stated above, defendants urge the administrative remedy is adequate and must be exhausted * * *. There are two aspects: the administrative remedy available (a) to review or revise assessments of taxable property and (b) to review the apportionment made by the county board of the cost of county government * * *.

With respect to the first, it is sufficient to say that the statutory right to equal treatment cannot effectively be achieved by an appeal to supervisory statutory agencies or by a multitude of petitions to raise the properties of others to full true value. * * * Moreover, retroac-

tive reassessments of all property would entail disorder hurtful to the
public interest. ＊ ＊ ＊

Defendants correctly challenge plaintiffs' attempt to attack directly
in these proceedings the equalization table (R.S. 54:3–17 to 19, N.J.S.A.),
the apportionment valuation (N.J.S.A. 54:4–49), and the table of aggregates (N.J.S.A. 54:4–52) made and prepared by the county board for the
purpose of allocating the cost of county government for the year 1959
＊ ＊ ＊. The reason is not the adequacy of an administrative review
＊ ＊ ＊. Rather the compelling reason is that government must function and to that end must have funds. ＊ ＊ ＊

＊ ＊ ＊

With respect to real property, defendants contend the equalization
of the aggregates thereof insures equality of treatment as among the
municipalities of the county. It is true that practical equality ＊ ＊ ＊
is thereby achieved with respect to the *pro rata* allocation of the county
burden among the municipalities as such. ＊ ＊ ＊ But unless all
municipalities thus deal equally with all real property within their
borders, there is discriminatory treatment as among the individual
taxpayers of the county with respect to the burden of county government which the equalization process does not correct. This was recognized in Switz.

＊ ＊ ＊

The concurring opinion stated (23 N.J. at pages 609–610, 130 A.2d at
page 31):

> "It seems clear to me that all of the taxpayers of a county are
> entitled to equal treatment with respect to the distribution of the cost
> of county government. ＊ ＊ ＊ purposes is concerned, each taxpayer is
> entitled to equality, not merely as against other taxpayers within his
> own municipality, but also as against all other taxpayers of the county.
> ＊ ＊ ＊

> "If the county tax were separately levied by the county itself, the
> right of each taxpayer to seek enforcement of the statutory scheme
> throughout the county would be apparent. ＊ ＊ ＊ If I am correct in
> this premise, then the right of a taxpayer of Middletown to relief as to
> the entire county with respect to the tax for county purposes should
> not be obscured and denied by the circumstance that the county tax is
> levied *via* municipalities and local assessors rather than directly by the
> county itself."

The views expressed above apply with equal force to personal
property. ＊ ＊ ＊

It is urged that assessment of personal property at true value
would be unpalatable. Perhaps so; indeed, probably so. But the
remedy lies with the legislative branch. ＊ ＊ ＊

One further question should be considered. Could the court
＊ ＊ ＊ refrain from acting ＊ ＊ ＊ if the municipalities each accomplished intramunicipal equality at a percentage of true value? The
answer, it seems to us, is that the statutory equality among taxpayers

with respect to county taxes (and school taxes where the burden is shared by municipalities) can be achieved only at full true value. If each municipality assessed all of its real and personal property at a single percentage of true value selected by it, there could be substantial equalization * * *, but there is no statutory authority or available technique for such equalization of the aggregates of personal property. If the aggregates of real property are equalized while the aggregates of personal property are not, then clearly the apportionment of the county tax (and school tax) would be discriminatory * * * as between the owners of real property and personal property within each municipality. And if all municipalities assessed personal property at full true value while each applied a percentage of true value to real property, then although, upon equalization of aggregates of real property, equality would substantially result with respect to the *county* tax (and school tax), yet real and personal property, being assessed upon an unequal basis for municipal purposes, would not share equally the cost of *municipal* government. Hence, we see no escape from the proposition that the existing legislative policy can be satisfied only by assessment of all taxable property at full true value.

III.

The county board urges it is entitled to judgment as a matter of law. In Switz it was noted that basically the problem in many, if not most, of the municipalities was that the assessment rolls were out of hand and hence nothing short of municipal-wide revaluations would bring order out of chaos; that the county board had neither the time nor the funds for so massive an effort; * * *. We have no reason to feel differently about the county board in the present case. However, the motion was based upon the pleadings, * * *. Hence the motion was properly denied. But we repeat that the board cannot be expected to assume the primary role of the assessors and hence a judgment should not run against it unless it appears that the board has either impeded the assessors or has evidenced an intent not to discharge its function * * *. And of course insofar as the complaint seeks to compel the county board to undo its work for the year 1959, we agree for the reasons given above that such relief may not be granted. The time for final action by the board and review thereof has long since passed. N.J.S.A. 54:4–55.

The orders are accordingly affirmed.

* * *

Notes

1. "Unless there is either full valuation or an explicit statutory mandate for a stated percentage of valuation, such as Iowa's 60 per cent, or Nebraska's 50 per cent, and these standards are followed by the assessors, no real assurance of fairness of treatment among taxpayers can be furnished. * * * The problems of establishing the actual percentages used have proved overwhelming. Only through publicly established standards

can inequalities and improprieties in assessment be kept at a minimum, and incompetence, favoritism, and corruption be at least subject to exposure to the public. * * * " J. Hellerstein, *State and Local Taxation* 103 (1969).

For an example of a constitutionally specified uniform percentage of true value assessment, see State v. Kinnear, supra. For an example of judicial imposition of a uniform percentage standard, see State ex rel. Park Investment Co. v. Board of Tax Appeals, 175 Ohio St. 410, 195 N.E.2d 908 (1964).

2. Until blunted by the California initiative (p. 590 supra), the New Jersey cases sparked a trend of decisions which require compliance with uniformity and true value standards. See e.g. State ex rel. Beggrow v. Atkisson, 170 So.2d 455 (Fla.App.1964); Russman v. Luckett, 391 S.W.2d 694 (Ky.1965); Bettigole v. Assessors of Springfield, 343 Mass. 223, 178 N.E.2d 10 (1961); State ex rel. Park Investment Co. v. Board of Tax Appeals, 175 Ohio St. 410, 195 N.E.2d 908 (1964); Union Pacific Railroad Co. v. Hoefke, 232 Or. 521, 376 P.2d 80 (1962); State ex rel. Barlow v. Kinnear, 70 Wash.2d 482, 423 P.2d 937 (1967). See also Note, *Inequality in Property Tax Assessments: New Cures For An Old Ill,* 75 Harv.L.Rev. 1374 (1962).

After Ridgefield, legislative changes permitted personal property assessments at adjusted, rather than actual value. See Thomas v. Kingsley, 43 N.J. 524, 206 A.2d 161 (1965).

3. People ex rel. Schaeger v. Allyn, 393 Ill. 154, 65 N.E.2d 392 (1946) involved a tract of land situate in two counties, each of which applied different percentages of true value for taxation purposes. There the court observed:

> "There is nothing in the briefs to indicate or suggest how uniformity might be maintained as between properties located in different counties but included within one park or school district. If he be correct in his position, it would necessitate all the property throughout the State being valued alike before absolute uniformity in overlapping districts, located partially in two or more counties, could be accomplished. In such situations, as long as the assessment and levy of taxes is based upon the judgment of the assessing officers in each separate county, absolute uniformity cannot be achieved. This matter is one exclusively for the legislature, and the relief, if any, * * * must come from the legislature and not from the courts. People ex rel. Hempen v. Baltimore & Ohio R. Co., 379 Ill. 543, at page 546, 42 N.E.2d 69." Id. at 160–61, 65 N.E.2d at 395–96.

4. **Valuation Techniques.** "Most of the inequities are attributes of the assessment process * * *. * * * The local [assessment] officials * * * often occupy positions of unique autonomy, partly because they may enjoy political independence from local spending authorities, and partly because they invariably function under imprecise state legislation which leaves them free to devise their own valuation standards. As a result, assessors can frequently manipulate their valuations to favor individual taxpayers, to reduce the local incidence of state and county realty taxes, to govern the revenue-raising power of municipalities, and to subvert

state grant-in-aid requirements expressed in terms of local assessed valuations. * * * Tax exemptions favoring farmers, veterans and home owners have partially compensated for the tax's regressivity * * *. Since such exemptions provide irresponsible legislators a means of distributing state gratuities by diminishing local revenues, exemption provisions frequently assume pork-barrel dimensions * * *. The techniques by which assessors and courts currently translate abstract legislative statements of value into dollar amounts are the three standard methods developed * * * for other purposes. The market-comparison approach utilizes the actual sales prices of realty parcels comparable to the one being appraised. Alternatively, depreciated reproduction cost measures present value by subtracting total depreciation from the hypothetical current cost of reproducing the improvements in question. Or thirdly, realty can be valued by capitalizing anticipated future income. * * * Even when a single method is applied to a given parcel at a given time, several values may be found, for appraisal rests on commercial and economic assumptions which can vary because they are not susceptible of empirical proof. * * * Regardless of statutory language, however, courts in 47 states have interpreted their realty tax laws to authorize assessors to consider all relevant facts, standards and assumptions. Consequently, the taxpayer's ability to predict his property's taxable value has been sacrificed in the interest of judicial and administrative flexibility. * * * Real estate taxation has long suffered from the legislature's abdication of their responsibilities to courts and administrators who manipulate empty statutory intonations on 'value' in order to implement policies of their own selection. * * * Consequently, detailed statutes delineating the procedures as well as the goals of realty tax assessment should replace the present legislative pronouncements directing assessors to find 'true value', 'actual value', 'cash value', or 'market value'." See Note, *Tax Assessments of Real Property: A Proposal For Legislative Reform,* 68 Yale L.J. 335, at 336, 339, 344–347, 369–370, 384 (1958).*

5. **What Is Taxable "Property"?** Is a long term leasehold taxable "property" to the lessee of a tax exempt municipal lessor? Should it be valued at the market value of the property or at the difference between such market value and the term rentals which lessee must pay? See People ex rel. Korzen v. American Airlines, Inc., 39 Ill.2d 11, 233 N.E.2d 568 (1968).

In Ampco Printing-Adv. Offset Corp. v. New York, 14 N.Y.2d 11, 247 N.Y.S.2d 865, 197 N.E.2d 285 (1964) the court upheld a business occupancy tax, measured by leasehold rental, over the objection that the tax was either an unlawful tax on "real" property, or an unauthorized tax on intangible property. The court held that the tax was neither a tax on real or intangible property. What then was the nature and subject of the tax?

6. **Avoidance of Local Property Tax Limits.** Most state limits on local tax rates or revenues stimulate unsound avoidance practices, *viz.* juggling property assessments; creating special districts as new taxing

* Reprinted by permission of The Yale Law Journal Company and Fred B. Rothman & Company copyright © 1958.

units; enforced borrowing; and fictional special assessments. While some relief from tax restrictions is provided by legislative exemptions or exceptions (such as electorally approved tax levies) the limitations remain too inflexible to operate effectively. See generally, ACIR, *State Constitutional and Statutory Restrictions On Local Taxing Powers,* 1–9, 39–48, 60–67 (1962).

7. **Assessment Discrimination.** On discriminatory property tax assessment against low-income areas, see Baar, "Property Tax Assessment Against Low-Income Neighborhoods," 13 Urban Lawyer 333 (1981).

8. **Property Tax Refund Claims.** On procedures, see Rosewell v. LaSalle Nat'l Bank, 450 U.S. 503, 101 S.Ct. 1221, 67 L.Ed.2d 464 (1981). Absent preservation of rights by payment under protest, or under specific statutory authorization for refund of illegal collections, courts refuse to order refunds of payments for taxes subsequently declared illegal. Carl v. Southern Columbia Area School District, 41 Pa.Cmwlth. 527, 400 A.2d 650 (1979).

ROBINSON v. CAHILL

Supreme Court of New Jersey, 1973.
62 N.J. 473, 303 A.2d 273.

[Following the line of decisions initiated by Serrano v. Priest, 5 Cal. 3d 584, 96 Cal.Rptr. 601, 487 P.2d 1241 (1971), the New Jersey Superior Court in 1972 invalidated the state system of financing public education, through local school district taxation, as violative of equal protection under federal and state constitutions. While the matter was being considered by the New Jersey Supreme Court, the federal question was resolved by the United States Supreme Court in San Antonio Independent School District v. Rodrigues, 411 U.S. 1, 93 S.Ct. 1278, 36 L.Ed.2d 16 (1973). By a five to four vote, the Supreme Court there held that the prevalent state systems of financing public education by local school district property taxes did not violate the federal equal protection clause notwithstanding the disparities in educational expenditures between tax rich and tax poor school districts. The New Jersey Supreme Court nevertheless held the New Jersey system was unlawful under other provisions of the state constitution.

The following excerpt is a very small part of that comprehensive opinion.]

WEINTRAUB, C.J.

＊   ＊   ＊

There emerges from the majority opinion [of the United States Supreme Court] an evident reluctance to say the Federal Constitution supplies single solutions by which all the States are bound. Although obviously not applauding the existing scene, the majority would leave the problem to the processes of the several States. ＊   ＊   ＊

The question whether the equal protection demand of our State Constitution is offended remains for us to decide. Conceivably a State Constitution could be more demanding. ＊   ＊   ＊

We hesitate to turn this case upon the State equal protection clause. The reason is that the equal protection clause may be unmanageable if it is called upon to supply categorical answers in the vast area of human needs, choosing those which must be met and a single basis upon which the State must act. The difficulties become apparent in the argument in the case at hand.

*   .*   *

*   *   * The case now before us was not tried or argued in terms that local government as a political institution denies equal protection in New Jersey because unequal demands upon unequal tax bases result in statewide inequality as to benefits or as to tax burden. In these circumstances we will not pursue the equal protection issue in the limited context of public education.

*   *   *

The remaining question is whether certain provisions of our State Constitution, two dealing with public education and a third with the general subject of property taxation, impose the tax burden upon the State's own revenues.

*   *   *

The obligation being the State's to maintain and support a thorough and efficient system of free public schools, the State must meet that obligation itself or if it chooses to enlist local government it must do so in terms which will fulfill that obligation. But plaintiffs say that although the operation of schools may be delegated, the fiscal responsibility may not. *   *   * Alternatively they say the amendment assures equality among the pupils of the State and that such equality is not achieved and cannot be achieved by a system of taxation which depends upon the existing local tax base.

We cannot say the amendment of 1875 was intended to bar the delegation of the taxing responsibility to local government. *   *   *

*   *   *

In the light of the foregoing, it cannot be said the 1875 amendments were intended to insure statewide equality among taxpayers. But we do not doubt that an equal educational opportunity for children was precisely in mind. *   *   * A system of instruction in any district of the State which is not thorough and efficient falls short of the constitutional command. Whatever the reason for the violation, the obligation is the State's to rectify it. If local government fails, the State government must compel it to act, and if the local government cannot carry the burden, the State must itself meet its continuing obligation.

*   *   *

The trial court found the constitutional demand had not been met and did so on the basis of discrepancies in dollar input per pupil. We agree. We deal with the problem in those terms because dollar input is plainly relevant and because we have been shown no other viable

criterion for measuring compliance with the constitutional mandate.
* * *

* * * Indeed the State has never spelled out the content of the educational opportunity the Constitution requires. Without some such prescription, it is even more difficult to understand how the tax burden can be left to local initiative * * *. The 1871 statute embraced a statewide tax because it was found that local taxation could not be expected to yield equal educational opportunity. Since then the State has returned the tax burden to local school districts to the point * * * the State was meeting but 28% of the current operating expenses. * * *

* * *

We have outlined the formula of the 1970 Act to show that it is not demonstrably designed to guarantee that local effort plus the State aid will yield to all the pupils in the State that level of educational opportunity which the 1875 amendment mandates. * * *

* * *

We repeat that if the State chooses to assign its obligation under the 1875 amendment to local government, the State must do so by a plan which will fulfill the State's continuing obligation. To that end the State must define in some discernible way the educational obligation and must *compel* the local school districts to raise the money necessary to provide that opportunity. The State has never spelled out the content of the constitutionally mandated educational opportunity. Nor has the State *required* the school districts to raise moneys needed to achieve that unstated standard. Nor is the State aid program designed to compensate for local failures to reach that level. It must be evident that our present scheme is a patchy product reflecting provincial contests rather than a plan sensitive only to the constitutional mandate.

* * *

Upon the record before us, it may be doubted that the thorough and efficient system of schools required by the 1875 amendment can realistically be met by reliance upon local taxation. The discordant correlations between the educational needs of the school districts and their respective tax bases suggest any such effort would likely fail, * * *.

Although we have dealt with the constitutional problem in terms of dollar input per pupil, we should not be understood to mean that the State may not recognize differences in area costs, or a need for additional dollar imput to equip classes of disadvantaged children * * *. Nor do we say that if the State assumes the cost of providing the constitutionally mandated education, it may not authorize local government to go further and to tax to that further end, provided that such authorization does not become a device for diluting the State's mandated responsibility.

The present system being unconstitutional, we come to the subject of remedies. We agree * * * that relief must be prospective. The judiciary cannot unravel the fiscal skein. Obligations incurred must not be impaired. And since government must go on, and some period of time will be needed to establish another statutory system, obligations hereafter incurred pursuant to existing statutes will be valid in accordance with the terms of the statutes. In other respects we desire the further views of the parties as to the content of the judgment, including argument as to whether the judiciary may * * * order that moneys appropriated by the Legislature * * * shall be distributed upon terms other than the legislated ones. A short date for argument will be fixed.

Note

The *Robinson* case marked a trend toward judicial invalidation of state school finance laws under state constitutions in California, Connecticut, New Jersey, New York, Washington, West Virginia and Wyoming. That trend has been blunted by cases upholding such laws against like challenges in Arizona, Colorado, Georgia, Idaho, Montana, Ohio, Oregon and Pennsylvania. See W.D. Valente, Education Law—Public and Private, Vol. 2, pp. 287–88 at n. 25 (1985); Danson v. Casey, 484 Pa. 415, 399 A.2d 360 (1979).

a. Tax Exemptions

The subject of tax exemption is complex. General and selective exemptions vary, with the type and the subject of tax, from mandatory to permissive or optional exemptions. Tax exemption differs from exclusion from the class of taxable subjects. Different policies govern different subjects of exemption. Veterans and homestead exemptions are not rationalized on the same policy grounds as business and charitable exemptions. The exemption of religious institutions may also rest on the policy of encouraging religious freedom. Intergovernmental tax immunities rest upon policies other than those affecting private taxpayer exemptions.

The purpose of the particular tax exemption influences judicial construction of its scope. Courts are not uniformly strict or liberal in their construction and classification of particular exempt classifications. See e.g., the opinions in Amarillo Lodge No. 731, A.F. & A.M. v. Amarillo, 473 S.W.2d 264 (Tex.Civ.App.1971); 16 McQuillin, *Municipal Corporations,* ch. 44 (3rd ed. 1972).

The subject of tax exemption is too large for brief commentary, but it is clear that local government finances suffer huge dollar losses under loose, jerry-built aggregations of state tax exemption laws. Many of these laws are vaguely worded, and unjustified. See ACIR, *The Role of the States in Strengthening the Property Tax,* Vol. 1, Ch. 8, 76–87 (1963).

The following questions touch some possible lines of revision. Should exemptions rest upon the extent of public benefits resulting from the subject's operation, rather than the social approval of that activity? Should foundations, which pursue narrow, sometimes selfish or ideosyncratic goals of dominant economic groups enjoy total exemption? As a form of "private government," do foundations unjustly serve narrow segments of society at general taxpayer expense? Can formulae be devised to tax excessive, (often luxurious) real estate improvements which house exempt foundations? At one time, the Ford Foundation headquarters in New York City, with an assessed value of $14,400,000 was fully tax exempt, according to departmental response to this author's letter inquiry. Should profit-making property and activity be taxed to avoid unfair competition between charities and taxed enterprises?

Tax exemptions have long been used to promote local business and industry. About one-fourth of the states, by constitutional or statutory provision, authorize a variety of local tax exemptions to new and expanding industry. With few exceptions, they have been sustained against constitutional challenges that they serve a private, rather than public purpose; and that they violate the requirement of uniformity of taxation. See the authorities in Note, *Legal Limitations on Public Inducements to Industrial Location,* 59 Colum.L.Rev. 18, 625–29 (1959); Note, *Municipal Inducements to Private Industry,* 40 Minn.L.Rev. 681, 691 (1956). On the grant of a partial exemption from increased assessments of property improvements, to encourage urban renewal improvements, see City of Dayton v. Cloud, 30 Ohio St.2d 295, 285 N.E. 42 (1972).

Many commentators question whether local tax incentives produce enough jobs and economic growth to offset the loss in tax revenue, or to warrant the resentment of non-exempt businesses. See e.g. Break, *Intergovernmental Fiscal Relations In The United States,* 121 (Brookings Inst.1967).

2. INCOME TAXATION

MARKET PLACE v. ANN ARBOR
Court of Appeals of Michigan, 1984.
134 Mich.App. 567, 351 N.W.2d 607.

HOOD, PRESIDING JUDGE.

* * *

The Market Place, a delicatessen, commenced business in Ann Arbor in September, 1980. In April, 1981, the city sent the Market Place a bill for $164 as a license fee imposed pursuant to * * * the City's Ordinance Code. The ordinance mandates that, in order to engage in business, all new businesses in the city must pay a fee equal to the tax rate that would be assessed on that business's personal property for *ad valorem* taxes, but pro rated for the months prior to December 31, or tax day.

* * *

The circuit court granted the city's motion for accelerated judgment and denied plaintiff's motion for rehearing.

The issues we must address in this appeal are: (1) what is the nature of the transient trader or new business license fee, a property or excise tax? and (2) does the city have the authority to impose the tax?

I

In *Dooley v. Detroit,* 370 Mich. 194, 121 N.W.2d 724 (1963), the Court was asked to determine whether Detroit's city income tax was a property or excise tax. The Court stated, pp. 205–206, 121 N.W.2d 724:

"Excises have been variously defined, sometimes in very general language and sometimes in language more specific. In 51 Am.Jur., Taxation, § 24, it is said that:

" 'Taxes fall naturally into 3 classes, namely, capitation or poll taxes, taxes on property, and excises. In general, it may be said that all taxes fall into one or the other of the foregoing classes, any exaction which is clearly not a poll tax or a property tax being an excise.'

"And at section 33, it is said:

" 'In its modern sense an excise tax is any tax which does not fall within the classification of a poll tax or a property tax, and embraces every form of burden not laid directly upon persons or property. The affirmative definitions of excise or excise tax found in the later decisions exhibit some variety in phraseology.'

"See, also, 16 McQuillin, Municipal Corporations (3d ed), § 44.190.

"Our own decisions offer some assistance. For instance, in a line of decisions determining the nature of our corporate franchise tax, * * * we held that the corporate franchise tax was an excise tax on the franchise to do business as a corporation within the State. In support, we relied, first in *Union Steam Pump* ([216 Mich] p 264 [185 NW 353]) and in the other cases cited, upon the broad definition of an excise, which we accepted, found in 26 RCL, Taxation, § 209, at p 236:

" 'An excise is a tax imposed upon the performance of an act, the engaging in an occupation, or the enjoyment of a privilege.' " (footnote omitted).

While we agree with the city and the trial court that the tax in question here is, in part, measured upon the value of business property and is imposed in a sense in lieu of property taxes, we find the new business license fee to be an excise tax within the meaning of *Dooley, supra,* rather than a property tax. We find support in cases from this and other jurisdictions.

In *Continental Motors Corp. v. Muskegon Twp.,* 376 Mich. 170, 135 N.W.2d 908 (1965), the Court determined the validity of a state law imposing a tax on a business possessing interest in property otherwise exempt from property taxes. The tax was measured by the value of the property in a manner similar to *ad valorem* property taxes. The Court stated:

"While the legislature in imposing the new tax has utilized the language of ad valorem taxation, the tax nonetheless in its operation and practical effect is a tax upon the privilege of possession and use for profit of another's tax-exempt personal property and, therefore, it is an excise and not an ad valorem property tax." *Continental*, p. 178, 135 N.W.2d 908.

Thus, the fact that a tax is measured by the value of property, like an *ad valorem* tax, does not mean that the tax is a property tax.

In *Storaasli v. Minnesota*, 283 U.S. 57, 51 S.Ct. 354, 75 L.Ed. 839 (1931), the Supreme Court determined that a state tax imposed upon motor vehicles using that state's highways was not a property tax although the tax was measured by the value of each automobile and was assessed in lieu of all other taxes on those vehicles. The Court placed particular importance on the statute's language denominating the fee as a privilege tax.

In *Ingels v. Riley*, 5 Cal.2d 154, 53 P.2d 939 (1936), the court was asked to determine the nature of a similar tax on motor vehicles, whether a property or excise tax. That court said:

* * *

"It is impossible to lay down any positive rule by means of which the character of any given tax may be ascertained. In each case the character of the given tax must be ascertained by its incidents, and from the natural and legal effect of the language employed in the statute. * * *

"[W]e are of the opinion that the better rule is that the mode of ascertaining the amount of the tax is not conclusive. We are of the opinion that if a tax in its nature is a privilege tax, it does not become a property tax simply because it is proportioned in amount to the value of the property used in connection with the privilege which is taxed.

* * *

The ordinance plaintiff challenges in this case prohibits the privilege of operating as a new business in Ann Arbor until the business pays the license fee. Therefore, although the fee is measured in most part by the value of personal business property, the nature of the tax Ann Arbor imposes is that of a revenue raising excise or privilege tax.

Aside from the language of the ordinance itself, there are other indices that this license fee is not a property tax. First, the fee is assessed only in part by the value of personal business property. There is also a minimum and maximum amount levied. Second, the city does not treat the taxes raised pursuant to the new business ordinance in the same manner as *ad valorem* property taxes. The city disburses most of the *ad valorem* property tax revenues it collects to the county and school district(s) according to state law. However, the city deposits the new business license fees it collects directly into the city's general fund without any such disbursement. Third, the transient trader or new business tax is not computed on the value of any real property a new business may have on hand when the business starts up. Thus, the amount of value taxed is not as comprehensive as an *ad valorem* property tax.

We conclude that the trial court erred by finding the transient trader or new business license fee to be a property tax rather than an excise tax. We find the fee to be an excise tax because it is primarily imposed on the privilege of operating a new business in Ann Arbor.

* * *

II

The next question with which we are presented is whether Ann Arbor has the authority to impose the new business or transient trader license fee as an excise tax.

Local units of government may impose only those taxes expressly authorized by state statute. *Berkley v. Royal Oak Twp.*, 320 Mich. 597, 601, 31 N.W.2d 825 (1948). The home rule cities act mandates that a home rule city charter include: (1) a provision limiting the subjects of municipal taxation to those recognized under general law, M.C.L. § 117.3(f); M.S.A. § 5.2073(f); (2) a provision stating tax limitations, M.C.L. § 117.3(g); M.S.A. § 5.2073(g); (3) a provision for an annual appropriation of money for municipal purposes, M.C.L. § 117.3(h); M.S.A. § 5.2073(h); and (4) a provision outlining a procedure for the levy and collection of taxes in conformity with general laws, or in other words, general property taxes, M.C.L. § 117.3(i); M.S.A. § 5.2073(i).

The home rule cities act also *permits* a home rule city charter to provide, "For laying and collecting rents, tolls and excises", M.C.L. § 117.4i(1); M.S.A. § 5.2082(1), if it desires. * * *. Thus, a home rule city may empower itself to impose excise taxes. However, a city may also decline to empower itself with such permissive authority. Such is the case here.

The Ann Arbor home rule city charter does not include the permissive power to impose excise taxes. We presume that the city intended to restrict its authority in this respect for two reasons. First, our review of the Ann Arbor charter shows that it provides for all of the statutorily permitted powers enumerated in the subsection of the home rule cities act except that for the laying of rents, tolls, or excises. Second, as the Market Place correctly argues, the history of the drafting of Ann Arbor's charter proves that the permissive authority to impose excise taxes was expressly excluded. * * *

At the Charter Commission's open meeting held January 21, 1955, the commission amended the draft by striking all authority to assess, levy, and collect specific taxes, rents, tolls, excises and license fees. The Ann Arbor voters approved the final draft of the charter with the power to tax limited to taxation of real and personal property.

* * * The city argues that the trial court correctly found in its original opinion * * * that the city retained the authority to impose this license fee pursuant to § 2 of the home rule cities act, M.C.L. § 117.2; M.S.A. § 5.2072. We disagree. Even if some such authority did carry over under Ann Arbor's home rule charter, that authority would not include the power to impose fees on businesses such as the Market Place.

* * *

Moreover, "a change in a charter depriving a municipality of previously existing power to enact an ordinance has been held to effect a repeal of the ordinance". 6 McQuillan, Municipal Corporations, § 21.26. See also *People v. Brill,* 120 Mich. 42, 78 N.W. 1013 (1899). Because the Ann Arbor voters adopted a home rule charter expressly precluding license fees or excise taxes under the city's powers to tax, and because the adoption in 1956 of the home rule charter acted to repeal the transient trader ordinance at issue in this case, the city no longer had the authority to impose such tax.

We address the remainder of the city's argument summarily. There is no doubt that the Michigan Constitution and state statutes permit a municipality to impose excise taxes of this nature. However the home rule cities act permits a home rule charter city to accept or reject this authority. Ann Arbor rejected the authority and may not now argue that the state laws should be read into its charter. * * * We also disagree with the city's contention that its general power in Chapter 3 of its home rule charter authorizes the new business license fees. While we agree that the powers of home rule cities must be liberally construed, * * * the rejection by the Charter Commission and Ann Arbor voters of the city's power to impose license fees or excise taxes precludes any construction at all in this case. Certainly, had Ann Arbor adopted the power to impose excise taxes we would broadly construe that term generically to include the license fee at issue here. See *Dooley, supra.*

In conclusion, we find that the trial court erred by finding Ann Arbor's new business transient trader ordinance a valid exercise of the city's power to impose property taxes. Rather, the tax at issue in this case is an excise tax which the city does not have the authority to impose. * * *

* * *

Notes

1. **Classifying the Nature of the Tax.** Compare with the principal case, Arnold v. Berra, 366 S.W.2d 321 (Mo.1963) which upheld a city "earnings" tax upon nonresidents, but rejected the claim that it was a "privilege" or excise tax.

2. **Graduated Income Taxes.** The authorities are divided on the treatment of graduated income taxes. Viewed as a "property" tax, graduation may violate the state's uniformity requirements. See e.g., Bachrach v. Nelson, 349 Ill. 579, 182 N.E. 909 (1932). Viewed as an excise, it may still run afoul of uniformity provisions in states where the provision is construed to apply to "all" taxes (Kelley v. Kalodner, 320 Pa. 180, 181 A. 598 (1935); cf. Saulsbury v. Bethlehem Steel Co., note 3 below), but not in states

where uniformity provisions do not extend to nonproperty taxes, nor where graduated taxes are permitted by constitutional amendment. See e.g. Reynolds Metal Co. v. Martin, 269 Ky. 378, 107 S.W.2d 251 (1937); Miles v. Department of Treasury, 209 Ind. 172, 199 N.E.2d 372 (1935); Hellerstein, *Book Review*, 9 Buffalo L.Rev. 402 (1960), Prentiss-Hall, *State and Local Tax Service—All States Unit,* ¶ 91.121.

3. **Occupation Taxes.** In Saulsbury v. Bethlehem Steel Co., 413 Pa. 316, 196 A.2d 664 (1964) exemption of persons with low income (below $6,000 per year) from the city's annual occupation tax was voided as a violation of the constitutional provision that "all taxes shall be uniform * * *." The court noted that unlike other Pennsylvania constitutional restrictions, the uniformity clause section was not confined to property taxation. The dissent argued that the classification of taxable subjects was reasonable, and, therefore, consistent with uniformity. A similar result was reached in Pharr Road Investment Co. v. Atlanta, 224 Ga. 403, 162 S.E.2d 333 (1968).

Could exemption of members of the armed forces from a city wage tax withstand a uniformity attack? See City of Philadelphia v. Farrell, 205 Pa. Super. 263, 209 A.2d 867 (1965).

4. **Nonresident Tax Liability.** The "incident" of the income tax may be "residence," or business activity within the city. Where a nonresident conducts business outside as well as within the city, the tax may only be assessed against income attributable to activity in the city. There is no narrow rule for such allocation. Courts only require that allocation formulae be "reasonable." See Los Angeles v. Moore Business Forms, Inc., 247 Cal.App.2d 353, 55 Cal.Rptr. 820 (1966).

Problem: An accounting partnership with the home office in the taxing city, consisted of resident and nonresident partners, with the nonresident partners servicing out of city clients. Should the partnership be taxed, as a resident entity, upon all of its income? If not, how should the income be allocated? See Tax Review Board of City of Philadelphia v. D.H. Shapiro Co., 409 Pa. 253, 185 A.2d 529 (1962).

Problem: Where Doe, a resident of Suburban Village, works in Center City, and both the Village and the City levy an income tax of 1% on all income of residents, and on nonresidents' income earned within their respective bounds, is Doe liable for either tax, both taxes, or partially for both taxes? The answer may be provided by legislation which allocates tax liability, or provides a credit of one tax payment against the other. See e.g. 53 Pa.Stat. § 6908; Mich.Comp.Laws Ann. §§ 141.611, 141.665. Absent legislation, courts may fashion an adjustment, but the shape and content of such adjustments is not dictated by any objective standard. See e.g. Morgan v. Glen Alden Coal Co., 165 Pa.Super. 203, 67 A.2d 756 (1949). See generally, Annotation, *Commuter Tax-Validity,* 48 A.L.R.3d 343 (1973).

3. SALES TAXES

"New York City adopted the first local sales tax in 1934. New Orleans followed in 1938. Due to revenue problems that developed after World War II, local sales taxes were adopted by various cities in

California, and also in Illinois, Mississippi, and Utah. About one-half of the incorporated cities in California had adopted sales taxes prior to the enactment of the Bradley-Burns Act. Presently, both counties and cities may impose the tax and nearly all do.

"At the beginning of 1968, local sales taxes were in effect in approximately 2400 cities and 370 counties in 16 states, including Alaska, Arizona, California, Colorado, New Mexico, and Utah in the west. The rates ranged between one-half of one per cent and three per cent." See Multnomah Kennel Club v. Department of Revenue, 295 Or. 279, 666 P.2d 1327, 1331 n. 5 (1983).

4. SPECIAL ASSESSMENTS

Whereas tax levies are geared to the requirements of general government, special assessments are primarily "one-shot" apportionments of public improvement costs to properties that are deemed to derive a primary, special or local benefit from that improvement. Not being taxes in a strict constitutional sense, special assessments are not governed by statutory and constitutional restrictions on local taxation. They must, however, be authorized by state or charter laws.

The principal issues in special assessment cases concern (a) their validity, i.e. whether an improvement constitutes an assessable special "benefit," or a general improvement requiring uniform tax support; (b) the method of apportioning improvement costs among benefited parcels; and (c) the legality of assessment procedures, i.e. their conformity with constitutional or statutory mandates.

MULLINS v. EL DORADO
Supreme Court of Kansas, 1968.
200 Kan. 336, 436 P.2d 837.

O'CONNOR, JUSTICE. This action was instituted by the owners of three tracts of land to enjoin the City of El Dorado from proceeding to levy and collect special assessments made against plaintiffs' properties for financing the construction of a sanitary sewer system. * * *

In May 1962, the plaintiffs * * * joined other landowners in petitioning the city governing body to provide their properties with sanitary sewers. Thereupon, the city, acting pursuant to K.S.A. 12–618 (now K.S.A.1967, Supp. 12–618), created sewer districts 103, 106 and 107. The system was eventually constructed and completed at a total cost of $44,483.68. The trial court found the districts were legally created and that the city complied with all statutory requirements in constructing the sewers. * * * The cost attributable to each district was apportioned to the various parcels of land therein, * * *.

* * *

In essence, the plaintiffs' petition alleged the special assessments against their individual tracts were excessive; that the actions of the defendant city, in determining the boundaries of the districts and apportioning the cost of the system, were arbitrary, capricious, unreasonable, oppressive, unlawful, confiscatory and void; and that the levy and collection of said special assessments should be enjoined. A restraining order was issued against the defendant city * * *. However, we were told in oral argument that the city has proceeded to collect the assessments made against other tracts in each of the districts. * * *

* * *

Taxation and assessment proceedings are fundamentally administrative or legislative in character and not judicial. Assuming that the petition states a claim * * * the power of the courts under K.S.A. 60–907(a) to grant relief * * * is confined to those situations where the action taken by the governing body is without authority, or permeated with fraud, corruption or conduct so oppressive, arbitrary or capricious as to amount to fraud. [Citations omitted]

In our recent decision of Schulenberg v. City of Reading, 196 Kan. 43, 410 P.2d 324, which was an action * * * to enjoin the collection of special assessments * * * for financing the construction of a sewer system, we said:

"* * * Courts can only interfere to curb action which is *ultra vires* because of some constitutional impediment, or lack of valid legislative authority, or unlawful acts under a valid statute, or because action under a valid statute is so arbitrary, capricious, unreasonable and subversive of private rights as to indicate a clear abuse rather than a *bona fide* exercise of power. * * *

The foundation of the power to make a special assessment for a local improvement of any character * * * is that the property against which the assessment is levied derives some special benefit from the improvement. * * *

The whole theory of special assessments is demonstrated by the language found in the early and oft cited case of Norwood v. Baker, 172 U.S. 269, 19 S.Ct. 187, 43 L.Ed. 443:

"* * * the principle underlying special assessments to meet the cost of public improvements is that the property upon which they are imposed is peculiarly benefited, and, therefore the owners do not, in fact, pay anything in excess of what they receive by reason of such improvement. * * *

"* * * the exaction from the owner of private property at the cost of a public improvement in substantial excess of the special benefits accruing to him is, *to the extent of such excess,* a taking, under the guise of taxation, of private property for public use without compensation. We say 'substantial excess,' because exact quality of taxation is not always attainable, and for that reason the excess of cost over special benefits, unless it be of a material character, ought not to be regarded by a court of equity, when its aid is invoked to restrain the enforcement of a special assessment." (pp. 278, 279, 19 P.2d p. 190.)

The inability to always balance with exactitude the assessment with the benefits was further recognized by Mr. Justice Holmes, speaking for the majority of the court in Louisville & N.R.R. Co. v. Barber Asphalt Co., 197 U.S. 430, 25 S.Ct. 466, 49 L.Ed. 819:

"* * * There is a look of logic when it is said that special assessments are founded on special benefits, and that a law which makes it possible to assess beyond the amount of the special benefit attempts to rise above its source. But that mode of argument assumes an exactness in the premises which does not exist. The foundation of this familiar form of taxation is a question of theory. The amount of benefit which an improvement will confer upon particular land— indeed whether it is a benefit at all—is a matter of forecast and estimate. In its general aspects, at least, it is peculiarly a thing to be decided by those who make the law. * * * " (p. 433, 25 S.Ct. p. 467.)

Ordinarily, the question of the existence and extent of special benefits resulting from a public improvement for which a special assessment is made is a question of fact to be determined by the governing body authorized to act in the premises, and is considered conclusive on the property owners and the courts. Inherent in this rule, however, is the requirement that an assessment so made be fair, just and equitable. Only if palpable injustice results in applying the method of apportionment and assessment so that the burden imposed is entirely disproportionate to benefit received, will courts, under their equity power, grant relief. (Schulenberg v. City of Reading, *supra;* Hurley v. Board of County Commissioners, 188 Kan. 60, 360 P.2d 1110; 14 McQuillin, Municipal Corporations § 38.124; 48 Am.Jur., Special or Local Assessments § 29.) The action of municipal authorities in making a special assessment is presumed to be legal, equitable and just, and the assessment is prima facie evidence of the regularity and correctness of all prior proceedings. [Citations omitted] Thus, in establishing grounds justifying intercession by the courts, a property owner has the burden of proof. [Citations omitted]

Turning to the crucial points of this appeal, we find the defendant city contending that the method used in allocating the cost of the sewer system was fair and reasonable. It asserts * * * that costs were apportioned upon a plan expressly approved by this court, that is, in proportion to the value of the lots taxed without improvements thereon. The point is well taken.

* * *

The statute makes no requirement for the appointment of appraisers, yet there is precedent for such procedure. (See, St. Louis & S.F. Ry. Co. v. City of Pleasanton, 121 Kan. 559, 247 P. 447.) Neither does the statute prescribe a specific method for apportioning costs. Where such is the case, the municipality may adopt any plan that is fair and equitable and such that will bring about an assessment in proportion to the benefits accruing. * * * A similar plan of apportionment was also approved in Ransom v. Minnick, 92 Kan. 953, 142 P. 934. Thus, the assessment of costs in proportion to the value of the properties without improvements thereon is a proper method of apportionment under K.S.A. 12–618 (now K.S.A.1967 Supp. 12–618) as long as the burden imposed on each of the tracts is not entirely disproportionate to benefits accruing thereto.

The defendant city admits that the market value of the tracts was less than that fixed by the appraisers; however, it aptly points out that the result would be the same regardless of the valuations determined if the frontage values were uniform for all properties. That is, each tract would bear a portion of the costs in relation to its frontage with the total frontage in the district.

The city also concedes the correctness of the lower court's finding that the special assessments made against the properties involved were greater than or substantially equivalent to their actual market value, but urges that this fact alone does not compel a conclusion that the assessments were confiscatory, unreasonable and oppressive. We are inclined to agree. In Buckwalter v. Henrion, 111 Kan. 781, 208 P. 645, certain lots belonging to the plaintiffs were subjected to special assessments for street improvements which aggregated more than the market value of the property. In holding there was no confiscation or breach of constitutional law, this court stated:

> " * * * But while such a result is to be avoided by city officials wherever possible, and if such result can be traced to their willful injustice, oppression, or sheer disregard of property rights, the strong hand of a court of equity would promptly reach out and set it at naught, and do it, too, with more concern for righteousness than for logic [citing Norwood v. Baker, *supra*] * * * yet where the special assessments are fairly made, and made according to equitable principles, and pursuant to statutory authority, the fact that the proportionate cost of the improvement is greater than the property will readily sell for on the current market does not make a case for the interference of a court of equity. [Citations omitted]"

Also, see, 14 McQuillin, Municipal Corporations § 38.183.

In support of the trial court's findings and conclusions that the assessments were confiscatory, unreasonable and oppressive, the plaintiffs strongly urge that the city governing body, in making the assessments on a uniform front-foot-valuation basis, disregarded the special benefit of the sewer to each tract, the size of the tract and its particular use. Defendant city argues there was no discrimination in assessing the tracts, that the tracts within the districts were of uniform depth and were equally benefited. The only property that merits attention on this point is that of Mrs. Mullins. She testified her tract consisted of 240 feet frontage on Sixth street with a north-south depth of 318 feet, that the Cities Service Company had an easement across the entire south frontage, that there was a fenced area for a pressure station consisting of 100 feet east and west by 50 feet in depth, and that the remaining frontage of 142 feet consisted of a pipeline easement 33 feet in depth. * * * One of the three appraisers testified * * * that the particular area could not be utilized as far as frontage was concerned; but in considering the manner and method in which driveways and approaches were used, they assumed this could be worked around and would have no appreciable effect on the ground whatever, and they appraised it as having none. The appraisers apparently gave little or no consideration to the easement in making their appraisal of the property. It would appear the entire Mullins tract located in the sewer district was subject to being served by the sewer without regard to the burden of the easement.

Mrs. Mullins' home, a tavern and two outbuildings were located on her tract. * * *

It is a matter of common knowledge that a sewer system ordinarily enhances the value of the property it is designed to serve. * * * While present use may properly be considered in determining benefits, it is not controlling. * * * Thus, the test is not whether the property is enhanced in value for the particular purpose to which it is devoted at the time of assessment but whether it is enhanced in value for any purpose. (See, Village of Edina v. Joseph, 264 Minn. 84, 119 N.W.2d 809.)

In light of the foregoing discussion, we are of the opinion the easement did not substantially affect the value or use of the Mullins property to such an extent that it did not receive the same benefits from the construction of the sewer as other properties in the districts.

To support their position that the uniform front-foot-valuation basis ignored the size of each tract, the plaintiffs cite Weed v. City of Boston, 172 Mass. 28, 51 N.E. 204. We have examined the decision and find it is not particularly helpful to plaintiffs' cause. * * * The court held that inasmuch as lots adjacent to the sewer constructed on a strip of private land taken for the purpose may vary greatly in size or depth and value per foot and may be inadequate to bear the burden of assessment, the method of assessment was unreasonable and disproportionate and, thus, the statute in such respect was unconstitutional. * * * The statute in the *Weed* case required the assessment of cost on a frontage basis in all instances, whereas here we are called on to consider only whether under the facts a frontage basis of apportionment was palpably inequitable and unreasonable. * * *

The law does not require that a special assessment correspond exactly with the benefits received. Seldom can precise mathematical accuracy be obtained. The most that can be expected of a governing body * * * is to estimate the benefits to each tract of land upon as uniform plan as possible so that the assessment against a particular piece of property is substantially proportionate to the benefits received. We have carefully examined the entire record and have concluded that the plaintiffs failed to sustain the burden of showing that the application of a uniform front-foot-valuation formula in apportioning costs has led to assessments that are entirely disproportionate to the benefits received by their individual properties.

* * * the plaintiffs also contend they were entitled to the relief granted because the action of the governing body, in determining the size of the sewer districts, resulted in unreasonable and oppressive assessments against the property. They maintain the system was capable of handling sewerage from other areas or districts, and the cost of the system was relatively large; therefore, it should have been considered as a main sewer, in which case a substantial portion of the cost could have been paid by the city at large, pursuant to K.S.A. 12–619 (now K.S.A.1967 Supp. 12–619). * * * While it was acknowledged the lines were of sufficient capacity to serve other areas outside the district, the city engineer testified that as future development took place in those areas, they would be served by main sewers from other directions rather than the system in question.

* * * Throughout all the proceedings the city proceeded on the theory the sewer was a lateral system except as to that portion designated as a pressure main and lift station. * * * The adoption of an appropriate plan in accordance with applicable statutory authority conferred by the legislature called for the exercise of discretion and judgment by the municipal authorities, whose decision, rendered in good faith, free from fraud, must be regarded as final and not subject to review by the courts. [Citations omitted] From the record we are unable to find any grounds which, under the authorities cited, justify disturbing the determination made by the city as to the size of the districts and the assessment of costs to the properties in the districts on the basis of a lateral system.

The judgment of the district court is reversed.

* * *

FONTRON, J., dissents.

FATZER, JUSTICE (concurring in part and dissenting in part):

I concur in this court's judgment of reversal, but I must respectfully dissent from the judgment denying the plaintiffs injunctive relief. I would direct the district court to make additional findings. It is manifest from the judgment rendered below that the district court was of the opinion the plaintiffs should be given some relief from the onerous assessments. Inherent in the judgment is the implied finding the system installed was a main sewer since the court ordered the city at large to absorb a much larger portion of the assessments. For the city at large to be assessed a substantial portion of the cost of the system in accordance with the judgment, the district court would have been required to find the system was a main sewer. (K.S.A.1967 Supp. 12–619.) Despite the fact both parties requested the court to make a specific finding whether the system was main or lateral * * *—the court refused to specifically find either way, and denied both motions. The evidence on the point was highly conflicting and until a specific finding is made, it is my judgment the case is not ripe for decision, and this court may not assume the sewers installed were all "lateral."

* * *

Notes

1. Compare: Mullins *with* Quality Homes, Inc. v. New Brighton, 289 Minn. 274, 183 N.W.2d 555 (1971) where the assessments for a sewer trunk line only against properties actually taken into the system was held invalid in view of the fact that the line was designed to be used by other properties in the near future. Plaintiffs attacking special assessments have a poor rate of success. See Nichols, Comment: *How Not To Contest Special Assessments in California, or You Can't Fight City Hall,* 17 Stanford L.Rev. 247 (1965).

The determination of the group or zone of properties specially benefited is complicated where an existing usable facility is reconstructed, extended, or connected to new utilities. The cases do not fall into any neat pattern. See the next case and 14 McQuillin, *Municipal Corporations* § 38.34 (3rd rev. ed. 1970).

2. **The Standard of Reasonableness.** This standard is not very exacting. Crocker v. Albany, 241 Ore. 180, 405 P.2d 364 (1965) upheld assessments for construction costs that proved to be 40% higher than the estimated assessments that were noticed to the property owners. In Schulenberg v. Reading, 196 Kan. 43, 410 P.2d 324 (1966) a city-wide sewer improvement district charged 93% of the total improvement cost against two school districts, and the court voided the assessments as unreasonable.

3. **Legislatively Formed Districts.** As the principal opinion indicates, court use of economic-effect arguments to find property benefit from a proposed improvement is especially evident in legislatively created special improvement districts, even though many included properties are benefited only indirectly or remotely. See e.g. Duncan Development Corp. v. Crestview Sanitary Dist., 22 Wis.2d 258, 125 N.W.2d 617 (1964). In Los Angeles County Flood Control District v. Hamilton, 177 Cal. 119, 169 P. 1028 (1917), the owners of high elevation land objected to its inclusion in a flood control district. They met the following response: "[T]he Act was designed to conserve the flood waters for beneficial and useful purposes by storing them, or otherwise, and to protect from damage by flood the harbors, waterways and public highways in the district. To say, therefore, that any given possible tract of land is not directly subject to overflow is not to say that it cannot be benefited. * * * We should, under the decisions, be required to hold that the benefits * * * need not be so direct and immediate as is assumed in the argument of counsel opposing the validity of the Act. * * * An examination of these cases will show that the courts have regarded an incidental or indirect benefit as sufficient to justify the imposition of a part of the burden of the improvement. Such indirect benefit may result from the improvement of the neighboring and surrounding land, and the consequent increase in the value of all land within the district. * * * At least, it is impossible, * * * to say that the Legislature could not fairly so determine. * * * Apart from any other consideration, the protection of the roads in any one of the water sheds, and the maintenance of communication with the others might be a matter of very direct concern to all of the land embraced within the district." Id. at 126–27, 169 P. at 1031.

Equitable considerations may underlie the legislative and judicial judgment as to what properties should be included in an improvement district. "The fact that certain properties are situated on high ground and in no danger from flood damage is not to say that such property should not pay its share of the cost of flood control. It is quite apparent, * * * that the density of population of these higher areas * * * causing the surplus rain waters to run off to the lower area, materially contributes to the flood condition. * * * The contention that such property owners who contribute to the problem are deprived of their property by due process of law by reason of being taxed to control that condition is untenable." See Albuquerque Metropolitan Arroyo Flood Control Authority v. Swinburne, 74 N.M. 487, 493–494, 394 P.2d 998, 1002–1003 (1964). Contra: Day v. Mummey, 200 N.E.2d 785 (Ohio App.1963).

The argument that potential as well as present use of particular land may properly be considered, was echoed in Atchison, T. & S.F. Ry. Co. v. Kings County Water District, 47 Cal.2d 140, 146–147, 302 P.2d 1, 5 (1956): "In the final analysis, it is therefore the potential rather than the present use of the particular land which must control. To hold otherwise, and permit the present non-agricultural use of the land to determine the right to its exclusion from the district, would result in the creation of excluded 'islands' * * * within an integrated county water district, * * * merely because of lack of need for the water in the present use, * * * rather than because of lack of benefit to, and consequent enhancement of the value of, the land itself."

In Crutchfield v. Nash, 84 Mont. 556, 569, 276 P. 938, 943 (1929) the court noted: "An assessment cannot be predicated upon future action of the public authorities or future legislation, and hence, if property cannot be benefited by a proposed improvement, unless subsequent work is done for which no provision is made, the property cannot be specially assessed."

Artificial rationalizations for special assessments by regional districting support the view that special assessment districts are poor substitutes for general regional government. Such districts compound interlocal conflict, viz. in the competition for water supply. See e.g. Central Basin Municipal Water District v. Fossette, 235 Cal.App.2d 689, 45 Cal.Rptr. 651 (1965). They unnecessarily duplicate municipal functions. A property owner may be forced into an improvement district even though the district's water service is already provided by a neighboring municipality. DeLoreto v. Goleta County Water District, 234 Cal.App.2d 164, 44 Cal.Rptr. 137 (1965).

SEILER v. BOARD OF SEWER COMMISSIONERS OF HINGHAM

Supreme Judicial Court of Massachusetts, 1968.
353 Mass. 452, 233 N.E.2d 306.

SPIEGEL, JUSTICE. This is an appeal from an order of the Superior Court dismissing a petition * * * to quash the assessments made by the respondent board of sewer commissioners of Hingham against the petitioners' estates for a proportional part of the cost of a new sewer system in the town of Hingham. * * *

* * * We state the agreed facts as summarized by the trial judge in his memorandum and order. "In 1900 common sewers were constructed in the public ways, on which the several estates of the petitioners now abut, by the Town pursuant to authorization granted at the annual town meeting of that year. These sewers all discharged through an outflow sewer constructed in Hingham Bay. The outflow sewer emptied into a channel in the Bay about 700 feet from shore. The houses served by the sewers in 1900 were used almost exclusively for seasonal occupancy. At said annual meeting it was determined that the cost of the sewers and outflow sewer, estimated at $4800., should be met by the Town paying $2500. and that 'every person who uses the common sewer to be constructed at Crow Point shall pay for the permanent privilege to his estate such reasonable sum as the Selectmen shall determine.' This latter determination was pursuant to P.S.C. 50, s. 8, which authorized the Town to provide 'that, instead of paying an assessment under section four every person who uses such * * * common sewers in any manner shall pay for the permanent privilege to his estate such reasonable sum' as the Selectmen shall determine. See now General Laws C. 83, ss. 17, 14. The selectmen determined upon the sum of $75.00. No new construction of said common sewers or changes in design thereof or method of operation occurred until the work done by the Board and described * * * [below]. Meanwhile, beginning about 1934, the discharge of raw sewage through the outflow pipe * * * was causing a health menace in the judgment of the Board of Health of the Town, and, in the judgment of the respondent Board, the pollution in Hingham Harbor caused by such raw sewage had to be brought to an end. * * * Commencing in 1955 the Town has constructed * * * a system of common sewers for the North Sewer District, which includes as part thereof the Crow Point section and the public ways on which the several estates of the petitioners abut. Among the changes wrought by the Board in the sewers constructed in 1900 was the elimination of the outflow sewer and the substitution for it of the newly constructed means and method of discharge * * *. By such change sewage now deposited in the 1900 sewer system no longer discharges into Hingham Bay, but, by the system newly constructed by the Town since 1955, flows * * * ultimately to the Metropolitan District Sewer System. With the exception of the rights claimed by petitioners by reason of the 1900 sewer construction and the determination that every person who used such 1900 sewers should pay $75. for the permanent privilege to his estate of such user, petitioners agree that all actions of the respondent in constructing the sewers commencing in 1955 and in making the assessments in relation to such construction were in accordance with the applicable statutes and votes of the Town. * * * The vote of the Town at the 1955 annual meeting determined that the Town shall pay 65% of the whole cost of the system of sewers for the North Sewer District, and that the 'remaining portion of the cost * * * shall be provided for by assessments upon the owners of lands abutting on that part of any way in which a sewer

is constructed according to the frontage of land on such way at the rate of $5.00 per linear foot of such frontage, provided that in no case shall any sewer assessment be made in excess of the actual benefit.' The estates of petitioners constitute a small number of the estates assessed * * *, and have been assessed in the same manner 'for the remaining portion of the cost of the system' as the owners of other estates on Crow Point situated on public ways where new sewers have been constructed since 1955."

The judge stated that the "Substitution of the newly constructed mains, sewers and pumping stations * * * for the old outflow sewer, (1) eliminated that part of the 1900 sewer system which had fallen into disrepair, (2) eliminated the health menace caused by the presence of raw sewage in Hingham Bay, * * * and (3) provided that 1900 sewer system with up-to-date means and methods for discharge of sewage collected in it." He concluded that the foregoing constituted a special benefit to the petitioners which justifies the assessments in question. The main thrust of the petitioners' appeal appears to be directed at this last conclusion.

* * *

The petitioners' position is that the only benefit conferred on them by the new sewer system is the abatement of pollution in Hingham Harbor. They maintain that this benefits them less than the rest of the residents of Hingham, since the petitioners' lands front on Hingham Bay which the tidal currents keep free of pollution from the discharge pipe of the 1900 sewer system. At most they are benefited equally with all other residents of Hingham. The continued existence and functioning of the 1900 system, it is contended, rebuts any other special benefit to them from the new construction.

Whether the pollution adversely affects the petitioners' frontage on Hingham Bay is not the controlling factor. It is not contested that the pollution problem existed, and that the further discharge of raw sewage into Hingham Bay from the 1900 sewer system could not be tolerated. It follows that prior to the new construction the 1900 sewer system on which the petitioners' estates abut was not functioning properly, in that it had no usable outlet. The respondent could have chosen to repair and extend the old discharge pipe into the bay. This might also have required other efforts to prevent the continued discharge of raw sewage. Such a project, exclusively for the benefit of the users of the 1900 system, could undenially have been assessed to the petitioners and to their fellow abutters. That the respondent chose to solve this problem by tying the 1900 system into a new and general plan for the disposal of sewage through the Metropolitan District System does not diminish the special benefit to the petitioners.

We agree with the judge that "The Town was not bound to maintain the design of the 1900 sewer system in perpetuity by the vote taken at the annual meeting of 1900. Neither that vote nor any payments made or to be made thereunder are a bar to assessments otherwise validly made for any changes in the design of that system or improvements thereto which result in special and peculiar benefits to the estates owned by the petitioners."

The petitioners also argue that general town revenues and Federal grants used for the North Sewer District project should have been allocated to cover that portion of the construction from which they derive benefit, with the remainder assessed against only those estates abutting on new sewer laterals. * * * There is nothing to compel the respondent to allocate funds so as to put the general burden exclusively on abutters other than on the petitioners. In view of the difficulty of attempting to estimate benefits to the estates individually, it is necessary only that the principle by which the expenditures are apportioned provide for reasonable and proportional assessments, not substantially in excess of the benefits received. There is nothing to show that the assessments have not been made in conformity with these requirements.

There was no error in refusing to quash the assessments.

Order affirmed.

Notes

1. **User Charges and Special Assessments.** Was the original $75 fee in the principal case a user charge or a special assessment? User or consumer charges, e.g. fees, fares, tolls, water and sewer rents, cover *operating* expenses, while special assessments cover *capital* improvements that benefit property value. Special assessments are "compelled," while user charges are optionally incurred. The distinction is, of course, inexact. A city may also compel non-owners to use and pay for city sewerage service. Some jurisdictions permit the capitalizing of service expenses through assessments on abutting property, e.g. for street sprinkling and sweeping services. See 14 McQuillin, *Municipal Corporations,* § 38.22 (3rd rev. ed. 1970).

2. **Classified Improvement Benefits.** Public parks are generally held to qualify either as general benefits, supportable by taxes; or as special benefits, supportable by special assessments. 14 McQuillin, supra, § 38.28 (3rd rev. ed. 1970). But a library or an auditorium, though it enhances nearby property values, may be held to be a nonassessable, general benefit project. See Heavens v. King County Rural Library Dist., 66 Wash.2d 558, 404 P.2d 453 (1965). In the absence of legislative declaration, courts draw their own conclusions on general and local benefit.

(a) Where a street improvement includes special facilities required by state law, *viz.* a railroad crossing gate, may the abutting owners be specially assessed for them, as well as the street work? See Sisters of St. Mary, Inc. v. Beaverton, 4 Or.App. 297, 478 P.2d 412 (1970).

(b) Where a special district is formed to widen a street in connection with development of a commercial mall, are all properties abutting the widened street specially benefitted? See Mueller v. Roseville, 38 Mich.App. 170, 195 N.W.2d 882 (1972).

3. **Intergovernmental Assessments.** The ability of one local unit to levy special assessments upon other government property varies from state to state. Compare e.g. City of Titusville v. Board of Public Instruction of Brevard County, 258 So.2d 836 (Fla.1970) (upholding city assessments of school district property) with City of Garland v. Garland Independent School Dist., 468 S.W.2d 110 (Tex.Civ.App.1971) (exempting school property). See Annot., 15 A.L.R.3d 847 (1967). But a school district which is exempt from special assessments cannot avoid user charges that are levied as part of the municipal police power, even though the district has no need or desire to employ the municipal service. Southwest Delaware County Municipal Authority v. Aston, 413 Pa. 526, 198 A.2d 867 (1964); Murray City v. Board of Education of Murray City School Dist., 16 Utah 2d 115, 396 P.2d 628 (1964).

On immunity of state property from local special assessments, see State ex rel. Londerholm v. Topeka, 201 Kan. 729, 443 P.2d 240 (1968). Here also, state statutes and decisions differ.

AXTELL v. PORTAGE

Court of Appeals of Michigan, 1971.
32 Mich.App. 491, 189 N.W.2d 99.

T.M. BURNS, JUDGE. Plaintiffs filed suit * * * against the City of Portage and its treasurer, Donald Gage, seeking a circuit court judgment declaring a special assessment to improve Kilgore Road unlawful, and an injunction against both defendants from collecting such special assessment. * * * After a six-day nonjury trial, judgment was entered November 7, 1969, dismissing plaintiffs' complaint. Plaintiffs appeal to this court as of right.

Sometime in 1966, the Kalamazoo County Road Commission approached the cities of Portage and Kalamazoo with the idea of widening and improving the most westerly section of Kilgore Road. * * *

Kilgore Road is a straight east-west one, largely residential in character, separating the City of Kalamazoo on the north from the City of Portage on the south. Presently the road is two-lane with a bituminous surface and is 22 feet wide. The road is in very poor condition * * *. The visibility is poor due to frequent hills and the road shoulders are presently in very poor condition. Complaints have also been registered about dust and drainage problems by abutting property owners.

Due to the above problems, the three governmental units (Kalamazoo County, City of Portage, and City of Kalamazoo) decided to improve the road by widening it to four lanes; repaving with reinforced concrete; regrading; and installing curbs, gutters, and a storm sewer to prevent further damage from water drainage. The total cost of the project, to be shared by all three governmental units, was estimated to be about $411,481.93. About one-fourth of this cost was to be borne by the property owners abutting Kilgore Road.

Plaintiffs contended below that the special assessment is void because no special benefit will be conferred upon them as abutting property owners due to the widening and improving of Kilgore Road. Plaintiffs cite the fact that all of the old trees lining both sides of the road will have to be removed and replaced with young small ones. They also contend that living next to a new four-lane road rather than the present two-lane road with the consequent increase in traffic is a detriment rather than an improvement. Plaintiffs also contend that the proposed changes in Kilgore Road will have a detrimental effect on property values. Defendants' position at the trial was that traffic would not significantly increase because Kilgore Road "dead-ends" at Oakland Drive; and, therefore, the function of the road would remain a "collector" road rather than an "arterial" road. Defendants also pointed out several other nearby artery routes which would continue to service the through traffic.

* * *

Municipal corporations may, of course, levy special assessments upon property "abutting upon and adjacent to" an improvement M.C. L.A. § 104.1 (Stat.Ann.1949 Rev. § 5.1825), based upon the theory that a special benefit, over and above the general benefit conferred upon the city as a whole, is being conferred upon such property. Although the benefit must be peculiar to them because of their proximity to the improvement, the benefit may exist in a number of forms:

> "Special benefits require an increase in value, relief from a burden, or the creation of a special adaptability in the land. 63 C.J.S. Municipal Corporations § 1371 [, p. 1128]." Soncoff v. City of Inkster (1970), 22 Mich.App. 358, 361, 177 N.W.2d 243, 245.

The Michigan Supreme Court has held that the widening of a residential street into a four-lane main artery would not confer the type of benefit which would subject the abutting owners to a special assessment. Brill v. City of Grand Rapids (1970), 383 Mich. 216, 174 N.W.2d 832; Fluckey v. City of Plymouth (1960), 358 Mich. 447, 100 N.W.2d 486. However, both of the Supreme Court cases cited dealt with the situation where a residential street was converted, more or less, into a highway. The whole character of the street and the neighborhoods had been changed as a result of the improvements, causing a great deal of deterioration in the quality of life experienced by abutting land owners.

In the instant case, Kilgore Road is hardly capable of being transformed into a through highway since it "dead-ends" at Oakland Drive. There are also in existence other thoroughfares in the Kilgore Road area which presently accommodate through traffic traveling east and west. We therefore find *Brill* and *Fluckey* distinguishable on the facts from the situation presented here.

The trial judge found that the improvements would make Kilgore Road safer, give the abutting land owners easier ingress and egress, and also that the value of the homes would increase due to the improvements. Our review of the record leads us to the conclusion that the trial court's findings of fact are fully supported by the evidence.

* * * Therefore, since the abutting land owners will be the recipients of special benefits as a result of the improvements, the trial court was correct in upholding the special assessment.

Plaintiffs also contend that the formula used by the cities to arrive at the amount of the special assessment is improper. Defendants have one formula for all special assessment situations based upon the theory that any street is of about equal benefit to the frontage owner. It is plaintiffs' position that the assessors must employ a "balancing test", *i.e.,* weighing special benefits against special detriments, to compute the amount of the assessment.

We cannot agree with the plaintiffs' position. * * *

In the instant case the trial court found that the proposed improvement would confer a special benefit on the abutting land owners. Our review of the evidence leads us to the same conclusion. We will not, therefore, substitute our judgment for that of the assessors upon the worth of the benefits conferred. Absent some showing that the assessment is unreasonable or out of proportion to the benefits conferred, we will not set aside the assessor's judgment.

Affirmed.

* * *

Notes

1. In Axtell, special benefit arose from improved ingress and egress to the widened street. Would such a benefit equally support assessment against non-abutting properties? The authorities are divided. See Snyder Realty Co. v. Overland Park, 208 Kan. 273, 492 P.2d 187 (1971); Annot., 46 A.L.R.3d 127 at 143–147 (1972). As to parking facilities, see the *Wing* case, p. 644, infra.

2. **Street Improvements.** Special assessments on abutting properties for street improvements are generally upheld. See also Eilender v. Pontiac, 371 Mich. 671, 124 N.W.2d 806 (1963). Where there is a legislative determination of special benefits, courts will not interfere unless the legislative determination is clearly unreasonable. Should a court imply a legislative finding of special benefit from the bare fact that a statute authorized special assessments for street improvements? Compare Aquarium Properties, Inc. v. Hayman, 38 Pa.D. & C.2d 1 (1965) with Mueller v. Roseville, 38 Mich.App. 170, 195 N.W.2d 882 (1972). As the Axtell opinion indicates, the issue of "special benefit," in the absence of any legislative determination of benefit, is one of fact.

Local governments may elect to use taxes rather than special assessments for street improvements. See e.g. Gaut v. Southfield, 388 Mich. 189, 200 N.W.2d 76 (1972).

3. **New and Reconstructed Improvements.** Generally, maintenance or repair is not considered capital improvement that specially benefits local properties; but reconstruction, e.g. street resurfacing or

repaving, as well as original construction, is deemed a capital improvement. The difference between repair and renovation is only one of degree, so that the issue becomes a question of fact. In a number of states, special assessments statutes apply strictly to original construction. See e.g. Mount Lebanon Township v. Scheck, 159 Pa.Super. 189, 48 A.2d 53 (1946); 14 McQuillin, *Municipal Corporations,* § 38.16 (3rd rev. ed. 1970); Annot., 41 A.L.R.2d 613 (1955). How should the widening of a street, involving construction of new shoulders and resurfacing of the old be treated? See Mount Lebanon Township case, supra.

CITY OF PLYMOUTH v. SUPERIOR COURT

Court of Appeal, Third District, California, 1970.
7 Cal.App.3d 188, 86 Cal.Rptr. 535.

JANES, ASSOCIATE JUSTICE.

The facts alleged in the petition for prohibition are uncontroverted. Petitioner is a municipal corporation. In July, 1968, petitioner's city council adopted a resolution determining to construct sewer improvements, to issue bonds to finance that project under the Improvement Bond Act of 1915 (Sts. & Hy.Code, § 8500 et seq.), and to undertake assessment proceedings under the Municipal Improvement Act of 1913 (Sts. & Hy.Code, § 10000 *et seq.*). (See § 10600.) On October 30, 1968, the city council adopted a resolution overruling protests, confirming the assessments, and ordering the work.

On November 27, 1968, the property owners timely filed * * * a complaint alleging that their lands located in the city had been placed within the new assessment district and had been assessed, but that such assessment was "arbitrary, fraudulent and confiscatory" and "without due process" in that their lands would receive "no benefit whatever" from the improvements. The complaint also alleged that the property owners had duly protested the assessments * * * that the council had confirmed and levied the assessments, that the assessments were void, and that petitioner, "unless restrained" by the court would sell the bonds. The prayer of the complaint sought a declaratory judgment invalidating the assessments as well as an injunction * * *

On the same day the action was filed—November 27, 1968—petitioner was served with summons and a copy of the property owners' complaint * * *. On December 17, 1968, however, petitioner awarded the sale of the assessment bonds to an agency of the federal government. Payment by that agency and delivery of the bonds to it were effected the next day. The property owners at no time attempted to temporarily restrain or preliminarily enjoin the sale and delivery of the bonds, nor did they post any form of security to protect petitioner if the bond sale was postponed or delayed during the pendency of the action.

After sale and delivery of the bonds, petitioner, in February, 1969, filed a motion to dismiss the superior court action on the ground that further proceedings were moot and barred by the operation of sections 8625 and 8655 of the Streets and Highways Code. * * *

Section 8625 * * * provides: "If bonds cannot be issued upon the security of any particular unpaid assessments because of a *restraining order, injunction or other cause* * * * the issuance of bonds upon the security of the assessments not affected by such *restraining order, injunction or other cause,* shall not be delayed, and such bonds may be issued in advance of the issuance of the bonds so affected." (Italics ours.) As we have pointed out, no restraining order or preliminary injunction was sought by the property owners in this case. * * * Petitioner cites no statutory or decisional authority, however, which *requires* that a temporary restraining order or preliminary injunction be sought by a property owner who seeks to permanently enjoin his assessment; and our own research has disclosed no such requirement. * * *

* * *

Streets and Highways Code, section 8655, which is part of the Improvement Bond Act of 1915, provides: "The bonds, by their issuance, shall be *conclusive evidence of the regularity of all proceedings* had prior thereto under this division [the 1915 Act] and under the law pursuant to which the work was done [here, the Municipal Improvement Act of 1913]." (Italics ours.) The 1913 Act declares that, where bonds are to be issued under the 1915 Act, all of the "curative clauses" and "powers of reassessment" of the latter are applicable. (Sts. & Hy. Code, § 10609.)

The sole ground urged in petitioner's motion to dismiss was that further proceedings in the action were "moot and barred by the operation of sections 8625 and 8655 of the Streets and Highways Code. * * *" * * *

* * *

It is questionable whether petitioner's assertion in the trial court that the action was "moot and barred" directly raised the issue of *jurisdiction,* and there is nothing else before us to show that the question was presented to the trial court as a jurisdictional issue. * * *

We have noted that under section 8655 of the Streets and Highways Code the issuance of the bonds for petitioner's sewer assessment district constituted "conclusive evidence of the regularity of all proceedings had prior thereto" under the Municipal Improvement Act of 1913 as well as under the Improvement Bond Act of 1915. Petitioner contends that this statutory provision bars the property owners from proving * * * if they can, their allegations * * *. We disagree.

Petitioner's misconstruction of the meaning of the pivotal language of section 8655 is based upon its erroneous interpretations of Chase v. Trout (1905) 146 Cal. 350, 80 P. 81; Noyes v. Chambers & DeGolyer (1927) 202 Cal. 542, 261 P. 1006, and Crangle v. City Council of Crescent City (1933) 219 Cal. 239, 26 P.2d 24. Although no dispositive construction of section 8655 appears in any California precedent, guidance is found in the principle recognized in Hoffman v. City of Red Bluff (1965) 63 Cal.2d 584, 591–592, 47 Cal.Rptr. 553, 557, 407 P.2d 857, 861: "Under the holding in Chase v. Trout (1905) 146 Cal. 350, 80 P. 81, reiterated in many subsequent cases [citations], a curative statute may validate all defects in proceedings *except* those which have resulted in violation of constitutional rights." (Italics ours.)

In Chase v. Trout, *supra,* the court had before it Section 4 of the Street Bond Act of 1893, * * *. Recognizing that this curative statute could not validate noncompliance with due process, and *speaking only of the "part of that proceeding" which occurred "before the assessment is issued,"* the court held that due process was satisfied by notice to the property owners and an opportunity to be heard in protest. (*Id.,* pp. 361–362, 80 P. 81.) (Italics ours.)

Chase did not address itself to questions of fraud, manifest abuse of discretion, or the absence of benefits to an assessed owner. * * *

* * *

Other cases cited by petitioner are distinguishable in that, with one exception, none of them coupled an allegation of "no benefit" *with other allegations* of fraud or manifest abuse of discretion on the part of the assessing entity, * * *. And, with one exception, those cases involved a failure of the assessed property owners to protest to the assessing entity before seeking judicial relief—an omission not present here. * * *

Our construction of the "conclusive evidence" provision of section 8655 is consistent with the many cases which state that the determination of the city council on the question of benefits is not conclusive where the evidence before it plainly shows that no benefit could reasonably be expected to accrue to the property in question, where the council's determination is infected by fraud, or where on the face of the council's proceedings there appears such an abuse of discretion as is equivalent to fraud. [Citations omitted].

Special assessment without benefits is a denial of due process. [Citations omitted] In the context of curative statutes such as section 8655, a taking of property without due process is considered a jurisdictional defect. [Citations omitted]

California law shields bond buyers by a variety of validation provisions. A ruling which permits attack on the assessment proceedings notwithstanding sale of the bonds is rare indeed. The present ruling deals with a unique set of facts where, according to the record before us, the seller, a municipal corporation, sold the bonds with full knowledge of the pending lawsuit. Whether the bond buyer, a federal agency, requested a "no litigation" certificate does not appear. Bond buyers customarily demand such a certificate. We do not, of course, anticipate the outcome of the trial. The actions of petitioner in issuing and selling (and of the buyer in purchasing) the bonds, in the face of the pending suit below, must also be evaluated in the light of the facts yet to be adduced at trial. We hold only that the property owners, who properly recorded their objections before the council and then—prior to petitioner's issuance and sale of the bonds—filed their timely suit and served petitioner, are entitled to a factual determination of the issues posed by their complaint, and that the superior court has jurisdiction to proceed further with the action.

* * *

WING v. EUGENE
Supreme Court of Oregon, 1968.
249 Or. 367, 437 P.2d 836.

LANGTRY, JUSTICE PRO TEM. Plaintiffs have appealed from a circuit court decree * * * The decree upheld the proceedings of Eugene's city council in levying special assessments for an off-street parking facility in downtown Eugene. The area determined to be specially benefited consists of several blocks and half blocks surrounding the proposed facility.

The special assessments are levied in four zones, the closest paying the heaviest and the farthest the least assessment. Plaintiff's property is in the outer zone. Estimated cost of the facility is two million dollars. Within the assessed area are several parcels which the council found to be public parking lots operated for profit. They were not required to pay special assessments. After the proposed assessments were made, plaintiffs and another owner, whose property was described as the Fisk property, brought separate circuit court writs of review seeking to void the proposed assessments. Further consideration by the council resulted in the Fisk property being given a substantially reduced assessment proportionate to parts of it found to be used as parking lots for the public, and Fisk dropped its court proceeding.

Initially, notice of the proposed improvement and assessment required by statute was given. When the Fisk property's proposed assessment was reduced no additional notices were given. The result of Fisk's reduction is that other proposed assessments will rise substantially in proportion.

* * *

Plaintiffs assign a number of errors, * * *.

* * *

The first, second, and fourth assignments of error will be considered together. Under ORS 223.810 and 223.815, a city may establish parking facilities and acquire property therefor. * * * Broad powers conferred by the statutes allow planning, construction, financing and method of operation. Financing methods include:

> "Special or benefit assessments * * * such assessment to be levied against property benefited in proportion to the benefit derived * * *." ORS 223.825(2).

Parking fees and other facility income are included as a financing method. * * *

* * *

ORS 223.825(2) quoted *supra*, does not specifically give the city authority to exempt any property in the district; consequently, plaintiffs assert the exemption of public parking lots is without authority. But the statute does require assessments levied to be against property benefited "in proportion to the benefit derived." If the city council determines that particular property or properties, by reason of use, derive no benefit, the statutory language indicates that it cannot be assessed. * * *

* * *

No evidence is needed to support the proposition that a two million dollar parking lot built near a presently operated commercial parking lot is of no benefit to the latter's profit prospects. This obviously was the reasoning of the California court in Safeway Stores, Inc. v. City of Burlingame, 170 Cal.App.2d 637, 339 P.2d 933 (1959), where a Safeway store had a parking lot capable of handling 119 vehicles and for its own purposes used only 71 spaces at its peak need. The lot was, and was required to be, available to the public. The city sought to assess it for a public parking facility in the general area. It was held not benefited and the attempted assessment voided. * * *

* * *

The assessments in the instant case are heavy in relation to the value of the property assessed. Plaintiff argues the cost should be more widely spread—there is a wider field of benefit. This is a matter for the city council, acting in its representative and legislative capacity, to consider rather than the court. More than one-half the owners of property in the assessment district * * * petitioned the council to initiate this project. * * *

Inevitably, some land uses will be more benefited than others, and some presently not at all. But if the city council's plan for assessing the cost reasonably takes into consideration these differences, a court will not strike it down because it is not exactly fitted to the prospective benefit of each. * * * " * * * It is not necessary to refine the concept of benefit so as to make it serve equally each of the lots in the area * * *." Raz et al. v. City of Portland et al., 226 Or. 515, 521, 360 P.2d 549, 552 (1961).

* * *

The third assignment of error is that the city council erred in failing to follow procedural requirements when it reduced the Fisk assessment. * * * Other assessed property, as a result, will have assessments increased about four percent. The reason for the Fisk reduction was a finding that part of this property was being used as a commercial parking lot and should not have been assessed.

The city claims this was a mere error which could be corrected without new procedural notices, but plaintiffs claim it was a reassessment requiring the procedures of ORS 223.405 through ORS 223.485. ORS 223.410 provides:

"Whenever all or part of any assessment for improvements was or is declared * * * set aside for any reason * * * or when the council is in doubt as to the validity of all or part of any such assessment by reason of such defects in procedure, the council may * * * make a new assessment or reassessment with respect to all or part * * *."

Following sections require that if a reassessment is to be made, the proposal shall be filed in the recorder's office and he shall publish and serve specified notices of time and place for a hearing on objections. These provisions are also in the city's ordinances. Such notices were not given in the proceedings resulting in the Fisk assessment reduction.

* * * The plain intention of the statute is to require notice so any interested property owner adversely affected may have an opportunity to be heard.

"The notice and hearing required under the statute is necessary to confer jurisdiction on the municipality and must be strictly observed." Rhyne, Municipal Law 723–724, § 29–6 (1957).

Here, no mere clerical or arithmetical error was involved; the council exercised judgment upon facts.

The statutory notices were required; the Fisk reduction proceedings are consequently invalid and will require new proceedings if pursued further. Judgment of the trial court is affirmed in all other respects.

Affirmed in part; reversed in part.

a. Special Assessment Procedures

Special assessment procedures vary under the laws of different states. Such laws may authorize improvement and assessments by citizen petition, initiative and referendum; by resolution or by ordinance. See e.g. Chesebro v. Los Angeles County Flood Control District, 306 U.S. 459, 59 S.Ct. 622, 82 L.Ed. 921 (1939); Browning v. Hooper, 269 U.S. 396, 46 S.Ct. 141, 70 L.Ed. 330 (1926). Whichever means are used, they must comply with governing statutes, and satisfy minimal constitutional requirements of procedural due process. Affected owners are entitled to fair notice and an opportunity to be heard at two, possibly three, stages of the assessment process. Affected owners are entitled to fair notice and an opportunity to be heard at two, possibly three, stages of the assessment process. Where a legislative determination is made that a particular capital improvement is needed, notice and hearing on the issue of need is not required. In the absence of such determination, the owners may be entitled to notice and an opportunity to be heard on the question of the need for the public improvement. They are also entitled to be heard on the question whether they are "specially benefitted"; and to notice and hearing on the apportionment of improvement costs to their respective properties. These rights may be waived and are often subjected to cut-off by short statutes of limitations. George A. Fuller Co. v. Rainey, 235 Cal.App.2d 379, 45 Cal.Rptr. 187 (1965).

Procedural requirements of state law may be jurisdictional prerequisites, so that procedural deficiencies could destroy the local unit's authority to make the improvement. Each case will depend upon the intent of governing statutes and the nature or effect of departure from statutory procedures. Cf. Roznos v. Slater, 254 Iowa 77, 116 N.W.2d 471 (1962) (technical noncompliance did not destroy validity of assessment where constructive notice to property owners satisfied the statute).

Special assessment practice usually includes a notice or notices of (a) intention to make the improvement and to finance it by special assessment; (b) the method and plan of calculating and apportioning special assessments; and (c) the procedures by which owners may raise objections. Before or after the work is completed, project costs are apportioned to individual properties and the interested parties are notified of the plan of assessment. After hearings or waivers of such hearings, the assessments are officially approved and issued under procedures which create a lien on each property to secure payment of its assessment. The exact order and manner in which these steps occur vary with different laws.

Special assessments do not generally create personal liability in the property owner. Where personal liability for special assessments was enacted, a conflict of authority developed on the validity of such legislation. See various authorities noted in 14 McQuillin, Municipal Corporations, § 38.323 (3rd rev. ed. 1970).

Insofar as special assessments are collectible solely from the benefited property, the pressure to cure defective special assessments by validation legislation, where constitutionally possible, is commonplace. For if private contractors who make improvements on the credit of those assessments, or if purchasers of capital improvement bonds secured by such assessments, are not paid, those financing sources will be lost to local governments.

5. BORROWING

The enterprise of local government requires a steady flow of cash that far exceeds current receipts. Financing government operations requires various forms of borrowing but public debt, like taxation, is subject to many legal controls. The controls vary according to the form of debt incurred, and directly influence official choices between short or long-term loans; between guaranteed or nonguaranteed loans; between electoral or nonelectoral borrowing; and the kinds of security offered for debt repayment (*viz.* the full faith and credit of the government, pledge of specified revenues, mortgage on real property). The following excerpt outlines the major forms of local government borrowing, and the loan documents which distinguish different loan arrangements.

"III. Types of Municipal Bonds

The most traditional type of municipal financing is the *general obligation (sometimes called G.O.) bond.**** These bonds are backed by the "full faith and credit" of the issuer. This language has been interpreted to mean that the municipality gives an unlimited guarantee to its investors that it will raise funds by whatever means necessary and to the fullest extent of its ability in order to honor its obligation. The most widely used security for these bonds is the *ad valorem* property tax levied by the municipality, although income and sales tax revenues, or any other source of revenue, can also be used. Ultimately, the security for all general obligation bonds must be the ability of the municipality to earn or to raise by taxation sufficient funds to pay the interest and principal on its debt. General obligation bonds are usually underwritten by large commercial banks and sold pursuant to competitive bidding. Negotiated transactions are used only when there is an unusual circumstance in the financing. * * *

"*Limited guarantee bonds* (or limited tax bonds) are those obligations which are not backed by the unlimited taxing power of the municipality. Hence, limited guarantee bonds are those obligations issued by municipalities which have a legal limit on the amount of taxes they can levy. * * * The weakness of these bonds lies in the inability of the municipality to raise tax rates in times of economic downturn when tax revenues are inadequate to service the debt.

"*Special tax bonds* are bonds payable only from the proceeds of a particular tax or fund such as a gasoline tax (and are sometimes classified as revenue bonds because they are payable solely from a special fund). *Special assessment* bonds are payable only from assessments against those who benefit from the improvements financed.******
* * * *Revenue bonds* are payable solely from the revenue from a specified income-generating facility acquired or constructed with the proceeds of the bonds.******* These bonds are issued by the municipality itself or by a public agency. They are not payable out of taxes, but are payable only from revenues received from the operation of a revenue-producing government-related activity. * * *

"Terminology characterizing revenue bonds is not uniform. Some of them may be described as user charge bonds (issued to finance projects such as turnpikes), lease rental bonds (issued to finance construction of school dormitories), and pollution control bonds (issued to finance facilities leased to private industry). If bonds payable from revenues of certain facilities are also secured by the full faith, credit, and taxing power of the issuer, the bonds are classified as general obligation bonds. Such bonds are sometimes described as "double barreled" securities. Among the most common projects for which these

---

* See e.g., State v. Spring City, p. 655, infra.

** See e.g., Patterson v. City of Bismark, p. 669, n. 1, infra.

*** See e.g., note 1, p. 670, infra.

securities are issued include roads, bridges, electric utilities, tunnels, housing, and airports. The development of this kind of financing was enhanced by a new type of government agency usually called an "authority," but often denominated "commission," "district," or similar name. Regardless of the name, these government agencies are essentially of the same character; that is, each is a public agency authorized to initiate or assume a revenue-producing activity and sell debt securities for this purpose, payable solely out of the revenues derived from the activity. Authorities possess no power of taxation since they are intended to finance public improvements without undermining the taxing capabilities of other government branches. The sources of revenues for these bonds as indicated above are as follows: (1) user charges (e.g., re utility facilities for water, sewers, electricity, gas); (2) tolls, concessions, fees (e.g., re turnpikes [including concessions]), docks, warehouses, airports, rapid transit systems); (3) special taxes (e.g., tobacco and alcoholic beverages); (4) rental payments (e.g., the bond financed facility is leased to the municipality at a rent sufficient to service debt); and (5) industrial revenue bonds (e.g., the bond financed facility is leased to a private corporation at a rent sufficient to service debt).

"Since authorities are established to finance revenue-producing enterprises rather than to carry out purely governmental functions, they can be regarded essentially as business enterprises. Investors purchase these bonds in reliance on the authority's operating such business enterprise at a profit. * * * Presumably the investor realizes that when he purchases such bonds he does not depend upon the taxing power of the municipality where the project is located to pay the principal and interest. * * *

"In 1975, revenue bonds represented about 49 percent of new tax-exempt issues; about $14.2 billion in revenue bonds were issued out of a total of $29.2 billion in tax-exempt financing. Because a revenue bond usually has a narrower base from which to draw funds * * * than does a general obligation bond, historically the revenue bond has yielded a higher return (to the lender and, therefore, a high cost to the public) than an otherwise comparable general obligation bond. The principal attractions of revenue bonds appear to be the ability of the municipality to bypass constitutional and statutory ceilings on debt issuance, the avoidance of requirements that new public debt be approved by the legislature and/or the voters and the placement of the burden of paying for the improvements directly on those benefited. * * * Despite their narrower source of funds, these bonds have become increasingly attractive. * * *

"Municipalities have also issued so-called *industrial revenue (or development) bonds* * for the benefit of private corporations to finance such projects as plant construction and pollution control equipment.

---

* See e.g., Basehore v. Hampden Industrial Development Auth., p. 704, infra.

The municipality issues the securities to finance the project, and then it leases the plant and equipment to the corporation with the lease payments synchronized to cover the debt service requirements. Consequently, this allows the corporation to benefit from the lower borrowing costs available to the municipality due to the tax-exempt status of the securities, and the public interest is presumably served by fostering industrial development, promoting a cleaner environment in the area, or otherwise promoting the common weal.

* * *

"Revenue bonds are usually sold through a negotiated transaction by a syndicate of investment banking firms. * * * A new development worthy of note, however, is the sale of bonds through a so-called "Dutch auction." This procedure involves an authority issuing its bonds directly to the public with principal and interest guaranteed by a major industrial corporation with an excellent credit rating. * * *

"*Public housing authority bonds* are used to raise funds for public housing projects and are backed by an agreement between the local housing authority and the Department of Housing and Urban Development (HUD). HUD guarantees unconditionally to lend the local housing authority sufficient funds to pay the principal and interest on the bonds until maturity. * * *

"*Moral obligation bonds* are used to finance a wide variety of projects and are backed by the moral, rather than the legal obligation of the state to provide financial assistance to meet debt service requirements not covered by the project's revenues. For this reason, a moral obligation security is not a debt of the state. Issuance of the security needs no approval by the legislature or by the voters. In theory, this should not jeopardize the credit rating of the state; however, in practice, the state serves as the insurer of the interest and principal for the agency issuing the moral obligation securities. * * * New York became the first state in recent years to issue moral obligation bonds in the mid–1960s, and it has since been followed by some thirty states. Agencies of the State of New York had approximately six billion dollars in moral obligation bonds outstanding early in 1975. *Refunding bonds* are bonds the proceeds of which are used to refund outstanding debt.

"IV. Types of Short-Term Municipal Notes

"Short-term borrowing by municipalities functions to smooth out cash flows and to match revenue and expenditure patterns over the year. The need for such borrowing arises for many reasons, particularly when revenues such as real estate taxes may be collected annually or quarterly, but expenses such as payroll and maintenance must be paid almost daily. Meeting the incongruities of revenues and expenses has forced many municipalities to rely on the issuance of short-term debt to cover such cash flow deficits. * * *

"New York authorizes municipalities to issue various kinds of notes such as: (1) tax anticipation notes, (2) revenue anticipation notes, (3) bond anticipation notes, (4) urban renewal notes, (5) budget notes, (6) capital notes, and (7) deferred payment notes. Without attempting to provide a complete listing of the characteristics of these notes, the New York securities laws associated with these notes are considered to be of general interest because of their national distribution.

"*Tax anticipation notes* (TANs) are short-term municipal notes which are sold in advance of receiving some specific taxes such as real estate taxes. * * * Such notes are secured by taxes collected during the current fiscal year or by taxes receivable for the preceding four fiscal years. These notes will permit the municipality to borrow against expected tax receipts in order to fund current operating expenses. Of course, proceeds must be used only for purposes for which taxes were authorized (namely, for the municipality's budget). Although these notes should be paid from tax revenues as received, they may be issued to mature up to one year after the revenue is received. These notes may be renewed up to five years after issuance if there are uncollected taxes to cover them. * * * The effect of so issuing (or rolling over) these notes on the eve of a new fiscal year is to provide a budgetary supplement which, if irresponsibly used, can result in tax anticipation note obligations equal to the entire budget for one fiscal year. * * *

"*Revenue anticipation notes* (RANs) are issued against various kinds of municipal revenue (except real estate taxes) to raise funds until special receipts are collected. These notes are issued in anticipation of the collection of rents, charges, taxes (other than real estate taxes), and other revenue or moneys to be received (1) for utility or other services rendered by the municipality or (2) from the state or the federal government. They cannot be issued for more than one year and are not renewable beyond the close of the second fiscal year after they were issued.

"*Bond anticipation notes* (BANs) are issued to raise funds until a long-term bond issue can be floated, that is, in anticipation of the sale of bonds. Prior to New York City's financial crises, BANs were considered an especially safe investment because of a presumption that they would surely be paid from the proceeds of a future bond issue. These notes may be issued whenever bonds have been authorized, and the proceeds of the notes must be used for the authorized purposes. * * * These notes must be replaced by bonds within five years of original issuance.

"*Urban renewal notes* (URNs) are a species of revenue anticipation notes issued against moneys to be received from an urban renewal project, from the United States under the Federal Housing Act, or from the various states pursuant to a statutory subsidy. These notes mature within one year but may be renewed for additional one-year periods up to seven years. The extended maturity was found to be necessary because of the delay experienced in receiving funds. These notes do not

benefit from the pledge of the municipality's full faith and credit,
* * *

"*Budget notes* (BUNs) are issued when an unforeseeable public
emergency occurs such as a storm, flood, earthquake, epidemic, riot, or
any other unusual peril to lives and property within the municipality.
These notes must be repaid by the end of the fiscal year succeeding the
one in which they are issued. * * *

"VIII. Underwriting Municipal Issues

"New bond issues are underwritten in many parts of the country,
usually by competitive bidding. Smaller issues are still underwritten
near the municipality issuing them, while the larger issues are underwritten and traded in the New York market, the dominant market in
size and influence. * * *

"There are very few private placements of municipal issues. The
underwriting of municipal securities is usually on a "firm commitment" basis * * *. The underwriting syndicate buys the whole issue
and attempts to resell it to the public * * *." Ronald David Greenberg, *Municipal Securities: Some Basic Principles and Practices,* The
Urban Lawyer, Vol. 9, No. 2, 338 at 340–349, 356 (1977).

For a review of existing limits on debt creation, as well as on tax
and spending limits, see Gelfand, *Seeking Local Government Financial
Integrity Through Debt Ceilings, Tax Limits, and Expenditure Limits:
The New York City Fiscal Crisis, The Taxpayer Revolt and Beyond,* 63
Minn.L.Rev. 545 (1979).

a. Short-Term Debt

Short-term loans are controlled both by budget law and special
statutes. "Some confusion has arisen in the cases as to the extent of
the right to anticipate the collection of taxes. We think, however, it is
fairly well settled that, as applied to ordinary revenues, that right
undoubtedly does not extend beyond the current year, nor can it be
exercised as to such revenues for any purpose beyond the payment of
ordinary expense. * * * For the current year, the rate having been
fixed, and levy made, the receipt of the revenue * * * is 'legally
certain' and is treated as cash actually in the treasury, and therefore,
* * * an appropriation thereof * * *. If, then, a city * * *
provides a special or extraordinary fund * * * by tax contemporane-
ously levied for that purpose alone * * * is not the receipt of such
revenue 'legally certain' * * * without the incurring of an indebtedness?" Swanson v. Ottumwa, 118 Iowa 161, 185–6, 91 N.W. 1048, 1056–
1057 (1902).

Some statutes codify the principle that short-term loans must
mature and be redeemed in the same fiscal year of their creation, out of
revenues that are due or collectable in that year (e.g., 53 P.S. § 6780–
201), while others liberalize the rule to permit such borrowing over

succeeding budget years, e.g., N.Y.—McKinney's Cons.Laws, Local Finance Law §§ 24:00, 25:00.

A recent study by the U.S. Advisory Commission produced the following comments and recommendations on short-term debt:

"At present, State attention to regulation of short-term municipal operating debt varies widely, ranging from New Mexico [where all such debt must be approved by specified State agencies] to the great majority of states which have no controls at all over short-term municipal operating debt."

"The inability to repay several years' accumulation of short-term operating loans has been the most important single factor in throwing a city into a financial crisis. Cities may find it tempting to 'roll over' short-term debt from year to year in ever-increasing amounts."

"The Commission recommends therefore that the States enact legislation to regulate the use of short-term operating debt that carries beyond the end of the fiscal year. At a minimum, such laws should require that any short-term operating debt remaining unliquidated at the end of the fiscal year should be charged against general debt limits and provision for its retirement be automatically included in the next year's budget." ACIR, *City Financial Emergencies* pp. 5, 6 (1973).

The following chart registers the increasing use of short-term, as well as long-term, debt to finance municipal operations.

FIGURE 6
ANNUAL DOLLAR VOLUME OF STATE AND LOCAL BORROWING—LONG–TERM VERSUS SHORT–TERM

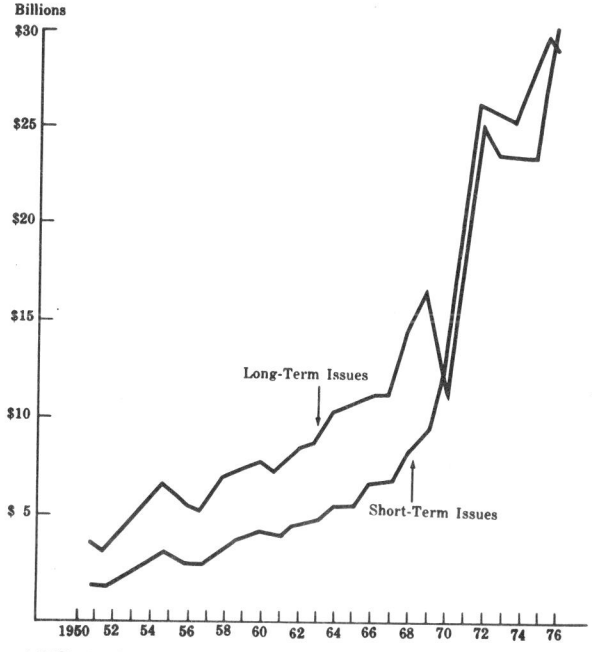

Source: ACIR, Understanding the Market for State and Local Dept 12 (1976).

b. *Long-Term Debt*

Short term loans are used almost exclusively to supply funds for current operational needs. Long term borrowing is "the" means by which general and special function units undertake costly capital improvements such as roads, schools, bridges and water, sewerage, power and transit facilities. Such borrowing has risen at an even faster rate than increases in ordinary spending and taxes.

The fiscal strains of capital expansion are exacerbated by debt limitation laws that are rooted in 19th century experience. Compare the following:

California Constitution, Article 11, § 18—"No county, city, township, board of education or school district shall incur any indebtedness * * * exceeding in any year the income and revenue provided for such year, without the assent of two-thirds of the qualified electors thereof * * *."

Iowa Constitution, Article 11, § 3—"No county, or other political or municipal corporation shall be allowed to become indebted * * * exceeding five percentum on the value of the taxable property within such county or corporation * * *."

Pennsylvania Constitution, Article 9, §§ 10, 12—"Subject only to the restrictions imposed by this section, the General Assembly shall prescribe the debt limits of all units of local government including municipalities and school districts. For such purposes, the debt limit base shall be a percentage of the total revenue, as defined by the General Assembly, of the unit of local government computed over a specific period immediately preceding the year of borrowing. The debt limit * * * shall exclude all indebtedness (1) for any project to the extent that it is self liquidating or self supporting * * *, or (2) which has been approved by referendum held in such manner as shall be provided by law. The provision of this paragraph shall not apply to the city and county of Philadelphia. * * *

"The debt of the City of Philadelphia may be increased in such amount that the total debt of said city shall not exceed 13½ percent of the average of the annual assessed valuations of the taxable realty therein, during the ten years immediately preceding the year in which such increase is made, but said city shall not increase its indebtedness to an amount exceeding 3 percent upon such average * * * without the consent of the electors thereof * * *. In ascertaining the debt-incurring capacity of the City of Philadelphia at any time, there shall be deducted from the debt of said city so much of the debt as shall have been incurred, and the proceeds thereof expended * * * upon any public improvement * * * if such public improvement * * * whether separately, or in connection with any other public improvement * * * may reasonably be expected to yield revenue in excess of operating expenses sufficient to pay the interest and sinking fund charges thereon. The method of determining such amount, so to be deducted, shall be as ＊ ＊ ＊ prescribed by law. ＊ ＊ ＊"

The source and standards of debt limitation vary greatly from state to state. See, e.g., City of Pocatello, p. 679, infra; R. Bowmar, *The Anachronism Called Debt Limitation,* 52 Iowa L.Rev. 863–868 (1967). Debt limitation laws have been repeatedly criticized but the criticism has not produced any consensus or model revision to reform them. The problems that are common to the debt limitation laws tend to be obscured by a case analysis of particularized applications. These will be better perceived by keeping the following points in mind.

"[T]he framers had in mind the great and ever growing evil to which the municipalities ＊ ＊ ＊ were subjected by the creation of a debt in one year, which debt was not, and was not expected to be paid out of the revenue of that year, but was carried on into the next year increasing like a rolling snowball as it went until the weight of it became almost unbearable upon the taxpayers. It was to prevent this abuse that the constitutional provision was enacted." McBean v. Fresno, 112 Cal. 159, 164, 44 P. 358, 359 (1896).

"＊ ＊ ＊ [I]n substantially every jurisdiction the word 'debt' or 'indebtedness,' as used in the limitation placed upon municipal power, is given a meaning much less broad ＊ ＊ ＊ than it bears in general language. This tendency has been more marked in some states than in others, with the result that the decisions are sufficiently at variance to fairly justify the statement of an eminent court that, 'in view of the warring among the adjudged cases, it is not easy to affirm that the word 'debt' has a firmly settled meaning.' " Swanson v. Ottumwa, 118 Iowa 161, 170–71, 91 N.W. 1048, 1051–52 (1902).

Since "debt", as here used, does not cover all future repayment obligations, but only those that commit the general credit and assets of government to secure repayment, attention must be given to the particular financing aspects of each scheme. See generally, R. Bowmar, *The Anachronism Called Debt Limitation,* 52 Iowa L.Rev. 863 (1967); ACIR, 1972 ed. *State and Local Finances,* Table 70, pp. 150–159.

(1) Debt Limitations

STATE v. SPRING CITY

Supreme Court of Utah, 1953.
123 Utah 471, 260 P.2d 527.

McDONOUGH, JUSTICE. ＊ ＊ ＊ On January 15, 1948, defendant Spring City, a municipal corporation, through defendant city officials, issued a series of bonds with a total face value of $12,000. The State of Utah, plaintiff ＊ ＊ ＊ purchased the entire issue for the sum of $13,498.67, representing principal, premium and accrued interest. The bonds were issued to raise funds "for the purpose of extending and improving the power and light plant to be owned and controlled by the city." * * * None of the bonds were to mature until the year 1961. Defendant Spring City paid all interest payments as they came due to and including January 15, 1950. On January 15, 1951, the state treasurer presented coupons for payment * * *. Payment was refused and no payments have since been made. Defendant Spring City maintains that the bonds and coupons are void.

* * *

Article XIV Section 3 of the Constitution of the State of Utah reads as follows:

"No debt in excess of the taxes for the current year shall be created by any county or subdivision thereof, or by any school district therein, or by any city, town or village, or any subdivision thereof in this State; unless the proposition to create such debt, shall have been submitted to a vote of such qualified electors as shall have paid a property tax therein, in the year preceding such election, and a majority of those voting thereon shall have voted in favor of incurring such debt."

No election was held * * *. The trial court found that in 1948 the expenditures of Spring City exceeded its revenues by $2,067.90. The court concluded therefore that the municipality had created a debt in excess of its revenues which was unconstitutional and void.

The plaintiff argues that the validity of such a contracted indebtedness should be determined as of the time when it is incurred, rather than at the end of the year. * * *

It is true that the validity of an indebtedness should be determined as of the time when it is incurred. Scott v. Salt Lake County, 58 Utah 25, 196 P. 1022; and see numerous cases collected at 159 A.L.R. 1263. Municipalities can and often do borrow or otherwise contract in anticipation of revenues to be received during the year. Dickinson v. Salt Lake City, 57 Utah 530, 195 P. 1110. It would be manifestly unfair to permit persons who entered into a valid contract with a municipality to be deprived of their rights by later acts of the officers of the municipality. * * * If the debt is valid when incurred, there is no objection to payment from the income of a subsequent year. Carl R. Miller Tractor Co. v. Hope, 218 Iowa 1235, 257 N.W. 312; Nelson County Fiscal Ct. v. McCrocklin, 175 Ky. 199, 194 S.W. 323.

If, therefore, the bonds in question were valid when issued, they did not become invalid because of the fact that the defendant Spring City ended the year 1948 with a deficit. We are of the opinion, however, that the bonds were void when they were issued.

The provisions of Article XIV Section 3 were placed in the Constitution to protect the taxpayers against an abuse of their credit. The evident purpose is that municipalities be required to operate each year within their revenues for that year; they must "pay-as-they-go" unless the voters enlarge that limit. [Citations omitted] In this instance, the city officials of Spring City apparently decided that the city needed an electric plant pipeline which it could not well afford out of revenues for the current year. They nevertheless decided to purchase the facilities and to pay for them in future years. This was an attempt by the municipality to live beyond its income for the current year, which violates the purpose of Article XIV Section 3. The city did not "pay-as-it-went." Whether the revenues of Spring City for 1948 exceeded or were less than the amount of the bonds at the time they were issued should not determine the validity of the indebtedness. It would be unreasonable to suppose that bonds issued in 1948 with principal payable in 1961 were to be paid out of 1948 revenues merely because on January 15, when they were issued, prospective revenues for the year exceeded their amount. On the contrary the bonds were never intended to be paid out of revenues for 1948; they represent an indebtedness incurred in anticipation of the income of future years. * * *

Plaintiff relies in his argument on Muir v. Murray City, 55 Utah, 368, 186 P. 433. This was a suit to recover payment from Murray City of money borrowed to build a power line, payable in four annual installments. The court stated that Article XIV Section 3 was not a defense to the action because no evidence showed that the debt was in excess of potential revenues for the current year. It is conceivable that the decision is not inconsistent with the views expressed above since there was no evidence to show that the moneys * * * to pay the indebtedness in question, were not from the revenues of the year in which the obligation was incurred. To the extent, however, that the Muir case can be viewed as holding that a municipality can incur indebtedness, absent an election authorizing it, in anticipation of the income of future years, it is overruled.

The trial court also held that the bonds are invalid under Article XIV Section 4 of the Constitution * * * Article XIV Section 4 provides that, when authorized to create indebtedness under Section 3, a city may incur an original aggregate indebtedness of four per cent of the value of taxable property within the corporate limits of the municipality. An additional eight per cent is permitted "for supplying such city or town with water, artificial lights or sewers." Since Spring City supplied the city with artificial lights, it qualified to indebt the city to the extent of 12 per cent.

The value of the taxable property is "to be ascertained by the last assessment for State and County purposes, previous to the incurring of such indebtedness." The County Assessor's figure for the valuation of the taxable property in Spring City for 1947 was $179,407. If this figure is used to compute the debt limit, Article XIV Section 4 would limit the power to obligate the city to the sum of $21,528.84, including existing indebtedness. At the time plaintiff purchased the bonds in question, plaintiff already held unpaid bonds issued by defendant city in the sum of $14,500. Thus the issue of the additional bonds in the value of $12,000 would exceed a debt limit of $21,528.84. Plaintiff argues, however, that the limitation refers to the actual value of the property and not the assessor's figure. As an original proposition, the standard referred to in the Constitution appears to be the assessor's figure and some states with similar provisions so hold. City of Chicago v. Fishburn, 189 Ill. 367, 59 N.E. 791.

Prior to 1947, statutes of Utah provided for assessment of all taxable property at its full cash value. See Section 80–5–1, Utah Code Annotated 1943. Section 59–5–1, Utah Code Annotated 1953 as amended by Chapter 102, Laws of Utah, 1947, provides, however:

> "All taxable property must be assessed at forty percent of its reasonable fair cash value. * * *"

In the light of this statute, this court, in Board of Education, Rich County School District v. Passey, Utah, 246 P.2d 1078, held that the figure to be used in determining the debt limitation is the full value of the property computed from the assessor's forty per cent figure. (That is, that figure, forty per cent of which equals the assessor's figure.) This view is in accord with decisions in Iowa, N.W. Halsey & Co. v. City of Belle Plaine, 128 Iowa 467, 104 N.W. 494, and Washington, Hansen v. City of Hoquiam, 95 Wash. 132, 163 P. 391, where similar constitutional and statutory provisions prevail.

* * *

* * * The full value of the taxable property in Spring City, $448,517.50, would permit a total indebtedness under Article XIV Section 4 of $53,822.10, which is $27,322.10 in excess of the then existing debt of the municipality. The trial court therefore erred in holding that this bond issue violated Article XIV Section 4 of the Constitution.

Even though the bonds are invalid under Article XIV Section 3 of the Constitution, plaintiff contends that plaintiff is entitled to recover upon the theory of money had and received. Plaintiff argues that the bonds were purchased under mutual mistake, that defendant Spring City used the money for a legitimate purpose for its benefit and that plaintiff is therefore entitled to restitution apart from any express contract. Although it results in a hardship on the purchasers of such invalid bonds, neither reason nor authority support this position.

The constitutional provisions were enacted as a protection for the taxpayers against an abuse of their credit. The protection is absolute in nature. If recovery is allowed against the municipality on a theory of money had and received, the entire purpose for which the provision exists is contravened. Although the legal theory is changed, the practical result would be payment by the taxpayers of an obligation against which the Constitution specifically attempts to protect them.

This situation should be distinguished from cases where, although the city was authorized to incur the indebtedness, bonds issued by the municipality were found to be invalid because certain procedural requirements were not met or because the city was not authorized to issue bonds negotiable in form or payable in the manner adopted. In such situations, justice may well require restitution on a theory of money had and received. Where a constitutional prohibition against indebtedness is involved however, most courts will not permit any such recovery. Litchfield v. Ballou, 114 U.S. 190, 5 S.Ct. 820, 29 L.Ed. 132; Town of Belleair v. Olds, 5 Cir., 127 F.2d 838; Fairbanks-Morse Co. v. City of Geary, 59 Okl. 22, 157 P. 720.

The plaintiff also contends that the trial court erred in denying recovery against the individual city authorities responsible for the invalid bond issue on a theory of negligence. This claim is without substance. There is no evidence of negligence on the part of the officials in the performance of their duties. The invalidity of these bonds results from the fact that they were issued in anticipation of the income of future years. Defendant city officials were entitled to rely on the advice of counsel and the opinion of the Attorney General, which opinion was issued prior to disposition of the bonds, as to the validity of such bonds. It would be unfair and unjust to require the city officials to guess at their peril what the opinion of this court as to the validity of the indebtedness would be.

Judgment affirmed.

* * *

Notes

1. **Actual vs. Assessed Property Value.** Where debt ceiling is set by a specified ratio of debt-to-property value, authorities are divided on the question whether property value should be based upon its full or actual value, or upon assessed value. Compare the principal case with People v. Doyle, infra p. 679; and with Breslow v. School District of Baldwin Tp., 408 Pa. 121, 182 A.2d 501 (1962), in which debt ceilings were held to be controlled by assessed values, rather than higher actual values. By Amendment 55 to the Washington Constitution (1972), that state substituted actual for assessed value in its debt limit formula.

The authorities are also divided on the question whether, for debt computation purposes, property value should include tax exempt property. See Zobel v. Schau, 260 Iowa 796, 150 N.W.2d 626 (1967) for a review of the cases.

2. **Variable Debt Limitations.** Do the following means of adjusting debt computation adequately solve the problem of inflexibility: different debt-to-property ratios for different types of capital improvement (as noted in the principal case); total exclusion of certain types of improvement financing from debt computation (see Ohio Rev.Code § 133.03); different debt limitations for different sizes and classes of local governmental units (see Pennsylvania Constitution quoted p. 653, supra)?

3. **Date of "Debt" Determination.** The Spring City rule that the debt ceiling is applied when the bonds are issued, i.e. when sent out,

delivered or put into circulation, (Accord: Baker v. Unified School District No. 346 Linn County, 206 Kan. 581, 480 P.2d 409 (1971); Karsh v. Denver, 176 Colo. 406, 490 P.2d 936 (1971)) is not universal. Where bonds are valid when authorized, but exceed the debt limit at the time of issue (due to additional debt creation in the interim), some courts hold them valid and enforceable. See Bilardi Construction Inc. v. Spencer, 6 Cal.App.3d 771, 86 Cal.Rptr. 406 (1970); Tulsa v. Langley, 196 Okl. 680, 168 P.2d 116 (1946); Fisher v. Philadelphia, 382 Pa. 607, 116 A.2d 735 (1955). *Fisher* also indicated that bonds which exceed debt limits when authorized, could not be made valid by later increases in assessed property valuations. Id. at 612, 116 A.2d at 737.

Are the foregoing problems avoided by making the loan authorization effective only at such future time as the proposed borrowing will fall within the legal debt limit? Safer methods are provided by statutory procedures for pre-issuance validation of bonds. See p. 692 et seq.

Where the validity of bonds turns on issues other than computation of debt, the date for determining validity may vary. Consider the following:

(a) The statute which enables a local unit to issue bonds is repealed after the bonds were authorized, but before any bonds were issued.

(b) The enabling statute was repealed after some, but not all, of the bonds were issued.

(c) The enabling statute was not repealed, but was declared unconstitutional after some of the bonds were issued.

The case law on such questions is sparse and not very current. See 15 McQuillin, *Municipal Corporations* § 43.28 (1970 rev. ed.).

ROCHLIN v. STATE

Supreme Court of Arizona, 1975.
112 Ariz. 171, 540 P.2d 643.

HONOHAN, JUSTICE.

[Suit by city and resident taxpayers seeking to nullify uniform state retirement system on ground (inter alia) that it created "debt" in excess of state constitutional limits]. * * *

The facts were stipulated * * * and motions for judgment were filed by the parties. The trial judge granted the defendants' motion for judgment * * *. A timely appeal was filed by the plaintiffs.

The parties agree that there are no issues of fact, and the issues to be resolved are solely matters of law.

Prior to 1968, the legislature had established separate pension systems for firemen, policemen, and highway patrolmen. Each system varied somewhat in the manner of funding and the amount of benefits. In 1968, the legislature enacted the statute in question in order to provide a uniform statewide pension system. Funding included the transfer of the monies in the previous independent systems into a single investment agency, a continuation of employee and employer (State and political subdivisions) current contributions, and contributions by the employer sufficient in amount to pay the prescribed interest rate on what is later defined as the past service cost. The act was amended in 1971 to liberalize the pension system by providing for earlier retirement by employees without reduction in benefits.

Appellants question the constitutionality of the Public Safety Personnel Retirement System on four grounds: First, that the unfunded liability of the State and political subdivisions is a debt subject to the limitations in Article 9, Sections 5 and 8 of the Arizona Constitution; second, that the act permits the State and local governments to postpone indefinitely the payment of an annual necessary expense contrary to the provisions of Article 9, Sections 3 and 7; third, that the giving of increased benefits grants extra compensation after services were rendered in violation of Article 4, Part 2, Section 17 of the Arizona Constitution; and fourth, that the method of funding the pension system creates non-uniformity in taxation, contrary to Article 9, Section 1 of the Arizona Constitution.

The Appellants are * * * challenging the system as created in 1968 and amended in 1971. They maintain that the several pensions systems in existence before the 1968 Act required fully funded systems. The 1968 Act and its amendments created a system which would have a constantly growing "unfunded liability." * * * This unfunded liability is the core of the issue of the constitutionality of the statute. * * *

The term "unfunded liability" is not used in the statute. A.R.S. § 38–843(B) uses the term "past service cost," but the effect is the same so that the terms may be said to be synonymous. The term unfunded liability is best described as the difference between the amount of money *actually* paid into the retirement fund and the amount required to provide retirement benefits for employees covered by the system based upon their past service. * * * This liability is unfunded, but the statutes require that each political unit pay into the retirement fund an amount representing the interest on the amount of the unfunded liability for that political unit.

Appellants contend that the unfunded liability * * * amounted to over thirty million dollars on July 1, 1972. While Appellees do not contest the figures of Appellants, they contend that the fund is sound even though partially funded because government is continuous and there will always be a steady supply of persons entering the system, some staying, some leaving, and * * * is actuarially sound if the contributions to the system each year are sufficient to cover normal cost plus interest on the unfunded liability. Dombrowski v. City of Philadelphia, 431 Pa. 199, 245 A.2d 238 (1968).

The arguments between Appellant and Appellees on the fiscal soundness of the retirement system are legislative considerations. * * * The Constitution of Arizona has placed such matters within the exclusive province of the legislature. Industrial Development Authority v. Nelson, 109 Ariz. 368, 509 P.2d 703 (1973). * * *

To overcome the presumption in favor of the constitutionality of a legislative enactment, Appellants have the burden of establishing beyond a reasonable doubt that the act violates some provision of the Constitution. * * *

I.

Appellants contend that the unfunded liability * * * under the Retirement System is a "debt" under Article 9, Sections 5 and 8 of the Arizona Constitution, and the unfunded liability exceeds the debt limitations by those sections. This is a question of first impression in Arizona.

* * *

* * * The question presented is whether an unfunded liability is a debt in the constitutional sense.

["Debt" as commonly understood includes every obligation by which one person is bound to pay money to another, but when used in the constitutional sense it is given a meaning much less comprehensive.] Hubbell v. Herring, 216 Iowa 728, 249 N.W. 430 (1933). A debt in the constitutional sense arises when the State or a political subdivision borrows money. * * *

Under Section 5 of Article 9, a debt can be either direct or contingent. A direct debt occurs when the State borrows money, pledging its credit as the sole source of payment. A contingent or secondary debt occurs when the governmental unit guarantees payment of revenue bonds, pledging its credit in the event that the revenues derived from the funded project prove inadequate to meet the bond obligations. Alan v. County of Wayne, 388 Mich. 210, 200 N.W.2d 628 (1972).

Appellants contend that the term "debt" has a broader meaning than simply borrowed money. They argue that this Court has so held in City of Phoenix v. Phoenix Civic Auditorium and Convention Center Association, 99 Ariz. 270, 408 P.2d 818 (1965) and American-La France and Foamite Corporation v. City of Phoenix, 47 Ariz. 133, 54 P.2d 258 (1936). The cited cases do not apply to state debt. Both cases deal with the question of debt of political subdivisions of the state, and neither of the cases is applicable to Article 9, Section 5.

There are significant differences in the language of Sections 5 and 8 of Article 9. Section 5 speaks in terms of "contracting debts to supply the casual deficits or failures in revenues, or to meet expenses not otherwise provided for." Section 8 provides that political subdivisions shall not "become indebted in any manner." In City of Phoenix v. Phoenix Civic Auditorium and Convention Center Association, supra, this Court held that Section 8 included not only borrowed money but also any pecuniary obligation created by contract or by express agreement. This holding construed the intent of the broad language of Section 8.

Due to the difference in the language between Sections 5 and 8, the cases construing Section 8 are not authority for the construction of Section 5. This difference in language must be respected. * * * We believe that Section 5 was meant to apply to borrowing money for the operation of state government.

In the instance of the retirement system the State has not borrowed any money. Any liability which has arisen is not due to borrowing funds; hence it is not "debt" in the sense of Section 5, Article 9 of the constitution.

In the instance of political subdivisions of the state the debt limitation is stated differently than that for the state. Section 8, Article 9 limits the amount which such units "shall for any purpose become indebted in any manner." Despite this broad language the courts have limited the meaning in several instances. Obligations of political subdivisions which are payable from a special fund and not from the general revenue have been held not to be debts within the meaning of the constitutional limitation. Guthrie v. City of Mesa, 47 Ariz. 336, 56 P.2d 655 (1936); Industrial Development Authority v. Nelson, supra. Obligations which have not been voluntarily incurred but which have been imposed by state law have been held not to be debts in the constitutional sense. Columbia County v. Board of Trustees, 17 Wis.2d 310, 116 N.W.2d 142 (1962).

In *Columbia County*, the Wisconsin Supreme Court held that a retirement system similar to that in issue did not violate the Wisconsin debt limitation provisions for counties because the obligation was not voluntarily incurred by the county. While the Wisconsin Constitution (Sec. 3, Art. 11) uses the phrase "incurring any indebtedness" in the debt limitation provision, it is sufficiently similar to our Section 8, Article 9 to be considered persuasive. * * *

We believe that the object of Section 8, Article 9 of our constitution was meant to apply to acts of the political subdivision in voluntarily becoming indebted, and it does not apply to obligations created and mandated by the state. As thus construed the constitutional section does not prohibit the manner of funding the pension system which the state has required of its political subdivisions.

II.

Appellants' second contention is that the unfunded liability is either a necessary ordinary expense which the statute permits the State and political subdivisions to postpone indefinitely, contrary to Article 9, Section 3 of the Arizona Constitution or it constitutes a gift by the State and local government which is forbidden by Article 9, Section 7 of the State Constitution.

* * *

Appellants argue that the expenses of operating the Highway Patrol including compensation of the employees, are part of the ordinary necessary expenses of the State and that the amount of the pension being earned by each member, including the unfunded liability, is also part of the ordinary necessary expenses of the State which must be provided for annually.

Appellants concede that the pension provisions have been held not to be gifts but a part of the contemplated compensation for employee services. Yeazell v. Copins, 98 Ariz. 109, 402 P.2d 541 (1965). Since the pension is not a gift appellants maintain that the full cost of the pension, like the salary, must be paid annually.

This position overlooks the basic fact that employees do not receive, nor is anything due, from the pension system until the employee has qualified and actually retired. Only upon retirement do the benefit payments become a current expense of the State. The expenses of the State governed by Section 3 of Article 9 are those which are required to be paid out during the fiscal year for the operation of government. The so-called "unfunded liability" amount is not part of the necessary ordinary expenses of the State. It is by its very nature a future cost not a current one.

III.

Appellants' third contention is that the liberalization of benefits * * * constitutes the granting of extra compensation after services were rendered, in violation of Article 4, Part 2, Section 17 of the Arizona Constitution. We reject that contention.

* * *

The nature of a pension was discussed in Yeazell v. Copins, supra. This Court held that a pension is not a gratuity but deferred compensation for services rendered. * * * The nature of a pension under Arizona statutes does not provide extra compensation for services already rendered.

The issue presented by appellants was considered in Gubler v. Utah State Teachers' Retirement Board, 113 Utah 188, 192 P.2d 580 (1948). Utah has a constitutional provision similar to the above quoted Arizona provision. The Utah Supreme Court held constitutional a 1945 amendment to the Teachers Retirement Act which allows teachers to have credit for services performed prior to 1937 which provision would result in increased pension benefits for those teachers who qualified. * * *

A pension even though based on past service is not intended to be compensation for past services. It is an inducement to experienced personnel to remain in service for continued performance. A promise of pension looks to the future and depends upon continued performance of service. Wright v. Craig, 202 App.Div. 684, 195 N.Y.S. 391 (1922); State v. Levitan, 181 Wis. 326, 193 N.W. 499 (1923); Dombrowski v. City of Philadelphia, supra.

The 1971 amendment to the act allowed earlier retirement than that formerly provided, and it is argued that, as to those who took advantage of early retirement, the retirement benefits were a payment for past services because it was certainly not an inducement for their continued service. With respect to such employees the payment was not for past services. The act had a dual purpose: to induce younger experienced officers to remain in service and to induce older officers to *Policy* retire to provide opportunity for replacement by younger personnel. Either purpose is constitutional and not payment for past service.

IV.

Appellants' final contention is that the method of funding the pension system creates non-uniformity in taxation, contrary to Article *A4* 9, Section 1 of the Arizona Constitution. We hold that it does not.

* * *

Appellants argue that when the Legislature requires an expenditure for a primary function of the State, then the above constitutional *ARG.* provision requires that the ad valorem property tax rate to fund the expenditure must be uniform throughout the State, and unless it is, the act is unconstitutional. This contention was rejected in substance by Shofstall v. Hollins, 110 Ariz. 88, 515 P.2d 590 (1973), which dealt with taxation for education. * * *

* * *

It is also pertinent to point out that the contributions to the pension system by the municipalities and counties need not necessarily come from the ad valorem tax revenue. Nothing in the statute requires that any particular source of revenue be used.

Having fully considered the issues presented by appellants we hold that the Public Safety Personnel Retirement System is constitutional, and the judgment of the superior court is affirmed.

(2) Bonded Debt—General or Special Obligations?

BOARD OF SUPERVISORS OF FAIRFAX COUNTY
v. MASSEY

Supreme Court of Appeals of Virginia, 1969.
210 Va. 253, 169 S.E.2d 556.

I'ANSON, JUSTICE. These cases are * * * upon separate petitions for writs of mandamus filed by the Board of Supervisors of Fairfax County (County) and City of Falls Church (City), petitioners, * * * to compel Carlton C. Massey, County Executive, and Harry E. Wells, City Manager, respondents, to execute on behalf of their respective County and City a contract designated "Transit Service Agreement" (Agreement), to which Washington Metropolitan Area Transit Authority (Authority) and other public bodies of Virginia, Maryland, and the District of Columbia are also parties.

The Authority was created * * * by the Washington Metropolitan Area Transit Authority Compact (Compact), an interstate agreement between Virginia, Maryland, and the District of Columbia, as an agency and instrumentality of each of the signatory parties thereto, to plan, develop, finance, and provide improved transit facilities and service for the Washington Metropolitan Area Transit Zone (Zone). The Zone encompasses the District of Columbia; the counties of Arlington and Fairfax, and the cities of Alexandria, Falls Church and Fairfax in Virginia and Montgomery and Prince George's counties in Maryland.

In contemplation of the Compact the General Assembly of Virginia adopted the Transportation District Act of 1964 * * *. It authorizes the creation of transportation districts to cooperate and participate with an agency such as the Authority in planning and financing an interstate regional transit system. In order to take advantage of this Act, the Northern Virginia Transportation District, consisting of the counties of Arlington and Fairfax and the cities of Alexandria, Fairfax and Falls Church, was created by Chapter 630, Acts of 1964, p. 933.

The Authority has adopted a mass transit plan for the Zone. It proposes to construct a combination subway and surface rapid rail system, 97.7 miles in length, with stations to serve the most densely populated areas of the Zone.

The estimated cost of constructing the transit system is $2,494,600,000. Funds are to be obtained from the following sources: The Authority will issue tax-exempt gross revenue bonds in the amount of $835,000,000; the federal government will contribute $1,147,044,000; and political subdivisions in the Zone will contribute the sum of $573,522,000. Of this amount, $149,900,000 will come from political subdivisions in Virginia. The shares of the County and City are $61,900,000 and $800,000, respectively. The County and City have authorized the issuance of general obligation bonds in these amounts, and have entered into a capital contributions agreement with the Authority for the payment of these sums during the estimated ten-year construction period.

* * *

Article VII, § 18(a), of the Compact, and Code § 15.1–1357(b)(3) of the Transportation Act authorize the County and City to enter into contracts with the Authority to contribute to the capital for construction and/or acquisition of facilities, and for meeting expenses and obligations *in the operation of such facilities.* See also, Code § 15.1–1359, as amended, 1968 Cum.Supp.

The Transit Service Agreement states in its preamble, *inter alia,* that the Authority's engineering studies estimate that fare box receipts and other transit system revenues will be more than sufficient to pay debt service and reserves on the Authority's transit revenue bonds as well as to meet operating and maintenance expenses, but it is nevertheless considered that the financing of the transit system on favorable terms requires each of the political subdivisions to agree to make payments for services to be provided by such transit systems.

Under the Agreement, the County and City will underwrite their proportionate shares of any deficits incurred in the operating expenses of the transit system by making monthly service payments in advance to the Authority, beginning with the first day of the fiscal year next

succeeding the initial operation date and ending June 30, 2040.
* * *

* * *

Each year the Authority is required to make a complete review of its financial condition, rate and fare structure, and the procedures, schedules and standards of transit service. * * * The Authority is also required to determine whether the estimated revenues of the transit system, after making provision for debt service and reserve requirements * * * will be sufficient to cover the cost of operation and maintenance incurred. The extent to which the revenues are insufficient for this purpose is the "operating deficiency requirement" for the ensuing year. * * * The "operating deficiency requirement" as thus adjusted constitutes the aggregate service payment.

The aggregate service payment is allocated among the political subdivisions in the Zone in accordance with a prescribed formula. The amounts thus allocated constitute the service payment to be made by each political subdivision. * * *

The obligation of each political subdivision to make its service payment is conditioned upon transit service being rendered to it. If no transit service is rendered in any particular year, no service payment is required for that year * * *.

* * *

The questions presented are:

(1) Will the obligations of the County and City under the Agreement constitute debt or indebtedness within the meaning of §§ 115a or 127 of the Constitution of Virginia, or §§ 7.03 or 7.06 of the charter of the City of Falls Church?

(2) Will the obligations of the County and City under the Agreement constitute a grant or loan of credit, in violation of § 185 of the Constitution of Virginia?

(3) Does the Agreement comply with the Compact and the Transportation Act of 1964?

I.

Sections 115a and 127 of the Constitution of Virginia are designed to control indebtedness of localities, but each approaches the problem in a different way. Section 115a limits county debt by requiring a referendum approved by the qualified voters. * * *

Section 127 limits the indebtedness of cities and towns to eighteen percent of local taxable real estate values. * * *

Section 7.03 of the Falls Church charter applies the limitation of § 127 of the Constitution to the issuance of "bonds and notes." Section 7.06 of the charter prescribes the procedure for the issuance of bonds and requires that bond ordinances be approved by a referendum.

Petitioners recognize that while § 127 refers to "bonds or other interest-bearing obligations," the language includes any unconditional obligation requiring the payment of money and has the same meaning as "debt" as used in § 115a, and that the Falls Church charter provisions rest upon the same determination. See, Button v. Day, 205 Va. 629, 642, 139 S.E.2d 91, 100 (1964).

Hence the paramount inquiry here is whether by executing the contract designated "Transit Service Agreement" the County and City will incur debts in violation of the constitutional limitations.

Petitioners say that to constitute a debt within the meaning of constitutional limitations, there must be a present obligation; and that since the Agreement requires the County and City to make the service payments when, as, and if transit service is rendered, and then only if available revenues of the transit system are inadequate, this creates nothing more than a contingent liability and not a present indebtedness.

Petitioners rely on the principle that a local government may lawfully contract for necessary services such as water, electricity, or sewerage, over a period of years and agree to pay therefor in periodic installments as the services are furnished. In such cases the amounts to be paid as the services are rendered under such contracts do not give rise to a present indebtedness of such local governments, and such contracts are not rendered invalid by the fact that the aggregate of the installments exceeds the debt limitation. City of Walla Walla v. Walla Walla Water Co., 172 U.S. 1, 19, 20, 19 S.Ct. 77, 43 L.Ed. 341 (1898); Struble v. Nelson, 217 Minn. 610, 15 N.W.2d 101, 104 (1944); 64 C.J.S. Municipal Corporations § 1852(b), p. 374; 38 Am.Jur., Municipal Corporations, § 463, pp. 144–146; Annotation, 103 A.L.R. 1160, 1161, and the numerous cases there cited.

We do not think, however, that the principle relied on is applicable in the present cases. Our examination of the authorities cited by the petitioners did not reveal a single case in which the local governments underwrote or guaranteed the deficit incurred in the operation of the facilities furnishing the services under their contracts.

* * *

It is true that in *Button* we said: "It is not a contract to furnish water, electricity or other public service utilities to the City, the furnishing of which is a condition of the obligation." This dictum was a mere recognition of the general rule that a continuing service contract, for which the municipality agrees to pay in installments as the services furnished, does not create a present debt for the aggregate amount of all the installments throughout the term of the contract within the meaning of constitutional limitations of municipal indebtedness. However, it cannot be concluded from the dictum in *Button* that all contracts which are called service agreements are in fact such, irrespective of the provisions contained therein.

* * * The obligations of the County and City under the Agreement are for more than just payments for transit service. They agree to pay that amount by which the "operating expenses" exceed the revenues from the transit system * * *. The obligations of the County and City to underwrite and guarantee an unknown "operating expense" deficit of the transit system are fixed and absolute and constitute a present debt within the meaning of the constitutional limitations on County and City debt or indebtedness.

There are no facts in the record, by stipulation or evidence, to show that the County's obligation under the Agreement can be paid out of current revenues or that there has been an election by the people of the County authorizing the obligation to be incurred. In the case of the City, there is nothing showing the value of its taxable property, or what is the aggregate amount of its indebtedness, or the amount of its constitutional debt limit.

Thus we hold that the obligations of the County and City under the Agreement constitute debt or indebtedness within the meaning of the constitutional prohibitions of §§ 115a and 127 and under the charter provisions of the City of Falls Church.

* * *

Notes

1. **Guarantees Which Do or Do Not Create Debt.** How could the contract in *Massey* be revised to become a service contract and not create debt? See the sequel to *Massey,* Board of Supervisors of Fairfax County v. Massey, 210 Va. 680, 173 S.E.2d 869 (1970). In accord with the principal case are Hink v. Board of Directors of Beaver Water District, 235 Ark. 107, 357 S.W.2d 271 (1962); Alan v. Wayne County, 388 Mich. 210, 200 N.W.2d 628 (1972); Bachtell v. Waterloo, 200 N.W.2d 548 (Iowa 1972). In Alan, the Wayne County Stadium Authority sought approval of bonds to construct a stadium, for lease to the county, which would sublease to the Detroit Tigers Baseball Club. The county undertook to levy taxes to make up for any difference between its stadium revenues and the rental charged by the Authority to meet its bond obligations. Though the bonds were denominated "revenue" bonds, the court found that the bonds were backed by the county's credit and created a general obligation in excess of the county debt limit. Some courts, however, strain to uphold such authority financing. In Conrad v. Pittsburgh, 421 Pa. 492, 218 A.2d 906 (1966) where the court, under circumstances substantially similar to Bachtell, supra, upheld the transaction as not resulting in local government debt. See also State ex rel. Brennan v. Bowman, 88 Nev. 582, 503 P.2d 454 (1972); Annot. *Government Expenditure, Athletic Stadium,* 67 A.L.R.3d 1186 (1975).

The decisions as to when a covenant to raise funds constitutes "guaranteed debt" are not harmonious. The following cases provide some guidance. A covenant to levy user charges or special assessments in amounts sufficient to pay for contracted services or lease rentals is generally held not to create debt. The fact that the rates levels or user charges coincide with payment schedules does not evidence debt-creation, unless such charges are clearly unreasonable. See e.g., Patterson v. Bismarck, 188 N.W.2d 734 (N.D.1971) (use of special assessments to repay bonds); Municipality of Metro Seattle v. Seattle, 57 Wash.2d 446, 357 P.2d 863 (1960) (city covenant to set sewer rates at level sufficient to meet annual sewer charges); Hillard v. Mobile, 253 Ala. 676, 47 So.2d 162 (1950) (city contract to pay annual water service fees sufficient to enable corporation to sell and repay revenue bonds for new water facilities).

2. **General Obligation Bonds and Revenue Bonds.** As all bonds are basically promissory notes, i.e., contractual promises to repay loans, but the sources and security for their repayment are important not only to their collectability and credit rating, but to their legal classification as "debt" or not "debt" for limitation purposes. Revenue bonds are excluded from debt limitations on the theory that the financed facilities are self-supporting, and that the local government is not exposed to liability. Bonds repayable solely from parking fees, tolls, transit fares or utility charges are held not to create debt. Petition of Philadelphia, 435 Pa. 193, 254 A.2d 628 (1969); Laverents v. Cheyenne, 67 Wyo. 187, 217 P.2d 877 (1950).

In strictly financial terms, distinctions between general obligation and "special fund" obligations may be deceptive. "Nonguaranteed bonds now take up more than half of state, and ⅓ of local debt: * * *. By obscuring what state and local governments are doing, they stimulate imprudent borrowing; they impose interest charges * * * higher by .5–.6 per cent than those of full faith and credit bonds." James A. Maxwell, *Financing State and Local Governments,* 7 (rev. ed. 1969).

The logic of self-supporting, special fund obligations breaks down where the pledged revenues fall short or exceed scheduled bond payments; where the pledged revenues are drawn partly from sources other than the new construction; and where the pledged revenues are levies of special improvement taxing districts. See, Note 6, below.

3. **Involuntary Liability.** The black letter proposition, that debt limitation laws do not govern contingent liability, is a misleading half-truth. Some contingent liabilities qualify for debt exclusion, but others do not. The significance of "contingent" liability may be more safely expressed in terms of whether the liability was voluntarily or involuntarily incurred.

Tort liability is not included in computation of debt, either because it is a "contingent" or "involuntary" obligation, or because the policy of holding local units accountable for tort injury outweighs debt limitation policy. Where, however, a potential tort liability is voluntarily assumed, as by a promise to indemnify a builder in a construction contract, the indemnity obligation may be held void as an unlawful assumption of debt. Brown v. Jefferson County, 406 S.W.2d 185 (Tex.1966); Columbia County v. Board of Trustees, *supra;* Keller v. Scranton, 200 Pa. 130, 49 A. 781 (1901).

While courts are not agreed on what constitutes mandatory and discretionary spending, the weight of authority favors the rule that only voluntary debts fall within debt ceilings. 2 Antieau, *Municipal Corporation Law* § 15.27 (1971); 15 McQuillin, *Municipal Corporations* § 41.28 (1970 rev. ed.). Thus, where a state imposes a mandatory duty upon a local unit to raise monies for a specific capital project, e.g. to build a courthouse, courts have ruled that such is not a local government debt. See e.g., Los Angeles County v. Byram, 36 Cal.2d 694, 227 P.2d 4 (1951); cf. Columbia

County v. Board of Trustees of Wisconsin Retirement Fund, 17 Wis.2d 310, 331, 116 N.W.2d 142, 153 (1962).

Where a municipality retained plaintiff to provide engineering services for a sewer project, which was thereafter aborted by electoral rejection of a proposed borrowing to finance the project, the court denied recovery for the engineering services performed. The obligation was held to be an unconstitutional "debt." Hancock v. Hazel Crest, 318 Ill.App. 170, 47 N.E.2d 557 (1943). Some years later a town in the same state, acting pursuant to an authorizing statute, issued a contract for engineering services for road improvements, and duly appropriated funds to cover the contract. The enabling statute was later held unconstitutional and the Town refused to pay for services rendered under the contract. May the engineer recover for services rendered prior to nullification of the statute? On the contract? On implied contract for the reasonable value of his services? See Mathew v. Allgonquin, 3 Ill.App.3d 429, 279 N.E.2d 91 (1972).

4. **Pledge of Physical Assets.** Where public debt is secured by a lien on the capital improvement as well as by revenues from its use, the local unit could lose its title to the property by foreclosure in the event of default. Does the likelihood that the government will employ its general assets and taxing power to avoid such loss import debt creation? Cf. the Basehore opinion at p. 704 infra. Where a mortgage is given on a preexisting facility as well as new improvements, the debt creation rationale is fortified. See McNichols v. Denver, 123 Colo. 132, 140, 230 P.2d 591, 595 (1951). Some courts prefer to ignore the significance of property encumbrance where the bonds are primarily secured by facility revenues. See e.g. People ex rel. City of Salem v. McMackin, 53 Ill.2d 347, 291 N.E.2d 807 (1972).

5. **Special Taxing Districts.** The operation of legislatively created special taxing districts is described in the following excerpt from Dortch v. Lugar, 255 Ind. 545, 266 N.E.2d 25, 42 (1971):

> "Suffice it to say that the Legislature may create such special taxing districts for local public improvements and provide for the levy of special ad valorem taxes throughout the district based upon the benefit accruing to the property holders therein situated; the Legislature may determine the boundaries of such districts or delegate to an agency the power to so determine them, *conforming or not* to the political or governmental subdivision there located; the Legislature may designate the agency to perform the administrative functions necessary on behalf of the district; and obligations so incurred by such a district payable out of the special benefit ad valorem tax are not debts of a municipal corporation within the provisions of Art. 13, § 1 of the Indiana Constitution.

> " * * * Appellant and intervenor's objection to the plan appears to center on the fact that the agency designated by the Legislature to administer the taxing districts is, in all cases, a department of the consolidated city. However, it is not the agency designated to administer the functions of the taxing district that determines its validity. * * * That the city officials may act as fiscal agents of the special taxing district was confirmed by the case of Book v. Board of Flood

Control Commissioners, supra. We are not prepared to reverse a long line of judicial authority relative to special taxing districts in order to hold the schematic plan under consideration unconstitutional. * * *" Accord: Barlow v. Clearfield City Corporation, 1 Utah 2d 419, 268 P.2d 682 (1954).

6. **Overlying Debt and Interlocal Contracts.** Absent contrary legislation, each local government unit may borrow up to its debt limit without affecting the debt limit of other units, however overlapping their territory or functions may be. See Albuquerque Metropolitan Arroyo Flood Control Authority v. Swinburne, 74 N.M. 487, 394 P.2d 998 (1964); Dortch v. Lugar, supra. Hence, the borrowing capacity of other local units may be tapped through interlocal service contracts to avoid submission of unpopular loan proposals to an uncooperative electorate. See Eastern Municipal Water District v. Scott, 1 Cal.App. 3d 129, 81 Cal.Rptr. 510 (1960).

In Goreham v. Des Moines Metropolitan Area Solid Waste Agency, 179 N.W.2d 449 (Iowa 1970) several local governments created an independent public service agency to issue revenue bonds and construct service facilities. The agreement creating the Agency bound each unit to continue the service contract with the Agency until the latter's revenue bonds were repaid. The court ruled that the agreement did not create general obligation debts for the participating units.

CITY OF OXNARD v. DALE

Supreme Court of California, 1955.
45 Cal.2d 729, 290 P.2d 859.

GIBSON, CHIEF JUSTICE. Petitioner, a municipal corporation of the sixth class, seeks a writ of mandate requiring respondent city treasurer to sign, and respondent city clerk to countersign, certain revenue bonds which the city proposes to issue * * *.

The sole question presented is whether the proposed bonds, and the statute under which they were authorized by the voters and the city council, are contrary to section 18 of article XI of the California Constitution, which provides, insofar as pertinent here: "No county, city, town, township, board of education, or school district, shall incur any indebtedness or liability in any manner or for any purpose exceeding in any year the income and revenue provided for such year, without the assent of two-thirds of the qualified electors thereof, * * * nor unless before or at the time of incurring such indebtedness provision shall be made for the collection of an annual tax sufficient to pay the interest on such indebtedness as it falls due, and also provision to constitute a sinking fund for the payment of the principal thereof * * *."

The city has owned a sanitary sewer system since 1905. The system and its additions and improvements were financed largely by the issuance of general obligation bonds, of which a total amounting to $795,200 remains outstanding and unpaid. Charges for use of the sewer system were first imposed in 1946, and since that time all expenses of operation and maintenance have been paid from sewer revenues. The revenues have been used, further, to pay part of the interest and principal on general obligation sewer bonds issued in 1949, but the city does not presently intend to continue to apply sewer revenues toward the retirement of these bonds.

A treatment plant, financed by a portion of the general obligation bonds referred to above, is now being constructed, and the city proposes to construct interceptor sewers to transport sewage to the treatment plant. Pursuant to the Revenue Bond Law of 1941 the city council, in March 1954, called a special election to submit to the voters the issuance of sewer revenue bonds in the amount of $450,000 to finance the construction of the interceptor sewers. It was specified that the bonds were to be payable exclusively from the revenues of the entire sewer system of the city, together with all additions and improvements thereafter made, and that the bonds were not to be secured by the taxing power of the city. . * * * The bonds were approved at the ensuing election.

Subsequently the city council adopted a resolution authorizing the proposed bonds * * *.

The resolution further provides that the city is to covenant, among other things, that it will * * * prescribe sufficient charges for the services of the system to pay interest and principal on the bonds and the expenses of operation. * * *

It is settled in California and recognized in almost all of the other states that, as a general rule, a constitutional provision such as section 18 of article XI is not violated by revenue bonds or other obligations which are payable solely from a special fund, provided the governmental body is not liable to maintain the special fund out of its general funds, or by tax levies, should the special fund prove insufficient. [Citations omitted] As pointed out in the case of California Toll Bridge Authority v. Wentworth, *supra*, 212 Cal. at page 302, 298 P. at page 486, such an obligation is not considered to be an indebtedness or liability of the political subdivision or agency issuing the bonds, within the meaning of the constitutional limitation.

The cases in California are not entirely clear as to the extent of the operation of the special fund doctrine, and there is a conflict of authority on the subject in other states. Some of the courts in other jurisdictions have held that revenue bonds payable solely from a special fund will not be free from the constitutional limitation unless the fund is restricted to the revenues from the particular improvement which is to be constructed out of the proceeds of the bonds in question, but under the prevailing view the doctrine may be applicable where the revenues of the entire existing system, as well as those of the proposed improvement, are pledged. See Joint Report of Committees of the American Society of Civil Engineers, the Section of Municipal Law of the American Bar Association and others (1951), 12 Ohio State L.J. 147, 182 *et seq.*; 38 Am.Jur. 155–156.

The first case in California discussing this problem is Garrett v. Swanton, 216 Cal. 220, 13 P.2d 725, where a city agreed to purchase a pumping plant on a conditional sales plan, with payments to be in installments over a period of years out of a special fund maintained by profits from the entire water system. There, as here, the city had previously issued general obligation bonds to finance the system, and, by ordinance, water revenues were being used for the payments on the bonds. It was held that the special fund doctrine was inapplicable under the facts of the case and that the contract was in violation of section 18 of article XI. The court said that the contract indirectly created a general liability of the city, and it reasoned that any deficiency of revenue would require the taxpayers to contribute to the water fund, from which both the contract and the bonds were being paid, in order to make the payments on the bonds. The court also stated, in effect, that the possibility of a forfeiture under the conditional sales contract might make it necessary for the city, if it wished to protect its investment, to pay contract installments from general funds and that the creation of this inducement amounted to a violation of the Constitution. [Citations omitted] In the present case, however, the resolution authorizing the proposed revenue bonds specifies that the bondholders shall have no right to cause the forfeiture of any property of the city.

Two subsequent decisions of this court, while distinguishing the Garrett case on its facts, have departed from its reasoning insofar as it may be applicable here. Department of Water and Power of City of Los Angeles v. Vroman, 218 Cal. 206, 22 P.2d 698; California Toll Bridge Authority v. Kelly, 218 Cal. 7, 21 P.2d 425; see also City of Glendale v. Chapman, 108 Cal.App.2d 74, 80, *et seq.*, 238 P.2d 162, *cf.* Board of State Harbor Com'rs for San Francisco Harbor v. Dean, 118 Cal.App.2d 628, 632 *et seq.*, 258 P.2d 590. * * *

* * *

As we have seen, an obligation which is payable out of a special fund is not an "indebtedness or liability" of a governmental body within the meaning of section 18 of article XI of the Constitution if the governmental body is not required to pay the obligation from its general funds, or by exercise of its powers of taxation, should the special fund prove insufficient. Respondents concede, as they must, that the special fund doctrine would be applicable and controlling here if the revenues pledged to secure the proposed bonds were secured by the revenues to be produced from the interceptor lines alone. Insofar as concerns the constitutional limitation, we can see no sound reason to distinguish between that situation and the one presented here where the pledge consists of the revenues of the entire system and where those revenues had formerly been used to make payments on the city's general obligation bonds. Garrett v. Swanton, 216 Cal. 220, 13 P.2d 725, is overruled to the extent that it is inconsistent with the views expressed herein. Accordingly, the proposed bonds, and the statutes under which they were authorized, are valid, and respondents are required to sign the bonds as demanded by petitioner.

It is ordered that a peremptory writ of mandate issue as prayed.

Notes

1. **Variants on the "special fund" doctrine.** "Courts which have dealt with special-fund financing are split into two groups. Some limit the governmental unit involved to those projects which will be completely self-liquidating from the income obtained from the new construction itself. Others also permit the use of income from already existing facilities to defray the new construction costs.

"Plaintiff is asking us to adopt the first or *strict* special-fund doctrine rather than the last or *broad* theory. He relies most heavily on Boe v. Foss, 76 S.D. 295, 77 N.W.2d 1, 10, which accepted the strict theory * * * Several other jurisdictions follow this formula. We make no attempt to distinguish this case from the present one. We only say it represents the minority view and one with which we cannot agree. As said in Lacher v. Board of Trustees of State Colleges, 243 Md. 500, 221 A.2d 625, 630, the South Dakota doctrine is followed by only 'a small minority of courts.' The overwhelming weight of authority is to the contrary. Most courts hold that financing such as the Board proposes here * * * does not create a debt * * *." Brack v. Mossman, 170 N.W.2d 416, 422 (Iowa 1969).

In Petition of City of Philadelphia, 435 Pa. 193, 254 A.2d 628 (1969), the city sought to exclude from its debt limit the amount of its subway extension bonds which were backed by the unqualified promise of the Southeast Pennsylvania Transit Authority to lease the system and to pay sufficient rentals to cover the bond obligations. Noting that Pennsylvania follows the broad special fund doctrine, the court permitted the exclusion. It held that the city did not have to prove that the Transit Authority would generate sufficient income to meet the bond payments, because the legislative creation of the Authority imported a finding that the Authority would be financially responsible.

In Davis v. Pueblo, 158 Colo. 319, 406 P.2d 671 (1965), the pledge of on-street parking meter fees (which would normally go into the city's general treasury) and of revenue from new off-street parking facility, was held not to create a general obligation on the city, even though the pledge of parking meter fees would result in increased property taxes. Accord: State ex rel. Gordon v. Rhodes, 158 Ohio St. 128, 107 N.E.2d 206 (1952); Town of Medley v. State, 162 So.2d 257 (Fla.1964). The conflicting authorities are noted in Laverents v. Cheyenne, 67 Wyo. 187, 217 P.2d 877 (1950).

2. **Surplus Project Revenues.** Should project revenues in excess of current bond obligations be transferable to the city treasury, especially where pledged revenues were derived from sources other than the new improvement? See State ex rel. City of Charleston v. Hutchinson, 154 W.Va. 585, 176 S.E.2d 691 (1970).

PEOPLE v. DOYLE AND ASSOCIATES, INC.

Supreme Court of Michigan, 1965.
374 Mich. 222, 132 N.W.2d 99.

SOURIS, JUSTICE. Late in 1962 the defendant county of Berrien entered into a series of transactions with defendant Doyle and Associates, Inc., whereby Doyle constructed and equipped, on land owned by the county, a large building suitable for the care of sick or aged people. As modified by stipulation of the contracting parties made on the record in open court by their attorneys, the county and Doyle agreed that the county would occupy and use the building and equipment for which it would pay Doyle monthly a specified sum and, as well, pay all other operating expenses and costs which normally are payable by the owner of a building, and at the end of 10 years, title to the building and equipment would be in the county free and clear of any incumbrances. The agreement was evidenced by a ground lease of the land * * * running to Doyle from the county and an agreement, labeled a "lease agreement", running to the county from Doyle.

Shortly after construction commenced, the attorney general filed this suit for injunctive and other relief claiming the transactions were void because they constituted the incurring of debt by the county in excess of the limitation then contained in article VIII, § 10 of the Constitution of 1908 and because the county had failed to comply with statutory requirements relating to debt financing by a county, [Citations omitted] A restraining order was issued *ex parte* upon filing of the complaint, * * *. A week or so later, * * *, a preliminary injunction was granted enjoining Doyle from furnishing medical or hospital care or medical facilities to or for the county and enjoining the county from payment of any of its funds for any purpose related to the construction or use of the building under construction. In granting the preliminary injunction in such fashion that construction of the building could continue, the chancellor expressly noted that, if the corporate defendant continued the project, it would act at its own peril. The building was completed shortly after hearing on the merits. The chancellor * * * entered a decree dismissing the complaint, from which decree this appeal has been taken. Pending the appeal, the county has occupied the building and has operated it as a hospital pursuant to a provisional certification therefor by the state health commissioner executed in accordance with a stipulation of the parties.

We cannot read the documents executed by the county and Doyle as other than an agreement for the construction and equipping of a medical facility by Doyle and its purchase by deferred payments by the county. By such agreement the county has incurred a debt in the total amount of the monthly sums it has agreed to pay to Doyle over a 10-year period plus the other expenses it has assumed to pay * * *. Labeling the monthly payments required to be made by the county as "rentals" does not affect their essential nature as purchase payments.

The experts, in reaching their conclusions that the monthly payments were reasonable in amount, did so with full understanding that the county would at the end of the 10-year period own the building and its equipment.

It is of interest to note that one of the experts concluded that in the event Doyle retained a reversionary interest in the building upon expiration of the county's 10-year "lease", then a reasonable "rental" (from a prudent investor's viewpoint) for the county's occupancy during its 10-year term would be very substantially less than the monthly payments agreed to be paid * * *. The record made demonstrates conclusively that the agreement was nothing less than an agreement by the county to purchase a fully equipped building [from] Doyle * * * over a 10-year period. The ground lease and lease-back agreement were devices of convenience to secure Doyle and to permit it to arrange financing for the project. It is not an unfamiliar practice in private commercial affairs nor is it unknown in government-purpose financing. See Magnusson, "Lease-Financing by Municipal Corporations as a Way Around Debt Limitations", 25 Geo.Wash.L.Rev. 377 (1957).

That the county undertook to incur an indebtedness cannot be questioned seriously. It agreed to make monthly payments * * * for a 10-year period certain during which time it forswore termination of the agreement. It pledged it would budget sufficient funds each year for the monthly payments * * * and, indeed, it pledged to levy sufficient taxes and to collect sufficient revenues from other sources to make such payments. In short, it assumed an indebtedness to Doyle repayable in installments over a 10-year term.

As this Court said in School Dist. No. 9 v. McLintock, 255 Mich. 197, at 201, 237 N.W. 539, to incur indebtedness is to borrow money. The constitutional provision * * * limited the borrowing power of counties to one-tenth of one mill on their assessed valuation, a maximum limitation in this case far below the indebtedness assumed by the county for each year to say nothing of the county's total obligation for the 10-year term. The record discloses that the electors of the county did not approve exceeding the stated limit, as the constitutional provision expressly authorized they could, and in fact, it appears that the county's electors several years earlier had rejected a financing proposal submitted to them for acquisition of similar facilities.

In Putnam v. Grand Rapids, 58 Mich. 416, 25 N.W. 330, this Court invalidated a contract entered into by a city for the time purchase of street lighting equipment for an aggregate sum in excess of the city's charter limitation upon its borrowing power. * * * We conclude that the agreement between the county and Doyle is invalid. * * *. Thus, we are required to reverse and remand for further proceedings.

In the peculiar circumstances of this case our reversal and remand should not be without some indication as to what further proceedings may be had. The leaseback agreement which imposed the excessive obligation upon the county is void. This being so, Doyle may not claim compensation under it, nor under the settled law of this State, may Doyle make claim against the county in *quantum meruit* for the facility it erected upon the lease ground. See, *inter alia*, Stratton v. City of Detroit, 246 Mich. 139, 224 N.W. 649.

The ground lease, however, remains valid, for while by its terms it contemplated the erection of a medical facility and a lease-back agreement to the county, its validity was not made dependent in any way upon the successful execution of such projects. * * * Thus, while Doyle has no rights it may enforce against the county arising from the invalid lease-back agreement nor may it invoke *quantum meruit* principles to recover its expenditures, it does have a completed and fully equipped building on land validly leased to it. It is a building the county presently is occupying and in the continued availability of which the public has an interest. Furthermore, our Constitution of 1963 has become effective. That constitution does not contain any limitation upon counties such as was in article VIII, § 10 of the Constitution of 1908. In view of the significant constitutional changes which now free the county and Doyle to contract as they attempted unsuccessfully to do and considering the public's interest, and Doyle's, in the continued use of the facilities involved in this litigation as a publicly operated hospital facility, this cause shall be remanded to the chancellor with instructions to retain jurisdiction until a new agreement can be made between the county and Doyle in compliance with existing law and to render such assistance as may be necessary to effectuate such agreement. Failing such agreement the chancellor shall entertain such cross-claim or cross-claims as the county and Doyle may be advised to make. GCR 1963, 203.3.

We do not decide other claims made by the attorney general in support of his request for injunctive relief in view of the disposition we make of this appeal. However, on remand, the chancellor shall, by order if necessary, compel compliance by the county and its appropriate agencies with all applicable statutory requirements for approval, licensing or certification of the building and its use.

Reversed and remanded for further proceedings in accordance herewith. No costs, there being public questions involved.

Notes

1. **Accord:** State ex rel. Kitchen v. Christman, 31 Ohio St.2d 64, 285 N.E.2d 362 (1972); City of Phoenix v. Phoenix Civic Auditorium and Convention Center Association, Inc., 99 Ariz. 270, 408 P.2d 818 (1965); Marine-Midland Trust Co. v. Waverly, 42 Misc.2d 704, 248 N.Y.S.2d 729 (1963). The prevailing trend, however, is to uphold long-term leases with the right to acquire title at the end thereof. See e.g., Schull Construction Co. v. Webster Ind. School Dist. No. 101 of Day, et al. Counties, 198 N.W.2d 512 (S.D.1972); Dean v. Kuchel, 35 Cal.2d 444, 218 P.2d 521 (1950), and the authorities reviewed in City of Phoenix, supra. Some case divisions may rest on fact differences, e.g. purchase prices to be paid over and above fixed

lease rentals; the relationship of that price to the depreciated value of the leased property; the status of the lessor as a private or public, profit-making or nonprofit entity; and whether the taking of title is automatic or optional with the lessee unit.

2. **Relief in Equity.** The principal case, and State v. Spring City, p. 655 supra, denied restitutionary relief on public policy to deter contracts which violate debt limitations. In Doyle, the plaintiff could recoup its investment by making another, lawful deal with the county for the use of the hospital, but in Spring City the lenders only had a government promise for their money. Yet the court went on to deny recovery against the public officials who issued the void contract on the advice of government counsel. Query, why should the individual lenders be prejudiced by like reliance? Had outside (private) bond counsel vouched for the validity of the bonds, should the lender be permitted recovery against them? See the Johns-Manville opinion, p. 688 infra.

While courts permit restitutionary recovery where bond defects are "procedural" (see the *Spring City* and *Edwards* opinions, supra), how does one determine whether a particular defect is sufficiently serious to be considered "substantive?"

CITY OF POCATELLO v. PETERSON

Supreme Court of Idaho, 1970.
93 Idaho 774, 473 P.2d 644.

[The majority upheld a contract whereby the city leased land for construction of an airport terminal building by private developers, which leased the terminal building back to the city.]

* * *

MCFADDEN, CHIEF JUSTICE (dissenting).

The majority opinion deals solely with the issue as to what constitutes "ordinary and necessary expenses" within the proviso clause of Idaho Const. art. 8, § 3. * * *

At the outset it is to be noted that the issue here is whether the rental payments of $6,000 per month for twenty years violate the constitutional provision, and not whether the repair and improvement of the airport facility were "ordinary and necessary expenses" * * *. This case does not deal with "*repair and improvement*" of existing facilities, but does deal with *rental payments* for a wholly new terminal building.

Inasmuch as I disagree with the conclusion reached by the majority opinion, an additional issue must be discussed. This additional issue * * * is whether the rental payments provided in the twenty-year lease * * * create a "debt or liability" within the prohibition of Idaho Const. art. 8 § 3.

Respondent, * * * contends that the plan whereby the city sells the land to appellants who construct the airport terminal facility and lease it back to the city is one that has generally been accepted in other jurisdictions. Throughout these cases runs the thought that where the lease is in fact a lease and the rentals are intended as rentals, rather than as a subterfuge for installment payments on the purchase price under a conditional sales contract, the lease, even if it contains an option to purchase the property, does not create an *indebtedness* within the meaning of a constitutional limitation on indebtedness. See 71 A.L.R. 1318 at 1321; 145 A.L.R. 1364; 15 McQuillin, Municipal Corporations § 41.38, pp. 392–393 (3d ed.). The reasoning used to support this result is that a lease calling for periodic rentals does not create any indebtedness for the aggregate of future rentals, but rather only creates indebtedness for the installment of rent currently owing, because rent is not a current obligation until it has accrued under the terms of the lease. [Citations omitted] * * *

* * *

Examination of the constitutions of those states from which opinions are cited by respondent * * * reveals that their constitutions do not contain a phrase "shall incur any *indebtedness, or liability*" (emphasis added) as used in Idaho Const. art. 8, § 3. Rather, most of those constitutions only prohibit governmental bodies from incurring "debts" or "indebtedness." Only the California, Missouri and New Jersey constitutions contain the word "liability." The New Jersey prohibition is applicable only against the state and does not mention counties or municipalities.

* * *

The Missouri constitution originally contained a reference to both "debt" and "liability," but was later amended to delete the reference to "debt," leaving only the word "liability." The Missouri case cited by respondent, Petition of Bd. of Public Bldgs. v. Crowe, 363 S.W.2d 598 (Mo.1962), discussed in detail the difference between "debt" and "liability" and upheld a revenue bond issue. The factual situation in that case, however, was quite different from the case before this court.

The Minnesota case cited by respondent, Ambrozich v. City of Eveleth, 200 Minn. 473, 274 N.W. 635 (1937), upholds a lease arrangement such as is involved here, stating that rent is not a "debt" or "liability," but it does not involve the interpretation of a constitutional debt limitation. That case dealt only with a debt limitation contained in a city charter.

This court has previously had occasion to consider the use of the terms "indebtedness" and "liability" in Idaho Const. art. 8, § 3. Williams v. City of Emmett, supra, dealt with an agreement under which the city had the use of street sprinklers for which it contracted to make annual payments. * * * Recognizing that numerous other states had held that a lease of property did not create a present indebtedness for the aggregate amount of the rentals, this court held that while there may have been no present indebtedness within the meaning of the constitution, there was a *liability* for the aggregate payment and that the agreement therefore violated the constitutional provision. The court thus gave a broader definition to the term "liability" than to "indebtedness."

* * * See also Feil v. City of Coeur d'Alene, 23 Idaho 32, 129 P. 643 (1912); School Dist. No. 8 v. Twin Falls County Mut. Fire Ins. Co., 30 Idaho 400, 164 P. 1174 (1917). Regardless of whether this lease agreement created an indebtedness * * * it is evident that upon execution of the agreement there was created within the meaning of the Idaho constitution a "liability" for the aggregate rentals to become due.

* * *

The next issue for consideration is the one which is the rationale of the majority opinion which accepts the contention of both parties, as well as amicus curiae, that the expenditures in this case are to be considered "ordinary and necessary expenses" within the meaning of the constitutional proviso which states:

"provided, that this section shall not be construed to apply to the ordinary and necessary expenses authorized by the general laws of the state." Idaho Const. art. 8, § 3. * * *

* * *

The words "ordinary and necessary" as used in their constitutional context have been considered by this court in several other cases. In Williams v. City of Emmett, 51 Idaho 500, 6 P.2d 475 (1931), this court held that payments by the city on an agreement to acquire use of and title to a street sprinkler were not ordinary or necessary expenses. In Dunbar v. Board of Com'rs, 5 Idaho 407, 49 P. 409 (1897), this court held that building of a bridge and the payment of scalp bounties were not within the contemplation of those terms. * * *

* * *

It is to be noted, however, that this court held in the following cases that where expenditures or liabilities exceed income for the current year, they are in violation of the constitution. [Citations omitted]

The majority opinion discards the reasoning of the North Carolina court in the cases of Goswick v. City of Durham, 211 N.C. 687, 191 S.E. 728 (1937); Sing v. City of Charlotte, 213 N.C. 60, 195 S.E. 271 (1938); Greensboro-Highpoint Airport Authority v. Johnson, 226 N.C. 1, 36 S.E.2d 803 (1946); Vance County v. Royster, 271 N.C. 53, 155 S.E.2d 790 (1967); in which series of cases that court held expenditures for municipal airport facilities were not "ordinary and necessary" expenses under that state's constitutional debt limitations. In Henderson v. City of Wilmington, 191 N.C. 269, 132 S.E. 25 (1926), the Supreme Court of North Carolina stated:

"The decisions heretofore rendered by the court make the test of a 'necessary expense' the purpose for which the expense is to be incurred. If the purpose is the maintenance of the public peace or the administration of justice, if it partakes of a governmental nature or purports to be an exercise by the city of a portion of the state's delegated sovereignty, if in brief, it involves a necessary governmental expense—in these cases the expense required to effect the purpose is necessary * * *." 132 S.E. at 30–31.

The reasoning of the North Carolina court seems valid. An airport terminal facility is not such an integral part of governmental function that an expenditure for renting of a terminal facility is a "necessary" expense. There are a wide variety of facilities that are frequently supplied by city government, such as municipal libraries, auditoriums, golf courses, museums and many more. Yet it is difficult to say in precisely which instance an expenditure for such facilities would be "necessary."

* * *

* * * When a city obligates itself to pay $1,440,000 at $6,000 per month for a twenty year term it is difficult to see how that is an "ordinary and necessary" expense. * * * Particularly is this so in the instant case, inasmuch as the city of Pocatello held a general obligation bond election in 1968 for the purpose of the city construction of aviation facilities including a municipal airport terminal building (Bogert v. Kinzer, 93 Idaho 515, 465 P.2d 639 (1970)), which did not pass by the necessary majority.

* * *

Sympathetic as we may be for the problem facing the city and understanding the need the city council in its good faith desires to alleviate by this arrangement, yet the regular method of proceeding for acquisition of such a large and expensive facility should be followed.

c. Protection of Bond Investors

(1) Partial Validation

CITY OF LAREDO v. LOONEY
Supreme Court of Texas, 1916.
108 Tex. 119, 185 S.W. 556.

PHILLIPS, C.J. In this action a mandamus is sought against the Attorney General to compel his approval of a proposed issue of bonds of the City of Laredo in the amount of $31,000.00 for the purpose of refunding in like amount bonds of an original issue, in 1883, of $75,000.00, for street improvement, city hall, and market house purposes.

The individual bonds of the original issue, so far as is disclosed by the record, were all sold and delivered at the same time. The issue was void to the extent of approximately $39,000.00, being that much in excess of the amount for which the city could at the time have lawfully issued its bonds for the purposes named under the amendment of Section 9, Article 8 of the Constitution then in force. The city has paid off and retired forty-two bonds of the original issue, aggregating

$42,000.00, and has available funds sufficient to retire two other bonds of the issue. This would leave $31,000.00 of the original issue outstanding, for which amount the refunding issue is proposed.

The contention of the relator is that although the original issue was partly void, * * * it is lawful for the city to refund the issue in the amount of $31,000.00, since the bonds could, originally, have been lawfully issued in that amount.

The power to issue refunding bonds can be exercised only where the original debt was valid. If it was partly invalid, it may be refunded only to the extent that it was valid. If bonds of a partly invalid issue are shown to have been delivered at different times, those first delivered, up to the amount of the debt that could have been lawfully created, should be paid, and the remainder be treated as nullities. The bonds of such an issue thus representing the valid part of the debt could be lawfully refunded. But if all of the bonds of the partly invalid issue were delivered at the same time, as appears to have been the case here, none of them could have any right of priority over the others, and the amount of the valid debt should be distributed equally between them. Citizens Bank v. City of Terrell, 78 Tex. 460, 14 S.W. 1003. Each bond now outstanding of this original issue, to the extent of its proportionate excess above the amount for which the debt could be lawfully created, was therefore invalid in its inception, and is still so invalid. Each of them being but a part of the whole debt created, partakes alike of its validity and invalidity. If they may be refunded for their full amount, the result is a clear evasion of the Constitution. * * *

The writ of mandamus is refused.

(2) Estoppel by Recital

NEWBERRY LIBRARY v. BOARD OF EDUCATION OF CITY OF CHICAGO

Supreme Court of Illinois, 1945.
390 Ill. 48, 60 N.E.2d 552.

SMITH, JUSTICE. * * * The purpose of the suit was to recover the amount represented by interest coupons attached to certain refunding bonds issued by the board of education.

* * * The facts are not in dispute. * * *

The record discloses that in the years 1928 and 1929, the board of education issued and sold certain tax anticipation warrants, anticipating the collection of taxes levied in those years. On December 11, 1931, the board * * * issued the bonds of the district for the payment of such outstanding tax anticipation warrants. In Berman v. Board of Education, 360 Ill. 535, 196 N.E. 464, 99 A.L.R. 1029, we held a similar act * * * invalid, * * *.

By an act approved on February 28, 1934, * * * the Legislature attempted to authorize school districts having a population exceeding

500,000 inhabitants to issue refunding bonds, * * * for the purpose of paying and discharging "outstanding bonds which are binding and subsisting legal obligations" * * *. Acting under this statute, the board of education, as of September 1, 1934 issued its bonds for the purpose of refunding certain outstanding bonds in the sum of $5,500,000. Included in the bonds refunded were bonds Nos. 1 to 500, in the aggregate amount of $500,000. The proof shows that bonds Nos. 1 to 500, being one-eleventh, or $500,000 of the total issue of the refunded bonds, were issued in 1931, for the purpose of paying and discharging outstanding tax anticipation warrants. * * * In People ex rel. Toman v. Granada Apartment Hotel Corporation, 381 Ill. 41, 44 N.E.2d 606, it was stipulated by the parties in that case that the bonds issued in 1931, for the payment of tax anticipation warrants, and one-eleventh of the refunding bonds issued September 1, 1934, in the amount of $5,500,000 for the purpose of refunding the bonds issued in 1931, were invalid. They were so treated in that case by this court.

* * *

* * *

The record shows that the two issues of refunding bonds here involved, * * * were purchased by a syndicate of banks. The banks in turn sold the bonds in the open market to their customers. Some of the present holders of the bonds * * * were furnished with copies of the opinion of the attorneys approving the proceedings of the board and the bonds issued. Interest was paid on the whole issue * * * until the due date of the second installment of interest in 1943. When the coupons * * * were presented for payment in 1943, being coupons No. 17, the board * * * and refused to pay one-eleventh part of each coupon. It based its refusal on the fact that, * * * there was an item of $500,000 of refunded bonds which were issued to pay tax anticipation warrants. Hence, it declined to pay interest on the one-eleventh part of such issue. As to the $900,000 of refunding bonds issued February 1, 1935, it refused to pay any part of the second installment of interest due in 1943 * * *. This refusal was based on the ground that all of said bonds were issued for the purpose of refunding bonds in a like amount which were issued for the payment of tax anticipation warrants.

* * * The issue involved is the liability of the board of education for the payment of those interest coupons. While only the coupons are here directly involved, the liability of the board of education to pay such coupons depends upon its liability to pay the bonds to which the coupons were attached.

In view of our decisions * * * the invalidity of the bonds involved cannot be regarded as an open question. While it is true that appellants were not parties to those cases * * * those decisions, until overruled, are the law of this State and binding upon this court. In those cases we definitely held that tax anticipation warrants are not liabilities of the municipality or school district by which they are issued. * * * Those cases further hold that the changing of tax anticipation warrants into bonds issued * * * does not make them corporate liabilities. * * * They further hold that even a judgment entered on tax anticipation warrants cannot be paid with the corporate funds of the school district. If the supposed liability has its inception in a tax anticipation warrant, such liability is still based upon such warrant in whatever form the claim may thereafter assume. * * *

Realizing the force of these decisions, appellants do not contend that the bonds here involved are legal liabilities of the school district. Their contention is that inasmuch as the board of education of the city of Chicago is an independent corporate body in which the statute has vested the power to issue bonds, it also has the power to determine when the conditions exist which authorize it to exercise the authority granted and to issue bonds. Otherwise stated the contention is that where there is lawful power to issue bonds under some state of facts, the board has the power to determine the existence of the necessary precedent facts and is estopped, as against bona fide holders of its bonds, to deny the existence of such precedent facts, represented by it to exist. * * *

In support of this contention, appellants rely upon a recital contained in the bonds themselves. This recital is as follows: "It is hereby certified and recited that this bond is authorized by and is issued in conformity with all requirements of the Constitution and laws of the State of Illinois; that all acts, conditions and things required to be done precedent to and in the issue of this bond and precedent to and in the issuance of the bonds hereby refunded have been properly done, happened and been performed in regular and due form and time as required by law. That the indebtedness represented by the bonds hereby refunded was a valid and legal obligation of said Board of Education of the City of Chicago and that the total indebtedness of said Board of Education of the City of Chicago including this bond did not at the time of the issuance of the bonds hereby refunded and does not now exceed any constitutional or statutory limitations, and that provision has been made for the collection of a direct annual tax upon all the taxable property in said School District sufficient to pay the interest hereon and the principal hereof when the same matures." It is insisted that, by this recital, the board is estopped from asserting that the bonds refunded were not valid and legal obligations of the board of education.

In support of their able and plausible argument on the application of the doctrine of estoppel, appellants cite and rely upon many Federal decisions and also the decisions of a number of the courts of foreign jurisdictions. A careful examination and analysis of the cases cited in connection with the particular facts involved in each case demonstrates, however, that they do not carry the doctrine of estoppel to the extent to which appellants would apply it. * * *

In Katzenberger v. City of Aberdeen, 121 U.S. 172, 7 S.Ct. 947, 949, 30 L.Ed. 911, it was said: "But it is insisted that the city is estopped, by the recital in the bonds, from denying that they were lawfully issued. The recital is, in effect, that they were issued 'under and pursuant' to law, the charter of the city, and the ordinance of April 26, 1870. * * * It is in effect nothing more than a recital that bonds issued under such circumstances were 'under and pursuant' to law and the charter of the city. Such a recital does not estop the city from asserting the contrary. To hold otherwise would be to invest a municipal corporation with full legislative power, and make it superior to the laws by which it was created."

In Board of County Commissioners v. Graham, 130 U.S. 674, 9 S.Ct. 654, 656, 32 L.Ed. 1065, the bonds contained a recital quite similar to that contained in the bonds in this case. It was there said: " * * * All parties are equally bound to know the law; and a certificate reciting the actual facts, and that thereby the bonds were conformable to the law, when, judicially speaking, they are not, will not make them so, nor can it work an estoppel upon the county to claim the protection of the law. Otherwise it would always be in the power of a municipal body, to which power was denied, to usurp the forbidden authority, by declaring that its assumption was within the law. This would be the clear exercise of legislative power, and would suppose such corporate bodies to be superior to the law itself."

In Sutliff v. Board of County Commissioners, 147 U.S. 230, 13 S.Ct. 318, 319, 37 L.Ed. 145, the rule was stated as follows: " * * * In those cases in which this court has held a municipal corporation to be estopped by recitals in its bonds * * * the statutes, as construed by the court, left it to the officers issuing the bonds to determine whether the facts existed which constituted the statutory or constitutional condition precedent, and did not require those facts to be made a matter of public record."

* * *

It will thus be seen that the rule as announced by the Federal courts is that the doctrine of estoppel may not be invoked where there is a lack of constitutional authority to issue the bonds involved. * * *

* * *

Numerous Illinois cases cited by appellants like Maxcy v. County Court of Williamson County, 72 Ill. 207; Burr v. City of Carbondale, 76 Ill. 455, and other similar cases, where the question involved was as to an irregular exercise of a granted power and not the existence of the power itself, are not in conflict with the rule announced in the cases above cited.

* * *

The rule deducible from the above authorities is that recitals contained in bonds issued by a municipal or quasi-municipal corporation, in so far as such recitals relate to the existence of facts, where the authority to determine the existence of such facts is expressly or by necessary implication conferred upon the officers issuing the bonds by the statute conferring the power, are binding upon the municipality. The rule is further that recitals as to questions of law are beyond the powers of the authority issuing the bonds and cannot operate as an estoppel. Where there is an absolute lack of power to issue the bonds, no recitals of either law or fact contained therein can be availed of even by bona fide holders.

Turning to the act of February 28, 1934, we find that the power conferred upon the school board to issue refunding bonds was limited to the purpose of refunding outstanding bonds which were binding and subsisting legal obligations of the board of education. * * * The power to issue refunding bonds was granted only when the district, as a matter of fact, had outstanding bonds which were binding and subsisting legal obligations of the district. Whether the outstanding bonds were binding and subsisting legal obligations of the district was a question of law. * * *

* * *

The rule contended for by appellants, if adopted, would result in placing in the hands of the board of education the power to circumvent all restrictions of the Constitution. * * *

The doctrine of estoppel cannot be invoked in this case. * * *

In reaching this conclusion, we are not unmindful of the position in which the purchasers of the refunding bonds now find themselves involved. Nevertheless, this court cannot disregard constitutional restrictions or settled rules of law in the interest of sympathetic inclinations and appeals. * * *

Judgment affirmed.

Notes

1. **Effect of Different Recitals.** Reliance alone does not support an estoppel; it must be "reasonable." In deciding which recitals a party may reasonably accept at face value, and which recitals he is bound to verify at his peril, courts weigh divergent policies of municipal, commercial and equity law. Doctrines fashioned to protect taxpayers collide with those developed to protect investors, particularly bona fide purchasers.

Estoppel-by-recital cases fall into several classes. It is settled that a recital which is constitutionally prohibited cannot give rise to an estoppel. Cf. Marshall Field case, p. 702, infra. But courts may disagree as to whether any particular recital is unconstitutional in a strict sense. Further, they may construe a general recital as a misrepresentation of unascertainable fact, or a misrepresentation of ascertainable law. They may disagree as to what facts are reasonably ascertainable by an investor. They may disagree as to how specific a recital must be to induce reasonable reliance thereon as fact, rather than opinion. Finally, their strictness in applying the estoppel doctrine may vary according to the subject of the recital. Those relating to debt limitations are not as generally accepted for estoppel purposes as those relating to electoral or councilmanic authorization for a bond issue. For these reasons, the decisions on estoppel by recital are narrow in scope. Recital decisions are categorized in 15 McQuillin, *Municipal Corporations* §§ 43.99, 43.100 (3rd ed.1970). Case development on estoppel by recital is not complete in many jurisdictions, probably due to improved financing practices, i.e. state supervision of local bond issues, and curative statutes. To the extent that the doctrine still proves useful, courts retain broad discretion as to its application.

2. **Bonds Issued by De Facto Officers.** The policy of protecting bond investors who rely upon ostensible government authority is also advanced by de facto doctrines. See e.g. Platte v. Dortch, 255 Ind. 157, 263 N.E.2d 266 (1970). But this mitigating doctrine has its perils, as indicated by the cases—Bowman v. Moorhead, Ocean Beach Heights v. Investment Co., and Norton v. Shelby (reported in Chapter II).

(3) Bona Fide Purchasers

JOHNS–MANVILLE CORPORATION
v. DeKALB, MO.

United States Court of Appeals, Eighth Circuit, 1971.
439 F.2d 656.

GIBSON, CIRCUIT JUDGE. This is an interlocutory appeal from a declaratory judgment * * * holding that $505,000 principal amount of waterworks revenue bonds issued and sold by the Village of DeKalb, Missouri, are "invalid, null and void, and of no force and effect."

The alignment of the parties in this case is highly unusual. The suit was commenced as a declaratory judgment action * * * by plaintiff, Johns-Manville Corporation, the current holder of the DeKalb waterworks revenue bonds. Plaintiff joined as defendants the Village of DeKalb and all parties and sureties who were in any way involved with the issuance of the bonds or the construction of the waterworks. The appellants in this Court are the 30 partners of the Chicago, Illinois law firm of Chapman and Cutler. Chapman and Cutler was joined as a defendant because it had issued a legal opinion that the municipal proceedings showed lawful authority for the issuance of the bonds * * * and that the form of the bonds revealed them to be valid and legally binding * * *. Upon motion * * * the case was removed to the federal district court under 28 U.S.C.A. § 1441(c).

Plaintiff's Complaint * * * requested specified relief against certain defendants in the event of a finding of validity and, alternatively, prayed for relief against other defendants, including Chapman and Cutler, if the bonds should be determined to be invalid. The Answer filed by the Village neither admitted nor denied the validity of the bonds. Thus, we have a bondholder challenging the validity of bonds it holds when the issuer of the bonds has not denied their validity.

The District Court severed for trial the issue of the bonds' validity, reserving all other issues for later determination. * * *

The facts surrounding the authorization and issuance of the bonds are basically not in dispute. In April 1962 a substantial number of buildings in the Village of DeKalb were destroyed by fire, primarily because the Village did not have a water system. * * *

Research and testing indicated that a supply of good quality water in sufficient quantity did not exist in or close to the Village. The nearest adequate supply of water was located in the Missouri River bottoms immediately to the west of the Village of Rushville * * * It was obvious that the Village of DeKalb with about 300 inhabitants could not support a system of the type needed to transport water from that low an elevation and over that distance. Due to these economic realities, engineer Lamb drew up plans for a waterworks system which would serve not only the Village of DeKalb, but also the incorporated Village of Rushville, the unincorporated communities of Sugar Lake and Winthrop, and certain adjacent farm areas. * * * The proposed project encompassed an area of approximately 33 square miles, contained more than 40 miles of water transmission lines and included approximately 550 potential customers (about 300 of whom were residents of DeKalb). Another advantage to this "loop" system was to insure that in the event of a breakdown in one line of supply, the other would still be operative.

* * *

In a special election held April 2, 1963, the voters of the Village adopted the proposed ordinance. * * * On January 7, 1964, the Board of Trustees, * * * enacted a bond ordinance authorizing the issuance of revenue bonds in the principal amount of $505,000 "for the purpose of paying the costs of constructing a waterworks for said Village."

The Village issued and sold the bonds to Audsley * * *. On November 20, 1964, Johns-Manville purchased the entire issue from Audsley, allegedly relying upon the opinion letter issued by Chapman and Cutler on September 25, 1964, that the bonds were legally valid revenue obligations.

Construction was begun on the project but the system was never placed into operation since the bond proceeds were depleted before the project was fully completed. The Village did make several semi-annual interest payments to Johns-Manville from the bond proceeds, but at the present time interest payments on the indebtedness have been in default for several years.

When the system was 70 per cent completed a suit seeking a declaratory judgment on the validity of the bonds and the construction contracts was heard * * *. The suit was brought by Elbert F. Spencer, a resident, property owner and taxpayer in the Village of DeKalb. * * * On November 26, 1965, the State Court enjoined the Village from further construction of the waterworks system and from paying any sums on the bonds or to the construction company or the engineers. On appeal, the Supreme Court of Missouri, on November

14, 1966, reversed the trial court on the ground that the plaintiff lacked standing to sue because he did not have a legally protectible interest at stake, * * *.

On April 22, 1968, plaintiff Johns-Manville filed the instant suit * * *. The District Court found that the only water system planned at the time of the bond election, the one described above, was illegal. * * * the Court held that the validity of the revenue bonds is dependent upon the legality of the contemplated project * * * and expressly rejected the argument that the validity of the bonds is determined solely by the regularity of the bond authorization and issuance process.

* * * The regularity of the ordinance calling the election and the election is not disputed, * * *.

The question then presented is whether the validity of revenue bonds, which have been issued and are held by a bona fide purchaser for value, is to be determined by the validity of the contemplated project * * *

Having stated the issue, we feel it advisable to comment that this case reflects how critical is the timing of litigation challenging the validity of municipal bonds or the expenditure of bond proceeds. Were the bond proceeds unexpended at this juncture, this case might have a completely different posture for the expenditure of funds on an illegal project obviously can be enjoined. But those facts unfortunately are not before us for the bonds have been issued and the proceeds spent. In light of these realities, our resolution of the issue in the instant case must be guided by the sound principle laid down long ago by the Missouri Supreme Court that legal defects which might have application in a proceeding to prevent the issuance and negotiation of municipal bonds will not be allowed to authorize the repudiation of bonds which have come into the possession of bona fide holders. Rose v. Springfield & Brookline Special Road Dist., 275 Mo. 590, 205 S.W. 54, 56 (1918); Steines v. Franklin County, 48 Mo. 167, 175–176, 8 Am.Rep. 87 (1871). It has also been held that where the municipality has repeatedly recognized the validity of its bonds and has paid interest on them for a series of years, as in the instant case, all questions of doubt in relation to their validity should be answered in favor of their legality. [Citations omitted]

There is a dearth of case law on the precise question of whether we look beyond the stated purpose in the ordinances and municipal proceedings to the contemplated project in making a determination on the validity of revenue bonds. The rule in Missouri with regard to general obligation bonds seems to be that the court should not look beyond a general statement of public purpose in the pertinent ordinances unless they contain a specific reference to a particular plan or project.

* * *

The case of Sager v. City of Stanberry, 336 Mo. 213, 78 S.W.2d 431 (1934), involving the validity of what apparently were general obligation bonds, provides further support for the proposition that a bond issue is valid when there is a proper statement of purpose in the pertinent ordinances even though the contemplated usage of the proceeds is illegal. * * * Although the Court did enjoin performance of the contract because it would result in a total municipal indebtedness in excess of the constitutional debt limitation, the Court did not invalidate the bond issue or restrain the sale of the bonds. * * *

* * *

If these principles which apply to general obligation bonds are equally applicable to a determination on the validity of revenue bonds, the Village of DeKalb waterworks revenue bonds are valid for the ordinances and ballot do state a proper general purpose and no mention is made of any specific plan or project. We perceive no reason for a distinction between general obligation and revenue bonds on this issue. The case law, while not abundant, supports this position. See State v. Florida State Turnpike Authority, 134 So.2d 12 (Fla.1961); Spencer v. Mayor & Board of Aldermen of Yazoo City, 215 Miss. 160, 60 So.2d 562 (1952). * * * for the proposition that valid ownership of a revenue-producing source is an "essential prerequisite to the practical validity of enforceability of revenue bonds." It is pointed out that unless there is a lawful revenue-producing project, revenue bonds are merely unsecured pieces of paper; in contrast, general obligation bonds constitute a valid governmental obligation even though there may be collateral issues relating to the use of the proceeds.

We take no exception to these comments but they have no bearing on the question before us. The lone case cited by plaintiff which provides tacit support for its position, Williamson v. City of High Point, 213 N.C. 96, 195 S.E. 90 (1938), does not reach the question of whether the validity of revenue bonds which have been issued and negotiated to a bona fide purchaser for value is to be determined by the legality of the contemplated project * * *.

Furthermore, there are important policy reasons which militate against determining the validity of revenue bonds on the legality of the contemplated project when no particular project is specified in the ordinances calling the election, the ballot, the ordinances authorizing the issuance of the bonds, or the bonds themselves. First, such a rule would seriously retard the marketability of revenue bonds. * * * Secondly, while a specific plan or plans are frequently developed prior to bond elections and prior to the issuance of the bonds, it is not uncommon for such plans to be changed as the planning progresses. Adoption of the rule urged by plaintiff would create substantial uncertainty as to the validity of all revenue bonds issued when a final plan had not been decided upon prior to the issuance of the bonds. * * * It is obvious that very few bondholders would be willing to undertake the policeman's role such a rule would require.

A court determining the validity of revenue bonds must look to the statements of public purpose in the ordinance calling the election, the election ballot, the ordinance authorizing the bond issuance, and the bonds. In the instant case, all of these legal documents * * * made no reference to a specific contemplated project. * * * While this is dispositive of the question before us, because this area is so uncharted, we think it advisable to add that had the ordinance authorizing the issuance of these bonds referred to the plan submitted to the state Division of Health, the validity of the bonds would have turned on the legality of the specific project submitted. * * * But that is not the situation in this case.

Although the Uniform Commercial Code has no application in this case since the DeKalb bonds were issued and purchased by plaintiff prior to July 1, 1965, the effective date in Missouri of the Code, we note that our conclusion is in accord with § 8–202(2) of the Code * * *. Consequently, the DeKalb bonds would be valid in the hands of Johns-Manville under the UCC though they contained a defect going to their validity if (a) there was substantial compliance with the legal requirements governing the issuance of the bonds or if (b) the Village had received substantial consideration for the issue and a stated purpose of the issue was for a proper municipal purpose. The bonds in question would be valid under both tests. * * *

* * * Since the ordinances and election procedures were unquestioned, a proper general statement of public purpose was made in the bonds and ordinances in question, and no reference was made to a specific contemplated project, we find the waterworks revenue bonds issued by the Village of DeKalb to be valid.

The case is reversed and remanded for proceedings consistent with this opinion.

(4) Pre-Issuance Validation

HAMILTON COUNTY v. CLOUD

Court of Common Pleas of Ohio, Hamilton County, 1967.
236 N.E.2d 803.

MATTHEWS, JUDGE. Hamilton County * * * has filed an action * * * to determine the validity of an issue of $42,250,000 of revenue bonds to be issued for the purpose of constructing a stadium as part of an Urban Renewal project of the City of Cincinnati, a municipal corporation, located in Hamilton County. The City and County have entered into an agreement under which the City agrees to sell the real estate upon which the stadium is to be built to the County for which the County will pay a fair price.

The County will then construct the stadium * * *. Then the City will lease the stadium from the County, the annual rental being the amount required to pay the taxes and meet the debt obligations created by the issuance of the bonds in question in this action. After the indebtedness has been eradicated, the lease would be renewed in perpetuity and the rent to be paid by the City to the County would be the amount necessary to pay taxes. During the entire lease period the City will rent the stadium to professional athletic teams and other users, the City maintaining the stadium, with all maintenance and operating costs being borne by the City. For all practical purposes the City will be exercising all of the incidents of ownership except bare legal title.

No part of the money to pay the indebtedness created by the issuance of the bonds in question will be from taxes levied by the issuer of the bonds, that is by Hamilton County, but it is possible that a portion of the rent paid by the City to the County will be derived from income received from the levy taxes.

* * *

The demurrer filed by Graham P. Hunt, Jr. recites that the petition does not state facts which show a cause of action. In argument he claimed that Sections 133.71 *et seq.* are unconstitutional because the expense for a taxpayer to participate constitutes a violation of due process of law. * * *

A portion of the argument regarding a lack of due process was based on the fact that if this Court finds the bonds valid, no future action may be brought by a taxpayer to contest the validity.

Naturally one of the purposes of this group of statutes is to avoid such an action, both to make the bonds more salable and to avoid a multiplicity of suits. The statutes in question provide that a decree of validation is effective only if proceedings subsequent to that decree are properly taken in accordance with the applicable provisions of law and the decree. The argument as to expenses of a taxpayer in contesting is without merit.

* * *

CONCLUSIONS OF LAW

1. This action to validate the issue of $42,250,000.00 of Stadium Revenue Bonds authorized by resolution of the Board of County Commissioners of Hamilton County, Ohio, * * * is properly brought under the provisions of Sections 133.71 to 133.79 of the Ohio Revised Code and all procedural requirements thereof have been properly met and all necessary parties have been properly served. The United States of America is not a necessary party hereto.

2. This Court has jurisdiction of the subject matter of this action.

3. The issuer, Hamilton County, Ohio, is authorized by Section 133.06 Ohio Revised Code, to issue revenue bonds to build a stadium and related parking facilities.

* * *

5. The Cooperative Agreement between the City of Cincinnati and Hamilton County and the proposed lease of the stadium by the county to the city are proper and are authorized by Section 153.61 of the Ohio Revised Code.

6. The acts and proceedings taken and proposed to be taken by the City of Cincinnati, * * * do not and will not create "net indebtedness" of the City as defined by Section 133.02 of the Ohio Revised Code, nor bonded indebtedness under any other statutory or constitutional provision.

7. The acts and proceedings taken by the City of Cincinnati and by Hamilton County, specifically the execution of the Cooperative Agreement, the proposed execution of the Lease and the bond resolution of Hamilton County, do not constitute a loan of credit by said City nor Hamilton County in violation of Article VIII, Section 6, of the Ohio Constitution.

8. The acts and proceedings taken by the City of Cincinnati and by Hamilton County, * * * do not show any abuse of discretion by the Council of said City or the Board of County Commissions of said County.

9. An issue has been joined with respect to the right of the City to convey the site of the public stadium to Plaintiff.

No evidence was offered regarding the rights of the people to the use of the portion of the river bank known as the public landing, so the Court finds that the City, by virtue of its home rule powers under Article XVIII, Section 3, has power to convey in fee simple the site, including a portion of the public square or common, or public landing described in the proposed Lease to Plaintiff, for the purpose of constructing thereon a public stadium with related parking facilities, and that no breach of trust will result from said conveyance.

Notes

1. **Statutory Pre-Issuance Validation.** "Exacting statutory requirements typically precede the issuance of bonds or securities by a public body to finance public works. Alleged defects in complying with such requirements may affect the validity of the issue and thus impair the marketability of the securities or tie up the project in litigation, unless there is some procedure by which to obtain an adjudication which binds all interested persons and forecloses a multiplicity of suits. That is the purpose of this statute." Practice Commentary to Michigan bond validation statute, Mich.Comp.Law Ann. § 600.2942. See also West's Fla.Stat. Ann. § 75.01 et seq.

The Pennsylvania Local Government Unit Debt Act of 1972 mandates administrative pre-issuance clearance of bond issues by the State Department of Community Affairs. "Section 801—The governing body of each local government unit shall, before any bonds or notes * * * are actually delivered * * * or before becoming bound on any lease evidencing the acquisition of a capital asset, cause to be certified to the department, * * * a complete and accurate copy of the proceedings had for the incurring of debt * * *." "Section 804—The department shall, * * * carefully examine the same to determine whether the debt * * * is within the applicable limitations imposed by this act, * * * for issuing and selling the bonds or notes * * *. If upon completion of its examination, a transcript or filing is found by the department to be in conformity with the Constitution and existing laws, * * * the department shall certify its approval to the local government unit." "Section 808—Bonds or notes sold and delivered to the initial purchasers prior to an approval * * * under Section 804 * * * shall be invalid and of no effect in the hands of the initial purchasers except to the extent provided in this section * * *. In the hands of a bona fide purchaser * * * for value without actual notice of a lack of a prior approval by the department, any bonds or notes containing a recital that the series had been approved by the department shall be valid and subsisting instruments enforceable in accordance with their terms, and any applicable borrowing base shall be deemed increased to the extent necessary to validate and keep such bonds valid * * *. Notwithstanding the invalidity of the instruments as to them, the initial purchasers shall be entitled to credit, in any action determining such invalidity or for the recovery provided by the preceding sentence where the amount of: (1) any proceeds * * * still held unexpended by the local government units; and (2) the lesser of either: (i) the cost or fair market value * * * of any capital project * * * or interest therein acquired by the local government unit by an expenditure of * * * the proceeds of the bonds or notes; or (ii) the remaining non electoral borrowing capacity of the local government unit." "Section 809—Where a certificate of approval has been issued by the department or has been deemed issued under Section 806, and no appeal has been taken, or when after appeal, the proceedings have been approved finally by the court, * * * the validity and due enforceability of the bonds or notes in accordance with their terms shall not thereafter be inquired into judicially * * * either directly or collaterally except where a constitutional question is involved. The effect of the approval by the department, or by the court on appeal, shall be to ratify, validate and confirm, so far as good faith purchasers * * * are concerned, such proceedings absolutely, including the lawful nature of the project, notwithstanding any defect or error in such proceedings, except as specifically provided hereinafter * * *. Nothing herein contained shall, however, free an initial purchaser of bonds or notes from liability to a local government unit for the payment of a consideration agreed in contract of sale, or make all such bonds or notes valid and enforceable in the hands of an initial purchaser unless the issuer shall have received a substantial consideration for the series as a whole. Nothing herein contained shall, however, relieve any person participating in such proceedings from liability for knowingly participating in an ultra vires act of a local government unit, * * *." "Section 810—The department shall have the power to prescribe rules and regulations * * * and to prescribe forms for, reports and filings to be submitted to the department * * *. Such definitions, rules and regulations when published and made available to the public shall have the force of law." 53 Pa.Stat. §§ 6780–351, 6780–354, 6780–358, 6780–360. Further refinements have been added by amendments since 1975.

2. **Alternatives to Statutory Validation.** Where the validation statute is not the exclusive method to test legality of proposed bond issues, other proceedings, such as declaratory judgment actions, may be used. North Shore Bank v. Surfside, 72 So.2d 659 (Fla.1954). In Lipford v.

Harris, 212 So.2d 766 (Fla.1968), the court rejected a challenge raised after a statutory proceeding, stating: "Public policy demands that we adhere to our many holdings that a validation decree ∗ ∗ ∗ puts at rest all questions which were raised ∗ ∗ ∗ as well as all questions which could have been raised." Id. at 768.

3. **Post-Issuance Validation.** Defective bond issues may be validated, after issuance, either by blanket ratification of the government acts or by ratification of specific proceedings relating to bond issuance. "A legislature may pass a retroactive law which could validate any act which it could in the first instance have authorized, subject to the restriction that it could not impair the obligation of a contract or a vested right." See Northern Wasco County Peoples Utility Dist. v. Wasco County, 210 Or. 1, 12, 305 P.2d 766, 772 (1957) (upholding retroactive validation of tax assessments that were invalidly made); Ventura Port District v. Taxpayers, Property Owners, etc., 53 Cal.2d 227, 1 Cal.Rptr. 169, 347 P.2d 305 (1959) (upholding legislative validation of local government debt); Osage National Bank v. Oakes Special School District, 72 N.D. 457, 7 N.W.2d 920 (1943) (upholding legislative validation of warrants previously issued in excess of the debt limit). "Bonds issued without authority of law may be validated by a subsequent statute, provided the legislature could have authorized the issuance of such bonds in the first place." Id. at 466, 7 N.W.2d at 922.

4. **State Supervisory Programs.** A good state by state summary of supervision of local government bonding practices is presented in ACIR, *Understanding the Market For State and Local Debt* p. 46 *et seq.* (1976).

(5) Constitutional Protection Against Impairment of Contracts

UNITED STATES TRUST CO. v. NEW JERSEY

Supreme Court of the United States, 1977.
431 U.S. 1, 97 S.Ct. 1505, 52 L.Ed.2d 92, reh. denied 431 U.S. 975, 97 S.Ct. 2942.

[Suit by Trustee and holders of bonds issued by New York and New Jersey Port Authority, to invalidate statutes of New York and New Jersey which repealed prior statute which covenanted the states not to allow the Port Authority to use its revenues for rail transit operations. The prior statute read:

"The 2 States covenant and agree with each other and with the holders of any affected bonds, as hereinafter defined, that so long as any of such bonds remain outstanding and unpaid and the holders thereof shall not have given their consent as provided in their contract with the port authority, (1) ∗ ∗ ∗ and (b) neither the States nor the port authority nor any subsidiary corporation incorporated for any of the purposes of this act will apply any of the rentals, tolls, fares, fees, charges, revenues or reserves, which have been or shall be pledged in whole or in part as security for such bonds, for any railroad purposes whatsoever other than permitted purposes hereinafter set forth."

The plaintiffs argued that the repeal of the statutory covenant by the states impaired the security of the Port Authority bonds, in violation of the Contracts Clause of the federal constitution, which reads: "No state shall * * * pass any * * * law impairing the Obligation of Contracts * * *" U.S. Const. Art. I, § 10, cl. 1. The Supreme Court divided 5–4 on this important question.]

MR. JUSTICE BLACKMUN delivered the opinion of the Court.

* * *

III

We first examine appellant's general claim that repeal of the 1962 covenant impaired the obligation of the States' contract with the bondholders. It long has been established that the Contract Clause limits the power of the States to modify their own contracts as well as to regulate those between private parties. [citations] Yet the Contract Clause does not prohibit the State from repealing or amending statutes generally, or from enacting legislation with retroactive effects. Thus, as a preliminary matter, appellant's claim requires a determination that the repeal has the effect of impairing a contractual obligation.

In this case the obligation was itself created by a statute, the 1962 legislative covenant. * * * As a security provision, the covenant was not superfluous; it limited the Port Authority's deficits and thus protected the general reserve fund from depletion. Nor was the covenant merely modified or replaced by an arguably comparable security provision. Its outright repeal totally eliminated an important security provision and thus impaired the obligation of the States' contract.

* * *

Having thus established that the repeal impaired a contractual obligation of the States, we turn to the question whether that impairment violated the Contract Clause.

IV

Although the Contract Clause appears literally to proscribe "any" impairment, this Court observed in *Blaisdell* that "the prohibition is not an absolute one and is not to be read with literal exactness like a mathematical formula." 290 U.S., at 428, 54 S.Ct., at 236. Thus, a finding that there has been a technical impairment is merely a preliminary step in resolving the more difficult question whether that impairment is permitted under the Constitution. In the instant case, as in *Blaisdell*, we must attempt to reconcile the strictures of the Contract Clause with the "essential attributes of sovereign power," * * * necessarily reserved by the States to safeguard the welfare of their citizens. * * *

The trial court concluded that repeal of the 1962 covenant was a valid exercise of New Jersey's police power because repeal served important public interests in mass transportation, energy conservation, and environmental protection. 134 N.J.Super., at 194–195, 338 A.2d, at 873. Yet the Contract Clause limits otherwise legitimate exercises of state legislative authority, and the existence of an important public interest is not always sufficient to overcome that limitation. * * * Legislation adjusting the rights and responsibilities of contracting parties must be upon reasonable conditions and of a character appropriate to the public purpose justifying its adoption. *Id.,* at 445–447, 54 S.Ct. at 242–43. * * *

When a State impairs the obligation of its own contract, the reserved power doctrine has a different basis. * * * It is often stated that "the legislature cannot bargain away the police power of a State." Stone v. Mississippi, 101 U.S. 814, 817, 25 L.Ed. 1079 (1879). * * * In short, the Contract Clause does not require a State to adhere to a contract that surrenders an essential attribute of its sovereignty.

* * *

The instant case involves a financial obligation and thus as a threshold matter may not be said automatically to fall within the reserved powers that cannot be contracted away. * * *

The Contract Clause is not an absolute bar to subsequent modification of a State's own financial obligations. As with laws impairing the obligations of private contracts, an impairment may be constitutional if it is reasonable and necessary to serve an important public purpose. * * *

The only time in this century that alteration of a municipal bond contract has been sustained by this Court was in Faitoute Iron & Steel Co. v. City of Asbury Park, 316 U.S. 502, 62 S.Ct. 1129, 86 L.Ed. 1629 (1942). That case involved the New Jersey Municipal Finance Act, which provided that a bankrupt local government could be placed in receivership by a state agency. * * *

Under the specific composition plan at issue in *Faitoute,* the holders of revenue bonds received new securities bearing lower interest rates and later maturity dates. This Court, however, rejected the dissenting bondholders' Contract Clause objections. The reason was that the old bonds represented only theoretical rights; as a practical matter the city could not raise its taxes enough to pay off its creditors under the old contract terms. The composition plan enabled the city to meets its financial obligations more effectively. * * * Thus, the Court found that the composition plan was adopted with the purpose and effect of protecting the creditors, * * *

It is clear that the instant case involves a much more serious impairment than occurred in *Faitoute.* No one has suggested here that the States acted for the purpose of benefiting the bondholders, and there is no serious contention that the value of the bonds was enhanced by repeal of the 1962 covenant. * * * We therefore conclude that repeal of the 1962 covenant cannot be sustained on the basis of this Court's prior decisions in *Faitoute* and other municipal bond cases.

V.

* * * Appellees contend that these goals are so important that any harm to bondholders from repeal of the 1962 covenant is greatly outweighed by the public benefit. We do not accept this invitation to engage in a utilitarian comparison of public benefit and private loss. * * * We can only sustain the repeal of the 1962 covenant if that impairment was both reasonable and necessary to serve the admittedly important purposes claimed by the State.

The more specific justification offered for the repeal of the 1962 covenant was the States' plan for encouraging users of private automobiles to shift to public transportation. The States intended to discourage private automobile use by raising bridge and tunnel tolls and to use the extra revenue from those tolls to subsidize improved commuter railroad service. * * * We reject this justification because the repeal was neither necessary * * * nor reasonable in light of the circumstances. * * * First, it cannot be said that total repeal of the covenant was essential; a less drastic modification would have permitted the contemplated plan without entirely removing the covenant's limitations on the use of Port Authority revenues and reserves to subsidize commuter railroads. Second, without modifying the covenant at all, the States could have adopted alternative means of achieving their twin goals of discouraging automobile use and improving mass transit. * * *

In the instant case the State has failed to demonstrate that repeal of the 1962 covenant was similarly necessary.

* * *

We therefore hold that the Contract Clause of the United States Constitution prohibits the retroactive repeal of the 1962 covenant. The judgment of the Supreme Court of New Jersey is reversed.

It is so ordered.

* * *

MR. JUSTICE BRENNAN, with whom MR. JUSTICE WHITE and MR. JUSTICE MARSHALL join, dissenting.

* * *

Notes

1. **Impairment of Bond Obligations and Security** in Ruano v. Spellman, 81 Wash.2d 820, 505 P.2d 447 (1973) the court enjoined, as an impairment of contract and bondholder security, a citizen initiative to revoke a prior bond approval, and to terminate construction of the facility financed by the approved bond issue. Similarly, in Canal National Bank v. School Administrative District No. 3, 160 Me. 309, 203 A.2d 734 (1964) the court held unconstitutional a statute which withdrew three towns from a school district *after* the school district had issued bonds that were secured by its power to levy taxes on all real and personal property within the district. The majority concluded that the shift in the risk and burdens of collection impaired contract rights. But see Jacksonville Port Authority v.

State, 161 So.2d 825 (Fla.1964) (take-over of city financed terminal facilities by the state-created authority, and assumption of bond obligations by the authority, held not to impair bondholder rights, where the city was not discharged from obligation to repay the bonds, in the event that the authority did not do so).

2. **State Constitutions.** Many state constitutions also prohibit government impairment of bond obligations. See, e.g., Flushing Nat. Bank v. Municipal Assistance Corp., 40 N.Y.2d 731, 390 N.Y.S.2d 22, 358 N.E.2d 848 (1976) where the New York Emergency Moratorium Act that required holders of New York City short term notes to either exchange them for other long terms bonds, or suffer a freeze on the note payments and at lesser interest, was held void under the New York state constitution.

3. **Diversion of Bond Proceeds.** Courts generally prohibit diversion of bond proceeds from the purposes for which the bonds were issued. Bell v. Board of Education of Barren County School Dist., 343 S.W.2d 804 (Ky. 1961). In determining whether an expenditure diverts from bond purposes, however, courts give broad deference to the judgment of local officials.

C. EXPENDITURE CONTROLS

1. PUBLIC PURPOSE LIMITATIONS

BOARD OF SUPERVISORS OF FAIRFAX COUNTY v. MASSEY

Supreme Court of Appeals of Virginia, 1969.
210 Va. 253, 169 S.E.2d 556.

* * *

[Facts reported at p. 665]

II.

Respondents say that the Agreement violates the credit clause of § 185 of the Constitution of Virginia in that the County and City lend their credit to a private contractor who will operate the transit system to the holders of the transit bonds, and to residents outside the jurisdictional limits of the County and City.

Section 185, so far as pertinent, reads as follows:

"Neither the credit of the State, nor of any county, city or town, shall be directly or indirectly, under any device or pretense whatsoever, granted to or in aid of any person, association, or corporation * * *."

In Almond v. Day, 197 Va. 782, 790, 91 S.E.2d 660, 667 (1956), we said: "Whether or not a transaction contravenes the 'credit clause' in § 185 depends upon its animating purpose and the object that it is designed to accomplish."

In Holston Corp. v. Wise County, 131 Va. 142, 157, 158, 109 S.E. 180, 184 (1921), the county agreed to guarantee payment for crushed stone furnished on credit to any contractor to whom the county might award a contract for road work. We held that the contract or guarantee did not grant the credit of the county to or in aid of any person, association or corporation because the contract was solely for the benefit of the county.

In Button v. Day, 208 Va. 494, 158 S.E.2d 735 (1968), the Virginia Industrial Authority was created to guarantee loans to stimulate development of industry, a public purpose, solely through guaranteeing payment of future default of a private debtor with no public ownership involved. We held that since the objective of the Authority was to enable a private firm to obtain loans on public credit when not available on the private firm's credit, it was impermissible under § 185.

Here the publicly conceived, owned and controlled Authority was created under the Compact as an instrumentality and agency of Virginia, Maryland and the District of Columbia to solve the transportation needs of northern Virginia and the entire Washington, D.C., metropolitan area. Courts of other States had recognized that an authority created and vested with power to establish and maintain subway or street railway projects in a large metropolitan area, in the interest of health, safety and public welfare, exercises a governmental function for public purposes. See, People v. Chicago Transit Authority, 392 Ill. 77, 64 N.E.2d 4 (1945); Cleveland v. City of Detroit, 322 Mich. 172, 33 N.W.2d 747 (1940); Sun Printing and Pub. Ass'n v. Mayor of New York, 152 N.Y. 257, 46 N.E. 499, 37 L.R.A. 788 (1897).

We have held that payments of money by the State and a city to aid an authority in exercising its governmental function do not violate § 185. Button v. Day, *supra,* 205 Va. at 639, 139 S.E.2d at 98; Harrison v. Day, 200 Va. 764, 775, 107 S.E.2d 594, 601 (1961).

The mere fact that others might incidentally profit from the operation, financing and use of a facility established by an authority for a public purpose, in the exercise of a governmental function, does not destroy its public purpose. [Citations omitted]

Thus we hold that the Agreement of the County and City does not extend the credit of the County or City "to or in aid of any person, association or corporation" within the letter or spirit of the credit clause of § 185.

Note

1. **Public Expenditure To Influence Election Outcomes.** The courts uniformly disapprove use of government funds to influence a partisan election: "Indeed every court which has addressed the issue to date has found the use of public funds for partisan campaign purposes improper, either on the ground that such use was not explicitly authorized or on the broader ground that such expenditures are never appropriate." See Stanson v. Mott, 17 Cal.3d 206, 130 Cal.Rptr. 697, 704–705, 551 P.2d 1, 8, 9 (1976). Accord: Anderson v. Boston, 376 Mass. 178, 380 N.E.2d 628 (1978), appeal dismissed 439 U.S. 1060, 99 S.Ct. 822, 59 L.Ed.2d 26 (1979); Moun-

tain States Legal Foundation v. Denver School District No. 1, 459 F.Supp. 357 (D.Colo.1978). The *Anderson* case addressed the constitutional claims, and distinguished the cases wherein election campaign contributions by private corporations were held to be constitutionally protected activities. 380 N.E.2d at 636 et seq. Anderson contains an extensive survey of cases from California, Oregon, Arizona and New York which also disapproved public appropriations to advance a partisan view in public elections (most of which involved referenda on bond proposals and constitutional amendments). 380 N.E.2d at 635 n. 2.

MARSHALL FIELD & CO. v. VILLAGE OF SOUTH BARRINGTON

Appellate Court of Illinois, First District, 1981.
92 Ill.App.3d 360, 47 Ill.Dec. 964, 415 N.E.2d 1277.

[Facts reported at p. 108, supra]

As a second and separable basis for declaring the bond issues invalid, South Barrington asserts that the financing scheme fails to serve the public purposes as is required by the constitution. * * *

The constitution mandates that public funds, property, or credit be used solely for public purposes. (Ill. Const.1970, art. VIII, § 1(a).) The determination of whether a proposed public expenditure serves the public purposes is initially to be made by the legislative body empowered to expend the funds. Such a legislative decision is not to be lightly set aside upon judicial review. However, a self-serving recitation that the public purposes are served is not conclusive of that question. (*People ex rel. City of Salem v. McMackin* (1972), 53 Ill.2d 347, 354–55, 291 N.E.2d 807; * * * The courts look to the goals sought by and the actual effects of the expenditure of the public funds in deciding the issue. * * * The consensus of modern legislative and judicial thinking is to broaden the scope of activities which may be classified as involving a public purpose, especially in the area of economic welfare. *McMackin* at 53 Ill.2d 356, 291 N.E. 807.

Field's initial response to this contention is an assertion of the doctrine of estoppel. According to Field's argument, South Barrington should be estopped from refuting its original legislative finding that the proposed bond issues serve the public purposes. In other circumstances, this theory has been deemed meritorious, most often where a bona fide holder of already issued bonds is seeking payment on them from the issuer, who then attempts to deny a prior representation as to the legality of the bonds. (See *e.g., Harter v. Kernochan* (1880), 103 U.S. 562, 26 L.Ed. 411; *Hackett v. Ottawa* (1878), 99 U.S. 86, 25 L.Ed. 363.) We find the present situation to be distinguishable. Both *Harter* and *Hackett* appear to turn upon the fact that the bonds there contained representations *on their face* that they complied with the law, and such representations were likely to foster reliance thereupon by a bona fide purchaser. In contrast, here no bonds have issued and therefore no bona fide purchaser exists. Field has not directed its financial resources, as a purchaser would, into the hands of the bond issuer with the expectation that repayment would eventually be forthcoming as specified in the transaction. We do not believe that the policy behind the estoppel doctrine found in the bona fide purchaser cases extends to such circumstances.

There is, further, another reason to reject the estoppel argument. If the proposed bond issues here were found to lack a valid public purpose, they would be void under the constitution. (Ill. Const.1970, art. VIII, § 1(a).) South Barrington has no power to issue revenue bonds lacking in this requisite public purpose. In such a situation, no recitals of law or fact made by a legislative body are available to work an estoppel as to the validity of that particular attempted exercise of governmental power. (*Newberry Library v. Board of Education of the City of Chicago* (1945), 390 Ill. 48, 63, 60 N.E.2d 552.) The estoppel doctrine cannot be used to validate a void bond proposal. (See McQuillin, Municipal Corporations § 43.74 (3rd Ed.1970).) Although South Barrington's action is inconsistent, we do not believe that the estoppel doctrine should be applied to the particular facts present here.

* * *

There yet remains the question of whether the trial court erred in implicitly ruling that the proposed bond issues serve the public purposes. As the appellant in this case, South Barrington bears the onus of demonstrating that its initial legislative finding on this question was erroneous. In neither the record before this court, which we have exhaustively examined, nor in the representations of the parties made in response to our inquiries at oral argument, have we found a *factual* basis for setting aside South Barrington's legislative determination. Rather, we see the minimal amount of factual material relevant to this matter as being insufficient to overcome the deference given to that legislative declaration. Therefore, we are constrained to accept the legislative judgment made by the village on this question, and we affirm the decision of the trial court which ruled that the proposed financing scheme was proper under Illinois law.

As a final note to this decision, we make this *caveat*. Our determination that the trial court did not err in finding the issues to be consonant with the law is made solely because we have been presented with nothing of record to warrant an exception to the traditional judicial deference to be given to legislative determinations on such matters.

* * *

The record before this court is wholly lacking in the specifics of the revenue bond issues and the financing agreements. Therefore, our decision does in no way foreclose later judicial scrutiny when those facts become apparent, should such scrutiny be required. Today's decision merely approves and is limited to the actions of South Barrington as evidenced in the record before us.

For the above reasons, the decision of the circuit court of Cook County is affirmed.

Affirmed.

BASEHORE v. HAMPDEN INDUSTRIAL DEVELOPMENT AUTHORITY

Supreme Court of Pennsylvania, 1969.
433 Pa. 40, 248 A.2d 212.

JONES, JUSTICE. * * * In effect, these are taxpayers' suits to test the constitutionality of the Industrial Development Authority Law, supra and the Amendment to the County Code and to test the constitutionality and legality of Agreements entered into between the Butler County Industrial Development Authority and Armco Steel Corporation and between the Hampden Industrial Development Authority and Ralston Purina Company. In both cases, the parties have stipulated the facts. * * *

The two Agreements here in question are similar in their provisions. The Hampden Authority was formed pursuant to an ordinance * * * of Hampden Township for the purpose of constructing or acquiring industrial development projects. On January 16, 1968, the Authority and Ralston entered into an Acquisition Agreement under which the Authority agreed to buy the industrial site on which the proposed factory will be built and the site would be leased to Ralston for a term of 30 years and the Authority will provide funds for the construction of the new industrial plant by floating revenue bonds issued by the Authority in the principal amount of $8 million. Ralston agreed to construct the industrial plant with the funds and to lease it from the Authority at an annual rent sufficient to pay the interest on and amortization of the principal of all bonds and other obligations incurred by the Authority in setting up the project; if the amount raised by the bonds does not cover the cost of construction. Ralston agreed to complete the project and, in addition, to pay all costs of maintaining and operating the project once it is completed. Moreover, Ralston agreed to pay annually *in lieu of taxes an amount equal to the taxes it would have to pay if the project were not owned by a tax-exempt authority.*

* * * Under the Agreement, Ralston has the right to assign or sublet the project once it is completed, but, if it does so, it will remain primarily liable for the performance of the Agreement.

* * *

The bonds to be issued will be revenue bonds. It will be stated on the bonds that all principal and interest will be payable exclusively from the income, rentals and revenues of the project and that neither the general credit nor the taxing power of the township or the Commonwealth is pledged for payment of the bonds. * * * All bonds will mature before the life of the Authority expires. The bond indenture prohibits foreclosure or execution on any property involved in the project.

The project envisages the construction of a new plant which will employ 100 persons at the outset and will not replace a plant already in existence in Pennsylvania. * * *

* * *

Industrial development authorities are not new, the first such authority having been set up in Mississippi in 1936. Today over 40 states have established such authorities. The principle behind the projects is relatively simple. Tax-exempt authorities are established to build plants for private manufacturing companies and the funds used to construct the projects come from revenue bonds which are tax-exempt under Section 103(a)(1) of the Internal Revenue Code of 1954. Obviously, the projects are enticing to private manufacturers since the authority can build the plant at a lower cost utilizing tax-exempt revenue bonds than the company could by utilizing its own non-tax-exempt bonds. The projects are enticing to the Commonwealth since presumbly they will attract industry to the state or encourage industries already located in Pennsylvania to increase their facilities and increase employment. In effect, the federal government subsidizes the construction of plants for private manufacturers to enhance and increase employment.

In most states having such projects, taxpayers have brought suits to test their constitutionality and, in most instances, the courts have held that the projects are constitutional. As in most of these suits, the taxpayers in the present suit have alleged that the Act and the Agreements violate several provisions of the State and National Constitutions. We will deal with their major contentions in turn.

I

* * *

The Act details legislative findings that unemployment is a serious problem in the state and that industrial development projects are effective means to fight unemployment.[8] The taxpayers argue that it is for the courts and not the legislature to evaluate the public purpose of a statute when that statute's constitutionality is attacked. * * *

All parties are agreed that unemployment is a problem which falls within the police power of the state. See: Commonwealth v. Perkins, 342 Pa. 529, 21 A.2d 45, aff'd, 314 U.S. 586, 62 S.Ct. 484, 86 L.Ed. 743 (1941). The legislature has found that the unemployment problem is

8. Industrial Development Authority Law, Act of August 23, 1967, § 2, P.L. 1609, 73 P.S. § 372(2). Some commentators have argued that industrial development bonds have not been nearly as successful as hoped. See: Note, The Proliferation of Industrial Revenue Bond Financing: Ban the Bond? 41 Temple L.Rev. 289 (1968); Comment, Financing Industrial Development with Municipal Revenue Bonds, 1967 Ill.L.Forum 331; 7 CCH 1968 Stand.Fed.Tax.Rep. ¶ 6128A. See also: Abbey, Municipal Industrial Development Bonds, 19 Vand.L.Rev. 25 (1965); Pinsky, State Constitutional Limitations on Public Industrial Financing: An Historical and Economic Approach, 111 U.Pa.L. Rev. 265 (1963).

sufficiently serious now to warrant that steps be taken to remedy the problem * * *. The taxpayers have not convinced us that the legislative findings are unrealistic * * *. Even if their characterization of the legislature's findings were correct, the taxpayers have not cited any cases holding that it is not within the police power to prevent a *potentially* serious problem from developing in the future. * * *

The taxpayers' main concern is that the party who is really benefiting from this program is the private manufacturer * * *. It is beyond question that private manufacturers receive a very large benefit from this program; however, this fact alone should not invalidate the program. If the legislative program is reasonably designed to combat a problem within the competence of the legislature and if the public will benefit from the project, then the project is sufficiently public in nature to withstand constitutional challenge.

* * * There is another important factor to consider. Industrial development authorities are so prevalent throughout the country that Pennsylvania is at a competitive disadvantage in attracting industry to this state should we declare this act unconstitutional. * * *

* * *

We conclude, therefore, the Agreements entered into by the Authorities pursuant to the Act are for a public purpose, a conclusion which effectively answers several of the taxpayers' objections. * * * Second, the taxpayers maintain that the Act violates the State Constitution in that the plants are tax-exempt * * * but that in reality it is the private manufacturers who are receiving the benefit of the tax exemption. The taxpayers rely on a line of cases holding that public bodies may not use their property for private purposes and still receive a tax exemption. [Citations omitted] The Authorities counter with a series of cases holding that, if the public body is acting for a public purpose, it does not lose the tax exemption even though the activity in question seems to be non-governmental in nature. [Citations omitted] * * * Since we conclude that the instant Authorities are acting for a public purpose in erecting the plants, the line of cases cited by the Authorities must control. * * *

The taxpayers place great reliance on our decision in Price v. Philadelphia Parking Authority, 422 Pa. 317, 221 A.2d 138 (1966). In *Price* the parking authority agreed with two private concerns to build combination parking garages and high rise apartments and, under the project as planned, * * * very little additional parking space would have been made available to the public. "This net increment to the public, in light of the magnitude of the garage project and the substantial benefits accruing to [public] therefrom, is not sufficient to warrant the public involvement here proposed." *Price,* supra, at 338, 221 A.2d at 150. Not only will there be a *substantial* benefit to the public in the instant projects but *Price* is inapposite in another respect. We held that the agreements in *Price* violated the enabling act and not the State Constitution * * *.

* * * The taxpayers maintain that the right to mortgage the Authorities' property makes the bonds debts of the municipalities, relying on Lesser v. Warren Borough, 237 Pa. 501, 85 A. 839, 43 L.R.A., N.S., 839 (1912). In *Lesser* we held that the constitutional debt limit was violated when the borough floated bonds to buy the water works and used the property of the water works as security for the bonds.

The Authorities counter with the arguments * * * that while the Act permits the Authorities to mortgage the property, both Agreements in the instant cases specifically state that the Authorities shall not have this right. In view of this factual posture of the instant litigation we need not consider this contention of the taxpayers because it is clearly irrelevant.

III

The taxpayers argue that the Act and the Agreements violate Sections 6 and 7 of Article IX which prohibit the Commonwealth and any municipality from pledging or loaning their credit to "any individual, company, corporation or association * * *." * * *

The Act specifically states that the Authorities shall not have the power to pledge the credit of the Commonwealth or any political subdivision of the Commonwealth. However, we need not rest on the language of the Act alone for there is a fatal flaw in the taxpayers' chain of logic. The money raised by the bonds will go to the Authorities and not to the industrial corporations; the Authorities will own the factories; the corporations will lease the plants from the Authorities. Therefore, if credit is being lent to anyone, it is being lent to the Authorities. * * *

The Authorities have also directed our attention to Section 9, Article IX, Proposition 6 of the newly-adopted Constitutional Amendments. The second sentence of that Section states: "The General Assembly may provide standards by which municipalities or school districts may give financial assistance or lease property to public service, industrial or commercial enterprises if it shall find that such assistance or leasing is necessary to the health, safety or welfare of the Commonwealth or any municipality or school district." The taxpayers do not maintain that this Section does not control the present situation but they argue instead that this Section should only be applied prospectively. However, since we have already determined that the Act does not violate old Sections 6 and 7 of the Constitution, we need not consider the impact of the newly adopted Section 9, Article IX, Proposition 6 of the new Constitutional Amendments. * * *

IV

The taxpayers allege that the Act, bond ordinances and Agreements all violate Section 31 of Article III of the State Constitution in three particulars. Section 31 states: "The General Assembly shall not delegate to any special commission, private corporation or association, any power to make supervise or interfere with any municipal improvement, * * *."

The taxpayers argue initially that the Authorities are special commissions within the meaning of Section 31 because the primary beneficiaries of the Act are private corporations and not the public. * * * we have held on several occasions that authorities similar to these Industrial Development Authorities are not special commissions in the sense that term is used in Section 31. [Citations omitted]

* * *

V

The taxpayers allege that the provisions in the Agreements permitting the two companies to purchase the properties for $1000 after all debts have been paid violates Sections 1 and 9 of Article I, Section 31 of Article III and Section 7 of Article IX of the State Constitution. In effect, they argue that a sale for such a small sum amounts to a wasting of public assets * * *.

* * * In the redevelopment cases, we have approved the sale of homes acquired by the redevelopment authorities to private individuals. [Citations omitted]

* * *

In *Basehore,* (Appeal No. 91 Misc.Dkt. 16) injunction is denied.

In *Walker,* (Appeal No. 167 March Term, 1968) decree affirmed.

Each party pay own costs.

MUSMANNO, J., did not participate in the decision of this case.

COHEN, J., dissents.

* * *

ROBERTS, JUSTICE (concurring).

* * *

Our conclusion that the legislation and projects serve a "public purpose" in part reflects an evolution in attitude prompted by the changing nature of our public needs. It also reflects the deference courts must accord to the legislative branch where fundamentally at issue is the appropriate role of government in meeting those needs.

* * *

Appellants have relied heavily on Price v. Philadelphia Parking Authority, 422 Pa. 317, 221 A.2d 138 (1966). As the majority correctly points out, that case is narrowly speaking inapposite because it was decided not on constitutional grounds, * * * Yet in a broad sense, we deal here with the same basic problem. If the instant projects were determined not to be essentially "public," * * * then our conclusion must necessarily be in accord with that reached in *Price.*

* * *

In the instant case, although the immediate beneficiary is intended to be the industrial lessee, it acts solely as a conduit by which the public may realize the ultimate benefit of local economic growth * * * Thus, within the confines of this specific program and its objectives * * * industrial lessees are functionally only incidental beneficiaries, necessary to the realization of an essentially public objective.

* * *

Today's decision will not preclude the courts from preventing an abuse of an authority's discretion in participating in a specific project. What would constitute such abuse within the confines of this program need not be here specified. * * * For these reasons, I concur in the result reached by the majority.

Notes

1. **Other States.** The overwhelming majority of states uphold these bonds. See e.g. Mitchell v. North Carolina Ind. Dev't, Fin. Auth., note 1 above; People ex rel. City of Salem v. McMackin, 53 Ill.2d 347, 291 N.E.2d 807 (1972); State v. Jacksonville Port Authority, 266 So.2d 1 (Fla.1972); State ex rel. Hammermill Paper Co. v. LaPlante, 58 Wis.2d 32, 205 N.W.2d 784 (1973); City of Gaylord v. Beckett, 378 Mich. 273, 144 N.W.2d 460 (1966).

2. **The Ambit of Public Purposes.** "A slide-rule definition to determine public purpose for all time cannot be formulated; the concept expands with the population, economy, scientific knowledge, and changing conditions. As people are brought closer together, * * * the public welfare requires governmental operation of facilities which were once considered exclusively private enterprises (Fawcett v. Mt. Airy, 134 N.C. 125, 45 S.E. 1029, 63 L.R.A. 870) and necessitates expenditures * * * for purposes which, in an earlier day, were not classified as public. Keeter v. Town of Lake Lure, 264 N.C. 252, 141 S.E.2d 634. Often public and private interests are so commingled that it is difficult to determine which predominates." Mitchell v. North Carolina Indus. Dev't, Fin. Auth., 273 N.C. 137, 144, 159 S.E.2d 745, 750 (1968).

3. **Curtailment of Tax Exempt Industrial Bonds.** The federal Tax Relief Act of 1986 severely curtailed the advantages and use of industrial development bonds by limiting the dollar amount of such bonds for tax exemption purposes, and by eliminating most of the interest deductions of bank borrowings for the purpose of purchasing them.

2. CONTROLS ON THE PROCESSES OF CONTRACTING

Special controls over expenditures are provided by legislation governing public contracts, and by many rules for the execution and administration of public contracts. Contracts may not be forged to barter away police powers; or to advance personal interests of public officials; or improperly to bind future governments; or to grant "unlawful" monopolies; or to confer rights of unreasonable duration. These principles are not applied as easily as they are stated. Each calls for line-drawing judgments that balance practical necessity with the need for strong prophylactic measures to protect public interests.

a. Required Authorization and Procedure

CITY OF JONESBORO v. SHAW–LIGHTCAP, INC.

Court of Appeals of Georgia, 1966.
112 Ga.App. 890, 147 S.E.2d 65.

BELL, PRESIDING JUDGE.

* * *

"As a general rule of law, when authority is delegated by the legislature to a municipality to enter into contracts in a certain specified manner, it becomes the duty of any person dealing with such municipality in a contractual relation to see that there has been a compliance with the mandatory provisions of the law limiting and prescribing its powers. It would follow from this principle that, when a suit is instituted by one against a municipality upon a contract, it should be clearly shown in the petition setting forth the cause of action that the contract was valid, under the charter powers conferred upon the city." [Citations omitted]

Construing the petition most strongly against the pleader * * * the inference is demanded that in dealing with plaintiff, the Mayor of Jonesboro acted as the city's agent individually and separately from the council without concurrence by that body either formal or informal. However, the charter of the City of Jonesboro vests authority for governmental action of the kind in question in the mayor *and* council as a body. *Cf.* Mayor, etc., of Sugar Valley v. Mills, supra. The Mayor acting alone was without authority to bind the city. "[W]hile generally an allegation of agency is sufficient to withstand both general and special demurrer (see Conney v. Atlantic Greyhound Corp., 81 Ga.App. 324, 58 S.E.2d 559), such is not true in cases involving the powers and duties of public officials (See Code § 89–903), where the agent is without authority of law to act." Ingalls Iron Works Co. v. City of Forest Park, 99 Ga.App. 706, 707, 109 S.E.2d 835, 836.

Since the petition here fails to show that the express contract sued upon was entered into on behalf of the city by the mayor and council as a body and as required by the city charter, it stated no cause of action, and the trial court erred in overruling defendant's oral motion to dismiss.

* * *

Judgment reversed.

* * *

Notes

1. **Equitable Relief.** Recovery on the theory of unjust enrichment, has been allowed for improperly let contracts, under the reasoning indicated by the *Hudson* case p. 42, supra. See also, McCuistion v. Siloam Springs, 268 Ark. 148, 594 S.W.2d 233 (1980).

2. **Ratification.** Requisite authorization may, under proper circumstances, be supplied retroactively by ratification: "However, even if it be held that the business administrator had no authority to enter into the contract in question, the governing body could ratify his act, since, as was previously stated, the contract was one which the corporation could lawfully make. * * *

"The principle of ratification has been said to apply to a municipal corporation the same as to an individual, as to the contracts which have been unauthorizedly entered into in its behalf, if it could have originally authorized such contracts. Campbell v. City of Hackensack, 115 N.J.L. 209, 178 A. 794, 98 A.L.R. 1225 (E. & A.1935). The making of contracts by an unauthorized agent are said to be *ultra vires* in the secondary sense, whereas contracts entirely beyond the municipal jurisdiction are *ultra vires* in the primary sense. Johnson v. Hospital Service Plan of N.J., 25 N.J. 134, 135 A.2d 483 (1957). The former can be ratified, while the latter may not be. Ratification may be by inaction, as well as by affirmative action. Such inaction may consist of the acceptance of benefits under the contract. City Affairs Committee of Jersey City v. Board of Commissioners of Jersey City, 132 N.J.L. 552, 41 A.2d 798 (Sup.Ct.1945), affirmed 134 N.J.L. 180, 46 A.2d 425 (E. & A.1946). In the instant case it must be found that there was such a ratification, at least as to the making of the contract by an unauthorized agency, both by the absence of any disavowal of the contract and by the acceptance of benefits under the contract at a time when all the material facts were known by the responsible officials." Riddlestorffer v. Rahway, 82 N.J.Super. 36, 53–54, 196 A.2d 550, 559–60 (1963). To like effect, see Lathrop Co. v. Toledo, 5 Ohio St.2d 165, 214 N.E.2d 408 (1966); School Admin. Dist. # 3 v. Maine School Dist. Com'n, 158 Me. 420, 185 A.2d 744, 747 (1962).

Ratification arises from inaction of an official who has notice of the transaction and accepts its benefits without objection. Johnson v. Hospital Service Plan of N.J., 25 N.J. 134, 135 A.2d 483 (1957). Such conduct might also fit the theory of promissory estoppel but, as noted elsewhere, courts are hesitant to raise estoppels against municipalities.

3. **The Elements of Good Faith and Fault.** In Lathrop Co. v. Toledo, 5 Ohio St.2d 165, 214 N.E.2d 408 (1966), the court permitted recovery, over the city's defense that a written order for the extra work, as required by the city charter, had not been issued. The court ruled that the city's duty to issue the written order was, under the circumstances, not a discretionary act, but a binding contract obligation. Similarly, in M. De Matteo Const. Co. v. Maine Turnpike Authority, 184 F.Supp. 907 (S.D.Me. 1960) the court rejected the Authority's defense that the work was not accepted by its engineer, whose certification, per the contract, was to be final and binding. The court ruled that the engineer did not act reasonably and in good faith. The Stahelin case, p. 714, reflects the same sentiments, though cast in a different legal rationale.

Where the contract makes the city engineer or architect the final arbiter of disputed performance or compensation, what rule should govern:—that the engineer's decision is not reviewable; that it is subject to independent reconsideration by the court; that it will be set aside only if it is manifestly arbitrary and unreasonable? See J.H. Jenkins Contractor, Inc. v. Denham Springs, 216 So.2d 549 (La.App.1968); Stahelin, p. 714, infra.

CAHN v. HUNTINGTON

Court of Appeals of New York, 1972.
29 N.Y.2d 451, 278 N.E.2d 908.

JASEN, JUDGE. This is an action to recover the reasonable value of legal services performed by plaintiff as attorney for the Planning Board of the Town of Huntington in litigation instituted against the Planning Board by the Town Board of Huntington.

The Town Board, in January, 1969, commenced an article 78 proceeding to prohibit the Planning Board * * * from interfering with the person named by the Town Board to sit on said Planning Board, and to require the planning Board to recognize that person as Chairman. This lawsuit was the culmination of a dispute * * * as to which agency had the power to appoint a Chairman of the Planning Board. In this litigation, the Town Attorney * * * represented the Town Board. Consequently, the Planning Board concluded that the Town Attorney, * * * could not, under the circumstances, also represent the Planning Board. Thereupon, the Planning Board duly adopted a resolution retaining plaintiff to act as its attorney in the lawsuit instituted by the Town Board.

* * *

Several months later, plaintiff submitted statements * * * to the Planning Board for the services rendered the Planning Board in the article 78 proceeding. The Planning Board then adopted resolutions approving the payment of the amount billed. When the Town of Huntington failed to authorize the payment of the claim, * * * plaintiff instituted this action against the Town of Huntington. * * *

The issue thus presented on this appeal is whether the Planning Board was authorized to employ private legal counsel to represent it respecting the litigation between it and the Town Board. The town contends * * * the Planning Board had no authority to bind the Town Board for the payment of legal fees. Plaintiff, on the other hand, concedes that the statute does not specifically confer upon the Planning Board the right to employ counsel, but argues that the Planning Board possesses implied authority to employ special counsel, under the circumstances present here.

It is well-settled law that an attorney may not be compensated for services rendered a municipal board or officer unless he has been retained in accordance with statutory authority. [Citations omitted] In other words, the power to employ counsel by a municipal board or officer is not deemed to be incidental to such board or officer. Rather, express authority, either by statute or by appropriate resolution of the governing body, must be shown to justify the retention of an attorney by a municipal board or officer. [Citations omitted] * * *

Notwithstanding lack of specific statutory authority, a municipal board or officer possesses implied authority to employ counsel in the good faith prosecution or defense of an action undertaken in the public interest, and in conjunction with its or his official duties where the municipal attorney refused to act, or was incapable of, or was disqualified from, acting. [Citations omitted] This authority is necessarily implied in order to enable the board to effect the purposes of its creation and to allow it to properly function. [Citations omitted] It should be abundantly clear that in view of the stringent requirements that must be satisfied, the policy underlying the general rule of express authority is certainly not compromised by this exception.

Under the facts and circumstances of the case before us, we conclude that the Planning Board had implied authority to engage the services of an attorney for which the Town Board should be held liable. In the article 78 proceeding instituted by the Town Board against the Planning Board, the Huntington Town Attorney represented the Town Board. He could not, therefore, under the circumstances, represent the Planning Board. The only possible recourse for the Planning Board was to employ special counsel, which it did. Only in this manner could the legal issues raised in said proceeding be properly resolved.

Section 65 (subd. 1) of the Town Law did not negative this implied authority of the Planning Board to employ counsel. * * * The statute certainly does not apply to litigation between two town officers or boards concerning the proper performance of their duties. If it did, a situation would be created in which the Town Board could prevent the board it sued from engaging counsel. We should not, of course, ascribe to the Legislature an intent to have such a result ensue. [Citations omitted]

Accordingly, the order appealed from should be affirmed, with costs.

* * *

Notes

1. **Implied Authority.** Should the Planning Board have sought a court ruling on its right to engage separate counsel *before* pursuing extensive litigation? Could it not have sued preliminarily for a decree that the town had the duty to provide independent counsel for this special purpose?

One of the complaints often raised by administrators, especially in home rule jurisdictions, is that courts hold them bound by rulings of the municipality's solicitor who tends to favor the elected official who appoints him. But see Krahmer v. McClafferty, 282 A.2d 631 (Del.Super.1971) where the court held that city council of a home rule city was entitled to independent representation in defending a suit to enforce the city solicitor's opinion that council must amend an allegedly unlawful budget ordinance.

STAHELIN v. BOARD OF ED., SCHOOL DIST. NO. 4, DuPAGE COUNTY

Appellate Court of Illinois, Second District, 1967.
87 Ill.App.2d 28, 230 N.E.2d 465.

DAVIS, PRESIDING JUSTICE. This is a suit by the plaintiff, Leland Stahelin, against the Board of Education, * * * for a declaratory judgment that he had fully performed his contract to construct a new junior high school, * * *

* * * it is abundantly clear that the present dispute, in a large part, was the result of the acts of the architect. There were some errors in the plans, which was not an unusual circumstance. These errors were the basis of some of the plaintiff's claim for extras.

However, the architect assumed an arbitrary and unreasonable attitude in his dealings with the contractor; and, it must be said * * * that the architect had the support and approval of a majority of the defendant board in this respect. * * *

* * *

The most serious legal dispute arises with reference to the question of the extras claimed by the contractor, in the sum of $60,000. * * * The court, ultimately allowed the plaintiff's claim for extras in the sum of $44,196.34. * * * It claimed, however, that the plaintiff was not entitled to be reimbursed for the extras because of the manner in which they were authorized.

The defendant contends that sections 10–6 and 10–7 of the School Code * * * preclude the plaintiff from recovering for the extras. Section 10–6 provides that no official business shall be transacted by the school board except at a regular or special meeting, and section 10–7 specifies that: "On all questions involving the expenditure of money, the yeas and nays shall be taken and entered on the records of the proceedings of the board." It is conceded that the expenditure for extras was not authorized by the school board by the taking of yea and nay votes nor was the payment of the claim for extras, as finally submitted, authorized in any manner.

The defendant also contends that the construction contract itself, bars the plaintiff from the right to recover for extras. The relevant portions of the contract are found in the General Conditions, and they are:

* * *

"A1–17 EXTRAS: It is distinctly understood that no extra of any kind will be allowed, except such extra or extras as ordered by the Architect in Writing * * *."

The defendant contends * * * that the extras were not ordered "in writing" and were ordered without the prior specific approval of the board.

Soon after the inception of the work, there were changes made in the plans. The architect advised the plaintiff to keep a record of all such "extras and credits" and that there would be an adjudication at the end of the job. Lester Przewlocki, the school board superintendent and ex-officio member of the board, was the board representative most often at the construction site. * * * He was not authorized to give instructions or directions to the contractor, but he kept informed on matters relating to the construction and reported to the board.

Several other members of the board also went to the construction site * * * and attempted to give the plaintiff instructions. As to the latter persons, the school board president wrote to the contractor, in June of 1963, advising the plaintiff, "Your instructions will be received from the architect's office only. Should you choose to follow instructions of anyone other than the architect, or member of his staff, you do so at your own risk and peril."

With rare exception, all of the modifications and alterations in the plans and specifications were made at the request of the architect. However, only a few requests were made in writing. * * * It is unbelievable that the board was not aware that the contractor was called upon from time to time throughout the construction to do work not called for in the contract and for which he would claim an extra charge.

* * *

As to the provisions of paragraph A1–17 * * * these provisions are for the benefit of the owner and may be waived by it. City of Elgin v. Joslyn, *supra,* 307; County of Cook v. Harms, 108 Ill. 151, 164 (1833). * * *

* * * If it can be said that paragraph A1–17 required the directions of the architect to be in writing and the prior approval of the board to be a condition precedent to the plaintiff's right to collect for the extras he furnished, then it must also be said that defendant waived these requirements by its conduct.

The defendant is in the unenviable position of also asserting that it is entitled to a number of credits which were to be adjudicated upon completion of the job, but that it is not obligated for any of the extras to be adjudicated in the same manner because it did not vote by yeas and nays on the expenditures for these extras, and that this was required by statute. * * *

At the time of the litigation stage of the dispute, it was too late in the day for the defendant to assert that it could not be estopped, under appropriate circumstances, from asserting a position inconsistent with its actions. * * *

The doctrine of estoppel may be applied against school boards or districts. [Citations omitted] Whether the doctrine of estoppel may be applied against a municipal corporation in a given case will be determined from a consideration of all the circumstances of the case. If under all of the circumstances, the affirmative acts of the public body have created a situation where it would be inequitable and unjust to permit it to deny what it has done or permitted to be done, the doctrine of estoppel may be applied against it. [Citations omitted]

* * *

Contracts entered into by a municipality which are expressly prohibited by law, and which under no circumstances can be entered into, are void and ultra vires. They may not be rendered valid thereafter by estoppel or ratification on the part of the municipality. However, there is another class of municipal contracts, distinct from the void type heretofore referred to, wherein the municipality has the power to enter into the contract, but where a portion thereof may be beyond its power, or its power may have been irregularly exercised. As to this class of contracts, a municipality may not assert its want of authority or power, or the irregular exercise thereof, where to do so would give it an unconscionable advantage over the other party. Municipal corporations, as well as private corporations and individuals, are bound by principles of common honesty and fair dealing. [Citations omitted]

In the present case the defendant had the general power to contract as it did. Apart from this it had the power to authorize expenditure of funds for the extras. It permitted the plaintiff to incorporate these extras into its building. The evidence established that the defendant had knowledge that it was intended that the amount of the extras and credits was to be adjudicated upon the completion of the work. It accepted the benefits resulting from this work and it cannot now be permitted to deny its obligation to pay for these items * * *. Under the circumstances of this case and the contract provisions in question, the trial court was correct in holding that the defendant was liable for the extras.

* * *

Note

1. **Ratification, Waiver and Estoppel.** The long indulged confusion of these three doctrines in contract law blurs legal reasoning. See 3A Collier, Contracts § 752 (1960). The court in *Stahelin* could have found a ratification by conduct (knowing acceptance of benefits). If the court were correct in finding a "waiver" of a contract term, why discuss estoppel? But should a court empower a Board to "waive" a provision of the School Code? Rather than "estop" the Board from asserting the School Code, could it have found or implied a contract duty to effect formal approval of the extras? Compare State Engineering Service Inc. v. Kevin, 148 Mont. 312, 420 P.2d 433 (1966); cf. Flora Crane case, p. 580, supra.

In Delta Construction Co. of Jackson v. Jackson, 198 So.2d 592 (Miss. 1967) suit for work authorized by the city engineer, but not by its governing body, was brought on the theory that the city waived the requirement of formal authorization. The court recognized the feasibility of such a waiver, but rejected the contention as "inappropriate" under the circumstances of that case.

The case for estoppel is very weak where the contract is "void" and against public policy. Whatcom County Water District v. Century Holdings, Ltd., 29 Wash.App. 207, 627 P.2d 1010 (1981).

ERICKSEN v. SIOUX FALLS
Supreme Court of South Dakota, 1944.
70 S.D. 40, 14 N.W.2d 89.

VAN BUREN PERRY, CIRCUIT JUDGE.

[Taxpayer suit to void a contract entered into between the city and an industrial corporation for the joint improvement of a sanitary sewer system whereby, in exchange for its contribution, the company was given the right to use the improved sewer system for its industrial sewerage for a period of 15 years. The court held that the contract was unauthorized and void.]

* * *

* * * The city does not grant to an individual householder any such contract for a period of years, nor does it assume any obligation or possible liability, but merely grants the privilege of connecting to the sewers, and it is a license which may be revoked for sufficient cause at any time. The contract purports to grant far more than is embraced in the license or permit which the city is authorized to grant. Were it valid, it might form the basis for a damage suit against the city for nonperformance. It attempts to grant a vested right for the 15–year term. The city cannot assume such liabilities, nor grant such rights.

The mere fact that one has expended considerable money to make the connection gives him no vested right to retain the connection. 4 McQuillin, Municipal Corporations, 2d Ed.Rev. § 1566.

The contract between the city and the company seems to treat the sewage disposal plant as property subject to joint control, a sort of partnership affair, to be supervised by engineers paid by and owing allegiance to both parties. The law does not authorize such. The plant belongs to the city. The city cannot part with any of its control thereof, nor should it share the allegiance of any of its employees. The company is not compelled to use it. It may use it only by permit from the governing board of the city. If the company wishes to use the city plant, it must conform to the requirements which the governing board may lawfully impose.

* * *

In the present state of our statutes we are compelled to hold that the amended contract of March 1, 1940 between the City of Sioux Falls and John Morrell & Company is wholly unauthorized and void.

* * *

Notes

1. **Bargaining Away Government Power.** A local unit can no more agree not to exercise responsibility than to act *ultra vires.* In Midtown Properties, Inc. v. Madison, 68 N.J.Super. 197, 172 A.2d 40 (1961) a contract between a township board and a developer, entered as a consent judgment by the parties, provided that the township board would refrain from exercising its zoning powers in a way prohibited by the contract. It was held void. A city cannot enforce a contract which requires it to zone land in a particular way? See City of Knoxville v. Ambrister, 196 Tenn. 1, 263 S.W.2d 528 (1953). Accord: Moskovitz v. St. Paul, 218 Minn. 543, 16 N.W.2d 745 (1944) (city cannot barter away by contract its police power control of liquor licenses). Neither can a city by contract relieve a company of duties required by state law, *viz.* to maintain a bridge. Connersville Hydraulic Co. v. Connersville, 95 Ind.App. 234, 173 N.E. 641 (1930). The delegation principle is not, however, strictly applied to intergovernmental contracts. See Town of Highlands, p. 722, infra.

2. **Arbitration.** It is generally established that a provision submitting local government contract disputes to arbitration is valid and not an unlawful restraint on legislative discretion. City of Madison v. Frank Lloyd Wright Foundation, 20 Wis.2d 361, 122 N.W.2d 409 (1963).

b. Limits on Contract Duration

Statutory rules on contract duration are neither comprehensive nor uniform. In the absence of a fixed statutory time limit, courts apply rules of reason to determine the outer durational limits of local government contracts. The nature and subject matter of each transaction govern the issue of reasonable duration.

DUGGAN v. TAUNTON

Supreme Judicial Court of Massachusetts, 1971.
360 Mass. 644, 277 N.E.2d 268.

CUTTER, JUSTICE. Mr. Duggan and Mr. Phillipe * * * each an attorney, brought separate actions of contract against the city and Taunton Municipal Light Plant Commission * * * to recover amounts allegedly owed them for legal services to the commission under written contracts, each dated December 14, 1965 * * *.

* * *

* * * In the record of the commission's meeting on December 14, 1965, the following entry appeared, "Legal contracts for retaining Attorneys Duggan and Phillipe were submitted to the [c]ommission. In order to protect the taxpayers, Mr. Farrell made a motion, seconded by Mr. Guglielmo to retain both attorneys for a period of three years. Mr. Phillipe to be paid $3,500.00 per year; Mr. Duggan to be paid $8,500.00 per year. Mr. Quinn no. Motion carried." The motion thus carried by two votes to one.

The commission then consisted of three members. After January 1, 1966, as a consequence of St.1965, c. 289 ＊ ＊ ＊, the mayor appointed two additional commission members. There was thus reasonable basis for the suspicion that two of the three commission members, in December of 1965, were anxious to make contracts for legal services which would bind the five-man board of commissioners to be in office in 1966. The two contracts were in fact executed on December 14, 1965, and Messrs. Duggan and Phillipe continued to serve as counsel and associate counsel.

On February 1, 1966, Messrs. Duggan and Phillipe were asked to appear before the newly constituted five-member commission in executive session. They were requested to resign and refused to do so. By a three to two vote, Messrs. Duggan and Phillipe were discharged as attorneys. A bill ($741.77) from Mr. Duggan for services rendered in January, 1966, and one ($291.67) from Mr. Phillipe for the same month were paid. On February 7, 1966, a new attorney was appointed pursuant to a vote of the commission.

＊ ＊ ＊

2. Substantial reasons exist for questioning any recovery by these plaintiffs beyond the value of the work in fact done by them. ＊ ＊ ＊

＊ ＊ ＊ The contracts appear to have been made ＊ ＊ ＊, at a time when its members must have known that a five-man commission (possibly with different views concerning counsel) would come into existence within a month or two. There is in the record evidence which would permit, and perhaps require, the finder of the facts to conclude that two members of the old commission were deliberately forcing the augmented five-man commission to allow Messrs. Duggan and Phillipe (a) to finish at least their then pending cases and (b) to furnish *all* legal advice and services to the commission until December 31, 1968 ＊ ＊ ＊.

A general principle, applicable to municipal corporations and their agencies, is that, under the "common law apart from statute ＊ ＊ ＊ a public officer cannot give an appointee a tenure of office beyond his own." [Citations omitted]

＊ ＊ ＊ Except where a valid contract, a clearly expressed statutory policy, or some special exigency requires a different result, we should be slow to permit a "lame duck" municipal body to dictate to its successors the choice of the attorneys who are to advise them.

No precisely applicable Massachusetts decision governs this case. We rely on the trend of authorities outside Massachusetts. Contracts made with attorneys in good faith by one board to handle ＊ ＊ ＊ a particular piece of litigation or other legal matter are much more likely to be sustained against attack (on grounds of public policy) by a successor board than arrangements for a more general representation. See Pima County v. Grossetta, 54 Ariz. 530, 538, 97 P.2d 538; Denio v. Huntington Beach, 22 Cal.2d 580, 590–591, 140 P.2d 392 (contract appearing to be "fair, just, and reasonable" when executed, not voidable although some executory features may extend beyond the terms of the municipal body executing the contract); Douglas v. City of Dunedin (Fla.Dist.Ct. of App.), 202 So.2d 787, 789. With respect to more general retainers, however, the rule is different and appears to us to be more appropriate in the public interest. See Willett & Willett v. Calhoun County, 217 Ala. 687, 688, 117 So. 311 ("Tying the hands of the succeeding board" in the selection of a confidential legal adviser "contrary to public policy"); Board of Commissioners of Jay County v. Taylor, 123 Ind. 148, 152–153, 23 N.E. 752; McCormick v. Hanover Township, 246 Pa. 169, 173–178, 92 A. 195 (but cf. Light v. Lebanon County, 292 Pa. 494, 497–500, 141 A. 291, where a contract was made at the beginning of a board's term, was unlikely to last beyond the term, and was justified by special circumstances). See also Jessup (Board of Commissioners of Hancock County) v. Hinchman, 77 Ind.App. 460, 463–465, 133 N.E. 853; Parent v. Woonsocket Housing Authority, 87 R.I. 444, 447–450, 143 A.2d 146; annotations, 70 A.L.R. 794, 799–802; 149 A.L.R. 336, 342–343. Compare cases where a contract for services or supplies (extending beyond the term of the appointing body) was reasonable, was made in good faith, and was for the public benefit, such as Rockhill Iron & Coal Co. v. City of Taunton, 273 F. 96, 100 (1st Cir.1921), purchase, in good faith, of coal by the manager of this Taunton municipal light plant, covering a year and a half beyond the term of his office, held to be a valid contract). See also Gray v. Joseph J. Brunetti Constr. Co. Inc., 266 F.2d 809, 818–819 (3d Cir.—application of New Jersey law to a contingent fee agreement with an attorney); annotation, 43 A.L.R.2d 677, 679–683.

We are not disposed to lay down any inflexible rule about contracts for attorneys' services made by municipal or other public boards for periods extending beyond the period when the board making the contract can control the actions of the board. Some such contracts made, pursuant to specific statutory or other authority, or made in good faith for particular and necessary services at an appropriate time and for reasonable compensation, may involve no substantial question of public policy and should be enforced. On the other hand, grounds of public policy may invalidate a contract for legal services made for an unduly long period, or to commence or to be in effect at a date unreasonably after the contracting body will cease to control the choice of counsel (see *e.g.* Pashman v. Friedbauer, Director of Pub. Safety of Passaic, 1 N.J.Super. 616, 620, 63 A.2d 838), or in circumstances which indicate either an unconscionable effort to bind a successor board or officers or lack of good faith. Much will depend upon the particular facts and circumstances. We conclude that this record squarely presents the issue whether these contracts were against public policy and should be denied enforcement on that ground.

* * * We think that, on this record, a verdict should have been directed for the commission on the basis of what seems to us the better reasoned authorities already cited.

Exceptions sustained. Judgments for the defendants.

Notes

1. **Accord:** Edsall v. Wheler, 29 A.D.2d 622, 285 N.Y.S.2d 306 (1967). Where city council retains an attorney to collect delinquent taxes for a fee of 10% of actual collections or 10% of the sale price received on tax foreclosures by the city, is the contract void if not limited to the term of the existing council? Should it make a difference that such an attorney is not providing personal, confidential counsel to government officials? See Douglas v. Dunedin, 202 So.2d 787 (Fla.App.1967).

2. **Legislators With Staggered Terms.** Where the legislative body is composed of members whose terms of office are staggered, a long term contract may begin or end beyond the expiration of the term of a minority or a majority of the officers. When do such contracts invalidly bind future legislative bodies? Compare Daly v. Stokell, 63 So.2d 644 (Fla.1953) (held that a city commission composed of members serving staggered terms was a continuing body) with Board of Education of Vocational School of Union County v. Finne, Lyman & Finne, 88 N.J.Super. 91, 210 A.2d 794 (1965) (treating a school board composed of members serving staggered terms as not being "continuous".) Is the policy of preserving legislative integrity meaningfully advanced by an absolute exemption of "continuous bodies" from the restrictions against binding successor legislatures? The authorities are divided. As in *Duggan,* some courts will nullify long term contracts or appointments motivated by an upcoming election which may oust the existing majority. Board of Education of Pendleton County v. Gulick, 398 S.W.2d 483 (Ky.1966); Thomas v. Board of Education of Morris Twp., 89 N.J.Super. 327, 215 A.2d 35 (1965). *A fortiorari,* where the new contract term is totally within the term of a succeeding board, it should be voided (Independent School Dist. of Liberty v. Pennington, 181 Iowa 933, 165 N.W. 209 (1917), but there is authority contra. King City Union H.S. Dist. v. Waibel, 2 Cal.App.2d 65, 37 P.2d 861 (1934).

A rule of reason, as advanced by the principal case, seems far more preferable than the artificial logic that a board with staggered terms is a "continuous" body. In Board of Education v. Finne, Lyman & Finne, supra, the court rejected any absolute rule based on classifying the body as continuous vel non, or on classifying the contract as governmental or proprietary, where the practical necessities of the single project, namely, planning and constructing a new school, made the duration of an architect's contract reasonable and, therefore, valid.

3. **Franchise Contracts.** Aside from antitrust problems discussed in chapter VI, special problems attend the grant of exclusive rights in governed territory. A five year exclusive franchise to operate an ambulance service may be voided (Macon Ambulance Service, Inc. v. Snow Properties, 218 Ga. 262, 127 S.E.2d 598 (1962)), while the grant of exclusive lease concessions to low bidders at municipal facilities (airports, stadia) may be upheld as both necessary and reasonable. Absent a governing statute, may a city contract with a nonprofit corporation, to operate a city zoo? See City of Cleveland v. Lausche, 70 Ohio App. 273, 49 N.E.2d 207 (1943).

4. **Intergovernmental Contracts.** The rules against surrender of legislative power are avoided by saving constructions in many interlocal

contracts between local government units. See City of Big Spring v. Board of Control, 404 S.W.2d 810 (Tex.1966); and Town of Highlands, which follows.

TOWN OF HIGHLANDS v. WEYANT

Supreme Court, Appellate Division, Second Department, New York, 1972.
38 A.D.2d 256, 329 N.Y.S.2d 58.

GULOTTA, JUSTICE. This is an appeal * * * from a declaratory judgment which held four contracts made by two water districts and two sewer districts with the respondent Village * * * to be void and unenforceable. The term of each of the contracts is for "so long as the said district exists".

The trial court held that, since these contracts might be operative for more than 40 years and sections 118–a and 119–a of the General Municipal Law, which deal with water supply and sewage disposal, respectively, limit such contracts to a period not in excess of 40 years, they were void *ab initio* and unenforceable, although only about 10 years have elapsed since the contracts were made in 1961 and 1962.

I believe this reaching out by the trial court so as to declare void contracts * * * which deal with a subject matter for which the municipality has the undoubted right to contract, simply because the contracts *might* extend for too long a period, is unwarranted and unnecessary. We may assume that the municipal officials intended to contract in conformity with the legislative mandate. The statutory purpose will be served by limiting the contracts to the permissible statutory period.

No New York case in point is cited by the Special Term. The indication in both Corpus Juris Secundum (63 C.J.S. Municipal Corporations § 979) and McQuillin on Municipal Corporations (3d ed., vol. 10, § 29.100, p. 490) is that in other jurisdictions the problem has been handled in a variety of ways, but the following cases squarely hold such contracts valid for the permissible statutory period: State ex rel. Attorney General v. Ironton Gas Co., 37 Ohio St. 45; Cartersville Improvement, Gas and Water Co. v. Mayor, 89 Ga. 683, 16 S.E. 25. An early New Jersey case, Board of Finance of Jersey City v. Mayor, 55 N.J.L. 230, 26 A. 92, held a contract to be void because it might exceed the allowed statutory period, but on appeal (57 N.J.L. 452, 31 A. 625) the basis for the ultimate decision was on a different ground. Contrariwise, an old Federal court case, Manhattan Trust Co. v. City of Dayton, (6 Cir., 59 F. 327), held that a contract for an indefinite term would not be valid even for the permissible 10–year period. No persuasive reason was advanced for this approach.

Additionally, it should be noted that the New York statutory provisions and how they apply to our fact situation are not free from doubt. Section 234 of the Village Law, which deals with contracts by a village with other districts for the purchase and sale of water, limits such contracts for the sale of water to 10 years, but permits the village to contract for the purchase of water for 40 years. Section 276 of the same law, relating to contracts between villages and sewer districts for operation and maintenance of sewer systems, in contrast to section 119–a of the General Municipal Law, has no time limit.

Furthermore, section 120 of the General Municipal Law authorizes contracts for the purification of a water supply and for sewerage between villages and improvement districts without prescribing any time limit; and section 120–a of that law specifically authorizes a contract between municipalities and sewer districts for sewerage disposal "upon such terms and for such consideration and *length of time* as may be mutually agreed upon between all the contracting municipalities" (emphasis added).

Thus the legislative purpose would seem to be somewhat clouded and certainly there is no clear-cut reason to allow a repudiation of these entire contracts to the detriment of the inhabitants of the improvement districts, simply because they might exceed a statutory term. The aim would seem to be to encourage these co-operative contracts between municipalities rather than to discourage them.

* * *

It is our opinion, therefore, that the ordinance of April 20, 1971 of the respondent Village, purporting to abrogate the contracts in question, is void and of no effect.

Were this the only issue, we might well finally dispose of this case now as a matter of law. However, there are two factual questions which can be determined only after a plenary trial, namely, (1) whether any binding contract exists obligating the respondent Village to supply sewerage services to the appellant Satterlee Grove Sewer District and (2) whether there existed a conflict of interest sufficient to vitiate the contracts, by reason of the simultaneous representation of all the parties to the contracts by the same firm of attorneys and by further reason of an undisclosed financial interest of said attorneys in the land developers who were the beneficiaries of these water and sewer agreements.

The judgment should be reversed, on the law, and the case remanded to the Special Term for trial of the factual issues, * * *.

Notes

1. **Long Term Procurement Contracts.** Beverly Sewerage Authority v. Delanco Sewerage Auth., 65 N.J.Super. 86, 167 A.2d 46 (1961) upheld, as reasonable in duration, a 40–year interlocal service contract. The reasonableness of a long term procurement contract depends upon the item or service procured. Future availability, price fluctuation, block purchasing economics, and other variables determine the propriety of forward commitments. "The true test is whether the contract itself deprives a governing body, or its successor, of a discretion which public policy de-

mands should be left unimpaired." See Plant Food Co. v. Charlotte, 214 N.C. 518, 520, 199 S.E. 712, 714 (1938).

2. **Governmental v. Proprietary Powers.** The difficulty of classifying particular activities as governmental or proprietary also muddles the issue of the legality of contracts, especially in utility service transactions. It is possible to classify municipal utility services as proprietary in nature; while at the same time classifying the rate-setting function as governmental in nature. In City of Warm Springs v. Bulloch, 212 Ga. 149, 91 S.E.2d 13 (1956) the court ruled that the setting of water rates could not be fixed by contract or ordinance beyond the term of the authorizing officials, and that a contract obligating the city to provide free water in exchange for an assignment of water rights would be void. Accord: Incorporated City of Humboldt v. Knight, 255 Iowa 22, 120 N.W.2d 457 (1963). Where, however, the city contracted to supply water at reduced rates to grantors of easements for its water mains, another court held the contract binding so long as the city continued to use the easements. Boiles v. Abilene, 276 S.W.2d 922 (Tex.Civ.App.1955). A Georgia court took a more restrictive view in voiding an agreement beyond the term of the city council, in which the city agreed to indemnify the grantor of a sewer easement from damages incurred in its use. City of Douglas v. Cartrett, 109 Ga.App. 683, 137 S.E.2d 358 (1964).

The uneven application of governmental-proprietary concepts was noted in Town of Lovell v. Menhall, 386 P.2d 109 (Wyo.1963). There the court refused to nullify a contract, involving parking meters, which was admittedly governmental in nature, and which extended beyond the legislative term of its authorizing body. It observed that courts ignore the rule when practical necessity requires long-term commitment and when the transaction is essentially fair and beneficial to the public interest.

Problems on duration are avoided by statutory authorization. See City of Big Spring v. Board of Control, 404 S.W.2d 810 (Tex.1966) (long-term fixed-rate water supply contract between city and state hospital agency upheld as legislatively authorized, and as a proprietary transaction); Water Works & Sanitary Sewer Board of City of Montgomery v. Campbell, 267 Ala. 561, 103 So.2d 165 (1958) (grant of free city water service in exchange for sewer line easement—upheld as authorized by state law).

3. **Post-Contract Nullification of Enabling Statutes.** Where the authorizing statute is declared unconstitutional *after* a contract was executed, but not completed, the contract may nevertheless be held void. Mathew v. Algonquin, 3 Ill.App.3d 429, 279 N.E.2d 91 (1972). Even where the parties raised no issue of *"ultra vires,"* one appellate court on its own initiative found that a contract for supplies, based upon a statute which authorized only contracts for services and facilities, was void. Sinclair Refining Co. v. Bergen, 103 N.J.Super. 426, 247 A.2d 484 (1968).

c. *Conflicts of Interest in Public Contracts*

"It is a wise and well established principle of public policy * * * that a public official may not use his official power to further his own interests." Genkinger v. New Castle, 368 Pa. 547, 551–52, 84 A.2d 303, 305 (1951).

HUSZAGH v. OAKBROOK TERRACE
Supreme Court of Illinois, 1968.
41 Ill.2d 387, 243 N.E.2d 831.

KLINGBIEL, JUSTICE.   The executor of the will of a deceased city attorney brought suit against the City of Oakbrook Terrace seeking to recover the balance of fees allegedly due under a contract for special legal services.   *   *   *

The contract ordinance, *   *   *, required plaintiff's decedent to perform certain services for the City *   *   *.   He was to handle "all legal matters" relating to certain annexation proceedings then pending in the county court *   *   *.   The contract ordinance expressly provided that the specified services "are to be considered for all legal purposes as 'special legal services' which are in addition to and not covered by his employment and retention as City Attorney in representing the city in handling all routine legal matters related to the general administrative affairs of the city."   As compensation he was to receive (subject to a limit of $80,000) one third of the revenues accruing to the City during the period May 1, 1962, to May 1, 1965, "from municipal retail occupation taxes, municipal retail service occupation taxes, and related taxes and revenues" from business and commercial activities located on or conducted from the annexed territory.

*   *   *

In affirming the judgment the appellate court did not consider on its merits the City's contention that the contract was illegal.   *   *   * In this we think the court was mistaken.   *   *   * Where a court is called upon to enforce a contract, the matter of its illegality may be inquired into whether or not it is set up as a defense in the answer. [Citations omitted]

*   *   * And it is urged, *inter alia,* that the contract violates section 3–14–4 of the Revised Cities and Villages Act which provides in part that "No municipal officer shall be interested, directly or indirectly, in any contract, work, or business of the municipality, or in the sale of any article, whenever the expense, price, or consideration of the contract, work, business or sale is paid either from the treasury or by any assessment levied by any statute or ordinance." (Ill.Rev.Stat.1961, ch. 24, par. 3–14–4.)   After careful consideration we think this bargain *   *   * contravenes the spirit if not the letter of the statutory provisions—which are merely declaratory of the common law—prohibiting municipal officers from becoming interested, directly or indirectly, in any business of the City.   We conclude that a similar result must follow.   Municipal authorities cannot, under a general grant of power, adopt ordinances which infringe the spirit of a State law or are repugnant to the general policy of the State.   (City of Marengo v.

Rowland, 263 Ill. 531, 534, 105 N.E. 285.) The ordinance in the case at bar is contrary to public policy and void.

* * *

Note

1. Should the executor have sued in quantum meruit for the reasonable value of the services rendered? See the *Polk* case, note 5, p. 730 infra.

DELTA ELECTRIC CONSTRUCTION COMPANY, INC. v. SAN ANTONIO

Court of Civil Appeals of Texas, 1969.
437 S.W.2d 602.

KLINGEMAN, J. [Delta, a Texas corporation, executed a contract on May 14, 1968, with the City of San Antonio to construct improvements in the city's water system. R.E. Shullanberger, a stockholder and president of Delta, served as a member of the Electrical Examining and Supervising Board of the City from August, 1965 to July, 1969. The conflict of interest provisions of the City Charter and state law prohibited any officer of the city from having any financial interest in any contract with the city. There was no irregularity in the bidding or procedures leading up to the Delta contract, and it was stipulated that Shullanberger, as a member of the Electrical Board, did not in any manner influence the procedures and award of the Delta contract. After the contract was awarded, the city and its Water Board learned of Shullanberger's membership on the Electrical Board and suspended the contract pending judicial determination as to whether there was a conflict of interest which would void the contract.]

* * *

Delta asserts three basic contentions on this appeal: (1) the contract was not made with the City; (2) Delta's president was not an officer or employee of the City of San Antonio; (3) no conflict of interests existed under the applicable conflicts of interest statutes or charter provisions.

Delta * * * asserts that the City was not a party to such contract, that the City is not obligated under such contract, that it was not approved by ordinance of the City, as required under certain charter provisions, that the Water Works Board has full management and control of the water works system, and that the Water Works Board is such a legal entity as can sue and be sued.

* * *

We hold that the Water Board is an agency and department of the City and therefore the contract in question was a contract with the City.

* * *

* * * It would appear that the Electrical Board performs sovereign functions of the City for the benefit of the public, and it is our opinion that members of the Electrical Board are officers of the City of San Antonio.

* * *

Delta contends that unless a contract is made "by the city" (Article 373, V.A.P.C.) "consideration of which is paid from the city treasury" (Article 988, V.A.C.S.) or is "with the City" or "with the Council" (Section 141, City Charter) the conflict of interest statutes and Charter provision have no application to it. It is our opinion that the contract involved was a contract with the City. Delta asserts that since it was stipulated that Delta's president did not in any way influence the award of such contract, no conflict of interest existed. The fact that no influence was exercised is not determinative of whether the contract was violative of the conflict of interest ordinance and statutes. * * *. It has long been the public policy of this state to prohibit officers of a city from having a personal pecuniary interest in contracts with the city and this policy is specifically expressed in both the penal and civil statutes. * * *

In McQuillin, Municipal Corporations, Vol. 10, § 29.97, p. 467 et seq., it is stated: "It is well settled that municipal officers cannot be interested in contracts of any character with the municipality * * * In many states and cities this has been adopted by statutory or charter provisions, which are, however, mostly declaratory of the rule at common law * * * Although under some statutes and charters, such an agreement is voidable only, it is generally held that whenever a public officer enters into a contract, the execution of which may make it possible for his personal interests to become antagonistic to his faithful discharge of a public duty, such contract will be held void as against public policy. It is the existence of such interest which is decisive and not the actual effect or influence, if any of the interest: if there is a potential conflict, the contract is invalid."

We hold that Delta's president was an officer of the City of San Antonio within the meaning of the conflict of interest provision of the City Charter and Art. 373, V.A.P.C., at the time of the execution of the contract; that such contract was in contravention of such Charter provision and the State Statute and is against public policy, and that the trial court did not err in declaring such contract null and void.

Notes

1. **Accord:** State Board of Accounts v. Holovachka, 236 Ind. 565, 142 N.E.2d 593 (1951). The policy of preventing, rather than the fact of, self dealing or dual agency is, for many courts, the true ground for voiding public contracts. Under this prophylactic rule, the absence of fraud or public injury is legally irrelevant. City of Miami v. Benson, 63 So.2d 916 (Fla.1953) (voiding sale by city of its bonds to its financial adviser); United States v. Mississippi Valley Generating Co., 364 U.S. 520, 81 S.Ct. 294, 5 L.Ed.2d 268 (1961) (voiding federal contract where employee of interested

corporation engaged in preliminary contract negotiations on behalf of the federal government).

Should persons serving in advisory positions be subject to conflicts statutes? Compare United States v. Mississippi Valley Generating Co., note 1, supra; with Tonkins v. Greensboro, N.C., 276 F.2d 890 (4th Cir. 1960).

The law governing conflicts of interest in government contracts is very unsettled, with some courts eschewing any absolute rule. "We deem it best to decide the instant case upon the facts presented to us without attempting to reconcile the conflicting decisions from other jurisdictions. The facts in this case would indicate that the plaintiffs, having submitted a low bid * * * would have resulted in an arms length transaction if accepted by the State. It is quite apparent that the proposed transaction was not influenced nor governed by Senator Brockbank's holding public office. The facts reveal no interest which conflicted with the Senator's public duty. We are of the opinion that the facts in this case do not show a conflict of interest situation which should have precluded the acceptance of the plaintiff's bid * * *. As stated above, we can only decide this case upon the facts presented to the court, and it is not our intention to speak in respect to other cases which might arise under the conflict of interest doctrine." Brockbank v. Rampton, 22 Utah 2d 19, 21–22, 447 P.2d 376, 378 (1968).

2. **Degree of Official Involvement.** The cases make clear that the conflict of interest or dual agency need not be direct or immediate. The question then arises, how direct or significant must the financial stake or participation of the interested individual be in order to invoke conflicts doctrine. This issue remains largely a matter of judicial discretion. In Conley v. Ipswich, 352 Mass. 201, 224 N.E.2d 411 (1967) a pharmacist, who was a town selectman, filled prescriptions for welfare recipients which were paid for by the town. In holding that he violated the state conflict of interest statute, the court defined the term "contract" broadly to include an implied contract on the part of the town to pay druggists for services rendered to its welfare recipients. In Baker v. Marley, 8 N.Y.2d 365, 208 N.Y.S.2d 449, 170 N.E.2d 900 (1960) a member of the village board of trustees owned one lot of a large tract of land which the board voted to condemn. The lot value, approximately $250, amounted to less than 1% interest in the larger condemned tract. The court voided the transaction, as falling within the conflict statute.

Some jurisdictions apply conflict of interest policy to public employees, as well as officials, and to indirect, as well as direct financial interests. See e.g. Norrell v. Judd, 374 S.W.2d 192 (Ky.1964).

The difficulties posed by broad conflicts doctrine in widely varied situations are discussed in M. Kaplan and R. Lillich, *Municipal Conflicts of Interest: Inconsistencies and Patchwork Prohibitions,* 58 Col.L.Rev. 157, 174, 181 (1958). See also Note, *Conflicts of Interest of Government Personnel: An Appraisal of the Philadelphia Situation,* 107 U.Pa.L.Rev. 985, 992–96 (1959).

3. **The Time Points When "Conflicts" Arise.** In United States v. Mississippi Generating Co., note 1, supra, the court found that a conflict

arose at the planning and preliminary negotiation stage by a dual agent who did not participate in the final contract decision. Similar reasoning is found in the lead case of Stigall v. Taft, 58 Cal.2d 565, 375 P.2d 289 (1962), where a member of the city council participated in preliminary steps toward the letting, on low bid, of a city plumbing contract to the company in which he had some financial interest. The councilman resigned from the city council prior to that body's vote to accept the low bid. The conflict statute referred specifically to contracts made by officials in their official capacity or by boards of which they were members. Hence it could have been construed strictly, as not applying to the case, but the court construed the statute to include "any interest * * * which would prevent the officials involved from exercising absolute loyalty and undivided allegiance to the best interests of the city." Accordingly it reversed the lower court's dismissal of an action to void the contract. See also Millbrae Association for Residential Survival v. Millbrae, 262 Cal.App.2d 222, 69 Cal.Rptr. 251 (1968).

Other courts reject this expansive view. In Eways v. Reading Parking Authority, 385 Pa. 592, 124 A.2d 92 (1956) the Authority passed a resolution to acquire land owned by a corporation in which an Authority board member was an officer. The transaction was challenged due to the dual position of the interested Authority member who also voted on the resolution. While disapproving the action of the interested board member, the court nevertheless upheld the transaction on the ground that the member having the adverse interest did not cast the deciding vote on the Authority resolution. In accord with Eways, on the effect of an unnecessary vote by an official in a conflict position, see Mayor, etc., of City Ensley v. J.E. Hollingsworth & Co., 170 Ala. 396, 54 So. 95 (1909); Tucker v. Howard, 122 Mass. 529 (1877). But see contra: State ex rel. West Jersey Traction Co. v. Board of Public Works of City of Camden, 29 A. 163 (1894); People ex rel. Plugger v. Township Board of Overyssel, 11 Mich. 222 (1863).

4. **Effect of Statutes on Common Law Doctrine.** Where conflicts legislation does not cover all contracts, a court is free to apply the common law. See e.g. Haynes v. Strange, 232 Ark. 374, 337 S.W.2d 661 (1960).

5. **Remedial Problems.** Case disparities concerning conflict of interest may be due, in part, to the fact that some cases involve potential criminal liability as well as the enforceability of contracts. Should the law relating to civil and criminal responsibility be separated out in order to foster liberal construction of conflicts principles for the purpose of protecting the public, while allowing strict construction of conflicts definitions in criminal cases for the purpose of protecting individuals who act in good faith? Since official conflicts constitute a deep sore in American politics, this issue of legal process is hardly academic, and warrants much more attention than it has received heretofore.

Whether an unlawful conflict renders the contract totally "void" or only "voidable" depends upon the nature of the violation, and the stage of contract execution. Where a township sued to recover sums paid to a township board member for grading and repairing township roads, the court held that, absent express statutory prohibition, the contract was not void but voidable; and that the township could not recover, since the benefits of the contracts were received and accepted. Polk Township Sullivan County v. Spencer, 364 Mo. 97, 259 S.W.2d 804 (1953). Where, however, suit was brought to recover contract payments for petroleum delivered by a corporation, in which one councilman was an employee, stockholder and other councilmen knew of that interest when they approved the contract, the court held the contract void. Miller v. Martinez, 28 Cal.App.2d 364, 82 P.2d 519 (1938). Some courts permitted quasi contractual recovery in the face of express legislative prohibitions, apparently on the view that such recovery would not defeat the statutory policy. See Town of Hartley v. Floete Lumber Co., 185 Iowa 861, 171 N.W. 183 (1919); City of Bristol v. Dominion National Bank, 153 Va. 71, 149 S.E. 632 (1929). In deciding how a particular policy should affect the consequences of an unlawful contract, distinctions may be drawn between contracts for services, supplies or property (see the Comment in 34 Minn.L.Rev. 46 at 50–51); between normal and emergency circumstances; and between inadvertent and knowing or intentional violations.

6. Conflicting interests in official actions other than public contracts are taken up in the next chapter.

d. Bidding Requirements

The common law did not mandate competitive bidding on government contracts. Wiener v. Reno, 494 P.2d 277 (Nev.1972). "The object of statutory bidding requirements * * * is to prevent fraud, collusion, favoritism, and improvidence in the administration of public business, as well as to insure that the municipality receives the best work or supplies at the most reasonable price practicable." Blum v. Hillsboro, 49 Wis.2d 667, 671, 183 N.W.2d 47, 49 (1971); 10 McQuillin, *Municipal Corporations*, § 29.29 (3rd ed. 1966). While the foregoing policy is universally acknowledged, its implementation in the several states varies. The public interest may or may not turn the purely monetary aspects of a bid. For this reason, exemptions from competitive bidding are specified in many statutes, as well as "judicially engrafted" onto statutory obligations. In certain circumstances, courts allow public officials discretion to award contracts to non-low bidders on findings that an award to the lowest monetary bidder would not serve the public interest.

The lawyer's task is to determine when discretionary exemption satisfies legislative intent and when it frustrates that intent. Some discretion must be exercised to answer the questions (1) what bid is actually lowest in net cost price; (2) who is the lowest "qualified" and "responsible" bidder; (3) when have the statutory procedural safeguards been fairly met? Finally, public officials are usually authorized to reject all bids. These issues of administrative discretion are not defined by legislation, but must be gleaned from case law.

CITY OF NEW YORK v. BEAME

Supreme Court, Appellate Div. 1st Dept., New York, 1971.
37 A.D.2d 89, 322 N.Y.S.2d 503.

PER CURIAM. Chapter 343 of the New York City Charter says, in effect, that if a contract for work, labor, supplies, materials or equipment involves more than the sum of Twenty-five hundred Dollars ($2,500), it must be founded on a sealed bid public letting, "except that *in a special case* the Board of Estimate by a two-thirds vote may order otherwise".

At issue here is a management consulting contract for $250,000, awarded by the Mayor without competitive bidding and without Board of Estimate approval. The Comptroller has refused to register it as a valid contract or to certify it against an appropriation pursuant to the Administrative Code (93c–3.0). Special term has upheld the Comptroller. We agree, but for additional reasons.

Special Term found that the work was irregularly done pursuant to a "letter of intent" dated March 4, 1969, calling for a fee of $100,000, but that the Assistant Director of the Budget did not issue a certificate of approval—in the sum of $250,000, or 150% beyond the letter of intent—until June 23, 1970, or long after the work was completed; that procedures and designated forms were not followed, and the Comptroller, not being a "rubber stamp", did not have to blindly register an illegal contract.

We go further. We find that the Charter, having been adopted by popular vote, should be interpreted by "the meaning which the words would convey to an intelligent, careful voter". * * * And the Charter explicitly mandates that contracts, in a generic sense, involving more than $2,500, are to be public, "except in a special case". In the latter situation, the Board of Estimate must approve. Arcane case law is not helpful, nor needed, when the statute's purpose is so unmistakable.

The cases relied upon by the petitioner-appellant, City of New York, * * * are entirely distinguishable. * * * In Potts v. City of Utica, the contract there involved was unanimously approved by the appropriate bodies, which, pursuant to statute had authority to exempt contracts which it found inappropriate to submit to public bidding. All that the court held was that those provisions of the statute requiring public bidding were, in the circumstances, rendered inapplicable (2 Cir., 86 F.2d 616 at p. 618).

* * * The cases relied upon by the appellant are inapplicable in that they simply dealt with competitive bidding statutes containing no "special case" provision and where it was held, although a strict reading of the pertinent statute would preclude the municipality from contracting for work for which competitive bidding was impossible, the courts would read into a statute an exception for such contracts. This is not the situation here presented, for § 343(a) of the Charter is

specially designed to take care of any "special case" in which competition is not an acceptable method of obtaining work by empowering the Board of Estimate to determine that a particular kind of work constitutes a "special case". * * *

 * * * The "special case" requiring approval by a two-thirds vote of the Board of Estimate cannot be severed from and has direct applicability to those situations where the "work or labor to be done" exceed a cost of $2,500, in which case competitive bidding is required, *unless* the Board of Estimate makes an exception.

 * * *

Notes

1. Does the blanket statutory authorization for a "special case," undercut the policy of precluding political patronage?

2. **Exempted Products and Services.** Some laws authorize administrative waiver of bid requirements in specified situations. Even in the absence of legislative exemption, courts exclude many specialty service and material contracts from the operation of bidding statutes. See generally 10 McQuillin, *Municipal Corporations,* 29.35 (1966 rev. ed.). But the discretion permitted to public officials to select specialist contractors is not unlimited. Rules of reason, rather than doctrinal formulae determine when requisite confidentiality, artistic talent, proven experience, financial capacity or reliability are sufficiently scarce to exempt contracts from competitive bidding. See the *Inglewood* opinion, p. 753 infra; and cases in Annot., Waiver of Competitive Bidding, 40 A.L.R. 968 (1985).

A contract for expert property appraisals may be let without competitive bidding (Parker v. Panama City, 151 So.2d 469 (Fla.App.1963)) as may long term leases to nonprofit institutions that are uniquely fit to manage certain public facilities. Hiller v. Los Angeles, 197 Cal.App.2d 685, 17 Cal. Rptr. 579 (1961) (public zoo); Accord: City of Cleveland v. Lausche, 70 Ohio App. 273, 49 N.E.2d 207 (1943).

Turnkey construction contracts invite developers to prepare their own design, finance, and construction plans (often on land sites which the developers, rather than the government, select and acquire). Such contracts are intended to promote flexibility and innovation in competing proposals for new projects, with the government agreeing only to purchase the approved package, upon completion. To achieve these benefits, government must forego construction specifications which are necessary for bid competition, namely, comparable sites, common design and building specifications, and uniform financing terms. Once the benefits of Turnkey construction are assumed, the rationale of public convenience supports exemption. Marino v. Ramapo, 68 Misc.2d 44, 326 N.Y.S.2d 162 (1971).

3. **Professional Canons of Ethics.** Canons of ethics adopted by professional societies, may be voided as anti-competitive under anti-trust laws, and under bidding laws. See generally, National Society of Professional Engineers v. United States, 435 U.S. 679, 98 S.Ct. 1355, 55 L.Ed.2d 637 (1978) where the society's canon of ethics which prohibited members from submitting competitive bids was held to violate the Sherman Act.

4. Bid Exemptions for Affirmative Action in Government Projects. Congressional exemption from low bid requirements for certain minority subcontractors in federally funded projects was sustained against constitutional challenge in Fullilove v. Klutznick, 448 U.S. 448, 100 S.Ct. 2758, 65 L.Ed.2d 902 (1980). While that case was carefully restricted to the statutory conditions, it would seem to support parallel state statutory exemptions from low bid requirements to overcome the effects of past discrimination. As shown by the following opinion and notes, affirmative action remains constitutionally doubtful in cases that do not fit the rationale of Fullilove.

ASSOCIATED GENERAL CONTRACTORS v. SAN FRANCISCO UNIFIED SCHOOL DISTRICT

United States Court of Appeals, Ninth Circuit, 1980.
616 F.2d 1381 (1980), cert. denied 449 U.S. 1060, 101 S.Ct. 783, 66 L.Ed.2d 603 (1980).

CHOY, CIRCUIT JUDGE:

Associated General Contractors (AGC) sued to challenge the "affirmative action policy" adopted by the San Francisco Board of Education (Board). Under the policy, bidders for construction contracts let by the San Francisco Unified School District (School District) must be minority general contractors or must utilize minority subcontractors for 25% in dollar volume of the contract work. AGC asserts that this policy violates 42 U.S.C. §§ 1981 and 1983 and the Fourteenth Amendment, and California law as well.

The district court held that such a set-aside for minority contractors on public works was illegal, except as to projects funded with federal money given on condition that 10% or more of the money would go to minority contractors. We agree.

* * * Relief from the policy was available only when the Board was satisfied that an ineligible contractor had "taken every possible measure to comply" with the policy, or that it was "not practicable in the best interests of the District to require compliance in the specific case."

The policy declared that noncomplying contractors were not "responsible bidders" under California Education Code § 15951 (now § 39640). That statute requires school construction contracts to be awarded to the "lowest responsible bidder."

The district court enjoined the School District from enforcing the policy, on the ground that "responsibility" under the state law referred only to a bidding contractor's financial and physical ability to do the work. * * * Associated General Contractors v. San Francisco Unified School District, 431 F.Supp. 854 (N.D.Cal.1977) * * *

At about the same time, the federal government granted the School District $8,000,000 in public works funds under the Public Works Employment Act of 1977, Pub.L. No. 95–28, 42 U.S.C. §§ 6701–6710, which requires that the recipient entity give "satisfactory assurance to the Secretary [of Commerce] that at least 10 per centum of the amount of each grant shall be expended for minority business enterprises," 42 U.S.C. § 6705(f)(2).

The Board then adopted a second affirmative action policy nearly identical to the first * * * except that it applies only to projects financed with Public Works Employment Act funds.

AGC applied for a contempt order to vindicate the earlier injunction. The district court dismissed the proceeding without prejudice. However, it issued an order changing the Board's 25% minority participation requirement on federally-aided projects to a 10% requirement. The court then modified its earlier injunction so as not to prohibit the new policy, as altered.

* * *

II. ISSUES

This appeal raises five issues: (1) whether the district court had jurisdiction * * * (2) whether the manner in which the court reduced the set-aside on Public Works Employment Act projects violated due process; (3) whether California Education Code § 39640 prohibits the Board's affirmative action policy; (4) if state law does prohibit it, whether the state law is unconstitutional as applied to do so; and (5) if the affirmative action policy is not prohibited by any valid state law, whether the policy itself violates the Constitution.

A. JURISDICTION

The district court had jurisdiction to enter its injunction and order. AGC's attacks on the set-aside policy based on the Fourteenth Amendment and 42 U.S.C. §§ 1981 and 1983 are substantial federal claims * * * The district court also had pendent jurisdiction over the state-law question whether the Board had authority under state law to adopt and enforce its affirmative action policy. See Hagans v. Lavine, 415 U.S. 528, 536, 94 S.Ct. 1372, 1378, 39 L.Ed.2d 577 (1974). * * *

* * *

C. AUTHORITY UNDER STATE LAW

The district court held that under state law the affirmative action program was void because the Board had no authority to adopt it. * * * We agree with the district court.

The authority of school boards in California derives from California Education Code § 35160, which authorizes the adoption of any program that * * * "is not in conflict with or inconsistent with, or preempted by, any law."

Because the Board's affirmative action program conflicts with California Education Code § 39640, we hold that § 35160 does not authorize it. Section 39640, the "low bid law," reads:

"The governing board of any school district shall let any contracts involving an expenditure of more than eight thousand dollars ($8,000) for work * * * or more than twelve thousand dollars ($12,000) for materials or supplies * * * to the lowest responsible bidder" * * * the California Supreme Court has circumscribed the meaning of "lowest responsible bidder" in another context.

In Inglewood-Los Angeles County Civic Center Authority v. Superior Court, 7 Cal.3d 861, 500 P.2d 601, 103 Cal.Rptr. 689 (1972), the court held that California Government Code § 25454, a statute requiring that counties award public contracts to the "lowest responsible bidder," did not embody a concept of "relative superiority" which would allow the county to award the contract to the next-to-lowest bidder because he was "more qualified" than the lowest bidder. The court said, "a contract must be awarded to the lowest bidder unless it is found that he is not responsible, i.e., *not qualified to do the particular work under consideration.*" 7 Cal.3d at 867, 500 P.2d at 604, 103 Cal.Rptr. at 692 (emphasis added). * * *

We do not think that the California Supreme Court would construe the term "lowest responsible bidder" as used in Education Code § 39640 differently from the construction it gave the same language in *Inglewood*; the statutes are virtually identical. Therefore, we hold that § 39640 must be construed to prohibit the Board from considering any factor other than the amount of the bid, the minimum qualifications of the bidder as to financial ability and skills to complete the job successfully, and the quality of the bidder's past work.

* * *

1. DUTY OF AFFIRMATIVE ACTION

a. *United States Constitution*

Appellants boldly claim that the Constitution imposes upon the School District a legal duty to take affirmative action to remedy the effects of past discrimination, and that any state law that prevents such action therefore violates the Supremacy Clause.

We think it is useful and necessary to distinguish between the two major types of positive governmental action taken on behalf of minorities. First, there are "reshuffle" programs, in which the state neither gives to nor withholds from anyone any benefits because of that person's group status, but rather ensures that everyone in every group enjoys the same rights in the same place. The most common examples are school desegregation cases and programs.

Second, there are "stacked deck" programs, in which the state specifically favors members of minorities * * * for benefits that the state can give to some citizens but not to all. This category includes affirmative action programs of both the quota and "positive-factor" varieties [8] (but not programs that merely encourage more minority persons to apply for state-conferred benefits).

8. See, e.g., Regents of the Univ. of California. v. Bakke, 438 U.S. 265, 98 S.Ct. 2733, 57 L.Ed.2d 750 (1978), which struck down a program that limited whites to 84% or fewer of the positions in a medical school class, but approved a program that made a

It is well established that the state has an affirmative constitutional duty to use "reshuffle" programs to cure the effects of past or present *de jure* segregation. * * * Where such a duty exists, remedies that merely avoid further overt state discrimination are inadequate if they fail to effect an immediate reshuffle. * * *

On the other hand, there is no constitutional duty to engage in "stacked deck" affirmative action.[9] In our view, the reason for this is that "stack deck" programs trench on Fourteenth Amendment values in ways that "reshuffle" programs do not. For example:

(1) "Stacked deck" programs offer the possibility that the official discrimination is or may become invidious. "Reshuffle" programs are inherently not invidious.

* * *

(3) In the short run, a "stacked deck" program works wholly to the benefit of certain members of one group, and correspondingly to the harm of certain members of another group. "Reshuffle" programs theoretically provide some benefits also to the whites, for their exposure to the minorities is expected to bring understanding and wisdom. See Trafficante v. Metropolitan Life Insurance Co., 409 U.S. 205, 93 S.Ct. 364, 34 L.Ed.2d 415 (1972). But "stacked deck" programs do not provide even collateral benefits to the disadvantaged whites.

(4) A "stacked deck" program arguably deprives citizens of rights (*e.g.*, the right to make contracts, free from racial discrimination; *cf.* 42 U.S.C. § 1981), whereas a "reshuffle" program does not (*e.g.*, no "right" to attend a segregated school).

It is true that courts, * * * have sometimes imposed "stacked deck" affirmative action remedies on public bodies for Fourteenth Amendment violations. But the basis for such remedies is the broad powers of equity, not an initial duty of those bodies to have undertaken affirmative action; it is not true that the substance of a post-verdict remedy necessarily was "constitutionally or legally required" before verdict. United States v. Montgomery County Board of Education, 395 U.S. 225, 236, 89 S.Ct. 1670, 1676, 23 L.Ed.2d 263 (1969).

minority applicant's race one of several positive factors that could be considered in the admissions process.

9. To the extent that the Sixth Circuit has relied on "reshuffle" cases to find a constitutional duty of states to take "stacked deck" affirmative action to eliminate the effects of past discrimination, see Detroit Police Officers' Assn. v. Young, 608 F.2d 671, 691 (6th Cir.1979), petition for cert. filed, ___ U.S. ___, 101 S.Ct. 3079, 69 L.Ed.2d 951, we disagree.

Some cases uphold or impose "stacked deck" affirmative action under federal statutes such as Title VII of the Civil Rights Act of 1964 and the Public Works Employment Act of 1977; these cases are irrelevant to our discussion of constitutional duty.

We also think that United Jewish Organizations v. Carey, 430 U.S. 144, 97 S.Ct. 996, 51 L.Ed.2d 229 (1977), is not adverse to our position. * * * However, close examination proves that this was just another "reshuffle" case, because no individual Hasid was placed in a district that violated the one-person-one-vote rule, and the petitioners denied that there was a right to maintain permanently in a single district the community's bloc voting power, id. at 154 n. 14, 97 S.Ct. at 1004 n. 14. It is well established that competent agencies may take race into account in "reshuffle" contexts.

No authority impels us to find a constitutional duty to take "stacked deck" affirmative action. If the Supreme Court believed that such a duty existed, it surely would have said so in Regents of the University of California v. Bakke, 438 U.S. 265, 98 S.Ct. 2733, 57 L.Ed. 2d 750 (1978). * * * Similarly, we think it significant that in all cases in recent years where the *permissibility* of "stacked deck" programs was sharply attacked, no court has ventured to still all the controversy by proclaiming that not only is such affirmative action permitted, it is actually *required* by the Constitution.

There is no doubt that the enactors of the Fourteenth Amendment did not intend it to require "stacked deck" affirmative action programs. * * * [W]e decline to import into the Amendment a "stacked deck" affirmative-action requirement. The pluses and minuses of "stacked deck" programs are far too uncertain and controversial for us to remove the question from the legislative sphere without grossly overstepping the appropriate limits of the judiciary in the American system.

* * *

Moreover, even if the argued-for constitutional duty exists, it could not come into play until proper findings were made of discrimination and the need for affirmative action to redress it. Such findings were not and could not be made in this case, as we show *infra*.

b. California Constitution

Nor is "stacked deck" affirmative action required by the California Constitution. It is true that Crawford v. Board of Education, 17 Cal.3d 280, 551 P.2d 28, 130 Cal.Rptr. 724 (1976), held that school boards have an affirmative duty under the *state* constitution to take "reshuffle" affirmative action to alleviate racial segregation in the public schools, regardless of whether its root cause was *de facto* or *de jure* segregation or anything else. However, *Crawford* (1) confined itself to the alleviation of disproportionate minority-student enrollment in public schools; (2) refused to set numerical quotas even in the "reshuffle" desegregation context; and (3) did not authorize "stacked deck" affirmative action in any context. Therefore, there is no reason to think that the California Constitution compels school boards to engage in "stacked deck" affirmative action geared to numerical quotas, especially in areas other than school enrollment.

Appellants assert that the affirmative action program is necessary to ensure equal educational opportunities for minority students in vocational work/study programs. * * * Schools teach; what happens to the graduates is the province of other agencies. * * *

Besides, if the Board truly were concerned with education, rather than employment, its affirmative action policy would merely compel contractors to offer work experience to all vocational education students, regardless of race. Instead, the policy says nothing about the education or hiring of any minority workers, student or non-student; its concern is that *employers* be minority. Even if the Board's policy might have the effect of enhancing education opportunities for minority students, we find that the previous inequality was not so great, and the ameliorative effect would not be so pronounced, that the policy is constitutionally compelled.

c. *Irretractability*

Appellants argue further that once a program is proven in practice to dispel discrimination, it is unconstitutional to withdraw from it.
* * *

Apparently, the Supreme Court's position is that it is a constitutional violation for a school board to rescind previous action if and only if the board was under a constitutional duty to take the action initially. Dayton Board of Education v. Brinkman, 433 U.S. 406, 414, 97 S.Ct. 2766, 2772, 53 L.Ed.2d 851 (1977). Because we hold that the Board here had no constitutional duty to adopt its affirmative action policy, the Constitution does not forbid the Board to return to its former race-neutral policy.

In support of their argument, appellants cite only Ethridge v. Rhodes, 268 F.Supp. 83 (S.D.Ohio 1967). There the state proposed to withdraw a requirement that contractors sign assurances that they would not discriminate against black workers. Given the state's knowledge that this would result in only whites being hired, the court properly found unconstitutional state action. But in this case no state agency is signalling private parties that they may disregard statutory antidiscrimination laws, so *Ethridge* is inapposite.

* * *

2. POWER TO PROHIBIT AFFIRMATIVE ACTION

Appellants argue that, even if the affirmative action policy is not constitutionally compelled, the state law prohibiting it is nonetheless unconstitutional.

a. *Legislative Incompetence Per Se*
* * *

Whether courts might think that voluntary affirmative action should be a favored policy is of no moment. There is no constitutional duty for the state or the Board to take affirmative action here. * * *

Appellants' position boils down to an assertion that if a state legislature and a state agency disagree about the wisdom of affirmative action, the agency should prevail (if it is the entity in favor of affirmative action). This we cannot accept. The competent entity in such a situation is always the legislature, whose members are charged with responsibility and accountable to the people for such decisions. The Supreme Court has insisted that "explicit [legislative or Presidential] action, especially in areas of doubtful constitutionality, requires careful and purposeful consideration by those responsible for enacting and implementing our laws. Without explicit action by lawmakers, decisions of great constitutional import and effect would be relegated by default to administrators who, under our system of government, are not endowed with authority to decide them." Greene v. McElroy, 360 U.S. 474, 507, 79 S.Ct. 1400, 1419, 3 L.Ed.2d 1377 (1959).

"Stacked deck" affirmative action, the constitutionality and wisdom as social policy of which are sharply debatable, is precisely the kind of policy decision in which legislatures have the greatest advantage in competence over local agencies such as school boards. Therefore, we hold that it is constitutionally acceptable for a legislative determination to foreclose, as it does in this case, the Board from voluntarily adopting an affirmative action policy.[14]

b. Discriminatory Impact and Intent

Even if the low bid law is not unconstitutional per se because it removes the Board's authority under state law to take "stacked deck" affirmative action, it still must be tested under Washington v. Davis, 426 U.S. 229, 96 S.Ct. 2040, 48 L.Ed.2d 597 (1976).

Under *Washington,* "a law, neutral on its face and serving ends otherwise within the power of government to pursue, is [not] invalid under the Equal Protection Clause simply because it may affect a greater proportion of one race than of another." Id. at 242, 96 S.Ct. at 2049. Even in cases involving so-called discriminatory impact, "the invidious quality of a law claimed to be racially discriminatory must ultimately be traced to a racially discriminatory purpose." Id. at 240, 96 S.Ct. at 2048.

The requirement of California Education Code § 39640 that school construction contracts go to the "lowest responsible bidder" obviously is on its face race-neutral. Although the low bid law may have a disproportionate impact on minorities, this is not a case where the disparity of a law's impact "may for all practical purposes demonstrate unconstitutionality because * * * the discrimination is very difficult to explain on nonracial grounds," thus permitting an inference of discriminatory purpose. See 426 U.S. at 242, 96 S.Ct. at 2049. Nor, as we understand it, has the Board itself ever applied (or failed to apply) the low bid law with an invidious intent.

Obviously, when the low bid law was passed in 1917, its purpose was not to disadvantage racial minorities. It was designed to protect the public fisc by preventing public officials from awarding contracts uneconomically on the basis of special friendships. * * * If anything, the purpose of the low bid law was to help such outsider contractors.

---

14. Moreover, the contrary legislative determination fatally undermines the propriety of the Board's findings in support of its affirmative action policy. However, the Supreme Court has held that quota-type affirmative action is unconstitutional where not supported by "appropriate findings * * * made by judicial, legislative, or administrative bodies with competence to act." Regents of the Univ. of Calif. v. Bakke, 438 U.S. 265, 325, 98 S.Ct. 2733, 2766, 57 L.Ed.2d 750 (Brennan, J., dissenting); accord, id. at 307, 98 S.Ct. at 2757 (opinion of Powell, J.). See also id. at 421, 98 S.Ct. at 2815 (Stevens, J., concurring in the judgment) (interpreting the federal legislative determination, Title VI, to prohibit the University's voluntary affirmative action program). * * *

Therefore, the low bid law passes the Washington v. Davis test, and must be upheld.

E. Constitutionality of the Policy

Even if the Board's policy was permissible under state law, or if the state law that prohibited the policy was unconstitutional, we would still have to test the policy itself against the standard of the United States Constitution before we could reverse the district court. * * *

III. CONCLUSION

The Board lacked authority to adopt its affirmative action policy because the policy was inconsistent with the California low bid law. This application of the low bid law is constitutional.

Note

Affirmative Action Balancing Factors. See discussions at pp. 357–733, 829, supra; and notes following Petrozello, p. 751, infra.

HYLTON v. MAYOR AND CITY COUNCIL OF BALTIMORE

Court of Appeals of Maryland, 1972.
268 Md. 266, 300 A.2d 656.

MURPHY, CHIEF JUDGE. This appeal presents the question whether a contract between the Mayor and City Council of Baltimore (the City) and Monsanto Enviro-Chem Systems, Inc. (Enviro-Chem) for the construction of a resource recovery solid waste disposal system was concluded in violation of the competitive bidding requirements contained in § 4 of Article VI of the City's Charter. * * *

By the terms of the contract, Enviro-Chem agreed, for $14,742,000, to construct a resource recovery solid waste disposal plant for the City utilizing its "Landgard" non-patented proprietary process for disposing of one thousand tons per day of garbage and trash by pyrolysis and recovering saleable by-products therefrom (resource recovery), viz., usable steam, glassy aggregate and ferrous metals. The agreement specified that $6,000,000 of the contract price would be paid by the City from grant funds which it would receive from the Environmental Protection Agency (EPA) of the United States; that $4,000,000 would be paid from funds received by the City through the Maryland Environmental Service (MES), an agency of the State of Maryland; and that the remainder of the contract price would be paid by the City from its own resources.

The contract, * * * was executed against this factual background: In an effort to find a satisfactory solution to its problem of disposing annually of approximately 540,000 tons of garbage and trash, the City initiated an in-depth study in early 1970 of all available technology in the field of solid waste disposal; the study included on-site investigations of operational facilities throughout the nation. As a result, the City prepared specifications and sought competitive bids in 1970 for a seventeen-year service contract for a one thousand ton per day solid waste disposal system, operational within State pollution control requirements. The five bids received by the City failed to comply with the specifications * * * and all bids were rejected. The City thereafter explored the possibility that under the Solid Waste Disposal Act of 1965, as amended by the Resource Recovery Act of 1970, 42 U.S.C.A. § 3251 *et seq.* (1970), it could obtain a grant of funds from the federal government to assist it in constructing its own solid waste disposal system. * * * Acting through EPA the federal government was empowered to make grants to selected municipalities for the demonstration of resource recovery solid waste disposal systems, the grants being limited in amount to 75% of project cost, including costs of design, construction, operation and maintenance. 42 U.S.C.A. § 3254b. * * * Under EPA standards, the proposed project could not duplicate a resource recovery system that had already been developed and operated at full scale; however, it could not be an untested system because the EPA Instructions provided that:

> "The feasibility of the unit processes of the proposed system must have been satisfactorily demonstrated in a pilot plant application at a sufficient rate to enable a reliable projection of the technical and economic performance of the proposed systems to be made. The operation must have been documented in a formal technical report."

* * * that a minimum of 60% (by dry weight) of the solid waste input must be converted to usable energy or recovered as saleable materials; * * *.

The action taken by the City to obtain an EPA demonstration grant was thoroughly documented by F. Pierce Linaweaver, the City's Director of Public Works, * * *.

* * *

The substance of Linaweaver's affidavit was confirmed and amplified by Dale Chapman, Vice President in charge of operations for Enviro-Chem, * * *. Both Linaweaver and Chapman unequivocally stated that Enviro-Chem was unique, of the some seventy companies investigated by the City, in possessing all the characteristics that the City was seeking.

Based on this evidence, the City selected Enviro-Chem's "Landgard" pyrolysis process as the subject of its demonstration grant application. In enumerating the reasons for the City's selection of Enviro-Chem, Linaweaver said in his affidavit: * * *

> *"This system was the only one which was technologically advanced to meet all the requirements of Baltimore City."* (Emphasis supplied.)

The City's application was one of sixty-six received by EPA; * * *.

Subsequent to the award, on November 30, 1972, EPA notified the City that:

" ＊ ＊ ＊ the awarded EPA funds can only be expended to demonstrate the Landgard solid waste pyrolysis system developed by Monsanto Enviro-Chem Systems, Inc.

＊ ＊ ＊

" ＊ ＊ ＊ the subject application was approved by EPA to demonstrate the Landgard system. No evidence has come to our attention that would indicate that anyone other than Monsanto Enviro-Chem Systems, Inc. could satisfactorily design and construct the Landgard system."

On condition that the project be that of Enviro-Chem, as specified in the EPA grant award, MES awarded $4,000,000 to the City to be applied to the contract price, as authorized by the provisions of Maryland Code (1957, 1971 Repl.Vol.), Article 33B, § 4.

I

It is undisputed that the contract between the City and Enviro-Chem is a contract for a public work, that it involves an expenditure of more than $5,000 and that the City neither advertised nor received bids in accordance with its Charter (1964 Rev.), Article VI, § 4(b), ＊ ＊ ＊.

Appellants contend that the charter requirements are mandatory. ＊ ＊ ＊ Appellants contend that there can be no exception to the competitive bid requirements other than those expressly outlined in § 4(d) of the Charter ＊ ＊ ＊. Clearly, the § 4(d) exceptions from the competitive bidding requirements do not expressly cover contracts for public works involving expenditures of $5,000 or more. The relevant inquiry, therefore, is whether § 4(b) admits of any exceptions other than those enumerated in § 4(d).

＊ ＊ ＊

＊ ＊ ＊ [C]ourts have allowed exceptions to a seemingly mandatory requirement of competitive bids in diverse types of unique situations. One line of cases concerns the purchase of patented objects: Consentino v. City of Omaha, 186 Neb. 407, 183 N.W.2d 475 (1971) (City's choice of patented process for waste treatment not subject to competitive bids); Hodgeman v. City of San Diego, 53 Cal.App.2d 610, 128 P.2d 412 (1942) (parking meters, each covered by a patent, were not standardized to point where competitive bidding was feasible or necessary); Cf. Worthington v. City of Boston, 152 U.S. 695, 704–705, 14 S.Ct. 737, 740, 38 L.Ed. 603, 606 (1894) (nothing could have been gained by competition among bidders, only one of whom was entitled to use the patented engine the City desired to obtain). Our predecessors recognized the futility of insisting on competitive bids where patented articles were involved ＊ ＊ ＊.

Judicially recognized exceptions to competitive bid statutes have not been limited to patented articles. See 10 McQuillin, *supra*, § 29.34 at 339–40; 1 Antieau, Municipal Corporation Law 757–60, § 10.28 (cum.supp.1972). In Whelan v. N.J. Power & Light Co., 45 N.J. 237, 212 A.2d 136 (1965), the competitive bid statute was held not to apply to the sale of City land to a utility for use as a power station since by contract, the only permissible buyer was the utility. In Mullen v. Town of Louisburg, 225 N.C. 53, 33 S.E.2d 484 (1945), it was held that the competitive bid statute did not apply to the wholesale purchase of electricity for there could be but one bidder and one price, the rate fixed by law. To the same effect, see Marino v. Town of Ramapo, 68 Misc.2d 44, 326 N.Y.S.2d 162 (1971); Kingsley v. City & County of Denver, 126 Colo. 194, 247 P.2d 805 (1952).

All of these cases are, of course, factually distinguishable from the instant case; however, a common thread runs through them all, namely, that where the object to be acquired is truly unique it would constitute a futile act, in the name of a policy which would not be served, to require competitive bidding. There are, as this court stated in Mayor and City Council of Baltimore v. Flack, *supra,* "two kinds of competition [underlying the competitive bidding policy]—the one, competition between different *things* which will equally answer the same general purpose; and the other, competition between the prices bid respectively upon *each* of those distinct things." 104 Md. at 128, 64 A. at 710. Where, therefore, the thing sought to be obtained by a municipality can by its nature be furnished by one and only one source, competition simply is not possible.

In contracting with Enviro-Chem, the City recognized that that company had no monopoly on pyrolysis as a technology for disposal of solid waste. On the contrary, the City always recognized that a number of other companies have such processes in various states of development. But, as reflected by the record, the processes differ materially in the extent to which they have been proven, in the equipment that they use, in the order in which the equipment is arranged, in the manner in which they operate, in the resources they recover, and in the results which they achieve. The City was not merely seeking a system by which to dispose of its solid wastes, with a wide range of alternatives open to it based upon differing characteristics between available systems; what it required was a particular system, materially different from all others, enabling it successfully to compete with other municipalities for a demonstration grant. * * * As so cogently observed by the City in its brief:

"To be eligible for a grant the process must meet requirements that reduce the [competing] candidates to a few. * * *

"Beyond that, it would obviously reduce the City's chance to win a grant if the City were to propose a particular process that was already the subject of a rival application by another city, because EPA would be unlikely to make two grants to demonstrate the same project * * *."

The singular nature of the contract between the City and Enviro-Chem, created by the factors hereinbefore enumerated, and particularly the immediate needs of the City to dispose of solid waste in large quantity (1,000 tons per day), to recover resources saleable in the area, to meet the pollution requirements of State law, and the need to obtain funding assistance through an EPA demonstration grant, narrowed the "competitiors" capable of fulfilling the City's need to one. * * * The trial judge found from the evidence that the City made a determination "that the proprietary process of Monsanto [Enviro-Chem] best suits the needs of the City"; that there was no evidence or suggestion of favoritism or corruption; that the circumstances presented not only the clear impracticability, but "the virtual impossibility" of competitive bidding; and that the policy behind the competitive bid statute— avoidance of corruption and economy to the taxpayers of Baltimore— had been met without competitive bids.

Appellants argue that since the municipal power to contract must be strictly construed [citations omitted] any reasonable doubt as to the existence of municipal power must be resolved against the City. They maintain that courts should not attempt, under the guise of construction, to imply the existence of exclusions in Charter provisions in addition to those expressly stated, citing Town of Somerset v. Montgomery County Board of Appeals, 245 Md. 52, 71–72, 225 A.2d 294, 306 (1966); State Insurance Commissioner v. Nationwide Mutual Ins. Co., 241 Md. 108, 117, 215 A.2d 749, 754–755 (1966).

While we agree with appellants' statement of the law, we find it inapplicable to the present case. * * * We do not think that the mere omission of "public works" from the express exceptions contained in § 4(d) represents an expression of deliberate exclusion calculated to require, under all circumstances, that competitive bids be obtained for all public works even where, by the nature of the project, no competition exists; * * *. Indeed, when the § 4(d) exceptions were first inserted in the 1946 revision of the Charter as § 37(b), there was little reason for anyone to foresee technological advances which could make public works as unique as supplies, materials, equipment and services.

We recognize the important protection provided by competitive bid provisions. We hold only that in the peculiarly unique factual situation of this case, competitive bidding was not required by the Charter.
* * *

* * *

Notes

1. **Experimental Procurement.** Courts are inclined to uphold awards to non-low bidders for projects that involve frontier technology. "With the development of technology the idea of what competition should be has changed. It is frequently difficult to determine which of several similar, complicated machines will serve the public at the lowest cost. * * * The contracting agency needs a wider latitude for the exercise of reasonable discretion." Rewco, Inc. v. Cleveland, 183 N.E.2d 646, 649 (Ohio Com.Pl.1961).

2. **Sole Source Procurement.** Sole source procurement is justified only where there is no adequate alternative: "We decline to rule flatly that competitive bidding requirements literally control every situation. Should

we do so, we would compel governing authorities at times to act against the public interest. Where a process or article is patented, public authorities may specify its use * * * in these circumstances. The process or article in their judgment possesses such exceptional superiority that it would be a public injury for the authorities not to use it [citations]. Similarly, a contract with an operator of a facility may be let without competitive bidding where highly specialized technical skills possessed only by him are required to operate the facility. See Potts v. City of Utica, 86 F.2d 616 (2d Cir.1936)." Cosentino v. Omaha, 186 Neb. 407, 413, 183 N.W.2d 475, 479 (1971). A court may refuse bidding exemption for patented or proprietary items where the patentee or owner is willing to provide such items to all bidders, or where other products or processes are equally satisfactory for the proposed work. See also Wurdeman v. Columbus, 100 Neb. 134, 158 N.W. 924 (1916).

Brand name products—Bid restriction to brand name products may be upheld because of proven reliability or special interchangeability with existing products. No problems arise where the product is generally available to all bidders on substantially equal terms, but some courts have discountenanced brand specifications as a violation of competitive bidding requirements. Specifications of a brand "or equal" item have been upheld where the "or equal" standard is not a sham. See e.g. City of Springfield v. Haydon, 216 Ky. 483, 288 S.W. 337 (1926); Hillig v. St. Louis, 337 Mo. 291, 85 S.W.2d 91 (1935); Hodge and Hammond, Inc. v. Burns, 23 Misc.2d 318, 202 N.Y.S.2d 133 (1960); 10 McQuillin, *Municipal Corporations* § 29.29 (3rd ed. 1966).

NATIONAL ELECTRICAL CONTRACTORS ASS'N v. BELLEVUE

Court of Appeals of Washington, 1969.
1 Wash.App. 81, 459 P.2d 420.

FARRIS, JUDGE.

In 1966, the City of Bellevue * * * determined to install several traffic control installations. No firm schedule was set, the installations to be completed at the discretion of the City.

* * * This action was commenced to enjoin the City from proceeding without public bids.

At issue is the operation of RCW 35.23.352:

"Any city or town of the second, third or fourth class may construct any public work or improvement by contract or day labor without calling for bids therefor whenever the estimated cost of such work or improvement, including cost of materials, supplies and equipment will not exceed the sum of five thousand dollars. Whenever the cost * * * will exceed five thousand dollars, the same shall be done by contract. All such contracts shall be let at public bidding * * *"

All parties agree that the issue is whether a third class city can, under RCW 35.23.352, separate work and material in determining whether an improvement exceeds the cost of $5,000.

The essential facts are not in dispute. The total cost of each traffic control installation (including the cost of material and labor) exceeds $5,000. As to one intersection now complete, the following took place:

In 1967, the City purchased signal control equipment

without taking bids $2,327.13

In 1967, the City purchased additional equipment with

bids... 1,746.00

In 1968, the City negotiated with a contractor to install

the equipment 2,434.85

In 1968, the City used its own personnel to complete

the installation................................. 565.15

Thus the total cost of the intersection was: $7,073.13

Upon these facts, the trial court entered judgment in favor of the City * * *

The Association contends that the trial court erred * * * In response, the City maintains that the statute allows it to acquire material in one year under one contract and install the equipment in another year under a separate contract. * * *

* * *

The City contends that an "improvement" may be divisible into several contracts under certain circumstances. It is argued that where equipment is acquired in one year and not installed until the next, it is unrealistic to require public bids. We do not agree.

A public project, for the purpose of applying RCW 35.23.352, is not divisible into cost of materials, equipment and labor, but is necessarily whole by the terms of the statute. The phrase "improvement, including cost of materials, supplies and equipment" leaves no room for construction. (Compare the school district purchasing statute RCW 28.58.135 considered by the Washington Supreme Court in National Elec. Contractors Ass'n etc. v. Seattle School Dist. No. 1, 66 Wash.2d 14, 400 P.2d 778 (1965) where the disjunctive language of the statute allowed the separation of the contract for purchase and the contract for installation.)

We do not find that the language of the statute prevents the City from completing an improvement phase by phase, if for reasons of budget or otherwise the City desires not to complete an entire project at once. However, the statute does require that the City put each phase out for public bid where the total estimated cost of an improvement *exceeds* $5,000.

A final question * * * is whether a city may decline to put any phase of an improvement up for public bid and do the work with its own personnel. This statute was enacted to effect the sound public policy that by competitive bidding, the public may receive the greatest benefit for the least expenditure. Reiter v. Chapman, 177 Wash. 392,

31 P.2d 1005, 92 A.L.R. 828 (1934). The city counsel is empowered by the statute to reject all bids

> " * * * if in its judgment the improvement * * * can be done by the city at less cost than the lowest bid submitted * * *." RCW 35.23.352

The City may then do the job itself. This provision of the statute bolsters our conclusion that the statute means what it says and that *whenever* the total cost exceeds $5,000 public bids must be called for. Therefore, even when the City would do a phase of the job with its own personnel, it must first call for public bids on that phase and reject the bids only if it can do the job at a lower cost than the lowest bid submitted.

The judgment is reversed, and the case remanded with instructions to enjoin the City of Bellevue from proceeding with the planned traffic control installations except in a manner consistent with this opinion.

Notes

1. **Split or Series Procurement.** Whether several contracts are truly separate or independent must be decided case by case. Where a series of contracts all go to the same contractor, and involve common subject matter or a common work project, courts tend to scrutinize them more strictly. Thus three separate orders for corrugated metal from the same supplier, although of different dimensions and used in different parts of the county, were held void for lack of bidding, where their accumulated value exceeded the statutory floor for competitive bidding. Armco Drainage and Metal Products v. Pinellas, 137 So.2d 234 (Fla.App.1962). *Accord:* Fonder v. South Sioux Falls, 76 S.D. 31, 71 N.W.2d 618 (1955) (series of gravel supply contracts to same supplier for maintenance of city streets over a period of time). But see Board of Educ. v. Hall, 353 S.W.2d 194 (Ky. 1962) where unbid supply contracts for diverse items from a common supplier were held to be separate and not governed by the bidding statutes, even though the items covered by those contracts were intended for the same public project. The case authorities are collected in Annots., *Public Contracts—Competitive Bidding,* 53 A.L.R.2d 498 (1957); 33 A.L.R.3d 397 (1970).

2. **Lawful Avoidance or Unlawful Evasion.** Courts lack hard guidelines to determine whether a transaction stems from unlawful favoritism in violation of bidding policy, or from a lawful judgment that a negotiated contract would better serve public convenience and need. A few illustrations follow.

Contracts Terminable at Will—Contracts for services at a specified hourly or weekly rate that were terminable on short notice by the city were held exempt from bidding requirements, even though their continuation for a sufficient period of time would accumulate charges in excess of the dollar minimum for competitive bids in a unitary contract. Lance Investigation Service, Inc., v. New York, 88 Misc.2d 119, 387 N.Y.S.2d 32 (1976) (security guard services); City of Evanston ex rel. Johnson v. Risinger, 116 Ill.App.2d 420, 253 N.E.2d 918 (1969) (tree pruning services). Similarly, equipment rentals of indefinite duration, at per diem rates, terminable at will, were held exempt from bid requirements. Sanitary Dist. of Chicago v. George F. Blake Mfg. Co., 179 Ill. 167, 53 N.E. 627 (1899).

Combination and Package Deals—Bid work may not be packaged to exclude competition. "By compelling bids on a combination basis * * * available bidders were necessarily restricted. * * * We think the situation, as a whole, tended too much to favor monopoly, deny equal opportunity of bidding, restrict competitive bidding, and add unnecessary burdens upon those who, in the last analysis, will be required to pay for this public improvement." Weiss v. Incorporated Town of Woodbine, 228 Iowa 1, 13, 289 N.W. 469, 475 (1940). Since package deals can result in economies of time and cost, and in assured quality, their validity, like splitting, often comes down to the issue of reasonable exercise of administrative discretion.

Noncomparable Bids—Where courts permit bid specifications which invite similar, alternate or assortment bids, a broader range of discretion to reject low bids may be justified, depending upon the subject matter of the proposed contract. Thus, a more efficient, but higher priced offer may be preferred. Austin v. Housing Authority of City of Hartford, 143 Conn. 338, 122 A.2d 399 (1956) (dividend-paying insurance policy preferred over lower cost non-dividend policy); Mayer Brothers Const. Co. v. Erie Parking Authority, 187 Pa.Super. 1, 149 A.2d 495 (1959) (bid for concrete paving preferred over lower bid for blacktop paving); Paul Goldman, Inc. v. Burns, 109 R.I. 236, 283 A.2d 673 (1971) (higher priced bid for automobiles of same manufacture and model as existing fleet, preferred over lower bid for automobiles of different make, which would require a new stock of spare maintenance parts). But see Schwartz and Nagle Tires v. Board of Chosen Freeholders of Middlesex County, 6 N.J.Super. 79, 69 A.2d 805 (1949) (township could not prefer non-low bid for tire supply contract, based upon difference in the brand and manufacture of tires).

Emergencies—"To state what constitutes an emergency is not an easy task. The term depends greatly upon the special circumstances of each case, and the authorities are not very helpful in the present inquiry. By definition, the term emergency implies a sudden or unexpected necessity requiring speedy action." Los Angeles Dredging Co. v. Long Beach, 210 Cal. 348, 356, 291 P. 839, 843 (1930); see also Rodin v. Director of Purchasing of Town of Hempstead, 38 Misc.2d 362, 238 N.Y.S.2d 2 (1963).

Cases requiring prompt action to protect the public health and safety, *viz.* to cure disruption in essential power, water, transit or sanitation services, easily qualify as emergencies, but there are grey areas where courts may disagree. This is especially true where the emergency exception is created judicially and not by express legislation. Some bid statutes expressly require a judicial finding of emergency as a precondition of awarding contracts without bidding. Scatuorchio v. Jersey City Incinerator Authority, 14 N.J. 72, 100 A.2d 869 (1953).

Legislative findings of emergency command respect but not blind adherence by the courts. In Grimm v. Troy, 60 Misc.2d 579, 303 N.Y.S.2d 170 (1969) a taxpayer challenged an unbid contract for garbage disposal equipment pursuant to City Council resolution. The city charter required bidding on such contracts * * * "unless the city council, by ordinance, determines that it is impossible or impractical to purchase or sell in such manner." The State General Municipal Law also authorized award of unbid contracts in cases of emergency "by the appropriate officer, board or agency." The court upheld the contract. But in Raynor v. Commissioners for Town of Louisburg, 220 N.C. 348, 352, 17 S.E.2d 495, 498 (1941), the court stated:

> "The governing body of a municipality cannot declare an emergency where none exists and thus defeat the provisions of a law. While we may treat their determination with some degree of liberality * * * its findings are not beyond review. [citations] Judicial opinion differs somewhat as to the consideration which should be given to the declaration of municipal authority that an emergency exists and the manner in which the evidence upon which the findings are made may be reviewed. Los Angeles Dredging Co. v. City of Long Beach, 210 Cal. 348, 291 P. 839, 71 A.L.R. 161 (1930); Continental Construction Co. v. City of Lawrence, 297 Mass. 513, 9 N.E.2d 550, 111 A.L.R. 699 (1937). The city council * * * is not a court whose findings of fact are binding upon appellate courts where there is evidence to support them. [Citation] Administrative boards, although necessarily called upon to find facts * * * are not usually immune from review of their conclusions * * * unless the law of their creation or some supplemental statute makes them so."

The emergency exception applies as well to contract amendments: "In the course of a construction contract, *bona fide* emergencies may well arise * * * Where the resulting additional expenditures are reasonable and are conscientiously viewed as being in fulfillment of the original undertaking rather than as departing therefrom [citations] it would clearly be contrary to the public interest to halt the undertaking and call for bidding with respect to the additional work entailed by the emergency * * *. It may fairly be assumed that the Legislature did not contemplate the halting of the undertaking pending a further specific appropriation for the additional work required by the emergency. * * *" Home Owners Const. Co. v. Glen Rock, 34 N.J. 305, 315, 169 A.2d 129, 134 (1961).

3. **Amendments to Properly Awarded Contracts.** "We recognize that a generally accepted rule is that where a statute requires that a contract * * * be let to the lowest responsible bidder, municipal corporations * * * cannot evade the law by making a substantial change in the contract after it had been awarded pursuant to the law. If the deviations * * * vary so substantially from the original plan as to constitute a new undertaking, the contract could be let only by competitive bidding. However, in order to render the contract void because of the changes or deviations, the same must be substantial." City of Crockett v. Murdock, 440 S.W.2d 864, 867 (Tex.Civ.App.1969).

Which of the following changes qualifies as a "substantial" deviation within the foregoing rule? Changes escalating the original contract price due to (a) increased contractor costs caused by the city's default in providing preparatory arrangements for the contractor's work; (b) cost escalations due to unforeseeable land conditions, *viz.* poor drainage or subsoil conditions; (c) city "add-on" of work area or materials requirements; (d) changes in city engineering or design specifications. As to (b) and (c) see Thomsen-Abbott Construction Co. v. Wausau, 9 Wis.2d 225, 100 N.W.2d 921 (1960); the *Blum* case, p. 765 infra.

Where the original contract provides that the same may be extended or renewed upon terms to be negotiated and agreed upon in the future, viz. in long term lease and concession agreements, may they be upheld as reasonable solutions to practical problems? Cf. Wiener v. Reno, 88 Nev. 127, 494 P.2d 277 (1972).

4. **Attempted Ratification of Unbid Contracts.** Under the better authority, contracts issued in violation of competitive bidding legislation cannot be validated by ratification. Since municipal officials would lack authority to approve such a contract at the outset, they could not claim authority to give it legal effect retrospectively. Board of Education of Floyd County v. Hall, 353 S.W.2d 194 (Ky.1962); Zottman v. San Francisco, 20 Cal. 96 (1862).

(1) Administrative Requirements

JAMES PETROZELLO CO. v. CHATHAM TP.

Superior Court of New Jersey, Appellate Div., 1962.
75 N.J.Super. 173, 178–80, 182 A.2d 572, 575–76.

KILKENNY, J.A.D.

* * *

To conform with statutory requirements, N.J.S.A. 40:50–1, specifications in an invitation to bid "must be as definite, precise and full as practicable in view of the character of the work, the quality and quantity of the materials to be furnished." Waszen v. Atlantic City, 137 N.J.L. 535, 537, 61 A.2d 85, 86 (Sup.Ct.1948), reversed on other grounds 1 N.J. 272, 63 A.2d 255 (1949). The specifications must "furnish the same information to all prospective bidders, so that there may be intelligent bidding." Phifer v. Bayonne, 105 N.J.L. 524, 525, 146 A. 463, 464 (Sup.Ct.1929). To invalidate an award for a deficiency in the specifications, "the irregularity must be of a substantial nature—such as will operate to affect fair and competitive bidding." Phifer v. Bayonne, supra, 105 N.J.L. at p. 527, 146 A. 463, 465. Invitations for bids in the form of unit prices, under proper circumstances, are not objectionable. Browning v. Freeholders of Bergen, 79 N.J.L. 494, 76 A. 1054 (E. & A.1910); Armaniaco v. Cresskill, 62 N.J.Super. 476, 163 A.2d 379 (App.Div.1960). However, where the unit price method is employed, fair estimates of the quantities to be ordered should wherever possible, be specified in advance of the bidding to avoid any possible juggling of the figures in aid of a favorite bidder. Browning v. Freeholders of Bergen, supra. The giving of the estimates is for the express purpose of forming a basis for the "uniform comparison of bids." Walter v. McClellan, 113 App.Div. 295, 99 N.Y.S. 78, 79 (App.Div.1906); Interstate Power Co. v. Forest City, 225 Iowa 490, 281 N.W. 207 (Sup.Ct.

1938); Best v. City of Omaha, 138 Neb. 325, 293 N.W. 116 (Sup.Ct.1940); 10 McQuillin, Municipal Corporations (3d ed.1950), § 29.54, p. 316.

Plaintiffs do not attack the propriety of seeking unit price bids. Rather, they rely mainly on the failure of the township to furnish in advance of the receipt of bids any estimates of quantities, upon the basis of which there could be a uniform comparison of the bids and determination of the lowest responsible bidder. * * *

In the instant case, by failing to indicate estimates before bids were received, it lay within the arbitrary power of the township committee to favor either of these two low bidders. If it were desired that Petrozello should get the contract, expected future growth and the times thereof in the several categories could have been minimized so that the $5000 differential in Petrozello's lump sum bid for removal of garbage from existing structures would not have been offset by his higher unit price bids on future buildings. Justification for such a pessimistic viewpoint could have been found in local statistics showing a diminishing of building permits issued for new residences; in the absence of garden-type apartments in the community and the unlikelihood of such development unless liberal zoning amendments were adopted; in the need for a central sewerage system whose cost might present a local financial problem; and by regarding the construction of a new office building, municipal building, and an elementary school as not probable during the life of this garbage contract. Conversely, future development could have been viewed optimistically, if the committee wanted to favor Roselle with his lower unit prices as to future buildings to whatever extent needed to overcome Petrozello's differential of $5000 on the base bid.

* * *

Notes

1. **Advertisement.** Invitations to bid must give sufficient facts to enable bidders intelligently to submit their bids. A bidder who fails to meet the material conditions of the advertising proposal is not entitled to consideration of his bid, and it must be rejected. Parks & Sons v. Pocatello, 91 Idaho 241, 419 P.2d 683 (1966).

The rule on conformity of bids to specifications may also be tested negatively. "Whether or not there is a material variance 'is determined largely with reference to whether the bidder's proposal gives him an advantage or benefit which is not enjoyed by other bidders.'" Claus v. Badiarz, 40 Del. Ch. 500, 507, 185 A.2d 283, 287 (1962); cf. Duffy v. Princeton, 240 Minn. 9, 60 N.W.2d 27 (1953) (holding a departure from engine repair specifications to be insubstantial).

2. **Rigging the Bid Via Specifications.** Where a bid specification is drawn to match the product or services exclusively of one supplier, without apparent justification courts will invalidate the action as a violation of the statutory mandate. Resco Equipment & Sup. Corp. v. City Council of Watertown, 34 A.D.2d 1088, 313 N.Y.S.2d 74 (1970); Gamewell Co. v. Phoenix, 216 F.2d 928 (9th Cir.1954); Gerzof, infra, p. 769.

Given the discretion accorded to contracting officials, it is often difficult to determine whether narrowly drawn specifications are objective and neutral, or are discriminatory. This is particularly true of architect and engineering work. Some 12 states have attempted to deter bid-rigging by criminal and civil penalties. See Kandell, Pennsylvania's Antibid-Rigging Statute, 30 Vill.L.Rev. 63, n. 2 (1985).

3. **Restricting the Bid Group—Exclusion of Aliens; and Local Preference Requirements.** In earlier decisions some courts upheld bid limitations which excluded aliens or newly resident bidders (10 McQuillin, *Municipal Corporations,* § 29.45 et seq. (3rd ed. 1966), but such restrictions are undercut by decisions which constitutionally bar official discrimination against aliens and new residents. See e.g. Sugarman v. Dougall, 413 U.S. 634, 93 S.Ct. 2842, 37 L.Ed.2d 853 (1973); Salla v. Monroe, 48 N.Y.2d 514, 423 N.Y.S.2d 878, 399 N.E.2d 909 (1979).

Where bidding disqualification or preference is indirectly effected by legislation that authorizes price preference or differential to domestic taxpayers, or requires the use of local labor and materials for the contract under bid, other policies must be adjusted. Local preference requirements, may promote public interest, by assurance of adequate and prompt delivery. But, such preferences restrict competition, and may violate the federal constitution, *viz.* by burdening or discriminating against interstate commerce. See 10 McQuillin, *Municipal Corporations,* § 29.47 (3rd ed. 1966) or travel. After finding no antitrust violation in a city requirement of 50% resident workforce on city funded projects (White v. Massachusetts Council of Construction Employers, 460 U.S. 204, 103 S.Ct. 1042, 75 L.Ed.2d 1 (1983)), the Supreme Court held that a similar requirement by Camden City, New Jersey, would violate the privileges and immunities clause of the federal constitution unless the city could demonstrate a substantial justification for preferring its residents. United Bldg. & Const. v. Mayor and Council of Camden, 465 U.S. 208, 104 S.Ct. 1020, 79 L.Ed.2d 249 (1984). See Annot., Public Works—Residence Preferred, 36 A.L.R. 4th 941 (1985).

4. **Other Bidders.** In City Council of City of Beverly Hills v. Superior Court for County of Los Angeles, 272 Cal.App.2d 876, 77 Cal.Rptr. 850 (1969), the court upheld the requirement that the bidder must hold a special, as well as general, license relating to the type of work being bid upon, even though the requirement incidentally reduced the number of competing bidders.

Wage Standards—Requirements that bidders on public work pay specified minimum wages clash with the policy of obtaining public work at the lowest possible cost. The courts are divided on the resolution of these policy conflicts. See the authorities reviewed in Parish Council of East Baton Rouge v. Louisiana Highway and Heavy Branch of Ass'n Gen. Contractors, Inc., 131 So.2d 272 (La.App.1961).

Where federal subsidies for a local government project are conditioned upon compliance with federal minimum wage policy, what dispositions may a court make in a state where a minimum wage term had been struck down as violating bidding legislation? Cf. Marino v. Ramapo, 68 Misc.2d 44, 326 N.Y.S.2d 162 (1971).

Union Labor and Products—In the absence of countervailing federal or state laws, courts have held that municipal authorities may not discriminate between union and non-union sources in the award of competitively bid contracts. Upchurch v. Adelsberger, 231 Ark. 682, 332 S.W.2d 242 (1960); Van Campen v. Building and Construction Trades Council, 202 Pa. Super. 118, 195 A.2d 134 (1963). The rule is subject to exception in certain circumstances, e.g. where the threat of strike delays or interference justifies a determination that a non-union bidder is not "responsible," in terms of assuring timely completion. Pallas v. Johnson, 100 Colo. 449, 68 P.2d 559 (1937).

(2) Lowest "Responsible" Bidder

CITY OF INGLEWOOD—L.A. COUNTY CIVIC CENTER AUTHORITY v. SUPERIOR COURT

Supreme Court of California, 1972.
7 Cal.3d 861, 500 P.2d 601.

MOSK, JUSTICE.

Petitioners seek mandate to compel respondent superior court to annul its judgment * * *. The respondent court's judgment restrained petitioner City of Inglewood—Los Angeles County Civic Center Authority (Authority) from executing or performing a contract awarded to Swinerton & Walberg Co. (Swinerton) relating to the construction of a civic center project. The mandate proceeding * * * was instituted by real party in interest, Argo Construction Co., Inc. (Argo), to have the contract award annulled and set aside.

Section 25454 of the Government Code provides that a contract for a "construction project" exceeding $6,500 must be awarded to the "lowest responsible bidder." Argo was the lowest bidder and it claims that the contract was improperly issued to Swinerton. The primary issues involved in this proceeding are (1) whether the section is applicable to the type of contract awarded here; (2) whether, if so, the Authority applied the appropriate standard in determining that Swinerton was the lowest responsible bidder, and (3) whether a contractor who has submitted the lowest monetary bid is entitled to a full judicial hearing to determine if he is responsible. The trial court found in Argo's favor, * * *.

Petitioner Authority was constituted pursuant to a "joint exercise of powers agreement" entered into in February 1970 by the City of Inglewood and the County of Los Angeles. * * * The Authority is a separate and distinct public entity. * * * It was established to construct the City of Inglewood—Los Angeles County Civic Center, which was planned to include both city and county buildings. * * *

Charles Luckman Associates (Luckman) was retained by the Authority as architects, and prepared preliminary plans for the civic center buildings, a $12,000,000 project. Luckman recommended that the Authority proceed with the construction of the project by means of a management contract. The operation of the management contracting method was summarized by Luckman as follows:

> "Under the traditional lump sum method of bidding, contractors enter the project process upon the completion of working drawings. At this point in time they have little opportunity or incentive to contribute to cost reduction.

> "The Management Contracting Method * * * differs from this traditional lump sum method in that the contractor is brought into the building project through competitive bidding at or shortly after, the completion of preliminary plans, rather than working drawings. He is then called upon to contribute his practical expertise during the development of the working drawings, and subsequently apply this expertise during construction, in order to achieve maximum economies. He is expected to provide cost estimates * * * to determine that the project is within budget so that some of the early phases of construction can proceed prior to completion of all of the drawings. This makes it possible to save a significant amount of time in the total building process." The management contractor performs none of the construction itself unless he is awarded a separate contract therefor as the lowest responsible bidder in subsequent bidding under the traditional "lump sum" bidding procedures.

The management contracting procedure was approved by the Inglewood City Council, and Swinerton was awarded the contract * * *.

I

Petitioners urge that the management contract here at issue was basically a contract for services as a consultant and supervisor-manager rather than a contract for a "construction project" and thus did not fall within the competitive bidding requirements upon which Argo relies. Those requirements are found in the Government Code and in the charter of the City of Inglewood as well as in the joint exercise of powers agreement. They provide that public construction of the magnitude here involved shall be accomplished by contract let to the lowest responsible bidder.

It is true that the management contractor was to perform services and to lend his * * * expertise in the preparation of the final plans, and in that respect may be likened to an engineer or an architect whose services may be procured without strict compliance with competitive bidding requirements. * * * However, our review of the other duties and obligations which were required of the management contractor in this case, * * * persuades us that the management contracting procedure as * * * is too closely akin to traditional lump sum general construction contracting to be held exempt from the statutory competitive bidding requirements. To hold otherwise as a broad principle would open the door to possible favoritism, fraud or corruption in the letting of other public construction contracts.

II

The next issue is whether petitioners applied the proper standards in determining that Swinerton was the lowest responsible bidder. * * * It bears emphasis that the word "responsible" in the context of the statute is not necessarily employed in the sense of a bidder who is trustworthy so that a finding of nonresponsibility connotes untrustworthiness. Rather, while that term includes the attribute of trustworthiness, it also has reference to the quality, fitness and capacity of the low bidder to satisfactorily perform the proposed work. (See West v. Oakland (1916), 30 Cal.App. 556, 560, 159 P. 202.) Thus, a contract must be awarded to the lowest bidder unless it is found that he is not responsible, *i.e.,* not qualified to do the particular work under consideration. * * *

The parties are in agreement that factors such as those set forth above may be considered in determining whether a bidder is responsible. Argo challenges the award of the management contract to Swinerton not because petitioners employed such criteria but because petitioners made no determination, either express or implied, that Argo was not responsible. Instead, it is asserted, petitioners found Swinerton to be the relatively superior bidder and awarded the contract on this basis. Argo cogently argues: "To permit a local public works contracting agency to expressly or impliedly reject the bid of a qualified and responsible lowest monetary bidder in favor of a higher bidder deemed to be more qualified frustrates the very purpose of competitive bidding laws and violates the interest of the public in having public works projects awarded without favoritism, without excessive cost, and constructed at the lowest price consistent with the reasonable quality and expectation of completion."

We agree with these assertions, and we hold that the contract for a public construction project must be awarded to the lowest monetary bidder * * * unless it is found that the lowest bidder is not responsible, in the sense defined above. There is no basis for the application of a relative superiority concept, * * * and if petitioners applied such standard in selecting Swinerton rather than Argo as the contractor, the award cannot stand.

The trial court found that petitioners chose to award the contract to Swinerton because they viewed Swinerton as more qualified than Argo and that the qualifications of Argo to perform the contract were never questioned. An examination of the procedure followed in making the award lends credence to the trial court findings.

* * *

Twelve bids were received. They were reviewed, analyzed, and evaluated by Luckman as architect and by the staff of the director of public works of the city (reviewing panel). The bids of nine were rejected, and it was ultimately determined that Argo and Swinerton were among the three lowest bidders. Under the formula applied to determine the total bid cost Argo's bid was some $70,000 lower than that of Swinerton. Swinerton achieved 34 on the financial responsibility information questionnaire, while Argo obtained a score of 30, the minimum necessary for qualification.

Thereafter, each of the three lowest bidders was interviewed by the reviewing panel, * * * The three contractors were evaluated in terms of their construction experience, completion ability, personnel, work load, and client relationships. Again, a uniform point system was applied, this time to reflect the performance capabilities of the three low bidders. Out of a maximum of 61 points, Swinerton rated highest with 55 points, while Argo scored second with 42 points.

The reviewing panel * * * recommended that Swinerton be awarded the contract as the lowest responsible bidder. The report did not state that Argo was unqualified to perform the job but pointed out that, based upon the evaluation scores and the interviews, the panel believed that by selecting Swinerton the city would obtain excellent construction talent, experience, and other qualities important to the successful completion of the project. The architect representative on the panel, in a separate report to the Authority, stated that while Argo was considered capable within its field of construction, Swinerton's qualifications were considered to be so superior as to justify its selection as the lowest responsible bidder.

The recommendations of the reviewing panel were discussed by members of the Authority on December 17, 1970. At that meeting, the public works director * * * explained the panel's choice of Swinerton. He emphasized, for example, that Argo was primarily a school contractor and the maximum height it had built was four stories, whereas Swinerton had experience with high rise structures (the city's project was deemed a high rise building). * * * Representatives of Argo contended at the meeting that the contract could only be awarded to Swinerton if the Authority found Argo to be irresponsible, and that Argo was in fact qualified to do the job.

The Authority adopted a resolution awarding the contract to Swinerton. * * *

It is evident from the procedure followed by the Authority that, as Argo charges and the trial court found, petitioner merely determined that Swinerton was superior to Argo in its ability to perform the contract, and that no determination was made whether in fact Argo, the lowest bidder, was also qualified to perform the contract. Since petitioners did not comply with the mandate of section 25454 that the contract be awarded to the lowest responsible bidder, the award must be set aside. (Miller v. McKinnon (1942), 20 Cal.2d 83, 87–88, 124 P.2d 34.)

III

Finally, it is contended that the award to Swinerton must be set aside because Argo was not afforded a full evidentiary hearing as to whether it was a responsible bidder. Due process requires, asserts

Argo, that prior to awarding a contract to one who is not the low monetary bidder, the Authority must conduct a hearing, which shall include a full panoply of judicial trial procedures, including pleadings, cross-examination of witnesses, and formal findings. No case so holding is called to our attention, and Housing Authority of Opelousas, La. v. Pittman Const. Co. (5th Cir.1959) 264 F.2d 695, upon which Argo places great reliance, is to the contrary.

In that case, Louisiana law provided that a public works contract must be awarded to the lowest responsible bidder, but a higher bidder had received the award primarily on the basis of evidence received by the awarding authority from the higher bidder casting doubt upon the low bidder's responsibility. The contractor submitting the low bid was not present at the meeting and was not afforded an opportunity to rebut the charges prior to the award. It was held that the low bidder was entitled to be informed of the charges made against him and to reply to those charges. However, opined the court, the awarding authority was not required to "conduct FBI investigations, hold elaborate hearings, adhere to legal rules of evidence, and function as a judicial body." (264 F.2d at p. 704.)

We hold that prior to awarding a public works contract to other than the lowest bidder, a public body must notify the low monetary bidder of any evidence reflecting upon his responsibility received from others or adduced as a result of independent investigation, afford him an opportunity to rebut such adverse evidence, and permit him to present evidence that he is qualified to perform the contract. We do not believe, however, that due process compels a quasi-judicial proceeding prior to rejection of the low monetary bidder as a nonresponsible bidder.

Let a peremptory writ of mandate issue directing the trial court to vacate its judgment * * * and to make new findings and conclusions of law and enter a new judgment in accordance with the principles set forth herein.

PETERS, TOBRINER and SULLIVAN, JJ., concur.

BURKE, JUSTICE (dissenting).

I dissent. If this case had involved an ordinary municipal construction contract, I would concur without reservation in the view that a "relative superiority" test is inappropriate to determine the "lowest responsible bidder," as that phrase is used in applicable charter or statutory provisions. It seems evident to me, however, that the management contract here at issue was more in the nature of a contract for services as a consultant and supervisor-manager, and that in the award of such contracts the governing board may properly consider a number of factors in addition to the amount bid in discharging its responsibility.

* * *

As the majority acknowledge, strict compliance with competitive bidding requirements need not be maintained in procuring an expert's services to prepare plans and specifications. * * * As noted in San Francisco v. Boyd, 17 Cal.2d 606, 620, 110 P.2d 1036, 1044: "The employment of a person who is highly and technically skilled in his science or profession is one which may properly be made without competitive bidding." In *San Francisco,* the approved employment was of a civil engineer to aid in the solution of traffic and transit problems. (See also Cobb v. Pasadena City Bd. of Education, 134 Cal.App.2d 93, 95, 285 P.2d 41.) * * * I would emphasize that every bidder was given advance notice of the bid evaluation system; bidders were told that an award would be made on the basis of the bidder's financial resources, surety and insurance experience, construction experience, completion ability, personnel, equipment and work load, as well as the amount of the bid. * * * It is significant that at no time prior to the bid opening did Argo or any of the bidders object to the method of evaluating or awarding bids or to the method of bid solicitation. And nothing in the record suggests that the Authority may have acted with an improper motive in awarding the contract to Swinerton.

As the majority concede, the term "lowest responsible bidder" is broad enough to include the attributes of quality, fitness and capacity to perform. * * * In the context of the "hybrid" management contract involved herein, I see no reason whatever for denying the Authority the right to evaluate, on the basis of objective criteria selected and announced in advance of bid solicitation, the quality, fitness and capacity of the respective bidders, and to award that contract to the bidder shown by application of those criteria to be the best qualified.

Notes

1. Compare: Vellaco v. Derby, 27 Conn.Sup. 135, 232 A.2d 335 (1966) (favoring higher bidder with substantially more prompt completion schedule); with Guerriero v. Board of Contract and Supply, 60 Misc.2d 22, 301 N.Y.S.2d 103 (1969), where the court upheld an award to an inexperienced second lowest bidder which assigned its contract to an experienced company. "The fact that the judgment may have been erroneous or naive would not justify the interference of the Court in the Board's decision in the absence of proof of illegality, fraud, collusion, corruption or bad faith." Id. at 27, 301 N.Y.S.2d at 108; accord: Slocum v. Medford, 302 Mass. 251, 18 N.E.2d 1013 (1939).

The better view is that courts will overturn a capricious, though not fraudulent, exercise of discretion as to who is the lowest "responsible" bidder. See 10 McQuillin, *Municipal Corporations* § 29.73 (3rd ed. 1966). Brown v. Phoenix, 77 Ariz. 368, 272 P.2d 358 (1954) disapproved an award to the second lowest bidder on the basis of its past reliable service. "The problem under consideration is the extent and nature of the powers vested in the council * * * where the charter provides that such leases shall be made * * * to the highest responsible bidder and then grants to the council discretion 'to reject any and all bids.' * * * [A]s between two bidders equally responsible the municipality cannot reject the lower bid.

∗   ∗   ∗ The cases agree that the power to grant the contract to the highest (or, in the ordinary situation, the lowest) *responsible* bidder, implies an exercise of discretion in determining responsibility, for that word embraces such elements as the bidder's integrity, skill, capacity, experience, and facilities for doing the work. ∗   ∗   ∗ Likewise the power to reject any or all bids is a further grant of discretionary power. ∗   ∗   ∗ Can it be said that this high trust was here fulfilled? We think not. If a lease may be granted to the lower bidder because ∗   ∗   ∗ the council has a sense of loyalty to him for past services ∗   ∗   ∗ or because he pioneered in the business, or is recommended ∗   ∗   ∗ then by a reductio ad absurdum the lease might be granted to one ∗   ∗   ∗ because he had six children to support ∗   ∗   ∗. Such nonsense serves only to illustrate that the word 'discretion' does not mean 'caprice' ∗   ∗   ∗. ∗   ∗   ∗ Nor does the fact that there is no evidence of fraud or corruption on the part of the city council, and that what they did was done openly ∗   ∗   ∗ cure the evil complained of, i.e. favoritism ∗   ∗   ∗." Id. at 372–76, 272 P.2d at 361–64; accord: Pensacola v. Kirby, 47 So.2d 533 (Fla.1950). Criteria for exercising discretion regarding bidder responsibility seldom are, expressly stipulated by statute law. See e.g. Vernon's Ann.Tex.Civ.St. art. 644–3, § 8(e).

2. **Measures of "Responsibility".** Contrary to the principal case, some courts adopt the relative-superiority test. See Commercial Cleaning Corp. v. Sullivan, 47 N.J. 539, 222 A.2d 4 (1966); Jerry's Rides, Inc. v. Mayor and City Council of Baltimore, 226 Md. 161, 172 A.2d 487 (1961).

(a) *Moral Integrity.* The quantum of requisite moral responsibility bidder must have is not defined by statute, but must be discerned from judicial opinions. See e.g. Trapp Rock v. Kohl, 59 N.J. 471, 284 A.2d 161 (1971) (temporary disqualification based upon the bidder's indictment for bribery); Zara Contracting Co. v. Cohen, 45 Misc.2d 497, 257 N.Y.S.2d 479 (1964), affirmed 23 A.D.2d 718, 257 N.Y.S.2d 118 (1965) (bidder disqualified for indictment regarding theft of building supplies from a highway project); Venneri Co. v. Housing Authority of City of Paterson, 29 N.J. 392, 149 A.2d 228 (1959) (holding irresponsible a bidder who was previously barred from federal contracting for violating anti-gratuity regulations); Kayfield Const. Corp. v. Morris, 15 A.D.2d 373, 225 N.Y.S.2d 507 (1962) (bidder disqualified for gifts to public employees in violation of the city charter).

(b) *Potential Conflict of Interest.* Noting that saving money is not the exclusive test in competitive bidding, W. Paynter Sharp & Son, Inc. v. Heller, 280 A.2d 748 (Del.Ch.1971) upheld denial of award to a member of a state agency whose work related to the agency that awarded the contract. Another court upheld a specification which disqualified any bidder which was in litigation with the contracting authority. Reed Const. Co. v. Jackson Municipal Airport Authority, 227 So.2d 466 (Miss.1969).

(c) *Reliability.* Reliability includes financial soundness, business skill and experience, product quality, and past performance of public contracts. See e.g. Kandel v. Greene, 236 App.Div. 607, 260 N.Y.S. 502 (1932) (rejection of low bidder for lack of operating experience—upheld); J.N. Futia Co. v. Office of General Services, 39 A.D.2d 136, 332 N.Y.S.2d 261 (1972) (rejection based upon record of past delays and lack of cooperation in other public contracts—upheld); Raymond v. Fresno City Unified School Dist.,

123 Cal.App.2d 626, 267 P.2d 69 (1954) (similar rejection, based upon prior poor work—upheld); *semble:* Automatic Laundries v. Housing Authority of City of Bayonne, 45 N.J.Super. 266, 132 A.2d 42 (1957).

The potential weight of financial resources is illustrated by Hillside Township, Union County v. Sternin, 25 N.J. 317, 136 A.2d 265 (1957) where the court sustained a requirement that bids be accompanied by a deposit of funds, even though the rejected bidder was willing to provide a performance bond.

3. **Administrative Discretion.** Since the prescription of "lowest responsible bidder" embraces several characteristics, the scope of administrative discretion as to each characteristic is crucial. There is no rule on the limits of discretion in such situations—other than the broad pronouncement that discretion must be "reasonable."

4. **Procedural Due Process in Bidder Disqualificiation.** The right to a hearing by a bidder whose responsibility has been questioned may be expressly conferred by statutes. Seacoast Construction Corp. v. Lockport Urban Renewal Agency, 72 Misc.2d 372, 339 N.Y.S.2d 188 (1972).

SWINERTON & WALBERG CO. v. CITY OF INGLEWOOD—L.A. COUNTY CIVIC CENTER AUTHORITY

Court of Appeal, Second District, Division 3, 1974.
40 Cal.App.3d 98, 114 Cal.Rptr. 834.

[Appeal from dismissal of suit by Argo Construction Co. Inc., low bidder, seeking damages and declaratory relief for misaward of contract to second low bidder.]

COBEY, J. * * *

We shall now consider whether Argo stated in this pleading facts sufficient to constitute any of the foregoing causes of action it alleged.

THE FIRST CAUSE OF ACTION—TORT

The first question posed is whether the misaward by a public entity (the Authority) of a public works contract to one (Swinerton) other than the lowest responsible bidder (Argo) gives to the latter a cause of action in tort for monetary damages against the public entity. This precise question has been answered in the negative by the Third District of the statewide court less than four years ago in Rubino v. Lolli, 10 Cal.App. 3d 1059 [89 Cal.Rptr. 320]. That decision, of course, is not binding upon us. (See Danley v. Superior Court, 64 Cal.App. 594, 599, 222 P. 362; 6 Witkin, Cal. Procedure (2d ed. 1971) Appeal, § 667, p. 4580.) But we find its rationale quite persuasive. There the court pointed out that competitive bidding requirements appear to have been imposed solely for the benefit and protection of the public rather than for the benefit of the bidders. (*Rubino,* p. 1062.) The court consequently held that the misaward of a public works contract to one other than the lowest responsible bidder constitutes only an abuse of discretion by the awarding entity in determining the identity of such bidder and therefore the making of the misaward comes within the discretionary immunity to tort liability established by sections 815, 815.2, subdivision (b), and 820.2. (*Id.,* pp. 1063–1064.) Thus, in *Rubino* recovery of monetary damages in tort by the lowest responsible bidder was denied on the basis of discretionary immunity.

Argo urges us not to follow *Rubino,* but instead to follow, in part at least, Southern Cal. Acoustics Co. v. C.V. Holder, Inc., 71 Cal.2d 719, 79 Cal.Rptr. 319, 456 P.2d 975, where our Supreme Court held that a listed subcontractor may enforce his statutory right under section 4107 to perform the subcontract by an action for monetary damages against the prime contractor to recover the benefit of the bargain the listed subcontractor would have realized if he had not been wrongfully deprived of the subcontract. (*Id.,* p. 727.) In this case our Supreme Court determined that the purpose of the basic statute involved (Subletting and Subcontracting Fair Practices Act) was to protect both the public and subcontractors from the proscribed evils of unfair bid peddling and bid shopping. (*Id.*) Its basis for so determining was the just-stated title of the statute and section 4101. * * *

We have no quarrel with this determination, but in our view, it has no application to the competitive bidding requirements involved in this case. There is nothing in these requirements, as there was in the construction industry's Fair Practices Act * * * to lead one to infer reasonably that competitive bidding requirements were imposed for the benefit of the bidders as well as for the benefit of the public. * * *

Accordingly, we hold that Argo did not state facts in its cross-complaint sufficient to constitute a cause of action in tort for breach of a statutory duty against the Authority, the City and County.

THE SECOND CAUSE OF ACTION—CONTRACT

Generally speaking, there are three types of relief available to one who has been damaged—preventive, specific and monetary. Argo in the prior litigation obtained preventive relief. As pointed out in the cases cited in *Rubino,* at page 1062, specific relief has been held to be unavailable to one in Argo's position because of the privilege (as here) of the public entity to reject all bids. In any event, in this case it is now too late for such relief to be effective. This leaves only monetary relief and we have just held that Argo may not have monetary relief in tort.

Therefore, the second question we must answer is whether Argo may recover such monetary relief in contract from the Authority, the City, and the County. It seeks monetary damages of approximately $141,500, consisting largely in (a) the expenses it incurred in its unsuccessful participation in the competitive bidding process, (b) the monies it expended in its successful aforementioned prior litigation to set aside the award of the contract to Swinerton, and (c) in the profits, etc. it allegedly lost by reason of its failure to obtain the award of the contract.

The cause of action in promissory estoppel alleged is apparently based on section 814 [6] and Restatement of Contracts, section 90.[7] If the requirements of the Restatement section have been met in the instant case, an informal contract (requiring neither assent nor consideration) between the Authority and Argo to award the public works contract to Argo as the "lowest responsible bidder" resulted (Rest., Contracts (1932) § 85) and Argo became entitled at least in some part to the damages that ensued from the Authority's breach of this informal contract. (See Drennan v. Star Paving Co., 51 Cal.2d 409, 413, 333 P.2d 757.) Clearly, the Authority promised in its solicitation of bids to award the contract to the lowest responsible bidder and Argo's reasonable and detrimental reliance upon this promise brings section 90 into play unless the final clause of the section prevents this result.

In this connection Restatement section 90 provides that a promise, meeting its other requirements, is binding "if injustice can be avoided only by enforcement of the promise." The public entities contend that such a cause of action against them cannot be recognized in Argo in view of our conclusion that the competitive bidding requirements on contracts for public works exist to protect the public rather than the bidders. They point out (as we indicated earlier) that Argo could not have compelled the Authority to award the contract to it because of the provision in the notice soliciting bids that any and all bids might be rejected. (See Rubino v. Lolli, *supra,* 10 Cal.App.3d 1059, 1062, and cases there cited.) To them the preventive relief that Argo obtained in the prior litigation was granted to protect the public interest and not that of Argo.

We disagree. It seems to us that injustice to Argo, the promisee, can be avoided only by at least the partial enforcement of the Authority's promise to it to award the contract to it as the lowest responsible bidder. As we have already stated earlier, Argo's reliance upon this promise was both reasonable and detrimental to it. To hold that Argo was not entitled to rely upon this promise because of the just-mentioned reservation of the right to reject any and all bids would make the Authority's promise an illusory one and render the whole competitive

---

6. Section 814, a portion of the Governmental Tort Liability Act of 1963, provides that nothing in the act affects liability based on contract.

7. Section 90 reads: "A promise which the promisor should reasonably expect to induce action or forbearance of a definite and substantial character on the part of the promisee and which does induce such action or forbearance is binding if injustice can be avoided only by enforcement of the promise."

In the current proposed Restatement Second of Contracts (Tent. Drafts Nos. 1–7 (1973)), section 90 has been reworded slightly. Subdivision (1) of the proposed section now reads: "A promise which the

promisor should reasonably expect to induce action or forbearance on the part of the promisee or a third person and which does induce such action or forbearance is binding if injustice can be avoided only by enforcement of the promise. *The remedy granted for breach may be limited as justice requires.*" (Italics supplied.)

This doctrine may be applied against public entities in appropriate circumstances. (See Youngman v. Nevada Irrigation Dist., 70 Cal.2d 240, 249–251, 74 Cal. Rptr. 398, 449 P.2d 462; Hilltop Properties v. State of California, 233 Cal.App.2d 349, 364–365, 43 Cal.Rptr. 605, 37 A.L.R.3d 109; Annot. (1956) Promissory Estoppel, 48 A.L.R.2d 1069, 1086.)

bidding process nugatory. In contract law generally monetary damages for breach of contract may be awarded where specific relief is unavailable because of the discretionary nature of the latter relief. (See Rest., Contracts, *supra,* § 358, *et seq.*) * * * An award of monetary damages to the lowest responsible bidder for the misaward of a public works contract would be in the public interest as well as that of the injured bidder because such an award would deter such misconduct by public entities in the future. * * *

It would seem, however, that the damages that Argo may recover in promissory estoppel might well be limited to those it sustained directly by reason of its justifiable reliance upon the Authority's promise—in other words to the expenses it incurred in its fruitless participation in the competitive bidding process. Professor Corbin has suggested this as an equitable measure of damages in certain promissory estoppel cases. (1A Corbin, Contracts (1963) § 200, p. 221.) * * * Other courts have taken this view in cases which were really promissory estoppel cases. (See Wheeler v. White (Tex.1965) 398 S.W.2d 93, 97; Goodman v. Dicker (1948) 169 F.2d 684, 685 [83 App.D.C. 353]; *cf.* Terre Haute Brewing Co. v. Dugan (8th Cir.1939) 102 F.2d 425, 427.) On the other hand, the opinions of the commentators regarding the justice of limited as opposed to complete contractual recovery (see Civ.Code, § 3300) in promissory estoppel is divided. (See Note, *Promissory Estoppel—Measure of Damages* (1960) 10 Vand.L.Rev. 705, 708.) But in any event the decision as to the proper measure of damages for breach of the promissory estoppel contract in this case must initially be that of the trial court.

We hold that Argo stated in its cross-complaint facts sufficient to constitute a cause of action in promissory estoppel against the public entities. What recovery Argo may attain on such cause of action will have to await the trial of the action and the trial court's consideration of what is just under all of the circumstances—including Swinerton's possible recovery in *quantum meruit.*

THE THIRD CAUSE OF ACTION

The general demurrers of the Authority, the City and Swinerton to the third cause of action (declaratory relief) in Argo's cross-complaint should have been overruled. * * * Argo also alleged on information and belief * * * that Swinerton and the public entities conspired to make the misaward of the contract to Swinerton with resulting damage to Argo. These allegations of conspiracy are sufficient to constitute a cause of action therefor. * * * For the purpose of determining the correctness of the trial court's ruling on Swinerton's general demurrer we must accept these allegations of conspiracy as true. (Hauger v. Gates, 42 Cal.2d 752, 755, 269 P.2d 609.) This being so, Argo has pled facts sufficient to constitute a cause of action in declaratory relief against Swinerton as well.

DISPOSITION

The judgment of dismissal of Argo's cross-action is reversed except as to the sustaining of the general demurrer of the Authority and the City to the first cause of action alleged in Argo's cross-complaint. * * * The trial court is further directed then to overrule the aforesaid general demurrers to the second and third causes of action alleged in Argo's cross-complaint.

Note

1. The Supreme Court of Arkansas also overruled prior law, to permit suit for alleged wrongs by an unsuccessful bidder. Walt Bennett Ford Inc. v. Pulaski County Special School District, 274 Ark. 208, 624 S.W.2d 426 (1981).

2. **Standing to Sue.** Taxpayer standing to sue for relief against contracts in violation of bidding requirements is well established. The authorities, however, do not agree on the standing of nontaxpaying, disappointed bidders. See generally, 1 Antieau, *Municipal Corporation Law*, § 10.44 (1972). In some states disgruntled low bidders are denied a judicial hearing, either on the ground that bidders lack standing to complain. (Austin v. Housing Authority of City of Hartford, 143 Conn. 338, 122 A.2d 399 (1956) or that the state statutes limit appeals to "quasi-judicial" administrative actions, and that bid rejection is not a quasi judicial action. Kelley Co. v. Cleveland, 32 Ohio St.2d 150, 290 N.E.2d 562, 61 O.O.2d 394 (1972). Contra Seacoast Constr. Co. v. Lockport Urban Renewal Agency, 72 Misc.2d 372, 339 N.Y.S.2d 188 (1972). The more permissive view on bidder standing is expressed in the following excerpt from M.A. Stephen Constr. Co. v. Borough of Rumson, 118 N.J.Super. 523, 288 A.2d 873 (1972). "* * * Statutes requiring competitive bidding are for the benefit of taxpayers, not for the benefit or enrichment of the bidders. * * * The public interest is served by permitting suits to enforce the policy of competitive bidding. A low bidder is entitled to be heard by the public authority before his bid is rejected; and if his bid is rejected, to sue. * * * A rejected low bidder has 'an interest of some character which will support a claim to be heard.' * * * The interest is conferred on him to the end that the public will obtain all that is due it in the process of procuring public contracts rather than for the bidder's individual aggrandizement. * * * The general rule is that an improper award of a public contract to one other than the low bidder does not entitle the low bidder to a recovery of damages from the public body. * * * Where there is no statute requiring that the award be made to the low bidder, damages have been denied on the ground that a bid does not give to the bidder any contractual rights. Where there is such a statutory requirement, damages have been disallowed on the grounds that such statutes are enacted for the benefit of the public, and that to allow a bidder to recover damages would aggravate the injury to the public. * * * Plaintiff M.A. Stephen Construction Co., Inc. has no basis for a claim for damages." Similar views were expressed in North Country Development Corp. v. Massena Housing Authority, 65 Misc.2d 105, 316 N.Y.S.2d 894 (1970); Electronics Unlimited, Inc. v. Burnsville, 289 Minn. 118, 182 N.W.2d 679 (1971).

(3) Withdrawal and Rejection of Bids

Local officials are often authorized by statute or local charter to reject all bids. Such action is generally upheld in the absence of proof of fraud or capricious action. Weber v. Philadelphia, 437 Pa. 179, 262 A.2d 297 (1970); Bielec Wrecking & Lumber Co. of Syracuse v. McMorran, 21 A.D.2d 949, 251 N.Y.S.2d 331 (1964); Harney, Inc. v. Durkee, 107 Cal.App.2d 570, 237 P.2d 561 (1951); cf. Cardell, Inc. v. Woodbridge Twp., 115 N.J.Super. 442, 280 A.2d 203 (1971).

Low bid awards may be subject to special legislated conditions, *viz.* that a contract not be let unless city council formally approve the contract. Samios v. Joliet, 101 Ill.App.2d 210, 242 N.E.2d 322 (1968) (high bidder on a proposed sale of city surplus land held not entitled to complain that the city council refused to approve the sale, as required by law). Would the policy against political favoritism be better protected by requiring official authorization *before* bids are opened?

The bidder's power to withdraw or rescind a submitted bid depends upon the legislation, regulations, contract and equity law in the governing jurisdiction. Acceptance of a bid normally creates binding contract obligations. See e.g. Cataldo Construction Co. v. Essex County, 110 N.J.Super. 414, 265 A.2d 842 (1970). In many jurisdictions the bid becomes irrevocable, as to create an option contract, upon its submission. Even in such jurisdictions, rescission may be granted where an excusable, material mistake in the bid preparation would render its acceptance by the government unconscionable, i.e. where the government received timely express or constructive notice of the mistake, and where it would suffer no unfair disadvantage by withdrawal of the bid. See e.g. M.F. Kemper Construction Co. v. Los Angeles, 37 Cal.2d 696, 235 P.2d 7 (1951). Courts may, however, differ in the judgment whether particular circumstances justify such relief. See the authorities collected in Annot., *Right of Bidder for State or Municipal Contract To Rescind Bid* [on ground of mistake] 2 A.L.R.4th 991–1041 (1980), Keys, *Consideration Reconsidered—The Problem of the Withdrawn Bid,* 10 Stan.L.Rev. 441 (1958).

(4) Equitable Relief Under Improperly Let Contracts

BLUM v. HILLSBORO
Supreme Court of Wisconsin, 1971.
49 Wis.2d 667, 183 N.W.2d 47.

CONNOR T. HANSEN, JUSTICE.

* * * the plaintiff alleged that after acceptance of the contract, the defendant through its Mayor and council members inquired whether the plaintiff would be willing to do additional lake bottom excavation at the bid price of 40¢ per cubic yard; that the plaintiff advised he was willing to do so; and that the defendant, through its Mayor, city council members acting in their official capacity and through council action, outlined additional areas of the lake to be excavated, prepared a written map of the areas, and drew an amendment to the contract requiring the plaintiff to excavate the additional areas of the lake.

The complaint further alleges that the plaintiff performed all the services requested by the defendant pursuant to the contract, as modified and supplemented, and that the total amount of the services performed is $153,902.50; that defendant has made payment in the sum of $81,840, but refused to pay the balance of $72,062.50.

The defendant's answer alleged that the services performed by the plaintiff under the contract total $47,438.50; and that it paid plaintiff $81,400, and counterclaims for $38,700, the amount paid the plaintiff in excess of the amount due under the contract.

The defendant does not deny that the procedure required by sec. 62.15, Stats., was followed with respect to the original contract, but alleges it was not followed in contracting for the extra work to be done by the plaintiff. The issue raised on this appeal is whether a cause of action will lie against the city under theories of unjust enrichment, equitable estoppel, or promissory estoppel, for additional work done on a public works contract which was not let in compliance with the statutory requirements relating to competitive bidding.

Unjust Enrichment

* * * The object of statutory bidding requirements in connection with the letting of municipal contracts is to prevent fraud, collusion, favoritism, and improvidence in the administration of public business, as well as to insure that the municipality receives the best work or supplies at the most reasonable price practicable. 10 McQuillin, Mun. Corp. (3d ed.), p. 321, sec. 29.29, (1966 Revised Vol.). Thus recovery has been denied on the theory of unjust enrichment. This was because to permit recovery on principles of quasicontract would seriously impair the protection intended to be afforded by the bidding statutes.

However, there is a growing body of authority to the effect that to permit recovery on the theory of unjust enrichment would not lead to the evils once imagined. Although the majority of jurisdictions still deny quasi-contractual recovery, the trend is toward permitting recovery. It is now recognized that the limitation of a recovery under the theory of unjust enrichment to the value of the benefits conferred, while denying profits, will insure that the municipality receives the services at a reasonable price and prevent deliberate violations of the statute.

"* * * there are many well-reasoned cases permitting quasi-contract relief, and the trend of the law is clearly this way. * * *

"* * * It is suggested that quasi-contract recovery here is proper. * * *." 1 Antieau, Municipal Corporation Law, pp. 755, 756, sec. 10.27.

It has also been stated that an effective remedy to protect the taxpayer has been established by the device of taxpayers' actions to vindicate a public right; and that judicial remedies in equity are more likely to prevent injustice than delegation to the municipality of the discretionary power to pay moral claims.

* * *

Therefore, this decision will result in a modification of case law of this state * * *.

We here conclude that when work has been performed for a municipality under a contract which is malum prohibitum and not malum in se, which contract is entered into in good faith and is devoid of any bad faith, fraud or collusion, and where the statute imposes no penalty, a cause of action based upon the equitable doctrine of unjust enrichment can be maintained. This is upon the principle that courts will always try to do justice between parties where they can do so consistently with adherence to law. Equity would favor the placing of the parties in the positions that they occupied prior to the carrying out of their engagements. However, it would appear from the pleadings in this case that such would be impossible. If the facts are as alleged, both parties are guilty of failing to respect the mandate of the bidding statute. When a municipality has received the benefits of work performed, or materials furnished, in good faith, it is not just to permit the municipality to retain those benefits without paying the reasonable value thereof.

Thus, any recovery allowed the plaintiff does not rest on the void or unenforceable contract; it must rest, if at all, upon a theory of quasi-contract or unjust enrichment. This view leaves no room to say that a promise to pay is implied where no valid contract existed, or to prove a cause of action on quantum meruit for such a view would have the effect of recognizing the unrestricted right of the parties to disregard the bidding statutes.

The jurisdictions which have recognized the quasi-contract or unjust enrichment theory of recovery have established various measures for the recovery of damages.[1]

We are of the opinion that in an action such as this, * * * the measure of recovery is expressed by the amount which the court considers the defendant has been unjustly enriched at the expense of the plaintiff, subject to certain prescribed limitations. The question is not how much the plaintiff has parted with, but how much has the municipality benefited.

In this case, the measure of damages should be limited by at least two factors: (1) Recovery should be limited to an amount which represents the actual cost to the plaintiff, without allowing profits including overhead expense, and (2) in no event should it exceed the unit cost of the original contract. Subject to these limitations, any recovery would be limited to the value of the actual benefit conferred, as distinguished

1. Annot. (1970), 33 A.L.R.3d 1164, Municipality—Quasi-Contract Liability.

from the reasonable value of the work performed and materials furnished by the plaintiff.

Such a measure of damages does equity in that it will prohibit the municipality from benefiting at another's expense; will provide the protection to the taxpayers that the bidding statutes contemplate; and will also alert municipal officials, contractors, and furnishers of material that the bidding statutes must be recognized.

*   *   *

The order sustaining the demurrer as to the alternative cause of action, based on unjust enrichment, is reversed.

EQUITABLE ESTOPPEL AND PROMISSORY ESTOPPEL

This court has held that a municipality may become bound by principles of equitable estoppel under some circumstances. [Citations omitted] However, it is generally held that a municipality is not estopped to deny the invalidity of a contract let without complying with competitive bidding requirements. 1 Antieau, Municipal Corporation Law, p. 753, sec. 10.27.

The measure of recovery under the doctrines of equitable estoppel and promissory estoppel differs from that of unjust enrichment. Where a contractor is permitted to recover on the theory of unjust enrichment, he is permitted to recover only the value of the benefits conferred and denied profits. Under the doctrines of equitable estoppel and promissory estoppel, the municipality would be estopped to deny the validity of the contract—thus, application of these doctrines would permit recovery at the contract price. *   *   *

The creation of an exception where, as in this case, extra work is done under a supplement to a contract which was not let in compliance with competitive bidding requirements, but at the same unit price as a valid contract awarded to the lowest responsible bidder, may not have the effect of impairing the protection intended to be afforded by statutes requiring competitive bidding. However, with regard to recovery on the contract for extra work, this court has held that changes are valid only where they do not substantially change the character of the work or unreasonably increase its cost, and are made pursuant to a provision in the contract permitting such changes. Thomsen-Abbott Construction Co. v. Wausau (1960), 9 Wis.2d 225, 100 N.W.2d 921. Moreover, sec. 62.15(1c), Stats., permits an increase in the quantity of work to be done under contract but only to the extent of 15 percent of the cost of the original contract price, and then, only when the contract contains a clause providing for such increase. The demurrer to the alternative causes of action on equitable estoppel and promissory estoppel was properly sustained.

Order affirmed in part; reversed in part.

GERZOF v. SWEENEY

Court of Appeals of New York, 1968.
22 N.Y.2d 297, 239 N.E.2d 521.

FULD, C.J.

[After Village received and paid for generator equipment, a taxpayer sued for return of the price. He proved that the Village officials, in defiance of prior court order and bidding statute, refused to purchase generator from a prior low bidder, and with the help of defendant, drafted a new bid specification which precluded any competitor from bidding the second contract.]

* * *

We have not previously been called upon to fashion a remedy appropriate to a case such as this, where an illegal and void contract for public work, entered into in defiance of the competitive bidding statute (General Municipal Law, Consol.Laws, c. 24, § 103) has been performed in full on both sides. We have, however, dealt with the situation, one step removed, in which the municipality has consumed or had the full benefit of illegally purchased goods or services but the vendor or supplier has not been paid. We have repeatedly refused, in such cases, to allow the sellers to recover payment either for the price agreed upon or in quasi-contract. One of our salient purposes in adopting this rule has been to deter violation of statutes governing the spending of public moneys for goods and services. The restrictions imposed by such legislation, we recognized, are designed as a safeguard against the extravagance or corruption of officials as well as against their collusion with vendors. If we were to sanction payment of the fair and reasonable value of items sold in contravention of the bidding requirements, the vendor, having little to lose, would be encouraged to risk evasion of the statute; by the same token, if public officials were free to make such payments, the way would be open to them to accomplish by indirection what they are forbidden to do directly. [Citations omitted] [2]

There should, logically, be no difference in ultimate consequence between the case where a vendor has been paid under an illegal contract and the one in which payment has not yet been made. * * * In neither case can the usual concern of equity to prevent unjust enrichment be allowed to overcome and extinguish the special safeguards which the Legislature has provided for the public treasury. Although this court has not had occasion to pass on the question,

---

2. This prophylactic policy found expression in the rule which underlay our 1965 decision in the present case. As we then had occasion to declare, once a contract is proved, as it was here, to have been awarded in violation of the statute—either without competitive bidding or by the manipulation of specifications so as to shut out such competitive bidding—"a waste of public funds is presumed and a taxpayer is entitled to have the contract set aside without showing that the municipality suffered any actual injury" (16 N.Y.2d, at p. 208, 264 N.Y.S.2d, at p. 378, 211 N.E.2d, at p. 827). The vice in such a situation, we said (p. 209, p. 379 of 264 N.Y.S.2d, p. 827 of 211 N.E.2d), is that "the public 'has been deprived of the protection which the law was intended to afford.' (Matter of Emigrant Ind. Sav. Bank, 75 N.Y. 388, 396.)"

appellate courts of at least two other states have so decided, holding that the vendor must pay back the amount received from the purchaser even though the items sold are not capable of being returned (see County of Shasta v. Moody, 90 Cal.App. 519, 523–524, 265 P. 1032; McKay v. Town of Lowell, 41 Ind.App. 627, 638, 84 N.E. 778),[3] and we strongly favor this view. Only thus can the practical effectiveness and vigor of the bidding statutes be maintained.[4]

There was, therefore, justification—and precedent—for Special Term's decision directing Nordberg to repay the full purchase price of $757,625 and allowing the Village to retain the machinery which had been installed and was in operation. We conclude, nevertheless, though the patently illegal conduct of the defendants entitles them to little consideration, that the amount to be awarded should be less than that. We may adopt this course, in the unusual circumstances of the present case, without disturbing the salutary rationale and policy underlying such decisions as Albany Supply & Equip. Co. v. City of Cohoes, 18 N.Y.2d 968, 224 N.E.2d 716, affg. 25 A.D.2d 700, *supra,* 268 N.Y.S.2d 42. The sheer magnitude of the forfeiture that would be suffered by the defendant Nordberg, as well as the corresponding enrichment that would enure to the Village of Freeport, under Special Term's determination adds an element to this case not to be found in any of those in which the principles we have been discussing have been applied.

Ordinarily, the application of the law to particular cases may not, of course, vary with the sums involved. But we must recognize that the rule with which we are concerned has unique aspects that make it appropriate for us to take into account the severity of its impact in cases as extreme as the present one. The purposes of our competitive bidding statutes may be fully vindicated here without our rendering so Draconian a decree as to subject the defendant Nordberg to a judgment for over three quarters of a million dollars. Justice demands that even the burdens and penalties resulting from disregard of the law be not so disproportionately heavy as to offend conscience. * * * In our view, though, there is no warrant for allowing Nordberg this opportunity to recoup its loss or for subjecting the Village power system to the disruption and uncertainty that would result from dismantling the present installation. The courts should not invite unpredictable consequences of this kind. We must regard the machinery as unreturnable,

3. The courts of several other jurisdictions have reached a contrary result. (See Vincennes Bridge Co. v. Board of County Comrs., 8 Cir., 248 F. 93, 98–102; Grady v. City of Livingston, 115 Mont. 47, 141 P.2d 346; Scott Twp. School Dist. Auth. v. Branna Constr. Corp., 409 Pa. 136, 185 A.2d 320.)

4. In contrast, however, in real property cases, where the property which had been illegally sold was capable of ready return to the vendor—by the simple device of voiding the deed upon refund of the purchase price—we have sanctioned such return. (See Spadanuta v. Incorporated Vil. of Rockville Centre, 15 N.Y.2d 755, 257 N.Y.S.2d 329, 205 N.E.2d 525, affg. 20 A.D. 2d 799, 248 N.Y.S.2d 405; Bauer v. City of Niagara Falls, 293 N.Y. 896, 60 N.E.2d 29, affg. 267 App.Div. 801, 47 N.Y.S.2d 286.) It should be noted, also, that these cases did not, and could not, involve competitive bidding.

as were the goods or services for which payment was denied in the cases cited above (22 N.Y.2d p. 304, 292 N.Y.S.2d 644, 239 N.E.2d 523).

* * *

A more appropriate alternate remedy is available on the record before us, a remedy which takes into account both the wrong done to the village by the defendants' callous disregard of the competitive bidding statutes and our policy of depriving sellers of any incentive to participate in such a violation. In point of fact, the remedy, lying well within the domain of equity, impresses us as one uniquely suited to the circumstances of this case.

The Board of Trustees, it is to be noted, had originally decided that a 3,500 kilowatt generator—such as the one for which specifications had been prepared—met the Village's reasonable needs, and bona fide competitive bidding established that such an engine could be purchased for the sum of $615,685. The Village was diverted from that purchase by the persistent efforts of Nordberg to persuade the trustees, * * * to rewrite the specifications in a way that would prevent any other manufacturer from submitting a competing bid. The successful result of this cynical maneuver * * * was the illegal purchase of the far more costly Nordberg engine.

We may estimate the ensuing loss to the Village by taking the difference between the $757,625 paid to Nordberg and the $615,685 which the Village would have paid if it had accepted the low bid of Enterprise for the 3,500 kilowatt engine the Village had earlier set out to procure. That difference is $141,940. To the sum just mentioned we should add the difference between what it cost the Village to install the Nordberg machine and what it would have cost it to install the one offered by Enterprise. * * * The total of the two items mentioned is $178,636, and the judgment against the defendant Nordberg should be modified so as to direct payment of this sum to the Village, together with interest at the rate of 3% per annum * * *—computed from December 16, 1964, the date on which Nordberg received the final installment of the purchase price.

Whether the individual defendants—the Mayor and the trustees—should have been held liable (along with Nordberg) for the damages awarded, as the plaintiff urges, was a matter resting in the sound discretion of the courts below (General Municipal Law, § 51). Since Special Term found—and the Appellate Division affirmed the finding—that nothing of value had been received by the individual defendants and since it evidently decided that judgment against Nordberg alone would afford the Village sufficient redress, we perceive no basis for interfering with this exercise of discretion.

We agree, too, that the plaintiff, having succeeded in the action for the benefit of the Village, is entitled to an allowance of counsel fees—in the amount fixed by the courts below—out of the fund created by his efforts. * * *

The order appealed from should be modified, without costs, in accordance with this opinion and, as so modified, affirmed.

Chapter IX

STAFFING LOCAL GOVERNMENT

Government requires sound administrative structures and procedures, but it ultimately relies upon the competence and integrity of individuals. The law classifies government personnel as officers and employees.

A. OFFICERS

Officers may be classified as constitutional or legislative; elective or appointive; executive, administrative or judicial, but all officers are differentiated from public employees by the level and character of their duties. It is possible for a holder of a given position to be an officer with respect to certain functions, and an employee with respect to other functions. The authorities agree upon the general criteria of public office and officer status, but there is no universally adopted definition of "officer." As shown by the cases that follow, the criteria are inexact. Provisions governing officers are found in state constitutions, statutes, charters and ordinances.

PEOPLE v. FREEDLAND
Supreme Court of Michigan, 1944.
308 Mich. 449, 14 N.W.2d 62.

BUTZEL, JUSTICE.

* * *

We must first determine whether defendant was an executive officer of the State of Michigan within the meaning of section 118 under which Freedland was indicted, or whether he was merely an employee having neither the duties nor powers of an executive officer. Section 118 of the Penal Code provides that any executive, legislative or judicial officer guilty of accepting a bribe shall be punished by imprisonment in the State prison for not more than 10 years, or a fine of not more than $5,000, and shall forfeit his office and be forever disqualified to hold any public office, trust or appointment under the Constitution or laws of this State.

* * *

* * * It would seem that an auditor whose business was solely to check books would thus be an employee.

We find but little can be gained by examining the vast number of authorities cited on the question of whether one having the duties of defendant is an officer or not. The peculiar facts in each case distinguish it from the others. Many cases could be cited where persons holding offices similar to the one in the instant case were held to be employees. State ex rel. Barney v. Hawkins, 79 Mont. 506, 257 P. 411, 53 A.L.R. 583; Hudson v. Annear, 101 Colo. 551, 75 P.2d 587; State ex rel. Gibson v. Fernandez, 40 N.M. 288, 58 P.2d 1197. A very large number of cases have been annotated in 53 A.L.R. 595; 93 A.L.R. 333; 140 A.L.R. 1076. * * *

The cases indicate that duties of a public officer must be more than those of a mere agent or servant. He must be endowed by law with power and authority to use his own discretion. Freedland could not exercise independent discretion; his duties were largely that of a bookkeeper and consisted of checking over the books of retailers to ascertain whether they had paid a correct tax or not. The work was mainly clerical and could have been performed in the office of the State board of tax administration had the retailer brought his books and records there. Freedland could not exercise any discretion in omitting sales from his report; if he did so, he was guilty of a neglect of duty, not an abuse of discretion. His figures were subject to rechecking at the main office. This was seldom done. The dishonesty of a bookkeeper does not constitute an abuse of discretion.

* * *

We find a few cases which tend to uphold the State's contention that defendant was a public officer. McGrath v. United States, 2 Cir., 275 F. 294; Attorney General v. Tillinghast, 203 Mass. 539, 89 N.E. 1058, 17 Ann.Cas. 449; State v. Duncan, 153 Ind. 318, 54 N.E. 1066; People v. Kerns, 9 Cal.App.2d 72, 48 P.2d 750. From the very large number of cases, we quote a very recent one as it seems to state the rule expressed in the majority. In Scofield v. Strain, 142 Ohio St. 290, 51 N.E.2d 1012, 1014, the court again stresses the rule stated in State ex rel. Hogan v. Hunt, 84 Ohio St. 143, 95 N.E. 666:

"Manifestly, however, each case should be decided on its peculiar facts, and involves necessarily a consideration of the legislative intent in framing the particular statute by which the position, whatever it may be, is created."

The rule is accurately stated in State ex rel. Barney v. Hawkins, 79 Mont. 506, 257 P. 411, 418, 53 A.L.R. 583, where the court said:

"After an exhaustive examination of the authorities, we hold that five elements are indispensable in any position of public employment, in order to make it a public office of a civil nature: (1) It must be created by the Constitution or by the Legislature or created by a municipality or other body through authority conferred by the Legislature; (2) it must possess a delegation of a portion of the sovereign power of government, to be exercised for the benefit of the public; (3) the powers conferred, and the duties to be discharged, must be defined, directly or impliedly, by the Legislature or through legislative authority; (4) the duties must be performed independently and without control of a superior power, other than the law, unless they be those of an inferior or subordinate office, created or authorized by the Legislature, and by it placed under the general control of a superior officer or body; (5) it must have some permanency and continuity, and not be only temporary or occasional."

This rule is recognized by both appellants and appellees in their briefs.

In People ex rel. Throop v. Langdon, 40 Mich. 673, Mr. Justice Cooley said: "The officer is distinguished from the employee in the greater importance, dignity and independence of his position; in being required to take an official oath, and perhaps to give an official bond; * * *." These factors, while not controlling, are of assistance in doubtful cases.

Applying the rules thus stated to the instant case, we are impressed with the fact that defendant neither had the dignity nor the discretion usually vested in one holding a public office.

We agree with the defendant in his contention that the entire chapter 17 of the Penal Code (Stat.Ann. § 28.312, *et seq.*) should be examined. Section 117 provides that any person who shall corruptly give, offer or promise to any public *officer, agent, servant or employee* after the election or appointment of such *officer, agent, servant* or *employee,* etc., a bribe, shall be guilty of a felony. On the other hand, section 118 of the same chapter of the Penal Code (Stat.Ann. § 28.313) under which defendant was indicted, definitely limits the operation of the statute to any executive, legislative or judicial officer who shall corruptly accept any gift or gratuity, etc. We are impressed with the fact that the legislature saw fit to use the words "agent, servant or employee" in section 117 but omitted them in section 118. It seems to have been the legislative intent as far as it can be ascertained to punish more severely any executive, legislative or judicial officer who shall accept a bribe. Section 125 of the same chapter makes it unlawful for any agent or employee to *accept* a bribe and declare it to be a misdemeanor. It is unnecessary to hold that this would grant to an assistant or agent, an alter ego of the main officers, clothed with high discretionary powers, immunity from section 118, which refers to executive, legislative or judicial officers, but we do not believe that defendant's position as an accounts examiner without any discretionary power was a public office. * * *

Notes

The five factors cited by the principal case are drawn from the widely cited authority of Barney v. Hawkins, supra. See, e.g., Black v. Sutton, p.

820, infra; State v. Taylor, 260 Iowa 634, 144 N.W.2d 289 (1966); Bredice v. Norwalk, 152 Conn. 287, 206 A.2d 433 (1964); State v. Hord, 264 N.C. 149, 141 S.E.2d 241 (1965). It is generally recognized that the use of the words "officer" and "employee" in a statute does not necessarily determine the status issue. The legislative intent to treat a position as an office may be drawn from other statutory language and circumstances. See Advisory Opinion to Senate, 108 R.I. 551, 277 A.2d 750 (1971); and the *Mosby, Naef* and *Reilly* opinions which follow.

There is considerable variation in statutory and decisional treatment of particular positions. Compare e.g., City of Jackson v. Little, 248 So.2d 795 (Miss.1971) (policeman held an employee and not an officer) with State v. Hord, supra (policeman held an officer and not an employee); State ex rel. Beck v. Carter, 2 Wash.App. 974, 471 P.2d 127 (1970) (fireman held an officer); with Devillier v. Opelousas, 247 So.2d 412 (La.App.1971) (fireman held an employee and not an officer). Is a school district tax assessor and collector an "officer?" See Aldine Ind. School Dist. v. Standley, 154 Tex. 547, 280 S.W.2d 578 (1955). A parking fee collector? See State v. Perla, 21 N.Y.2d 608, 289 N.Y.S.2d 957, 237 N.E.2d 215 (1968), reversed 392 U.S. 296, 88 S.Ct. 2062, 20 L.Ed.2d 1108 (1968).

1. INCIDENTS OF OFFICE

MOSBY v. BOARD OF COMMISSIONERS OF VANDERBURGH COUNTY

Appellate Court of Indiana, 1963.
134 Ind.App. 175, 186 N.E.2d 18.

AX, JUDGE.

* * *

The allegations of fact are as follows: In accordance with Ind.Ann. Stat. § 26–1558 (Burns' 1960), the Park Board had appointed Mr. Mosby as Park Manager for three years, the term expiring February 23, 1959. On November 7, 1958, appellant Mosby was given another three year contract which was to begin the same day—three and one-half months before his original term was to expire * * *. On February 23, 1959, when appellant's original term would have expired, he was discharged. Appellant brought this action for lost wages occasioned by the alleged wrongful discharge to which a demurrer was sustained for lack of sufficient facts to constitute a cause of action.

The main question presented by the appeal is whether appellant was an officer or an employee. This involves interpretation of Ind.Ann. Stat. § 26–1558 (Burns' 1960), which reads as follows:

> "The county park board shall appoint a park manager for a term not exceeding four [4] years and shall further prescribe the duties and fix the compensation of such park manager and such other employees as may be necessary for the discharge of the duties and responsibilities of such board * * *."

Appellant contends that the position of Park Manager is that of an "employee," not an officer, and that it is immaterial whether a vacancy existed in the office at the time of the contract. He asserts in the alternative that the Park Board is an agent for the county, possessing contracting powers.

Appellee counters that the position of Park Manager is that of an "officer" and that an appointment to fill the office is void since there was no vacancy. Appellee denies that the Park Board can act as an agent since it has no legal entity apart from the county. This latter contention does not avail appellee because his argument was based on a case which has since been reversed on other grounds: [citations omitted].

It is true that "an appointment to fill a vacancy in an office is void when there is no vacancy." McGurik v. State ex rel. Gottschalk (1930), 201 Ind. 650, 659, 169 N.E. 521, 524. One can not forestall the rights of his successor by making an appointment to fill an office which would be vacated during the term of the appointing officer's successor. Hansen v. Town of Highland (1958), 237 Ind. 516, 147 N.E.2d 221.

This rule originated in Indiana over section 3, article 15 of the State Constitution which provides that an officer shall hold his office during his term "and until his successor shall have been elected and qualified." The Supreme Court, in Kimberlin v. State ex rel. Tow (1892), 130 Ind. 120, 29 N.E. 773, 14 L.R.A. 858, held that if the officer-elect dies before he qualifies for the office, the office is not vacant so as to allow an appointment, but that the incumbent continues in office until a successor is elected and qualified. The rule that an appointment to fill a vacancy in an office is void when there is no vacancy has never been applied to employees. All of the cases cited by the appellee concern public officers: [citations omitted].

An office, as opposed to an employment, is a position for which the duties include the performance of some sovereign power for the public's benefit, are continuing, and are created by law instead of contract. Wells v. State ex rel. Penden, *supra*.

Generally, one who holds an elective or appointive position for which public duties are prescribed by law is a "public officer." Brinson v. Board of Commissioners of Owen County (1933), 97 Ind.App. 354, 186 N.E. 891. In the Brinson case, an assistant county highway superintendent was held to be a public officer. His *duties, as defined in the statute,* consisted of executing a bond, making monthly inspection of roads, repairing breaks and defects and keeping the road bed free from ruts, chuck holes and depressions, and keeping ditches open for proper drainage. No specific duties, other than executing a bond, are mentioned in the statute concerning the Park Manager in the instant case.

An officer is also distinguished by his power of supervision and control and by his liability to be called to account as a public offender in case of malfeasance in office. State ex rel. Wickens, Prosecutor v. Clark (1935), 208 Ind. 402, 196 N.E. 234.

The superintendent of the county asylum was held to be an employee in State ex rel. Wickens, supra, primarily because the Board of the County Commissioners retained supervision and control. The superintendent was merely an agent who advised the Board and exercised no sovereign power himself. Again, in State ex rel. Black v. Burch (1948), 226 Ind. 445, 80 N.E.2d 294, 560, rehearing denied 226 Ind. 445, 81 N.E.2d 850, the Superintendent of Maintenance of the Highway Commission was held not to be a public officer because he was "acting under the direction of the commission."

In the instant case, the "county park board * * * when established, shall have the management and control of the * * * park." Ind.Ann.Stat. § 26–1552 (Burns' 1960). The park board is then to appoint a park manager and "further prescribe the duties * * * of such park manager and such *other employees* as may be necessary for the discharge of the *duties and responsibilities* of such board." (Italics added.) Ind.Ann.Stat. § 26–1558 (Burns' 1960). It is apparent that the board, not the manager, has supervision and control over the park.

The Park Manager, as well as other "employees" had to execute a bond, but did not take an oath. Judge Treanor, in State ex rel. Wickens, supra, ruled that the superintendent of a county asylum was an employee because, as in the instant case, although he executed a bond, he took no oath and exercised no sovereign power. The oath and bond, being mere incidents, and not requirements, of public office, do not serve as absolute guides in determining the character of a position. However, their absence is strong evidence, when considered with other criterion, that the position is one of employment rather than public office. [Citations omitted]

The title of Ind.Ann.Stat. § 26–1558 (Burns' 1960) is "Counties of 140,000 to 170,000 population—Park manager—Term of *office—Employees* compensation." (Italics added.) The appellee argues that the word "office" in the title labels the Park Manager an officer. Nomenclature in a statute designating a position an officer or employee is not controlling. Coulter v. Pool (1921), 187 Cal. 181, 201 P. 120. It is merely evidence of the title and not controlling on the character of the position which depends upon the power granted and duties performed. Besides, the title also reads "*employees* compensation," and the substantive text of the statute refers to the "park manager and such *other employees* as may be necessary." (Italics added.)

The appellee further argues that the word "appoint" in the statute indicates that the position is that of an office. In State ex rel. Coffing v. Abolt (1934), 206 Ind. 218, 222, 189 N.E. 131, 133, the Supreme Court held:

> "* * * while the word *'appointed'* as used in the statute is sometimes, if not generally, used in connection with the designation of one to an office, it is not always so used. It is often used to *designate employment,* as the appointment of a secretary, building custodian, janitor, etc. The duties of relator under his agreement were profes-

sional and technical, but so would be the duties of an architect employed by the board of county commissioners, or, perhaps, the *manager of a county farm,* and still these would not be officers, but *employees.* * * * " (Italics added.)

Consequently it is our opinion that appellant is an employee and is not subject to the rule that "an appointment to fill a vacancy in an office is void when there is no vacancy." Since an "appointment" may refer to the hiring of an employee, the park board has the power to hire a park manager under the statute.

Having disposed of the main question presented herein, upon examination it appears that the complaint contains sufficient facts to constitute a cause of action.

Judgment is reversed.

Notes

1. **Status v. Contract.** Among the different legal consequences that flow from officer status vis a vis employee contract, are the following: De jure officers may be elected, appointed and removed only in the manner authorized by law. Vacancies must be filled in accordance with governing laws and only for the term permitted by law.

Compensation attaches to the office as a matter of law, hence an agreement to pay an official compensation other than that fixed by law is void. Grace v. Douglas County, 178 Neb. 690, 134 N.W.2d 818 (1965); State ex rel. Beck v. Carter, 2 Wash.App. 974, 471 P.2d 127 (1970); Vallet v. City of Seattle, 77 Wash.2d 12, 459 P.2d 407, 410 (1969).

Many state constitutions and statutes prohibit new self-serving enactments that take effect during the term of the enacting officials to increase their salary or extend their term of office. Consumers Education and Protective Association v. Schwartz, 495 Pa. 10, 432 A.2d 173 (1981); Delardas v. County Court of Monongalia County, 155 W.Va. 776, 186 S.E.2d 847 (1972); cf. State ex rel. Mikus v. Roberts, 15 Ohio St.2d 253, 239 N.E.2d 660 (1968). The *Naef* opinion which follows also points up the decisive distinction between elective and appointive status of officers in compensation claims.

2. **Holding Office Beyond the Prescribed Term.** Courts and many statutes adopt the holdover rule whereby officers remain in office beyond their normal term (unless otherwise removed) until their successors are duly elected or appointed, and qualified. Youngblood v. Marr, 253 Ind. 412, 254 N.E.2d 868 (1970); Reed v. President and Commissioners of Town of North East, 226 Md. 229, 172 A.2d 536 (1961). But holdover may be prohibited by statute. Alcorn ex rel. Hoerle v. Thomas, 127 Conn. 426, 17 A.2d 514 (1941). For various applications of the holdover rule, see 3 McQuillin, *Municipal Corporations,* §§ 12.105, 12.110 (3rd ed. 1973).

NAEF v. ALLENTOWN

Supreme Court of Pennsylvania, 1967.
424 Pa. 597, 227 A.2d 888.

EAGEN, JUSTICE. The question posed by these appeals is, whether or not the city solicitor and assistant city solicitors of a third class city in Pennsylvania may be removed from office and deprived of the emoluments thereof at the pleasure of the city council, and, without cause shown, at any time prior to the expiration of the four-year terms for which the appointments were made. The lower court answered the question in the affirmative. We agree and affirm.

Article VI § 4 of the Constitution of Pennsylvania, P.S. provides in part: "Appointed officers, other than judges of the courts of record and the Superintendent of Public Instruction, may be removed at the pleasure of the power by which they shall have been appointed."

In a multitude of decisions, this Court has ruled that, under the above constitutional provision, appointed public officers are removable from office at the pleasure of the appointive power even though the appointments were made for a statutorily fixed term. [Citations omitted] Moreover, in Mitchell v. Chester Housing Authority, 389 Pa. 314, 132 A.2d 873 (1957), such right of removal was upheld, even though the statute under which the appointments * * * were made provided for a system of rotated or staggered terms.

However, in Watson v. Pennsylvania Turnpike Commission, 386 Pa. 117, 125 A.2d 354 (1956), this Court held that Article VI § 4 of the Pennsylvania Constitution, supra, must be read in conjunction with Article XII § 1 thereof, which provides in part as follows, "[a]ll officers whose selection is not provided for in this Constitution, shall be elected or appointed as may be directed by law * * *," and ruled that where the legislature creates a public office, it may impose such terms and limitations with reference to tenure or removal of an incumbent as it sees fit. In *Watson, supra,* the Court concluded that where public officers are appointed to a legislatively created commission or board, for a statutorily fixed term with staggered expiration dates, the presence of the staggered term provision indicates a legislative intent that the holders of the office are not to be removed at the pleasure of the appointer. This ruling in *Watson* was subsequently followed in Bowers v. Penna. Labor Relations Board, 402 Pa. 542, 167 A.2d 480 (1961); and, Commonwealth ex rel. Hanson v. Reitz, 403 Pa. 434, 170 A.2d 111 (1961).

In the instant case the city solicitor and assistant solicitors were appointed for a term of four years under the provisions of the Third Class City Code, Act of June 28, 1951, P.L. 662 §§ 16 & 16.1, 53 P.S. §§ 36601 & 36609. No staggered terms are involved, and likewise no appointments to a board or commission. Nevertheless, appellants contend that the history and changes in the provisions of the Third Class City Code, * * * indicates a strong legislative intent that such appointees are not now removable at the will of the appointing power. * * * They note that the pertinent sections in the Acts of 1913 and 1931, supra, specifically included a provision stating that the city solicitor could be removed at the pleasure of the appointer, but no such reference or provision is included in Section 16 of the Act of 1951. * * *

What the appellants overlook is that at the same time the legislature was deleting the removal language in Section 16 of the Act of 1951, they re-enacted another section of the Third Class City Code dealing with precisely the same subject. * * * As re-enacted and amended in 1951, this portion of the act provides: "*Council shall have the power of appointment and dismissal of all city officers and employes other than elected officers* * * *." Act of June 28, 1951, P.L. 662 § 9, 53 P.S. § 35901. (Emphasis added.)

The above quoted section of the Act of 1951, and Section 16 thereof, both deal with the appointment of municipal officers and must be read in conjunction with each other. See, 1 Sutherland Statutory Construction § 1935 (3d ed. Horack 1943). So read, the conclusion is inevitable that the legislature clearly intended that all appointive city officers, including the city solicitor, were subject to the council's dismissal power.

Both public policy considerations and common sense dictate the wisdom of the legislature in vesting such control in the council. The solicitor is an important confidant of the council and the mayor in the administration of the city's business. To hold that one who is unacceptable must be retained in such a position would lead to a seriously disturbed municipal situation. *Cf.* Commonwealth ex rel. Schofield v. Lindsay, *supra.*

Since we rule that the appellants have no right to reinstatement to the posts involved, their claims for the emoluments of the office must also be denied. An appointment to a public office for a fixed term and salary is not a contract within the protection of the Constitution. See, Vega v. Burgettstown Borough, 394 Pa. 406, 147 A.2d 620 (1958). The compensation is incidental to the office and is governed by the right thereto. The emoluments are annexed to the office and not to the person; hence the salary belongs to the officer, de jure. If the officer is properly dismissed, the salary ceases. See, 4 McQuillin, Municipal Corporations § 12.205 (3d ed. 1949).

We have primarily directed our attention in this opinion to the right of the city solicitor to continue in office for the term fixed by his appointment. Our ruling in reference thereto necessarily determines the right of the assistant solicitors to also continue in office. In view of this, we deem it unnecessary to determine whether or not an assistant city solicitor is a constitutional public officer or merely enjoys the status of a professional employee. But see, Commonwealth ex rel. Foreman v. Hampson, 393 Pa. 467, 143 A.2d 369 (1958).

Judgments affirmed.

*   *   *

ROBERTS, JUSTICE (dissenting). I dissent from the Court's conclusion that sections 16 and 16.1 of the Third Class City Code make the city solicitor and assistant city solicitors of third class cities removable at the pleasure of the body appointing them. My dissenting opinion in Schluraff v. Rzymek, 417 Pa. 144, 147–152, 208 A.2d 239, 240–243 (1965), a case involving a question of statutory interpretation closely analogous to this one, contains most of the reasons for my dissent here. I would add, however, that the instant statutes' specification of the day on which the terms of the city solicitors and assistant city solicitors begin, when coupled with the specified length of the term, makes me even more certain that I was in *Schluraff* that the Legislature did not intend such officers to be removable at the pleasure of the body appointing them.

Notes

1. **Term of Appointive Offices.** In the absence of a statutory term (which is to be distinguished from "tenure"—note 4, below), the power to appoint includes the power to remove an officer. In re Schwartz, 219 Pa. Super. 245, 275 A.2d 666 (1971); Annot., 91 A.L.R. 1097 (1934). Subjecting officers to the pleasure of the appointing authorities whom they serve is easily defended, but the threshold question remains: did the legislature intend an officer to serve at the pleasure of the appointing authority, or to have tenure for the term mentioned in the statute?

2. **Abolition or Change in Terms of Office.** The legislative body that creates an office may abolish or change its term, except where the incidents of office are fixed by the constitution. Kennon v. Schlesinger, 182 S.W.2d 373 (Tex.Civ.App.1944); Cawood v. Hensley, 247 S.W.2d 27 (Ky.App. 1952) (statutory modification of constitutional term of office held invalid); Sueppel v. City Council of Iowa City, 257 Iowa 1350, 136 N.W.2d 523 (1965) (municipal council having control over an office may terminate and abolish it).

3. **Vacancy Appointments.** There is no general rule on the length of term of one appointed to fill a vacated office. 3 McQuillin, *Municipal Corporations,* § 12.109 (3rd rev. ed. 1973). Legislation varies from office to office and from jurisdiction to jurisdiction. Thus, a vacancy appointment may run: for the unexpired term of the original incumbent (State v. Ramaker, 57 Wash.2d 767, 359 P.2d 813 (1961)); to the expiration of the term of the appointing authority (Rawlins v. Levy Court of Kent County, 235 A.2d 840 (Del.1967); Powers ex rel. Davis v. Palmer, 83 R.I. 80, 113 A.2d 374 (1955)); or until the ensuing general or special election (Austin v. Welch, 480 S.W.2d 273 (Tex.Civ.App.1972)).

A familiar ploy to perpetuate officeholding is seen where an incumbent resigns his office shortly before it expires, in order to be reappointed to another vacant office, whose unexpired term will run for a longer period. Where the switch is made between like offices, e.g. between seats in a multi-member council or board, some courts hold the vacancy appointment to be invalid. Bernstein v. Krom, 108 N.J.Super. 176, 260 A.2d 269 (1969).

Other constitutional and statutory disqualifications from vacancy appointments of persons holding the same or different office are noted in Annot., 59 A.L.R.2d 716 (1958).

4. **Tenure.** "The word 'tenure' and the word 'term' are not synonymous although frequently so used. * * * Tenure is the right to hold office for an indefinite time. Term denotes a period of time. * * * The statute having granted relator a specific tenure of office, any interference therewith * * * for any reason other than those specified in the statute is invalid." State ex rel. Daly v. Toledo, 142 Ohio St. 123, 129–30, 50 N.E.2d 338, 342 (1943). Tenure does denote term of service (whether for a fixed period or doing good behavior), but also the right to retain the office and to claim its emoluments. Tenure rights cannot be terminated except for reasons and in the manner prescribed by law. Since tenure rights attach to the office, and do not rest on contract rights, they cease to exist when the office is lawfully abolished. Cawood v. Hensley, note 2 supra. But an incumbent cannot complain of legislative modification of official duties or compensation. Redwood City v. Grimmenstein, 68 Cal. 512, 9 P. 560 (1886).

5. **Removal From Office.** Removal processes differ from termination by abolition; from vacation of office by resignation, abandonment, death, or incompetence; and from automatic disqualifications by reason of proscribed dual office holding (see p. 785, et seq. infra); or of personal conflict of interest (see p. 803, et seq. infra). Removal from office may occur in several ways, i.e. by recall elections. (Campbell v. Johnson, 182 So.2d 244 (Fla.1966)); Batchelor v. Eighth Judicial District Ct., in and for County of Clark, Dept. No. 4, 81 Nev. 629, 408 P.2d 239 (1965); by ouster for specified causes, (State ex rel. Stokes v. Probate Court of Cuyahoga County, 17 Ohio App.2d 247, 246 N.E.2d 607 (1969); People ex rel. Ward v. Tomek, 54 Ill.App.2d 197, 203 N.E.2d 744 (1964)). See generally 3 Antieau, *Municipal Corporations* § 22.25 (1967).

6. **Trying Disputed Title to Office.** As pointed out in Chapter II (p. 46), the title to an office is normally tested only by a direct attack in *quo warranto* proceedings, in which standing to sue is limited to the state attorney general, the local district attorney, or some person having a direct or special interest in the office itself. Country Clubs, Inc. v. Knoxville, 217 Tenn. 104, 395 S.W.2d 789 (1965). Some statutes permit citizen suits to try title to an office where the attorney general fails to act on the question. See State ex rel. Genz v. Thomas, 185 Neb. 637, 177 N.W.2d 607 (1970). Others adopt the general rule but permit suits for other relief that raise substantially the same issue. Thus, in Pennsylvania a taxpayer may sue to enjoin improper spending of public funds, on the ground that the person asserting officer status to make the expenditure is not a legally qualified officer. Mayer v. Hemphill, 411 Pa. 1, 190 A.2d 444 (1963). *But see* McCamant v. Denver, 31 Colo.App. 287, 501 P.2d 142 (1972). In some states title to an office may be challenged in mandamus proceedings. Housing Authority of City of Needles v. City Council of City of Needles, 208 Cal.App.2d 599, 25 Cal.Rptr. 493 (1962).

2. QUALIFICATION AND ELIGIBILITY FOR OFFICE

Many conditions that are prescribed by law to qualify for office may not be waived.

Qualifying and Loyalty Oaths—Where the law requires a putative officer to take an oath of office, in order to qualify (McCue v. Antisell, 105 N.J.Super. 128, 251 A.2d 308 (1969)) failure to do so may result in a vacancy of that office. Entwistle v. Murtaugh, 44 Misc.2d 1022, 255 N.Y.S.2d 422 (1964); City of Colonial Heights v. Loper, 208 Va. 580, 159 S.E.2d 843 (1968).

A state may constitutionally require its officers, and even employees, to take a loyalty oath promising to "support" the state and federal constitutions, and to "oppose" the overthrow of government by unlawful means (Cole v. Richardson, 405 U.S. 676, 92 S.Ct. 1332, 31 L.Ed.2d 593 (1972)). But the scope and wording of loyalty oaths must be carefully narrowed to avoid infringement of First Amendment freedoms of expression, belief and association. Vague or overbroad oath language that might chill such freedoms is unconstitutional. See also, Communist Party of Indiana v. Whitcomb, 414 U.S. 441, 94 S.Ct. 656, 38 L.Ed.2d 635 (1976).

Citizenship and Residence—See the discussion on citizenship eligibility requirements in chapter VI at p. 356 supra.

Residence—While the practice is not universal, local governments increasingly require their officers and employees to take residence within their territory, and such requirements have been upheld.

A state legislature may, either generally, or for selective positions, forbid local government units from requiring in-district residence. E.g., City of Atlanta v. Myers, 240 Ga. 261, 240 S.E.2d 60 (1977) (general prohibition); 24 Pa.Stat. § 11–1106 (selective prohibition); Wierenga v. Board of Fire and Police Comm'rs, 40 Ill.App.3d 270, 352 N.E.2d 322 (1976); cf. Labouisee v. Koppel, 229 So.2d 161 (La.App.1969). Such statutory limitations are, however, the exception and not the rule. See, e.g., People ex rel. Adamowski v. Wilson, 20 Ill.2d 568, 170 N.E.2d 605 (1960); McCarthy v. Philadelphia Civil Service Comm'n, 424 U.S. 645, 96 S.Ct. 1154, 47 L.Ed.2d 366 (1976); Meyers v. Newport Consolidated School Dist., 31 Wash.App. 145, 639 P.2d 853 (1982) and the authorities hereafter noted with respect to the constitutional issues.

An indirect state limitation on local government power to require residency may arise under new state public employee bargaining statutes. If those statutes authorize local government employers to toll in-district residency requirement in a collectively bargained agreement, the issue will be governed by labor law.

Challenges to residency conditions, as infringing federal constitutional rights (liberty, right to travel) have been rejected by a majority of federal and state courts. McCarthy v. Civil Service Comm'n, supra; Meyers v. Newport Consolidated School Dist., supra; Wardwell v. Board of Education, 529 F.2d 625 (6th Cir.1976); City of Memphis v. International Bhd. of Elec. Workers, 545 S.W.2d 98 (Tenn.1976); Miller v. Police Board, 38 Ill.App.3d 894, 349 N.E.2d 544 (1976). The courts have also sustained grandfather-type exemptions from in-district residency requirements for employees who acquired outside residence prior to the effective date of the new law. See, e.g., Pittsburgh Federation of Teachers v. Aaron, 417 F.Supp. 94 (W.D.Pa.1976). The cases hold that new regulations need only be uniform in their prospective operation. The federal constitutional test for *current* residency requirements (as distinguished from "durational" residency requirements to be noted shortly) requires only that there be a reasonable relationship between the duties of office and employment and the requirement of current residency. Courts have no difficulty in finding this rational relationship since local residents will have a greater familiarity with and community of interest in matters of public interest affecting their work. But see contra: Lanam v. Civil Service Comm'n, 80 Cal.App.3d 315, 145 Cal.Rptr. 590 (1978).

To be distinguished from bare residency requirement is the requirement of prior residence for a specified period of time within the local government territory. If such a requirement is deemed to "penalize" the right of interstate travel, courts may, under heightened "strict scrutiny", nullify the durational residency requirement. Cf. Memorial Hospital v. Maricopa County, 415 U.S. 250, 94 S.Ct. 1076, 39 L.Ed.2d 306 (1974) (eligibility for public welfare services). The justification for durational residency is clearly stronger for officers and for employees in policymaking positions, and the courts, to date, have had no difficulty upholding durational residency requirements. Sununu v. Stark, 383 F.Supp. 1287 (D.N.H.1974), affirmed 420 U.S. 958, 95 S.Ct. 1346, 43 L.Ed.2d 435 (1975) (seven-year requirement for public office—upheld); Daves v. Longwood, 423 F.Supp. 503 (M.D.Fla.1976) (one-year residency requirement for office—upheld). Since duration of residence is relevant to preparation to serve as an officer in a local government unit, courts will be slow to find that legislated time periods unreasonably burden and penalize the right of interstate travel. See Annots., 4 A.L.R. 4th 380 (1981), 65 A.L.R.3d 1048 (1975).

The majority of states have sustained residency requirements under their state constitutions, but at least one state has interpreted its state constitution to prohibit that requirement. Angwin v. Manchester, 118 N.H. 336, 386 A.2d 1272 (1978).

Where a qualified officer removes his residence outside the legally required residential zone, he may be disqualified and ousted from office. State ex rel. Repay v. Fodeman, 30 Conn.Sup. 82, 300 A.2d 729 (1972); Berg v. Minneapolis, 274 Minn. 277, 143 N.W.2d 200 (1966). Some jurisdictions permit nonresident incumbents to qualify and take office, subject to the condition that they obtain the required residence within a specified time following entry into office. Appeal of Gagliardi, 401 Pa. 141, 163 A.2d 418 (1960). Where, however, the requirement is unreasonably restrictive, it may be stricken as unconstitutional. Martinez v. Newton, 8 Cal.3d 756, 106 Cal.Rptr. 105, 505 P.2d 529 (1973) (five-year residency requirement held void).

Other Qualifications—The Supreme Court has recently declared property ownership qualifications to be unconstitutional in the absence of a demonstrated "rational state interest" to justify such a condition of eligibility. Turner v. Fouche, 396 U.S. 346, 90 S.Ct. 532, 24 L.Ed.2d 567 (1970); accord: Sorenson v. Bellingham, 80 Wash.2d 547, 496 P.2d 512 (1972). While that decision undercut much of the older law, it recognizes the possibility that property ownership may, for certain offices, be a justified prerequisite.

Laws disqualifying from public office persons who are convicted of crime are commonplace, but vary greatly. Some disqualify only for felonies; others for crimes that are "infamous" or involve "moral turpitude." Upshaw v. McNamara, 435 F.2d 1188 (1st Cir.1970) (convicted felons ineligible to be policemen); Elder v. County Election Bd. of Cherokee County, 326 P.2d 776 (Okl.1958) (misdemeanant held eligible for county commissioner office); Walsh v. Watson, 198 Misc. 643, 99 N.Y.S.2d 805 (1950) (misdemeanant held ineligible for police position); Raphalides v. New Jersey Department of Civil Service, 80 N.J.Super. 407, 194 A.2d 1 (1963) (petit larceny held a disqualifying crime of "moral turpitude"). The law of each jurisdiction must be consulted. See generally Annot., 39 A.L.R.3d 303 (1971); 71 A.L.R.2d 593 (1960); People ex rel. Ward v. Tomek, 54 Ill.App.2d 197, 203 N.E.2d 744 (1964).

Minimum age requirements of eligibility, particularly for offices requiring professional or special training are generally upheld. Since age classifications are not deemed suspect under the Equal Protection Clause, courts uphold age qualifications for office so long as they have a rational basis. See Manson v. Edwards, 482 F.2d 1076 (6th Cir.1973) (age eligibility requirement for city council office); Annot., Age Requirement of State Public Officer, 90 A.L.R.3d 900 (1985).

The effect of multiple office-holding upon eligibility or qualification for office is taken up in the following section.

3. PLURAL OFFICE HOLDING

Ethical perspectives regarding the fiduciary duty in the conduct of public office vary considerably. Courts and legislatures have fashioned rules and remedies to reduce the risks of conflicts between the duties of different offices or between the duties of a particular office and the personal interests of its incumbent. At common law one person could not hold incompatible offices, and an officer could not advance his personal interests through the use of official power. These common law principles are declared in many statutes, but some modern statutes go further to prohibit plural office holding, irrespective of their compatibility, and to strengthen the common law restrictions on personal conflicts. Others, however, abrogate all or part of the common law. Each jurisdiction must, therefore, be consulted on the extent to which it presses the ideal of "undivided loyalty" for given offices.

Imperfections in the law are sometimes dictated by practical needs for some plural office holding. Ex officio membership of elected officers on many boards and commissions may be the only effective means of coordinating official policies. In some municipalities, plural office holding may be the only fiscally feasible way of conducting government business.

"The restrictions against holding more than one office fall into two classes: forbidden offices and incompatible offices. The acceptance of an incompatible office ipso facto vacates the first office; while a forbidden office cannot be accepted (*i.e.* the first office is retained while the second office remains vacant)." Conklin, *Plural Office Holding,* 28 Ore.L.Rev. 332, 346 (1949). Although commentators do not agree on how conflicts rules should be classified, the foregoing distinction may be conveniently expressed as follows: The forbidden office rule is a rule of presumed ineligibility, while the incompatibility rule is one of presumed resignation. Id. at 346–7, 358. These and other distinctions are treated in the following materials.

REILLY v. OZZARD

Supreme Court of New Jersey, 1960.
33 N.J. 529, 166 A.2d 360.

WEINTRAUB, C.J. The ultimate question is whether the common law doctrine prohibiting dual holding of incompatible offices bars a member of the State Senate from holding the post of township attorney.

* * *

I

We must first consider constitutional objections advanced by defendant. One is that since the Constitution defines eligibility for membership in the Legislature (Art. IV, § I, par. 2), no further requirement may be added, Imbrie v. Marsh, 3 N.J. 578, 71 A.2d 352, 18 A.L.R.2d 241 (1950), and an application of the common law doctrine to a member of the Legislature would have that forbidden effect. Another is that, if the common law doctrine does apply, nonetheless the Judiciary may not act since each house of the Legislature is "the judge of the elections, returns and qualifications of its own members" (Art. IV, § IV, par. 2) and has the power of expulsion (Art. IV, § IV, par. 3).

* * *

An individual does not move beyond the restraints of law, common or statutory, when he accepts membership in the Legislature. * * * Prohibiting a legislator to hold another office neither denies eligibility for legislative membership nor frustrates the discharge of the duties of a legislator. Eligibility for office is one thing; the right to pursue governmental activities extraneous to the office of legislator is something else. *Cf.* In re Hess, 128 N.J.L. 387, 26 A.2d 277 (Sup.Ct.1942).

B

We do not doubt the jurisdiction and duty of the courts to decide controversies of this character. A judicial determination that a legislator may not hold another office does not trench upon the authority of each house to judge the elections and qualifications of its members or to expel them. * * *

* * *

We can find no grant to the Senate of exclusive authority to deal with the external activities of its members. * * *

* * * As the facts then were, defendant had first been elected to the Senate and thereafter had accepted the post of township attorney. Under the conventional statement of the common law doctrine, acceptance of the later office vacates the earlier. Kobylarz v. Mercer, 130 N.J.L. 44, 46, 31 A.2d 208 (E. & A. 1943). * * *

Next, defendant contends the Constitution itself exhausts the subject of dual officeholding by legislators and thus supersedes any common law doctrine which otherwise might have applied. Reference is made to several provisions.

* * * More specifically, Article IV, § V, par. 3 provides:

"3. If any member of the Legislature shall become a member of Congress or shall accept any Federal or State office or position, of profit, his seat shall thereupon become vacant."

and par. 4:

"4. No member of Congress, no person holding any Federal or State office or position, of profit, and no judge of any court shall be entitled to a seat in the Legislature."

Defendant says the post of township attorney is not a "*State* office or position" (emphasis added) within the meaning of these provisions, and plaintiff does not disagree. Defendant points out that the Convention received specific proposals that legislators be barred from holding office under local government (3 Constitutional Convention of 1947, pp. 689, 851, 898) and a monograph upon the subject expressly referred to a provision in the constitution of Arizona to that effect (Vol. 2, p. 1477). In this setting, defendant urges the Constitution deals completely with the problem and bars any further restraint upon dual officeholding by members of the Legislature.

The most that can be said from the record of the Convention is that a more sweeping ban was suggested but not accepted. We see no basis to invoke the maxim, *expressio unius est exclusio alterius.* The maxim at best is a mere aid to interpretation. Perhaps more accurately, it usually serves to describe a result rather than to assist in reaching it. * * *

* * *

Where, as here, the constitutional provision is prohibitory in nature, it surely can not mechanically be inferred that what was not prohibited was thereby affirmatively guaranteed. The decision to prohibit is simply a decision to foreclose a contrary view as to the area dealt with. What is left untouched remains within the jurisdiction of government. * * *

* * *

It is convenient to consider at this point the claim that R.S. 19:3–5, N.J.S.A., exhausts the subject. The statute reads in part:

> "No person shall hold at the same time more than one of the following offices: elector of president and vice president of the United States, member of the United States senate, member of the house of representatives of the United States, member of the senate or of the general assembly of this state, county clerk, register, surrogate, sheriff or coroner."

It has been held that this enactment did not authorize dual office-holding beyond the terms of its interdiction and thus erase the common law doctrine. Kobylarz v. Mercer, *supra* (130 N.J.L., at p. 48, 31 A.2d at p. 212). * * * We can not say the Legislature thereby intended to abolish the common law elsewhere by implication.

II

Hence we reach the issue whether the office of senator and the post of township attorney are incompatible under the common law.

A

It is contended the doctrine applies only to "offices" and the post of township attorney is not of that character.

* * * We need not however pursue the matter since, as we shall presently develop, the post of township attorney is an "office" within the purpose of the doctrine.

B

It is argued that from the nature of his profession an attorney can be only an independent contractor. Reliance is placed upon Ewart v. Commissioner, 98 F.2d 649 (3 Cir.1938). * * * The case does not hold the inherent nature of an attorney's service is such as to preclude the creation of an office for their rendition. * * * Government needs professional services of many types, * * * and if the need is sufficient to induce the creation of a post for their rendition, the incumbent is not an independent contractor merely because the services are professional in nature. * * *

The definition of an office depends upon the context. See 2 Antieau, Municipal Corporation Law (1955), § 13.00, at p. 209. For present purposes, it may be sufficiently defined as a post created or authorized by constitution or statute for the continuous exercise of a portion of governmental power or authority. * * * The role of the lawyer is threaded throughout government. It includes advice, the preparation of indispensable instruments, and the prosecution of the civil and criminal business of the public. The need is so apparent that the Legislature either directed or authorized the creation of a legal post in local government. And in so doing it has consistently characterized the post as an "office." [citations omitted] * * * And the weight of authority elsewhere holds the municipal attorney to be an officer. Rhyne, Municipal Law (1957), § 8–2, at p. 118.

We see no reason to deny the post the status of an office within the purpose of the doctrine of incompatible offices. If a member of a governing body attempted simultaneously to serve in the subordinate role of municipal attorney, quite obviously there would arise the evil at which the common law doctrine was aimed. * * *

C

We come accordingly to the question whether the office of municipal attorney is incompatible with the office of senator. Incompatibility is usually understood to mean a conflict or inconsistency in the functions of an office. It is found where in the established governmental scheme one office is subordinate to another, or subject to its supervision or control, or the duties clash, inviting the incumbent to prefer one obligation to another. Jones v. MacDonald, 33 N.J. 132, 162 A.2d 817 (1960); Annotation, 1917A L.R.A. 216. There is no conflict between senator and township attorney in any of the conventional applications of the doctrine. * * *

Plaintiff suggests a conflict in duties would arise whenever legislation is considered which may affect the interests of the municipality. The assumption is that the municipal attorney, as such, has a duty to lobby, which duty would conflict with the duty to legislate.

Lobbying is not a part of the practice of law. * * *

That local government has the *right* to seek or to oppose legislation affecting its interests is settled. City Affairs Committee of Jersey City v. Jersey City, 134 N.J.L. 180, 46 A.2d 425 (E. & A.1946); In re Carrick, 127 N.J.L. 316, 22 A.2d 561 (Sup.Ct.1941). Whether a municipality is under a *duty* to do so is another matter, and whether that duty, if it exists, attaches to a specific office in local government, we need not inquire. It is enough to say that it is not inherently a lawyer's role and that in the present case the ordinance defining the duties of the township attorney does not impose that obligation and we know of no statute which does.

We do not suggest a legislator may accept an engagement for pay on behalf of a municipality to introduce or oppose legislative proposals. Quite obviously a legislator, whether or not a lawyer, could not lawfully be so engaged by any interests, public or private. And if the office of municipal attorney (or any other local office) were specifically charged with the duty thus to lobby, that obligation would plainly be incompatible with the duty of a legislator and would bar dual holding of the offices. Here, however, the office of township attorney does not hold that duty and hence defendant does not face the prospect as legislator of passing upon a position advanced in discharge of a duty of his other office.

It is here appropriate to explore the theme of the dissenting opinion to be filed in this matter. The dissent starts with a discussion of the subject of *conflict of interests* as distinguished from *conflict of duties*. It quotes a passage from DeFeo v. Smith, *infra* (17 N.J., at pp. 188–189, 110 A.2d, at p. 556), in which successive paragraphs speak of "the possibility of *conflicting interests*" and "the possibility of a *conflict in the obligations* of the positions in relation to the public interest." (Emphasis added.) The dissent does not suggest DeFeo holds a possible *conflict of interests* results in incompatibility of offices at common law, and quite clearly DeFeo did not intend to convey that thought. The question was not involved, and the case turned upon a finding of a conflict in *duties*.

The dissent here does not conclude, as we read it, that a possibility of a *conflict of interests* results in incompatibility of offices. We will discuss that subject more fully in "D" below. That a possible conflict of interests inheres in the present scene is obvious. It, however, is by no means indigenous to the roles of legislator and municipal attorney. On the contrary, it inheres in any local officeholding by a legislator. Indeed it is more pronounced if the legislator holds a local office which has the authority to make the policy decision to seek or to oppose legislation, a power which does not repose in the municipal attorney. It exists also with respect to the possible direct impact of legislation upon a local office itself, a possibility equally evident if the legislator be a municipal attorney or a school teacher or an assessor or a member of a planning board, etc. Even local *residence* (not required of a municipal attorney, N.J.S.A. 40:46–14) spells out a possible conflict of interests if the welfare of the municipality should become pitted against the welfare of others in the county or state. * * *

If the possibility of a *conflict of interests* were the touchstone for decision, the office of municipal attorney would be indistinguishable from any other local office. The dissent, as we have said, does not adopt that test, but rather adheres to the standard we apply. It is the application of that standard, *i.e.*, a conflict of *duties*, that the opinions in this case part company.

The dissent finds a conflict in the *duty* of a municipal attorney with the *duty* of a legislator in these respects: (1) rendition of legal advice to the municipality, (2) drafting of proposed legislation, and (3) the processing of bills in the legislative hall.

As to the first, we are unable to detect any conflict between the duty to legislate and the duty to advise with respect to the meaning of bills or statutes.

As to the second, many bills are prepared * * * by the Division of Law Revision and Bill Drafting, a part of a legislative agency (L.1954, c. 254, § 13c; N.J.S.A. 52:11–18c), at the behest of individual legislators. Doubtless, however, some are prepared by the municipal attorney and we agree it is his duty to do so if his superiors so direct. But if he should draw a bill, there is no conflict with the *duty* of a legislator.

The conflict involved in legislation revolves about the *policy* issue which a bill projects, and as to that issue the authority to decide to advocate or oppose legislation clearly is not within the office of the municipal attorney. He acts only after the policy decision is made by others; * * *. Just as the draftsman of a will may deplore the testator's wishes, so a municipal attorney may disagree with the policy decision he is asked to embody in a proposed bill. * * * The point is that the duty to act as a scrivener is not incompatible with a legislator's duty to pass upon the merits of a bill. If the dissent means that a municipal attorney may feel some compulsion to prefer his client's interests when he acts as legislator, we of course agree the possibility is evident, but it is no more or less so whether the bill is prepared by the attorney or by someone else. That conflict is one of *interests*. * * *

Finally the dissent finds it is the municipal attorney's duty to represent his client in the legislative process. It obviously is not the attorney's duty to introduce a bill; * * *. And with respect to persuading legislators for or against a bill or appearing at legislative hearings (a rare event in our State), the function is not inherently that of an attorney and hence is not impliedly the obligation of that office. * * * As we have already said, that role *may* be assigned to the municipal attorney (or to another local officer), and *if it is,* that office would then become incompatible with the office of legislator, but the duty not being the inherent obligation of the attorney's office, incompatibility in terms of *duties* cannot be found * * *.

Hence we are satisfied that here the possibility of a conflict lies in the area of interests rather than in the duties of office. If the common law prohibited local officeholding by a legislator because of the possibility of a conflict of interests, a remedy exists and it is within the authority of the courts to enforce it. If however the common law ban did not reach the subject, then the Legislature alone can cut the knot; the court could but nibble at it in those instances in which the possibility of some incidental conflict of duties might be detected. * * * It is well to be mindful that an indirect approach to the basic problem of conflict of interests may hinder a forthright solution, for if it suggests to others that a solution is already on hand, it may obscure the responsibility of the legislative branch to deal with the total problem in a comprehensive and decisive manner.

D

Although plaintiff rests his attack upon a claim of conflict in *duties* of the offices, the argument before us branched into the larger question, whether under the common law a legislator may hold *any* local office in view of a possible conflict of *interests* with respect to legislation affecting either his office or the municipality's welfare.

A ready answer can not be found in the traditional definition of the common law doctrine. As we have said, the doctrine in its specific applications has been applied to incompatibility in the *functions* or *duties* of office. The doctrine, however, is also expressed more vaguely to embrace an "inconsistency of *nature,* duty, or function which, from considerations of sound policy, cannot be lodged in one and the same functionary at one and the same time." DeFeo v. Smith, 17 N.J. 183, 187, 110 A.2d 553, 555 (1955) (emphasis added). Does a possibility of a conflict in interests come within the concept?

This much is clear. The doctrine does not denounce *all* dual officeholding. * * *

There is a difference between the subject of incompatible offices and the subject of conflict in *interests.* In the former, a clash of *duties* inheres in the very relationship of one office to the other * * *. On the other hand, a conflict in interests by virtue of a dual officeholding by a legislator will not inevitably arise as an incident of the relationship of the two offices. It may arise depending upon what bills are introduced. If it should, the incumbent is not put to a choice of duties. Rather the conflict relates to the duty of one office, the legislative seat. It is true that, if a conflict of interests should arise, it may cast a cloud upon the objectivity of the exercise of legislative discretion. Yet the possibility of a conflict of interests is not peculiar to the case of duality of officeholding by a legislator. Rather it is part of a larger problem which inheres in the nature of the legislative authority and confronts all members of that department of government. This is so because the police power and the taxing power range so widely that every legislator, whether he be in a private calling or in another public post or in neither, must inevitably have some interest which may conceivably be affected by some legislative proposal at some time.

We are not discussing the effect of an *actual* conflict of interests. Plainly the common law dealt with that subject and forbade an officer from acting in a particular matter permeated by an *actual* conflict. See, for example, Griggs v. Princeton, 33 N.J. 207, 62 A.2d 862 (1960). Rather, the question is whether the common law forbade the holding of office because of a possibility of a future conflict of interests. * * * Of course conflicts of that kind vary in intensity from the distant and inconsequential to the immediate and severe. And it may well be that public policy warrants excising from the total scene the possibility of a conflict of interests generated by additional public officeholding and employment. Indeed in some jurisdictions, organic law expressly forbids a legislator to hold local office. We referred above to the constitution of Arizona. See also Goodloe v. Fox, 96 Ky. 627, 29 S.W. 433 (Ct. App.1895); cf. Padron v. People of Puerto Rico ex rel. Castro, 142 F.2d 508 (1 Cir.1944), certiorari denied 323 U.S. 791, 65 S.Ct. 427, 89 L.Ed. 630 (1945). And as we have already said, our Legislature, which is the ultimate authority with respect to this issue, may constitutionally prohibit it. The question before us, however, is not whether it is unsound for a legislator to hold local office but rather whether the common law doctrine of incompatibility reached into the area of possible conflicts of interests and forbade such dual officeholding because of it.

No precedent in our State suggests a legislator is barred from local office by the common law doctrine. Elsewhere there is little discussion of the subject. In New York, it was expressly held there is no common law incompatibility. People ex rel. Ryan v. Green, 58 N.Y. 295 (Ct.App. 1874); People ex rel. Gilchrist v. Murray, 73 N.Y. 535 (Ct.App.1878); Stewart v. Mayor, etc., of City of New York, 15 App.Div. 548, 44 N.Y.S. 575 (App.Div.1897). A contrary conclusion was reached by a majority of the court in Weza v. Auditor General, 297 Mich. 686, 298 N.W. 368 (Sup.Ct.1941). There the office of county school commissioner was held to be "subordinate" to that of a member of the legislature because (298 N.W. at p. 368): * * * No authority was cited to support the proposition that the office is "subordinate" to the office of legislator as the term is used in the statement of the common law doctrine. * * * The case seems never to have been cited.

It is not disputed that historically legislators in our State have held local office as some now do. If illegality were clear, prior practice could not excuse it, State ex rel. Rogers v. Taggart, 118 N.J.L. 542, 547, 194 A. 164 (Sup.Ct.1937), affirmed 120 N.J.L. 243, 199 A. 47 (E. & A. 1938), but in ascertaining the sweep of a common law doctrine of uncertain limits, we can not wholly ignore what transpired without challenge, * * *. We know of no instance in our State in which it was suggested that under the common law a legislator may not hold a local office. * * * And in other jurisdictions in which the state constitution or statute was held not to bar legislators from local office, the possibility that the common law might be a barrier was not discussed. Carpenter v. People ex rel. Tilford, 8 Colo. 116, 5 P. 828 (Sup.Ct.1885); Commonwealth ex rel. Woodruff v. Joyce, 291 Pa. 82, 139 A. 742 (Sup.Ct.1927); Phillips v. West, 187 Tenn. 57, 213 S.W.2d 3 (Sup.Ct.1948); Boswell v. Powell, 163 Tenn. 445, 43 S.W.2d 495 (Sup.Ct.1931); cf. State ex rel. Baca v. Otero, 33 N.M. 310, 267 P. 68 (Sup.Ct.1928).

* * *

The matter is of obvious public interest and hence we should add a word about the respective responsibilities of the several branches of government under our Constitution. Except as to offices created by the Constitution, public offices and employments are ultimately the creatures of legislation. The Legislature alone may determine the duties and the interrelation of the public posts it establishes or authorizes to be established. Within the constitutional framework, the Legislature is the architect of the structure of government. The Judiciary has no creative power in that area. * * * Whether a further ban would be wise or unwise is not a subject upon which we may properly venture a view, and this opinion should not be understood to do so. We hold only that the common law did not bar the dual officeholding involved in this case, and that the question whether it should be barred in the public interest reposes in the power and responsibility of the legislative department.

The judgment is affirmed.

Notes

1. **Strict and Broad Construction of Incompatibility.** The *Reilly* view of the restricted operation of the incompatibility doctrine is widely followed. O'Malley v. Macejka, 44 N.Y.2d 530, 378 N.E.2d 88 (1978); McCabe v. Kane, 101 R.I. 119, 221 A.2d 103 (1966); Lillich and Linton, *Incompatible Municipal Offices in New York,* 28 Fordham L.Rev. 463 (1959). In Ahto v. Weaver, 39 N.J. 418, 189 A.2d 27 (1963), the New Jersey court held that a town mayor could lawfully serve on the staff of attorneys of the County Counsel even though "situations can arise where the interests of the county and his municipality will be at odds, with a consequent conflict of duties * * *." The court found that "it is not requisite that he be barred from holding office * * *" since the County Counsel could always avoid the mayor's conflicts problem by assigning other lawyers on his staff to matters affecting the mayor's town. Id. at 432–33, 189 A.2d at 34–35. Does this reasoning undermine the central purpose of the incompatibility rule? See Jones v. MacDonald, 33 N.J. 132, 162 A.2d 817, 819 (1960); Schear v. Elizabeth, 41 N.J. 321, 196 A.2d 774 (1964).

2. **Elements of Incompatibility.** "What constitutes incompatibility of officer functions is a difficult question. No standard rule can be laid down." Poynter v. Walling, 54 Del. (4 Storey) 409, 413, 177 A.2d 641, 644 (1962).

Under a strict reading, "physical impossibility is not the incompatibility of the common law" (see People v. Green, note 1 *supra,* at 304; People on Complaint of Chapman v. Rapsey, 16 Cal.2d 636, 107 P.2d 388 (1940)), but some courts consider physical impossibility relevant. State ex rel. Welty v. Outland, 149 Ohio St. 13, 77 N.E.2d 245 (1948); Perkins v. Manning, 59 Ariz. 60, 122 P.2d 857 (1942).

Incompatibility clearly arises from a supervising and a subordinate, supervised office. State ex rel. Hover v. Wolven, 175 Ohio St. 114, 191 N.E.2d 723 (1963); Welsch v. Wilson, 218 Ga. 843, 131 S.E.2d 194 (1963); Byrd v. State, 240 Ark. 743, 402 S.W.2d 121 (1966); State v. Thompson, 193 Tenn. 395, 246 S.W.2d 59 (1952). But courts often differ on whether a given office is "subordinate" to another. See generally 3 McQuillin, *Municipal Corporations,* § 12.67 (3rd ed. 1963).

3. **Modifications of the Common Law Rule.** A minority of jurisdictions permit an incumbent who holds impermissible plural offices to elect which one he may retain. McDonough v. Roach, 35 N.J. 153, 171 A.2d 307 (1961); Commonwealth ex rel. Crow v. Smith, 343 Pa. 446, 23 A.2d 440 (1942).

Where the incumbent is disqualified from taking a second position, a vacation rule cannot apply, since the condition of losing the first office never arises. State v. Thompson, 193 Tenn. 395, 246 S.W.2d 59 (1952). The automatic vacation rule is also inapplicable to offices which, by legislative mandate, may not be abandoned. State ex rel. Welty v. Outland, note 2, *supra.* For other instances of legislative supersedure of the rule vacating the first office, see generally Conklin, *Plural Office Holding,* 28 Ore.L.Rev. 332 (1949).

4. **Abrogation of Incompatibility Rule.** Concurrent holding of incompatible offices may be authorized by legislation. Schear v. Elizabeth, 41 N.J. 321, 196 A.2d 774 (1964); cf. Ahto v. Weaver, *supra*, note 1. Nor does incompatibility apply where two offices involving inconsistent duties are merged in one office. Davis v. Hale, 96 Ariz. 219, 393 P.2d 912 (1964). An extreme application of the abrogation principle was made in Commonwealth ex rel. Fox v. Swing, 409 Pa. 241, 186 A.2d 24 (1962). The court there held that constitutional authorization of legislative control over plural office holding removed all judicial power to declare offices incompatible, even where the legislature remained silent on that subject. But see Childs v. Moses, 265 App.Div. 353, 38 N.Y.S.2d 704 (1942) where the court held that legislation on plural office holding should be construed as intended to supplement, but not to destroy, the common law or the power of courts to advance common law policy.

5. **Incompatibility and Separation of Powers.** While the law on incompatible offices advances the principle of separating executive, legislative and judicial powers (Kaufman v. Pannuccio, 121 N.J.Super. 27, 295 A.2d 639 (1972)), the two should not be confused. In some cases the separation of powers principle has no application *viz.* in commission forms of municipal government which combine legislative and executive powers. See Poynter v. Walling, 54 Del. (4 Storey) 409, 177 A.2d 641 (1962).

DOYLE v. DEARBORN

Supreme Court of Michigan, 1963.
370 Mich. 236, 121 N.W.2d 473.

SMITH, JUSTICE. Plaintiff was a member of the State legislature from 1945 through 1962, serving in both the house and senate. Both positions paid a salary and expenses. While a member of the State senate, he was elected councilman of the city of Dearborn, taking the oath of office on November 22d, 1955. He resigned from the council September 10, 1957. No salary was paid him as councilman, although the Dearborn city charter provided for an annual salary of $2000. On September 21, 1961, he filed his declaration in assumpsit, claiming the city of Dearborn had refused and neglected to pay his salary as required by the city charter. Defendant city admits that plaintiff was elected to the office of councilman, but denies he is entitled to salary. Defendant claims that plaintiff was ineligible to enter upon duties as councilman because the city charter expressly prohibits anyone from holding elective office under the charter who occupies, at the time, any other public office except member of the Wayne county board of supervisors (to which the city is entitled to certain seats).

* * * The city charter of Dearborn specifies that it is unlawful for any elective official to hold any position on another public payroll.
* * *

The obvious and essential question is whether plaintiff is entitled to a salary in view of the language of the charter. Plaintiff claims on appeal that the charter provisions are no defense to his action because, in effect, the charter imposes restrictions on membership in the State legislature and that, in this regard, the State Constitution preempts the field.

It hardly need be said that the only valid limitations upon qualifications for membership in the State legislature are those imposed by state law. However, home-rule cities are mandated to establish in their charters the qualifications of its officers. The word "qualifications" as used in the statute is used in the generic sense and includes qualifications to be elected to office and also qualifications to hold the office, sometimes referred to as eligibility. Defendant city concedes that plaintiff was qualified to be elected to the office of councilman but denies that he was qualified to serve without first having resigned his office as a member of the State legislature. With this we agree. We think it is within the express authority of the home-rule act to impose such a restriction in the city charter. The restriction is not upon a person becoming a member of the State legislature but upon becoming city councilman. A person such as plaintiff, serving in the legislature at the time of his election to the council had an option, either to resign from the legislature and qualify as councilman, or to refuse the oath as councilman and stay in the legislature. As to the public policy considerations, manifest in the charter, two citations are of general import in this connection. In Mechem, Public Offices and Officers, bk. 2, ch. 4, § 427, p. 271, the statement is made:

"From motives of public policy, it is frequently provided in the state constitutions and statutes that a person shall not at the same time hold an office of trust or profit both under the State and under the Federal government; that persons holding judicial offices shall not at the same time hold other offices of trust or profit; that a person shall not at the same time hold two offices of trust or profit, and the like.

"These provisions often cover substantially the same ground as the common law prohibition against incompatible offices; but they also, in many cases, go further than that and arbitrarily prohibit the holding of two offices which the common law might not declare incompatible."

The author concludes in section 431, page 275, that:

"* * * a fortiori, where the charter of a city prohibits an alderman from holding any other office, and provides that by his election to and acceptance of another, his office as alderman shall immediately become vacant, any alderman who is elected to Congress and accepts the office ipso facto vacates his office of alderman." See People ex rel. Kelly v. Common Counsel of City of Brooklyn, 77 N.Y. 503, 33 Am.Rep. 659.

In a later exposition on the subject, 42 Am.Jur. § 58, p. 926, the following appears:

"Since a public office is a public agency or trust * * *, the holder of such an office is subject to such regulations and conditions as the law may impose. He cannot, therefore, complain of any restrictions which public policy may dictate on his holding of more than one office. The common law recognizes certain limitations on double office holding, and there are provisions in the Constitutions and statutes of the various states declaring or extending the common-law rule. Their manifest purpose is to prevent multiple office holding so that offices and places of public trust will not accumulate in a single person."

In this case, the charter provision is in line with the general public policy. Not offending either the State Constitution or the home-rule statute, necessarily, we conclude therefore that the charter restrictions are valid. * * * By its terms, the disqualification occurs by operation of law.

Regrettably, no one challenged the privilege of plaintiff to serve on the council while he was colorably a member. This, however, in no way negates the effect of the will of the electors validly to adopt such a provision in the charter. The same charter upon which plaintiff now expressly relies to create the claimed obligation negates any possibility of recovery through its automatic forfeiture provisions. We conclude therefore that the order granting summary judgment to defendant should be affirmed. Costs to defendant.

Notes

1. See also State ex rel. Corrigan v. Wheeler, 27 Ohio St.2d 9, 271 N.E.2d 862 (1971) (city commissioner seeking county employment); State ex rel. Platz v. Mucci, 10 Ohio St.2d 60, 225 N.E.2d 238 (1967) (teacher elected to office of councilman, held ineligible to take office). But see City of Kingsport v. Lay, 62 Tenn.App. 145, 459 S.W.2d 786 (1970) (school superintendent, elected alderman, held entitled to both salaries but only for term of the school district contract that was in effect at the time of his election). The proscription against dual office holding is often written into local charters and in state constitutions. See e.g. Smith v. State ex rel. Mayor and Town Council of Citronelle, 276 Ala. 378, 162 So.2d 473 (1964); cf. Kereiakes v. Graham, 458 S.W.2d 162 (Ky.App.1970). But legislative exemptions are often authorized. Mott v. Horstmann, 36 Cal.2d 388, 224 P.2d 11 (1950).

2. *Seeking Nomination or Election to a Second Office.* Absent legislative prohibition, an incumbent of an existing office may retain his office while seeking nomination or election to another office. Wilson v. Niesse, 251 Ind. 639, 244 N.E.2d 436 (1969); Kelly v. Reed, 76 Nev. 389, 355 P.2d 969 (1960); Burton v. Graham, 242 S.W.2d 855 (Ky.1951). But, the common law rule may be changed by legislation to provide for automatic resignation or ouster of an officer who seeks another office. Yonts v. Commonwealth ex rel. Armstrong, 700 S.W.2d 407 (Ky.1985); Morial v. Judiciary Comm'n, 565 F.2d 295 (5th Cir.1977), cert. denied 435 U.S. 1013, 98 S.Ct. 1887, 56 L.Ed.2d 395 (1978); Willis v. Fort Worth, 380 S.W.2d 814 (Tex.Civ.App. 1964); cf. Chalfin v. Specter, 426 Pa. 464, 233 A.2d 562 (1967). The Supreme Court has upheld such laws as constitutional. Clement v. Fashing, 457 U.S. 957, 102 S.Ct. 2836, 73 L.Ed.2d 508 (1982).

In some jurisdictions the conditions of vacating an office is not nomination or election, but actual assumption of the second office. See e.g., People ex rel. Kraemer v. Bagshaw, 55 Cal.App.2d 155, 130 P.2d 243 (1942) (first office not vacated at time of filing oath or bond); McCue v. Antisell, 105 N.J.Super. 128, 251 A.2d 308 (1969) (election victor held not to become officer until he qualified therefor).

4. SELF–APPOINTMENT AND NEPOTISM

Self-appointment and nepotism may involve both the evils of conflicting duties in plural positions (Ehlinger v. Clark, 117 Tex. 547, 8 S.W.2d 666 (1928)), and of personal interest conflicts (Haislip v. White, 124 W.Va. 633, 22 S.E.2d 361 (1942)). The fact that the opportunities and temptations to abuse official * * * power are so strong may explain why nepotism and self-appointment receive separate treatment in the law.

STATE v. THOMPSON

Supreme Court of Tennessee, 1952.
193 Tenn. 395, 246 S.W.2d 59.

TOMLINSON, JUSTICE. * * * The bill charges the defendant, J.J. Thompson, with having forfeited his office as a member of the Board of Commissioners * * *, and charges Thompson with unlawfully holding or exercising its office of City Manager. The bill seeks a judgment so holding as to both offices.

* * *

The Chancellor held that Thompson vacated his office as a Commissioner by accepting and assuming the office of City Manager, but that his appointment as City Manager was valid. Both sides have appealed. * * *

"The rule at common law is that, where one accepts a second office incompatible with one already held by him, the office first held is thereby ipso facto terminated without judicial proceedings of any kind". State ex rel. Little v. Slagle, 115 Tenn. 336, 341, 89 S.W. 326, 327. However, if Thompson's appointment to the second office was void it follows that his attempted acceptance of that second office was likewise legally ineffective. In this plight of the case the question arises as to whether this common law rule would apply. It is necessary, therefore, to first determine whether the Council had the authority to appoint one of its own members its City Manager.

The Charter of Paris provides that "the Board of Commissioners shall appoint and fix the salary of the City Manager". * * *

Of course, it was not the intention of the Legislature to permit the City Manager to be one of the five members of the Board which determines whether or not he shall be discharged for cause, or without cause after twelve months, or, as a member of the Board, to accept or reject or modify his own recommendation made as City Manager, or, as a member of the Board, to direct and supervise himself as City Manager in the administration of the affairs of the City. This statement of the situation seems conclusive of the fact that the two offices are completely incompatible.

As heretofore stated, the statute (the Charter of Paris) expressly provides that "the board of commissioners shall appoint and fix the salary of the city manager". The Legislature, in enacting this statute, knew that each commissioner is a trustee charged with the utmost fidelity to his cestui que trust, the City of Paris, and that each commissioner probably could not with due fidelity mingle his personal interests and affairs with his duties as such trustee, human nature being what it is. Therefore, when this statute provided that the commissioners should fix the salary of the City Manager it did by necessary implication forbid the Board from appointing one of its own members to that office. No other effect can logically be given this provision of the statute.

The immediately above stated necessary implication of the statute (Charter of Paris) is in accord with the common law rule on the subject. The text of 42 American Jurisprudence, page 955, Section 97, in so far as pertinent here, is this: "So, it is contrary to public policy to permit an officer having an appointing power to use such power as a means of conferring an office upon himself, or to permit an appointing body to appoint one of its own members."

* * *

There are a number of decisions of this court dealing with Board members voting * * * for a contract in which they were personally interested. But those decisions are not applicable to the question with which we are dealing since the rights and obligations of a public office are created by law, not by contract. Cornett v. City of Chattanooga, 165 Tenn. 563, 567, 56 S.W.2d 742. Nor have we been able to find any decision of this court dealing with this question, but we are referred to or find a number of such decisions in other States. Those decisions are fairly uniform in holding that a council or board which has the power and duty of appointment to an office cannot select one of its own members. Some that seem quite in point are Snipes v. City of Winston, 126 N.C. 374, 35 S.E. 610; Meglemery v. Weissinger, 140 Ky. 353, 131 S.W. 40, 31 L.R.A., N.S., 575; Gaw v. Ashley, 195 Mass. 173, 80 N.E. 790; Board of Commissioners v. Montgomery, 170 Ga. 361, 153 S.E. 34, 37; Arbogast v. Shields, 123 W.Va. 167, 14 S.E.2d 4.

* * *

Although we are keenly aware of an individual hardship that may result, we are compelled to conclude that both (1) under a proper construction of the statute (Charter of the City of Paris) and (2) under the common law, the Board of Commissioners of the City of Paris was without authority to appoint one of its own members to the office of City Manager of that City, and that the attempted appointment of Thompson was void; therefore, ineffective to place him in that office.

* * * In as much as Thompson's attempted acceptance of the second office (City Manager) was legally ineffective, it results that Thompson has not, legally speaking, held a second office while holding his first and incompatible office of Commissioner. Compare Reckner v. School District, 341 Pa. 375, 19 A.2d 402, 133 A.L.R. 1254. We think, therefore, that the remedy, if any, against Thompson with reference to his retention of the office of City Commissioner under the circumstances is under the provisions of the Ouster Statute carried in the code at section 1877 et seq., rather than under the quo warranto statute. The decree of the Circuit Court holding that Thompson has vacated his office as commissioner must, therefore, be reversed.

The bill seeks a judgment against Thompson for the use and benefit of the City of Paris in an amount equal to all of the funds of the City paid to him as City Manager.

* * *

As heretofore pointed out the attempted appointment of Thompson to this office was illegal and void, and against public policy. If he is allowed to retain the money so paid him under this illegal and void act it would be very detrimental to the effectiveness of the public policy involved, and quite contrary to the public interest. The extent of profit which a person would then receive from the illegal receipt of public funds in this manner would depend only upon how long it would take in court proceedings to get him out of the office. That would be much to the detriment of the public interest, as well as to the public policy involved. For that reason, perhaps among others, it is generally held that the public funds of a municipality paid out under appointment to office that is void, * * * may be recovered back from the person to whom it was paid, and that this rule is of general application, and "is so inflexible that no inquiry into the good or bad intention of the officer * * * is permitted." 63 C.J.S., Municipal Corporations, §§ 989–990, pp. 552–554. The principle upon which recovery is allowed is one of prevention, rather than remedial justice. Its purpose is to remove from a public official the temptation to so violate his office of trust for personal benefit. Compare Tisdale v. Tisdale, 34 Tenn. 596.

It results that the petitioner is entitled to a judgment against Thompson for the use and benefit of the City of Paris in an amount equal to the total amount paid him out of the public funds of the City for salary as City Manager. * * *

* * *

NEIL, CHIEF JUSTICE (dissenting).

* * *

I concur in the view that J.J. Thompson, being a City Commissioner, was ineligible to hold the office of City Manager; that under the circumstances his election to that office was in violation of law. But he was a *de facto* officer * * *. Moreover no other person claimed any right or title to the office, or the emoluments thereof.

If he had brought suit to recover compensation for his services as de facto officer, I would hold that, by the possible weight of authority, his right of action would fail. He is not here seeking any affirmative relief in that regard.

I base my dissent from the majority opinion upon the following authorities.

In 67 C.J.S., Officers, § 145, p. 446, it is said: "Since the collection of the salary annexed to the office is an incident to the title, a de facto officer has no legal right to the emoluments of the office. It has, however, been held that an actual incumbent of a public office who is an officer de facto is entitled to the compensation attached to the office, *where there is no adverse contestant or de jure officer,* and he has acted in good faith with prima facie evidence of a right to perform the duties." (Emphasis supplied).

* * *

I think public policy has much to do in forbidding the election of Thompson to the office of City Manager, but it is not a controlling principle in determining the right of the City of Paris to compel the refund of his salary. He was performing the duties of the office under a mistaken view of the law, and his right to do so was not questioned from any source until the present suit was instituted. With all deference to the view of the majority I cannot agree that the refusal by the court to require a refund by a de facto officer would "encourage the occupant of the office to continue to hold it in violation of law."

Notes

1. **The Not-So-Common Law.** The principal case appears to represent the majority view. See State ex rel. Bove v. McDaniel, 52 Del. (2 Storey) 304, 157 A.2d 463 (1960); and the authorities tabulated in Raynovich v. Romanus, 450 Pa. 391, 402–3, 299 A.2d 301, 307–8 (1973) (dissenting opinion). *But see* Jackson v. Maypearl Ind. Sch. District, p. 802, infra, which takes the position of dissent in the principal case. In Raynovich, supra, the majority upheld the borough council appointment of one of its members to the vacated office of mayor, "We start with the premise that absent a statutory prohibition, a borough council may select one of its members to fill a mayoral vacancy. * * * It would indeed seem counterproductive and contrary to the public interest to establish for the first time a rule that one who has been elected by his fellow citizens, served on the council, and presumably has knowledge and experience in local government affairs is per se ineligible to fill a vacancy in the mayor' office. We are not disposed to fashion such a categorical rule." Id. at 394, 299 A.2d at 303. Connecticut has also refused to recognize an absolute common law prohibition against self-appointment. See State ex rel. Kenney v. Ranslow, 21 Conn.Sup. 294, 154 A.2d 526 (1959). Cf. Ehlinger v. Clark, 117 Tex. 539, 8 S.W.2d 666 (1928).

The incomplete development of common law policy has been noted officially: "We are not entirely sure that there is no California public policy against self-appointment. * * * We state only our own opinion.

Our opinion is partly a matter of ascertaining the law and partly a matter of prognosticating a judicially-acceptable result. * * * In view of the overwhelming weight of judicial authority in other states * * * we do not believe the California courts would reject the rule against self-appointment as an expression of California public policy." 23 Op.Cal.Atty.Gen. 75 (1954).

2. **Legislative Variants.** Many statutes enact a firm rule against self-appointment. See e.g. Mass.Gen. Laws Ann. c. 268A, § 8A. Absent constitutional restraint, however, self-appointment may be authorized by local charter or by legislation. Cf. Kopczynski v. Schriber, 194 Mich. 553, 161 N.W. 238 (1917) (upholding charter provision which authorized election of mayor by and from the ranks of the city commission).

Where legislation is not clear on self-appointment, courts may follow the "common law" policy: "[W]hen a statute confers appointing power and does not expressly authorize self-appointment, the appointment of someone other than self is always contemplated." Welsch v. Wilson, 218 Ga. 843, 844, 131 S.E.2d 194, 196 (1963).

3. **Indirect Forms of Self-Appointment.** In Welsch v. Wilson, supra, the court enjoined payment to the mayor for services rendered pursuant to a councilmanic resolution which authorized special payments to the mayor for services that were normally covered by the duties of the city manager,—a position which could be filled by appointment of the mayor and council. But see Baillie v. Medley, 262 So.2d 693 (Fla.App.1972). In People ex rel. Scott v. Grivetti, 50 Ill.2d 156, 277 N.E.2d 881 (1971) the court held that a constitutional authorization to the legislature to appoint members of a redistricting committee did not authorize the legislature to appoint either its own members, or their subordinate aides.

Nepotism

"Nepotism has been defined as the bestowal of patronage by public officers in appointing others to offices or position by reason of their blood or marital relationship to the appointing authority, rather than because of the merit or ability of the appointee." State ex rel. Robinson v. Keefe, 111 Fla. 701, 149 So. 638 (1933). Anti-nepotism provisions appear in constitutional, charter and statutory law to disqualify appointment of persons who are related in specified degrees to appointive officials even though no personal conflict of interest could be proved. Such provisions sometime impose stronger sanctions than those prescribed for conflicts of interest. See e.g. State ex rel. McKittrick v. Whittle, 333 Mo. 705, 63 S.W.2d 100 (1933) (school board director held to forfeit office by appointing a relative as a teacher in violation of anti-nepotism provisions of the state constitution); *accord:* Haislip v. White, 124 W.Va. 633, 22 S.E.2d 361 (1942); State ex inf. Ellis ex rel. Patterson v. Ferguson, 333 Mo. 1177, 65 S.W.2d 97 (1933).

While anti-nepotism statutes abound, the case law is very sparse. Consequently few generalizations can be made with respect to varied statutes.

In Jackson v. Maypearl Independent School District, 392 S.W.2d 892 (Tex.Civ.App.1965) the court refused to overturn actions taken by **tax** officials who were appointed in violation of anti-nepotism statutes. Since the appointees were deemed to be *de facto* officers, their actions were held to be binding. In State v. Keefe, supra, the court construed the anti-nepotism statute as inapplicable to certified teachers since their qualifications were established by general state certification laws. Further exception to the anti-nepotism statute was made in Baillie v. Medley, 262 So.2d 693 (Fla.App.1972) for a lightly populated town: "In these small communities of less than three hundred voters, the probability is that many of the residents are related ' * * * within the fourth degree, either by consanguinity or by affinity * * *' * * * the application of section 116.10 or 116.111 to 'towns' might render the municipal corporation inoperative for lack of qualified persons to serve as elected or appointed officials. The common weal would not be served." Id. at 697. Exception may be made where application of anti-nepotism statute would be constitutionally suspect. In Backman v. Bateman, 1 Utah 2d 153, 263 P.2d 561 (1953) the court held an anti-nepotism statute inapplicable to a principal and to a teacher whose brother was elected to the school board long after they were first employed by the district. Cf. People v. Simpkins, 45 Ill.App.3d 202, 3 Ill.Dec. 969, 359 N.E.2d 828 (1977).

5. CONFLICTS OF INTEREST

It has long been recognized that "[T]he best security for the fidelity of mankind is to make their interest coincide with their duty." The Federalist No. 23 at 437 (Mentor ed. 1961 A. Hamilton).

"Conflict of interest" broadly indicates the occasions in which the personal interest of an officer (or an employee) may exert a compromising or adverse influence upon the objective exercise of official duties and discretion. The abuse of official power or influence for personal gain cannot be eliminated by any law, but various prophylactic rules and codes have been developed to minimize such hazards.

The ways in which the public trust can be undermined by personal conflicts are too numerous to canvass, especially where the connection between official obligation and personal interest is not direct, immediate or monetary. The more familiar examples of conflicts of interests include self dealing, self appointment, or nepotism, selling of official favors (whether by extortion, bribery, campaign contributions, legal retainers or post-term employment), and the use or disclosure of confidential official information for private gain. The subject of conflicts in awarding public contracts, discussed in chapter VIII, § C, is but one aspect of this much broader problem of personal conflicts.

The separation of adverse official and personal interest cannot be ideally achieved. In many instances persons with the expertise required by government would decline public service if required to surrender and sever all outside income, employment, and business connections. The practical task is to strike a fair balance between preventing "dangerous" conflicts and preserving legitimate personal interest of officeholders. Where guidelines cannot be fashioned for such balancing, alternative safeguards, such as public disclosure of the finances of elected officials, may serve to heighten an official's sensitivity to potential conflicts.

Conflicts problems vary with the office held. Officials with greater power, such as legislators, encounter greater difficulty in reconciling personal and political interests with official duty. They are expected to represent constituents, as well as the general public, but being mostly attorneys, they also expect to be paid for legal services, even when it draws them into client representation involving government agencies. On the many difficulties encountered in shaping conflicts laws and codes of behavior, see generally *Developments—Conflict of Interests,* 94 Harv.L.Rev. 1244 (1981); Eisenberg, *Conflicts of Interests Situations and Remedies,* 13 Rutgers L.Rev. 666 (1959); Feinberg and Porro, *Ethics, Incompatibility and Conflict of Interests of Public Officials,* 7 Current Municipal Problems 393 (1966); Note, *Conflicts of Interest of State and Local Legislators,* 55 Iowa L.Rev. 450 (1969); Comment, *Legislative Conflicts of Interest—An Analysis of the Pennsylvania Legislative Code of Ethics,* 19 Vill.L.Rev. 82, particularly 83, notes 7 and 8 (1973).

ANDERSON v. PARSONS

Supreme Court of Kansas, 1972.
209 Kan. 337, 496 P.2d 1333.

PRAGER, JUSTICE.

* * *

The appellants, Mr. and Mrs. Anderson, raise a number of points on this appeal which attack the validity of various proceedings in the development of the urban renewal program in Parsons. * * *

The appellants' first point involves an alleged conflict of interest arising from the fact that City Commissioners Myer S. Freshman and Barton Dean and all of the five urban renewal commissioners owned property within the general urban renewal area at the time they voted on various resolutions during the progress of the urban renewal program. The legislature provided in the urban renewal law for a special conflict of interest section to disqualify any officer or employee of the city or of the urban renewal board who owned property included or planned to be included in an urban renewal project. * * *

It is undisputed * * * that * * * at the time the resolutions were passed by the city commission declaring certain areas of Parsons to be "slum and blight areas" and creating and appointing the urban renewal agency, two of the three Parsons city commissioners owned real estate in the slum or blight areas. The same two commissioners continued to own their properties at the time the urban renewal plan was adopted. The two commissioners mentioned were Myer S. Freshman and Barton Dean. On January 22, 1969, the city commission by resolution approved the urban renewal project. At that time commissioners Freshman and Dean owned property within the urban renewal *area* but did not own any land within the area covered by the urban renewal project. As pointed out heretofore, at all stages in the development of the urban renewal program, all of the five urban renewal commissioners had an interest in property located within the general urban renewal area. The first issue to be determined is whether or not the various actions ＊ ＊ ＊ of the Parsons city commissioners in approving the urban renewal plan and in approving the urban renewal project were so tainted with conflict of interest within the meaning of K.S.A. 17–1758 as to completely invalidate *ab initio* all of the actions and steps taken by the urban renewal board and by the city commissioners in developing the Parsons urban renewal program. It should be emphasized that each of the commissioners made a full disclosure of his property interest in the urban renewal area before participating in any action of his board.

We, of course, recognize the common law principle that a public officer owes an undivided duty to the public whom he serves and is not permitted to place himself in a position that will subject him to conflicting duties or cause him to act other than for the best interests of the public. If he acquires any interest adverse to those of the public, without a full disclosure it is a betrayal of his trust and a breach of confidence. (United States v. Carter, 217 U.S. 286, 30 S.Ct. 515, 54 L.Ed. 769.)

The law, however, does not forbid the holding of an office and exercising powers thereunder because of a *possibility* of a future conflict of interest. (Reilly v. Ozzard, 33 N.J. 529, 66 A.2d 360, 89 A.L.R.2d 612.) It has generally been held that the vote of a council or board member who is disqualified because of interest or bias in regard to the subject matter being considered may not be counted in determining the necessary majority for valid action. There are many cases cited ＊ ＊ ＊ in support of this principle. It is also the rule that where the required majority exists without the vote of the disqualified member, his presence and vote will not invalidate the result and further that a majority vote need not be invalidated where the interest of a member is general or of a minor character. [Citations omitted]

The difficult problem which is often presented in conflict of interest cases is in determining whether or not the personal interest of the commissioner or board member is of a nature justifying disqualification to act. Usually this is a question to be determined under the peculiar facts and circumstances of the particular case presented to the court for determination.

＊ ＊ ＊

As pointed out heretofore in the case at bar the claim of disqualification of the urban renewal commissioners and the city commissioners arises from the specific statute, K.S.A. 17–4758, ＊ ＊ ＊. The first paragraph of the statute deals with public officers who voluntarily *acquire* an interest in property included or planned to be included in an urban renewal project. This paragraph is not applicable here since all of the property interests of the various commissioners were owned long prior to the beginning of the urban renewal program in Parsons. The second paragraph, however, might reasonably be applicable since it is directed toward public officers who own or control property included or planned to be included in any urban renewal project.

When a close analysis of paragraph two of the statute is made it is clear that before a public officer is disqualified two elements are necessary: (1) He must own, or within the preceding two years have owned, an interest in property included or planned to be included *in any urban renewal project.* (2) Such officer is precluded from participating in any action of his board "affecting such property."

The term "Urban Renewal Project" is specifically defined in K.S.A. 17–4760(j) to include "undertakings or activities of a municipality in an urban renewal area for the elimination and for the prevention of the development of spread of slums and blight, * * *." In K.S.A. 17–4760(m) the term "Urban Renewal Area" is defined as "a slum area or a blighted area or a combination thereof which the local governing body designates as appropriate for an urban renewal project." We have concluded that the conflict of interest statute, K.S.A. 17–1758, disqualifies a commissioner only where the property interest of the commissioner exists in property included or planned to be included in a specific urban renewal project and does not apply where the commissioner owns property in the general urban renewal area not included within the specific urban renewal project upon which action is being taken. It seems obvious to this court that there may be a number of specific urban renewal projects which are developed from time to time under the general urban renewal plan. The disqualification is not a blanket disqualification covering *all* actions of a city commissioner or urban renewal commissioner who owns property in the urban renewal area. The disqualification is limited to actions where the officer or employee has an interest in property which is included or planned to be included in the specific urban renewal project under consideration. Until there is a specific urban renewal project to be voted on the statute does not come into play.

In the case at bar the record does not disclose that any city commissioner or urban renewal commissioner participated in voting on any urban renewal project in which he owned an interest in property included or planned to be included in the specific urban renewal project under consideration. * * *

The appellants in this case have relied upon Wilson v. Iowa City, 165 N.W.2d 813. In *Wilson* the Supreme Court of Iowa had before it a statute which was practically identical with K.S.A. 17–4758. There is language in this Iowa case which might well justify a court in taking the position that an urban renewal commissioner or city commissioner owning property within the general urban renewal area is disqualified from participating in the voting on a resolution establishing an urban renewal project even though the property of such commissioner was not included within the specific urban renewal project area being voted on. The decision in the *Wilson* case was handed down by the Supreme Court of Iowa on March 11, 1969. We note that following this decision the legislature of Iowa took immediate action to amend the conflict of interest statute effective April 26, 1969, and thereby nullified the *Wilson* decision. * * *

We believe that the interpretation of K.S.A. 17–4758 which we have adopted is sound and is consistent with the rationale contained in City of Topeka v. Huntoon, supra. We adhere to the rule that members of a public board are disqualified to vote as such on proposals on which they have a prime interest adverse to the municipality they represent. This rule should not be applied, however, under the circumstances presented in the case before us. We hold that K.S.A. 17–4758 is not applicable to disqualify any of the urban renewal commissioners or the city commissioners in acting upon the resolutions complained of by the appellants in this case.

Note

Tenants of public housing authorities were held ineligible to serve on the authorities in control of their tenancies. Brown v. Kirk, 64 Ill.2d 144, 355 N.E.2d 12 (1976); Housing Authority of City of New Haven v. Dorsey, 164 Conn. 247, 320 A.2d 820 (1973).

* * *

DALY v. TOWN PLAN AND ZONING COMMISSION OF TOWN OF FAIRFIELD

Supreme Court of Errors of Connecticut, 1963.
150 Conn. 495, 191 A.2d 250.

ALCORN, ASSOCIATE JUSTICE.

[The Supreme Court of Errors held that commission approval of zoning amendment permitting erection of radio broadcasting antenna was invalid because one of its members participated in the decision and was an officer of a group which had contracted to sell land to the broadcasting company if the zoning change could be obtained.]

Under the zoning regulations of the town of Fairfield, originally adopted in 1925, no provision was made for radio towers in any zone. This limitation continued until 1960, when the defendant, the town plan and zoning commission, initiated and adopted an amendment to permit radio towers to be erected in residence zones under restrictions not now material. * * * The single question is whether the court was correct in deciding that the commission's action is invalid because one of its members, Elbert S. Overbaugh, was disqualified.

* * *

The record is silent as to what part, if any, Overbaugh took either in initiating the proposal for the amendment or in the discussions among the members of the commission prior to its ultimate decision to adopt the change. This information is unnecessary, however, because the action of the commission, taken under the circumstances disclosed, leaves Overbaugh's part in it open to misinterpretation or question by interested property owners. It is unnecessary to repeat here the standards we said in Low v. Madison, 135 Conn. 1, 60 A.2d 774, were to be required in such cases. We there pointed out (135 Conn. p. 7, 60 A.2d p. 777) that our decisions over the years have involved "a common and unifying philosophy of public official conduct in which fairness and impartiality [are] fundamental." While recognizing that we will not indulge in any assumption that public officers have acted dishonorably, we have declared it to be the policy of the law to keep public officials "so far from temptation as to insure the exercise of unselfish public interest." 135 Conn. 8, 60 A.2d 777.

Following the declaration of policy in Low v. Madison, the General Assembly gave it legislative support by enacting what is now § 8–11 of the General Statutes, which provides: "No member of any zoning commission or board and no member of any zoning board of appeals or of any municipal agency exercising the powers of any zoning commission or board of appeals, whether existing under the general statutes or under any special act, shall appear for or represent any person, firm, corporation or other entity in any matter pending before the planning or zoning commission or board or said board of appeals or any agency exercising the powers of any such commission or board in the same municipality, whether or not he is a member of the board or commission hearing such matter. No member of any zoning commission or board and no member of any zoning board of appeals shall participate in the hearing or decision of the board or commission of which he is a member upon any matter in which he is directly or indirectly interested in a personal or financial sense." Clearly, Overbaugh's appearance before the zoning board of appeals was a violation of that statute. The limited question on this appeal—whether it was a violation of that statute for him to participate in the hearing and the decision of the town plan and zoning commission, of which he was a member—is only incidental to whether such participation by him transgressed our public policy as declared in the Low case. There is nothing before us to indicate that any improper influence was exerted by Overbaugh on his associates, and we impute no such influence to him by our decision in this case. The evil lies not in influence improperly exercised but rather in the creation of a situation tending to weaken public confidence and to undermine the sense of security of individual rights which the property owner must feel assured will always exist in the exercise of zoning power. Mills v. Town Plan & Zoning Commission, 144 Conn. 493, 499, 134 A.2d 250. Involved, as Overbaugh was, in the action which he had advocated before the zoning board of appeals concerning the use of what was then described as the only suitable property in the town of Fairfield for the erection of a radio tower, he should have disqualified himself from any participation in action by the commission, of which he was a member, to amend the zoning regulations in a manner which would open the door to the very use he had unsuccessfully advocated before the board of appeals. See Lage v. Zoning Board of Appeals, 148 Conn. 597, 604, 172 A.2d 911. Overbaugh's participation in the action taken renders the attempted amendment invalid.

* * *

Note

1. **Effects of Participation by Disqualified Officer.** The two preceding opinions evidence the division of authority on the consequences of conflict of interest. *Daly* applies a strict rule of disqualification based upon the bare fact of participation, while Anderson voices the rule that the participation must have been necessary to produce the challenged resolution. In accord with *Daly,* see Baker v. Marley, 8 N.Y.2d 365, 170 N.E.2d 900 (1960); cf. Singewald v. Minneapolis Gas Co., 274 Minn. 556, 142 N.W.2d 739 (1966).

Where the mayor, as a private attorney, represents a client before a zoning board, whose members are appointed by the mayor, should the proceeding be nullified? See Place v. Board of Adjustment Borough of Saddle River, 42 N.J. 324, 332, 200 A.2d 601, 605 (1964). Where a township commissioner votes to appoint his law partner as township solicitor, is the action unlawful? Cf. Snyderwine v. Craley, 434 Pa. 349, 254 A.2d 16 (1969); Graham v. McGrail, 370 Mass. 133, 345 N.E.2d 888 (1976).

S & L ASSOCIATES, INC. v. WASHINGTON

Superior Court of New Jersey, Appellate Division, 1960.
61 N.J.Super. 312, 160 A.2d 635.

GOLDMANN, S.J.A.D.

* * *

V

Plaintiff's final point is that the ordinance and its amendment should be set aside because tainted with the self-interest of the officials who participated in their preparation and adoption, * * *.

* * * As we said in Aldom v. Roseland, 42 N.J.Super. 495, at pages 502, 503 and 507, 127 A.2d 190 (1956), the interest which disqualifies need not be a direct, pecuniary one: it may be indirect. Basically, the question is whether the public official, by reason of a personal interest in the matter, is placed in a situation of temptation to serve his own purposes, to the prejudice of those for whom the law authorizes him to act. The validity of his action does not rest upon proof of fraud, dishonesty, loss to the municipality, or whether he was in fact influenced by his personal interest. We take note, also, of the prohibition contained in the Municipal Planning Act, N.J.S.A. 40:55–1.4: "No member of the planning board shall be permitted to act on any matter in which he has, either directly or indirectly, any personal or financial interest."

In this connection, see, generally, Note, "The Doctrine of Conflicting Interests Applied to Municipal Officials in New Jersey," 12 Rutg.L. Rev. 582 (1958); * * *. But *cf.* Wilson v. Long Branch, 27 N.J. 360, 142 A.2d 837 (1958), certiorari denied 358 U.S. 873, 79 S.Ct. 113, 3 L.Ed. 2d 104 (1958), where our Supreme Court refused to upset resolutions of the governing body and planning board declaring a certain area to be blighted. The chairman of the planning board was the president, a director and stockholder of a bank holding mortgages on property in the area; another member was a director and stockholder of the same bank; a third was municipal health officer and resided some 300 feet from the blighted area. The court held their interests "so remote and contingent as not to warrant disqualification."

The most recent case dealing with the question under discussion is Van Itallie v. Franklin Lakes, 28 N.J. 258, 146 A.2d 111 (1958), involving an attack upon two zoning ordinances because two councilmen had allegedly conflicting interests. In holding these too remote to call for disqualification the court said:

> "Local governments would be seriously handicapped if every possible interest, no matter how remote and speculative, would serve as a disqualification of an official. If this were so, it would discourage capable men and women from holding public office. Of course, courts should scrutinize the circumstances with great care and should condemn anything which indicates the likelihood of corruption or favoritism. But in doing so they must also be mindful that to abrogate a municipal action at the suggestion that some remote and nebulous interest is present, would be to unjustifiably deprive a municipality in many important instances of the services of its duly elected or appointed officials. * * *"

The decision whether a specific interest is sufficient to disqualify a public official is necessarily a factual one, depending upon the circumstances of the particular case.

In passing upon plaintiff's claim of conflict of interest the Law Division judge took into account the very limited population of the township, remarking that "where a small group of persons in a small municipality undertakes to achieve anything as broad in scope as a zoning ordinance, it is inevitable that there will be some conflict of interest in the sense that they would have some personal interest which would be affected by the ordinance, and that is all I see here." He found that the officials involved had acted fairly and without venality, so that there was no ground for plaintiff's charge of self-interest. This would support a finding that there was no fraud or collusion, and would also seem dispositive of the claim that the township committee and the planning board showed favoritism toward Umstadter, who was on the Industrial Development Commission.

That commission, as we have noted, is a purely advisory, unofficial body, * * *. It did not propose any of the legislation in question. Commission member Umstadter, who would appear to be the prime target of plaintiff's charge of self-interest, is not a township official. He had no part in the actions taken by the planning board or governing body. Such personal interest as he might have is therefore without significance in the present setting.

The question remains whether the interests of the township officials under attack fit the test laid down in our cases. * * * Those officials are Spencer, Guerin and Hemmings, of the planning board; Harrison, the township engineer; and Andrews, one of the three members of the township committee.

Spencer was on the planning board until December 1957, when he resigned. In May 1958, a year after plaintiff's tract was denied classification as industrial, Spencer, representing a group who desired to purchase plaintiff's tract, offered it a price higher than it had paid. We perceive no conflicting private interest on his part. There is nothing in the record indicating any interest in that tract, or for that matter in any other, by Spencer while still a planning board member.

* * *

Andrews, of the township committee, was an officer and stockholder in the Hager Water Co., as was Umstadter. The company supplied potable water to that part of the township which, it would appear from the testimony, lies east of Middle Valley Road and Route 24, which respectively lead southwest and east away from the central, developed Long Valley section. * * * Plaintiff argues that it is not too much to assume that had its tract been zoned for industry, it would compete with the Scott-Umstadter tract and might well affect the water revenues received by Hager Water Co. From this it spells out a self-interest on the part of Andrews which vitiated his participation as one of the three township committeemen in the adoption of the ordinances.

We find the argument entirely too tenuous. There is an available water supply on that portion of Umstadter's land which lies within the enlarged Scott-Umstadter industrial zone. Umstadter has a relatively new pump house and equipment on his remaining premises close by. * * * Presently Umstadter can pump 1,200,000 gallons a day. There is a place on his lands that would permit of the storage of water through damming. The water system is now used for irrigation, but Umstadter testified that if industry came to the Scott-Umstadter tract, it could be supplied by water from his pumping station, permission first having been obtained from the Public Utility Commission.

In light of this available water supply, the possibility of Hager Water Co. furnishing water to plants that might come to the industrial park is very problematical. Since it already supplies residences and farms in what we have described as the eastern section of the township, a new supply of water would have to be obtained. New and larger lines would have to be installed. State agency permission would have to be obtained. Most important, and before any of these steps were undertaken, industries would have to locate on the Scott-Umstadter tract and contracts entered into with them to supply industrial water. Accordingly, we find Andrews' interest entirely too remote and contingent to affect the validity of the ordinances.

In considering whether the participation of Guerin and Hemmings in the proceedings leading to the ordinance under attack invalidated it, a distinction should be drawn between the decision to place their own properties in the industrial zone and the decision to exclude plaintiff's tract therefrom. If only the former were implicated, a conclusion to condemn the ordinance on grounds of self-interest would be questionable. It is to be emphasized that original zoning was being effectuated. * * * Since presumably all or most planning board members in municipalities of the general size and character of Washington Township own property therein, a general rule disqualifying owners from participating in an act of original zoning would not seem to be practicable or desirable. * * * In the present case Guerin and Hemmings merely offered to make their properties available for industrial zoning. There is no presumption that this was necessarily favorable treatment of such property, it appearing that those who volunteered land for industrial purpose were few in number.

We therefore need not decide whether, without more, the placement of the Guerin and Hemmings properties in the industrial zone would of itself have been fatal to the ordinance on grounds of conflict of interest. However, insofar as the exclusion of plaintiff's property from the industrial zone is concerned, we conclude that their participation did involve invidious self-interest, calling for disqualification of the resulting official action. Once it was officially decided that the Guerin and Hemmings parcels were to be zoned industrial, those individuals had a natural economic stake in the exclusion of a tract like plaintiff's from that category. That tract, with its freight railroad, high tension lines, roads and river, was of a size fairly comparable to those of Guerin and Hemmings, and obviously competitive. The Scott-Umstadter tract could not reasonably be considered competitive; it was in a class by itself—the only property suitable for the industrial park which the township so much desired in order to attract substantial industry.

The number of tracts eventually zoned industrial were relatively few. Consequently, owners like Guerin and Hemmings had a competitive interest in restricting the number of tracts similar to theirs which might be so classified, and therefore an appreciable self-interest in the exclusion of plaintiff's property therefrom. The matter of their actual good faith becomes immaterial in such circumstances. The crucial question is merely one of the existence of a potential conflicting interest in the matter being debated and decided, to an extent which can be considered more than remote or contingent. Such, we think, was the case here.

Although Guerin was not a member of the planning board when he offered his tract for consideration as an industrial zone, he, together with Hemmings, was a member when the board voted to exclude plaintiff's property from the industrial zone. * * * Both participated in the discussions and action taken by the planning board in rejecting plaintiff's application to have its tract approved for industrial use. This was enough to bring their activity within the proscribed sphere established by the Aldom case. It is of little moment that there were sufficient votes, apart from their own, to have effected these results. Aldom v. Roseland, above, 42 N.J.Super., at page 507, 127 A.2d 190; Pyatt v. Mayor, etc., of Dunellen, 9 N.J. 548, 557, 89 A.2d 1 (1952), * * *.

We conclude that since the participation of Guerin and Hemmings in the action of the planning board affected or may have affected the recommendation of that body in a material respect, the recommendation must be set aside. There being absent the statutory prerequisite of planning board recommendation for the zoning action of the governing body, [citations omitted] the ordinance and its amendment must be set aside. Upon any future new consideration of a zoning ordinance by the planning board, Guerin and Hemmings should refrain from participation in its deliberations or recommendation.*

Notes

1. **Ascertainment of Conflict of Interest.** The cases recognize that the determination of a conflict often involves questions of fact. Compare e.g. Warren v. Leesburg, 203 So.2d 522 (Fla.App.1967) (voiding conveyance by city to one of its officials) with City of Coral Gables v. Weksler, 164 So.2d 260 (Fla.App.1964) (upholding city lease to its employee). The view that the personal interest need not be direct or pecuniary to create a disqualifying conflict, has a respectable following. United States v. Mississippi Valley Generating Co., 364 U.S. 520, 81 S.Ct. 294, 5 L.Ed.2d 268 (1961); Schaefer v. Berinstein, 140 Cal.App.2d 278, 295 P.2d 113 (1956); Delta Elec. Const. Co. v. San Antonio, 437 S.W.2d 602 (Tex.Civ.App.1969). But that view is not universal. "[T]o disqualify, the personal pecuniary interest of the official must be immediate, definite and capable of demonstration; not remote, uncertain, contingent and speculative, that is, such 'that men of ordinary capacity and intelligence would not be influenced by it.' * * * [O]nly a direct personal and pecuniary interest on the part of an official in the matter under consideration requires his disqualification to act thereon." Atherton v. Concord, 109 N.H. 164, 165–66, 245 A.2d 387, 388–89 (1968); *semble:* Brown v. Kirk, p. 807, supra.

Even in jurisdictions which disapprove indirect personal conflicts, there are divergent opinions on the degree of proximity that gives rise to impermissible conflicts. Compare e.g. Griggs v. Princeton, 33 N.J. 207, 162 A.2d 862 (1960) (action affecting property of Princeton University, by two members of council, who were also employed by Princeton University, held invalid by reason of conflict of interest) with Katz v. Brandon, 156 Conn. 521, 245 A.2d 579 (1968) (action by city council to support a redevelopment project upheld though one councilman served as union agent in a company

---

* This case was reversed in part as to facial validity of the ordinance. 35 N.J. 224, 172 A.2d 657 (1961).

that was interested in the redevelopment). "While personal advantage * * * is one of the elements to be considered, it is not the only test * * *. * * * The decision to redevelop the area was made in the public interest, and the interests of Cronin and Olivette, were neither greater than nor in any way different from the interest of any other citizen of Hartford. On the facts of this case, we can find no conflict of interest which would reflect on, or interfere with, the performance by Cronin of his duty as a public officer." Id. at 535–37, 245 A.2d at 587–88. But see Singewald v. Minneapolis Gas Co., supra (member of Village council participating in resolution to grant franchise to gas company of which he was an employee, held to have acted improperly, notwithstanding his good faith and the reasonableness of the resolution).

At least one court has further restricted the application of conflicts doctrine to "legislative acts": "Under existing law the personal interest of councilman Halperin and the fact that he stood to receive substantial gain from the action of city council in which he took part did not operate to disqualify him or destroy the effectiveness of his vote. * * * Such a disqualification of a member of the city council would have to be provided by legislation." City of Miami Beach v. Schauer, 104 So.2d 129, 133 (Fla. App.1958). But see Piggott v. Hopewell, 22 N.J.Super. 106, 91 A.2d 667 (1952); Baker v. Marley, supra.

The suggestion in S & L Associates, Inc. that a person serving in an advisory position is not subject to the same conflicts rules as an official (p. 809) was rejected in United States v. Mississippi Valley Generating Co., supra; and in Schaefer v. Berinstein, supra.

A California court overturned dismissal of a union officer, who was also an officer of the City Airport Commission because he expressly encouraged his union members to engage in a five-month strike at the Airport; and he rejected the mayor's appeal for aid in having the strikers repair a broken water-main that was disrupting public services. The court concluded that his abstention from any Airport Commission action involving labor negotiations, removed any basis for a finding of "official misconduct," and declared: "To accept [the city's] theory [of official misconduct] would be tantamount to stating that union officials may serve as city officials only so long as they do not discharge their duties to local unions." Mazzola v. San Francisco, 112 Cal.App.3d 141, 169 Cal.Rptr. 127, 136 (1980). Was there a conflict?

2. **Legislative Problems.** The attempt to find a common formula to solve essentially disparate conflicts problems may be futile. Personal interests that may conflict with public interests may be harmless, even necessary, in some but not other positions or government units. On the other hand, special laws narrowly directed to particular classes of government or employment often resulted in scattershot statutes that leave wide gaps in the regulatory scheme. " * * * [I]t is apparent that these patchwork prohibitions are both highly confusing and highly contradictory. Different groups of public servants are covered to a different extent by each general statute. Each general statute has exceptions differing in scope from the exceptions to other general statutes. Many have strayed far from the common law conception of the prohibition against conflicts of interest.

In this respect, the legislature must hare equal blame with the courts and administrative agencies for the confusion which exists in this area of New York law. The ramifications of this confusion can best be illustrated by the case of an average citizen considering public service. Depending upon his residence, he may be qualified to enter the service of his village, town, city, county, school district or fire district. The strength of his moral fiber would undoubtedly remain the same, but because of New York's divergent conflicts of interest statutes and rules the extent of the trust reposed in him by the public would depend on the government he serves and the public position he holds * * *." Kaplan and Lillich, *Municipal Conflicts of Interest: Inconsistencies and Patchwork Prohibitions*, 58 Colum.L.Rev. 157, 174 (1958).*

3. **Disclosure Requirements.** Perhaps the best deterrent to conflicts temptations are laws that require public officials and employees to disclose by written certification (1) those matters coming before them for action which present an actual or potential conflict of interest, and (2) periodic, personal financial reports showing, *inter alia,* sources of their assets, income, investment information, and financial transactions. The extent to which a constitutional claim of privacy may limit disclosure laws is not fully settled, but financial disclosure laws were held to be constitutional in New York and Pennsylvania. Barry v. New York, 712 F.2d 1554 (2d Cir.1983); Snider v. Shapp, 45 Pa.Cmwlth. 337, 405 A.2d 602 (1979). See Annot, Public Officers—Financial Disclosure, 22 A.L.R. 4th 237 (1983).

B. PUBLIC EMPLOYEES

ADAMCZYK v. CALEDONIA

Supreme Court of Wisconsin, 1971.
52 Wis.2d 270, 190 N.W.2d 137.

HEFFERNON, JUSTICE.

[The plaintiff sought reinstatement to employment as a policeman, following his discharge without a notice or hearing. The judgment below, dismissing the complaint, was affirmed.]

* * *

* * * In the absence of civil service regulations or properly authorized statutory rules governing labor relations, a municipal employee has no tenure in his public service.

In the case of State ex rel. Wattawa v. Manitowoc Public Library Board (1949), 255 Wis. 492, 39 N.W.2d 359, a city librarian sought to have her discharge vacated. This court pointed out:

"In the absence of tenure rights the right to hire carries the concomitant of the right to fire. This power may be exercised by the board arbitrarily and without cause. * * *" (P. 493, 39 N.W.2d p. 360)

---

* Reprinted by permission of Columbia Law Review copyright © 1958.

* * *

The question remaining is whether the 1966 contract, which provided that employees were to be removed only for just cause, abrogated the town board's unfettered right to terminate the services of an appointed employee.

We conclude that, in the absence of statutory authority authorizing the employment contract of 1966, the town board was powerless to abrogate its authority to terminate the services of an employee at its pleasure. * * *

* * *

We conclude that the complaint failed to state a cause of action. * * *

Note

1. **Residency and Citizenship Requirements.** See pp. 783–785, supra.

Tenure —The traditional state law rule "that government employment, in the absence of legislation, can be revoked at the will of the appointing officer [citations omitted]." (Nebraska Department of Roads Employees Ass'n v. Department of Roads, 189 Neb. 754, 205 N.W.2d 110, 114 (1973)), has been narrowed by the following case, to exclude political patronage dismissals.

BRANTI v. FINKEL

Supreme Court of the United States, 1980.
445 U.S. 507, 100 S.Ct. 1287, 63 L.Ed.2d 574.

Mr. Justice Stevens delivered the opinion of the Court.

The question presented is whether the First and Fourteenth Amendments to the Constitution protect an assistant public defender who is satisfactorily performing his job from discharge solely because of his political beliefs.

Respondents, * * * commenced * * * to preserve their positions as assistant public defenders in Rockland County, New York. * * *

The critical facts can be summarized briefly. The Rockland County Public Defender is appointed by the County Legislature for a term of six years. He in turn appoints nine assistants who serve at his pleasure. The two respondents have served as assistants since their respective appointments in March 1971 and September 1975; they are both Republicans.

Petitioner Branti's predecessor, a Republican, was appointed in 1972 by a Republican-dominated County Legislature. By 1977, control of the legislature had shifted to the Democrats and petitioner, also a Democrat, was appointed to replace the incumbent when his term expired. As soon as petitioner was formally appointed * * * he began executing termination notices for six of the nine assistants then in office. Respondents were among those who were to be terminated. With one possible exception, the nine who were to be appointed or retained were all Democrats.

* * *

The District Court found that Finkel and Tabakman had been selected for termination solely because they were Republicans and thus did not have the necessary Democratic sponsors: * * * The court rejected petitioner's belated attempt to justify the dismissals on nonpolitical grounds. Noting that both Branti and his predecessor had described respondents as "competent attorneys," the District Court expressly found that both had been "satisfactorily performing their duties as Assistant Public Defenders." * * * The District Court held that those discharges would be permissible under this Court's decision in Elrod v. Burns, 427 U.S. 347, 96 S.Ct. 2673, 49 L.Ed.2d 547, only if assistant public defenders are the type of policymaking, confidential employees who may be discharged solely on the basis of their political affiliations. He concluded that respondents clearly did not fall within that category. Although recognizing that they had broad responsibilities with respect to particular cases that were assigned to them, the court found that respondents had "very limited, if any, responsibility" with respect to the overall operation of the public defender's office. They did not "act as advisors or formulate plans for the implementation of the broad goals of the office" and, although they made decisions in the context of specific cases, "they do not make decisions about the orientation and operation of the office in which they work." 457 F.Supp. at 1291.

The District Court also rejected the argument that the confidential character of respondents' work justified conditioning their employment on political grounds. He found that they did not occupy any confidential relationship to the policymaking process, and did not have access to confidential documents that influenced policymaking deliberations. Rather, the only confidential information to which they had access was the product of their attorney-client relationship with the office's clients; to the extent that such information was shared with the public defender, it did not relate to the formulation of office policy.

In light of these factual findings, the District Court concluded that petitioner could not terminate respondents' employment as assistant public defenders consistent with the First and Fourteenth Amendments. On appeal, a panel of the Second Circuit affirmed. * * *

Petitioner advances two principal arguments for reversal: First, that the holding in Elrod v. Burns is limited to situations in which government employees are coerced into pledging allegiance to a political party that they would not voluntarily support and does not apply to a simple requirement that an employee be sponsored by the party in power; and, second, that, even if party sponsorship is an unconstitutional condition of continued public employment for clerks, deputies, and janitors, it is an acceptable requirement for an assistant public defender.

I

In Elrod v. Burns the Court held that the newly elected Democratic Sheriff of Cook County, Ill., had violated the constitutional rights of certain non-civil-service employees by discharging them "because they did not support and were not members of the Democratic Party and had failed to obtain the sponsorship of one of its leaders." 427 U.S. at 351, 96 S.Ct. 2673, 49 L.Ed.2d 547. That holding was supported by two separate opinions.

Writing for the plurality, Mr. Justice Brennan identified two separate but interrelated reasons supporting the conclusion that the discharges were prohibited * * * First, he analyzed the impact of a political patronage system on freedom of belief and association. Noting that in order to retain their jobs, the Sheriff's employees were required to pledge their allegiance to the Democratic Party, work for or contribute to the party's candidates, or obtain a Democratic sponsor, he concluded that the inevitable tendency of such a system was to coerce employees into compromising their true beliefs. * * *

Second, apart from the potential impact of patronage dismissals on the formation and expression of opinion, Mr. Justice Brennan also stated that the practice had the effect of imposing an unconstitutional condition on the receipt of a public benefit and therefore came within the rule of cases like Perry v. Sindermann, 408 U.S. 593, 92 S.Ct. 2694, 33 L.Ed.2d 570. * * *

Mr. Justice Stewart's opinion concurring in the judgment avoided comment on the first branch of Mr. Justice Brennan's analysis, * * *

Petitioner argues that Elrod v. Burns should be read to prohibit only dismissals resulting from an employee's failure to capitulate to political coercion. Thus, he argues that, so long as an employee is not asked to change his political affiliation or to contribute to or work for the party's candidates, he may be dismissed with impunity—even though he would not have been dismissed if he had had the proper political sponsorship and even though the sole reason for dismissing him was to replace him with a person who did have such sponsorship. Such an interpretation would surely emasculate the principles set forth in Elrod. * * *

In sum, there is no requirement that dismissed employees prove that they, or other employees, have been coerced into changing, either actually or ostensibly, their political allegiance. To prevail in this type of an action, it was sufficient, as Elrod holds, for respondents to prove that they were discharged "solely for the reason that they were not affiliated with or sponsored by the Democratic Party." Id., at 350, 96 S.Ct., at 2678.

II

Both opinions in Elrod recognize that party affiliation may be an acceptable requirement for some types of government employment. Thus, if an employee's private political beliefs would interfere with the discharge of his public duties, his First Amendment rights may be required to yield to the State's vital interest in maintaining governmental effectiveness and efficiency. Id., at 366, 49 L.Ed.2d 547, 96 S.Ct. 2673. In Elrod, it was clear that the duties of the employees— * * *—were not of that character, for they were, as Mr. Justice Stewart stated, "nonpolicymaking, nonconfidential" employees. Id., at 375, 96 S.Ct., at 2690.

As Mr. Justice Brennan noted in Elrod, it is not always easy to determine whether a position is one in which political affiliation is a legitimate factor to be considered. * * * Under some circumstances, a position may be appropriately considered political even though it is neither confidential nor policymaking in character. As one obvious example, if a State's election laws require that precincts be supervised by two election judges of different parties, a Republican judge could be legitimately discharged solely for changing his party registration. That conclusion would not depend on any finding that the job involved participation in policy decisions or access to confidential information. Rather, it would simply rest on the fact that party membership was essential to the discharge of the employee's governmental responsibilities.

It is equally clear that party affiliation is not necessarily relevant to every policymaking or confidential position. The coach of a state university's football team formulates policy, but no one could seriously claim that Republicans make better coaches than Democrats, or vice versa, no matter which party is in control of the state government. On the other hand, it is equally clear that the Governor of a State may appropriately believe that the official duties of various assistants who help him write speeches, explain his views to the press, or communicate with the legislature cannot be performed effectively unless those persons share his political beliefs and party commitments. In sum, the ultimate inquiry is not whether the label "policymaker" or "confidential" fits a particular position; rather, the question is whether the hiring authority can demonstrate that party affiliation is an appropriate requirement for the effective performance of the public office involved.

Having thus framed the issue, it is manifest that the continued employment of an assistant public defender cannot properly be conditioned upon his allegiance to the political party in control of the county government. The primary, if not the only, responsibility of an assistant public defender is to represent individual citizens in controversy with the State.[13] * * *

13. This is in contrast to the broader public responsibilities of an official such as a prosecutor. We express no opinion as to whether the deputy of such an official

Thus, whatever policymaking occurs in the public defender's office must relate to the needs of individual clients and not to any partisan political interests. Similarly, although an assistant is bound to obtain access to confidential information arising out of various attorney-client relationships, that information has no bearing whatsoever on partisan political concerns. Under these circumstances, it would undermine, rather than promote, the effective performance of an assistant public defender's office to make his tenure dependent on his allegiance to the dominant political party. ＊ ＊ ＊

Accordingly, the judgment is affirmed.

[STEWART, POWELL and REHNQUIST, JJ. dissented.]

Note—The problem raised by *Branti,* i.e. what criteria satisfy the new test for patronage firings, is illuminated by the opinion in Ness v. Marshall, 660 F.2d 517 (3d Cir.1981). The court there upheld the firing of city solicitors (Republicans) by a newly elected mayor (Democratic Party).

1. CIVIL SERVICE—MERIT EMPLOYMENT

Most local governments, by local option or by state mandate, adopt merit systems which establish specific classes of public employment to be filled by objective merit standards. The use of competitive examinations tends to minimize political favoritism and encourage qualified persons to seek public employment. Civil service laws protect civil servants from discharge, except "for cause," upon a fair hearing. Fair administration, and judicial review of civil service decisions constitute an essential part of the system.

BLACK v. SUTTON

Court of Appeals of Kentucky, 1945.
301 Ky. 247, 191 S.W.2d 407.

SIMS, JUSTICE.

＊ ＊ ＊

We have now confronting us the question of whether or not a third class city operating under a commission form of government which has abolished ＊ ＊ ＊ all nonelective offices, including that of city attorney, can then under a civil service ordinance pursuant to KRS 90.300 to 90.990 appoint a city attorney in the guise and under the name of an employee so that he may be perpetuated in office. ＊ ＊ ＊.

The answer to this question requires us to determine whether or not the appointment of a city attorney under the civil service ordinance made him an officer or an employee of the city, since an officer can have no vested right in the office he holds while an employee does have a vested right in the position he holds under the civil service ordinance.

could be dismissed on grounds of political party affiliation or loyalty. Cf. Newcomb v. Brennan, 558 F.2d 825 (CA7 1977), cert. denied, 434 U.S. 968, 98 S.Ct. 513, 54 L.Ed. 2d 455 (dismissal of deputy city attorney).

In this country offices are not held by grant or contract but are created by the law-making power and no person has a vested right in them. [Citations omitted] * * *

While an office established by the Constitution may not be abolished by the General Assembly, yet one established by statute may be abolished by statute. [Citations omitted]. Since the General Assembly created the office of city attorney * * * it cannot be doubted that under these authorities it had the right to abolish it, thus leaving such cities to secure counsel by contract. In abolishing that office by KRS 89.040 no provision seems to have been made for a city attorney and certainly KRS Chapter 89 authorizing a commission form of government in cities of the third class did not affect the duties of city attorney as they were not mentioned.

It is provided in KRS 89.020 that all laws, applicable to and governing cities, by-laws, ordinances and resolutions not inconsistent with Chapter 89, KRS, shall continue in force until altered or repealed in the manner provided for in that chapter.

Therefore, that part of KRS 69.480 providing the city attorney must be a qualified voter of the city and shall have been a licensed practicing attorney for five years, and shall not be a stockholder, officer, agent, attorney or employee of any corporation or person holding a franchise under or with the city, seems to have been left intact. Certainly, KRS 69.490 fixing his duties as general law officer of the city and KRS 69.500 relative to his salary, were not repealed * * *.

Thus, it appears that the General Assembly abolished the office of city attorney in name only. In City of Lexington v. Thompson, 250 Ky. 96, 61 S.W.2d 1092, we expressly held that the General Assembly could not convert the office of city manager into a position of employment merely by designating him as an employee when as a matter of fact he possessed the attributes of an officer. Likewise, the General Assembly may not convert the office of city attorney into that of an employee merely by calling the city attorney by the latter name while leaving all his qualifications and duties those of an official.

The line of demarcation between public office and public employment is oftentimes dim and the distinction between them as marked by judicial expression is not always clear. [Citations omitted]. However, we have had but little difficulty in deciding the question on the facts in this record. * * * It will suffice to say that a public office is created by law and the incumbent is usually required to be an inhabitant of the political unit he serves; the powers conferred and the duties to be performed must be defined directly or impliedly and they must be continuing in their nature and not occasional or intermittent; and the powers thus conferred must be a portion of the sovereign power of government to be performed for the public benefit. On the other hand, a public employment is a position which lacks one or more of the foregoing elements.

The city attorney is made the general law officer of the city
* * *. In so doing he is exercising a sovereign power for the benefit
of the public. That part of KRS 69.480 requiring him to be a qualified
voter of the city and a licensed practicing attorney for five years was
unaffected by KRS 89.040, * * *. While the office was abolished in
name, in effect it was not abolished. The city attorney still remained
the general law officer of the city and his qualifications remained the
same and he took the oath required of all officers by § 228 of our
Constitution. The fact that the civil service ordinance referred to him
as an employee no more makes him such than did the Act of the
General Assembly applicable to the Lexington case make Thompson an
employee when in fact he was an official. The Attorney General is the
chief law officer of this State and if the Legislature should abolish the
title to his office but leave his qualifications and duties the same and
call him an employee of the State, his status would not be changed from
that of an official to an employee.

* * * It may be helpful to public service to put employees under
the merit system, usually referred to as civil service, but that statute
should not be extended to officers under the guise that they are
employees for the all too apparent purpose of perpetuating them in
office.

We are of the opinion that the General Assembly in authorizing
cities of the third class to organize under a commission form of
government did not abolish the office of city attorney and that such
office has not become one of employment merely because the civil
service ordinance referred to it as such. The chancellor should have
entered a judgment to the effect that the city attorney is an officer and
not an employee and does not come within the provisions of the civil
service ordinance.

The judgment is reversed.

ZIOMEK v. BARTIMOLE

Supreme Court of Connecticut, 1968.
156 Conn. 604, 244 A.2d 380.

COTTER, ASSOCIATE JUSTICE. The plaintiffs, officers in the Derby
police department, took an appeal * * * from the action of the board
of police commissioners of the city of Derby in making certain promotions in the police department of the city. [Citations omitted] The
defendants have appealed to this court from a judgment of the Court of
Common Pleas, which sustained the appeal * * *, vacated the actions
of the board and ordered that new examinations be held for the ranks
of lieutenant * * *.

* * *

Membership or promotion in the police department is governed by
the charter of the city of Derby which provides in part as follows:
"Applicants for membership or promotion in the police department

shall submit to civil service examinations based on the Connecticut state police entrance examinations. Such examination shall be conducted by the board of police commissioners under the supervision of the state police." Derby Charter § 49(a) (1960); 26 Spec.Laws, p. 1077, No. 549 § 1, as amended by 28 Spec.Laws, p. 483, No. 383. The board of police commissioners cannot abrogate the force of positive statutory provisions where the statute does not specifically grant it that power, and it was required to comply with those provisions without modification, abridgment or change. [Citations omitted] * * * Strict statutory compliance in such a case is required in order to support the validity of the action of a municipal board concerned with promotions under civil service. Resnick v. Civil Service Commission, 156 Conn. 28, 32, 238 A.2d 391; Kenney v. McDonough, 315 Mass. 689, 693, 53 N.E.2d 1006.

The object of providing for civil service examinations is to secure more efficient employees, promote better government, eliminate as far as practicable the element of partisanship and personal favoritism, protect the employees and the public from the spoils system and secure the appointment to public positions of those whose merit and fitness have been determined by proper examination. Civil Service Board of City of Phoenix v. Warren, 74 Ariz. 88, 90, 91, 92, 244 P.2d 1157. "Therefore any violation of an ordinance enacted for the purpose of preserving that efficiency is fatal because it weakens the system of competitive selection which is the basis of civil service legislation." *Id.*, 91, 244 P.2d 1159. The findings of the court, supported by the evidence, that "[t]here was no uniformity in the so-called oral examinations as each member of the Board of Police Commissioners and the Mayor asked different questions of each candidate and same were thus noncompetitive"; that "[n]o uniform list of questions for the so-called oral examination was prepared or agreed upon by the Board of Police Commissioners in advance of said examinations"; and that "[n]o arrangements had been established by the Board of Police Commissioners prior to the oral examinations as to the method to be used in scoring the examination or as to the weight to be given therefor" demonstrate the manifest infirmity in the proceedings conducted by the board not only as to the content of the examinations but also the mode of procedure. There was testimony that the commissioners were informed by the mayor that they could ask the applicants any questions they wanted, any questions that came into their minds, and no uniform list of questions was selected, discussed or prepared. "A test or examination, to be competitive, must employ an objective standard or measure. Where the standard or measure is wholly subjective to the examiners it differs in effect in no respect from an uncontrolled opinion of the examiners and cannot be termed competitive. * * * An examination cannot be classed as competitive unless it conforms to measures or standards which are sufficiently objective to be capable of being challenged and reviewed, when necessary, by other examiners of equal ability and experience." Matter of Fink v. Finegan, 270 N.Y. 356, 361,

362, 1 N.E.2d 462, 464; Matter of Cowen v. Reavy, 283 N.Y. 232, 237, 28 N.E.2d 390; 15 Am.Jur.2d 484, Civil Service, § 22. Where the board acts capriciously upon the individual notions of the members of the board in conducting the oral examination, its action will be invalidated. Matter of Cohen v. Fields, 298 N.Y. 235, 242, 82 N.E.2d 23. The examinations as prepared and conducted did not meet the requirements of the charter.

It was improper for the mayor to preempt the functions and authority of the board of police commissioners. His authority was clearly defined and limited in the charter of the city of Derby, which provides in part as follows: "The mayor shall be ex officio, a member of the board of police commissioners * * *. In case of disagreement between the members of the board of police commissioners in any matter pertaining to the department of police service, or pertaining to the duties and powers of the police commissioners, * * * the mayor shall vote to dissolve such tie, and thereupon such action shall be deemed to be the action of a majority of the board of police commissioners * * *." Derby Charter, p. 12 (1960); 21 Spec.Laws, p. 357, No. 390. The board did not meet as such at any time in connection with the examinations prepared and conducted for the promotions under consideration. Consequently, there was no vote and no tie which the mayor was called upon to dissolve under the provisions of the charter. Members of a municipal board cannot exercise their powers and duties separately. They must meet and act as a board at authorized meetings duly held. Jack v. Torrant, 136 Conn. 414, 420, 71 A.2d 705; 2 Am.Jur. 2d Administrative Law, § 227. An informal discussion is not a formally convened session as required by law. State Tax Commission v. El Paso Natural Gas Co., 73 Ariz. 43, 46, 236 P.2d 1026.

There is no error.

Notes

1. **The Rule of Strict Compliance and Administrative Discretion.** Failure to comply strictly with the requirements of civil service laws or regulations could render certain appointments or promotions ultra vires and void. Walker v. Jankura, 162 Conn. 482, 294 A.2d 536 (1972); Tuscaloosa v. Markum, 283 Ala. 440, 218 So.2d 254 (1969). But the doctrine of strict compliance has little use in the civil service field. Snizaski v. Zaleski, 410 Pa. 548, 189 A.2d 284 (1963); State ex rel. Kos v. Adamson, 226 Minn. 177, 32 N.W.2d 281 (1948). Once action is lawfully authorized, the judgments of administrators concerning methods and procedures for implementing civil service programs is subject only to limited judicial scrutiny. "The Courts have held that it is the function of a civil service agency to use methods it deems best adapted for the determination of fitness for a position and even if reasonable men could differ as to the soundness and appropriateness of the scope and character of the examination, the judgment of the agency must prevail and is not to be interfered with by the courts in the absence of proof of bad faith or arbitrary, capricious or illegal action." Deyesu v. Baltimore, 232 Md. 601, 610, 194 A.2d 783, 788 (1963);

semble: Lindgren v. Crystal, 295 Minn. 557, 204 N.W.2d 444 (1973); Civil Service Board of City of Charlotte v. Page, 2 N.C.App. 34, 162 S.E.2d 644 (1968).

2. **Competition Requirements.** "[I]t is usually required that the examinations be competitive * * *, if practicable, because selection of the most competent through competitive examination is the heart and purpose of civil service laws." 3 McQuillin, *Municipal Corporations* § 12.78(a) (3rd rev. ed. 1973). Objective and uniform testing standards provide courts with a rational basis for reviewing the propriety of administrative decisions. It is most stringently applied to written examinations. Elliott v. Hoberman, 61 Misc.2d 411, 306 N.Y.S.2d 627 (1969).

Competition may be required, although in diluted form, in less objective forms of testing. Where several policemen are examined for a promotional opening and 10% of their scores is based upon service ratings of departmental superiors, such ratings must be made upon comparable standards, and not in the unrestricted discretion of each candidate's superior. Spickard v. Civil Service Commission of City and County of Denver, 31 Colo.App. 450, 505 P.2d 32 (1972). These rules do not apply to nonobjective evaluations. See the following case.

STOOR v. SEATTLE

Supreme Court of Washington, 1954.
44 Wash.2d 405, 267 P.2d 902.

MALLERY, JUSTICE. Appellants commenced this action to annul an oral civil service examination from which a list was certified of those eligible for promotion from lieutenant to captain in the Seattle fire department.

The duties of a captain * * * are delineated in exhibit No. 1, p. 3, "Official Bulletin For Fire Promotional Examinations," as follows:

"Duties: Under general direction of a Battalion Chief, to direct the activities of a fire company; and to perform related work as required.

"Desired Qualifications: Two years' experience as a Lieutenant; high school graduation; good knowledge of Fire Department methods and apparatus; familiarity with fire laws, regulations, general and special fire hazards; *ability to assume full responsibility for the personnel and equipment of his company; initiative; supervisory ability, including ability to train, instruct and organize.*" (Italics ours.)

The civil service commission believing that the qualities italicized above could not be ascertained by the written examination, found it necessary to give an oral one too.

Appellants are lieutenants in the Seattle fire department. They took the oral examination and received grades that were unsatisfactory to them. No complaint is made as to their grades in the written part of the examination.

The oral examination consisted of a group performance test. One or two problems were given to a group of six or seven applicants, who were allowed a limited time to study the problems and make notes. They then entered the examination room and were seated at a conference table, where they commenced a discussion of the problems in the presence of three examiners, who asked them no questions. The conference lasted forty-two minutes. The examiners graded the applicants on the following qualifications: Voice and speech, ability to present ideas, comprehension of problems, judgment, emotional stability, self-confidence, diplomacy, cooperation, and overall estimate of value. The examiners were prominent business people in Seattle and not members of the commission.

Appellants contend that the oral part of the examination violates Art. XVI, § 10, of the charter of the city of Seattle, which provides, in part:

> "The Commission shall by its rules provide, that whenever possible vacancies shall be filled by promotion; on the basis of service credit and standing upon *written competitive examination, except where tests of manual or professional skill are necessary.* * * * *" (Italics ours.)

Appellants argue that the oral examination was (1) not written, (2) not competitive, and (3) inept.

(1) Appellants contend that * * * an examination for captain of the fire department must be written because that position is not a profession. * * *

We agree that only when it is necessary to discover a *professional skill* is an oral examination permissible under the charter. We do not agree with appellants' contention that the vocation of a captain of the fire department is not a profession in the sense in which the word is used in the charter. * * *

We think that the context in which words "professional skill" are used in the charter, clearly indicates that it refers to a position * * * which requires education, training, experience, ability, and personality characteristics of a specialized nature not possessed by persons generally.

* * *

We hold that a captaincy in the fire department is a profession, and that the charter of the city of Seattle permits an oral examination to discover certain qualifications for it.

(2) Appellants contend that the oral examination was not competitive. They rely upon the rule announced in Fink v. Finegan, 270 N.Y. 356, 1 N.E.2d 462, 464, which is as follows:

> "A test or examination, to be competitive, must employ an objective standard or measure. Where the standard or measure is wholly subjective to the examiners, it differs in effect in no respect from an uncontrolled opinion of the examiners and cannot be termed competitive. * * *

> " * * * An examination cannot be classed as competitive unless it conforms to measures or standards which are sufficiently objective to

be capable of being challenged and reviewed, when necessary, by other examiners of equal ability and experience."

Obviously, no oral examination can meet this test of objectivity and opportunity for review. This question of what constitutes a competitive examination is one of first instance in this state.

In Almassy v. Los Angeles County Civil Service Commission, 34 Cal.2d 387, 210 P.2d 503, 510, it is said:

"* * * So pertinent is the following language in the case of State ex rel. King v. Emmons, 128 Ohio St. 216, 190 N.E. 468, at page 471, where a similar requirement contained in the state constitution with reference to the Ohio civil service law was before the court for interpretation: 'What, then, is meant by "competitive examination"? In a competitive examination, the candidates match their qualifications each against the others, and the final determination is made by rating and comparison. It is open to all who are eligible. In contrast, a noncompetitive examination is one in which the examining authority selects at pleasure such candidates as he may choose and subjects them to examination as he deems necessary.' See Vol. 8, Words and Phrases, Perm.Ed., pp. 253–254. Consistent with these observations, the candidates for the positions here in question were all tested by oral interviews for the same personality factors—each candidate was pitting his personality traits against those of every other candidate incident to the examiner's process of making comparative evaluations—so that the ratings in consequence of such 'open' contest may properly be said to rest on a competitive basis."

We prefer the logic of the Almassy case, *supra,* to that of the Fink case, *supra,* and, accordingly, hold that the test given was competitive within the purview of the charter.

(3) Appellants contend that the oral examination was inept because the candidates were graded upon the subjective impressions made upon the examiners by admittedly intangible qualities; that "total personality" cannot be judged within the forty-two minutes allotted for the examination; and that these qualities can be better evaluated by observations of actual performance on the job by a person's qualified superior rather than under simulated conditions for a brief moment by a stranger with no experience in the fire department. These are matters of opinion, and, as such, might well have some appeal if directed to the commission.

The commission has a wide discretion in the examination of applicants with regard to the manner of performing its duties and exercising its powers. State ex rel. Hearty v. Mullin, 198 Wash. 99, 87 P.2d 280.

In discussing the discretionary powers of the commission in job classification, we said in State ex rel. Reilly v. Civil Service Commission of City of Spokane, 8 Wash.2d 498, 112 P.2d 987, 988, 134 A.L.R. 1100, the following:

"Again, in State ex rel. Farmer v. Austin, 186 Wash. 577, 59 P.2d 379, 381, we stated: 'Courts will not by mandamus attempt to control the discretion of subordinate bodies acting within the limits of discretion vested in them by law. Where courts do interfere, it is upon the theory that the action is so capricious and arbitrary as to evidence a total failure to exercise discretion, and is, therefore, not a valid act.'

"Our search of the authorities makes it clear to us that civil service commissions come within this rule and have a discretionary power in the matter of classification, * * *."

See, also, Adams v. City of Seattle, 31 Wash.2d 147, 195 P.2d 634; 3 McQuillin, Municipal Corporations (3d ed.) 303, § 12.78.

We do not think the civil service commission of the city of Seattle was guilty herein of actions so "capricious and arbitrary as to evidence total failure to exercise discretion."

The judgment is affirmed.

Notes

1. The Compass of Administrative Discretion.

(a) *Classification of Civil Service Positions.* Other than positions fixed by law, civil service classification is determined administratively. Courts will not disturb them except for abuse of discretion or errors of law. 3 McQuillin, *Municipal Corporations,* § 12.77 (3rd rev. ed. 1973).

(b) *The Nature, Scope and Procedures of Examination.* Commission discretion establishing examinations is also subject to narrow judicial review. See Zicherman v. Department of Civil Service, 40 N.J. 347, 351, 192 A.2d 566, 568 (1963); Elliott v. Hoberman, 61 Misc.2d 411, 414, 306 N.Y.S.2d 627, 631 (1969); Short v. Kissinger, 184 Neb. 491, 168 N.W.2d 917 (1969).

(c) *Rating and Evaluating Applicants.* Courts will not disturb administrative ratings and grades except for illegal, arbitrary, or fraudulent action. Meaney v. Kaplan, 19 A.D.2d 680, 241 N.Y.S.2d 725 (1963); Ferguson v. Civil Service Commission, 344 Mass. 484, 182 N.E.2d 826 (1962).

(d) *Establishing Promotion Critera.* Commission discretion on promotional standards was strongly supported in Cash v. Houston, 426 S.W.2d 624 (Tex.Civ.App.1968).

(e) *Establishing Non-objective Rating Criteria and Credits.* In addition to establishing conditions of eligibility to compete for a civil service position, civil service commissions may, in their discretion, give special rating credit for particular training experience and seniority, so long as the allowed credits are reasonably relevant to the position in question. Kenmore Club, Police Benevolent Association v. Civil Service Commission, 61 Misc.2d 685, 307 N.Y.S.2d 63 (1969); cf. People ex rel. Dragel v. O'Connor, 10 Ill.App.2d 196, 134 N.E.2d 624 (1956) (nullifying seniority credit where the seniority involved experience unrelated to the position covered by the examination). State legislatures may grant or authorize fixed preference credits for armed service veterans as a recompense for military service. Personnel Adm'r. of Massachusetts v. Feeney, 442 U.S. 256, 99 S.Ct. 2282, 60 L.Ed.2d 870 (1979).

(f) *Eligibility Lists.* The preparation and use of eligibility lists, unless restricted by law, also rests in the broad discretion of civil service officers. Thus, where the statutory limit for the duration of an eligibility list was four years, the Commission could establish the list for only two years, and later extend its use up to the four year limit. (Uniformed Fireman's Benevolent Association v. Herten, 23 A.D.2d 788, 259 N.Y.S.2d 51 (1965)).

The Commission does not make appointments from the list, but must certify to appointing authorities the ranking names on the list that qualify for appointment. Governing law may limit certification to the persons at the top of the list, or may require certification of a specified number at the top. In many cases the appointing authority is authorized to choose any one of the certified eligibles. Unless otherwise required by statute, the appointing authority has the discretion to leave the vacancy unfilled. Marranca v. Harbo, 41 N.J. 569, 197 A.2d 865 (1964).

(g) *Dismissal "for Cause".* Where an employee may be discharged only "for cause," the Commission's finding will not be disturbed except for error of law, bad faith, or capricious action. Stueve v. Everett, 11 Or.App. 18, 500 P.2d 491 (1972).

2. **Standing to Sue.** Civil service candidates have standing to challenge the legality of the examination process. Those eligible for appointment may protest being passed over, and may challenge the certification and appointment of rivals, but they have the burden of proving that a rival is not qualified. Bingham v. Department of Civil Service, 77 N.J.Super. 459, 187 A.2d 10 (1962). However, certified eligibles may not force municipal authorities to fill vacancies.

a. Civil Service Testing and Affirmative Action

As noted in chapter VI (p. 357, et seq.), the validity of affirmative action programs, other than as of constitutional remedies for adjudicated de jure discrimination, remains to be fully developed. Assuming the constitutionality of a particular affirmative action program, there remain basic problems of reconciling civil service policies laws with those of affirmative action goals.

The standard of individual merit for job placement collides with group assistance aims. Civil service tests evaluate and rank qualifications of particular individuals. This process has been attacked as "unfair." The issue of employment test validation is further confused by the inability or refusal of politicians, courts, administrators and advocates to acknowledge the limits of testing science and their inadequacy to satisfy both the demand of individual merit evaluation, and of compensatory treatment of minority groups. The shifting burdens of proof on validating tests or employment practices under federal antidiscrimination statutes confused lawyers as well as laymen. See, e.g., Texas Department of Community Affairs v. Burdine, 450 U.S. 248, 101 S.Ct. 1089, 67 L.Ed.2d 207 (1981). Bridgeport Guardians, Inc. v. Members of Bridgeport Civil Service Comm'n, 482 F.2d 1333 (2d Cir.1973). Even more controversial than merit selection-affirmative action conflicts, are the conflicts between civil service laws and the new public employee labor relations laws (which are discussed at p. 884 et seq., infra).

The difficulties regarding civil service testing techniques were recently summarized by a psychologist who noted the following problems:

(1) the "fairness" of tests when viewed as an objective measure of individual abilities is radically different from fairness as judged by results, e.g., when the test produces disproportionate exclusion of minority candidates.

(2) Test score differentials within a narrow range do not demonstrate superiority of the higher graded candidate, since "on the job" relationships cannot be objectively measured with great precision in the current stage of testing science.

(3) No single test or series of tests has been developed (or suggested by legal authority) to cover the concerns of both individual merit competition and affirmative action goals.

(4) Psychological tests are often administered inexpertly by nonspecialist supervisors who disregard both the limited significance of particular tests, and the limits of conclusions to be drawn therefrom with respect to different classes of public employment. The problem of relating and properly "weighting" test results for particular positions requires expert judgments which are, at best, less than perfect predictions. "There is probably no test able to discriminate with any reliability among persons within one or two score points of each other." Using different tests for different minority groups has proved equally troublesome and unsatisfactory.

(5) Imprecise evaluations are aggravated by civil service laws which require job placement of the person at the top, or within the top three or four ranks of the civil service list.

(6) The jargon of testing theory, statistics and validation is often misunderstood, misinterpreted, or downright distorted by public officials, courts, and partisan advocates of different interest groups. Clarification and common definitions are sorely needed to prevent the obfuscation.

(7) Legally imposed guidelines, whether of affirmative action administrators, or of psychological associations have been too readily "taken as law" by the courts, which intertwine them with technical standards of psychonometrics.

(8) Test validations made on the basis of selected experiences, i.e. case-by-case, ignore the overall rate of success of a particular test. No clear choice between these two approaches is dominant in the law, perhaps because data on overall reliability of particular tests have not been sufficiently established. See *Civil Service Testing and Affirmative Action*, 44 U.Conn.L.Rev. 690 (1975).

Professor Hunt concluded: "Discrimination * * * is a social ailment. * * * The rejection of measuring instruments which register the consequences of such deprivation is merely a modern version of killing the messenger who brings bad news. Since psychonometrics, * * *, cannot alone resolve the tensions between evaluating specific individuals and overcoming the effects of past group discrimination, the reconciliation of these divergent, if not incompatible, public policies will require closer collaboration between politicians, lawyers, psychologists, and social activists."

2. LABOR MANAGEMENT RELATIONS IN THE PUBLIC SECTOR

a. *The Growth of Government Employment*

As of 1983, the rapidly expanding work force in government totalled about 16 million workers, of whom more than 9.3 million worked for local governments. See 1985 Statistical Abstract of the United States, Table 472, at p. 292 (U.S. Bureau of the Census). The unionization of public employees under state labor laws has been equally dramatic although local government employees were excluded from the National Labor Relations Act. Individual state laws on public employee relations continue to be enacted, but no discernible nation-wide pattern has emerged from the collective labor activities by local government employees.

As of 1976 some 32 states enacted such legislation. Collective bargaining is mandated for most state and local employees in 19 states, including Alaska, Connecticut, Delaware, Hawaii, Maine, Massachusetts, Michigan, Minnesota, Nebraska, Nevada, New Jersey, New York, Oklahoma, Pennsylvania, Rhode Island, South Dakota, Vermont, Washington and Wisconsin. A few states require a "meet and confer" type arrangement with employees. Many states have special laws for selected groups such as teachers, firemen, policemen, etc. For a detailed report on the statutes, attorney general's opinions and selected court decisions, state by state, see Summary of Public Sector Labor Relations Policies (U.S. Department of Labor; Labor-Management Services Administration, 1979). See generally, Baird & Walters, *Recent Developments in Public Sector Labor Law,* 4 Urban Lawyer 869 (1982); Note, *Developments in Public Employment,* 77 Harv.L.Rev. 1161 (1984).

The Pennsylvania Public Employe Relations Act of 1970 (hereinafter cited as Pa. Law) is one of the landmark enactments that confer broad collective bargaining powers, including the right to strike, upon public employees (other than police, fire and security officers) in all units of state and local government. Excerpts of this law, reproduced in Appendix A, p. 990 infra, provide a point of reference to measure variations in the laws of other states.

b. *Public Employee Labor Relations Patterns*

(1) *The Right to Organize*

Public employees have a constitutional right to associate for labor relations purposes. Atkins v. Charlotte, 296 F.Supp. 1068 (W.D.N.C. 1969). Any interference with that right is not only unlawful, but also remediable under civil rights statutes. AFSCME, AFL–CIO v. Woodward, 406 F.2d 137 (8th Cir.1969); McLaughlin v. Tilendis, 398 F.2d 287 (7th Cir.1968). But the right of association is not absolute, and it may be limited by overriding state interests. The right to unionize has been withheld from employees in sensitive, investigatory, and confidential positions. At the state and local levels, restrictions upon certain employee classes, viz. policemen, firemen and guards, confidential employees and supervisors whose duties may be adverse to unionized employees have been upheld. Greenfield v. Local 1127, 35 Wis.2d 175, 150 N.W.2d 476 (1967); 1970 Pa.Laws § 301. Some governments prohibit policemen from joining a union that represents private employees, since the police may be called upon to take enforcement action against the union. Local No. 201, AFSCME (AFL–CIO) v. Muskegon, 369 Mich. 384, 120 N.W.2d 197 (1963); City of Medford v. Local No. 446, 42 Wis.2d 581, 167 N.W.2d 414 (1969); see also Annot., *Right of Public Employees to Form or Join a Labor Organization Affiliated with a Federation of Trade Unions or Which Includes Private Employees*, 40 A.L.R.3d 728 (1971); but see City of Escanaba v. Michigan Labor Mediation Board, 19 Mich.App. 273, 172 N.W.2d 836 (1969).

Nor does the constitutional right to organize and join associations include the right to strike, or to compel government representatives to meet, confer or to collectively bargain with them. See Smith v. Arkansas State Highway Employees, Local 1315, 441 U.S. 463, 99 S.Ct. 1826, 60 L.Ed.2d 360 (1979); Winston-Salem/Forsythe County Unit, N.C. Assn. of Educators v. Phillips, 381 F.Supp. 644 (M.D.N.C.1974); Atkins v. Charlotte, supra; Zeluck v. Board of Education of City School Dist. of City of New Rochelle, 62 Misc.2d 274, 307 N.Y.S.2d 329 (1970). Such rights must be granted by the law of the governing state.

(2) *The Right to Bargain Collectively*

There is no common law foundation for public employees to claim a right to *bargain* collectively. The assumption that government employees have no such right has been implicitly recognized in labor laws that originally limited the grant of collective bargaining rights to employees in the private sector. See Railway Mail Ass'n v. Murphy, 180 Misc. 868, 44 N.Y.S.2d 601, 607 (1943).

> "Wherever the issue has been raised, it has been held laws governing the rights of public employees to engage in Union activities, collective bargaining, strikes and other coercive practices, not equally applicable to private employees, and vice versa, are premised on a

constitutionally approved classification; and, for this reason, are not violative of the constitutional guarantee of equal protection of the law. (Railway Mail Ass'n v. Corsi, 326 U.S. 88, 94–95, 65 S.Ct. 1483, 1488, 89 L.Ed. 2072; [citations omitted]; City of Evanston v. Buick (1970), 7 Cir., 421 F.2d 595; City of New York v. De Lury, supra (1968), 23 N.Y.2d 175, 185, 295 N.Y.S.2d 901, 903–909, 243 N.E.2d 128—appeal to U.S. Supreme Court dismissed for want of a properly presented federal question, De Lury v. City of New York, 394 U.S. 455, 89 S.Ct. 1223, 22 L.Ed.2d 414; * * *)."

See City of San Diego v. American Federation of State, County and Municipal Employees, Local 127, 8 Cal.App.3d 308, 87 Cal.Rptr. 258, 262 (1970).

As the following case demonstrates, however, some courts have allowed non-statutory bargaining as a managerial option of public employers.

STATE BOARD OF REGENTS v. UNITED PACKING HOUSE FOOD AND ALLIED WORKERS, LOCAL NO. 1258

Supreme Court of Iowa, 1970.
175 N.W.2d 110.

STUART, JUSTICE. Sometime prior to February 20, 1968, the non-academic personnel who operate the physical plant of the University of Northern Iowa (UNI) organized themselves into a union and received a charter as Local No. 1258 United Packing House Food and Allied Workers of America AFL–CIO (UPWA). On February 20, 1968 the union and its members struck against plaintiff, * * *. Plaintiff brought this action which ultimately resulted in a permanent injunction:

* * *

Plaintiff appealed from that part of the Ruling and Order and Decree which holds the Board of Regents has the power to enter into collective bargaining and collective bargaining agreements.

Defendants appealed from that portion of the injunctive order which prohibits them from picketing the campus * * *.

Because of the narrow questions presented by this appeal, it might be helpful to point out that the following propositions are accepted as the law of the case. (1) Public employees have the right to organize and join labor organizations. (2) Public employees do not have the right to strike. (3) Defendants have the right to picket for informational purposes if the picketing does not interfere with or impede the operation of the university.

I. Does the Board of Regents, * * * have the power and authority to bargain collectively with defendant union?

The employer-employee relationship in public employment "is governed by statutory law and administrative regulation, it is not fixed, either in whole or in part, by contract, as in the field of private industry." City of Los Angeles v. Los Angeles Bldg. & C. Tr. Council, 94 Cal.App.2d 36, 210 P.2d 305, 310. Defendants concede there is no specific legislation giving the board such authority. They rely on the rule of statutory construction that whenever a power is conferred by statute, everything necessary to carry out the power and make it effectual and complete will be implied. [Citations omitted] They claim the authority is necessarily implied in section 262.9(2) (4) (7) (11), Code of Iowa which gives the Regents the general power to hire employees, fix their salaries and wages, direct the expenditure of money and to perform all other acts necessary and proper for the execution of the powers and duties conferred by law upon it.

The answer to the question depends upon the definition of the term "collective bargaining". Neither party nor the trial court defines the term. There is a vast difference between implying authority in the Regents to meet with selected representatives of a group of employees to discuss wages, working conditions and grievances on behalf of those who have agreed to such representation and implying authority in the Regents to recognize the union as the exclusive employee representative for collective bargaining on behalf of all employees.

It is not clear for which concept of collective bargaining the parties are contending. Plaintiff seems to take the position that all sort of representative bargaining and discussion is improper without specific authority. * * * However, their brief contains extensive quotes from Richard F. Dole, Jr., State and Local Public Employee Collective Bargaining in the Absence of Explicit Legislative Authorization, 54 Iowa L.Rev. 539, 542–543, which is focused "on the legality of negotiating and contracting with an exclusive employee representative * * *."

* * * We hold the Regents have authority to engage in collective bargaining in this context.

* * *

The Board of Regents has the power and authority to meet with representatives of an employee's union to discuss wages, working conditions and grievances if it so desires. It can do so without becoming obligated to meet with the representatives of any other group of employees. The agreed terms could be adopted by the Regents in a proper legislative manner. Such action does not involve an improper delegation of legislative powers to private persons as there is no compulsion to sign an agreement and the final decision remains in the Board of Regents.

On the other hand, if the legislature desires to give public employees the advantages of collective bargaining in the full sense as it is used in private industry, it should do so by specific legislation to that effect. We cannot imply authority under these general powers to agree to exclusive representation, depriving other employees of the right to be represented by a group of their choosing or an individual the right to represent himself. * * * The power to fix the terms and conditions of public employment is a legislative function which, with proper guidelines from the legislature, can be delegated to its administrative agencies.

" * * *

"The existence of a statute in the field of public employee bargaining is of major significance. As has been indicated, courts may sanction voluntary bargaining in the absence of statute but this will not always insure the desired result. For instance, a statute can spell out election procedure to be used in the determination of a majority representative in an appropriate unit. It can make clear that bargaining is to be on an exclusive basis with the organization that represents the majority of the employees in an appropriate unit. It can express other intents. If there is no statute, whatever attempts are made at bargaining may break down in arguments over procedure and over such questions as exclusive representation." Seitz, *ibid*, 49 Marquette Law Review 498–499.

The following cases from other jurisdictions support our position.

* * *

In N.J. Turnpike Auth. v. Amer. Fed. of State, etc., Emp. (1964), 83 N.J.Super. 389, 200 A.2d 134, 138–139, the New Jersey Supreme Court said:

* * *

"The right to organize does not carry with it the right to collective bargaining. The term 'collective bargaining' is conspicuously absent from the rights conferred upon public employees by virtue of the N.J. Const., Art. I, par. 19. * * *

"Although the Turnpike is not obliged to engage in collective bargaining, it is under an affirmative duty to meet with its employees or their chosen representatives and consider in good faith the 'grievances and proposals'. However, any decision reached must be the result of the independent judgment of Turnpike, taking into consideration, *inter alia*, the 'grievances and proposals' of its employees.

"It should be emphasized that any one or more representatives may speak only for those employees who chose them. The Turnpike has no right to recognize a representative of only a segment of its employees as agent for all of the employees of the Turnpike."

The Minnesota Supreme Court also considered this issue:

" * * * Public employees do not have collective bargaining rights in the same sense that private or industrial employees enjoy them. There must be some statutory provision authorizing collective bargaining. * * *

"There is nothing to prevent the heads of governmental agencies from meeting with, or discussing wages, hours, and conditions of employment with groups or individuals representing groups of the employee class. * * *

"It would appear that even without express statutory authority, there is nothing to prevent collective bargaining when it is entered into voluntarily and no prohibitory state statute exists. Even though courts may sanction voluntary bargaining in the absence of statute, satisfactory results can hardly be expected. A statute is needed to spell out procedures to be used in the determination of majority representatives in an appropriate unit. But this is a legislative concern. * * * In the meantime, there is nothing to prevent the school board from meeting with representatives of both teacher groups. Certainly in the past the school board has not dealt individually with its more than 3,000 teachers. Until the legislature provides a better method, the parties must resort to the former methods employed to solve their differences." Minneapolis Fed. of Teachers Local 59 v. Obermeyer (1969) 275 Minn. 347, 147 N.W.2d 358, 366–367.

Norwalk Teachers' Ass'n v. Board of Education (1951) 138 Conn. 269, 83 A.2d 482, 486, 31 A.L.R.2d 1133, which is cited as approving of collective bargaining, does not use the term in the full industrial sense.

* * *

The following cases hold the public employer has no authority to engage in collective bargaining or enter into collective bargaining contracts without specific legislation to that effect. They contain no reference to the power to meet and consult with representatives of groups of employees. * * *

Most of the cases cited by defendants * * * involve employees working for the government in its corporate or proprietary capacity. * * *

We are not, by pointing out this distinction in the instant case indicating we would follow this line of authority if a proprietary function were involved. There is a strong line of authority to the contrary. * * *

Chicago Div. of Ill. Ed. Ass'n v. Board of Education (1966), 76 Ill. App.2d 456, 222 N.E.2d 243, is the only case cited which implies authority to enter into a collective bargaining agreement with a sole collective bargaining agency selected by employees working in a governmental capacity. We prefer the logic and reasoning behind those cases which hold this is a matter for specific legislation.

II. There is also confusion about the meaning of collective bargaining agreements. In the industrial sense they are not contracts of employment but trade agreements * * *. J.I. Case Co. v. Nat. Lab. Rel. Board (1944), 321 U.S. 332, 64 S.Ct. 576, 88 L.Ed. 762, 766. Almost without exception they include a provision making the union the exclusive bargaining agent. Dole, ibid. at 543. Under our holding in Division I, it is obvious that the Regents would have no authority to enter into a collective bargaining agreement in the sense recognized in private industry.

However, we can see no reason why the Regents, if they so desire, could not enter into one written contract with the union binding all members of the union agreeing to such representation as long as the terms of the contract are within the statutory authority of the board and contains no terms of employment which could not be included in a standardized contract for individual employees.

III. Defendants cross-appeal from that portion of the trial court's order which prohibits them from picketing even when not in furtherance of a strike "for the purpose of coercing plaintiff to bargain collectively with defendant union * * *.

We agree with the trial court.

* * *

We have heretofore held that the Board of Regents has no authority to enter into collective bargaining or collective bargaining agreements in the industrial context. We have also held the Board of Regents may voluntarily meet and consult with representatives of groups of employees to discuss wages, working conditions and grievances. The decision whether to do so or not remains that of the Board of Regents. Therefore, any picketing to coerce the Board of Regents to bargain collectively against its better judgment would either be illegal, against public policy or both.

In support of this position see: International Brotherhood of Teamsters, Local 695, AFL v. Vogt (1957), 354 U.S. 284, 77 S.Ct. 1166, 1 L.Ed. 2d 1347; Hughes v. Superior Court of State of California, *supra;* International Brotherhood of Teamsters, Local No. 309 v. Hanke (1950), 339 U.S. 470, 70 S.Ct. 773, 94 L.Ed. 995; Giboney v. Empire Storage and Ice Co. (1948), 336 U.S. 490, 69 S.Ct. 684, 93 L.Ed. 834; Bakery and Pastry Drivers and Helpers, Local 802, etc. v. Wohl (1942), 315 U.S. 769, 62 S.Ct. 816, 86 L.Ed. 1178; City of Los Angeles v. Los Angeles Bldg. & C. Tr. Council, 94 Cal.App.2d 36, 210 P.2d 305, 311; Board of Education of Community Unit Sch. Dist. v. Redding (1965) 32 Ill.2d 567, 207 N.E.2d 427, 431–432; Board of Education, Borough of Union Beach v. New Jersey Education Association (1967), 96 N.J.Super. 371, 233 A.2d 84, 92–93; Delaware River & Bay Auth. v. International Org., etc. (1965) 45 N.J. 138, 211 A.2d 789; Ind. Dairy Workers, etc. v. Milk Drivers, etc., Local No. 680, *supra. But see:* City of Rockford v. Local No. 413, Int. Ass'n of Fire (1968), 98 Ill.App.2d 36, 240 N.E.2d 705, 708.

In arriving at the final determination of this case we have considered that the trial court treated collective bargaining as meeting with and discussing wages, working conditions and grievances rather than the full industrial sense. We have therefore modified the trial court's order and decree only insofar as we have attempted to spell out in more detail the limitations on the power of the Board of Regents in this particular area. For the reasons set out we modify and affirm the decision of the trial court.

* * *

Notes

1. **The Governmental—Proprietary Rationale.** In the absence of controlling legislation, some courts find an implied authority for governments to bargain collectively with employees who perform proprietary

functions. See International Broth. of Elec. Workers, Local Union No. 611, AFL–CIO v. Farmington, 75 N.M. 393, 405 P.2d 233 (1965). Subjecting labor law to the governmental-proprietary distinction compounds practical as well as legal problems. In Amalgamated Transit Union Local Division 1338 v. Dallas Public Transit Board, 430 S.W.2d 107 (Tex.Civ.App.1968), the city took over and operated a private transportation company which had executed collective bargaining contracts with the plaintiff union. The labor agreement created a pension plan to be administered by a board consisting of company and union members. The city agreed to contribute to the pension plan, but refused to assume the obligations of the collective bargaining agreement or to recognize the union as a bargaining representative. The pension plan trustee sued for declaratory judgment to determine who had the power to deal with the pension trust. The appellate court upheld the city's refusal to deal with the union on the ground that collective bargaining by the city was specifically forbidden by statute. Since the pension plan was a "term and condition" of employment and the product of collective bargaining, the court held that the contract design for pension plan administration was thwarted by supervening illegality. It further held that the pension plan could be administered by a board consisting of city members and of representatives elected by the employees, provided that the employees did not assert any right to strike.

2. **"Meet and Discuss" v. "Bargaining".** The authority or duty to "meet and discuss" employment conditions with employees, unlike the authority and duty to "bargain", imposes no obligation on the employer to arrive at a mutual agreement with the employees, but leaves the employer with the unilateral decision to accept or reject employee demands. The crucial distinction drawn by the principal case, in implying authority to "meet and discuss" in the absence of statutory direction, but denying such implied authority to "bargain" with an exclusive union representative, is widely followed. The distinction gets blurred, however, when, as in the principal case, a court suggests that subsequent adoption of "meet and discuss" terms for all employees, as a matter of unilateral employer discretion, is lawful, even without an enabling statute. Is the court indulging a "fiction" to empower an employer to achieve the same result as one authorized by statutory exclusive bargaining?

3. **Construing Ambiguous Statutes.** Statutes authorizing public employee collective activity are often vague on the scope of authority to bargain. They may merely give local government a discretion to accept or decline the opportunity. (See *Tremblay,* p. 852, infra). Or they may oblige such governments to deal with collective employee groups. See State College case, *infra.* The authority or duty may be limited to "meet and discuss," or extended to "bargain collectively," on particular subjects. Compare, e.g. Nichols v. Bolding, note 4, infra with National Ed. Association of Shawnee Mission, Inc. v. Board of Education of Shawnee Mission Unified School, No. 512, Johnson County, 212 Kan. 741, 512 P.2d 426 (1973) (obliging public employer to bargain collectively); semble: West Hartford Education Association, Inc. v. DeCourcy, 162 Conn. 566, 295 A.2d 526 (1972).

4. "It seems to be established in this jurisdiction that a public governing body cannot enter into a valid labor contract with a labor organization concerning * * * conditions of employment in the absence of express constitutional or statutory authority to do so. * * * There has been a division of authority as to whether or not such contracts are permissible. Some have held they are permissible in certain limits if not prohibited by constitutional or statutory impediments. Our Alabama Court has held * * * that there must be authorization by constitutional statute in order to justify such binding contract. In so holding our Court cited as a general rule that public employers cannot abdicate or bargain away their continuing legislative discretion with reference to the subject matter of any labor contract. It is said that public officials have no authority to surrender any of their responsibilities as public officials at a negotiating conference." Nichols v. Bolding, 291 Ala. 50, 55, 277 So.2d 868, 870 (1973).

"Of course, collective bargaining contracts with municipalities, when authorized, are surrounded by many limitations because they deal with public employment, public budgets, and public funds. The legislative body cannot surrender policy making powers * * *. The validity of each collective bargaining contract, therefore, depends upon its precise term and the subject matter covered." Fellows v. LaTronica, 151 Colo. 300, 305, 377 P.2d 547, 551 (1962) (concurring opinion).

MINNESOTA STATE BD. FOR COM. COLLEGES v. KNIGHT

Supreme Court of the United States, 1984.
465 U.S. 271, 104 S.Ct. 1058, 79 L.Ed.2d 299.

JUSTICE O'CONNOR delivered the opinion of the Court.

The State of Minnesota authorizes its public employees to bargain collectively over terms and conditions of employment. It also requires public employers to engage in official exchanges of views with their professional employees on policy questions relating to employment but outside the scope of mandatory bargaining. If professional employees forming an appropriate bargaining unit have selected an exclusive representative for mandatory bargaining, their employer may exchange views on nonmandatory subjects only with the exclusive representative. The question presented in this case is whether this restriction on participation in the nonmandatory-subject exchange process violates the constitutional rights of professional employees within the bargaining unit who are not members of the exclusive representative and who may disagree with its views. We hold that it does not.

I

A

In 1971, the Minnesota legislature adopted the Public Employment Labor Relations Act (PELRA), Minn.Stat. §§ 179.61 et seq. (1982), to establish "orderly and constructive relationships between all public employers and their employees. * * *" Id., § 179.61. * * * In its amended form, as in its original form, PELRA provides for the division of public employees into appropriate bargaining units and establishes a procedure, based on majority support within a unit, for the designation of an exclusive bargaining agent for that unit. *Id.,* §§ 179.67, 179.71, 179.741. The statute requires public employers to "meet and negotiate" with exclusive representatives concerning the "terms and conditions of employment," * * *. The employer's and employees' representatives must seek an agreement in good faith. *Id.,* § 179.63, subd. 16.

PELRA also grants professional employees, * * * the right to "meet and confer" with their employers on matters related to employment that are outside the scope of mandatory negotiations. *Id.,* §§ 179.63, 179.65. * * * There is no statutory provision concerning the "meet and confer" process, however, that requires good faith efforts to reach agreement. * * *

PELRA requires professional employees to select a representative to "meet and confer" with their public employer. Minn.Stat. § 179.73. If professional employees in an appropriate bargaining unit have an exclusive representative to "meet and negotiate" with their employer, that representative serves as the "meet and confer" representative as well. Indeed, the employer may neither "meet and negotiate" nor "meet and confer" with any members of that bargaining unit except through their exclusive representative. *Id.,* § 179.66, subd. 7. This restriction, however, does not prevent professional employees from submitting advice or recommendations to their employer as part of their work assignment. *Ibid.* Moreover, nothing in PELRA restricts the right of any public employee to speak on any "matter related to the conditions or compensation of public employment or their betterment" as long as doing so "is not designed to and does not interfere with the full, faithful and proper performance of the duties of employment or circumvent the rights of the exclusive representative if there be one." *Id.,* § 179.65, subd. 1.

* * *

Following enactment of PELRA, appellant Minnesota Community College Faculty Association (MCCFA) was designated the exclusive representative of the faculty of the state's community colleges, which had been deemed a single bargaining unit. MCCFA has "met and negotiated" and "met and conferred" with the State Board since 1971. The result has been the negotiation of successive collective bargaining agreements in the intervening years and, in order to implement the "meet and confer" provision, a restructuring of governance practices in the community college system.

* * *

C

Appellees are twenty Minnesota community college faculty instructors who are not members of MCCFA. In December 1974, they filed suit * * * challenging the constitutionality of MCCFA's exclusive representation of community college faculty in both the "meet and negotiate" and "meet and confer" processes. * * *

The court rejected appellees' attack on the constitutionality of exclusive representation in bargaining over terms and conditions of employment, relying chiefly on *Abood v. Board of Education,* 431 U.S. 209, 97 S.Ct. 1782, 52 L.Ed.2d 261 (1977). The court agreed with appellees, however, that PELRA, * * * infringes First and Fourteenth Amendment speech and associational rights of faculty who do not wish to join MCCFA. * * *

Appellees, the State Board, and MCCFA all filed appeals with this Court, invoking jurisdiction under 28 U.S.C. § 1253. The Court summarily affirmed the judgment insofar as the District Court held the "meet and negotiate" provisions of PELRA to be valid. __ U.S. __, 103 S.Ct. 1493, 75 L.Ed.2d 927 (1983). The Court thus rejected appellees' argument, * * * that PELRA unconstitutionally delegated legislative authority to private parties. The Court's summary affirmance also rejected the constitutional attack on PELRA's restriction to the exclusive representative of participation in the "meet and negotiate" process.

On March 28, 1983, the Court noted probable jurisdiction in the appeals by the Board and MCCFA. __ U.S. __, 103 S.Ct. 1496, 75 L.Ed.2d 928. * * *

Appellees do not and could not claim that they have been unconstitutionally denied access to a public forum. A "meet and confer" session is obviously not a public forum. It is a fundamental principle of First Amendment doctrine, articulated most recently in *Perry Education Assn. v. Perry Local Educators' Assn.,* 460 U.S. __, __, __, 103 S.Ct. 948, 954, 74 L.Ed.2d 794 (1983), that for government property to be a public forum, it must by long tradition or by government designation be open to the public at large for assembly and speech. * * *

The rights at issue in this case are accordingly wholly unlike those at stake in *City of Madison Joint School District v. Wisconsin Public Employment Relations Comm'n,* 429 U.S. 167, 97 S.Ct. 421, 50 L.Ed.2d 376 (1976). The Court in that case upheld a claim of access to a public forum, * * *. The school board meetings at issue there were "opened [as] a forum for direct citizen involvement," 429 U.S., at 175, 97 S.Ct., at 426, and "public participation [was] permitted," *id.,* at 169, 97 S.Ct., at 423. The First Amendment was violated when the meetings were suddenly closed to one segment of the public even though they otherwise remained open for participation by the public at large. This case, by contrast, involves no selective closure of a generally open forum and hence any reliance on the *City of Madison* case would be misplaced.

* * * Appellees here make a claim quite different from those made in the nonpublic forum cases. They do not contend that certain government property has been closed to them for use in communicating with private individuals or public officials not acting as such who might

be willing to listen to them. Rather, they claim an entitlement to a government audience for their views.

"Meet and confer" sessions are occasions for public employers, acting solely as instrumentalities of the state, to receive policy advice from their professional employees. Minnesota has simply restricted the class of persons to whom it will listen in its making of policy. Thus, appellees' principal claim is that they have a right to force officers of the state acting in an official policymaking capacity to listen to them in a particular formal setting. * * *

The District Court agreed with appellees' claim to the extent that it was limited to faculty participation in governance of institutions of higher education. * * *

* * * the District Court concluded, "when the state compels creation of a representative governance system in higher education and utilizes that forum for ongoing debate and resolution of virtually all issues outside the scope of collective bargaining, it must afford every faculty member a fair opportunity to participate in the selection of governance representatives." Id., at A–22, A–23.

This conclusion is erroneous. Appellees have no constitutional right to force the government to listen to their views. They have no such right as members of the public, as government employees, or as instructors in an institution of higher education.

The Constitution does not grant to members of the public generally a right to be heard by public bodies making decisions of policy. * * *

* * * As public employees, of course, they have a special interest in public policies relating to their employment. * * * Appellees' status as public employees, however, gives them no special constitutional right to a voice in the making of policy by their government employer.

* * *

The academic setting of the policymaking at issue in this case does not alter this conclusion. To be sure, there is a strong, if not universal or uniform, tradition of faculty participation in school governance, and there are numerous policy arguments to support such participation. See American Association for Higher Education—National Education Association, Faculty Participation in Academic Governance (1967); Brief Amicus Curiae of American Association of University Professors 3–10. But this Court has never recognized a constitutional right of faculty to participate in policymaking in academic institutions.

In several cases the Court has recognized that infringement of the rights of speech and association guaranteed by the First and Fourteenth Amendment " 'in the case of teachers brings the safeguards of those amendments vividly into operation.' " Shelton v. Tucker, 364 U.S. 479, 487, 81 S.Ct. 247, 251, 5 L.Ed.2d 231 (1960) (quoting Wieman v. Updegraff, 344 U.S. 183, 195, 73 S.Ct. 215, 220, 97 L.Ed. 216 (1952) (Frankfurter, J., concurring)). Those cases, however, involved individuals' rights to express their views and to associate with others for communicative purposes. * * * These rights do not entail any government obligation to listen. * * * Even assuming that speech rights guaranteed by the First Amendment take on a special meaning in an academic setting, they do not require government to allow teachers employed by it to participate in institutional policymaking. Faculty involvement in academic governance has much to recommend it as a matter of academic policy, but it finds no basis in the Constitution.

Although there is no constitutional right to participate in academic governance, the First Amendment guarantees the right both to speak and to associate. Appellees' speech and associational rights, however, have not been infringed by Minnesota's restriction of participation in "meet and confer" sessions to the faculty's exclusive representative. The state has in no way restrained appellees' freedom to speak on any education-related issue or their freedom to associate or not to associate with whom they please, including the exclusive representative. Nor has the state attempted to suppress any ideas.

It is doubtless true that the unique status of the exclusive representative in the "meet and confer" process amplifies its voice in the policymaking process. But that amplification no more impairs individual instructors' constitutional freedom to speak than the amplification of individual voices impaired the union's freedom to speak in *Smith v. Arkansas State Highway Employees, Local 1315, supra.* Moreover, the exclusive representative's unique role in "meet and negotiate" sessions amplifies its voice as much as its unique role in "meet and confer" sessions, yet the Court summarily affirmed the District Court's approval of that role in this case. Amplification of the sort claimed is inherent in government's freedom to choose its advisers. * * *

Nor is appellees' right to speak infringed by the ability of MCCFA to "retaliate" for protected speech, as the District Court put it, by refusing to appoint them to the "meet and confer" committees. * * *

* * * Appellees are free to form whatever advocacy groups they like. They are not required to become members of MCCFA, and they do not challenge the monetary contribution they are required to make to support MCCFA's representation activities. Appellees may well feel some pressure to join the exclusive representative in order to give them the opportunity to serve on the "meet and confer" committees or to give them a voice in the representative's adoption of positions on particular issues. That pressure, however, is no different from the pressure they may feel to join MCCFA because of its unique status in the "meet and negotiate" process, * * *. Moreover, the pressure is no different from the pressure to join a majority party that persons in the minority always feel. Such pressure is inherent in our system of government; it does not create an unconstitutional inhibition on associational freedom.

Unable to demonstrate an infringement of any First Amendment right, appellees contend that their exclusion from "meet and confer" sessions denies them equal protection of the laws in violation of the

Fourteenth Amendment. This final argument is meritless. The interest of appellees that is affected—the interest in a government audience for their policy views—finds no special protection in the Constitution. There being no other reason to invoke heightened scrutiny, the challenged state action "need only rationally further a legitimate state purpose" to be valid under the Equal Protection Clause. *Perry Education Assn. v. Perry Local Educators' Assn., supra,* 460 U.S., at ___, 103 S.Ct., at 960. PELRA certainly meets that standard. * * *

The District Court erred in holding that appellees had been unconstitutionally denied an opportunity to participate in their public employer's making of policy. Whatever the wisdom of Minnesota's statutory scheme for professional employee consultation on employment-related policy, in academic or other settings, the scheme violates no provision of the Constitution. The judgment of the District Court is therefore *Reversed.*

(3) Bargainable Subjects

PENNSYLVANIA LABOR RELATIONS BD. v. STATE COLLEGE AREA SCHOOL DIST.

Supreme Court of Pennsylvania, 1975.
461 Pa. 494, 337 A.2d 262.

NIX, JUSTICE.

The subject of this appeal is the relatively recent enactment of the Public Employee Relations Act. The dispute centers upon the tension evoked between what the legislature has specifically made bargainable and what the legislature has also specifically allowed management to reserve to its unilateral decision-making. * * *

The State College Area Education Association (Association) filed with the Pennsylvania Labor Relations Board (Board) an unfair labor charge consisting of twenty-three items on which the Board of School Directors of State College Area School District (School District) refused to bargain, allegedly in violation of section 701. * * * The School District filed a timely answer, * * * admitting refusal to bargain on the remaining items contending that these items were not matters where they were mandated to bargain. * * *

* * *

I.

It is argued that the absence of precedent interpreting the relatively new Act 195 in this area and the similarity of language between section 701, now under consideration, and section 8(d) of the National Labor Relations Act, 29 U.S.C.A. 158(d), * * * that the National Labor Relations Board's cases and federal decisions interpreting section 8(d) should provide compelling authority for the resolution of the current dispute. * * *

Although these decisions may provide some guidance, we are mindful of the distinctions that necessarily must exist between legislation primarily directed to the private sector and that for public employes. The distinction between the public and private sector cannot be minimized. Employers in the private sector are motivated by the profit to be returned from the enterprise whereas public employers are custodians of public funds and mandated to perform governmental functions as economically and effectively as possible. The employer in the private sector is constrained only by investors who are most concerned with the return for their investment whereas the public employer must adhere to the statutory enactments which control the operation of the enterprise. * * *

We also recognize the wisdom of refraining from attempting to fashion broad and general rules that would serve as a panacea. The obviously wiser course is to resolve disputes on a case-by-case basis until we develop, through experience in the area, a sound basis for developing overall principles.

Guided by these preliminary observations, we will now proceed * * *. Section 701 provides:

"Collective bargaining is the performance of the mutual obligation of the public employer and the representative of the public employes to meet at reasonable times and confer in good faith with respect to wages, hours and other terms and conditions of employment, or the negotiation of an agreement or any question arising thereunder and the execution of a written contract incorporating any agreement reached but such obligation does not compel either party to agree to a proposal or require the making of a concession."

That the right to collective bargaining as to "wages, hours and other terms and conditions of employment" is not unlimited, is made clear by the two succeeding sections. Section 702 states:

"Public employers shall not be required to bargain over matters of inherent managerial policy, which shall include but shall not be limited to such areas of discretion or policy as the functions and programs of the public employer, standards of services, its overall budget, utilization of technology, the organizational structure and selection and direction of personnel. Public employers, however, shall be required to meet and discuss on policy matters affecting wages, hours and terms and conditions of employment as well as the impact thereon upon request by public employe representatives."

Section 703 states:

"The parties to the collective bargaining process shall not effect or implement a provision in a collective bargaining agreement if the implementation of that provision would be in violation of, or inconsistent with, or in conflict with any statute or statutes enacted by the General Assembly of the Commonwealth of Pennsylvania or the provisions of municipal home rule charters."

The conflict in the Commonwealth Court centered upon the extent the legislature intended to limit the scope of negotiation made mandatory under section 701 by its inclusion of sections 702 and 703 within this act. The majority of that court concluded that any item of wages, hours, and other terms and conditions of employment affecting policy determinations or the impairment of other performance of the duties and responsibilities imposed upon public employers by statute are not bargainable. Pa. L.R.B. v. State College Area School District, 9 Pa.Cmwlth. 229, 306 A.2d 404 (1973). Judge Kramer, in a dissent joined by two other members of the court, took a different view.
* * *

Where provisions of a statute appear to be ambiguous or inconsistent, the intention of the legislature may be determined by examining the occasion, reason or necessity for the law. * * * Prior to the passage of Act 195 the prior law prohibited all strikes by public employes and did not require collective bargaining by public employers. The chaotic climate that resulted from this obviously intolerable situation occasioned the creation of a Governor's Commission to Revise the Public Employe Law of Pennsylvania. This commission, which is commonly referred to as the Hickman Commission, issued a report recommending * * * passage of new law which would permit the right of all public employes to bargain collectively. In recommending this change the commission suggested the need for collective bargaining to restore harmony in the public sector and to eliminate the numerous illegal strikes and the widespread labor unrest. * * * The declaration of policy contained in Act 195, section 101 clearly establishes that the legislature concurred with the commission's belief * * *.

In this setting we are forced to conclude that the legislature at the time of the passage of Act 195 fully recognized that the right of collective bargaining was crucial to any attempt to restore harmony in the public sector. It would be absurd to suggest that the legislature deliberately intended to meet this pressing need by providing an illusory right of collective bargaining. * * *

II.

Section 702, when read in conjunction with section 701, requires us to distinguish between the area of managerial prerogative and the areas of vital concern to employes. The Commonwealth Court's premise that any interpretation of sections 701 and 702 must recognize the dominance of a legislative intention to preserve the traditional concept of inherent managerial policy emasculates section 701 and thwarts the fulfillment of the legislative policy sought to be achieved by the passage of the Act. * * * The introduction of a concept of mandatory collective bargaining, regardless of how narrowly the scope of negotiation is defined, necessarily represents an encroachment upon the former autonomous position of management. * * *

The majority in the Commonwealth Court and some of the briefs filed in this Court attempt to equate the preservation of the inherent managerial policy as synonymous with the public interest and the concern of the employes as a private interest. * * * This argument fails to perceive that the true public interest is the effective and efficient operation of public employment and that collective bargaining as well as managerial prerogatives are only significant insofar as they further this objective. * * *

A determination of the interrelationship between sections 701 and 702 calls upon us to strike a balance * * *. In striking this balance the paramount concern must be the public interest in providing for the effective and efficient performance of the public service in question. The Supreme Court of Kansas was recently required to consider this problem. National Education Ass'n. of Shawnee Mission, Inc. v. Board of Education of Shawnee Mission Unified School District No. 512, 212 Kan. 741, 512 P.2d 426 (1973). In that decision the Court was confronted with a dispute between a teachers' association and the board of education. In resolving questions relating to the scope of negotiations provided under their statute they recognized that "terms and conditions" which were negotiable under the terms of the statute as something more than minimal economic terms of wages and hours, but something less than the basic educational policies of the board of education. That Court suggested that the courts of that jurisdiction should resolve these issues on a case-by-case basis. * * * Further, the Kansas Court suggested:

> "The key, as we see it, is how direct the impact of an issue is on the well-being of the individual teacher, as opposed to its effect on the operation of the school system as a whole." *Id.* at 753, 512 P.2d at 435.

We believe that the suggested test is helpful in attempting to strike the balance between sections 701 and 702 of our statute. We recognize that in many instances the line will be difficult to draw, however, if we remain ever mindful that our paramount concern in this area is the public interest, no situation will be insoluble.

Thus we hold that where an item of dispute is a matter of fundamental concern to the employes' interest in wages, hours and other terms and conditions of employment, it is not removed as a matter subject to good faith bargaining under section 701 simply because it may touch upon basic policy. It is the duty of the Board in the first instance and the courts thereafter to determine whether the impact of the issue on the interest of the employe in wages, hours and terms and conditions of employment outweighs its probable effect on the basic policy of the system as a whole. If it is determined that the matter is one of inherent managerial policy but does affect wages, hours and terms and conditions of employment, the public employer shall be required to meet and discuss such subjects upon request by the public employe's representative pursuant to section 702.

III.

The relationship between sections 701 and 703 is particularly significant in a highly regulated area such as public education. * * * The majority of the Commonwealth Court reasoned that the duties and prerogatives imposed upon and granted to school boards under the Public School Code of 1949, and other pieces of legislation could not be the subject of collective bargaining under the terms of section 703. We cannot agree.

The mere fact that a particular subject matter may be covered by legislation does not remove it from collective bargaining under section 701 if it bears on the question of wages, hours and conditions of employment. We believe that section 703 only prevents the agreement to and implementation of any term which would be in violation of or inconsistent with any statutory directive. The distinction between this view and that expressed by the majority of the Commonwealth Court (as we understand it) is best illustrated by an example. Under section 1142 of the Public School Code, a minimum salary scale is set forth. Section 1151 provides that school boards may pay salaries in excess of the minimum salary. * * * Clearly, the parties are precluded from agreeing to a rate lower than the minimum scale but even though the statute vested in the public employer the prerogative to pay a higher rate, to do so as a result of collective bargaining is not "in violation of, or inconsistent with, or in conflict with" the statute in question. The mere fact that the General Assembly granted the prerogative to the employer does not exclude the possibility that the decision to exercise that prerogative was influenced by the collective bargaining process.

* * * The purpose of section 703 was not to further define "inherent managerial policy" but to recognize that Act 195 did not affect the continuing vitality of existing law at the time of that Act's passage. * * * Section 703 merely prevents a term of a collective bargaining agreement from being in violation of existing law. * * * If however the General Assembly mandates a particular responsibility to be discharged by the board and the board alone, then the matter is removed from bargaining under section 701 even if it has direct impact upon "wages, hours and other terms or conditions of employment." The removal from collective bargaining results not because it necessarily falls within the purview of section 702 (in fact it may clearly be within the scope of section 701), but rather because to do otherwise would be in direct violation of a statutory mandate and thus excluded under section 703. *Cf.* West Hartford Education Ass'n v. DeCourcy, *supra,* 162 Conn. at 577, 295 A.2d at 533.

We therefore conclude that items bargainable under section 701 are only excluded under section 703 where other applicable statutory provisions explicitly and definitively prohibit the public employer from making an agreement as to that specific term or condition of employment.

IV.

The areas of bargaining that are in issue in this lawsuit provide a wide spectrum of concern [11]. It is, however, clear that there has been significant disagreement as to the principles to be applied in determining the applicability of section 701. * * * It is clear that many of the items were framed in terms of the objective sought to be obtained as opposed to the issue sought to be negotiated. We assume the reason for the artless framing of the issues was as a result of the general confusion which prevailed in the area. We also believe that the Pennsylvania Labor Relations Board should have an opportunity to again re-assess the respective positions of the parties in light of the principles set forth herein.

We therefore remand the cause to the Pennsylvania Labor Relations Board for further proceedings consistent herewith, granting leave to each party to modify and amend their position as they may wish.

* * *

POMEROY, JUSTICE (concurring).

I agree in general with the opinion of the Court, but write this separate statement in an attempt to place in perspective certain aspects of the problems presented as they appear to me.

John Chipman Gray well said that interpretation of statutes is "one of the most difficult of a judge's duties." Gray, Nature and Sources of Law, Section 370. * * *

In this case the legislature, through its declaration of policy, did make clear its general intent, * * *. The specific intent, however, as

11. The items in issue are as follows: (1) The availability of proper and adequate classroom instructional printed material; (2) The provision for time during the school day for team planning of required innovative programs; (3) The timely notice of teaching assignment for the coming year; (4) Providing separate desks and lockable drawer space for each teacher in the district; (5) Providing cafeteria for teachers in the senior high school; (6) Eliminating the requirement that teachers perform non-teaching duties such as but not limited to hall duty, bus duty, lunch duty, study hall, and parking lot duties; (7) Eliminating the requirement that teachers teach or supervise two consecutive periods in two different buildings; (8) Eliminating the requirement that teachers substitute for other teachers during planning periods and teaching in noncertificated subject areas; (9) Eliminating the requirement that teachers chaperone athletic activities; (10) Eliminating the requirement that teachers unpack, store, check or otherwise handle supplies; (11) Providing that there shall be one night each week free for Association meetings; (12) Providing that a teacher will, without prior notice, have free access to his personnel file; (13) Permitting a teacher to leave the building any time during the school day unless he has a teaching assignment; (14) Providing special teachers with preparation time equal to that provided for other staff members; (15) Provision for maximum class sizes; (16) Provision that the Association will be consulted in determining the school calendar; (17) Provision that school will officially close at noon of the last day of classes for Thanksgiving, Christmas, Spring and Summer vacation; (18) Provision that at least one-half of the time requested for staff meetings be held during the school day; * * * (20) a provision that the present Tuesday afternoon conference with parents be abolished and teachers hold conferences with parents by appointment at a mutually convenient time; (21) Provision that secondary teachers not be required to teach more than 25 periods per week and have at least one planning period per day; and (22) a provision that elementary teachers shall have one period or fifteen minutes per day for planning purposes.

to what subjects are within the scope of collective bargaining, is, to say the least, elusive. * * * [T]he text of the Act on this subject seems to speak with two voices. * * * The precise question presented by these appeals is the scope of Sec. 702, which in turn, of course, affects the scope of Sec. 701.

Given the vagueness of the terms with which we must deal, there is no room, as I see it, for dogmatism; the courts can but strive as best they can to reach a result which comes closest to giving effect to what they find to be the legislative intent. This the courts below sought to do, and I cannot subscribe to the majority's characterization of the painstaking opinion of the Commonwealth Court as one which "emasculates" the legislative intent. * * *

As to the main thrust of the Court's opinion, that Act No. 195 should be so construed as to afford a viable framework for meaningful collective bargaining in the public sector, I am in complete agreement, * * *. I also agree that this requires a balancing approach, and that in striking the balances undue emphasis must not be placed on either Sec. 702 or Sec. 703 of the Act, lest the innovative provision of Sec. 701 be lost in the shuffle. * * * I have difficulty, however, with the Court's statement that the Board is to "determine whether the impact of the issue on the interest of the employe * * * outweighs its probable effect on the basic policy of the system as a whole." Opinion of the Court, *ante* at 268, for I fear that in application this directive may prove no more lucid than the words of the Act of which we strive to give meaning. * * * I venture to suggest that the governing test might preferably be formulated as follows:

"As to each item of potential dispute, (*i.e.*, the items put forward in a request for bargaining) the factors to be balanced in determining the susceptibility of an item to collective bargaining are the probable effects of the granting or refusal of the item upon (a) the individual performance by the teachers of their duties as such, and upon (b) the school board's overall operation of an educational system within its district. If the effect of the granting or denial of a request would be more direct, immediate and substantial upon the teachers' individual performance of their duties than it would be upon the school board's overall operation of an educational system, the item should be considered negotiable. On the other hand, if the effect would bear more directly, immediately and substantially upon the school board's overall operation of an educational system, the opposite result should obtain— *i.e.*, the item should be considered non-negotiable. * * *"

* * *

EAGEN, JUSTICE (dissenting).

I cannot subscribe to the views expressed in Part II or Part III of the opinion filed by Mr. Justice Nix. He fails to give proper weight to Section 702 of Act 195 and, in effect, nullifies it. In fact, if the Legislature intended to give public employees the sweeping, all-encompassing collective bargaining rights that Mr. Justice Nix indicates, enactment of Section 702 was the height of futility.

"After reviewing the instant record, it is my personal view that the conclusions and ruling of the Pennsylvania Labor Relations Board reasonably comport with the intent of the Legislature when it enacted Act 195. Moreover, the expertise of the Board in this class of case should be recognized and its conclusions sustained absent substantial error. I, therefore, would reverse the Order of the Commonwealth Court and reinstate and affirm the Order of the Board.

Notes

1. See generally Sackman, *Redefining the Scope of Bargaining in Public Employment*, 19 Boston College L.Rev. 155 (1977); Annot.: 83 A.L.R.3d 242 (1972).

2. The difficulty of separating working conditions from managerial rights is evidenced by two other Pennsylvania cases, one proceeding and one following the principal case. In Canon-McMillan School Bd. v. Commonwealth, 12 Pa.Cmwlth. 323, 316 A.2d 114 (1973) the Court held that a school board must bargain all union demands of extra pay for extra curricular work, even though the decision to conduct extra-curricular activities was non-bargainable. The dissent objected that this decision gave unions a back-door avenue to frustrate management policy decisions. Five years later the Supreme Court ruled that once a board bargained an agreement on paid teacher aides, it could not refuse to bargain its decision to terminate and replace them with unpaid volunteers, as a management right to control costs. Pennsylvania Labor Relations Bd. v. Mars Area School Dist., 480 Pa. 295, 389 A.2d 1073 (1978). Could the Board have refused in the first instance to negotiate employment of teacher aides? Compare Board of Educ. v. Murphy, 56 Ill.App.3d 981, 14 Ill.Dec. 620, 372 N.E.2d 899 (1978), where the Court voided a collective bargaining agreement whereby the Board agreed to grant a minimum number of sabbatical leaves.

3. **Scope of Bargaining Issues.** The right to bargain on particular subjects depends upon several separate, related issues and upon the construction of labor statutes in each state. Courts must determine whether the agreement in question represents an exercise rather than a surrender of official duty or discretion. Pertinent statutes, other than the labor laws (viz., those dealing with the civil service administration, and special classes of employees, may allow or prohibit the employing agency to relegate a particular decision to the bargaining context. Where inconsistency is found between the labor statute and other relevant statutes, courts must determine which statutory terms and policies take precedence. For example, the New York Education Law was construed to void a bargained agreement regarding the grant of tenure to probationary teachers, but not to void a bargained agreement on the procedures the school board must follow before its final action on the grant or denial of such tenure. Cohoes City School Dist. v. Cohoes Teachers' Ass'n, 40 N.Y.2d 774, 390 N.Y.S.2d 53, 358 N.E.2d 878 (1976).

Since the different relevant statutes vary from state to state, as does judicial appraisal of operative facts, case variations on the bargainability of specific items are to be expected.

Some of the more common distinctions courts draw to reconcile labor statutes with other pertinent statutes include: the distinction between statutes which specifically limit or prohibit official decisions by legislative standards, vis a vis those that merely impose procedural requirements on the process of decisionmaking; the difference between enabling and mandatory statutes; the difference between statutes that set minimum requirements, and permit discretionary action beyond those minimums vis a vis statutes which set fixed requirements which cannot be altered by executive or administrative action. See Blair, *State Legislative Control over the Conditions of Public Employment: Defining the Scope of Collective Bargaining for State and Municipal Employees,* 26 Vanderbilt L.Rev. 1 (1973); Summers, Public Employee Bargaining, A Political Perspective, 83 Yale L.J. 1156 (1974); Wellington and Winter, *The Limits of Collective Bargaining in Public Employment,* 78 Yale L.J. 1107 (1969); W.D. Valente, *Education Law—Public and Private,* § 14.8 (1985).

4. **Permissive v. Mandatory Bargaining.** Another critical difference to be found in public employee bargaining statutes is that between provisions that mandate local governments to bargain, and provisions that enable, but do not compel, local governments to engage in collective bargaining, as a matter of local discretion.

TREMBLAY v. BERLIN POLICE UNION

Supreme Court of New Hampshire, 1968.
108 N.H. 416, 237 A.2d 668.

PER CURIAM. The "right of public employees to join or become members of labor unions is becoming increasingly recognized." * * * The corresponding right of a municipality to enter into a collective bargaining contract with a labor union has been recognized by statute since the enactment of Laws 1955, ch. 255. Manchester v. Manchester Teachers Guild, 100 N.H. 507, 511, 131 A.2d 59. That statute, which is a constitutional exercise of legislative power [citations omitted] reads as follows: "Towns * * * may recognize unions of employees and make and enter into collective bargaining contracts with such unions." RSA 31:3 (supp). In 1962 the city of Berlin passed an ordinance which expressly empowered all present and future city boards and commissions to recognize unions of their employees and to enter into collective bargaining contracts with such unions.

* * * The power of municipalities to recognize unions of their employees is discretionary and not compulsory and the power resides in the mayor and city council. American Federation of State &c. Employees v. City of Keene, 108 N.H. 68, 70, 227 A.2d 602. This discretionary power was exercised by the mayor and city council of Berlin by its ordinance of December 3, 1962, whereby the city expressly accepted the provisions of RSA 31:3 (supp) and validly conferred upon all city boards

and commissions the authority to place those provisions into effect. Therefore we conclude that the Berlin police commissioners had authority to enter into a collective bargaining contract with the union.

* * *

This collective bargaining agreement is assailed as being an abdication and surrender of municipal sovereignty and "completely contrary to the public interest." As we read and interpret the collective bargaining agreement it contains certain overriding provisions which are designed to make all delegation of authority to the union consistent with and subject to the ultimate authority of the police commission and mayor and council to manage the police department consistently with the statutory directives. Under the contract the union has agreed that there shall be no strikes, slowdowns, stoppage of work "or any interference with the efficient management of the Police Department." Art. 20, section 1. Thus the interest of the public in having uninterrupted police protection is explicitly preserved. See Manchester v. Manchester Teachers Guild, 100 N.H. 507, 511, 131 A.2d 59. Article 2, section 1 provides that the "Union unreservedly accepts and recognizes the necessity of the Police Department to operate within its budget as set by the City Council." This is an express recognition that the union must operate within the municipal fiscal system and that it is bound by the discretion of the city council. Article 17, section 1 relating to the disposition grievance procedures and providing for arbitration was specifically amended as follows: "Notwithstanding any provision of the within arbitration clause, the said clause and all provision[s] thereof shall comply with and be subordinate to the N.H. State Law." Additionally in Article 20, section 1 it is provided that "nothing in the * * * paragraph shall be construed so as to conflict with applicable state laws." These quoted provisions of the contract demonstrate the objective of both the union and the city to enter into a collective bargaining agreement that is legal and consistent with all governing state laws.

The plaintiffs contend that police commissioners have lost the power to make rules and regulations. Article 19, section 3 places the responsibility for making regulations for the health and safety of the employees in the police department and the union members agree to comply with them. The provision that either party to the agreement may request a meeting "to discuss such regulations" is unobjectionable. Article 19, section 2 makes explicit what is already implicit in the agreement which is that the police commissioners will abide by the terms of the contract and that other rules and regulations shall not conflict therewith. The commissioners still have "full authority to make and enforce all rules and regulations for the government of the police force." Laws 1963, 275:5.

The grievance procedure clause of the agreement (Article 17, section 1) is attacked as an unlawful delegation of municipal authority to the union. This clause provides, after a series of preliminary procedures, for an impartial arbitrator to be appointed by the state board of arbitration whose decision is to be final and binding on the parties. If that were the end of the matter, it would present a serious question. But, as previously noted, the clause was specifically amended to provide that it "shall comply and be subordinate to N.H. State Law." This amendment subjects the grievance and arbitration procedure to Laws 1963, 275:5 as well as the state arbitration statute (RSA 273:12–27) which contains a provision that a party may give a notice in writing not to be bound by the arbitrator's decision. RSA 273:22. We conclude that Article 17, section 1 is not an unlawful delegation of the city's authority to control the police department. See Norwalk Teachers Ass'n. v. Board of Education, 138 Conn. 269, 279–280, 83 A.2d 482, 31 A.L.R.2d 1133; * * *.

* * *

Petition dismissed.

(4) Exclusive Representation

The Bargaining Unit —The bargaining unit consits of those employees who are to elect the bargaining agent which is to bargain on their collective behalf. To assure fair representation of the unit employees, statutes commonly prescribe various standards for determining the composition of the bargaining unit. Among these, the most pervasive requirement is that the unit employees have a "community of interest." Stated negatively, there should be no conflicting labor relations interests among employees who are represented by a common agent. See e.g. 1970 Pa. Law § 604, Appendix A, infra.

ALAMEDA COUNTY ASSISTANT PUBLIC DEFENDERS ASSOCIATION v. ALAMEDA

Court of Appeals of California, First District, Division 4, 1973.
33 Cal.App.3d 825, 109 Cal.Rptr. 392.

BRAY, ASSOCIATE JUSTICE.

* * *

QUESTION PRESENTED

Does the establishment of Unit XI illegally deny the Assistant Public Defenders of the right to representation by a professional organization of their own choice?

RECORD

Pursuant to the provisions of Government Code section 3500 et seq., the Alameda County Board of Supervisors on October 13, 1970, enacted the Alameda County Employee Relations Ordinance (Ord. 70-68) which provided rules and regulations for the organization and operation of organizations for the administration of county employer-employee relations. On February 23, 1971, appellant Public Defenders Association petitioned the county to recognize the association as the

representative of attorneys employed in the public defender's office
* * *.

On March 9, 1971, respondent county through respondent board of
supervisors established Representation Unit XI, consisting of all non-
health-related professional employees working for respondent county
for the purposes of meeting and conferring with regard to wages,
salaries, hours and working conditions. Unit XI includes approximately 360 county professional employees in various occupations, to wit,
librarians, planners, agricultural inspectors, auditors, buyers, systems
and procedures analysts, appraisers and engineers, as well as attorneys
in the public defender's office.

Appellant alleges that because Representation Unit XI consists of
employees of such diverse and varied job functions and classifications,
the attorneys of the public defender's office will be denied their right
under Government Code section 3507.3 to be represented by an employee organization of their own choice consisting of professional employees.

Shortly after the establishment of Unit XI, the Alameda County
Public Defenders Association and the Western Council of Engineers,
together with the American Federation of State, County and Municipal
Employees and United Public Employees Union, Local 390, formed a
coalition employee organization known as the Coalition of Professional
Employees. This coalition * * * filed with the board of supervisors a
petition for its certification as the recognized employee organization for
the non-health-related professional employees. A secret ballot election
was then conducted involving a majority of all county employees voting
for 14 different representation units, including the unit consisting of
non-health-related professional employees. The results of the election
were announced on May 7, 1971, with 162 votes cast for the Alameda
County Employees Association and 131 votes cast for the Coalition of
Professional Employees. Apparently none of the public defenders voted
at the election. Appellant's brief states that 92 percent of the attorneys in the public defender's office have indicated that they want
appellant Public Defenders Association to represent them.

* * *

THE EFFECT OF SECTION 3500 ET SEQ., GOVERNMENT CODE
(THE BROWN ACT)

Appellant contends that * * * assistant public defenders are
entitled to have a bargaining organization limited to them.

While under section 3507 of the Government code, Unit XI might
be an "appropriate" employee bargaining association for professional
employees of the county who do not have an organization of their own,
the real question is whether, in view of the fact that the assistant
public defenders had an organization of their own and chose to have it
as their sole bargaining body, the county could deny organization
representation and force the public defenders into Unit XI. Another
way of stating the issue is whether requiring all professional employees,

regardless of their type, to be in one organization for the administration of employer-employee relations is reasonable and appropriate, in view of section 3507, providing that the county may adopt "reasonable rules and regulations" and may create "appropriate" units for this purpose.

The language of "an appropriate unit" in Government Code section 3507 parallels the language of the National Labor Relations Act, section 9(a), allowing the National Labor Relations Board to certify labor organizations selected by the majority of employees in a "unit appropriate for such purposes * * *" (29 U.S.C.A. § 159.) * * *

In International Assn. of Fire Fighters v. County of Merced (1962) 204 Cal.App.2d 387, 392, 22 Cal.Rptr. 270, the court stated that the construction placed by the United States Supreme Court on the provisions of the federal Labor Management Relations Act was helpful in determining the connotation of similar language in Labor Code section 1962. In Board v. Hearst Publications (1944) 322 U.S. 111, 134, 64 S.Ct. 851, 862, 88 L.Ed. 1170, the United States Supreme Court said: "Wide variations in the forms of employee self-organization and the complexities of modern industrial organization make difficult the use of inflexible rules as the test of an appropriate unit. Congress was informed of the need for flexibility in shaping the unit to the particular case and accordingly gave the Board wide discretion in the matter."

The discretion given the county under section 3507 appears to be as broad as that given to the Labor Relations Board under the National Labor Relations Act. The standard by which the county is to be governed in determining the appropriate bargaining unit is whether or not such determination is "reasonable." * * *

* * *

Government Code section 3507, subdivision (d), provides that the rules of a public agency may provide for "exclusive recognition of employee organizations formally recognized pursuant to a vote of the employees of the agency or *an appropriate unit thereof* * * *" (Emphasis added.) Alameda County apparently attempted to set standards for determining an appropriate unit when it enacted Ordinance 70–68, section 7–8.05, which provides in part: "The Director shall be guided by the policy of the Board that any single representation unit shall encompass as many position classifications as possible consistent with the full use by employees of the privileges of organization and representation established by this ordinance. Within the limits of this policy, criteria used in recommending representation units may include, but shall not be limited to *such factors as community of interest among employees,* history of representation and the general field of work." (Emphasis added.)

* * * Section 3507 further provides: "No public agency shall unreasonably withhold recognition of employee organizations."

* * *

Certainly attorneys have a distinct function from librarians, planners, etc. Public defenders have separate supervision, place of work and hiring procedures. There is very little if any interchange between public defenders and the other professions grouped together in Unit XI.

"Unit determinations are as critical to the bargaining process as districting is to the political process. Such determinations affect not only the number but also the character of the organizations which represents an agency's employees. The definition of units may determine, for example, such matters as whether traditional civil service employees associations gain or lose strength in comparison to unions, whether craft unions gain or lose strength in comparison to unions seeking to represent employees on departmental or cross-departmental bases, and the like. The procedures by which such decisions are made, and the criteria brought to bear upon the decisions, are among the most significant factors in any industrial relations system." (J. Grodin, Public Employee Bargaining in California: The Meyers-Milias-Brown Act in the Courts, *supra*, 23 Hastings L.J. 719, 738.)

It does seem incongruous that assistant public defenders should be grouped in a bargaining unit with auditors, planners, rodent and weed inspectors. The attorneys in the public defender's office are *sui generis*, having little community of interest with the other professional groups which Unit XI tries to place in one organization. This conclusion does not place a greater burden on the County of Alameda, given Government Code section 3502, which provides in relevant part: "Public employees also shall have the right to refuse to join or participate in the activities of employee organizations and shall have the right to represent themselves individually in their employment relations with the public agency."

* * *

Denying recognition to appellant violates section 3507 of the Government Code in that thereby professional employees with common interests and having an organization of their own choice, are unreasonably forced into an organization with other employees with whom there exists little, if any, community of interest.

The judgment denying appellant's petition is reversed and the superior court is directed to issue a writ of mandamus as prayed for by appellant.

Notes

1. **Unit Determination.** Unit determination may be vested in state labor relations boards (9 N.Y.—McKinneys Cons.Laws § 207; 1970 Pa.Law § 604 (Appendix A, Infra)); in local government officials (see *Tremblay,* p. 852 supra); or may be preempted by direct legislative rule (Hawaii Rev. Stat. § 89–6(a)).

The law of many states prohibits the inclusion of supervisory and nonsupervisory employees within the same bargaining unit (e.g., Elk Grove Firefighters Local 2340 v. Willis, 400 F.Supp. 1097 (N.D.Ill.1975); Local 2263, Int'l Ass'n of Fire Fighters v. Tupelo, 439 F.Supp. 1224 (N.D.Miss. 1977)) and mandates separate units for policemen and firemen. The classification of employees as "supervisors" is largely delegated to administrative and judicial discretion. See Annot, Who Are Supervisors, 96 A.L.R.3d 723 (1980).

2. **Exclusive Representation.** The statute and case law on the grant or permissibility of exclusive bargaining is varied.

In Dade County Classroom Teachers' Association v. Ryan, 225 So.2d 903 (Fla.1969) the court held that the "right-to-work" provision of the Florida constitution prohibited a school district (a) from recognizing a union as an exclusive bargaining agent for unit employees who were not members of the union; and (b) from granting, by agreement, check-off privileges (the right to collect union dues from union members through payroll deductions) unless such privileges were granted similarly to all other employee labor associations. The court allowed that the majority union could bargain for its own members and that such members could individually authorize the district to deduct from their paychecks sums to be transferred to the union. But see *contra*, Lullo v. International Association of Fire Fighters, Local 1066, 55 N.J. 409, 262 A.2d 681 (1970) where the court rejected the contention that the state legislature was powerless to force individual or minority employees to accept majority union representation in collective bargaining. The Supreme Court recently confirmed that minority union employees do not have a constitutional right to force employers to meet with them to hear their views. Minnesota State Bd. for Community Colleges v. Knight, 465 U.S. 271, 104 S.Ct. 1058, 79 L.Ed.2d 299 (1984).

3. **Public Access to Negotiation and Arbitration Proceedings.** Parents and taxpayers have sought without success to open union-management proceedings to public view. Ghiglione v. School Committee of Southbridge, 376 Mass. 70, 378 N.E.2d 984 (1978); Burlington Community School Dist. v. Public Employment Relations Bd., 268 N.W.2d 517 (Iowa 1978). Amendments to statutes in Wisconsin and California, however, require that the initial bargaining proposals must be made at a meeting that is open to the public. Wis.Stat.Ann. § 111.70; West's Ann.Cal.Gov.Code § 3547.

(a) Union Security

CHICAGO TEACHERS UNION, LOCAL NO. 1
v. HUDSON

Supreme Court of the United States, 1986.
—— U.S. ——, 106 S.Ct. 1066, 89 L.Ed.2d 232.

JUSTICE STEVENS delivered the opinion of the Court.

In *Abood v. Detroit Board of Education*, 431 U.S. 209, 97 S.Ct. 1782, 52 L.Ed.2d 261 (1977), "we found no constitutional barrier to an agency shop agreement between a municipality and a teacher's union insofar as the agreement required every employee in the unit to pay a service fee to defray the costs of collective bargaining, contract administration, and grievance adjustment. The union, however, could not, consistently with the Constitution, collect from dissenting employees any sums for the support of ideological causes not germane to its duties as collective-bargaining agent." *Ellis v. Railway Clerks*, 466 U.S. 435, 447, 104 S.Ct. 1883, 1892, 80 L.Ed.2d 428 (1984). The *Ellis* case was primarily concerned with the need "to define the line between union expenditures that all employees must help defray and those that are not sufficiently related to collective bargaining to justify their being imposed on dissenters." *Ibid.* In contrast, this case concerns the constitutionality of the procedure adopted by the Chicago Teachers Union, with the approval of the Chicago Board of Education, to draw that necessary line * * *.

I

The Chicago Teachers Union has acted as the exclusive collective-bargaining representative of the Board's educational employees continuously since 1967. Approximately 95% of the 27,500 employees in the bargaining unit are members of the Union. Until December 1982, the Union members' dues financed the entire cost of the Union's collective bargaining and contract administration. Nonmembers received the benefits of the Union's representation without making any financial contribution to its cost.

In an attempt to solve this "free rider" problem, the Union made several proposals for a "fair share fee" clause in the labor contract. Because the Illinois School Code did not expressly authorize such a provision, the Board rejected these proposals until the Illinois General Assembly amended the School Code in 1981.[1] In the following year, the Chicago Teachers Union and the Chicago Board of Education entered into an agreement requiring the Board to deduct "proportionate share payments" from the paychecks of nonmembers. The new contractual provision authorized the Union to specify the amount of the payment; it stipulated that the amount could not exceed the members' dues. The contractual provision also required the Union to indemnify the Board for all action taken to implement the new provision.

For the 1982–83 school year, the Union determined that the "proportionate share" assessed on nonmembers was 95% of union dues. * * *

Union officials computed the 95% fee on the basis of the Union's financial records for the fiscal year ending on June 30, 1982. They identified expenditures unrelated to collective bargaining and contract administration (which they estimated as $188,549.82). They divided this amount by the Union's income for the year ($4,103,701.58) to

---

1. The statute, which became effective on August 1, 1981, provided:

"Where a collective bargaining agreement is entered into with an employee representative organization, the school board may include in the agreement a provision requiring employees covered by the agreement who are not members of the representative organization to pay their proportionate share of the cost of the collective bargaining process and contract administration,

* * *

produce a percentage of 4.6%; the figure was then rounded off to 5% to provide a "cushion" to cover any inadvertent errors.

The Union also established a procedure for considering objections by nonmembers. Before the deduction was made, the nonmember could not raise any objection. After the deduction was made, a nonmember could object to the "proportionate share" figure by writing to the Union President within 30 days after the first payroll deduction. The objection then would meet a three-stage procedure. First, the Union's Executive Committee would consider the objection and notify the objector within 30 days of its decision. Second, if the objector disagreed with that decision and appealed within another 30 days, the Union's Executive Board would consider the objection. Third, if the objector continued to protest after the Executive Board decision, the Union President would select an arbitrator from a list maintained by the Illinois Board of Education. The Union would pay for the arbitration, and, if there were multiple objections, they could be consolidated. If an objection was sustained at any stage of the procedure, the remedy would be an immediate reduction in the amount of future deductions for all nonmembers and a rebate for the objector.

In October 1982, the Union formally requested the Board to begin making deductions and advised it that a hearing procedure had been established for nonmembers' objections. The Board accepted the Union's 95% determination without questioning its method of calculation and without asking to review any of the records supporting it. The Board began to deduct the fee from the paychecks of nonmembers in December 1982. The Board did not provide the nonmembers with any explanation of the calculation, or of the Union's procedures. The Union did undertake certain informational efforts. It asked its member delegates at all schools to distribute flyers, display posters, inform nonmembers of the deductions, and invite nonmembers to join the Union with an amnesty for past fines. It also described the deduction and the protest procedures in the December issue of the Union newspaper, which was distributed to nonmembers.

Three nonmembers—Annie Lee Hudson, K. Celeste Campbell, and Walter Sherrill—sent identical letters of protest to the Union stating that they believed the Union was using part of their salary for purposes unrelated to collective bargaining and demanding that the deduction be reduced. A fourth nonmember—Beverly Underwood—objected to any deduction from her paycheck. The Union's response to each of the four briefly explained how the proportionate share fee had been calculated, described the objection procedure, enclosed a copy of the Union Implementation Plan, and concluded with the advice that "any objection you may file" would be processed in compliance with that procedure. None of the letters was referred to the Executive Committee. Only Hudson wrote a second letter; her request for detailed financial information was answered with an invitation to make an appointment for an "informational conference" at the Union's office, at which she could review the Union's financial records. The four nonmembers made no further effort to invoke the Union procedures; instead, they challenged the new procedure in court.

II

In March 1983, the four nonmembers, joined by three other nonmembers who had not sent any letters, filed suit in Federal District Court. * * * They objected to the Union procedure for three principal reasons: it violated their First Amendment rights to freedom of expression and association; it violated their Fourteenth Amendment due process rights; and it permitted the use of their proportionate shares for impermissible purposes.

The District Court rejected the challenges. 573 F.Supp. 1505 (ND Ill.1983). * * *

The posture of the case changed significantly in the Court of Appeals. The plaintiffs no longer focused on the claim that particular expenditures were inappropriate; they concentrated their attack on the procedures used by the Union to determine the amount of the deductions and to respond to their objections. The Union also modified its position. Instead of defending the procedure upheld by the District Court, it advised the Court of Appeals that it had voluntarily placed all of the dissenters' agency fees in escrow, and thereby avoided any danger that respondents' constitutional rights would be violated.

The Court of Appeals was unanimous in its judgment reversing the District Court. 743 F.2d 1187 (CA7 1984). * * *

The importance of the case, and the divergent approaches of other courts to the issue, led us to grant certiorari, 472 U.S. ___, 105 S.Ct. 2700, 86 L.Ed.2d 716 (1985). We affirm the judgment of the Court of Appeals, but we do not find it necessary to resolve all of the questions discussed in its opinion.

III

In *Abood v. Detroit Board of Education,* 431 U.S. 209, 97 S.Ct. 1782, 52 L.Ed.2d 261 (1977), we recognized that requiring nonunion employees to support their collective-bargaining representative "has an impact upon their First Amendment interests," *id.,* at 222, 97 S.Ct., at 1792–1793, and may well "interfere in some way with an employee's freedom to associate for the advancement of ideas, or to refrain from doing so, as he sees fit," *ibid.* See also *id.,* at 255, 97 S.Ct., at 1809–1810 (POWELL, J., concurring in judgment). We nevertheless rejected the claim that it was unconstitutional for a public employer to designate a union as the exclusive collective-bargaining representative of its employees, and to require nonunion employees, as a condition of employment, to pay a fair share of the union's cost of negotiating and administering a collective-bargaining agreement. * * *

The question presented in this case is whether the procedure used by the Chicago Teachers Union and approved by the Chicago Board of

Education adequately protects the basic distinction drawn in *Abood*. "[T]he objective must be to devise a way of preventing compulsory subsidization of ideological activity by employees who object thereto without restricting the Union's ability to require every employee to contribute to the cost of collective-bargaining activities." *Abood*, 431 U.S., at 237, 97 S.Ct., at 1800.

Procedural safeguards are necessary to achieve this objective for two reasons. First, although the government interest in labor peace is strong enough to support an "agency shop" notwithstanding its limited infringement on nonunion employees' constitutional rights, the fact that those rights are protected by the First Amendment requires that the procedure be carefully tailored to minimize the infringement. Second, the nonunion employee * * * must have a fair opportunity to identify the impact of the governmental action on his interests and to assert a meritorious First Amendment claim.

In *Ellis v. Railway Clerks*, 466 U.S. 435, 443, 104 S.Ct. 1883, 1889, 80 L.Ed.2d 428 (1984), we determined that, under the Railway Labor Act, a "pure rebate approach is inadequate." We explained that, under such an approach, in which the union refunds to the nonunion employee any money to which the union was not entitled, "the union obtains an involuntary loan for purposes to which the employee objects." *Id.*, at 444, 104 S.Ct., at 1890. We noted the possibility of "readily available alternatives, such as advance reduction of dues and/or interest-bearing escrow accounts," *ibid.*, but, for purposes of that case, it was sufficient to strike down the rebate procedure.

In this case, we must determine whether the challenged Chicago Teachers Union procedure survives First Amendment scrutiny. * * *

The procedure that was initially adopted by the Union contained three fundamental flaws. First, as in *Ellis*, a remedy which merely offers dissenters the possibility of a rebate does not avoid the risk that dissenters' funds may be used temporarily for an improper purpose. * * * The amount at stake for each individual dissenter does not diminish this concern. For, whatever the amount, the quality of respondents' interest in not being compelled to subsidize the propagation of political or ideological views that they oppose is clear. In *Abood*, we emphasized this point * * *.

Second, the "advance reduction of dues" was inadequate because it provided nonmembers with inadequate information about the basis for the proportionate share. In *Abood*, we reiterated that the nonunion employee has the burden of raising an objection, but that the union retains the burden of proof: " 'Since the unions possess the facts and records from which the proportion of political to total union expenditures can reasonably be calculated, basic considerations of fairness compel that they, not the individual employees, bear the burden of proving such proportion.' " *Abood*, 431 U.S., at 239–240, n. 40, 97 S.Ct., at 1801–1802, n. 40, * * * Basic considerations of fairness, * * * also dictate that the potential objectors be given sufficient information to gauge the propriety of the union's fee. Leaving the nonunion employees in the dark about the source of the figure for the agency fee—and requiring them to object in order to receive information—does not adequately protect the careful distinctions drawn in *Abood*.

In this case, the original information given to the nonunion employees was inadequate. Instead of identifying the expenditures for collective bargaining and contract administration * * *—the Union identified the amount that it admittedly had expended for purposes that did not benefit dissenting nonmembers. An acknowledgment that nonmembers would not be required to pay any part of 5% of the Union's total annual expenditures was not an adequate disclosure of the reasons why they were required to pay their share of 95%.

Finally, the original Union procedure was also defective because it did not provide for a reasonably prompt decision by an impartial decisionmaker. Although we have not so specified in the past, we now conclude that such a requirement is necessary. The nonunion employee, whose First Amendment rights are affected by the agency shop itself and who bears the burden of objecting, is entitled to have his objections addressed in an expeditious, fair, and objective manner.

The Union's procedure does not meet this requirement. As the Seventh Circuit observed, the "most conspicuous feature of the procedure is that from start to finish it is entirely controlled by the union, which is an interested party, since it is the recipient of the agency fees paid by the dissenting employees." 743 F.2d, at 1194–1195. * * * The third step—review by a Union-selected arbitrator—is also inadequate because the selection represents the Union's unrestricted choice from the state list.

Thus, the original Union procedure was inadequate because it failed to minimize the risk that nonunion employees' contributions might be used for impermissible purposes, because it failed to provide adequate justification for the advance reduction of dues, and because it failed to offer a reasonably prompt decision by an impartial decisionmaker.

The Union has not only created an escrow of 100% of the contributions exacted from the respondents, but has also advised us that it would not object to the * * * entry of a judgment compelling it to maintain an escrow system in the future. The Union does not contend that its escrow has made the case moot. Rather, it takes the position that because a 100% escrow completely avoids the risk that dissenters' contributions could be used improperly, it eliminates any valid constitutional objection to the procedure and thereby provides an adequate remedy in this case. We reject this argument.

Although the Union's self-imposed remedy eliminates the risk that nonunion employees' contributions may be temporarily used for impermissible purposes, the procedure remains flawed in two respects. It does not provide an adequate explanation for the advance reduction of dues, and it does not provide a reasonably prompt decision by an impartial decisionmaker. * * *

We need not hold, however, that a 100% escrow is constitutionally required. Such a remedy has the serious defect of depriving the Union of access to some escrowed funds that it is unquestionably entitled to retain. * * * On the record before us, there is no reason to believe that anything approaching a 100% "cushion" * * * would be constitutionally required. * * *

Thus, the Union's 100% escrow does not cure all of the problems in the original procedure. * * *

We hold today that the constitutional requirements for the Union's collection of agency fees include an adequate explanation of the basis for the fee, a reasonably prompt opportunity to challenge the amount of the fee before an impartial decisionmaker, and an escrow for the amounts reasonably in dispute while such challenges are pending.

The determination of the appropriate remedy in this case is a matter that should be addressed in the first instance by the District Court. The Court of Appeals correctly reversed the District Court's original judgment and remanded the case for further proceedings. That judgment of reversal is affirmed, and those further proceedings should be consistent with this opinion.

It is so ordered.

Notes

1. **Union Security Via Union Dues and Charges.** Unions representing the bargaining unit have sought to strengthen their efforts by a variety of revenue insuring devices. The strongest, namely, the union or "closed shop" arrangement, requires all bargaining unit members to join, and pay dues to, the union. It is not authorized by public employee labor relations statutes in most states, although it prevails in the private sector under the National Labor Relations Act. See, e.g., Board of Education v. Cahokia Dist. Council, 93 Ill.App.3d 376, 48 Ill.Dec. 749, 417 N.E.2d 151 (1981).

The next strongest device is the "agency shop" whereby unit employees, though not required to join the union, are nevertheless required to pay union dues. As indicated by the principal case, the constitutional rights of dissident unit members confines the power of states—to mandate or authorize union fee charges to government employees only for such amounts that are reasonably related to union costs of representation in contract negotiation and administration. As so limited, union charges to all members of the bargaining unit have been authorized and upheld in a growing number of states, including California, Connecticut, Indiana, Maine, Minnesota, New York, Oregon, Rhode Island and Wisconsin. See, e.g., the New Prairie Classroom Teachers Ass'n v. Stewart, 460 N.E.2d 149 (Ind.App.1983); Carlson v. Portland, 45 Or.App. 439, 608 P.2d 1198 (1980). Generally speaking, fees-for-services legislation has been held to be consistent with, and therefore not superseded by, statutes granting "tenure" to covered employees; so that a tenured employee who refuses to pay authorized representation charges to the bargaining representative may be discharged. E.g., White Cloud Education Association v. Board of Education, 101 Mich.App. 309, 300 N.W.2d 551 (1980).

A further variant on the modified agency shop arrangement is the "maintenance of membership" requirement in a minority of states, such as Pennsylvania. Under that system, a person who voluntarily joins the bargaining agent union must remain a member and pay dues for the duration of the negotiated contract, and may only withdraw from the union within a relatively short time period prior to the expiration of the union-negotiated contract. E.g., Burse v. Commonwealth, 56 Pa.Cmwlth. 555, 425 A.2d 1182 (1981); cf. Stines v. Oregon State Employees Association, 37 Or. App. 707, 588 P.2d 97 (1978), reversed 287 Or. 643, 601 P.2d 799 (1979).

A sizeable number of states, mostly in the South and West, have enacted "right to work" laws which prohibit employer-union agreements that compel dissident employees to accept union affiliation. The precise interaction of those laws with fair share fee arrangements is not fully settled. Variants of the agency shop or maintenance of membership provisions will probably be construed to be barred by such laws in some of those states. Still, as was found in Rhode Island, a court might construe fair-share fee arrangements to be consistent with right to work statutes. Town of North Kingstown v. North Kingstown Teachers Association, 110 R.I. 698, 297 A.2d 342 (1972). See generally, Annots, Public Employment Union Security, 95 A.L.R.3d 1102 (Supp.1985); Note, Developments in Public Employment, 77 Harv.L.Rev. 1161 (1984).

2. **Checkoff Arrangements.** Unions may not unilaterlly require public employers to "checkoff" (deduct and forward to union offices dues or fees from employee paychecks). They may, where authorized by state law, bargain for such accommodations. City of Charlotte v. Local 660, Internat'l Ass'n of Firefighters, 426 U.S. 283, 96 S.Ct. 2036, 48 L.Ed.2d 636 (1976); 1970 Pa. Law § 705 (Appendix A, infra); Bauch v. New York, 21 N.Y.2d 599, 289 N.Y.S.2d 951, 237 N.E.2d 211 (1968); cf. Board of School Directors, City of Milwaukee v. Wisconsin Employment Relations Comm'n, 42 Wis.2d 637, 168 N.W.2d 92 (1969). While the law in many states either requires or permits collective bargaining on checkoff, some states, prohibit checkoff practices without the consent of the affected individual employee. NEA v. Unified School District, 227 Kan. 541, 608 P.2d 415 (1980); cf. Kentucky Educators Public Affairs Council v. Kentucky Registry of Election Finance, 677 F.2d 1125 (6th Cir.1982); Dade County Classroom Teachers Ass'n v. Ryan, 225 So.2d 903 (Fla.1969).

3. **Exclusive Privileges and Access to Employer Facilities.** In 1983, the Supreme Court addressed a question on which the lower courts were not in agreement, namely, the legality of excluding minority unions from access to employer facilities for labor-related communications purposes; and of exclusive special privileges, for labor relations purposes, to agents of the majority union. In Perry Education Association v. Perry Local Educators' Association, 460 U.S. 37, 103 S.Ct. 948, 74 L.Ed.2d 794 (1983), the Court held that school district grant of exclusive access to bargaining representatives of certain school communications facilities, and

the grant of special privileges to bargaining representative agents for labor relations purposes (e.g., time off with pay) did not violate the constitutional rights of minority unions or their members, so long as other channels of communication remained available to the minority group. So long as the grant of exclusive privileges was labor-related, and did not exclude all opportunity for First Amendment expression; and so long as it was not "content-based," this form of union-security arrangement was upheld. Cf. Ysleta Federation of Teachers v. Ysleta Independent School District, 720 F.2d 1429 (5th Cir.1983) (striking down restriction on access to employer facilities, under rules based upon communication content, rather than labor-relations status).

(5) Dispute Resolution

Methods of dispute resolution vary with the context of the dispute. At the contract negotiation stage, the principal method of settling disputes involves various forms of mediation and "interest arbitration, while disputes regarding the proper interpretation and performance under executed contracts, following negotiations, are usually settled by "grievance arbitration." Under appropriate circumstances, a party may seek relief from the state Labor Board directly on complaint of an unfair labor practice. The ultimate weapon of unions to force employer concessions, namely to strike, is closely controlled by public sector bargaining statutes. Where all else fails, judicial review remains available, usually by way of injunctions to terminate unfair labor practices or strikes, or by decision on contested procedures or arbitration awards.

The following materials will not cover the multifarious, specialized law regarding unfair labor practices. See, e.g., authorities in lengthy Annot., Unfair Labor Practices—State Acts, 9 A.L.R. 4th 20 (1981; Supp.1985).

(a) Arbitration

Arbitration in public sector labor relations (both "interest" arbitration dealing with negotiation disputes, and "grievance" arbitration dealing with performance disputes) takes many forms. It may be voluntary or compulsory, and advisory only or binding, depending upon governing state law and the arbitration agreements between the parties. Many state laws compel interest arbitration for designated employees, e.g., police, fire, transit or security personnel, while allowing, but not compelling, the use of interest arbitration for other employees. See, e.g., Township of Moon v. Police Officers of Twp. of Moon, 508 Pa. 495, 498 A.2d 1305 (1985); Annot., Statutory Arbitration for Public Employees, 68 A.L.R.3d 885 (1976, Supp.1985); Armbrust, Impasse Resolution Procedures in Public Employment Negotiations, 8 Urban Lawyer, 449, 453 et seq. (1976). Statutory arbitration for public sector labor disputes has been generally sustained against challenges that such arbitration improperly delegates government authority, or denies due process or equal protection rights to affected groups. See Annot., supra, 68 A.L.R.3d at 893–4; Westbrook, *Nondelegation in Public Sector Law,* 30 St. Louis L.J. 331, 379–80 (1986). As noted in the *Tremblay* case, p. 852, supra, the delegation issue is avoided where such arbitration is "advisory" only, and where the arbitration decision is contrary to law or requires further legislative action. Many issues of procedure, arbitrability of particular subjects, and scope of arbitrator's awards are contested in the arbitration context, but they must be left to more specialized texts. While divisions persist among the states on many issues, recent cases from the industrialized states project a clear trend toward judicial deference to decisions of arbitrators concerning the interpretation of bargained arbitration agreements and the characterization of the fact circumstances and issues submitted to arbitration, e.g., Mahoning County Bd. of Mental Retardation v. Mahoning County TMR Ed. Ass'n, 22 Ohio St.3d 80, 488 N.E.2d 872 (1986); Board of Education v. Dover-Wingdale Teachers Ass'n, 61 N.Y.2d 913, 474 N.Y.S.2d 716, 463 N.E.2d 32 (1984) (holding any matter arbitrable that is not expressly excluded by agreement, statute or public policy).

The overlaps of labor statute provisions on arbitration with other special statutes, viz. civil service laws, and codes regulating professional groups, add issues of interstatutory construction, especially on subjects such as employee tenure or discipline. The nature of those issues is outlined in the following excerpt (supporting footnotes deleted) which, though addressed to public school teacher bargaining, is generally apt for most local government bargaining units:

"Jurisdictional variations on grievance process arise in part from differences in statutes and in bargained contracts; in part from variant case circumstances; and in part from the liberal or conservative bent of different state courts. The tendency to confine arbitration decisions to their narrow facts adds to the wide diversity of arbitration rulings.

*   *   *

"The states have not developed any uniform criteria of arbitrability, but the majority has generally favored arbitration, and resolved doubts in favor of arbitration. Some courts uphold arbitrability of any matter affecting a term or condition of employment, so long as it is not expressly excluded by the arbitration agreement, or is not otherwise preempted by state statute or public policy. Except in minority states, (which bar arbitration of any matter that is not mandatorily negotiated) the recognized authority of school committees to arbitrate most disputes arising out of negotiated agreements, leads courts to focus upon the intent of the negotiated contract. The construction of arbitration clauses is often critical to the scope of arbitration. Where clauses are broadly worded, or contain catchall language that defines grievances to include all matters of dispute, including matters not specified in the agreement, the scope of arbitration has been drastically widened. Courts have, however, denied arbitration where the particular grievance was expressly excluded from, or not covered by, arbitration provisions. On the other hand, in jurisdictions which adopt the 'essence test,' the parties' intention to include or exclude particular subjects from arbitration is drawn not only from the contract language, but from the entire negotiating context, 'and other indicia of the parties' intentions.'

"The interpretive latitude provided by the essence test is exceeded only by the discretion accorded to arbitrators in deciding arbitrability: * * * In many states, the arbitrator's interpretation of arbitrability is well nigh conclusive: * * *. The majority of courts thus tend to view arbitration decisions as presumptively valid and binding, so long as the proceedings were regular and fair, and the decision is not patently unreasonable.

* * *

"Where a dispute implicates rights redressable by grievance or by other proceedings, the question arises whether the parties are confined to one exclusive route, or whether they may elect to pursue either administrative or legal relief, or both. As to exclusivity of arbitration, or at least its exhaustion as a precondition to suit, the answer may depend upon the directive statutes in each state; and the particular matter in dispute. In circumstances where arbitration and other proceedings are deemed alternative and not exclusive, there remains the question whether and when the election to pursue either of them would operate as a waiver or bar to the other. The law on elections remains largely undeveloped. The filing of a statutory appeal was held to bar arbitration in one case, but in others, participation in a school board discharge hearing did not foreclose the dismissed employee's right to pursue *de novo* arbitration, where he expressly reserved that right at the board hearing. * * * It would appear, however, that the unqualified pursuit of one remedy to completion, however completion might be defined, would bar all other remedies as inconsistent.

"The form of *relief* granted in arbitration must also conform to the arbitration agreement and to state law. Generally speaking, the award need only be rationally derived from the agreement: * * *. However, even awards intra vires the arbitration clause may be vacated if found to be inconsistent with governing law. Different mechanisms and approaches have been taken by state legislatures and courts to avoid or cure such conflicts.

* * *

"Under the pressure of avoiding impasses and strikes, school boards often adopt the expedient of accepting inconsistent contract and arbitration terms, i.e. reserving management rights in one clause and limiting their exercise in other clauses, e.g. by 'just cause' and special procedural conditions that submit board actions to grievance arbitration. An alternative expedient is to accept ambiguous language which postpones to the grievance arbitration stage, negotiation disputes regarding board-control over certain decisions. In either case, the board's gamble, * * * often misfires. Arbitrators tend more often to interpret ambiguities, or conflicting contract language to support rather than destroy arbitration jurisdiction. Since courts usually refuse to reconsider contract constructions by labor expert arbitrators, in the absence of gross errors or misconduct by arbitrators, the odds do not favor school boards in any game of 'pick and choose' between alternative contract interpretations.

"The use of grievance arbitration as a backdoor method for settling, by postponement, issues not confronted in contract negotiations, may thus constitute a disguised form of 'interest' arbitration under the guise of 'grievance' arbitration. * * *" See W.D. Valente, *Education Law—Public and Private*, § 14.19 (1985).

POOLE v. LITTLE VALLEY CENTRAL SCHOOL DIST.

Supreme Court of New York, 1984.
114 Misc.2d 901, 452 N.Y.S.2d 829 (1982), affirmed 99 A.D.2d 650, 472 N.Y.S.2d 226.

JOSEPH P. KUSZYNSKI, JUSTICE.

In this CPLR Article 78 proceeding, petitioner Little Valley School District ("School District"), seeks a permanent stay of an application for arbitration filed by the respondent Donald H. Poole ("Poole") and the Little Valley Teachers Association ("Teachers Association"). Respondents cross-move to compel the arbitration.

When charges were filed against Poole, a teacher employed by the petitioner School District which accused him of conduct evidencing immoral character, conduct unbecoming a teacher and insubordination, Poole requested a hearing as provided for in Section 3020–a Education Law.

A statutorily prescribed three member panel was then convened * * *. The Panel unanimously found Poole guilty of the charges of conduct unbecoming a teacher and insubordination. He was acquitted, however, of the charges of conduct evidencing immoral character. The Panel imposed the penalty of "immediate termination from service", and three days later, on April 9, 1981, respondent Poole's employment with the School District was terminated.

Thereafter, Poole, and the respondent Teachers Association did not avail themselves of a review either by an appeal to the State Commissioner of Education or by a CPLR Article 78 proceeding as provided in Section 3020–a(5) Education Law, but filed a grievance with the District's Superintendent of Schools alleging Poole had been dismissed without "just cause" demanding arbitration as described in the 1980 Collective Bargaining Agreement ("Agreement") entered into by the School District and the Teachers Association.

Petitioner School District, submits that the filing of a grievance under the Agreement's arbitration procedure is an impermissible attempt to circumvent the statutorily prescribed appeal process provided for in Section 3020–a(5) Education Law, for review of a determination made by a hearing panel.

Petitioner sets forth that the arbitration provisions of the Agreement assign for resolution through the arbitral process, disputes arising from the violation, misinterpretation or from an inequitable application of any portion of the agreement. The School District points out that Poole's dismissal arises not from a contract violation, but from acts spelled out in Education Law Section 3020, as to which charges were filed and processed through a 3020–a Education Law panel hearing.

Petitioner contends also that the respondents no longer have any recourse to the Agreements grievance procedure, no matter how broad the contract definition may be of a grievance, after a 3020–a Panel hearing.

Respondents on the other hand contend Poole is entitled to a review of the panel's determination by means of the arbitration route in reliance upon *Board of Education of Union Free School District # 3 v. Associate Teachers of Huntington, Inc.,* 30 N.Y.2d 122, 331 N.Y.S.2d 17, 282 N.E.2d 109 (1972) and *Liverpool Central School District v. United Liverpool Faculty Association,* 42 N.Y.2d 509, 399 N.Y.S.2d 189, 369 N.E.2d 746 (1976). * * *

The posited issue before this Court is whether Section 3020–a Education Law as amended by Chapter 82 of the Laws of 1977 allows for the submission by a School District of a determination made by a Section 3020–a hearing panel to arbitration under the grievance procedure contained in a Collective Bargaining Agreement between a school district and a teachers association.

The 1977 amendment changed the effect of Section 3020–a hearing Panel's determinations. Previously a Panel's determination served only as a recommendation to the Board of Education. Now the amendment makes such determinations binding upon a school district.

Petitioner School District argues that a submission of a Section 3020–a Panel's determination to a review by way of the arbitration procedure contained in a collective bargaining agreement would interdict public policy considerations, as § 3020–a(5) Education Law limits review to an appeal to the Commissioner of Education or to the Courts by way of an Article 78 proceeding.

Petitioner contends also that the change brought about by the 1977 amendment which makes binding upon it the recommended penalty of the hearing panel, forecloses any review by arbitration where a different result could conceivably be reached.

The rationale advanced by *Huntington, supra,* decided in 1972 and *Liverpool, supra,* decided in 1976 favoring an arbitral review no longer has any application after 1977, when by legislative fiat only two (2) methods are available to a chastised teacher for a review of the adverse determination of charges by a 3020–a Education Law hearing panel. Once the issues have been submitted to such a hearing, the binding aspects of the panel's determination upon the School District have stripped the School District of any discretion to agree to a submission of the controversy to any processing under the grievance procedures of the Agreement. In *South Colonie Central School District v. South Colony Teachers Assoc.,* 46 N.Y.2d 521, 415 N.Y.S.2d 403, 388 N.E.2d 727, the Court of Appeals has stamped Section 3020–a(5) Education Law, as "a statutorily mandated procedure for review".

The amendment to Section 3020–a of the Education Law changed the three way option previously available to a disciplined teacher under the *Huntington* and *Liverpool, supra* cases. Here, respondent Poole, having invoked the panoply of the statutorily provided hearing forum afforded him under the Education Law, is bound to a review of its determination only by the two statutorily provided for avenues, an appeal to the State Commissioner of Education or the Courts in a CPLR Article 78 setting.

*   *   *

Abramovich v. Board of Education, 46 N.Y.2d 450, 414 N.Y.S.2d 109, 386 N.E.2d 1076 (1979), cited by respondents, concerns itself with arbitration absent any 3020–a Education Law Panel determination.

Clearly, once a 3020–a Education Law Panel has been convened and has decided charges filed against a teacher, the recommended penalty is binding upon a school district barring any claim of irregularity. It follows then, that a school district cannot agree to a resubmission of the same issues or the penalty imposed, which would be tantamount to a retrial of the issues, to an arbitral processing as a grievance under the Agreement. The decision of the hearing panel is res judicata upon the School District unless modified or set aside either by an Order of the State Commissioner of Education or a Court in a CPLR Article 78 decision.

The arbitration is permanently stayed and the motion to compel arbitration is denied in its entirety.

Notes

1. **Exclusivity or Election of Statutory or Arbitration Procedure.** As the principal case indicates, a choice of an authorized procedure, other than arbitration, may preclude later resort to arbitration, where such is intended by alternate legislation. Conversely, resort to arbitration may preclude other statutory hearings. As to exclusivity of either alternative, the answer will also depend upon directive statutes in each state. Where an employee participated in a school board (statutory) hearing, but reserved the right to pursue arbitration de novo, the courts of Wisconsin and Pennsylvania held that arbitration was not precluded. Fortney v. School District of West Salem, 108 Wis.2d 167, 321 N.W.2d 225 (1982); West Middlesex Area Sch. District v. Commonwealth, 55 Pa.Cmwlth. 404, 423 A.2d 781 (1980). It may be doubted, however, that the same result would obtain if the employee in those cases had pursued and exhausted all appeals from the school board hearing. See e.g. Commonwealth, Pennsylvania Labor Relations Board v. Neshaminy Sch. District, 43 Pa.Cmwlth. 377, 403 A.2d 1003 (1979). A similar bar (waiver) of alternative proceed-

ings was found where the employee elected to pursue arbitration. Pederson v. South Williamsport Area Sch. District, 677 F.2d 312 (3d Cir.1982). The law on exclusivity of alternative procedures (as a matter of statutory directive and intent), and on the preclusive effect of an election to pursue one of alternative procedures, remains unsettled in most states. Within any one state it may well vary with the subject matter in dispute, (as it affects legislative and judicial policies) and with the appeal of the circumstances of each case to judicial use of equitable principles.

2. **Voluntary vs. Compulsory Arbitration.** While voluntary arbitration has been generally favored, a recent statutory trend toward compulsory arbitration has appeared. Between 1970 and 1977, the states allowing compulsory arbitration for certain departments grew from 4 to 19, though courts in Colorado, Maryland, South Dakota, and Utah voided compulsory arbitration provisions. See, e.g., Greeley Police Union v. City Council, 191 Colo. 419, 553 P.2d 790 (1976); Bales, Public Employee Labor Relations, 10 Urban Lawyer 504 (1978).

(b) Strikes—Their Use, Abuse and Control

W.D. VALENTE, EDUCATION LAW—PUBLIC AND PRIVATE, § 14.20 (1985). "The most powerful union weapons to induce concessions from employers is the organized stoppage of work, commonly termed a strike. Strikes by government employees are prohibited by law in the great majority of states, either under the common law rule to that effect, or under statutes that expressly adopt that rule. * * *

"A thorough compilation of cases covering all facets of a public employee's right to strike can be found in Annot., 37 A.L.R.3d 1147 (1971). A study of this Annotation makes it perfectly clear that a judicial or legislative interdiction against strikes by public employees does not constitute involuntary servitude or an unwarranted impingement of one's constitutional rights, be they of free speech, assembly, due process, or equal protection. [See School Committee v. Westerly Teachers Association, 111 R.I. 96, 299 A.2d 441, 444 (1973).]

"A growing minority of states by legislation authorize public sector strikes for certain classes of employees under specified statutory conditions and restrictions. Even in those states, the strike prohibition has been retained with respect to certain employee groups which are legislatively classified as performing 'essential services,' viz., policemen, firefighters, and certain security and maintenance personnel. Strike enabling statutes generally limit the right to strike to impasses concerning contract negotiations; and still prohibit strikes on grievances disputes under existing contracts, or on unfair labor practices. For the latter class of disputes, arbitration or labor board proceedings remain the exclusive mode of settlement. Statutory preconditions on the right to strike typically involve prior exhaustion of mandated procedures for third-party mediation and fact-finding efforts to resolve negotiation impasses. The extent to which these legislative qualifications on the right to strike apply to public school employees in any state, must be determined by reference to the applicable statute in that state. Where strike activity is lawful, an employer's interference with it will, in turn, constitute an unfair labor practice.

* * *

"The application of strike prohibitions or limitations is often contested on the ground that a challenged work stoppage or action does not, in legal contemplation, amount to a strike. Generally speaking, a 'strike' includes any *concerted* stoppage, absence, or obstruction of school work and work routines by all or a substantial number of employees for the purpose of inducing employer concessions; or any individual act in support thereof. Courts must decide whether a particular stoppage is the product of unlawfully motivated collective action or whether it is attributable to other lawful causes and motives. In order to clarify the issue, statutes often define 'strike' very broadly. The following definition is illustrative:

> 'Strike means concerted action in failing to report for duty, the willful absence from one's position, the stoppage of work, slow down, or the abstinence in whole or in part from the full, faithful, and proper performance of the duties of employment for the purpose of inducing, influencing or coercing a change in the conditions or compensation for the rights, privileges or obligations of employment.'

"Equally condemned are strike support activities * * * viz., by refusing to cross picket lines or by sympathy support of the strike. Courts look to the nature and context of each alleged strike action, rather than to its particular form. * * *

"Kindred problems of fact characterization appear in picketing activities, the legality of which depends upon its purposes and effects. * * * Purely informational picketing that is not related to an illegal activity cannot be enjoined. It is not always clear, however, whether certain forms of picketing, (e.g. off-site strike sympathy picketing or recognition picketing) will be protected as informational, or enjoined as an unlawful labor action. It is clear, however, that picketing in support of an illegal strike can be enjoined.

* * *

"The minority states which authorize a limited strike have not adopted any uniform scheme on the proceedings prerequisite to initiating a strike; or on the allowable scope and duration of a strike; or on the procedures and standards for terminating a strike, once legally commenced; or on the sanctions that may be imposed against unions, union officials and employees for violating strike controls. Those jurisdictions generally do require exhaustion of statutory settlement procedures before any strike is commenced. Some nice questions may be anticipated, however, as to when an impasse exists, or has been broken. * * *

"The standard strike-termination method is by court injunction. The overwhelming weight of authority holds that public employee strikes are not subject to barriers of state anti-injunction statutes:

> 'While this court has not previously considered this issue, nearly all courts which have, have concluded that the provisions of

state Little Norris-LaGuardia Acts are inapplicable to suits brought by states or their political subdivisions against governmental employees.' [See Joint School District of Wisconsin Rapids v. Education Association, 70 Wis.2d 292, 234 N.W.2d 289, 298 (1975).]

"Any illegal strike is subject to summary termination by court injunction, without reference to the circumstances leading to the strike, but the legality vel non of the strike must be adjudicated in the forum, and under the criteria prescribed by the government statute.

* * *

"Jurisdiction aside, the general standard for terminating a lawfully commenced strike, is harm or danger to public welfare. Unlike the common law, some public inconvenience and disruption is envisaged by strike-enabling statutes, so that the nature and severity of the inconvenience prohibited by particular statutes rests with judicial construction of legislative intent and judicial discretion in evaluating the impact of each strike. * * * The courts of sister states have not assumed or exercised the same latitude of discretion in addressing the foregoing problems. Some have enjoined imminent strikes not yet begun, while others have refused to enjoin the threat of a strike before it is actually in progress" [Supporting footnotes omitted.]

COUNTY SANI. DIST. v. LOS ANGELES COUNTY EMPLOY. ASS'N

Supreme Court of California, 1985.
38 Cal.3d 564, 214 Cal.Rptr. 424, 699 P.2d 835, cert. denied ___ U.S. ___, 106 S.Ct. 408, 88 L.Ed.2d 359.

BROUSSARD, JUSTICE.

Defendants appeal from a judgment awarding plaintiff sanitation district damages and prejudgment interest in connection with defendant union's involvement in a labor strike against plaintiff. The case squarely presents issues of great import to public sector labor-management relations, * * *. After careful review of a long line of case law and policy arguments, we conclude that the common law prohibition against all public employee strikes is no longer supportable. Therefore, the judgment for the plaintiff finding the strike to be unlawful and awarding damages, interest and costs must be reversed.

* * *

On July 5, 1976, approximately 75 percent of the District's employees went out on strike after negotiations between the District and the union for a new wage and benefit agreement reached an impasse * * * The District promptly filed a complaint for injunctive relief and damages and was granted a temporary restraining order. The strike continued for approximately 11 days, during which time the District was able to maintain its facilities and operations through the efforts of management personnel and certain union members who chose not to strike. * * *

The District then proceeded with the instant action for tort damages. The trial court found the strike to be unlawful and in violation of the public policy of the State of California and thus awarded the District $246,904 in compensatory damages, prejudgment interest in the amount of $87,615.22 and costs of $874.65.

II. THE TRADITIONAL PROHIBITION AGAINST PUBLIC EMPLOYEE STRIKES

Common law decisions in other jurisdictions at one time held that no employee, whether public or private, had a right to strike in concert with fellow workers. In fact, such collective action was generally viewed as a conspiracy and held subject to both civil and criminal sanctions. Over the course of the 20th century, however, courts and legislatures gradually acted to change these laws as they applied to private sector employees * * *.

By contrast, American law continues to regard public sector strikes in a substantially different manner. A strike by employees of the United States government may still be treated as a crime, and strikes by state and local employees have been explicitly allowed by courts or statute in only 11 states.

Contrary to the assertions of the plaintiff as well as various holdings of the Court of Appeal, this court has repeatedly stated that the legality of strikes by public employees in California has remained an open question. * * * While we had ample reason for deciding the aforementioned cases without determining the broader question of the right of public employees to strike, the instant case presents us with the proper circumstances for direct consideration of this fundamental issue.

Before commencing our discussion, however, we must note that the Legislature has also chosen to reserve judgment on the general legality of strikes in the public sector. As Justice Grodin observed in his concurring opinion in *El Rancho Unified School Dist. v. National Education Assn., supra,* 33 Cal.3d 946, 964, 192 Cal.Rptr. 123, 663 P.2d 893, "the Legislature itself has steadfastly refrained from providing clearcut guidance." With the exception of firefighters (Lab.Code, § 1962), no statutory prohibition against strikes by public employees in this state exists. The MMBA, the statute under which the present controversy arose, does not directly address the question of strikes.

The MMBA sets forth the rights of municipal and county employees in California. (Gov.Code, §§ 3500–3511.) The MMBA protects the right of such employees "to form, join, and participate in the activities of employee organizations * * * for the purpose of representation on all matters of employer-employee relations." It also requires public employers to "meet and confer" in good faith with employee representatives on all issues within the scope of representation. * * *

On its face, the MMBA neither denies nor grants local employees the right to strike. This omission is noteworthy since the Legislature has not hesitated to expressly prohibit strikes for certain classes of

public employees. * * * Thus, the absence of any such limitation on
other public employees covered by the MMBA at the very least implies
a lack of legislative intent to use the MMBA to enact a general strike
prohibition.

Plaintiffs have suggested that section 3509 of the MMBA must be
construed as a general prohibition on the right to strike because it
specifically precludes the application of Labor Code section 923 to
public employees.   Labor Code section 923 has been construed by this
court to protect the right of private sector employees to strike (see *Petri
Cleaners, Inc. v. Automotive Employees, etc. Local No. 88* (1960) 53 Cal.
2d 455, 2 Cal.Rptr. 470, 349 P.2d 76); yet, an examination of other
California statutes governing public employees makes it perfectly clear
that section 3509 was *not* included in the MMBA as a means for
prohibiting strikes.

* * *

In sum, the MMBA establishes a system of rights and protections
for public employees which closely mirrors those enjoyed by workers in
the private sector.   The Legislature, however, intentionally avoided the
inclusion of any provision which could be construed as either a blanket
grant or prohibition of a right to strike, thus leaving the issue shrouded
in ambiguity.   In the absence of clear legislative directive on this
crucial matter, it becomes the task of the judiciary to determine
whether, under the law, strikes by public employees should be viewed
as a prohibited tort.

III.   THE COMMON LAW PROHIBITION AGAINST PUBLIC EMPLOYEE STRIKES

As noted above, the Court of Appeal and various lower courts in
this and other jurisdictions have repeatedly stated that, absent a
specific statutory grant, all strikes by public employees are per se
illegal. * * * The various justifications for the common law prohibition can be summarized into four basic arguments.   First—the traditional justification—that a strike by public employees is tantamount to
a denial of governmental authority/sovereignty.   Second, the terms of
public employment are not subject to bilateral collective bargaining, as
in the private sector, because they are set by the legislative body
through unilateral lawmaking.   Third, since legislative bodies are responsible for public employment decision making, granting public employees the right to strike would afford them excessive bargaining
leverage, resulting in a distortion of the political process and an
improper delegation of legislative authority.   Finally, public employees
provide essential public services which, if interrupted by strikes, would
threaten the public welfare.

Our determination of the legality of strikes by public employees
necessarily involves an analysis of the reasoning and current viability
of each of these arguments.   The first of these justifications, the
sovereignty argument, asserts that government is the embodiment of

the people, and hence those entrusted to carry out its function may not impede it. * * *

The sovereignty concept, however, has often been criticized in recent years as a vague and outdated theory * * *. As Judge Harry T. Edwards has cogently observed, "the application of the strict sovereignty notion—that governmental power can never be opposed by employee organizations—is clearly a vestige from another era, an era of unexpanded government. * * * With the rapid growth of the government, both in sheer size as well as in terms of assuming services not traditionally associated with the 'sovereign,' government employees understandably no longer feel constrained by a notion that 'The King can do no wrong.' The distraught cries by public unions of disparate treatment merely reflect the fact that, for all intents and purposes, public employees occupy essentially the same position vis a vis the employer as their private counterparts." (Edwards, *The Developing Labor Relations Law in the Public Sector* (1972) 10 Duq.L.Rev. 357, 359–360.

In recent years, courts have rejected the very same concept of sovereignty as a justification for governmental immunity from tort liability. * * *

The second basic argument underlying the common law prohibition of public employee strikes holds that since the terms of public employment are fixed by the Legislature, public employers are virtually powerless to respond to strike pressure, or alternatively that allowing such strikes would result in "government by contract" instead of "government by law." (See *City of L.A. v. Los Angeles etc. Council* (1949) 94 Cal.App.2d 36, 46, 210 P.2d 305.) This justification may have had some merit before the California Legislature gave extensive bargaining rights to public employees. However, at present, most terms and conditions of public employment are arrived at through collective bargaining under such statutes as the MMBA.

* * *

* * * While the MMBA does not directly address the issue of such strikes, its implications regarding the traditional common law prohibition are significant.

This argument was eloquently explained by Justice Grodin in his concurring opinion in *El Rancho Unified Sch. Dist. v. National Education Assn., supra*, 33 Cal.3d at page 963, 192 Cal.Rptr. 123, 663 P.2d 893, where he pointed out that "[t]he premise underlying the court's opinion in *City of L.A.* [94 Cal.App.2d 36, 210 P.2d 305]—that it is necessarily contrary to public policy to establish terms and conditions of employment for public employees through the bilateral process of collective bargaining rather than through unilateral lawmaking—has since been rejected by the Legislature. The heart of the statute under consideration in this case [the Educational Employment Relations Act], for example, contemplates that matters relating to wages, hours, and certain other terms and conditions of employment for teachers will be the subject of negotiation and agreement between a public school employer and organizations representing its employees. (Gov.Code, §§ 3543.2, 3543.3, 3543.7.) Thus, the original policy foundation for the 'rule' that public employee strikes are illegal in this state has been substantially undermined, if not obliterated."

The remaining two arguments have not served in this state as grounds for asserting a ban on public employee strikes * * *.

The first of these arguments draws upon the different roles of market forces in the private and public spheres. This rationale suggests that because government services are essential and demand is generally inelastic, public employees would wield excessive bargaining power if allowed to strike. Proponents of this argument assume that economic constraints are not present to any meaningful degree in the public sector. Consequently, in the absence of such constraints, public employers will be forced to make abnormally large concessions to workers, which in turn will distort our political process by forcing either higher taxes or a redistribution of resources between government services.

There are, however, several fundamental problems with this "distortion of the political process" argument. For one, as will be discussed more fully below, a key assumption underlying the argument—that all government services are essential—is factually unsupportable. Modern governments engage in an enormous number and variety of functions, which clearly vary as to their degree of essentiality. * * * The recent case of the air-traffic controllers' strike is yet another example that governments have the ability to hold firm against a strike for a considerable period, even in the face of substantial inconvenience. As this court concluded in *Los Angeles Met. Transit Authority v. Brotherhood of Railroad Trainmen, supra,* "Permitting employees to strike does *not* delegate to them authority to fix their own wages to the exclusion of the employer's discretion. In collective bargaining negotiations, whether or not the employees strike, the employer is free to reject demands if he determines that they are unacceptable." (54 Cal. 2d at p. 693, 8 Cal.Rptr. 1, 355 P.2d 905, italics added.)

Other factors also serve to temper the potential bargaining power of striking public employees and thus enable public officials to resist excessive demands: First, wages lost due to strikes are as important to public employees as they are to private employees. Second, the public's concern over increasing tax rates will serve to prevent the decision-making process from being dominated by political instead of economic considerations. A third and related economic constraint arises in such areas as water, sewage and, in some instances, sanitation services, where explicit prices are charged. * * * A fourth economic constraint on public employees exists in those services where subcontracting to the private sector is a realistic alternative. For example, Warren, Michigan resolved a bargaining impasse with an American Federation of State, County and Municipal Employees (AFSCME) local by subcontracting its entire sanitation service; Santa Monica, California, ended a strike of city employees by threatening to subcontract its sanitation operations; in fact, San Francisco has chosen to subcontract its entire sanitation system to *private* firms. If this subcontract option is preserved, wages in the public sector clearly need not exceed the rate at which subcontracting becomes a realistic alternative.

The proponents of a flat ban on public employee strikes not only ignore such factors as the availability of subcontracting, but also fail to adequately consider public sentiment towards most strikes and assume that the public will push blindly for an early resolution at any cost.
* * *

In sum, there is little, if any empirical evidence which demonstrates that governments generally capitulate to unreasonable demands by public employers in order to resolve strikes. The result of the strike in the instant case clearly suggests the opposite. During the 11–day strike, negotiations resumed, and the parties subsequently reached an agreement on a new MOU, the terms of which were *precisely the same* as the District's last offer prior to the commencement of the strike. Such results certainly do not illustrate a situation where public employees wielded excessive bargaining power and thereby caused a distortion of our political process.

The fourth and final justification for the common law prohibition is that interruption of government services is unacceptable because they are essential. As noted above, in our contemporary industrial society the presumption of essentiality of most government services is questionable at best. In addition, we tolerate strikes by private employees in many of the same areas in which government is engaged, such as transportation, health, education, and utilities; in many employment fields, public and private activity largely overlap.

* * *

We of course recognize that there are certain "essential" public services, the disruption of which would seriously threaten the public health or safety. In fact, defendant union itself concedes that the law should still act to render illegal any strikes in truly essential services which would constitute a genuine threat to the public welfare. Therefore, to the extent that the "excessive bargaining power" and "interruption of essential services" arguments still have merit, specific health and safety limitations on the right to strike should suffice to answer the concerns underlying those arguments.

In addition to the various legal arguments advanced to persuade the courts to impose a judicial ban on public employee strikes—* * * there is the broader concern that permitting public employees to strike may be, on balance, harmful to labor-management relations in the public sector. This is essentially a political argument, best addressed to the Legislature. We review the matter only to point out that the issue is not so clear cut as to justify judicial intervention, since the Legislature could reasonably conclude that recognizing public employees' right to strike may actually enhance labor-management relations.

At least 10 states have granted most of their public employees a right to strike; and the policy rationale behind this statutory recognition further undercuts several of the basic premises relied upon by strike-ban advocates. * * *

It is unrealistic to assume that disputes among public employees and their employers will not occur; in fact, strikes by public employees are relatively frequent events in California. * * * Although the circumstances behind each individual strike may vary somewhat, commentators repeatedly note that much of the reason for their occurrence lies in the fact that without the right to strike, or at least a credible strike threat, public employees have little negotiating strength. This, in turn, produces frustrations which exacerbate labor-management conflicts and often provoke "illegal" strikes.

* * *

In the absence of some means of equalizing the parties' respective bargaining positions, such as a credible strike threat, both sides are less likely to bargain in good faith; this in turn leads to unsatisfactory and acrimonious labor relations and ironically to more and longer strikes. Equally as important, the possibility of a strike often provides the best impetus for parties to reach an agreement at the bargaining table, because *both* parties lose if a strike actually comes to pass. Thus by providing a clear incentive for resolving disputes, a credible strike threat may serve to avert, rather than to encourage, work stoppages.

* * *

Plaintiff's argument that only the Legislature can reject the common law doctrine prohibiting public employee strikes flies squarely in the face of both logic and past precedent. Legislative silence is not the equivalent of positive legislation and does not preclude judicial reevaluation of common law doctrine. If the courts have created a bad rule or an outmoded one, the courts can change it. * * *

For the reasons stated above, we conclude that the common law prohibition against public sector strikes should not be recognized in this state. Consequently, strikes by public sector employees in this state as such are neither illegal nor tortious under California common law. We must immediately caution, however, that the right of public employees to strike is by no means unlimited. Prudence and concern for the general public welfare require certain restrictions.

The Legislature has already prohibited strikes by firefighters under any circumstance. It may conclude that other categories of public employees perform such essential services that a strike would invariably result in imminent danger to public health and safety, and must therefore be prohibited.

While the Legislature may enact such specific restrictions, the courts must proceed on a case-by-case basis. Certain existing statutory standards may properly guide them in this task. As noted above, a number of states have granted public employees a limited right to strike, and such legislation typically prohibits strikes by a limited number of employees involved in clearly essential services. In addition, several statutes provide for injunctive relief against other types of striking public employees when the state clearly demonstrates that the continuation of such strikes will constitute an imminent threat or "clear and present danger" to public health and safety.[33] Such an approach guarantees that essential public services will not be disrupted so as to genuinely threaten public health and safety, while also preserving the basic rights of public employees.

After consideration of the various alternatives before us, we believe the following standard may properly guide courts in the resolution of future disputes in this area: strikes by public employees are not unlawful at common law unless or until it is clearly demonstrated that such a strike creates a substantial and imminent threat to the health or safety of the public. This standard allows exceptions in certain essential areas of public employment (e.g., the prohibition against firefighters and law enforcement personnel) and also requires the courts to determine on a case-by-case basis whether the public interest overrides the basic right to strike.

Although we recognize that this balancing process may impose an additional burden on the judiciary, it is neither a novel nor unmanageable task. Indeed, an examination of the strike in the instant case affords a good example of how this new standard should be applied. The 11–day strike did not involve public employees, such as firefighters or law enforcement personnel, whose absence from their duties would clearly endanger the public health and safety. * * * That is not to say that had the strike continued indefinitely, or had the availability of replacement personnel been insufficient to maintain a reasonable sanitation system, there could not have been at some point a clear showing

---

33. See, e.g., Alaska Statutes section 23.40.200(c) (strikes by most public employees may not be enjoined unless it can be shown that it has begun to threaten the health, safety and welfare of the public); Oregon Revised Statutes section 243.726(3)(a) (injunctive relief available when strike creates a clear and present danger or threat to the health, safety or welfare of the public); Pennsylvania Statutes Annotated title 43, section 1101.1003 (injunctive relief available when strike creates a clear and present danger or threats to the health, safety or welfare of the public); Wisconsin Statutes Annotated section 111.70(7m)(b) (injunctive relief available if strike poses an imminent threat to the public health or safety). See also *School District for City of Holland v. Holland Educ. Ass'n* (1968) 380 Mich. 314, 157 N.W. 2d 206, 210 (Mich.Supreme Ct., in teachers strike cases, declaring state's policy is not "to issue injunctions in labor disputes absent a showing of violence, irreparable injury, or breach of the peace"); *Timberlane Reg. Sch. Dist. v. Timberlane Reg. Ed. Ass'n* (1974) 114 N.H. 245, 317 A.2d 555, 559 (N.H.Supreme Ct. refused to rule on the legality of teachers' strikes but stated that in determining whether to issue a strike injunction, a court should consider "whether the public health, safety and welfare will be substantially harmed if the strike is allowed to continue."). The Federal Labor Management Relations Act of 1947 [29 U.S.C. §§ 141–187], follows a similar approach with respect to private sector strikes. It empowers the President to direct the Attorney General to enjoin a threatened or actual strike if it affects an industry involved in interstate commerce and if permitted to occur or continue would imperil the national health or safety. (29 U.S.C. §§ 176–180.)

of a substantial threat to the public health and welfare. However, such was not the case here, and the legality of the strike would have been upheld under our newly adopted standard.

Defendant union has also urged this court to find that a per se prohibition of all public employee strikes violates the California Constitution's guarantees of freedom of association, free speech, and equal protection. They do not contend that such a constitutional infringement is present when a court exercises its equitable authority to enjoin a strike based on a showing that the strike represents a substantial and imminent danger to the public health or safety. * * * As yet, however, the right to strike has not been accorded full constitutional protection, the prevailing view being that "[t]he right to strike, because of its more serious impact upon the public interest, is more vulnerable to regulation than the right to organize and select representatives for lawful purposes of collective bargaining which this Court has characterized as a 'fundamental right. * * *'" (*Auto Workers v. Wis. Board* (1949) 336 U.S. 245, 259, 69 S.Ct. 516, 524, 93 L.Ed. 651.)

Further, the federal ban on public employee strikes has been specifically upheld as constitutionally permissible. (See *United Federation of Postal Clerks v. Blount, supra,* 325 F.Supp. 879, 884; affd. (1971) 404 U.S. 802, 92 S.Ct. 80, 30 L.Ed.2d 38.) In the absence of any explicit constitutional protection of the right to strike, the *Blount* court reasoned that the law prohibiting only public employees from striking need only have a rational basis to avoid offending constitutional guarantees. The court then easily found that the common law policy justifications (discussed in detail above) did indeed provide a rational basis for the per se prohibition. (See, *United Federation of Postal Clerks v. Blount, supra,* at p. 883.)

* * *

We are not persuaded that the personal freedoms guaranteed by the United States and California Constitutions confer an *absolute right* to strike, but the arguments above may merit consideration at some future date. * * *

Since we have already concluded that the traditional per se prohibition against public employee strikes can no longer be upheld on common law grounds, we do not find it necessary to reach the issue in constitutional terms. Although we are not inclined to hold that the right to strike rises to the magnitude of a fundamental right, it does appear that associational rights are implicated to a substantial degree. As such, the close connection between striking and other constitutionally protected activity adds further weight to our rejection of the traditional common law rationales underlying the per se prohibition.

* * *

We conclude that it is not unlawful for public employees to engage in a concerted work stoppage for the purpose of improving their wages or conditions of employment, unless it has been determined that the work stoppage poses an imminent threat to public health or safety.

Since the trial court's judgment for damage in this case was predicated upon an erroneous determination that defendants' strike was unlawful, the judgment for damages cannot be sustained.

The judgment is reversed.

BURNS JACKSON MILLER SUMMIT & SPITZER v. LINDNER

Court of Appeals of New York, 1983.
59 N.Y.2d 314, 464 N.Y.S.2d 712, 451 N.E.2d 459

MEYER, JUDGE. * * *

This appeal involves separate action by two New York City law firms to recover damages resulting from the April, 1980 transit strike. The first, * * * is a class action against the Transport Workers Union of America, AFL–CIO (TWU), the Amalgamated Transit Union, AFL–CIO (ATU), * * * Local 100 of TWU, Locals 726 and 1056 of ATU and their respective officers. It alleges that the strike was intentional and in violation of both section 210 of the Civil Service Law and of a preliminary injunction issued March 31, 1980 by the Supreme Court and seeks damages of $50,000,000 per day for each day of the strike. The complaint sets forth two causes of action: prima facie tort and public nuisance.

The second action, * * * likewise alleges an intentional strike in violation of the statute and preliminary injunction. It was, however, brought only against the TWU and its Local 100, and officers of both, sought but $25,000 in damages, and did not ask class action status. It declared on six causes of action: for violation of the Taylor Law, prima facie tort, intentional interference with plaintiff's business, willful injury, conspiracy and breach of plaintiff's rights as third-party beneficiary of the contract between defendant unions and the New York City Transit Authority (NYCTA) and the Manhattan and Bronx Surface Transit Operating Authority (MABSTOA).

* * * We conclude (1) that the Taylor Law was neither intended to proscribe private damage actions by persons caused injury by a strike by public employees nor to establish a new private right of action for such damages, and (2) that the complaints fail to state a cause of action for (a) prima facie tort, (b) public nuisance, (c) intentional interference with business, or (d) breach of plaintiffs' rights as third-party beneficiary of defendants' contracts with NYCTA or MABSTOA.

* * *

Notes

1. **Strikes.** The minority of states that authorize public employee strikes do so with many limitations. See e.g. Annot., 84 A.L.R.3d 336 (1978, Supp.1985). The state may limit particular employees, *viz.* policemen and firemen, to mandatory arbitration while permitting other public employees to strike. It may prohibit strikes until prescribed mediation and grievance

settlement procedures are exhausted. It may authorize judicial termination of a lawful strike on a finding that the strike endangers public welfare.

2. **Picketing.** In City of Rockford v. Local 413, I.A.F., 98 Ill.App.2d 36, 240 N.E.2d 705 (1968) the court refused to enjoin peaceful picketing which firemen continued after their strike was enjoined and ended. While expressing some doubt as to its legality, the court reasoned that such picketing did not interfere with government functions as to justify injunction. But *cf.* Board of Education of Community Unit School Dist. No. 2 v. Redding, 32 Ill.2d 567, 207 N.E.2d 427 (1965) where the court enjoined picketing related to an enjoined strike on the ground that, however peaceful, it supported illegal activity and interfered with school functions. See generally, Staudahor, *Rights and Limitations of Picketing by Public Employees*, 25 Labor Law Journal, 623 (1974).

c. Civil Service—Collective Bargaining Conflicts

"The recent growth of public employee unionism poses a serious challenge to the control which Civil Service Commissions have traditionally exercised over the terms and conditions of public employment. * * * Union attempts to supplant civil service may be attributable to several considerations, including alleged civil service bias against employees, union confidence in its ability to make better decisions than civil service concerning working conditions, and the possible desire by unions to assume greater importance in the eyes of their members. * * * At stake is final decision-making power over many aspects of the employment relationship.

"To reconcile civil service laws and public sector collective bargaining, and to assign distinct roles to each, is not an easy task. Any resolution of the conflict necessarily involves making assumptions concerning a plethora of issues * * *.

* * *

"In those states with both collective bargaining laws and civil service regulations, the response to the conflict has been uneven. One group of 14 state legislatures has attempted to reconcile the conflict by statute—six of these states give absolute primacy to civil service, four give primacy to civil service only on certain specifically defined issues, and four leave the public employer free to determine whether to pursue collective bargaining or to preserve civil service. * * * In another group of 19 states, however, no statutory attempt has been made to resolve the conflict. As a result, the parties are left in an uncertain and often confused position.

" * * * The central problem has been the failure of legislatures to define the respective parameters of the civil service commission and the collective bargaining process. This abdication of responsibility has placed the courts in the position of having to decide issues which involve subtle policy judgments concerning the purpose and function of the civil service system. It is understandable, therefore, that courts have usually attempted to avoid the problem by applying the traditional, if formalistic, rules of judicial construction." Comment, *The Civil Service-Collective Bargaining Conflict in the Public Sector: Attempts at Reconciliation,* 38 U.Chi.L.Rev. 826–7, 829–30, 848 (1971).

The mere fact that a subject is covered by the state civil service statute does not automatically exempt it from compulsory bargaining under the labor statutes, unless the civil service legislation "contained specific and mandatory provisions relating to such matters." AFSCME v. County of Lancaster, 200 Neb. 301, 263 N.W.2d 471 (1978).

d. Unionization and Municipal Finance

"The basic reason that prices rise more rapidly for State and local governments is that public services are labor intensive. Labor-related costs, including both salary costs and provisions for fringe benefits constitute 70 to 80 percent of most city budgets. Productivity gains are difficult to achieve where labor is the main factor of production.

Pressures of External Forces

"Because of the high labor component in city expenditures, the forces that influence labor costs throughout the economy exert extraordinary pressure on city finances. For example, salary and wage expectations of city employees are elevated by Federal and private employees salary increases. City outlays are pushed upward by rivalry among unions and organizations representing city employees, rivalry between functional city employee groups, emphasis on fringe benefits in addition to wages in collective bargaining, and increasing reliance on arbitration to settle wage disputes.

"These external forces working in concert, may generate tremendous leverage on city costs in the long-run while remaining hidden in the short-run. For example, the combination of wage expectations and sharp bargaining among rival unions and functional groupings has often resulted in wage packages with fringe benefits that are prohibitively expensive to the cities. In their labor negotiations, some municipalities have not yet adopted the practice of fully costing out fringe benefits in dollars-and-cents terms thereby temporarily hiding the full cost of a labor settlement. In some cases, the failure to cost out a wage settlement is intentional. City officials and, for that matter, union officials may want to minimize the immediate cost implications for the city. Under the circumstances, city officials take credit with taxpayers for a low dollars-and-cents settlement and union officials take credit for improvement in the workers' benefits package on an item-by-item basis that their membership understands. The net result from the standpoint of the city is an ever-increasing cost in terms of retirement payments, health and hospitalization payments, and decreasing productivity from employees because of longer vacations, more holidays, and generally shortened work weeks.

"Improvements in pension benefits have particularly insidious effects on city cost levels because these improvements can be passed forward many years into the future." ACIR, *City Financial Emergencies* 33 (1973).

Integrating Collective Bargaining Into the Budget Process—The management of local government finances requires a reasonably accurate forecast of revenue needs; the timely levy of taxes to meet those needs; and the advance allocation, by appropriations, of sums required for specified expenditures. Each of these steps presuppose reasonably accurate knowledge of public employment wage rates and costs. Therefore, unless labor negotiations and settlements are reached, or nearly firmed, prior to budget adoption dates, essential elements of intelligent budgeting will be lost. State legislatures have attempted to induce timely completion of labor negotiations by enacting deadlines for mediation or arbitration in the event of impasses (e.g. Pa.Law Art. VIII, Appendix A, infra). These efforts to assure timely agreement have failed.

Chapter X

LOCAL GOVERNMENT TORTS—
STATE LAW

Governmental tort law has several different branches. Some arise out of federal law, and these are discussed in the next chapter. Most arise out of state law which varies considerably from state to state. At the state level, significant distinctions exist between *private* tort law where the liability and defenses of principals and agents rest upon common standards, on one hand; and *public* tort law where the liability and defenses of government units may differ materially from those of their officers and employees. The reasons for these distinctions, which are unique to government processes, will appear shortly. In dealing with local government torts, particular attention is given to the defenses of privilege, immunity, and to preclusive requirements of timely claim notices and short statutes of limitations, as well as to statutory ceilings on the amount of recoverable damages against local government units.

Detailed coverage of the foregoing subjects must be left to specialized texts. The following materials sketch the issues one may expect to encounter, with the caveat that the courts and legislatures of each state have developed tort principles and limitations that are in some respects unique to that state. Further, modern tort claim statutes continue to undergo legislative amendments, and have not been fully construed or tested, making all the more necessary a careful check of current developments in each state.

A. TRENDS IN GOVERNMENTAL TORT LAW

As of 1982, all jurisdictions, save two (Maryland and Virginia) have either abrogated or substantially modified the common law doctrine of governmental immunity. These changes were wrought in a majority of states by judicial decision, and in the remaining states by legislative enactments. There persists, however, considerable variation among the states on the extent to which governmental or individual immunity is preserved, and on the conditions which give rise to the removal or limitation of such immunity. Different theories of abrogation or waiver of immunity, total or partial, are indicated in the following materials. The nature and extent of immunity waiver adopted by each state is listed in Restatement, Law of Torts 2d, Appendix §§ 895B, 895C (1982). The grant of immunity to government units and their officials was recently held by the Supreme Court to be valid constitutionally, both as to due process and equal protection. Martinez v. California, 444 U.S. 277, 100 S.Ct. 553, 62 L.Ed.2d 481 (1980).

AYALA v. PHILADELPHIA BOARD OF PUBLIC EDUCATION

Supreme Court of Pennsylvania, 1973.
453 Pa. 584, 305 A.2d 877.

ROBERTS, JUSTICE. Appellants, William Ayala and William Ayala, Jr., instituted this action to recover damages for injuries suffered by William, Jr., when his arm was caught in a shredding machine in the upholstery class of the Carrol School in Philadelphia. As a result of these injuries, the 15 year old student's arm was amputated.

Appellants alleged that appellee school district, through its employees, was negligent in failing to supervise the upholstery class, in supplying the machine for use without a proper safety device, in maintaining the machine in a dangerous and defective condition, and in failing to warn the children of the dangerous condition. Appellee, the Philadelphia Board of Public Education, interposed preliminary objections asserting the defense of governmental immunity. These objections were sustained and the Superior Court affirmed in a per curiam order. * * *

We now hold that the doctrine of governmental immunity—long since devoid of any valid justification—is abolished in this Commonwealth. In so doing, we join the ever-increasing number of jurisdictions which have judicially abandoned this antiquated doctrine. See, *e.g.,* Spencer v. General Hospital of District of Columbia, 138 U.S.App.D.C. 48, 425 F.2d 479 (1969); Campbell v. State, 284 N.E.2d 733 (Ind.1972) (citing with approval Klepinger v. Board of Commissioners, 143 Ind. App. 155, 239 N.E.2d 160 (1968) and Brinkman v. City of Indianapolis, 141 Ind.App. 662, 231 N.E.2d 169 (1967)); Evans v. Board of County Commissioners, 174 Colo. 97, 482 P.2d 968 (1971); Flournoy v. School District No. 1, 174 Colo. 110, 482 P.2d 966 (1971); Smith v. State, 93 Idaho 795, 473 P.2d 937 (1970); Willis v. Department of Conservation and Econ. Dev., 55 N.J. 534, 264 A.2d 34 (1970); Becker v. Beaudoin, 106 R.I. 562, 261 A.2d 896 (1970); Johnson v. Municipal University of Omaha, 184 Neb. 430, 160 N.W.2d 805 (1968); Parish v. Pitts, 244 Ark. 1239, 429 S.W.2d 45 (1968); Veach v. City of Phoenix, 102 Ariz. 195, 427 P.2d 335 (1967) (relying on Stone v. Arizona Highway Commission, 93 Ariz. 384, 381 P.2d 107 (1963)); Haney v. City of Lexington, 386 S.W.2d 738 (Ky.1964); Sherbutte v. Marine City, 374 Mich. 48, 130 N.W.2d 920 (1964); Rice v. Clark County, 79 Nev. 253, 382 P.2d 605 (1963); Scheele

v. City of Anchorage, 385 P.2d 582 (Alaska 1963); City of Fairbanks v. Schaible, 375 P.2d 201 (Alaska 1962); Spanel v. Mounds View School District No. 621, 264 Minn. 279, 118 N.W.2d 795 (1962); Holytz v. City of Milwaukee, 17 Wis.2d 26, 115 N.W.2d 618 (1962); Muskopf v. Corning Hospital District, 55 Cal.2d 211, 11 Cal.Rptr. 89, 359 P.2d 457 (1961); Williams v. City of Detroit, 364 Mich. 231, 111 N.W.2d 1 (1961); Molitor v. Kaneland Community Unit District No. 302, 18 Ill.2d 11, 163 N.E.2d 89 (1959); Hargrove v. Town of Coca Beach, 96 So.2d 130 (Fla.1957).

I.

It is generally agreed that the historical roots of the governmental immunity doctrine are found in the English case of Russell v. Men of Devon, 2 T.R. 667, 100 Eng.Rep. 359 (1788). [Citations omitted]. There, the court, in extending immunity to an unincorporated county, expressed the fear that if suits against such political subdivisions were permitted, there would be "an infinity of actions." * * * That court was also influenced by the absence of a fund "out of which satisfaction is to be made." *Id.* Finally, Justice Ashurst, expressing the eighteenth century societal evaluation of the individual and local governmental interests, observed that "it is better that an individual should sustain an injury than that the public should suffer an inconvenience." Id.

While some attribute the immunity of municipal corporations and quasi-corporations to an extension of the theory that "the King can do no wrong", it has been noted that in Russell v. Men of Devon there is no mention of that phrase. * * *

> "[e]very reason assigned by the court [in *Russell*] is born of expediency. The wrong to plaintiff is submerged in the convenience of the public. No moral, ethical, or rational reason for the decision is advanced by the court except the practical problem of assessing damages against individual defendants." *Id.*

* * *

Whatever may have been the actual basis for Russell v. Men of Devon, the doctrine it advanced was soon applied in the United States. * * *

Pennsylvania joined the numerous states adopting the immunity doctrine and, in Ford v. School District, 121 Pa. 543, 15 A. 812 (1888), held that school districts, as quasi-corporations, are not liable for the tortious conduct of employees. The Court's decision was motivated by factors similar to those which influenced the English court in *Russell.*

Although the English courts abandoned the doctrine and permitted suits against municipalities and school districts, this Commonwealth continued to deny recovery. * * *

Thus, until the present action, we have retained the archaic and artificial distinction between tortious conduct arising out of the exercise of a proprietary function and tortious conduct arising out of exercise of a governmental function.

Today we conclude that no reasons whatsoever exist for continuing to adhere to the doctrine of governmental immunity. Whatever may have been the basis for the inception of the doctrine, it is clear that no public policy considerations presently justify its retention.

* * *

Moreover, we are unwilling to perpetuate the notion that "it is better that an individual should sustain an injury than that the public should suffer an inconvenience." Russell v. Men of Devon, *supra* at 673, 100 Eng.Rep. at 362. This social philosophy of nonliability is "an anachronism in the law of today." Flagiello v. Pennsylvania Hospital, 417 Pa. 486, 502, 208 A.2d 193, 201 (1965). * * *

* * *

Thus, we must agree with Chief Justice Traynor of the California Supreme Court that "the rule of governmental immunity for tort is an anachronism, without rational basis, and has existed only by the force of inertia." Muskopf v. Corning Hospital District, *supra* 55 Cal.2d at 216, 11 Cal.Rptr. at 92, 359 P.2d at 460. Moreover, the distinction between governmental and proprietary functions "is probably one of the most unsatisfactory known to the law, for it has caused confusion not only among the various jurisdictions but almost always within each jurisdiction." Davis, Administrative Law Treatise § 25.07 at 460 (1958).

This Court recognized the general dissatisfaction with this distinction when we stated, "Perhaps there is no issue known to the law which is surrounded by more confusion than the question whether a given municipal operation is governmental or proprietary in nature." Morris v. Mount Lebanon Township School District, *supra* 393 Pa. at 637, 144 A.2d at 739. Compare Shields v. Pittsburgh, supra (operation of playground during vacation is a governmental function) with Morris v. Mount Lebanon Township School District, *supra,* decided four years earlier, (operation of summer recreation program is a proprietary function).

Recently, the Indiana Supreme Court echoed the widespread displeasure with the governmental-proprietary distinction: * * * Campbell v. State, *supra* 284 N.E.2d at 735.

* * *

* * * Indeed, appellee does not attempt to justify retention of immunity on policy grounds. Rather, it contends that abrogation, if it is to be achieved, should be accomplished by legislative direction rather than by judicial determination.

In response to arguments that the Court should defer to legislative action, we stated in Flagiello v. Pennsylvania Hospital, *supra,* 417 Pa. at 503, 208 A.2d at 202: "[T]he controverted rule [charitable immunity] is not the creation of the Legislature. *This Court fashioned it, and, what it put together, it can dismantle.*" (Emphasis added.)

* * *

Similarly, here, the doctrine of governmental immunity—judicially imposed—may be judicially terminated. "Having found that doctrine to be unsound and unjust under present conditions, we consider that we have not only the power, but the duty, to abolish that immunity. 'We closed our courtroom doors without legislative help, and we can likewise open them.'" Molitor v. Kaneland Community Unit District No. 302, *supra,* 18 Ill.2d at 25, 163 N.E.2d at 96. * * *

* * *

Finally, it is suggested that if we abolish governmental immunity, our decision to do so should not apply to the instant case.[9] We refused to adopt that suggestion in Falco v. Pados, *supra,* as well as numerous other cases. [Citations omitted] On the basis of these decisions, appellee's argument that we do not apply our newly adopted rule to the facts of this case must be rejected.

Having concluded that local governmental units—municipal corporations and quasi-corporations—are no longer immune from tort liability, the crder sustaining appellee's preliminary objections is reversed and the record remanded for proceedings consistent with this opinion.

Notes

1. **The Extent of Abrogation.** Abrogation of common law immunity does not necessarily imply that government tort duties are the same as those of private individuals. See Wilson v. Tucson, 8 Ariz.App. 398, 446 P.2d 504 (1968). Judicial abrogation has not been absolute in all states. Many preserve immunity for legislative, quasi-legislative, judicial, or quasi-judicial functions (Gorrell v. Parsons, 223 Kan. 645, 576 P.2d 616 (1978)) and modern tort claims statutes of many states limit the amount of damages that may be recovered. See p. 923, et seq., infra.

2. **Privilege Distinguished From Immunity.** Some government activities are so essential that they are excluded as "privileged" from the scope of tort duties. Immunity arises from the status of the party defendant, irrespective of the facts of the case, e.g. government, charity, infancy or incompetence. Subject to narrow exceptions, this status provides a defense without reference to particular circumstances. The defenses of privilege and justification, however, are generally grounded in the particular facts of each case. Thus, while these concepts are related, they should not be confused. Judges, prosecutors and legislators enjoy common law immunity, while policemen do not; although the latter may defend actions in the nature of tort by the limited privilege of acting in good faith even though the action is misconceived under technical law. Re immunity, see Stump v. Sparkman, 435 U.S. 349, 98 S.Ct. 1099, 55 L.Ed.2d 331 (1978); Imbler v. Pachtman, 424 U.S. 409, 96 S.Ct. 984, 47 L.Ed.2d 128 (1976); Scheuer v. Rhodes, 416 U.S. 232, 94 S.Ct. 1683, 40 L.Ed.2d 90 (1972).

9. In Great Northern Ry. Co. v. Sunburst Oil and Refining Co., 287 U.S. 358, 364, 53 S.Ct. 145, 148, 77 L.Ed. 360 (1932), the United States Supreme Court stated:

"A state in defining the limits of adherence to precedent may make a choice for itself between the principle of forward operation and that of relation backward."

Compare Bivens v. Six Unknown Named Agents of Federal Bureau of Narcotics, 456 F.2d 1339 (2d Cir.1972).

3. **State Sovereign Immunity Distinguished From Local Government Immunity.** Immunity from suits of all kinds, as an aspect of sovereignty, applies to states as sovereigns, but not to their political subdivisions and local governments, (except in the unusual instances where the act of the local government is deemed to be the direct act of the state itself). An unusual *judicial* abrogation of state sovereign immunity, (see Mayle v. Pennsylvania Department of Highways, 479 Pa. 384, 388 A.2d 709 (1978)) was reversed by legislative restoration, Safeguard Mut. Ins. Co. v. Commonwealth of Pa. Ins. Comm'r, 48 Pa.Cmwlth. 235, 410 A.2d 84 (1980).

1. EXCEPTIONAL CASES AFFECTING IMMUNITY DEFENSES

At common law, several situations were excepted from immunity defenses, i.e. proprietary activities, nuisance conditions, and ministerial acts which do not involve "discretion." To varying extents, these exceptions are adopted by the public tort claim statutes of some states which partially preserve governmental immunity. Therefore, the classification of particular activities as proprietary or governmental, negligent or nuisance, and ministerial or discretionary, remains crucial to tort liability in those states.

a. Proprietary Activities

Municipal entities are no more immune for proprietary enterprises than private corporations. Schwartz v. Borough of Stockton, 32 N.J. 141, 160 A.2d 1 (1960). This basis for nonimmunity ill suits the multifarious character of modern local governments. The confusion among authorities on the classification of governmental or proprietary activities has led one expert to abandon any attempt to explain them. "[L]ittle can be said about it here, and the reader must be referred to the detailed consideration in texts on the law of municipal corporation." W. Prosser, Law of Torts 979 (4th ed.1971). See generally 18 McQuillin, *Municipal Corporations,* §§ 53.01–53.144 (3d rev. ed. 1963).

HATTEN v. MASON REALTY CO.
Supreme Court of Appeals of West Virginia, 1964.
148 W.Va. 380, 135 S.E.2d 236.

CALHOUN, JUDGE. This case involves an action for wrongful death * * * arising from the drowning of an eight-year old boy in a pool of water. The pool of water was created in connection with the installation of a sewer line in a residential development area within the City of Point Pleasant. * * * The sewer line was being installed by the employees of the municipality and at its expense.

* * *

As stated previously, the defendant city asserted in its answer that it cannot be held liable in any event because the construction or installation of the sewer line within the municipality was a governmental function. If such was a governmental function, the city, of course, may not be held liable in damages for the death of the boy, * * *. [Citations omitted] It is equally clear, however, that a city may be held liable in damages for personal injuries or a death resulting from the negligence of its officers, agents or employees in the performance of proprietary functions. [Citations omitted]

The principles relating to the liability or nonliability of a municipality, as stated above, are clear and well settled; but courts experience difficulty in determining what functions are governmental and what functions are merely proprietary.

An annotation dealing with liability of a municipality arising from negligence in the construction or repair of sewers or drains is found in 61 A.L.R.2d 874. According to decisions of appellate courts listed on pages 877 to 880, inclusive, it appears that they are sharply divided on the question whether the cloak of governmental immunity is available to a municipal corporation in cases of this character. * * *

We believe that prior decisions of this Court tend to sustain the proposition that the construction or installation of the sewer line by the city represented the performance of a proprietary function. McCabe v. City of Parkersburg, 138 W.Va. 830, 79 S.E.2d 87. The Court holds, therefore, that, to the extent that the municipality was engaged in the construction or installation of the sewer line in this case, it was engaged in the performance of a proprietary function; and that it may be held liable in damages for the death of the boy if the death resulted proximately from the negligence of the officers, agents or employees of the city while engaged in the performance of such function.

* * *

Notes

1. See People v. Mission Brook Sanitary District opinion at p. 31, Chapter II of this text. Where in the course of constructing a viaduct, the city severs a water main causing property damage, would the activity be deemed governmental and thus immune? See Chavez v. Laramie, 389 P.2d 23 (Wyo.1964). On the attempt to define and distinguish the concepts of governmental and proprietary acts, see Antieau, Municipal Corporations Law, §§ 11.40–11.46 (1985); Ross v. Consumers Power Co., 420 Mich. 567, 363 N.W.2d 641 (1984) (legislative definitions).

2. **Criteria for Distinguishing Proprietary and Governmental Activity.** "We now come to the most troublesome problem of what constitutes a proprietary function. We are mindful of what was said in 60 A.L.R.2d at page 1204:

> 'The general tests provided by the courts * * * have not proved adequate for the resolution of particular questions; and as a result the courts have frequently treated such questions on their individual merits, often reaching at least superficially conflicting results.'

It should be stated as elementary that each case must be governed by its own particular facts. * * * It may be said that when a state by itself, or through its corporate creations, embarks on an enterprise which is commercial in character or which is usually carried on by private individuals or private companies, it is engaged in a proprietary enterprise (Stadler v. Curtis Gas, Inc., 182 Neb. 6, 151 N.W.2d 915). * * *

"We have no hesitancy in concluding that in the operation of the hospital at the University Medical Center the Board of Regents was engaged in a proprietary rather than a governmental function. The operation of a hospital is usually carried on by private individuals or private companies; * * *

"It is not necessary that an actual net profit result.

"The courts of our sister states are not in accord on the question of the character of a hospital operation. It would serve no useful purpose to review the decisions of other states in this opinion. * * *" See Carroll v. Kittle, 203 Kan. 841, 847–851, 457 P.2d 21, 27–29 (1969).

2. In Grover v. Manhattan, 198 Kan. 307, 424 P.2d 256 (1967), the court noted that no single test of classification of activity is decisive. It concluded that the operation of a city zoo was more like the operation of a public park and a governmental activity. Can you suggest arguments to refute the analogy of a zoo to a public park? Compare Byrnes v. Jackson, 140 Miss. 656, 105 So. 861 (1925).

In Sarmiento v. Corpus Christi, 465 S.W.2d 813 (Tex.Civ.App.1971) school crossing guards were held to be engaged in governmental activity: "Municipalities have the right, under the police power, reasonably to control and regulate the use of their streets, and this, including traffic regulation, is a governmental function. Id. at p. 815.

Municipal liability for traffic control activities is the subject of proliferated special rules:

"The determination of the liability of the municipality in a case involving the obstruction of view at an intersection must commence with the subject of the duty owed by the municipality to persons traveling on its streets. First, there is no duty on the city to maintain unobstructed-view intersections. McGough v. City of Edmonds, 1 Wash.App. 164, 460 P.2d 302 (1969); Barton v. King County, 18 Wash.2d 573, 139 P.2d 1019 (1943). Second, there is no duty on the city to regulate traffic by posting signs or otherwise. Rodgers v. Ray, supra. Third, there is a duty to warn of dangerous conditions in a public road. City of Glendale v. Bradshaw, supra; Rodgers v. Ray, supra. Fourth, although there is no duty to regulate traffic by posting signs or otherwise, once the city undertakes to control traffic with signs or warning devices, it cannot create a dangerous condition in doing so, Teall v. City of Cudahy, 60 Cal.2d 431, 34 Cal.Rptr. 869, 386 P.2d 493 (1963); Hilts v. County of Solano, 265 Cal.App.2d 161, 71 Cal.Rptr. 275 (1968), and must properly maintain the signs, Dudum v. City of San Mateo, 167 Cal.App.2d 593, 334 P.2d 968 (1959)." Slavin v. Tucson, 17 Ariz.App. 16, 495 P.2d 141, 143 (1972). See also Resnik v. Michaels, infra, p. 901. Do these factors on "duty" confuse other grounds for nonimmunity, i.e. nuisances (per following case) and "ministerial" acts (per Resnik, p. 901, infra)?

b. *Nuisances*

The classic conception of a "nuisance" in the early common law involved a condition of property that caused a continuing injury to other property or its enjoyment, i.e. a continuing trespass based on property conditions and not on activity (which might create the condition.) The distinction between wrongful activity and damaging property conditions has not always been maintained in case law, and has been subject to legislative revision, so that the term nuisance has taken on varied meanings in different circumstances and different jurisdictions. Nevertheless, the term maintains its significance as an exceptional ground for local government tort liability.

> "A municipality like any other individual or private corporation may be liable for damages it causes to a third party from the operation or maintenance of a nuisance, irrespective of whether it is exercising a governmental or a ministerial function, Ingram v. City of Acworth, 90 Ga.App. 719, 720, 84 S.E.2d 99; Archer v. City of Austell, 68 Ga.App. 493, 497, 23 S.E.2d 512. While it is true that a municipal corporation is not liable for its acts of negligence in discharging a governmental function, yet a municipal corporation cannot under the guise of performing a governmental function create a nuisance dangerous to life or health. Delta Air Corp. v. Kersey, 193 Ga. 862, 870, 20 S.E.2d 245, 140 A.L.R. 1352. Anything that works hurt, inconvenience or damage to another is a nuisance. Code § 72–101. An action may be brought against a municipality for the creation or maintenance of a nuisance where the municipality is negligent in carrying out a lawful act which it was authorized to do. Southland Coffee Co. v. City of Macon, 60 Ga. App. 253, 257, 258, 3 S.E.2d 739; City of Atlanta v. Due, 42 Ga.App. 797, 803, 157 S.E. 256. See Town of Fort Oglethorpe v. Phillips, 224 Ga. 834, 165 S.E.2d 141, 144 (1968); 1A Antieau, Municipal Corporation Law § 11.08 (1985).

The distinction between immune negligence and non-immune nuisance is troublesome. "It seems reasonable to say that there is no sound argument behind the distinction itself, and that resort to the more or less undefined concept of nuisance is merely one method by which the courts have retreated from municipal non-liability." W. Prosser, *Law of Torts* 983 (4th ed. 1971).

What facts constitute a nuisance depends upon particular case or statutory law. Compare, e.g., Brainard et al. v. West Hartford, p. 479 supra, with Osborn v. Akron, 171 Ohio St. 361, 171 N.E.2d 492 (1960) where the city operation of a dump was held not to be a nuisance. The court declared: "Irrespective of what the rule is in other jurisdictions, that is not the rule in Ohio. The liability of a municipality for a nuisance in Ohio is defined in Section 723.01, revised code * * *. The General Assembly by the enactment of Section 723.01, revised code, has set forth those instances in which a municipality may become liable for a nuisance, and, * * * has thereby excluded liability for nuisance not encompassed by such statute. Therefore, a municipality's liability for the creation or maintenance of a nuisance exists only in those cases provided for in Section 723.01, revised code." Id. 171 N.E.2d at 493–94. To like effect see Vater v. Glenn County, 49 Cal.2d 815, 323 P.2d 85, 88 (1958).

In some jurisdictions the nuisance doctrine may support tort recovery even where the statute preserving governmental tort immunity does not list nuisance as one of the express exceptions. In Nestle v. Santa Monica, 6 Cal.3d 920, 101 Cal.Rptr. 568, 496 P.2d 480 (1972) the court construed the state torts claims act to impliedly exclude nuisances from its general preservation of tort claims immunity.

TOWN OF FORT OGLETHORPE v. PHILLIPS

Supreme Court of Georgia, 1968.
224 Ga. 834, 165 S.E.2d 141.

ALMAND, PRESIDING JUSTICE. Alvin Doyle Phillips, Jr., * * * brought an action seeking to recover damages for personal injuries against Earl and Sylvia Hamilton, * * * and the Town of Fort Oglethorpe wherein the collision occurred. Plaintiff in his petition alleged that: The Town of Fort Oglethorpe maintains and operates a traffic control light at the intersection where the collision took place. On the date of the collision and for two weeks beforehand, the Mayor, Chief of Police and Aldermen of Fort Oglethorpe had knowledge that this traffic light was not working correctly and failed to correct it. This traffic light was defective in that it would flash either red or green on all four sides of the intersection simultaneously. Numerous accidents resulted from the defective condition of the traffic light, and on the day the plaintiff was injured there were six collisions at this crowded intersection because the defective traffic light flashed green in all directions causing approaching vehicles to collide. The mayor and chief of police knew of these six collisions * * * and did not repair the defective traffic light. Through the negligent acts of the Town of Fort Oglethorpe a traffic hazard was created obstructing the intersection and producing a condition injurious to the plaintiff. The Town of Fort Oglethorpe's negligent and careless operation of the traffic light at the intersection in question constituted a nuisance * * *.

The Town of Fort Oglethorpe filed a general demurrer to the plaintiff's petition. After hearing argument of counsel of the parties, the trial court sustained the municipality's demurrer and dismissed the petition as to the Town of Fort Oglethorpe. Plaintiff appealed to the Court of Appeals which reversed the trial court * * *.

The Court of Appeals regarded the main issue in the case as being "whether the maintenance of a defective traffic light by the city, * * * constitutes negligence in the exercise of a governmental or ministerial function." Certainly, we view this issue as being one of the decisive questions in this case; however, we would arrive at a different conclusion from that drawn by the Court of Appeals.

The Court of Appeals took the position that the maintenance of a traffic light is a ministerial function and that the failure to properly maintain a traffic light creates a defect or obstruction in the street in violation of Code § 69–303. With these conclusions we cannot agree.

The general rule is that in the maintenance and operation of a traffic light system a city functions in a governmental capacity thereby relieving the city of liability for failure to keep traffic lights functioning properly. 18 McQuillin, Municipal Corporations (3d Ed. revised) p. 234, § 53.42. * * * We are of the opinion that the maintenance and operation of the traffic light by the Town of Fort Oglethorpe was a governmental function and the municipality is not liable for negligent performance.

Secondly, we are of the opinion that the improper operation of a traffic light by a municipality is not such a defect or obstruction of the streets as to bring this function within the scope of Code § 69–303, which would result in this function becoming ministerial. * * * Obstructions or defects in the streets within the meaning of Code § 69–303 are physical obstructions or defects in the streets. * * *

* * *

While we disagree that the maintenance and operation of a traffic light is a ministerial function and that the municipality's failure to properly maintain such traffic light constitutes an obstruction or defect in the street within the context of Code § 69–303, we do agree with the judgment of the Court of Appeals but for other reasons.

We are limited in our ruling in the instant case exclusively to the allegations of the petition and under these particular allegations the plaintiff sets forth facts sufficient to state a cause of action based on nuisance as against the municipality's general demurrer.

* * *

The allegations of the petition take the instant case beyond mere negligence and into a situation which constitutes a nuisance. The allegations that the Mayor, Chief of Police and Aldermen of Fort Oglethorpe had knowledge for more than two weeks of the defective condition of the traffic light at the intersection in question causing numerous collisions and these officials did not repair this defect but continued to allow it to operate defectively; and further, that the mayor and chief of police knew that six collisions took place at the intersection on the day plaintiff was injured and did nothing to correct the situation, set forth the operation and maintenance of a defective condition that could work damage to anyone who came in proximity to it. Certainly, the petition states facts sufficient to show the active operation and maintenance of a dangerous condition and knowingly allowing such condition to continue to the injury of the plaintiff. Accordingly, the particular allegations of the instant petition set forth a cause of action for the operation and maintenance of a nuisance.

Judgment affirmed.

Notes

1. Had the traffic standard in the principal case broken down one hour prior to the plaintiff's accident and had there been no intervening accidents, would the condition have amounted to a nuisance? Cf. Borden v. Salem, 249 Or. 39, 436 P.2d 734 (1968).

CITY OF DENTON v. VAN PAGE

Supreme Court of Texas, 1986.
701 S.W.2d 831.

CAMPBELL, JUSTICE.

This is a suit for damages under the Texas Tort Claims Act. Tex. Rev.Civ.Stat.Ann. art. 6252–19 (Vernon 1970). Michael Van Page sued Frances Melton and the City of Denton for injuries received from a fire in a building owned by Melton. Page alleged that the fire was caused by an unsafe or dangerous condition in the building. Page further alleged that the city was liable because its fire marshal was negligent in his investigation of previous arson attempts on the building thereby contributing to its dangerous condition. Page's wife joined in the suit and sought damages for mental anguish, loss of consortium and loss of household services.

Following a jury trial, the trial court rendered judgment for the Pages against Melton and the City of Denton, jointly and severally. On appeal, the city contended that it was not liable for the dangerous condition of the building because it did not own, occupy, furnish or control the property in question. The court of appeals rejected this argument and, with minor reformation, affirmed the judgment of the trial court. 683 S.W.2d 180. We reverse the judgment of the court of appeals and render judgment that the Pages take nothing from the City of Denton.

Page rented a house from Melton. On a lot in back of the rental house was an old building used by Melton for storage. A short time after Page and his family moved into the rental house, the storage building was set on fire. On three separate occasions an arsonist attempted to burn the building and its contents. On each occasion the fire department for the City of Denton extinguished the fire. The fire marshal also investigated the scene and filed a report in which he concluded kerosene had been used to set the fires.

With this history in mind, Page was understandably suspicious when one evening he heard strange noises coming from the storage building. He went to investigate. As Page entered the building, he was met with an explosion and what he described as a "tornado of flames." He was severely burned, but able to crawl from the shed and run to his house for help.

The fire department responded again to extinguish the fire. The fire marshal also arrived to investigate. He discovered some empty five-gallon cans inside the storage building and several unopened cans of gasoline both inside and outside the building. A matchbook was found just inside the door of the building and the smell of gasoline was in the air.

Page sued Melton and the City of Denton * * *. Page's theory was that the city, through its fire marshal, was negligent in its investigation of the arson in failing to discover and remove the gasoline stored in the building or in failing to warn Page of the building's dangerous condition. Page alleged that the dangerous condition of the storage building was a "condition" of real property for which the city was liable under section 3 of the Tort Claims Act.

* * *

The issue before us is whether the dangerous condition of the storage building is a condition of real property on which Page may base a waiver of the City of Denton's governmental immunity. Governmental immunity generally shields a municipality from liability in the performance of governmental functions such as fire protection. Section 3 of the Tort Claims Act, however, waives immunity in three general areas: (1) claims arising out of the use of motor driven vehicles and motor driven equipment, (2) claims arising from some condition or use of personal property, and (3) claims arising from some condition or use of real property. Tex.Rev.Civ.Stat.Ann. art. 6252–19 (Vernon 1970). That part of section 3 that applies to our question provides for liability for negligence.

* * *

Section 3 does not create new duties. It simply waives the common law doctrine of governmental immunity under circumstances where a private person similarly situated would be liable. As in any other tort case, a plaintiff relying on section 3 of the Act must prove the existence and violation of a legal duty owed him by the defendant. *Abalos v. Oil Development Company of Texas,* 544 S.W.2d 627, 631 (Tex.1976). The threshold issue is what duty did the City of Denton owe Page with respect to the dangerous condition of the storage building.

The court of appeals held that the city owed Page the same duty of care as Melton, the owner of the property, owed Page. * * * The court of appeals recognized that the city did not own or occupy the storage building, but analogized the city's duty to that of an independent contractor hired to remedy a known defect on the premises.

* * *

We agree that a person put in control of premises by the owner, such as an independent contractor, is under the same duty as the owner to keep the premises under his control in safe condition. *Smith v. Henger,* 148 Tex. 456, 226 S.W.2d 425, 431 (1950). It is the element of control, however, which distinguishes the independent contractor cases from this case. The City of Denton did not assume control over the storage building and did not assume a duty to discover any dangerous condition existing on the premises.

* * *

As previously observed, section 3 waives immunity under circumstances where a private person similarly situated would be liable. Ordinarily a person who does not own the real property must assume control over and responsibility for the premises before there will be liability for a dangerous condition existing on the real property. It is possession and control which generally must be shown as a prerequisite to liability. 62 Am.Jur.2d *Premises Liability* §§ 12 and 14 (1972). Additionally, a private person who has created the dangerous condition may be liable even though not in control of the premises at the time of injury. *Strakos v. Gehring, supra.* Also, a private person who agrees to make safe a known, dangerous condition of real property may be liable for the failure to remedy the condition. *Gundolf v. Massman-Johnson, supra.*

The conduct of the City of Denton does not satisfy any of these circumstances. The City of Denton did not exercise control over the storage building, nor did it expressly or impliedly contract to remedy any dangerous condition on the property. The fire marshal did not create the dangerous condition, nor did he promise to find and remedy any unsafe condition in the building, nor did he promise to make the storage building safe from arson. We hold that the City of Denton is not liable for the dangerous condition of the storage building because it neither owned, occupied nor controlled the premises, nor did it create the dangerous condition.

These facts do not present a case of waiver of governmental immunity within the meaning of section 3 of the Tort Claims Act. Because the City of Denton is not liable for the dangerous condition of the storage building, it is unnecessary to discuss any of the other points attacking the judgment. * * * The judgment of the court of appeals as it pertains to the City of Denton is reversed and judgment is rendered that Michael Van Page and his wife, Ida Louise Page, take nothing from the City of Denton.

Notes

1. **Negligence v. Nuisance.** The principal case not only highlights the importance of control factors to impute a nuisance condition to the City, but also suggests the later developed distinction between governmental duties that are "general" for which immunity exists, and those that are "special" for which immunities are tolled. See the materials at p. 905 et seq., infra.

For another demonstration of the elusive nature of the negligence-nuisance distinction, see City of Texarkana v. Taylor, 490 S.W.2d 191 (Tex. Civ.App.1973). There the court denied recovery for property damage that was caused by negligent city operation of its sewer system, on the ground that while the damages caused by the city's negligence were nuisance damages, and while the city would have been liable even for its "non-negligent" creation of a nuisance, it remained immune for negligent sewer operation. "So far as the distinction that leads to this result is concerned, the language of Prosser * * * is worth pondering: 'There is little that can be said except that they exist; that they are highly artificial; and that they make no great amount of sense.'" Id., 490 S.W.2d at 194.

2. **Failure to Abate Privately Created Nuisance.** Local government liability for nuisances of its own creation does not encompass the government's failure to abate nuisance conditions created by other parties. Galleher v. Wichita, 179 Kan. 513, 296 P.2d 1062 (1952). "The distinction between nuisance to which governmental immunity does not attach and negligence as to which it is available, turns upon whether the condition was one created by the municipality itself or was one otherwise created * * * which the municipality has failed to use the requisite care in remedying." Id., 296 P.2d at 1067.

3. **Affirmative Statutory Duties.** The problem of distinguishing negligence and nuisance is avoided where affirmative duties are placed upon local government units by statutes which also provide remedies for the city's failure to perform such duties. The most common of such statutes are those dealing with the maintenance of streets. See e.g. Hales v. Wauwatosa, 275 Wis. 445, 82 N.W.2d 301 (1957); 2 Antieau, *Municipal Corporation Law,* §§ 12.13–12.20 (1973).

c. Ministerial Actions

Both common law and, to some extent, tort statutes distinguish between "discretionary", i.e. policy-making decisions, and "ministerial" acts, for the purpose of excepting ministerial acts from the immunity rule. See 18 McQuillin, *Municipal Corporations* § 53.33 (3rd rev. ed. 1963); 1A Antieau, *Municipal Corporation Law* § 11.46. Applying this distinction is difficult. "The expression, discretionary function, is clearly a standard, requiring measured judgment in its application, and its meaning cannot be reduced to a set of specific rules." *A.L.I. Restatement of the Law 2d, Torts,* § 895D, comment d, p. 413. The Restatement observation reflects a hopeless conflict in the cases because the discretionary-ministerial dichotomy more often hinges upon specific circumstances rather than departmental function. Given the disarray in the case law, counsel will best rely upon the proximate precedents of the involved jurisdiction.

RESNIK v. MICHAELS

Appellate Court of Illinois, First District, Third Division, 1964.
52 Ill.App.2d 107, 201 N.E.2d 769.

DEMPSEY, JUSTICE. The plaintiff was injured in an automobile collision * * * The plaintiff's complaint charged Michaels with willful and wanton misconduct and charged Parker and the Village of Park Forest with negligence. The court granted the Village's motion for summary judgment, from which judgment the plaintiff prosecutes the present appeal, * * *.

The gist of the complaint against the Village is its failure to provide two-way stop signs on Tampa Street at the intersection with Talala. The Village trustees had approved the installation of the signs * * * because "there is heavy traffic at this corner," and had instructed the Village Manager to proceed with the installation, but at the time of the accident the stop signs had not yet been put up. The plaintiff contends that once the municipality passed the resolution or ordinance directing the installation of stop signs, it then assumed an obligation to act with reasonable diligence to complete its undertaking, and that the failure to do so constituted negligence in the performance of a ministerial duty. The position of the Village is that it was exercising a governmental function when it authorized the erection of the stop signs and that it was not subject to liability until it began to carry out the ministerial function of putting up the signs and maintaining them.

It has been uniformly held that municipal corporations are not subject to liability for governmental functions but are liable for torts arising from ministerial or proprietary functions. Ludwig v. Board of Education, 35 Ill.App.2d 401, 183 N.E.2d 32. The classification of the activities of municipal corporations into governmental and ministerial or proprietary functions has been criticized as arbitrary, incapable of uniform application and productive of incongruities. (See Molitor v. Kaneland Com. Unit Dist., 18 Ill.2d 11, 163 N.E.2d 89, and the legal articles cited therein at page 17, 163 N.E.2d 89). * * *

There have been numerous cases in Illinois involving the liability of municipal corporations for injuries resulting from the development, maintenance and improvement of streets, sidewalks, bridges and sewers. A municipality is responsible for the negligent construction of public works and for its failure to maintain them, but it is not obligated, and is not liable for its neglect or refusal, to undertake such projects. * * *

There are several decisions which delineate the extent of a city's liability. In Buckley v. City of Chicago, 3 Ill.App.2d 39, 120 N.E.2d 375, the City was held liable for an accident caused by its failure to maintain stop signs at an intersection. * * * Stop signs had been installed, but for some reason there was no sign there at the time of the accident, nor had there been any for many months before. * * *

The City of East Moline was held liable for the negligent maintenance of a stop light, which became defective and caused a collision between two automobiles traveling through the intersection. Johnston v. City of East Moline, 405 Ill. 460, 91 N.E.2d 401. The court discussed the City's liability in terms of the distinction between governmental and ministerial functions and concluded that after the City had constructed the signal system and put it into operation it was imposed with the duty of keeping it in such condition that it would not create a hazard for the citizens. * * *

In the Buckley and Johnston cases, the municipalities were found liable for negligently maintaining traffic regulators; in the present case the Village of Park Forest had done nothing except authorize the placement of stop signs. As far as the plaintiff and all other motorists using the streets in the Village of Park Forest were concerned, there had been no change in the regulation of traffic at the corner of Tampa and Talala; no motorist could have relied upon the protection that would have been afforded by the signs.

In Locigno v. City of Chicago, 32 Ill.App.2d 412, 178 N.E.2d 124, an automobile accident occurred at an intersection containing no stop signs; as in the present case, none had been put up. * * * In reversing the judgment against the City, the court stated:

> " * * * Johnston v. City of East Moline, 405 Ill. 460, 91 N.E.2d 401, and City of Chicago v. Seben, 165 Ill. 371, 46 N.E. 244, indicate that until the city acts it cannot be held liable. In the case at bar the City was under no obligation to post signs at the intersection. The Johnston case involved traffic-control lights that were in operation at the time of the accident."

Liability follows negligence. The Village of Park Forest certainly would not be liable for not passing an ordinance providing for traffic signs on Tampa Street * * *. It follows that the Village was not negligent and could not be liable for not installing the signs after the ordinance was passed. The legal obligation and the ministerial function of the Village did not commence until the signs were erected. * * *

The summary judgment granted by the trial court is affirmed.

Notes

1. **Accord:** Bowen v. Little, 139 Ga.App. 176, 228 S.E.2d 159 (1976) (failure to erect traffic light).

2. **The Relation of Duty to Discretion-Ministerial Classifications.** Where there is no duty, but only discretion to act, the immunity exception cannot apply. This conceptual distinction is murky in many situations. A duty of supervision often is admitted, but its scope is undefined and contested. For example, the acts of a school class instructor, whose student drowned in the school pool were held to be discretionary in his removing the student from the water, but ministerial in failing to warn parents of conditions in the swimming class; and in attempting to resuscitate the child. Weber v. Yeo, 147 Mich.App. 453, 383 N.W.2d 230 (1985).

The duty-discretion issue is also mirrored in the conceptual distinction between a "general" (due to the public only) duty vis-a-vis a "special" (due to the injured individual) duty. Absent a "special relationship" giving rise to a special duty, the immunity defense obtains. "It is somewhat unfortunate that the terms 'public' duty and 'special' duty have been used, inasmuch as they give the misleading impression that the distinction applies only to governmental tortfeasors. Perhaps 'no duty' and 'assumed duty' would be more appropriate." See Cracraft v. St. Louis Park, 279

N.W.2d 801, 806 (Minn.1979). Modern developments on the general-special duty dichotomy are reviewed at pp. 905–916 infra.

HIGBY ENTERPRISES, INC. v. UTICA

Supreme Court, Special Term, Oneida County, 1967.
54 Misc.2d 405, 282 N.Y.S.2d 583.

CARDAMONE, J.

* * *

The facts appear to be as follows: On January 15, 1964, the Common Council in the City of Utica rezoned the plaintiff's premises at 10 Higby Road in the City from A to B–1. * * * Thereafter the plaintiff began preparation for the construction of a modern luxury apartment building on its premises. In January of 1965 plaintiff learned that the City Clerk's Office of the City had failed to give the proper legal and required notice of a hearing regarding the proposed change in zoning to neighboring property owners. The plaintiff also learned that the City Clerk's Office had negligently advised the Common Council that all the necessary rules and regulations had been complied with. It is these acts by the City Clerk that are the gravamen of the plaintiff's complaint and the defendant's motion for a dismissal of the same.

The state, its counties, cities, towns and villages are answerable in civil suits for the wrongs of their officers and employees (Bernardine v. City of New York, 294 N.Y. 361, 62 N.E.2d 604, 161 A.L.R. 364 (1945); Bloom v. Jewish Board of Guardians, 286 N.Y. 349, 352–353, 36 N.E.2d 617, 618 (1941)). Immunity is no longer bestowed on the municipality because it was engaged in the performance of a governmental function (Holmes v. County of Erie, 266 App.Div. 220, 42 N.Y.S.2d 243, (Fourth Dept.1943), aff'd 291 N.Y. 798, 53 N.E.2d 369 (1944), or because the negligence alleged consisted in nonfeasance rather than misfeasance (McCrink v. City of New York, 296 N.Y. 99, 71 N.E.2d 419 (1947); Meistinsky v. City of New York, 309 N.Y. 998, 132 N.E.2d 900 (1956)).

Where the act is a discretionary or quasi-judicial act, however, no liability is imposed upon the public official whose act or failure to act caused the plaintiff damages; nor does any liability fall upon the municipality for whom the public official served either as agent or employee. (Rottkamp v. Young, 21 A.D.2d 373, 375, 377, 249 N.Y.S.2d 330, 333, 335 (Second Dept.1964); aff'd 15 N.Y.2d 831, 257 N.Y.S.2d 944, 205 N.E.2d 866 (1965); Pansa v. Damiano, 21 A.D.2d 974, 252 N.Y.S.2d 890).

Here, however, the duty imposed upon the City Clerk of the defendant City was merely ministerial, i.e., it was his duty to give notice to those whose real property was within one hundred (100) feet of the premises proposed to be rezoned. No judgment or discretion on his part was involved; nor does immunity attach to the municipality for his actions in this connection. (Bernardine v. City of New York (*supra*); Holmes v. County of Erie, (*supra*)).

Defendant's motion is denied without costs.

Notes

1. **The Limits of Respondeat Superior.** The rule in *Higby,* that the liability of a government employer can rise no higher than that of its officers and employees is widely followed. Arnolt v. Highland Park, 52 Ill. 2d 27, 282 N.E.2d 144 (1972); McCorkle v. Los Angeles, infra, p. 932. This does not mean that the liability of government and of its agents will always be co-terminal. An officer may be liable where a municipality is not; and conversely, the municipality may be liable where the officer is not. See e.g. Wicks v. Milzoco Builders, 25 Pa.Cmwlth. 340, 360 A.2d 250 (1976); aff'd, 481 Pa. 554, 393 A.2d 300 (1978); DePalma v. Rosen, infra, p. 931. Further, statutes may limit the remedies against local government units, without similar limitations against individual officers and employees.

The authorities are in conflict on the question whether a local government is liable for the intentional torts of its officers and employees. See Carter v. Carlson, infra, p. 925.

d. *"Special Duty" Doctrines*

It is important to note that the issue of immunity is conceptually distinct from the issue of liability and that waiver of immunity does not create liability where none existed for lack of some cognizable tort duty upon which to raise a cause of action. A broader ground (than immunity) exists for avoiding local government liability for negligent performance of governmental functions, i.e. where the local unit owes only a "general" duty to the public, and not a "special" duty to the injured individual by reason of a "special" relationship to that party. What circumstances or statutory interests give rise to a special relationship and duty, are questions which the cases have only begun to explore. Despite some confusion and conflicts on the meaning and limits of the special duty doctrine, it appears to have gathered strength with the expansion of specialized governmental services. The task of courts and counsel, to develop the parameters of "special" duty and to clarify their application to varied situations, has hardly begun. The following materials serve more as points of departure than of definition for this still developing area.

CRACRAFT v. ST. LOUIS PARK

Supreme Court of Minnesota, 1979.
279 N.W.2d 801.

Todd, Justice.

* * * This suit involves the alleged negligent failure of a city inspector to discover a violation of the municipal fire ordinance at Benilde-St. Margaret's High School, St. Louis Park, Minnesota. After argument by the parties, the trial judge granted summary judgment in favor of the city. Plaintiffs appeal from that judgment. We affirm.

On October 27, 1974, a 55–gallon drum of duplicating fluid, an extremely volatile and highly flammable liquid, ignited on the loading dock of Benilde High School. * * *

As a result of the explosion, three youths received first, second, and third-degree burns over their entire bodies. Two of the boys died, including Kenneth Kasper. A third boy, plaintiff John Cracraft, received severe burns over 50 percent of his body.

The city fire inspector, Gerald Hines, inspected the entire premises on September 13, 1974. This inspection was conducted pursuant to a city ordinance. The presence of a drum of duplicating fluid on the dock would be a violation of the fire code. Mr. Hines testified, in deposition, that he did not see the drum at the time of his inspection. He stated that if it was there at the time of the examination, it would have been noticed and removed.

Plaintiffs contend that the city must conduct an inspection with due care, that the city's inspection was negligently performed, and the negligence was a substantial causal factor of the injuries and damages. Defendant municipality, on the other hand, contends that it owed no duty of care for the purposes of a negligence action. Thus, the question in this case becomes: Under what conditions is a duty of care imposed on a municipality which seeks to enforce the law by inspecting for fire code violations? It is important to distinguish the issue presented by this case from confusingly similar issues. We are not concerned with the legal duties owed by municipalities as owners and operators of buildings, roadways, or other facilities.[1] Nor are we concerned with the duty of a municipality to comply with its own safety codes as we were in Lorshbough v. Township of Buzzle, 258 N.W.2d 96 (Minn.1977). These duties to comply with the law are analogous to those owed by private persons, and a breach of such duties can be the basis of a lawsuit against the municipality just as it can be the basis of a lawsuit against private tortfeasors. We are, instead, considering the municipality's unique duty to enforce the law by taking steps to assure that third persons comply with the law.

To hold a municipality liable for negligently inspecting the conduct of third persons for fire code violations, plaintiffs must establish that the municipality has a common-law duty to provide a reasonable inspection. In 1972, this court decided Hoffert v. Owatonna Inn Towne Motel, Inc., 293 Minn. 220, 199 N.W.2d 158 (1972). In Hoffert, plaintiffs were guests at a motel that had been recently remodeled. * * * The building inspector also examined the premises during construction. Two weeks after the last inspection, a fire broke out in the motel and the plaintiffs alleged they were trapped on the second floor because of

1. See, Ondarko v. Village of Hibbing, 256 Minn. 17, 96 N.W.2d 865 (1959) (duty of care when operating a gas service line); Diker v. City of St. Louis Park, 268 Minn. 461, 130 N.W.2d 113 (1964) (duty of care when operating a hockey rink).

improper stairway enclosures constructed in violation of the building code.

This court affirmed the dismissal of the complaint against the city. Although recognizing that the Minnesota Legislature had abolished the doctrine of sovereign immunity as it applied to the political subdivision of the state, we held (293 Minn. 222, 199 N.W.2d 159):

"* * * [T]hese statutory provisions [abolishing immunity] merely removed the defense of immunity. They did not create any new liability for a municipality. In order to recover against the city, appellants must show a breach of some duty owed them in their individual capacities and not merely a breach of some obligation owed the general public."

"The purpose of a building code is to protect the public." * * * Because the building code ordinances did not create a duty owed to plaintiffs as individuals, they could not recover for the alleged negligence of the city's employees.

The *Hoffert* decision is controlling in this case. Recently, however, significant criticism has been launched against the distinction between a duty owed to the public in general (which cannot be the basis of a negligence action) and a duty owed to individual members of the public (which can be the basis of a negligence action). See, Adams v. State, 555 P.2d 235 (Alaska 1976); Coffey v. City of Milwaukee, 74 Wis.2d 526, 247 N.W.2d 132 (1976). * * * The distinction, say the critics, is a relic of sovereign immunity and should be discarded * * *. Plaintiffs contend that the distinction should be discarded and *Hoffert* should be overruled.

We disagree. By abolishing the distinction between public duty and special duty, this court would depart from vast precedent and traditional common-law principles of negligence. * * *

To demonstrate that the distinction between public duty and special duty is not a doctrine unique to governmental torts, we start our analysis of the duty to enforce the law by placing municipalities on the same footing as any other person.

The common-law rule, of course, is that generally there is no duty to prevent the misconduct of a third person. * * * At the outset then, there is no common-law duty imposed on any individual or any municipality to inspect and correct the fire code violations of a third person unless there is a "special relation" between the parties.

If there were no additional considerations in this case, it could be concluded at this point that the defendant municipality had no duty, public or special, to inspect and correct fire code violations. There are additional considerations, however. The municipality's own ordinances require that it undertake inspections for fire code violations. However, such inspections are required for the purpose of protecting the interests of the municipality as a whole * * *. The inspections are not undertaken for the purpose of assuring either the person inspected or third persons that the building is free from all fire hazards, just as the state's issuance of a driver's license is no assurance that the licensed person will be a safe driver. Because the ordinances are designed to protect the municipality's own interests, rather than the interests of a particular class of individuals, only a "public" duty to inspect is created. It is a basic principle of negligence law that public duties created by statute cannot be the basis of a negligence action even against private tortfeasors. * * * This distinction, therefore, is neither a fiction, nor artificial, nor a relic of the days of sovereign immunity. It is a well-established principle of negligence law applicable to tort actions against individuals as well as governments.

We hold, therefore, that a municipality does not owe any individual a duty of care merely by the fact that it enacts a general ordinance requiring fire code inspections or by the fact that it undertakes an inspection for fire code violations. A duty of care arises only when there are additional indicia that the municipality has undertaken the responsibility of not only protecting itself, but also undertaken the responsibility of protecting a particular class of persons from the risks associated with fire code violations. * * * This rule, or a similar rule, is recognized by all but two courts that have considered the issue.[6] It is also the rule in the context of other law enforcement activities.[7] Only two cases, Adams v. State, *supra*, and Coffey v. City of Milwaukee, *supra*, have abolished this time-honored distinction between public duty and special duty. We find these cases unpersuasive.

We refuse, therefore, to abolish the distinction between public duty and special duty. The concept of a special duty is not unique to government torts. "Special duty" is nothing more than convenient terminology, in contradistinction to "public duty," for the ancient doctrine that once a duty to act for the protection of others is voluntarily assumed, due care must be exercised even though there was no duty to act in the first instance. Isler v. Burman, 305 Minn. 288, 232

6. See, Duran v. City of Tucson, 20 Ariz. App. 22, 509 P.2d 1059 (1973); Modlin v. City of Miami Beach, 201 So.2d 70 (Fla. 1967); Dufrene v. Guarino, 343 So.2d 1097 (La.App.), writ denied, 343 So.2d 1069 (La. 1977); Smullen v. City of New York, 28 N.Y.2d 66, 320 N.Y.S.2d 19, 268 N.E.2d 763 (1971); Campbell v. City of Bellevue, 85 Wash.2d 1, 530 P.2d 234 (1975), second appeal on other grounds, 86 Wash.2d 572, 546 P.2d 922 (1976). See, generally, Note, 13 Columbia L.J. & Soc.Prob. 303; Note, 23 Loyola L.Rev. 458.

Some other courts have denied recovery on the grounds that the municipality's inspection was governmental rather than proprietary, or discretionary rather than ministerial. See, E. Eyring & Sons Co. v. City of Baltimore, 253 Md. 380, 252 A.2d 824 (1969); Fiduccia v. Summit Hill Constr. Co., 109 N.J.Super. 249, 262 A.2d 920

(1970). Such analysis is inappropriate in this case. Municipalities are subject to tort liability even if the activity is governmental rather than proprietary. Minn.St. 466.02. And although municipalities cannot be held liable for discretionary acts, Minn.St. 466.03(6), the distinction between ministerial and discretionary acts relates to the municipality's defense of immunity rather than the question of whether it even has a duty of care.

7. Ordinarily, a municipality is not liable for failure to provide police protection unless a special duty to the plaintiff is created. See, Massengill v. Yuma County, 104 Ariz. 518, 456 P.2d 376 (1969); Henderson v. St. Petersburg, 247 So.2d 23 (Fla. App.), certiorari denied, 250 So.2d 643 (Fla. 1971); Huey v. Town of Cicero, 41 Ill.2d 361, 243 N.E.2d 214 (1968). See, generally, Annotation, 46 A.L.R.3d 1084.

N.W.2d 818 (1975). "Special duty," therefore, could also effectively be termed "assumed" duty. It is somewhat unfortunate that the terms "public" duty and "special" duty have been used, inasmuch as they give the misleading impression that the distinction applies only to governmental tortfeasors. Perhaps "no duty" and "assumed" duty would be more appropriate.

At what point, then, does the municipality assume to act for the protection of others as distinguished from acting merely for itself when it inspects the activities of third parties for fire code violations? There is no bright line. But, without intending to be exhaustive, there are at least four factors which should be considered. First, actual knowledge of the dangerous condition is a factor which tends to impose a duty of care on the municipality.[8] Second, reasonable reliance by persons on the municipality's representations and conduct tends to impose a duty of care.[9] Of course, reliance on the inspection in general is not sufficient. Instead, the reasonable reliance must be based on specific actions or representations which cause the persons to forego other alternatives of protecting themselves. Third, a duty of care may be created by an ordinance or statute that sets forth mandatory acts clearly for the protection of a particular class of persons rather than the public as a whole.[10] Finally, the municipality must use due care to avoid increasing the risk of harm.

8. In Hansen v. City of St. Paul, 298 Minn. 205, 214 N.W.2d 346 (1976), plaintiff was bitten by dogs that were known by the city officials to be vicious and prone to unprovoked attacks. This court held the city had a duty to impound the dogs because the government clearly had knowledge of the dogs' vicious propensities.

Cases in other jurisdictions indicate that the government officials' knowledge of the code violations may create a special duty to the plaintiff. For example, the Washington Supreme Court in Campbell v. City of Bellevue, 85 Wash.2d 1, 530 P.2d 234 (1975), second appeal on other grounds, 86 Wash.2d 572, 546 P.2d 922 (1976), held that the city had a special duty to an area resident who reported to the city officials that her neighbor had improper electrical wiring in an underwater lighting system at a nearby creek. The court found that a special duty had been created because the inspector had knowledge of the neighbor's code violations and yet did not disconnect the wiring as required specifically by statute. See, also, Annotation, 46 A.L.R.3d 1084, § 7 (reporting cases which impose a special duty on police to protect the plaintiff when the police have knowledge of threatened criminal activity against the plaintiff).

9. The factor of reliance is present, for example, in Smullen v. City of New York,

28 N.Y.2d 66, 320 N.Y.S.2d 19, 268 N.E.2d 763 (1971). In that case, a city sewer inspector had told plaintiff's decedent that a trench was "pretty solid there" and that it did not need to be shored. The trench collapsed, killing the decedent. The New York Court of Appeals held these utterances established a special duty.

Similarly, Restatement, Torts (2d), § 324A, provides: "One who undertakes, gratuitously or for consideration, to render services to another which he should recognize as necessary for the protection of a third person or his things, is subject to liability to the third person for physical harm resulting from his failure to exercise reasonable care to protect [sic] his undertaking, if

* * *

"(c) the harm is suffered because of reliance of the other or the third person upon the undertaking." See, also, Restatement, Torts (2d), § 323(b).

10. The statute considered in McCorkell v. City of Northfield, 266 Minn. 267, 123 N.W.2d 367 (1963), affirmed second appeal on other grounds, 272 Minn. 24, 136 N.W.2d 840 (1965), is illustrative of the type which may create a special duty to the plaintiff. In that case, a prisoner died from asphyxiation caused by a smoldering fire in an unattended jail. A statute con-

Applying these factors to this case, we find no evidence in the record indicating that a duty was assumed or a special duty was created. The inspector, without contradiction, stated that he had no actual knowledge of the 55–gallon drum on the loading dock. With regard to the factor of reliance, the inspection had resulted in the discovery of some problems and a letter was sent by the municipality to the school, listing several problems which had to be corrected immediately and several problems which had to be corrected as soon as possible. No reference was made to the 55–gallon drum of duplicating fluid. * * * [N]o grounds for reasonable reliance exist with regard to hazards not set forth in the letter.

We have already indicated that the applicable codes, ordinances, or statutes have not been drawn with sufficient specificity to create an inspection duty in favor of a class of individuals rather than the public as a whole. Finally, the municipality did nothing to increase the risk. Even assuming the 55–gallon drum was on the dock at the time of the inspection, the risk of explosion prior to the inspection was the same as after the inspection. Because the record fails to show the creation of an assumed or special duty, summary judgment for defendants must be affirmed.

* * *

KELLY, JUSTICE (dissenting).

* * *

The determination of whether and under what standard a city should be held liable for negligent inspection of premises under a municipal fire ordinance is a difficult question involving far-reaching considerations of social and political significance. In most cases, however, the determination that a given duty under a statute is a "public" one is merely a shorthand statement of a conclusion rather than an aid to analysis. A court's holding that a given duty is "public" or "special" generally stops short of necessary inquiry into the specific effects and other considerations which bear on the root policy issue involved.

* * *

That injuries to a third person as a result of a negligent building inspection are foreseeable is without doubt. * * * By adopting the ordinance in question, the city set certain minimum fire safety requirements and established itself as the enforcement agent thereby inducing reliance upon the reports of its inspector. * * * It does not seem to be

tained in Minn.St. c. 642 required certain maintenance activities in prisons for the health and safety of prisoners. Because the statute was clearly designed to impose a duty of care for the benefit of prisoners, this court found a cause of action was stated against the municipality for failure to comply with the mandatory provisions of the statute.

Other courts have found a special duty to the plaintiff based on a statute contain-

ing mandatory acts for the benefit of a class of persons. See, Runkel v. City of New York, 282 App.Div. 173, 123 N.Y.S.2d 485 (1953), affirmed on second appeal on other grounds sub nom., Runkel v. Homelsky, 286 App.Div. 1101, 145 N.Y.S.2d 729 (1955); Campbell v. City of Bellevue, 85 Wash.2d 1, 530 P.2d 234 (1975), second appeal on other grounds, 86 Wash.2d 572, 546 P.2d 922 (1976).

unreasonable for the school to assume that other than the specific violations cited in the report, the condition of the building was safe. Not only do the landowners come to rely on the reports of the inspectors, but the public for whose benefit the inspections are made does so as well. Yet the majority tells us that members of the public cannot rely on services of the municipality performed pursuant to statute or ordinance because it owes them no duty to use due care. * * *

* * *

The artificiality of the public duty-special duty distinction is further demonstrated by the facility with which courts that recognize this distinction are able to find a special duty in cases wherein they wish to allow recovery. See, *e.g.,* Foley v. State of New York, 294 N.Y. 275, 62 N.E.2d 69; *Id.,* 177 Misc. 443, 30 N.Y.S.2d 998 (1945); Serpas v. Margiotta, 59 So.2d 492 (La.App.1952). Campbell v. City of Bellevue, 85 Wash.2d 1, 530 P.2d 234 (1975). * * *

It is obvious that the majority opinion does not make the tort liability of the state and local governments co-equal with that of private entities. There may be a reluctance to permit such liability, presumably based on the fear of the crushing burden of limitless liability which may be placed on the political subdivisions of the state if such suits were allowed to be brought. * * * The possibility that a municipality may be held liable for the breach of every building code or zoning ordinance within the city, and the consequent enormous potential drain of the public coffers, is often raised as the prime justification for the "public duty doctrine." See, Lorshbough v. Township of Buzzle, 258 N.W.2d 96 (Minn.1977); and Hoffert v. Owatonna Inn Towne Motel, Inc., *supra.*

Such arguments, however, were raised a decade ago in opposition to the proposal that the state waive its defense of sovereign immunity. * * * These contentions proved to be false then and they are just as likely to be false now. * * *

Moreover, by allowing suits of this type against the state, the state does not assume an absolute duty to enforce its laws and ordinances. * * * Rather, cities will be held only to a standard of due and reasonable care, liability being limited by such principles as proximate cause and foreseeability.

Finally, there are many defenses to municipal tort liability already set out by our legislature in Minn.St. c. 466.[2] These exceptions provide

2. Minn.St. 466.03 provides: "Subdivision 1. Section 466.02 does not apply to any claim enumerated in this section. As to any such claim every municipality shall be liable only in accordance with the applicable statute and where there is no such statute, every municipality shall be immune from liability.

"Subd. 2. Any claim for injury to or death of any person covered by the worker's compensation act.

"Subd. 3. Any claim in connection with the assessment and collection of taxes.

"Subd. 4. Any claim based on snow or ice conditions on any highway or other public place, except when the condition is affirmatively caused by the negligent acts of the municipality.

"Subd. 5. Any claim based upon an act or omission of an officer or employee, ample protection to political subdivisions of the state, and no further exceptions to tort liability need be judicially created.

* * *

YETKA, JUSTICE (dissenting).

I join in the dissent of Mr. Justice Kelly.

SCOTT, JUSTICE (dissenting).

I agree with the dissent of Mr. Justice Kelly. * * *

* * *

PIPPIN v. CHICAGO HOUSING AUTHORITY

Supreme Court of Illinois, 1979.
78 Ill.2d 204, 35 Ill.Dec. 530, 399 N.E.2d 596.

THOMAS J. MORAN, JUSTICE:

This is an action for the wrongful death of Frederick Douglas Pippin, brought by his mother, Mollie Pippin, the administratrix of his estate, against the Chicago Housing Authority (Authority), a municipal corporation, and Interstate Service Corporation (Interstate) * * *.

At issue is the extent of the Authority's duty, if any, to protect plaintiff's decedent, Frederick Pippin, a social guest, from criminal conduct which occurred on premises owned and managed by the Authority, and the duty of Interstate to protect the deceased from such conduct.

On January 10, 1973, around 6 p.m., in the lobby of a housing project owned and operated by the Authority, Lorretta Haywood approached Willie Torrence and Willie Butler, employed as security guards at the project by Interstate. She asked the two guards, * * * to remove Pippin, an acquaintance and apparently a licensee (Restatement (Second) of Torts sec. 330, comment *h* (3) (1965)) from her apartment in the project building. They explained they were not permitted, by Interstate's policy, to become involved in any "domestic problem," and suggested she call the Chicago police. She thereupon left the building but returned to the lobby in three or four minutes. About the same time, Pippin entered the lobby from the building's stairway. Haywood, in an audible voice, told him to "go * * * and don't come back." At that, Pippin walked over to Haywood and struck her on the head more than once. The guards stopped their work at the mailboxes and, within seconds of the start of the altercation, separated the couple. Upon pulling them apart, the guards for the first time saw that Haywood was in possession of a knife and that Pippin was bleeding.

exercising statute, charter, ordinance, resolution, or regulation.

"Subd. 6. Any claim based upon the performance or the failure to exercise or perform a discretionary function or duty, whether or not the discretion is abused.

"Subd. 7. Any claim against a municipality as to which the municipality is immune from liability by the provisions of any other statute."

According to both guards, at no time prior to the beating and knifing did either Haywood or Pippin display haste, excitement or hysteria.

At the time of the incident, a contract for security or "protective services" existed between the Authority and Interstate, and included the following language.

> "WHEREAS, the party of the second part [(Authority)] is desirous of securing from the party of the first part [(Interstate)] the services of armed guards and other protective services *for the purpose of guarding its properties * * * and the protection of persons thereon * * *.*

> *   *   *   *   *   *   *   *   *

> "It is expressly understood and agreed that the party of the first part is an *independent contractor, * * * that neither party of the first part nor any of its employees, * * * shall under any circumstances whatsoever be considered as employees of the party of the second part." (Emphasis added.)

The Authority contends that it had no legal duty to protect Pippin from criminal conduct because the common law imposes no such duty; that Pippin had no special relationship with the Authority that would justify placing a burden of protection on the Authority; and that it had not assumed a duty of protection by contracting for protective services. The appellate court agreed there was no duty to protect the victim, but held that the Authority and Interstate, "by the terms of their contract * * * assumed a duty to exercise reasonable care in protecting persons lawfully on the premises from foreseeable criminal attacks and other foreseeable dangers." 58 Ill.App.3d 1029, 1037, 16 Ill.Dec. 280, 285, 374 N.E.2d 1055, 1060.

"It is fundamental that there can be no recovery in tort for negligence unless the defendant has breached a duty owed to the plaintiff." * * * The appellate court correctly states the common law in Illinois: a landlord does not owe a tenant or social guest (licensee) a duty to protect the latter from criminal acts. * * * Moreover, this case does not fall into the "special relationship" exception to the general rule above. *Fancil v. Q.S.E. Foods, Inc.* (1975), 60 Ill.2d 552, 559–60, 328 N.E.2d 538. *Cf. McCoy v. Chicago Transit Authority* (1977), 69 Ill.2d 280, 13 Ill.Dec. 690, 371 N.E.2d 625 (common law liability existed because the defendant was a common carrier, a "special relationship" classification).

*   *   *

Although the Authority had no independent duty to protect against criminal acts on its premises, it voluntarily entered into a contract with Interstate, an independent contractor, by which the latter agreed to provide guard services on Authority premises. In *Nelson v. Union Wire Rope Corp.* (1964), 31 Ill.2d 69, 74, 199 N.E.2d 769, this court gave its recognition to the established principle that liability can arise from the negligent performance of a voluntary undertaking. * * * Although the principle is applicable here, the extent of the Authority's undertaking was different than that of the insurer in *Nelson.* Because the

Authority did not undertake to perform the guard services itself, it cannot be held to have had a duty to protect Pippin. The Authority's duty was limited by the extent of the undertaking, *viz*, to use reasonable care in engaging Interstate to provide the guard services. The Authority can therefore be liable at most for the negligent hiring of Interstate. (Restatement (Second) of Torts sec. 411 (1965); Prosser, Torts sec. 71, at 469–70 (4th ed. 1971).) We note that plaintiff's complaint, which alleges that the Authority employed Interstate without proper investigation and with negligence, raises a question of fact relevant to the issue of the Authority's liability. Thus, summary judgment should not have been granted in favor of the Authority.

* * *

Notes

1. **General vs. Special Duty.** Notwithstanding criticism of the rule—that negligent performance of governmental functions, even those intended to protect the general public, does not render the local government liable, absent a special duty to the injured claimant—a majority of jurisdictions adopt it. The rule has, however, been rejected in Arizona, Alaska, Colorado, Louisiana, Oregon, and Wisconsin as either superseded by modern tort statutes or as a confusing restatement of the common law immunity for discretionary actions. See the authorities in Annot, Governmental Tort—General Duty, 38 A.L.R. 4th 1194 (1985).

Where the majority rule is applied, the finding of a "special duty" may be based on several grounds, namely, legislation that directly creates that duty qua the claimant; or a specific undertaking by the local government to protect or benefit the claimant not as a member of the general public, but as a member of a special class; or peculiar circumstances whereunder courts find that peculiar circumstances give rise to a special relationship and special duty toward the claimant. Absent an express undertaking, courts must decide what situations and factors give rise to the requisite special relationship. School authorities may have a special duty to notify parents of assault patterns by other students that threaten a parent's child. Phyllis P. v. Superior Ct., 228 Cal.Rptr. 776 (1986). On the latter issue the limited case law provides only limited guidance, but the following reports point to the more prominent factors that influence decision.

(a) *Code Inspections and Enforcement.* Routine safety inspections are not deemed to create or assume any special duty to affected individuals. *Cracraft,* p. 905, supra; *City of Denton,* p. 898, supra.

(b) *Public Operated Housing.* The rule, approved in *Pippin,* supra, that a landlord owes no special duty to protect tenants may be avoided on several grounds. Treating such operations as "proprietary," courts may well hold local governments liable for dangerous conditions that fall within the "implied warranty of habitability." Cf. Trentacost v. Brussel, 82 N.J. 214, 412 A.2d 436 (1980) (negligent failure to secure common entrances to apartments in known high crime district).

(c) *Service Buildings.* The mere fact that local governments operate buildings to which the public is invited to receive public services does not give rise to any special duty.

> "Special Term correctly held that the mere act of hiring additional front-door security guards did not create a special duty to protect plaintiff against the criminal acts of third parties upon its premises. Absent indicia that the additional security guards were hired specifically to protect plaintiff or a limited class of teachers of which plaintiff was a member, security provisions at a public school do not create a special duty upon which governmental liability may be predicated." See Corcoran v. Community School District, 111 A.D.2d 835, 494 N.Y.S. 2d 747, 748 (1985).

(d) *Public Transit Facilities.* Government provision of public transit gives rise to a special relationship to transit riders and to liability for negligent failure to protect rider safety. See also, Lopez v. Southern California Rapid Transit District, 40 Cal.3d 780, 221 Cal.Rptr. 840, 710 P.2d 907 (1985) (failure of driver to act or seek help to control disorderly passengers); Kenny v. Southeastern Pa. Trans. Authority, 581 F.2d 351 (3d Cir.1978) (failure to minimize passenger danger in known high crime area).

(e) *Police Protection.* It is generally recognized that under ordinary circumstances, i.e. absent some special duty, local government units may not be held liable for failure to provide police protection. See Annot, Police Protection—Governmental Liability, 46 A.L.R.3d 1084 (1972, Supp.1985).

Even in the face of an impending riot, decisions regarding deployment of police were held to be discretionary [sic general and not special duty] and not a basis for tort claim under a Minnesota statute. Silver v. Minneapolis, 284 Minn. 266, 170 N.W.2d 206 (1969). *Semble:* Cadmus v. Long Branch Bd. of Educ., 155 N.J.Super. 42, 382 A.2d 98 (1977) (Board failure to supervise vocational training activities). Compare: Sorichetti v. New York, 95 Misc.2d 451, 408 N.Y.S.2d 219 (1978), affirmed 70 A.D.2d 573, 417 N.Y.S. 2d 202 (1978) where the city was subject to liability for injuries to a child by an estranged father, after police declined to arrest the father for making death threats, although the father was under a court protection order for past threats to his spouse. Obviously the court order focused more specifically on these family members and could be construed as effecting an official committment to protect specific individuals.

While the authorities are agreed that government has no special duty to the public to provide police protection (Warren v. District of Columbia, 444 A.2d 1 (D.C.App.1981)), they are not agreed on the point at which official assurance that protection will be given and individual reliance on such assurance will create a special duty and support tort liability. Compare, e.g., Doe v. Hendricks, 92 N.M. 499, 590 P.2d 647 (1979) (no liability for negligent failure to report and respond to telephone call for help to assault victim) with Chambers-Castanes v. King County, 100 Wash.2d 275, 669 P.2d 451 (1983) (finding special duty where police officers negligently failed to assist assault victims after receiving calls and assuring victims that help was on the way). A stronger case for liability arises where the local government establishes a special telephone line for emergency assistance calls, and then negligently fails to respond to such calls. In such instances, courts have held the municipality liable. Barth v. Board of Education and City of Chicago, 141 Ill.App.3d 266, 95 Ill.Dec. 604, 490 N.E.2d 77 (Ill.1986); DeLong v. Erie, 60 N.Y.2d 296, 469 N.Y.S.2d 611, 457 N.E.2d 717 (1983). See Annot., Emergency Call-Police Nonresponse, 39 A.L.R. 4th 691 (1985).

(f) *Failure to Warn of Dangerous Individual.* Failure-to-warn cases involve three distinct situations, namely, where the threat victim can be any member of the general public; where the potential victim is identified; and where, regardless of those factors, the tort immunity statute grants absolute immunity for failure to warn. In the latter instance, the issue of general-special duty becomes moot. See, e.g., Martinez v. California, 444 U.S. 277, 100 S.Ct. 553, 62 L.Ed.2d 481 (1980); Cairl v. State, 323 N.W.2d 20 (Minn.1982); Coppola v. State, 177 N.J.Super. 37, 424 A.2d 858 (1981). Where the potential victim of a known dangerous person is not identified, there arguably arises no special duty to any individual, but the case law is not sufficiently developed to indicate probable outcomes. In the situation where the intended victim of a dangerous person is identified and known to public officials, a stronger case for special duty arises, by analogy to private tort law whereunder psychotherapists have been held liable for failure to warn. See, e.g., McIntosh v. Milano, 168 N.J.Super. 466, 403 A.2d 500 (1979); Tarasoff v. Regents, Univ. of California, 17 Cal.3d 425, 131 Cal.Rptr. 14, 551 P.2d 334 (1976). Cf. Currie v. United States, 111 F.R.D. 56 (M.D N.Car.1986). Whether that analogy is sufficiently strong to overcome countervailing common law precedents is also unsettled. See generally, Annots., Liability of Government Officer or Entity for Failure to Warn— Release of Potentially Dangerous Individual, 12 A.L.R. 4th 722 (1985); Tort Claims—Assault by Released Prisoner, 6 A.L.R. 4th 1155 (1981); Immunity—Injuries Caused by Negligently Released Individual, 5 A.L.R. 4th 773 (1981).

2. PUBLIC TORT CLAIMS STATUTES

a. *Limited Restoration or Abolition of Common Law Immunity*

Following judicial abrogation, many states enacted immunity, but with variations that did not exist at common law. See Restatement, Torts 2d, Appendix § 895B for a listing and description of the individual state statutes. These laws blanket all or most classes of local government units. See e.g. Susman v. City of Los Angeles, 269 Cal. App.2d 803, 75 Cal.Rptr. 240 (1969); Comment, *Illinois Tort Claims Act: A New Approach to Municipal Tort Immunity in Illinois,* 61 Nw.L.Rev. 265, 281 (1966). Tort claim administration takes several forms. In some states, tort claims are adjudicated as civil suits, and in others, special tribunals and procedures are established for such claims.

The task of considering what risks and costs should be spread between injured citizens and the government was aptly summarized by Professor Van Alstyne:

"The widespread consensus that the immunity doctrine should be ended, * * * has tended to obscure a more difficult question: what system of public tort responsibility should supplant the regime of immunity? It seems rather obvious that legal concepts appropriate to private tort liability administration may not, in all respects, be adequate for allocating tort responsibilities of governmental agencies. Public entities typically engage in a wide spectrum of activities which have no obvious private counterparts. Many governmental functions involve inherent exposure to potential injurious consequences far in excess of the risks normally encountered in the private sector. Indeed, many of the most typical and routine duties of governmental entities (including, for example, most if not all of the functions embraced by the compendious term, "police power") require the making of policy determinations and operational decisions which involve the taking of calculated risks of injury to persons and property in the interest of better serving the larger public welfare. Moreover, the ever-expanding range of public services being performed by governmental agencies suggests that private enterprise may be either unwilling or incapable of undertaking, upon terms of economic feasibility, certain kinds of activities beset with substantial loss exposures (including tort risks). * * * Yet, it must be remembered that public entities charged with such duties and responsibilities cannot simply avoid the risk by refusing to act; unlike the private entrepreneur, the public officer is ordinarily not free to terminate an unduly risky enterprise. Considerations of this sort suggest that governmental tort liability, * * * may tend to develop rationally grounded functional distinctions quite different from those which characterize private tort liability systems." Van Alstyne, *Government Tort Liability: A Decade of Change,* 1966 U.Ill. L.F. 919, 922–23.

The legislative response has been scattered and disuniform. Most tort claims statutes restore or preserve common law immunities or exceptions on a selective and partial basis only; and contain unclear provisos that will require further construction and clarification by the courts. The power of state legislatures to limit immunity on a selective basis has generally been upheld against constitutional challenges. See *Martinez v. California,* p. 934, supra; Annot., Government Tort Damages Statute, 43 A.L.R. Fed. 19 (1986).

Waiver by Insurance. In the absence of legislative mandate or authorization to take out liability insurance, as the predicate for waiving immunity, courts divided on the (implied waiver) effect of local government liability insurance. Those courts finding a waiver of the immunity defense do so on the reasoning that such insurance removes the foundation for immunity, namely, the threat of ruinous judgments. Others reject that reasoning, on the view that the authority to waive immunity does not exist for local governments without state legislative or constitutional authorization. See generally, Annot, Public Employee-Liability Insurance, 71 A.L.R.3d 6 (1975).

A number of states resolved the issue of implied immunity by enacting statutes that promulgate a rule of waiver or that permit local governments to waive immunity. Some statutes required insurance coverage for specified acts, while others merely authorize the purchase of insurance at the option of local units. See Ill.—S.H.A. ch. 85, ¶ 9–103; Utah Code Ann. §§ 63–30–28 to 63–30–34; 5 Wyo.Stat. § 15.1–4; Davis v. Macon, 122 Ga.App. 665, 178 S.E.2d 557 (1970); Flowers v. Board of Comm'rs of Vanderburgh County, 240 Ind. 668, 168 N.E.2d 224 (1960); Ballew v. Chattanooga, 205 Tenn. 289, 326 S.W.2d 466 (1959); Taylor v. Knox County Bd. of Education, 292 Ky. 767, 167 S.W.2d 700 (1943); Schoening v. United States Aviation Underwriters, 265 Minn. 119, 120 N.W.2d 859 (1963); Marshall v. Green Bay, 18 Wis.2d 496, 118 N.W.2d 715 (1963); cf. Steelman v. New Bern, 279 N.C. 589, 184 S.E.2d 239 (1971) (recovery denied for lack of insurance coverage).

3. STATUTORY RESTRICTIONS ON TORT REMEDIES

a. Time Bars—Claim Notices and Suit

Unlike the common law, statutes, charters and ordinances precondition tort recovery from local governments by requiring notice of a tort claim to the defendant unit within a specified time deadline (usually within three to six months following an injury), including information regarding the injury and claim. Subject to the limited exceptions hereafter noted, the power to impose these notice requirements, as mandatory, nonwaivable conditions of government liability is universally sustained. See Cornett v. Neodesha, 187 Kan. 60, 353 P.2d 975, 977 (1960); Heck v. Knoxville, 249 Iowa 602, 88 N.W.2d 58, 63 (1958); Annot., 59 A.L.R.3d 93 (1974).

The adequacy of notice turns on two basic problems, to wit, the strict or liberal application of notice legislation, and the quantum of information that is given. Notice provisions vary in detail, but commonly require the following basic information: identity of claimant by name and address; the time, place and circumstances of the tortious event; the nature of the injuries sustained and the amount of the claim. See e.g. Ill.—S.H.A. ch. 85, ¶ 8–102; West's Ann.Cal.Gov.Code § 910.

CITY OF DAWSON SPRINGS v. REDDISH
Court of Appeals of Kentucky, 1961.
344 S.W.2d 826.

MILLIKEN, J.

[Held that notice of claim which did not contain the name of a plaintiff, barred that plaintiff from recovery, despite actual notice of plaintiff's injury, which the city received independently of the notice.]

* * *

On the other hand, the appellees assert that the City had actual notice of the accident because the Mayor of the City came to the scene shortly after it occurred and one of the City policemen took the plaintiff, Wanda Lee Reddish, to a doctor's office.

It is the consensus of the Court that the notice adequately sets out the time, place, character and circumstances of the accident and the nature of the injuries of all the claimants except Wanda Lee Reddish for whose injuries the judgment awarded $2,000 in accordance with the verdict of the jury. Since there was no statutory notice given at all of the claim of Wanda Lee Reddish, the judgment in her favor must be set aside because the giving of such a notice is a mandatory prerequisite. Wellman v. City of Owensboro, Ky., 282 S.W.2d 628; Berry v. City of Louisville, Ky., 249 S.W.2d 818; Treitz v. City of Louisville, 292 Ky. 654, 167 S.W.2d 860; Ballinger v. City of Harlan, 294 Ky. 72, 170 S.W.2d 912. Cases holding actual notice is not enough: Hall v. City of Los Angeles, 19 Cal.2d 198, 120 P.2d 13; Harding v. City of Chicago, 1937, 290 Ill.App. 598, 7 N.E.2d 918.

BUSCH v. ALBANY

Court of Appeals of Georgia, Division No. 2, 1972.
125 Ga.App. 558, 188 S.E.2d 245.

CLARK, J.

[In holding that a notice of claim against the city was not rendered defective by inadvertent omission of the claimant's name, since the same could have readily been obtained from the attorney who submitted the notice, the court made the following observations.]

* * *

The requirements contained in § 69–308 which are prerequisite to a suit against a municipality for injuries to person or property state explicitly the following condition precedent: "[W]ithout first, and within six months of the happening of the event upon which such claim is predicated, presenting in writing such claim to the governing authority of said municipality for adjustment, stating the time, place, and extent of such injury, as nearly as practicable, and the negligence which caused the same." It is significant that these requirements do not include the name and address of the claimant as is done in many other jurisdictions.

* * *

As is stated in 17 McQuillin on Municipal Corporations, Section 48.02, page 60 of the 1967 Revised Volume: "the principal purpose of the requirement that claims be presented or filed is to provide the City with full information of the rights asserted against it, enable it to make proper investigation concerning the merits of the claim, and to settle those of merit without the expense of litigation."

Our courts have ruled that this statute requiring this notice is in derogation of the common law, and must be strictly construed against the municipality. [Citations omitted] The result is as stated in Taylor v. King, 104 Ga.App. 589, 591, 122 S.E.2d 265, 267, that "it has been held many times that a substantial compliance with this section is all that is necessary, the purpose of the notice requirement being to apprize the city of the claim in order that it may determine whether or not to adjust the claim without suit."

* * *

In the light of these authorities * * * substantial compliance with the requirements of Code Ann. § 69–308 is all that is required. The specified elements are "the time, place, and extent of such injury, as nearly as practicable, and the negligence which caused the same." The notice given in this case contains these specified elements. Even if it fails to give the name of the petitioner, it is signed by the attorney for the petitioner. It would have been a simple matter for the city's representatives to telephone the attorney and obtain the name and address of his client. "Where the claim requirement demands the address of the claimant, it is deemed satisfied if an address is given at which or through which the claimant may be found, in order that the local government officials may make such investigation of the merits of the claim as may be desired." 2 Antieau, *Municipal Corporation Law,* Section 16.06, page 474.

In our great country the citizen looks upon the government as his friend and not as his adversary. This philosophy undoubtedly underlies our giving the aggrieved citizen the right to sue his government as contrasted with the ancient maxim "The King Can Do No Wrong." In claims against others than municipalities notice is not required. * * * An injured citizen should not have his grievance disregarded without any consideration by his government because of an inadvertent omission where the notice represents substantial compliance and gives the city sufficient information to make inquiry and determine if the claim is meritorious. * * *

Notes

1. **Technical Versus Substantial Compliance.** In accord with *Busch,* see Magee v. Jacksonville, 87 So.2d 589, 591 (Fla.1956). *Busch* and *City of Dawson* could be reconciled on the distinction between a total absence of the required notice, and an imperfect but sufficient statement of notice. However, they reflect a more fundamental division of opinion as to how rigorously notice statutes should be applied. The following cases illustrate this division.

Nelson v. Dunkin, 69 Wash.2d 726, 732, 419 P.2d 984, 988 (1966)—"It is not for the courts to decide whether a claimant's failure to comply with the statutory requirement * * * is prejudicial to the county in any particular case. * * * If this requirement is no longer meaningful, it is for the legislature and not for this court to take it out of the statute." Accord: Peck v. Modesto, 181 Cal.App.2d 465, 5 Cal.Rptr. 482 (1960).

Boone v. District of Columbia, 294 F.Supp. 1156 (D.D.C.1968) barred a wife's suit for loss of consortium because the husband's claim notice did not mention her. Cf. Cornett v. Neodesha, 187 Kan. 60, 353 P.2d 975 (1960) (notice by an injured housewife that her injury resulted in loss of services to her family was sufficient to support an action for her husband's loss of consortium).

City of Houston v. Glover, 355 S.W.2d 757 (Tex.Civ.App.1962) upheld recovery in a wrongful death action for decedent's pain and suffering, although the notice did not claim damages for pain and suffering. "We think the notice was sufficient to apprise the City of this element of damage." Id. 760.

2. **Requisite Compliance for Particular Elements of Notice.** The degree of compliance that will satisfy a court necessarily relates to how the case is affected by notice discrepancies, and to the importance of the notice element in question. Courts are generally more insistent upon time deadlines. See e.g. Gale v. Santa Barbara County, 118 Cal.App.2d 451, 257 P.2d 1000 (1953) where suit was barred because the notice was filed one day beyond the statutory limit. For cases dealing with separate elements of notice, see Annots.: 7 A.L.R.4th 1063 (1981, Supp.1985) (actual notice as satisfying statute); 63 A.L.R.2d 863 (1959) (sufficiency of notice regarding injury); 63 A.L.R.2d 911 (sufficiency of notice regarding identity of claimant); 24 A.L.R.3d 965 (sufficiency of notice re claimed damages) (1969). The following cases treat some of the more commonly litigated notice discrepancies.

(a) *Place and Time of Accident.* In Hartley v. Tacoma School District No. 10, 56 Wash.2d 600, 354 P.2d 897 (1960) the court upheld, as substantial compliance, a claim which erroneously placed the accident on the north side of the street, when it took place on the south side. But a claim which misplaced the accident one block from its occurrence constituted a fatal variance, leading to dismissal of suit in Gardner v. Houston, 320 S.W.2d 715 (Tex.Civ.App.1959). Where the location misdescription was not misleading, and provided a reasonable basis for accurate investigation, the variance did not bar recovery. City of Wichita Falls v. Williams, 342 S.W.2d 588 (Tex. Civ.App.1961); *accord:* Parodi v. San Francisco, 160 Cal.App.2d 577, 325 P.2d 224 (1958).

Discrepancies as to the accident date are more prejudicial, and are commonly held to be fatal. Williams v. Gibson, 129 Ill.App.2d 431, 263 N.E.2d 138 (1970) (error of one day held not to be substantial compliance); accord: Benton v. Kansas City, 237 Mo.App. 385, 168 S.W.2d 476 (1943); *but see* Kling v. Kansas City, 227 Mo.App. 1248, 61 S.W.2d 411 (1933) which held a one-day date discrepancy not to be fatal where other circumstances of the notice enabled the city to make a reasonable investigation of the accident.

(b) *Specification of Injuries and the Amount of Claim.* Provision is normally made for description of injuries sustained, and specification of the amount demanded. Although related, these elements are distinct. The specification of the one (injury) does not satisfy the other requirement (damages). Gardner v. Houston, 320 S.W.2d 715 (Tex.Civ.App.1959). In describing personal injuries, a bare statement that one suffered personal injury will not suffice (Armijo v. Denver, 123 Colo. 304, 228 P.2d 989 (1951)), but a claimant is not required to describe personal injuries with the precision of a professional expert, or to forecast the future course of those

injuries. Flynn v. First National Bank and Trust Company of New Haven,
131 Conn. 430, 40 A.2d 770 (1944). Courts have held sufficient, statements
relating to the body parts injured, and to the general nature of the harm,
e.g. fracture, sprain, cuts, internal injuries. As to unascertainable injuries,
the courts are equally indulgent: "Where a claimant, * * * does not or
cannot know the full extent of his injuries within the sixty day period
provided by the charter for giving notice, he is not precluded from showing
that his injuries were more extensive than known at the time of giving
notice, * * *." See Dowell v. Schisler, 143 Colo. 438, 443, 354 P.2d 152,
154 (1960). Similar standards have been applied to notice of property
damage. Olson v. King County, 71 Wash.2d 279, 428 P.2d 562 (1967). *But
see* City of Atlanta v. Scott, 66 Ga.App. 257, 18 S.E.2d 76 (1941); Hudon v.
Butte, 111 Mont. 210, 107 P.2d 882 (1940) where damages for personal
injuries and property damage were limited to the amounts indicated in the
claim notices.

3. **Excuses for Noncompliance.** In some jurisdictions, courts temper notice requirements by mitigating doctrines, e.g. impossibility of compliance, incompetence of the claimants, waiver and estoppel. See Annots.:
65 A.L.R.2d 1278 (1959) (Waiver and Estoppel); 44 A.L.R.3d 1108 (1972)
(Incapacity). An Illinois court went so far as to hold that the statutory
notice requirement was waived by the municipality's procurement of insurance. Crowe v. Doyle, 6 Ill.App.3d 1098, 287 N.E.2d 99 (1972). On the
waivability of notice requirements, the authorities appear to be in hopeless
conflict. See 18 McQuillin, Municipal Corporations § 53.156 (3rd rev. ed.
1963).

Where a party is incapable of filing the required notice by reason of his
injuries, many courts preserve the claim by construing the notice statutes
as not intending action by incapacitated persons. City of Miami Beach v.
Alexander, 61 So.2d 917 (Fla.1952). In other jurisdictions, disability does
not excuse failure to comply with the statute. Johnson v. Fresno County,
64 Cal.App.2d 576, 149 P.2d 38 (1944); Waite v. Orgill, 203 Tenn. 146, 310
S.W.2d 179 (1958); Daniel v. Richmond, 199 Va. 490, 100 S.E.2d 763 (1957)
"The legislature may make any exception it chooses, * * * and, whether
or not an exception exists, for instance in favor of infants, insane persons or
others, is to be determined by the statutory law. If exceptions are made by
statute, they exist; if not, they do not exist." Id. 100 S.E.2d at 765–66.

Whether a statute may *constitutionally* cut off a claim for lack of
notice by an incompetent or incapacitated person is the subject of a split of
authority. The view that such a cut-off would be unconstitutional is
expressed in O'Neill v. Parkesburg, 160 W.Va. 694, 237 S.E.2d 504 (1977);
Turner v. Staggs, 89 Nev. 230, 510 P.2d 879 (1973), cert. denied 414 U.S.
1079, 94 S.Ct. 598, 38 L.Ed.2d 486 (1973); Grubaugh v. St. Johns, 384 Mich.
165, 180 N.W.2d 778 (1970); City of Waxahachie v. Harvey, 255 S.W.2d 549
(Tex.Civ.App.1953). That view was rejected in states where notice is
considered essential to the very existence of any right to recover. Johnson
v. Fresno County, supra; Waite v. Orgill, supra; Workman v. Emporia, 200
Kan. 112, 434 P.2d 846 (1967). See the cases in Annot., 59 A.L.R.3d 93
(1974).

Where incapacity excuses noncompliance, the questions remain as to what constitutes "incapacity," and what period of time following removal of incapacity is allowed for the filing of a notice claim. See the cases in Annot., 44 A.L.R.3d 1108 (1972).

Subject to qualifications discussed elsewhere on the estoppel doctrine, courts may estop a municipality from raising the defense of noncompliance with notice statutes. See e.g. City of Fairburn v. Clanton, 102 Ga.App. 556, 117 S.E.2d 197 (1960); Tillman v. Pompano Beach, 100 So.2d 53 (Fla.1957); Kirchmann v. Anaheim, 137 Cal.App.2d 216, 289 P.2d 817 (1955).

4. **Statutory Exceptions from Notice Requirements.** Grounds for excuse and exception are often provided by statutes, charters and ordinances. See e.g. Rost v. Board of Educ., 137 N.J.Super. 79, 347 A.2d 811 (1975) (statute tolling filing deadline in case of minors). One approach is to prevent extinguishment of any claim in the absence of a showing by the government that it was prejudiced by noncompliance. Zack v. Saxonburg, 386 Pa. 463, 126 A.2d 753 (1956). Another approach is to place upon the local unit the burden of demanding information not contained in the notice, as a prerequisite to defeating the claim for nonproduction of required information. See Goodwin v. Bloomfield, 203 N.W.2d 582, 584 (Iowa 1973); 26A Minn.Stat.Ann. § 466.05; West's Ann.Cal.Gov.Code §§ 910.8, 911; but see Hirth v. Long Prairie, 274 Minn. 76, 143 N.W.2d 205 (1966).

A third method is to authorize relief, upon a petition, to permit a late filing or corrected notice of claim. N.Y.—McKinney's General Municipal Law § 50–e(5). In Pennsylvania: "No cause of action may be validly entered * * * where there was a failure to file such notice within the time required * * * except leave of court to enter such action upon a showing of reasonable excuse * * * shall first have been secured." 53 Pa.S. § 5301.

b. Short Limitations for Instituting Suit

Tort claimants must also be wary of short statutes of limitations that apply specially to government torts. See, *e.g.*, City of Rock Falls v. Chicago Title & Trust Company, 13 Ill.App.3d 359, 300 N.E.2d 331 (1973).

c. Dollar Limits on Recoveries

In many states, statutes impose specific dollar limits on tort recoveries against government. See the authorities collected in Annot., Government Tort Damage Statutes, 43 A.L.R.4th 19 (1986). While limits vary widely from state to state, Oregon's statute is fairly illustrative.

"30.270 *Amount of liability.* (1) Liability of any public body or its officers, employes or agents acting within the scope of their employment or duties on claims within the scope of ORS 30.260 to 30.300 shall not exceed:

'(a) $50,000 to any claimant for any number of claims for damage to or destruction of property, including consequential damages, arising out of a single accident or occurrence.'

'(b) $100,000 to any claimant for all other claims arising out of a single accident or occurrence.'

'(c) $300,000 for any number of claims arising out of a single accident or occurrence.'

"(2) No award for damages on any such claim shall include punitive damages. The limitation imposed by this section on individual claimants includes damages claimed for loss of services or loss of support arising out of the same tort.

"(3) Where the amount awarded to or settled upon multiple claimants exceeds $300,000, any party may apply to any circuit court to apportion to each claimant his proper share of the total amount limited by subsection (1) of this section. * * *

"(4) Liability of any public body and one or more of its officers, employes or agents, or two or more officers, employes or agents of a public body, on claims arising out of a single accident or occurrence, shall not exceed in the aggregate the amounts limited by subsection (1) of this section."

Some statutes also exclude recovery of damages for certain classes of injury, *viz.,* recovery for pain and suffering; permanent loss of bodily function; and require set-off of amounts collectible from outstanding insurance. The states are not in agreement on the recovery of exemplary or punitive damages from local government units. See the cases collected in Annot.: *Recovery of Exemplary or Punitive Damages From Municipal Corporation,* 1 A.L.R. 4th 448 (1980). Some statutes also establish different dollar recovery ceilings for personal injury *vis-a-vis* property damage and wrongful death. Statutory dollar ceilings are avoided in certain states for claims arising out of proprietary activity, or where available insurance coverage exceeds the otherwise applicable recovery limit. See Utah Code Ann. 63–30–30.

Constitutional Issues. The selective differentiation of dollar recovery ceilings for different classes of tort claim must have a rational basis to withstand constitutional challenge. If the classifications of torts subjected to different limitations have some reasonable basis, they will survive challenge; otherwise they may violate equal protection or due process standards. See, e.g., Smith v. Philadelphia, __ Pa. __, 516 A.2d 306 (1986); Haymes v. Catholic Bishop of Chicago, 41 Ill.2d 336, 243 N.E.2d 203 (1968); Harvey v. Clyde Park Dist., 32 Ill.2d 60, 203 N.E.2d 573 (1964).

B. LIABILITY OF INDIVIDUAL OFFICERS AND EMPLOYEES

CARTER v. CARLSON

United States Court of Appeals, District of Columbia Circuit, 1971.
447 F.2d 358.

BAZELON, CHIEF JUDGE. * * *

The complaint alleged that in 1968 one police officer Carlson arrested appellant Carter without probable cause in a bar and, * * * proceeded to beat him with brass knuckles. The complaint further alleged that Carlson's precinct captain, and the Chief of Police, and the District of Columbia each negligently failed to train, instruct, supervise, and control Carlson with regard to the circumstances in which (1) an arrest may be made, and (2) various degrees of force may be used in making an arrest.

Carter sought to hold Carlson liable * * *. He sought to hold precinct captain Prete and Police Chief Layton liable for negligence in failing to give Carlson adequate training and supervision. Finally, he sought to hold the District of Columbia liable either for its own negligence in failing to train and supervise Carlson, or for the torts of Carlson, Prete, and Layton on a theory of *respondeat superior*. In each case, he asserted both a common law tort theory of liability, and an action for deprivation of civil rights under 42 U.S.C.A. § 1983.

Officer Carlson was never found for service of process. Captain Prete and Chief Layton moved to dismiss * * *. Their supporting memorandum argued that no tort on their part had been alleged, and that in any event they were protected by the doctrine of official immunity. The District of Columbia moved to dismiss the complaint for failure to state a claim, and also on the ground of sovereign immunity. The district court dismissed the complaint against all defendants without explanation.

The common law liability of the individual officers and of the District for police misconduct is similar in many respects to their liability under § 1983, but the two theories of liability are by no means coextensive. The federal statute provides:

"Every person who, under color of any statute, ordinance, regulation, custom, or usage, of any State or Territory, subjects, or causes to be subjected, any citizen of the United States or other person within the jurisdiction thereof to the deprivation of any rights, privileges, or immunities secured by the Constitution and laws, shall be liable to the party injured in an action at law, suit in equity, or other proper proceeding for redress."

When a police officer makes an arrest without probable cause, or uses excessive force in making an arrest, his action is sufficiently cloaked with official authority to satisfy the limitation of the statute to wrongs performed under color of law. Such conduct invades an interest ordinarily protected both by the common law of torts, and by the Constitutional guarantee against unreasonable searches and seizures. The common law, however, may create immunities that do not apply to an action under § 1983. Conversely, the developing law of torts may extend potential liability to some defendants beyond the reach of the federal statute. Accordingly, for each ground of liability asserted in the complaint, it will be necessary to consider separately the relevant principles at common law and under § 1983.

I. THE INDIVIDUAL OFFICERS

We start with the premise that a government officer, like any other person, is liable at common law for his torts, even if they are committed within the scope of his employment. A government officer, however, is protected by the doctrine of official immunity if the alleged tort was committed in the performance of a "discretionary" rather than a "ministerial" function.[5]

The distinction between discretionary and ministerial functions in this context must be drawn primarily with reference to its purpose. Official immunity, like the related doctrine of sovereign immunity, is designed to protect government officers from the inhibiting fear of damages suits, and the time-consuming duty to defend them; its purpose is to encourage "fearless, vigorous, and effective administration of policies of government." Barr v. Matteo, 360 U.S. 564, 571, 79 S.Ct. 1335, 1339, 3 L.Ed.2d 855 (1959). Accordingly, in determining whether a particular government function falls within the scope of official immunity, it does not suffice to consider simply whether the officer has "discretion" in the sense that he exercises judgment in choosing among alternative courses of action. The proper approach is to consider the precise function at issue, and to determine whether an officer is likely to be unduly inhibited in the performance of that function by the threat of liability for tortious conduct.[7]

---

5. Barr v. Matteo, 360 U.S. 564, 79 S.Ct. 1335, 3 L.Ed.2d 855 (1959); David v. Cohen, 132 U.S.App.D.C. 333, 407 F.2d 1268 (1969). While many jurisdictions recognize official immunity only for negligence, others extend immunity to malicious acts as well, so long as they fall within the general scope of a discretionary function. *Compare, e.g.,* Bedrock Foundations, Inc. v. Geo. H. Brewster & Son, 31 N.J. 124, 140, 155 A.2d 536, 545 (1959) (immunity limited to negligence) *with* Adams v. Tatsch, 68 N.M. 446, 362 P.2d 984 (1961) (immunity for malice). The immunity of federal officers is governed by federal common law, Howard v. Lyons, 360 U.S. 593, 597, 79 S.Ct. 1331, 3 L.Ed.2d 1454 (1959), and extends to malicious as well as negligent acts, Barr v. Matteo, *supra.*

It is not clear whether the District of Columbia follows the federal rule. * * * Nevertheless, it appears that officers of the District, unlike federal officers, may lose their immunity when there are allegations of malice. Gager v. "Bob Seidel," 112 U.S. App.D.C. 135, 139–140, 300 F.2d 727, 731–732 (dictum), cert. denied, 370 U.S. 959, 82 S.Ct. 1612, 8 L.Ed.2d 825 (1962). In this case, of course, there are no allegations of malice on the part of the supervisory officers; and Officer Carlson, whose duties were ministerial, lacks immunity in any event. Consequently, any distinction between the immunity of federal officers and that of local officers would seem to be irrelevant for present purposes.

7. This approach to the problem of discretion and immunity has been elaborated

Under this standard, it is clear that an action could be maintained against Officer Carlson at common law * * *. An arrest without probable cause constitutes a tort at common law, as does the use of excessive force to make an arrest. And the law is clear that an arresting officer has no immunity from suit for torts committed in the course of making an arrest.[9]

Officer Carlson would likewise be subject to suit under the federal statute. * * *

The arresting officer, however, is not at present a party to this litigation. Accordingly, we turn to the more difficult question of the possible liability of Carlson's superior officers. The claim against Chief Layton and Captain Prete is based on the allegation that they were each negligent in the exercise of duties to train, instruct, supervise, and control Carlson. At this stage, of course, we have no way of knowing the extent, if any, to which such duties may have rested upon them instead of others. Likewise, we cannot now determine whether a breach of such duties occurred, or had any causal relationship to appellant's injuries. We are confronted only with the threshold claim that the suit is barred by the doctrine of official immunity.

In our view, even that claim cannot be resolved in this case on the basis of the bare pleadings before us. The functions of training, supervising, and controlling police officers subsume a variety of distinct duties, * * *. No doubt some of these duties should be regarded as discretionary for the purposes of official immunity, but others are clearly ministerial for that purpose. * * * Either Chief Layton or Captain Prete will prevail in his claim of immunity if he can establish that his responsibility, if any, for the training and supervision of Officer Carlson was wholly discretionary in character. He may be able to

by the California Supreme Court in a thoughtful opinion, in the case of Johnson v. State, 69 Cal.2d 782, 73 Cal.Rptr. 240, 447 P.2d 352 (1968). We agree with that court in refusing "to enmesh ourselves deeply in the semantic thicket of attempting to determine, as a purely literal matter, 'where the ministerial and imperative duties end and the discretionary powers begin.'" Id. at 788, 73 Cal.Rptr. at 245, 447 P.2d at 357, quoting Ham v. County of Los Angeles, 46 Cal.App. 148, 162, 189 P. 462, 468 (1920). Instead we think the inquiry should be guided by the underlying purposes of the immunity doctrine. We have already adopted essentially this approach to the immunity of government units, see Spencer v. General Hospital, 138 U.S.App.D.C. 48, 425 F.2d 479 (1969) (en banc); Graham v. District of Columbia, 139 U.S.App.D.C. 378, 433 F.2d 536 (1970). It is equally appropriate when the issue is the immunity of government officers.

9. See sources cited note 8 *supra*. Official immunity does not extend to the ar-

resting officer, despite the fact that a high degree of discretion is clearly involved in deciding when and how to make an arrest without a warrant. See *e.g.,* Sherbutte v. Marine City, 374 Mich. 48, 130 N.W.2d 920 (1964), explicitly rejecting the argument that an arrest is discretionary for the purposes of official immunity. This rule presumably reflects a longstanding judgment that the threat of damage suits does not significantly impede the effective operation of a police department, when the impediment is weighed against the public interest in a tort remedy for police misconduct. See Jaffe, Suits Against Governments and Officers: Damage Actions, 77 Harv.L.Rev. 209, 218–219 (1963).

While the arresting officer has no immunity, he may nevertheless assert, as a defense on the merits, that he made the arrest in good faith, with probable cause, under a statute that he reasonably believed to be valid. Pierson v. Ray, 386 U.S. at 555–558, 87 S.Ct. 1213.

establish that fact by reference to police department regulations delegating the crucial responsibility to another officer, or by means of uncontroverted affidavits in support of a motion for summary judgment. Alternatively, Mr. Carter may be able to defeat one or both claims of official immunity after he has had the opportunity through pretrial discovery to ascertain how the relevant responsibilities are allocated within the police department, and how, if at all, they were fulfilled in this case. When the necessary factual information emerges, either officer may of course again invoke his claim of immunity; in the absence of the relevant information, however, it was error to dismiss the common law claims against the officers.

Even if Captain Prete or Chief Layton is protected by official immunity from suit at common law, they are both subject to suit under § 1983 for any negligent breach of duty that may have caused appellant to be subjected to a deprivation of constitutional rights. Indeed, Mr. Justice Frankfurter maintained that § 1983 was designed for precisely such a case, i.e., the case in which the State shields a police officer from liability for conduct which would subject a private citizen to liability. While the Supreme Court has read into the statute immunity for legislators and judges, it has not read into the statute a broad common law immunity for all government officers exercising discretionary functions.[19] In particular, various supervisory officers have been held subject to suit under § 1983 for negligence in supervising their subordinates.

In Roberts v. Williams, the Fifth Circuit affirmed a judgment against a prison superintendent for injuries resulting from the careless use of a shotgun by a prisoner-guard, or "trusty." The superintendent's liability was based on the finding that he had negligently failed to train or supervise the guard in the safe use of the weapon. (No. 28,829, Apr. 1, 1971) (slip opinion at 6–20). Similarly in this case appellant will be entitled to prevail if he can show that Captain Prete or Chief Layton was negligent in performing his own duty to supervise or train Officer Carlson, and that the negligence caused appellant to be deprived by Carlson of his constitutional rights. The showing may well be difficult, but if it succeeds then no local rule of immunity can bar recovery under the federal statute.

II. The District of Columbia

We turn now to appellant's claim against the government of the District of Columbia. That claim may rest on a theory of vicarious liability for the torts of the individual police officers, or on the theory that the District itself was negligent in the performance of its own duty to supervise and control police officers. In either case, the first ques-

---

19. Several federal courts have held that official immunity is more limited under § 1983 and related statutes than at common law. *E.g.*, Roberts v. Williams, (5th Cir. No. 28,829, Apr. 1, 1971) (slip op. at 26–27); McLaughlin v. Tilendis, 398 F.2d 287, 290–291 (7th Cir.1968); Jobson v. Henne, 355 F.2d 129, 133–134 (2d Cir.1966).

tion is whether the District is protected from suit by the doctrine of sovereign or governmental immunity.

Sovereign immunity serves essentially the same function as the distinct doctrine of official immunity discussed above. Thus it is not surprising to find that in this jurisdiction, * * * the common law has developed the same criteria for both kinds of immunity. The District of Columbia is immune from suit only for acts committed in the exercise of discretionary functions. Spencer v. General Hospital, 138 U.S.App. D.C. 48, 425 F.2d 479 (1969) (*en banc*). A function is discretionary under *Spencer* if it is "of such a nature as to pose threats to the quality and efficiency of government in the District if liability in tort was made the consequence of negligent act or omission." *Id.* at 51, 425 F.2d at 482. * * *

A. *Vicarious liability at common law for Carlson's conduct.* The alleged tort of arresting officer Carlson is one possible basis for imposing vicarious liability on the District. * * * If the arresting officer himself is subject to suit for his tort, it is hard to conceive of any substantial additional threat to the efficiency of government that would result from subjecting the District to suit as well. Accordingly, we hold that the act of making an arrest is ministerial for the purposes of the *Spencer* doctrine of sovereign immunity.

The District urges us to limit the rule of *Spencer* to cases involving negligence, and to hold the municipal government completely immune from suit for the intentional torts of its employees.

* * *

* * * When a tort is made possible only through the abuse of power granted by the government, then the government should be held accountable for the abuse, whether it is negligent or intentional in character. Accordingly, we reject the suggestion that the District is immune from suit for the intentional torts of its employees.

At one time the intentional character of Officer Carlson's alleged tort might have been a barrier to suit, not because of any quirk in the doctrine of immunity, but because many courts would not impose vicarious liability for an intentional tort. Today, however, it is widely recognized that a master may be held liable for the intentional torts of his servants in appropriate circumstances. In particular, a servant authorized to make arrests ordinarily subjects his master to liability for using excessive force to make an arrest, or for making an unlawful arrest. Since Officer Carlson was authorized by the District of Columbia to make arrests, misuse of that authority, even though intentional, may nevertheless result in vicarious liability on the part of the District.

B. *Vicarious liability at common law for the conduct of supervisory officers.* The alleged negligence of Captain Prete and Chief Layton is another possible basis for imposing vicarious liability on the District. As we have previously noted, the present record does not disclose the precise character of either officer's supervisory functions. Thus at this stage it is impossible to determine whether the District is immune to suit with respect to their conduct, even as it is impossible to determine whether the officers themselves are immune at common law.

If it develops that either officer is subject to individual liability, then his negligence should subject the District to liability as well, * * *.

If, on the other hand, it develops that the officers themselves are immune, we think that should not necessarily foreclose the question of the District's vicarious liability for their conduct.[26] With respect to some government functions, the threat of individual liability would have a devastating effect, while the threat of government liability would not significantly impair performance. If the trial court determines that this is such a case, then the officers, but not the District, will be entitled to immunity at common law.[27]

C. *Direct liability of the District for negligence at common law.* Appellant also claims that the District may be liable for its own negligence in failing adequately to supervise, train, and control Carlson. * * * The claim of direct government liability will be important, however, if no individual officer can be charged with the alleged failure of training and supervision, either because the District has never delegated to any officer the relevant supervisory functions, or because appellant is unable to discover which officer is responsible.

Here the threshold question is whether the common law imposes on the District such a duty of supervision, with potential liability in tort for its breach.[28] We think this question was correctly answered by

26. There is perhaps a conceptual difficulty with the notion of imposing vicarious liability on the District for the conduct of officers who are not themselves subject to liability. It is generally recognized, however, that the master can assert only the servant's substantive defenses, and not his immunity to suit. *E.g.,* Schubert v. August Schubert Wagon Co., 249 N.Y. 253, 164 N.E. 42 (1928) (servant's immunity from suit of spouse no bar to master's vicarious liability); see Harper & James, *supra* note 23, § 26.17.

27. In concluding that the common law immunity of the government may sometimes be narrower in scope than the immunity of government officers, we are in accord with the views of several leading commentators. See, *e.g.,* K. Davis, Administrative Law Treatise, § 25.17 (1958, Supp. 1970); 2 Harper & James, *supra* note 23, comment to § 29.10 n. 29 (Supp.1968); Mathes & Jones, Toward a "Scope of Official Duty" Immunity for Police Officers in Damage Actions, 53 Geo.L.J. 889 (1965). When the California Supreme Court embarked on its pioneering effort to update the law of the immunity of governments and of officers, the court similarly concluded that the immunity of a government unit

for discretionary conduct should be narrower than that of an officer. Lipman v. Brisbane Elem. School Dist., 55 Cal.2d 224, 230, 11 Cal.Rptr. 97, 99, 359 P.2d 465, 467 (1961). The reasons given by the court are essentially those stated in text, *infra.* The California Legislature subsequently rejected that approach, however, making the two immunities for the most part coextensive. Calif. Tort Claims Act of 1963, § 1 Calif.Gov't Code § 815.2(b) (West 1966).

28. *Compare* Westminster Investing Corp. v. G.S. Murphy Co., 140 U.S.App.D.C. 247, 434 F.2d 521 (1970) (D.C. has no duty to protect citizens from riot damage, unnecessary to decide question of immunity). * * * the immunity of governments and of officers, the court similarly concluded that the immunity of a government unit for discretionary conduct should be narrower than that of an officer. Lipman v. Brisbane Elem. School Dist., 55 Cal.2d 224, 230, 11 Cal.Rptr. 97, 99, 359 P.2d 465, 467 (1961). The reasons given by the court are essentially those stated in text, *infra.* The California Legislature subsequently rejected that approach, however, making the two immunities for the most part coextensive. Calif. Tort Claims Act of 1963, § 1 Calif.Govt.Code § 815.2(b) (West 1966).

the District Court in Thomas v. Johnson, 295 F.Supp. 1025, 1030–1033 (D.D.C.1968). In a carefully reasoned opinion, the court held that the District of Columbia as a corporate entity has a duty to supervise, train, and control its police officers.

A breach of that duty might involve either ministerial or discretionary aspects of supervising police officers. Accordingly, a claim of negligence based on a breach of that duty cannot be dismissed at this stage on the ground of sovereign immunity.

* * *

DePALMA v. ROSEN

Supreme Court of Minnesota, 1972.
294 Minn. 11, 199 N.W.2d 517.

TODD, J.

[Actions by owner, whose premises were razed, against members of city council and against city. The District Court dismissed the action against members of council and granted summary judgment for city. On appeal, the Supreme Court held that individual members of city council could not be held responsible for damages in the exercise of discretionary acts, but held that failure by city to conform to its code requirements rendered the razing a taking of property without due process, and entitled owner to damages.]

* * *

1. With regard to the judgment dismissing the action against the individual members of the city council, we must affirm. The general rule of law is that a municipal officer is not liable for his discretionary acts. 4 McQuillin, Municipal Corporations (3 ed.) § 12.208. The judgments of the individual members of the city council in this matter were clearly discretionary and not ministerial. A public officer whose functions are judicial or quasi-judicial cannot be called upon to respond in damages for the honest exercise of his judgment * * *, however erroneous his judgment may be. Stewart v. Case, 53 Minn. 62, 54 N.W. 938 (1893), cited with approval in Roerig v. Houghton, 144 Minn. 231, 175 N.W. 542 (1919). * * *

The council had no authority to order the razing of plaintiff's home, since it failed to follow the procedures outlined in its legislative code, and its purported action was a nullity. The subsequent destruction of plaintiff's property was thus a taking of plaintiff's property without due process of law, and he is entitled to have the issue of damages litigated by the trial court.

The summary judgment for the city is therefore reversed, and the case is remanded for trial. At the time of trial, the matter will have to be tried in the nature of a condemnation, * * *.

Notes

1. **Licensing Decisions.** Legislative immunity has been applied to licensing decisions. Thus, where a legislative body exercises discretion to deny a license application, and there is no mandatory duty to issue the same, the legislative officers cannot be held liable, no matter how erroneous or negligent their action, *unless* they are shown to have acted in bad faith. But where administrators are required by law to ascertain and report certain facts as conditions to licensing, their failure to do so would be considered a negligent, ministerial act, and not an immune discretionary act. Puffer v. Binghamton, 59 Misc.2d 856, 301 N.Y.S.2d 274 (1969).

Courts have protected license applicants from fraudulent, bad faith and malicious official action, by excepting such action from the scope of official immunity. The exception was strong enough to lead courts of Illinois to read such an exception into the tort claim statute. Young v. Hansen, 118 Ill.App.2d 1, 249 N.E.2d 300 (1969). Another means of recovering for official bad faith is to broaden the complaint allegations to charge a conspiracy and a tort of "interference." See e.g., City of Rock Falls v. Chicago Title and Trust Co., 13 Ill.App.3d 359, 300 N.E.2d 331 (1973).

Where refusal to issue a license is clearly illegal, should the applicant nevertheless be denied damage recovery against the government entity on the ground that the applicant should be charged with knowledge of the law? Compare: Anderson v. Minneapolis, 287 Minn. 287, 178 N.W.2d 215 (1970), with Puffer v. Binghamton, note 1, supra.

2. **Other Discretionary Actions.** Disclosure of investigative information that was inaccurate and embarrassing to a homicide victim's family, were held immune from tort liability, as a performance of a discretionary function. Moloney v. Tribune Publishing Co., 26 Wash.App. 357, 613 P.2d 1179 (1980).

Qualified immunity for discretionary acts was construed to cover professional employees who negligently permitted students to carry jars full of acid. Wagner v. Alvarado Independent School District, 598 S.W.2d 51 (Tex.Civ.App.1980). Do you agree?

McCORKLE v. LOS ANGELES

Supreme Court of California, 1969.
70 Cal.2d 252, 74 Cal.Rptr. 389, 449 P.2d 453.

TOBRINER, J.

[In the course of an auto accident investigation, plaintiff was asked by the police officer to go onto the highway and point out skid marks at the place of the accident. When plaintiff complied, he was struck by another automobile. He sued the city and obtained a judgment for $45,000. The city appealed.]

* * *

DISCRETIONARY IMMUNITY

The City contends that Officer Lombardo was immune from liability for his act or omission during the investigation of the Phillips accident, under the provisions of Government Code, section 820.2;[6] and that, this being so, the City is immune, as his employer under subdivision (b) of section 815.2.[7] The argument rests upon the premise that Lombardo had no duty to investigate the accident, but undertook to do so in the exercise of "discretion vested in him."

Whether or not a public employee is immune from liability under section 820.2 depends in many cases upon whether the act in question was "discretionary" or "ministerial," respectively. [Citations omitted] For this reason, contentions such as the City makes here have frequently required judicial determination of the category into which the particular act falls: *i.e.,* whether it was ministerial because it amounted "only to an obedience to orders, or the performance of a duty in which the officer is left no choice of his own," or discretionary because it required "personal deliberation, decision and judgment." [Citations omitted]

However, classification of the act of a public employee as "discretionary" will not produce immunity under section 820.2 if the injury to another results not from the employee's exercise of "discretion vested in him" to undertake the act, but from his negligence in performing it after having made the discretionary decision to do so. [Citations omitted]

Accordingly, if we were to accept the City's premise that Officer Lombardo exercised his discretion in undertaking his investigation of the Phillips accident, section 820.2 did not clothe him with immunity from the consequences of his negligence in conducting it. He would have been immune if plaintiff's injury had been the *result* of his—Lombardo's—exercise of discretion. [Citations omitted] It was not: it resulted from his negligence after the discretion, if any, had been exercised. Because the essential requirement of section 820.2—a causal connection between the exercise of discretion and the injury—did not exist, the statutory immunity does not apply.

Since Lombardo was not immune from liability under section 820.2, the City (1) is not immune under subdivision (b) of section 815.2 and (2) is liable under subdivision (a) thereof. (See section 815.2, quoted in footnote [7], *ante.*)

*   *   *

6. Except where otherwise indicated, all statutory references hereinafter are to the Government Code. Section 820.2 states that "Except as otherwise provided by statute, a public employee is not liable for an injury resulting from his act or omission where the act or omission was the result of the exercise of the discretion vested in him, whether or not such discretion be abused."

7. Section 815.2 provides in full as follows: "815.2. * * * (b) Except as otherwise provided by statute, a public entity is not liable for an injury resulting from an act or omission of an employee of the public entity where the employee is immune from liability."

MARTINEZ v. CALIFORNIA

Supreme Court of the United States, 1980.
444 U.S. 277, 100 S.Ct. 553, 62 L.Ed.2d 481.

MR. JUSTICE STEVENS delivered the opinion of the Court.

The two federal questions that appellants ask us to decide are (1) whether the Fourteenth Amendment invalidates a California statute granting absolute immunity to public employees who make parole-release determinations, and (2) whether such officials are absolutely immune from liability in an action brought under the federal Civil Rights Act of 1871, 42 U.S.C. § 1983. We agree with the California Court of Appeal that the state statute is valid when applied to claims arising under state law, and we conclude that appellants have not alleged a claim for relief under federal law.

The case arises out of the murder of a 15–year-old girl by a parolee. Her survivors brought this action in a California court claiming that the state officials responsible for the parole-release decision are liable in damages for the harm caused by the parolee.

The complaint alleged that the parolee, one Thomas, was convicted of attempted rape in December 1969. He was first committed to a state mental hospital as a "Mentally Disordered Sex Offender not amenable to treatment" and thereafter sentenced to a term of imprisonment of 1 to 20 years, with a recommendation that he not be paroled. Nevertheless, five years later, appellees decided to parole Thomas to the care of his mother. They were fully informed about his history, his propensities, and the likelihood that he would commit another violent crime. Moreover, in making their release determination they failed to observe certain "requisite formalities." Five months after his release Thomas tortured and killed appellants' decedent. We assume, as the complaint alleges, that appellees knew, or should have known, that the release of Thomas created a clear and present danger that such an incident would occur. Their action is characterized not only as negligent, but also as reckless, willful, wanton and malicious. Appellants prayed for actual and punitive damages of $2 million.

The trial judge sustained a demurrer to the complaint and his order was upheld on appeal. 85 Cal.App.3d 430, 149 Cal.Rptr. 519 (1978). After the California Supreme Court denied appellants' petition for a hearing, we noted probable jurisdiction. 441 U.S. 960, 99 S.Ct. 2403, 60 L.Ed.2d 1064.

I

Section 845.8(a) of the Cal.Gov't Code Ann. (West Supp.1979) provides:

"Neither a public entity nor a public employee is liable for:

"(a) Any injury resulting from determining whether to parole or release a prisoner or from determining the terms and conditions of his parole or release or from determining whether to revoke his parole or release."

The California courts held that this statute provided appellees with a complete defense to appellants' state-law claims. They considered and rejected the contention that the immunity statute as so construed violates the Due Process Clause of the Fourteenth Amendment to the Federal Constitution.

Like the California courts, we cannot accept the contention that this statute deprived Thomas' victim of her life without due process of law because it condoned a parole decision that led indirectly to her death. The statute neither authorized nor 'immunized the deliberate killing of any human being. It is not the equivalent of a death penalty statute which expressly authorizes state agents to take a person's life after prescribed procedures have been observed. This statute merely provides a defense to potential state tort-law liability. At most, the availability of such a defense may have encouraged members of the parole board to take somewhat greater risks of recidivism in exercising their authority to release prisoners than they otherwise might. But the basic risk that repeat offenses may occur is always present in any parole system. A legislative decision that has an incremental impact on the probability that death will result in any given situation—such as setting the speed limit at 55–miles-per-hour instead of 45—cannot be characterized as state action depriving a person of life just because it may set in motion a chain of events that ultimately leads to the random death of an innocent bystander.

Nor can the statute be characterized as an invalid deprivation of property. Arguably, the cause of action for wrongful death that the State has created is a species of "property" protected by the Due Process Clause. On that hypothesis, the immunity statute could be viewed as depriving the plaintiffs of that property interest insofar as they seek to assert a claim against parole officials.[5] But even if one characterizes the immunity defense as a statutory deprivation, it would remain true that the State's interest in fashioning its own rules of tort law is paramount to any discernible federal interest, except perhaps an interest in protecting the individual citizen from state action that is wholly arbitrary or irrational.

We have no difficulty in accepting California's conclusion that there "is a rational relationship between the state's purposes and the statute." In fashioning state policy in a "practical and troublesome area" like this, * * * the California Legislature could reasonably conclude that judicial review of a parole officer's decisions "would

---

5. It is arguable, however, that the immunity defense, like an element of the tort claim itself, is merely one aspect of the State's definition of that property interest. Recently, in considering a lawyer's claim of immunity in a state malpractice action, we noted that "when state law creates a cause of action, the State is free to define the defenses to that claim, including the defense of immunity, unless, of course, the state rule is in conflict with federal law." Ferri v. Ackerman, 444 U.S. 193, 198, 100 S.Ct. 402, 406, 62 L.Ed.2d 355.

inevitably inhibit the exercise of discretion," * * * Whether one agrees or disagrees with California's decision to provide absolute immunity for parole officials in a case of this kind, one cannot deny that it rationally furthers a policy that reasonable lawmakers may favor. As federal judges, we have no authority to pass judgment on the wisdom of the underlying policy determination. We therefore find no merit in the contention that the State's immunity statute is unconstitutional when applied to defeat a tort claim arising under state law.

* * *

[The balance of the opinion dealing with the federal claim issue is discussed infra, page reference 961.]

1. INDEMNIFICATION STATUTES

Statutes which authorize or mandate local entities to indemnify their officers or employees for tort damages incurred in the course of government service achieve the practical effect of waiving government immunity, as well as insuring the indemnified individual against personal loss. See generally, Annotation on statutes providing governmental indemnity to officers and employees for liability arising out of performance of public duties, 71 A.L.R.3d 90 (1976). The range of these statutes are illustrated by the following.

§ 7–465. Assumption of liability for damage caused by employees

"Any town, city or borough, * * * shall pay on behalf of any employee of such municipality, except firemen covered under the provisions of section 7–308, all sums which such employee becomes obligated to pay by reason of the liability imposed upon such employee by law for physical damages to person or property, except as hereinafter set forth, if the employee, * * * was acting in the performance of his duties and within the scope of his employment, and if such occurrence, * * * was not the result of any wilful or wanton act of such employee * * *. This section shall not apply to physical injury * * * to a fellow employee while both employees are engaged in the scope of their employment for such municipality if the employee suffering such injury * * * has a right to benefits or compensation under chapter 568 by reason of such injury. * * * This section shall not apply to libel or slander proceedings brought against any such employee and, in such cases, there is no assumption of liability by any town, city or borough. * * * Such municipality may arrange for and maintain appropriate insurance or may elect to act as a self-insurer to maintain such protection. * * * Governmental immunity shall not be a defense in any action brought under this section. In any such action the municipality and the employee may be represented by the same attorney if the municipality, * * * files a statement with the court * * * that it will pay any verdict rendered in such action against such employee. * * *" 7 Conn.Gen.Stat.Ann. § 465; See also West's Ann.Cal.Gov.Code § 825.

§ 2–301. Indemnification or insurance of employees

"Nothing in this Part 3 relieves a local public entity of its duty to indemnify or insure its employees as provided in Sections 1–4–5 and 1–4–6 of the "Illinois Municipal Code", * * * Sections 10–20.20 and 34–18.1 of "The School Code", * * * and in Section 22.1 of "An Act to revise the law in relation to counties", * * *.

§ 2–302. Actions against employee—Election by entity

"If any claim or action is instituted against an employee or former employee of a local public entity based on an injury allegedly arising out of an act or omission occurring within the scope of his employment as such employee, the entity may elect to do any one or more of the following:

(a) Appear and defend against the claim or action;

(b) Indemnify the employee or former employee for his court costs incurred in the defense of such claim or action;

(c) Pay, or indemnify the employee or former employee for a judgment based on such claim or action, or

(d) Pay, or indemnify the employee or former employee for, a compromise or settlement of such a claim or action. Illinois—S.H.A. ch. 85, ¶¶ 2–301, 2–302; see also Mich.Comp.Laws Ann. §§ 691, 1408; 20A Minn.Stat.Ann. § 466.07 (1963); W.Va.Code, § 8–12–7(b); Pa.Stat. Ann. tit. 53, § 5311.304.

Chapter XI

LOCAL GOVERNMENT TORTS— FEDERAL LAW

A. THE CHECKERBOARD OF FEDERAL CIVIL RIGHTS STATUTES

The monetary tort liability of local government units and their personnel has literally exploded in the past two decades, due largely to the decisions of federal courts that implied new private causes of action under federal civil rights statutes and newly articulated constitutional rights. These include the Civil War civil rights statutes (42 U.S.C.A. §§ 1981–1988); the Civil Rights Act of 1964 (especially Titles VI, VII, and IX (42 U.S.C.A. § 2000 et seq.)), the Equal Pay Act of 1963 (29 U.S.C.A. § 206(d)), the Rehabilitation Act of 1973 (29 U.S.C.A. § 794), The Education For All Handicapped Children Act of 1975 (29 U.S.C.A. § 1401); and the Age Discrimination Act of 1964, (29 U.S.C.A. § 621), all as expanded and amended, to name but a few. Each statute provides independent grounds for suit by different classes of individuals, and its respective language and intent requires separate judicial construction. The operation of each is by no means parallel to the other statutes with regard to procedures, substantive elements, and authorized remedies.

The new sources will be increasingly litigated and require extensive, specialized study. They are of growing concern, especially since many questions remain unanswered regarding their operation and interplay. Traditional state tort law provides only limited guidance, because Congress and federal courts are not bound to adopt state tort standards for federal causes of action. Since multiple federal torts may arise from a common occurence, under separate civil rights statutes; and since neither Congress nor the courts have attempted to dovetail or integrate the various branches of civil rights law, the analysis of federal tort liability continues to be developed on a case-by-case, statute-by-statute basis.

The core provisions of major federal statutes that support monetary recoveries are set forth in the Appendix, *B*, infra. While their operation cannot be adequately surveyed here, two recent publications provide a good outline of the coverage, defenses and procedural requisites of those laws. See Federal Civil Rights Laws: A Source Book, U.S. Senate Committee on the Judiciary, 98th Cong., 2d Sess. (1984); C.R. Richey, Manual on Employment Discrimination and Civil Rights Actions in the Federal Courts (Attorney's Edition 1986).

Perhaps the best sources for a general overview on developing federal tort law as it affects local government, are the cases arising under those provisions of the Civil Rights Act of 1871 known as [42 U.S. C.A. § 1983]. Unlike the other above mentioned statutes which create independent substantive rights:

"Section 1983 is a remedial statute which does not create substantive rights. Chapman v. Houston Welfare Rights Organization, 441 U.S. 600, 616–18, 99 S.Ct. 1905, 1915–16, 60 L.Ed.2d 508 (1979). It provides a remedy for the violation of rights created elsewhere. As the Supreme Court made clear in Maine v. Thiboutot, 448 U.S. 1, 100 S.Ct. 2502, 65 L.Ed.2d 555 (1980), § 1983 provides a remedy for actions under color of law which contravene federally protected rights, whether those rights derive from the Constitution or from a federal statute."

See Day v. Wayne County Bd. of Auditors, 749 F.2d 1199, 1202 (6th Cir. 1984). But for exceptions hereafter noted, § 1983 acts as an umbrella statute to remedy deprivation of rights under many federal laws. Only where the Supreme Court has found that the invoked substantive federal law was deemed not to create individually enforceable rights, or where Congress intended remedies under a statute other than § 1983 to be exclusive, has relief been denied under this general remedial statute. See notes, p. 946, infra.

The attractiveness of § 1983 to civil rights grievants lies in the facts that its procedures and prelitigation requirements are more favorable and less burdensome to claimants than those afforded by other federal laws. The following materials illustrate how federal tort claims are decided within the framework of a § 1983 proceeding, first with respect to local government entities, and thereafter with respect to individuals and officials.

B. LOCAL GOVERNMENT LIABILITY UNDER § 1983

MONELL v. NEW YORK CITY DEPT. OF SOC. SERV.

Supreme Court of the United States, 1978.
436 U.S. 658, 98 S.Ct. 2018, 56 L.Ed.2d 611.

[Suit against City Department of Social Services and Board of Education alleging, inter alia, deprivation of constitutional rights of plaintiff employees by forcing them to take maternity leave before leave was medically indicated. The City defended that it was not a "person" within the coverage of § 1983, citing Supreme Court prior holding to that effect.]

MR. JUSTICE BRENNAN delivered the opinion of the Court.

I

In Monroe v. Pape, we held that "Congress did not undertake to bring municipal corporations within the ambit of [§ 1983]." 365 U.S., at 187, 81 S.Ct. at 484. The sole basis for this conclusion was an inference drawn from Congress' rejection of the "Sherman amendment" to the bill which became Civil Rights Act of 1871, 17 Stat. 13—the precursor of § 1983—* * *

* * *

II

Our analysis of the legislative history of the Civil Rights Act of 1871 compels the conclusion that Congress *did* intend municipalities and other local government units to be included among those persons to whom § 1983 applies. Local governing bodies, therefore, can be sued directly under § 1983 for monetary, declaratory, or injunctive relief where, as here, the action that is alleged to be unconstitutional implements or executes a policy statement, ordinance, regulation, or decision officially adopted and promulgated by that body's officers. Moreover, although the touchstone of the § 1983 action against a government body is an allegation that official policy is responsible for a deprivation of rights protected by the Constitution, local governments, like every other § 1983 "person," * * * may be sued for constitutional deprivations visited pursuant to governmental "custom" even though such a custom has not received formal approval through the body's official decisionmaking channels. * * *

On the other hand, the language of § 1983, read against the background of the same legislative history, compels the conclusion that Congress did not intend municipalities to be held liable unless action pursuant to official municipal policy of some nature caused a constitutional tort. In particular, we conclude that a municipality cannot be held liable *solely* because it employs a tortfeasor—or, in other words, a municipality cannot be held liable under § 1983 on a *respondeat superior* theory.

We begin with the language of § 1983 as passed:

"[*A*]*ny person who,* under color of any law, statute, ordinance, regulation, custom, or usage of any State, *shall subject, or cause to be subjected,* any person * * * to the deprivation of any rights, privileges, or immunities secured by the Constitution of the United States, shall, any such law, statute, ordinance, regulation, custom, or usage of the State to the contrary notwithstanding, be liable to the party injured in any action at law, suit in equity, or other proper proceeding for redress * * *." Globe App., at 335 (emphasis added).

The italicized language plainly imposes liability on a government that, under color of some official policy, "causes" an employee to violate another's constitutional rights. At the same time, that language cannot be easily read to impose liability vicariously on governing bodies solely on the basis of the existence of an employer-employee relationship with a tortfeasor. * * *

* * *

We conclude, therefore, that a local government may not be sued for an injury inflicted solely by its employees or agents. Instead, it is when execution of a government's policy or custom, whether made by its lawmakers or by those whose edicts or acts may fairly be said to represent official policy, inflicts the injury that the government as an entity is responsible under § 1983. Since this case unquestionably involves official policy as the moving force of the constitutional violation found by the District Court, * * * we must reverse the judgment below. In so doing, we have no occasion to address, and do not address, what the full contours of municipal liability under § 1983 may be. * * *

III

* * *

* * * Finally, in the Civil Rights Attorneys' Fees Award Act of 1976, 90 Stat. 2641, which allows prevailing parties (in the discretion of the court) in § 1983 suits to obtain attorneys fees from the losing party, the Senate stated:

> "[D]efendants in these cases are often State or local *bodies* or State or local officials. In such cases it is intended that the attorneys' fees, like other items of costs, will be collected either directly from the official, *in his official capacity,* from funds of his agency or under his control, or *from the State or local government (whether or not the agency or government is a named party)."* S.Rep. No. 94–1011, at 5; U.S.Code Cong. & Admin.News 1976, pp. 5908, 5913 (emphasis added; footnotes omitted).

Far from showing that Congress has relied on *Monroe,* therefore, events since 1961 show that Congress has refused to extend the benefits of *Monroe* to school boards and has attempted to allow awards of attorneys' fees against local governments even though *Monroe,* City of Kenosha v. Bruno, *supra,* and Aldinger v. Howard, 427 U.S. 1, 96 S.Ct. 2413, 49 L.Ed.2d 276 (1976), have made the joinder of such governments impossible.

Third, municipalities can assert no reliance claim which can support an absolute immunity. * * *

* * *

For reasons stated above, therefore, we hold that *stare decisis* does not bar our overruling of *Monroe* insofar as it is inconsistent with Parts I and II of this opinion.

IV

Since the question whether local government bodies should be afforded some form of official immunity was not presented as a question to be decided on this petition and was not briefed by the parties nor addressed by the courts below, we express no views on the scope of any municipal immunity beyond holding that municipal bodies sued under § 1983 cannot be entitled to an absolute immunity, lest our decision that such bodies are subject to suit under § 1983 "be drained of meaning," Scheuer v. Rhodes, 416 U.S. 232, 248, 94 S.Ct. 1683, 40 L.Ed. 2d 90 (1974). *Cf.* Bivens v. Six Unknown Federal Narcotics Agents, 403 U.S. 388, 397–398, 91 S.Ct. 1999, 29 L.Ed.2d 619 (1971).

V

For the reasons stated above, the judgment of the Court of Appeals is

Reversed.

* * *

Note

1. **Argumentative Elements of § 1983 Liability.** In establishing the critical elements for § 1983 liability, the *Monnell* opinion raised a host of questions that require judicial elaboration, to wit: What "rights" and what kinds of "deprivation" of those rights are protected by § 1983? Do all acts of public officials or employees satisfy the "color of law" requirement of § 1983? What actions constitute a government policy or custom vis-a-vis mere negligence? What degree of connection is required to prove that a policy or custom caused the alleged injury? What immunity defenses, if any, would apply to federal law torts? What damages are available under § 1983 with respect to different constitutional and statutory rights deprivations? Each of these questions will be considered in the following sections.

1. THE RANGE OF FEDERAL RIGHTS PROTECTED BY 42 U.S.C. § 1983

MAINE v. THIBOUTOT

Supreme Court of the United States, 1980.
448 U.S. 1, 100 S.Ct. 2502, 65 L.Ed.2d 555.

MR. JUSTICE BRENNAN delivered the opinion of the Court.

* * * Respondents brought this suit in the Maine Superior Court alleging that petitioners, the State of Maine and its Commissioner of Human Services, violated § 1983 by depriving respondents of welfare benefits to which they were entitled under the federal Social Security Act, * * *. The petitioners present two issues: (1) whether § 1983 encompasses claims based on purely statutory violations of federal law, and (2) if so, whether attorney's fees under § 1988 may be awarded to the prevailing party in such an action.

I

Respondents, Lionel and Joline Thiboutot, are married and have eight children, three of whom are Lionel's by a previous marriage. The Maine Department of Human Services notified Lionel that, in computing the Aid to Families with Dependent Children (AFDC) benefits * * * it would no longer make allowance for the money spent to support the other five children, even though Lionel is legally obligated to support them. * * * By amended complaint, respondents also claimed relief under § 1983 for themselves and others similarly situated. * * *

II

Section 1983 provides:

> "Every person who, under color of any statute, ordinance, regulation, custom, or usage, of any State or Territory, subjects, or causes to be subjected, any citizen of the United States or other person within the jurisdiction thereof to the deprivation of any rights, privileges, or immunities secured by the Constitution *and laws,* shall be liable to the party injured in an action at law, suit in equity, or other proper proceeding for redress." (Emphasis added.)

The question before us is whether the phrase "and laws," as used in § 1983, means what it says, or whether it should be limited to some subset of laws. Given that Congress attached no modifiers to the phrase, the plain language of the statute undoubtedly embraces respondents' claim that petitioners violated the Social Security Act.

Even were the language ambiguous, however, any doubt as to its meaning has been resolved by our several cases suggesting, explicitly or implicitly, that the § 1983 remedy broadly encompasses violations of federal statutory as well as constitutional law. * * *

While some might dismiss as dictum the foregoing statements * * *, our analysis in several § 1983 cases involving Social Security Act (SSA) claims has relied on the availability of a § 1983 cause of action for statutory claims. Constitutional claims were also raised in these cases, providing a jurisdictional base, but the statutory claims were allowed to go forward, and were decided on the merits, under the court's pendent jurisdiction. * * *

In the face of the plain language of § 1983 and our consistent treatment of that provision, petitioners nevertheless persist in suggesting that the phrase "and laws" should be read as limited to civil rights or equal protection laws. Petitioners suggest that when § 1 of the Civil Rights Act of 1871, which accorded jurisdiction and a remedy for deprivations of rights secured by "the Constitution of the United States," was divided by the 1874 statutory revision into a remedial section, § 1979, and jurisdictional sections, §§ 563(12) and 629(16), Congress intended that the same change made in § 629(16) be made as to each of the new sections as well. Section 629(16), the jurisdictional provision for the circuit courts and the model for the current jurisdictional provision, 28 U.S.C. § 1343(3), applied to deprivations of rights secured by "the Constitution of the United States, or of any right secured by any law providing for equal rights." On the other hand, the remedial provision, the predecessor of § 1983, was expanded to apply to deprivations of rights secured by "the Constitution and laws," and § 563(12), the provision granting jurisdiction to the district courts, to deprivations of rights secured by "the Constitution of the United States, or of any right secured by any law of the United States."

We need not repeat at length the detailed debate over the meaning of the scanty legislative history concerning the addition of the phrase "and laws." See Chapman v. Houston Welfare Rights Organization, 441 U.S. 600, 99 S.Ct. 1905, 60 L.Ed.2d 508 (1979); ibid. (Powell, J., concurring); ibid. (White, J., concurring in judgment); ibid. (Stewart, J., dissenting). One conclusion which emerges clearly is that the legislative history does not permit a definitive answer. Id., at 610–611, 99 S.Ct., at 1912–1913; id., at 674, 99 S.Ct., at 1945 (Stewart, J., dissenting). There is no express explanation offered for the insertion of the phrase "and laws." On the one hand, a principal purpose of the added language was to "ensure that federal legislation providing specifically for equality of rights would be brought within the ambit of the civil action authorized by that statute." Id., at 637, 99 S.Ct., at 1926 (Powell, J., concurring). On the other hand, there are no indications that that was the only purpose, and Congress' attention was specifically directed to this new language. * * * Petitioners' arguments amount to the claim that had Congress been more careful, and had it fully thought out the relationship among the various sections, it might have acted differently. That argument, however, can best be addressed to Congress, which, it is important to note, has remained quiet in the face of our many pronouncements on the scope of § 1983. * * *

* * *

MR. JUSTICE POWELL, with whom THE CHIEF JUSTICE, and MR. JUSTICE REHNQUIST, join dissenting.

The Court holds today, almost casually, that 42 U.S.C. § 1983 creates a cause of action for deprivations under color of state law of any federal statutory right. Having transformed purely statutory claims into "civil rights" actions under § 1983, the Court concludes that 42 U.S.C. § 1988 permits the "prevailing party" to recover his attorney's fees. These two holdings dramatically expand the liability of state and local officials * * *.

The Court's opinion reflects little consideration of the consequences of its judgment. It relies upon the "plain" meaning of the phrase "and laws" in § 1983 and upon this Court's assertedly "consistent treatment" of that statute. * * * But the reading adopted today is anything but "plain" when the statutory language is placed in historical context. Moreover, until today this Court never had held that § 1983 encompasses all purely statutory claims. Past treatment of the subject has been incidental and far from consistent. The only firm basis for decision is the historical evidence, which convincingly shows that the phrase the Court now finds so clear was—and remains—nothing more than a shorthand reference to equal rights legislation enacted by Congress. To read "and laws" more broadly is to ignore the lessons of history, logic, and policy.

* * *

Blind reliance on plain meaning is particularly inappropriate where, as here, Congress inserted the critical language without explicit discussion when it revised the statutes in 1874. * * * Indeed, not a single shred of evidence in the legislative history of the adoption of the 1874 revision mentions this change. Since the legislative history also shows that the revision generally was not intended to alter the meaning of existing law * * * this Court previously has insisted that apparent changes be scrutinized with some care. As Mr. Justice Holmes observed, the Revised Statutes are "not lightly to be read as making a change. * * *" United States v. Sischo, 262 U.S. 165, 168–169, 43 S.Ct. 511, 512, 67 L.Ed. 925 (1923).

* * *

A

Section 1983 derives from § 1 of the Civil Rights Act of 1871, which provided a cause of action for deprivations of constitutional rights only. "Laws" were not mentioned. Act of Apr. 20, 1871, 17 Stat. 13. The phrase "and laws" was added in 1874, when Congress consolidated the laws of the United States into a single volume under a new subject-matter arrangement. See 2 Cong.Rec. 827 (Jan. 21, 1874) (remarks of Rep. Lawrence). Consequently, the intent of Congress in 1874 is central to this case.

* * *

In my view, the legislative history unmistakably shows that the variations in phrasing introduced in the 1874 revision were inadvertent, and that each section was intended to have precisely the same scope. * * *

* * *

The Court's opinion does not consider the nature or scope of the litigation it has authorized. In practical effect, today's decision means that state and local governments, officers, and employees now may face liability whenever a person believes he has been injured by the administration of *any* federal-state cooperative program, whether or not that program is related to equal or civil rights.

1

Even a cursory survey of the United States Code reveals that literally hundreds of cooperative regulatory and social welfare enactments may be affected. The States now participate in the enforcement of federal laws governing migrant labor, noxious weeds, historic preservation, wildlife conservation, anadromous fisheries, scenic trails, and strip mining. Various statutes authorize federal-state cooperative agreements in most aspects of federal land management. In addition, federal grants administered by state and local governments now are available in virtually every area of public administration. Unemployment, Medicaid, school lunch subsidies, food stamps, and other welfare benefits may provide particularly inviting subjects of litigation. Federal assistance also includes a variety of subsidies for education, housing, health care, transportation, public works, and law enforcement. Those who might benefit from these grants now will be potential § 1983 plaintiffs.

No one can predict the extent to which litigation arising from today's decision will harass state and local officials; nor can one foresee the number of new filings in our already overburdened courts. But no one can doubt that these consequences will be substantial. And the Court advances no reason to believe that any Congress—from 1874 to the present day—intended this expansion of federally imposed liability on state defendants.

Moreover, state and local governments will bear the entire burden of liability for violations of statutory "civil rights" even when federal officials are involved equally in the administration of the affected program. Section 1983 grants no right of action against the United States, and few of the foregoing cooperative programs provide expressly for private actions to enforce their terms. * * *

* * *

Today's decision confers upon the courts unprecedented authority to oversee state actions that have little or nothing to do with the individual rights defined and enforced by the civil rights legislation of the Reconstruction era. This result cannot be reconciled with the purposes for which § 1983 was enacted. * * *

Notes

1. **State Law Violations.** To come within § 1983, a party must allege deprivation of a *federal* right. Violation of state law does not constitute a § 1983 cause of action (Williams v. Treen, 671 F.2d 892 (5th Cir.1982, cert. denied 459 U.S. 1126, 103 S.Ct. 762, 74 L.Ed.2d 977 (1983) unless that violation gives rise to a deprivation of a constitutional liberty or property right or of a federal statutory right. For example, deprivation of a property right created by state law that is protection by constitutional due process requirements which are not met, would give rise to a federal due process deprivation that qualifies for § 1983 protection. Goss v. Lopez, 419 U.S. 565, 95 S.Ct. 729, 42 L.Ed.2d 725 (1975).

2. **Federal Law Violations Not Reached by § 1983.** Notwithstanding its broad language in *Monell*, the Supreme Court later ruled that not every federal statute violation is remediable under § 1983. As the Supreme Court declared in the following principal case: "The crucial consideration is what Congress intended" with respect to each substantive statute. 468 U.S. at 1012, 104 S.Ct. at 3469–70, 82 L.Ed.2d 746 at 765. Where the statutory source (of the right allegedly deprived) reveals a Congressional intent to make the remedies provided by that statute exclusive of all others, and not to be

supplemented by § 1983 remedies, the Court has held § 1983 to be inapplicable. The authorities make clear, however, that the issue of exclusivity between § 1983 and substantive rights statutes is not an "all or none" proposition, i.e., that for certain violations the Court may find a congressional intent to exclude § 1983 remedies, whereas for other violations of the same or similar statutes, it may find congressional intent to permit supplemental § 1983 remedies. The question of intent to exclude alternate remedies may thus turn on two factors, namely: (a) intent to exclude *all* 1983 causes of action under a given statute; or (b) intent to preclude recovery for certain kinds of deprivation or for certain elements of damages under a particular statute while permitting § 1983 recovery for other classes of deprivation or damages under that same statute. The sorting out of these issues will vary from statute to statute. The following *Smith* opinion provides some illustration of the complexity of the ad hoc approach taken by the United States Supreme Court in implying or denying private causes of § 1983 actions. Compare e.g., Smith v. Robinson (which follows these notes), denying § 1983 relief for violations of the Education for the Handicapped Children Act; Day v. Wayne County Bd. of Auditors, 749 F.2d 1199 (6th Cir.1984), holding Title VII remedies to be exclusive; *semble,* Great American Federal Savings & Loan Assn. v. Novotny, 442 U.S. 366, 99 S.Ct. 2345, 60 L.Ed.2d 957 (1979) (Title VII remedies excluded remedies under § 42 U.S.C.A. § 1985(3)); Middlesex County Sewerage Authority v. National Sea Clammers Assn., 453 U.S. 1, 101 S.Ct. 2615, 69 L.Ed.2d 435 (1981) (federal environmental and conservation statutes excluded remedies under § 1983), with Johnson v. Railway Exp. Agency, 421 U.S. 454, 95 S.Ct. 1716, 44 L.Ed.2d 295 (1975) (availability of Title VII remedy for racial employment discrimination did not exclude remedy for racial discrimination under 42 U.S.C.A. § 1981); Grano v. Department of Development of City of Columbus, 637 F.2d 1073 (6th Cir.1980) (Concurrent violation of constitutional and Title VII rights may be remedied as to constitutional rights, under § 1983).

Given the Supreme Court rulings regarding the application of § 1983 remedies, to other federal statutes, the full import of § 1983 will take years to determine. For more extensive discussion of the relation of § 1983 causes of action to specific violations under specific federal civil rights statutes, see W.D. Valente, *Education Law—Public and Private,* chs. 17 and 18 (1985); Annot, Title VII and § 1983, 78 A.L.R.Fed. 492 (1986).

SMITH v. ROBINSON

Supreme Court of the United States, 1984.
468 U.S. 992, 104 S.Ct. 3457, 82 L.Ed.2d 746.

[Suit seeking § 1983 equitable and monetary relief, arising from alleged deprivation of educational rights, under the Education For All Handicapped Children Act (EHA), and the Rehabilitation Act, as well as deprivation of due process and equal protection under the federal constitution. In view of hopeless conflicts in the lower courts, the Supreme Court undertook review.]

BLACKMUN, J.

* * *

As petitioners emphasize, their § 1983 claims were not based on alleged violations of the EHA, but on independent claims of constitutional deprivations. As the Court of Appeals recognized, however, petitioners' constitutional claims, a denial of due process and a denial of a free appropriate public education as guaranteed by the Equal Protection Clause, are virtually identical to their EHA claims. The question to be asked, therefore, is whether Congress intended that the EHA be the exclusive avenue through which a plaintiff may assert those claims.

We have little difficulty concluding that Congress intended the EHA to be the exclusive avenue through which a plaintiff may assert an equal protection claim to a publicly financed special education. The EHA is a comprehensive scheme set up by Congress * * *. Both the provisions of the statute and its legislative history indicate that Congress intended handicapped children with constitutional claims to a free appropriate public education to pursue those claims through the carefully tailored administrative and judicial mechanism set out in the statute.

* * *

In light of the comprehensive nature of the procedures and guarantees set out in the EHA and Congress' express efforts to place on local and state educational agencies the primary responsibility for developing a plan to accommodate the needs of each individual handicapped child, we find it difficult to believe that Congress also meant to leave undisturbed the ability of a handicapped child to go directly to court with an equal protection claim to a free appropriate public education. Not only would such a result render superfluous most of the detailed procedural protections outlined in the statute, but, more important, it would run counter to Congress' view that the needs of handicapped children are best accommodated by having the parents and the local education agency work together to formulate an individualized plan for each handicapped child's education. No federal district court presented with a constitutional claim to a public education can duplicate that process.

We do not lightly conclude that Congress intended to preclude reliance on § 1983 as a remedy for a substantial equal protection claim. * * * Nevertheless, § 1983 is a statutory remedy and Congress retains the authority to repeal it or replace it with an alternative remedy. The crucial consideration is what Congress intended. * * *

* * * We conclude, therefore, that where the EHA is available to a handicapped child asserting a right to a free appropriate public education, based either on the EHA or on the Equal Protection Clause of the Fourteenth Amendment, the EHA is the exclusive avenue through which the child and his parents or guardian can pursue their claim.

Petitioners also made a due process challenge to the partiality of the state hearing officer. The question whether this claim will support an award of attorney's fees has two aspects—whether the procedural safeguards set but in the EHA manifest Congress' intent to preclude resort to § 1983 on a due process challenge and, if not, whether petitioners are entitled to attorney's fees for their due process claim. We find it unnecessary to resolve the first question, because we are satisfied that even if an independent due process challenge may be maintained, petitioners are not entitled to attorney's fees for their particular claim.

* * *

We turn, finally, to petitioners' claim that they were entitled to fees under § 505 of the Rehabilitation Act, because they asserted a substantial claim for relief under § 504 of that Act.

Much of our analysis of petitioners' equal protection claim is applicable here. The EHA is a comprehensive scheme designed by Congress as the most effective way to protect the right of a handicapped child to a free appropriate public education. * * *

* * *

We emphasize the narrowness of our holding. We do not address a situation where the EHA is not available or where § 504 guarantees substantive rights greater than those available under the EHA. We hold only that where, as here, whatever remedy might be provided under § 504 is provided with more clarity and precision under the EHA, a plaintiff may not circumvent or enlarge on the remedies available under the EHA by resort to § 504.

* * *

Notes

1. **Niches for § 1983 Damages.** The above opinion left two doors ajar for monetary recovery, notwithstanding the exclusive remedial scheme of the Education for the Handicapped Act (E.H.A.) namely, (1) for monetary losses directly under the E.H.A. statute; and (2) for § 1983 monetary recovery for deprivations that could not be redressed under E.H.A.

As to the first ground, see, e.g., Burlington School Committee v. Department of Education, 471 U.S. 359, 105 S.Ct. 1996, 85 L.Ed.2d 385 (1985), where the Court found that the Education for Handicapped Act authorized courts to order monetary reimbursement to parents who were required to incur private school expenses for their child's education which was improperly denied by the state education authorities under EHA.

For an illustration of the second exception, see, e.g., Manecke v. School Board, 762 F.2d 912 (11th Cir.1985), wherein the court held that a § 1983 action for due process violation would lie where the local education agency totally denied that child access to any administrative hearings proceedings required by the EHA. After carefully reviewing many pertinent authorities and noting the complexity of the issues, the court declared: "Lest our holding be broadly construed, we now emphasize its narrowness. We do not hold that § 1983 may be employed whenever a procedural deprivation occurs in the EHA context. We simply conclude that, under the facts of the instant case, the plaintiff properly invoked § 1983." Id. at p. 924.

The cases do not provide a uniform answer to the question—when does a due process deprivation under a substantive rights statute leave no adequate remedy under the substantive statute as to justify an independent § 1983 remedy? That issue must continue to be decided ad hoc particular actions as well as ad hoc particular statutes.

2. THE COLOR OF LAW REQUIREMENT

POLK COUNTY, et al. v. DODSON

Supreme Court of the United States, 1981.
454 U.S. 312, 102 S.Ct. 445, 70 L.Ed.2d 509.

JUSTICE POWELL delivered the opinion of the Court.

The question in this case is whether a public defender acts "under color of state law" when representing an indigent defendant in a state criminal proceeding.

I

* * * Dodson brought the action in federal court under 42 U.S.C. § 1983. As the factual basis for his lawsuit Dodson alleged that Martha Shepard, an attorney in the Polk County Offender Advocate's office, had failed to represent him adequately in an appeal to the Iowa Supreme Court.

A full-time employee of the County, Shepard had been assigned to represent Dodson in the appeal of a conviction for robbery. After inquiring into the case, however, she moved for permission to withdraw as counsel on the ground that Dodson's claims were wholly frivolous. Shepard accompanied her motion with an affidavit explaining this conclusion. She also filed a memorandum summarizing Dodson's claims and the supporting legal arguments. On November 9, 1979, the Iowa Supreme Court granted the motion to withdraw and dismissed Dodson's appeal.

In his complaint in the District Court the respondent alleged that Shepard's actions, * * * had deprived him of his right to counsel, subjected him to cruel and unusual punishment, and denied him due process of law. He sought injunctive relief as well as damages in the amount of $175,000. To establish that Shepard acted "under color of state law," a jurisdictional requisite for a § 1983 action, Dodson relied on her employment by the county. Dodson also sued Polk County, the Polk County Offender Advocate, and the Polk County Board of Supervisors. He alleged that the Offender Advocate and the Board of Supervisors had established the rules and procedures that Shepard was bound to follow in handling criminal appeals.

The District Court dismissed Dodson's claims against all defendants. * * * It held that the relevant actions by Shepard had not occurred under color of state law. Canvassing the leading authorities, it reasoned that a public defender owes a duty of undivided loyalty to his client. A public defender therefore could not be sued as an agent of the State. The District Court dismissed the Offender Advocate's Office from the suit on the same theory. It also held that Dodson's complaint failed to allege the requisite personal involvement to state a § 1983 claim against Polk County and the Board of Supervisors.

The Court of Appeals for the Eighth Circuit reversed. * * *

* * *

We granted certiorari to resolve the division among the Courts of Appeals over whether a public defender acts under color of state law when providing representation to an indigent client. We now reverse.

II

In United States v. Classic, 313 U.S. 299, 326, 61 S.Ct. 1031, 1043, 85 L.Ed. 1368 (1941), this Court held that a person acts under color of state law only when exercising power "possessed by virtue of state law and made possible only because the wrongdoer is clothed with the authority of state law." In this case the Offender Advocate for Polk County assigned Martha Shepard to represent Russell Dodson in the appeal of his criminal conviction. This assignment entailed functions and obligations in no way dependent on state authority. From the moment of her appointment Shepard became Dodson's lawyer, and Dodson became Shepard's client. Except for the source of payment, their relationship became identical to that existing between any other lawyer and client. * * *

* * *

The respondent argues that a public defender's employment relationship with the State, rather than his function, should determine whether he acts under color of state law. We take a different view.

A

In arguing that the employment relationship establishes that the public defender acts under color of state law, Dodson relies heavily on two cases in which this Court assumed that physicians, whose relationships with their patients have not traditionally depended on state authority, could be held liable under § 1983. See O'Connor v. Donaldson, 422 U.S. 563, 95 S.Ct. 2486, 45 L.Ed.2d 396 (1975); Estelle v. Gamble, 429 U.S. 97, 97 S.Ct. 285, 50 L.Ed.2d 251 (1976). * * * Like the physicians in O'Connor and Estelle, a public defender is paid by the State. Further, like the institutionalized patients in those cases, an indigent convict is unable to choose the professional who will render him traditionally private services. These factors, it is argued, establish that public defenders—like physicians in state hospitals—act under color of state law and are amenable to suit under § 1983.

In our view O'Connor and Estelle are distinguishable from this case. O'Connor involved claims against a psychiatrist who served as the superintendent at a state mental hospital. Although a physician

* * * he was sued in his capacity as a state custodian and administrator. Unlike a lawyer, the administrator of a state hospital owes no duty of "undivided loyalty" to his patients. On the contrary, it is his function to protect the interest of the public as well as that of his wards. Similarly, *Estelle* involved a physician who was the medical director of the Texas Department of Corrections and also the chief medical officer of a prison hospital. He saw his patients in a custodial as well as a medical capacity.

Because of their custodial and supervisory functions, the State-employed doctors in *O'Connor* and *Estelle* faced their employer in a very different posture than does a public defender. * * *

* * * Because public defenders are paid by the State, it is argued that they are subject to supervision by persons with interests unrelated to those of indigent clients. Although the employment relationship is certainly a relevant factor, we find it insufficient to establish that a public defender acts under color of state law within the meaning of § 1983.

First, a public defender is not amenable to administrative direction in the same sense as other employees of the State. * * * State decisions may determine the quality of his law library or the size of his caseload. But a defense lawyer is not, and by the nature of his function cannot be, the servant of an administrative superior. * * *

Second, and equally important, it is the constitutional obligation of the State to respect the professional independence of the public defenders whom it engages. * * *

* * · *

In concluding that Shepard did not act under color of state law * * * we do not suggest that a public defender never acts in that role. In Branti v. Finkel, 445 U.S. 507 (1980), for example, we found that a public defender so acted when making hiring and firing decisions on behalf of the State. It may be—although the question is not present in this case—that a public defender also would act under color of state law while performing certain administrative and possibly investigative functions. Cf. Imbler v. Pachtman, 424 U.S. 409, 430–431 and n. 33, 96 S.Ct. 984, 995–996 and n. 33, 47 L.Ed.2d 128 (1976). And of course we intimate no views as to a public defender's liability for malpractice in an appropriate case under state tort law. See Ferri v. Ackerman, 444 U.S. 193, 198, 100 S.Ct. 402, 406, 62 L.Ed.2d 355 (1979). With respect to Dodson's § 1983 claims against Shepard, we decide only that a public defender does not act under color of state law when performing a lawyer's traditional functions as counsel to a defendant in a criminal proceeding. Because it was based on such activities, the complaint against Shepard must be dismissed.

V

In his complaint in the District Court, Dodson also asserted § 1983 claims against the Offender Advocate, Polk County, and the Polk

County Board of Supervisors. Section 1983 will not support a claim based on a *respondeat superior* theory of liability. Monnell v. Department of Social Services, 436 U.S. 658, 694, 98 S.Ct. 2018, 2037, 56 L.Ed. 2d 611 (1978). To the extent that Dodson's claims rest on this basis, they fail to present a federal claim.

* * *

* * * In Monell v. Department of Social Services, supra, we held that official policy must be "the moving force of the constitutional violation" in order to establish the liability of a government body under § 1983. *Id.*, at 694. See Rizzo v. Goode, 423 U.S. 362, 370–377, 96 S.Ct. 598, 603–607, 46 L.Ed.2d 561 (1976). * * * In this case the respondent failed to allege any policy that arguably violated his rights under the Sixth, Eighth, or Fourteenth Amendments. He did assert that assistant public defenders refused to prosecute certain appeals on grounds of their frivolity. But a policy of withdrawal from frivolous cases would not violate the Constitution. Anders v. California, 386 U.S. 738, 87 S.Ct. 1396, 18 L.Ed.2d 493 (1967). * * * Respondent further asserted that he personally was deprived of a Sixth Amendment right to effective counsel. Again, however, he failed to allege that this deprivation was caused by any constitutionally forbidden rule or procedure.

* * * Accordingly, his claims against them must be dismissed.

Notes

1. **§ 1983 "Color of Law" Coverage.** The holding that local government action is taken under "color of law" was recently extended to include a regional bi-state agency created by interstate compact. Since there was considerable involvement of counties and cities in the funding and staffing of the agency board; and since its land use function was one normally performed by local governments, the court ruled that it should be treated as a local government entity, and not as "an arm of the state" as to bar suit under the Eleventh Amendment. Lake Country Estates, Inc. v. Tahoe Regional Planning Agency, 440 U.S. 391, 99 S.Ct. 1171, 59 L.Ed.2d 409 (1979). That opinion, however, recognized the possibility of so arranging an interstate compact, its structure and operations—to show a clear intent by the participating states and Congress to create a system of state governance that might qualify for Eleventh Amendment sovereign immunity.

2. **Private Actions That Qualify as "Color of Law" Action.** The fact that an individual is not a government agent does not always exempt him from the "color of law" coverage of § 1983. See Tower v. Glover, 467 U.S. 914, 104 S.Ct. 2820, 81 L.Ed.2d 758 (1984) reported at p. 972, infra, wherein a Public Defender was held to act under color of law when conspiring with public officials to deprive a party of constitutional rights. Accord: Dennis v. Sparks, 449 U.S. 24, 101 S.Ct. 183, 66 L.Ed.2d 185 (1980).

The nature and degree of private involvement with official action that gives color of law to private conduct is (like "state action") not objectively defined, but rests upon the quantum of interdependence between private and official parties. Compare e.g. Lugar v. Edmonson Oil Co., 457 U.S. 992,

102 S.Ct. 2744, 73 L.Ed.2d 482 (1982) with Rendell-Baker v. Kohn, 457 U.S. 830, 102 S.Ct. 2764, 73 L.Ed.2d 418 (1982).

3. **Municipal Liability for Acts of Private Parties.** For possible municipal liability for acts performed by non-government entities under contract, license or franchise, see Little, McPherson & Healy, *Section 1983 Liability of Municipalities and Private Entities Operating Under Color of Municipal Law,* 14 Stetson L.Rev. 565 (1985).

4. **Alternatives to § 1983 in Absence of Color of Law.** While a local government entity cannot be held for acts that lack "color of law", it may still be subject to remedies directly under other civil rights statutes which impose no "color of law" requirement. See e.g. Johnson v. Railway Express Agency, Inc., 421 U.S. 454, 95 S.Ct. 1716, 44 L.Ed.3d 295 (1975) (direct action under civil war statute, 42 U.S.C.A. § 1981).

3. THE POLICY OR CUSTOM REQUIREMENT

"An allegation that city officials were acting in furtherance of their duty to enforce the Philadelphia Code * * * only establishes that they were acting under color of law. In order to create liability for deprivation of civil rights on the part of the municipality, it is necessary to establish that the unconstitutional actions taken by the City's representatives were the product of official policy, or represented customary behavior * * *." See Hassell v. Philadelphia, 507 F.Supp. 814, 816 (E.D.Pa.1981)

"Color of law" only shows that the actor somehow involved government authority. It does not establish that the actor's conduct was directed by official policy or custom. The issue then becomes one of identifying parties who qualify as policymakers for specified challenged conduct; and of ascertaining when and how (other than official written directives) policies arise from individual acts. As the following cases demonstrate, these questions are extremely fact-sensitive.

PEMBAUR v. CINCINNATI et al.

Supreme Court of the United States, 1986.
475 U.S. ___, 106 S.Ct. 1292, 89 L.Ed.2d 452.

[*Decision:* County prosecutor's instructions to deputy sheriffs to force entry into medical clinic to serve process on grand-jury witnesses—held to constitute an official policy decision and to subject county to § 1983 liability.]

* * *

Monell is a case about responsibility. In the first part of the opinion, we held that local government units could be made liable under § 1983 for deprivations of federal rights, * * *. In the second part of the opinion, we recognized a limitation on this liability and concluded that a municipality cannot be made liable by application of the doctrine of *respondeat superior.* * * *

The conclusion that tortious conduct, to be the basis for municipal liability under § 1983, must be pursuant to a municipality's "official

policy" is contained in this discussion. The "official policy" requirement was intended to distinguish acts of the *municipality* from acts of
employees of the municipality, and thereby make clear that municipal
liability is limited to action for which the municipality is actually
responsible. *Monell* reasoned that recovery from a municipality is
limited to acts that are, properly speaking, acts "of the municipality"—
that is, acts which the municipality has officially sanctioned or ordered.

With this understanding, it is plain that municipal liability may be
imposed for a single decision by municipal policymakers under appropriate circumstances. No one has ever doubted, for instance, that a
municipality may be liable under § 1983 for a single decision by its
properly constituted legislative body—whether or not that body had
taken similar action in the past or intended to do so in the future—
because even a single decision by such a body unquestionably constitutes an act of official government policy. See, *e.g., Owen v. City of
Independence,* 445 U.S. 622, 100 S.Ct. 1398, 63 L.Ed.2d 673 (1980) (city
council passed resolution firing plaintiff without a pretermination
hearing); *Newport v. Fact Concerts, Inc.,* 453 U.S. 247, 101 S.Ct. 2748, 69
L.Ed.2d 616 (1981) (city council cancelled license permitting concert
because of dispute over content of performance). But the power to
establish policy is no more the exclusive province of the legislature at
the local level than at the state or national level. *Monell*'s language
makes clear that it expressly envisioned other officials "whose acts or
edicts may fairly be said to represent official policy," *Monell, supra,* 436
U.S., at 694, 98 S.Ct., at 2037–2038, and whose decisions therefore may
give rise to municipal liability under § 1983.

 * * * To be sure, "official policy" often refers to formal rules or
understandings—often but not always committed to writing—that are
intended to, and do, establish fixed plans of action to be followed under
similar circumstances consistently and over time. That was the case in
Monell itself, * * *. However, as in *Owen* and *Newport,* a government frequently chooses a course of action tailored to a particular
situation and not intended to control decisions in later situations. If
the decision to adopt that particular course of action is properly made
by that government's authorized decisionmakers, it surely represents
an act of official government "policy" as that term is commonly
understood. More importantly, where action is directed by those who
establish governmental policy, the municipality is equally responsible
whether that action is to be taken only once or to be taken repeatedly.
To deny compensation to the victim would therefore be contrary to the
fundamental purpose of § 1983.

Having said this much, we hasten to emphasize that not every
decision by municipal officers automatically subjects the municipality
to § 1983 liability. Municipal liability attaches only where the decisionmaker possesses final authority to establish municipal policy with
respect to the action ordered. The fact that a particular official—even
a policymaking official—has discretion in the exercise of particular

functions does not, without more, give rise to municipal liability based on an exercise of that discretion. See *e.g., Oklahoma City v. Tuttle,* 471 U.S., at ___, 105 S.Ct., at ___. The official must also be responsible for establishing final government policy respecting such activity before the municipality can be held liable.[12] Authority to make municipal policy may be granted directly by a legislative enactment or may be delegated by an official who possesses such authority, and of course, whether an official had final policymaking authority is a question of state law. However, like other governmental entities, municipalities often spread policymaking authority among various officers and official bodies. As a result, particular officers may have authority to establish binding county policy respecting particular matters and to adjust that policy for the county in changing circumstances. To hold a municipality liable for actions ordered by such officers exercising their policymaking authority is no more an application of the theory of *respondeat superior* than was holding the municipalities liable for the decisions of the city councils in *Owen* and *Newport.* In each case municipal liability attached to a single decision to take unlawful action made by municipal policymakers. We hold that municipal liability under § 1983 attaches where—and only where—a deliberate choice to follow a course of action is made from among various alternatives by the official or officials responsible for establishing final policy with respect to the subject matter in question. See *Tuttle, supra,* at ___, 105 S.Ct., at 2436 ("'policy' generally implies a course of action chosen from among various alternatives").

C

Applying this standard to the case before us, we have little difficulty concluding that the Court of Appeals erred in dismissing petitioner's claim against the county. The Deputy Sheriffs who attempted to serve the capiases at petitioner's clinic found themselves in a difficult situation. Unsure of the proper course of action to follow, they sought instruction from their supervisors. The instructions they received were to follow the orders of the County Prosecutor. The Prosecutor made a considered decision based on his understanding of the law and commanded the officers forcibly to enter petitioner's clinic. That decision directly caused the violation of petitioner's Fourth Amendment rights.

* * *

12. Thus, for example, the County Sheriff may have discretion to hire and fire employees without also being the county official responsible for establishing county employment policy. If this were the case, the Sheriff's decisions respecting employment would not give rise to municipal liability, although similar decisions with respect to law enforcement practices, over which the Sheriff *is* the offical policymaker, *would* give rise to municipal liability. Instead, if county employment policy was set by the Board of County Commissioners, only that body's decisions would provide a basis for county liability. This would be true even if the Board left the Sheriff discretion to hire and fire employees and the Sheriff exercised that discretion in an unconstitutional manner; the decision to act unlawfully would not be a decision of the Board. However, if the Board delegated its power to establish final employment policy to the Sheriff, the Sheriff's decisions *would* represent county policy and could give rise to municipal liability.

Notes

1. **Single Act as "Policy" Making.** *Pembaur* cited with approval the Court's earlier decision (*Oklahoma City v. Tuttle*) that a policy of inadequate police training could not be inferred from a single shooting incident. The question thus becomes, not whether a single action can create policy, but whether: (1) the actor is "responsible for establishing final government policy; (2) the actor made a "deliberate choice to follow a course of action ＊ ＊ ＊ from among various alternatives . . . with respect to the subject matter in question. Cf. Rhode v. San Jacinto County, 776 F.2d 107 (5th Cir. 1985) (County held not liable for civil rights violation of County Constable who lacked official policy power with respect to his tortious decisions).

2. **Discretion v. Policy.** As the text, and particularly footnote 12 of *Pembaur* makes clear, "discretion" is not the same as policymaking authority. What distinguishes the two—level of delegated authority? If so, how are lawyers, judges, (and worse, juries) to decide when policymaking authority is reserved at one level of office or has been "redelegated" down to a lower level, so that a city has plural "ultimate" policymaking sources? The answers to these questions by lower court cases that preceded *Pembaur* and *Oklahoma City* may be unreliable, inasmuch as the latter opinions place arguably limiting glosses on the prior decisions.

3. **A Troublesome Supreme Court Footnote.** Footnote 7 to the *Oklahoma City plurality* opinion, casts a cloud on lower court decisions regarding "training" liability.

> "7. We express no opinion on whether a policy that itself is not unconstitutional, such as the general 'inadequate training' alleged here, can ever meet the 'policy' requirement of *Monell*. In addition, even assuming that such a 'policy' would suffice, it is open to question whether a policymaker's 'gross negligence' in establishing police training practices could establish a 'policy' that constitutes a 'moving force' behind subsequent unconstitutional conduct, or whether a more conscious decision on the part of the policymaker would be required." See 471 U.S. at ＿, 105 S.Ct. at 2436.

Compare the above dicta with the following opinion.

GRANDSTAFF v. BORGER, TEX.

United States Court of Appeals, Fifth Circuit, 1985.
767 F.2d 161.

REAVLEY, CIRCUIT JUDGE:

The City of Borger police mistook James C. Grandstaff for a fugitive and killed him. The estate and family of Grandstaff sued and recovered $1,430,000, together with attorneys fees and expenses, from four of the officers as well as the City. We uphold the liability of the officers on both the federal and state claims and the damages award because of Texas law; we sustain the 42 U.S.C. § 1983 liability of the City but modify the damages recovered against it.

* * *

III. Municipal Liability

The City of Borger enjoys governmental immunity from the state tort claim. The liability of the City therefore depends upon the scope of 42 U.S.C. § 1983. * * * There must be (1) a policy (2) of the city's policymaker (3) that caused (4) the plaintiff to be subjected to a deprivation of constitutional right. *Monell v. Department of Social Services,* 436 U.S. 658, 98 S.Ct. 2018, 56 L.Ed.2d 611 (1978); *Bennett v. City of Slidell,* 728 F.2d 762 (5th Cir.1984) (en banc), *cert. denied,* ___ U.S. ___, 105 S.Ct. 3476, 87 L.Ed.2d 612 (1985); *Webster v. City of Houston,* 735 F.2d 838 (5th Cir.) (en banc), *rev'd on other grounds,* 739 F.2d 993 (5th Cir.1984) (en banc).

There was a deprivation of a constitutional right, as held above, when the officers took the life of James Grandstaff without due process of law. And the policymaker for the City is clearly identified; the City does not deny that the police chief was its sole policymaker. Our remaining inquiry is this: was there some policy or custom or action attributable to the police chief that was a cause of Grandstaff's death? By properly identifying the policy, we decide the inquiry in the affirmative.

(a) Inadequate training as cause: In *Rizzo v. Goode,* 423 U.S. 362, 96 S.Ct. 598, 46 L.Ed.2d 561 (1976), the Supreme Court held that past constitutional violations by subordinates are not necessarily sufficient to prove a policy of the supervisor causally linked to subsequent constitutional deprivations. The Court could find "no affirmative link between the occurrence of the various incidents of police misconduct and the adoption of any plan or policy by [certain named defendants]—express or otherwise—showing their authorization or approval of such misconduct." *Id.* at 371, 96 S.Ct. at 604, 46 L.Ed.2d at 569. The Supreme Court has elaborated on the causal requirement by holding that the connection must be more than de facto; the policy must be "the moving force of the constitutional violation." *Monell,* 436 U.S. at 694, 98 S.Ct. 2037, 56 L.Ed.2d at 638; *see also Polk County v. Dodson,* 454 U.S. 312, 326, 102 S.Ct. 445, 454, 70 L.Ed.2d 509 (1981).

An "inadequate" training program alone is not ordinarily the moving force behind an injured plaintiff's harm, because the police officer who injures the plaintiff does not rely upon inadequate training as tacit approval of his conduct. It is not enough that the city could, but does not, reduce the risk of harm to the plaintiff. *See Milligan v. City of Newport News,* 743 F.2d 227 (4th Cir.1984); *Dunn v. Tennessee,* 697 F.2d 121, 128 (6th Cir.1982), *cert. denied,* 460 U.S. 1086, 103 S.Ct. 1778, 76 L.Ed.2d 349 (1983); *Wilson v. Beebe,* 612 F.2d 275 (6th Cir. 1980); *Watson v. Interstate Fire & Casualty Co.,* 611 F.2d 120 (5th Cir. 1980); *Kostka v. Hogg,* 560 F.2d 37 (1st Cir.1977). Nor does it satisfy the causal link/moving force requirement to prove that a supervisor has failed to satisfy a general responsibility to supervise employees imposed by state law. *But see Sims v. Adams,* 537 F.2d 829 (5th Cir. 1976).

* * *

The Supreme Court last spoke on the policy requirement of § 1983 in *Tuttle v. Oklahoma City,* ___ U.S. ___, 105 S.Ct. 2427, 85 L.Ed.2d 791 (1985). In *Tuttle,* inadequate training was asserted as a basis of municipal liability under section 1983. *Id.* at ___, 105 S.Ct. at 2433. Justice Rehnquist, writing for the plurality, reserved the question whether a policy not itself unconstitutional, such as inadequate training, could be a policy under *Monell. Id.* at ___ n. 7, 105 S.Ct. at 2436 n. 7. Justice Rehnquist, however, wrote that until the Court answered that question a plaintiff relying on a policy not itself unconstitutional must have considerable proof that the policy was causally related to the constitutional deprivation, *id.* at ___ & n. 8, 105 S.Ct. at 2436 & n. 8, and that to be a policy, inadequate training must be a product of a conscious choice, *id.* at ___ & n. 7, 105 S.Ct. at 2436 & n. 7. Justice Brennan, writing for three justices, would not require that the city policy in itself be unconstitutional so long as the city is at fault for the damage suffered. He sees a more indirect causal link permitted by the statutory language * * *.

We cannot know what conscious choices on the part of the city policymaker would carry the Court's policy/cause hurdle. It may not be enough that the policymaker demonstrates a conscious lack of concern whether the police force is well trained or poorly trained. We doubt that a finding of "gross" negligence in that training will always be the ticket to municipal liability. *But see Turpin v. Mailet,* 619 F.2d 196, 201–02 (2d Cir.), *cert. denied,* 449 U.S. 1016, 101 S.Ct. 577, 66 L.Ed. 2d 475 (1980); *Reeves v. City of Jackson,* 608 F.2d 644, 652–53 (5th Cir. 1979); *Owens v. Haas,* 601 F.2d 1242, 1246–47 (2d Cir.), *cert. denied,* 444 U.S. 980, 100 S.Ct. 483, 62 L.Ed.2d 407 (1979).

(b) The city policy/custom of dangerous recklessness: If there is a reckless disregard for human life and safety prevalent among the city's police officers which threatens the life and security of those whom they encounter, and if that recklessness is attributable to the instruction or example or acceptance of or by the city policymaker, the policy itself is a repudiation of constitutional rights. Where police officers know at the time they act that their use of deadly force in conscious disregard of the rights and safety of innocent third parties will meet with the approval of city policymakers, the affirmative link/moving force requirement is satisfied.

That was the rationale of this court in *Languirand v. Hayden,* 717 F.2d 220 (5th Cir.1983), *cert. denied,* ___ U.S. ___, 104 S.Ct. 2656, 81 L.Ed.2d 363 (1984). Conscious indifference to widespread incompetence or misbehavior may be more than a matter of extreme negligence and more than a failure to instruct or train. If it is the deliberate police policy to demand instant compliance, heedless of rights and risks, abuses—i.e., incompetence and misbehavior—will occur when officers of varying judgment and stability encounter resistance. * * * Where the city policymaker knows or should know that the city's police officers are likely to shoot to kill without justification and without restraint, so as to endanger innocent third parties, the city should be liable when the inevitable occurs and the officers do so.

* * *

Notes

1. **Semble:** Kibbe v. Springfield, 777 F.2d 801 (1st Cir.1985). Cf. Berry v. McLemore, 670 F.2d 30 (5th Cir.1982) (Town not liable for use of excessive police force absent proof of policy or custom on such practice).

2. **Negligence v. Unconstitutional Policy or Custom.** The ambit of governmental liability under § 1983 for due process violations was narrowed further by very recent Supreme Court decisions. In Daniels v. Williams, ___ U.S. ___, 106 S.Ct. 662, 88 L.Ed.2d 662 (1986), and in Davidson v. Cannon, ___ U.S. ___, 106 S.Ct. 668, 88 L.Ed.2d 677 (1986), the Court held that prison inmates had no cognizable § 1983 civil rights action for injuries arising from negligent conduct of prison officials.

> "We conclude that the Due Process Clause is simply not implicated by a negligent act of an official causing unintended loss of or injury to life, liberty or property." 106 S.Ct. at p. 663.

These decisions were viewed as overruling an earlier case (Parratt v. Taylor, 451 U.S. 527, 101 S.Ct. 1908, 68 L.Ed.2d 420 (1981)) which suggested that a negligent act could work a constitutional due process deprivation. See, e.g., Williams v. Boston, 784 F.2d 430 (1st Cir.1986), at p. 434, n. 4. *Williams* held that negligent failure to provide adequate security at racially tense school events did not effect a due process violation, notwithstanding allegation that policy making officials negligently established a custom or policy of providing inadequate security.

The foregoing cases do not fully answer the question—when does official neglect create an official policy or custom?

3. **Negligent Supervision v. Custom.** The courts are not agreed on the line separating nonactionable negligence from custom arising from inaction. In Bowen v. Watkins, 669 F.2d 979 (5th Cir.1982), the court observed: "Usually, a failure to supervise gives rise to § 1983 liability only in those situations in which there is a history of widespread abuse." Id. at p. 988. But the court there also cited Knight v. Colorado, 496 F.Supp. 779 (D.Colo.1980), wherein the court found no liability, in spite of history of abuses, because supervisors took action to prevent further abuses. The Eighth Circuit, however, found a custom, or informal policy, from municipality's continuing failure to remedy known unconstitutional conduct of police offers. Herrera v. Valentine, 653 F.2d 1220 (8th Cir.1981). In a case falling between the two prior cases, the Eleventh Circuit held that failure of supervisors to correct an unconstitutional practice of booking arrestees presented a question for the jury as to whether the practice ripened into a "custom" to support § 1983 recovery. Trezevant v. Tampa, 741 F.2d 336 (11th Cir.1984). Cf. Alberts v. New York, 549 F.Supp. 227 (S.D.N.Y.1982);

Ybarra v. Reno Thunderbird Mobile Home Village, 723 F.2d 675 (9th Cir. 1984).

4. **Administrative Regulation as Policy.** A regulation delaying disciplinary investigation of officers' misconduct was held sufficient to create a policy giving rise to § 1983 liability. Black v. Stephens, 662 F.2d 181 (3d Cir.1981).

4. THE CAUSATION REQUIREMENT

A custom or policy that authorizes deprivation of civil rights will not be actionable under § 1983 if the official acting thereunder did not, *in fact,* deprive the claimant of any federal right:

> "[N]either Monell v. New York City Department of Social Services
> * * * nor any other of our cases authorizes the award of damages
> against a municipal corporation based on the actions of one of its
> officers when in fact the jury has concluded that the officer inflicted no
> constitutional harm. If a person has suffered no constitutional injury
> * * * the fact that the departmental regulation might have *authoriz-
> ed* the use of constitutional excessive force is quite beside the point."
> See City of Los Angeles v. Heller, ___ U.S. ___, 106 S.Ct. 1571, 89 L.Ed.
> 2d 806 (1986).

In Martinez v. California, 444 U.S. 277, 100 S.Ct. 553, 62 L.Ed.2d 481 (1980), the Supreme Court affirmed dismissal of a § 1983 suit against parole officers who released a prisoner with dangerous characteristics where that prisoner, five months after release, murdered the plaintiff's kin.

> " * * * we hold that * * * appellees did not 'deprive' appel-
> lants' decedent of life within the meaning of the Fourteenth Amend-
> ment. * * *. We * * * do not decide that a parole officer could
> never be deemed to 'deprive' someone of life by action taken in
> connection with the release of a prisoner on parole. But we do hold
> that at least under particular circumstances of this parole decision,
> appellants' decedent's death is too remote a consequence of the parole
> officers' action to hold them responsible under the federal civil rights
> law. * * * [I]t is perfectly clear that not every injury in which a
> state official has played some part is actionable under that [§ 1983]
> statute." 444 U.S. at 285, 100 S.Ct. at 559.

5. IMMUNITY DEFENSES—GOVERNMENTAL UNITS

OWEN v. CITY OF INDEPENDENCE
445 U.S. 622, 63 L.Ed.2d 673, 100 S.Ct. 1398 (1980)

[Suit for deprivation of constitutional rights against City and City officials by discharged police chief. Lower courts discharged suits, holding that city and its officials enjoyed immunity under § 1983. The Supreme Court reversed as to the City].

* * *

Because the question of the scope of a municipality's immunity from liability under § 1983 is essentially one of statutory construction, see *Wood v. Strickland,* 420 U.S. 308, 314, 316, 95 S.Ct. 992, 996, 998, 43 L.Ed.2d 214 (1975); *Tenney v. Brandhove,* 341 U.S. 367, 376, 71 S.Ct. 783, 788, 95 L.Ed. 1019 (1951), the starting point in our analysis must be the language of the statute itself. * * * Its language is absolute and unqualified; no mention is made of any privileges, immunities, or defenses that may be asserted. * * *

However, notwithstanding § 1983's expansive language and the absence of any express incorporation of common-law immunities, we have, on several occasions, found that a tradition of immunity was so firmly rooted in the common law and was supported by such strong policy reasons that "Congress would have specifically so provided had it wished to abolish the doctrine." *Pierson v. Ray,* 386 U.S. 547, 555, 87 S.Ct. 1213, 1218, 18 L.Ed.2d 288 (1967). * * *

Subsequent cases have required that we consider the personal liability of various other types of government officials. Noting that "[f]ew doctrines were more solidly established at common law than the immunity of judges from liability for damages for acts committed within their judicial jurisdiction," *Pierson v. Ray, supra,* 386 U.S., at 553–554, 87 S.Ct., at 1217, held that the absolute immunity traditionally accorded judges was preserved under § 1983. In that same case, local police officers were held to enjoy a "good faith and probable cause" defense to § 1983 suits similar to that which existed in false arrest actions at common law. 386 U.S., at 555–557, 87 S.Ct., at 1218– 1219. Several more recent decisions have found immunities of varying scope appropriate for different state and local officials sued under § 1983. See *Procunier v. Navarette,* 434 U.S. 555, 98 S.Ct. 855, 55 L.Ed. 2d 24 (1978) (qualified immunity for prison officials and officers); *Imbler v. Pachtman,* 424 U.S. 409, 96 S.Ct. 984, 47 L.Ed.2d 128 (1976) (absolute immunity for prosecutors in initiating and presenting the State's case); *O'Connor v. Donaldson,* 422 U.S. 563, 95 S.Ct. 2486, 45 L.Ed.2d 396 (1975) (qualified immunity for superintendent of state hospital); *Wood v. Strickland,* 420 U.S. 308, 95 S.Ct. 992, 43 L.Ed.2d 214 (1975) (qualified immunity for local school board members); *Scheuer v. Rhodes,* 416 U.S. 232, 94 S.Ct. 1683, 40 L.Ed.2d 90 (1974) (qualified "good-faith" immunity for state Governor and other executive officers for discretionary acts performed in the course of official conduct).

In each of these cases, our finding of § 1983 immunity "was predicated upon a considered inquiry into the immunity historically accorded the relevant official at common law and the interests behind it." *Imbler v. Pachtman, supra,* at 421, 96 S.Ct., at 990. Where the immunity claimed by the defendant was well established at common law at the time § 1983 was enacted, and where its rationale was compatible with the purposes of the Civil Rights Act, we have construed the statute to incorporate that immunity. But there is no tradition of immunity for municipal corporations, and neither history nor policy supports a construction of § 1983 that would justify the qualified immunity accorded the city of Independence by the Court of Appeals. We hold, therefore, that the municipality may not assert the good faith of its officers or agents * * *.

* * *

Our rejection of a construction of § 1983 that would accord municipalities a qualified immunity for their good-faith constitutional violations is compelled both by the legislative purpose in enacting the statute and by considerations of public policy. The central aim of the Civil Rights Act was to provide protection to those persons wronged by the " '[m]isuse of power, possessed by virtue of state law and made possible only because the wrongdoer is clothed with the authority of state law.' " * * * By creating an express federal remedy, Congress sought to "enforce provisions of the Fourteenth Amendment against those who carry a badge of authority of a State and represent it in some capacity, whether they act in accordance with their authority or misuse it." *Monroe v. Pape, supra,* 365 U.S., at 172, 81 S.Ct., at 476.

How "uniquely amiss" it would be, therefore, if the government itself—* * *—were permitted to disavow liability for the injury it has begotten. * * * A damages remedy against the offending party is a vital component of any scheme for vindicating cherished constitutional guarantees, and the importance of assuring its efficacy is only accentuated when the wrongdoer is the institution that has been established to protect the very rights it has transgressed. Yet owing to the qualified immunity enjoyed by most government officials, see *Scheuer v. Rhodes,* 416 U.S. 232, 94 S.Ct. 1683, 40 L.Ed.2d 90 (1974), many victims of municipal malfeasance would be left remediless if the city were also allowed to assert a good-faith defense. Unless countervailing considerations counsel otherwise, the injustice of such a result should not be tolerated.

* * * The knowledge that a municipality will be liable for all of its injurious conduct, whether committed in good faith or not, should create an incentive for officials who may harbor doubts about the lawfulness of their intended actions to err on the side of protecting citizens' constitutional rights. Furthermore, the threat that damages might be levied against the city may encourage those in a policymaking position to institute internal rules and programs designed to minimize the likelihood of unintentional infringements on constitutional rights.

* * *

We believe that today's decision, together with prior precedents in this area, properly allocates these costs among the three principals in the scenario of the § 1983 cause of action: the victim of the constitutional deprivation; the officer whose conduct caused the injury; and the public, as represented by the municipal entity. The innocent individual who is harmed by an abuse of governmental authority is assured that he will be compensated for his injury. The offending official, so long as he conducts himself in good faith, may go about his business secure in the knowledge that a qualified immunity will protect him from personal liability for damages that are more appropriately chargeable to the populace as a whole. And the public will be forced to bear only the costs of injury inflicted by the "execution of a government's policy or custom, whether made by its lawmakers or by those whose edicts or acts may fairly be said to represent official policy."

* * *

Notes

1. **Unconstitutional Ordinances.** Municipalities are absolutely liable for unconstitutional ordinances, though their officials may enjoy qualified immunity. See e.g. Pesticide Public Policy v. Wauconda, 622 F.Supp. 423, 433 (N.D.Ill.1985).

2. **Eleventh Amendment Immunity.** The Eleventh Amendment does not apply to local governments or their officials, but only to state entities and their officials. See Papasan v. Allain, ___ U.S. ___, 106 S.Ct. 2932, 90 L.Ed.2d 209 (1986), and authorities there reviewed; Nahmod, *Damages and Injunctive Relief Under Section 1983,* 16 Urban Lawyer, 201, 210 (1984). Possible exceptions to the foregoing general rule are explained in Gary A. v. New Trier H.S. District, 796 F.2d 940 (7th Cir. 1986).

FAIR ASSESSMENT IN REAL ESTATE ASSOCIATION, INC. v. McNARY

Supreme Court of the United States, 1981.
454 U.S. 100, 102 S.Ct. 177, 70 L.Ed.2d 271.

JUSTICE REHNQUIST delivered the opinion of the Court.

In this action we are required to reconcile two somewhat intermittent and conflicting lines of authority as to whether a damages action may be brought under 42 U.S.C. § 1983 to redress the allegedly unconstitutional administration of a state tax system. The United States District Court for the Eastern District of Missouri held that such suits were barred by both 28 U.S.C. § 1341 (the Tax Injunction Act) and the principle of comity, and the Court of Appeals for the Eighth Circuit affirmed by an equally divided court sitting en banc. We granted certiorari to resolve a conflict among the Courts of Appeals, and we now affirm. * * *

I

This Court, even before the enactment of § 1983, recognized the important and sensitive nature of state tax systems and the need for federal court restraint when deciding cases that affect such systems. * * *

After this Court conclusively decided that federal courts *may* enjoin state officers from enforcing an unconstitutional state law, Ex Parte Young, 209 U.S. 123, 28 S.Ct. 441, 52 L.Ed. 714 (1908), Congress also recognized that the autonomy and fiscal stability of the States survive best when state tax systems are not subject to scrutiny in federal courts. Thus, in 1937 Congress provided:

> "The district courts shall not enjoin, suspend or restrain the assessment, levy or collection of any tax under State law where a plain, speedy and efficient remedy may be had in the courts of such State." 28 U.S.C. § 1341 (hereinafter "§ 1341" or "the Act").

This legislation, * * * reflect the fundamental principle of comity between federal courts and state governments that is essential to "Our Federalism," particularly in the area of state taxation. * * *

Contrasted with this statute and line of cases are our holdings with respect to 42 U.S.C. § 1983. * * *

Obviously § 1983 cut a broad swath. * * * The combined effect of this newly created federal cause of action and the absence of an express exhaustion requirement was not immediately realized. * * *

The immediacy of federal relief under § 1983 was reemphasized in McNeese v. Board of Education, 373 U.S. 668, 83 S.Ct. 1433, 10 L.Ed.2d 622 (1963), where the Court stated that "[i]t is immaterial" whether [the state official's] conduct is legal or illegal as a matter of state law. * * * And in the unargued Per Curiam opinion of Wilwording v. Swenson, 404 U.S. 249, 92 S.Ct. 407, 30 L.Ed.2d 418 (1971), the Court concluded that "[p]etitioners were * * * entitled to have their actions treated as claims for relief under the Civil Rights Acts, not subject * * * to exhaustion requirements." Id., at 251. * * *

Thus, we have two divergent lines of authority. * * * Both cannot govern this case. On one hand, the Tax Injunction Act, 28 U.S.C. § 1341, with its antecedent basis in the comity principle * * * bars at least federal injunctive challenges to state tax laws. Added to this authority is our decision in Great Lakes Dredge & Dock Co. v. Huffman, supra, holding that declaratory judgments are barred on the basis of comity. On the other hand is the doctrine originating in Monroe v. Pape, supra, that comity does not apply where § 1983 is involved, and that a litigant challenging the constitutionality of any state action may proceed directly to federal court. With this divergence of views in mind, we turn now to the facts of this case, a § 1983 challenge to the administration of state tax laws which implicates both lines of authority. We hold that at least as to such actions, which is all we need decide here, the principle of comity controls.

II

Petitioner * * * is a non-profit corporation formed by taxpayers in St. Louis County ("County") to promote equitable enforcement of property tax laws in Missouri. Petitioners J. David and Lynn F. Cassilly own real property with recent improvements in the County. Petitioners filed suit under § 1983 alleging that respondents, the County's Tax Assessors, Supervisors, and Director of Revenue, and three members of the Missouri State Tax Commission, had deprived them of equal protection and due process of law by unequal taxation of real property.

* * * First, petitioners allege that County properties with new improvements are assessed at approximately 33⅓% of their current market value, while properties without new improvements are assessed at approximately 22% of their current market value. This disparity allegedly results from the respondents' failure to reassess old property on a regular basis, the last general reassessment having occurred in 1960. Second, petitioners allege that property owners who successfully appeal their property assessments, as did the Cassillys in 1977, are specifically targeted for reassessment the next year.

* * * In 1977, the Cassillys appealed the tax assessed on their home to the County Board of Equalization and received a reduction in assessed value from 33⅓% to 29%. When their home was again assessed at 33⅓% in 1978, the Cassillys once more appealed to the Board of Equalization. That appeal was pending at the commencement of this litigation.

The Cassillys brought this § 1983 action in federal court seeking actual damages in the amount of overassessments from 1975 to 1979, and punitive damages of $75,000.00 from each respondent. Petitioner Fair Assessment sought actual damages in the amount of expenses incurred in efforts to obtain equitable property assessments for its members. As in all other § 1983 actions, the award of such damages would first require a federal court declaration that respondents, in administering the state tax, violated petitioners' constitutional rights.

III

As indicated by our discussion in Part I, the Tax Injunction Act and our comity cases have thus far barred federal courts from granting injunctive and declaratory relief in state tax cases. Because we decide today that the principle of comity bars federal courts from granting damages relief in such cases, we do not decide whether the Act, standing alone, would require such a result. * * *

A

Prior to enactment of § 1341, virtually all federal cases challenging state taxation sought equitable relief. Consequently, federal court restraint in state tax matters was based upon the traditional doctrine that courts of equity will stay their hand when remedies at law are plain, adequate, and complete. * * * Even with this basis in equity law, these cases recognized that the doctrine of equitable restraint was of "notable application," * * * and carried "peculiar force," * * * in suits challenging the constitutionality of state tax laws. * * *

* * *

D

The principle of comity has been recognized and relied upon by this Court in several recent cases dealing with matters other than state taxes. Its fullest articulation was given in the now familiar language of Younger v. Harris, 401 U.S. 37, 91 S.Ct. 746, 27 L.Ed.2d 669 (1971), a case in which we held that traditional principles of equitable restraint bar federal courts from enjoining pending state criminal prosecutions except under extraordinary circumstances: * * *

The principles of federalism recognized in *Younger* have not been limited to federal court interference in state criminal proceedings, but have been extended to some state civil actions. E.g., Huffman v. Pursue, Ltd., 420 U.S. 592, 95 S.Ct. 1200, 43 L.Ed.2d 482 (1975). Although these modern expressions of comity have been limited in their application to federal cases which seek to enjoin state judicial proceedings, a limitation which we do not abandon here, they illustrate the principles that bar petitioners' suit under § 1983. * * * As will be seen in the next section, petitioners' § 1983 action would be no less disruptive of Missouri's tax system than would the historic equitable efforts to enjoin the collection of taxes, * * *

IV

* * * [P]etitioners contend that damages actions are inherently less disruptive of state tax systems than injunctions or declaratory judgments, and therefore should not be barred by prior decisions of this Court. Petitioners emphasize that their § 1983 claim seeks recovery from individual state officers, not from state coffers, and that the doctrine of qualified immunity will protect such officers' good faith actions and will thus avoid chilling their administration of the Missouri tax scheme.

We disagree. Petitioners will not recover damages under § 1983 unless a district court first determines that respondents' administration of the County tax system violated petitioners' constitutional rights. In effect, the district court must first enter a declaratory judgment like that barred in *Great Lakes.* We are convinced that such a determination would be fully as intrusive as the equitable actions that are barred by principles of comity. Moreover, the intrusiveness of such § 1983 actions would be exacerbated by the nonexhaustion doctrine of Monroe v. Pape, supra. Taxpayers such as petitioners would be able to invoke federal judgments without first permitting the State to rectify any alleged impropriety.

In addition to the intrusiveness of the judgment, the very maintenance of the suit itself would intrude on the enforcement of the state scheme. * * *

This intrusion, although undoubtedly present in every § 1983 claim, is particularly highlighted by the facts of this case. Defendants are not one or two isolated administrators, but virtually every key tax official in St. Louis County. * * * In addition, the actions challenged in the complaint—unequal assessment of new and old property and retaliatory assessment of property belonging to those who successfully appeal to the Board of Equalization—may well be the result of policies or practicalities beyond the control of any individual officer. * * * There is little doubt that such officials, faced with the prospect of personal liability to numerous taxpayers, not to mention the assessment of attorney's fees under 42 U.S.C. § 1988, would promptly cease the conduct found to have infringed petitioners' constitutional rights, whether or not those officials were acting in good faith. In short, petitioners action would "in every practical sense operate to suspend collection of the state taxes * * *," *Great Lakes,* 319 U.S., at 299, 63 S.Ct., at 1073, a form of federal court interference previously rejected by this Court on principles of federalism.

V

* * * And damages actions, no less than actions for an injunction, would hale state officers into federal court every time a taxpayer alleged the requisite elements of a § 1983 claim. * * *

Therefore, despite the ready access to federal courts provided by *Monroe* and its progeny, we hold that taxpayers are barred by the principle of comity from asserting § 1983 actions against the validity of state tax systems in federal courts. Such taxpayers must seek protection of their federal rights by state remedies, provided of course that those remedies are plain, adequate, and complete, and may ultimately seek review of the state decisions in this Court. See Huffman v. Pursue, 420 U.S., at 605, 95 S.Ct., at 1208–1209; Matthews v. Rodgers, supra, at 526, 52 S.Ct., at 220.

The adequacy of available Missouri remedies is not at issue in this case. * * *

* * *

Accordingly, the judgment of the Court of Appeals is

Affirmed.

JUSTICE BRENNAN, with whom JUSTICE MARSHALL, JUSTICE STEVENS, and JUSTICE O'CONNOR, join, concurring in the judgment.

I agree that the judgment of the district court dismissing petitioners' complaint should be affirmed. But I arrive at that conclusion by a different route for I cannot agree that this case, and the jurisdiction of the federal courts over an action for damages brought pursuant to express congressional authority, is to be governed by applying a "principle of comity" grounded solely on this Court's notion of an appropriate division of responsibility between the federal and state judicial systems. * * *

* * *

While the "principle of comity" may be a source of judicial policy, it is emphatically no source of judicial *power* to renounce jurisdiction. * * * Only where a federal court is asked to employ its historic powers as a court of equity, and is called upon to decide whether to exercise the broadest and potentially most intrusive form of judicial authority, does "comity" have an established and substantial role in informing the exercise of the court's discretion. * * *

* * *

The jurisdiction of the federal courts over cases such as the present one reflects a considered Congressional judgment. As the Court acknowledges, § 1983 "gave a federal cause of action to prisoners, taxpayers, or anyone else who was able to prove that his constitutional or federal rights had been denied by any State." Ante, at 187. * * * Where Congress has granted the federal courts jurisdiction, we are not free to repudiate that authority. * * *

The power to control the jurisdiction of the lower federal court is assigned by the Constitution to Congress, not to this Court. In its haste to rid the federal courts of a class of cases that it thinks unfit for federal scrutiny, the Court today departs from this fundamental precept.

III

* * * As pointed out above, supra, at 7–8, and n. 11, this case appears to fall squarely within the jurisdictional grant of 28 U.S.C. § 1343, and perhaps of 28 U.S.C. § 1331 as well. The question, then, is whether Congress has anywhere contradicted that presumptive grant of judicial authority. Only one possible source of that contradiction having been suggested, I begin my analysis of the jurisdictional question with the Tax Injunction Act itself.

* * *

The conclusion is thus inescapable that Congress did *not* intend to bar actions such as this one from the federal courts. On the contrary, Congress clearly intended that the federal forum would continue to remain available in state tax cases for monetary relief despite passage of the Tax Injunction Act.

* * *

IV

Petitioners argue that since their federal claim is brought pursuant to 42 U.S.C. § 1983, it was not necessary to exhaust administrative remedies before commencing this action.

* * *

More importantly, while this Court has repeatedly reaffirmed that exhaustion of administrative remedies is not a precondition to a suit brought under the Civil Rights Acts, * * * that conclusion rests firmly on the understanding that such was the intention of Congress in enacting § 1983. Where Congress has provided that in a particular class of cases the federal courts should refrain from hearing suits brought under § 1983 until administrative remedies have been exhausted, see e.g., 42 U.S.C.A. § 1997e (Supp.1981), there is no doubt that the federal courts are bound by that limitation. Cf. Preiser v. Rodriguez, 411 U.S. 475, 489–490, 93 S.Ct. 1827, 1836–1837, 36 L.Ed.2d 439 (1973). My view has always been that displacement of § 1983 remedies can only "be justified by a clear statement of congressional intent, or, at the very least, by the presence of the most persuasive considerations of policy." * * *

We surely have sufficient evidence of such congressional policy here * * *. Where administrative remedies are a precondition to suit for monetary relief in state court, absent some substantial consideration compelling a contrary result in a particular case, those remedies should be deemed a precondition to suit in federal court as well.

V

* * *

Because petitioners failed to exhaust their administrative remedies in each tax year for which they seek damages, their complaint was properly dismissed. To the extent today's judgment affirms that dismissal, I concur.

Note

1. **Non-Immunity to Other Injunctive Relief.** The above case is limited to federal interference with state and local taxation. Equitable, sic injunctive, relief under § 1983 is not barred generally. See the later authorities p. 980 infra, et seq.

C. INDIVIDUAL AND OFFICIAL LIABILITY UNDER § 1983

In addition to the general distinction drawn between governmental and personal immunity under § 1983, a broader distinction must be made. Any individual acting under "color of law" may be liable under § 1983 (assuming no immunity) irrespective of the presence or absence of an underlying governmental policy or custom in support of the individual's act. All local government officers and employees are deemed to act under "color of law" since their action constitutes "state action" even when not following official policy. See e.g. Herrera v. Valentine, 653 F.2d 1220 (8th Cir.1981) (personal liability of police officer Black v. Stephens, 662 F.2d 181 (3d Cir.1981) (undercover agent, personally liable); Cf. Rendell-Baker v. Kohn, 457 U.S. 830, 838, 102 S.Ct. 2764, 2769, 73 L.Ed.2d 418 (1982). Indeed, individuals who are not public officers or employees may still be held to act under "color of law" where action is clothed with official authority by combination with public officials. See Tower v. Glover, infra, p. 972.

For the foregoing reasons, it is possible that, depending upon circumstances, a municipality alone may be liable, with the individual escaping liability by way of an immunity; an individual may be liable, with the municipality escaping liability for lack of a causative policy or custom; or liability may be visited upon both the municipality and the individual personally where neither immunity applies. For this reason, suits against individuals usually name them as individuals and as defendants in their official capacity. Recovery against defendants in their official capacity results in entity liability only.   See Brandon v. Holt, 469 U.S. 464, 105 S.Ct. 873, 83 L.Ed.2d 878 (1985).

1. THE COLOR OF LAW REQUIREMENT

[Compare, Polk County v. Dodson, p. 950, supra, with Tower v. Glover, infra]

2. LIABILITY OF SUPERVISORS

Where individuals are sued not for their direct action, but as supervisors of the tortious actor, the plaintiff must prove a causal relationship between the supervisor's action and the subordinate's misconduct.   Thus the same rule against government § 1983 liability based solely on the respondeat superior doctrine, applies to relieve superior officials from acts of their subordinates.   See, e.g. Baskin v. Parker, 602 F.2d 1205 (5th Cir.1979), (holding that a sheriff could not be held vicariously liable in the § 1983 action for a deputy sheriff's unlawful procurement of a search warrant); Annotation: Vicarious Liability of Superiors Under 42 U.S.C.A. § 1983 for Subordinate's Acts in Deprivation of Civil Rights, 51 A.L.R.Fed. 285 (1981).

"Even if Chief of Police Watkins is held liable for the transfer under the *Mt. Healthy* test, the City Councilmen cannot be held liable for his tortious action solely on the basis of respondeat superior.

*   *   *

"Although supervisory officials cannot be held liable solely on the basis of their employer-employee relationship with a tortfeasor, they may be liable when their own action or inaction, including a failure to supervise that amounts to gross negligence or deliberate indifference, is a proximate cause of the constitutional violation.

*   *   *

"The City Councilmen would not be liable if they delegated their authority to the Chief of Police and he committed a constitutional tort, unless the delegation itself caused the tort.   Thus, in Watson v. Interstate Fire & Casualty Co., 5 Cir.1980, 611 F.2d 120, this court held that a sheriff who delegated responsibility to his subordinates and was not aware of an allegedly illegal incarceration and commitment until after the fact was not liable to the injured party where he did not fail to supervise properly.   Accordingly, we conclude that, to impose liability on a supervisory official, section 1983 requires more than a simple ratification of an impermissible act when the ratification is based on independent legitimate reasons.   To prevail against the City Councilmen, the plaintiffs must show a failure to supervise properly that caused the harm.   See Sims v. Adams, 5 Cir.1976, 537 F.2d 829. Usually, a failure to supervise gives rise to section 1983 liability only in those situations in which there is a history of widespread abuse.   Then knowledge may be imputed to the supervisory official, and he can be found to have caused the later violation by his failure to prevent it.
*   *   * See Bowen v. Watkins, 669 F.2d 979, 988 (5th Cir.1982).

Accord: Ybarra v. Reno Thunderbird Mobile Home Village, 723 F.2d 675 (9th Cir.1984).

While most courts agree on the principles above expressed, they appear to be quite divided on its application to like situations, and on the characterization of inaction by supervisors before the alleged deprivation took place. Compare e.g. Clark v. Taylor, 710 F.2d 4 (1st Cir. 1983) with Allman v. Coughlin, 577 F.Supp. 1440 (S.D.N.Y.1984); cf. Trotter v. Chicago, 573 F.Supp. 1269 (N.D.Ill.1983). The authorities are collected in Annots, Liability for Failure to Train, 70 A.L.R.Fed. 17 (1984, Supp.1985); Arrest—Excessive Force, 60 A.L.R.Fed. 204 (1982) Until the Supreme Court addresses these diverse judgments more thoroughly, supervisory officers remain at risk on hindsight versions and proofs of faulty oversight.

3. OFFICIAL AND INDIVIDUAL IMMUNITY

In denying § 1983 tort immunity to local government entities, while recognizing various categories of official immunity, the *Owen* case, supra, raises a new set of problems. When, if ever, may a local government entity be deemed to act directly for the state as to qualify for Eleventh Amendment immunity? Courts must decide which individuals and individual actions are entitled to absolute or qualified immunity; and the nature of proofs required to establish such immunity. The answers to these questions will vary depending upon the public position held and the actions giving rise to the § 1983 claim. Therefore, resort must be had to the decided cases.

a. *Scope of Immunized Functions*

TOWER v. GLOVER

Supreme Court of the United States, 1984.
467 U.S. 914, 104 S.Ct. 2820, 81 L.Ed.2d 758.

[Suit alleging public defender conspired with state officials to deprive plaintiff of federal rights stated § 1983 cause of action for which public defender could not claim immunity.]

* * *

In *Polk County v. Dodson, supra,* we held that appointed counsel in a state criminal prosecution, though paid and ultimately supervised by the State, does not act "under color of" state law in the normal course of conducting the defense. See also *Ferri v. Ackerman, supra.* In *Dennis v. Sparks,* 449 U.S. 24, 27–28, 101 S.Ct. 183, 186, 66 L.Ed.2d 185 (1980), however, the Court held that an otherwise private person acts "under color of" state law when engaged in a conspiracy with state officials to deprive another of federal rights. Glover alleges that petitioners conspired with state officials, and his complaint, therefore, includes an adequate allegation of conduct "under color of" state law.

On its face § 1983 admits no immunities. But since 1951 this Court has consistently recognized that substantive doctrines of privilege and immunity may limit the relief available in § 1983 litigation. See *Imbler v. Pachtman,* 424 U.S. 409, 417–419, 96 S.Ct. 984, 47 L.Ed.2d 128, (1976); *Pulliam v. Allen,* 466 U.S. ___, 104 S.Ct. 1970, 80 L.Ed.2d ___ (1984). The Court has recognized absolute § 1983 immunity for legislators acting within their legislative roles, *Tenney v. Brandhove,* 341 U.S. 367, 71 S.Ct. 783, 95 L.Ed. 1019 (1951), for judges acting within their judicial roles, *Pierson v. Ray,* 386 U.S. 547, 554–555, 87 S.Ct. 1213, 1217–1218, 18 L.Ed.2d 288 (1967), for prosecutors, *Imbler v. Pachtman, supra,* and for witnesses, *Briscoe v. LaHue,* 460 U.S. 325, 103 S.Ct. 1108, 75 L.Ed.2d 96 (1983), and has recognized qualified immunity for state executive officers and school officials, see *Scheuer v. Rhodes,* 416 U.S. 232, 94 S.Ct. 1683, 40 L.Ed.2d 90 (1974), *Wood v. Strickland,* 420 U.S. 308, 95 S.Ct. 992, 43 L.Ed.2d 214 (1975).

Section 1983 immunities are "predicated upon a considered inquiry into the immunity historically accorded the relevant official at common law and the interests behind it." *Imbler v. Pachtman, supra,* 424 U.S., at 421, 96 S.Ct., at 990; *Pulliam v. Allen, supra,* at ___, 104 S.Ct., at ___. If an official was accorded immunity from tort actions at common law when the Civil Rights Act was enacted in 1871, the Court next considers whether § 1983's history or purposes nonetheless counsel against recognizing the same immunity in § 1983 actions. See *Imbler v. Pachtman, supra,* 424 U.S., at 424–429, 96 S.Ct., at 992–994; *Briscoe v. Lahue, supra,* 460 U.S., at ___ – ___, 103 S.Ct., at ___ – ___. Using this framework we conclude that public defenders have no immunity from § 1983 liability for intentional misconduct of the type alleged here.

No immunity for public defenders, as such, existed at common law in 1871 because there was, of course, no such office or position in existence at that time. * * * Our inquiry, however, cannot stop there. Immunities in this country have regularly been borrowed from the English precedents, and the public defender has a reasonably close "cousin" in the English barrister. Like public defenders, barristers are not free to pick and choose their clients. * * * It is therefore noteworthy that English barristers enjoyed in the 19th century, as they still do today, a broad immunity from liability for negligent misconduct. * * *

In this country the public defender's only 19th-century counterpart was a privately retained lawyer, and petitioners do not suggest that such a lawyer would have enjoyed immunity from tort liability for intentional misconduct. * * * Indeed, few state supreme courts have addressed the question of public defender immunity, none to our knowledge has concluded that public defenders should enjoy immunity for intentional misconduct. * * *

Finally, petitioners contend that public defenders have responsibilities similar to those of a judge or prosecutor, and therefore should enjoy similar immunities. The threat of § 1983 actions based on alleged conspiracies among defense counsel and other state officials may deter counsel from engaging in activities that require some degree of cooperation with prosecutors—negotiating pleas, expediting trials and appeals, and so on. * * *

Petitioners' concerns may be well founded, but the remedy petitioners urge is not for us to adopt. We do not have a license to establish immunities from § 1983 actions in the interests of what we judge to be sound public policy. It is for Congress to determine whether § 1983 litigation has become too burdensome to state or federal institutions and, if so, what remedial action is appropriate. We conclude that state public defenders are not immune from liability under § 1983 for intentional misconduct, "under color of" state law, by virtue of alleged conspiratorial action with state officials that deprives their clients of federal rights. * * *

Notes

1. **Titles v. Functions Test.** Unlike the common law immunity which focussed upon political status and authority of a given office, § 1983 immunity, as construed by the Supreme Court focusses upon the particular function in which the alleged tortious act occurred. Thus an official in the legislative, judicial, enforcement or administrative agencies of government may or may not enjoy immunity or a particular class of immunity. As the following notes illustrate, this approach to immunity raises line-drawing issues as to whether particular acts fall within the scope of absolute or qualified immunity.

(a) *Legislative Acts.* Local government officers acting in a legislative capacity have *absolute* immunity under § 1983 (Lake Country Estates v. Tahoe Planning Agency, 440 U.S. 391, 99 S.Ct. 1171, 59 L.Ed.2d 401 (1979)), but one does not have to hold a formal "legislative" office to enjoy such immunity. Board members appointed to a compact agency, when employing legislative powers, qualify for legislative immunity (*Lake Country Estates,* supra) Callaway v. Hafeman, 628 F.Supp. 1478 (W.D.Wis.1986) (School Board Budget Decisions). So does a mayor when exercising veto powers over city legislation. (Hernandez v. Lafayette, 643 F.2d 1188 (5th Cir.1981). Even state judges, when adopting disciplinary rules for the legal profession, enjoy absolute legislative immunity. Supreme Court of Virginia v. Consumer's Union, 446 U.S. 719, 100 S.Ct. 1967, 64 L.Ed.2d 641 (1980). But mayors, board members, and judges, when acting in an executive or enforcement capacity are not *absolutely* immune.

(b) *Judicial Acts.* In *Supreme Court of Virginia,* supra, the court indicated that judges could be held liable to § 1983 suit for injunction and declaratory relief, when acting to *enforce* their legislated disciplinary rules, the same as any other administrative enforcement officers. 466 U.S. at 735–36, 100 S.Ct. at 1976, 1977. Nevertheless, it protected the judges from liability and attorneys' fee assessments (under 42 U.S.C.A. § 1988) though they refused to repeal unconstitutional disciplinary rules—(as a legislative act). The case left judges vulnerable to payment of attorneys' fees (as well as liability for deprivations they caused) in enforcing those rules. Id. 739,

100 S.Ct. at 1978. These distinctions may seem fine, but they clearly forewarn attorneys that, not titles, but the nature of the officer's activity governs § 1983 immunity. How the above rulings will affect local government tribunals (e.g. traffic courts) remains to be seen.

(c) *Prosecutors, Public Defenders and Court Appointed Counsel.* The absolute immunity granted to state public prosecutors, Imbler v. Pachtman, 424 U.S. 409, 96 S.Ct. 984, 47 L.Ed.2d 128 (1976), even covered a fraudulent inducement of a plea bargain. Taylor v. Kavanagh, 640 F.2d 450 (2d Cir. 1981). Nevertheless, exceptions to prosecutorial absolute immunity remain a possibility:

> "2. Hamilton County Prosecutor Leis was not made a defendant because counsel for petitioner believed that Leis was absolutely immune. Tr. Mar. 14–Mar. 17, p. 267. We express no view as to the correctness of this evaluation. Cf. *Imbler v. Pachtman*, 424 U.S. 409, 430–31, 96 S.Ct. 984, 995, 47 L.Ed.2d 128 (1976) (leaving open the question of a prosecutor's immunity when he acts 'in the role of an administrator or investigative officer rather than that of an advocate')."

See Pembaur v. Cincinnati, 475 U.S. ___, ___, 106 S.Ct. 1292, 1295, 89 L.Ed. 2d 452 (1986). Cf. Higgs v. District Court, 713 P.2d 840 (Colo.1985) (district attorneys not absolutely immune for pre-charge investigative acts). Should court-appointed attorneys (by state courts) enjoy § 1983 immunity, absolute or qualified, in performing their assigned duties?

Absolute immunity has been extended to local units and agency officials whose functions were deemed analogous to prosecutors. Whelehan v. Monroe, 558 F.Supp. 1093 (W.D.N.Y.1983); accord: Pepper v. Alexander, 599 F.Supp. 523 (D.N.M.1984).

(d) *Witness Immunity.* The general rule of absolute witness immunity applies to § 1983 suits for monetary damages. Briscoe v. LaHue, 460 U.S. 325, 103 S.Ct. 1108, 75 L.Ed.2d 96 (1983) (police officer immune from § 1983 damage claim for lying at criminal trial).

2. **Discretion and Reason to Know.** The opinions in *Owen*, supra, as well as *Tower* list classes of official immunity which include subordinate, non-elected officials who carry out discretionary functions, e.g. parole officers.

"We therefore hold that government officials performing discretionary functions generally are shielded from liability for civil damages insofar as their conduct does not violate clearly established statutory or constitutional rights of which a reasonable person should have known." See Harlowe v. Fitzgerald, 457 U.S. 800, 817, 102 S.Ct. 2727, 2738, 73 L.Ed.2d 396, 410 (1982). This standard, as applied to a police officer proved treacherous when the Supreme Court later held that the objective reason to know test required the officer to exercise independent judgment and his good faith mistake and his reliance also upon a magistrate's decision, that the warrant applied for was constitutional, did not afford him qualified immunity under § 1983 because the Supreme Court thought his action not "reasonable." Malley v. Briggs, ___ U.S. ___, 106 S.Ct. 1092, 89 L.Ed.2d 271 (1986).

See also Williams v. Treen, 671 F.2d 892 (5th Cir.1982) (prison official belief, contrary to state law, held per se unreasonable).

Not all of the actions of each individual necessarily involves an immunized function; and this fact raised issues that are unique to § 1983 immunity.

b. Qualified Immunity—The Applicable Standard

DAVIS v. SCHERER

Supreme Court of the United States, 1984.
468 U.S. 183, 104 S.Ct. 3012, 82 L.Ed.2d 139.

[Plaintiff highway patrolman resigned his position following a dispute concerning his outside employment and an order of termination which he succeeded in having reversed through administrative settlement. After the resignation, he sued the superior officers for damages alleging deprivation of constitutional rights to a hearing before or after issuance of the termination order.]

POWELL J.

* * *

In the present posture of this case, the District Court's decision that appellants violated appellee's rights under the Fourteenth Amendment is undisputed. This finding of the District Court—based entirely upon federal constitutional law—resolves the merits of appellee's underlying claim for relief under § 1983. It does not, however, decide the issue of damages. Even defendants who violate constitutional rights enjoy a qualified immunity that protects them from liability for damages unless it is further demonstrated that their conduct was unreasonable under the applicable standard. The precise standard for determining when an official may assert the qualified immunity defense has been clarified by recent cases, see *Wood v. Strickland,* 420 U.S. 308, 95 S.Ct. 992, 43 L.Ed.2d 214 (1975); *Butz v. Economou,* 438 U.S. 478, 98 S.Ct. 2894, 57 L.Ed.2d 895 (1978); *Harlow v. Fitzgerald,* 457 U.S. 800, 102 S.Ct. 2727, 73 L.Ed.2d 396 (1982). The present case requires us to consider the application of the standard where the official's conduct violated a state regulation as well as a provision of the federal Constitution.

The District Court's analysis of appellants' qualified immunity, written before our decision in *Harlow v. Fitzgerald, supra,* rests upon the "totality of the circumstances" surrounding appellee's separation from his job. This Court applied that standard in *Scheuer v. Rhodes,* 416 U.S., at 247–248, 94 S.Ct., at 1691–1692. As subsequent cases recognized, *Wood v. Strickland, supra,* 420 U.S., at 322, 95 S.Ct., at 1000, the "totality of the circumstances" test comprised two separate inquiries: an inquiry into the objective reasonableness of the defendant official's conduct in light of the governing law, and an inquiry into the official's subjective state of mind. *Harlow v. Fitzgerald, supra,* rejected the inquiry into state of mind in favor of a wholly objective standard. Under *Harlow,* officials "are shielded from liability for civil damages insofar as their conduct does not violate clearly established statutory or constitutional rights of which a reasonable person would have known." 457 U.S., at 818, 102 S.Ct., at 2739. Whether an official may prevail in his qualified immunity defense depends upon the "objective reasonableness of [his] conduct as measured by reference to clearly established law." *Id.* (footnote deleted). No other "circumstances" are relevant to the issue of qualified immunity.

Appellee suggests, however, that the District Court judgment can be reconciled with *Harlow* in two ways. First, appellee urges that the record evinces a violation of constitutional rights that were clearly established. Second, in appellee's view, the District Court correctly found that, absent a violation of clearly established constitutional rights, appellants' violation of the state administrative regulation—although irrelevant to the merits of appellee's underlying constitutional claim—was decisive of the qualified immunity question. In our view, neither submission is consistent with our prior cases.

* * *

* * * As the District Court recognized in rejecting appellee's contention, *Weisbrod v. Donigan,* 651 F.2d 334 (CA5 1981), is authoritative precedent to the contrary. The Court of Appeals in that case found that the State had violated no clearly established due process right when it discharged a civil service employee without *any* pretermination hearing.

Nor was it unreasonable in this case, under Fourteenth Amendment due process principles, for the Department to conclude that appellee had been provided with the fundamentals of due process. * * * We conclude that the District Court correctly held that appellee has demonstrated no violation of his *clearly established* constitutional rights.

Appellee's second ground for affirmance in substance is that upon which the District Court relied. * * *

Appellee makes no claim that the appellants' violation of the state regulation either is itself actionable under § 1983 or bears upon the claim of constitutional right that appellee asserts under § 1983. * * * Nonetheless, in appellee's view, official conduct that contravenes a statute or regulation is not "objectively reasonable" because officials fairly may be expected to conform their conduct to such legal norms. * * * Appellee urges therefore that a defendant official's violation of a clear statute or regulation, although not itself the basis of suit, should deprive the official of qualified immunity from damages for violation of other statutory or constitutional provisions.

On its face, appellee's reasoning is not without some force. We decline, however, to adopt it. * * * Officials sued for constitutional violations do not lose their qualified immunity merely because their conduct violates some statutory or administrative provision.

We acknowledge of course that officials should conform their conduct to applicable statutes and regulations. For that reason, it is an appealing proposition * * * But in determining what circumstances a court may consider in deciding claims of qualified immunity, we choose "between the evils inevitable in any available alternative." * * * Appellee's submission, if adopted, would disrupt the balance that our cases strike between the interests in vindication of citizens' constitutional rights and in public officials' effective performance of their duties. The qualified immunity doctrine recognizes that officials can act without fear of harassing litigation only if they reasonably can anticipate when their conduct may give rise to liability for damages and only if unjustified lawsuits are quickly terminated. * * * Yet, under appellee's submission, officials would be liable in indeterminate amount for violation of *any* constitutional right—one that was not clearly defined or perhaps not even foreshadowed at the time of the alleged violation—merely because their official conduct also violated some statute or regulation. And, in § 1983 suits, the issue whether an official enjoyed qualified immunity then might depend upon the meaning or purpose of a state administrative regulation, questions that federal judges often may be unable to resolve on summary judgment.

* * *

Nor is it always fair, or sound policy, to demand official compliance with statute and regulation on pain of money damages. Such officials as police officers or prison wardens, to say nothing of higher-level executive levels who enjoy only qualified immunity, routinely make close decisions in the exercise of the broad authority that necessarily is delegated to them. These officials are subject to a plethora of rules, "often so voluminous, ambiguous, and contradictory, and in such flux that officials can comply with them only selectively." See P. Schuck, Suing Government 66 (1983). In these circumstances, officials should not err always on the side of caution. "[O]fficials with a broad range of duties and authority must often act swiftly and firmly at the risk that action deferred will be futile or constitute virtual abdication of office." *Scheuer v. Rhodes,* 416 U.S., at 246, 94 S.Ct., at 1691.

A plaintiff who seeks damages for violation of constitutional or statutory rights may overcome the defendant official's qualified immunity only by showing that those rights were clearly established at the time of the conduct at issue. As appellee has made no such showing, the judgment of the Court of Appeals is reversed and the case remanded for proceedings consistent with this opinion.

It is so ordered.

* * *

Notes

1. Recent lower court cases are collected in Annot, Civil Rights—Immunity, 63 A.L.R.Fed. 744 (1983, Supp.1985).

2. **Nonimmunity from Equitable Relief.** Officials who are entitled to absolute immunity from § 1983 *legal* relief in the form of damages, are not immune from *equitable* relief by way of prospective injunction. See Pulliam v. Allen, infra. But equitable relief can be denied under the grounds asserted in the majority and concurring opinions in Fair Assessment Real Estate Assn. v. McNary, p. 964, supra.

3. **Burden of Pleading.** A § 1983 plaintiff need only plead conclusory allegations of deprivation of federal rights under color of law, to withstand a pleading challenge, but the burden of pleading immunity defenses rests with defendant parties. Gomez v. Toledo, 446 U.S. 635, 100 S.Ct. 1920, 64 L.Ed.2d 572 (1980).

PULLIAM v. ALLEN

Supreme Court of the United States, 1984.
466 U.S. 522, 104 S.Ct. 1970, 80 L.Ed.2d 565.

JUSTICE BLACKMUN delivered the opinion of the Court.

This case raises issues concerning the scope of judicial immunity from a civil suit that seeks injunctive and declaratory relief under § 1 of the Civil Rights Act of 1871, as amended, 42 U.S.C. § 1983 (1976 ed., Supp. V), and from fee awards made under the Civil Rights Attorney's Fees Awards Act of 1976, 90 Stat. 2641, as amended, 42 U.S.C. § 1988 (1976 ed., Supp. V).

Petitioner Gladys Pulliam is a state magistrate in Culpeper County, Va. Respondents Richmond R. Allen and Jesse W. Nicholson were plaintiffs in a § 1983 action against Pulliam * * * They claimed that Magistrate Pulliam's practice of imposing bail on persons arrested for nonjailable offenses under Virginia law and of incarcerating those persons if they could not meet the bail was unconstitutional. The District Court agreed and enjoined the practice. That court also awarded respondents $7,691.09 in costs and attorney's fees under § 1988. * * *

* * *

We granted certiorari in this case, * * * to determine, as petitioner phrased the question, "[w]hether Judicial Immunity Bars the Award of Attorney's Fees Pursuant to 42 U.S.C. § 1988 Against a Member of the Judiciary Acting in his Judicial Capacity." * * * As the Court of Appeals recognized, the answer to that question depends in part on whether judicial immunity bars an award of injunctive relief under § 1983. The legislative history of § 1988 clearly indicates that Congress intended to provide for attorney's fees in cases where relief properly is granted against officials who are immune from damages awards. * * * There is no indication, however, that Congress intended to provide for a fee award if the official was immune from the underlying relief on which the award was premised. See *Supreme Court of Virginia v. Consumers Union of the United States, Inc.,* 446 U.S. 719, 738–739, 100 S.Ct. 1967, 1977–1978, 64 L.Ed.2d 641 (1980). Before addressing the specific provisions of § 1988, therefore, we turn to the more fundamental question, that is, whether a judicial officer acting in her judicial capacity should be immune from prospective injunctive relief.

*   *   *

As illustrated above, there is little support in the common law for a rule of judicial immunity that prevents injunctive relief against a judge. There is even less support for a conclusion that Congress intended to limit the injunctive relief available under § 1983 in a way that would prevent federal injunctive relief against a state judge.

*   *   *

*   *   *

We conclude that judicial immunity is not a bar to prospective injunctive relief against a judicial officer acting in her judicial capacity.

*   *   *

D. ALLOWABLE REMEDIES

Section 1983 expressly refers to civil rights liability "in an action at law, suit in equity, or other proper proceeding for redress." Three principal forms of redress are provided, i.e., equitable and declaratory relief; monetary damages; and (by interaction with the Civil Rights Attorney's Fees Awards Act (42 U.S.C.A. § 1988)) awards for attorneys fees. Each of these forms of redress is subject to certain limitations which do not apply equally to all claims, or to all classes of litigant.

1. EQUITABLE RELIEF

While it is settled that a local government entity and officer can be sued for injunctive relief under § 1983, the usual precondition to equitable relief, namely, that there is no adequate legal remedy, applies:

> "The equitable remedy is unavailable absent a showing of irreparable injury, a requirement that cannot be met where there is no showing of any real or immediate threat that the plaintiff will be wronged again.
>
> *   *   *
>
> "Nor will the injury *   *   * go unrecompensed; for that injury, he has an adequate remedy [damages] at law.
>
> *   *   *
>
> "We decline the invitation to slight the preconditions of equitable relief. Mitchum v. Foster *   *   * held that suits brought under 42 U.S.C. § 1983 are exempt from the flat ban against the issuance of injunctions directed to state court proceedings. *   *   * But this holding did not displace the normal principles of equity, comity or federalism. *   *   * " See City of Los Angeles v. Lyons, 461 U.S. 95, 103 S.Ct. 1660, 75 L.Ed.2d 675 (1983).

While the federal Anti-Injunction Act, per the Mitchum case, **supra**, did not bar § 1983 injunctions generally, the federal Tax Injunction Act and comity principles (per the Fair Assessment Case, p. 964, supra) did bar § 1983 injunctions specifically with respect to state and local taxation practices.

2. LEGAL RELIEF

MEMPHIS COMMUNITY SCHOOL DISTRICT v. STACHURA

Supreme Court of the United States, 1986.
___ U.S. ___, 106 S.Ct. 2537, 91 L.Ed.2d 249.

[A tenured teacher in Michigan public schools was suspended following parents' complaints about his teaching methods in a 7th-grade life science course that included the showing of allegedly sexually explicit pictures and films. He brought suit under 42 U.S.C. § 1983 against petitioner School District, Board of Education, Board Members, school administrators, and parents, alleging that his suspension deprived him of liberty and property without due process of law and violated his First Amendment right to academic freedom. The jury found petitioners liable, awarding compensatory damages against all defendants and punitive damages against individual defendants.]

JUSTICE POWELL delivered the opinion of the Court.

* * *

We have repeatedly noted that 42 U.S.C. § 1983 [8] creates " 'a species of tort liability' in favor of persons who are deprived of 'rights, privileges, or immunities secured' to them by the Constitution." *Carey v. Piphus,* 435 U.S. 247, 253, 98 S.Ct. 1042, 1047, 55 L.Ed.2d 252 (1978), quoting *Imbler v. Pachtman,* 424 U.S. 409, 417, 96 S.Ct. 984, 988, 47 L.Ed.2d 128 (1976). See also *Smith v. Wade,* 461 U.S. 30, 34, 103 S.Ct. 1625, 1628, 75 L.Ed.2d 632 (1983); *Newport v. Fact Concerts, Inc.,* 453 U.S. 247, 258–259, 101 S.Ct. 2748, 2755, 2756, 69 L.Ed.2d 616 (1981). Accordingly, when § 1983 plaintiffs seek damages for violations of constitutional rights, the level of damages is ordinarily determined according to principles derived from the common law of torts. * * *

Punitive damages aside, damages in tort cases are designed to provide "*compensation* for the injury caused to plaintiff by defendant's breach of duty." * * * To that end, compensatory damages may include not only out-of-pocket loss and other monetary harms, but also such injuries as "impairment of reputation * * *, personal humiliation, and mental anguish and suffering." *Gertz v. Robert Welch, Inc.,* 418 U.S. 323, 350, 94 S.Ct. 2997, 3012, 41 L.Ed.2d 789 (1974). See also *Carey v. Piphus, supra,* 435 U.S., at 264, 98 S.Ct., at 1052 (mental and emotional distress constitute compensable injury in § 1983 cases). Deterrence is also an important purpose of this system, but it operates through the mechanism of damages that are *compensatory*—damages grounded in determinations of plaintiffs' actual losses. * * * Congress adopted this common-law system of recovery when it established liability for "constitutional torts." Consequently, "the basic purpose" of § 1983 damages is "to *compensate persons for injuries* that are caused by the deprivation of constitutional rights." *Carey v. Piphus*, 435 U.S., at 254, 98 S.Ct., at 1047 (emphasis added). See also *id.*, at 257, 98 S.Ct., at 1049 ("damages awards under § 1983 should be governed by the principle of compensation").

Carey v. Piphus represents a straightforward application of these principles. *Carey* involved a suit by a high school student suspended for smoking marijuana; the student claimed that he was denied procedural due process because he was suspended without an opportunity to respond to the charges against him. * * * We held * * * that the student could recover compensatory damages only if he proved actual injury caused by the denial of his constitutional rights. *Id.*, at 264, 98 S.Ct., at 1052. * * * Where no injury was present, no "compensatory" damages could be awarded.

The instructions at issue here cannot be squared with *Carey*, or with the principles of tort damages on which *Carey* and § 1983 are grounded. The jurors in this case were told that, in determining how much was necessary to "compensate [respondent] for the deprivation" of his constitutional rights, they should place a money value on the "rights" themselves by considering such factors as the particular right's "importance * * * in our system of government," its role in American history, and its "significance * * * in the context of the activities" in which respondent was engaged. App. 96. These factors focus, not on compensation for provable injury, but on the jury's subjective perception of the importance of constitutional rights as an abstract matter. *Carey* establishes that such an approach is impermissible. The constitutional right transgressed in *Carey*—the right to due process of law—is central to our system of ordered liberty. * * * We nevertheless held that *no* compensatory damages could be awarded for violation of that right absent proof of actual injury. *Carey*, 435 U.S., at 264. *Carey* thus makes clear that the abstract value of a constitutional right may not form the basis for § 1983 damages.

Respondent nevertheless argues that *Carey* does not control here, because in this case a *substantive* constitutional right—respondent's First Amendment right to academic freedom—was infringed. The argument misperceives our analysis in *Carey*. That case does not establish a two-tiered system of constitutional rights, with substantive rights afforded greater protection than "mere" procedural safeguards. We did acknowledge in *Carey* that "the elements and prerequisites for recovery of damages" might vary depending on the interests protected by the constitutional right at issue. *Id.*, at 264–265, 98 S.Ct., at 1053. But we emphasized that, whatever the constitutional basis for § 1983 liability, such damages must always be designed "to *compensate injuries* caused by the [constitutional] deprivation." *Id.*, at 265, 98 S.Ct. at 1053 * * *. * * * That conclusion simply leaves no room for noncompensatory damages measured by the jury's perception of the abstract "importance" of a constitutional right.

Nor do we find such damages necessary to vindicate the constitutional rights that § 1983 protects. * * * Section 1983 presupposes that damages that compensate for actual harm ordinarily suffice to deter constitutional violations. *Carey, supra,* 495 U.S., at 256–257, 88 S.Ct., at 1048 * * *. Moreover, damages based on the "value" of constitutional rights are an unwieldy tool for ensuring compliance with the Constitution. History and tradition do not afford any sound guidance concerning the precise value that juries should place on constitutional protections. Accordingly, were such damages available, juries would be free to award arbitrary amounts without any evidentiary basis, or to use their unbounded discretion to punish unpopular defendants. * * * Such damages would be too uncertain to be of any great value to plaintiffs, and would inject caprice into determinations of damages in § 1983 cases. We therefore hold that damages based on the abstract "value" or "importance" of constitutional rights are not a permissible element of compensatory damages in such cases.

B

Respondent further argues that the challenged instructions authorized a form of "presumed" damages—a remedy that is both compensatory in nature and traditionally part of the range of tort law remedies. Alternatively, respondent argues that the erroneous instructions were at worst harmless error.

Neither argument has merit. Presumed damages are a *substitute* for ordinary compensatory damages, not a *supplement* for an award that fully compensates the alleged injury. When a plaintiff seeks compensation for an injury that is likely to have occurred but difficult to establish, some form of presumed damages may possibly be appropriate. See *Carey, supra,* 435 U.S., at 262, 98 S.Ct., at 1051, cf. *Dun & Bradstreet, Inc. v. Greenmoss Builders,* 472 U.S. ___, ___, 105 S.Ct. 2939, ___, 86 L.Ed.2d 593 (1985) (opinion of Powell, J.); *Gertz v. Robert Welch, Inc., supra,* 418 U.S., at 349, 94 S.Ct., at 3011. In those circumstances, presumed damages may roughly approximate the harm that the plaintiff suffered and thereby compensate for harms that may be impossible to measure. As we earlier explained, the instructions at issue in this case did not serve this purpose, but instead called on the jury to measure damages based on a subjective evaluation of the importance of particular constitutional values. Since such damages are wholly divorced from any compensatory purpose, they cannot be justified as presumed damages. Moreover, no rough substitute for compensatory damages was required in this case, since the jury was fully authorized to compensate respondent for both monetary and non-monetary harms caused by petitioners' conduct.

* * *

The judgment of the Court of Appeals is reversed, and the case is remanded for further proceedings consistent with this opinion.

* * *

JUSTICE BRENNAN and JUSTICE STEVENS join the opinion of the Court and also join JUSTICE MARSHALL'S opinion concurring in the judgment.

JUSTICE MARSHALL, with whom JUSTICE BRENNAN, JUSTICE BLACKMUN, and JUSTICE STEVENS join, concurring in the judgment.

I agree with the Court that this case must be remanded for a new trial on damages. Certain portions of the Court's opinion, however, can be read to suggest that damages in § 1983 cases are necessarily limited to "out-of-pocket loss," "other monetary harms," and "such injuries as 'impairment of reputation * * *, personal humiliation, and mental anguish and suffering.'" See *ante*, at 2542. I do not understand the Court so to hold, and I write separately to emphasize that the violation of a constitutional right, in proper cases, may itself constitute a compensable injury.

The appropriate starting point of any analysis in this area is this Court's opinion in *Carey v. Piphus*, 435 U.S. 247, 98 S.Ct. 1042, 55 L.Ed. 2d 252 (1978). In *Carey*, we recognized that "the basic purpose of a § 1983 damages award should be to compensate persons for injuries caused by the deprivation of constitutional rights." *Id.*, at 254, 98 S.Ct., at 1047, see *ante*, at 2542–2543. We explained, however, that application of that principle to concrete cases was not a simple matter. 435 U.S., at 257, 98 S.Ct., at 1048. "It is not clear," we stated, "that common-law tort rules of damages will provide a complete solution to the damages issue in every § 1983 case." *Id.*, at 258, 98 S.Ct., at 1049. Rather, "the rules governing compensation for injuries caused by the deprivation of constitutional rights should be tailored to the interests protected by the particular right in question—just as the common-law rules of damages themselves were defined by the interests protected in various branches of tort law." *Id.*, at 259, 98 S.Ct., at 1050.

Applying those principles, we held in *Carey* that substantial damages should not be awarded where a plaintiff has been denied procedural due process but has made no further showing of compensable damage. We repeated, however, that "the elements and prerequisites for recovery of damages appropriate to compensate injuries caused by the deprivation of one constitutional right are not necessarily appropriate to compensate injuries caused by the deprivation of another." *Id.*, at 264–265, 98 S.Ct., at 1053. We referred to cases that support the award of substantial damages simply upon a showing that a plaintiff was wrongfully deprived of the right to vote, without requiring any further demonstration of damages. *Id.*, at 264–265, n. 22, 98 S.Ct., at 1052–1053, n. 22.

Following *Carey*, the courts of appeals have recognized that invasions of constitutional rights sometimes cause injuries that cannot be redressed by a wooden application of common-law damages rules. In *Hobson v. Wilson*, 237 U.S.App.D.C. 219, 275–281, 737 F.2d 1, 57–63 (1984), cert. denied, 470 U.S. ___, 105 S.Ct. 1843, 85 L.Ed.2d 142 (1985), which the Court cites, *ante*, at 2544, and n. 13, plaintiffs claimed that defendant FBI agents had invaded their First Amendment rights to assemble for peaceable political protest, to associate with others to engage in political expression, and to speak on public issues free of unreasonable government interference. The District Court found that the defendants had succeeded in diverting plaintiffs from, and impeding them in, their protest activities. The Court of Appeals for the District of Columbia Circuit held that that injury to a First Amendment-protected interest could itself constitute compensable injury wholly apart from any "emotional distress, humiliation and personal indignity, emotional pain, embarrassment, fear, anxiety and anguish" suffered by plaintiffs. 237 U.S.App.D.C., at 280, 737 F.2d, at 62 (footnotes omitted). The court warned, however, that that injury could be compensated with substantial damages only to the extent that it was "reasonably quantifiable"; damages should not be based on "the so-called inherent value of the rights violated." *Ibid.*

I believe that the *Hobson* court correctly stated the law. When a plaintiff is deprived, for example, of the opportunity to engage in a demonstration to express his political views, "[i]t is facile to suggest that no damage is done." *Dellums v. Powell,* 184 U.S.App.D.C. 275, 303, 566 F.2d 167, 195 (1977). Loss of such an opportunity constitutes loss of First Amendment rights " 'in their most pristine and classic form.' " *Ibid.*, quoting *Edwards v. South Carolina,* 372 U.S. 229, 235, 83 S.Ct. 680, 683, 9 L.Ed.2d 697 (1963). There is no reason why such an injury should not be compensable in damages. At the same time, however, the award must be proportional to the actual loss sustained.

The instructions given the jury in this case were improper because they did not require the jury to focus on the loss actually sustained by respondent. * * *

Note

1. **Punitive Damages.** A different rule applies to government entities and to individuals. City of Newport v. Fact Concerts, Inc., 453 U.S. 247, 101 S.Ct. 2748, 69 L.Ed.2d 616 (1981) held that § 1983 does not authorize recovery of punitive damages against municipalities, and its rationale would apply to all local government units. Smith v. Wade, 461 U.S. 30, 103 S.Ct. 1625, 75 L.Ed.2d 632 (1983) held that § 1983 does authorize recovery of punitive damages against individuals "when the defendant's conduct is shown to be motivated by evil motive or intent, or when it involves reckless or callous indifference to the federally protected rights of others." Id. at 56, 103 S.Ct. at 1640.

3. ATTORNEY'S FEE AWARDS

The Civil Rights Attorney's Fees Awards Act, p. 1000, infra, (hereafter cited as § 1988) authorizes courts to award attorney's fees to the prevailing party in individual and class actions to enforce federal rights via § 1983. Blum v. Stenson, 465 U.S. 886, 104 S.Ct. 1541, 79 L.Ed.2d 891 (1984). § 1988 applies to claims of statutory as well as of constitutional rights deprivation; to suits seeking equitable relief as well as to damage suits; and to legal counsel drawn from public interest organizations and government practice, as well as to private practitioners. See Washington v. Seattle School District, 458 U.S. 457, 487–88 n. 31, 102 S.Ct. 3187, 3204 n. 31, 73 L.Ed.2d 896 (1982); Maine v. Thiboutot, 448 U.S. 1, 100 S.Ct. 2502, 65 L.Ed.2d 555 (1980); Maher v. Gagne, 448 U.S. 122, 100 S.Ct. 2570, 65 L.Ed.2d 653 (1980).

While § 1988 vests discretion in trial courts on fee allowance and amounts, the Supreme Court has adopted dual standards for fee allowance, one for prevailing plaintiffs and the other for prevailing defendants: "[A] prevailing plaintiff should ordinarily recover an attorney's fee unless special circumstances would render such an award unjust." See Hensley v. Eckerhart, 461 U.S. 424, 429, 103 S.Ct. 1933, 1937, 76 L.Ed.2d 40 (1983). But, "[A] plaintiff should not be assessed his opponent's attorney's fees unless a court finds that his claim was frivolous, unreasonable or groundless or that the plaintiff continued to litigate after it clearly became so." See Hensley v. Eckerhart, supra, 461 U.S. at 429 n. 2, 103 S.Ct. at 1937 n. 2. A counterclaiming individual grievant would appear to fall under the plaintiff's rule. See Kingsville Ind. School District v. Cooper, 611 F.2d 1109 (5th Cir.1980) (teacher defendant prevailing on counterclaim).

The Supreme Court and lower courts have been almost as occupied by a host of issues regarding fee awards, as they have with the supporting § 1983 claims, and the issues are by no means exhausted. The following is a sampling of issues to be anticipated in § 1983 suits at the local government level. City of Riverside v. Rivera, ___ U.S. ___, 106 S.Ct. 2686, 91 L.Ed.2d 466 (1986) (no majority opinion, with court rejecting award on a "contingent fee" basis; but Justices splitting 5–4 in rejecting rule that fee awards should be proportional to amounts recovered by the plaintiff); Kentucky v. Graham, ___ U.S. ___, 105 S.Ct. 3099, 87 L.Ed.2d 114 (1985) (Recovery against official in individual capacity cannot support fee award against the government); Marek v. Chesny, ___ U.S. ___, 105 S.Ct. 3012, 87 L.Ed.2d 1 (1985) (Police officer not liable for plaintiff's attorney fees incurred after plaintiff rejected pretrial settlement offer, where plaintiff's judgment was less than the offer); Evans v. Jeff D., ___ U.S. ___, 106 S.Ct. 1531, 89 L.Ed.2d 747 (1986) (trial court denial of fees to prevailing class action plaintiff, pursuant to fee waiver as part of court approved settlement-held not to be an abuse of discretion under § 1988); Bond v. Keck, 629 F.Supp. 225 (E.D.Mo.1986) (fee award to prevailing defendant upheld where plaintiff's action was frivolous).

For a general review of the issues arising in fee award disputes in § 1983 cases, see Webb v. Board of Education, 471 U.S. 234, 105 S.Ct. 1923, 85 L.Ed.2d 233 (1985); W.D. Valente, Education Law—Public and Private, § 18.52 (1985); Annot, Civil Rights Attorney's Fees, 43 A.L.R. Fed. 243 (1979, Supp.1985). Other statutes directly authorizing attorney's fees in designated claims are not covered here and must be separately consulted.

PULLIAM v. ALLEN

Supreme Court of the United States, 1984.
466 U.S. 522, 104 S.Ct. 1970, 80 L.Ed.2d 565.

[Reported at p. 979, supra]

* * *

* * * We proceed, therefore, to the question whether judicial immunity bars an award of attorney's fees, under § 1988, to one who succeeds in obtaining injunctive relief against a judicial officer.

Petitioner insists that judicial immunity bars a fee award because attorney's fees are the functional equivalent of monetary damages and monetary damages indisputably are prohibited by judicial immunity. She reasons that the chilling effect of a damages award is no less chilling when the award is denominated attorney's fees.

There is, perhaps, some logic to petitioner's reasoning.

The weakness in it is that it is for Congress, not this Court, to determine whether and to what extent to abrogate the judiciary's common-law immunity. See *Pierson v. Ray*, 386 U.S., at 554, 87 S.Ct., at 1217. Congress has made clear in § 1988 its intent that attorney's fees be available in any action to enforce a provision of § 1983. See also *Hutto v. Finney*, 437 U.S. 678, 694, 98 S.Ct. 2565, 2575, 57 L.Ed.2d 522 (1978). * * * See also *Supreme Court of Virginia v. Consumers Union of the United States, Inc.*, 446 U.S. 719, 738–739, 100 S.Ct. 1967, 1977–1978, 64 L.Ed.2d 641 (1980) ("The House Committee Report on [§ 1988] indicates that Congress intended to permit attorney's fees awards in cases in which prospective relief was properly awarded against defendants who would be immune from damages awards").

Congress' intent could hardly be more plain. Judicial immunity is no bar to the award of attorney's fees under 42 U.S.C. § 1988.

The judgment of the Court of Appeals, allowing the award of attorney's fees against petitioner, is therefore affirmed.

It is so ordered.

E. OTHER DEFENSES

The law concerning procedural and process prerequisites to suit under § 1983 is also incomplete. In addition to prerequisites expressly imposed by substantive statutes (e.g. Title VII prior notice and complaints to designated federal agencies) courts have had to develop rules and standards regarding the effects, if any, of doctrines regarding time bars to exhaustion of administrative remedies, abstention pending state proceedings, and preclusive effect of decisions by state courts or agencies. On many such topics there is no universal rule for all civil rights suits. It will, therefore, be necessary to consult specialized texts on prelitigation requirements for specific classes of civil rights lawsuits. See e.g. C.R. Richey, Manual On Employment Discrimination and Civil

Rights Actions In The Federal Courts (1986); S. Nahmod, Civil Rights and Civil Liberties Litigation (1979); W.D. Valente, Education Law— Public and Private (1985).

The prelitigation requirements that appear in the mass of § 1983 suits cannot be adequately summarized here. The following sampling of fairly common issues provides a general indication of the kinds of process problems that must be anticipated by counsel engaged in civil rights cases.

Proper Forum for § 1983 Suits. It is now settled that suits for redress under § 1983 may be brought in state as well as federal courts. See Maine v. Thiboutot, 448 U.S. 1, 10, 100 S.Ct. 2502, 2507, 65 L.Ed.2d 555, 563 (1980).

Statutes of Limitations. Section 1983 is silent on time bars to suit. In Wilson v. Garcia, 471 U.S. 261, 105 S.Ct. 1938, 85 L.Ed.2d 254 (1985), the Supreme Court adopted the rule that § 1983 suits would be subject to the statute of limitation of the state where the action was deemed to arise, for "personal injury". Courts must still resolve issues as to which state was the locus of the claim, and as to which of its several limitations statutes is applicable. Even then, federal courts may find it necessary in exceptional cases to reject state court decisions on the applicable statute of limitations, i.e. when the state decision frustrates or contravenes the very purposes of § 1983, e.g., where state law imposes a very short limitations period for suits against local governments and their officials. See e.g. Johnson v. Railway Express Agency, Inc., 421 U.S. 454, 464, 95 S.Ct. 1716, 1722, 44 L.Ed.2d 295 (1975); Knoll v. Springfield Twp. School District, 699 F.2d 137 (3d Cir.1983), vacated 471 U.S. 288, 105 S.Ct. 2065, 85 L.Ed.2d 275 (1985).

Exhaustion of State Administrative Proceedings. Subject to exceptions hereafter noted, exhaustion of state remedies is not generally required for suit under § 1983. Patsy v. Board of Regents, 457 U.S. 496, 102 S.Ct. 2557, 73 L.Ed.2d 172 (1982). Dicta in *Patsy* suggests that if the claim is based on a substantive statute which requires exhaustion, then the exhaustion rule would apply. Lower courts are, however, in conflict on the scope of the *Patsy* decision. Some view the ruling as a general one, while others read it as waiving exhaustion only where the state remedy is futile or inadequate, with further variations on the question whether state remedies can ever be adequate if the claimed deprivation is of substantive constitutional rights. See the case authorities in Annot.: Exhaustion of State Remedies, 47 A.L.R.Fed. 15 (1980, Supp.1985); C.R. Richey, supra; S. Nahmod, supra; W.D. Valente, supra, §§ 18.26–18.35.

Abstention. While some federal courts disfavor abstention, to avoid interference with state administration of state and local affairs, (e.g. Devlin v. Sosbe, 465 F.2d 169 (7th Cir.1972); Kohler v. Hirst, 460 F.Supp. 412 (E.D.Va.1978); compare: Caleb Stowe Ass'n Ltd. v. Albemarle County, 724 F.2d 1079 (4th Cir.1984)), the application of abstention principles turns on the circumstances and nature of particular cases. See, e.g., Ohio Civil Rights Commission v. Dayton Christian Schools, Inc., ___ U.S. ___, 106 S.Ct. 2718, 91 L.Ed.2d 512 (1986), wherein the Court ruled that the trial court should have abstained under Younger v. Harris (criminal case) from trying a First Amendment claim against a state civil rights agency.

Effect of Prior State Adjudications. Issues that are litigated to final decision in state forums may not be relitigated in federal court under § 1983. Allen v. McCurry, 449 U.S. 90, 101 S.Ct. 411, 66 L.Ed.2d 308 (1980); Clark v. Yosemite Comm'y College District, 785 F.2d 781 (9th Cir.1986); Takahashi v. Board of Trustees of Livingston Un. School District, 783 F.2d 848 (9th Cir.1986). Preclusion by state law of a federal claim also applies where a party pursued a state law claim to judgment in state court, without raising the federal claim arising out of the same situation. Migra v. Warren City School District Board of Education, 465 U.S. 75, 104 S.Ct. 892, 79 L.Ed.2d 56 (1984). The Supreme Court recently ruled further that for § 1983 claims, findings on disputed facts by a state agency acting in a judicial capacity have the same preclusive effect in federal as in the state court. University of Tennessee v. Elliott, ___ U.S. ___, 106 S.Ct. 3220, 92 L.Ed.2d 635 (1986). These decisions giving preclusive effect to state court decisions do not apply to arbitration awards. Finally, as the Supreme Court observed in *Migra,* supra, the impact of state law and state court judgments upon federal civil rights claims must be analyzed and determined by specific reference to the civil right in question. 465 U.S. at 84–88, 104 S.Ct. at 898–899.

Waivability of § 1983 Claims. Whether an agreement not to sue the government or its officers or employees under § 1983 in exchange for some benefit, or waiver of public prosecution, is contrary to § 1983 remains unsettled. Some courts found such waivers to be contrary to the policy and intent of § 1983 (e.g. Rumery v. Newton, 778 F.2d 66 (1st Cir.1985), but the Supreme Court in upholding a court approved fee waiver in § 1983 actions, used broad dicta supportive of court approved waivers on substantive issues, as well as on fee claims. See Evans v. Jeff D., p. 986, supra. Whether the rationale of the *Evans* case will be extended remains to be seen.

Appendix A

PUBLIC EMPLOYEE RELATIONS ACT NO. 195, 43 P.S. 1101.101

Table of Contents

The General Assembly of the Commonwealth of Pennsylvania hereby enacts as follows;

ARTICLE I. PUBLIC POLICY

* * *

ARTICLE III. DEFINITIONS

Section 301.

As used in this act:

(1) "Public employer" means the Commonwealth of Pennsylvania, its political subdivisions including school districts and any officer, * * * agency, or other instrumentality thereof * * * but shall not include employers covered or presently subject to coverage under the act of June 1, 1937 (P.L. 1168), as amended, known as the "Pennsylvania Labor Relations Act," the act of July 5, 1935, Public Law 198, 74th Congress, as amended, known as the "National Labor Relations Act."

(2) "Public employe" or "employe" means any individual employed by a public employer but shall not include elected officials, appointees of the Governor * * *, management level employes, confidential employes, * * * and those employes covered under the act of June 24, 1968 (Act No. 111), entitled "An act specifically authorizing collective bargaining between policemen and firemen and their public employers; providing for arbitration in order to settle disputes, and requiring compliance with collective bargaining agreements and findings of arbitrators."

(3) "Employe organization" means an organization of any kind, or any agency or employe representation committee or plan * * * which exists for the purpose, * * * of dealing with employers * * *.

(4) "Representative" means any individuals acting for public employers or employes and shall include employe organizations.

(5) "Board" means the Pennsylvania Labor Relations Board.

(6) "Supervisor" means any individual having authority in the interests of the employer to hire, transfer, suspend, layoff, recall, promote, discharge, assign, reward or discipline other employes or responsibly to direct them or adjust their grievances; * * *.

* * *

(9) "Strike" means concerted action in failing to report for duty, the wilful absence from one's position, the stoppage of work, slowdown, or the abstinence in whole or in part from the full, faithful and proper performance of the duties of employment for the purpose of inducing, influencing or coercing a change in the conditions or compensation or the rights, privileges, or obligations of employment.

* * *

(12) "Budget submission date" means the date by which under the law or practice a public employer's proposed budget, or budget containing proposed expenditures applicable to such public employer is submitted to the Legislature or other similar body for final action. For the purposes of this act, the budget submission date for the Commonwealth shall be February 1 of each year and for a nonprofit organization or institution, the last day of its fiscal year.

* * *

(16) "Management level employe" means any individual who is involved directly in the determination of policy or who responsibly directs the imple-

mentation thereof and shall include all employes above the first level of supervision.

(17) "Meet and discuss" means the obligation of a public employer upon request to meet at reasonable times and discuss recommendations submitted by representatives of public employes: Provided, That any decisions or determinations on matters so discussed shall remain with the public employer and be deemed final on any issue or issues raised.

* * *

ARTICLE IV. EMPLOYE RIGHTS

Section 401.

It shall be lawful for public employes to organize, form, join or assist in employe organizations or to engage in lawful concerted activities for the purpose of collective bargaining or other mutual aid and protection or to bargain collectively through representatives of their own free choice and such employes shall also have the right to refrain from any or all such activities, except as may be required pursuant to a maintenance of membership provision in a collective bargaining agreement.

ARTICLE V. PENNSYLVANIA LABOR RELATIONS BOARD

* * *

ARTICLE VI. REPRESENTATION

* * *

Section 602.

(a) A public employer may recognize employe representatives for collective bargaining purposes, provided the parties jointly request certification by the board which shall issue such certification if it finds the unit appropriate.

* * *

Section 604.

The board shall determine the appropriateness of a unit which shall be the public employer unit or a subdivision thereof. In determining the appropriateness of the unit, the board shall:

(1) Take into consideration but shall not be limited to the following: (i) public employes must have an identifiable community of interest, and (ii) the effects of over-fragmentization.

(2) Not decide that any unit is appropriate if such unit includes both professional and nonprofessional employes, unless a majority of such professional employes vote for inclusion in such unit.

(3) Not permit guards at prisons and mental hospitals, employes directly involved with * * * the courts * * * or any individual employed as a guard to enforce against employes and other persons, rules to protect property of the employer or to protect the safety of persons * * * to be included in any unit with other public employes, each may form separate homogenous employe organizations with the proviso that organizations of the latter designated employe group may not be affiliated with any other organization representing or including as members, persons outside of the organization's classification.

(4) Take into consideration that when the Commonwealth is the employer, it will be bargaining on a Statewide basis * * *. This section, however, shall not be deemed to prohibit multi-unit bargaining.

(5) Not permit employes at the first level of supervision to be included with any other units of public employes but shall permit them to form their own separate homogenous units. * * *

* * *

Section 606.

Representatives selected by public employes in a unit appropriate for collective bargaining purposes shall be the exclusive representative of all the employes in such unit to bargain on wages, hours, terms and conditions of employment: Provided, That any individual employe or a group of employes shall have the right at any time to present grievances to their employer and to have them adjusted without the intervention of the bargaining representative as long as the adjustment is not inconsistent with the terms of a collective bargaining contract then in effect: And, provided further, That the bargaining representative has been given an opportunity to be present at such adjustment.

ARTICLE VII. SCOPE OF BARGAINING

Section 701.

Collective bargaining is the performance of the mutual obligation * * * to meet * * * and confer in good faith with respect to wages, hours and other terms and conditions of employment, or the negotiation of an agreement or any question arising thereunder and the execution of a written contract incorporating any agreement reached but such obligation does not compel either party to agree to a proposal or require the making of a concession.

Section 702.

Public employers shall not be required to bargain over matters of inherent managerial policy, which shall include but shall not be limited to such areas of discretion or policy as the functions and programs of the public employer, standards of services, its overall budget, utilization of technology, the organizational structure and selection and direction of personnel. Public employers, however, shall be required to meet and discuss on policy matters affecting wages, hours and terms and conditions of employment as well as the impact thereon upon request by public employe representatives.

Section 703.

The parties to the collective bargaining process shall not effect or implement a provision in a collective bargaining agreement if the implementation of that provision would be in violation of, or inconsistent with, or in conflict with any statute or statutes enacted by the General Assembly of the Commonwealth of Pennsylvania or the provisions of municipal home rule charters.

Section 704.

Public employers shall not be required to bargain with units of first level supervisors or their representatives but shall be required to meet and discuss with first level supervisors or their representatives, on matters deemed to be bargainable for other public employes covered by this act.

Section 705.

Membership dues deductions and maintenance of membership are proper subjects of bargaining with the proviso that as to the latter, the payment of dues and assessments while members, may be the only requisite employment condition.

Section 706.

Nothing contained in this act shall impair the employer's right to hire employes or to discharge employes for just cause consistent with existing legislation.

ARTICLE VIII.   COLLECTIVE BARGAINING IMPASSE

Section 801.

If after a reasonable period of negotiation, a dispute or impasse exists * * * the parties may voluntarily submit to mediation but if no agreement is reached between the parties within twenty-one days after negotiations have commenced, but in no event later than one hundred fifty days prior to the "budget submission date," * * * both parties shall immediately, in writing, call in the service of the Pennsylvania Bureau of Mediation.

Section 802.

Once mediation has commenced, it shall continue for so long as the parties have not reached an agreement. If, however, an agreement has not been reached within twenty days after mediation has commenced or in no event later than one hundred thirty days prior to the "budget submission date," the Bureau of Mediation shall notify the board of this fact. Upon receiving such notice the board may in its discretion appoint a fact-finding panel * * *. If during this time the parties have not reached an agreement, the panel shall make findings of fact and recommendations:

(1) * * *

(2) Not more than ten days after the findings and recommendations shall have been sent, the parties shall notify the board and each other whether or not they accept the recommendations of the fact-finding panel and if they do not, the panel shall publicize its findings of fact and recommendations.

(3) Not less than five days nor more than ten days after the publication of the findings of fact and recommendations, the parties shall again inform the board and each other whether or not they will accept the recommendations of the fact-finding panel.

(4) * * *

* * *

Section 804.

Nothing in this article shall prevent the parties from submitting impasses to involuntary binding arbitration with the proviso the decisions of the arbitrator which would require legislative enactment to be effective shall be considered advisory only.

Section 805.

Notwithstanding any other provisions of this act where representatives of units of guards at prisons or mental hospitals or units of employes directly involved with and necessary to the functioning of the courts * * * have reached an impasse in collective bargaining * * * the impasse shall be submitted to a panel of arbitrators whose decision shall be final and binding upon both parties with the proviso that the decisions of the arbitrators which would require legislative enactment to be effective shall be considered advisory only.

* * *

ARTICLE IX. COLLECTIVE BARGAINING AGREEMENT

Section 901.

Once an agreement is reached * * * the agreement shall be reduced to writing and signed by the parties. Any provisions of the contract requiring legislative action will only be effective if such legislation is enacted.

Section 902.

If the provisions of the constitution or bylaws of an employe organization requires ratification of a collective bargaining agreement by its membership, only those members who belong to the bargaining unit involved shall be entitled to vote on such ratification notwithstanding such provisions.

Section 903.

Arbitration of disputes or grievances arising out of the interpretation of the provisions of a collective bargaining agreement is mandatory. The procedure to be adopted is a proper subject of bargaining with the proviso that the final step shall provide for a binding decision by an arbitrator or a tri-partite board of arbitrators as the parties may agree. Any decisions of the arbitrator or arbitrators requiring legislation will only be effective if such legislation is enacted: * * *

ARTICLE X. STRIKES

Section 1001.

Strikes by guards at prisons or mental hospitals, or employes directly involved with and necessary to the functioning of the courts * * * .

Section 1002.

Strikes by public employes during the pendency of collective bargaining procedures set forth in sections 801 and 802 of Article VIII are prohibited. * * *

Section 1003.

If a strike by public employes occurs after the collective bargaining processes set forth in sections 801 and 802 of Article VIII of this act have been completely utilized and exhausted, it shall not be prohibited unless or until such a strike creates a clear and present danger or threat to the health, safety or welfare of the public. In such cases the public employer shall initiate, in the court of common pleas of the jurisdiction where such strike occurs, an action for equitable relief including but not limited to appropriate injunctions and shall be entitled to such relief if the court finds that the strike creates a clear and present danger or threat to the health, safety or welfare of the public. * * *

Section 1004.

An unfair practice by a public employer shall not be a defense to a prohibited strike. * * *

Section 1005.

If a public employe refuses to comply with a lawful order of a court of competent jurisdiction issued for a violation of any of the provisions of this article the public employer shall initiate an action for contempt and if the public employe is adjudged guilty of such contempt, he shall be subject to suspension, demotion or discharge at the discretion of the public employer, provided the public employer has not exercised that discretion in violation of clauses (1), (2), (3) and (4) of subsection (a) of section 1201, Article XII.

Section 1006.

No public employe shall be entitled to pay or compensation from the public employer for the period engaged in any strike.

Section 1007.

In the event any public employe refuses to obey an order issued by a court of competent jurisdiction for a violation of the provisions of this article, the punishment for such contempt may be by fine or by imprisonment in the prison of the county where the court is sitting or both in the discretion of the court.

Section 1008.

Where an employe organization wilfully disobeys a lawful order of a court of competent jurisdiction issued for a violation of the provisions of this article, the punishment for each day that such contempt persists may be by a fine fixed in the discretion of the court.

Section 1010.

Nothing in this article shall prevent the parties from voluntarily requesting the court for a diminution or suspension of any fines or penalties imposed. Any requests by employe representatives for such participation by the public employer shall be subject to the requirements of "meet and discuss."

ARTICLE XI.   PICKETING

Section 1101.

Public employes, other than those engaged in a nonprohibited strike, who refuse to cross a picket line shall be deemed to be engaged in a prohibited strike and shall be subject to the terms and conditions of Article X pertaining to prohibited strikes.

ARTICLE XII.   UNFAIR PRACTICES
* * *

ARTICLE XIII.   PREVENTION OF UNFAIR PRACTICES

Section 1301.

The board is empowered, as hereinafter provided, to prevent any person from engaging in any unfair practice listed in Article XII of this act. This power shall be exclusive and shall not be affected by any other means of adjustment or prevention that have been or may be established by agreement, law, or otherwise.

* * *

ARTICLE XV.   JUDICIAL REVIEW

* * *

Section 1504.

When granting appropriate temporary relief, a restraining or mandamus order * * * the jurisdiction of courts sitting in equity shall not be limited by acts pertaining to equity jurisdiction of courts. The act of June 2, 1937 (P.L. 1198), known as the "Labor Anti-Injunction Act," shall not be applicable to orders of the board, or to court orders enforcing orders of the board, or any provision of this act, * * *.

* * *

ARTICLE XVI.   INVESTIGATORY POWERS

* * *

ARTICLE XVII.   EMPLOYE ORGANIZATIONS

Section 1701.

No employe organization shall make any contribution out of the funds of the employe organization either directly or indirectly to any political party or organization or in support of any political candidate for public office.

* * *

ARTICLE XVIII.   CONFLICT OF INTEREST

Section 1801.

(a) No person who is a member of the same local, State, national or international organization as the employe organization with which the public employer is bargaining or who has an interest in the outcome of such bargaining which interest is in conflict with the interest of the public employer, shall participate on behalf of the public employer in the collective bargaining processes with the proviso that such person may, where entitled, vote on the ratification of an agreement.

* * *

ARTICLE XIX.   PENALTIES

* * *

ARTICLE XX. SAVINGS PROVISIONS

Section 2001.

The rights granted to certain public employes by the following acts or parts thereof shall not be repealed or diminished by this act:

(1) Section 24 of the act of August 14, 1963 (P.L. 984), known as the "Metropolitan Transportation Authorities Act of 1963."

(2) The act of November 27, 1967 (P.L. 628), entitled "An act protecting the rights of employes of existing transportation systems which are acquired by cities of the third class or any authority thereof or certain joint authorities; *   *   *.

(3) Section 13.2 of the act of April 6, 1956 (P.L. 1414), known as the "Second Class County Port Authority Act."

Section 2002.

This act shall not be construed to repeal the act of June 24, 1968 (Act No. 111), entitled "An act specifically authorizing collective bargaining between policemen and firemen and their public employers; providing for arbitration in order to settle disputes, and requiring compliance with collective bargaining agreements and findings of arbitrators."

Section 2003.

Present provisions of an ordinance of the City of Philadelphia approved April 4, 1961, entitled "An Ordinance to authorize the Mayor to enter into an agreement with District Council 33, American Federation of State, County and Municipal Employes, A.F.L.–C.I.O., Philadelphia and vicinity regarding its representation of certain City Employes," which are inconsistent with the provisions of this act shall remain in full force and effect so long as the present provisions of that ordinance are valid and operative.

*   *   *

ARTICLE XXII. REPEALS

Section 2201.

The act of June 30, 1947 (P.L. 1183), entitled "An act relating to strikes by public employes; prohibiting such strikes; providing that such employes by striking terminate their employment; providing for reinstatement under certain conditions; *   *   * is hereby repealed as to those public employes covered by the provisions of this act, *   *   *.

*   *   *

Appendix B

FEDERAL CIVIL RIGHTS STATUTES

A. 42 U.S.C. § 1981—Civil Rights Acts of 1866, 1870

Section 1981 provides:

"All persons within the jurisdiction of the United States shall have the same right * * * to make and enforce contracts, to sue, be parties, give evidence, and to the full and equal benefit of all laws and proceedings for the security of persons and property as is enjoyed by white citizens, and shall be subject to like punishments, pains, penalties, taxes, licenses, and exactions of every kind, and to no other."

B. 42 U.S.C. § 1983—The Civil Rights Act of 1871

Section 1983 provides:

"Every person who, under color of any statute, ordinance, regulation, custom or usage, of any State or Territory, subjects, or causes to be subjected, any citizen of the United States or other person within the jurisdiction thereof to the deprivation of any rights, privileges or immunities secured by the Constitution and laws, shall be liable to the party injured in an action at law, suit in equity, or other proper proceeding for redress."

C. 42 U.S.C. §§ 1985 and 1986—The Civil Rights Act of 1871

Section 1985(3) provides:

"If two or more persons in any State or Territory conspire or go in disguise on the highway or on the premises of another, for the purpose of depriving, either directly or indirectly, any person or class of persons of the equal protection of the laws, or of equal privileges and immunities under the laws: or for the purpose of preventing or hindering the constituted authorities of any State or Territory from giving or securing to all persons within such State or Territory the equal protection of the laws * * *: in any case of conspiracy set forth in this section, if one or more persons engaged therein do, or cause to be done, any act in furtherance of the object of such conspiracy, whereby another is injured in his person or property, or deprived of having and exercising any right or privilege of a citizen of the United States, the party so injured or deprived may have an action for the recovery of damages, occasioned by such injury or deprivation, against any one or more of the conspirators."

Section 1986 provides:

"Every person who, having knowledge that any of the wrongs conspired to be done, and mentioned in Section 1985 of this title, are about to be committed, and having the power to prevent or aid in preventing the commission of the same, neglects or refuses so to do, if such wrongful act be committed, shall be liable to the party injured, or his legal representatives, for all damages caused by such wrongful act, which such person by reasonable diligence could have prevented; and such damages may be recovered in an action on the case; and any number of persons guilty of such wrongful neglect or refusal may be joined as defendants in the action. ＊ ＊ ＊ "

D.　42 U.S.C. § 1988—Civil Rights Acts of 1866, 1870

As amended 1976, § 1988 provides:

Proceedings in vindication of civil rights. The jurisdiction in civil and criminal matters conferred on the district courts by the provisions of this chapter and Title 18, for the protection of all persons in the United States in their civil rights, and for their vindication, shall be exercised and enforced in conformity with the laws of the United States, so far as such laws are suitable to carry the same into effect; but in all cases where they are not adapted to the object, or are deficient in the provisions necessary to furnish suitable remedies and punish offenses against law, the common law, as modified and changed by the constitution and statutes of the State wherein the court having jurisdiction of such civil or criminal cause is held, so far as the same is not inconsistent with the Constitution and laws of the United States, shall be extended to and govern the said courts in the trial and disposition of the cause, and, if it is of a criminal nature, in the infliction of punishment on the party found guilty. In any action or proceeding to enforce a provision of sections 1981, 1982, 1983, 1985, and 1986 of this title, title IX of Public Law 92–318, or in any civil action or proceeding, by or on behalf of the United States of America, to enforce, or charging a violation of, a provision of the United States Internal Revenue Code, or title VI of the Civil Rights Act of 1964, the court, in its discretion, may allow the prevailing party, other than the United States, a reasonable attorney's fee as part of the costs.

As amended Pub.L. 94–559, § 2, Oct. 19, 1976, 90 Stat. 2641.

E.　42 U.S.C. § 2000(d)—Civil Rights Act of 1964, Title VI

Section 601 of Title VI provides:

"No person in the United States shall, on the ground of race, color, or national origin, be excluded from participation in, be denied the benefits of, or be subjected to discrimination under any program or activity receiving Federal financial assistance."

F. 42 U.S.C. § 2000(e)—Civil Rights Act of 1964, Title VII

Section 702 of Title VII provides:

"This title shall not apply to ＊ ＊ ＊ a religious corporation, association, educational institution, or society with respect to the employment of individuals of a particular religion to perform work connected with the carrying on by such corporation, association, educational institution, or society of its activities."

Section 703(a) provides in part that:

"It shall be an unlawful employment practice for an employer—(1) ＊ ＊ ＊ to discriminate against any individual with respect to his compensation, terms, conditions, or privileges of employment because of such individual's race, color, religion, sex, or national origin; or (2) to limit, segregate, or classify his employees ＊ ＊ ＊ in any way which would deprive or tend to deprive any individual of employment opportunities or otherwise adversely affect his status as an employee, because of such individual's race, color, religion, sex, or national origin."

Section 703(e) provides:

"Notwithstanding any other provision of this [title], (1) it shall not be an unlawful employment practice for an employer to hire and employ employees, for an employment agency to classify or refer for employment any individual, for a labor organization to classify its membership or to classify or refer for employment any individual, or for an employer, labor organization, or joint labor-management committee controlling apprenticeship or other training or retraining programs to admit or employ any individual in any such program, on the basis of his religion, sex, or national origin *in those certain instances where religion, sex, or national origin is a bona fide occupational qualification reasonably necessary to the normal operation of that particular business or enterprise.* ＊ ＊ ＊ " (Emphasis supplied.)

Section 703(h) reads in relevant part:

"Notwithstanding any other provision of this title, it shall not be an unlawful employment practice for an employer to apply different standards of compensation, or different terms, conditions, or privileges of employment *pursuant to a bona fide seniority or merit system,* ＊ ＊ ＊ provided that such differences are not the result of an intention to discriminate because of race, color, religion, sex, or national origin. ＊ ＊ ＊ " (Emphasis supplied.)

G. 20 U.S.C. § 1681—Education Amendments of 1972, Title IX

Section 901 of Title IX provides in part:

SEC. 901. (A) No person in the United States shall, on the basis of sex, be excluded from participation in, be denied the benefits of, or be subjected to discrimination under any education program or activity receiving Federal financial assistance, except that:

(1) in regard to admissions to educational institutions, this section shall apply only to institutions of vocational education, professional

education, and graduate higher education, and to public institutions of undergraduate higher education. * * *

(3) this section shall not apply to an educational institution which is controlled by a religious organization if the application of this subsection would not be consistent with the religious tenets of such organization. * * *

(5) in regard to admissions this section shall not apply to any public institution of undergraduate higher education which is an institution that traditionally and continually from its establishment has had a policy of admitting only students of one sex.

H. 29 U.S.C. § 206(d)—Equal Pay Act

§ 206 provides:

"No employer having employees subject to [the minimum wage provisions of the FLSA] shall discriminate, within any establishment * * *, between employees on the basis of sex by paying wages to employees in such establishment at a rate less than the rate at which he pays wages to employees of the opposite sex in such establishment for equal work on jobs the performance of which requires equal skill, effort, and responsibility, and which are performed under similar working conditions. * * * "

The Act nevertheless permits differences in wages if paid pursuant to:

"(i) a seniority system; (ii) a merit system; (iii) a system which measures earnings by quantity or quality or production; or (iv) a differential based on any factor other than sex. * * * "

I. 29 U.S.C. § 621—Age Discrimination Act (§ 623)

(a) It shall be unlawful for an employer—

(1) to fail or refuse to hire or to discharge any individual or otherwise discriminate against any individual with respect to his compensation, terms, conditions, or privileges of employment, because of such individual's age. * * *

(c) It shall be unlawful for a labor organization—

(1) to exclude or to expel from its membership, or otherwise to discriminate against, any individual because of his age. * * *

(3) to cause or attempt to cause an employer to discriminate against an individual in violation of this section. * * *

(f) It shall not be unlawful for an employer, employment agency, or labor organization—

(1) to take any action otherwise prohibited under subsections (a), (b), (c), or (e) of this section where age is a bona fide occupational qualification reasonably necessary to the normal operation of the particular business, or where the differentiation is based on reasonable factors other than age. * * *

(3) to discharge or otherwise discipline an individual for good cause. * * *

J. 20 U.S.C. § 1703—Equal Education Opportunities Act

§ 1703 provides:

No State shall deny equal educational opportunity to an individual on account of his or her race, color, sex, or national origin, by—

(a) the deliberate segregation by an educational agency of students on the basis of race, color, or national origin among or within schools.

   *   *   *

(c) the assignment by an educational agency of a student to a school, other than the one closest to his or her place of residence within the school district in which he or she resides, if the assignment results in a greater degree of segregation of students on the basis of race, color, sex, or national origin. *   *   *

(d) discrimination by an educational agency on the basis of race, color, or national origin in the employment, employment conditions, or assignment to schools of its faculty or staff, except to fulfill the purposes of subsection (f) below. *   *   *

(e) the transfer by an educational agency, whether voluntary or otherwise, of a student from one school to another if the purpose and effect of such transfer is to increase segregation of students on the basis of race, color, or national origin among the schools of such agency; or

(f) the failure by an educational agency to take appropriate action to overcome language barriers that impede equal participation by its students in its instructional programs.

K. 29 U.S.C. § 794—Rehabilitation Act of 1973 (§ 504)

The Act provides in part:

"No otherwise qualified handicapped individual *   *   * shall, solely by reason of his handicap, be excluded from the participation in, be denied the benefits of, or be subjected to discrimination under any program or activity receiving Federal financial assistance."

L. 29 U.S.C. § 1401—Education For All Handicapped Children Act

This Act provides in part:

§ 1401. Definitions

As used in this chapter—

(1) The term "handicapped children" means mentally retarded, hard of hearing, deaf, speech impaired, visually handicapped, seriously emotionally disturbed, orthopedically impaired, or other health impaired children, or children with specific learning disabilities, who by reason thereof require special education and related services.

§ 1412. Eligibility requirements

In order to qualify for assistance under this subchapter in any fiscal year, a State shall demonstrate to the Commissioner that the following conditions are met:

(1) The State has in effect a policy that assures all handicapped children the right to a free appropriate public education.

(2) The State has developed a plan pursuant to section 1413(b) of this title in effect prior to November 29, 1975, and submitted not later than August 21, 1975, which will be amended so as to comply with the provisions of this paragraph. Each such amended plan shall set forth in detail the policies and procedures which the State will undertake or has undertaken in order to assure that—

(A) there is established (i) a goal of providing full educational opportunity to all handicapped children, (ii) a detailed timetable for accomplishing such a goal, and (iii) a description of the kind and number of facilities, personnel, and services necessary throughout the State to meet such a goal;

(B) a free appropriate public education will be available for all handicapped children between the ages of three and eighteen within the State not later than September 1, 1978, and for all handicapped children between the ages of three and twenty-one within the State not later than September 1, 1980, except that, with respect to handicapped children aged three to five and aged eighteen to twenty-one, inclusive, the requirements of this clause shall not be applied in any State if the application of such requirements would be inconsistent with State law or practice, or the order of any court, respecting public education within such age groups in the State;

(C) all children residing in the State who are handicapped, regardless of the severity of their handicap, and who are in need of special education and related services are identified, located, and evaluated, and that a practical method is developed and implemented to determine which children are currently receiving needed special education and related services and which children are not currently receiving needed special education and related services;

(D) policies and procedures are established in accordance with detailed criteria prescribed under section 1417(c) of this title; and

(E) the amendment to the plan submitted by the State required by this section shall be available to parents, guardians, and other members of the general public at least thirty days prior to the date of submission of the amendment to the Commissioner.

(3) The State has established priorities for providing a free appropriate public education to all handicapped children, which priorities shall meet the timetables set forth in clause (B) of paragraph (2) of this section, first with respect to handicapped children who are not receiving an education, and second with respect to handicapped children, within each disability, with the most severe handicaps who are receiving an inadequate education,

and has made adequate progress in meeting the timetables set forth in clause (B) of paragraph (2) of this section.

(4) Each local educational agency in the State will maintain records of the individualized education program for each handicapped child, and such program shall be established, reviewed, and revised as provided in section 1414(a)(5) of this title.

(5) The State has established (A) procedural safeguards as required by section 1415 of this title, (B) procedures to assure that, to the maximum extent appropriate, handicapped children, including children in public or private institutions or other care facilities, are educated with children who are not handicapped, and that special classes, separate schooling, or other removal of handicapped children from the regular educational environment occurs only when the nature or severity of the handicap is such that education in regular classes with the use of supplementary aids and services cannot be achieved satisfactorily, and (C) procedures to assure that testing and evaluation materials and procedures utilized for the purposes of evaluation and placement of handicapped children will be selected and administered so as not to be racially or culturally discriminatory. Such materials or procedures shall be provided and administered in the child's native language or mode of communication, unless it clearly is not feasible to do so, and no single procedure shall be the sole criterion for determining an appropriate educational program for a child.

(6) The State educational agency shall be responsible for assuring that the requirements of this subchapter are carried out and that all educational programs for handicapped children within the State, including all such programs administered by any other State or local agency, will be under the general supervision of the persons responsible for educational programs for handicapped children in the State educational agency and shall meet education standards of the State educational agency.

(7) The State shall assure that (A) in carrying out the requirements of this section procedures are established for consultation with individuals involved in or concerned with the education of handicapped children, including handicapped individuals and parents or guardians of handicapped children, and (B) there are public hearings, adequate notice of such hearings, and an opportunity for comment available to the general public prior to adoption of the policies, programs, and procedures required pursuant to the provisions of this section and section 1413 of this title.

*

Index

References are to pages

†